PLUNKETT'S AUTOMOBILE INDUSTRY ALMANAC 2020

The only comprehensive
guide to automotive companies and trends

Jack W. Plunkett

Published by:
Plunkett Research®, Ltd., Houston, Texas
www.plunkettresearch.com

PLUNKETT'S AUTOMOBILE INDUSTRY ALMANAC 2020

Editor and Publisher:
Jack W. Plunkett

Executive Editor and Database Manager:
Martha Burgher Plunkett

Senior Editor and Researchers:
Isaac Snider

Editors, Researchers and Assistants:
Jeremy Amorin
Michael Cappelli
Annie Paynter
Anoosh Saidi
Jorden Smith
Gina Sprenkel

Information Technology Manager:
Rebeca Tijiboy

Special Thanks to:
American Automobile Association (AAA)
IHS Markit
Kelly Blue Book
National Automobile Dealers Association (NADA)
National Highway Transportation Safety Administration (NHTSA)
Scotiabank Group
U.S. Bureau of Economic Analysis
U.S. Bureau of Transportation Statistics
U.S. Census Bureau
U.S. Department of Commerce
U.S. Department of Energy
U.S. Department of Transportation
U.S. Energy Information Administration
U.S. Environmental Protection Agency
U.S. Federal Highway Administration

Plunkett Research®, Ltd.
P. O. Drawer 541737, Houston, Texas 77254 USA
Phone: 713.932.0000 Fax: 713.932.7080
www.plunkettresearch.com

Plunkett Research®, Ltd.
P. O. Drawer 541737
Houston, Texas 77254-1737
Phone: 713.932.0000, Fax: 713.932.7080 www.plunkettresearch.com

ISBN13 # 978-1-62831-545-5 (eBook Edition # 978-1-62831-852-4)

Limited Warranty and Terms of Use:

Users' publications in static electronic format containing any portion of the content of this book (and/or the content of any related Plunkett Research, Ltd. online service to which you are granted access, hereinafter collectively referred to as the "Data") or Derived Data (that is, a set of data that is a derivation made by a User from the Data, resulting from the applications of formulas, analytics or any other method) may be resold by the User only for the purpose of providing third-party analysis within an established research platform under the following conditions: (However, Users may not extract or integrate any portion of the Data or Derived Data for any other purpose.)

a) Users may utilize the Data only as described herein. b) User may not export more than an insubstantial portion of the Data or Derived Data, c) Any Data exported by the User may only be distributed if the following conditions are met:

   i) Data must be incorporated in added-value reports or presentations, either of which are part of the regular services offered by the User and not as stand-alone products.
   ii) Data may not be used as part of a general mailing or included in external websites or other mass communication vehicles or formats, including, but not limited to, advertisements.
   iii) Except as provided herein, Data may not be resold by User.

"Insubstantial Portions" shall mean an amount of the Data that (1) has no independent commercial value, (2) could not be used by User, its clients, Authorized Users and/or its agents as a substitute for the Data or any part of it, (3) is not separately marketed by the User, an affiliate of the User or any third-party source (either alone or with other data), and (4) is not retrieved by User, its clients, Authorized Users and/or its Agents via regularly scheduled, systematic batch jobs.

LIMITED WARRANTY; DISCLAIMER OF LIABILITY: While Plunkett Research, Ltd. ("PRL") has made an effort to obtain the Data from sources deemed reliable, PRL makes no warranties, expressed or implied, regarding the Data contained herein. This book and its Data are provided to the End-User "AS IS" without warranty of any kind. No oral or written information or advice given by PRL, its employees, distributors or representatives will create a warranty or in any way increase the scope of this Limited Warranty, and the Customer or End-User may not rely on any such information or advice. Customer Remedies: PRL's entire liability and your exclusive remedy shall be, at PRL's sole discretion, either (a) return of the price paid, if any, or (b) repair or replacement of a book that does not meet PRL's Limited Warranty and that is returned to PRL with sufficient evidence of or receipt for your original purchase.

NO OTHER WARRANTIES: TO THE MAXIMUM EXTENT PERMITTED BY APPLICABLE LAW, PRL AND ITS DISTRIBUTORS DISCLAIM ALL OTHER WARRANTIES AND CONDITIONS, EITHER EXPRESSED OR IMPLIED, INCLUDING, BUT NOT LIMITED TO, IMPLIED WARRANTIES OR CONDITIONS OF MERCHANTABILITY, FITNESS FOR A PARTICULAR PURPOSE, TITLE AND NON-INFRINGEMENT WITH REGARD TO THE BOOK AND ITS DATA, AND THE PROVISION OF OR FAILURE TO PROVIDE SUPPORT SERVICES. LIMITATION OF LIABILITY: TO THE MAXIMUM EXTENT PERMITTED BY APPLICABLE LAW, IN NO EVENT SHALL PRL BE LIABLE FOR ANY SPECIAL, INCIDENTAL OR CONSEQUENTIAL DAMAGES WHATSOEVER (INCLUDING, WITHOUT LIMITATION, DAMAGES FOR LOSS OF BUSINESS PROFITS, BUSINESS INTERRUPTION, ABILITY TO OBTAIN OR RETAIN EMPLOYMENT OR REMUNERATION, ABILITY TO PROFITABLY MAKE AN INVESTMENT, OR ANY OTHER PECUNIARY LOSS) ARISING OUT OF THE USE OF, OR RELIANCE UPON, THE BOOK OR DATA, OR THE INABILITY TO USE THIS DATA OR THE FAILURE OF PRL TO PROVIDE SUPPORT SERVICES, EVEN IF PRL HAS BEEN ADVISED OF THE POSSIBILITY OF SUCH DAMAGES. IN ANY CASE, PRL'S ENTIRE LIABILITY SHALL BE LIMITED TO THE AMOUNT ACTUALLY PAID BY YOU FOR THE BOOK.

PLUNKETT'S AUTOMOBILE INDUSTRY ALMANAC 2020

CONTENTS

Continued on next page

Continued from previous page

INTRODUCTION

PLUNKETT'S AUTOMOBILE INDUSTRY ALMANAC is designed to be used as a general source for researchers of all types.

The data and areas of interest covered are intentionally broad, ranging from the trends relating to automotive sales, to emerging technology, to an in-depth look at the major for-profit firms (which we call "THE AUTOMOBILE 400") within the many industry sectors that make up the automotive arena.

This reference book is designed to be a general source for researchers. It is especially intended to assist with market research, strategic planning, employment searches, contact or prospect list creation and financial research, and as a data resource for executives and students of all types.

PLUNKETT'S AUTOMOBILE INDUSTRY ALMANAC takes a rounded approach for the general reader. This book presents a complete overview of the entire automobile and truck industry (see "How To Use This Book"). For example, you will find trends in the passenger car, light truck and heavy truck markets, along with easy-to-use charts and tables on all facets of automobiles in general, from the sales and profits of the automakers, to fuel efficiency, to manufacturing output.

THE AUTOMOBILE 400 is our unique grouping of the biggest, most successful corporations in all segments of the global automotive industry, including cars, trucks, components, parts, dealerships, specialty vehicles and related services. Tens of thousands of pieces of information, gathered from a wide variety of sources, have been researched and are presented in a unique form that can be easily understood. This section includes thorough indexes to THE AUTOMOBILE 400, by geography, industry, sales, brand names, subsidiary names and many other topics. (See Chapter 4.)

Especially helpful is the way in which PLUNKETT'S AUTOMOBILE INDUSTRY ALMANAC enables readers who have no business background to readily compare the financial records and growth plans of large automotive companies and major industry groups. You'll see the mid-term financial record of each firm, along with the impact of earnings, sales and strategic plans on each company's potential to fuel growth, to serve new markets and to provide investment and employment opportunities.

No other source provides this book's easy-to-understand comparisons of growth, expenditures, technologies, corporations and many other items of great importance to people of all types who may be studying this, one of the largest industries in the world today.

By scanning the data groups and the unique indexes, you can find the best information to fit your personal research needs. The major companies in the automobile field are profiled and then ranked using several different groups of specific criteria. Which firms are the biggest employers? Which companies earn the most profits? These things and much more are easy to find.

In addition to individual company profiles, an overview of automotive markets and trends is provided. This book's job is to help you sort through easy-to-understand summaries of today's trends in a quick and effective manner.

Whatever your purpose for researching the automotive field, you'll find this book to be a valuable guide. Nonetheless, as is true with all resources, this volume has limitations that the reader should be aware of:

- Financial data and other corporate information can change quickly. A book of this type can be no more current than the data that was available as of the time of editing. Consequently, the financial picture, management and ownership of the firm(s) you are studying may have changed since the date of this book. For example, this almanac includes the most up-to-date sales figures and profits available to the editors as of mid-2018. That means that we have typically used corporate financial data as of the end of 2018.

- Corporate mergers, acquisitions and downsizing are occurring at a very rapid rate. Such events may have created significant change, subsequent to the publishing of this book, within a company you are studying.

- Some of the companies in THE AUTOMOBILE 400 are so large in scope and in variety of business endeavors conducted within a parent organization, that we have been unable to completely list all subsidiaries, affiliations, divisions and activities within a firm's corporate structure.

- This volume is intended to be a general guide to a vast industry. That means that researchers should look to this book for an overview and, when conducting in-depth research, should contact the specific corporations or industry associations in question for the very latest changes and data. Where possible, we have listed contact names, toll-free telephone numbers and Internet site addresses for the companies, government agencies and industry associations involved so that the reader may get further details without unnecessary delay.

- Tables of industry data and statistics used in this book include the latest numbers available at the time of printing, generally through the end of 2018. In a few cases, the only complete data available was for earlier years.

- We have used exhaustive efforts to locate and fairly present accurate and complete data. However, when using this book or any other source for business and industry information, the reader should use caution and diligence by conducting further research where it seems appropriate. We wish you success in your endeavors, and we trust that your experience with this book will be both satisfactory and productive.

Jack W. Plunkett
Houston, Texas
September 2019

HOW TO USE THIS BOOK

The two primary sections of this book are devoted first to the automotive industry as a whole and then to the "Individual Data Listings" for THE AUTOMOBILE 400. If time permits, you should begin your research in the front chapters of this book. Also, you will find lengthy indexes in Chapter 4 and in the back of the book.

Video Tip
For our brief video introduction to the Automobile industry, see www.plunkettresearch.com/video/automobile.

THE AUTOMOBILE INDUSTRY

Chapter 1: Major Trends Affecting the Automobile Industry. This chapter presents an encapsulated view of the major trends that are creating rapid changes in the automotive industry today.

Chapter 2: Automobile Industry Statistics. This chapter presents in-depth statistics on car sales, manufacturing import/export and more.

Chapter 3: Important Automobile Industry Contacts – Addresses, Telephone Numbers and Internet Sites. This chapter covers contacts for important government agencies, automotive organizations and trade groups. Included are numerous important Internet sites.

THE AUTOMOBILE 400

Chapter 4: THE AUTOMOBILE 400: Who They Are and How They Were Chosen. The companies compared in this book were carefully selected from the automobile industry, largely in the United States. Many of the firms are based outside the U.S. For a complete description, see THE AUTOMOBILE 400 indexes in this chapter.

Individual Data Listings:

Look at one of the companies in THE AUTOMOBILE 400's Individual Data Listings. You'll find the following information fields:

Company Name:

The company profiles are in alphabetical order by company name. If you don't find the company you are seeking, it may be a subsidiary or division of one of the firms covered in this book. Try looking it up in the Index by Subsidiaries, Brand Names and Selected Affiliations in the back of the book.

Industry Code:

Industry Group Code: An NAIC code used to group companies within like segments.

Types of Business:

A listing of the primary types of business specialties conducted by the firm.

Brands/Divisions/Affiliations:

Major brand names, operating divisions or subsidiaries of the firm, as well as major corporate affiliations—such as another firm that owns a significant portion of the company's stock. A complete Index by Subsidiaries, Brand Names and Selected Affiliations is in the back of the book.

Contacts:

The names and titles up to 27 top officers of the company are listed, including human resources contacts.

Growth Plans/ Special Features:

Listed here are observations regarding the firm's strategy, hiring plans, plans for growth and product development, along with general information regarding a company's business and prospects.

Financial Data:

Revenue (2018 or the latest fiscal year available to the editors, plus up to five previous years): This figure represents consolidated worldwide sales from all operations. These numbers may be estimates.

R&D Expense (2018 or the latest fiscal year available to the editors, plus up to five previous years): This figure represents expenses associated with the research and development of a company's goods or services. These numbers may be estimates.

Operating Income (2018 or the latest fiscal year available to the editors, plus up to five previous years): This figure represents the amount of profit realized from annual operations after deducting operating expenses including costs of goods sold, wages and depreciation. These numbers may be estimates.

Operating Margin % (2018 or the latest fiscal year available to the editors, plus up to five previous years): This figure is a ratio derived by dividing operating income by net revenues. It is a measurement of a firm's pricing strategy and operating efficiency. These numbers may be estimates.

SGA Expense (2018 or the latest fiscal year available to the editors, plus up to five previous years): This figure represents the sum of selling, general and administrative expenses of a company, including costs such as warranty, advertising, interest, personnel, utilities, office space rent, etc. These numbers may be estimates.

Net Income (2018 or the latest fiscal year available to the editors, plus up to five previous years): This figure represents consolidated, after-tax net profit from all operations. These numbers may be estimates.

Operating Cash Flow (2018 or the latest fiscal year available to the editors, plus up to five previous years): This figure is a measure of the amount of cash generated by a firm's normal business operations. It is calculated as net income before depreciation and after income taxes, adjusted for working capital. It is a prime indicator of a company's ability to generate enough cash to pay its bills. These numbers may be estimates.

Capital Expenditure (2018 or the latest fiscal year available to the editors, plus up to five previous years): This figure represents funds used for investment in or improvement of physical assets such as offices, equipment or factories and the purchase or creation of new facilities and/or equipment. These numbers may be estimates.

EBITDA (2018 or the latest fiscal year available to the editors, plus up to five previous years): This figure is an acronym for earnings before interest, taxes, depreciation and amortization. It represents a company's financial performance calculated as revenue minus expenses (excluding taxes, depreciation and interest), and is a prime indicator of profitability. These numbers may be estimates.

Return on Assets % (2018 or the latest fiscal year available to the editors, plus up to five previous years): This figure is an indicator of the profitability of a company relative to its total assets. It is calculated by dividing annual net earnings by total assets. These numbers may be estimates.

Return on Equity % (2018 or the latest fiscal year available to the editors, plus up to five previous years): This figure is a measurement of net income as a percentage of shareholders' equity. It is also called the rate of return on the ownership interest. It is a vital indicator of the quality of a company's operations. These numbers may be estimates.

Debt to Equity (2018 or the latest fiscal year available to the editors, plus up to five previous years): A ratio of the company's long-term debt to its shareholders' equity. This is an indicator of the overall financial leverage of the firm. These numbers may be estimates.

Address:

The firm's full headquarters address, the headquarters telephone, plus toll-free and fax numbers where available. Also provided is the internet address.

Stock Ticker, Exchange: When available, the unique stock market symbol used to identify this firm's common stock for trading and tracking purposes is indicated. Where appropriate, this field may contain "private" or "subsidiary" rather than a ticker symbol. If the firm is a publicly-held company headquartered outside of the U.S., its international ticker and exchange are given.

Total Number of Employees: The approximate total number of employees, worldwide, as of the end of 2018 (or the latest data available to the editors).

Parent Company: If the firm is a subsidiary, its parent company is listed.

Salaries/Bonuses:

(The following descriptions generally apply to U.S. employers only.)

Highest Executive Salary: The highest executive salary paid, typically a 2018 amount (or the latest year available to the editors) and typically paid to the Chief Executive Officer.

Highest Executive Bonus: The apparent bonus, if any, paid to the above person.

Second Highest Executive Salary: The next-highest executive salary paid, typically a 2018 amount (or the latest year available to the editors) and typically paid to the President or Chief Operating Officer.

Second Highest Executive Bonus: The apparent bonus, if any, paid to the above person.

Other Thoughts:

Estimated Female Officers or Directors: It is difficult to obtain this information on an exact basis, and employers generally do not disclose the data in a public way. However, we have indicated what our best efforts reveal to be the apparent number of women who either are in the posts of corporate officers or sit on the board of directors. There is a wide variance from company to company.

Hot Spot for Advancement for Women/Minorities: A "Y" in appropriate fields indicates "Yes." These are firms that appear either to have posted a substantial number of women and/or minorities to high posts or that appear to have a good record of going out of their way to recruit, train, promote and retain women or minorities. (See the Index of Hot Spots For Women and Minorities in the back of the book.) This information may change frequently and can be difficult to obtain and verify. Consequently, the reader should use caution and conduct further investigation where appropriate.

Glossary: A short list of automotive industry terms.

Chapter 1

MAJOR TRENDS AFFECTING THE AUTOMOBILE INDUSTRY

1) Automobile Industry Introduction

Video Tip
For our brief video introduction to the Automobile industry, see www.plunkettresearch.com/video/automobile.

The automobile industry surged ahead worldwide in recent years, with particularly sharp growth in the U.S. and China. Analysts at IHS Automotive forecast the global market at 98.2 million units for 2019.

Car sales within North American markets have been running at very high rates. Total U.S. car and light truck sales for 2019 are projected by National Automobile Dealers Association (NADA) at 16.8 million units. U.S. car and light truck sales totaled 17.22 million units for 2018, according to NADA.

The biggest upward trend in auto sales has been in China. While estimates of its annual unit sales vary widely, China has clearly become the world's largest car market with about 23.5 million units sold in 2018. However, China's sales are subject to change due to such factors as economic growth, the availability of credit and the regulatory environment. China's government has a great deal of control over the market, as, at any time, it may increase sales by encouraging new auto loans, or decrease sales by adding new registration fees or restricting traffic in major cities in order to reduce congestion and pollution.

One of the biggest winners by far in today's highly competitive automobile market has been Korea, where Hyundai, along with its brand Kia, have enjoyed soaring global sales. Consumers are attracted to their reasonable prices, excellent warranties and world class quality.

There were approximately 278 million cars and light trucks in operation in the United States, as of 2019. Around the world, there were about 1.24 billion cars and light trucks on the road in 2018.

Most major car makers are aggressively pushing their crossover vehicles, which are an excellent compromise in design between sedans and SUVs. They offer large passenger and cargo compartments, good visibility and reasonably good gas mileage. Crossovers are essentially replacing sedans and some vans as the new family car. Ford, for example, is phasing out nearly all of its sedans in its U.S. market, including the Taurus, so that it can concentrate on its highly popular crossovers and pickup trucks. In sedans, Ford will offer only the Mustang and the upscale Lincoln sedans.

Engineers are pushing technological changes in their larger cars and light trucks in order to enhance their fuel efficiency. An excellent example is the launch of the Ford F150 full-size pickup truck that relies on the use of aluminum body panels and advanced engine/transmission combinations to dramatically reduce weight and improve mileage. This truck has been selling in very large numbers in the U.S., as have the Chevy Silverado and Chrysler Ram full-size pickups. Recent low gasoline prices have boosted this trend. Roughly one-third of all light vehicle sales in the U.S. were pickup trucks, as of 2019, with the Ford F-150 holding the greatest market share. Considering the popularity of such trucks, it isn't surprising that even Tesla has announced its intention to launch an electric pickup.

At the same time, manufacturers are forced to continue to invest in smaller, high efficiency vehicles due to government mandates that they meet high average miles-per-gallon rules. Over the mid- to long-term, manufacturers will emphasize hybrid and electric vehicles. Honda, Volkswagen, Toyota, Hyundai, Nissan and Peugeot all have invested in new, advanced small cars.

Most major luxury brands, such as Mercedes, BMW, Lexus and Audi, have relatively small cars on the market and will steadily introduce a wide range of fuel efficient designs, including electric and hybrid vehicles. BMW introduced its iSeries high efficiency all-electric, as well as hybrid cars.

Both VW and Toyota have announced very aggressive investment in the design and manufacture of advanced hybrids and electrics. These cars will be rolled out globally over the next several years.

There have historically been strong sales for Toyota's Prius gasoline-electric hybrid car. The company has also made investments that enable it to manufacture hybrid versions of many of its popular models, including the Camry and several models of the Lexus. Hybrids are available from a wide variety of other makers as well, and technology has steadily improved. Nonetheless, hybrids remain a very small fraction of the overall car and truck market due to their relatively high initial costs. Manufacturers have a significant challenge ahead of them in order to produce hybrids and electrics that will generate high demand from consumers. Better batteries with longer driving ranges will be a big help. The automobile industry is looking forward to the eventual development of advanced, long-range batteries at much lower cost. Many of the world's top research organizations are working steadily on this challenge.

Meanwhile, the use of ethanol as a gasoline additive in America has grown substantially over the long term, whether or not it makes any environmental or economic sense, thanks to requirements enacted by Congress. However, Congress recently dropped its financial subsidies to ethanol.

The rising affluence of consumers in China has been creating both huge opportunities and major problems. China has become the world's largest user of energy overall and one of the world's largest importers of petroleum products, partly to fuel its burgeoning fleet of cars and trucks. Streets and highways are clogged with vehicles, to the extent that traffic and smog are nightmarish. Automakers from abroad have raced to establish plants and partnerships in China.

India has also seen significant growth in its automotive manufacturing in recent years, and its auto exports are growing. India-based Tata now owns the prestigious Jaguar and Land Rover brands.

Not to be overlooked are the vast changes taking place in automobile manufacturing plants. Flexible factories have reduced man-hours and cut costs per car, while offering a much wider range of choices for customization by consumers. The wide use of robotics, advanced factory software and lean inventory methods have completely revamped the modern car factory. Today, more than ever, car manufacturers and their suppliers are cooperating in the design and manufacture of new cars in ways that are revolutionizing the entire process. Bankruptcies at GM and Chrysler in 2009 enabled these firms to shed debt, cut employees, renegotiate contracts and dramatically reduce operating costs.

Inexpensive cars manufactured in China are now on the market in many emerging nations. The question is not whether China will export cars and trucks, but whether consumers in advanced markets such as America will be convinced that they offer safety and reliability. Meanwhile, U.S. automakers have made intense demands on their component suppliers for lower prices—these suppliers are, in turn, looking to low-cost production in China, Mexico and elsewhere.

European manufacturers are facing challenges of their own. High costs, tough labor laws and daunting government regulations are constant challenges to manufacturers in Europe. Nonetheless, firms like Volkswagen and Daimler/Mercedes-Benz have found great success in the global market over a period of many decades, often locating plants in nations where their products sell well, including major plants in the U.S.

The thought of the next billion automobile owners/users is either the most intriguing or the most terrifying vision for the near future, depending on how you look at it. Future global demand for cars could possibly outstrip today's levels, creating immense business opportunities.

However, the combination of car sharing strategies like ZipCar, ride sharing systems like Uber and autonomous vehicles capable of driving themselves will have very profound effects on automobile manufacturing, usage, sales and ownership patterns. At least in dense urban environments, the result is very likely to be a large proportion of individuals who opt to use shared vehicles rather than user-owned cars.

Surveys show that many young adults have little interest in owning a car of their own, which is vastly different from the attitude that was held by previous generations. U.S transportation analysts reported that only about 25% of 16-year-olds had a driver's license in 2017, down from almost 50% in 1983. Car sharing is such a strong trend that car rental giant Avis acquired Zipcar, a pioneer in this area. Even major auto makers, like BMW with its DriveNow program, are starting their own car sharing schemes, hoping to develop strategies that are well in tune with changing consumer trends. Major automobile makers, when looking to the future, talk in terms of delivering "mobility services" as much as automobiles, while they consider the looming effects of car-sharing and ride-on-demand services.

Car safety has made dramatic progress in recent years, mainly by adopting technologies such as backup cameras, anti-skid, advanced brakes and collision avoidance systems. Now, all major car makers are heavily invested in technologies that will enable cars to essentially drive themselves.

The automobile and heavy truck sectors are rapidly forging ahead with remarkable technologies for self-driving (autonomous) vehicles. The first step is vehicles that communicate with each other while utilizing advanced technologies to safely stay in lanes, regulate speeds and apply emergency braking. (This is referred to as vehicle-to-vehicle communications, and is part of an overall digital strategy known as ITS, or intelligent transportation systems.)

Automobiles have become high-powered computers on wheels, as many automotive systems are now controlled by chips and software. At the same time, auto makers are finding innovative ways to use the latest in wireless and smartphone technologies, including apps, to enhance the entertainment, information and communications capabilities of vehicles. Automotive "infotainment" has become a dominant theme.

2) U.S. Auto Manufacturers Ford, Chrysler and GM Compete Head-On with Volkswagen, Toyota and Honda

Globally, during 2018, Volkswagen Group remained the top seller, reaching 10.9 million vehicles sold, followed by Toyota with 8.98 million and General Motors (GM) with 8.38 million. Hyundai (including Kia) was fourth with 7.27 million and Ford was fifth with 5.98 million. In the U.S. market, GM remained the leader for 2018 with a 16.7% market share over Ford's 14.1% and Toyota's 13.7%. Fiat/Chrysler achieved a 12.6% market share in America for 2018.

Recent U.S. Car Company History: Control of Chrysler was acquired by Italian car maker Fiat in 2009, with the firm now known as Fiat Chrysler Automobiles NV. The other major U.S. automakers, Ford and GM, have gone through their own vast changes. GM took bankruptcy in 2009 and accepted massive federal loans while it restructured. Meanwhile, Ford engineered its own reorganization, without government bailouts and without declaring bankruptcy. The company sold its Jaguar, Volvo and Land Rover brands, and in 2010 closed its Mercury division. Ford also closed several of its production plants and shuttered more than 600 dealerships. By 2011, the company began to radically simplify production by utilizing a small number of basic platforms for all its models (thereby working from the same basic components in plants that utilize the same types of tooling), down from 15 platforms five years earlier.

Market Share of Cars and Light Trucks sold in America, 2018

General Motors	16.7%
Ford	14.1%
Toyota	13.7%
Fiat/Chrysler	12.6%
Honda	9.1%
Nissan	8.4%
Hyundai/Kia	7.2%
Source: Fiat	

SPOTLIGHT: Hyundai Motor Company

Hyundai Motor Company, headquartered in South Korea, is one of the world's leading automobile manufacturers. The firm designs and manufactures passenger cars; recreational vehicles; commercial vehicles, including trucks, buses and tractors; and specialty vehicles, including crane trucks, refrigerated vans and tank trucks for fuel and water transport. Popular export models include the Accent, a sub-compact; the Sonata, a mid-size sedan; the Elantra, a compact sedan; the Santa Fe SUV; and the Tucson SUV. Light commercial vehicles include the H-1 cargo van, the Xcient truck and a variety of mini buses. Heavy commercial vehicles include small/medium size HD36L, HD35-78 and HD120 trucks and busses as well as cargo, dump, mixer and tractor trucks. Hyundai's i30 N vehicle offers the feeling of driving a racecar with up to 275 horsepower and high-performance cornering capabilities; KONA is a compact SUV; and the IONIQ model offers a line of electric and hybrid sedans.

Genesis is the firm's luxury car unit. Hyundai also makes machine tools for factory automation and material handling and owns approximately 34% of Kia Motors Corporation. Subsidiary Hyundai Motor America oversees U.S. operations, including primary facilities in Alabama, Michigan and California. The subsidiary also distributes Hyundai vehicles in the U.S. In addition to its U.S. operations, the firm has other overseas plants in Brazil, Turkey, the Czech Republic, Russia, India and China, as well as research and development centers in North America, Japan and Europe. The company offers automotive financing services to European customers through joint venture Hyundai Capital Germany GmbH.

Total car and light truck sales in the U.S. during 2018 hit 17.2 million vehicles, roughly the same as in 2017. 2016 hit a record with 17.6 million units sold, boosted by buyers driving new, bigger vehicles to take advantage of cheap gasoline prices.

Production at American plants owned by foreign manufacturers is on the rise. Companies including Honda, Toyota, BMW and Volkswagen are major manufacturers at U.S. locations, particularly in the Southeastern states. Toyota had invested more than $20 billion in its American plants by 2016 and employed more than 33,000 people in those plants. Toyota recently budgeted approximately $2 billion to increase its U.S.-made output by 145,000 units per year. The company announced another $1.3 billion investment in 2017 to retool its factory in Georgetown, Kentucky.

Elsewhere in North America, major car manufacturers headquartered from many nations are investing heavily in auto production at state of the art plants in Mexico, largely for the export market, and many car makers have long had significant manufacturing operations in Canada.

SPOTLIGHT: Auto Manufacturing Plants May Miniaturize

With the advent of new software and 3-D printing, some automotive plants of the future may be significantly smaller in scale. Startup Divergent 3D (www.divergent3d.com) has developed a patented digital technology that utilizes 3-D metal printing to create two prototype vehicles: the Dagger, a motorcycle and the Blade, a sports car. The firm plans to create additional prototypes, including a van. While traditional automotive factories cost between $500 million and $1 billion to build (and must produce hundreds of thousands of units to be profitable), Divergent 3D believes it can build factories for as little as $50 million using large-scale 3-D metal printers, laser cutters and robots for assembly, with a capacity of about 20,000 vehicles per year.

3) U.S. Automobile Sales Level Off/ Consumers Want Pickup Trucks and Crossovers

America's car manufacturers have benefitted greatly in recent years with the rebound in the willingness of Americans to buy cars and light trucks, with 17.2 million sold during 2018, roughly the same as 2017's amount, and down from 2016's 17.6 million.

At the same time, automobile exports have been very good in recent years. For 2018, exports rose to $130.7 billion, up from $130.4 billion in 2017 and $124.6 billion in 2016.

This growth in sales and exports is a huge benefit to domestic makers and foreign-owned plants alike. In addition to plants operated by U.S. brands like Chrysler, Ford and GM, America is home to highly automated, extremely efficient plants owned by foreign companies including Mercedes Benz, Toyota, BMW and Honda.

American manufacturers are shifting away from making sedans to focus on better-selling SUVs and pickup trucks. Ford Motor Co. announced plans to discontinue production of its Fiesta compact by 2019, and also plans to halt production of the Taurus sedan. The only sedans made by Ford in America may be the Mustang and the upscale Lincoln sedans. General Motors (GM) ceased production of the Chevrolet Sonic subcompact in 2018 and may stop building the Chevy Impala sedan in 2020. Cars, including sedans, coupes and compacts accounted for only 31% of U.S. sales in 2018, compared to 51% in 2012. FiatChrysler's (maker of the highly popular Jeeps and Ram pickups) U.S. sales for 2018 were up 8.5% over the previous year, largely due to its Jeep brand which was up 17%. Ford's overall sales were down 3.5% for 2018, but its F-Series pickup sales rose 1.4% (remaining the top selling vehicle in the U.S.) Extra-large models such as Ford's Lincoln Navigator SUV are undergoing luxury redesigns that take advantage of cheaper gasoline prices and lower emissions standards expected in the near term from the Trump Administration. The new Navigator is priced higher than the previous year's model, but was selling at almost twice the rate of its predecessor as of early 2018.

4) Fuel Efficiency Continues to Improve/ Trump Administration Expected to Delay Increases in MPG Standards

The recent plunge in the retail price of gasoline caused many consumers to reconsider the types of vehicles they are willing to drive. The light truck market, including pickups and vans, is of vital importance due to automakers several factors. To begin with, for manufacturers, gross profits per light truck unit can be many times higher than the profits made from small, highly fuel-efficient cars. Next, light trucks will always burn more fuel than smaller cars, having an effect on both a manufacturer's total CAFE average fuel efficiency and on the total demand for gasoline.

Strong light truck sales are due to many factors, including a surge in new home construction, where building contractors rely on their pickups, a reduction in unemployment, plummeting gasoline prices and, importantly, excellent improvement in the fuel efficiency of pickup trucks thanks to changes in engineering, design and materials.

CAFE (corporate average fuel economy) standards were first issued by U.S. federal regulators in the 1970s as a method of setting average fuel economy standards for carmakers. Current standards call for manufacturers to sell a portfolio of light-duty cars and trucks averaging 54.5 miles per gallon (mpg) by 2025. The Trump administration has announced plans to reduce these standards, and made a first step in August 2018 with a proposal to freeze fuel economy standards at 37 mpg by 2020. Nonetheless, the state of California may maintain its own, more stringent mpg regulations. In July 2019, Ford, BMW, Honda and Volkswagen signed a deal with California to increase gas mileage and emissions standards. It remains to be seen what will happen on a national level.

Higher fuel efficiency requires higher manufacturing costs, and thus impacts retail car prices. CAFE rules are also likely to force manufacturers to offer more electric vehicles, and may give a boost to the eventual entry of hydrogen fuel cell-powered vehicles, although the technical and logistical problems remain high for fuel cells.

When considering the effect of CAFE rules, bear in mind that they are an average of sorts (a "harmonic mean") for a manufacturer's entire line of cars and light trucks, and that number is arrived at by a circuitous calculation, with separate considerations for a company's domestic cars, imported cars and light trucks. The more that a car maker offers ultra-efficient cars, such as electrics and hybrids, the closer it comes to meeting the rules. As with all federal regulations, CAFE rules (at 700 pages published in one year alone) are immense and intricate. For example, firms can earn various "credits" that enable them to temporarily avoid penalties if they do not meet the standards.

In general, meeting such high average fuel efficiency will require a combination of several things. To begin with, manufacturers will be forced to build much lighter vehicles. This means that in some cases they will go so far as to eliminate the spare tire and wheel in order to save 100 to 150 pounds. At the same time, they will engineer lighter engines, use plastic where possible as a replacement for metals, and look for weight savings in everything from seats to bumpers. For example, Ford designed a new EcoBoost three-cylinder engine. Utilizing turbocharging, this much lighter powerhouse produces 118 horsepower per liter, compared to about 70 horsepower for current four-cylinder models. Fuel efficiency is greatly enhanced.

Ford released an aluminum-bodied F-150 pickup truck in 2015. The lighter metal cuts the popular truck's weight by 700 pounds, making it much more fuel efficient. Other light weight material alternatives include carbon fiber composites (BMW's i3 electric car has a carbon fiber composite frame) and magnesium, which is 50% lighter that steel and 30% lighter than aluminum. GM plans to use carbon fiber for the beds of premium versions of its pickup trucks to boost fuel efficiency.

A proven gas-saving measure is an inexpensive shift from a five-speed to a six- or eight-speed automatic transmission. The cost for the enhancement is in the neighborhood of $400 to $800, but the measure can add as much as two miles per gallon in efficiency.

GM claims that an improvement of between 6% and 12% in fuel economy can be achieved through cylinder deactivation technology. In these systems, one-half of an engine's cylinders stop firing once a steady cruising speed is reached. Other small changes, such as those incorporated in the Chevrolet Malibu sedan, can add up. For example, the hood is made of aluminum instead of steel and rounded front corners reduce drag (saving 0.4 mpg on the highway); active shutters behind the grill open and close as needed to cool the engine (savings of 0.3 mpg); and the car has no spare tire but includes an inflator kit for temporary tire fixes (savings of 0.4 mpg).

Johnson Controls, a manufacturer in Wisconsin, retrofitted one of its factories to produce advanced batteries that allow traditional engines to start and stop repeatedly without wearing out the battery. Just as in hybrids, where engines stop when the vehicle comes to a halt and then restart to accelerate, the advanced batteries allow traditional engines to do the same. Mileage is improved by about 4% to as much as 10%, depending on the vehicle and its usage.

Another bright spot on the fuel efficiency horizon is a new hydraulic-hybrid system that is in use on large service vehicles such as garbage trucks and UPS delivery vans. The EPA's National Vehicle and Fuel Emissions Laboratory in Ann Arbor, Michigan has designed a hybrid garbage truck that uses a diesel engine, assisted by a hydraulic pump and storage tank system that replaces the drivetrain and transmission. The pump and tanks make it possible to store and reuse energy normally lost when brakes are applied, thereby increasing fuel efficiency as much as 60% and reducing carbon monoxide emissions by more than 40%. UPS placed an order with hydraulic manufacturer Eaton Corporation and truck builder Navistar for 200 hybrid electric vehicles which hit the streets in cities across the U.S.

Internet Research Tip: Hybrid Commercial Trucks:
Hybrid trucks and buses will soon be in high demand by major truck fleet operators such as UPS. For the latest information on pilot projects, technologies and fleet purchases, see Calstart's web site at www.calstart.org.

Another new technology of note is an artificial neural network. The network detects cylinder misfires and controls idle speeds, thus increasing fuel efficiency. Serious measures such as these will have to be taken across the board by automakers in their vehicle designs in order to meet future emissions and efficiency stipulations. The aforementioned National Highway Traffic Safety Administration 2015 report found that lightweight materials, better transmissions, turbochargers and other improvements already made or in the development pipeline for current car and truck models may be enough for manufacturers to meet CAFE standards.

SPOTLIGHT: Motor Scooters

Don't be surprised to see more and more of your neighbors zipping around on stylish motor scooters. The motor scooter dates back to post-war Europe, where Piaggio made the first Vespa in 1946. While scooters have long been extremely popular in densely-populated cities outside the U.S., such as Rome and Bangkok, Americans have rarely been scooter buyers, turning instead to cars, light trucks and powerful motorcycles.

However, the difficulty of parking in some U.S. cities and attractive new scooter models are lighting a fire under U.S. consumers. For example, the Vespa has extremely peppy new models that have room for two people and perhaps a shopping bag, get more than 60 mpg and cost about $4,400. Honda and Yamaha have jumped into the market with scooters that feature storage compartments for groceries or helmets along with engines that are powerful enough for highway cruising. Lighter, new scooters with small engines that get up to 120 mpg are offered by other makers for about $3,000.

Electric scooters are also proliferating. The Swagtron Swagger is a 17-pound carbon fiber scooter with a range of 15 miles and a top speed of 15 mph. A Taiwanese startup called Gogoro (www.gogoro.com) is marketing a stylish electric motorbike called the Smartscooter. Launched in mid-2015 in Taiwan, the bike has an electric motor equivalent in power to a 125cc gasoline engine, can accelerate from zero to 30 mph in 4.2 seconds and has a top speed of 60 mph. Riders can purchase the bikes but don't own the batteries. Instead, portable batteries are swapped out as-needed from a charging station network of "GoStations" for a monthly fee. Batteries must be authenticated using a smartphone app in order to work.

The Gogoro has a growing number of competitors. Manufacturers include Zero Motorcycles (www.zeromotorcycles.com), Polaris Industries' Victory Motorcycles (which acquired the Brammo Empulse model in 2015, www.victorymotorcycles.com) and Yamaha (www.yamaha-motor.com). Harley Davidson (www.harley-davidson.com) announced plans to sell a production electric motorcycle by 2020.

5) Electric Cars and Plug-in Hybrids (PHEVs) to See Massive New Investments by Auto Makers

Electric cars range from 100% electric power vehicles that have relatively short ranges and are plugged-in at home overnight to recharge—to cars like the Chevrolet Volt that will run primarily on an electric motor only, but include a small gasoline-powered generator engine that will recharge the batteries when needed and give an occasional boost to the drivetrain as well. The Volt has the ability to be recharged by plug-in at home, and has a range of more than 400 miles using gas and electric combined.

A little history is in order: An all-electric car has long sounded logical to many people. GM launched the EV1, an all-electric vehicle, in 1996. Unfortunately, the car was a complete flop, and the $1-billion project was abandoned in 1999. In 2002, Ford announced that it would give up on the Think, an electric car model in which it had invested $123 million. These efforts were an attempt to satisfy government demands, not an attempt to fill early consumer needs. Today, stringent U.S. government average fuel efficiency requirements continue to push manufacturers to offer electric vehicles, in order to bring down their brand's overall average mpg.

Plug-in hybrids (PHEVs) are similar to standard hybrids, but they enable the owner the option of plugging-in at home overnight to recharge the battery. This will eliminate the need to run the car's gasoline engine, using only battery power as long as the relatively short range isn't exceeded. (Standard hybrids recharge only by running the gasoline-powered side of the car, and by drawing on the drag produced by using the brakes.)

Initial PHEV sales have been low in market share. InsideEVs.com reported U.S. sales rose from 199,826 vehicles in 2017 to 361,307 million in 2018. Global sales were 2.01 million in2018, up from 1.21 million in 2017. Sales will be helped by the nine U.S. states that have announced plans to require 15% of new car purchases to be made up of zero-emission vehicles by 2025. While sales have grown, electric cars accounted for only 2% of 2018's vehicle sales in the U.S. Despite the low numbers, global car manufacturers, as of 2018, had plans to invest more than $70 billion in electric vehicle and battery development over the mid-term.

Toyota previously decided to limit its production of electric vehicles to very small numbers for the near term. To explain these decisions, Vice Chairman Takeshi Uchiyamada stated, "The current capabilities of electric vehicles do not meet society's needs, whether it may be the distance the cars can run, or the costs, or how it takes a long time to charge." However, after sales of electric vehicles soared in China and in Europe in 2016, Toyota announced plans to create a unit dedicated to the production of a battery-powered car. The company expects to sell vehicles equipped with a new lithium-ion battery that could significantly cut charging time and double driving range based on patent filings made in 2017. By the early 2020s, Toyota plans to offer electric vehicles powered by solid-state batteries instead of lithium ion.

For now, large numbers of U.S. consumers remain skeptical about electric or hybrid cars in general. That may change, however, with the passages of laws such as California's Senate Bill 350, which calls for cutting greenhouse gas emissions to 40% below 1990 levels by 2030. Southern California Edison hopes to install 30,000 electric vehicle chargers in commercial buildings, parking lots and apartment complexes by 2019 (at a cost of $355 million).

Nine other states are following California's lead in requiring 15% of all cars sold to be either electric or hydrogen powered by 2025. However, many of these states, such as Vermont, are in locations that have much colder weather than that of California, and batteries based on current technology lose performance in colder temperatures. The vast majority of electric vehicles sold in the U.S. are sold in California and in the Southern states, where weather is comparatively warm.

Some states are voting to halt tax credits for electric vehicles, since the credit costs are high. Other states are imposing fees of up to $200 per year on electric car buyers since they do not pay gasoline taxes. (Gasoline taxes help state agencies to pay for road maintenance and other expenses, vital to drivers of gasoline and electric vehicles alike.) It is also possible that the Trump administration could roll back tax credits and electric or hydrogen requirements on a national level.

How electric vehicles will eventually gain significant market share:

1) Technical breakthroughs in batteries will eventually make all-electric vehicles more affordable while providing longer range. Nanotechnology may be the key. Government requirements for higher miles-per-gallon ratings on cars over the mid-term may force automakers to focus on electrics, in order to lower each maker's overall average. Similarly, several U.S. states have announced aggressive requirements that 15% of cars sold annually be zero-emission by the year 2025.

2) Electricity is user-friendly, easy to understand, and easy to obtain. Electric utility companies are generally in favor of the electric car trend. Governments have been extremely enthusiastic and supportive (including financial support for manufacturers and incentives for consumers).

3) Innovative entrepreneurs remain committed to electric vehicles. Meanwhile, virtually all of the world's major automobile manufacturers are investing heavily in new all-electric and hybrid models.

4) Electric vehicle maker Tesla is setting the standard in electric vehicles, selling sizable quantities of its high-end cars, and boosting consumer acceptance of electric cars in general.

Source: Plunkett Research, Ltd.

Tesla is the rock star of the electric car industry, albeit with significant production problems. Its sales have been impressive, despite the relatively high price of its initial models, and the company's own stock has soared, thrilling early investors. Tesla's high-end Model S sedan has a range of 370 miles per charge and can go from zero to 60 miles per hour in 2.4 seconds. It also offers the Model X SUV and has a Model Y compact crossover set for release in 2020. The Model 3 sedan, first released in 2017, has a base price significantly lower than its luxury models, capable of traveling about 310 miles per charge. The company has also announced plans to launch an electric pickup truck.

Tesla has taken a simple route to solve the problem of batteries: each car has thousands of small, lithium-ion batteries linked together, similar to the batteries found in consumer electronics. The firm also has a global system of convenient chargers in high traffic areas, called Tesla Superchargers, where Tesla owners can recharge at no cost.

As of mid-2019, Tesla was facing serious problems with production and deliveries, especially for the Model 3 and the Model X. The company hoped to deliver thousands of vehicles in China and Europe, but is having to rely solely on its Fremont, California production plant until a new facility is completed in China (which was planned for year-end 2019). Tesla cut 7% of its workforce in January 2019. In the first quarter of 2019, Model 3 deliveries fell to 50,900 from the previous quarter's 63,150 due to difficulties in shipping the cars to overseas destinations. Overall deliveries for the quarter fell 31%.

Tesla has also developed heavy-duty electric trucks capable of hauling major loads up to 600 miles at a price of $180,000 (about twice what a traditional diesel-powered truck costs). Originally slated for delivery starting in 2019, the company recently delayed production until 2020. Other firms such as Cummins, are developing their own electric heavy trucks. Daimler delivered its first Freightliner eCascadia all-electric semi in August 2019. Its rig has a range of 250 miles per charge. The problem with electrifying 18-wheeled trucks is weight. A diesel-powered engine weighs about two tons while an electric version with its batteries would weigh between four and nine tons, depending on range.

For those with thinner wallets, the BMW i3 electric compact has a base price of about $42,400. The i3 is making headlines for its lightweight, two-module carbon fiber architecture. GM hopes to begin delivery of 20 fully-electric models between 2019 and 2023. Volkswagen launched the ID.3 hatchback, the first built on the brand's new standardized electric vehicle platform, in August 2019. The firm plans a fleet of 20 models built on this platform, hopefully resulting in the sale of up to 1 million electric cars by 2025.

Volvo, which is owned by China's Geely Holding Group, started taking orders for its all-electric XC40 SUV in late 2019. It joined six other new Volvo electric models. Going forward, all cars manufactured by Volvo will be either all-electric or hybrids.

China has imposed an increasingly strict mandate boosting zero-emission vehicles due to a massive air pollution problem. As of early 2018, there were 487 electric vehicle manufacturers in China. There is likely to be significant consolidation and some failures. GM announced in April 2017 that it planned to build 10 electric or plug-in hybrid models in China by 2020.

The nation of India is also boosting sales of electric vehicles. India, China and the EU are all likely to see very high ratios of electric car sales by 2030.

Electric SUVs from a variety of manufacturers were hitting the market or in the planning stages starting in 2017 in competition with Tesla's Model X. Jaguar's I-Pace was available in 2018, while Audi's e-tron was released in 2019 as was Mercedes-Benz's EQC. An electric version of BMW's X3 is planned for 2020. Prices for these luxury vehicles start in the $75.000-$80,000 range.

Internet Research Tip: Electric Cars

For the latest on electric car manufacturers see:
Electric Drive Transportation Association, www.goelectricdrive.org
Global Electric Motorcars, www.gemcar.com
Tesla Motors, www.teslamotors.com

6) Major Research and Advancements in Lithium Batteries/Tesla and Panasonic Operate the Gigafactory

Although all-electric vehicles still make up only a fraction of the automotive market, the battery industry is expected by some analysts to boom. However, the extreme drop in gasoline prices that began in late 2014 and continued into 2019 is tempering near-term demand for hybrids and all-electric vehicles. Historically, battery-powered vehicles have been more costly when compared to gasoline-powered cars.

There remain many obstacles to all-electric vehicles: a shortage of battery charging stations available to the driving public, battery cost and driving range. Another challenge is the increasing demand for lithium. Cobalt is also used in lithium-ion batteries.

According to Bloomberg, batteries accounted for 57% of the price of a medium-sized electric vehicle in 2015. By 2030, the cost is projected to fall to 14%. When and if electric vehicles become cheaper than internal combustion engine-powered cars and trucks, which might happen by 2030, electrics are expected to account for between 20% and 50% of all vehicle sales.

There is concern as to whether lithium producers can keep up with demand. Most manufacturers enter into long-term contracts with lithium miners including Ganfreng Lithium, Kidman Resources, Nemaska Lithium and Pilbara Minerals. Ganfreng, for example, had long-term contracts with Tesla, BMW and Volkswagen as of 2019. Chilean lithium producer SQM reported that global lithium demand was expected to grow by at least 20% in 2019 compared to 2018's approximately 270,000 metric tons.

For electrics to gain such high market share, there are several logistical challenges. Electric vehicles in such massive numbers would not only require vastly higher numbers of charging stations, but could also require a very significant increase in the generation of electricity.

The biggest news in advanced batteries for automobiles is being made at Tesla, the U.S.-based maker of high end, all-electric vehicles. Tesla's automobiles are unique on several counts. To begin with, the firm has been very successful in attracting buyers for its Model S sedan and Model X crossover, as well as its Model 3, launched in 2017. Next, Tesla's unique technology ties together thousands of small lithium-ion batteries, similar to cellphone batteries, in each car, as opposed to the normal use of one or two giant batteries per vehicle. This has enabled Tesla's cars to have more power and a range in the neighborhood of 200 to 300 miles per charge. Tesla has also increased the power density of its batteries, meaning more storage per kilogram.

In 2014, Tesla broke ground on a massive battery factory, known as the Gigafactory, near Reno, Nevada. The long-term plan is for a 10 million square foot plant capable of manufacturing enough batteries to power 500,000 cars per year. The factory had a soft opening in 2016, and began commercial production in early 2017. A facility known as Gigafactory 2 in the state of New York manufactures solar panels and solar roof tiles.

The company's next major project was the construction of the world's largest lithium-ion system in Australia. The 100-megawatt system will collect power from a wind farm built by Neoen that will be three times more powerful than any other battery system. CEO Elon Musk made headlines when announcing the project, promising to complete it within 100 days of signing an agreement or it would be paid for with $50 million of his own money. The battery bank was completed in November 2017, 40 days before deadline, and will supply power to more than 30,000 homes. This was a significant proof-of-concept for large-scale energy storage systems.

A Chinese leader in advanced batteries is BYD Company Limited. BYD is already a global leader in contract manufacturing of batteries and handsets for mobile phones. For example, BYD manufactures batteries for iPhones and iPods.

However, another Chinese leader in battery manufacturing is CATL (Contemporary Amperex Technology Ltd). Its strategy includes a vast increase in production capacity through the opening of a new megafactory in southeast China, as early as 2020.

The holy grail of electric car research is the development of battery technology that will enable a car to go 400 to 500 miles between recharges, while maintaining a competitive retail price for the car. The expensive Tesla Model S already claims a relatively long range of 370 miles.

Wireless Battery Charging for Electric Buses

In the city of Gumi, South Korea, a small number of electric buses are utilizing exciting new technology that enables to them to recharge their batteries, while moving or parked, wirelessly—that is, without being plugged in. The technology is capable of focusing an electromagnetic field towards a specific direction (the bus). The field recharges the battery with little energy loss during transmission. While expensive (Gumi's small system cost nearly $5 million, including two advanced, carbon fiber buses), the technology is very promising as a means of promoting zero-emission public transit.

IBM is working on a radical new lithium battery that could be far lighter than current batteries and have a vehicle range of as much as 500 miles. The Battery 500 Project is researching a lithium-air battery that, instead of shuttling ions back and forth between two metal electrodes, moves them between one metal electrode and air. The concept is similar to zinc-air batteries used to power hearing aids. The problem is that zinc-air batteries are not rechargeable and limited to a very small size.

Samsung Electronics is working to incorporate graphene into a lithium-ion battery. This ultra-thin form of carbon could increase a battery's capacity by as much as 45% and significantly reduce recharging time.

Lithium-ion batteries are also in use to store power electric utilities. In early 2017, AES Corp. began utilizing a bank of 400,000 batteries in Escondido, California built by Samsung SDI Co. for Sempra Energy.

Startups including Sila Nanotechnologies (silanano.com), Angstron Materials (a unit of Global Graphene Group, www.theglobalgraphenegroup.com), Enovix (enovix.com)and Enevate (www.enevate.com) produce materials for lithium-silicon batteries which have the potential to increase capacity by as much as 40%. German automaker BMW plans to use Sila's silicon anode technology in a plug-in electric vehicle by 2023.

Innolith AG (innolith.com) , a Swiss startup, announced in 2019 that it had built the world's first rechargeable battery capable of powering a vehicle for more than 600 miles between charges. The firm hopes to have the battery commercially available by 2022.

Top Producers of Lithium-Ion Batteries Include:
Panasonic Corporation, www.panasonic.com
LG Chem. www.lgchem.com
Samsung SDI Co., www.samsungsdi.com
BYD, www.byd.com
CATL, www.catlbattery.com

7) Natural Gas-Powered Vehicles Gain in Popularity/Long Term Potential Is Bright Thanks to Low Shale Gas Prices

Natural gas vehicles (NGVs), that is cars and trucks that run on either compressed natural gas (CNG) or liquid natural gas (LNG), are already in use around the world, especially in municipal fleets and buses. The International Association of Natural Gas Vehicles publishes detailed numbers for NGV markets yearly. It states that Iran, Pakistan, Argentina and Brazil are the world's leaders, followed by China and India. Each of these nations have more than 1 million NGVs. A large percentage of all new public transit buses run on natural gas, and 60% of the 8,000 new trash trucks sold annually in the U.S. run on CNG.

Natural gas is an attractive fuel for vehicles, not only because it enjoys a highly developed production and pipeline infrastructure, but also because it is economically and environmentally friendly. While initially costing substantially more per vehicle than standard fuel equivalents, natural gas engines save 30% or more on fuel costs, making the investment potentially very worthwhile over the long term, especially for commercial vehicles that drive long total distances each year. Emissions are significantly lower overall, and have much lower concentrations of polluting particles and harmful gases. Recognizing the possible economic benefits, UPS has put about natural gas trucks in service to haul its packages, including test trucks running on compressed natural gas, liquefied natural gas or propane. (UPS announced plans to invest $70 million in propane infrastructure, including 1,000 new trucks and 50 fueling stations largely in Louisiana and Oklahoma. UPS already operated a fleet of 900 propane trucks in Canada at the time.) GE, FedEx, AT&T, PepsiCo, Budweiser and Waste Management have converted parts of their fleets to natural gas starting.

As for LNG, Shell Oil is helping to install LNG filling units at dozens of Travel Centers of America and Petro Stopping Center truck stop locations on Interstate highways in the U.S., aimed at the long-haul truck market. Shell is interested also in greater use of LNG for trains and ships in America.

Some proponents, including financier T. Boone Pickens (who partly owns Clean Energy Fuels, a company that installs natural gas fueling stations), believe natural gas is a viable alternative for diesel fuel for semi-trailer trucks. Unlike switching to electric batteries or fuel cells, natural gas-powered trucks that travel primarily on major highways would not need as many new fueling stations. Clean Energy Fuels had more than 530 LNG and/or CNG fueling stations in early 2019, across the U.S. and in British Columbia, Canada.

Meanwhile, a natural gas-powered Honda Civic GX was on the U.S. market in selected locations. State and federal tax credits were available. Honda removed the natural gas version of the Civic from the market starting with the 2015 model year, citing low gasoline prices as the reason. Chrysler built its first CNG powered Ram pickup in 2012 (which is only available to fleet and commercial customers), and General Motors offers bi-fuel Chevrolet Silverado and GMC Sierra trucks as well as CNG vans and a CNG Impala sedan.

There are detractors who say that natural gas is as bad a pollutant as crude oil. However, the U.S. Department of Energy sponsored a "well-to-wheel" study which found that total emissions related to natural gas were 6% to 11% lower than gasoline. Another report by the nonprofit Center for Climate and Energy Solutions found that LNG reduces lifecycle carbon emissions by 13% compared with gasoline, and CNG lowers them by 29%.

Up until recently, cost was a factor when considering trucks powered by natural gas, since they were as much as $80,000 more expensive than diesel models. However, costs are dropping, and more filling stations were opening, making it possible for 18-wheel trucks to operate with one tank (as opposed to the two that used to be necessary for the long trips between refueling stations). New LNG heavy trucks are expected to go for $30,000 to $40,000 more than diesels, which can be made up in fuel costs savings within one year for heavily used trucks.

Truck manufacturers are taking notice of the trend. New natural gas engines are hitting the market such several engine options from Cummins Westport,

Inc. Heavy duty truck manufacturers Navistar and Volvo are producing 13-liter and 14-liter LNG-fueled engines.

After-market NGV conversion kits for trucks are made by firms that include NGV Motori USA and Landi Renzo. They allow standard diesel engines to run on a 60/40 blend of natural gas and diesel, which is blended on-demand at the engine. If the natural gas supply empties, the truck switches seamlessly to diesel only.

Ford offers natural gas-ready trucks in its F150 through F650 lines, as well as certain vans, as an option. This enables a Ford-certified after-market company to install a natural gas system to the truck without voiding the warranty. GM offers a similar feature on certain truck models.

8) Ethanol Production Soared, But U.S. Federal Subsidy Expires

High gasoline prices, effective lobbying by agricultural and industrial interests, and a growing interest in cutting reliance on imported oil put a high national focus on bioethanol in America in recent years. Corn and other organic materials, including agricultural waste, can be converted into ethanol through the use of engineered bacteria and superenzymes manufactured by biotechnology firms. This trend gave a boost to the biotech, agriculture and alternative energy sectors. At present, corn is almost the exclusive source for bioethanol in America. This is a shift of a crop from use in the food chain to use in the energy chain that is unprecedented in all of agricultural history—a shift that had profound effects on prices of corn for consumers, livestock growers (where corn has long been a traditional animal feed) and food processors.

Ethanol is an alcohol produced by a distilling process similar to that used to produce liquors. A small amount of ethanol is added to much of the gasoline sold in America, and most U.S. autos are capable of burning "E10," a gasoline blend that contains 10% ethanol. E85 is an 85% ethanol blend that may grow in popularity due to a shift in automotive manufacturing.

Yet, despite the millions of vehicles on the road that can run on E85 and billions of dollars in federal subsidies to participating refiners, many oil companies seem unenthusiastic about the adoption of the higher ethanol mix. E85 requires separate gasoline pumps, trucks and storage tanks, as well as substantial cost to the oil companies (the pumps alone cost about $200,000 per gas station to install). The plants needed to create ethanol cost $500 million or more to build. Many drivers who have tried filling up with E85 once revert to regular unleaded when they find as much as a 25% loss in fuel economy when burning the blend.

Ethanol is a very popular fuel source in Brazil. In fact, Brazil is one of the world's largest producers of ethanol, which provides a significant amount of the fuel used in Brazil's cars. This is due to a concerted effort by the government to reduce dependency on petroleum product imports. After getting an initial boost due to government subsidies and fuel tax strategies beginning in 1975, Brazilian producers developed methods (typically using sugar cane) that enable them to produce ethanol at moderate cost. The fact that Brazil's climate is ideally suited for sugarcane is a great asset. Also, sugar cane can be converted with one less step than corn, which is the primary source for American ethanol. Brazilian automobiles are typically equipped with engines that can burn pure ethanol or a blend of gasoline and ethanol. Brazilian car manufacturing plants operated by Ford, GM and Volkswagen all make such cars.

In America, partly in response to the energy crisis of the 1970s, Congress instituted federal ethanol production subsidies in 1979. Corn-based grain ethanol production picked up quickly, and federal subsidies amounted to several billion dollars. The size of these subsidies and environmental concerns about the production of grain ethanol produced a steady howl of protest from observers through the years. Nonetheless, the Clean Air Act of 1990 further boosted ethanol production by increasing the use of ethanol as an additive to gasoline. Meanwhile, the largest producers of ethanol, such as Archer Daniels Midland (ADM), have reaped significant subsidies from Washington for their output. However, Congress allowed the subsidy to expire on December 31, 2011.

In March 2014, the United Nations Intergovernmental Panel on Climate Change released two Working Group reports that questioned biofuels' cost to the environment, the food chain and ultimately their direct and indirect production of harmful emissions. Ethanol production requires enormous amounts of water. To produce one gallon of ethanol, up to four gallons of water are consumed by ethanol refineries. Add in the water needed to grow the corn in the first place, and the number grows to as much as 1,700 gallons of water for each gallon of ethanol. Meanwhile, Brazil has clear-cut as much as 1 million acres of tropical forest per year to produce sugarcane for ethanol.

In 2000, over 90% of the U.S. corn crop was used for human and animal consumption (much was exported to undeveloped countries), and less than 5% was used to make ethanol. By 2017/2018, 38.3% was used for ethanol, according to the Agricultural Marketing Resource Center.

A bright note for ethanol proponents is an increase in production efficiency, due to improvements in process technology (such as finer corn grinding to release more starch) and improved temperature control of fermentation to optimize yeast productivity. Better enzymes and yeast strains are also boosting output per bushel of corn.

On the negative side, other concerns regarding the use of corn to manufacture ethanol include the fact that a great deal of energy is consumed in planting, reaping and transporting the corn in trucks. In Brazil alone, the devastation of the rainforest and the need to ship ethanol to other countries emits about 50% more carbon than using petroleum fuels, according to agricultural nonprofit Food First.

9) Cellulosic Ethanol Makes Slow Commercial Progress

Traditional grain ethanol is typically made from corn or sugarcane. In contrast to grain ethanol, "cellulosic" ethanol is typically made from agricultural waste like corncobs, wheat husks, stems, stalks and leaves, which are treated with specially engineered enzymes to break the waste down into its component sugars. The sugars (or sucrose) are used to make ethanol. Since agricultural waste is plentiful, turning it into energy seems a good strategy. Cellulosic ethanol can also be made from certain types of plants and grasses.

The trick to cellulosic ethanol production is the creation of efficient enzymes to treat the agricultural waste. The U.S. Department of Energy is investing heavily in research, along with major companies such as Dow Chemical, DuPont and Cargill. A joint venture between U.S. ethanol producer POET and Royal DSM of the Netherlands is also betting on cellulosic ethanol, building a plant in Iowa next to a traditional corn-fed ethanol plant. Another challenge lies in efficient collection and delivery of cellulosic material to the refinery. It may be more costly to make cellulosic ethanol than to make it from corn. In any event, the U.S. remains far behind Brazil in cost-efficiency, as Brazil's use of sugar cane refined in smaller, nearby biorefineries creates ethanol at much lower costs per gallon.

Iogen, a Canadian biotechnology company has been operating a demonstration plant to determine how economical the process may be. Since 2004, Iogen has produced more than 500,000 gallons of cellulosic ethanol. Iogen developed and patented a new method to manufacture drop-in cellulosic biofuels from biogas using existing refinery equipment and operations in early 2014. Also in 2014, the company partnered with Raizen to open a $100 million, 10 million gallons per year cellulosic plant next to Raizen's Costa Pinto sugar cane mill in Brazil in late 2014.

In the U.S., by late 2014, two new commercial-scale plants opened, with another completed in 2015. The $275 million Project Liberty plant in Emmetsburg, Iowa is a joint venture of corn ethanol producer POET and Royal DSM of The Netherlands. It opened in September 2014.

Biofuel production in the U.S. was seriously impacted by an EPA ruling that significantly reduced both the total renewable fuel targets and the advanced biofuels blending targets. Specifically, the target for cellulosic ethanol would drop from 1.75 billion gallons to a mere 123 million in 2015 and 230 million in 2016, with 311 million gallons set for 2017. A proposal for 2018 called for 238 million gallons, while 2019's requirement was up to 420 million gallons. Most of the cellulosic ethanol plants have gone out of business due to lack of demand and high production costs. As of mid-2019, only Project Liberty was still in operation.

Meanwhile, the Canadian government plans to support the Canadian biofuel industry with up to 500 million Canadian dollars for construction of next-generation plants. Iogen is expected to receive part of those funds for construction of a commercial scale cellulosic ethanol plant.

SPOTLIGHT: Biofuels

Corn and sugar cane are not the only sources for creating biofuels.

Municipal/Agricultural Waste: Might be cheaply produced, but could be in limited supply compared to the billions of gallons of fuel needed in the market place.

Wood: Easily harvested and in somewhat healthy supply; however, cellulose can be more difficult to extract from wood than from other biosources.

Algae: The slimy green stuff does have the potential for high yields per acre, but the process for distilling its cellulose is complex, requiring a source of carbon dioxide to permeate the algae.

Grasses/Wheat: Including switchgrass, miscanthus and wheat straw, the supply could be almost limitless. The challenge here is creating efficient methods for harvesting and infrastructure for delivering it to biorefineries.
Vegetable Oils: Including soybean, canola, sunflower, rapeseed, palm or hemp. It is difficult to keep production costs of these oils low.

10) Fuel Cell and Hydrogen Power Research Continue/Fuel Cell Cars Enter Market

The fuel cell is nothing new, despite the excitement it is now generating. It has been around since 1839, when Welsh physics professor William Grove created an operating model based on platinum and zinc components. Much later, the U.S. Apollo space program used fuel cells for certain power needs in the Apollo space vehicles that traveled from the Earth to the Moon.

In basic terms, a fuel cell consists of quantities of hydrogen and oxygen separated by a catalyst. Inside the cell, a chemical reaction within the catalyst generates electricity. Byproducts of this reaction include heat and water. Several enhancements to basic fuel cell technology are under research and development at various firms worldwide. These include fuel cell membranes manufactured with advanced nanotechnologies and "solid oxide" technologies that could prove efficient enough to use on aircraft. Another option for fuel cell membranes are those made of hydrocarbon, which cost about one-half a much as membranes using fluorine compounds.

Fuel cells require a steady supply of hydrogen. Therein lies the biggest problem in promoting the widespread use of fuel cells: how to create, transport and store the hydrogen. At present, no one has been able to put a viable plan in place that would create a network of hydrogen fueling stations substantial enough to meet the needs of everyday motorists in the U.S. or anywhere else.

Many current fuel cells burn hydrogen extracted from such sources as gasoline, natural gas or methanol. Each source has its advantages and disadvantages. Unfortunately, burning a hydrocarbon such as oil, natural gas or coal to produce the energy necessary to create hydrogen results in unwanted emissions. Ideally, hydrogen would be created using renewable, non-polluting means, such as solar power or wind power. Also, nuclear or renewable sources could be used to generate electricity that would be used to extract hydrogen molecules from water.

The potential market for fuel cells encompasses diverse uses in fixed applications (such as providing an electric generating plant for a home or a neighborhood), portable systems (such as portable generators for construction sites) or completely mobile uses (powering anything from small hand-held devices to automobiles). The likely advantages of fuel cells as clean, efficient energy sources are enormous. The fuel cell itself is a proven technology—fuel cells are already in use, powering a U.S. Post Office in Alaska, for example. (This project, in Chugach, Alaska, is the result of a joint venture between the local electric association and the U.S. Postal Service to install a one-megawatt fuel cell facility.) Tiny fuel cells are also on the market for use in powering cellular phones and laptop computers.

FuelCell Energy of Danbury, Connecticut (www.fuelcellenergy.com), built a 59-megawatt fuel cell complex in Hwasung City, South Korea. The plant, which went online in 2014, is the world's largest to date. In 2017, the company announced a 20-megawatt fuel cell project with Korea Southern Power Company, with completion expected in 2018.

Shipments of fuel cell-equipped mobile devices may be very useful to certain types of customers as they can eliminate the need for frequent recharging of current battery-powered models. The Medis 24/7 Power Pack is a portable, disposable power source for small electronic devices such as cell phones and MP3 players. Manufactured by Medis Technologies, it is based on Direct Liquid Fuel cell technology, and may be of particular utility in military applications. Elsewhere, MeOH Power (formerly MTI MicroFuel Cells) manufactures a power pack for portable electronics that is based on direct methanol fuel cell technology.

In Bridgeport, Connecticut, a 14.9-megawatt fuel-cell complex generates enough electricity to power 15,000 homes (out of a total 51,000 in the city). In April 2015, a 1.4-megawatt cell went online at the University of Bridgeport.

Internet Research Tip: Micro Fuel Cells
For more information on research involving fuel cells for small applications, visit:
MeOH Power www.meohpower.com

Electric Vehicles vs. Fuel Cells

1) While the potential for fuel cell-powered vehicles seems promising, the majority of the automobile industry has focused instead on plug-in electric hybrids and all-electric vehicles as the alternative fuel base of choice for the near-term.

2) An important factor in that decision is the tremendous success and wide consumer acceptance of Toyota's Prius hybrid car. This success gave Toyota early dominance in the electric car field while other makers were still dreaming about fuel cells. A vital feature of the Prius is its very affordable price.

3) For fuel cells, the technical hurdles of distributing, storing and transporting hydrogen as a fuel are challenging. A massive investment in hydrogen filling stations would be required to make fuel cell vehicles practical for consumers.

4) Consumers, bureaucrats, investors and legislators already understand and trust the safety and ease of use of electricity, whether fixed or portable. This cannot be said for hydrogen.

5) Despite these obstacles, major automakers are continuing significant investments in fuel cell technology, with promising results. The costs of manufacturing fuel cells are dropping, to the point that they may eventually become affordable for passenger cars.

6) In the U.S., federal and state requirements for ever-higher average fuel efficiency ratings, and in some cases zero-emission vehicles, will encourage continued investment in fuel-cells. By 2016, limited numbers of fuel-cell powered vehicles were on the market in the U.S. and Japan.

Source: Plunkett Research, Ltd.

GM invested $1 billion in fuel cell vehicle research. The company leased 199 fuel cell-equipped Equinox crossover vehicles to customers as a test called Project Driveway in three U.S. markets, starting in early 2008. Despite the setback of the financial problems of 2008-09 that led to bankruptcy and a government bailout, GM managed to keep Project Driveway going, in which more than 5,000 drivers provided feedback on Chevrolet Equinox FCV sedans. Some of those vehicles accumulated more than 120,000 miles each.

GM began a long-term collaboration with Honda in July 2013 to co-develop next generation fuel cells and hydrogen storage systems. Honda leased test models of its "FCX" fuel cell-powered car to small numbers of customers in the U.S. and Japan. In 2017, Honda launched a new generation of its fuel cell vehicle, to be called Clarity. (See automobiles.honda.com/clarity.) GM is expected to follow with its own new FCV, per the companies' agreement. In January 2017, the two companies announced plans to invest a total of $85 million to form a joint venture called Fuel Cell System Manufacturing, where production is expected to begin as early 2020. Meanwhile, Hyundai Motor Co. began limited sales of a hydrogen-powered SUV in California in mid-2014.

Toyota unveiled a fuel cell car at the Tokyo automobile show in November 2013. The vehicle, a $57,500 FVC sedan with a 312-mile range called the Mirai, launched in Japan and in California in the U.S. in 2015. The Japanese government has committed to creating a network of 100 hydrogen filling stations. In the U.S., as of early 2018, there were only 39 retail hydrogen fueling stations (and all were in the state of California), a serious stumbling block for Toyota, which was planning to build another 12 stations in the northeastern U.S. in conjunction with Air Liquide.

In a bid to boost sales, Toyota and Honda offer fuel cell customers credit cards for up to $15,000 in fuel over the first three years of ownership. They also provide a rental car for up to three weeks per year in case a customer needs a car for a long trip outside of the range of existing hydrogen fueling stations.

Another problem is that many people still have concerns about the safety of hydrogen. Naturally gaseous at room temperature, storing hydrogen involves using pressurized tanks that can leak and, if punctured, could cause explosions. It is also difficult to store enough hydrogen in a vehicle to take it the 300+ miles that drivers are used to getting on a tank of gasoline. To do so, hydrogen must be compressed to 10,000 pounds per square inch and stored on board in bulky pressure tanks.

In 2010, U.S. President Obama signed a Nationwide Hydrogen Highway Initiative hoping to provide subsidies for up to 200,000 hydrogen fueling stations not more than five miles apart. In June 2013, the California Energy Commission approved $18.7 million to expand its hydrogen fueling station program. As of early 2017, California had 30 operational stations for vehicles.

Meanwhile, governments are facing up to the economic and technical difficulties of boosting alternative fuels through loans and subsidies, and car makers have received no return on their massive investments in fuel cells. Nonetheless, a 2012 survey of automotive industry executives by global accounting firm KPMG found that 20% of respondents thought fuel cell vehicles could attract more consumer demand than electric vehicles by 2025. Fuel cells or hydrogen-powered engines may eventually gain traction, but the technological challenges and investment required remain daunting.

Ten states, led by California, have set serious goals for zero-emission vehicles within their borders. The end game is to have 15% of vehicles to be running on electric or hydrogen power sold within each state by 2025. The additional states (including New York, Massachusetts, Maine, New Jersey, Oregon, Vermont, Maryland, Connecticut and Rhode Island) hope to have tens of thousands of additional zero-emission vehicles on the roads by then. Combined, these states total about 23% of the U.S. car market. While these mandates will undoubtedly evolve to some extent, they put a serious burden on car makers. Using hydrogen as a fuel may become a prime method of fulfilling the mandates, especially if financial incentives and tax credits are substantial enough and a massive network of hydrogen fueling stations emerges. California's mandate begins with small numbers of vehicles in 2018, growing to 15.4% of total car sales by 2025. Car makers are fighting to have the mandate modified or overturned, as they are greatly alarmed over the potential development costs and deterred by the fact that consumers have responded poorly to-date to offerings of electric cars other than the Tesla.

11) China Becomes the World's Largest Auto Market

The continuous growth of the middle class in is creating a vast and lucrative market for automobiles and trucks worldwide. China's most affluent residents have been eager buyers of expensive imported cars, while a mass market is growing for inexpensive, China-built family cars and vans. In addition, consumers in rural areas are buying their first vehicles, which are typically small, low-cost domestic cars or vans. Beijing's accession to the World Trade Organization brought about a steep reduction in tariffs on vehicle imports. For 2017, LMC Automotive reported 28.6 million new vehicles sold in China, compared to 28.03 million passenger vehicles sold in 2016, per the China Association of Automobile Manufacturers (CAAM). China had clearly become the world's largest car market, surpassing the U.S.

However, starting in mid-2018 China's car market was suffering a downturn, with sales falling 3% for the year compared to 2017 according to Chinese consulting firm ZoZoGo. China remains the largest car market in the world, with approximately 28 million vehicles sold in 2018 compared to about 17 million in the U.S.

Major automotive companies such as GM, Toyota, Honda, Volkswagen and others are exporting large numbers vehicles into China. These companies have also invested directly in manufacturing operations within China through government mandated joint ventures with Chinese firms. GM operates several automotive joint ventures in China including Shanghai General Motors (a partnership with Shanghai Automotive Industry Corp.) and Shanghai GM (Shenyang) Norsom Motors Co. As of mid-2019, GM had four manufacturing plants in China that produce Cadillac, Buick and Chevrolet vehicles.

Ford is investing $5 billion in the Chinese market and is hoping to increase its production capacity to 1.2 million passenger cars per year. Unfortunately, Ford's sales sin China fell by 37% in 2018 over 2017. The slump in the Chinese auto market extended to its 12th month in June 2019, which puts Ford in a tough situation. It arrived late in China compared to other Western manufacturers.

BMW has a manufacturing facility in China located in Shenyang. The German automaker is partnering with Chinese firm Brilliance in a joint venture called BMW Brilliance Automotive Co., Ltd.

China still offers relatively low costs, although wage rates have been growing substantially. A number of U.S. auto parts companies such as American Axle & Manufacturing Holdings, Inc. and ArvinMeritor, Inc. operate manufacturing plants in China.

A number of local Chinese manufacturers are vying for market share. Geely, which began as a refrigerator builder, first made and sold cars in 1998, with sales of a meager 200 vehicles. In March 2010, a much larger Geely agreed to purchase Ford Motor Company's Volvo Cars unit for $1.8 billion. China currently exports automobiles to 190 countries and regions, with Russia, Brazil and Iran being among the largest markets.

For the U.S. and European markets, there is the potential for exports from Chinese companies allied with industry leaders such as GM, Ford, Toyota, Honda and Volkswagen. For years, Chinese automakers have been on the receiving end of Western automotive know-how, which will come back to haunt the Westerners. As Chinese cars and trucks hit the global market, China's manufacturers will be in direct competition with their partners. For example, state-run Shanghai Automotive Industry

Corp. (SAIC), which has partnered with GM and Volkswagen, plans to sell its products in Europe as well as the U.S. Extremely low-priced, Chinese-built models could eventually have a major impact on sales of U.S. and European cars, but only if consumers can be convinced that they represent high quality and reliability.

By 2019, Chinese manufacturers were branching out into production and sales outside of China. SAIC, for example, it promptly sold out of its MG Hector SUV (which is made by the firm's Indian subsidiary MG Motor India). SAIC has also opened plants in Indonesia and Thailand, from which it is exporting vehicles throughout southeast Asia. Its goal is to reach 1 million overseas sales by 2025. Great Wall Motors Co. opened its first overseas manufacturing facility in Russia in Mid-2019, while BAIC Motor Corp. began production in South Africa in 2018 in a new $772 million plant.

Meanwhile, China has become one of the world's largest importers of oil, thanks to rapidly rising demand for gasoline. Watch for the Chinese Government to become a leading innovator in alternative fuel vehicles. For example, the city of Beijing converted its entire 120,000 vehicle bus fleet to run on compressed natural gas. Automakers in China, including BYD, are already pioneers in the manufacture of electric vehicles.

China offers compelling tax incentives to buyers of electric vehicles and requires manufacturers to fill an electric quota. Major automotive companies have committed to investing $150 billion in China's electric car market over the mid-term. German companies such as BMW and Volkswagen account for more than 50% of that investment. BMW is spending $4 billion to take full control of its BMW Brilliance Automotive joint venture, and plans to begin production of an all-electric iX3 SUV in China for export to foreign markets. Tesla broke ground on a new plant in Shanghai in January 2019, the first wholly foreign-owned car plant in China.

As for domestic electric vehicle production, Beijing Electric Vehicle (BJEV) is the largest manufacturer in China and the second largest in the world behind Tesla as of mid-2019. BJEV is a unit of BAIC Group.

12) India Sees Automobile Export Growth

Total passenger vehicle sales (including imports) for India reached 3.29 million units April-March 2018 over the same period in the previous year, up 7.89% according to the Society of Indian Automobile Manufacturers. The market has the potential to grow to much higher numbers over the mid-term. The Society of Indian Automobile Manufacturers reported that 4.0 million new passenger vehicles were built in that nation during the 2017-2018 fiscal year, up from 38.0 million the previous year, and a large portion were exported to other nations. (In addition, the nation builds millions of motor scooters, motorcycles and three-wheelers each year, plus a modest number of commercial vehicles.) The Indian government has committed to building 30 kilometers of new roads per day. Although India is nowhere near as large a market as China, it is attracting the attention of leading global manufacturers.

GM has two factories in India with a production capacity of 300,000 units per year. In mid-2015, the company announced plans to invest $1 billion over several years to make India into a global export hub. Plans include reducing manufacturing capacity in the country to 220,000 by 2025 ceasing production at one plant raising capacity at the second.

The port city of Chennai has attracted a number of automobile and parts manufacturers in recent years. Hyundai, Ford, Nissan/Renault and Daimler have invested large sums (in the case of Hyundai, $2 billion) in new manufacturing facilities.

Tata Group, an Indian industrial conglomerate, is another large presence in the car market. While selling steel to giants such as Honda and Toyota, the company also has its own major automobile venture in India, Tata Motors, which makes the Indica economy model. The company manufactures commercial and passenger vehicles and also provides automobile financing services. Tata Motors is also among the world's leading bus manufacturers, and it has expanded these activities through strategic partnerships with Tata Hispano Motors Carrocera SA, a Spanish bus and coach manufacturer, as well as Marcopolo, a Brazil-based company engaged in the manufacture of bodies for buses and coaches. The firm has also expanded its international presence through such activities as the manufacture and marketing of pick-up trucks in Thailand and the marketing of Fiat-branded cars in India, as well as through vehicle sales in several countries in Europe, Africa, the Middle East, Australia and Asia. Tata Motors also owns the Jaguar and Land Rover brands, an operation encompassing roughly 26 major vehicle subsidiaries worldwide

13) Mexico Is a Leading Automotive Maker and Exporter

Over the past several years, Mexico has grown to become a major producer and exporter of cars, trucks and other vehicles. Mexico's economic growth is expected to continue over the mid-term, fueled by its relatively young population (between 2000 and 2030, Boston Consulting Group expects the labor force there to grow by 18%, while China's will fall by 3%). Manufacturing wages are relatively low, at about $2.60 per hour as of May 2019. (Proposed changes to the NAFTA trade agreement with the U.S. and Canada may cause wages to rise substantially.) Mexico is home to a variety of advanced manufacturing industries. Automotive production, for example, has catapulted Mexico to be the world's 4th-largest exporter of cars behind Germany, South Korea and Japan. About 80% of Mexican-built vehicles are exported, and the majority go to the U.S. American-manufacturing gets some benefit, since roughly 40% of the parts found in Mexican imports were manufactured in the U.S. (compared to only 4% for imports from China) according to the Natural Bureau of Economic Research.

Automotive manufacturers have invested heavily in plants in Mexico. Between 2010 and 2016, manufacturers including Nissan, Honda, Volkswagen and Mazda invested $24 billion in automotive production. In 2018, production reached 3.9 million light vehicles, up 2.5% from 2017, according to the Mexican Automotive Industry Association.

Although automobile-related manufacturing is spread across much of central and northern Mexico, the greatest concentration is in the Bajio region, incorporating the Mexican states of Guanajuato, Queretaro, Aguascalientes and Jalisco. In this industrial heartland of the nation, which some observers refer to as "Mexico's Detroit," Mexican plants compete very effectively with their peers in the world's other auto centers.

The State of Queretaro alone employed more than 50,000 auto industry workers in roughly 80 factories in 2018. Excellent transportation networks nearby make it easy to ship finished products to other countries.

Visitors to the Leon airport, in the State of Guanajuato in the heart of the auto manufacturing district, are immediately struck by the enormous impact of the car and pickup manufacturing sector. Massive, modern plants line the highways, including one of GM's most important pickup truck plants close to the airport. Nearby, there are large numbers of modern hotels, attractive housing districts and good highways.

Mexico is a powerhouse of high-value manufacturing and a major export machine. Its close proximity to the American market, growing middle class, highly desirable workforce, reasonable costs and government support will continue to boost major manufacturing investments there. Mexico's strategy of entering into free trade agreements around the world will boost this trend even further. As of late 2018, the Trump administration was focused on renegotiating NAFTA, the main trade agreement between the U.S., Mexico and Canada. The outcome of these negotiations is likely to have a significant impact on Mexico's automotive industry.

14) Focus on Safety Improvements by Automakers

Today, advanced technologies are having a dramatic impact on vehicle safety records. Adaptive cruise control adjusts a car's speed relative to the speed of the vehicles nearby. Electronic stability control adjusts pressure on individual brakes if a sensor picks up wheel, steering wheel or brake data that suggests a loss of control. The U.S. government required this technology on all new vehicles. Collision sensors read tire, steering wheel and brake data and make adjustments such as closing sunroofs or adjusting seats to increase safety factors in the moments before a crash. Lane-drift systems utilize a rear-view mirror camera to detect unusual movement beyond the boundaries of the current lane. A warning sounds or the driver's seat vibrates to alert the driver. All of these options, with the exception of the lane-drift warning system, are currently available on many luxury vehicles, and on a growing number of mid-priced vehicles.

Many new vehicles are equipped with rear-view cameras, with images appearing on monitors installed in the dash board or in the central rear-view mirror. The cameras show anything or anyone directly behind the vehicle. In the spring of 2014, the U.S. National Highway Traffic Safety Administration finalized a ruling that will require all vehicles under 10,000 pounds and manufactured after May 1, 2018 to be equipped with rear visibility technology.

An immense issue is caused by texting on cellphones while driving. Studies show that it is common for 18 to 24-year-olds to send more than 100 texts per day. However, the combination of driving and texting is deadly. As of mid-2018, 47 U.S. states had passed laws prohibiting texting while driving. However, enforcement of such laws is nearly impossible, short of clear evidence that someone caused an accident while texting.

New applications are emerging that limit a cellphone or digital device's ability to receive or send calls and messages while a vehicle is moving, but they are selling slowly and are utilized at the cellphone owner's option. For example, Safe Driving Systems Corp. has developed an application that overrides a cellphone display when its owner is driving. Cogosense offers bSafeMobile, a software system for smartphones and tablets automatically places devices in safe mode while driving. Although many organizations, including leading cellphone service provider AT&T, are calling for restrictions on texting in moving vehicles, little is being done to actually enforce what is a rapidly growing safety problem.

Mercedes-Benz engineered a Mercedes S-Class that uses a stereo camera, radar and an infrared camera to follow nearby vehicles and objects on the road ahead. When potential problems are detected, the car's computers take control of the brakes, acceleration and steering from the driver. BMW has a 5-Series sedan with similar technology. GM has a similar concept, calling it a "super-cruise" system that takes temporary control of the vehicle when dangers are sensed. The Cadillac CT6 and CTS models have super-cruise installed, which Cadillac states can enable hands-free driving.

Adaptive cruise control is in use in many high-end vehicles. For example, Mercedes' Pre-Safe system uses its radar to scan for distances to nearby vehicles and, when a collision seems imminent, primes the braking system, tightens the seat belts and adjusts the car seats to optimum protection positions. Mercedes-Benz claims the system can reduce rear collisions by 75%. Another example of adaptive cruise control is the Acura collision-mitigation braking system. When a driver approaches another vehicle too quickly, a warning light flashes on the dashboard, followed by a tightening of the driver's seat belt and ultimately the braking system is engaged (if the driver has yet to put on the brakes). Similar systems are available from Volvo, which emit loud beeps and flash red lights on the dashboard; and from Infiniti, where a system beeps and pushes back on the accelerator. In a recent study, the Insurance Institute for Highway Safety reports that forward collision warning/avoidance technology may be able to prevent or mitigate up to 2.3 million police-reported crashes in the U.S. each year. In September 2015, U.S. government regulators announced that 10 auto manufacturers had agreed to install automatic braking systems using sensors to detect potential collisions as standard equipment on new vehicles over the mid-term.

15) Car Sharing Programs Like Zipcar and Autolib, AKA Mobility Services, Proliferate

Car sharing has become a big business in North America and Europe. This practice is called car sharing because the organizations providing the cars enable short-term, on-demand use, without the burdens of car ownership.

The costs of buying, operating, insuring and parking a personal automobile are extremely high. At the same time, consumer attitudes and behavior regarding transportation are evolving rapidly. Surveys in mature economies such as Japan show that a relatively large number of young people have no interest in purchasing a car. The percentage of people in major cities in the U.S. and UK who do not own cars is rising. The term Mobility Services is widely used to describe car sharing strategies like ZipCar, ride-on-demand systems like Uber and other alternative personal transportation systems.

Autonomous vehicles capable of driving themselves will have very profound effects on automobile manufacturing, usage, sales and ownership patterns. At least in dense urban environments, the result is very likely to be a large proportion of individuals who opt to use shared vehicles rather than user-owned cars.

A car sharing pioneer called Zipcar (www.zipcar.com) offers drivers inexpensive alternatives to owning their own cars. Zipcar members are issued smart cards that allow them to unlock Zipcar vehicles with a wave of the card over the windshield. The cars are equipped with pre-paid cards for use at gas stations and insurance coverage; and drivers are allowed 180 miles of driving per day. Business boomed during the firm's early years, as gas prices escalated to dizzying heights and then again at the onset of the global economic crisis. In March 2013, Avis Budget Group completed its acquisition of Zipcar for $491 million.

Zipcar is utilizing innovative, densely populated locations as pick up spots, such as garages in major hotels and university campuses. The firm spawned a number of similar offerings from competitors, including rental car firm Hertz Corp.'s Hertz 24/7 (formerly Hertz on Demand and Connect by Hertz) and Enterprise Rent-A-Car's CarShare (formerly WeCar). Hertz is taking the car sharing business so seriously that all vehicles in its U.S. fleet are equipped with devices that allow customers to use the internet to reserve and unlock a rental car from Hertz 24/7. There are no membership or annual fees, and users earn points in the Hertz Gold frequent renter program.

Luxury versions of car sharing are also available in select cities, offering vehicles for manufacturers such as Mercedes-Benz and Porsche. For example, Turo Go is an app for startup rental company Turo for luxe car shares in Los Angeles, San Francisco and San Diego. A number of car share companies use automotive subscription service software from Clutch Technologies (www.driveclutch.com). Many of these services provide forums in which owners can list their personal vehicles for rent.

An initiative in France is Autolib, a car sharing program which has about 2,000 electric vehicles. Along with commissioning the vehicles (designed by CEO Vincent Bolloré), Autolib is building a total of 4,000 electric charging stations for parking and recharging.

BMW offers the BMW on Demand program. Available vehicles range from its 1 Series of compacts up to its luxury 7 Series. Cars can be picked up and dropped off at the BMW Welt, the company's exhibition and event center next to its headquarters in Munich. BMW is betting that the trend of younger urban drivers choosing not to own vehicles will continue. The project is similar to other European initiatives, including Daimler's car2go (which offered service in 26 locations in eight countries as of 2019). BMW also has a European rental program called DriveNow in partnership with German car rental company Sixt AG. Electric cars are accessed by a computer chip embedded in driver's licenses, and can be left at any location without having to return it to a specific drop off point. In 2019, BMW and Daimler announced plans to merge their car-sharing businesses into one firm, with services to include Uber-like ride-hailing, as well as parking space locator apps. The two companies are investing about $1.1 billion in the joint venture.

16) Wireless Information Systems Surge Ahead in Vehicles: Telematics, Intelligent Transportation (ITS) and Real Time Traffic Information

Telematics: Many near-term advances in car and truck technology will lie in on-board software, wireless communications and convenience features known broadly as "telematics." Using cellular telephone technology, fee-based telematics networks, which allow drivers to check e-mail and online services for weather, stock quotes or driving directions merely by voicing a command, are already in place. Many other features are also provided. GM's OnStar is a leading telematics system. Such systems offer varying degrees of networked services linking cars to external systems such as global positioning systems (GPS). The external systems monitor the position of each vehicle and perform tasks such as unlocking doors or switching off lights remotely upon request. They also dispatch service vehicles or medical aid when necessary. More recent innovations include ultrasonic rear sensors that warn drivers when they are about to back into something, and voice-activated phone dialing and navigation plotting.

OnStar services (www.onstar.com) are available in GM cars worldwide. The OnStar RemoteLink App affords users the ability to view vehicle diagnostics, such as tire pressure, oil life and gasoline levels, start the vehicle remotely and get navigation assistance.

Significant improvements to OnStar's accident-reporting system have been developed. The system is able to notify 911 of further details regarding automobile accidents, including the force and direction of impact and whether the car has rolled over. Through an Advanced Automatic Crash Notification (AACN) system, such data travels in real time to an internet database that alerts hospitals, police and similar emergency responders.

OnStar's 4G LTE service is standard equipment on all new GM vehicles. Most other major car manufacturers are following suit with similar products. As the technology grows, it will be able to provide more and more options, both safety- and entertainment-related.

Apple's CarPlay software displays an iPhone's screen on a vehicle's dashboard, offering access to apps such as Apple's mapping tool.

Porsche's Porsche Communication Management (PCM) system uses Wi-Fi, Bluetooth and cable to connect smartphones with its vehicles. Dashboard touchscreens are sensitive to handwriting, and links written letters or numbers to contacts or addresses automatically.

Car rental giant Avis reported it had 100,000 vehicles connected to the internet as of late 2018. It uses a device located on the underside of a vehicle's hood that senses the car's location, fuel level, tire pressure and break pad status. This data is vital for Avis to maintain its fleet efficiently. It also affords the company the ability to make its cars more accessible to customers by creating self-service, counter-free hubs away from airports.

Predictive Diagnostics: Telematics systems that include sensors connected to engines and transmissions are now capable of providing real time diagnostics to fleet headquarters. This can be particularly valuable to owners of truck fleets, where diesel engines represent immense investments, and predictive software can alert owners to potential failures and the need for preventive maintenance. PACCAR, a major maker of trucks, is working with Sprint Nextel to create an onboard package that includes telematics, navigation, GPS location reporting and predictive analytics.

ITS (Intelligent Transportation Systems): The FCC set aside the 5.9-gigahertz spectrum for wireless networks providing in-car services known as Intelligent Transportation Systems (ITS). ITS includes a broad number of information technologies that can provide an electronic communications link to cars and trucks, enabling drivers to be alerted to road hazards, delays, construction and accidents. At the same time, ITS can transmit driving directions and a wealth of additional driving-related information. (Services such as this have been available to drivers in Japan for a few years.)

The U.S. Department of Transportation has a serious effort underway to cooperate with a variety of industries to develop ITS. (See its ITS-specific web site at www.its.dot.gov.)

In August 2012, the U.S. government launched a $25 million study in which 3,000 cars, trucks and buses in Michigan were outfitted with data recorders and Wi-Fi transmission equipment to communicate changes in traffic patterns such as collisions and road work. Displays mounted on vehicle dashboards warn drivers of potential hazards. The NHTSA reports that intervehicle communication has the ability to reduce as much as 80% of vehicle crashes involving non-impaired drivers. The concept may be close to reality. The NHTSA estimated that vehicle-to-vehicle transmitters will add about $350 to a car's cost by 2020.

In a similar vein, Europe's eCall initiative will require all new cars to be equipped with wireless transmitters for sending and receiving data regarding nearby traffic hazards and informing emergency personnel (in the same manner utilized by GM's OnStar system). The requirement took effect in April 2018.

"V2V" or vehicle-to-vehicle communications systems and "V2I" (vehicle-to-infrastructure) systems are under intense development and research. The 2017 Cadillac CTS sedan was the first vehicle on the road with the technology which can transmit data such as hard braking in the vehicle ahead. They may soon be required in all new vehicles as a basis for collision avoidance.

Advanced Onboard Traffic Information: Satellite Radio provider Sirius XM, though best known for satellite-based music, has jumped into advanced onboard traffic information provided by satellite. Previously, GPS navigation systems calculated routes to a destination, with no knowledge of true traffic conditions along the planned route. Sirius XM NavTraffic provides detailed traffic information overlaid on the navigation road map, allowing the navigation system to show the traffic conditions between the driver and his or her destination. The display can show traffic delays, such as accidents or construction, and the average speed of vehicles along the way.

Waze, Inc. offers a social driving app through which drivers share traffic data, maps and other travel information, such as where to find the cheapest gas, or a friend's location on route to common destinations. Google acquired Waze in 2013.

The ever-increasing amounts of data, known as "big data," require more and more sophisticated technology for tracking and analysis. Take, for example, Inrix, Inc. (inrix.com), which gathers data from a community of millions of vehicles, including locations, speeds, weather conditions and nearby events such as highly attended concerts or sporting events. Inrix crunches the data and produces detailed maps used by drivers, city and state authorities and emergency services providers. Drivers can use Inrix to avoid congested areas, traffic authorities are able to post information on highway signs relating to problems and emergency services can respond more quickly when needed. The state of New Jersey's transportation department spends approximately $540,000 per year on an Inrix system. Inrix acquired automotive services and software provider OpenCar, Inc. in 2016.

17) Embedded LTE Wi-Fi and Onboard Apps Incorporated by Auto Makers in New Car Infotainment Systems

The AAA Foundation for Traffic Safety reports that the average American driver spends 51 minutes per day in a car, making those drivers captive audiences every day for the "fourth screen," that is, devices viewed in vehicles. The fourth screen (following the television, the personal computer and the cellphone as the first three screens) may be any portable device such as a tablet or portable media player. At the same time, automakers are increasingly focused on enhancing the screens embedded into a vehicle's dashboard.

Advanced information systems in automobiles, such as the Ford Sync system, utilize Wi-Fi to receive their initial software customization at the factory. For example, Wi-Fi may be used at the plant to load one type of emergency response package for cars intended for sale in the U.S., and another for cars that will be sold in other nations. Now, Tesla and other makers use Wi-Fi to install software updates to their vehicles. As a next step, several car makers, including Ford, GM, Chrysler and Volkswagen are turning their vehicles into Wi-Fi hotspots, so that passengers can use their laptops, tablet computers and other devices on the road.

As advanced wireless broadband systems, such as LTE, are ultrafast, such systems can offer passengers access to conduct business, watch videos, listen to music of their choice and send emails. The GENIVI Alliance (www.genivi.org) has been formed by several auto industry leaders in order to create an open standard for "In-Vehicle Infotainment" or IVI. Members include GM, BMW, Volvo, Honda, Nissan and parts maker Visteon.

One way to enable onboard internet hotspots is to create a system whereby an owner's smartphone becomes a single internet connection for all passengers and all of their devices. However, auto makers are now embedding independent wireless receivers into their cars—systems that require their own wireless service contracts. GM is offering embedded 4G broadband provided by AT&T for onboard Wi-Fi. (GM's popular OnStar telematics system has long featured built-in wireless communications for directions and emergency phone calls.)

Meanwhile, car makers are rushing to develop sophisticated smartphone apps and onboard apps that enable owners to customize and communicate with their cars. Ford's AppLink service is available on most Ford models, including the Mustang, Fusion Hybrid, Focus, F-150 pickup and the E-Series van. Ford's SYNC already offers real-time traffic information, turn-by-turn directions and personalized sports and weather reports, in addition to hands-free operation of cellphones and sound systems.

Under new developments in AppLink, car owners will be able to download entertainment of their choice to SYNC for listening while they drive. The wildly popular Pandora music service was among the first offerings. But this is just the beginning of the services apps will bring to onboard SYNC infotainment systems. Owners will be able to download travel and time management apps, such as systems that will alert them to changes in the status of flights while in route to the airport. Voice-activated apps may even enable drivers to update their social media such as Facebook or Twitter.

Meanwhile, Ford wants apps to enable owners to better manage their cars remotely. Such apps will include systems to diagnose car performance and maintenance. SYNC Destination enables owners to enter a destination into a smartphone at their convenience, and then beam it to the car for turn-by-turn guidance later. A car maker's ability to offer the maximum synchronization with a consumer's smartphone in a safe and entertaining manner is rapidly becoming one of the most hotly contested fields in the automobile market.

Toyota, GM, Tesla and Mercedes-Benz, among others, are also jumping on the app access wagon in varying degrees. At Tesla, for example, new models sport 17-inch video monitors in the dashboard with USB plugs for internet access. At GM, the touch screen measures eight inches and can be activated by voice, touch or controls mounted on the steering wheel. Mercedes has developed an app called DriveStyle as well as a voice activated assistant called Hey Mercedes, and BMW offers an app program called ConnectedDrive.

Google's Android Auto as well as Apple's CarPlay stream phone data through a car's USB port to a monitor set into the dashboard. Proponents say the displays keep drivers from looking down at their smartphones or dashboards. Detractors are concerned that the displays are simply more distractions from the road.

An advanced system is installed in the new BMW 7-series sedan which includes the ability for the car to park itself when a driver exits the vehicle and presses a button on a remote control. The 7-series also has a color heads-up display that projects information on the windshield with 75% more display area than previous models, and the infotainment center offers its own app store. In addition, the vehicle has gesture control, allowing drivers to accept or reject phone calls and adjust sound system volume by waving their hands.

Apple has agreements with a number of auto manufacturers including Audi, BMW, GM, Honda and Toyota to install its Siri voice command service in new vehicles. The service utilizes "eyes free" buttons that engage Siri so that the driver can request information from the internet on everything from weather to navigation to nearby restaurant reviews.

The use of digital assistants such as Amazon's Alexa is expanding into vehicles. BMW announced in late 2016 that its "Connected" services would enable Alexa users to lock car doors or check tire pressures remotely. Ford is also integrating Alexa into its Fusion and Escape models. While driving, users can receive alerts regarding shopping lists and nearby stores that offer the necessary items. Mercedes-Benz offers a similar feature called In Car Office, which integrates Microsoft Exchange calendars into vehicles.

Google offers telematic software that was in 19% of all in-car operating systems as of early 2019. IHS Markit forecasts that Google systems will be in one-third of car operating systems by 2024. Volkswagen has developed its own operating system that can run apps from the cloud, as has BMW.

Samsung Electronics, with its subsidiary Harman International Industries (which Samsung acquired in 2016 for $2 billion), is working on a fully digital vehicle cockpit design featuring a bank of screens stretching from one side of the car to the other. Drivers will be able to adjust controls in the vehicle or use smart apps to command changes via digital assistants at home or at the office. Passengers will be able to watch streaming video or surf the internet. Samsung hopes to have the system installed in vehicles by the 2021-2022 model year.

There is some concern that connectivity opens the door for hackers who might take control of crucial systems such as braking, steering or engine startup and shutdown. Hackers also might be able to unlock doors and drive off using cellular, Bluetooth or other wireless connections. Manufacturers are working on ways to secure automotive computer systems. Toyota, for example, programs its onboard computers to recognize outside commands and reject them.

18) Technology Drives Insurance Efficiencies/Policy Holders Allow Their Habits to Be Tracked for Lower Insurance Rates

Like other financial services sectors, the insurance industry has undergone major changes due to the internet and advanced data networks. The internet and the development of e-commerce have delivered more expedient operations and cost efficiency to the insurance industry, while enabling customers to get pricing and to order policies online. Now, very fast cellphone networks, smartphones and tablets will be the biggest drivers of change in terms of interfacing with customers and with agents in the field. At the same time, the advent of "big data," that is, vast databases of customer activity, claims data, environmental data and more, is enabling underwriters to better evaluate risks and thereby adjust pricing correctly on an individual customer basis.

State of the art software is also providing powerful risk modeling and management tools to insurance underwriters. Such software makes it easier and faster for underwriters to rate customers according to risk and thereby quickly determine the most appropriate (and profitable) price for a given policy. Adopting risk modeling technology can enable an underwriter to confidently enter new areas of risk and write new types of specialty insurance.

Meanwhile, savvy underwriters are utilizing advanced communications systems and software to make their sales systems—both direct- and agency-based—more efficient. Their goals are faster response to the customer and higher productivity. The benefits of getting all agents onto an underwriter's computer network are worth the expense. The internet makes it possible for an agent to log in, submit a request for an underwriting, a binder (a preliminary agreement to provide immediate coverage), or a firm quote, and then receive the fastest possible response. It wasn't very long ago that such functions were handled by snail mail and printed forms. Advanced communications systems enable both underwriters and agents to achieve much greater productivity. As a result, profits can be improved and savings can be passed along to the consumer.

Growing numbers of drivers are choosing to install data-logging devices into ports in their cars that transmit information about driving habits from car computers to insurance companies via cellphone networks. Sometimes called "user-based insurance," the technology affords insurance companies the ability to offer drivers individualized pricing based on data collected.

The Progressive Corporation offers a program called Snapshot (formerly called MyRate), which utilizes on-board telematics. Drivers receive periodic reports about their driving habits and those who drive cautiously and log fewer miles are offered discounts, depending on which state they are in. Progressive collects and analyzes data for a period of six months, after which the customer can remove the device. GMAC Insurance, a subsidiary of American Capital Acquisition Corporation, offers a similar program using the OnStar telematics system. Unlike

Progressive's Snapshot program, the GMAC version includes GPS data on a driver's whereabouts.

Conversely, drivers who opt into telematic measurements of their driving habits can face surcharges for reckless driving (such as excessive miles, high speeds and hard braking) in some states. Using smartphones while driving is also leading to soaring insurance rates. Star Farm Mutual Auto Insurance Co. conducted a survey in 2015 which found that 36% of those surveyed admitted to texting while driving and 29% access the internet (up from 31% and 13% respectively in 2009). The percentages are even higher for Millennials, of which 64% reported that they text while driving and 54% use the internet. Allstate reported that vehicle-related deaths rose 8% in the first nine months of 2016, largely due to smartphone use while driving. Consequently, a number of insurers have raised rates by as much as 8%.

At present, careful drivers are the customers who will be the most motivated to participate in monitoring programs. As the use of telematics grows by car insurance underwriters, all drivers may eventually be required to participate in programs like Snapshot in order to obtain insurance. This would essentially be forced, automatic, ever-present surveillance of driving habits.

SPOTLIGHT: Car Insurance by the Mile

San Francisco-based Metromile offers pay-as-you drive auto insurance measured through an onboard sensor called Metronome that plugs into a vehicle's data port. Drivers who log more miles pay higher rates than those who drive less. Policies are underwritten by National General Insurance Group.

Teenaged and young adult drivers are also eligible for special rate programs that utilize telematics. Although these age groups have traditionally been difficult and costly to insure, programs such as Safeco Corp.'s Teen Safety Rewards (formerly called Teensurance) and American Family Mutual Insurance Co.'s Teen Safe Driver Program use on-board surveillance technology to track driver locations and driving habits. Young drivers who consistently drive safely get a substantial break on their auto insurance premiums. Teen Safety Rewards, for example, is GPS-based and offers drivers up to age 25 as much as a 15% discount. Other companies such as Nationwide Mutual Insurance Co. and State Farm Mutual Automobile Insurance Co. offer discounts to young drivers who complete safety courses (some may be taken online). Also of note is Fireman's Fund Insurance Co.'s offer to independent young adults up to age 27 who can qualify for their parents' multiline, multicar and long-term customer discounts of between 35% and 50%.

SPOTLIGHT: DriveCam

In an effort to monitor commercial vehicle drivers, Lytx (formerly DriveCam, Inc.), www.lytx.com is marketing a video camera with audio that records activity both inside and outside moving vehicles. Sudden movements trigger the DriveCam device to send digital feed to the company's central monitoring station for analysis. Alerts are e-mailed to parents within 24 hours and weekly reports on driving skills are sent as well. The cost for the camera and a one-year monitoring contract is relatively expensive, but many insurance companies are willing to pay for in order to attract new business. The company also offers products that assist in truck fleet fuel management and tracking.

In a similar vein, life insurance premiums may be discounted for certain policy holders who agree to have their habits tracked by smartphone or wearable devices such as the Fitbit. John Hancock was the first U.S. insurer to institute such a policy, which it calls Vitality, in 2015. Under the policy, customers earn points for healthy habits such as not smoking, maintaining low cholesterol levels and regular exercise. There are three point levels: silver, gold and platinum. Gold level participants, for example, enjoy about a 9% discount on a 20-year, $500,000 term life insurance policy.

Another twist on habit-tracking is the use of algorithms to analyze a variety of data, including customer survey responses, data pulled from prescription pharmaceutical databases and motor vehicle records. Startup Haven Life (which is owned by Massachusetts Mutual Life Insurance Co.) offers some of the lowest rates available for life insurance to individuals who rate highly in healthy habits, spend less on prescription drugs and have clean driving records.

Meanwhile, technology is now on the market to assist corporate insurance buyers in managing the purchasing process and attempting to receive the best prices. For example, HighRoads, www.highroads.com, sells software that enables corporate health insurance purchasing managers to bypass brokers and send requests for bids directly to major companies. The insurance firms are able to submit their bids online. The software has been used by customers including Dell, Pfizer, IBM, Bristol-Myers Squibb and Verizon.

19) Uber and Didi Dominate the Car on Demand (Raid Hailing) Industry

Uber, Inc. is a California-based creator of the Uber mobile app which connects drivers and ridesharing services with passengers. The application serves over 600 cities in 65 countries throughout the Americas, Europe, the Middle East, Africa and Asia Pacific. Upon receiving a ride request, Uber sends the closest driver to fulfill it. Riders can rate their experiences with drivers for other riders to view. The company retains a fee from each ride that it books and then passes the balance of the fare to the drivers.

Uber has expanded very aggressively on a worldwide basis, although it merged its operations in China with local competitor Didi Chuxing, after Uber incurred massive losses in China. This enabled the firm to concentrate its expansion efforts and cash in other markets, including the vast market in India where it is investing heavily. Uber is a major competitor in India, where it has been purchasing cars and leasing them out to local drivers who want to work with the firm.

Uber is also expanding into delivery services of many types. UberEATS is a restaurant-prepared meal delivery service that is available in dozens of cities worldwide. Uber, through its cutting-edge technologies and industry-leading experience base, is in a position to potentially revolutionize the freight trucking dispatch industry. UberPOOL matches riders heading in the same direction to save on fares based on a car pool-like service. In 2016, the firm launched Uber Freight, which connects shippers with trucks. Also during 2016, it acquired the self-driving truck technology firm Otto. While the company remains privately held, it has attracted several billion dollars in investment capital and has been able to maintain a sufficient cash balance to enable it to fund its global expansion. In 2017, Uber announced a joint venture with Russia's Yandex.Taxi, in which the Russian firm will hold a 59.3% majority stake. By 2018, Uber had largely abandoned its solo efforts in Russia, China and Southeast Asia. The company held an IPO in 2019.

Lyft, Inc. is a major competitor to Uber in the U.S. and Canada and is based in San Francisco. The firm hit its 1 billionth ride in September 2018. According to a 2018 Raymond James report, Lyft had about 23% of the U.S. ride-hailing market share while Uber had about 60%. Lyft also held an IPO in 2019.

Meanwhile, China's Didi Chuxing is working to push into new markets and invest in developing driverless technology. It recently expanded into Japan and Latin America. The firm is a member of a loose alliance of ride sharing companies including Lyft.

Other ride hailing services include India's Ola, Korea's Kakao Taxi, Singapore's Grab (which acquired Uber's Southeast Asia ride sharing and food delivery business in March 2018) and the EU's Gett. Gett acquired U.S. rival Juno for $200 million in April 2017. The ride hailing industry is expected to rise from $36 billion in 2016 to $285 billion in 2030, according to Goldman Sachs.

The industry, and especially Uber which has been particularly aggressive in its expansion, faces many challenges. Uber has skirted a number of regulatory issues in many countries by claiming that it is an online service company rather than a transportation provider. For example, in the EU during late 2017, The European Court of Justice ruled to restrict Uber's activities through stricter licensing requirements for Uber drivers and vehicles because the service was deemed a transportation service rather than a digital platform. Taxi drivers in cities around the world have protested against Uber and its competitors for similar reasons.

One study found that Uber drivers generate on average $15.58 per hour before expenses such as fuel and maintenance. Uber drivers are classified as contractors, who do not enjoy the same protections and compensations as employees. Some Uber rivals, such as Juno (which was acquired by Gett in 2017) and Lyft, offer drivers better pay. Juno also offers equity ownership stakes to drivers who book high numbers of rides.

As of September 2019, the state of California appeared close to passing landmark legislation that would require firms, such as Uber and Lyft, that rely on gig (contract) workers to consider these workers to be classified as employees. This would create massive changes within gig-based companies of all types. Multiple laws and regulations that protect employees and regulate the ways in which firms must treat them would come into play, such as minimum wage, unemployment coverage, employer's liability, OSHA, EEOC and a long list of additional rules. Unions are extremely excited at the prospect of unionizing the gig industry's hundreds of thousands of California workers. If the bill is passed, it could take effect as early as January 1, 2019. Uber, Lyft and food delivery firm DoorDash vowed to invest a joint $90 million to put a ballot in front of voters in 2020, aimed at overturning the law.

In the EU, Uber offers some health benefits, including maternity and paternity leave as well coverage for injuries while driving and sick pay for illnesses unrelated to driving. The company is partnering with AXA SA to pay for these benefits. In the U.S., drivers are insured with vehicle-accident coverage of up to $1 million while on the job.

According to Lyft in its "2018 Economic Impact Report," a survey of its customers found that one-half of passengers interviewed said they use their personal cars less frequently, and 250,000 Lyft passengers reported eliminating a personal household vehicle because they are able to use ride-hailing services. Lyft surveyed a total of 30,000 passengers and 37,000 drivers.

20) Self-Driving, Autonomous Cars Receive Massive Investments in Research and Development Worldwide

In September 2016, the U.S. National Highway Traffic Safety Administration (NHTSA)announced a 15-point safety assessment guideline to be used by manufacturers planning to produce self-driving vehicles. The list covers data sharing, data privacy, safety systems, crashworthiness and consumer education, among other things. A car's systems must be able to easily switch from machine driving to human driving when needed. All features must be submitted to the NHTSA for certification.

The Levels of Self-Driving Technologies

Level 0: The driver is always in total control, with no assistance. However most new cars today come with automated safety features that may adjust traction and braking under certain circumstances.

Level 1: Very simple driver assistance, such as cruise control and parking assist. The driver always controls the direction of the car on the road.

Level 2: The car can steer itself under certain situations, such as a slow-moving traffic jam. Requires constant monitoring by the driver.

Level 3: The car can largely steer, brake and adjust speed by itself. However, the car realizes its own limitations and may ask the driver to retake control at any moment. Technologies employed may include such items as adaptive cruise control and automatic lane centering.

Level 4: This is the lowest level of truly autonomous driving. The car is able to perform all driving tasks under most driving conditions.

Level 5: This is full automation, as no driver is required at all. The vehicle may be operated unoccupied.

Today, self-driving technology is largely a reality, although it will require continuous refinement to make it capable of meeting the demands of day-to-day transportation in a safe manner. Armed with sensors, cameras and cutting-edge software, these vehicles can navigate themselves completely. Machine learning and artificial intelligence are key to the development and operation of reasonably safe, practical autonomous vehicles. The more that such vehicles are tested on the road, the greater the ability of their systems to learn the endless variations of road conditions, traffic flow, pedestrian activities and highway hazards. Ford Motor Co. acquired Argo AI, an artificial intelligence research and development firm that had grown to 330 employees by 2019. GM has invested in Cruise Automation, a similar firm that grew from 40 employees in 2016 to 740 by 2019. The company hoped to deploy autonomous service by late 2019, but announced a delay until it can log more test miles.

The technology also relies on maps that are constantly updated as roads and conditions change. A company called Here (originally owned by Nokia but acquired by BMW, Daimler and Audi) is mapping roads in the U.S. and Europe using data acquired from truckers equipped with scanners. Google's self-driving unit is also working on precise mapping using technology that uses lasers transmitted from specially outfitted cars that create images of roads and their surroundings. Another company, Mobileye, makes camera systems that enable vehicles to detect obstacles and apply the brakes to avoid collisions. Volkswagen and BMW are equipping models with Mobileye, and will gather and analyze the images to create maps in a crowdsourcing model.

By 2030, Boston Consulting Group estimates that one-quarter of the miles driven in the U.S. will be by shared, self-driving vehicles. Costs associated with driving will drop accordingly, as will the percentage of people in America who own personal vehicles. In a recent study, Deloitte Consulting found that the cost of personal car ownership was on average 97 cents per mile in 2017, but was expected to fall by as much as two-thirds when shared, self-driving vehicles become the norm.

Tesla led the pack with software updates for its popular Model S that allow the cars to operate largely by themselves on highways. The firm hopes to have a self-driving taxi fleet to be on the roads by late 2020 pending regulatory approval. Tesla drivers could eventually use a smartphone app to put their vehicles into this service, collecting 25% to 30% of the fee charged from riders. Daimler-Benz unveiled its F015 autonomous vehicle (AV) concept car in early 2015, while Audi launched a road-legal AV about the same time. Chevrolet introduced its FNR fully-autonomous concept car at the Shanghai motor show.

Google has been testing its driverless cars, which have logged millions of road miles. (A driver/observer is in each car when it is on the road.) The onboard equipment includes an $80,000 3-D video camera that watches for things like pedestrians and traffic lights, radar and car position sensors. Equipment costs will plummet when these units go into volume production.

Google's self-driving effort has been placed into a special subsidiary named Waymo. It has been conducting tests of self-driving cars for several years, and in 2017 it announced plans to add 500 customized Chrysler minivans to its existing fleet of 100 cars. Passengers have the use of buttons to start the vehicle, pull the vehicle over, lock or unlock doors and contact a call center. Waymo is partnering with Lyft to offer rides in the Phoenix metro area in 10 driverless Waymo One vehicles (with human safety observers onboard). In July 2019, the firm received permission from California legislators to transport passengers as part of the state's Autonomous Vehicle Passenger Service pilot.

Uber instituted a test program for driverless vehicles in Pittsburgh, Pennsylvania in September 2016, and later launched tests in the Phoenix, Arizona area. Tragically, in March 2018, an Uber self-driving car (while under minimal supervision by an observer riding in the car) struck and killed a woman who was pushing a bicycle in a street in Arizona. Uber has realigned its effort by agreeing to work with Toyota in the self-driving field. Toyota announced that it would invest $500 million in Uber and that technology from both firms will be integrated into Toyota vehicles to be built for use on Uber's ride-sharing platform. Uber resumed self-driving car tests in Pittsburgh in late 2018.

Industry analysts estimate that the cost of driving a mile in an owner-driven vehicle is between 60 cents and $1.00, while rides with Uber or Lyft drivers cost between $2.50 and $3.00. Taking the driver out of the vehicle would save approximately two-thirds of the cost. It's no surprise that Uber, Lyft and Didi Chuxing (in addition to Google and Chinese search engine firm Baidu) are all investing in driverless technology.

Proponents of driverless cars argue that they are infinitely safer than traditional vehicles. Such automated cars may be able to react to potential crashes and safety hazards much more quickly and effectively than human drivers. In addition, their constant communication with nearby vehicles would enable more cars to be safely moving at a steady speed on a given stretch of road at one time, cutting traffic jams and enhancing transportation efficiency. McKinsey & Co. estimated that a widespread adoption of self-driving cars and trucks could eliminate 90% of all auto accidents in the U.S. and prevent up to $190 billion in damages and health care costs yearly. Boston Consulting Group expects the market for driverless technology (including vehicles, equipment and software) to reach $42 billion by 2025, and that AVs will account for 25% of global automotive sales by 2035.

A $6.5 million, 23-acre testing site opened at the University of Michigan in early 2015 where AVs are tested in simulated congested urban conditions. Robotic pedestrians and cyclists dart into traffic while vehicles navigate any number of potentially hazardous conditions including traffic circles, bridges, tunnels, gravel roads and obstructed views.

Texas A&M University's Transportation Institute oversees the Center for Transportation Safety, an organization that conducts research and outreach programs funded at approximately $5 million per year. The school has recently launched its new RELLIS campus on 2,000 acres for research, testing, training and development related to advanced transportation.

Driverless trucks (18-wheelers) are also on the horizon. Although truckers and the firms they drive for tend to be slow to adopt new technologies, some are using automation to enable "platooning," or a caravan of two to three trucks equipped with video cameras, advanced cruise control systems and radar-based braking systems. The lead truck on a convoy controls acceleration and braking for all trucks in the line which are precisely spaced at distances as close as 30 feet. A real-time video camera beams a feed to the following truck drivers so that they can see the road ahead. Traveling single file affords aerodynamic drag reduction resulting in fuel savings of up to 10%. Peloton Technology developed the technology which saw highway trials beginning in 2015. Consultants Frost & Sullivan anticipate that widespread use of platooning could start as early as 2020, however the current cost, at about $30,000 per truck, may prove too high for most trucking companies.

Uber acquired Otto, a driverless truck startup founded in early 2016. Otto developed a system that allows big rigs to steer themselves, allowing long haul drivers to rest while on the road. The system has been tested on U.S. highways. Uber recruited a number of researchers from the robotics department at Carnegie Mellon University to develop self-driving taxis at its Advanced Technology Center. Uber also agreed to a partnership with Daimler in early 2017 to build self-driving vehicles to operate on Uber's transportation network.

The U.S. Postal Service (USPS) tested self-driving trucks on five 1,000-mile routes between Phoenix and Dallas in May 2019. The trucks were provided by TuSimple, an autonomous trucking firm that recently raised $95 million to expand its fleet.

Driverless vehicles raise significant safety concerns. The software necessary to run the vehicles is vulnerable to hacking.

21) Gig Economy and Self-Driving Cars Pose Insurance Challenges and Underwriting Opportunities

Transportation industry analysts believe that, over the mid- to long-term, more and more consumers will forgo car ownership in favor of ride-hailing services (such as Uber, Didi and Lyft) and car sharing services (such as ZipCar). This has profound implications for the future of the automobile insurance industry, in the same way that it will deeply affect the automobile manufacturing sector. Consumers are expected to switch, to a large extent, to "mobility services" (that include a number of ride service options) from traditional car ownership.

Consequently, insurers are scrambling to devise policy options that cover drivers (or riders, which may include paying passengers) in a wide variety of transportation scenarios. Allstate subsidiary Arity is working to analyze staggering amounts of telematics (digital automobile trip records) data on personal driving habits to help develop such insurance options for the future. Arity says it has access to more than 1 billion miles of new driver information per month on top of 10 years of archival data from Drivewise, another Allstate subsidiary. Analysis of this data may help Allstate form a benchmark for future rates in emerging mobility services trips.

Insurance coverage for ride-hailing companies such as Uber and Lyft currently rely on different auto polices depending on the circumstances of an accident. In the event of an accident while off duty, these drivers rely on personal auto insurance. On duty, but before accepting a passenger, drivers typically have liability insurance from their ride sharing companies (however, damage to drivers' vehicles is often not covered). On the way to pick up customers, drivers may have liability and physical damage insurance from their standard insurance company. Finally, while transporting passengers, may drivers have liability and physical damage insurance from the ride-sharing company. The Holy Grail for insurance companies will be the ability to sell more expensive and more comprehensive policies to these drivers for Uber and similar firms. However, Uber and similar drivers are on limited budgets and may be resistant to higher operating costs.

There are business opportunities for insurance startups that hope to serve the ride-hailing market. Zego, for example, brokers third-party liability insurance for food and package couriers working in Britain, including those carrying orders for firms ranging from Deliveroo to Amazon to Quiqup. In the U.S., Uber offers insurance coverage to a number of its drivers through major insurance company Aon, which has policies covering illness, disability and death for as little as $0.04 per mile driven. Meanwhile, French long-distance carpooling provider BlaBlaCar works through insurance industry giant AXA to provide coverage for repairs and for the provision of alternative transport while the repairs are being done. Another company, Clutch (an Atlanta-based car subscription service), covers drivers not only when they are in Clutch vehicles but also in vehicles owned by others.

While ride-hailing poses challenges to insurers, self-driving vehicles are even more complicated to insure. Auto manufacturers, including Volvo and Mercedes-Benz, as of early 2018 were already accepting certain types of liability in some cases where a vehicle's self-driving system is found to be at fault in an accident. Some experts believe that self-driving cars will reduce accidents, citing data that indicates that as much as 94% of all accidents are caused by human error. This may create significant drops in revenues for insurance underwriters. For example, there may be fewer automobile-related wrecks, fatalities and personal injuries in the future, not to mention fewer individual car owners. It is possible that insurance premiums will become much more competitive and drop if accidents become rarer. This will drive insurance industry innovation and force insurance firms to create new types of products aimed at multiple types of consumers: traditional car owners, makers of self-driving vehicles and the software and other technologies that guide them, ride-hailing firms such as Uber, and individual consumers who want better personal coverage when they are riding in vehicles that they do not own.

Chapter 2

AUTOMOBILE INDUSTRY STATISTICS

Tables and Charts:

Automobile Industry Statistics and Market Size Overview

	Quantity	Unit	Date	Source
Sales				
Global Unit Sales, Cars & Light Trucks (estimate)	98.20	Mil.	2019	IHS
Volkswagen	10.90	Mil.	2018	Volkswagen
Toyota	8.98	Mil.	2019*	Toyota
General Motors	8.38	Mil.	2018	GM
Ford	5.98	Mil.	2018	Ford
Nissan	5.52	Mil.	2018	Nissan
Honda	5.30	Mil.	2019*	Honda
Fiat/Chrysler	4.84	Mil.	2018	Fiat
Hyundai	4.58	Mil.	2018	Hyundai
Peugeot Citroen	3.90	Mil.	2018	PSA Group
Daimler (Mercedes-Benz)	2.38	Mil.	2018	Daimler
U.S. New Car & Truck Sales				
Cars & Light Trucks Unit Sales	16.80	Mil.	2018	NADA
Cars & Light Trucks Unit Sales	17.22	Mil.	2018	NADA
Average Transaction Price (ATP) for Light Vehicles	36,590	US$	Feb-19	KBB
Total Number of New-Car Dealerships	16,753		2018	NADA
Total Revenue: New-Car & Light Truck Dealers	1	Tril. US$	2018	NADA
Car Service & Parts Sales, Franchised Dealerships	116	Bil. US$	2018	NADA
Market Share:				
General Motors	16.7	%	2018	Fiat
Ford	14.1	%	2018	Fiat
Toyota	13.7	%	2018	Fiat
Fiat/Chrysler	12.6	%	2018	Fiat
Honda	9.1	%	2018	Fiat
Nissan	8.4	%	2018	Fiat
Hyundai/Kia	7.2	%	2018	Fiat
Electric Vehicles Sold	361.3	Thous.	2018	gtm
Car Sales by Selected Country/Region (forecast)				
Total Sales	78.70	Mil.	2019	Scotiabank
North America[1]	20.10	Mil.	2019	Scotiabank
Canada	1.93	Mil.	2019	Scotiabank
U.S.	16.80	Mil.	2019	Scotiabank
Mexico	1.36	Mil.	2019	Scotiabank
Asia	37.10	Mil.	2019	Scotiabank
China	23.50	Mil.	2019	Scotiabank
India	2.47	Mil.	2019	Scotiabank
Western Europe	14.20	Mil.	2019	Scotiabank
Germany	3.43	Mil.	2019	Scotiabank
Eastern Europe	3.50	Mil.	2019	Scotiabank
Russia	1.86	Mil.	2019	Scotiabank
South America	3.80	Mil.	2019	Scotiabank
Brazil	1.82	Mil.	2019	Scotiabank
Operations and Transportation				
Total Vehicles in Operation, Cars & Light Trucks, Worldwide	1.24	Bil.	2018	PRE
Total Vehicles in Operation, Cars & Light Trucks, U.S.	278	Mil.	2019	IHS
Average Age of Passenger Cars & Light Trucks, U.S.	11.8	Years	2019	IHS

* Fiscal year ending March 31. [1]Includes light trucks; IHS = IHS Markit; NADA = National Automobile Dealers Association; KBB= Kelley Blue Book; gtm = greentechmedia.com; Scotiabank = Estimates by Scotia Economics, "Global Auto Report," released April 2019; PRE = Plunkett Research Estimate.

General Motors Corporation Overview

(Sales in Thousands of Units)

U.S. Car & Truck Sales

Vehicle	2016		2017		2018	
	Units	As a % of Industry	Units	As a % of Industry	Units	As a % of Industry
Cars	890	12.9%	709	11.5%	560	10.4%
Trucks	1,325	27.0%	1,328	26.4%	1,360	25.4%
Crossovers	828	13.6%	965	15.1%	1,034	14.8%
Total U.S.	**3,043**	**17.0%**	**3,002**	**17.1%**	**2,954**	**16.7%**

Note: Figures may not equal total due to rounding.

Worldwide Sales

Sales Division	2016		2017		2018	
	Units	As a % of Industry	Units	As a % of Industry	Units	As a % of Industry
GM North America	3,630	16.6%	3,576	16.6%	3,490	1.2%
N.A. excluding U.S.	587	14.7%	574	14.4%	536	14.0%
GM Europe	1,161	6.2%	685	3.6%	4	--
Asia/Pacific, Middle East and Africa	4,634	9.5%	4,670	9.5%	4,200	8.6%
China	3,914	13.8%	4,041	14.3%	3,645	13.8%
Other	720	3.5%	629	3.0%	555	2.5%
GM South America	583	15.9%	669	16.1%	690	15.4%
Brazil	346	16.9%	394	17.6%	434	16.9%
Other	237	14.6%	275	14.3%	256	13.3%
Total Worldwide	**10,008**	**10.8%**	**9,600**	**10.2%**	**8,384**	**8.9%**

GMIO = General Motors International Operations

Number of Dealerships as of December 31

Sales Division	2016	2017	2018
GM North America	4,857	4,809	4,793
GM International	8,598	7,641	7,716
Total Worldwide	**13,455**	**12,450**	**12,509**

Note: Most dealerships are independently owned.

Source: General Motors Corporation
Plunkett Research,® Ltd.
www.plunkettresearch.com

Ford Motor Company Overview

Vehicles Sold at Wholesale by Automotive Segment (in Thousands of Units)

Segment	2014	2015	2016	2017	2018
Ford North America	2,842	3,073	3,019	2,967	2,920
Ford South America	463	381	325	373	365
Ford Europe	1,387	1,530	1,539	1,582	1,533
Ford Asia Pacific & Africa	1,439	1,464	1,607	1,566	1,055
Total	**6,323**	**6,635**	**6,651**	**6,607**	**5,982**

Revenues (in Billions of US$)

Unit	2014	2015	2016	2017	2018
Automotive	135.8	140.6	141.5	145.7	148.3
Financial Services	8.3	9.0	10.3	11.1	12.0

Ford Motor Company Plants

Regional Segment	2014	2015	2016	2017	2018
Ford North America	30	29	29	31	32
Ford South America	8	8	8	8	8
Ford Europe	12	16	16	16	15
Ford Middle East & Africa	2	2	2	2	2
Ford Asia Pacific and Africa	10	12	7	4	4
Total	**62**	**67**	**62**	**61**	**61**

Total Worldwide Number of Ford Dealerships by Vehicle Brands, End of Year

Brand	2014	2015	2016	2017	2018
Ford	10,938	10,727	10,608	10,345	10,466
Ford-Lincoln (combined)	869	884	915	820	858
Lincoln	173	360	214	263	210
Total	**11,980**	**11,971**	**11,737**	**11,428**	**11,534**

Note: Most dealerships are independently owned. Because many of these dealerships distribute more than one of Ford's brands from the same sales location, a single dealership may be counted under more than one brand.

Source: Ford Motor Company
Plunkett Research,® Ltd.
www.plunkettresearch.com

Volkswagen Group Overview

(Sales in Thousands of Units)

New Car Sales

Region	2016		2017		2018	
	Units	% of Global Car Market	Units	% of Global Car Market	Units	% of Global Car Market
Group Total	10,391	11.9%	10,777	12.1%	10,900	--
In Germany	1,257	--	1,264	--	1,236	--
Abroad	9,135	--	9,513	--	9,664	--

Worldwide Sales by Brand

Segment	2016		2017		2018	
	Units	% of Total Group	Units	% of Total Group	Units	% of Total Group
Volkswagen Passenger Cars*	4,347	41.8%	3,573	33.2%	3,715	34.1%
Audi	1,534	14.8%	1,530	14.2%	1,467	13.5%
SKODA	814	7.8%	937	8.7%	957	8.8%
SEAT	548	5.3%	595	5.5%	608	5.6%
Bentley	11	0.1%	11	0.1%	10	0.1%
Porsche Automotive	239	2.3%	248	2.3%	253	2.3%
Volkswagen Commercial Vehicles	478	4.6%	498	4.6%	469	4.3%
Scania	83	0.8%	92	0.9%	97	0.9%
MAN	102	1.0%	114	1.1%	137	1.3%
VW China	3,873	37.3%	4,020	37.3%	4,101	37.6%
Other	-1,638	-15.8%	-840	-7.8%	-912	-8.4%
Group Total	10,391	100.0%	10,777	100.0%	10,900	100.0%

Sales by Market

Region	2016		2017		2018	
	Units	% of Total Group	Units	% of Total Group	Units	% of Total Group
Europe/Remaining Markets	4,635	43.0%	4,731	43.9%	5,739	52.7%
North America	968	9.0%	992	9.2%	925	8.5%
South America	421	3.9%	526	4.9%	596	5.5%
Asia-Pacific	4,367	40.5%	4,527	42.0%	4,640	42.6%

* 2017, 2018 figures take account of the reclassification of companies; prior-year figures were not adjusted.

Source: Volkswagen Group
Plunkett Research,® Ltd.
www.plunkettresearch.com

Toyota Motor Corporation Overview

(Fiscal Year Ending March 31)

Worldwide Vehicle Unit Sales *(in Thousands)*

Region	2012	2013	2014	2015	2016	2017	2018	2019
Japan	2,071	2,279	2,365	2,154	2,059	2,274	2,255	2,226
North America	1,872	2,469	2,529	2,715	2,839	2,837	2,806	2,745
Europe	798	799	844	859	844	925	968	994
Asia	1,327	1,684	1,609	1,489	1,345	1,588	1,543	1,684
Other*	1,284	1,640	1,769	1,755	1,594	1,347	1,392	1,326
Total	**7,352**	**8,871**	**9,116**	**8,972**	**8,681**	**8,971**	**8,964**	**8,977**

* Includes Central and South America, Oceania, Africa and the Middle East, etc.

Toyota Motor Primary Facilities as of March 31, 2019

Region	Cars	Parts	R&D	Other
Japan	9	3	2	1
U.S. & Canada	2	0	0	2
Thailand	1	0	0	0

Note: figures do not include factories under construction in Japan, the U.S., Canada, China and Russia. Other joint ventures are not listed. Toyota has more than 50 manufacturing plants in 27 countries, but the table lists only the primary plants.

Source: Toyota Motor Corporation
Plunkett Research,® Ltd.
www.plunkettresearch.com

Daimler AG Overview

(Sales in Thousands of Units)

Mercedes Benz Worldwide Unit Sales

Region	2016	2017	2018
Europe	980	1,014	983
Germany	314	320	324
NAFTA*	406	403	393
United States	347	338	327
Asia	715	859	921
China	488	619	678
Total	2,198	2,374	2,383

Mercedes Benz Cars Unit Sales by Brand

Brand	2016	2017	2018
Mercedes-Benz	2,054	2,238	2,253
A-/B-Class (excluding GLA)	435	420	409
C-Class	490	493	478
E-Class	304	398	434
S-Class	84	79	84
SUVs (including GLA)	712	823	829
Sports cars	27	25	19
Smart	144	136	130
Mercedes-Benz Cars Total	**2,198**	**2,374**	**2,383**

Mercedes Benz Vans Worldwide Unit Sales

Region	2016	2017	2018
EU30	250	273	278
Germany	96	106	107
NAFTA*	43	45	51
United States	34	34	39
Latin America (excluding Mexico)	12	16	19
China	14	24	29
Other Markets	31	33	35
Total	**359**	**401**	**421**

* North American Free Trade Agreement.

Source: Daimler AG
Plunkett Research,® Ltd.
www.plunkettresearch.com

Hyundai Motor Group Overview

(Unit Sales in Thousands)

Worldwide Retail Vehicle Unit Sales *(Excluding Kia[1])*

	2013	2014	2015	2016	2017	2018
Korea	641	684	712	657	689	721
Overseas	3,980	4,151	4,130	4,258	3,817	3,866
North America	858	864	897	913	833	820
Europe	636	642	650	667	767	785
AMEA & APAC[2]	--	--	--	--	1,020	1,056
Total	**4,621**	**4,835**	**4,843**	**4,914**	**4,506**	**4,587**

Kia Worldwide Retail Sales

Region	2012	2013	2014	2015	2016	2017
Korea	481	458	465	527	533	518
Overseas	2,218	2,282	2,432	2,345	2,485	2,242
Total	**2,699**	**2,740**	**2,896**	**2,871**	**3,018**	**2,760**

[1] Hyundai holds an ownership stake of approximately 33.88% in Kia Motor Corp., as of 12/31/15.

[2] India, Middle East, Africa, Asian Pacific, Australia

Source: Hyundai Motor Co., Kia Motor Corp.
Plunkett Research,® Ltd.
www.plunkettresearch.com

Honda Motor Co. Overview

(Fiscal Year Ending March 31)

Worldwide Honda Group Unit Sales[1] in Thousands

Segment	2012	2013	2014	2015	2016	2017	2018	2019
Automobiles	**3,108**	**4,014**	**4,340**	**4,367**	**4,743**	**5,028**	**5,199**	**5,323**
Japan	588	692	818	761	668	668	696	719
North America	1,323	1,731	1,754	1,750	1,929	1,970	1,902	1,954
Europe	158	171	171	161	172	184	183	169
Asia	837	1,122	1,311	1,426	1,723	1,964	2,166	2,233
Other Regions[2]	202	298	286	269	251	242	252	248
Motorcycles[3]	**15,061**	**15,494**	**17,008**	**17,592**	**17,055**	**17,661**	**19,554**	**20,238**
Japan	220	217	226	199	180	156	167	207
North America	200	250	278	286	308	294	313	301
Europe	198	179	166	191	204	217	234	249
Asia	12,412	13,035	14,534	15,345	15,133	15,937	17,720	18,224
Other Regions[2]	2,031	1,813	1,804	1,571	1,230	1,057	1,120	1,257
Power Products[4]	**5,819**	**6,071**	**6,018**	**5,983**	**5,965**	**6,121**	**6,262**	**6,301**
Japan	392	314	314	338	363	301	300	336
North America	2,314	2,604	2,719	2,705	2,811	2,977	3,012	3,049
Europe	1,121	1,004	1,031	1,091	1,008	1,035	1,022	984
Asia	1,472	1,572	1,485	1,382	1,349	1,430	1,512	1,559
Other Regions[2]	520	577	469	467	434	378	416	373

[1] Honda Group Unit Sales is the total unit sales of completed products of Honda, its consolidated subsidiaries and its affiliates and joint ventures accounted for using the equity method.

[2] Includes Latin America, the Middle East & Africa and Oceania.

[3] The motorcycle segment includes all-terrain vehicles (ATVs) and multi utility vehicles (MUVs).

[4] Power Products include tillers, thin film solar cells for home use, portable generators, general-purpose engines, grass cutters, outboard marine engines, water pumps, snow throwers, power carriers, power sprayers, lawn mowers and lawn tractors (riding lawn mowers).

Source: Honda Motor Co. Ltd.
Plunkett Research,® Ltd.
www.plunkettresearch.com

U.S. New Car & Truck Market Shares by Company: 2014-2018

(In Percentages)

New Car Market Share	2014	2015	2016	2017	2018
General Motors	17.4	17.3	17.0	17.1	16.7
Ford	14.7	14.7	14.6	14.7	14.1
Toyota	14.1	14.0	13.7	13.9	13.7
Fiat/Chrysler	12.4	12.6	12.6	11.7	12.6
Honda	9.2	8.9	9.2	9.3	9.1
Nissan	8.2	8.3	8.8	9.1	8.4
Hyundai/Kia	7.8	7.8	8.0	7.3	7.2

Note: Includes sales of passenger cars, trucks and crossovers.

Source: Fiat Chrysler Automobiles
Plunkett Research,® Ltd.
www.plunkettresearch.com

Licensed Drivers, Vehicle Registrations & Resident Population, U.S.: 1960-2017

(In Millions; Latest Year Available)

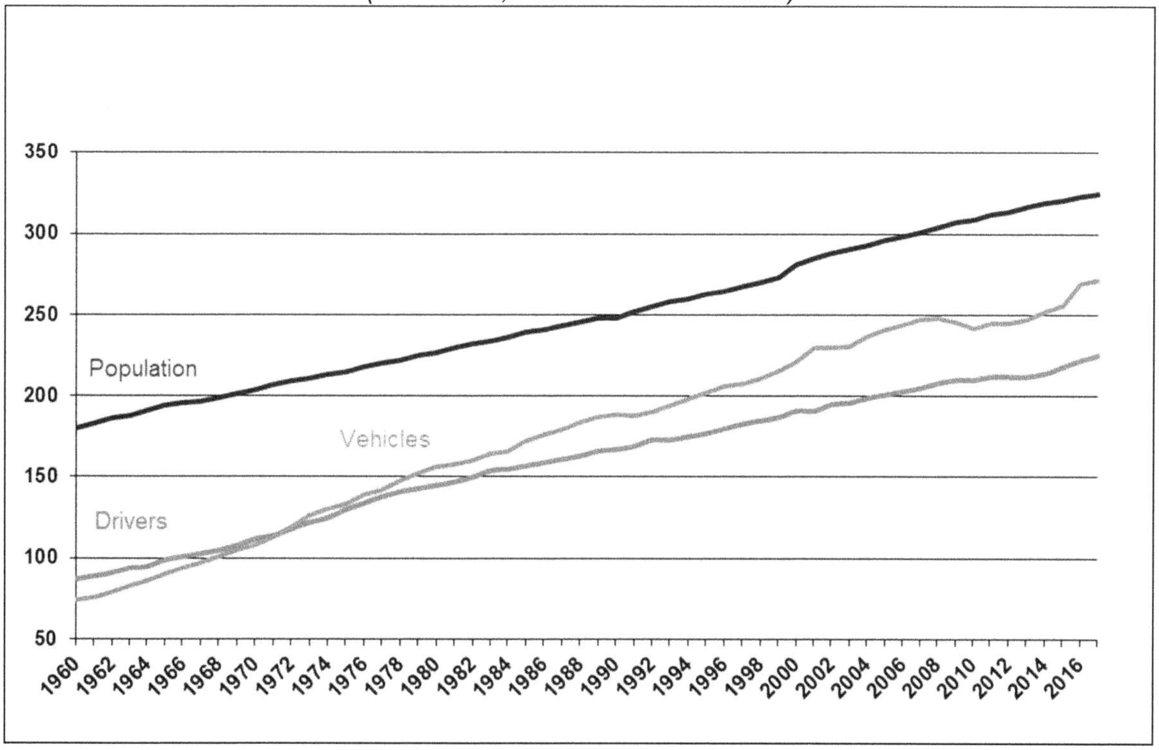

Source: Federal Highway Administration, U.S. Dept. of Transportation
Plunkett Research,® Ltd.
www.plunkettresearch.com

Highest Fuel Economy by Vehicle Class: 2019 Model Year

Class	Make/Model	MPG
Two Seater	smart EQ fortwo (coupe) (EV)	108
Minicompact Car	Fiat 500e (EV)	112
Subcompact Car	BMW i3 (EV)	113
	BMW i3s (EV)	113
Compact Car	Volkswagen e-Golf (EV)	119
Midsize Car	Hyundai Ioniq Electric (EV)	136
Large Car	Tesla Model S Long Range (EV)	111
Small Station Wagon	Chevrolet Bolt (EV)	119
Midsize Station Wagon	Volvo V90 FWD	27
Small Pickup Truck	Chevrolet Colorado 2WD (Diesel)	23
	GMC Canyon 2WD (Diesel)	23
Standard Pickup Truck	Ford F150 Pickup 2WD	25
Small Sport Utility Vehicle	Hyundai Kona Electric (EV)	120
	Toyota RAV4 Hybrid AWD	40
Standard Sport Utility Vehicle	Tesla Model X Long Range (EV)	96
	Lexus RX 450h AWD (Hybrid)	30
Minivan	Chrysler Pacifica Plug-in Hybrid (PHEV)	48
	Chrysler Pacifica	22
	Chrysler Pacifica (w / Stop-Start option)	22
	Honda Odyssey (S9)	22
	Honda Odyssey (S10)	22
	Toyota Sienna 2WD	22

Note: Vehicles are ranked by their combined rating (weighted by 55% city and 45% highway). Ties are listed alphabetically. In classes where the most fuel-efficient is a plug-in hybrid electric vehicle (PHEV) or an electric vehicle (EV), a conventional or regular hybrid is also listed. These lists were created using information available as of August 2019.

Source: U.S. Environmental Protection Agency (EPA)
Plunkett Research® Ltd.
www.plunkettresearch.com

Lowest Fuel Economy by Vehicle Class: 2019 Model Year

Class	Make/Model	MPG
Two Seater Car	Bugatti Chiron	11
	Lamborghini Aventador Coupe	11
	Lamborghini Aventador Roadster	11
Minicompact Car	Ferrari GTC4Lusso	13
Subcompact Car	Roush Performance Stage 3 Mustang	15
Compact Car	Rolls-Royce Dawn	14
Midsize Car	Bentley Mulsanne	12
Large Car	Rolls-Royce Ghost	14
	Rolls-Royce Ghost EWB	14
	Rolls-Royce Phantom	14
	Rolls-Royce Phantom EWB	14
Small Station Wagon	Buick Regal TourX AWD	24
Midsize Station Wagon	Rolls-Royce Cullinan	14
Small Pickup Truck	Chevrolet Colorado ZR2 4WD	17
	Nissan Frontier 4WD	17
	Nissan Frontier 4WD FFV	17
Standard Pickup Truck	Toyota Tundra 4WD	14
Small Sport Utility Vehicle	Jaguar F-Pace	18
Standard Sport Utility Vehicle	Jeep Grand Cherokee Trackhawk 4WD	13
Minivan	Dodge Grand Caravan	20
	Dodge Grand Caravan FFV	20
	Toyota Sienna AWD	20

Note: Vehicles are ranked by their combined rating (weighted by 55% city and 45% highway), then by their city rating. In the event of a tie, multiple vehicles may share the same ranking. These lists were created using information available as of August, 2019.

Source: U.S. Environmental Protection Agency (EPA)
Plunkett Research,® Ltd.
www.plunkettresearch.com

Gross Output in the Motor Vehicles & Transportation Equipment Manufacturing Industries: Selected Years, 2011-2017

(In Billions of US$; Latest Year Available)

Description	2011	2012	2013	2014	2015	2016	2017
Automobile mfg.	52.3	58.6	61.9	67.0	67.5	70.4	61.8
Light truck & utility vehicle mfg.	169.9	171.0	206.2	238.4	268.0	287.2	322.1
Heavy duty truck mfg.	30.0	31.5	30.9	32.1	35.5	28.8	31.2
Motor vehicle body mfg.	12.5	11.5	12.1	12.9	14.1	14.5	15.2
Truck trailer mfg.	6.9	8.2	8.2	9.4	10.3	9.5	10.0
Motor home mfg.	3.2	2.3	3.2	4.0	4.3	4.7	5.0
Travel trailer & camper mfg.	7.9	10.5	11.9	13.8	14.3	13.7	14.4
Motor vehicle gasoline engine & engine parts mfg.	33.5	29.9	32.3	33.1	34.9	34.7	36.1
Motor vehicle electrical & electronic equipment mfg.	21.1	19.6	21.5	24.1	25.3	25.2	26.1
Motor vehicle transmission & power train parts mfg.	30.5	35.5	36.2	38.5	38.4	38.6	40.1
Motor vehicle seating & interior trim mfg.	21.5	23.0	25.7	30.0	32.4	33.7	35.0
Motor vehicle metal stamping	29.3	30.2	32.6	35.5	37.8	38.5	39.9
Other motor vehicle parts mfg.	57.6	57.6	59.7	65.9	69.0	69.1	71.8
Motor vehicle steering, suspension component (except spring), and brake systems mfg.	21.8	23.6	22.8	25.3	26.0	26.3	27.5
Aircraft mfg.	101.2	117.7	124.5	132.5	137.4	126.0	128.0
Aircraft engine & engine parts mfg.	35.0	44.0	47.1	49.3	50.0	51.7	52.3
Other aircraft parts & auxiliary equipment mfg.	34.8	35.9	38.2	41.6	40.1	37.8	37.3
Guided missile & space vehicle mfg.	20.1	20.9	21.4	22.1	21.7	21.3	22.9
Propulsion units and parts for space vehicles and guided missiles	5.6	5.9	5.9	5.9	5.9	5.6	5.9
Railroad rolling stock mfg.	12.2	16.6	19.7	22.4	22.0	15.7	15.3
Ship building & repairing	21.1	22.7	22.6	22.5	23.1	22.1	23.2
Boat building	5.9	7.2	7.8	8.6	9.8	9.6	9.6
Motorcycle, bicycle, & parts mfg.	6.3	6.1	6.3	6.4	6.7	7.1	7.8
Military armored vehicle, tank, & tank component mfg.	7.1	6.1	4.5	3.4	4.3	5.0	5.0
All other transportation equipment mfg.	9.3	7.3	8.1	8.6	9.2	8.2	9.1

Source: U.S. Bureau of Economic Analysis
Plunkett Research,® Ltd.
www.plunkettresearch.com

Personal Transportation Expenditures, U.S.: 2011-2018

(in Billions of US$)

Category	2011	2012	2013	2014	2015	2016	2017	2018
Transportation	**1080.3**	**1,135.5**	**1,170.5**	**1,202.0**	**1,162.5**	**1,161.7**	**1,232.0**	**1,311.8**
Motor vehicles and parts	365.2	396.6	417.5	442.0	474.2	483.6	502.2	521.5
New motor vehicles	207.9	237.0	249.8	264.4	276.9	275.0	282.1	289.3
Net purchases of used motor vehicles	96.6	96.3	102.3	110.8	127.6	137.1	147.2	156.7
Motor vehicle parts and accessories	60.7	63.3	65.5	66.8	69.8	71.5	72.9	75.5
Tires	26.8	28.2	28.7	28.6	29.2	29.4	30.0	31.2
Accessories and parts	33.9	35.1	36.8	38.2	40.6	42.1	43.0	44.3
Public transportation	118.7	123.6	131.7	139.3	142.7	144.4	151.7	160.8
Ground transportation	37.6	38.8	41.8	44.8	47.8	50.0	52.3	53.2
Railway transportation	1.1	1.2	1.2	1.3	1.2	1.2	1.3	1.3
Road transportation	36.5	37.7	40.6	43.6	46.6	48.8	51.0	51.9
Air transportation	78.6	82.1	87.2	91.5	91.8	91.2	96.1	104.2
Water transportation	2.4	2.6	2.7	2.9	3.2	3.1	3.3	3.5

Source: U.S. Bureau of Economic Analysis
Plunkett Research,® Ltd.
www.plunkettresearch.com

Average Miles Per Gallon vs. Horsepower, U.S.: 1975-2018

(Latest Year Available)

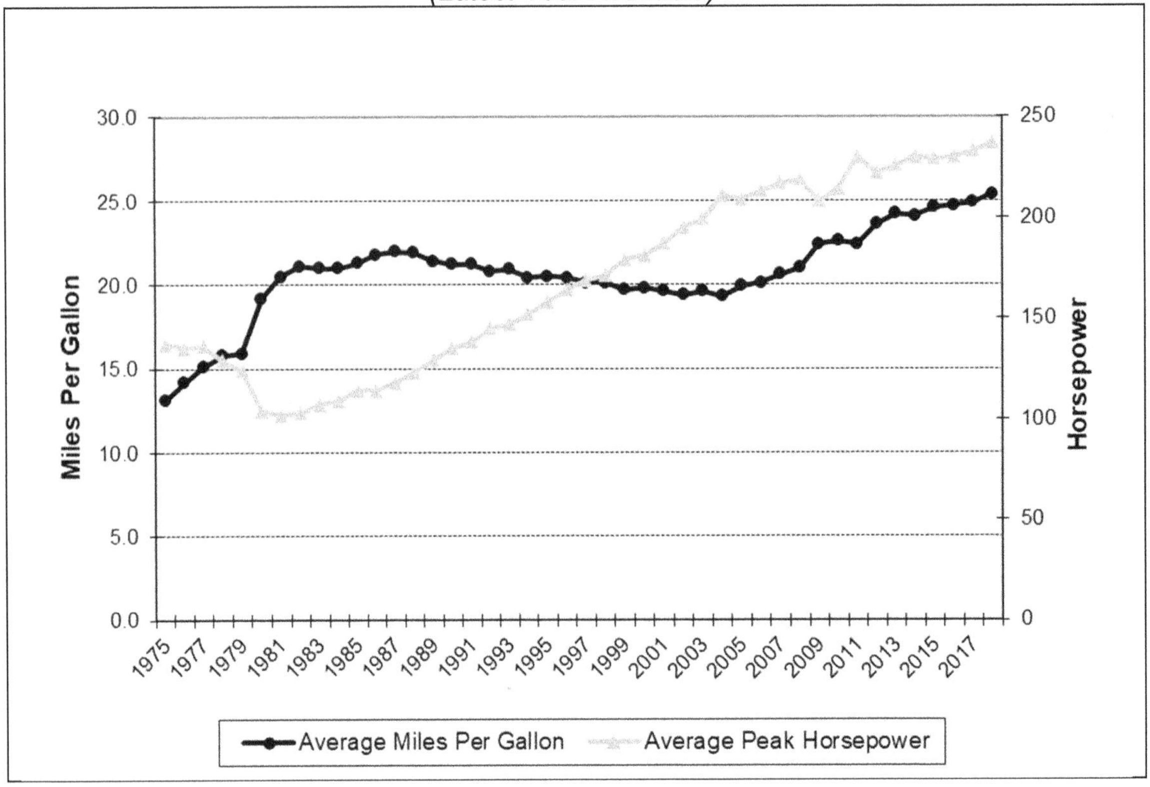

Notes: Motorcycles are not reflected as part of the light-duty fleet. The light truck data used in this series of reports includes vans, SUVs, and trucks with gross vehicle weight ratings (GVWR) up to 8,500 lbs. EPA adjusted the fuel economy figures to reflect real road conditions rather than lab conditions. 2018 values are preliminary.

Source: U.S. Environmental Protection Agency
Plunkett Research,® Ltd.
www.plunkettresearch.com

Automobile Driving Costs, U.S.: 2018

Category	Small Sedan	Midsize Sedan	Large Sedan	Small SUV (FWD)	Medium SUV (4WD)
Examples	Chevrolet Cruze, Ford Focus, Honda Civic, Hyundai Elantra and Toyota Corolla	Chevrolet Malibu, Ford Fusion, Honda Accord, Nissan Altima and Toyota Camry	Chevrolet Impala, Chrysler 300, Ford Taurus, Nissan Maxima and Toyota Avalon	Chevrolet Equinox, Ford Escape, Honda CR-V, Nissan Rogue and Toyota RAV4	Chevrolet Traverse, Ford Explorer, Honda Pilot, Jeep Grand Cherokee and Toyota Highlander
Operating Costs (Cents/Mile)					
Fuel	8.01	9.18	12.19	9.12	12.43
Maintenance, repair and tires	7.25	8.58	8.80	8.45	8.66
Cost per mile	**15.26**	**17.76**	**20.99**	**17.57**	**21.09**
Ownership Costs (US$/Year)					
Full-Coverage Insurance	1,315	1,232	1,209	1,074	1,102
License, Registration & Taxes	466	690	783	614	845
Depreciation (15,000 Miles Annually)	2,268	3,580	3,893	2,927	3,714
Finance Charge (10% down; national average interest rate for 5 years)	439	700	770	618	872
Cost per year	**4,488**	**6,202**	**6,655**	**5,233**	**6,533**
Cost per day	**12.30**	**16.99**	**18.23**	**14.34**	**17.90**
Total Annual Cost (US$)					
10,000 miles per year					
Cost per year	5,775	7,720	8,428	6,664	8,229
Cost per mile (in cents)	57.8	77.2	84.3	66.6	82.3
15,000 miles per year					
Cost per year	6,777	8,866	9,804	7,869	9,697
Cost per mile (in cents)	45.2	59.1	65.4	52.5	64.6
20,000 miles per year					
Cost per year	7,810	10,043	11,219	9,115	11,219
Cost per mile (in cents)	39.1	50.2	56.1	45.6	56.1

(Continued on next page)

Automobile Driving Costs, U.S.: 2018 (cont.)

Category	Minivan	1/2-Ton, CrewCab Pickup (4WD)	Hybrid Vehicle	Electric Vehicle	Average
Examples	Chrysler Pacifica, Dodge Grand Caravan, Kia Sedona, Honda Odyssey, and Toyota Sienna	Chevrolet Silverado 1500, Ford F-150, Nissan Titan, Ram 1500 and Toyota Tundra	Ford Fusion, Hyundai Ioniq, Kia Niro, Toyota Prius Liftback and Toyota RAV4	BMW i3, Chevrolet Bolt, Ford Focus, Kia Soul and Nissan Leaf	
Operating Costs (Cents/Mile)					
Fuel	11.87	15.05	5.70	3.68	11.05
Maintenance, repair and tires	8.23	8.13	7.49	7.60	8.21
Cost per mile	**20.10**	**23.18**	**13.19**	**11.28**	**19.26**
Ownership Costs (US$/Year)					
Full-Coverage Insurance	1,114	1,242	1,200	1,215	1,189
License, Registration & Taxes	769	996	617	-677	738
Depreciation (15,000 Miles Annually)	4,003	3,518	3,068	5,471	3,289
Finance Charge (10% down; national average interest rate for 5 years)	776	982	621	683	744
Cost per year	**6,662**	**6,738**	**5,506**	**6,692**	**5,960**
Cost per day	**18.25**	**18.46**	**15.08**	**18.33**	**16.33**
Total Annual Cost (US$)					
10,000 miles per year					
Cost per year	8,370	8,563	6,524	7,501	7,531
Cost per mile (in cents)	83.7	85.6	65.2	75.0	75.3
15,000 miles per year					
Cost per year	9,677	10,215	7,485	8,384	8,849
Cost per mile (in cents)	64.5	68.1	49.0	55.9	59.0
20,000 miles per year					
Cost per year	11,022	11,930	8,484	9,307	10,213
Cost per mile (in cents)	55.1	59.7	42.4	46.5	51.1

Source: American Automobile Association (AAA)
Plunkett Research,® Ltd.
www.plunkettresearch.com

Motor Vehicle Traffic Accidents in the U.S. by Type of Vehicle & Person: 2008-2017

(Latest Year Available)

Category	2017	2016	2015	2014	2013	2012	2011	2010	2009	2008
Fatal Vehicle Traffic Accidents	34,247	34,748	32,538	30,056	30,202	31,006	29,867	30,296	30,862	34,172
Vehicle Occupants										
Drivers	18,726	18,717	17,615	16,470	16,520	16,838	16,474	16,864	17,670	19,279
Passengers	6,174	6,485	6,213	5,766	5,896	6,106	5,972	6,451	6,793	7,441
Unknown	73	74	71	71	67	73	64	56	63	71
Total	24,973	25,276	23,899	22,307	22,483	23,017	22,510	23,371	24,526	26,791
Motorcycle Riders	5,172	5,337	5,029	4,594	4,692	4,986	4,630	4,518	4,469	5,312
Nonmotorist										
Pedestrians	5,977	6,080	5,494	4,910	4,779	4,818	4,457	4,302	4,109	4,414
Pedalcyclists	783	852	829	729	749	734	682	623	628	718
Other/Unknown	228	261	233	204	190	227	200	185	151	188
Total	6,988	7,193	6,556	5,843	5,718	5,779	5,339	5,110	4,888	5,320
Total	37,133	37,806	35,484	32,744	32,893	33,782	32,479	32,999	33,883	37,423
Other National Statistics										
Vehicle Miles Traveled (Billions)	3,212	3,174	3,095	3,026	2,988	2,969	2,950	2,967	2,957	2,977
Resident Population (Thousands)	325,719	323,406	321,040	318,623	316,235	313,993	311,644	309,338	306,772	304,094
Registered Vehicles (Thousands)	290,387	288,034	281,312	274,805	269,294	265,647	265,043	257,312	258,958	259,360
Licensed Drivers (Thousands)	225,346	221,712	218,084	214,092	212,160	211,815	211,875	210,115	209,618	208,321
National Rates: Fatalities										
Fatalities per 100 Million Vehicle Miles Traveled	1.16	1.19	1.15	1.08	1.10	1.14	1.10	1.11	1.15	1.26
Fatalities per 100,000 Population	11.40	11.69	11.05	10.28	10.40	10.76	10.42	10.67	11.05	12.31
Fatalities per 100,000 Registered Vehicles	12.79	13.13	12.61	11.92	12.21	12.72	12.25	12.82	13.08	14.43
Fatalities per 100,000 Licensed Drivers	16.48	17.05	16.27	15.29	15.50	15.95	15.33	15.71	16.16	17.96

Source: National Highway Transportation Safety Administration (NHTSA), Fatality Analysis Reporting System (FARS)
Plunkett Research,® Ltd.
www.plunkettresearch.com

Retail On-Highway Diesel vs. Regular Gasoline Prices, U.S.: January 1995-August 2019

(Weekly Data; Dollars per Gallon)

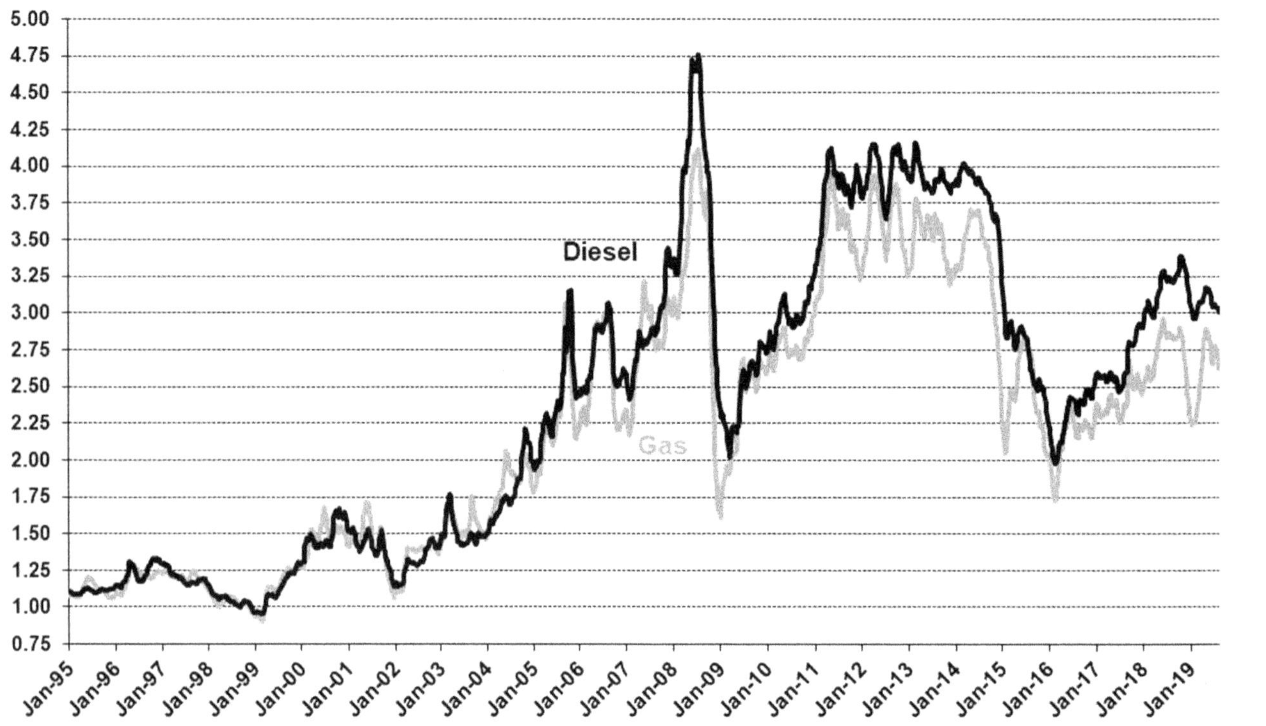

Retail Motor Fuel Prices	8/13/18	8/12/19
Average regular grade, all formulations (Current dollars per gallon, incl. taxes)	2.84	2.62
Percent change from previous month	-0.77%	-5.58%
Average on-highway diesel prices (Current dollars per gallon, incl. taxes)	3.22	3.01
Percent change from previous month	-0.19%	-0.69%

Notes: Motor fuel prices are an important cost component of highway transportation. Changes in motor fuel prices impact the behavior of both producers and consumers, and affect the demand for transportation in terms of level and modal mix. In the United States, motor gasoline prices follow world crude oil prices more closely than motor diesel prices. Changes in motor fuel prices affect the profit margin of transportation firms, particularly trucking firms.

Source: U.S. Bureau of Transportation Statistics
Plunkett Research,® Ltd.
www.plunkettresearch.com

Value of Imports of Vehicles to the U.S.: 2013-2nd Quarter 2019

(In Thousands of US$)

Partner	2013	2014	2015	2016	2017	2018	Q2 2018	Q2 2019
World Total	**249,017,543**	**261,647,463**	**279,909,020**	**280,571,079**	**289,636,340**	**300,501,509**	**145,470,581**	**153,806,659**
Mexico	59,597,907	68,041,013	74,685,050	74,734,143	83,531,116	93,248,193	43,217,743	50,620,937
Canada	55,703,872	56,193,328	55,564,944	57,939,819	55,873,680	53,271,360	27,560,237	26,799,781
Japan	49,762,338	45,263,281	46,087,550	49,554,648	50,616,132	51,340,081	25,524,852	25,438,971
Germany	32,594,878	33,434,175	34,113,550	28,589,116	27,003,549	25,412,999	11,746,257	12,197,613
South Korea	16,620,669	19,405,942	22,262,859	21,036,812	20,103,790	18,464,684	8,840,321	10,328,144
China	9,825,133	11,491,146	13,027,099	13,565,151	14,627,422	17,324,261	8,304,761	7,287,457
United Kingdom	6,209,736	6,573,338	8,027,963	9,698,781	9,641,399	10,865,453	5,168,948	5,116,852
Italy	2,754,262	3,555,439	5,141,720	5,096,536	5,971,319	5,747,605	2,874,647	2,192,660
Slovakia	953,905	1,130,445	1,358,033	1,624,912	2,064,687	3,053,672	961,963	2,535,082
India	926,961	1,113,767	1,379,899	1,174,549	1,387,844	2,809,638	1,468,011	1,480,756
Taiwan	2,365,874	2,446,568	2,696,060	2,502,567	2,605,634	2,801,768	1,393,742	1,473,651
Sweden	1,065,400	1,313,655	1,831,200	2,059,466	2,317,335	1,956,682	1,093,553	1,210,119
Finland	39,281	48,049	57,098	53,302	1,213,876	1,767,398	1,038,984	711,038
Austria	1,063,902	1,065,456	1,114,632	950,801	808,151	1,579,262	560,908	969,882
Spain	301,311	1,236,898	1,573,005	1,573,934	1,500,600	1,478,014	864,002	594,353
Turkey	818,513	482,917	844,075	718,034	1,333,810	1,087,913	524,610	533,150
Hungary	524,772	1,737,407	2,281,384	1,595,140	1,362,228	1,040,309	595,104	340,180
Thailand	601,369	694,962	847,304	895,618	1,013,929	1,034,479	519,168	695,813
Brazil	422,930	562,115	545,792	675,786	747,266	988,290	495,125	530,336
Netherlands	87,879	154,330	220,378	278,223	663,007	794,923	346,725	354,846
Belgium	1,369,671	936,854	1,279,716	1,017,168	690,905	608,249	331,913	630,293
France	872,413	1,108,053	1,046,304	842,007	730,781	605,575	317,614	307,315
South Africa	2,253,964	1,354,447	1,476,587	1,589,929	1,148,611	552,835	406,754	120,326
Poland	185,916	205,291	222,380	485,358	311,771	324,586	170,150	203,045
Viet Nam	155,153	182,826	226,649	230,760	260,167	301,761	135,383	206,867

Note: "Vehicles" refers to HS (Harmonized System) Code 87, "vehicles, except railway or tramway, and parts etc."

Source: Foreign Trade Division, U.S. Census Bureau
Plunkett Research,® Ltd.
www.plunkettresearch.com

Value of Exports of U.S. Vehicles: 2013-2nd Quarter 2019

(In Thousands of US$)

Partner	2013	2014	2015	2016	2017	2018	2Q 2018	2Q 2019
World	134,090,149	136,021,619	127,366,637	124,702,177	130,406,804	130,730,673	68,694,544	67,808,108
Canada	51,993,319	51,428,475	47,904,675	48,442,221	51,755,817	52,267,474	28,190,889	27,483,853
Mexico	21,607,458	21,250,784	22,406,835	21,399,327	21,181,035	22,153,042	10,889,533	11,094,581
China	10,330,141	13,268,974	10,808,810	11,066,438	12,862,665	9,381,114	5,605,669	4,201,151
Germany	6,050,402	6,670,519	7,198,379	7,691,189	7,320,039	7,182,369	3,952,671	3,907,812
Australia	3,484,424	3,648,551	3,364,151	2,702,529	3,244,686	3,503,753	1,828,686	1,763,508
United Kingdom	2,094,046	2,687,089	3,063,297	3,128,046	2,780,035	2,651,134	1,455,489	1,264,263
United Arab Emirates	3,555,034	3,334,534	3,170,716	2,486,582	2,260,082	2,631,467	1,268,891	1,396,003
South Korea	1,281,396	1,598,975	1,873,254	2,195,816	2,091,060	2,230,710	1,117,341	1,142,207
Saudi Arabia	5,762,407	4,895,798	4,799,099	3,604,644	2,572,014	2,115,335	1,009,120	970,994
Japan	1,585,433	1,447,808	1,324,493	1,309,008	1,359,446	1,691,955	898,818	783,672
Netherlands	686,542	874,107	986,578	1,122,818	1,244,310	1,550,510	767,636	555,641
Belgium	936,969	1,164,869	1,201,608	1,285,535	1,515,655	1,475,088	872,218	2,647,747
Chile	1,466,279	1,158,751	911,305	702,672	934,068	1,132,908	503,879	460,218
Brazil	1,268,567	1,280,686	1,067,051	925,468	1,939,129	1,103,275	571,588	526,880
Norway	307,807	541,473	243,770	369,685	672,768	910,189	378,289	50,628
Russian Federation	1,999,349	2,140,921	599,331	635,903	639,278	866,858	494,389	401,044
Kuwait	1,112,784	816,913	932,759	801,161	756,196	864,369	445,253	547,229
Nigeria	1,317,860	1,045,153	475,696	299,908	466,443	853,777	381,576	440,725
Italy	520,268	644,307	848,154	791,491	717,383	787,733	397,677	346,259
South Africa	1,035,465	1,114,177	650,976	446,060	550,823	692,417	315,550	332,002
Afghanistan	217,326	105,135	113,512	491,545	573,498	638,107	339,175	23,454
Jordan	670,855	429,651	363,713	350,104	476,692	554,934	263,031	218,580
Dominican Republic	349,833	387,942	451,646	506,519	476,812	545,494	265,116	298,224
Taiwan	396,537	420,097	325,369	319,253	391,135	532,863	287,542	350,500
France	606,175	541,621	465,951	521,020	480,267	517,500	256,374	264,013

Note: "Vehicles" refers to HS (Harmonized System) Code 87, "vehicles, except railway or tramway, and parts etc."

Source: Foreign Trade Division, U.S. Census Bureau
Plunkett Research,® Ltd.
www.plunkettresearch.com

Occupational Employment and Wages for Automotive Service Technicians and Mechanics: May 2018

Employment estimate and mean wage estimates for this occupation:

Employment[1]	Employment RSE[2]	Mean Hourly Wage	Mean Annual Wage[3]	Wage RSE[2]
648,050	0.7%	$21.02	$43,730	0.3%

Percentile wage estimates for this occupation:

Percentile	10%	25%	50% (Median)	75%	90%
Hourly Wage	$11.26	$14.53	$19.57	$26.31	$32.19
Annual Wage[3]	$23,420	$30,220	$40,710	$54,720	$66,950

Industries with the highest levels of employment in this occupation:

Occupation	Employment	Hourly Mean Wage	Annual Mean Wage
Automobile Dealers	244,040	$22.32	$46,420
Automotive Repair and Maintenance	230,100	$19.78	$41,140
Automotive Parts, Accessories, and Tire Stores	63,800	$18.42	$38,320
Local Government (OES Designation)	16,230	$19.17	$39,870
Gasoline Stations	15,860	$25.40	$52,820

Note: Category includes those who diagnose, adjust, repair, or overhaul automotive vehicles. Exclude "Automotive Body and Related Repairers" (49-3021), "Bus and Truck Mechanics and Diesel Engine Specialists" (49-3031), and "Electronic Equipment Installers and Repairers, Motor Vehicles" (49-2096).

[1] Estimates for detailed occupations do not sum to the totals because the totals include occupations not shown separately. Estimates do not include self-employed workers.

[2] The relative standard error (RSE) is a measure of the reliability of a survey statistic. The smaller the relative standard error, the more precise the estimate.

[3] Annual wages have been calculated by multiplying the hourly mean wage by a "year-round, full-time" hours figure of 2,080 hours; for those occupations where there is not an hourly mean wage published, the annual wage has been directly calculated from the reported survey data.

Source: U.S. Bureau of Labor Statistics
Plunkett Research,® Ltd.
www.plunkettresearch.com

Employment in the Automobile Industry, U.S.: 2013-June 2019

(Annual Estimates in Thousands of Employed Workers)

NAICS Code	Industry Sector	2013	2014	2015	2016	2017	2018	Jun-19*
Manufacturing								
3361,2,3	**Motor vehicles & parts**	**824.8**	**872.1**	**913.7**	**944.3**	**963.4**	**996.0**	**1,001.6**
3361	**Motor vehicles**	**181.5**	**194.0**	**200.8**	**211.8**	**218.9**	**233.6**	**241.1**
33611	Automobiles & light trucks	155.7	167.1	171.9	183.6	189.3	201.6	208.6
336111	Automobiles	113.5	117.4	114.5	117.5	121.8	133.8	138.3
336112	Light trucks & utility vehicles	42.2	49.6	57.4	66.2	67.5	67.8	70.3
33612	Heavy duty trucks	25.8	26.9	28.9	28.2	29.6	32.0	32.5
3362	**Motor vehicle bodies & trailers**	**134.6**	**141.1**	**148.0**	**151.3**	**155.3**	**165.3**	**168.9**
336211	Motor vehicle bodies	52.9	53.9	56.3	56.5	54.8	57.6	58.6
336212,3,4	Truck trailers, motor homes, travel trailers & campers	81.6	87.2	91.8	94.8	100.5	107.6	110.3
3363	**Motor vehicle parts**	**508.7**	**537.0**	**564.9**	**581.2**	**589.2**	**597.1**	**591.6**
33631	Motor vehicle gasoline engine & parts	58.9	61.1	63.2	64.3	63.0	62.9	62.0
33632	Motor vehicle electric equipment	54.0	55.6	58.8	61.0	62.6	62.8	61.0
33633	Motor vehicle steering & suspension parts	31.7	34.5	37.3	38.3	36.9	35.8	34.7
33634	Motor vehicle brake systems	23.8	24.5	25.1	25.1	26.2	26.2	25.9
33635	Motor vehicle power train components	67.8	74.6	79.7	79.6	81.1	83.3	80.4
33636	Motor vehicle seating & interior trim	61.4	66.0	70.1	73.1	75.7	77.1	73.7
33637	Motor vehicle metal stamping	74.1	78.3	81.9	86.3	88.7	89.8	87.5
33639	Other motor vehicle parts	137.0	142.4	148.8	153.4	155.2	159.1	166.4
Transportation & Warehousing								
484	**Truck transportation**	**1,382.6**	**1,417.7**	**1,452.7**	**1,448.1**	**1,457.0**	**1,491.9**	**1,534.0**
4841	General freight trucking	944.2	967.1	995.2	998.6	1,001.8	1,029.6	1,048.8
48411	Local	226.1	231.4	241.1	246.0	249.4	257.5	265.2
48412	Long-Distance	718.1	735.7	754.1	752.6	752.4	772.0	783.6
484121	Truckload	497.4	501.1	504.7	505.0	502.4	510.5	519.1
484122	Less-than-Truckload	220.7	234.6	249.4	247.6	250.0	261.6	264.5
4842	Specialized freight trucking	438.4	450.6	457.5	449.4	455.1	462.3	485.2
48421	Used household & office goods moving	94.9	95.3	96.9	98.3	99.4	98.8	102.8
48422	Other specialized trucking, local	216.6	223.7	224.2	216.5	222.1	226.0	239.6
48423	Other specialized trucking, long-distance	126.9	131.5	136.4	134.7	133.7	137.4	142.8
485	**Transit and ground passenger transportation**	**448.5**	**466.5**	**477.5**	**483.9**	**488.9**	**487.5**	**486.5**
4853	Taxi and limousine service	76.8	78.8	80.1	80.4	78.6	74.5	72.3
48531	Taxi service	34.8	35.8	36.8	37.3	37.2	35.9	34.5
48532	Limousine service	42.0	43.0	43.3	43.1	41.4	38.6	37.8
4854	School and employee bus transportation	184.2	193.2	195.5	198.5	200.0	199.7	195.3
4855	Urban, interurban, rural, and charter bus transportation	96.8	98.4	99.7	100.6	103.0	103.9	106.6
4859	Other ground passenger transportation	90.8	96.1	102.3	104.5	107.3	109.4	112.3
4884	**Support activities for road transportation**	**88.2**	**93.0**	**95.4**	**99.5**	**101.7**	**102.5**	**102.1**
48841	Motor vehicle towing	53.9	56.9	58.4	61.9	62.9	65.9	67.3

* Preliminary Estimate

Source: U.S. Bureau of Labor Statistics
Plunkett Research,® Ltd.
www.plunkettresearch.com

Chapter 3

IMPORTANT AUTOMOBILE INDUSTRY CONTACTS

Addresses, Telephone Numbers and Internet Sites

Contents:

1) Alternative Energy-Clean Transportation

ACEEE's Green Book Online
529 14th St. NW
Washington, DC 20045 US
Phone: 202-507-4000
Fax: 202-429-2248
E-mail Address: *greenercars@aceee.org*
Web Address: www.greenercars.org
Green Book Online is the official web site for the American Council for an Energy-Efficient Economy (ACEEE)'s Green Book publication, which rates cars on how they impact the environment.

Clean Cities Program
1000 Independence Ave. SW, Rm. 5G-030
Washington, DC 20585 USA
Phone: 202-586-8055
Fax: 202-586-7409
E-mail Address: linda.bluestein@ee.doe.gov
Web Address: cleancities.energy.gov
The Clean Cities Program, sponsored by the U.S. Department of Energy, is a federal program to promote the use of alternative transportation fuels in U.S. cities.

International Council on Clean Transportation (ICCT)
1225 I St. NW, Ste. 900
Washington, DC 20005 USA
Phone: 202-534-1600
Web Address: www.theicct.org
The International Council on Clean Transportation is an assembly of about 30 top government officials and policymakers from the 10 largest motor vehicle markets. Together, it accounts for 85% of the world's new car and truck sales, providing them and other interested parties with accurate information about research, best practices, and technical resources for improving the efficiency and environmental performance of cars, trucks and other vehicles. The Council hopes to support sustainable transportation.

2) Alternative Energy-Ethanol

Growth Energy Market Development
E-mail Address: SBrenden@growthenergy.org
Web Address: www.ethanolretailer.com
Growth Energy Market Development, created through the 2009 merger of the National Ethanol Vehicle Coalition and Growth Energy, is a nonprofit organization that is one of the leading advocates in the U.S. for expanding the use of 85% (E85) ethanol motor fuel. It also advocates the production of so-called flexible fuel vehicles, which can run on higher than conventional 10% ethanol fuels. Additionally, the firm promotes the installation of ethanol blender pumps, or flex fuel pumps.

Renewable Fuels Association (RFA)
425 3rd St. SW, Ste. 1150
Washington, DC 20024 USA
Phone: 202-289-3835
Fax: 202-289-7519
Web Address: www.ethanolrfa.org
The Renewable Fuels Association (RFA) is a trade organization representing the ethanol industry. It publishes a wealth of useful information, including a listing of biorefineries and monthly U.S. fuel ethanol production and demand.

Renewable Industries Canada
55 Murray St., Ste. 450
Ottawa, ON K1N 5M3 Canada
Phone: 613-594-5528
Fax: 613-594-3076
E-mail Address: w.meyer@ricanada.org
Web Address: www.greenfuels.org
Renewable Industries Canada is a nonprofit organization that represent producers of renewable fuels and value added products that reduce GHG emissions and provide economic opportunity to the benefit of all Canadians. Its mandate is to promote the use of value-added products made from renewable resources through consumer awareness and government liaison activities.

3) Alternative Energy-Fuel Cells

EERE Hydrogen, Fuel Cells & Infrastructure Technologies Program
1000 Independence Ave. SW
Washington, DC 20585 USA
Phone: 202-586-3388
E-mail Address: fuelcells@ee.doe.gov
Web Address:
www1.eere.energy.gov/hydrogenandfuelcells
The Hydrogen, Fuel Cells & Infrastructure Technologies Program of the Energy Efficiency and Renewable Energy (EERE), a division of the U.S. Department of Energy (DOE), works to develop and successfully introduce fuel cell technologies to the global market.

4) Automobile Finance and Loans Associations

National Automotive Finance Association (NAF)
7037 Ridge Rd., Ste. 300
Hanover, MD 21076 USA
Phone: 410-712-4036
Fax: 410-712-4038
Toll Free: 800-463-8955
E-mail Address: inquire@nafassociation.com
Web Address: www.nafassociation.com
The National Automotive Finance Association (NAF) is the only trade association exclusively serving the non-prime auto financing industry. Organized in the fall of 1996, the NAF Association supports its members and the industry with programs and education.

5) Automobile Purchasing-Online

Autobytel, Inc.
18872 MacArthur Blvd., Ste. 200
Irvine, CA 92612-1400 USA
Phone: 949-225-4500
Web Address: www.autobytel.com
Autobytel, Inc. is an Internet automotive marketing services company that helps retailers sell cars and manufacturers build brands through marketing and CRM (customer relationship management) tools and programs. Car purchasers can use this popular site to request bids on specific makes and models of new cars and trucks. Participating dealers will respond with detailed prices.

AutoTrader.com
3003 Summit Blvd., Ste. 200
Atlanta, GA 30319 USA
Phone: 404-568-8000
Toll Free: 800-353-9350
E-mail Address: julie.shipp@autotrader.com
Web Address: www.autotrader.com
AutoTrader.com is designed to give users more control of the buying process and make finding a used vehicle that meets your personal needs easier.

CARFAX, Inc.
5860 Trinity Pkwy., Ste. 600
Centreville, VA 20120 USA
Phone: 703-934-2664
Web Address: www.carfax.com
CARFAX, Inc.'s web site offers Vehicle History Reports that reveal important background information and unearth hidden problems in a vehicle's past that may affect its safety and resale value.

Cars.com
175 W. Jackson Blvd., Fl. 8
Chicago, IL 60604 USA
Phone: 312-601-5000
Fax: 312-601-5755
Toll Free: 888-780-1286
E-mail Address: feedback@cars.com
Web Address: www.cars.com
Cars.com, a division of Classified Ventures, LLC, provides users with complete local and national inventories of new and used vehicles, featuring automotive reviews, model reports, advice, a dealer locator, financing information and much more.

ClassicCar.com
4283 Express Ln., Ste. V5610
Sarasota, FL 34238 USA
E-mail Address: privacy@classiccar.com
Web Address: www.classiccar.com
ClassicCar.com, powered by Traffic Junction Ltd., is an online forum for buying, selling and discussing classic cars and their restoration.

eBay Motors
2065 Hamilton Ave.
San Jose, CA 95125 USA
Phone: 408-376-7400
Fax: 408-376-7401
Toll Free: 800-322-9266
E-mail Address: press@ebay.com
Web Address: www.ebay.com/motors
eBay Motors, part of eBay, Inc., is a provider of online car and truck vehicle auctions and services. It is an incredibly popular site that makes it possible for buyers and sellers to connect nationwide. It includes listings of used and classic cars and trucks.

Edmunds.com
1620 26th St., Ste. 400 S.
Santa Monica, CA 90404 USA
Phone: 310-309-6300
Fax: 310-309-6466
Toll Free: 855-782-4711
E-mail Address: pr@edmunds.com
Web Address: www.edmunds.com
Edmunds.com, launched in 1995, was one of the first web sites to offer automotive information to consumers. It provides a database of car values, car

reviews, ratings and expert advice to help consumers get a fair deal.

Kelley Blue Book
195 Technology Dr.
Irvine, CA 92618 USA
Toll Free: 800-258-2665
Web Address: www.kbb.com
Kelley Blue Book (KBB) is a respected source for pricing information on new and used vehicles. Its web site recently launched a new service, called KBBGreen, which offers information on environmentally friendly vehicles.

Motorplace.com
605 Fifth Ave. S., Ste. 800
Seattle, WA 98104-3889 USA
Toll Free: 800-908-8244
Web Address: www2.motorplace.com
Motorplace.com, a part of The Cobalt Group, Inc., is a leading provider of Internet-based automotive products and services.

MSN Autos
1 Microsoft Way
Microsoft Corp.
Redmond, WA 98052-6399 USA
Phone: 425-882-8080
Fax: 425-936-7329
Web Address: www.autos.msn.com
MSN Autos offers extensive information on new cars, used cars, warranties, finance, insurance and automotive news. Consumers will find extensive tools to help them make car-buying decisions.

NADAguides.com
P.O. Box 7800
Costa Mesa, CA 92628 USA
Toll Free: 800-966-6232
E-mail Address: information@NADAguides.com
Web Address: www.nadaguides.com
NADAguides.com are appraisal guides that serve as resources for pricing information on used vehicles. The site also has reviews and buying resources for new and used vehicles.

TrueCar
120 Broadway, Ste. 200
Santa Monica, CA 90401 USA
Toll Free: 888-878-3227
E-mail Address: feedback@truecar.com
Web Address: www.truecar.com
TrueCar.com is a transparent, visual publisher of new car transaction data. TrueCar.com price reports help dealers and consumers to agree on the parameters of a fair deal by providing an accurate, comprehensive and simple understanding of what others actually paid for the identically equipped new car over the last 30 days both locally and nationally.

Yahoo! Autos
701 1st Ave.
Yahoo! Inc.
Sunnyvale, CA 94089 USA
Phone: 408-349-3300
Fax: 408-349-3301
Web Address: autos.yahoo.com
Yahoo! Autos provides a vast amount of information on new and used cars, finance, insurance and car maintenance.

6) Automotive Industry Associations

Alliance of Automobile Manufacturers
803 7th St. NW, Ste. 300
Washington, DC 20001 USA
Phone: 202-326-5500
Fax: 202-326-5598
E-mail Address: info@autoalliance.org
Web Address: www.autoalliance.org
The Alliance of Automobile Manufacturers is a trade association composed of 9 car manufacturing companies including BMW Group, DaimlerChrysler, Ford Motor Company, General Motors, Mazda, Mitsubishi Motors, Porsche, Toyota and Volkswagen. Alliance members account for more than 90% of vehicles sold in the U.S.

American International Automobile Dealers Association (AIADA)
500 Montgomery St., Ste. 800
Alexandria, VA 22314 USA
Fax: 703-519-7810
Toll Free: 800-462-4232
Web Address: www.aiada.org
American International Automobile Dealers Association (AIADA) is the lobbying and communications force in Washington, D.C. for the 10,000 American automobile dealerships that sell and service international nameplate brands.

ANFAVEA (National Association of Automobile Manufacturers-Brazil)
Avenida Indianapolis, 496
Sao Paulo, 04062-900 Brazil

Phone: 55 11 2193-7800
Web Address: www.anfavea.com.br
ANFAVEA brings together automobile manufacturing companies and agricultural machinery manufacturers in Brazil, by sponsoring and supporting industry related events; and compiles and disseminates industry performance data.

ANFIA (Italian Association of the Automotive Industry)
Corso Galileo Ferraris 61
Torino, 10128 Italy
Phone: 39-011-55-46-511
Fax: 39-011-54-59-86
E-mail Address: anfia@anfia.it
Web Address: www.anfia.it
ANFIA - the Italian Association of the Automotive Industry - is one of the main Trade Associations within CONFINDUSTRIA (the Confederation of Italian Industry) and is the networking and strategic benchmark between the automotive trade and the Italian and international political and institutional scene.

Association of Global Automakers (Global Automakers)
1050 K St. NW, Ste. 650
Washington, DC 20001 USA
Phone: 202-650-5555
E-mail Address: info@globalautomakers.org
Web Address: www.globalautomakers.org
The Association of Global Automakers (Global Automakers), formerly the Association of International Automobile Manufacturers, Inc., is a trade association representing 14 international motor vehicle manufacturers. Members concentrate on improving the safety and efficiency of vehicles, as well as investing in American communities.

Automotive Industry Action Group (AIAG)
26200 Lahser Rd., Ste. 200
Southfield, MI 48033-7100 USA
Phone: 248-358-3570
Fax: 248-358-3253
E-mail Address: order_inquiry@aiag.org
Web Address: www.aiag.org
The Automotive Industry Action Group (AIAG) is an open forum for members to cooperate in developing and promoting solutions that enhance the prosperity of the automotive industry.

Automotive Service Association (ASA)
8190 Precinct Line Rd.
Colleyville, TX 76034-7675 USA
Phone: 817-514-2900
Fax: 817-514-0770
Toll Free: 800-272-7467
E-mail Address: asainfo@asashop.org
Web Address: www.asashop.org
The Automotive Service Association (ASA) is a leading organization for owners and managers of automotive service businesses that strive to deliver excellence in service and repairs to consumers.

Canadian Automobile Dealers Association (CADA)
85 Renfrew Dr.
Markham, ON L3R 0N9 Canada
Phone: 905-940-4959
Fax: 905-940-6870
Toll Free: 800-463-5289
Web Address: www.cada.ca
The Canadian Automobile Dealers Association (CADA) represents 3,200 automobile dealers across Canada.

Canadian Transportation Equipment Association (CTEA)
16 Barrie Blvd., Unit 3B
St. Thomas, ON N5P 4B9 Canada
Phone: 519-631-0414
Fax: 519-631-1333
E-mail Address: ccowell@atminc.on.ca
Web Address: www.ctea.ca
The Canadian Transportation Equipment Association (CTEA) standardizes the commercial vehicle equipment manufacturing industry in Canada.

Canadian Vehicle Manufacturers' Association (CVMA)
170 Attwell Dr., Ste. 400
Toronto, ON M9W 5Z5 Canada
Phone: 416-364-9333
Fax: 416-367-3221
Toll Free: 800-758-7122
E-mail Address: info@cvma.ca
Web Address: www.cvma.ca
The Canadian Vehicle Manufacturers' Association (CVMA) is the industry organization representing manufacturers of light and heavy duty motor vehicles in Canada. Association members collaborate to solve industry objectives in the way of consumer protection, the environment and vehicle safety.

China Association of Automobile Manufacturers (CAAM)
No. 46 SanLiHe Rd.
Xicheng District
Beijing, 100823 China
Phone: 86-10-68594182
Fax: 86-10-68595243
E-mail Address: caam@caam.org.cn
Web Address: www.caam.org.cn/english/
China Association of Automobile Manufacturers (CAAM) represents the automobile and vehicle manufacturers in China.

China Automotive Technology & Research Center (CATARC)
No. 68, E. Xianfeng Rd.
Dongli District
Tianjin, 300162 China
Phone: 86-22-84370000-1936
Fax: 86-22-24711970
E-mail Address: qianrui@catarc.ac.cn
Web Address: www.catarc.ac.cn
China Automotive Technology & Research Center (CATARC) serves as a technical administrative body with ties to China's State-Owned Assets Supervision and Administration Commission (SASAC) and to the automotive industry throughout China. CATARC works in conjunction with the Chinese government to formulate auto standards and technical regulations, and is also involved in overseeing product certification testing; quality system certification; industry planning and policy research; and automotive technology research. In addition to its headquarters, CATARC maintains various research and testing facilities, as well as offices in Beijing, Shanghai and Wuhan.

European Automobile Manufacturers Association (ACEA)
Avenye des Nerviens 85
Brussels, B-1040 Belgium
Phone: 32-2-732-55-50
Fax: 32-2-738-73-10
E-mail Address: info@acea.be
Web Address: www.acea.be
The European Automobile Manufacturers Association, or the Association des Constructeurs EuropÃ©ens d' Automobiles (ACEA), represents the automobile industry in Europe.

Federal Chamber of Automotive Industries (FACI)
59 Wentworth Ave., Level 1
Kingston, ACT 2604 Australia
Phone: 60-2-6247-3811
Fax: 61-2-6248-7673
E-mail Address: sheena.ireland@fcai.com.au
Web Address: www.fcai.com.au
FACI represents Australia's automobile manufacturing industry.

Federation of Automobile Dealers Associations (FADA)
805 Surya Kiran, 19 K G Marg
New Delhi, 110 001 India
Phone: 91-11-2332-0095
Fax: 91-11-2332-0093
Web Address: www.fadaindia.org
The Federation of Automobile Dealers Associations (FADA) represents Automobile Dealers of India. It supports and promotes the Indian retail automobile market and members include vehicle manufacturers, tire manufacturers, insurance and finance sectors and other allied industries.

German Association of the Automobile Industry (VDA)
Behrenstr. 35
Berlin, 10117 Germany
Phone: 49-30-897842-0
Fax: 49-30-897824-600
E-mail Address: info@vda.de
Web Address: www.vda.de
The German Association of the Automobile Industry (VDA) promotes the Germany automotive industry nationally and internationally.

Global Automakers of Canada (GAC)
2 Bloor St. W., Ste. 1804, Box 5
Toronto, ON M4W 3E2 Canada
Phone: 416-595-8251
Fax: 416-595-2864
E-mail Address: auto@globalautomakers.ca
Web Address: www.globalautomakers.ca
The Global Automakers of Canada (GAC) represents before federal, provincial and territorial governments the interests of members engaged in the manufacturing, importation, distribution and servicing of light duty vehicles. While GAC was initially dedicated to the interests of importers, it has broadened its focus as offshore-based companies have set up vehicle manufacturing plants in Canada. There are presently 15 members.

International Organization of Motor Vehicle Manufacturers (OICA)
4 rue de Berri
8 eme arrondissement
Paris, France
Web Address: www.oica.net
The International Organization of Motor Vehicle Manufacturers was founded in Paris in 1919. It is known as the Organisation Internationale des Constructeurs d'Automobiles (OICA). The organization's membership comprises 38 national trade associations around the world, including all major automobile manufacturing countries, thereby covering virtually the entire motor vehicle industry all over the world. It publishes an excellent list of global automobile manufacturing statistics on its web site.

Japan Automobile Manufacturers Association of Canada (JAMA Canada)
151 Bloor St. W., Ste. 460
Toronto, ON M5S 1S4 Canada
Phone: 416-968-0150
Fax: 416-968-7095
E-mail Address: jama@jama.ca
Web Address: www.jama.ca
The Japan Automobile Manufacturers Association of Canada (JAMA Canada) represents the interests of members in both the Canadian and Japanese auto industries by promoting closer industrial ties. The association provides up-to-date statistics, newsletters and industry links on its web site.

Japanese Automobile Manufacturers Association, Inc. (JAMA)
Shiba Daimon 1-chome, Minato-ku
Jidosha Kaikan (NBF Twr.), 16th Fl., 1-30
Tokyo, 105-0012 Japan
Phone: 81-3-5405-6126
Web Address: www.jama-english.jp
Japanese Automobile Manufacturers Association, Inc. (JAMA) is a nonprofit industry association that is made up of 14 manufacturers of passenger cars, trucks, buses and motorcycles in Japan. Besides its Tokyo headquarters, JAMA maintains offices in the U.S., Europe and Asia.

Mexican Automotive Industry Association (AMIA)
E-mail Address: comunicacion@amia.com.mx
Web Address: www.amia.com.mx
Mexican Automotive Industry Association (AMIA) is an industry group representing manufacturers of vehicles and related parts within the nation of Mexico. Its proper name in Spanish is ASOCIACION MEXICANA DE LA INDUSTRIA AUTOMOTRIZ A.C.

Motor Traders Association of Singapore
Phone: 65-6258-7210
Web Address: www.mta.org.sg
Motor Traders Association of Singapore represents the automotive industry in Singapore. It hosts the annual Singapore Motorshow.

National Automobile Dealers Association (NADA)
8400 Westpark Dr.
McLean, VA 22102 USA
Phone: 703-821-7000
Toll Free: 800-252-6232
Web Address: www.nada.org
The National Automobile Dealers Association (NADA) represents more than 17,000 new car and truck dealers, both import and domestic, operating more than 37,500 separate franchises.

National Institute for Automotive Service Excellence (ASE)
101 Blue Seal Dr. SE, Ste. 101
Leesburg, VA 20175 USA
Phone: 703-669-6600
Fax: 703-669-6123
Toll Free: 800-390-6789
E-mail Address: webmaster@ase.com
Web Address: www.ase.com
ASE's mission is to improve the quality of automotive service and repair through the voluntary testing and certification of automotive technicians.

North American Automobile Trade Association (NAATA)
10 Four Seasons Pl., Ste. 1000
Toronto, ON M9B 6H7 Canada
Toll Free: 877-227-8878
E-mail Address: naata@naata.org
Web Address: www.naata.org
The North American Automobile Trade Association (NAATA) is a nonprofit organization of automobile dealers that import and export vehicles across international borders.

Quebec Ground Transportation Cluster (The)
1418, rue Michaud
Drummondville, QC J2C 7V3 Canada
Phone: 819-472-4494
Fax: 819-472-6520

Toll Free: 866-499-4494
E-mail Address: vdugre@polet2.com
Web Address: www.transportail.com
The Quebec Ground Transportation Cluster was created by the merger of four of Quebec's ground transportation associations in the Monteregie, Centre-du-Quebec, Estrie and Laurentides regions, and of the Specialty Vehicles and Transportation Equipment Manufacturers Association. By organizing a range of special events, networking activities and trade missions, the Cluster looks to cultivate the development and growth of ground transportation sector companies in Quebec.

Society of Indian Automobile Manufacturers (SIAM)
Lodhi Rd.
Core 4-B, 5th Fl., India Habitat Ctr.
New Delhi, 110 003 India
Phone: 91-11-24647810-12
Fax: 91-11-24648222
E-mail Address: siam@siam.in
Web Address: www.siamindia.com
The Society of Indian Automobile Manufacturers (SIAM) represents 38 leading vehicle and vehicular engine manufacturers in India. The site contains industry statistics, technical regulations, fuel specifications, industry news and events.

Society of Motor Manufacturers and Traders (SMMT)
71 Great Peter St.
London, SW1P 2BN UK
Phone: 44-20-7235-7000
Fax: 44-20-7235-7112
E-mail Address: MVRISWeb@smmt.co.uk
Web Address: www.smmt.co.uk
Society of Motor Manufacturers and Traders (SMMT) represents the automotive and automotive manufacturing industry in the United Kingdom. The site has information regarding the industry's and United Kingdom's automotive statistics.

United States Council for Automotive Research Inc. (USCAR)
1000 Town Center Dr., Ste. 300
Southfield, MI 48075 USA
Phone: 248-223-9000
E-mail Address: sbairley@uscar.org
Web Address: www.uscar.org
The United States Council for Automotive Research (USCAR) was founded in 1992. Its goal is to further strengthen the technology base of the U.S. auto industry through cooperative research and development. Its main focus is to create, support and direct U.S. cooperative research and development to advance automotive technologies. USCAR is composed of a number of specialized groups that focus on specific research areas. USCAR is governed by the three-member USCAR Council, whose membership includes the R&D vice presidents from each of the U.S. automakers.

Used Car Dealers Association of Ontario (UCDA)
230 Norseman St.
Toronto, ON M8Z 2R4 Canada
Phone: 416-231-2600
Fax: 416-232-0775
Toll Free: 800-268-2598
E-mail Address: web@ucda.org
Web Address: www.ucda.org
The Used Car Dealers Association of Ontario (UCDA) is a nonprofit organization representing the interests of more than 4,400 used car dealers in the Ontario, Canada area.

7) Automotive Industry Resources

Automotive Center
1800 Crooks Rd.
Troy, MI 48084 USA
Phone: 248-244-8920
Web Address: www.plastics-car.com
The Automotive Center, sponsored by the American Chemistry Council's Plastics Division, strives to provide the automobile designer, stylist or engineer with up-to-the-minute research and information on plastics applications in cars.

Automotive Design & Production
6915 Valley Ave.
Cincinnati, OH 45244-3029 USA
Phone: 513-527-8800
Fax: 513-527-8801
E-mail Address: malbert@mmsonline.com
Web Address: www.autofieldguide.com
Automotive Design & Production is dedicated to the automotive design industry offering studies and reports; a magazine with online articles; a calendar of events; supply chain and electronics information and a forum.

Automotive Industries Online
Phone: 313-879-0887
E-mail Address: jal@autoindustry.us
Web Address: www.ai-online.com

Automotive Industries Online is a monthly publication devoted to providing global coverage of all aspects of the automobile marketplace, with an emphasis on the people, products and processes that shape the industry.

AutoRemarketing.com
301 Cascade Pointe Ln.
Westview at Weston
Cary, NC 27513 USA
Fax: 919-674-6027
Toll Free: 800-608-7500
E-mail Address: zadeits@autoremarketing.com
Web Address: www.autoremarketing.com
AutoRemarketing.com is an online magazine devoted to the auto remarketing industry.

Center for Automotive Research (CAR)
3005 Boardwalk, Ste. 200
Ann Arbor, MI 48108 USA
Phone: 734-662-1287
Fax: 734-662-5736
E-mail Address: lhart@cargroup.org
Web Address: www.cargroup.org
The Center for Automotive Research, a nonprofit organization, is focused on a wide variety of important trends and changes related to the automobile industry and society at the international, federal, state and local levels. CAR conducts industry research, develops new methodologies, forecasts industry trends, advises on public policy, and sponsors multi-stakeholder communication forums.

ConceptCar
P.O. Box 10339
Colchester, CO1 9HZ UK
E-mail Address: admin@conceptcar.co.uk
Web Address: www.conceptcar.co.uk
ConceptCar is a web site devoted to car design, which provides books, email, message boards and a search directory composed of hundreds of web sites.

Diesel Technology Forum
5291 Corporate Dr., Ste. 102
Frederick, MD 21703 USA
Phone: 301-668-7230
Fax: 301-668-7234
E-mail Address: dtf@dieselforum.org
Web Address: www.dieselforum.org
The Diesel Technology Forum, which was created by companies in the diesel technology, fuel systems manufacturing and petroleum refining industries, aims to create a new dialogue and encourage the open exchange of information on a range of issues concerning diesel technologies.

DieselNet
Ecopoint Inc.
P.O. Box 47055
Mississauga, ON L5K 2R2 Canada
Phone: 905-990-0775
Fax: 905-990-0776
E-mail Address: consult@dieselnet.com
Web Address: www.dieselnet.com
DieselNet is an online information service on diesel emissions, emission control, diesel engines, fuels and more. Ecopoint Inc. owns and publishes the site.

8) Automotive Parts, Repair & Supplies Associations

Auto Care Association, The
7101 Wisconsin Ave., Ste. 1300
Bethesda, MD 20814-3415 USA
Phone: 301-654-6664
Fax: 301-654-3299
E-mail Address: info@autocare.org
Web Address: www.autocare.org
The Auto Care Association, formerly the Automotive Aftermarket Industry Association (AAIA) consists of members, including independent manufacturers, marketers, repair shops, distributors and retailers in the auto care industry. The organization serves the interests of its members through promotion of technology, best practices, professional education and market intelligence.

Automotive Component Manufacturers Association of India (ACMA)
The Capital Ct., 6th Fl.
Olof Palme Marg, Munirka
New Delhi, 110 067 India
Phone: 91-11-2616-0315
Fax: 91-11-2616-0317
E-mail Address: acma@acma.in
Web Address: www.acmainfo.com
Automotive Component Manufacturers Association of India (ACMA) is the nodal agency for the Indian auto component industry.

Automotive Industries Association of Canada (AIA)
180 Elgin St., Ste. 1400
Ottawa, ON K2P 2K3 Canada
Phone: 613-728-5821
Fax: 613-728-6021

Toll Free: 800-808-2920
E-mail Address: info@aiacanada.com
Web Address: www.aiacanada.com
The Automotive Industries Association of Canada (AIA) is a national trade organization representing the Canadian automotive repair, accessories and tools aftermarket industry.

Automotive Parts Manufacturers' Association (APMA)
10 Four Seasons Pl., Ste. 801
Toronto, ON M9B 6H7 Canada
Phone: 416-620-4220
Fax: 416-620-9730
Web Address: www.apma.ca
The Automotive Parts Manufacturers' Association (APMA) is a leading national association representing OEM producers of parts and services for the worldwide automotive industry.

Automotive Recyclers Association
9113 Church St.
Manassas, VA 20110 USA
Phone: 571-208-0428
Fax: 571-208-0430
Toll Free: 888-385-1005
E-mail Address: michael@a-r-a.org
Web Address: www.a-r-a.org
The Automotive Recyclers Association is dedicated to the efficient removal and reuse of automotive parts and the safe disposal of inoperable motor vehicles.

Hong Kong Auto Parts Industry Association (HKAPIA)
5/F HKPC Bldg., 78 Tat Chee Ave.
Kowloon, Hong Kong Hong Kong
Phone: 852-278-85457
Fax: 852-2788-5543
E-mail Address: autopart@hkpc.org
Web Address: www.hkapia.com
The Hong Kong Auto Parts Industry Association (HKAPIA) represents the automotive components industry in Hong Kong. Its members are engaged in the design, manufacturing and business investment in the auto parts industry.

Motor & Equipment Manufacturers Association (MEMA)
10 Laboratory Dr.
Research Triangle Park, NC 27709-3966 USA
Phone: 919-549-4800
Fax: 919-406-1465
E-mail Address: info@mema.org
Web Address: www.mema.org
The Motor & Equipment Manufacturers Association (MEMA) exclusively represents and serves manufacturers of motor vehicle components, tools and equipment, automotive chemicals and related products used in the production, repair and maintenance of all classes of motor vehicles.

Specialty Equipment Market Association (SEMA)
1575 S. Valley Vista Dr.
Diamond Bar, CA 91765 USA
Phone: 909-610-2030
Web Address: www.sema.org
Specialty Equipment Market Association (SEMA) members offer innovative specialty equipment products and services that enhance a vehicle's style, utility and performance.

Transmission Rebuilders Network International (TRNI)
6501 E. Greenway Pkwy., Ste. 103/298
Scottsdale, AZ 85254 USA
Toll Free: 888-582-8764
E-mail Address: INFO@trannybuilder.com
Web Address: www.trannybuilder.com
Transmission Rebuilders Network International (TRNI) is a worldwide network of over 1,000 transmission technicians, interacting on topics related to transmission repair.

Truck and Engine Manufacturers Association (EMA)
333 West Wacker Dr., Ste. 810
Chicago, IL 60606 USA
Phone: 312-929-1970
Fax: 312-929-1975
E-mail Address: ema@emamail.org
Web Address:
www.truckandenginemanufacturers.org
The Truck and Engine Manufacturers Association (EMA) is the voice of the engine manufacturing and on-highway medium- and heavy-duty truck industries on domestic and international public policy, as well as regulatory and technical issues.

9) Automotive Publications

Auto Week Magazine
1155 Gratiot Ave.
Detroit, MI 48207-2997 USA
Phone: 313-446-6000
E-mail Address: customerservice@autoweek.com
Web Address: www.autoweek.com

Auto Week Magazine is a publication devoted to the automotive industry and motor sports. It is a service of Crain Communications, Inc.

Automobile Magazine
1995 Highland Dr.
Ann Arbor, MI 48108 USA
Phone: 734-994-3500
E-mail Address: Eric.Schwab@sorc.com
Web Address: www.automobilemag.com
Automobile Magazine is a monthly magazine featuring the latest automotive news. The magazine is a publication of Source Interlink Media, LLC, which is itself part of Source Interlink Companies, Inc.

Automotive Digest
425 32nd St.
Manhattan Beach, CA 90266 USA
Phone: 310-265-2225
E-mail Address: cparker@automotivedigest.com
Web Address: www.automotivedigest.com
Automotive Digest reviews the massive amount of printed and electronic material published every day for or about the automotive industry and its related market segments and industries in the U.S. and globally. The site is owned and operated by Automotive Information Network, Inc.

Automotive News Group
1155 Gratiot Ave.
Detroit, MI 48207-2997 USA
Phone: 313-446-0361
Fax: 313-446-0383
E-mail Address: customerservice@autonews.com
Web Address: www.autonews.com
The Automotive News Group, a part of the Crain Publishing Company, publishes the weekly magazine, Automotive News. Its web site provides a wealth of up-to-date auto industry news.

Car and Driver Magazine
1585 Eisenhower Pl.
Ann Arbor, MI 48108 USA
Phone: 212-649-2582
E-mail Address: editors@caranddriver.com
Web Address: www.caranddriver.com
Car and Driver Magazine publishes current information on automobiles and the automobile industry. It is published by Hearst Communications, Inc., one of the world's largest publishers of monthly magazines.

Motor Trend Online
831 S. Douglas St.
El Segundo, CA 90245 USA
Phone: 248-594-5999
Toll Free: 800-247-1971
E-mail Address: inquiries@automotive.com
Web Address: www.motortrend.com
Motor Trend Online is an online magazine providing previews on cars, a buyer's guide and current information on the auto industry. It is owned by New York-based Source Interlink Media, LLC.

Road & Track Magazine
1499 Monrovia Ave.
Newport Beach, CA 92663 USA
Phone: 949-720-5300
E-mail Address: RTLettersOnline@Hearst.com
Web Address: www.roadandtrack.com
Road & Track Magazine is an automotive magazine providing news and information relating to the auto industry. The company is operated by Hearst Communications, Inc. Hearst Magazines, a unit of Hearst Corporation, is one of the world's largest publishers of monthly magazines.

Velocity Automotive Journal
P.O. Box 476
Crystal Lake, IL 60039-0476 USA
Web Address: www.velocityjournal.com
Velocity Automotive Journal enables viewers to research all of the vehicles currently available in the U.S. domestic market. The group utilizes the Velocity Index tool, which measures 15 performance and drivability criteria and computes them into one easy-to-compare number.

Ward's Auto
3000 Town Ctr., Ste. 2750
Southfield, MI 48075 USA
Phone: 248-799-2622
Fax: 248-357-9747
E-mail Address: tduncan@wardsauto.com
Web Address: www.wardsauto.com
Ward's Auto is a highly popular company that provides auto news and in-depth data, in addition to publishing magazines such as Ward's AutoWorld and Ward's Dealer Business.

10) Automotive Safety

American Traffic Safety Services Institute (The) (ATSSA)
15 Riverside Pkwy., Ste. 100

Fredericksburg, VA 22406-1077 USA
Phone: 540-368-1701
Fax: 540-368-1717
Toll Free: 800-272-8772
E-mail Address: communications@atssa.com
Web Address: www.atssa.com
The American Traffic Safety Services Institute (ATSSA) is an international trade association whose members provide pavement markings, signage, work zone traffic control devices and other safety features on our nation's roadways.

Insurance Institute for Highway Safety (IIHS)
1005 N. Glebe Rd., Ste. 800
Arlington, VA 22201 USA
Phone: 703-247-1500
Fax: 703-247-1588
E-mail Address: rrader@iihs.org
Web Address: www.iihs.org
The Insurance Institute for Highway Safety (IIHS) is an independent nonprofit scientific and educational organization dedicated to reducing the numbers of deaths, injuries and property damage in crashes on U.S. highways.

National Safety Council (NSC)
1121 Spring Lake Dr.
Itasca, IL 60143-3201 USA
Phone: 630-285-1121
Fax: 630-285-1315
Toll Free: 800-621-7615
E-mail Address: info@nsc.org
Web Address: www.nsc.org
The National Safety Council (NSC) is a nonprofit, international organization that provides safety information and statistics in order to help to prevent accidental injury and death.

SaferCar.gov
1200 New Jersey Ave. SE, W. Bldg.
NHTSA Headquarters
Washington, DC 20590 USA
Phone: 202-366-4000
Toll Free: 888-327-4236
Web Address: www.safercar.gov
Safercar.gov offers crash test and rollover ratings for all automobiles manufactured since 1990. It also provides tools for checking for automobile recalls, to look into ongoing investigations and to file vehicle complaints. Additionally, safety information regarding child safety seats, electronic stability control, tires, air bags, rollover prevention and hybrid FAQs can all be found on the site. Safecar.gov is operated by the National Highway Traffic Safety Administration (NHTSA), a part of the U.S. Department of Transportation (DOT).

11) Battery Industry Associations

Consortium for Battery Innovation
2530 Meridian Pkwy., Ste. 115
Durham, NC 27713 USA
Phone: 919-361-4647
Fax: 919-361-1957
Web Address: www.batteryinnovation.org
The Consortium for Battery Innovation, formerly known as ALABC, has been carrying out research into lead batteries for a quarter of a century. Members have commissioned research into advanced lead batteries to help meet the needs of global energy storage.

12) Business Model Resources

Fraunhofer Institute for Industrial Engineering & Organization
Nobelstrasse 12
Stuttgart, 70569 Germany
Phone: 49-711-970-01
Web Address: www.iao.fraunhofer.de/lang-en/
The Fraunhofer Institute for Industrial Engineering & Organization assists companies and institutions in introducing new business models and efficient processes in Germany. Clients range from major corporations and SMEs to public sector bodies and institutions.

13) Careers-First Time Jobs/New Grads

CollegeGrad.com, Inc.
950 Tower Ln., Fl. 6
Foster City, CA 94404 USA
E-mail Address: info@quinstreet.com
Web Address: www.collegegrad.com
CollegeGrad.com, Inc. offers in-depth resources for college students and recent grads seeking entry-level jobs.

MonsterCollege
444 N. Michigan Ave., Ste. 600
Chicago, IL 60611 USA
E-mail Address: info@college.monster.com
Web Address: www.college.monster.com

MonsterCollege provides information about internships and entry-level jobs, as well as career advice and resume tips, to recent college graduates.

National Association of Colleges and Employers (NACE)
62 Highland Ave.
Bethlehem, PA 18017-9085 USA
Phone: 610-868-1421
E-mail Address: customer_service@naceweb.org
Web Address: www.naceweb.org
The National Association of Colleges and Employers (NACE) is a premier U.S. organization representing college placement offices and corporate recruiters who focus on hiring new grads.

14) Careers-General Job Listings

CareerBuilder, Inc.
200 N La Salle St., Ste. 1100
Chicago, IL 60601 USA
Phone: 773-527-3600
Fax: 773-353-2452
Toll Free: 800-891-8880
Web Address: www.careerbuilder.com
CareerBuilder, Inc. focuses on the needs of companies and also provides a database of job openings. The site has over 1 million jobs posted by 300,000 employers, and receives an average 23 million unique visitors monthly. The company also operates online career centers for 140 newspapers and 9,000 online partners. Resumes are sent directly to the company, and applicants can set up a special e-mail account for job-seeking purposes. CareerBuilder is primarily a joint venture between three newspaper giants: The McClatchy Company, Gannett Co., Inc. and Tribune Company.

CareerOneStop
Toll Free: 877-872-5627
E-mail Address: info@careeronestop.org
Web Address: www.careeronestop.org
CareerOneStop is operated by the employment commissions of various state agencies. It contains job listings in both the private and government sectors, as well as a wide variety of useful career resources and workforce information. CareerOneStop is sponsored by the U.S. Department of Labor.

LaborMarketInfo (LMI)
Employment Development Dept.
P.O. Box 826880, MIC 57
Sacramento, CA 94280-0001 USA
Phone: 916-262-2162
Fax: 916-262-2352
Web Address: www.labormarketinfo.edd.ca.gov
LaborMarketInfo (LMI) provides job seekers and employers a wide range of resources, namely the ability to find, access and use labor market information and services. It provides statistics for employment demographics on both a local and regional level, as well as career searching tools for California residents. The web site is sponsored by California's Employment Development Office.

Recruiters Online Network
E-mail Address: rossi.tony@comcast.net
Web Address: www.recruitersonline.com
The Recruiters Online Network provides job postings from thousands of recruiters, Careers Online Magazine, a resume database, as well as other career resources.

USAJOBS
USAJOBS Program Office
1900 E St. NW, Ste. 6500
Washington, DC 20415-0001 USA
Phone: 818-934-6600
Web Address: www.usajobs.gov
USAJOBS, a program of the U.S. Office of Personnel Management, is the official job site for the U.S. Federal Government. It provides a comprehensive list of U.S. government jobs, allowing users to search for employment by location; agency; type of work; or by senior executive positions. It also has special employment sections for individuals with disabilities, veterans and recent college graduates; an information center, offering resume and interview tips and other information; and allows users to create a profile and post a resume.

15) Careers-Job Reference Tools

Vault.com, Inc.
132 W. 31st St., Fl. 17
New York, NY 10001 USA
Fax: 212-366-6117
Toll Free: 800-535-2074
E-mail Address: customerservice@vault.com
Web Address: www.vault.com
Vault.com, Inc. is a comprehensive career web site for employers and employees, with job postings and valuable information on a wide variety of industries. Its features and content are largely geared toward MBA degree holders.

16) Construction Resources-Energy Efficient Buildings

Energy Efficiency Programme Office (E2PO)
40 Scotts Rd.
Environmental Bldg. #13-00
Singapore, 228231 Singapore
Fax: 65-6235-2611
Toll Free: 800-2255-632
E-mail Address: contact_NEA@nea.gov.sg
Web Address: www.e2singapore.gov.sg
To drive energy efficiency improvement in Singapore, the Energy Efficiency Programme Office (E2PO) has been established. The website includes information about energy programs, publications, incentives and development opportunities for power generation, industry, transport, green buildings and the public sector of Singapore.

17) Corporate Information Resources

bizjournals.com
120 W. Morehead St., Ste. 400
Charlotte, NC 28202 USA
Toll Free: 866-853-3661
E-mail Address: gmurchison@bizjournals.com
Web Address: www.bizjournals.com
Bizjournals.com is the online media division of American City Business Journals, the publisher of dozens of leading city business journals nationwide. It provides access to research into the latest news regarding companies both small and large. The organization maintains 42 websites and 64 print publications and sponsors over 700 annual industry events.

Business Wire
101 California St., Fl. 20
San Francisco, CA 94111 USA
Phone: 415-986-4422
Fax: 415-788-5335
Toll Free: 800-227-0845
E-mail Address: info@businesswire.com
Web Address: www.businesswire.com
Business Wire offers news releases, industry- and company-specific news, top headlines, conference calls, IPOs on the Internet, media services and access to tradeshownews.com and BW Connect On-line through its informative and continuously updated web site.

Edgar Online, Inc.
11200 Rockville Pike, Ste. 310
Rockville, MD 20852 USA
Phone: 301-287-0300
Fax: 301-287-0390
Toll Free: 888-870-2316
Web Address: www.edgar-online.com
Edgar Online, Inc. is a gateway and search tool for viewing corporate documents, such as annual reports on Form 10-K, filed with the U.S. Securities and Exchange Commission.

PR Newswire Association LLC
350 Hudson St., Ste. 300
New York, NY 10014-4504 USA
Fax: 800-793-9313
Toll Free: 800-776-8090
E-mail Address: MediaInquiries@prnewswire.com
Web Address: www.prnewswire.com
PR Newswire Association LLC provides comprehensive communications services for public relations and investor relations professionals, ranging from information distribution and market intelligence to the creation of online multimedia content and investor relations web sites. Users can also view recent corporate press releases from companies across the globe. The Association is owned by United Business Media plc.

Silicon Investor
E-mail Address: si.admin@siliconinvestor.com
Web Address: www.siliconinvestor.com
Silicon Investor is focused on providing information about technology companies. Its web site serves as a financial discussion forum and offers quotes, profiles and charts.

18) Economic Data & Research

Centre for European Economic Research (The, ZEW)
L 7, 1
Mannheim, 68161 Germany
Phone: 49-621-1235-01
Fax: 49-621-1235-224
E-mail Address: empfang@zew.de
Web Address: www.zew.de/en
Zentrum fur Europaische Wirtschaftsforschung, The Centre for European Economic Research (ZEW), distinguishes itself in the analysis of internationally comparative data in a European context and in the creation of databases that serve as a basis for scientific research. The institute maintains a special

library relevant to economic research and provides external parties with selected data for the purpose of scientific research. ZEW also offers public events and seminars concentrating on banking, business and other economic-political topics.

Economic and Social Research Council (ESRC)
Polaris House
North Star Ave.
Swindon, SN2 1UJ UK
Phone: 44-01793 413000
E-mail Address: esrcenquiries@esrc.ac.uk
Web Address: www.esrc.ac.uk
The Economic and Social Research Council (ESRC) funds research and training in social and economic issues. It is an independent organization, established by Royal Charter. Current research areas include the global economy; social diversity; environment and energy; human behavior; and health and well-being.

Eurostat
5 Rue Alphonse Weicker
Joseph Bech Bldg.
Luxembourg, L-2721 Luxembourg
Phone: 352-4301-1
E-mail Address: eurostat-pressoffice@ec.europa.eu
Web Address: ec.europa.eu/eurostat
Eurostat is the European Union's service that publishes a wide variety of comprehensive statistics on European industries, populations, trade, agriculture, technology, environment and other matters.

Federal Statistical Office of Germany
Gustav-Stresemann-Ring 11
Wiesbaden, D-65189 Germany
Phone: 49-611-75-2405
Fax: 49-611-72-4000
Web Address: www.destatis.de
Federal Statistical Office of Germany publishes a wide variety of nation and regional economic data of interest to anyone who is studying Germany, one of the world's leading economies. Data available includes population, consumer prices, labor markets, health care, industries and output.

India Brand Equity Foundation (IBEF)
Fl. 20, Jawahar Vyapar Bhawan
Tolstoy Marg
New Deli, 110001 India
Phone: 91-11-43845500
Fax: 91-11-23701235
E-mail Address: info.brandindia@ibef.org
Web Address: www.ibef.org
India Brand Equity Foundation (IBEF) is a public-private partnership between the Ministry of Commerce and Industry, the Government of India and the Confederation of Indian Industry. The foundation's primary objective is to build positive economic perceptions of India globally. It aims to effectively present the India business perspective and leverage business partnerships in a globalizing marketplace.

National Bureau of Statistics (China)
57, Yuetan Nanjie, Sanlihe
Xicheng District
Beijing, 100826 China
Fax: 86-10-6878-2000
E-mail Address: info@gj.stats.cn
Web Address: www.stats.gov.cn/english
The National Bureau of Statistics (China) provides statistics and economic data regarding China's economy and society.

Organization for Economic Co-operation and Development (OECD)
2 rue Andre Pascal
Cedex 16
Paris, 75775 France
Phone: 33-1-45-24-82-00
Fax: 33-1-45-24-85-00
E-mail Address: webmaster@oecd.org
Web Address: www.oecd.org
The Organization for Economic Co-operation and Development (OECD) publishes detailed economic, government, population, social and trade statistics on a country-by-country basis for over 30 nations representing the world's largest economies. Sectors covered range from industry, labor, technology and patents, to health care, environment and globalization.

Statistics Bureau, Director-General for Policy Planning (Japan)
19-1 Wakamatsu-cho
Shinjuku-ku
Tokyo, 162-8668 Japan
Phone: 81-3-5273-2020
E-mail Address: toukeisoudan@soumu.go.jp
Web Address: www.stat.go.jp/english
The Statistics Bureau, Director-General for Policy Planning (Japan) and Statistical Research and Training Institute, a part of the Japanese Ministry of Internal Affairs and Communications, plays the central role of producing and disseminating basic

official statistics and coordinating statistical work under the Statistics Act and other legislation.

Statistics Canada
150 Tunney's Pasture Driveway
Ottawa, ON K1A 0T6 Canada
Phone: 514-283-8300
Fax: 514-283-9350
Toll Free: 800-263-1136
E-mail Address: STATCAN.infostats-infostats.STATCAN@canada.ca
Web Address: www.statcan.gc.ca
Statistics Canada provides a complete portal to Canadian economic data and statistics. Its conducts Canada's official census every five years, as well as hundreds of surveys covering numerous aspects of Canadian life.

19) Engineering Industry Resources

Cornell Engineering Library (The)
Engineering Library Cornell University
Carpenter Hall, Fl. 1
Ithaca, NY 14853 USA
Phone: 607-254-6261
E-mail Address: engrref@cornell.edu
Web Address: engineering.library.cornell.edu
Cornell University's Engineering Library web site has a number of resources concerning engineering research, as well as links to other engineering industry information sources.

20) Engineering, Research & Scientific Associations

American National Standards Institute (ANSI)
1899 L St. NW, Fl. 11
Washington, DC 20036 USA
Phone: 202-293-8020
Fax: 202-293-9287
E-mail Address: info@ansi.org
Web Address: www.ansi.org
The American National Standards Institute (ANSI) is a private, nonprofit organization that administers and coordinates the U.S. voluntary standardization and conformity assessment system. Its mission is to enhance both the global competitiveness of U.S. business and the quality of life by promoting and facilitating voluntary consensus standards and conformity assessment systems and safeguarding their integrity.

American Society of Mechanical Engineers (ASME)
Two Park Ave.
New York, NY 10016-5990 USA
Phone: 973-882-1170
Fax: 973-882-1717
Toll Free: 800-843-2763
E-mail Address: CustomerCare@asme.org
Web Address: www.asme.org
The American Society of Mechanical Engineers (ASME) offers quality programs and activities in mechanical engineering. It also facilitates the development and application of technology in areas of interest to the mechanical engineering profession.

American Society of Safety Engineers (ASSE)
520 N. Northwest Hwy
Park Ridge, IL 60068 USA
Phone: 847-699-2929
E-mail Address: customerservice@asse.org
Web Address: www.asse.org
The American Society of Safety Engineers (ASSE) is the world's oldest and largest professional safety organization. It manages, supervises and consults on safety, health and environmental issues in industry, insurance, government and education.

ASM International
9639 Kinsman Rd.
Materials Park, OH 44073-0002 USA
Phone: 440-338-5151
Toll Free: 800-336-5152
E-mail Address: memberservicecenter@asminternational.org
Web Address: www.asminternational.org
ASM International is a worldwide network of materials engineers, aimed at advancing industry, technology and applications of metals and materials. It provides materials information, education and training, as well as networking opportunities for professionals within the materials industry.

ASTM International
100 Barr Harbor Dr.
P.O. Box C700
West Conshohocken, PA 19428-2959 USA
Phone: 610-832-9585
Toll Free: 877-909-2786
Web Address: www.astm.org
ASTM International, formerly the American Society for Testing & Materials, provides and develops voluntary consensus standards and related technical information that promote public health and safety. It

also contributes to the reliability of materials for industries worldwide.

European Industrial Research Management Association
rue de al Loi, 81 A
Brussels, 1040 Belgium
Phone: 33-2-233-11-80
Web Address: www.eirma.org
EIRMA is not-for-profit organization which focuses on the effective global management and organization of business R&D and innovation within a European perspective. EIRMA engages over 100 major companies which are based in over 20 countries and operate in a wide range of sectors.

Industrial Research Institute (IRI)
2300 Clarendon Blvd., Ste. 400
Arlington, VA 22201 USA
Phone: 703-647-2580
Fax: 703-647-2581
E-mail Address: information@iriweb.org
Web Address: www.iriweb.org
The Industrial Research Institute (IRI) is a nonprofit organization of over 200 leading industrial companies, representing industries such as aerospace, automotive, chemical, computers and electronics, which carry out industrial research efforts in the U.S. manufacturing sector. IRI helps members improve research and development capabilities.

Institute of Electrical and Electronics Engineers (IEEE)
3 Park Ave., Fl. 17
New York, NY 10016-5997 USA
Phone: 212-419-7900
Fax: 212-752-4929
Toll Free: 800-678-4333
E-mail Address: society-info@ieee.org
Web Address: www.ieee.org
The Institute of Electrical and Electronics Engineers (IEEE) is a nonprofit, technical professional association of more than 430,000 individual members in approximately 160 countries. The IEEE sets global technical standards and acts as an authority in technical areas ranging from computer engineering, biomedical technology and telecommunications, to electric power, aerospace and consumer electronics.

International Federation of Automotive Engineering Societies (FISITA)
29 M11 Business Link
Stansted, CM24 8GF UK
Phone: 44-0-1279-833-470
E-mail Address: info@fisita.com
Web Address: www.fisita.com
The Federation Internationale des Societes d'Ingenieurs des Techniques de l'Automobile (FISITA) was founded in Paris in 1948 with the purpose of bringing engineers from around the world together in a spirit of cooperation to share ideas and advance the technological development of the automobile. FISITA is the umbrella organization for the national automotive societies in 37 countries around the world. Its network of member societies represents more than 200,000 automotive engineers around the globe.

International Standards Organization (ISO)
Chemin de Blandonnet 8
1214 Vernier
Geneva, CP 401 Switzerland
Phone: 41-22-749-01-11
Fax: 41-22-733-34-30
E-mail Address: central@iso.org
Web Address: www.iso.org
The International Standards Organization (ISO) is a global consortium of national standards institutes from 162 countries. The established International Standards are designed to make products and services more efficient, safe and clean.

Materials Research Society (MRS)
506 Keystone Dr.
Warrendale, PA 15086-7573 USA
Phone: 724-779-3003
Fax: 724-779-8313
E-mail Address: info@mrs.org
Web Address: www.mrs.org
The Materials Research Society (MRS) is dedicated to basic and applied research on materials of technological importance. MRS emphasizes an interdisciplinary approach to materials science and engineering. It is responsible for the publication of the Journal of Materials Science, a peer-reviewed journal focused on printing advanced research in materials science.

Research in Germany, German Academic Exchange Service (DAAD)
Kennedyallee 50
Bonn, 53175 Germany
Phone: 49-228-882-743
Web Address: www.research-in-germany.de
The Research in Germany portal, German Academic Exchange Service (DAAD), is an information

platform and contact point for those looking to find out more about Germany's research landscape and its latest research achievements. The portal is an initiative of the Federal Ministry of Education and Research.

Royal Society (The)
6-9 Carlton House Ter.
London, SW1Y 5AG UK
Phone: 44-20-7451-2500
E-mail Address: science.policy@royalsociety.org
Web Address: royalsociety.org
The Royal Society, originally founded in 1660, is the UK's leading scientific organization and the oldest scientific community in continuous existence. It operates as a national academy of science, supporting scientists, engineers, technologists and researchers. Its web site contains a wealth of data about the research and development initiatives of its fellows and foreign members.

Society of Automotive Engineers (SAE)
755 W. Big Beaver, Ste. 1600
Troy, MA 48084 USA
Phone: 248-273-2455
Fax: 248-273-2494
Toll Free: 877-606-7323
E-mail Address: automotive_hq@sae.org
Web Address: www.sae.org
The Society of Automotive Engineers (SAE) is a resource for technical information and expertise used in designing, building, maintaining and operating self-propelled vehicles for use on land, sea, air or space.

Society of Manufacturing Engineers (SME)
One SME Dr.
Dearborn, MI 48121 USA
Phone: 313-425-3000
Fax: 313-425-3400
Toll Free: 800-733-4763
E-mail Address: communications@sme.org
Web Address: www.sme.org
The Society of Manufacturing Engineers (SME) is a leading professional organization serving engineers in the manufacturing industries.

Society of Plastics Engineers (SPE)
6 Berkshire Blvd., Ste. 306
Bethel, CT 06081 USA
Phone: 203-775-0471
Fax: 203-775-8490
Web Address: www.4spe.org
The Society of Plastics Engineers (SPE) is a recognized medium of communication among scientists and engineers engaged in the development, conversion and applications of plastics.

21) Hybrid & Electric Vehicles

Electric Drive Transportation Association (EDTA)
1250 Eye St. NW, Ste. 902
Washington, DC 20005 USA
Phone: 202-408-0774
E-mail Address: info@electricdrive.org
Web Address: www.electricdrive.org
The Electric Drive Transportation Association (EDTA) is an industry association working to advance electric vehicle transportation technologies and supporting infrastructure through policy, information and market development initiatives.

High-Efficiency Truck Users Forum (HTUF)
48 S. Chester Ave.
Pasadena, CA 91106 USA
Phone: 626-744-5600
Fax: 626-744-5610
E-mail Address: calstart@calstart.org
Web Address: www.calstart.org/Projects/htuf.aspx
The High-Efficiency Truck Users Forum, formerly known as the Hybrid Truck Users Forum (HTUF), operated by CALSTART, offers a wealth of information on technologies, pilot projects, test results, fleet purchasing plans and much more.

Vehicle Technologies Program
1000 Independence Ave. SW
EE-3V, Rm. 5G-030
Washington, DC 20585 USA
Phone: 202-586-8055
Fax: 202-586-7409
E-mail Address: connie.bezanson@ee.doe.gov
Web Address:
www1.eere.energy.gov/vehiclesandfuels
Vehicle Technologies Program of the Office of Energy Efficiency and Renewable Energy (EERE), a division of the U.S. Department of Energy, works with U.S. industries toward the development of emission- and petroleum-free cars and light trucks. The program focuses on high-risk technological research for fuel cells and advanced hybrid propulsion systems.

22) Industry Research/Market Research

Forrester Research
60 Acorn Park Dr.
Cambridge, MA 02140 USA
Phone: 617-613-5730
Toll Free: 866-367-7378
E-mail Address: press@forrester.com
Web Address: www.forrester.com
Forrester Research is a publicly traded company that identifies and analyzes emerging trends in technology and their impact on business. Among the firm's specialties are the financial services, retail, health care, entertainment, automotive and information technology industries.

Gartner, Inc.
56 Top Gallant Rd.
Stamford, CT 06902 USA
Phone: 203-964-0096
E-mail Address: info@gartner.com
Web Address: www.gartner.com
Gartner, Inc. is a publicly traded IT company that provides competitive intelligence and strategic consulting and advisory services to numerous clients worldwide.

MarketResearch.com
11200 Rockville Pike, Ste. 504
Rockville, MD 20852 USA
Phone: 240-747-3093
Fax: 240-747-3004
Toll Free: 800-298-5699
E-mail Address:
customerservice@marketresearch.com
Web Address: www.marketresearch.com
MarketResearch.com is a leading broker for professional market research and industry analysis. Users are able to search the company's database of research publications including data on global industries, companies, products and trends.

NPD Group (The)
900 W. Shore Rd.
Port Washington, NY 11050 USA
Phone: 516-625-0700
Toll Free: 866-444-1411
Web Address: www.npd.com
The NPD Group is one of the world's leading market research firms covering the retailing and related sectors. NPD covers industries including automotive, beauty, technology, entertainment, fashion, food & beverage, home, software, toys and wireless.

Plunkett Research, Ltd.
P.O. Drawer 541737
Houston, TX 77254-1737 USA
Phone: 713-932-0000
Fax: 713-932-7080
E-mail Address:
customersupport@plunkettresearch.com
Web Address: www.plunkettresearch.com
Plunkett Research, Ltd. is a leading provider of market research, industry trends analysis and business statistics. Since 1985, it has served clients worldwide, including corporations, universities, libraries, consultants and government agencies. At the firm's web site, visitors can view product information and pricing and access a large amount of basic market information on industries such as financial services, InfoTech, e-commerce, health care and biotech.

23) Labor Unions

United Automobile, Aerospace and Agricultural Implement Workers of America (UAW)
8000 E. Jefferson Ave.
Detroit, MI 48214 USA
Phone: 313-926-5000
Web Address: www.uaw.org
The United Automobile, Aerospace and Agricultural Implement Workers of America (UAW) is a diverse international union that represents workplaces ranging from multinational corporations, small manufacturers and state and local governments to colleges and universities, hospitals and private nonprofit organizations.

24) Manufacturing Associations-General

Confederation of Indian Industry (CII)
The Mantosh Sondhi Ctr.
23 Institutional Area, Lodi Rd.
New Delhi, 110 003 India
Phone: 91-11-24629994-7
Fax: 91-11-24626149
E-mail Address: info@cii.in
Web Address: www.cii.in
Confederation of Indian Industry (CII) works to develop industry in India. The site provides research reports, a library supporting members and other industry resources and information. CII organizes trade shows including the Auto Expo held biennially in India.

MAPI/Manufacturers Alliance
1600 Wilson Blvd., Fl. 11, Ste. 1100
Arlington, VA 22209-2594 USA
Phone: 703-841-9000
Web Address: www.mapi.net
Established in 1933, MAPI/Manufacturers Alliance was once known as the Machinery and Allied Products Institute. Today, it represents manufacturers of all types. The organization publishes extensive research on manufacturing in America; and offers webinars, live meeting opportunities, surveys and email discussion forums, education programs, economic forecasts and policy analyses to its members.

National Association of Manufacturers (NAM)
733 10th St. NW, Ste. 700
Washington, DC 20001 USA
Phone: 202-637-3000
Fax: 202-637-3182
Toll Free: 800-814-8468
E-mail Address: manufacturing@nam.org
Web Address: www.nam.org
The National Association of Manufacturers (NAM) is one of the largest industrial trade associations in the United States, representing manufacturers and employees in every industrial sector. The association lobbies Congress on behalf of its members and seeks economic growth through the promotion of manufacturing activities and legislation.

25) Manufacturing Associations-Machinery & Technology

Association for Manufacturing Technology (AMT)
7901 Westpark Dr.
McLean, VA 22102-4206 USA
Phone: 703-893-2900
Fax: 703-893-1151
Toll Free: 800-524-0475
E-mail Address: amt@amtonline.org
Web Address: www.amtonline.org
The Association for Manufacturing Technology (AMT) actively supports and promotes American manufacturers of machine tools and manufacturing technology.

National Center for Manufacturing Sciences (NCMS)
3025 Boardwalk Dr.
Ann Arbor, MI 48108-3230 USA
Fax: 734-995-0380
Toll Free: 800-222-6267
E-mail Address: info@ncms.org
Web Address: www.ncms.org
The National Center for Manufacturing Sciences (NCMS) is a non-profit membership organization dedicated to advancing the global competitiveness of North American manufacturing industry.

National Tooling and Machining Association (NTMA)
1357 Rockside Rd.
Cleveland, OH 44134 USA
Fax: 216-264-2840
Toll Free: 800-248-6862
E-mail Address: info@ntma.org
Web Address: www.ntma.org
The National Tooling and Machining Association (NTMA) helps members of the U.S. precision custom manufacturing industries achieve business success in a global economy through advocacy, advice, networking, information, programs and services.

Precision Metalforming Association (PMA)
6363 Oak Tree Blvd.
Independence, OH 44131-2500 USA
Phone: 216-901-8800
Fax: 216-901-9190
E-mail Address: info@pma.org
Web Address: www.pma.org
The Precision Metalforming Association (PMA) is a trade association representing the $117-billion metalforming industry of North America. The industry creates precision metal products using stamping, fabricating, spinning, slide forming and roll forming technologies, and other value-added processes. Its nearly 900 member companies also include suppliers of equipment, materials and services to the industry.

Singapore Institute of Manufacturing Technology (SIMTech)
73 Nanyang Dr.
Singapore, 637662 Singapore
Phone: 65-6793-8383
E-mail Address: ido@SIMTech.a-star.edu.sg
Web Address: www.a-star.edu.sg/simtech
The Singapore Institute of Manufacturing Technology (SIMTech) has completed more than 880 projects with more than 410 companies, big and small, in the electronics, semiconductor, precision engineering, aerospace, automotive, marine, logistics and other sectors.

26) MBA Resources

MBA Depot
Web Address: www.mbadepot.com
MBA Depot is an online community and information portal for MBAs, potential MBA program applicants and business professionals.

27) Metals & Steel Industry Associations

Aluminum Association (The)
1400 Crystal Dr., Ste. 430
Arlington, VA 22202 USA
Phone: 703-358-2960
E-mail Address: mmeenan@aluminum.org
Web Address: www.aluminum.org
The Aluminum Association is the trade association for producers of primary aluminum, recyclers and makers of semi-fabricated aluminum products, as well as suppliers to the industry.

28) Metals & Steel Industry Resources

American Iron and Steel Institute
25 Massachusetts Ave. NW, Ste. 800
Washington, DC 20001 USA
Phone: 202-452-7100
Web Address: www.steel.org
AISI provides an in-depth web site with statistics, news, links and various other features geared to members of the steel industry, as well as to students and researchers.

29) Motorcycle Industry Associations

Federation of Asian Motorcycle Industry
Wisma Indomobil I
Jl. M.T. Haryono Kav 8
Jakarta, 13330 Indonesia
Phone: 62-21-856-6181
Fax: 62-21-857-0618
E-mail Address: anyenquiry@fami-motorcycle.org
Web Address: www.fami-motorcycle.org
The Federation of Asian Motorcycle Industries (FAMI) is a non-profit association currently comprised of seven motorcycle associations in the Asia Pacific: Indonesia, Japan, Malaysia, The Philippines, Singapore, Taiwan, and Thailand.

International Motorcycle Manufacturers Association (IMMA)
20, Route de Pre-bois
Geneva, CH-1215 Switzerland
Phone: 41-22-920-2123
Fax: 41-22-920-2121
E-mail Address: info@immamotorcycles.org
Web Address: www.immamotorcycles.org
The International Motorcycle Manufacturers Association (IMMA) is the trade association which represents the motorcycle industry at the global level.

Motorcycle Industry Council (MIC)
2 Jenner St., Ste. 150
Irvine, CA 92618-3806 USA
Phone: 949-727-4211
Fax: 949-727-3313
E-mail Address: memberservices@mic.org
Web Address: www.mic.org
The Motorcycle Industry Council (MIC) is a not-for-profit, national trade association created to promote and preserve motorcycling and the U.S. motorcycle industry. This is accomplished through its activities in government relations, statistics, communications, technical, and aftermarket programs.

Singapore Motor Cycle Trade Association (SMCTA)
40 Sam Leong Rd.
Singapore, 207930 Singapore
Phone: 65-6297-1991
Fax: 65-6297-1313
E-mail Address: mail@smcta.org.sg
Web Address: www.smcta.org.sg
Singapore Motor Cycle Trade Association (SMCTA) represents the motorcycle trade and related industries in Singapore.

30) Natural Gas Vehicles

Asia Pacific Natural Gas Vehicles Association (ANGVA)
Lvl. 2, Block A, Lot 3288 & 3289,
Off Jalan Ayer Itam, Kawasan Institusi Bangi
Kajang, Selangor 43000 Malaysia
Phone: 603-2166-5137
Fax: 603-2166-5135
E-mail Address: angva@angva.org
Web Address: www.angva.org
Asia Pacific Natural Gas Vehicles Association (ANGVA) serves the needs of fleet operators, vehicle manufacturers, gas suppliers, equipment suppliers, refueling equipment providers, consultants, government representatives, non-governmental organizations (NGO) and others involved with the

natural gas vehicles industry by promoting the use of natural gas as the fuel for the transportation sector.

Natural Gas Vehicles for America (NGVAmerica)
400 N. Capitol St. NW
Washington, DC 20001 USA
Phone: 202-824-7360
E-mail Address: Syborra@ngvamerica.org
Web Address: www.ngvamerica.org
Natural Gas Vehicle for America (NGVAmerica) is a national organization dedicated to the development of a growing, sustainable and profitable market for vehicles powered by natural gas or hydrogen. NGVAmerica represents more than 230 companies interested in the promotion and use of natural gas and hydrogen as transportation fuels, including: engine, vehicle and equipment manufacturers; fleet operators and service providers; natural gas companies; and environmental groups and government organizations.

31) Outsourcing Industry Resources

Reshoring Initiative
Phone: 847-726-2975
E-mail Address: info@reshorenow.org
Web Address: www.reshorenow.org
The Reshoring Initiative is an industry led effort whose focus is the return of manufacturing jobs to the U.S. from overseas, namely China. The Initiative achieves this by demonstrating to manufacturers that local production may actually lead to a reduction in total cost by getting rid of superfluous costs such as inventory carrying costs, traveling costs to check on suppliers, intellectual property risks and opportunity costs from product pipelines being too long. Its website features a TCO, Total Cost of Ownership, calculation tool to help firms determine the feasibility of operating in the U.S. as opposed to offshoring.

32) Research & Development, Laboratories

Helmholtz Association
Anna-Louisa-Karsch-Strasse 2
Berlin, 10178 Germany
Phone: 49-30-206329-0
E-mail Address: info@helmholtz.de
Web Address: www.helmholtz.de/en
The Helmholtz Association is a community of 18 scientific-technical and biological-medical research centers. Helmholtz Centers perform top-class research in strategic programs in several core fields: energy, earth and environment, health, key technologies, structure of matter, aeronautics, space and transport.

National Research Council Canada (NRC)
1200 Montreal Rd., Bldg. M-58
Ottawa, ON K1A 0R6 Canada
Phone: 613-993-9101
Fax: 613-952-9907
Toll Free: 877-672-2672
E-mail Address: info@nrc-cnrc.gc.ca
Web Address: www.nrc-cnrc.gc.ca
National Research Council Canada (NRC) is comprised of 12 government organization, research institutes and programs that carry out multidisciplinary research. It maintains partnerships with industries and sectors key to Canada's economic development.

Program on Vehicle and Mobility Innovation (PVMI)
1050 Steinberg Hall-Dietrich Hall
3620 Locust Walk
Philadelphia, PA 19104-6371 USA
Phone: 215-746-4831
E-mail Address: mackinstitute@wharton.upenn.edu
Web Address: pvmi.wharton.upenn.edu
The Program on Vehicle and Mobility Innovation (PVMI), formerly the International Motor Vehicle Program (IMVP), is a research project, funded by leading global car makers as well as government agencies, focused on enhancing automotive design and manufacturing methods. In 2013, the IMVP changed its name to the PVMI and was integrated into the Mack Institute for Innovation Management at the Wharton School, University Pennsylvania.

Sloan Automotive Laboratory
60 Vassar St., Bldg. 31-153
Cambridge, MA 02139-4307 USA
Phone: 617-253-4529
Fax: 617-253-9453
Web Address: web.mit.edu/sloan-auto-lab
The Sloan Automotive Laboratory at MIT was founded in 1929 by Professor C.F. Taylor, with a grant from Alfred P. Sloan, Jr., CEO of General Motors, as a major laboratory for automotive research in the US and the world. The goals of the Laboratory are to provide the fundamental knowledge base for automotive engineering and to educate students to become technological leaders in the automotive industry.

33) Robotics & Automation Industry Associations

International Federation of Robotics (IFR)
Lyoner St. 18
Frankfurt am Main, 60528 Germany
Phone: 49-69-6603-1502
Fax: 49-69-6603-2502
E-mail Address: gl@ifr.org
Web Address: www.ifr.org
The International Federation of Robotics (IFR) promotes the robotics industry worldwide, including the fields of industrial robots for manufacturing and other purposes, service robots and robotics research. Among other things, it is focused on research, development, use and international co-operation in the entire field of robotics, and it seeks to act as a focal point for organizations and governmental representatives in activities related to robotics.

34) Rubber Industry Associations

Rubber Manufacturers Association (RMA)
1400 K St. NW, Ste. 900
Washington, DC 20005 USA
Phone: 202-682-4800
E-mail Address: info@rma.org
Web Address: www.rma.org
The Rubber Manufacturers Association (RMA) is the national trade association for the rubber products industry. Its members include companies that manufacture various rubber products, such as tires, hoses, belts, seals, molded goods and other finished rubber products.

Tire and Rubber Association of Canada (TRAC)
2000 Argentia Rd., Plz. 4, Ste. 100
Mississauga, ON L5N 1W1 Canada
Phone: 905-814-1714
Fax: 905-814-1085
E-mail Address: info@rubberassociation.ca
Web Address: www.tracanada.ca
The Tire and Rubber Association of Canada, formerly The Rubber Association of Canada (RAC) is the national association of tire and other rubber manufacturers, distributors, as well as importers of rubber goods in Canada.

35) RV & Motor Home Industry Associations

RV Industry Association
1896 Preston White Dr.
Reston, VA 20191 USA
Phone: 703-620-6003
Fax: 703-620-5071
Web Address: www.rvia.org
The RV Industry Association is the national trade association representing RV manufacturers and their component parts suppliers who together build more than 98 percent of all RVs produced in the U.S., and approximately 60 percent of RVs produced worldwide.

36) Sports Leagues

IndyCar
4551 W. 16th St.
Indianapolis, IN 46222 USA
Phone: 317-492-6526
E-mail Address: indycar@indycar.com
Web Address: www.indycar.com
IndyCar, formerly the Indy Racing League (IRL), is the official sanctioning body for Indy auto racing. It operates four racing series, the Verizon IndyCar Series, the Indy Lights, the Pro Mazda and the Cooper Tires USF2000. IndyCar is a subsidiary of Hulman and Co., the owner of the Indianapolis Motor Speedway complex.

National Association for Stock Car Auto Racing (NASCAR)
International Motorsports Center
One Daytona Blvd.
Daytona Beach, FL 32114 USA
Web Address: www.nascar.com
The National Association for Stock Car Auto Racing (NASCAR) is the organizing body for professional stock car racing. It sanctions over 1,200 races in 30 U.S. states, Canada, Mexico and Europe.

Singapore Motor Sports Association
20 Maxwell Rd.
10-18 Maxwell House
Singapore, 069113 Singapore
Phone: 65-6227-7889
Fax: 65-6227-0911
E-mail Address: smsa@smsa.org.sg
Web Address: www.smsa.org.sg

The Singapore Motor Sports Association is a nonprofit organization representing and promoting the motor sports and racing in Singapore.

37) Sustainable Transportation

Transportation Sustainability Research Center (TSRC)
University of California Richmond Field Station
1301 S. 46th St., Building 190
Richmond, CA 94804 USA
E-mail Address: sshaheen@berkeley.edu
Web Address: tsrc.berkeley.edu/
The Transportation Sustainability Research Center (TSRC) was formed in 2006 to combine the research forces of six campus groups at UC Berkeley: the University of California Transportation Center, the University of California Energy Institute, the Institute of Transportation Studies, the Energy and Resources Group, the Center for Global Metropolitan Studies, and the Berkeley Institute of the Environment. Research efforts are primarily concentrated in six main areas: advanced vehicles and fuels; energy and infrastructure; goods movement; innovative mobility; Mobility for special populations; and transportation and energy systems analysis.

38) Technology Transfer Associations

Association of University Technology Managers (AUTM)
One Parkview Plaza, Ste. 880
Oakbrook Terrace, IL 60015 USA
Phone: 847-686-2244
Fax: 847-686-2253
E-mail Address: info@autm.net
Web Address: www.autm.net
The Association of University Technology Managers (AUTM) is a nonprofit professional association whose members belong to over 300 research institutions, universities, teaching hospitals, government agencies and corporations. The association's mission is to advance the field of technology transfer and enhance members' ability to bring academic and nonprofit research to people around the world.

Federal Laboratory Consortium for Technology Transfer
950 N. Kings Hwy., Ste. 105
Cherry Hill, NJ 08304 USA
Phone: 856-667-7727
E-mail Address: support@federallabs.org
Web Address: www.federallabs.org
In keeping with the aims of the Federal Technology Transfer Act of 1986 and other related legislation, the Federal Laboratory Consortium (FLC) works to facilitate the sharing of research results and technology developments between federal laboratories and the mainstream U.S. economy. FLC affiliates include federal laboratories, large and small businesses, academic and research institutions, state and local governments and various federal agencies. The group has regional support offices and local contacts throughout the U.S.

Licensing Executives Society (USA and Canada), Inc.
11130 Sunrise Valley Dr., Ste. 350
Reston, VA 20191 USA
Phone: 703-234-4058
Fax: 703-435-4390
E-mail Address: info@les.org
Web Address: www.lesusacanada.org
Licensing Executives Society (USA and Canada), Inc., established in 1965, is a professional association composed of about 3,000 members who work in fields related to the development, use, transfer, manufacture and marketing of intellectual property. Members include executives, lawyers, licensing consultants, engineers, academic researchers, scientists and government officials. The society is part of the larger Licensing Executives Society International, Inc. (same headquarters address), with a worldwide membership of some 12,000 members from approximately 80 countries.

39) Textile & Fabric Industry Associations

Industrial Fabrics Association International (IAFI)
1801 County Rd. B W
Roseville, MN 55113-4061 USA
Phone: 651-222-2508
Fax: 651-631-9334
Toll Free: 800-225-4324
E-mail Address: generalinfo@ifai.com
Web Address: www.ifai.com
Industrial Fabrics Association International (IAFI) is a not-for-profit trade association that represents the entire range of the specialty fabrics industry.

40) Trade Associations-General

Associated Chambers of Commerce and Industry of India (ASSOCHAM)
5, Sardar Patel Marg
Chanakyapuri
New Delhi, 110 021 India
Phone: 91-11-4655-0555
Fax: 91-11-2301-7008
E-mail Address: assocham@nic.in
Web Address: www.assocham.org
The Associated Chambers of Commerce and Industry of India (ASSOCHAM) has a membership of more than 300 chambers and trade associations and serves members from all over India. It works with domestic and international government agencies to advocate for India's industry and trade activities.

BUSINESSEUROPE
168 Ave. de Cortenbergh 168
Brussels, 1000 Belgium
Phone: 32-2-237-65-11
Fax: 32-2-231-14-45
E-mail Address: main@businesseurope.eu
Web Address: www.businesseurope.eu
BUSINESSEUROPE is a major European trade federation that operates in a manner similar to a chamber of commerce. Its members are the central national business federations of the 34 countries throughout Europe from which they come. Companies cannot become direct members of BUSINESSEUROPE, though there is a support group which offers the opportunity for firms to encourage BUSINESSEUROPE objectives in various ways.

United States Council for International Business (USCIB)
1212 Ave. of the Americas
New York, NY 10036 USA
Phone: 212-354-4480
Fax: 212-575-0327
E-mail Address: azhang@uscib.org
Web Address: www.uscib.org
The United States Council for International Business (USCIB) promotes an open system of world trade and investment through its global network. Standard USCIB members include corporations, law firms, consulting firms and industry associations. Limited membership options are available for chambers of commerce and sole legal practitioners.

41) Trade Associations-Global

World Trade Organization (WTO)
Centre William Rappard
Rue de Lausanne 154
Geneva 21, CH-1211 Switzerland
Phone: 41-22-739-51-11
Fax: 41-22-731-42-06
E-mail Address: enquiries@wto.og
Web Address: www.wto.org
The World Trade Organization (WTO) is a global organization dealing with the rules of trade between nations. To become a member, nations must agree to abide by certain guidelines. Membership increases a nation's ability to import and export efficiently.

42) Trade Resources

Made-in-China.com - China Manufacturers Directory
Block A, Software Bldg. No. 9, Xinghuo Rd.
Nanjing New & High Technology Industry Development Zone
Nanjing, Jiangsu 210061 China
Fax: 86-25-6667-0000
Web Address: www.made-in-china.com
Made-in-China.com - China Manufacturers Directory, one of the largest business to business portals in China, helps to connect Chinese manufacturers, suppliers and traders with international buyers. Made-in-China.com contains additional information on trade shows and important laws and regulations about business with China.

43) Transportation Industry Associations

American Association of State Highway and Transportation Officials (AASHTO)
444 N. Capitol St. NW, Ste. 249
Washington, DC 20001 USA
Phone: 202-624-5800
Fax: 202-624-5806
E-mail Address: info@aashto.org
Web Address: www.transportation.org
The American Association of State Highway and Transportation Officials (AASHTO) advocates transportation-related policies and provides technical services to support states in their efforts to efficiently and safely move people and goods. The organization's special interests include Intelligent Transportation Systems (ITS), materials, bridges and structures.

American Highway Users Alliance
1920 L St. NW, Ste. 525
Washington, DC 20036 USA
Phone: 202-857-1200
Fax: 202-857-1220
E-mail Address: info@highways.org
Web Address: www.highways.org
The American Highway Users Alliance is a nonprofit advocacy organization serving as a united voice of the transportation community and promoting safe, uncongested highways and enhanced freedom of mobility.

Intelligent Transportation Society of America (ITS America)
1100 New Jersey Ave. SE, Ste. 850
Washington, DC 20003 USA
Phone: 202-484-4847
Toll Free: 800-374-8472
E-mail Address: info@itsa.org
Web Address: www.itsa.org
The Intelligent Transportation Society of America (ITS America) is a nonprofit organization made up of members interested in the development of intelligent transportation systems technologies.

National Association of City Transportation Officials (NACTO)
120 Park Ave., Fl. 23
New York, NY 10017 USA
Phone: 929-276-2286
E-mail Address: nacto@nacto.org
Web Address: www.nacto.org
The National Association of City Transportation Officials (NACTO) is a non-profit association that represents large cities on transportation issues of local, regional and national significance.

44) Transportation Industry Resources

Institute of Transportation Studies
University of California
109 McLaughlin Hall, MC1720
Berkeley, CA 94720 USA
Phone: 510-642-3585
E-mail Address: its@its.berkeley.edu
Web Address: its.berkeley.edu/
The UC Berkeley Institute of Transportation Studies is one of the world's leading centers for transportation research, education, and scholarship. Areas of research focus include: transportation planning, logistics, infrastructure management, safety, transportation economics and public transportation.

45) Travel-Local Transportation, Bus & Car Rental

American Automobile Association (AAA)
1000 AAA Dr., Box 28
Heathrow, FL 32746 USA
Phone: 407-44-7000
Fax: 407-444-8030
Toll Free: 800-222-1134
Web Address: www.aaa.com
The American Automobile Association (AAA) offers members roadside assistance, financial services, car rental, a travel agency and a variety of other services.

46) U.S. Government Agencies

Bureau of Economic Analysis (BEA)
4600 Silver Hill Rd.
Washington, DC 20233 USA
Phone: 301-278-9004
E-mail Address: customerservice@bea.gov
Web Address: www.bea.gov
The Bureau of Economic Analysis (BEA), an agency of the U.S. Department of Commerce, is the nation's economic accountant, preparing estimates that illuminate key national, international and regional aspects of the U.S. economy.

Bureau of Labor Statistics (BLS)
2 Massachusetts Ave. NE
Washington, DC 20212-0001 USA
Phone: 202-691-5200
Fax: 202-691-7890
Toll Free: 800-877-8339
E-mail Address: blsdata_staff@bls.gov
Web Address: stats.bls.gov
The Bureau of Labor Statistics (BLS) is the principal fact-finding agency for the Federal Government in the field of labor economics and statistics. It is an independent national statistical agency that collects, processes, analyzes and disseminates statistical data to the American public, U.S. Congress, other federal agencies, state and local governments, business and labor. The BLS also serves as a statistical resource to the Department of Labor.

International Trade Administration (ITA)
1401 Constitution Ave. NW
U.S. Department of Commerce
Washington, DC 20230 USA
Phone: 202-482-3809
Toll Free: 800-872-8723

E-mail Address: lorri.crowley@trade.gov
Web Address: www.trade.gov
The International Trade Administration (ITA) is a U.S. Government agency that provides a wealth of information regarding imports and exports. In addition, it publishes in-depth analyses and statistics on various industry sectors and provides assistance to U.S. firms that wish to increase their exports.

National Highway Traffic Safety Administration (NHTSA)
1200 New Jersey Ave. SE
Washington, DC 20590 USA
Phone: 202-366-4000
Toll Free: 888-327-4236
E-mail Address: nhtsa.webmaster@dot.gov
Web Address: www.nhtsa.gov
NHTSA was established by the Highway Safety Act of 1970 and is dedicated to achieving the highest standards of excellence in motor vehicle and highway safety. It works daily to help prevent crashes and their attendant costs, both human and financial.

National Institute of Standards and Technology (NIST)
100 Bureau Dr., Stop 1070
Gaithersburg, MD 20899-1070 USA
Phone: 301-975-6478
Toll Free: 800-877-8339
E-mail Address: inquiries@nist.gov
Web Address: www.nist.gov
The National Institute of Standards and Technology (NIST) is an agency of the U.S. Department of Commerce that works with various industries to develop and apply technology, measurements and standards.

Occupational Safety and Health Administration (OSHA)
200 Constitution Ave. NW
Washington, DC 20210 USA
Toll Free: 800-321-6742
Web Address: www.osha.gov
The Occupational Safety and Health Administration (OSHA), regulates safety within the workplace. Its web site provides information on laws and regulations, safety and health, statistics, compliance assistance and news. OSHA is a unit of the U.S. Department of Labor.

Recalls.gov
E-mail Address: webteam@cpsc.gov
Web Address: www.recalls.gov
Recalls.gov is a one-stop website where six different U.S. government agencies post announcements about governmental recalls in consumer products, motor vehicles, boats, food, medicine, cosmetics and environmental products.

U.S. Census Bureau
4600 Silver Hill Rd.
Washington, DC 20233-8800 USA
Phone: 301-763-4636
Toll Free: 800-923-8282
E-mail Address: pio@census.gov
Web Address: www.census.gov
The U.S. Census Bureau is the official collector of data about the people and economy of the U.S. Founded in 1790, it provides official social, demographic and economic information. In addition to the Population & Housing Census, which it conducts every 10 years, the U.S. Census Bureau numerous other surveys annually.

U.S. Department of Commerce (DOC)
1401 Constitution Ave. NW
Washington, DC 20230 USA
Phone: 202-482-2000
E-mail Address: TheSec@doc.gov
Web Address: www.commerce.gov
The U.S. Department of Commerce (DOC) regulates trade and provides valuable economic analysis of the economy.

U.S. Department of Labor (DOL)
200 Constitution Ave. NW
Washington, DC 20210 USA
Phone: 202-693-4676
Toll Free: 866-487-2365
Web Address: www.dol.gov
The U.S. Department of Labor (DOL) is the government agency responsible for labor regulations.

U.S. Department of Transportation (DOT)
1200 New Jersey Ave. SE
Washington, DC 20590 USA
Phone: 202-366-4000
Web Address: www.dot.gov
The U.S. Department of Transportation (DOT) is the Government agency in charge of all aspects of the U.S. transportation system. It has agencies dealing with all aspects of transportation, including highways; hazardous materials transportation; pipelines; railroads; marine transportation; aviation; and public transit systems, such as buses and subways. It also has agencies researching

transportation statistics, new transportation technologies and even the eventual impact of environmental change on transportation. The DOT web site has links to citizen traveler resource, as well as resources for transportation businesses and mainly transportation-related government grants.

U.S. Department of Transportation (US DOT)-Intelligent Transportation Systems (ITS)
1200 New Jersey Ave. SE, HOIT
Washington, DC 20590 USA
Toll Free: 866-367-7487
E-mail Address: ITSHelp@dot.gov
Web Address: www.its.dot.gov
The U.S. Department of Transportation's (US DOT) Intelligent Transportation System (ITS) program was established to support the development of intelligent transportation systems through the integration of intelligent vehicles and an intelligent infrastructure. The Federal ITS program supports the overall advancement of ITS through investments in major initiatives, exploratory studies and a crosscutting core program.

U.S. Environmental Protection Agency (EPA) On-road Vehicles and Engines
U.S. EPA, OAR/OTAQ/CISD.
2000 Traverwood Dr.
Ann Arbor, MI 48105 USA
Phone: 734-214-4200
E-mail Address: otaq@epa.gov
Web Address: www.epa.gov/vehicles-and-engines
The U.S. Environmental Protection Agency (EPA) On-road Vehicles and Engines site, part of the EPA's Office of Transportation and Air Quality (OTAQ), provides details about the best and worst cars and trucks in terms of exhaust emissions. Its web site allows people to instantly check the emission rating of any vehicle. The site also contains information about industry emission trends and goals.

U.S. Patent and Trademark Office (PTO)
600 Dulany St.
Madison Bldg.
Alexandria, VA 22314 USA
Phone: 571-272-1000
Toll Free: 800-786-9199
E-mail Address: usptoinfo@uspto.gov
Web Address: www.uspto.gov
The U.S. Patent and Trademark Office (PTO) administers patent and trademark laws for the U.S. and enables registration of patents and trademarks.

U.S. Securities and Exchange Commission (SEC)
100 F St. NE
Washington, DC 20549 USA
Phone: 202-942-8088
Toll Free: 800-732-0330
E-mail Address: help@sec.gov
Web Address: www.sec.gov
The U.S. Securities and Exchange Commission (SEC) is a nonpartisan, quasi-judicial regulatory agency responsible for administering federal securities laws. These laws are designed to protect investors in securities markets and ensure that they have access to disclosure of all material information concerning publicly traded securities. Visitors to the web site can access the EDGAR database of corporate financial and business information.

U.S. Trade Representative (USTR)
600 17th St. NW
Washington, DC 20508 USA
Phone: 202-395-3230
Fax: 202-395-6121
E-mail Address: media@ustr.eop.gov
Web Address: www.ustr.gov
The U.S. Trade Representative (USTR) is the nation's chief trade negotiator and the principal trade policy advisor to the President.

47) Wireless & Cellular Industry Associations

5G Automotive Association (5GAA)
E-mail Address: oflore@qti.qualcomm.com
Web Address: www.5gaa.org
The 5G Automotive Association (5GAA) is comprised ot AUDI AG, BMW Group, Daimler AG, Ericsson, Huawei, Intel, Nokia and Qualcomm. The association develops, tests and promotes communications solutions, support standardization and accelerate commercial availability and global market penetration. The goal is to address connected mobility and road safety needs with applications such as connected automated driving, ubiquitous access to services and integration into smart cities and intelligent transportation.

Chapter 4

THE AUTOMOBILE 400: WHO THEY ARE AND HOW THEY WERE CHOSEN

Includes Indexes by Company Name, Industry & Location

The companies chosen to be listed in PLUNKETT'S AUTOMOBILE INDUSTRY ALMANAC comprise a unique list. THE AUTOMOBILE 400 were chosen specifically for their dominance in the many facets of the automotive industry in which they operate. Complete information about each firm can be found in the "Individual Profiles," beginning at the end of this chapter. These profiles are in alphabetical order by company name.

THE AUTOMOBILE 400 includes leading companies from all parts of the United States as well as many other nations, and from all automobile and related industry segments: manufacturers; dealerships; financial services; and many others, including makers of trucks and specialty vehicles.

Simply stated, the list contains the largest, most successful, fastest growing firms in the automotive and related industries in the world. To be included in our list, the firms had to meet the following criteria:

1) Generally, these are corporations based in the U.S., however, the headquarters of many firms are located in other nations.
2) Prominence, or a significant presence, in automotive and supporting fields. (See the following Industry Codes section for a complete list of types of businesses that are covered).
3) The companies in THE AUTOMOBILE 400 do not have to be exclusively in the automotive field.
4) Financial data and vital statistics must have been available to the editors of this book, either directly from the company being written about or from outside sources deemed reliable and accurate by the editors. A small number of companies that we would like to have included are not listed because of a lack of sufficient, objective data.

INDEXES TO THE AUTOMOBILE 400, AS FOUND IN THIS CHAPTER AND IN THE BACK OF THE BOOK:

INDEX OF COMPANIES WITHIN INDUSTRY GROUPS

The industry codes shown below are based on the 2012 NAIC code system (NAIC is used by many analysts as a replacement for older SIC codes because NAIC is more specific to today's industry sectors, see www.census.gov/NAICS). Companies are given a primary NAIC code, reflecting the main line of business of each firm.

Industry Group/Company	Industry Code	2018 Sales	2018 Profits
Advertising/Marketing - Online			
CDK Global Inc	541810E	2,273,200,128	380,800,000
Air Transportation, Support Activities for			
Sequa Corporation	488190	2,625,000,000	
ATV, Snowmobile, Golf Cart, Gocart and Race Car Equipment Manufacturing			
Kawasaki Heavy Industries Ltd	336999	14,466,477,056	265,714,016
Polaris Industries Inc	336999	6,078,539,776	335,256,992
Automobile (Car) and Light Truck Dealers (New)			
Americas Car-Mart Inc	441110	612,201,024	36,509,000
Ancira Enterprises	441110	1,323,000,000	
Asbury Automotive Group Inc	441110	6,874,399,744	168,000,000
AutoNation Inc	441110	21,412,800,512	396,000,000
Berkshire Hathaway Automotive	441110	9,828,000,000	
Bilia AB	441110	3,050,000,000	
Bob Rohrman Auto Group	441110	1,103,592,881	
Braman Management Association	441110	2,156,744,676	
Brown Automotive Group Ltd	441110		
CFAO SA	441110	4,803,930,000	
Chapman Automotive Group LLC	441110	1,515,006,157	
Continental Motors Group	441110	523,687,500	
Darcars Automotive Group	441110	1,586,266,889	
David McDavid Auto Group	441110		
David Wilson Automotive Group	441110	2,629,558,770	
D'Ieteren SA/NV	441110	3,961,581,056	1,160,318,848
Earnhardt Auto Centers	441110	1,707,644,777	
Elder Automotive Group	441110	231,525,000	
Faulkner Organization (The)	441110		
Fletcher Jones Management Group Inc	441110	2,577,201,064	
Galpin Motors Inc	441110	1,349,574,632	
Group 1 Automotive Inc	441110	11,601,357,824	157,772,000
Hendrick Automotive Group	441110	9,427,756,576	
Herb Chambers Companies (The)	441110	2,898,436,267	
Holman Automotive Group Inc	441110	3,267,879,776	
Inchcape plc	441110	11,275,051,008	58,581,164
Jim Koons Automotive Companies Inc	441110	2,464,900,769	
Joe Rizza Auto Group	441110		
Jordan Automotive Group	441110		
Kelley Automotive Group LLC	441110		
Larry H Miller Group of Companies	441110	5,159,425,257	
Lithia Motors Inc	441110	11,821,400,064	265,700,000
Lupient Automotive Group Inc	441110	716,625,000	
Major Automotive Companies Inc	441110		

Industry Group/Company	Industry Code	2018 Sales	2018 Profits
Morse Operations Inc	441110	1,456,635,327	
Ourisman Automotive Enterprises	441110	1,400,000,000	
Pendragon PLC	441110	5,042,112,512	-61,376,532
Penske Automotive Group Inc	441110	22,785,099,776	471,000,000
Phil Long Dealerships Inc	441110	788,280,347	
Potamkin Automotive Group	441110	1,703,972,815	
Ricart Automotive Inc	441110	574,402,500	
Rosenthal Automotive Organization	441110	1,113,525,000	
Rush Enterprises Inc	441110	5,506,189,824	139,062,000
Russ Darrow Group Inc	441110	633,037,497	
Rybrook Holdings Limited	441110	780,404,625	
Rygor Group Limited	441110	329,053,000	-586,908
Sansone Auto Network	441110	358,098,938	
Santa Monica Ford Lincoln Mercury	441110		
Sheehy Auto Stores	441110	1,600,000,000	
Sonic Automotive Inc	441110	9,951,630,336	51,650,000
Spitzer Management Inc	441110		
Sytner Group Limited	441110	6,621,151,950	
Toresco Enterprises Inc	441110	722,137,500	
Tuttle-Click Automotive Group	441110	1,046,302,869	
Volvo Cars of North America Inc	441110		
Automobile (Car) and Light Truck Dealers (Used)			
ADESA Inc	441120	2,101,900,000	203,300,000
CarMax Inc	441120	17,120,208,896	664,112,000
Carvana Co	441120	1,955,467,008	-61,754,000
Copart Inc	441120	1,805,694,976	417,867,008
DriveTime Automotive Group Inc	441120	1,764,000,000	
Vroom	441120	1,155,000,000	
Automobile (Car) and Light, Heavy & Utility Truck Body Manufacturing			
Geely Automobile Holdings Limited	336211	15,485,825,024	1,823,692,672
JB Poindexter & Co Inc	336211	1,470,000,000	
Nissan Shatai Co Ltd	336211	4,825,000,000	
Supreme Industries Inc	336211	327,600,000	
Toyota Auto Body Co Ltd	336211	21,388,500,000	
Toyota Motor East Japan Inc	336211	6,812,477,697	
Automobile (Car) and Other Motor Vehicle Wholesale Distribution			
Beijing Automotive Import & Export Corporation	423110		
Gulf States Toyota Inc	423110	9,240,000,000	
JM Family Enterprises Inc	423110	16,300,000,000	
Suzuki Motor (Thailand) Co Ltd	423110		
TuanChe Limited	423110	94,577,240	-11,433,303
Zhongsheng Group Holdings Limited	423110	15,651,516,416	528,319,680
Automobile (Car) and Truck Brake System Manufacturing			
WABCO Holdings Inc	336340	3,831,000,064	394,100,000
Automobile (Car) and Truck Electrical and Electronic Equipment Manufacturing			
Sumitomo Electric Industries Ltd	336320	28,324,270,080	1,105,752,704

Industry Group/Company	Industry Code	2018 Sales	2018 Profits
YAZAKI Corporation	336320	18,435,012,750	
Automobile (Car) and Truck Gasoline Engine and Engine Parts Manufacturing			
BorgWarner Inc	336310	10,529,599,488	930,700,032
ElringKlinger AG	336310	1,881,089,536	48,532,996
Automobile (Car) and Truck Metal Stamping			
Shiloh Industries Inc	336370	1,139,943,936	11,479,000
Unipres Corporation	336370	3,040,709,376	146,563,136
Automobile (Car) and Truck Parts (including Air Bags, Air-Conditioners, Mufflers & Radiators) Manufacturing			
Accuride Corporation	336390	595,350,000	
Automobile (Car) and Truck Parts, Components and Systems Manufacturing, Including Gasoline Engines, Interiors and Electronics,			
ABC Technologies Inc	336300	960,109,865	
AGS Automotive Systems Inc	336300	540,225,000	
Aisan Industry Co Ltd	336300	2,000,210,000	42,399,800
Aisin Seiki Co Ltd	336300	35,921,125,376	1,236,454,784
American Axle & Manufacturing Holdings Inc	336300	7,270,400,000	-57,500,000
Applied Industrial Technologies Inc	336300	3,073,274,112	141,624,992
Aptiv PLC	336300	14,435,000,320	1,067,000,000
Autocam Corporation Inc	336300	353,694,600	
Autoliv Inc	336300	8,678,200,320	190,400,000
Benteler International AG	336300	9,232,690,000	35,686,300
BorgWarner Emissions Systems LLC	336300	6,163,085,250	
Brembo SpA	336300	2,929,170,688	263,893,936
Calsonic Kansei Corporation	336300	10,700,000,000	
Carlisle Companies Incorporated	336300	4,479,499,776	611,100,032
China Yuchai International Limited	336300	2,362,676,480	101,006,184
Commercial Vehicle Group Inc (CVG)	336300	897,737,024	44,512,000
Compagnie Plastic Omnium SA	336300	8,021,076,480	590,451,712
Cooper-Standard Holdings Inc	336300		
Cummins Filtration	336300	1,265,000,000	
Cummins Inc	336300	23,771,000,832	2,140,999,936
Dana Incorporated	336300	8,143,000,064	427,000,000
Delphi Technologies PLC	336300	4,857,999,872	358,000,000
Denso Corporation	336300	46,942,576,640	2,945,791,232
Dorman Products Inc	336300	973,705,024	133,602,000
Eagle Ottawa LLC	336300	1,215,506,250	
East Penn Manufacturing Company Inc	336300	1,714,387,500	
Eaton Corporation plc	336300	21,609,000,960	2,144,999,936
Edelbrock LLC	336300	51,266,250	
Exco Technologies Limited	336300	436,257,056	32,039,716
Faurecia SA	336300	19,402,899,456	775,907,904
Federal Signal Corporation	336300	1,089,500,032	94,000,000
Federal-Mogul LLC	336300	8,190,000,000	
Fisher & Company Inc	336300		
Gentex Corporation	336300	1,834,063,744	437,883,104
Gentherm Incorporated	336300	1,038,259,008	41,899,000

Industry Group/Company	Industry Code	2018 Sales	2018 Profits
Georg Fischer Ltd	336300	4,643,400,000	283,357,000
GKN plc	336300		
GT Technologies Inc	336300		
Hella GmbH & Co KGaA	336300	7,817,030,656	430,335,488
Hilite International Inc	336300	631,373,000	
Hyundai Mobis Co Ltd	336300	29,629,032,448	1,592,167,296
International Automotive Components Group SA	336300	4,620,000,000	
Jason Industries Inc	336300	612,947,968	-19,317,000
Joyson Safety Systems	336300	7,350,000,000	
Koito Manufacturing Co Ltd	336300	7,800,662,016	766,375,680
Lacks Enterprises Inc	336300	574,623,000	
Lear Corporation	336300	21,148,499,968	1,149,799,936
Linamar Corporation	336300	5,776,230,912	448,329,408
LKQ Corporation	336300	11,876,673,536	480,118,016
Lund International Inc	336300	155,452,500	
Magna International Inc	336300	40,826,998,784	2,296,000,000
Magna Mirrors	336300		
Magneti Marelli SpA	336300	10,313,604,000	
Martinrea International Inc	336300	2,776,396,288	140,895,168
Maxion Wheels USA LLC	336300	1,984,500,000	
Meritor Inc	336300	4,177,999,872	117,000,000
Miller Industries Inc	336300	711,705,984	33,746,000
Modine Manufacturing Company	336300	2,103,100,032	22,200,000
Montupet SA	336300	700,087,500	
Motorcar Parts of America Inc	336300	428,072,000	16,316,000
Nihon Plast Co Ltd	336300	1,079,420,000	18,964,600
Nippon Piston Ring Co Ltd	336300	537,089,000	17,769,300
Novares Group SA	336300	1,715,690,000	
NYX Incorporated	336300	471,870,000	
Orbital Corporation Limited	336300	15,508,900	1,638,030
Peterson Manufacturing Company	336300	358,312,500	
Rassini SAB de CV	336300		
Rheinmetall AG	336300	6,806,908,416	337,688,224
Rheinmetall Automotive AG	336300	3,351,310,000	299,673,000
Rieter Holding AG	336300	1,081,907,840	32,099,014
Robert Bosch GmbH	336300	88,321,400,000	6,008,870,000
Sogefi SpA	336300	1,857,260,000	16,018,800
Spartan Motors Inc	336300	816,163,968	15,012,000
Special Devices Inc	336300		
Spectra Premium Industries Inc	336300	482,343,750	
Stanadyne LLC	336300	281,137,500	
Standard Motor Products Inc	336300	1,092,050,944	43,003,000
Stoneridge Inc	336300	866,198,976	53,848,000
Strattec Security Corporation	336300	439,195,008	12,283,000
Superior Industries International Inc	336300	1,501,826,944	25,961,000
Tenneco Inc	336300	11,763,000,320	55,000,000
Titan International Inc	336300	1,602,407,936	16,087,000
Tokai Rika Co Ltd	336300	4,535,930,000	-40,809,200
Tower International Inc	336300	1,571,853,056	48,900,000

Industry Group/Company	Industry Code	2018 Sales	2018 Profits
Toyoda Gosei Co Ltd	336300	7,415,346,688	194,587,392
Unipart Group of Companies	336300	1,073,205,000	
Valeo SA	336300	21,173,606,400	604,517,312
Visteon Corporation	336300	2,984,000,000	164,000,000
Wanxiang Automotive Components LLC	336300		
Wanxiang Group Corporation	336300	2,050,000,000	
Wescast Industries Inc	336300	358,312,500	
Yazaki North America Inc	336300	5,300,000,000	
Automobile (Car) and Truck Seating and Interior Trim Manufacturing			
Autoneum Holding AG	336360	2,295,733,504	55,443,752
Grammer AG	336360	2,060,775,168	25,801,594
Lydall Inc	336360	785,897,024	34,944,000
MacNeil Automotive Products Limited (WeatherTech)	336360	551,250,000	
Automobile (Car) and Truck Transmission and Power Train Parts Manufacturing			
Allison Transmission Holdings Inc	336350	2,712,999,936	639,000,000
Grupo Kuo SAB de CV	336350	1,425,663,616	115,839,728
Stackpole International Inc	336350	647,400,000	
TI Fluid Systems plc	336350	3,972,390,000	160,245,000
ZF Friedrichshafen AG (ZF)	336350	42,236,100,000	1,103,760,000
Automobile (Car) Leasing			
Donlen Corporation	532112	748,000,000	
Automobile (Car) Manufacturing (incl. Autonomous or Self-Driving)			
American Honda Motor Co Inc	336111	53,823,840,000	
Aston Martin Lagonda Global Holdings PLC	336111	1,391,490,000	-72,461,300
Audi AG	336111	65,600,090,112	3,744,464,384
Audi of America Inc	336111	10,334,200,000	75,490,300
Automobili Lamborghini SpA	336111	1,505,230,000	
AvtoVAZ OAO	336111	3,477,130,000	97,222,300
BAIC BluePark New Energy Technology Co Ltd	336111	2,389,870,000	20,974,200
BAIC Motor Corporation Limited	336111	22,087,200,000	2,074,820,000
Bayerische Motoren Werke AG (BMW Group)	336111	107,927,371,776	7,879,761,408
Bentley Motors Limited	336111	1,770,590,000	-329,412,000
BMW of North America LLC	336111	18,000,000,000	3,053,920,000
Brilliance China Automotive Holdings Limited	336111	635,915,840	845,644,416
BYD Company Limited	336111	18,893,963,264	403,898,368
Changan Automobile (Group) Co Ltd	336111	9,638,930,000	105,167,000
Daihatsu Motor Co Ltd	336111	17,587,500,000	
Daimler AG	336111	185,298,944,000	8,025,908,224
Dongfeng Motor Corporation	336111	15,199,200,000	1,828,680,000
Dongfeng Motor Group Co Ltd	336111	15,187,697,664	1,885,550,720
DRB-HICOM Berhad	336111	3,308,720,000	76,396,300
FAW Group Corporation (First Automotive Works)	336111	69,524,000,000	2,855,800,000
FCA Canada Inc	336111	9,726,535,174	
FCA US LLC	336111	11,777,000,000	
Ferrari SpA	336111	3,786,892,288	868,775,488
Fiat Chrysler Automobiles NV	336111	122,245,349,376	3,994,685,696

Industry Group/Company	Industry Code	2018 Sales	2018 Profits
Ford Motor Company	336111	160,338,001,920	3,676,999,936
Ford Motor Company of Canada Limited	336111	10,541,000,000	
GAZ Group	336111	2,997,246,000	
General Motors Company (GM)	336111	147,049,005,056	8,014,000,128
General Motors of Canada Limited	336111		
GM Korea	336111	9,518,620,000	
Group Lotus plc	336111	130,710,000	1,122,500
Holden	336111	1,379,124,500	
Honda Motor Co Ltd	336111	141,161,054,208	9,734,764,544
Hyundai Motor America	336111	13,689,800,000	-295,529,000
Hyundai Motor Company Limited	336111	81,608,179,712	1,271,239,424
Isuzu Motors Limited	336111	19,025,539,072	970,988,800
Jaguar Land Rover Limited	336111	36,181,100,000	1,589,750,000
Jardine Cycle & Carriage Limited	336111	18,991,800,320	419,600,000
Jiangling Motors Corporation Ltd	336111	4,103,980,544	13,341,276
Karma Automotive LLC	336111		
Kia Motors Corporation	336111	45,662,441,472	974,402,112
Koenigsegg Automotive AB	336111		
Land Rover	336111	7,966,332,277	
Lucid Motors Inc	336111		
Mahindra & Mahindra Limited	336111	11,938,217,984	1,082,110,848
Maruti Suzuki India Limited	336111	11,510,311,936	1,136,473,472
Mazda Motor Corporation	336111	31,924,500,480	1,029,746,368
Mazda North American Operations	336111	12,784,900,000	254,116,000
Mercedes-Benz USA LLC	336111	48,171,422,250	
Mitsubishi Motors (Thailand) Co Ltd	336111	1,583,352,200	
Mitsubishi Motors Corporation	336111	20,146,931,712	988,963,456
Morgan Motor Company (The)	336111	42,893,000	4,060,880
NFI Group Inc	336111	2,519,021,056	159,942,000
NIO Inc	336111	719,291,456	-1,394,263,552
Nissan Motor Co Ltd	336111	109,825,114,112	6,863,554,560
Nissan North America Inc	336111	56,743,807,500	
Nuro Inc	336111		
Opel Automobile GmbH	336111	9,103,647,000	
Otokar Otomotiv ve Savunma Sanayi AS	336111		
Peugeot SA	336111	81,960,804,352	3,129,982,464
Porsche Automobil Holding SE	336111	114,038,976	3,845,217,024
Proton Holdings Berhad	336111	4,961,250,000	
PT Astra International TbK	336111	16,887,046,144	1,530,038,912
Renault SA	336111	63,572,856,832	3,655,890,432
Rivian Automotive LLC	336111		
Rolls-Royce Motor Car Limited	336111	749,981,000	80,604,600
SAIC Motor Corporation Limited	336111	198,711,000,000	5,233,940,000
SAIC-GM-Wuling Automobile Company	336111	2,154,951,960	
SEAT SA	336111	11,427,600,000	336,504,000
Skoda Auto AS	336111	18,486,200,000	1,281,760,000
Smart GmbH	336111		
SsangYong Motor Company	336111	3,316,450,000	-55,320,300
Subaru Corporation	336111	31,292,235,776	2,024,940,288

Industry Group/Company	Industry Code	2018 Sales	2018 Profits
Suzuki Motor Corporation	336111	34,526,916,608	1,982,448,128
Tata Motors Limited	336111	41,538,093,056	960,461,056
Tesla Inc	336111	21,461,268,480	-976,091,008
Tofas Turk Otomobil Fabrikasi AS	336111		
Toyota Motor Corporation	336111	269,982,629,888	22,918,424,576
Toyota Motor Sales USA Inc (TMS)	336111	95,578,770,000	
Toyota Motor Thailand Co Ltd	336111	6,174,000,000	
Vauxhall Motors Limited	336111	2,093,830,000	
Volkswagen AG (VW)	336111	235,849,000,000	12,136,000,000
Volkswagen Group of America Inc	336111	43,070,600,000	
Volvo Car Corporation	336111	28,113,500,000	1,098,380,000
WM Motor Technology Co Ltd	336111		
Xiaopeng Motors (Xpeng)	336111		
Yulon Motor Co Ltd	336111	2,649,000,000	125,633,000
Zoox Inc	336111		
Automobile (Car) Parts and Supplies Distributors (Wholesale Distribution)			
CARQUEST Auto Parts	423120	3,060,225,000	
Genuine Parts Company	423120	18,735,073,280	810,473,984
Hahn Automotive Warehouse Inc	423120	259,087,500	
Uni-Select Inc	423120	1,751,965,056	36,497,000
YHI International Limited	423120		
Automobile (Car) Parts Stores			
Advance Auto Parts Inc	441310	9,580,554,240	423,847,008
AutoZone Inc	441310	11,221,076,992	1,337,536,000
Car Monkeys Group	441310	902,226	
Halfords Group plc	441310	1,379,574,272	66,481,112
O Reilly Automotive Inc	441310	9,536,428,032	1,324,487,040
Pep Boys-Manny Moe & Jack (The)	441310	2,315,250,000	
Automobile (Car) Rental			
ADA SA	532111	6,349,907	
Avis Budget Group Inc	532111	9,123,999,744	165,000,000
Dollar Thrifty Automotive Group Inc	532111	1,620,000,000	
Enterprise Holdings Inc	532111	24,100,000,000	
Fair Financial Corp	532111		
Hertz Global Holdings Inc	532111	9,504,000,000	-225,000,000
Silvercar Inc	532111	80,000,000	
Sixt SE	532111	3,351,310,000	502,125,000
Zipcar Inc	532111	400,000,000	
Automotive (Car and Truck) Oil Change and Lubrication Shops			
Jiffy Lube International Inc	811191	275,000,000	
Ball Bearing and Roller Bearing Manufacturing			
Schaeffler AG	332991	15,767,272,448	975,420,736
Battery Manufacturing, Including Automobile (Car) and Truck Storage Batteries			
Yuasa Battery (Thailand) Public Company Limited	335910	73,693,900	3,922,120

Industry Group/Company	Industry Code	2018 Sales	2018 Profits
Battery Manufacturing, Including Energy Storage Technologies			
Automotive Energy Supply Corporation (AESC)	335911	599,173,050	
CODA Energy	335911		
EnerDel Inc	335911	51,000,000	
Interstate Battery System of America Inc	335911	1,890,000,000	
Primearth EV Energy Co Ltd	335911	1,562,001,000	
Boilers and Condensers (Including Nuclear Reactors) and Heat Exchangers Manufacturing			
Cool Technologies Inc	332410	0	-4,618,388
Car Repair (Repair and Maintenance of Automobiles and Trucks)			
AAMCO Transmissions Inc	811100		
Caliber Holdings Corporation	811100	253,575,000	
MAACO Franchising Inc	811100	540,225,000	
Midas Inc	811100	234,045,750	
Monro Muffler Brake Inc	811100	1,127,815,040	63,935,000
Ziebart International Corporation	811100	167,580,000	
Commercial and Industrial Machinery and Equipment (except Automotive and Electronic) Repair and Maintenance			
Titan Machinery Inc	811310	1,202,937,984	-7,049,000
Computer Software (Business and Consumer), Packaged Software, Artificial Intelligence (AI), Software as a Service (Saas) Industry			
Aurora Innovation Inc	511210		
GM Cruise LLC (Cruise)	511210		
Waymo LLC	511210		
Consumer Electronics Manufacturing, Including Audio and Video Equipment, Stereos, TVs and Radios			
Clarion Co Ltd	334310		
Diesel, Semidiesel, Locomotive, Marine and Other Non-Automotive or Aircraft Engine Equipment Manufacturing			
DEUTZ AG	333618	1,969,442,048	77,391,496
Weichai Power Co Ltd	333618	23,136,217,088	1,257,740,032
Electricity Control Panels, Circuit Breakers and Power Switches Equipment (Switchgear) Manufacturing			
Alps Alpine Co Ltd	335313	7,887,493,120	435,489,792
Engineering Services, Including Civil, Mechanical, Electronic, Computer and Environmental Engineering			
Pininfarina SpA	541330	120,472,000	2,485,460
Fluid Power Pump and Motor Manufacturing			
Danfoss Power Solutions	333996	2,412,260,000	
General Automotive (Car) Repair			
Precision Auto Care Inc	811111	30,425,631	
Glass Product Manufacturing Made of Purchased Glass			
AGC Inc	327215	13,994,706,944	823,313,792
Guardian Industries	327215	6,129,900,000	
Pilkington Group Limited	327215	102,716,000	317,004,000
Heavy Duty Truck (including Buses) Manufacturing			
AB Volvo	336120	40,448,454,656	2,576,656,896

Industry Group/Company	Industry Code	2018 Sales	2018 Profits
AM General LLC	336120	2,480,625,000	
ARBOC Specialty Vehicles LLC	336120	26,460,000	
Blue Bird Corporation	336120	1,024,976,000	30,820,000
Daimler Trucks North America LLC	336120	19,012,100,000	1,345,100,000
Hino Motors Ltd	336120	16,890,113,024	471,981,280
Hino Motors Manufacturing (Thailand) Ltd	336120		
Mack Trucks Inc	336120	2,870,000,000	
MAN SE	336120	13,402,347,520	747,342,784
Mitsubishi Fuso Truck of America Inc	336120		
Motor Coach Industries International Inc	336120	550,000,000	
Navistar International Corp (Holding Co.)	336120	10,250,000,384	340,000,000
Nikola Corporation	336120		
Nissan Diesel (Thailand) Co Ltd	336120		
Oshkosh Corporation	336120	7,705,500,160	471,900,000
PACCAR Inc	336120	23,495,700,480	2,195,099,904
REV Group Inc	336120	2,381,299,968	13,000,000
Scania AB	336120	15,258,400,000	1,083,130,000
Sinotruk (Hong Kong) Limited	336120	8,975,893,504	631,162,624
Traton SE	336120	29,655,100,000	
Tri Petch Isuzu Sales Co Ltd	336120	19,459,125,000	
UD Trucks Corporation	336120		
Utilimaster Corporation	336120		
Zhengzhou Yutong Bus Co Ltd	336120	4,615,440,000	338,517,000
Holding Companies			
Roark Capital Management LLC (Roark Caoital Group)	551112		
Industrial Truck, Tractor, Trailer and Stacker Machinery Manufacturing			
Hyster-Yale Materials Handling Inc	333924	3,174,400,000	34,700,000
KION Group AG	333924	8,852,635,648	442,759,104
Internet Search Engines, Online Publishing, Sharing, Gig and Consumer Services, Online Radio, TV and Entertainment Sites and Social Media			
AutoWeb Inc	519130	125,589,000	-38,816,000
Cox Automotive Inc	519130	7,780,500,000	
TrueCar Inc	519130	353,571,008	-28,321,000
Iron and Steel Mills and Ferroalloy Manufacturing			
Tata Group	331110	109,670,000,000	1,381,820,000
Light Truck and Utility Vehicle Manufacturing			
Great Wall Motor Company Limited	336112	14,208,073,728	756,503,168
Qingling Motors (Group) Co Ltd	336112	763,176,896	65,922,652
Market Research, Business Intelligence and Opinion Polling			
JD Power & Associates	541910	385,875,000	
Motor Home Manufacturing			
Newmar Corporation	336213	507,150,000	
Winnebago Industries Inc	336213	2,016,829,056	102,357,000
Motorcycle, Bicycle, and Parts Manufacturing			
Bajaj Auto Limited	336991	3,858,300,000	648,560,000
Ducati Motor Holding SpA	336991	680,556,000	

Industry Group/Company	Industry Code	2018 Sales	2018 Profits
Harley-Davidson Inc	336991	5,716,874,752	531,451,008
Hero MotoCorp Ltd	336991	4,689,151,488	536,565,440
KR Motors Co Ltd	336991	32,730,400	-20,924,800
LDI Ltd	336991	1,260,000,000	
Niu Technologies	336991	214,687,680	-50,705,680
Piaggio & C SpA	336991	1,538,469,888	39,941,320
Segway Inc	336991		
Yamaha Motor Company Limited	336991	15,375,270,912	857,985,728
Online Sales, B2C Ecommerce, Sharing Economy Platforms			
US Auto Parts Network Inc	454111	289,467,008	-4,889,000
Plastics (Including Packaging Materials, Pipe, Laminated & Unlaminated Film & Sheet, Foam and Bottles) Product Manufacturing			
SRG Global Inc	326100	546,000,000	
Trelleborg AB	326100	3,519,268,352	330,141,632
Plastics, Plastic Products, Chemicals and Related Products (Wholesale Distributors)			
FinishMaster Inc	424600	855,370,950	
Recreational Vehicle (RV) Trailer and Camper Manufacturing			
Gulf Stream Coach Inc	336214	180,258,750	
Jayco Inc	336214	1,934,887,500	
SAF-Holland SA	336214	1,439,941,376	53,311,560
Thor Industries Inc	336214	8,328,908,800	430,151,008
Recreational Vehicle Dealers			
Camping World Holdings Inc	441210	4,792,016,896	10,398,000
Rubber (Including Tires, Hoses and Belting) Product Manufacturing			
Bridgestone Corporation	326200	33,542,647,808	2,680,040,704
Continental AG	326200	49,163,419,648	3,207,816,704
Hankook Tire Co Ltd	326200		
Inoue Rubber (Thailand) Public Company Limited	326200	172,828,000	11,039,800
Kumho Tire Co Ltd	326200	2,156,840,192	-146,863,408
Marangoni SpA	326200	387,450,000	
Michelin (Compagnie Generale des Etablissements Michelin SCA)	326200	24,388,839,424	1,856,731,648
Pirelli & C SpA	326200	6,900,000,000	
Toyo Tire Corporation	326200	3,613,490,176	96,976,664
Sales Financing			
Ally Financial Inc	522220	6,662,000,128	1,263,000,064
Daimler Mobility AG	522220	30,045,100,000	1,583,010,000
Ford Motor Credit Company LLC	522220	11,977,000,000	2,224,000,000
Toyota Motor Credit Corporation	522220	10,717,000,000	3,410,000,000
Security, Detection, Burglar Alarms, Sensors & Intercom System Manufacturing			
LoJack Corporation	334290	126,000,000	
Tire and Tube Wholesale Distribution			
American Tire Distributors Inc	423130	5,565,000,000	

Industry Group/Company	Industry Code	2018 Sales	2018 Profits
Tire Manufacturing (except Retreading)			
Cooper Tire & Rubber Company	326211	2,808,061,952	76,586,000
Double Coin Holdings Ltd	326211		
Goodyear Tire & Rubber Company (The)	326211	15,475,000,320	693,000,000
Nokian Tyres plc	326211	1,766,607,616	326,837,920
Tire Retreading			
Bridgestone Bandag LLC	326212	1,819,125,000	
Tire Stores			
Canadian Tire Corporation Limited	441320	10,656,180,224	524,596,320
Discount Tire Company	441320	4,784,850,000	
Les Schwab Tire Centers	441320	1,786,050,000	
TBC Corporation	441320	3,570,000,000	
Truck Trailer Manufacturing			
Great Dane Limited Partnership	336212		
Utility Trailer Manufacturing Company	336212	1,391,505,503	
Wabash National Corporation	336212	2,267,278,080	69,421,000
Truck, Utility Trailer and RV (Recreational Vehicle) Rental and Leasing			
AMERCO (U-Haul)	532120	3,601,114,112	790,582,976
Penske Corporation	532120	27,000,000,000	
Wholesale Trade Agents and Brokers			
KAR Auction Services Inc	425120	3,769,600,000	328,000,000
Wireless Communications and Radio and TV Broadcasting Equipment Manufacturing, including Cellphones (Handsets) and Internet of Things (IoT)			
Mobileye NV	334220		
Wireless Telecommunications Carriers (except Satellite)			
Agero Inc	517210	735,000,000	
OnStar LLC	517210	2,100,000,000	

ALPHABETICAL INDEX

Earnhardt Auto Centers
East Penn Manufacturing Company Inc
Eaton Corporation plc
Edelbrock LLC
Elder Automotive Group
ElringKlinger AG
EnerDel Inc
Enterprise Holdings Inc
Exco Technologies Limited
Fair Financial Corp
Faulkner Organization (The)
Faurecia SA
FAW Group Corporation (First Automotive Works)
FCA Canada Inc
FCA US LLC
Federal Signal Corporation
Federal-Mogul LLC
Ferrari SpA
Fiat Chrysler Automobiles NV
FinishMaster Inc
Fisher & Company Inc
Fletcher Jones Management Group Inc
Ford Motor Company
Ford Motor Company of Canada Limited
Ford Motor Credit Company LLC
Galpin Motors Inc
GAZ Group
Geely Automobile Holdings Limited
General Motors Company (GM)
General Motors of Canada Limited
Gentex Corporation
Gentherm Incorporated
Genuine Parts Company
Georg Fischer Ltd
GKN plc
GM Cruise LLC (Cruise)
GM Korea
Goodyear Tire & Rubber Company (The)
Grammer AG
Great Dane Limited Partnership
Great Wall Motor Company Limited
Group 1 Automotive Inc
Group Lotus plc
Grupo Kuo SAB de CV
GT Technologies Inc
Guardian Industries
Gulf States Toyota Inc
Gulf Stream Coach Inc
Hahn Automotive Warehouse Inc
Halfords Group plc
Hankook Tire Co Ltd
Harley-Davidson Inc
Hella GmbH & Co KGaA
Hendrick Automotive Group
Herb Chambers Companies (The)
Hero MotoCorp Ltd
Hertz Global Holdings Inc
Hilite International Inc
Hino Motors Ltd
Hino Motors Manufacturing (Thailand) Ltd
Holden
Holman Automotive Group Inc
Honda Motor Co Ltd
Hyster-Yale Materials Handling Inc
Hyundai Mobis Co Ltd
Hyundai Motor America
Hyundai Motor Company Limited
Inchcape plc
Inoue Rubber (Thailand) Public Company Limited
International Automotive Components Group SA
Interstate Battery System of America Inc
Isuzu Motors Limited
Jaguar Land Rover Limited
Jardine Cycle & Carriage Limited
Jason Industries Inc
Jayco Inc
JB Poindexter & Co Inc
JD Power & Associates
Jiangling Motors Corporation Ltd
Jiffy Lube International Inc
Jim Koons Automotive Companies Inc
JM Family Enterprises Inc
Joe Rizza Auto Group
Jordan Automotive Group
Joyson Safety Systems
KAR Auction Services Inc
Karma Automotive LLC
Kawasaki Heavy Industries Ltd
Kelley Automotive Group LLC
Kia Motors Corporation
KION Group AG
Koenigsegg Automotive AB
Koito Manufacturing Co Ltd
KR Motors Co Ltd
Kumho Tire Co Ltd
Lacks Enterprises Inc
Land Rover
Larry H Miller Group of Companies
LDI Ltd
Lear Corporation
Les Schwab Tire Centers
Linamar Corporation
Lithia Motors Inc
LKQ Corporation
LoJack Corporation
Lucid Motors Inc
Lund International Inc
Lupient Automotive Group Inc
Lydall Inc
MAACO Franchising Inc
Mack Trucks Inc
MacNeil Automotive Products Limited (WeatherTech)
Magna International Inc
Magna Mirrors
Magneti Marelli SpA
Mahindra & Mahindra Limited

Major Automotive Companies Inc
MAN SE
Marangoni SpA
Martinrea International Inc
Maruti Suzuki India Limited
Maxion Wheels USA LLC
Mazda Motor Corporation
Mazda North American Operations
Mercedes-Benz USA LLC
Meritor Inc
Michelin (Compagnie Generale des Etablissements Michelin SCA)
Midas Inc
Miller Industries Inc
Mitsubishi Fuso Truck of America Inc
Mitsubishi Motors (Thailand) Co Ltd
Mitsubishi Motors Corporation
Mobileye NV
Modine Manufacturing Company
Monro Muffler Brake Inc
Montupet SA
Morgan Motor Company (The)
Morse Operations Inc
Motor Coach Industries International Inc
Motorcar Parts of America Inc
Navistar International Corp (Holding Co.)
Newmar Corporation
NFI Group Inc
Nihon Plast Co Ltd
Nikola Corporation
NIO Inc
Nippon Piston Ring Co Ltd
Nissan Diesel (Thailand) Co Ltd
Nissan Motor Co Ltd
Nissan North America Inc
Nissan Shatai Co Ltd
Niu Technologies
Nokian Tyres plc
Novares Group SA
Nuro Inc
NYX Incorporated
O Reilly Automotive Inc
OnStar LLC
Opel Automobile GmbH
Orbital Corporation Limited
Oshkosh Corporation
Otokar Otomotiv ve Savunma Sanayi AS
Ourisman Automotive Enterprises
PACCAR Inc
Pendragon PLC
Penske Automotive Group Inc
Penske Corporation
Pep Boys-Manny Moe & Jack (The)
Peterson Manufacturing Company
Peugeot SA
Phil Long Dealerships Inc
Piaggio & C SpA
Pilkington Group Limited
Pininfarina SpA
Pirelli & C SpA
Polaris Industries Inc
Porsche Automobil Holding SE
Potamkin Automotive Group
Precision Auto Care Inc
Primearth EV Energy Co Ltd
Proton Holdings Berhad
PT Astra International TbK
Qingling Motors (Group) Co Ltd
Rassini SAB de CV
Renault SA
REV Group Inc
Rheinmetall AG
Rheinmetall Automotive AG
Ricart Automotive Inc
Rieter Holding AG
Rivian Automotive LLC
Roark Capital Management LLC (Roark Caoital Group)
Robert Bosch GmbH
Rolls-Royce Motor Car Limited
Rosenthal Automotive Organization
Rush Enterprises Inc
Russ Darrow Group Inc
Rybrook Holdings Limited
Rygor Group Limited
SAF-Holland SA
SAIC Motor Corporation Limited
SAIC-GM-Wuling Automobile Company
Sansone Auto Network
Santa Monica Ford Lincoln Mercury
Scania AB
Schaeffler AG
SEAT SA
Segway Inc
Sequa Corporation
Sheehy Auto Stores
Shiloh Industries Inc
Silvercar Inc
Sinotruk (Hong Kong) Limited
Sixt SE
Skoda Auto AS
Smart GmbH
Sogefi SpA
Sonic Automotive Inc
Spartan Motors Inc
Special Devices Inc
Spectra Premium Industries Inc
Spitzer Management Inc
SRG Global Inc
SsangYong Motor Company
Stackpole International Inc
Stanadyne LLC
Standard Motor Products Inc
Stoneridge Inc
Strattec Security Corporation
Subaru Corporation
Sumitomo Electric Industries Ltd

Superior Industries International Inc
Supreme Industries Inc
Suzuki Motor (Thailand) Co Ltd
Suzuki Motor Corporation
Sytner Group Limited
Tata Group
Tata Motors Limited
TBC Corporation
Tenneco Inc
Tesla Inc
Thor Industries Inc
TI Fluid Systems plc
Titan International Inc
Titan Machinery Inc
Tofas Turk Otomobil Fabrikasi AS
Tokai Rika Co Ltd
Toresco Enterprises Inc
Tower International Inc
Toyo Tire Corporation
Toyoda Gosei Co Ltd
Toyota Auto Body Co Ltd
Toyota Motor Corporation
Toyota Motor Credit Corporation
Toyota Motor East Japan Inc
Toyota Motor Sales USA Inc (TMS)
Toyota Motor Thailand Co Ltd
Traton SE
Trelleborg AB
Tri Petch Isuzu Sales Co Ltd
TrueCar Inc
TuanChe Limited
Tuttle-Click Automotive Group
UD Trucks Corporation
Unipart Group of Companies
Unipres Corporation
Uni-Select Inc
US Auto Parts Network Inc
Utilimaster Corporation
Utility Trailer Manufacturing Company
Valeo SA
Vauxhall Motors Limited
Visteon Corporation
Volkswagen AG (VW)
Volkswagen Group of America Inc
Volvo Car Corporation
Volvo Cars of North America Inc
Vroom
Wabash National Corporation
WABCO Holdings Inc
Wanxiang Automotive Components LLC
Wanxiang Group Corporation
Waymo LLC
Weichai Power Co Ltd
Wescast Industries Inc
Winnebago Industries Inc
WM Motor Technology Co Ltd
Xiaopeng Motors (Xpeng)
Yamaha Motor Company Limited
YAZAKI Corporation
Yazaki North America Inc
YHI International Limited
Yuasa Battery (Thailand) Public Company Limited
Yulon Motor Co Ltd
ZF Friedrichshafen AG (ZF)
Zhengzhou Yutong Bus Co Ltd
Zhongsheng Group Holdings Limited
Ziebart International Corporation
Zipcar Inc
Zoox Inc

INDEX OF U.S. HEADQUARTERS LOCATION BY STATE

To help you locate the firms geographically, the city and state of the headquarters of each company are in the following index.

IOWA
Bridgestone Bandag LLC; Muscatine
Danfoss Power Solutions; Ames
Winnebago Industries Inc; Forest City

MARYLAND
Darcars Automotive Group; Silver Spring
Ourisman Automotive Enterprises; Marlow Heights

MASSACHUSETTS
Agero Inc; Medford
Herb Chambers Companies (The); Somerville
LoJack Corporation; Canton
Zipcar Inc; Boston

MICHIGAN
Ally Financial Inc; Detroit
American Axle & Manufacturing Holdings Inc; Detroit
Autocam Corporation Inc; Kentwood
BorgWarner Inc; Auburn Hills
Cooper-Standard Holdings Inc; Novi
Eagle Ottawa LLC; Southfield
Elder Automotive Group; Troy
FCA US LLC; Auburn Hills
Federal-Mogul LLC; Southfield
Fisher & Company Inc; St. Clair Shores
Ford Motor Company; Dearborn
Ford Motor Credit Company LLC; Dearborn
General Motors Company (GM); Detroit
Gentex Corporation; Zeeland
Gentherm Incorporated; Northville
GT Technologies Inc; Westland
Guardian Industries; Auburn Hills
Joyson Safety Systems; Auburn Hills
Lacks Enterprises Inc; Grand Rapids
Lear Corporation; Southfield
Maxion Wheels USA LLC; Novi
Meritor Inc; Troy
NYX Incorporated; Livonia
OnStar LLC; Detroit
Penske Automotive Group Inc; Bloomfield Hills
Penske Corporation; Bloomfield Hills
Rivian Automotive LLC; Plymouth
Spartan Motors Inc; Charlotte
SRG Global Inc; Troy
Stoneridge Inc; Novi
Superior Industries International Inc; Southfield
Tower International Inc; Livonia
Visteon Corporation; Van Buren Township
WABCO Holdings Inc; Auburn Hills
Yazaki North America Inc; Canton
Ziebart International Corporation; Troy

MINNESOTA
Lupient Automotive Group Inc; Minneapolis
Polaris Industries Inc; Medina

MISSOURI
Enterprise Holdings Inc; St. Louis
O Reilly Automotive Inc; Springfield
Peterson Manufacturing Company; Grandview

NEVADA
AMERCO (U-Haul); Reno
Fletcher Jones Management Group Inc; Las Vegas

NEW HAMPSHIRE
Segway Inc; Bedford

NEW JERSEY
Avis Budget Group Inc; Parsippany
BMW of North America LLC; Woodcliff Lake
Holman Automotive Group Inc; Maple Shade
Mitsubishi Fuso Truck of America Inc; Swedesboro
Sansone Auto Network; Avenel
Toresco Enterprises Inc; Springfield
Volvo Cars of North America Inc; Rockleigh

NEW YORK
Hahn Automotive Warehouse Inc; Rochester
Major Automotive Companies Inc; Long Island City
Monro Muffler Brake Inc; Rochester
Standard Motor Products Inc; Long Island City

NORTH CAROLINA
Advance Auto Parts Inc; Raleight
American Tire Distributors Inc; Huntersville
CARQUEST Auto Parts; Raleigh
Hendrick Automotive Group; Charlotte
MAACO Franchising Inc; Charlotte
Mack Trucks Inc; Greensboro
Sonic Automotive Inc; Charlotte

NORTH DAKOTA
Titan Machinery Inc; West Fargo

OHIO
Applied Industrial Technologies Inc; Cleveland
Commercial Vehicle Group Inc (CVG); New Albany
Cooper Tire & Rubber Company; Findlay
Dana Incorporated; Maumee
Goodyear Tire & Rubber Company (The); Akron
Hyster-Yale Materials Handling Inc; Cleveland
Ricart Automotive Inc; Columbus
Shiloh Industries Inc; Valley City
Spitzer Management Inc; Elyria

OKLAHOMA
Dollar Thrifty Automotive Group Inc; Tulsa

OREGON
Daimler Trucks North America LLC; Portland
Les Schwab Tire Centers; Bend

Lithia Motors Inc; Medford

PENNSYLVANIA
AAMCO Transmissions Inc; Horsham
Dorman Products Inc; Colmar
East Penn Manufacturing Company Inc; Lyon Station
Faulkner Organization (The); Trevose
Pep Boys-Manny Moe & Jack (The); Philadelphia

TENNESSEE
AutoZone Inc; Memphis
Cummins Filtration; Nashville
Miller Industries Inc; Ooltewah
Nissan North America Inc; Smyrna

TEXAS
Ancira Enterprises; San Antonio
Berkshire Hathaway Automotive; Irving
Caliber Holdings Corporation; Lewisville
Copart Inc; Dallas
David McDavid Auto Group; Irving
Group 1 Automotive Inc; Houston
Gulf States Toyota Inc; Houston
Interstate Battery System of America Inc; Dallas
JB Poindexter & Co Inc; Houston
Jiffy Lube International Inc; Houston
Rush Enterprises Inc; New Braunfels
Silvercar Inc; Del Valle
Toyota Motor Credit Corporation; Plano
Toyota Motor Sales USA Inc (TMS); Plano
Vroom; Grand Prairie

UTAH
Larry H Miller Group of Companies; Sandy
Nikola Corporation; Salt Lake

VIRGINIA
Audi of America Inc; Herndon
Brown Automotive Group Ltd; Fairfax
CarMax Inc; Richmond
Jim Koons Automotive Companies Inc; Vienna
Precision Auto Care Inc; Leesburg
Rosenthal Automotive Organization; Reston
Sheehy Auto Stores; Fairfax
Volkswagen Group of America Inc; Herndon

WASHINGTON
PACCAR Inc; Bellevue

WISCONSIN
Harley-Davidson Inc; Milwaukee
Jason Industries Inc; Milwauke
Modine Manufacturing Company; Racine
Oshkosh Corporation; Oshkosh
REV Group Inc; Milwaukee
Russ Darrow Group Inc; Menomonee Falls
Strattec Security Corporation; Milwaukee

INDEX OF NON-U.S. HEADQUARTERS LOCATION BY COUNTRY

INDONESIA
PT Astra International TbK; Jakarta

IRELAND
Eaton Corporation plc; Dublin

ISRAEL
Mobileye NV; Jerusalem

ITALY
Automobili Lamborghini SpA; Sant'Agata Bolognese
Brembo SpA; Curno
Ducati Motor Holding SpA; Bologna
Ferrari SpA; Maranello
Magneti Marelli SpA; Milano
Marangoni SpA; Rovereto
Piaggio & C SpA; Pisa
Pininfarina SpA; Cambiano
Pirelli & C SpA; Milano
Sogefi SpA; Milan

JAPAN
AGC Inc; Tokyo
Aisan Industry Co Ltd; Obu, Aichi
Aisin Seiki Co Ltd; Kariya
Alps Alpine Co Ltd; Tokyo
Automotive Energy Supply Corporation (AESC); Zama City
Bridgestone Corporation; Tokyo
Calsonic Kansei Corporation; Saitama
Clarion Co Ltd; Saitama
Daihatsu Motor Co Ltd; Osaka
Denso Corporation; Kariya
Hino Motors Ltd; Tokyo
Honda Motor Co Ltd; Tokyo
Isuzu Motors Limited; Tokyo
Kawasaki Heavy Industries Ltd; Kobe
Koito Manufacturing Co Ltd; Tokyo
Mazda Motor Corporation; Hiroshima
Mitsubishi Motors Corporation; Tokyo
Nihon Plast Co Ltd; Fujinomiya City
Nippon Piston Ring Co Ltd; Saitama City
Nissan Motor Co Ltd; Kanagawa
Nissan Shatai Co Ltd; Kanagawa
Primearth EV Energy Co Ltd; Shizuoka-ken
Subaru Corporation; Tokyo
Sumitomo Electric Industries Ltd; Osaka
Suzuki Motor Corporation; Hamamatsu
Tokai Rika Co Ltd; Aichi
Toyo Tire Corporation; Hyogo
Toyoda Gosei Co Ltd; Kiyosu
Toyota Auto Body Co Ltd; Aichi
Toyota Motor Corporation; Toyota
Toyota Motor East Japan Inc; Kurokawa-gun
UD Trucks Corporation; Saitama
Unipres Corporation; Kanagawa
Yamaha Motor Company Limited; Iwata-shi
YAZAKI Corporation; Tokyo

KOREA
GM Korea; Incheon
Hankook Tire Co Ltd; Seoul
Hyundai Mobis Co Ltd; Seoul
Hyundai Motor Company Limited; Seoul
Kia Motors Corporation; Seoul
KR Motors Co Ltd; Changwon-si, Gyeongnam
Kumho Tire Co Ltd; Seoul
SsangYong Motor Company; Gyeonggi Province

LUXEMBOURG
International Automotive Components Group SA; Findel
SAF-Holland SA; Bessenbach

MALAYSIA
DRB-HICOM Berhad; Shah Alam
Proton Holdings Berhad; Subang Jaya, Selangor Darul Ehsan

MEXICO
Grupo Kuo SAB de CV; Mexico DF
Rassini SAB de CV; Mexico

RUSSIA
AvtoVAZ OAO; Tolyatti
GAZ Group; Nizhny Novgorod

SINGAPORE
China Yuchai International Limited; Singapore
Jardine Cycle & Carriage Limited; Singapore
YHI International Limited; Singapore

SPAIN
SEAT SA; Martorell

SWEDEN
AB Volvo; Gothenburg
Autoliv Inc; Stockholm
Bilia AB; Gothenburg
Koenigsegg Automotive AB; Angelholm, Skane
Scania AB; Sodertalje
Trelleborg AB; Trelleborg
Volvo Car Corporation; Goteborg

SWITZERLAND
Autoneum Holding AG; Winterthur
Georg Fischer Ltd; Schaffhausen
Rieter Holding AG; Winterthur

TAIWAN
Yulon Motor Co Ltd; Sanyi

THAILAND

Hino Motors Manufacturing (Thailand) Ltd; Teparak, Muang Samutprakarn
Inoue Rubber (Thailand) Public Company Limited; Prachatipat
Mitsubishi Motors (Thailand) Co Ltd; Pathum Thani
Nissan Diesel (Thailand) Co Ltd; Ban Klang
Suzuki Motor (Thailand) Co Ltd; Bangkok
Toyota Motor Thailand Co Ltd; Samrong Tai
Tri Petch Isuzu Sales Co Ltd; Bangkok
Yuasa Battery (Thailand) Public Company Limited; Prakam

TURKEY

Otokar Otomotiv ve Savunma Sanayi AS; Istanbul
Tofas Turk Otomobil Fabrikasi AS; Istanbul

UNITED KINGDOM

Aptiv PLC; Dublin 2
Aston Martin Lagonda Global Holdings PLC; Gaydon
Bentley Motors Limited; Crewe
Delphi Technologies PLC; London
Fiat Chrysler Automobiles NV; London
GKN plc; Worcestershire
Group Lotus plc; Norwich
Halfords Group plc; Worcestershire
Inchcape plc; London
Jaguar Land Rover Limited; Coventry
Land Rover; Coventry
Morgan Motor Company (The); Malvern
Pendragon PLC; Annesley
Pilkington Group Limited; Lancashire
Rolls-Royce Motor Car Limited; Chichester
Rybrook Holdings Limited; Warwick
Rygor Group Limited; Westbury
Sytner Group Limited; Leicester
TI Fluid Systems plc; Oxford
Unipart Group of Companies; Oxford
Vauxhall Motors Limited; Luton

Individual Profiles
On Each Of
THE AUTOMOBILE 400

AAMCO Transmissions Inc

www.aamco.com

NAIC Code: 811100

TYPES OF BUSINESS:

Automotive Repair & Maintenance-Transmissions
Automatic Transmission Fluid
Bioethanol Conversion

BRANDS/DIVISIONS/AFFILIATES:

Icahn Enterprises LP
American Driveline Systems Inc
AAMCO Automatic Transmission Fluid
AAMCO Mercon V
AAMCO Synthetic Blend ATF
Eco-Green Auto Service
Flex-Box Smart Kit

CONTACTS: *Note: Officers with more than one job title may be intentionally listed here more than once.*

Jim Gregory, CEO

GROWTH PLANS/SPECIAL FEATURES:

AAMCO Transmissions, Inc. is a chain of auto transmission shops with approximately 600 independently owned and operated franchise locations in the U.S. and Canada. AAMCO's services include diagnostic, repair and maintenance services for automatic and standard transmissions in cars and trucks; free towing; external and multi-point inspections; and estimates. The company guarantees its services through a selection of six warranty packages from 90-day limited contracts to lifetime coverage. AAMCO also offers a national fleet program in which owners of large fleets of vehicles can contract transmission services at discounted prices. Moreover, the firm manufactures a branded automatic transmission fluid, AAMCO Automatic Transmission Fluid (ATF). Additional transmission fluid products include AAMCO Mercon V and AAMCO Synthetic Blend ATF. Transmission fluids are available through automotive product retailers across North America. The firm offers its Eco-Green Auto Service at several locations in the U.S., which meet eco-friendly standards such as solvent and waste fluid recycling. These locations offer, in addition to standard AAMCO services, a bioethanol fuel conversion kit called the Flex-Box Smart Kit, developed in partnership with Flex Fuel U.S. The company is a subsidiary of American Driveline Systems, Inc., which itself owned by Icahn Enterprises LP.

FINANCIAL DATA: *Note: Data for latest year may not have been available at press time.*

In U.S. $	2018	2017	2016	2015	2014	2013
Revenue						
R&D Expense						
Operating Income						
Operating Margin %						
SGA Expense						
Net Income						
Operating Cash Flow						
Capital Expenditure						
EBITDA						
Return on Assets %						
Return on Equity %						
Debt to Equity						

CONTACT INFORMATION:

Phone: 215-643-5885 Fax: 215-956-0340
Toll-Free: 800-462-2626
Address: 201 Gibraltar Rd., Horsham, PA 19044 United States

STOCK TICKER/OTHER:

Stock Ticker: Private
Exchange:
Employees: 1,778
Fiscal Year Ends: 12/31
Parent Company: Icahn Enterprises LP

SALARIES/BONUSES:

Top Exec. Salary: $ Bonus: $
Second Exec. Salary: $ Bonus: $

OTHER THOUGHTS:

Estimated Female Officers or Directors:
Hot Spot for Advancement for Women/Minorities:

AB Volvo

www.volvogroup.com

NAIC Code: 336120

TYPES OF BUSINESS:

Truck Manufacturer
Engines
Buses
Aerospace Products
Construction Equipment
Financial Services
Intelligent Transport Systems
Overhaul & Repair Services

BRANDS/DIVISIONS/AFFILIATES:

Volvo Group
Volvo
Renault Trucks
UD Trucks
Mack Trucks
Arquus
Volvo Penta
Volvo Financial Services

CONTACTS: *Note: Officers with more than one job title may be intentionally listed here more than once.*

Martin Lundstedt, CEO
Jan Gurander, Deputy CEO
Olof Persson, Pres.
Jan Ytterberg, Exec. VP-Group Finance
Kerstin Renard, Exec. VP-Group Human Resources
Sofia Frandberg, General Counsel
Mikael Bratt, Exec. VP-Group Truck Oper.
Karin Falk, Exec. VP-Corp. Strategy
Marten Wikforss, Exec. VP-Corp. Comm.
Anders Osberg, Exec. VP-Corp. Finance & Control
Niklas Gustavsson, Exec. VP-Public & Environmental Affairs
Martin Weissburg, Exec. VP-Volvo Construction Equipment
Torbjorn Homstrom, Exec. VP-Group Trucks Tech.
Dennis Slagle, Exec. VP-Group Trucks Sales & Mktg., Americas
Carl-Henric Svanberg, Chmn.
Peter Karlsten, Exec. VP-Group Trucks Sales & Mktg., EMEA

GROWTH PLANS/SPECIAL FEATURES:

AB Volvo, also called the Volvo Group, is a world leader in the manufacture of trucks and heavy machinery, including buses; construction equipment; and marine, industrial and aerospace components. The Volvo Group has ten product-related business areas: Volvo Trucks, UD Trucks, Renault Trucks, Mack Trucks, Group Trucks Asia and JV:s, Volvo Buses, Volvo Construction Equipment, Volvo Penta, Arquus and Volvo Financial Services. Volvo Trucks is the second-largest heavy-duty truck brand in the world, and its trucks are sold and serviced in more than 140 countries. UD Trucks markets heavy, medium and light duty trucks in Japan, growth markets in Asia and around the world. Renault Trucks is a France-based company that sells trucks and tools to transportation professionals throughout the world. Mack Trucks, based in America, makes durable, reliable and application-driven trucks. Group Trucks Asia and JV:s markets value trucks to customers and is responsible for the Group's Value Truck business. Volvo Buses develops, manufactures and sells hybrid, single-decker and double-decker buses, and also offers a network of services such as spare parts handling, financial, traffic information systems and repair contracts. Volvo Construction Equipment develops, manufactures and sells large road machinery, including hydraulic wheeled and crawler excavators; simulators; expander bolts; filters; lubricants; batteries; and other remanufactured products. Volvo Penta develops, manufactures and sells engines and drive systems for marine duties. It also supplies engines for various industrial applications. Arquus is responsible for the Group's sales to government authorities and organizations. Volvo Financial Services offers customer financing, insurance, treasury, real estate and related services operations. In May 2018, Volvo Group divested itself of a Chinese subsidiary that held a 25.2% stake in Inner Mongolia North Hauler Joint Stock Co., a Chinese mining truck manufacturer.

FINANCIAL DATA: *Note: Data for latest year may not have been available at press time.*

In U.S. $	2018	2017	2016	2015	2014	2013
Revenue	40,448,450,000	34,643,960,000	31,245,890,000	32,343,010,000	29,283,050,000	28,214,380,000
R&D Expense	1,645,430,000	1,666,025,000	1,514,201,000	1,590,475,000	1,723,774,000	1,565,223,000
Operating Income	3,436,681,000	2,972,827,000	2,379,710,000	2,109,802,000	1,210,450,000	953,167,600
Operating Margin %		.09%	.08%	.07%	.04%	.03%
SGA Expense	3,796,939,000	3,541,933,000	3,310,524,000	3,463,175,000	3,400,355,000	3,556,836,000
Net Income	2,576,657,000	2,171,380,000	1,360,618,000	1,558,393,000	217,231,100	370,814,200
Operating Cash Flow	3,227,626,000	3,891,221,000	1,817,228,000	2,676,114,000	904,215,500	1,147,734,000
Capital Expenditure	2,159,685,000	1,990,578,000	2,105,248,000	2,002,273,000	1,940,384,000	2,117,977,000
EBITDA	5,406,974,000	4,861,568,000	3,916,266,000	4,097,378,000	2,381,677,000	2,582,452,000
Return on Assets %		.05%	.03%	.04%	.01%	.01%
Return on Equity %		.21%	.15%	.19%	.03%	.04%
Debt to Equity		0.689	0.876	0.891	1.372	1.096

CONTACT INFORMATION:

Phone: 46 31660000 Fax: 46 31665170
Toll-Free:
Address: Volvo Bergegardsvag 1, Torslanda, Gothenburg, SE-405 08 Sweden

STOCK TICKER/OTHER:

Stock Ticker: VOLVF
Exchange: PINX
Employees: 105,175
Fiscal Year Ends: 12/31
Parent Company:

SALARIES/BONUSES:

Top Exec. Salary: $ Bonus: $
Second Exec. Salary: $ Bonus: $

OTHER THOUGHTS:

Estimated Female Officers or Directors: 5
Hot Spot for Advancement for Women/Minorities: Y

ABC Technologies Inc

www.abctechnologies.com

NAIC Code: 336300

TYPES OF BUSINESS:

Automotive Plastics
Design & Manufacturing Services
Plastic Packaging & Industrial Parts
Plastic Consumer Products
Decorating & Labeling Services

BRANDS/DIVISIONS/AFFILIATES:

Cerberus Capital Management LP
ABC Inoac Exterior Systems
ABCOR
NBHX
Inoac

CONTACTS: *Note: Officers with more than one job title may be intentionally listed here more than once.*

Todd Sheppelman, CEO
Ken Friedman, COO
David Smith, CFO
David Ellacott, Chief Human Resources Officer
Mark Poynton, Co-Managing Dir.

GROWTH PLANS/SPECIAL FEATURES:

ABC Technologies, Inc., an automotive Tier 1 supplier, is a Canadian company specializing in the design, development and production of complete plastic automotive systems as well as individual components for automotive OEMs (original equipment manufacturers). ABC Technologies operates manufacturing facilities within Canada, the U.S, Mexico, Brazil, Germany, Croatia, Spain, the U.K., Japan, China, India, Korea and Poland, and sales offices worldwide. Manufacturing techniques of the firm include extrusion blow molding, injection molding, thermoforming/sheet extrusion and continuous extrusion. Some of the services of the firm include design and engineering, machine building, research and development and painting. ABC Technologies' line of products include interior automotive systems such as instrument panels, seating systems, interior trim and HVAC (heating, ventilation and air conditioning) systems; exterior products such as bumper systems, spoilers and blow-molded running boards and exterior trim; under-hood components such as air induction and fluid management systems; and high-performance flexible products that include constant velocity joint (CVJ) boots, prop shaft boots and suspension dust covers. The company is also capable of manufacturing products that meet customer requirements and specifications such as impact, airflow, permeation, temperature and NVH (noise, vibration and harshness) requirements. In addition to its primary automotive line of business, the ABC Technologies provides industrial manufacturers throughout North America with sports, recreational and consumer goods. Products include computer enclosure doors, stadium seats, tool containers and composters. Joint ventures of the firm are primarily located in China, but also in the U.S., and include ABC Inoac Exterior Systems, NBHX, Inoac and ABCOR. The firm is owned by the Cerberus Capital Management LP.

FINANCIAL DATA: *Note: Data for latest year may not have been available at press time.*

In U.S. $	2018	2017	2016	2015	2014	2013
Revenue	960,109,865	914,390,348	870,847,950	829,379,000	859,927,000	816,930,650
R&D Expense						
Operating Income						
Operating Margin %						
SGA Expense						
Net Income						
Operating Cash Flow						
Capital Expenditure						
EBITDA						
Return on Assets %						
Return on Equity %						
Debt to Equity						

CONTACT INFORMATION:

Phone: 416-246-1782 Fax: 416-246-1552
Toll-Free:
Address: 2 Norelco Dr., Toronto, ON M9L 2X6 Canada

STOCK TICKER/OTHER:

Stock Ticker: Private Exchange:
Employees: 6,000 Fiscal Year Ends: 12/31
Parent Company: Cerberus Capital Management LP

SALARIES/BONUSES:

Top Exec. Salary: $ Bonus: $
Second Exec. Salary: $ Bonus: $

OTHER THOUGHTS:

Estimated Female Officers or Directors: 2
Hot Spot for Advancement for Women/Minorities:

Accuride Corporation

www.accuridecorp.com

NAIC Code: 336390

TYPES OF BUSINESS:

Vehicle Wheel Manufacturing
Wheels & Assemblies
Body & Chassis Parts
Seating Assemblies

BRANDS/DIVISIONS/AFFILIATES:

Crestview Partners
Accuride Wheels
Accuride Wheel End Solutions
Gunite
KIC
mefro wheels GmbH

CONTACTS: *Note: Officers with more than one job title may be intentionally listed here more than once.*

Robin Kendrick, CEO
John Risner, Chairman of the Board
Fritz Nelson, Sr. VP
Mark Cain, Sr. VP
Stephen Martin, General Counsel
Scott Hazlett, President, Divisional
Gregory Risch, President, Divisional
Mary Blair, Senior VP, Divisional
Michael Hajost, Senior VP

GROWTH PLANS/SPECIAL FEATURES:

Accuride Corporation, owned by private equity firm Crestview Partners, is a leading North American designer, manufacturer and distributor of commercial vehicle components. The company produces commercial vehicle wheels, wheel-end parts and assemblies, and ductile and gray iron castings. The firm operates through five divisions: Accuride Wheels, Accuride Wheel End Solutions, Gunite and KIC. Accuride Wheels provides a vast product line of both steel and forged aluminum wheels and wheel end components for heavy-duty and medium-duty vehicles and trailers. Accuride Wheel End Solutions is the industry's number one single-source wheel-end solutions provider capable of supplying a wide range of Gunite and KIC wheel end components. Gunite includes products such as brake drums, disc wheel hubs, spoke wheels, disc brake rotors and automatic slack adjusters for heavy-duty and medium-duty trucking. KIC supplies brake drums, disc wheel hubs, spoke wheels and rotors for the heavy-duty and medium-duty trucking, off-highway and bus markets and the aftermarket. Accuride's primary customers include commercial vehicle manufacturers, such as Daimler Truck North America, LLC; PACCAR, Inc.; Navistar, Inc.; and Volvo/Mack. During 2018, Accuride sold its interest in Gianetti Ruote Srl in order to secure the European Commission's approval of Accuride's June 2018 acquisition of mefro wheels GmbH.

The firm offers employees incentive plans, comprehensive health and welfare benefits, educational assistance, internal and external training programs and retirement plans.

FINANCIAL DATA: *Note: Data for latest year may not have been available at press time.*

In U.S. $	2018	2017	2016	2015	2014	2013
Revenue	595,350,000	567,000,000	540,000,000	685,574,016	705,177,984	642,883,008
R&D Expense						
Operating Income						
Operating Margin %						
SGA Expense						
Net Income				-7,634,000	-2,307,000	-38,313,000
Operating Cash Flow						
Capital Expenditure						
EBITDA						
Return on Assets %						
Return on Equity %						
Debt to Equity						

CONTACT INFORMATION:

Phone: 812 962-5000 Fax: 812 962-5400
Toll-Free:
Address: 7140 Office Cir., Evansville, IN 47715 United States

STOCK TICKER/OTHER:

Stock Ticker: Private
Exchange:
Employees: 2,290
Fiscal Year Ends: 12/31
Parent Company: Crestview Partners

SALARIES/BONUSES:

Top Exec. Salary: $ Bonus: $
Second Exec. Salary: $ Bonus: $

OTHER THOUGHTS:

Estimated Female Officers or Directors: 2
Hot Spot for Advancement for Women/Minorities: Y

ADA SA

www.ada.fr

NAIC Code: 532111

TYPES OF BUSINESS:

Automobile Rental

BRANDS/DIVISIONS/AFFILIATES:

Rousselet Group
Holiday Bikes
Homebox

CONTACTS:

Note: Officers with more than one job title may be intentionally listed here more than once.

Nicolas Rousselet, Chmn.

GROWTH PLANS/SPECIAL FEATURES:

ADA SA is a franchise car-rental company based in France and the French islands that also operates internationally in Morocco, Luxembourg, Senegal, the Dominican Republic, Germany, Canada and the U.S. As one of the largest private car-rental firms in the world, ADA has over 480 locations and offers economy-class cars, electric cars, wagons and minivans. Some agencies additionally offer commercial vehicles, such as moving vans, dump trucks, all-terrain vehicles and weight-bearing porters. Through ADA's partnership with Holiday Bikes, it also offers two-wheeled vehicles such as bicycles, motorcycles and scooters for rent at most agencies. The company's other partnerships include Homebox, which rents out storage boxes that are located within the company's facility. In addition, most of the firm's agencies offer special equipment, such as baby and child seats, boosters, GPS systems and snow chains. The company offers supplemental insurance. ADA provides car and scooter rental service to people without a license, with the possibility to book and pay directly online or by contacting an ADA agency. The company operates in-terminal locations in nearly all of the major airports in France, including Ajaccio, Bastia, Bordeaux, Brest, Lorient, Lyon, Marseille, Montpellier, Nantes, Nice, Paris Orly, Paris Roissy Charles de Gaulle, Perpignan, Toulouse, Guadeloupe, Guyana and La Reunion. ADA also has agencies at all major railway stations in France. ADA customers can locate the agency of their choice through the company's partnership with Via Michelin, a map, route planner and travel guide service for the U.S. and Europe. ADA is a subsidiary of the Rousselet Group, a global holding company with several subsidiaries. These include Europe's largest taxi company, a software company and numerous real estate holdings.

FINANCIAL DATA:

Note: Data for latest year may not have been available at press time.

In U.S. $	2018	2017	2016	2015	2014	2013
Revenue	6,349,907	60,475,300	48,688,200	47,420,000	50,529,848	39,164,539
R&D Expense						
Operating Income						
Operating Margin %						
SGA Expense						
Net Income		3,948,160	2,920,470	3,196,585	3,627,812	2,690,608
Operating Cash Flow						
Capital Expenditure						
EBITDA						
Return on Assets %						
Return on Equity %						
Debt to Equity						

CONTACT INFORMATION:

Phone: 41-27-46-00 Fax: 47-39-17-65
Toll-Free:
Address: 22-28 rue Henri Barbusse, Clichy, 92585 France

STOCK TICKER/OTHER:

Stock Ticker: ALADA
Employees: 97
Parent Company: Rousselet Group
Exchange: Paris
Fiscal Year Ends: 12/31

SALARIES/BONUSES:

Top Exec. Salary: $ Bonus: $
Second Exec. Salary: $ Bonus: $

OTHER THOUGHTS:

Estimated Female Officers or Directors:
Hot Spot for Advancement for Women/Minorities:

ADESA Inc

NAIC Code: 441120

www.adesa.com

TYPES OF BUSINESS:

Vehicle Auctions-Wholesale
Salvage Vehicle Auctions
Automobile Transportation
Automobile Reconditioning
Automotive Market Analysis
Publishing

BRANDS/DIVISIONS/AFFILIATES:

KAR Auction Services Inc
ADESA LiveBlock
ADESA Run Lists
ADESA DealerBlock
ADESA Market Guide
ADESA Virtual Inventory
ADESA Notify Me

CONTACTS:

Note: Officers with more than one job title may be intentionally listed here more than once.

John Hammer, Pres.
Paul Lips, COO
Scott Myer, VP-Finance
Bob Rauschenberg, Exec. VP-Sales, Mktg. & Special Svcs.
J. Marty Nowlin, VP-Human Resources
Richard Griskie, CIO
Michelle Mallon, VP-Legal
Sanjiv Agrawal, VP-Bus. Oper.
Mike Caggiano, Exec. VP-U.S. Oper., Eastern Region
Carol Sewell, VP-Mktg.
Jane Morgan, Pres., Specialty Auctions Div.
Lisa Scott, Sr. VP-ADESA Canada & OPENLANE

GROWTH PLANS/SPECIAL FEATURES:

ADESA, Inc., a wholly-owned subsidiary of KAR Auction Services, Inc., is primarily engaged in automotive auctions, transportation and cosmetic and mechanical reconditioning. The firm operates 75 used-vehicle auction sites across the U.S and Canada. It serves two main client types: institutional buyers and dealers. The firm's institutional customers include vehicle manufacturers; banks, credit unions and other financial institutions; vehicle finance companies; vehicle rental companies; and insurance companies. Dealers buying from ADESA include both licensed franchises and independent wholesale dealers. ADESA's online auction tools include ADESA LiveBlock, an online real-time bidding tool; ADESA Run Lists, a summary of consigned vehicles offered for auction sale; and ADESA DealerBlock, a bulletin board type online auction platform. The firm also offers ADESA Market Guide, a summary of wholesale auction prices, auction sales results, market data and condition reports; ADESA Virtual Inventory, a subscription-based service that allows dealers to embed ADESA Search technology into their web sites; and ADESA Notify Me, an email notification service for dealers looking for particular vehicles. The firm also offers analytical services via monthly, semi-annual and annual market analysis publications.

Employee benefits include medical, dental and vision coverage; a medical flexible spending account; short- and long-term disability; life and AD&D insurance; supplemental life insurance; an employee assistance program; a 401(k); and an employee stock purchase plan.

FINANCIAL DATA:

Note: Data for latest year may not have been available at press time.

In U.S. $	2018	2017	2016	2015	2014	2013
Revenue	2,101,900,000	1,937,500,000	1,765,300,000	1,427,800,000	1,218,500,000	1,118,600,000
R&D Expense						
Operating Income						
Operating Margin %						
SGA Expense						
Net Income	203,300,000	260,900,000	156,900,000	109,200,000	86,400,000	67,700,000
Operating Cash Flow						
Capital Expenditure						
EBITDA						
Return on Assets %						
Return on Equity %						
Debt to Equity						

CONTACT INFORMATION:

Phone: 317-815-1100 Fax: 317-249-4600
Toll-Free: 800-923-3725
Address: 13085 Hamilton Crossing Blvd., Carmel, IN 46032 United States

STOCK TICKER/OTHER:

Stock Ticker: Subsidiary
Exchange:
Employees: 11,000
Fiscal Year Ends: 12/31
Parent Company: KAR Auction Services Inc

SALARIES/BONUSES:

Top Exec. Salary: $ Bonus: $
Second Exec. Salary: $ Bonus: $

OTHER THOUGHTS:

Estimated Female Officers or Directors: 4
Hot Spot for Advancement for Women/Minorities: Y

Advance Auto Parts Inc

www.advanceautoparts.com

NAIC Code: 441310

TYPES OF BUSINESS:

Auto Parts & Accessories Stores
Online Sales

BRANDS/DIVISIONS/AFFILIATES:

Advance Auto Parts
Carquest
Worldpac
Autopart International

CONTACTS: *Note: Officers with more than one job title may be intentionally listed here more than once.*

Thomas Greco, CEO
Jeffrey Shepherd, CFO
Jeffrey Smith, Chairman of the Board
Andrew Page, Chief Accounting Officer
Natalie Schechtman, Executive VP, Divisional
Robert Cushing, Executive VP, Divisional
Reuben Slone, Executive VP, Divisional
Michael Broderick, Executive VP, Divisional
Tammy Finley, Executive VP

GROWTH PLANS/SPECIAL FEATURES:

Advance Auto Parts, Inc. is a leading specialty retailer of automotive aftermarket parts, accessories, batteries and maintenance items. The firm primarily operates in the U.S. and serves both do-it-yourself (DIY) and commercial customers. It operates in a single segment comprised of the company's store and branch operations. Advance Auto serves its customers through a variety of channels ranging from brick-and-mortar store locations to self-service eCommerce sites. The company operates under the following store names: Advance Auto Parts, consisting of 4,912 stores that average 7,500 square feet in size; Carquest, consisting of 1,250 stores that average 7,600 square feet in size; Worldpac, consisting of 150 stores that average 28,000 square feet in size; and Autopart International, consisting of 185 stores that offer approximately 41,000 SKUs. Primary categories of products offered by the company include: parts such as alternators, batteries, belts, hoses, brakes, brake pads, chassis parts, climate control parts, clutches, drive shafts, engines, engine parts, ignition parts, lighting, radiators, starters, spark plugs, wires, steering and alignment parts, transmissions, water pumps and windshield wiper blades; accessories such as air fresheners, auto paint, anti-theft devices, emergency road kits, floor mats, ice scrapers, mirrors, seat and steering wheel covers and vent shades; chemicals such as antifreeze, brake and power steering fluids, car wash fluids, car waxes, Freon, fuel additives and windshield washer fluid; and oil such as transmission fluid and other automotive petroleum products. The company's stores are primarily located in the U.S., and are also located throughout Canada, Puerto Rico and the Virgin Islands.

The firm offers employees comprehensive benefits, 401(k) and retirement options, as well as a variety to employee assistance programs.

FINANCIAL DATA: *Note: Data for latest year may not have been available at press time.*

In U.S. $	2018	2017	2016	2015	2014	2013
Revenue	9,580,554,000	9,373,784,000	9,567,679,000	9,737,018,000	9,843,862,000	6,493,814,000
R&D Expense						
Operating Income	604,275,000	570,212,000	787,598,000	825,780,000	851,710,000	660,318,000
Operating Margin %		.06%	.08%	.08%	.09%	.10%
SGA Expense	3,615,138,000	3,514,837,000	3,468,317,000	3,596,992,000	3,601,903,000	2,591,828,000
Net Income	423,847,000	475,505,000	459,622,000	473,398,000	493,825,000	391,758,000
Operating Cash Flow	811,028,000	600,805,000	500,874,000	689,642,000	708,991,000	545,250,000
Capital Expenditure	193,715,000	189,758,000	259,559,000	234,747,000	228,446,000	195,757,000
EBITDA	850,036,000	828,320,000	1,057,132,000	1,087,772,000	1,139,495,000	870,811,000
Return on Assets %		.06%	.06%	.06%	.07%	.08%
Return on Equity %		.15%	.17%	.21%	.28%	.29%
Debt to Equity		0.306	0.358	0.493	0.817	0.694

CONTACT INFORMATION:

Phone: 540-362-4911 Fax:
Toll-Free: 877-238-2623
Address: 2635 East Millbrook Rd., Raleight, NC 27604 United States

STOCK TICKER/OTHER:

Stock Ticker: AAP
Exchange: NYS
Employees: 74,000
Fiscal Year Ends: 12/31
Parent Company:

SALARIES/BONUSES:

Top Exec. Salary: $1,100,008 Bonus: $
Second Exec. Salary: $515,491 Bonus: $

OTHER THOUGHTS:

Estimated Female Officers or Directors: 3
Hot Spot for Advancement for Women/Minorities: Y

AGC Inc

NAIC Code: 327215

www.agc.com

TYPES OF BUSINESS:

Glass Manufacturing
Home & Office Window Glass Manufacturing
Automotive Glass Manufacturing
Specialty Glass Manufacturing
Chemicals Manufacturing
Electronics Components Manufacturing

BRANDS/DIVISIONS/AFFILIATES:

CONTACTS: *Note: Officers with more than one job title may be intentionally listed here more than once.*

Takuya Shimamura, CEO
Tomoya Takigawa, Gen. Mgr.-Research Center, Tech. Gen. Div.
Tadayuki Oi, Gen. Mgr.-Production Tech. Center
Shinichi Kawakami, Gen. Mgr.-Admin. Office
Eisuke Yanagisawa, Gen. Mgr.-Legal
Yuji Nishimi, Sr. Exec. VP-Bus. Dev. & Electronics Bus.
Takashi Fujino, Mgr.-Finance
Marehisa Ishiko, Pres., Glass Company
Jean-Francois Heris, Pres., Europe Glass Company
Yasumasa Nakao, VP-Tech.-Glass Company
Takuya Shimamura, Pres., Electronics Company
Kazuhiko Ishimura, Chmn.
Kei Yonamoto, Brazil Global Project Leader

GROWTH PLANS/SPECIAL FEATURES:

AGC, Inc. is a global supplier of products, materials and components for glass and related fields. The company operates through four business fields: glass, electronics, chemicals and ceramics. The glass segment is composed of architectural glass and automotive glass. Architectural glass includes float glass, insulating glass, polished wired glass, tempered glass and mirrors; and glass for industrial use include laminated glass, low-E insulating glass, heat-resistant tempered glass and figured glass. The automotive glass business provides laminated glass and tempered glass, providing features such as water repellency, safety/strength, ultra-violet protection, 2-sheet glass with radio wave permeability, privacy glass, acoustic glass (decreases noise), defog functionality and more. The electronics segment is composed of the display, electronic materials and applied glass materials groups. The display business produces glass for TFT-LCD displays (thin-film transistor liquid crystal display), as well as other display types, which help to improve image qualities, clarity and contrast. The electronic materials business provides technology to support the information and communication industry. Its expertise in glass, chemicals and ceramics embedded with advanced technology in materials, processing, forming and surface finishing enables the development and production of innovative electronic components. The applied glass materials business produces cover glass for electronic devices, including smartphones and tablet PC models, as well as glass substrates for photovoltaic modules. This division develops multiple applications that utilize AGC's thin, light-weight-yet-strong glass. The chemicals business produces soda ash, caustic soda, chlorine derivatives, fluorine resins, elastomers, refrigerants, solvents for industrial cleaners/coatings, polyether polyols, raw materials for agrochemical and pharmaceutical purposes, and a variety of fine chemicals such as fine silica. The ceramics segment produces high thermal insulation ceramics wall for furnaces, ceramics beads for casting and blasting, sputtering targets, abrasion-resistant ceramics, road pavement surface materials, alumina cement, fine ceramics engineering and ceramics molding agents for 3D printers, etc.

FINANCIAL DATA: *Note: Data for latest year may not have been available at press time.*

In U.S. $	2018	2017	2016	2015	2014	2013
Revenue	13,994,710,000	13,449,110,000	11,786,160,000	12,187,950,000	12,390,260,000	12,130,180,000
R&D Expense						
Operating Income	1,094,385,000	1,083,385,000	868,195,200	632,374,600	547,087,000	724,931,100
Operating Margin %		.08%	.07%	.05%	.04%	.06%
SGA Expense	2,763,334,000	2,619,473,000	2,338,440,000	2,432,917,000	2,502,252,000	2,481,961,000
Net Income	823,313,800	636,142,200	435,930,900	394,284,200	146,232,300	148,309,100
Operating Cash Flow	1,739,451,000	1,870,097,000	1,871,320,000	1,719,996,000	1,247,841,000	1,538,054,000
Capital Expenditure	1,942,382,000	1,444,836,000	1,087,842,000	1,162,387,000	1,047,289,000	1,364,428,000
EBITDA	2,391,261,000	2,301,066,000	1,808,188,000	2,107,627,000	1,717,295,000	1,715,889,000
Return on Assets %		.00%	.02%	.02%	.01%	.01%
Return on Equity %		.01%	.04%	.04%	.01%	.02%
Debt to Equity		0.297	0.302	0.34	0.361	0.361

CONTACT INFORMATION:

Phone: 81-3-3218-5741 Fax: 81-3-3218-7815
Toll-Free:
Address: 1-5-1, Marunouchi, Chiyoda-ku, Tokyo, 100-8405 Japan

STOCK TICKER/OTHER:

Stock Ticker: ASGLF Exchange: PINX
Employees: 58,853 Fiscal Year Ends: 12/31
Parent Company:

SALARIES/BONUSES:

Top Exec. Salary: $ Bonus: $
Second Exec. Salary: $ Bonus: $

OTHER THOUGHTS:

Estimated Female Officers or Directors:
Hot Spot for Advancement for Women/Minorities:

Agero Inc

www.agero.com

NAIC Code: 517210

TYPES OF BUSINESS:

Automotive Telematics
Emergency Response Systems
Stolen Vehicle Tracking
Automobile Operational Analysis
Navigation Tools

BRANDS/DIVISIONS/AFFILIATES:

Cross Country Automotive Services
ATX Group
VehicleAssist
ClaimsAssist
Drive360

CONTACTS: *Note: Officers with more than one job title may be intentionally listed here more than once.*

Dave Ferrick, CEO
George Horvat, COO
Bill Gerraughty, CFO
Sameer Bhalla, Co-Founder
Emma Barnes Brown, Chief People Officer
Bernie Gracy, Chief Digital Officer
Peter Necheles, Sr. VP-Corp. Dev.
Michael A. Saxton, Sr. Advisor
Tom Metzger, Sr. VP

GROWTH PLANS/SPECIAL FEATURES:

Agero, Inc., a product of the merger of Cross Country Automotive Services and the ATX Group, is a pioneer in the telematics (location-based voice and data communication services) industry as well as a provider of roadside assistance for motorists and claims management services for insurance carriers. With operations throughout North America, the firm serves more than 115 million drives each year, and its technology is incorporated into 70% of new passenger vehicles sold in the U.S. Agero divides its products and services into four segments: mobile offerings, information services, roadside assistance and claims and asset management. The mobile offerings segment offers products that connect customers with their insurance carriers and roadside assistance companies. Products include VehicleAssist, MobileCare, RoadsideConnect and ClientConnect. The information services segment leverages data and insights to increase process efficiencies. Agero's roadside assistance segment protects over 80 million drivers through its various scalable services and products, such as VehicleAssist. The firm maintains six geographically dispersed response centers. The claims management segment provides accident scene management and vehicle release services. Products include VehicleAssist and ClientConnect.

FINANCIAL DATA: *Note: Data for latest year may not have been available at press time.*

In U.S. $	2018	2017	2016	2015	2014	2013
Revenue	735,000,000	700,000,000	675,000,000	625,000,000	600,000,000	500,000,000
R&D Expense						
Operating Income						
Operating Margin %						
SGA Expense						
Net Income						
Operating Cash Flow						
Capital Expenditure						
EBITDA						
Return on Assets %						
Return on Equity %						
Debt to Equity						

CONTACT INFORMATION:

Phone: 781-393-9300   Fax: 781-393-6706
Toll-Free:
Address: One Cabot Rd., Medford, MA 02155 United States

STOCK TICKER/OTHER:

Stock Ticker: Private   Exchange:
Employees: 3,500   Fiscal Year Ends: 12/31
Parent Company: Cross Country Group

SALARIES/BONUSES:

Top Exec. Salary: $ Bonus: $
Second Exec. Salary: $ Bonus: $

OTHER THOUGHTS:

Estimated Female Officers or Directors: 1
Hot Spot for Advancement for Women/Minorities: Y

AGS Automotive Systems Inc

www.agsautomotive.com

NAIC Code: 336300

TYPES OF BUSINESS:

Automotive Products, Parts Manufacturing
Chrome Bumpers
Heavy Metal Stamping

BRANDS/DIVISIONS/AFFILIATES:

J2 Management Corp
Tiercon

CONTACTS:

Note: Officers with more than one job title may be intentionally listed here more than once.

Joe Loparco, Co-Pres.
Joseph Leon, Co-Pres.
Dan Reid, Dir.-Oper.
Maria Di Zio, Dir.-Communications
Joe Loparco, Co-Pres.

GROWTH PLANS/SPECIAL FEATURES:

AGS Automotive Systems, Inc. is an automotive parts manufacturer owned by private investor J2 Management Corp. AGS has operations in heavy metal stamping, welding, plating, coating, sequencing and assembly. The company's impact system assemblies and products include spring hangars, risers, brace rear bumper assemblies, wheelhouses, corner braces, panel rear wheelhouses, front panels, deck panels, assembled rear bumpers, H brackets, rail assemblies, bumper assemblies, crossmembers and floor pans. The company's stamping capabilities consist of over 130 stamping presses, and its stamped products include bumper products, cross members, oil pans, control arms and frame assemblies. The firm operates six plant facilities in Canada and the U.S., with nearly 2 million square feet of manufacturing space. AGS has provided bumper systems and body-in-white structural modules to several original equipment manufacturers (OEM) customers, including General Motors, Chrysler and International Truck. Its Tier 1 customers have included TRW Karmax, Johnson Controls, TI Automotive and Stant Corporation. The company owns and operates Canadian plants in Windsor, Oshawa and Cambridge, as well as two U.S. facilities in Sterling Heights, Michigan (plus a sales and engineering office in Sterling Heights). In addition, affiliate Tiercon, also owned by J2 Management Corp., supplies exterior components & systems to the automotive industry.

FINANCIAL DATA:

Note: Data for latest year may not have been available at press time.

In U.S. $	2018	2017	2016	2015	2014	2013
Revenue	540,225,000	514,500,000	490,000,000	400,000,000	388,000,000	368,000,000
R&D Expense						
Operating Income						
Operating Margin %						
SGA Expense						
Net Income						
Operating Cash Flow						
Capital Expenditure						
EBITDA						
Return on Assets %						
Return on Equity %						
Debt to Equity						

CONTACT INFORMATION:

Phone: 416-438-6650 Fax:
Toll-Free:
Address: 200 Yorkland Blvd., Ste. 800, Toronto, ON M2J 5C1 Canada

STOCK TICKER/OTHER:

Stock Ticker: Private
Exchange:
Employees: 1,500
Fiscal Year Ends: 12/31
Parent Company: J2 Management Corp

SALARIES/BONUSES:

Top Exec. Salary: $ Bonus: $
Second Exec. Salary: $ Bonus: $

OTHER THOUGHTS:

Estimated Female Officers or Directors: 1
Hot Spot for Advancement for Women/Minorities:

Aisan Industry Co Ltd

www.aisan-ind.co.jp

NAIC Code: 336300

TYPES OF BUSINESS:

Automobile Components Manufacturing
Engine Components
Industrial Devices

BRANDS/DIVISIONS/AFFILIATES:

Toyota Motor Corporation

GROWTH PLANS/SPECIAL FEATURES:

Aisan Industry Co., Ltd., founded in 1938, is a Japanese manufacturer of automotive engine components, including electronic fuel injection products, carbon canisters, engine valves and gaseous fuel systems. Aisan operates two factories and one technical center in Japan, as well as through seven domestic affiliates and 23 overseas affiliates. The firm's electronic fuel injection products include throttle bodies, fuel pumps, fuel pump modules, fuel injectors, intake modules, exhaust system products, emission control systems, valve train systems and electronic fuel injection (EFI) systems for motorcycles and other vehicles with small engines. Aisan also produces carbon canisters; both traditional steel engine valves and titanium alloy engine valves, which are 40% lighter than the steel version; and gaseous fuel systems, which accommodate either liquefied petroleum gas (LPG) or compressed natural gas (CNG). Toyota Motor Corporation owns 28.8% of the firm.

CONTACTS: *Note: Officers with more than one job title may be intentionally listed here more than once.*

Nomura Tokuyuki, Pres.
Michikatsu Sato, Sr. Managing Exec. Officer
Kunio Nakashima, Managing Exec. Officer
Masataka Nakano, Sr. Managing Exec. Officer
Shoji Kawakami, Sr. Managing Exec. Officer

FINANCIAL DATA: *Note: Data for latest year may not have been available at press time.*

In U.S. $	2018	2017	2016	2015	2014	2013
Revenue	2,000,210,000	1,816,285,000	1,839,326,250	1,769,793,000	1,595,600,000	1,408,400,000
R&D Expense						
Operating Income						
Operating Margin %						
SGA Expense						
Net Income	42,399,800	40,155,000	37,024,697	56,212,000	54,615,082	-7,688,531
Operating Cash Flow						
Capital Expenditure						
EBITDA						
Return on Assets %						
Return on Equity %						
Debt to Equity						

CONTACT INFORMATION:

Phone: 81-562-47-1131 Fax: 81-562-48-6357
Toll-Free:
Address: 1-1-1 Kyowa-cho, Obu, Aichi, 474-8588 Japan

STOCK TICKER/OTHER:

Stock Ticker: 7283 Exchange: Tokyo
Employees: 10,440 Fiscal Year Ends: 03/31
Parent Company:

SALARIES/BONUSES:

Top Exec. Salary: $ Bonus: $
Second Exec. Salary: $ Bonus: $

OTHER THOUGHTS:

Estimated Female Officers or Directors:
Hot Spot for Advancement for Women/Minorities:

Aisin Seiki Co Ltd

NAIC Code: 336300

www.aisin.co.jp

TYPES OF BUSINESS:

Automobile Parts Manufacturing
Sewing & Embroidery Machines
Air Conditioners
Hospital & Biotechnology Equipment
Lasers & Laser Imaging Technology

BRANDS/DIVISIONS/AFFILIATES:

Aisin Europe Manufacturing (UK) Ltd
Aisin Europe SA
Advics South Africa Pty Ltd
Aisin Asia Pte Ltd
AT India Auto Parts Pvt Ltd
Aisin Tianlin Body Parts Co Ltd
Aisin Al Brasil Industria Automotiva Ltda
Aisin Holdings of America Inc

CONTACTS: *Note: Officers with more than one job title may be intentionally listed here more than once.*

Kiyotaka Ise, Pres.
Shinzo Kobuki, Exec. VP
Takashi Morita, Exec. VP
Makoto Mitsuya, Exec. VP
Toshikazu Nagura, Exec. VP
Kanshiro Toyoda, Chmn.

GROWTH PLANS/SPECIAL FEATURES:

Aisin Seiki Co., Ltd. primarily develops and manufactures automotive parts and household appliance products. The firm operates in three business units: automotive parts, lifestyle- and energy-related products, and wellness-related products. The automotive parts business manufactures and sells drivetrains, auto body parts, brakes, chassis, engines and information technology auto-related products. The lifestyle- and energy-related business manufactures and sells sewing machines, beds, gas heat pumps and more. The wellness-related business manufactures and sells: fiber laser, a processing laser that uses a femto-second pulse to enable processing that minimally causes heat damage to the peripheral area and micro-fabrication of transparent and ultra-hard materials, which are traditionally difficult to work with. This division is also developing a 3-wheel personal mobility vehicle that resembles a combination of an upright scooter and a Segway. Aisin Seiki comprises 210 subsidiaries, approximately 82 in Japan and 128 overseas, including the Americas, Asia, Europe and Australia (as of mid-2018). Subsidiaries include: Aisin Europe Manufacturing (UK) Ltd.; Aisin Europe SA; Advics South Africa Pty. Ltd.; Aisin Asia Pte. Ltd.; AT India Auto Parts Pvt. Ltd.; Aisin Tianlin Body Parts Co., Ltd.; Aisin Al Brasil Industria Automotiva Ltda.; and Aisin Holdings of America, Inc. In December 2018, Aisin and Denso Corporation agreed to form a new company to develop and sell driving modules used for electric vehicles. The new company is to be named BluE Nexus, and scheduled to be founded in April 2019.

FINANCIAL DATA: *Note: Data for latest year may not have been available at press time.*

In U.S. $	2018	2017	2016	2015	2014	2013
Revenue	35,921,130,000	32,738,670,000	29,803,140,000	27,237,370,000	25,934,710,000	
R&D Expense						
Operating Income	2,332,375,000	2,101,562,000	1,621,375,000	1,523,203,000	1,573,222,000	
Operating Margin %	.06%	.06%	.10%	.10%	.11%	
SGA Expense	2,660,743,000	2,840,691,000	402,545,500	369,656,300	352,913,100	
Net Income	1,236,455,000	1,163,876,000	891,141,300	710,512,800	827,871,700	
Operating Cash Flow	2,862,911,000	3,628,120,000	2,685,104,000	2,203,373,000	2,633,762,000	
Capital Expenditure	2,437,502,000	2,588,072,000	2,450,993,000	2,210,375,000	1,795,571,000	
EBITDA	4,536,703,000	4,105,946,000	3,516,127,000	3,227,614,000	3,168,048,000	
Return on Assets %	.04%	.03%	.03%	.03%	.04%	
Return on Equity %	.11%	.09%	.09%	.07%	.10%	
Debt to Equity	0.329	0.319	0.29	0.276	0.305	

CONTACT INFORMATION:

Phone: 81-566-24-8441 Fax:
Toll-Free:
Address: 2-1, Asahi-machi, Kariya, Kariya, 448-8650 Japan

STOCK TICKER/OTHER:

Stock Ticker: ASEKF
Exchange: PINX
Employees: 148,359
Fiscal Year Ends: 03/31
Parent Company:

SALARIES/BONUSES:

Top Exec. Salary: $ Bonus: $
Second Exec. Salary: $ Bonus: $

OTHER THOUGHTS:

Estimated Female Officers or Directors:
Hot Spot for Advancement for Women/Minorities:

Allison Transmission Holdings Inc

www.allisontransmission.com

NAIC Code: 336350

TYPES OF BUSINESS:

Automobile Transmission & Power Train Parts Manufacturing

BRANDS/DIVISIONS/AFFILIATES:

CONTACTS: *Note: Officers with more than one job title may be intentionally listed here more than once.*

David Graziosi, CEO
G. Bohley, CFO
Lawrence Dewey, Chairman of the Board
Eric Scroggins, General Counsel
Michael Dick, Senior VP, Divisional
Randall Kirk, Senior VP, Divisional
John Coll, Senior VP, Divisional
Dana Pittard, Vice President, Divisional

GROWTH PLANS/SPECIAL FEATURES:

Allison Transmission Holdings, Inc. designs and manufactures fully-automatic transmissions for medium-and heavy-duty commercial vehicles, medium- and heavy-tactical U.S. military vehicles and hybrid-propulsion systems for transit buses. Although much of its revenues are generated in North America, the company has a global presence in Europe, Asia-Pacific, Middle East, India, South America and Africa, serving customers through an independent network of 1,400 independent distributor and dealer locations. In North America, Allison is one of the largest manufacturers of fully-automatic transmissions for the on-highway medium- and heavy-duty commercial vehicle market. Its core North American on-highway market includes Class 4-5, Class 6-7 and Class 8 straight trucks, conventional transit, shuttle and coach buses, school buses and motorhomes. Allison sells substantially all its transmissions in the North American on-highway market to OEMs, including Daimler AG, PACCAR, Inc. and many others. Off-highway products include products used in vehicles and equipment that serve energy, mining and construction applications. Off-highway energy applications include well-stimulation equipment; hydraulic fracturing equipment; pumping equipment; and well-servicing rigs, which often use a fully-automatic transmission to propel the vehicle and drive auxiliary equipment. During 2018, Allison sold approximately 60% of all fully-automatic transmissions for medium- and heavy-duty on-highway commercial vehicle applications. Allison has a long-standing relationship with the U.S. military, dating back to 1946, when it began developing its first-generation tank transmission. Today, it sells substantially all the transmissions for medium- and heavy-tactical wheeled vehicle platforms, including the family of medium tactical vehicles, armored security vehicles, heavy expanded mobility tactical trucks, heavy equipment transporters, palletized loading systems, M915 series trucks, medium tactical vehicle replacements and the logistic vehicle system replacement. During 2019, Allison acquired Vantage Power and AxleTech's electric vehicle systems division.

FINANCIAL DATA: *Note: Data for latest year may not have been available at press time.*

In U.S. $	2018	2017	2016	2015	2014	2013
Revenue	2,713,000,000	2,262,000,000	1,840,200,000	1,985,800,000	2,127,400,000	1,926,800,000
R&D Expense	131,000,000	105,000,000	88,800,000	92,500,000	103,800,000	97,100,000
Operating Income	923,000,000	679,000,000	452,300,000	527,100,000	530,100,000	415,100,000
Operating Margin %		.30%	.25%	.26%	.25%	.21%
SGA Expense	364,000,000	342,000,000	323,900,000	317,100,000	344,600,000	334,900,000
Net Income	639,000,000	504,000,000	214,900,000	182,300,000	228,600,000	165,400,000
Operating Cash Flow	837,000,000	658,000,000	590,800,000	579,900,000	556,900,000	453,500,000
Capital Expenditure						
EBITDA	1,090,000,000	800,000,000	618,800,000	614,700,000	700,000,000	603,800,000
Return on Assets %		.12%	.05%	.04%	.05%	.03%
Return on Equity %		.57%	.19%	.14%	.16%	.12%
Debt to Equity		3.678	1.987	1.979	1.79	1.849

CONTACT INFORMATION:

Phone: 317 242-5000 Fax:
Toll-Free:
Address: 1 Allison Way, Indianapolis, IN 46222 United States

STOCK TICKER/OTHER:

Stock Ticker: ALSN
Employees: 2,600
Parent Company:
Exchange: NYS
Fiscal Year Ends: 12/31

SALARIES/BONUSES:

Top Exec. Salary: $758,333 Bonus: $500,000
Second Exec. Salary: $418,333 Bonus: $75,000

OTHER THOUGHTS:

Estimated Female Officers or Directors: 2
Hot Spot for Advancement for Women/Minorities:

Ally Financial Inc

www.ally.com

NAIC Code: 522220

TYPES OF BUSINESS:

Automobile Financing
Banking
Corporate Financial Services

BRANDS/DIVISIONS/AFFILIATES:

Ally Bank
Ally CashBack Credit Card
Ally Invest

GROWTH PLANS/SPECIAL FEATURES:

Ally Financial, Inc. is a digital financial services company with $178.9 billion in assets, as of December 31, 2018. The firm offers a wide range of financial services and insurance products to automotive dealerships and consumers. Its online bank, Ally Bank, offers mortgage lending services and a variety of deposit and other banking products, including savings, money market accounts, checking accounts, certificates of deposits and individual retirement accounts (IRAs). Ally also supports the Ally CashBack Credit Card; offers securities brokerage and investment advisory services through Ally Invest; and offers capital for equity sponsors and middle-market companies.

CONTACTS: *Note: Officers with more than one job title may be intentionally listed here more than once.*

Jeffrey Brown, CEO
Jennifer LaClair, CFO
David Debrunner, Chief Accounting Officer
Jason Schugel, Chief Risk Officer
Franklin Hobbs, Director
Scott Stengel, General Counsel
Douglas Timmerman, President, Divisional
Diane Morais, President, Divisional

FINANCIAL DATA: *Note: Data for latest year may not have been available at press time.*

In U.S. $	2018	2017	2016	2015	2014	2013
Revenue	6,662,000,000	6,889,000,000	7,099,000,000	7,336,000,000	6,999,000,000	6,201,000,000
R&D Expense						
Operating Income						
Operating Margin %						
SGA Expense	2,525,000,000	2,418,000,000	2,245,000,000	2,134,000,000	2,298,000,000	2,449,000,000
Net Income	1,263,000,000	929,000,000	1,067,000,000	1,289,000,000	1,150,000,000	361,000,000
Operating Cash Flow	4,150,000,000	4,079,000,000	4,567,000,000	5,095,000,000	3,403,000,000	2,501,000,000
Capital Expenditure	3,709,000,000	4,052,000,000	3,274,000,000	4,685,000,000	9,884,000,000	9,196,000,000
EBITDA						
Return on Assets %		.01%	.01%	-.01%	.01%	.00%
Return on Equity %		.07%	.08%	-.10%	.07%	-.05%
Debt to Equity		3.277	4.065	5.198	4.706	5.363

CONTACT INFORMATION:

Phone: 866-710-4623 Fax: 815-282-6156
Toll-Free: 877-247-2559
Address: 500 Woodward Ave., 10/Fl, Ally Detroit Center, Detroit, MI 48226 United States

STOCK TICKER/OTHER:

Stock Ticker: ALLY
Employees: 7,600
Parent Company:
Exchange: NYS
Fiscal Year Ends: 12/31

SALARIES/BONUSES:

Top Exec. Salary: $1,000,000 Bonus: $3,000,000
Second Exec. Salary: $600,001 Bonus: $1,150,000

OTHER THOUGHTS:

Estimated Female Officers or Directors: 7
Hot Spot for Advancement for Women/Minorities: Y

Alps Alpine Co Ltd

www.alps.com

NAIC Code: 335313

TYPES OF BUSINESS:

Electronic Components Manufacturing
Automotive Parts Manufacturing

BRANDS/DIVISIONS/AFFILIATES:

GlidePoint
Alps Electric Co Ltd

CONTACTS: *Note: Officers with more than one job title may be intentionally listed here more than once.*

Toshihiro Kuriyama, Pres.
Nobuhiko Komeya, Sr. Managing Dir.
Shuji Takamura, Managing Dir.
Takashi Kimoto, Managing Dir.
Masataka Kataoka, Chmn.

GROWTH PLANS/SPECIAL FEATURES:

Alps Alpine Co., Ltd. (formerly Alps Electric Co., Ltd.) is primarily engaged in the manufacture and sale of more than 40,000 types of electronic components used in a variety of applications. The company operates in four divisions: automotive, home & mobile, healthcare and environment & energy. The automotive division provides custom products and modules such as control panels and steering modules for specific vehicle models, as well as components compatible for any vehicle. The home & mobile division provides switches, potentiometers, sensors and other components through to multi-input devices like touch panels and GlidePoint trackpad technology to home, mobile and personal computer (PC) markets. The healthcare division offers light, temperature, humidity and various other types of sensors for the detection of environmental changes to assist health maintenance. For example, the light, temperature and humidity products help prevent heat disorders; and switches, card connectors, switches and other components support the evolution of healthcare equipment. Last, the environment & energy division serves environment and energy markets with sensors that enable power usage visualization, as well as sensors for measuring parameters such as temperature, illuminance and carbon dioxide levels in indoor and outdoor environments. These can be combined with communication modules essential for xEMS to build smart networks. In January 2019, Alps Electric merged its departments under a single name, Alps Alpine Co., Ltd.

FINANCIAL DATA: *Note: Data for latest year may not have been available at press time.*

In U.S. $	2018	2017	2016	2015	2014	2013
Revenue	7,887,493,000	6,922,092,000	7,113,013,000	6,879,379,000	6,288,936,000	
R&D Expense						
Operating Income	660,797,600	407,774,300	480,867,500	491,950,000	262,166,900	
Operating Margin %	.08%	.06%	.07%	.07%	.04%	
SGA Expense						
Net Income	435,489,800	320,896,900	358,702,400	319,233,600	131,510,800	
Operating Cash Flow	646,820,400	382,310,200	495,846,400	598,336,700	530,261,000	
Capital Expenditure	618,526,000	436,326,000	328,395,500	280,830,800	223,534,300	
EBITDA	937,272,600	763,425,900	915,484,400	765,493,500	523,047,200	
Return on Assets %	.07%	.06%	.07%	.06%	.03%	
Return on Equity %	.17%	.14%	.19%	.22%	.11%	
Debt to Equity	0.111	0.101	0.085	0.251	0.621	

CONTACT INFORMATION:

Phone: 81-33726-1211 Fax: 81-33728-1741
Toll-Free:
Address: 1-7 Yukigaya Otsuka-cho, Ota-Ku, Tokyo, 145-8501 Japan

STOCK TICKER/OTHER:

Stock Ticker: APELY Exchange: PINX
Employees: 47,738 Fiscal Year Ends: 03/31
Parent Company:

SALARIES/BONUSES:

Top Exec. Salary: $ Bonus: $
Second Exec. Salary: $ Bonus: $

OTHER THOUGHTS:

Estimated Female Officers or Directors:
Hot Spot for Advancement for Women/Minorities:

AM General LLC

www.amgeneral.com

NAIC Code: 336120

TYPES OF BUSINESS:

Military Vehicle Manufacturing
Diesel Engines

BRANDS/DIVISIONS/AFFILIATES:

MacAndrews & Forbes Holdings Inc
Renco Group LLC
High Mobility Multipurpose Wheeled Vehicle
Humvee
Hummer
Mandus Group

CONTACTS: *Note: Officers with more than one job title may be intentionally listed here more than once.*

R. Andrew Hove, CEO
Stephen Zink, COO
Robert Gold, CFO
Kevin A. Rahrig, Exec. VP-Commercial
Mark Minne, Chief Admin. Officer
Ricky R. Smith, Pres., Comm. Bus.
Daniel J. Dell'Orto, Exec. VP-Gov't Rel.
Mark A. Whalen, Sr. VP-Oper.
Thomas R. Douglas, Sr. VP-Bus. Dev. & Strategy

GROWTH PLANS/SPECIAL FEATURES:

AM General, LLC designs, engineers and manufactures specialized vehicles for military and commercial customers worldwide. The company's most recognized product is the military High Mobility Multipurpose Wheeled Vehicle (HMMWV), called the Humvee, and its now discontinued civilian counterparts, the Hummer H1, H2 and H3. The Humvee is sold to the armed forces of over 70 countries and to domestic agencies like the National Guard and Border Patrol. AM General, General Motors and Mercedes-Benz were partners in the marketing and distribution of the company's commercial vehicles, as an original equipment manufacturer (OEM) and as a contract manufacturer. AM General's products and services are grouped into three segments: U.S. defense, international defense and commercial. The U.S. defense segment produces a complete line of M1100 series expanded capacity vehicles, as well as M997 ambulances and M1097 payload cargo and troop carriers for U.S. forces. This division also provides vehicle modernization/re-manufacturing services. The international defense segment offers the Humvee and other light tactical vehicles for export through AM General's direct purchase program or through the U.S. Foreign Military Sales program. This division also provides full lifecycle support, such as OEM parts, components, kits, training and technical services. The commercial vehicles segment assembles vehicles for U.S.-based vehicle OEMs who need help with rapid ramp-up of vehicles production, excess and carryover volume, specialty vehicles runs and other situations. In addition, Am General provides technical manuals, training, maintenance planning, parts, components, kits and more for its military and commercial vehicles. AM General is owned by MacAndrews & Forbes Holdings, Inc. and Renco Group, LLC. In late-2018, AM General announced that it made an investment in Mandus Group, an innovator of artillery solutions based on soft recoil technology.

FINANCIAL DATA: *Note: Data for latest year may not have been available at press time.*

In U.S. $	2018	2017	2016	2015	2014	2013
Revenue	2,480,625,000	2,362,500,000	2,250,000,000	2,100,000,000	1,900,000,000	1,868,740,000
R&D Expense						
Operating Income						
Operating Margin %						
SGA Expense						
Net Income						
Operating Cash Flow						
Capital Expenditure						
EBITDA						
Return on Assets %						
Return on Equity %						
Debt to Equity						

CONTACT INFORMATION:

Phone: 574-237-6222 Fax: 574-284-2819
Toll-Free:
Address: 105 N. Niles Ave., South Bend, IN 46617 United States

STOCK TICKER/OTHER:

Stock Ticker: Private Exchange:
Employees: 2,550 Fiscal Year Ends: 12/31
Parent Company: MacAndrews & Forbes Inc

SALARIES/BONUSES:

Top Exec. Salary: $ Bonus: $
Second Exec. Salary: $ Bonus: $

OTHER THOUGHTS:

Estimated Female Officers or Directors:
Hot Spot for Advancement for Women/Minorities:

AMERCO (U-Haul)

www.amerco.com

NAIC Code: 532120

TYPES OF BUSINESS:

Truck Rental & Leasing Services
Moving & Storage Services & Supplies
Property & Casualty Insurance
Life Insurance
Annuities
Self-Storage Properties
Propane Tank Refilling
Car Sharing Services

BRANDS/DIVISIONS/AFFILIATES:

U-Haul International Inc
Amerco Real Estate Company
Repwest Insurance Company
Oxford Life Insurance Company
Uhaul.com
Safemove
Safetow
Safestor

CONTACTS:
Note: Officers with more than one job title may be intentionally listed here more than once.

Jason Berg, CFO
Edward Shoen, Chairman of the Board
Samuel Shoen, Director
Laurence Derespino, General Counsel
Mark Haydukovich, President, Subsidiary
John Taylor, President, Subsidiary
Carlos Vizcarra, President, Subsidiary
Douglas Bell, President, Subsidiary

GROWTH PLANS/SPECIAL FEATURES:

AMERCO is a holding company operating through four primary subsidiaries: U-Haul International, Inc.; Amerco Real Estate Company; Repwest Insurance Company; and Oxford Life Insurance Company. Accordingly, the firm has three reportable business segments: moving and storage, property and casualty insurance and life insurance. Moving and storage consists of U-Haul, with its rental equipment fleet of trucks, trailers and tow dollies offered at 1,790 company operated locations and 20,000 independent dealer outlets. It also provides furniture pads, utility dollies and hand trucks; sells a wide selection of moving supplies; and offers protection packages for moving and storage. U-Haul owns more than 160,000 trucks, 118,000 trailers and 42,000 towing devices. The firm's Uhaul.com online reservation portal allows its self-storage customers to make reservations, access all U-Haul storage centers and affiliate partners. This segment is also operated by Amerco Real Estate Company, which manages 632,000 rentable rooms comprising 55.2 million square feet of rentable storage space located in North America. The property and casualty insurance segment, operated by Repwest Insurance Company, provides loss adjusting and claims handling for U-Haul through regional offices across North America. This segment also underwrites components of the Safemove, Safetow, Safestor and Safestor Mobile protection packages to U-Haul customers. The life insurance segment, operated by Oxford Life Insurance Company, provides life and health insurance products primarily to the senior market through the direct writing and reinsuring of life insurance, Medicare supplement and annuity policies.

FINANCIAL DATA:
Note: Data for latest year may not have been available at press time.

In U.S. $	2018	2017	2016	2015	2014	2013
Revenue	3,601,114,000	3,421,767,000	3,275,656,000	3,074,531,000	2,835,252,000	
R&D Expense						
Operating Income	568,905,000	742,263,000	866,814,000	663,024,000	630,214,000	
Operating Margin %	.16%	.22%	.26%	.22%	.22%	
SGA Expense						
Net Income	790,583,000	398,424,000	489,001,000	356,741,000	342,391,000	
Operating Cash Flow	936,328,000	1,020,061,000	1,041,063,000	808,190,000	709,504,000	
Capital Expenditure	1,363,745,000	1,419,505,000	1,509,154,000	1,111,899,000	999,365,000	
EBITDA	1,315,521,000	1,219,839,000	1,252,972,000	1,008,244,000	919,832,000	
Return on Assets %	.08%	.05%	.07%	.06%	.06%	
Return on Equity %	.26%	.16%	.24%	.21%	.25%	
Debt to Equity	1.031	1.245	1.194	1.163	1.272	

CONTACT INFORMATION:

Phone: 775-688-6300 Fax: 775 688-6338
Toll-Free:
Address: 5555 Kietzke Ln., Ste. 100, Reno, NV 89511 United States

STOCK TICKER/OTHER:

Stock Ticker: UHAL
Exchange: NAS
Employees: 28,300
Fiscal Year Ends: 03/31
Parent Company:

SALARIES/BONUSES:

Top Exec. Salary: $675,004 Bonus: $215,000
Second Exec. Salary: $410,777 Bonus: $200,000

OTHER THOUGHTS:

Estimated Female Officers or Directors: 1
Hot Spot for Advancement for Women/Minorities:

American Axle & Manufacturing Holdings Inc

www.aam.com

NAIC Code: 336300

TYPES OF BUSINESS:

Automotive Components Manufacturing
Driveline Systems
Chassis Systems
Forged Products

BRANDS/DIVISIONS/AFFILIATES:

CONTACTS:

Note: Officers with more than one job title may be intentionally listed here more than once.

David Dauch, CEO
Christopher May, CFO
James Zaliwski, Chief Accounting Officer
Michael Lynch, Controller
David Barnes, General Counsel
Michael Simonte, President
Timothy Bowes, President, Divisional
Norman Willemse, President, Divisional
Gregory Deveson, President, Divisional
David Buckley, President, Geographical
James Voeffray, Senior VP, Divisional
Tolga Oal, Senior VP, Divisional
Terri Kemp, Vice President, Divisional

GROWTH PLANS/SPECIAL FEATURES:

American Axle & Manufacturing Holdings, Inc. (AAM) is a Tier I supplier to the automotive industry. The company designs, engineers and manufactures driveline, metal forming, powertrain and casting products, operating at more than 90 facilities in 17 countries. AAM divides its operations into four reportable segments: driveline, metal forming, powertrain and casting. Driveline products consist primarily of axles, driveshafts, power transfer units, rear drive modules, transfer cases, and electric and hybrid driveline products and systems for light trucks, SUVs, crossover vehicles, passenger cars and commercial vehicles. Metal forming products consist primarily of axle and transmission shafts, ring and pinion gears, differential gears, transmission gears and shafts and suspension components for original equipment manufacturers (OEM) and Tier 1 automotive suppliers. The Powertrain segment products consist primarily of transmission module and differential assemblies, transmission valve bodies, connecting rod forging and assemblies, torsional vibration dampers and variable valve timing products for OEM and Tier I automotive suppliers. The Casting segment produces both thin wall castings and high strength ductile iron castings, as well as differential cases, steering knuckles, control arms, brackets, and turbo charger housings for the global light vehicle, commercial and industrial markets. AAM is the principal supplier of driveline components to General Motors Company (GM) for its full-size rear-wheel drive light trucks and SUVs manufactured in North America, supplying substantially all of GM's rear axle and front four-wheel drive/all-wheel drive axle requirements for these vehicle platforms. Sales to GM accounted for approximately 41% of the company's revenues in 2018. The company also supplies driveline system products to FCA US LLC for: the heavy-duty Ram full-size pickups and its derivatives; the AWD Jeep Cherokee; and a passenger car driveshaft program. Sales to FCA accounted for approximately 13% of the company's net sales in 2018.

AAM offers comprehensive benefits.

FINANCIAL DATA:

Note: Data for latest year may not have been available at press time.

In U.S. $	2018	2017	2016	2015	2014	2013
Revenue	7,270,400,000	6,266,000,000	3,948,000,000	3,903,100,000	3,696,000,000	3,207,300,000
R&D Expense						
Operating Income	655,300,000	653,700,000	406,900,000	358,100,000	267,600,000	240,300,000
Operating Margin %		.10%	.10%	.09%	.07%	.07%
SGA Expense	385,700,000	390,100,000	319,200,000	277,300,000	255,200,000	238,400,000
Net Income	-57,500,000	337,100,000	240,700,000	235,600,000	143,000,000	94,500,000
Operating Cash Flow	771,500,000	647,000,000	407,600,000	377,600,000	318,400,000	223,000,000
Capital Expenditure	525,200,000	491,000,000	227,600,000	193,500,000	206,500,000	251,900,000
EBITDA	631,200,000	964,100,000	594,200,000	570,300,000	476,500,000	379,200,000
Return on Assets %		.06%	.07%	.07%	.04%	.03%
Return on Equity %		.32%	.57%	1.11%	1.91%	
Debt to Equity		2.584	2.643	4.563	13.434	46.402

CONTACT INFORMATION:

Phone: 313 758-2000 Fax: 313 974-3090
Toll-Free: 800-299-2953
Address: 1 Dauch Dr., Detroit, MI 48211 United States

STOCK TICKER/OTHER:

Stock Ticker: AXL
Exchange: NYS
Employees: 9,200
Fiscal Year Ends: 12/31
Parent Company:

SALARIES/BONUSES:

Top Exec. Salary: $1,150,000 Bonus: $
Second Exec. Salary: $750,000 Bonus: $

OTHER THOUGHTS:

Estimated Female Officers or Directors: 2
Hot Spot for Advancement for Women/Minorities:

American Honda Motor Co Inc

www.hondainamerica.com

NAIC Code: 336111

TYPES OF BUSINESS:

Automotive Manufacturing
Motorcycles & ATVs
Power Equipment
Marine Engines
Parts Manufacturing & Retail
Research & Development

BRANDS/DIVISIONS/AFFILIATES:

Honda Motor Co Ltd
Honda of America Manufacturing Inc
Accord
Civic
CR-V
Insight
Ridgeline
HondaJet

CONTACTS: *Note: Officers with more than one job title may be intentionally listed here more than once.*

Mikoshiba Toshiaki, CEO
Tetsuo Iwamura, Pres.
Bruce Smith, Sr. VP-Parts & Svcs. Div.
Michael Accavitti, Sr. VP-Auto Oper.
Steven Center, VP-Environmental Bus. Dev. Office
Sage Marie, Sr. Mgr.-Public Rel.
Michael Ryan, VP-Finance
Robyn Eagles, Mgr.-Honda Public Rel.
Gary Robinson, Mgr.-Acura Advertising
Dave Speck, VP-Tech Coordination Product, Regulatory Office
Tom Peyton, Assistant VP-Auto Advertising

GROWTH PLANS/SPECIAL FEATURES:

American Honda Motor Co., Inc. manufactures and sells automobiles, motorcycles, ATVs, personal watercraft, marine engines, lawn care equipment, snow equipment, generators and water pumps. It is the U.S. subsidiary of Honda Motor Co., Ltd. The company's car models include the Accord, Civic, CR-V, Insight, Odyssey, Pilot and Ridgeline. In addition, Honda owns the Acura brand of vehicles, with nearly two-thirds of the Honda and Acura vehicles sold in the U.S. being manufactured in the U.S. Other Power Sport products include offroad bikes, ATVs, the Side by Side and scooters. Through Honda of America Manufacturing Inc., the firm operates engine, transmission, automobile, motorcycle, ATV and power equipment plants. Additionally, in North Carolina, American Honda manufactures the HondaJet aircraft. In 2018, the firm produced 1.24 million cars and light trucks, 1.44 million automobile engines, 1.185 million transmissions, 1.69 million general purpose engines, 535,000 power equipment products and 74,000 ATVs. Through Honda R&D Americas, Inc., American Honda operates office, testing and research/development facilities in North Carolina, Colorado, Ohio, California, Michigan and Toronto. Its 12 manufacturing plants are in Ohio, Alabama, Georgia, Indiana, South Carolina and North Carolina.

Employee benefits include tuition reimbursement, comprehensive health care plans, pre-tax spending accounts, retirement plans, same-sex domestic-partner benefits and onsite wellness/fitness facilities.

FINANCIAL DATA: *Note: Data for latest year may not have been available at press time.*

In U.S. $	2018	2017	2016	2015	2014	2013
Revenue	53,823,840,000	51,260,800,000	61,551,806,117	60,557,038,000	52,624,765,000	45,043,300,000
R&D Expense						
Operating Income						
Operating Margin %						
SGA Expense						
Net Income			1,525,529,259	1,801,247,748	3,330,926,576	2,052,150,000
Operating Cash Flow						
Capital Expenditure						
EBITDA						
Return on Assets %						
Return on Equity %						
Debt to Equity						

CONTACT INFORMATION:

Phone: 310-783-2000 Fax: 310-783-3023
Toll-Free: 800-999-1009
Address: 1919 Torrance Blvd., Torrance, CA 90501 United States

STOCK TICKER/OTHER:

Stock Ticker: Subsidiary
Exchange:
Employees: 31,000
Fiscal Year Ends: 03/31
Parent Company: Honda Motor Co Ltd

SALARIES/BONUSES:

Top Exec. Salary: $ Bonus: $
Second Exec. Salary: $ Bonus: $

OTHER THOUGHTS:

Estimated Female Officers or Directors: 2
Hot Spot for Advancement for Women/Minorities:

American Tire Distributors Inc

www.atd-us.com

NAIC Code: 423130

TYPES OF BUSINESS:

Tires & Related Products, Distribution

BRANDS/DIVISIONS/AFFILIATES:

American Tire Distributors Holdings Inc
ATDOnline
TireBuyer.com

CONTACTS: *Note: Officers with more than one job title may be intentionally listed here more than once.*

Stuart Schuette, CEO
Michael Gaither, General Counsel
Phillip Marrett, Exec. VP-Product Planning & Positioning
Daniel Brown, Pres., Tire Pros

GROWTH PLANS/SPECIAL FEATURES:

American Tire Distributors, Inc. (ATD) is one of the nation's largest suppliers of tires and wheels as well as tools and other automotive service equipment. The company serves the replacement tire market through approximately 140 distribution centers in Canada and the U.S., and a fleet of 1,500 delivery vehicles, delivering products to approximately 80,000 customers. ATD distributes more than 40 million replacement tires each year. ATD offers its tire retailers and service shop clients various tires for passenger vehicles and light trucks, tractor-trailers, buses, farm machinery and specialty and recreational vehicles. The company carries brands including Michelin, Continental, BFGoodrich and Bridgestone. Its wheel division offers rims in a range of sizes for passenger vehicles and light trucks. The firm maintains ATDOnline, which offers dealers access to prices, availability and the ability to place orders 24 hours a day, seven days a week; and TireBuyer.com, where customers can buy tires and wheels as well as choose a dealer location for installation. TireBuyer.com also allows potential purchasers to view tires and wheels on their particular vehicle, using the website's 3D visualizer. ATD operates as a subsidiary of American Tire Distributors Holdings, Inc. In December 2018, ATD announced that it had successfully completed its financial recapitalization and emerged from Chapter 11 bankruptcy protection.

FINANCIAL DATA: *Note: Data for latest year may not have been available at press time.*

In U.S. $	2018	2017	2016	2015	2014	2013
Revenue	5,565,000,000	5,300,000,000	5,000,000,000	4,800,000,000	5,030,698,000	3,839,269,000
R&D Expense						
Operating Income						
Operating Margin %						
SGA Expense						
Net Income			-92,256,933	-95,800,000	-94,599,999	-6,357,000
Operating Cash Flow						
Capital Expenditure						
EBITDA						
Return on Assets %						
Return on Equity %						
Debt to Equity						

CONTACT INFORMATION:

Phone: 704-992-2000 Fax: 704-992-1384
Toll-Free: 800-222-1167
Address: 12200 Herbert Wayne Ct., Ste. 150, Huntersville, NC 28070 United States

STOCK TICKER/OTHER:

Stock Ticker: Subsidiary Exchange:
Employees: 5,000 Fiscal Year Ends: 01/04
Parent Company: American Tire Distributors Holdings Inc

SALARIES/BONUSES:

Top Exec. Salary: $ Bonus: $
Second Exec. Salary: $ Bonus: $

OTHER THOUGHTS:

Estimated Female Officers or Directors:
Hot Spot for Advancement for Women/Minorities:

Americas Car-Mart Inc

www.car-mart.com

NAIC Code: 441110

TYPES OF BUSINESS:

Used Auto Dealers, Retail
Used Car Financing & Servicing

BRANDS/DIVISIONS/AFFILIATES:

America's Car-Mart of Arkansas
Colonial Auto Finance Inc

CONTACTS: *Note: Officers with more than one job title may be intentionally listed here more than once.*

Jeffery Williams, CEO
Vickie Judy, CFO
Ray Dillon, Chairman of the Board

GROWTH PLANS/SPECIAL FEATURES:

America's Car-Mart, Inc. is one of the largest publicly-held automotive retailers focused exclusively on the integrated auto sales and finance segment of the used car market. As of mid-2019, America's Car-Mart operates approximately 145 dealerships located primarily in small cities throughout the South-Central United States. However, the company does have several dealerships in larger cities such as Tulsa, Oklahoma; Lexington, Kentucky; Springfield; Missouri; and Little Rock, Arkansas. The firm operates primarily through its two subsidiaries, America's Car-Mart of Arkansas; and Colonial Auto Finance, Inc. The company targets credit-impaired borrowers living in small to midsize cities and towns who would typically not qualify for conventional financing. Stores are run on a decentralized basis, with each dealership responsible for purchasing (with the help of a corporate buyer), making credit decisions, servicing vehicles and collecting the installment loans it originates. The company operates both regular and satellite stores. Satellite stores tend to be smaller, sell fewer vehicles and have their financing reported with the corresponding regular stores that sponsor them. On average, the firm's dealerships typically maintain an inventory of between 20-90 vehicles. Most of the company's vehicles are purchased through wholesalers, new car dealers, individuals and from auctions. Generally, the firm's buyers purchase vehicles that are between five and 12 years old with 70,000-150,000 miles, paying anywhere from $4,000-$12,000 per vehicle. The company's most popular vehicles sold include the Chevrolet Impala, Chevrolet Malibu, Dodge Charger, Chrysler Minivan, Ford Focus, Ford Taurus, Ford Fusion, Dodge Ram Pickup and Ford F-150 pickup.

FINANCIAL DATA: *Note: Data for latest year may not have been available at press time.*

In U.S. $	2018	2017	2016	2015	2014	2013
Revenue	612,201,000	587,751,000	567,906,000	530,321,000	489,187,000	
R&D Expense						
Operating Income	38,997,000	33,446,000	18,867,000	47,051,000	33,748,000	
Operating Margin %	-.06%	-.06%	-.08%	-.02%	-.04%	
SGA Expense	99,023,000	91,940,000	92,242,000	83,802,000	78,591,000	
Net Income	36,509,000	20,205,000	11,596,000	29,490,000	21,129,000	
Operating Cash Flow	9,994,000	7,334,000	14,286,000	12,387,000	21,875,000	
Capital Expenditure	2,258,000	1,587,000	4,526,000	4,009,000	7,095,000	
EBITDA	43,247,000	37,718,000	23,075,000	50,881,000	37,033,000	
Return on Assets %	.08%	.05%	.03%	.08%	.06%	
Return on Equity %	.16%	.09%	.05%	.13%	.10%	
Debt to Equity	0.66	0.506	0.472	0.448	0.456	

CONTACT INFORMATION:

Phone: 497 464-9944 Fax: 479 273-7556
Toll-Free:
Address: 802 SE Plaza Ave., Ste. 200, Bentonville, AR 72712 United States

STOCK TICKER/OTHER:

Stock Ticker: CRMT
Employees: 1,504
Parent Company:
Exchange: NAS
Fiscal Year Ends: 04/30

SALARIES/BONUSES:

Top Exec. Salary: $440,962 Bonus: $
Second Exec. Salary: $232,308 Bonus: $75,000

OTHER THOUGHTS:

Estimated Female Officers or Directors:
Hot Spot for Advancement for Women/Minorities:

Ancira Enterprises

NAIC Code: 441110

www.ancira.com

TYPES OF BUSINESS:

Auto Dealers, Retail
Used Vehicle Sales
Truck & RV Sales
Body Shops

BRANDS/DIVISIONS/AFFILIATES:

Ancira Buick GMC
Ancira Chevrolet
Ancira Ford
Ancira Kia
Ancira Mitsubishi
Ancira Nissan
Ancira Volkswagen
Ancira RV

CONTACTS:

Note: Officers with more than one job title may be intentionally listed here more than once.

Diego Itrube, General Manager
Betty Ferguson, CFO
Greg Spence, Exec. VP

GROWTH PLANS/SPECIAL FEATURES:

Ancira Enterprises is a private car, truck and recreational vehicle dealer in Texas. The company has 10 car dealerships and a recreational vehicle dealership predominately located in the greater San Antonio area. Ancira's car dealerships include Ancira Buick GMC, Ancira Chevrolet, Ancira CJDR, Ancira Ford, Ancira Kia, Ancira Mitsubishi, Ancira Nissan and Ancira Volkswagen. The firm also has a used car and trucks division and a body shop, one of the largest in South Texas. Ancira RV, located in Boerne, Texas, sells new and used campers, motorhomes and recreational vehicles. These include diesel motorhomes, class A, B and C motorhomes, fifth wheels and travel trailers from Winnebago, Fleetwood, Itasca, Allegro and others. Ancira RV also sells parts and accessories for RVs, including bathroom parts, beds, kitchen items, lights, electronics, wheels and brakes as well as accessories such as camping and hiking gear, flags and flag holders, games, grills and accessories, outdoor furniture cleaners, patio accessories, picnic supplies, books, CDs, coffee makers and health and beauty products. Ancira accepts trade-in vehicles with financing and offers free 23-point vehicle inspections. The company's repair technicians are industry certified in the use of the Genesis System, a computerized and laser-based structure and frame measuring tool, and are also equipped with the Speis Hecker Paint Color Match System. Besides its Ancira dealerships in San Antonio, the firm also has dealerships in Boerne, Floresville, Laredo and Eagle Pass, Texas.

FINANCIAL DATA:

Note: Data for latest year may not have been available at press time.

In U.S. $	2018	2017	2016	2015	2014	2013
Revenue	1,323,000,000	1,260,000,000	1,200,000,000	1,100,000,000	1,078,000,000	975,750,000
R&D Expense						
Operating Income						
Operating Margin %						
SGA Expense						
Net Income						
Operating Cash Flow						
Capital Expenditure						
EBITDA						
Return on Assets %						
Return on Equity %						
Debt to Equity						

CONTACT INFORMATION:

Phone: 210-681-4900 Fax: 210-681-9413
Toll-Free: 800-972-5374
Address: 6111 Bandera Rd., San Antonio, TX 78241 United States

STOCK TICKER/OTHER:

Stock Ticker: Private
Employees: 870
Parent Company:
Exchange:
Fiscal Year Ends: 12/31

SALARIES/BONUSES:

Top Exec. Salary: $ Bonus: $
Second Exec. Salary: $ Bonus: $

OTHER THOUGHTS:

Estimated Female Officers or Directors: 2
Hot Spot for Advancement for Women/Minorities:

Applied Industrial Technologies Inc

www.applied.com

NAIC Code: 336300

TYPES OF BUSINESS:

Industrial Component Distribution
Automotive Parts & Products, Distribution
Engineering & Maintenance Services

BRANDS/DIVISIONS/AFFILIATES:

Olympus Controls Corp

CONTACTS:

Note: Officers with more than one job title may be intentionally listed here more than once.

Neil Schrimsher, CEO
David Wells, CFO
Peter Wallace, Chairman of the Board
Christopher Macey, Chief Accounting Officer
Warren Hoffner, General Manager, Subsidiary
Kurt Loring, Other Executive Officer
Fred Bauer, Vice President

GROWTH PLANS/SPECIAL FEATURES:

Applied Industrial Technologies, Inc. (AIT) is a North American industrial distributor with operating service centers, distribution centers and specialty repair shops. Its primary products include bearings, power transmission components, fluid power components and systems, industrial rubber products, linear motion components, tools, safety products, oilfield supplies and other industrial and maintenance supplies. AIT is divided into two segments: the service center-based distribution business and the fluid power business. The service center-based distribution segment supplies industrial products across North America, Canada, Australia and New Zealand. This division accounts for 71% of fiscal 2019 sales revenue and serves customers in the upstream oil and gas industry, applied maintenance and supplies industry, and also serves regional fabricated rubber shops. The fluid power business segment consists of specialized regional companies that distribute fluid power components and operate shops in order to assemble fluid power systems and perform equipment repair. This division primarily sells products and services directly to customers rather than through service centers. Its primary products include hydraulic, pneumatic, lubrication and filtration components and systems. AIT operates more than 600 facilities and 11 distribution centers in North America, Australia, New Zealand and Singapore, serving over 4,000 product manufacturers. In August 2019, AIT acquired Olympus Controls Corp., an automation solutions provider of motion control, machine vision and robotic technologies.

The firm offers employees medical, dental, vision and prescription drug coverage; short- and long-term disability; life insurance; retirement; incentive programs; and product discounts.

FINANCIAL DATA:

Note: Data for latest year may not have been available at press time.

In U.S. $	2018	2017	2016	2015	2014	2013
Revenue	3,073,274,000	2,593,746,000	2,519,428,000	2,751,561,000	2,459,878,000	2,462,171,000
R&D Expense						
Operating Income	225,827,000	174,590,000	153,595,000	184,619,000	164,358,000	176,399,000
Operating Margin %		.07%	.06%	.07%	.07%	.07%
SGA Expense	658,168,000	563,105,000	553,827,000	585,195,000	522,568,000	506,563,000
Net Income	141,625,000	133,910,000	29,577,000	115,484,000	112,821,000	118,149,000
Operating Cash Flow	147,304,000	164,619,000	160,992,000	154,538,000	110,110,000	111,397,000
Capital Expenditure	23,230,000	17,045,000	13,130,000	14,933,000	20,190,000	12,214,000
EBITDA	278,723,000	215,474,000	129,528,000	226,367,000	195,162,000	204,020,000
Return on Assets %		.10%	.02%	.08%	.09%	.12%
Return on Equity %		.19%	.04%	.15%	.14%	.17%
Debt to Equity		0.385	0.494	0.428	0.21	

CONTACT INFORMATION:

Phone: 216 426-4000 Fax: 216 426-4884
Toll-Free: 877-279-2799
Address: 1 Applied Plaza, Cleveland, OH 44115 United States

STOCK TICKER/OTHER:

Stock Ticker: AIT
Employees: 5,554
Parent Company:
Exchange: NYS
Fiscal Year Ends: 06/30

SALARIES/BONUSES:

Top Exec. Salary: $875,000 Bonus: $
Second Exec. Salary: $410,000 Bonus: $

OTHER THOUGHTS:

Estimated Female Officers or Directors: 1
Hot Spot for Advancement for Women/Minorities:

Aptiv PLC

www.aptiv.com

NAIC Code: 336300

TYPES OF BUSINESS:

Motor Vehicle Parts Manufacturing
Autonomous Vehicle Technologies
Self-Driving Cars
Robotic Taxis
Smart City Technologies
Internet of Things Technologies

BRANDS/DIVISIONS/AFFILIATES:

Delphi Automotive USA
Delphi Technologies PLC

CONTACTS: *Note: Officers with more than one job title may be intentionally listed here more than once.*

Kevin P. Clark, CEO
William H. Guggina, VP, Global Operations
Joseph R. Massaro, Sr VP, CFO
Wendy F. Miller, SVP, CMO
Matthew Peterson, CIO

GROWTH PLANS/SPECIAL FEATURES:

Aptiv PLC (formerly Delphi Automotive USA) is a technology company engaged in the manufacture of automotive components and systems, as well as developing solutions for next-generation autonomous vehicle, smart city and connectivity purposes. Aptiv operates in two business segments: signal and power solutions, and advanced safety and user experience. The signal and power solutions segment provides the design, manufacture and assembly of a vehicle's electrical architecture, including engineered component products, connectors, wiring assemblies, harnesses, cable management solutions, electrical centers and hybrid high-voltage and safety distribution systems. These signal distribution and computing power products support increased vehicle content, electrification and fuel economy, and reduced emissions. The advanced safety and user experience segment provides components, systems and advanced software for passenger safety, security, comfort and vehicle operation. This division's products and services include body controls, infotainment and connectivity systems, passive and active safety electronics, autonomous driving software and technologies, displays and systems integration. These products increase vehicle connectivity, reduce driver distraction and enhance vehicle safety. Aptiv operates 109 major manufacturing facilities and 14 major technical centers for its global customers, which includes all 25 of the largest automotive original equipment manufacturers (OEMs) in the world. The firm is present in 45 countries. In November 2017, Delphi Automotive USA was renamed Aptiv PLC after Delphi Automotive PLC spun off its powertrain business into a new, independent public company named Delphi Technologies PLC. Aptiv trades on the New York Stock Exchange under ticker symbol APTV. Aptiv has an autonomous vehicle center in Las Vegas where it has been conducting robotic taxi tests with Lyft.

FINANCIAL DATA: *Note: Data for latest year may not have been available at press time.*

In U.S. $	2018	2017	2016	2015	2014	2013
Revenue	14,435,000,000	12,884,000,000	16,661,000,000	15,165,000,000	17,023,000,000	16,463,000,000
R&D Expense						
Operating Income	1,582,000,000	1,545,000,000	2,275,000,000	1,900,000,000	1,991,000,000	1,829,000,000
Operating Margin %		.12%	.14%	.13%	.12%	.11%
SGA Expense	993,000,000	952,000,000	1,145,000,000	1,017,000,000	1,081,000,000	963,000,000
Net Income	1,067,000,000	1,355,000,000	1,257,000,000	1,450,000,000	1,351,000,000	1,212,000,000
Operating Cash Flow	1,628,000,000	1,468,000,000	1,941,000,000	1,703,000,000	2,135,000,000	1,750,000,000
Capital Expenditure	846,000,000	698,000,000	828,000,000	704,000,000	855,000,000	682,000,000
EBITDA	2,151,000,000	1,941,000,000	2,285,000,000	2,175,000,000	2,427,000,000	2,206,000,000
Return on Assets %		.11%	.10%	.13%	.12%	.11%
Return on Equity %		.48%	.54%	.61%	.50%	.46%
Debt to Equity		1.253	1.649	1.758	0.963	0.808

CONTACT INFORMATION:

Phone: 011-44163-423442 Fax:
Toll-Free:
Address: Courteney Rd., Oath Way, Dublin 2, Kent United Kingdom

STOCK TICKER/OTHER:

Stock Ticker: APTV
Employees: 145,000
Parent Company:
Exchange: NYS
Fiscal Year Ends: 12/31

SALARIES/BONUSES:

Top Exec. Salary: $1,375,000 Bonus: $
Second Exec. Salary: $790,500 Bonus: $

OTHER THOUGHTS:

Estimated Female Officers or Directors:
Hot Spot for Advancement for Women/Minorities:

ARBOC Specialty Vehicles LLC

www.arbocsv.com

NAIC Code: 336120

TYPES OF BUSINESS:

Buses (Except Trackless Trolley) Assembling on Chassis of Own Manufacture

BRANDS/DIVISIONS/AFFILIATES:

NFI Group Inc
Spirit of Freedom
Spirit of Mobility
Spirit of Liberty
Spirit of Independence
Spirit of Equess
Spirit of Legacy

CONTACTS: *Note: Officers with more than one job title may be intentionally listed here more than once.*

Don Roberts, Pres.
Del Herr, VP-Oper.
Mel Williams, Dir.-Parts & Svcs.

GROWTH PLANS/SPECIAL FEATURES:

ARBOC Specialty Vehicles, LLC produces specialty vehicles for the low-floor and mobility transportation markets. Its 112,000-square-foot facility in Middlebury, Indiana manufactures six product lines. The Spirit of Freedom ranges in size from 14 to 23 passengers and is equipped with a 34-by-62-inch accessibility ramp, with a single 41-inch exit. Of all the models, the Spirit of Freedom is more basic. The Spirit of Mobility ranges in size from 10 to 19 passengers and is designed with a cutaway chassis, in place of the conventional dropbox, with air-ride suspension and theater seating. It comes with an optional wheelchair ramp and has a standard kneeling feature to permit entrance of less than 5 inches from the curb. The Spirit of Liberty ranges in size from 17 to 29 passengers. This rear engine bus comes equipped with two entrances: a 1:6 Braun 1,000lbs ramp at the front of the bus and an 800-lb Ricon ramp situated between the front and rear tires. The Spirit of Independence is built on a fuel-efficient RAM ProMaster chassis, with a 96-inch-wide body for easy maneuverability inside for both ambulatory (up to 14) and wheelchair (up to 4) passengers. The Spirit of Equess is a low-floor rural transit bus built on ARBOC's chassis and can accommodate up to 33 seated passengers and six wheelchair passengers. There are no steps throughout the Equess bus. The Spirit of Legacy is built on an E450 strip chassis, contains no steps throughout, and accommodates up to 21 passengers and six wheelchair positions. It is offered in gasoline, compressed natural gas (CNG) and liquefied petroleum gas (LPG) propulsion. Dealers are located throughout North America as well as Hawaii. ARBOC operates as a subsidiary of NFI Group, Inc. (New Flyer Industries), a leading transit bus and motor coach manufacturer and parts distributor.

FINANCIAL DATA: *Note: Data for latest year may not have been available at press time.*

In U.S. $	2018	2017	2016	2015	2014	2013
Revenue	26,460,000	25,200,000	24,000,000	12,800,000	12,600,000	12,200,000
R&D Expense						
Operating Income						
Operating Margin %						
SGA Expense						
Net Income						
Operating Cash Flow						
Capital Expenditure						
EBITDA						
Return on Assets %						
Return on Equity %						
Debt to Equity						

CONTACT INFORMATION:

Phone: 574-825-4880 Fax: 574-825-1750
Toll-Free: 866-953-5555
Address: 51165 Greenfield Pkwy., Middlebury, IN 46540 United States

STOCK TICKER/OTHER:

Stock Ticker: Subsidiary
Employees: 100
Parent Company: NFI Group Inc
Exchange:
Fiscal Year Ends: 12/31

SALARIES/BONUSES:

Top Exec. Salary: $ Bonus: $
Second Exec. Salary: $ Bonus: $

OTHER THOUGHTS:

Estimated Female Officers or Directors:
Hot Spot for Advancement for Women/Minorities:

Asbury Automotive Group Inc

www.asburyauto.com

NAIC Code: 441110

TYPES OF BUSINESS:

Automotive Dealers, Retail
Finance & Insurance
Vehicle Maintenance & Repair Services
Replacement Parts

BRANDS/DIVISIONS/AFFILIATES:

Nalley Automotive Group
Courtesy Autogroup
Coggin Automotive Group
Crown Automotive Company
David McDavid Auto Group
Gray-Daniels Auto Family
Hare Automotive
Bill Estes

CONTACTS: *Note: Officers with more than one job title may be intentionally listed here more than once.*

Sean Goodman, CFO
Thomas Reddin, Chairman of the Board
William Stax, Chief Accounting Officer
George Villasana, General Counsel
Jed Milstein, Other Executive Officer
David Hult, President
John Hartman, Senior VP, Divisional

GROWTH PLANS/SPECIAL FEATURES:

Asbury Automotive Group, Inc. is one of the largest U.S. automotive retailers, with 106 vehicle franchises at 87 dealership locations, and 25 collision centers. Franchise brands include Nalley Automotive Group, Courtesy Autogroup, Coggin Automotive Group, Crown Automotive Company, David McDavid Auto Group, Gray-Daniels Auto Family, Hare Automotive Group and Plaza Motor Company. Asbury's stores offer a wide range of automotive products and services, including new and used vehicles, parts, services, as well as finance and insurance offerings. The dealerships sell 30 different brands of vehicles manufactured by American, European and Asian manufacturers. New vehicle sales generated 55.1% of the company's revenue in 2018, used vehicles generated 28.7%, parts and service generated 11.9% and finance and insurance generated 4.3%. Approximately 80% of sales are from import brands. During 2019, Asbury acquired Bill Estes Automotive Group's four locations: Bill Estes Chevrolet, Bill Estes Ford, Bill Estes Chrysler Dodge Jeep Ram and Bill Estes Chevy Buick GMC, all of which are located in Indiana.

Employee benefits include medical, dental and vision coverage; life insurance; short-and long-term disability; flexible spending accounts; a 401(k) plan; and an employee assistance program; company discount programs for cars, fitness and fun.

FINANCIAL DATA: *Note: Data for latest year may not have been available at press time.*

In U.S. $	2018	2017	2016	2015	2014	2013
Revenue	6,874,400,000	6,456,500,000	6,527,800,000	6,588,300,000	5,867,700,000	5,334,900,000
R&D Expense						
Operating Income	314,600,000	292,800,000	297,800,000	301,600,000	268,200,000	226,100,000
Operating Margin %		.05%	.05%	.05%	.05%	.04%
SGA Expense	755,800,000	729,700,000	732,500,000	729,900,000	671,600,000	619,300,000
Net Income	168,000,000	139,100,000	167,200,000	169,200,000	111,600,000	109,100,000
Operating Cash Flow	10,100,000	266,300,000	142,300,000	155,400,000	84,200,000	50,700,000
Capital Expenditure	62,300,000	53,500,000	111,600,000	102,000,000	63,300,000	86,900,000
EBITDA	344,600,000	319,800,000	374,000,000	366,000,000	262,700,000	243,600,000
Return on Assets %		.06%	.07%	.08%	.05%	.06%
Return on Equity %		.41%	.56%	.45%	.24%	.24%
Debt to Equity		2.188	3.263	2.99	1.526	1.107

CONTACT INFORMATION:

Phone: 770 418-8200 Fax:
Toll-Free:
Address: 2905 Premiere Pkwy., Ste. 300, Duluth, GA 30097 United States

STOCK TICKER/OTHER:

Stock Ticker: ABG
Employees: 7,900
Parent Company:
Exchange: NYS
Fiscal Year Ends: 12/31

SALARIES/BONUSES:

Top Exec. Salary: $1,000,000 Bonus: $
Second Exec. Salary: $600,000 Bonus: $

OTHER THOUGHTS:

Estimated Female Officers or Directors: 3
Hot Spot for Advancement for Women/Minorities: Y

Aston Martin Lagonda Global Holdings PLC

www.astonmartinlagonda.com

NAIC Code: 336111

TYPES OF BUSINESS:

Automobile Manufacturing
Sports Cars
Antique Vehicle Maintenance & Restoration
Clothing & Fashion Accessories
Automobile Racing

BRANDS/DIVISIONS/AFFILIATES:

Vantag
DB11
DBS Superleggera
Rapide AMR
Rapide E
Aston Martin Valkyrie
Lagonda
DBX

CONTACTS: *Note: Officers with more than one job title may be intentionally listed here more than once.*

Andy Palmer, CEO
Marek Reichman, Chief Creative Officer
Mark Wilson, CFO
Simon Sproule, CMO
Michael Kerr, Chief Human Resources Officer
Max Szwaj, CTO
Marek Reichman, Dir.-Design
Mark Kenworthy, Gen. Mgr.-India, Middle East & North Africa
Penny Hughes, Chmn.
Adham Charanoglu, CEO-Middle East & North Africa

GROWTH PLANS/SPECIAL FEATURES:

Aston Martin Lagonda Global Holdings PLC is a British manufacturer of sport cars marketed under the Aston Martin brand, and luxury cars marketed under the Lagonda brand. The firm has a global network of more than 150 dealerships on six continents. Its current Aston Martin models include the Vantage, DB11, DBS Superleggera, Rapide AMR, Rapide E and Aston Martin Valkyrie (as of mid-2019). These cars are hand-crafted, with the DB11 being a grand tourer and the Valkyrie being a limited production hybrid sports car. The Lagonda model is an all-terrain concept with a zero-emission platform. Aston Martin Lagonda operates a headquarters production facility in Gaydon, Warwickshire in the U.K. The firm offers a wide variety of customization options and a performance-driving course. It can collect and deliver cars for servicing at its Newport Pagnell, Buckinghamshire facility from anywhere in Europe and will send service teams to any location in the world, if necessary. The company operates a Heritage team dedicated to providing obsolete parts for repair of its older model and antique cars. In October 2018, Aston Martin completed its initial public offering on the London Stock Exchange under the ticker symbol AML. In mid-2019, the firm opened a new 90-acre factory in St. Athan for the production of its upcoming SUV, the DBX, and two new models under the Lagonda banner.

FINANCIAL DATA: *Note: Data for latest year may not have been available at press time.*

In U.S. $	2018	2017	2016	2015	2014	2013
Revenue	1,391,490,000	1,181,830,000	730,100,000	756,300,000	666,233,100	878,674,000
R&D Expense						
Operating Income						
Operating Margin %						
SGA Expense						
Net Income	-72,461,300	103,613,000	-60,582,000	93,320,458	75,712,047	142,890,370
Operating Cash Flow						
Capital Expenditure						
EBITDA						
Return on Assets %						
Return on Equity %						
Debt to Equity						

CONTACT INFORMATION:

Phone: 44-1926-644644 Fax: 44-1926-644733
Toll-Free: 866-278-6661
Address: Banbury Rd., Gaydon, Warwickshire CV35 0DB United Kingdom

STOCK TICKER/OTHER:

Stock Ticker: AML
Employees: 2,913
Parent Company:
Exchange: London
Fiscal Year Ends: 12/31

SALARIES/BONUSES:

Top Exec. Salary: $ Bonus: $
Second Exec. Salary: $ Bonus: $

OTHER THOUGHTS:

Estimated Female Officers or Directors:
Hot Spot for Advancement for Women/Minorities:

Audi AG

www.audi.com

NAIC Code: 336111

TYPES OF BUSINESS:

Automobile Manufacturing
Luxury & Sports Cars
Automobile Customization & Accessories
Engine Manufacturing
Automotive Electronics

BRANDS/DIVISIONS/AFFILIATES:

Lamborghini
Ducati
Audi Sport GmbH
A8
Audi e-tron
Audi Aicon
Q2
Volkswagen AG

CONTACTS:

Note: Officers with more than one job title may be intentionally listed here more than once.

Alexander Seitz, Dir.-Finance
Abraham Schot, Dir.-Mktg. & Sales
Wendelin Gobel, Dir.-Human Resources
Hans-Joachim Rothenpieler, Dir.-Tech. Dev.
Frank Dreves, Dir.-Prod.
Bernd Martens, Dir.-Procurement
Abraham Schot, Chmn.
Ulf Berkenhagen, Dir.-Purchasing

GROWTH PLANS/SPECIAL FEATURES:

Audi AG, a publicly-listed subsidiary of Volkswagen AG, is a Germany-based designer and manufacturer of high-end luxury cars. The firm participates in companies like sports car manufacturer Lamborghini, motorcycle manufacturer Ducati, and vehicle upgrade and technology firm Audi Sport GmbH. Audi AG's models include the A1, A3, A4, A5, A6, A7, A8, Q2, Q3, Q5, Q7, Q8, TT, e-tron and RS/R8 models. The A1 is a 4-door compact Sportback sedan; A3 comes in 2- or 4-door sedan Sportback, and convertible; A4 comes in 4-door sedan, extended length, and allroad quattro formats; A5 is an elegant 2-door sport-style vehicle in Sportback and convertible formats; A6 is a 4-door sedan; A7 is a 4-door Sportback sedan; A8 is a 4-door luxury vehicle; Q2 is a 4-door urban model with geometrical design elements; Q3 is a 4-door compact and agile vehicle; Q5 is a 4-door, all-wheel drive car; Q7 is a 4-door model with a focus on comfort; TT is a 2-door sports car; e-tron is the company's first fully electric SUV; and the RS/R8 series of sport vehicles in various formats and styles. Under current development is: the Audi Aicon, an autonomous model, with no steering wheel or pedals; and the Audi Elaine, an electric-powered SUV coupe that will also make highly-automated driving possible. Audi's quattro technology offers dynamics and safety in conditions where 2-wheel-drive vehicles lose traction, such as slippery or unpaved roads. In collaboration with Berlin-based PTScientists, the company plans to launch a private moon mission, scheduled for a 2019 touchdown. The Audi lunar quattro vehicles will be built with lightweight construction materials, equipped with quattro technology, and driven by a solar-supplied-e-tron engine. In September 2018, Audi launched a monthly subscription service in the Dallas-Ft. Worth area, where a customer receives access to five different models for $1,395 a month.

FINANCIAL DATA:

Note: Data for latest year may not have been available at press time.

In U.S. $	2018	2017	2016	2015	2014	2013
Revenue	65,600,090,000	66,572,190,000	65,675,380,000	64,680,030,000	59,552,700,000	55,224,760,000
R&D Expense						
Operating Income	7,113,596,000	5,745,129,000	5,376,439,000	6,872,232,000	5,453,942,000	5,442,870,000
Operating Margin %		.09%	.08%	.08%	.10%	.10%
SGA Expense	5,370,904,000	6,623,118,000	7,163,419,000	7,110,275,000	6,069,531,000	5,765,058,000
Net Income	3,744,464,000	3,936,005,000	2,197,741,000	4,654,562,000	4,835,031,000	4,385,518,000
Operating Cash Flow	7,764,615,000	6,834,589,000	8,322,631,000	7,974,978,000	8,216,343,000	7,504,429,000
Capital Expenditure	5,631,090,000	5,663,197,000	5,629,983,000	5,310,009,000	4,749,778,000	3,978,078,000
EBITDA	9,148,583,000	9,396,591,000	7,229,850,000	6,839,017,000	7,704,827,000	6,653,011,000
Return on Assets %		.06%	.03%	.08%	.09%	.09%
Return on Equity %		.14%	.09%	.21%	.24%	.24%
Debt to Equity		0.012	0.013	0.012	0.011	0.01

CONTACT INFORMATION:

Phone: 49-800-2834444 Fax:
Toll-Free:
Address: Ettinger StraÃŸe, Ingolstadt, D-85045 Germany

STOCK TICKER/OTHER:

Stock Ticker: AUDVF
Exchange: PINX
Employees: 91,674
Fiscal Year Ends: 12/31
Parent Company: Volkswagen AG

SALARIES/BONUSES:

Top Exec. Salary: $ Bonus: $
Second Exec. Salary: $ Bonus: $

OTHER THOUGHTS:

Estimated Female Officers or Directors:
Hot Spot for Advancement for Women/Minorities:

Audi of America Inc

www.audiusa.com

NAIC Code: 336111

TYPES OF BUSINESS:

Automobile Manufacturing
Automotive Accessories
Personal Accessories
Automotive Service

BRANDS/DIVISIONS/AFFILIATES:

Volkswagen Group of America Inc
A3
A4
S5
RS5
Q8
TT
R8 Spyder

CONTACTS: *Note: Officers with more than one job title may be intentionally listed here more than once.*

Scott Keogh, Pres.
Filip Brabec, Dir.-Prod. Planning
Ricky Hudi, Chief Exec. Eng. Electrics & Electronics
Reinhard Fischer, Dir.-Strategy
Joe Jacuzzi, Chief Communications Officer
Peter Donnellan, Dir.-After Sales
Pete Hamilton, Regional Dir.-Southern Region
Jeri Ward, Dir.-Customer Exper.
Jeff Tolerico, Dir.-Eastern Region

GROWTH PLANS/SPECIAL FEATURES:

Audi of America, Inc., a subsidiary of Volkswagen Group of America, Inc., is the U.S. sales and marketing branch of the Audi car brand. Audi's 2019 sedan models include the A3, S3, RS3, A4, S4, A5, S5, RS5, A6, A7 and A8. SUVs, crossovers and wagon models include the A4 allroad, Q3, Q5, SQ5, Q7, Q8 and e-tron. The models come with various body style options, including sedan, SUVs, crossovers, wagons, coupes and convertibles. Coupes and convertible models include the A3, A5, S5, RS5, TT, TTS, TT RS and R8. Audi vehicles are identifiable through the four-ring logo that appears prominently on the grills of all cars. S models have additional specially-stylized features compared to the A models. Audi equips its luxury cars with options such as Audi MMI Navigation with voice control system, Audi MMI touch, Audi connect, BOSE surround sound and keyless start. Models range in starting price from about $34,700 (the Q3) to $182,100 (the R8 Spyder). The Volkswagen Group manufactures a line of car and personal accessories that Audi of America then sells. This line of car accessories allows customers to customize a car at a local dealership as well as from the manufacturer through the company web site's Build Your Audi function. In addition to new cars, the company offers certified pre-owned models that are subject to a 300+ point inspection process. Service and support programs for these vehicles include roadside assistance, no-charge scheduled maintenance and extended warranties. Audi of America imports its cars from five main manufacturing facilities in Brazil, Germany, Italy, Hungary and China.

FINANCIAL DATA: *Note: Data for latest year may not have been available at press time.*

In U.S. $	2018	2017	2016	2015	2014	2013
Revenue	10,334,200,000	11,857,700,000	12,998,684,059	10,145,871,400	9,291,103,561	8,400,000,000
R&D Expense						
Operating Income						
Operating Margin %						
SGA Expense						
Net Income	75,490,300	-111,401,000	412,027,737	856,793,784	652,541,100	394,760,691
Operating Cash Flow						
Capital Expenditure						
EBITDA						
Return on Assets %						
Return on Equity %						
Debt to Equity						

CONTACT INFORMATION:

Phone: 703-364-7000 Fax:
Toll-Free: 800-822-8987
Address: 2200 Ferdinand Porsche Drive, Herndon, VA 20171 United States

STOCK TICKER/OTHER:

Stock Ticker: Subsidiary
Exchange:
Employees: 14,809
Fiscal Year Ends: 12/31
Parent Company: Volkswagen Group of America Inc

SALARIES/BONUSES:

Top Exec. Salary: $ Bonus: $
Second Exec. Salary: $ Bonus: $

OTHER THOUGHTS:

Estimated Female Officers or Directors:
Hot Spot for Advancement for Women/Minorities:

Aurora Innovation Inc

aurora.tech

NAIC Code: 511210

TYPES OF BUSINESS:

Technology for Self-Driving Vehicles
Artificial Intelligence

BRANDS/DIVISIONS/AFFILIATES:

GROWTH PLANS/SPECIAL FEATURES:

Aurora Innovation, Inc., founded in 2017, develops self-driving technology, including software and hardware, for the automotive, transportation and urban industries. The firm utilizes engineering and machine learning strategies to address autonomous ways of transporting people and goods. Aurora's goals are to increase safety, provide expanded access to individuals with disabilities and minimize congested parking garages and road traffic. The company has been working with Volkswagen to integrate its self-driving systems in custom-designed electric shuttles for VW's Moia brand. In early-2018, Aurora raised $90 million from Greylock Partners and Index Ventures, and in 2019 it raised $530 million from Amazon. Aurora was founded by former employees of Tesla and Waymo..

CONTACTS: *Note: Officers with more than one job title may be intentionally listed here more than once.*

Chris Urmson, CEO
Sterling Anderson, Chief Product Officer
Drew Bagnell, Chief Technology Officer

FINANCIAL DATA: *Note: Data for latest year may not have been available at press time.*

In U.S. $	2018	2017	2016	2015	2014	2013
Revenue						
R&D Expense						
Operating Income						
Operating Margin %						
SGA Expense						
Net Income						
Operating Cash Flow						
Capital Expenditure						
EBITDA						
Return on Assets %						
Return on Equity %						
Debt to Equity						

CONTACT INFORMATION:

Phone: 412-983-6681 Fax:
Toll-Free:
Address: 429 Acacia Ave, Palo Alto, CA 94306 United States

STOCK TICKER/OTHER:

Stock Ticker: Private Exchange:
Employees: Fiscal Year Ends:
Parent Company:

SALARIES/BONUSES:

Top Exec. Salary: $ Bonus: $
Second Exec. Salary: $ Bonus: $

OTHER THOUGHTS:

Estimated Female Officers or Directors:
Hot Spot for Advancement for Women/Minorities:

Autocam Corporation Inc

www.autocam.com

NAIC Code: 336300

TYPES OF BUSINESS:

Automobile Parts, Manufacturing
Metal Components
Medical Devices

BRANDS/DIVISIONS/AFFILIATES:

NN Inc

CONTACTS:

Note: Officers with more than one job title may be intentionally listed here more than once.

Richard D. Holder, CEO
John C. Kennedy, Pres.
Warren A. Veltman, Sec.
Warren A. Veltman, Treas.
John R. Buchan, COO-North American Oper.

GROWTH PLANS/SPECIAL FEATURES:

Autocam Corporation, Inc. manufactures highly engineered, precision-machined, metal alloy components for many of the world's Tier 1 automotive parts suppliers. With 10 facilities worldwide, in the U.S., Brazil, France, Germany, Poland and China, the company's primary focus is on precision-machined automotive components, sub-assemblies and complete assemblies. Autocam has the technological and manufacturing capacity to produce complex parts requiring extremely close tolerances in the single-digit micron range. The company manufactures its precision automotive components in three primary product categories: steering, which includes valve assemblies, sleeves, torsion bars, input shafts, pinions and worms; fuel delivery, which includes disk checks, pole pieces, valves, seat guides, diesel pump bodies, diesel cases, sleeves and inlet tubes; and electric motors products, which includes gears, gear sub-assemblies and worm shafts. The company also manufactures components and assemblies for other automotive applications and for medical devices, such as hand pieces for ophthalmic surgery; spinal, hip, knee and shoulder implant systems; blood cleaning and separation equipment, ultrasonic imaging equipment and DNA testing equipment; and laser cut coronary and aortic stents. Autocam makes its products through a variety of high-tech processes, including precision turning, grinding and milling, forging, plastic injection molding, rotary transfer, precision secondary and laser machining, finishing, heat treating and precision cleaning. Autocam Corporation, Inc. is a subsidiary of industrial metal and plastic components manufacturer NN, Inc.

FINANCIAL DATA:

Note: Data for latest year may not have been available at press time.

In U.S. $	2018	2017	2016	2015	2014	2013
Revenue	353,694,600	336,852,000	326,138,000	328,260,000	395,000,000	385,000,000
R&D Expense						
Operating Income						
Operating Margin %						
SGA Expense						
Net Income			20,210,265	31,700,000	15,732,000	15,986,000
Operating Cash Flow						
Capital Expenditure						
EBITDA						
Return on Assets %						
Return on Equity %						
Debt to Equity						

CONTACT INFORMATION:

Phone: 616-698-0707 Fax: 616-698-6876
Toll-Free: 800-747-6978
Address: 4180 40th Street, SE, Kentwood, MI 49512 United States

STOCK TICKER/OTHER:

Stock Ticker: Subsidiary
Employees: 2,000
Parent Company: NN Inc
Exchange:
Fiscal Year Ends: 06/30

SALARIES/BONUSES:

Top Exec. Salary: $ Bonus: $
Second Exec. Salary: $ Bonus: $

OTHER THOUGHTS:

Estimated Female Officers or Directors:
Hot Spot for Advancement for Women/Minorities:

Autoliv Inc

www.autoliv.com

NAIC Code: 336300

TYPES OF BUSINESS:

Automotive Safety Products Manufacturing
Seat Belts
Airbags
Seat Components
Steering Wheels
Child Seats
Safety Electronics
Anti-Whiplash Systems

BRANDS/DIVISIONS/AFFILIATES:

Veoneer Inc

GROWTH PLANS/SPECIAL FEATURES:

Autoliv, Inc. develops, manufactures and supplies automotive safety equipment and systems to the automotive industry. The company operates through one business segment, passive safety. Passive safety systems are primarily meant to improve vehicle safety, and include modules and components for frontal-impact airbag protection systems, side-impact airbag protection systems, seatbelts, steering wheels, inflator technologies, battery cable cutters, pedestrian protection systems and child seats. Including all of its joint venture operations, Autolive has more than 60 production facilities in 25 countries. Business is conducted in the following geographic regions: Europe, the Americas, China, Japan and the rest of Asia (ROA). In mid-2018, the firm completed the spin-off of its electronics business into a new company called Veoneer, Inc.

CONTACTS: *Note: Officers with more than one job title may be intentionally listed here more than once.*

Mikael Bratt, CEO
Christian Hanke, Interim CFO
Sherry Vasa, Exec. VP-Human Resources
Jan Olsson, VP-Research & Eng.
Jordi Lombarte, CTO
Johan Lofvenholm, VP-Eng.
Svante Mogefors, VP-Mfg. & Quality
Anthony J. Nellis, Interim General Counsel
Thomas Jonsson, VP-Corp. Comm.
Mats Wallin, VP-Finance
Steve Fredin, Pres., Autoliv Americas
Jonas Nilsson, Pres., Autoliv Europe
Steven Rode, Pres., Electronics
Jan Carlson, Chmn.
George Chang, Pres., Autoliv Asia
Henrick Arrland, VP-Purchasing

FINANCIAL DATA: *Note: Data for latest year may not have been available at press time.*

In U.S. $	2018	2017	2016	2015	2014	2013
Revenue	8,678,200,000	10,382,600,000	10,073,600,000	9,169,601,000	9,240,500,000	8,803,400,000
R&D Expense	412,600,000	740,900,000	651,000,000	523,800,000	535,600,000	489,300,000
Operating Income	686,000,000	839,500,000	847,700,000	727,800,000	722,600,000	761,400,000
Operating Margin %		.08%	.08%	.08%	.08%	.09%
SGA Expense	390,300,000	489,700,000	476,100,000	411,500,000	414,900,000	389,900,000
Net Income	190,400,000	427,100,000	567,100,000	456,800,000	467,800,000	485,800,000
Operating Cash Flow	590,600,000	935,900,000	868,400,000	750,500,000	712,700,000	837,900,000
Capital Expenditure	560,000,000	580,100,000	507,900,000	490,700,000	456,000,000	385,600,000
EBITDA	1,075,600,000	993,500,000	1,249,200,000	1,059,900,000	1,035,800,000	1,052,900,000
Return on Assets %		.05%	.07%	.06%	.06%	.07%
Return on Equity %		.11%	.16%	.13%	.13%	.13%
Debt to Equity		0.328	0.36	0.434	0.444	0.07

CONTACT INFORMATION:

Phone: 46-8-587-20-600 Fax:
Toll-Free:
Address: Klarabergsviadukten 70, Stockholm, SE-107 24 Sweden

STOCK TICKER/OTHER:

Stock Ticker: ALV
Employees: 70,300
Parent Company:
Exchange: NYS
Fiscal Year Ends: 12/31

SALARIES/BONUSES:

Top Exec. Salary: $986,646 Bonus: $
Second Exec. Salary: $875,957 Bonus: $

OTHER THOUGHTS:

Estimated Female Officers or Directors: 1
Hot Spot for Advancement for Women/Minorities:

Automobili Lamborghini SpA

www.lamborghini.com

NAIC Code: 336111

TYPES OF BUSINESS:

Automobile Manufacturing
Sports Cars
Powerboat Engines
Vehicle Accessories

BRANDS/DIVISIONS/AFFILIATES:

Volkswagen AG
Audi AG
Urus
Huracan
Aventador
Centenario
Terzo Millennio
Lamborghini Financial Services

CONTACTS: *Note: Officers with more than one job title may be intentionally listed here more than once.*

Stefano Domenicali, CEO
Stephan Winkelmann, Pres.
Paolo Poma, CFO
Katia Bassi, CMO
Umberto Tossini, Dir.-Human Resources
Maurizio Reggiani, CTO
Dominik Hoberg, Dir.-Corporate Image Div.
Max Welti, Head-Motorsport

GROWTH PLANS/SPECIAL FEATURES:

Automobili Lamborghini SpA is a subsidiary of Volkswagen AG's Audi business unit, Audi AG. The Italian company manufactures luxury super sports cars. Currently, Lamborghini markets three model lines: the Urus super sport utility vehicle (SUV); the Huracan all-wheel or rear-wheel drive, with a V10 engine; and the Aventador coupe or roadster, powered by a V12 engine. Few-Off Lamborghinis are exclusive, limited edition super cars for a select number of clients and include the Centenario and Centenario roadster models. Current concept cars by Lamborghini include the the Terzo Millennio sports car, the Asterion hybrid and the Estoque 4-door sedan. Lamborghini Financial Services offers purchase and lease finance options. Spare parts and related accessories are also manufactured and sold by Lamborghini, with more than 150 service assistance centers in more than 50 countries. Warranty and care packages are available for purchase. Lamborghini comprises 135 dealerships worldwide.

FINANCIAL DATA: *Note: Data for latest year may not have been available at press time.*

In U.S. $	2018	2017	2016	2015	2014	2013
Revenue	1,505,230,000	1,117,610,000	955,525,147	852,339,944	664,333,550	591,586,367
R&D Expense						
Operating Income						
Operating Margin %						
SGA Expense						
Net Income						
Operating Cash Flow						
Capital Expenditure						
EBITDA						
Return on Assets %						
Return on Equity %						
Debt to Equity						

CONTACT INFORMATION:

Phone: 39-051-6817-611 Fax:
Toll-Free:
Address: Via Modena 12, Sant'Agata Bolognese, 40019 Italy

STOCK TICKER/OTHER:

Stock Ticker: Subsidiary
Employees: 1,643
Parent Company: Volkswagen AG
Exchange:
Fiscal Year Ends: 12/31

SALARIES/BONUSES:

Top Exec. Salary: $ Bonus: $
Second Exec. Salary: $ Bonus: $

OTHER THOUGHTS:

Estimated Female Officers or Directors:
Hot Spot for Advancement for Women/Minorities:

Automotive Energy Supply Corporation (AESC) www.eco-aesc-lb.com/en/vision

NAIC Code: 335911

TYPES OF BUSINESS:

Batteries for Electric Automobiles

BRANDS/DIVISIONS/AFFILIATES:

Nissan Motor Co Ltd
NEC Corporation

CONTACTS: *Note: Officers with more than one job title may be intentionally listed here more than once.*

Yo Tsunashma, Pres.

GROWTH PLANS/SPECIAL FEATURES:

Automotive Energy Supply Corporation (AESC), a joint venture between Nissan Motor Co. Ltd. (owning 51%), NEC Corporation (42%) and NEC Energy Devices, Ltd. (7%), is a manufacturer of advanced lithium-ion battery technology. AESC's development and manufacturing operating divisions produce rechargeable lithium-ion batteries in laminate cells, modules and packs for EV and HEV applications. These are distributed to original equipment manufacturers (OEMs) and automotive parts suppliers worldwide. The company's other products include lithium-ion cells (for battery electric vehicles), high power cells (for hybrid electric vehicles), high energy modules (for battery electric vehicles), high power modules (for hybrid electric vehicles), high energy battery packs (for battery electric vehicles) and high-power battery packs (for hybrid electric vehicles). Applications for the firm's products include a battery-powered forklift manufactured by Nissan as well as several Nissan-branded electric vehicles (EVs), which operate solely on battery power, and hybrid vehicles, which use an electric motor and battery pack to augment a gasoline engine. AESC also performs research and development in-house. As of 2018, Nissan is actively looking for a buyer for its 51% stake.

FINANCIAL DATA: *Note: Data for latest year may not have been available at press time.*

In U.S. $	2018	2017	2016	2015	2014	2013
Revenue	599,173,050	570,641,000	332,108,979	358,173,521	366,620,878	372,163,516
R&D Expense						
Operating Income						
Operating Margin %						
SGA Expense						
Net Income						
Operating Cash Flow						
Capital Expenditure						
EBITDA						
Return on Assets %						
Return on Equity %						
Debt to Equity						

CONTACT INFORMATION:

Phone: 046-252-3211 Fax:
Toll-Free:
Address: 2-10-1 Hironodai, Zama City, 252-0012 Japan

STOCK TICKER/OTHER:

Stock Ticker: Joint Venture
Exchange:
Employees: 531
Fiscal Year Ends: 03/31
Parent Company: Nissan Motor Co Ltd

SALARIES/BONUSES:

Top Exec. Salary: $ Bonus: $
Second Exec. Salary: $ Bonus: $

OTHER THOUGHTS:

Estimated Female Officers or Directors:
Hot Spot for Advancement for Women/Minorities:

AutoNation Inc

www.autonation.com

NAIC Code: 441110

TYPES OF BUSINESS:

Auto Dealer
Online Auto Sales
Vehicle Maintenance & Repair Services
Vehicle Parts
Extended Service Contracts
Vehicle Protection Products

BRANDS/DIVISIONS/AFFILIATES:

CONTACTS:

Note: Officers with more than one job title may be intentionally listed here more than once.

Cheryl Miller, CFO
Michael Jackson, Chairman of the Board
Christopher Cade, Chief Accounting Officer
Marc Cannon, Chief Marketing Officer
James Bender, Executive VP, Divisional
H. Arnold, Executive VP, Divisional
C. Coleman Edmunds, Executive VP

GROWTH PLANS/SPECIAL FEATURES:

AutoNation, Inc. is one of the largest automobile retailers in the U.S. It owns and operates more than 300 new vehicle franchises from 239 stores located in major metropolitan markets, predominantly in the Sunbelt region of the U.S. The company offers a diversified range of automotive products and services, including new vehicles, which generated 54.9% of the firm's 2018 revenue; used vehicles, 23.9%; parts and automotive services, 16.1%; and automotive finance, insurance products and other 5.1%. The firm also arranges financing for vehicle purchases through third-party finance sources. The core brands of vehicles, representing approximately 92% of the new vehicles the firm sold in 2018, are manufactured by Toyota (including Lexus), Honda, Ford, General Motors, FCA US, Mercedes-Benz, Nissan, BMW and Volkswagen (including Audi and Porsche). The company also owns and operates 85 AutoNation-branded collision centers. AutoNation operates in three segments: domestic, import and premium luxury. Domestic is comprised of franchises that sell new Ford, Lincoln, Chevrolet, Buick, Cadillac, GMC, Chrysler, Dodge Jeep and Ram brands. Import includes franchises that sell Toyota, Honda, Nissan and other vehicles. Premium Luxury includes retailers that sell Mercedes-Benz, BMW, Lexus, Audi, Jaguar Land Rover and other franchises. In 2018, the domestic segment accounted for 28% of the company's total new vehicle unit sales; import, 34%; and premium luxury, 38%. AutoNation's website offers prospective buyers the ability to evaluate current trade-in values of vehicles, explore nearby car lots, read automotive reviews and even arrange for the purchase of an automobile online.

The firm offers employees health, dental, life and disability insurance; longevity bonuses; a 401(k) plan; and an employee vehicle purchase program.

FINANCIAL DATA:

Note: Data for latest year may not have been available at press time.

In U.S. $	2018	2017	2016	2015	2014	2013
Revenue	21,412,800,000	21,534,600,000	21,609,000,000	20,862,000,000	19,108,800,000	17,517,600,000
R&D Expense						
Operating Income	786,000,000	843,400,000	889,500,000	888,500,000	820,800,000	740,300,000
Operating Margin %		.04%	.04%	.04%	.04%	.04%
SGA Expense	2,509,800,000	2,436,200,000	2,349,400,000	2,263,500,000	2,079,600,000	1,935,000,000
Net Income	396,000,000	434,600,000	430,500,000	442,600,000	418,700,000	374,900,000
Operating Cash Flow	511,000,000	540,100,000	516,000,000	507,200,000	485,100,000	484,100,000
Capital Expenditure	400,800,000	313,400,000	249,500,000	257,800,000	209,600,000	202,700,000
EBITDA	945,400,000	1,012,300,000	1,037,700,000	999,300,000	929,200,000	841,400,000
Return on Assets %		.04%	.04%	.05%	.05%	.05%
Return on Equity %		.19%	.18%	.20%	.20%	.20%
Debt to Equity		0.827	0.697	0.746	1.015	0.878

CONTACT INFORMATION:

Phone: 954 769-6000 Fax:
Toll-Free:
Address: 200 SW 1st Ave., Ste.1600, Fort Lauderdale, FL 33301 United States

STOCK TICKER/OTHER:

Stock Ticker: AN
Exchange: NYS
Employees: 26,000
Fiscal Year Ends: 12/31
Parent Company:

SALARIES/BONUSES:

Top Exec. Salary: $1,293,750 Bonus: $
Second Exec. Salary: $771,875 Bonus: $

OTHER THOUGHTS:

Estimated Female Officers or Directors: 2
Hot Spot for Advancement for Women/Minorities:

Autoneum Holding AG

www.autoneum.com

NAIC Code: 336360

TYPES OF BUSINESS:

Motor Vehicle Seating and Interior Trim Manufacturing

BRANDS/DIVISIONS/AFFILIATES:

Tianjin Autoneum Nittoku Sound-Proof Co. Ltd
Autoneum Belgium NV
Autoneum France SAS
Autoneum India Pvt Ltd
Nihon Tokushu Toryo Co Ltd
Autoneum Mexico S de RL de CV
Autoneum Switzerland AG
Autoneum North America Inc

CONTACTS: *Note: Officers with more than one job title may be intentionally listed here more than once.*

Martin Hirzel, CEO
Martin Zwyssig, CFO
Matthais Holzammer, Bus. Group Europe
Richard Derr, Bus. Group North America
Uwe Trautmann, Bus. Group Asia
Volker Eimertenbrink, Bus. Group SAMEA
Hans-Peter Schwald, Chmn.

GROWTH PLANS/SPECIAL FEATURES:

Autoneum Holding AG provides innovative and cost-effective solutions for noise reduction and heat management to all major vehicle manufacturers worldwide. Operating in 55 locations across 25 countries, the firm divides its operations into four regions: Europe, North America, Asia and SAMEA (South America, Middle East and Africa). Its acoustics and thermal management units develop, test and produce vehicle components and integrate them into tailored, multifunctional systems and modules, as well as for thermal protection and comfort. Products include engine covers, hoodliners, outer dashes, water box shields, inner dashes, non-woven carpets, tufted carpets, floor insulators, floor mats, dampers/stiffeners, sealants, underbody shields, floor pans, heat shields, outer tunnel insulators and wheelhouse outer liners. Autoneum continuously develops innovative systems and equipment to measure the noise, vibration and harshness performance of component and material properties. In addition, Autoneum operates through partnerships with major light vehicle and heavy truck manufacturers, producing over 80 million vehicles annually. Primarily serving customers in Europe, the company also serves a significant population in North America. Subsidiaries include Tianjin Autoneum Nittoku Sound-Proof Co. Ltd., in China; Autoneum Belgium NV; Autoneum CZ sro, in Czech Republic; Autoneum France SAS; Autoneum Germany GmbH; Autoneum India Pvt. Ltd.; Nihon Tokushu Toryo Co. Ltd., in Japan; Autoneum Mexico S de RL de CV; Autoneum Switzerland AG; and Autoneum North America, Inc., in the U.S.

FINANCIAL DATA: *Note: Data for latest year may not have been available at press time.*

In U.S. $	2018	2017	2016	2015	2014	2013
Revenue	2,295,734,000	2,216,744,000	2,166,030,000	2,098,913,000	1,966,895,000	2,066,110,000
R&D Expense						
Operating Income	65,204,270	151,841,400	158,885,100	111,692,500	119,440,500	109,076,300
Operating Margin %		.08%	.08%	.06%	.07%	.06%
SGA Expense	126,685,500	118,937,400	112,900,000	117,830,600	46,588,850	41,054,540
Net Income	55,443,750	91,869,590	96,397,660	42,463,270	79,392,230	14,590,460
Operating Cash Flow	124,773,600	146,105,900	195,310,900	112,396,900	139,062,200	166,733,800
Capital Expenditure	167,438,100	179,110,500	139,263,400	121,352,400	102,435,100	81,304,090
EBITDA	197,021,500	264,640,800	281,243,700	187,462,300	200,543,400	148,118,300
Return on Assets %		.07%	.08%	.04%	.08%	.01%
Return on Equity %		.21%	.28%	.14%	.29%	.06%
Debt to Equity		0.506	0.199	0.567	0.443	0.70

CONTACT INFORMATION:

Phone: 41 522088282 Fax: 41 522088419
Toll-Free:
Address: Schlosstalstrasse 43, Winterthur, 8406 Switzerland

STOCK TICKER/OTHER:

Stock Ticker: ATNNF
Exchange: GREY
Employees: 12,946
Fiscal Year Ends:
Parent Company:

SALARIES/BONUSES:

Top Exec. Salary: $ Bonus: $
Second Exec. Salary: $ Bonus: $

OTHER THOUGHTS:

Estimated Female Officers or Directors:
Hot Spot for Advancement for Women/Minorities:

AutoWeb Inc

www.autoweb.com

NAIC Code: 519130

TYPES OF BUSINESS:

Automotive Media & Marketing Services
Online Car Sales Support

BRANDS/DIVISIONS/AFFILIATES:

Payment Pro
Autobytel
MyGarage
TextShield
iControl by Autobytel

CONTACTS: *Note: Officers with more than one job title may be intentionally listed here more than once.*

Jared Rowe, CEO
Joseph Hannan, CFO
Michael Fuchs, Chairman of the Board
Wesley Ozima, Chief Accounting Officer
Glenn Fuller, Chief Administrative Officer
Tim Branham, Chief Technology Officer
Daniel Ingle, COO
Sara Partin, Other Executive Officer

GROWTH PLANS/SPECIAL FEATURES:

AutoWeb, Inc. is a digital marketing company for the automotive industry that assists automotive retail dealers and automotive manufacturers in the marketing and selling of new and used vehicles to consumers. The company owns and operates a network of websites both for consumers and dealers. Consumer-facing automotive websites provide customers with information and tools to aid them with their automotive purchase decisions and the ability to submit inquiries requesting dealers to contact the consumers regarding purchasing or leasing vehicles. Leads are internally-generated from AutoWeb's online sites or acquired from third-parties (generating leads from their own websites). The firm's click traffic referral program provides consumers who are shopping for vehicles online with targeted offers based on make, model and geographic location. They are presented with relevant offers on a timely basis, and upon the consumer clicking on an ad or link, are redirected to the new website location. AutoWeb, therefore, sells internally-generated leads and non-internally-generated leads directly to dealers and indirectly to dealers through a wholesale market consisting of manufacturers and other third parties in the automotive lead distribution industry. Payment Pro is a dealer website conversion tool based on a third-party product that offers consumers real-time online monthly payment information based on an instant evaluation process. The lead goes directly into the dealer's management tool so that a salesperson can address the consumer's inquiry. Advertising accounted for 22% of 2018 revenues. Other products and trademarks of AutoWeb include Autobytel, MyGarage, TextShield and iControl by Autobytel.

FINANCIAL DATA: *Note: Data for latest year may not have been available at press time.*

In U.S. $	2018	2017	2016	2015	2014	2013
Revenue	125,589,000	142,125,000	156,684,000	133,226,000	106,278,000	78,361,000
R&D Expense						
Operating Income	-31,971,000	-1,000,000	6,078,000	7,649,000	5,999,000	2,527,000
Operating Margin %		-.01%	.04%	.06%	.06%	.03%
SGA Expense	28,496,000	26,425,000	32,781,000	29,145,000	25,942,000	19,166,000
Net Income	-38,816,000	-64,964,000	3,871,000	4,646,000	3,411,000	38,144,000
Operating Cash Flow	-2,920,000	11,488,000	18,242,000	12,200,000	7,890,000	4,332,000
Capital Expenditure	896,000	10,399,000	2,148,000	2,719,000	1,124,000	686,000
EBITDA	-23,427,000	6,653,000	13,381,000	11,670,000	8,226,000	4,402,000
Return on Assets %		-.50%	.02%	.04%	.04%	.59%
Return on Equity %		-.70%	.03%	.05%	.05%	.84%
Debt to Equity		0.134	0.138	0.201	0.188	0.143

CONTACT INFORMATION:

Phone: 949-225-4500 Fax:
Toll-Free:
Address: 18872 MacArthur Blvd., Ste. 200, Irvine, CA 92612 United States

STOCK TICKER/OTHER:

Stock Ticker: AUTO
Employees: 254
Parent Company:
Exchange: NAS
Fiscal Year Ends: 12/31

SALARIES/BONUSES:

Top Exec. Salary: $394,167 Bonus: $250,000
Second Exec. Salary: $341,500 Bonus: $

OTHER THOUGHTS:

Estimated Female Officers or Directors: 1
Hot Spot for Advancement for Women/Minorities:

AutoZone Inc

www.autozone.com

NAIC Code: 441310

TYPES OF BUSINESS:

Auto Parts, Retail
Automotive Software
Online Sales
General Automotive Service

BRANDS/DIVISIONS/AFFILIATES:

AutoZone
Duralast
Valucraft
SureBilt
ProElite
Loan-a-Tool
ALLDATA LLC

CONTACTS: *Note: Officers with more than one job title may be intentionally listed here more than once.*

William Rhodes, CEO
Domingo Hurtado, Sr. VP, Geographical
William Giles, CFO
Charlie Pleas, Chief Accounting Officer
Ronald Griffin, Chief Information Officer
Thomas Newbern, Executive VP, Divisional
Mark Finestone, Executive VP, Divisional
William Graves, Executive VP, Geographical
Kristen Wright, General Counsel
Philip Daniele, Senior VP, Divisional
William Hackney, Senior VP, Divisional
Richard Smith, Senior VP, Divisional
Albert Saltiel, Senior VP, Divisional

GROWTH PLANS/SPECIAL FEATURES:

AutoZone, Inc. is a leading specialty retailer and distributor of automotive parts, chemicals and accessories, targeting do-it-yourself (DIY) customers. With 5,618 stores in the U.S. and Puerto Rico, as well as 564 in Mexico and 20 in Brazil. Each AutoZone store carries an extensive product line for cars, sport utility vehicles (SUVs), vans and light trucks, including new and remanufactured automotive parts and maintenance items as well as non-automotive products. Many AutoZone stores have a commercial sales program that provides commercial credit and prompt delivery of parts and other products to local, regional and national repair garages, dealers and service stations. Although each of the company's stores carry the same basic product lines, the company tailors each store's parts inventory to the makes and models of the vehicles in their trade areas. Parts not kept in stock can be ordered and delivered to the store within a few days, or they can be ordered online. In-house brands AutoZone, Duralast, Valucraft, SureBilt and ProElite are offered at competitive value to customers. The company also has a Loan-a-Tool program, through which customers can borrow a specialty tool, such as a steering wheel puller, for which they would have little or no use other than for a single job. In addition, AutoZone provides other free services, including check engine light readings, collection of used oil for recycling, battery charging & installation assistance, as well as the testing of starters, alternators, batteries, sensors and actuators. Moreover, the company offers automotive diagnostic and repair software through its subsidiary, ALLDATA LLC. During 2018, AutoZone sold Interamerican Motor Corporation (IMC), including its 26 IMC branches, to Parts Authority.

AutoZone offers comprehensive employee benefits, retirement plans and employee assistance programs.

FINANCIAL DATA: *Note: Data for latest year may not have been available at press time.*

In U.S. $	2018	2017	2016	2015	2014	2013
Revenue	11,221,080,000	10,888,680,000	10,635,680,000	10,187,340,000	9,475,313,000	9,147,530,000
R&D Expense						
Operating Income	1,810,856,000	2,080,069,000	2,060,395,000	1,953,051,000	1,830,223,000	1,773,098,000
Operating Margin %		.19%	.19%	.19%	.19%	.19%
SGA Expense	4,162,890,000	3,659,551,000	3,548,341,000	3,373,980,000	3,104,684,000	2,967,837,000
Net Income	1,337,536,000	1,280,869,000	1,241,007,000	1,160,241,000	1,069,744,000	1,016,480,000
Operating Cash Flow	2,080,292,000	1,570,612,000	1,577,329,000	1,525,123,000	1,341,234,000	1,415,011,000
Capital Expenditure	522,247,000	550,881,000	496,137,000	488,838,000	445,028,000	404,686,000
EBITDA	2,161,576,000	2,406,622,000	2,360,163,000	2,224,575,000	2,083,340,000	2,001,955,000
Return on Assets %		.14%	.15%	.15%	.15%	.15%
Return on Equity %						
Debt to Equity						

CONTACT INFORMATION:

Phone: 901 495-6500 Fax: 901 495-8300
Toll-Free: 800-288-6966
Address: 123 S. Front St., Memphis, TN 38103 United States

STOCK TICKER/OTHER:

Stock Ticker: AZO
Exchange: NYS
Employees: 90,000
Fiscal Year Ends: 08/31
Parent Company:

SALARIES/BONUSES:

Top Exec. Salary: $1,000,000 Bonus: $
Second Exec. Salary: $641,923 Bonus: $

OTHER THOUGHTS:

Estimated Female Officers or Directors: 2
Hot Spot for Advancement for Women/Minorities: Y

Avis Budget Group Inc

www.avisbudgetgroup.com

NAIC Code: 532111

TYPES OF BUSINESS:

Automobile Rental
Franchising
Truck Rental

BRANDS/DIVISIONS/AFFILIATES:

Avis
Budget
ZipCar
Payless
Apex
Maggiore
FranceCars
Turiscar Group

CONTACTS: *Note: Officers with more than one job title may be intentionally listed here more than once.*

Larry De Shon, CEO
John North, CFO
Leonard Coleman, Chairman of the Board
David Calabria, Chief Accounting Officer
Michael Tucker, Chief Compliance Officer
Edward Linnen, Executive VP
Joseph Ferraro, President, Divisional
Mark Servodidio, President, Divisional
Cathleen DeGenova, Vice President, Divisional

GROWTH PLANS/SPECIAL FEATURES:

Avis Budget Group, Inc. (ABG) operates in the global vehicle rental industry through Avis, Budget, Zipcar, Payless, Apex, Maggiore and FranceCars. Avis is a rental car supplier to the premium commercial and leisure segments of the travel industry. Budget is a rental car supplier to the price-conscious segments of the travel industry. Its fleet of approximately 19,000 Budget trucks are rented through a network of approximately 925 dealer-operated and 450 company-operated locations throughout the U.S. Zipcar operates a membership-based car sharing network present in more than 500 cities and towns and on more than 600 college campuses across the U.S., Canada, Europe and Central America. Payless is a rental car supplier comprised of 280 vehicle rental locations worldwide. Apex operates in New Zealand and Australia via 25 locations. Maggiore operates in Italy through 140 rental locations. The FranceCars operates one of the largest light commercial vehicle fleets in France from more than 70 rental locations. On average, ABG's operations include approximately 11,000 car and truck rental locations throughout the world, with a fleet of more than 620,000 vehicles. Annually, it completes more than 39 million vehicle rental transactions worldwide. The company operates in two segments: Americas, which provides vehicle rentals and ancillary products and services throughout the Americas and the Caribbean, and operates the car sharing business in these markets; and International, which provides and licenses ABG's brands to third parties for vehicle rentals and ancillary products and services primarily in Europe, the Middle East, Asia, Australia and New Zealand, and operates the car sharing business in select markets. In October 2018, Avis Budget acquired Turiscar Group, a car rental company in Portugal.

The company offers its employees medical, dental and vision coverage; life insurance; flexible spending accounts; short-and long-term disability, AD&D; and 401(k).

FINANCIAL DATA: *Note: Data for latest year may not have been available at press time.*

In U.S. $	2018	2017	2016	2015	2014	2013
Revenue	9,124,000,000	8,848,000,000	8,659,000,000	8,502,000,000	8,485,000,000	7,937,000,000
R&D Expense						
Operating Income	830,000,000	776,000,000	843,000,000	974,000,000	978,000,000	881,000,000
Operating Margin %		.09%	.10%	.11%	.11%	.11%
SGA Expense	1,220,000,000	1,120,000,000	1,134,000,000	1,093,000,000	1,080,000,000	1,019,000,000
Net Income	165,000,000	361,000,000	163,000,000	313,000,000	245,000,000	16,000,000
Operating Cash Flow	2,609,000,000	2,648,000,000	2,629,000,000	2,584,000,000	2,579,000,000	2,253,000,000
Capital Expenditure	12,820,000,000	11,735,000,000	12,651,000,000	12,127,000,000	12,057,000,000	11,051,000,000
EBITDA	2,999,000,000	2,891,000,000	2,896,000,000	2,920,000,000	2,903,000,000	2,419,000,000
Return on Assets %		.02%	.01%	.02%	.01%	.00%
Return on Equity %		.91%	.49%	.57%	.34%	.02%
Debt to Equity		11.019	24.557	12.526	7.771	6.467

CONTACT INFORMATION:

Phone: 973 496-4700 Fax: 212 413-1924
Toll-Free:
Address: 6 Sylvan Way, Parsippany, NJ 07054 United States

STOCK TICKER/OTHER:

Stock Ticker: CAR
Employees: 30,000
Parent Company:
Exchange: NAS
Fiscal Year Ends: 12/31

SALARIES/BONUSES:

Top Exec. Salary: $1,100,000 Bonus: $
Second Exec. Salary: $650,000 Bonus: $

OTHER THOUGHTS:

Estimated Female Officers or Directors: 2
Hot Spot for Advancement for Women/Minorities:

AvtoVAZ OAO

www.lada-auto.ru

NAIC Code: 336111

TYPES OF BUSINESS:

Automobile Manufacturing
Insurance
Vehicle Transportation
Power Supply
Maintenance Services

BRANDS/DIVISIONS/AFFILIATES:

Renault SA
Rostec
Alliance Rostec Auto BV
GM-AvtoVAZ
Granta
Vesta
XRAY
Largus

CONTACTS: *Note: Officers with more than one job title may be intentionally listed here more than once.*

Yves Caracatzanis, Pres.
Alexey Bobrov, CFO
Vitaly Andreevich Vilchik, Exec. VP-Prod.
Oleg Vladimirovich Lobanov, Exec. VP-Corp. Dev.
Oleg Vladimirovich Lobanov, Exec. VP-Finance
Evgeny Nikolaevich Shmelev, VP-Tech. Dev.
Hugues Desmarchelier, VP-Prod. & Programs
Pavel Vladimirovich Zhukalin, VP-Safety & Regime
Damir Sayrinovich Kashapov, VP-Purchasing

GROWTH PLANS/SPECIAL FEATURES:

AvtoVAZ OAO is a leading manufacturer of passenger cars for the Russian market as well as for export to Georgia, Armenia, Azerbaijan and other Eastern European countries. The company's models include the 4-door Granta sedan, liftback and sport; the Vesta sedan; the XRAY crossover; the Largus 5-seat wagon and crossover, as well as the 7-seat wagon, crossover and van; and the 3-door, 5-door, urban and bronto four-wheel drives. The firm also has subsidiaries that specialize in: manufacturing components for the vehicles, distribution, vehicle maintenance, power supply, insurance and construction. AvtoVAZ produces more than 1 million automobiles and automobile kits annually. It occupies 20% of the Russian passenger car market. The company's joint venture with General Motors, GM-AvtoVAZ, produces the Chevrolet Niva, based on the Lada Niva 4x4 off-road vehicle. AvtoVaz OAO is part of the Renault-Nissan-Mitsubishi alliance. AvtoVAZ is owned by Alliance Rostec Auto BV, a joint venture (JV) between Renault SA, holding 67.61% of the JV, and Russian state conglomerate Rostec. In mid-2019, Rostec announced plans to reduce its stake in AvtoVAZ to 25%, selling it to Renault.

FINANCIAL DATA: *Note: Data for latest year may not have been available at press time.*

In U.S. $	2018	2017	2016	2015	2014	2013
Revenue	3,477,130,000	3,913,230,000	3,038,250,000	2,712,636,232	3,118,022,766	4,776,800,000
R&D Expense						
Operating Income						
Operating Margin %						
SGA Expense						
Net Income	97,222,300	-167,560,000	-735,679,000	-1,121,901,575	403,964,701	-207,500,000
Operating Cash Flow						
Capital Expenditure						
EBITDA						
Return on Assets %						
Return on Equity %						
Debt to Equity						

CONTACT INFORMATION:

Phone: 7-846-937-7125 Fax: 7-846-937-8221
Toll-Free:
Address: Yuzhnoye Shosse 36 Samarskaya, Tolyatti, 445633 Russia

STOCK TICKER/OTHER:

Stock Ticker: Subsidiary
Exchange:
Employees: 96,777
Fiscal Year Ends: 12/31
Parent Company: Renault SA

SALARIES/BONUSES:

Top Exec. Salary: $ Bonus: $
Second Exec. Salary: $ Bonus: $

OTHER THOUGHTS:

Estimated Female Officers or Directors:
Hot Spot for Advancement for Women/Minorities:

BAIC BluePark New Energy Technology Co Ltd www.bjev.com.cn

NAIC Code: 336111

TYPES OF BUSINESS:

Electric Automobile Manufacturing

BRANDS/DIVISIONS/AFFILIATES:

BAIC Motor Corporation Limited
BH Leasing Co Ltd

GROWTH PLANS/SPECIAL FEATURES:

BAIC BluePark New Energy Technology Co., Ltd. is a passenger vehicle manufacturer in China. Via joint ventures, the firm's models include premium passenger vehicles, multi-purpose passenger vehicles, mid- to -high-end passenger vehicles and proprietary brand passenger vehicles. BAIC BluePark also manufactures pure electric passenger vehicles. The company engages in the research and development, manufacture and sales and after-sales services of these vehicles. It also produces core parts and components of passenger vehicles, and provides vehicle financing and other related services and solutions. Brands of the firm include Beijing, Senova, BJ and Fujian Benz. BAIC BluePark and Hyuandai Motor Group (China) Ltd. formed a joint venture called BH Leasing Co., Ltd., which offers automobile leasing and lease financing services and solutions. BAIC BluePark operates as a subsidiary of BAIC Motor Corporation Limited.

CONTACTS: *Note: Officers with more than one job title may be intentionally listed here more than once.*

Heyi Xu, Chmn.

FINANCIAL DATA: *Note: Data for latest year may not have been available at press time.*

In U.S. $	2018	2017	2016	2015	2014	2013
Revenue	2,389,870,000	1,764,780,000				
R&D Expense						
Operating Income						
Operating Margin %						
SGA Expense						
Net Income	20,974,200	6,275,160				
Operating Cash Flow						
Capital Expenditure						
EBITDA						
Return on Assets %						
Return on Equity %						
Debt to Equity						

CONTACT INFORMATION:

Phone: 8628-6976-5187 Fax:
Toll-Free:
Address: No. 99, Shuanghe St., Beijing, 101300 China

STOCK TICKER/OTHER:

Stock Ticker: 600733 Exchange: Shanghai
Employees: 3,994 Fiscal Year Ends:
Parent Company: BAIC Motor Corporation Limited

SALARIES/BONUSES:

Top Exec. Salary: $ Bonus: $
Second Exec. Salary: $ Bonus: $

OTHER THOUGHTS:

Estimated Female Officers or Directors:
Hot Spot for Advancement for Women/Minorities:

BAIC Motor Corporation Limited

www.baicmotor.com/en/

NAIC Code: 336111

TYPES OF BUSINESS:

Automobile Manufacturing
Passenger Vehicles
Commercial Vehicles
Automotive Finance

BRANDS/DIVISIONS/AFFILIATES:

BAIC Motor Sales Co Ltd
Beijing Benz Automotive Co Ltd
Beijing Hyundai Motor Company
Fujian Benz Automotive Co Ltd
BAIC Senova
BJ

GROWTH PLANS/SPECIAL FEATURES:

BAIC Motor Corporation Limited is a Chinese passenger car manufacturer and service provider. The company comprises a range of brands, from middle-end to luxury to commercial luxury, including: the BAIC Senova and BJ brands of sedans, sport utility vehicles (SUVs) and off-road vehicles, all of which are marketed and sold through subsidiary BAIC Motor Sales Co., Ltd.; the Beijing Benz brand of engines and cars via joint venture company Beijing Benz Automotive Co., Ltd. (between BAIC and Daimler); the Bejing Hyundai brand of passenger vehicles via joint venture Beijing Hyundai Motor Company (BAIC and Korea Hyundai Motor Company); and the Fujian Benz brand of high-end passenger and commercial vehicles via joint venture Fujian Benz Automotive Co., Ltd. (BAIC and Fujian Motor Group). BAIC Motor Corporation also engages in research and development activities, and provides sales and after-sales services as well as automotive financing.

CONTACTS: *Note: Officers with more than one job title may be intentionally listed here more than once.*

Hongliang Chen, Pres.
Heyi Xu, Chmn.

FINANCIAL DATA: *Note: Data for latest year may not have been available at press time.*

In U.S. $	2018	2017	2016	2015	2014	2013
Revenue	22,087,200,000	20,599,700,000	16,721,000,000	12,958,700,000	9,160,630,000	2,090,620,000
R&D Expense						
Operating Income						
Operating Margin %						
SGA Expense						
Net Income	2,074,820,000	1,688,710,000	1,660,030,000	973,999,000	949,215,000	482,666,000
Operating Cash Flow						
Capital Expenditure						
EBITDA						
Return on Assets %						
Return on Equity %						
Debt to Equity						

CONTACT INFORMATION:

Phone: 86-10-5663-6000 Fax: 86-10-5663-6126
Toll-Free:
Address: 99 Shuanghe Ave., Shunyi Dist., Beijing, Beijing 101300 China

STOCK TICKER/OTHER:

Stock Ticker: 1958 Exchange: Hong Kong
Employees: 20,431 Fiscal Year Ends:
Parent Company:

SALARIES/BONUSES:

Top Exec. Salary: $ Bonus: $
Second Exec. Salary: $ Bonus: $

OTHER THOUGHTS:

Estimated Female Officers or Directors:
Hot Spot for Advancement for Women/Minorities:

Bajaj Auto Limited

www.bajajauto.com

NAIC Code: 336991

TYPES OF BUSINESS:

Motorcycle Manufacturer
Commercial Vehicle Manufacturer

BRANDS/DIVISIONS/AFFILIATES:

Bajaj Group
Dominar 400
Pulsar
Avenger
Platina
Compact
Maxima
Qute

CONTACTS: *Note: Officers with more than one job title may be intentionally listed here more than once.*

Rajiv Bajaj, Managing Dir.
J. Sridhar, Corp. Sec.
S. Ravikumar, Sr. VP-Bus. Dev. & Assurance
R.C. Maheshwari, Pres., Commercial Vehicle Bus.
K. Srinivas, Pres., Motorcycle Bus.
Eric Vas, Pres., Retail Finance
N.H. Hingorani, VP-Commercial
Rahul Bajaj, Chmn.
Rakesh Sharma, Pres., Int'l Bus.

GROWTH PLANS/SPECIAL FEATURES:

Bajaj Auto Limited is a leading India-based manufacturer of motorcycles and three-/four-wheeled commercial vehicles. Motorcycles come in seven models: Dominar 400, Pulsar, Avenger, V, Discover, Platina and CT. Intracity vehicles are compatible with all fuel types, including gas, liquefied petroleum gas (LPG), compressed natural gas (CNG) and diesel as well as for all categories such as small, medium and large. Intracity three-wheel models include Compact, Maxima and Maxima C, and the Qute model is a four-wheel quadricycle. Bajaj Auto markets its motorcycles and vehicles in 70 countries. The company also manufactures and sells spare parts and related accessories. It is the flagship of the Bajaj Group of companies, which is comprised of 34 companies.

FINANCIAL DATA: *Note: Data for latest year may not have been available at press time.*

In U.S. $	2018	2017	2016	2015	2014	2013
Revenue	3,858,300,000	3,745,590,000	3,539,197,518	3,294,728,419	3,210,943,037	3,302,300,000
R&D Expense						
Operating Income						
Operating Margin %						
SGA Expense						
Net Income	648,560,000	628,545,000	569,698,978	421,044,105	538,435,818	506,900,000
Operating Cash Flow						
Capital Expenditure						
EBITDA						
Return on Assets %						
Return on Equity %						
Debt to Equity						

CONTACT INFORMATION:

Phone: 91-20-2747-2851 Fax: 91-20-2747-3398
Toll-Free:
Address: Mumbai-Pune Rd., Bajaj Auto Complex, Akurdi, Pune, 411 035 India

STOCK TICKER/OTHER:

Stock Ticker: 532977
Employees: 8,013
Parent Company: Bajaj Group
Exchange: Bombay
Fiscal Year Ends: 03/31

SALARIES/BONUSES:

Top Exec. Salary: $ Bonus: $
Second Exec. Salary: $ Bonus: $

OTHER THOUGHTS:

Estimated Female Officers or Directors:
Hot Spot for Advancement for Women/Minorities:

Bayerische Motoren Werke AG (BMW Group) www.bmwgroup.com

NAIC Code: 336111

TYPES OF BUSINESS:

Automobile Manufacturing
Financial Services
Motorcycles
Software
Consulting Services
Fleet Management
IT Solutions
Engines

BRANDS/DIVISIONS/AFFILIATES:

MINI
Rolls-Royce Motor Cars
BMW Motoren
Bavaria Wirtschaftsagentur GmbH
BMW Technik
X1
HP4 RACE
C 650 GT

CONTACTS: *Note: Officers with more than one job title may be intentionally listed here more than once.*

Harald Krueger, CEO
Nicolas Peter, CFO
Ian Robertson, Dir.-Sales & Mktg.
Milagros Caina Carreiro-Andree, Dir.-Human Resources
Frank-Peter Arndt, Head-Prod.
Herbert Diess, Dir.-Dev.
Friedrich Eichner, Dir.-Finance
Harald Kruger, Dir.-MINI, Motorcycles, Rolls-Royce & After Sales
Peter Schwarzenbauer, Head-MINI, Rolly-Royce & Aftersales
Harald Krueger, Chmn.
Klaus Draeger, Chief Purchasing & Supplier Network Officer

GROWTH PLANS/SPECIAL FEATURES:

Bayerische Motoren Werke AG (BMW), based in Munich, Germany, is a leading vehicle manufacturer in Europe, with brands including BMW, MINI and Rolls-Royce Motor Cars. The company operates in three primary business segments: automobiles, motorcycles and financial services. The company's automobile models include the 2 through 8 series; the X1 through X7 sport utility series; the M series of performance vehicles; and the BMW i electric and hybrid vehicles, i3, i8 coupe and i8 roadster. The company also manufactures specialty vehicles such as the BMW X5 armored security vehicle. Additionally, BMW produces the MINI brand of cars (Cooper) and Rolls-Royce Motor Cars (Phantom, Ghost, Wraith, Dawn and Cullinan). BMW brand motorcycles include: Sport models HP4 RACE, S 1000 RR and R 1200 RS; Tour models K 1600 B, K 1600 Grand America, K1600 GTL, K 1600 GT, R 1200 RT and R 1250 RT; Roadster models R 1200 R, S 1000 R and G 310 R; Heritage model R nineT; Adventure models R 1200 GS,S 1000 XR, G 310 GS, R 1250 GS, F 750 GS and F 850 GS; and Urban Mobility models C 650 GT and C evolution. The financial services segment manages vehicle-related financial services, including financing and leasing, asset management, insurance, dealer financing and company car pools. Other group activities include Bavaria Wirtschaftsagentur GmbH, which provides insurance and other services to the firm; BMW Technik, which works to develop innovative automobile technologies; and BMW Motoren, which manufactures engines. The firm operates approximately 30 production and assembly facilities in 14 countries and has a global sales network in over 140 countries.

FINANCIAL DATA: *Note: Data for latest year may not have been available at press time.*

In U.S. $	2018	2017	2016	2015	2014	2013
Revenue	107,927,400,000	109,253,800,000	104,254,900,000	102,053,800,000	89,017,930,000	84,209,480,000
R&D Expense						
Operating Income	9,973,428,000	10,833,700,000	10,301,150,000	10,496,010,000	10,098,540,000	8,814,216,000
Operating Margin %		.10%	.10%	.10%	.11%	.10%
SGA Expense	10,582,370,000	10,584,590,000	10,139,500,000	9,558,237,000	8,737,821,000	8,032,551,000
Net Income	7,879,761,000	9,543,845,000	7,598,539,000	7,051,594,000	6,419,398,000	5,883,525,000
Operating Cash Flow	5,592,338,000	6,542,295,000	3,513,065,000	1,062,888,000	3,224,092,000	4,001,329,000
Capital Expenditure	8,610,497,000	7,874,225,000	6,447,077,000	6,520,151,000	6,752,657,000	7,383,747,000
EBITDA	16,955,270,000	17,591,900,000	16,775,910,000	16,085,030,000	15,001,110,000	13,485,390,000
Return on Assets %		.05%	.04%	.04%	.04%	.04%
Return on Equity %		.17%	.15%	.16%	.16%	.16%
Debt to Equity		0.902	1.051	0.999	1.014	0.988

CONTACT INFORMATION:

Phone: 49 89 3822 5858 Fax: 49 89 3821 4661
Toll-Free:
Address: BMW-HAUS, Petuelring 130, Munich, 80788 Germany

STOCK TICKER/OTHER:

Stock Ticker: BAMXF
Exchange: PINX
Employees: 134,682
Fiscal Year Ends: 12/31
Parent Company:

SALARIES/BONUSES:

Top Exec. Salary: $ Bonus: $
Second Exec. Salary: $ Bonus: $

OTHER THOUGHTS:

Estimated Female Officers or Directors: 5
Hot Spot for Advancement for Women/Minorities: Y

Beijing Automotive Import & Export Corporation

www.cccme.org.cn/shop/cccme0158/introduction.aspx

NAIC Code: 423110

TYPES OF BUSINESS:

Automobiles Import & Exports
Automotive Parts & Accessories
Vehicle Manufacturing

BRANDS/DIVISIONS/AFFILIATES:

Beijing Automotive Industry Holding Co Ltd

GROWTH PLANS/SPECIAL FEATURES:

Beijing Automotive Import & Export Corporation (BAIEC) is a leading supplier of automobiles in China, with capabilities ranging from auto manufacturing, parts supplies, technical solutions and import/export, as well as related financial services. Beijing Automotive Industry Holding Co., Ltd. is the holding company of BAIEC, with auto production bases throughout the country, producing approximately 300,000 cars per year in the jeep, light-duty trick and travelling van categories. BAIEC is present in key markets worldwide, including the U.S., Europe, Japan, Southeast Asia, Middle East, South America and Africa. The firm has numerous production bases and sales networks in 26 cities throughout China, and engages in auto sales, property management, license trading, tax reservation trading, materials trading and more.

CONTACTS: *Note: Officers with more than one job title may be intentionally listed here more than once.*

Wang Zhiming, Gen. Mgr.

FINANCIAL DATA: *Note: Data for latest year may not have been available at press time.*

In U.S. $	2018	2017	2016	2015	2014	2013
Revenue						
R&D Expense						
Operating Income						
Operating Margin %						
SGA Expense						
Net Income						
Operating Cash Flow						
Capital Expenditure						
EBITDA						
Return on Assets %						
Return on Equity %						
Debt to Equity						

CONTACT INFORMATION:

Phone: 86-10-66177658 Fax: 86-10-66177325
Toll-Free:
Address: No. 2 Xisi Dahongluochang, Xicheng District, Beijing, China

STOCK TICKER/OTHER:

Stock Ticker: Subsidiary Exchange:
Employees: Fiscal Year Ends:
Parent Company: Beijing Automotive Industry Holding Co Ltd

SALARIES/BONUSES:

Top Exec. Salary: $ Bonus: $
Second Exec. Salary: $ Bonus: $

OTHER THOUGHTS:

Estimated Female Officers or Directors:
Hot Spot for Advancement for Women/Minorities:

Benteler International AG

NAIC Code: 336300

www.benteler.com

TYPES OF BUSINESS:

Automotive Parts Manufacturing
Chassis & Structure Parts Manufacturing
Engine Parts Manufacturing
Exhaust Systems Manufacturing
Engineering Solutions
Design & Testing Services

BRANDS/DIVISIONS/AFFILIATES:

CONTACTS:

Note: Officers with more than one job title may be intentionally listed here more than once.

Ralf Gottel, CEO
Guido Huppertz, CFO

GROWTH PLANS/SPECIAL FEATURES:

Benteler Inernational AG is one of the largest industrial companies in Germany. The holding firm operates through three independent business divisions: automotive, steel/tube and distribution. The automotive division provides components and modules for chassis, body, engine and exhaust systems for nearly every major vehicle manufacturer. This segment also provides lightweight solutions for vehicle structures in steel and aluminum; mechanical engineering machines, systems and tools for the automotive industry; protective solutions for various customers and market segments; and innovative material composites for customized lightweight solutions. The steel/tube division develops and produces seamless and welded steel tubes for the automotive, energy and industry markets. The distribution division is a stockholding company for steel tubes with more than 1 million square feet of warehouse space. This segment offers a full range of carbon steel and stainless steel tubes, short and flexible delivery times, as well as customized services. Benteler's worldwide presence consists of locations in nearly 40 countries. In mid-2019, Benteler opened a new plant, a smart factory, in Mos, Spain, its eighth in the country. The plant is part of the company's automotive division and will produce rear axle components for a global automotive manufacturer.

FINANCIAL DATA:

Note: Data for latest year may not have been available at press time.

In U.S. $	2018	2017	2016	2015	2014	2013
Revenue	9,232,690,000	9,410,550,000	8,812,575,654	8,996,113,585	8,553,911,459	9,776,514,985
R&D Expense						
Operating Income						
Operating Margin %						
SGA Expense						
Net Income	35,686,300	120,697,000	130,127,444	75,481,302	114,569,833	4,127,033
Operating Cash Flow						
Capital Expenditure						
EBITDA						
Return on Assets %						
Return on Equity %						
Debt to Equity						

CONTACT INFORMATION:

Phone: 43-662-2283-0 Fax: 43-662-2283-0
Toll-Free:
Address: Schillerstranbe 25-27, Salzberg, 5020 Austria

STOCK TICKER/OTHER:

Stock Ticker: Private
Employees: 30,000
Parent Company:
Exchange:
Fiscal Year Ends: 12/31

SALARIES/BONUSES:

Top Exec. Salary: $ Bonus: $
Second Exec. Salary: $ Bonus: $

OTHER THOUGHTS:

Estimated Female Officers or Directors:
Hot Spot for Advancement for Women/Minorities:

Bentley Motors Limited

www.bentleymotors.com

NAIC Code: 336111

TYPES OF BUSINESS:

Automobile Manufacturing
Luxury Automobiles
Luxury Automobile Customization
Automobile Racing
Sports Competition Sponsorship

BRANDS/DIVISIONS/AFFILIATES:

Volkswagen AG
Mulsanne
Flying Spur
Continental GT
Bentayga

CONTACTS: *Note: Officers with more than one job title may be intentionally listed here more than once.*

Wolfgang Durheimer, CEO
Stefan Buscher, Dir.-Prod & Mktg.
Rolf Frech, Head-Eng.
Michael Straughan, Head-Mfg.
Wolfgang Glabus, Dir.-Comm.
Jan-Henrik Lafrentz, Head-Finance
Alice Wei, Dir.-Public Rel., Greater China
Andrea Baker, Head-Media Rel.
David Hilton, Head-Exterior Design

GROWTH PLANS/SPECIAL FEATURES:

Bentley Motors Limited, founded in 1919, designs and manufactures luxury automobiles. The company is a subsidiary of Volkswagen AG. Its current models include the Mulsanne, Flying Spur, Continental GT and Bentayga. The company also offers the option of custom-designed Bentleys and maintains a used car program. Its specialist commissioning department, Bentley Mulliner, allows clients to specify the degree of customization, including such options as a front wing vent, longer wheelbase or a specially tailored interior. Bentley also offers financial services, as well as a range of luxury consumer goods, including luggage and small leather accessories, apparel, books and prints, office accessories, gifts, model cars, camp chairs and umbrellas. Headquartered in the U.K., Bentley has global locations in the Americas, Europe, Russia, Middle East, India, Africa, Asia and Australasia.

Employee benefits include time off and gym and restaurant facilities.

FINANCIAL DATA: *Note: Data for latest year may not have been available at press time.*

In U.S. $	2018	2017	2016	2015	2014	2013
Revenue	1,770,590,000	2,156,150,000	2,315,665,432	2,168,019,758	2,613,240,000	2,172,380,649
R&D Expense						
Operating Income						
Operating Margin %						
SGA Expense						
Net Income	-329,412,000	65,882,500	156,258,411	123,180,541	261,324,000	217,368,273
Operating Cash Flow						
Capital Expenditure						
EBITDA						
Return on Assets %						
Return on Equity %						
Debt to Equity						

CONTACT INFORMATION:

Phone: 44-1270-255-155 Fax:
Toll-Free: 877-300-8803
Address: Pyms Ln., Crewe, Cheshire CW1 3PL United Kingdom

STOCK TICKER/OTHER:

Stock Ticker: Subsidiary
Employees: 4,000
Parent Company: Volkswagen AG
Exchange:
Fiscal Year Ends: 12/31

SALARIES/BONUSES:

Top Exec. Salary: $ Bonus: $
Second Exec. Salary: $ Bonus: $

OTHER THOUGHTS:

Estimated Female Officers or Directors: 3
Hot Spot for Advancement for Women/Minorities: Y

Berkshire Hathaway Automotive

www.berkshirehathawayautomotive.com

NAIC Code: 441110

TYPES OF BUSINESS:

New Car Dealer

BRANDS/DIVISIONS/AFFILIATES:

Berkshire Hathaway Inc

CONTACTS:

Note: Officers with more than one job title may be intentionally listed here more than once.

Jeff Rachor, CEO
Larry Van Tuyl, Chmn.

GROWTH PLANS/SPECIAL FEATURES:

Berkshire Hathaway Automotive operates approximately 185 automotive dealerships and franchises across 10 U.S. states. These states include Arizona, California, Florida, Georgia, Illinois, Indiana, Missouri, Nebraska, New Mexico and Texas. The company's automotive inventory comprises new, pre-owned and certified pre-owned cars and trucks. Some of the many brands of vehicles include Ford, Nissan, Chevrolet, Toyota, Honda, Hyundai, Jeep, Infiniti, Lexus, GMC, Acura, KIA, Dodge, Volkswagen, Mazda and Subaru. Moreover, Berkshire provides an extensive array of services and products, including web services, digital marketing, in-store consultation, extended warranty services, automotive protection plans, auctions, collision center resources and a premier bi-weekly payment program for the auto industry. Berkshire Hathaway Automotive is a subsidiary of Berkshire Hathaway, Inc., which engages in diverse business activities, including property and casualty insurance/reinsurance, utilities/energy, freight rail transportation, finance, manufacturing, retailing and services.

FINANCIAL DATA:

Note: Data for latest year may not have been available at press time.

In U.S. $	2018	2017	2016	2015	2014	2013
Revenue	9,828,000,000	9,513,000,000	9,389,331,000	8,300,000,000	9,000,000,000	8,000,000,000
R&D Expense						
Operating Income						
Operating Margin %						
SGA Expense						
Net Income						
Operating Cash Flow						
Capital Expenditure						
EBITDA						
Return on Assets %						
Return on Equity %						
Debt to Equity						

CONTACT INFORMATION:

Phone: 972-536-2900 Fax:
Toll-Free:
Address: 8333 Royal Ridge Pkwy, Ste.130, Irving, TX 75063 United States

STOCK TICKER/OTHER:

Stock Ticker: Subsidiary
Employees: 10,964
Parent Company: Berkshire Hathaway Inc
Exchange:
Fiscal Year Ends: 12/31

SALARIES/BONUSES:

Top Exec. Salary: $ Bonus: $
Second Exec. Salary: $ Bonus: $

OTHER THOUGHTS:

Estimated Female Officers or Directors:
Hot Spot for Advancement for Women/Minorities:

Bilia AB

www.bilia.com

NAIC Code: 441110

TYPES OF BUSINESS:

New Car Dealers
Used Car Dealers
Car Maintenance
Fuel

BRANDS/DIVISIONS/AFFILIATES:

GROWTH PLANS/SPECIAL FEATURES:

Bilia AB is Scandinavia's leading seller of new and used cars and transport vehicles. It also sells fuel in Sweden. The company manages more than 130 facilities throughout Sweden, Norway, Germany, Luxembourg and Belgium, as well as online auction sites in Sweden and Norway. Major brands Bilia offers include Volvo, Renault, Ford, Lexus, MINI, BMW, Toyota and Dacia. In addition to car sales, the firm offers supplementary services such as damage centers, spare parts, car washes, glass centers, oil & work shop services and offers financing and insurance to customers. In late-2018, Bilia acquired Furubakken Bilverksted AS, an authorized BMW service business in Norway; and acquired a BMW and MINI dealer in Belgium. During 2019, Bilia acquired Jensen & Scheele Bil AS, which operates three facilities in Norway, including a Volvo facility, a damage repair workshop and a facility for the sale of used cars and other services.

CONTACTS: *Note: Officers with more than one job title may be intentionally listed here more than once.*

Per Avander, CEO
Kristina Franzen, CFO

FINANCIAL DATA: *Note: Data for latest year may not have been available at press time.*

In U.S. $	2018	2017	2016	2015	2014	2013
Revenue	3,050,000,000	3,000,000,000	2,891,073,792	2,472,275,712	2,354,968,576	2,135,229,568
R&D Expense						
Operating Income						
Operating Margin %						
SGA Expense						
Net Income			76,914,704	78,244,992	46,560,000	35,071,168
Operating Cash Flow						
Capital Expenditure						
EBITDA						
Return on Assets %						
Return on Equity %						
Debt to Equity						

CONTACT INFORMATION:

Phone: 46 317095500 Fax:
Toll-Free:
Address: Norra Langebergsgatan 3, Gothenburg, SE 400 91 Sweden

STOCK TICKER/OTHER:

Stock Ticker: BILI-A
Employees: 4,327
Parent Company:
Exchange: Stockholm
Fiscal Year Ends: 12/31

SALARIES/BONUSES:

Top Exec. Salary: $ Bonus: $
Second Exec. Salary: $ Bonus: $

OTHER THOUGHTS:

Estimated Female Officers or Directors:
Hot Spot for Advancement for Women/Minorities:

Blue Bird Corporation

www.blue-bird.com

NAIC Code: 336120

TYPES OF BUSINESS:

Bus Manufacturer
Financial Services
School Buses
Bus Parts

BRANDS/DIVISIONS/AFFILIATES:

ASP Holdings LLC
Blue Bird Micro Bird

CONTACTS: *Note: Officers with more than one job title may be intentionally listed here more than once.*

Philip Horlock, CEO
Phillip Tighe, CFO
Kevin Penn, Chairman of the Board
Thomas Roberts, Chief Administrative Officer
Mark Terry, Other Executive Officer
Paul Yousif, Secretary
Daniel Hennessy, Vice Chairman of the Board

GROWTH PLANS/SPECIAL FEATURES:

Blue Bird Corporation designs and manufactures school buses, with more than 550,000 buses sold since its 1927 formation. ASP Holdings, LLC controls approximately 43% of Blue Bird's common stock. The company has approximately 180,000 buses in operation today. Blue Bird operates through two business segments: bus and parts. The bus segment designs, engineers, manufactures and sells school buses and extended warranties. The buses are sold through a network of 50 U.S. and Canadian dealers that are exclusive to Blue Bird's Type C and D school buses. This division also sells directly to major fleet operators, the U.S. government, state governments and authorized dealers in foreign countries. In fiscal 2018, the bus segment sold 11,659 buses worldwide. Specialty buses include school buses that are converted to suit applications required by local, state and federal U.S. governments, and various customers for commercial and export markets. The Blue Bird Micro Bird is a Type A bus produced by this division, and is smaller than the Type C and D models. The parts segment sells replacement bus parts. This division maintains a parts distribution center in Ohio that fills demand for Blue Bird's specific parts, as well as parts by other makers. The parts segment is linked to more than 40 suppliers that ship directly to dealers and independent service centers when demand for parts cannot be fulfilled at Blue Bird's distribution facility. In mid-2019, Blue Bird opened a new state-of-the-art paint facility at its Georgia assembly plant, which will provide paint coverage within the production line of the school bus manufacturer.

FINANCIAL DATA: *Note: Data for latest year may not have been available at press time.*

In U.S. $	2018	2017	2016	2015	2014	2013
Revenue	1,024,976,000	990,602,000	932,010,000	919,128,000		
R&D Expense						
Operating Income	33,233,000	54,537,000	26,645,000	35,834,000	-5,683,000	
Operating Margin %		.06%	.03%	.04%		
SGA Expense	88,755,000	72,831,000	102,711,000	84,561,000	5,683,000	
Net Income	30,820,000	28,801,000	6,900,000	14,932,000	-5,650,000	
Operating Cash Flow	48,353,000	47,641,000	25,105,000	23,366,000	-1,029,000	
Capital Expenditure	32,118,000	9,252,000	9,583,000	5,190,000		
EBITDA	42,576,000	52,716,000	34,798,000	44,737,000	-5,683,000	
Return on Assets %		.06%	.01%	.05%	-.10%	
Return on Equity %					-2.25%	
Debt to Equity						

CONTACT INFORMATION:

Phone: 478-822-2801 Fax:
Toll-Free: 800-486-7122
Address: 3920 Arkwright Rd., 2/Fl, Macon, GA 31210 United States

STOCK TICKER/OTHER:

Stock Ticker: BLBD
Exchange: NAS
Employees: 1,762
Fiscal Year Ends: 09/30
Parent Company: ASP Holdings LLC

SALARIES/BONUSES:

Top Exec. Salary: $800,000 Bonus: $
Second Exec. Salary: $475,000 Bonus: $

OTHER THOUGHTS:

Estimated Female Officers or Directors:
Hot Spot for Advancement for Women/Minorities:

BMW of North America LLC

www.bmwusa.com

NAIC Code: 336111

TYPES OF BUSINESS:

Automobile Manufacturing
Financial Services
Automobile Manufacturing
Automobile Design Services

BRANDS/DIVISIONS/AFFILIATES:

Bayerische Motoren Werke AG (BMW)
BMW Financial Services NA LLC
Designworks
BMW Manufacturing Co LLC
ALPINA
Z4 Roadster
MINI
Rolls-Royce

CONTACTS: *Note: Officers with more than one job title may be intentionally listed here more than once.*

Bernhard Kuhnt, CEO
Ludwig Willisch, Pres.
Peter Miles, Exec. VP-Oper.

GROWTH PLANS/SPECIAL FEATURES:

BMW of North America LLC (BMW NA), a subsidiary of Bayerische Motoren Werke AG, imports BMW, MINI and Rolls-Royce motor cars and motorcycles. The firm markets, sells and provides financial services for BMW car dealerships, BMW motorcycle retailers, MINI passenger car dealers and Rolls-Royce dealers. The BMW product line includes the 2 series (coupe and convertible); 3 series (sedan, sports wagon and gran turismo); 4 series (coupe, gran coupe and convertible); 5 series (sedan and gran turismo); 6 series (coupe, gran coupe, ALPINA gran coupe and convertible); 7 series (sedan); 8 series (coupe and convertible); the X models (sports activity vehicles and coupe); the Z4 Roadster; the M models (sedan, coupe, gran coupe, convertible, sports activity vehicle and coupe); and the all-electric BMW i3 and plug-in hybrid i8, as well as the 530e and 745e sedans. The BMW Motorcycle product line includes several models: sport, tour, roadster, heritage, adventure and urban mobility. These motorcycles range from about $6,000 to $78,000 in price. The MINI line of passenger vehicles include the Mini Cooper and the Mini Cooper S (both available in convertible, hardtop and clubman models), and the Rolls-Royce line includes Phantom, Ghost and Wraith. BMW NA's sister companies include BMW Financial Services NA, LLC, which provides financial tools for buying or leasing a new or used vehicle; and Designworks, a design consultancy firm. BMW Manufacturing Co., LLC is the exclusive plant for all X5 and X3 Sports Activity vehicles and X6 and X4 Sports Activity Coupes. The vehicles produced at the factory are shipped to more than 130 countries.

FINANCIAL DATA: *Note: Data for latest year may not have been available at press time.*

In U.S. $	2018	2017	2016	2015	2014	2013
Revenue	18,000,000,000	19,000,000,000	18,832,600,000	20,388,972,750	18,061,340,000	17,039,000,000
R&D Expense						
Operating Income						
Operating Margin %						
SGA Expense						
Net Income	3,053,920,000					
Operating Cash Flow						
Capital Expenditure						
EBITDA						
Return on Assets %						
Return on Equity %						
Debt to Equity						

CONTACT INFORMATION:

Phone: 201-307-4000 Fax: 201-307-0880
Toll-Free: 800-831-1117
Address: 300 Chestnut Ridge Rd., Woodcliff Lake, NJ 07677 United States

STOCK TICKER/OTHER:

Stock Ticker: Subsidiary Exchange:
Employees: 19,500 Fiscal Year Ends: 12/31
Parent Company: Bayerische Motoren Werke AG (BMW)

SALARIES/BONUSES:

Top Exec. Salary: $ Bonus: $
Second Exec. Salary: $ Bonus: $

OTHER THOUGHTS:

Estimated Female Officers or Directors:
Hot Spot for Advancement for Women/Minorities:

Bob Rohrman Auto Group

NAIC Code: 441110

www.rohrman.com

TYPES OF BUSINESS:

Auto Dealers, Retail
Auto Service
Financing

BRANDS/DIVISIONS/AFFILIATES:

GROWTH PLANS/SPECIAL FEATURES:

Bob Rohrman Auto Group is a new and used automobile sales company with more than 30 dealerships in Indiana, Illinois and Wisconsin, as well as a collision center in Indiana. The dealerships sell and service a wide variety of cars from most major automotive manufacturers, including Acura, Nissan, Honda, Hyundai, Kia, Lincoln, Mitsubishi, Scion, Subaru, Toyota, Lexus, Volkswagen, Infiniti and Ford. In addition to sales, the firm offers car and truck service as well as parts. Bob Rohrman Auto Group's website provides users with a complete search feature for new and used vehicles. Moreover, customers may book service appointments, order parts online and compare Blue Book values directly on the group's site. The company also offers leasing and financing.

CONTACTS: *Note: Officers with more than one job title may be intentionally listed here more than once.*

Bob Rohrman, CEO
Bob Rohrman, Pres.
Craig Gibson, Dir.-Oper.
Tom Hanlan, Comptroller

FINANCIAL DATA: *Note: Data for latest year may not have been available at press time.*

In U.S. $	2018	2017	2016	2015	2014	2013
Revenue	1,103,592,881	1,051,040,839	1,000,991,275	1,150,000,000	1,100,000,000	1,000,000,000
R&D Expense						
Operating Income						
Operating Margin %						
SGA Expense						
Net Income						
Operating Cash Flow						
Capital Expenditure						
EBITDA						
Return on Assets %						
Return on Equity %						
Debt to Equity						

CONTACT INFORMATION:

Phone: 765-448-1000 Fax: 765-449-2266
Toll-Free:
Address: 701 Sagamore Pkwy. S., Lafayette, IN 47905 United States

STOCK TICKER/OTHER:

Stock Ticker: Private
Exchange:
Employees: 1,750
Fiscal Year Ends: 12/31
Parent Company:

SALARIES/BONUSES:

Top Exec. Salary: $ Bonus: $
Second Exec. Salary: $ Bonus: $

OTHER THOUGHTS:

Estimated Female Officers or Directors:
Hot Spot for Advancement for Women/Minorities:

Sales, profits and employees may be estimates. Financial information, benefits and other data can change quickly and may vary from those stated here.

BorgWarner Emissions Systems LLC

www2.borgwarner.com/en/Emissions/default.aspx

NAIC Code: 336300

TYPES OF BUSINESS:

Automobile Parts, Manufacturing
Diesel Cold-Start Systems
Ignition Technology
Electronics & Sensors

BRANDS/DIVISIONS/AFFILIATES:

BorgWarner Inc

CONTACTS: *Note: Officers with more than one job title may be intentionally listed here more than once.*

Alexis Michas, Chmn.-Corporate

GROWTH PLANS/SPECIAL FEATURES:

BorgWarner Emissions Systems, LLC manufactures air management and emissions control systems for passenger cars, light trucks and commercial vehicles. The company's advanced technologies are designed to lower emissions, improve fuel economy and enhance vehicle performance. BorgWarner Emissions' products include: exhaust gas recirculation (EGR) modules, which consists of the valve, cooler, tubes and by-pass valve; and secondary air systems, tubular products, advanced actuators and integrated system solutions. BorgWarner Emissions' manufacturing facility in Ningbo, China, helps meet the demand for advanced emissions and thermal management systems in this country. The facility also produces gasoline and diesel ERG systems, ignition coils, exhaust heat recovery systems, high/low-voltage air heaters and high-voltage liquid heaters for combustion, hybrid and electric vehicles. Additional emissions and thermal systems plants are located in Spain, India and Brazil. BorgWarner Emissions operates as a subsidiary of BorgWarner, Inc.

FINANCIAL DATA: *Note: Data for latest year may not have been available at press time.*

In U.S. $	2018	2017	2016	2015	2014	2013
Revenue	6,163,085,250	5,869,605,000	5,590,100,000	5,500,000,000	5,076,000,000	5,022,000,000
R&D Expense						
Operating Income						
Operating Margin %						
SGA Expense						
Net Income						
Operating Cash Flow						
Capital Expenditure						
EBITDA						
Return on Assets %						
Return on Equity %						
Debt to Equity						

CONTACT INFORMATION:

Phone: 815-288-1462 Fax:
Toll-Free:
Address: 1350 Franklin Grove Rd., Dixon, IL 61021 United States

STOCK TICKER/OTHER:

Stock Ticker: Subsidiary
Employees:
Parent Company: BorgWarner Inc
Exchange:
Fiscal Year Ends: 03/31

SALARIES/BONUSES:

Top Exec. Salary: $ Bonus: $
Second Exec. Salary: $ Bonus: $

OTHER THOUGHTS:

Estimated Female Officers or Directors: 1
Hot Spot for Advancement for Women/Minorities:

BorgWarner Inc

www.borgwarner.com

NAIC Code: 336310

TYPES OF BUSINESS:

Gasoline Engine and Engine Parts Manufacturing
Motor Vehicle Transmissions
Power Train Parts
Turbochargers
Cooling Systems
Chain Systems
Industrial Equipment

BRANDS/DIVISIONS/AFFILIATES:

CONTACTS: *Note: Officers with more than one job title may be intentionally listed here more than once.*

Frederic Lissalde, CEO
Kevin Nowlan, CFO
Alexis Michas, Chairman of the Board
Thomas McGill, Chief Accounting Officer
Tonit Calaway, Chief Legal Officer
Brady Ericson, Chief Strategy Officer
Joseph Fadool, General Manager, Subsidiary
Joel Wiegert, General Manager, Subsidiary
Martin Fischer, General Manager, Subsidiary
Stefan Demmerle, General Manager, Subsidiary
Robin Kendrick, General Manager, Subsidiary
Anthony Hensel, Vice President, Divisional

GROWTH PLANS/SPECIAL FEATURES:

BorgWarner, Inc. manufactures and sells engineered systems and components, designed to improve fuel efficiency, air quality and vehicle stability, to original equipment manufacturers (OEMs) of passenger cars, SUVs, trucks, commercial transportation products and industrial equipment worldwide. BorgWarner's products fall into two operating segments: engine and drivetrain. The engine segment develops and manufactures products to improve fuel economy, reduce emissions and enhance performance. These products include combustion, hybrid and electric propulsion systems. Its technologies include turbo chargers, eBoosters, timing systems, emissions systems, thermal systems, gasoline ignition technology, cabin heaters, battery heaters and battery charging. The drivetrain segment develops and manufactures products to improve fuel economy, reduce emissions and enhance performance in combustion, hybrid and electric vehicles. This division's technologies include rotating electrical components, power electronics, clutching systems, control modules and all-wheel drive systems. Its mechanical products include friction, mechanical and controls products for automatic transmissions; and torque management products for all-wheel-drive vehicles. Rotating electrical components include starter motors, alternators and electric motors for hybrid and electric vehicles. BorgWarner operates manufacturing and technical facilities at 68 locations in 16 U.S. locations, nine in China, eight in Germany, seven in South Korea, four each in India and Mexico, three each in Brazil, Japan and the U.K., two in Italy, and one each in Canada, France, Hungary, Ireland, Poland, Portugal, Spain, Sweden and Thailand.

FINANCIAL DATA: *Note: Data for latest year may not have been available at press time.*

In U.S. $	2018	2017	2016	2015	2014	2013
Revenue	10,529,600,000	9,799,300,000	9,071,000,000	8,023,200,000	8,305,100,000	7,436,600,000
R&D Expense						
Operating Income	1,291,800,000	1,221,900,000	1,119,800,000	1,016,400,000	1,064,800,000	918,800,000
Operating Margin %		.12%	.12%	.13%	.13%	.12%
SGA Expense	945,700,000	898,500,000	817,500,000	687,700,000	702,000,000	645,600,000
Net Income	930,700,000	439,900,000	118,500,000	609,700,000	655,800,000	624,300,000
Operating Cash Flow	1,126,500,000	1,180,300,000	1,035,700,000	867,900,000	801,800,000	718,800,000
Capital Expenditure	546,600,000	560,000,000	500,600,000	577,300,000	563,000,000	417,800,000
EBITDA	1,685,900,000	1,541,900,000	666,500,000	1,307,400,000	1,346,900,000	1,202,900,000
Return on Assets %		.05%	.01%	.08%	.09%	.09%
Return on Equity %		.13%	.03%	.17%	.18%	.19%
Debt to Equity		0.566	0.635	0.598	0.198	0.287

CONTACT INFORMATION:

Phone: 248 754-9200 Fax:
Toll-Free:
Address: 3850 Hamlin Rd., Auburn Hills, MI 48326 United States

STOCK TICKER/OTHER:

Stock Ticker: BWA
Exchange: NYS
Employees: 27,000
Fiscal Year Ends: 12/31
Parent Company:

SALARIES/BONUSES:

Top Exec. Salary: $1,108,945 Bonus: $
Second Exec. Salary: $946,235 Bonus: $

OTHER THOUGHTS:

Estimated Female Officers or Directors: 4
Hot Spot for Advancement for Women/Minorities: Y

Braman Management Association

www.braman.com

NAIC Code: 441110

TYPES OF BUSINESS:

Auto Dealers, Retail
Parts & Service

BRANDS/DIVISIONS/AFFILIATES:

Bentley Palm Beach
Braman BMW of Jupiter
Braman BMW West Palm Beach
Braman MINI of Palm Beach
Braman Porsche
Rolls-Royce Motor Cars Palm Beach

GROWTH PLANS/SPECIAL FEATURES:

Braman Management Association operates a chain of dealerships that primarily sells upscale vehicles in Florida. New and used vehicles sold at the dealerships include Audi, Bentley, BMW, Bugatti, Cadillac, Honda, Hyundai, KIA, Mercedes-Benz, MINI, Porsche, Rolls Royce, Sprinter and Acura, among many others. The Bentley Palm Beach dealership sells exotic vehicles as well. Braman offers vehicle specials every day to online and offline customers, and provides parts and services, finance options and more. Dealerships include Bentley Palm Beach, Braman BMW of Jupiter, Braman BMW West Palm Beach, Braman MINI of Palm Beach, Braman Porsche and Rolls-Royce Motor Cars Palm Beach.

CONTACTS: *Note: Officers with more than one job title may be intentionally listed here more than once.*

Alex Shack, COO
Norman Braman, Pres.
Matt Gilmore, Dir.-IT

FINANCIAL DATA: *Note: Data for latest year may not have been available at press time.*

In U.S. $	2018	2017	2016	2015	2014	2013
Revenue	2,156,744,676	2,054,042,550	1,956,231,000	1,800,000,000	1,799,665,100	1,771,846,800
R&D Expense						
Operating Income						
Operating Margin %						
SGA Expense						
Net Income						
Operating Cash Flow						
Capital Expenditure						
EBITDA						
Return on Assets %						
Return on Equity %						
Debt to Equity						

CONTACT INFORMATION:

Phone: 305-438-2789 Fax:
Toll-Free:
Address: 2060 Biscayne Blvd., 2/Fl, Miami, FL 33137-5024 United States

STOCK TICKER/OTHER:

Stock Ticker: Private
Employees:
Parent Company:
Exchange:
Fiscal Year Ends: 12/31

SALARIES/BONUSES:

Top Exec. Salary: $ Bonus: $
Second Exec. Salary: $ Bonus: $

OTHER THOUGHTS:

Estimated Female Officers or Directors:
Hot Spot for Advancement for Women/Minorities:

Brembo SpA

www.brembo.com

NAIC Code: 336300

TYPES OF BUSINESS:

Automobile Parts Manufacturing
Brake Components & Systems
Racing Brake Systems
Seatbelts

BRANDS/DIVISIONS/AFFILIATES:

Brembo SGL Carbon Ceramic Brakes
AP Racing Ltd
Brembo Czech sro
Brembo Deutschland GmbH
Brembo Scaninavia AB
Lavorazioni Camune srl
Brembo Japan Co Ltd
Brembo North America Inc

CONTACTS: *Note: Officers with more than one job title may be intentionally listed here more than once.*

Daniele Schillaci, Managing Dir.
Alberto Bombassei, Pres.
Monica Michelini, Head-Media Rel.
Cristina Bombassei, Exec. Dir.
Alberto Bombassei, Chmn.

GROWTH PLANS/SPECIAL FEATURES:

Brembo SpA, based in Italy, designs, develops, produces and manufactures brake discs, components and systems for cars, motorcycles and commercial vehicles, as well as clutches and other components for the automotive racing market. The company's products are sold to various automotive manufacturers and original equipment manufacturers, and are also made for racing vehicles engaged in major motorsport competitions. Within the racing sector, the firm has won more than 300 championships, including car and motorcycle racing vehicles. Brembo also provides aftermarket replacement parts and vehicle maintenance services. The company is the owner of the Brembo, Breco, AP, Bybre and Marchesini brands. Brembo SGL Carbon Ceramic Brakes is a joint venture between Brembo and SGL Group, and was established to design, develop and produce carbon ceramic brakes. Brembo sells its products in 70 different countries, and has production sites in Italy, the U.K., Poland, Czech Republic, Spain, Germany, Brazil, the U.S., Mexico, China and India. Just a few of the company's wholly-owned subsidiaries include AP Racing Ltd., Brembo Czech sro, Brembo Deutschland GmbH, Brembo Scandinavia AB, Lavorazioni Camune srl, Brembo Japan Co. Ltd. and Brembo North America, Inc.

FINANCIAL DATA: *Note: Data for latest year may not have been available at press time.*

In U.S. $	2018	2017	2016	2015	2014	2013
Revenue	2,929,171,000	2,734,514,000	2,530,693,000	2,307,053,000	2,007,135,000	1,747,171,000
R&D Expense						
Operating Income	363,228,500	367,490,000	350,065,300	270,999,800	193,598,300	134,628,000
Operating Margin %		.13%	.14%	.12%	.10%	.08%
SGA Expense						
Net Income	263,893,900	291,660,800	266,421,600	203,678,000	142,885,300	98,556,250
Operating Cash Flow	495,560,300	424,911,400	399,535,000	345,750,700	234,824,000	184,713,200
Capital Expenditure	318,576,200	399,340,100	291,818,000	172,617,400	140,363,200	147,340,600
EBITDA	550,723,000	533,344,800	489,117,600	407,464,600	314,340,100	234,929,200
Return on Assets %		.12%	.14%	.12%	.09%	.07%
Return on Equity %		.28%	.31%	.30%	.27%	.22%
Debt to Equity		0.308	0.246	0.311	0.511	0.59

CONTACT INFORMATION:

Phone: 39 35-605-2111 Fax: 39 35605518
Toll-Free:
Address: Via Brembo 25, Curno, 24035 Italy

STOCK TICKER/OTHER:

Stock Ticker: BRBOF Exchange: GREY
Employees: 10,247 Fiscal Year Ends: 12/31
Parent Company:

SALARIES/BONUSES:

Top Exec. Salary: $ Bonus: $
Second Exec. Salary: $ Bonus: $

OTHER THOUGHTS:

Estimated Female Officers or Directors: 2
Hot Spot for Advancement for Women/Minorities: Y

Bridgestone Bandag LLC

www.bandag.com

NAIC Code: 326212

TYPES OF BUSINESS:

Auto Parts, Tire Treads
Retreading Equipment
Management & Outsourcing Services

BRANDS/DIVISIONS/AFFILIATES:

Bridgestone Corporation

CONTACTS:

Note: Officers with more than one job title may be intentionally listed here more than once.

Masaaki Tsuya, CEO-Bridgestone Corp.
Masaaki Tsuya, Chmn.-Corp.

GROWTH PLANS/SPECIAL FEATURES:

Bridgestone Bandag, LLC, a subsidiary of Bridgestone Corporation, manufactures and markets tire retreading materials, equipment and tire management services. The company has more than 650 franchise dealers on six continents. In North America, Bandag franchise dealers operate a network of repair and service facilities via more than 240 retread manufacturing plants and 1,700 points of service. Bandag has been retreading tires for 60 years and prides itself in producing retreads that perform like new tires at a fraction of the price. Its products are comprised of next-generation compounds that resist wear and tear, innovative designs that lower rolling resistance, increase fuel efficiency and reduce total cost of ownership. The Bandag retread process is patented, and its retread manufacturing network is ISO 9001:2000 certified. More than 800 tires per hour are retreaded with Bandag, which amounts to approximately 7 million tires in one year's time. In addition, the company offers fleet services such as emergency road service and assistance, as well as National Warranty fleet service. Bandag's international operations are organized under other Bridgestone Corporation international subsidiaries.

FINANCIAL DATA:

Note: Data for latest year may not have been available at press time.

In U.S. $	2018	2017	2016	2015	2014	2013
Revenue	1,819,125,000	1,732,500,000	1,650,000,000	1,410,000,000	1,230,000,000	1,200,000,000
R&D Expense						
Operating Income						
Operating Margin %						
SGA Expense						
Net Income						
Operating Cash Flow						
Capital Expenditure						
EBITDA						
Return on Assets %						
Return on Equity %						
Debt to Equity						

CONTACT INFORMATION:

Phone: 563-262-2511 Fax:
Toll-Free:
Address: 2000 Bandag Dr., Muscatine, IA 52761 United States

STOCK TICKER/OTHER:

Stock Ticker: Subsidiary
Employees: 235
Parent Company: Bridgestone Corporation
Exchange:
Fiscal Year Ends: 12/31

SALARIES/BONUSES:

Top Exec. Salary: $ Bonus: $
Second Exec. Salary: $ Bonus: $

OTHER THOUGHTS:

Estimated Female Officers or Directors:
Hot Spot for Advancement for Women/Minorities:

Bridgestone Corporation

NAIC Code: 326200

www.bridgestone.com

TYPES OF BUSINESS:

Plastics & Rubber, Manufacturing
Tires
Building Materials
Adhesive Films
Industrial Products
Marine Products
Sporting Goods
Bicycles

BRANDS/DIVISIONS/AFFILIATES:

Bridgestone Americas Inc
Bridgestone Europe NV/SA
Bridgestone Asia Pacific Pte Ltd

GROWTH PLANS/SPECIAL FEATURES:

Bridgestone Corporation is a major producer of tires and rubber products. The firm, along with its subsidiaries and affiliates, manufacture a variety of tires, tire materials and other products at 180 plants across the globe. Bridgestone operates in two principal business segments: tires and diversified products. The tire business manufactures and markets tires for passenger vehicles, aircraft, construction and mining vehicles, agricultural and industrial machinery, motorcycles and scooters. This division also provides retreading products and services, automotive maintenance and repair work, raw materials for tires and other tire-related products. The diversified products unit supplies chemical and industrial products, including vehicle parts, polyurethane foam seat pads, anti-vibration rubber, conveyor belts, multi-rubber bearings, films used in plasma display panels and civil engineering and construction materials and equipment; sporting goods, such as golf balls and clubs; and bicycles and related accessories. Some of the company's larger subsidiaries include: Bridgestone Americas, Inc., which oversees the company's operations in the Americas; Bridgestone Europe NV/SA, overseeing the European operations; and Bridgestone Asia Pacific Pte. Ltd., overseeing the tire operations in Asia and Oceania. In early-2019, Bridgestone announced that it had ceased all EVA-related operations (electric vehicle approved); and transferred its ultra-high-purity fine ceramics silicon carbide (SiC) component operations to MARUWA CO., LTD.

CONTACTS: *Note: Officers with more than one job title may be intentionally listed here more than once.*

Masaaki Tsuya, CEO
Akihiro Eto, Pres.
Yuichiro Takenami, VP-Central Research & Global Innovation
Masato Banno, CTO
Masato Hiruma, VP-Prod. Dev.
Shingo Kubota, General Counsel
Asahiko Nishiyama, VP-Original Equipment Tire Sales
Narumi Zaitsu, Sr. VP-Intl. Tire Bus. Oper.
Franco Annunziato, CEO
Minoru Shimizu, Chmn.
Masaaki Tsuya, Chmn.
Gary Garfield, CEO
Masakazu Sekiguchi, VP-Global Prod. Admin. & Logistics

FINANCIAL DATA: *Note: Data for latest year may not have been available at press time.*

In U.S. $	2018	2017	2016	2015	2014	2013
Revenue	33,542,650,000	33,481,230,000	30,665,480,000	34,830,460,000	33,761,850,000	32,788,930,000
R&D Expense	951,580,600	917,028,200	876,704,600	872,790,000	865,162,700	818,755,800
Operating Income	3,700,937,000	3,850,873,000	4,131,162,000	4,753,281,000	4,392,961,000	4,026,245,000
Operating Margin %		.12%	.21%	.21%	.20%	.19%
SGA Expense	2,753,869,000	2,663,426,000	2,469,491,000	2,652,187,000	2,538,403,000	2,439,993,000
Net Income	2,680,041,000	2,649,100,000	2,440,269,000	2,612,516,000	2,762,259,000	1,856,763,000
Operating Cash Flow	3,316,991,000	3,842,180,000	4,085,049,000	5,090,406,000	3,938,835,000	4,335,325,000
Capital Expenditure	2,419,601,000	1,879,746,000	1,770,943,000	2,382,071,000	2,673,856,000	2,523,121,000
EBITDA	5,932,853,000	5,857,958,000	5,695,819,000	6,384,452,000	6,267,157,000	4,880,555,000
Return on Assets %		.08%	.07%	.07%	.08%	.06%
Return on Equity %		.12%	.12%	.13%	.15%	.13%
Debt to Equity		0.128	0.073	0.129	0.175	0.156

CONTACT INFORMATION:

Phone: 81 335670111 Fax:
Toll-Free:
Address: 1-1 Kyobashi 3-chome, Chuo-ku, Tokyo, 104-8340 Japan

STOCK TICKER/OTHER:

Stock Ticker: BRDCY
Exchange: PINX
Employees: 143,509
Fiscal Year Ends: 12/31
Parent Company:

SALARIES/BONUSES:

Top Exec. Salary: $ Bonus: $
Second Exec. Salary: $ Bonus: $

OTHER THOUGHTS:

Estimated Female Officers or Directors: 3
Hot Spot for Advancement for Women/Minorities: Y

Brilliance China Automotive Holdings Limited

www.brillianceauto.com

NAIC Code: 336111

TYPES OF BUSINESS:

Automobile Manufacturing
Minibus Manufacturing
Engine & Components Manufacturing

BRANDS/DIVISIONS/AFFILIATES:

Huachen Automotive Group Holdings Co Ltd
Renault SAS
BMW Brilliance Automotive Ltd
Renault Brilliance Jinbei Automotive Co Ltd
Brilliance-BEA Auto Finance Co Ltd
Xinchen China Power Holdings Limited

CONTACTS: *Note: Officers with more than one job title may be intentionally listed here more than once.*

Bingzhe Yan, CEO
Qi Yumin, Pres.
Zuming Qian, CFO
Lisa Ng, Sr. VP
Xiao An Wu, Chmn.

GROWTH PLANS/SPECIAL FEATURES:

Brilliance China Automotive Holdings Limited (Brilliance) is a leading manufacturer of autos and passenger vehicles in China. Brilliance principally manufactures and sells passenger vehicles, including minibuses, sport utility vehicles (SUVs), multi-purpose vehicles (MPVs) and sedans through its many subsidiaries and joint ventures. During 2018, Brilliance sold 23.71 million passenger vehicles, an approximate 4.1% decrease from the year before. Minority-owned BMW Brilliance Automotive Ltd. sold 466,182 BMW vehicles in 2018, and offers a variety of model architectures and drivetrains. The minibus division is operated by joint venture company Renault Brilliance Jinbei Automotive Co., Ltd. (with Renault SAS), offering light commercial vehicles. Renault Brilliance sold 43,000 minibuses and MVPs in 2018. Brilliance-BEA Auto Finance Co., Ltd. is the company's auto finance subsidiary in China, and supports the group's vehicle sales and provides finance options for other brands. Brilliance also manufactures and sells automotive parts and components, including engines, moldings, seats, axles, safety/airbag systems, interior decorations and more. In addition, Brilliance holds a 31.20% equity stake in Xinchen China Power Holdings Limited, which develops, manufactures and sells light-duty gasoline and diesel engines used by various domestic and international passenger vehicle and light commercial vehicle manufacturers. Brilliance's major shareholders are Huachen Automotive Group Holdings Co., Ltd. and Renault SAS. In 2019, Brilliance announced that BMW Brilliance would be commencing domestic and export production for the electrified version of the X3 model, to be called iX3, in 2020.

FINANCIAL DATA: *Note: Data for latest year may not have been available at press time.*

In U.S. $	2018	2017	2016	2015	2014	2013
Revenue	635,915,800	770,654,500	744,562,000	706,461,200	801,174,400	886,696,500
R&D Expense						
Operating Income	-125,788,400	-213,280,800	-107,717,500	-94,685,910	-46,500,420	-32,691,400
Operating Margin %		-.28%	-.14%	-.13%	-.06%	-.04%
SGA Expense	187,950,700	256,383,300	144,559,400	136,718,900	143,353,000	146,403,100
Net Income	845,644,400	635,749,700	534,920,800	507,704,500	784,994,900	490,193,800
Operating Cash Flow	-411,182,400	-369,988,800	-135,460,200	-148,300,400	111,804,600	-22,344,910
Capital Expenditure	66,942,500	90,642,260	69,784,110	88,100,070	107,107,800	89,518,400
EBITDA	835,400,600	626,953,500	556,018,200	530,712,400	819,147,600	523,355,000
Return on Assets %		.13%	.13%	.14%	.26%	.19%
Return on Equity %		.17%	.17%	.19%	.36%	.29%
Debt to Equity		0.003				

CONTACT INFORMATION:

Phone: 852 25237227 Fax: 852 25268472
Toll-Free:
Address: 8 Connaught Rd. Central, Charter House, Ste 1602-05, Hong Kong, Hong Kong

STOCK TICKER/OTHER:

Stock Ticker: BCAUF Exchange: PINX
Employees: 6,541 Fiscal Year Ends: 12/31
Parent Company:

SALARIES/BONUSES:

Top Exec. Salary: $ Bonus: $
Second Exec. Salary: $ Bonus: $

OTHER THOUGHTS:

Estimated Female Officers or Directors: 1
Hot Spot for Advancement for Women/Minorities: Y

Brown Automotive Group Ltd

www.brownscar.com

NAIC Code: 441110

TYPES OF BUSINESS:

Auto Dealers, Retail
Maintenance & Repair Services

BRANDS/DIVISIONS/AFFILIATES:

GROWTH PLANS/SPECIAL FEATURES:

Brown Automotive Group Ltd. sells new and pre-owned vehicles. The company offers brands such as Toyota, Honda, Nissan, Mazda, KIA, Hyundai, Volkswagen and Subaru through its network of 15 dealerships. These dealerships are primarily located in Washington, D.C., Virginia and Maryland. Additionally, Brown offers finance options, vehicle protection plans, as well as maintenance, collision and repair services. The company's website contains information regarding its dealerships and the makes and models for sale. Customers are also able to view vehicle inventories and current specials offered by the dealerships.

CONTACTS: *Note: Officers with more than one job title may be intentionally listed here more than once.*

William Schuiling, Chmn.

FINANCIAL DATA: *Note: Data for latest year may not have been available at press time.*

In U.S. $	2018	2017	2016	2015	2014	2013
Revenue						
R&D Expense						
Operating Income						
Operating Margin %						
SGA Expense						
Net Income						
Operating Cash Flow						
Capital Expenditure						
EBITDA						
Return on Assets %						
Return on Equity %						
Debt to Equity						

CONTACT INFORMATION:

Phone: 703-222-2412 Fax:
Toll-Free:
Address: 12500 Fair Lakes Cir., Fairfax, VA 22033 United States

STOCK TICKER/OTHER:

Stock Ticker: Private
Employees:
Parent Company:
Exchange:
Fiscal Year Ends: 12/31

SALARIES/BONUSES:

Top Exec. Salary: $ Bonus: $
Second Exec. Salary: $ Bonus: $

OTHER THOUGHTS:

Estimated Female Officers or Directors:
Hot Spot for Advancement for Women/Minorities:

BYD Company Limited

www.byd.com.cn

NAIC Code: 336111

TYPES OF BUSINESS:

Automobile Manufacturing
Cellular Telephone Equipment Manufacturing
Battery Manufacturing
Advanced Battery Technologies
Hybrid and Electric Cars
Contract Electronics Manufacturing

BRANDS/DIVISIONS/AFFILIATES:

Berkshire Hathaway Inc

CONTACTS: *Note: Officers with more than one job title may be intentionally listed here more than once.*

Chuan-Fu Wang, CEO
Chuan-Fu Wang, Pres.
Jing-Sheng Wu, CFO
Lian Yubo, VP
Chuan-Fu Wang, Chmn.

GROWTH PLANS/SPECIAL FEATURES:

BYD Company Limited, based in China, is involved in the design and production of automobiles as well as contract electronics manufacturing. The company operates in three divisions: automobiles, new energy and IT. The automobile division, operating as BYD Auto Company Limited, manufactures low to high-end vehicles, auto molding, auto parts, Dual Mode (DM) electric cars and all-electric cars. BYD's all-electric compact crossover, the BYD e6, can travel about 250 miles and has zero emissions. Through Shenzhen BYD Automobile Company Limited, the firm manufactures buses and coaches for the Chinese market. In addition to the development of BYD's electric vehicles, the new energy division has developed energy storage solutions based on its Fe battery technology and solar energy stations. Additionally, it has developed solar farms, LED lighting and electric forklifts. BYD's IT division produces rechargeable batteries, battery chargers, electro acoustic components, connectors, keypads, microelectronics, cell phone accessories and opto-electronics. It is a major manufacturer of cell phone handsets as well as batteries for iPods and iPhones. BYD has manufacturing facilities located across China and branch offices in the U.S. (Illinois and California), Europe, Japan, South Korea, India, Taiwan and Hong Kong. Berkshire Hathaway, Inc., owns a 24.6% stake in the company.

FINANCIAL DATA: *Note: Data for latest year may not have been available at press time.*

In U.S. $	2018	2017	2016	2015	2014	2013
Revenue	18,893,960,000	15,386,970,000	15,031,820,000	11,623,470,000	8,454,525,000	7,679,821,000
R&D Expense	724,839,500					
Operating Income	1,891,841,000	1,212,614,000	1,237,529,000	573,122,400	208,549,200	230,645,200
Operating Margin %		.07%	.08%	.05%	.02%	.03%
SGA Expense	1,233,386,000	1,701,393,000	1,603,709,000	1,203,337,000	967,404,000	773,828,600
Net Income	403,898,400	590,765,900	733,961,900	410,181,100	62,981,230	80,346,780
Operating Cash Flow	1,819,291,000	925,107,700	-268,119,100	558,168,100	5,530,552	353,919,400
Capital Expenditure	2,592,089,000	2,146,695,000	1,896,367,000	1,785,478,000	1,246,206,000	837,370,400
EBITDA	2,455,629,000	2,186,049,000	2,236,625,000	1,558,620,000	956,740,400	795,599,400
Return on Assets %		.03%	.04%	.03%	.01%	.01%
Return on Equity %		.08%	.12%	.10%	.02%	.03%
Debt to Equity		0.197	0.182	0.348	0.433	0.399

CONTACT INFORMATION:

Phone: 86-755-89888888 Fax: 86-755-84202222
Toll-Free:
Address: BYD Rd., No. 3009, Pingshan, Shenzhen, Guangdong 518118 China

STOCK TICKER/OTHER:

Stock Ticker: BYDDF
Exchange: PINX
Employees: 194,000
Fiscal Year Ends: 12/31
Parent Company:

SALARIES/BONUSES:

Top Exec. Salary: $ Bonus: $
Second Exec. Salary: $ Bonus: $

OTHER THOUGHTS:

Estimated Female Officers or Directors:
Hot Spot for Advancement for Women/Minorities:

Caliber Holdings Corporation

calibercollision.com

NAIC Code: 811100

TYPES OF BUSINESS:

Automotive Repair & Maintenance
Body Shops

BRANDS/DIVISIONS/AFFILIATES:

Hellman & Friedman LLC
OMERS Private Equity
Leonard Green & Partners LP
Caliber Collision Centers
CaliberCare Limited Lifetime Warranty
Abra

CONTACTS: *Note: Officers with more than one job title may be intentionally listed here more than once.*

Steve Grimshaw, CEO
Mark Sanders, Pres.
Bob Gary, CFO
Dave Goldstein, Chief Talent Officer
Ashley Denison, CIO
Greg Nichols, Chief Admin. Officer
Greg Nichols, General Counsel
Ron Davis, Chief Dev. Officer
Ty Gammill, VP-Sales

GROWTH PLANS/SPECIAL FEATURES:

Caliber Holdings Corporation, one of the largest independent body shop companies in the U.S., operates a chain of over 1,100 automotive repair centers across 37 states. The company offers comprehensive collision repair, which includes the equipment necessary to repair composites, high-strength steel, aluminum, safety systems, on-board computers and complex finishes. Repair services also include paint-less dent repair and auto glass repair. Caliber Collision Centers work with 24-hour-a-day towing agencies and rental car networks, with many of its locations featuring on-site Enterprise Rent-A-Car offices. In addition, the firm has partnered with most insurance companies in order to expedite and simplify repair. Caliber warrantees repair work against defects in materials and workmanship with its CaliberCare Limited Lifetime Warranty for as long as the customer owns the vehicle. The company also keeps its service centers open year-round, 24-hours-a-day. Caliber is majority-owned by OMERS Private Equity. In February 2019, OMERS Private Equity sold a majority share of Caliber Holdings to Hellman & Friedman, LLC. OMERS and Leonard Green & Partners LP are minority shareholders in the combined company. Hellman & Friedman merged its auto body repair division (Abra) with Caliber's, with each keeping their individual brands and locations until further notice.

Caliber offers its employees comprehensive benefits, retirement options and various employee assistance programs.

FINANCIAL DATA: *Note: Data for latest year may not have been available at press time.*

In U.S. $	2018	2017	2016	2015	2014	2013
Revenue	253,575,000	241,500,000	230,000,000	222,500,000	222,000,000	221,000,000
R&D Expense						
Operating Income						
Operating Margin %						
SGA Expense						
Net Income						
Operating Cash Flow						
Capital Expenditure						
EBITDA						
Return on Assets %						
Return on Equity %						
Debt to Equity						

CONTACT INFORMATION:

Phone: 469-948-9500 Fax:
Toll-Free: 888-225-4237
Address: 401 E. Corporate Dr., Ste. 150, Lewisville, TX 75057 United States

STOCK TICKER/OTHER:

Stock Ticker: Private
Exchange:
Employees: 4,100
Fiscal Year Ends: 12/31
Parent Company: Hellman & Friedman LLC

SALARIES/BONUSES:

Top Exec. Salary: $ Bonus: $
Second Exec. Salary: $ Bonus: $

OTHER THOUGHTS:

Estimated Female Officers or Directors: 1
Hot Spot for Advancement for Women/Minorities:

Calsonic Kansei Corporation

www.calsonickansei.co.jp

NAIC Code: 336300

TYPES OF BUSINESS:

Automobile Parts Manufacturing
Modular Assemblies
Retail Parts & Accessories
Industrial & Construction Equipment

BRANDS/DIVISIONS/AFFILIATES:

KKR & Co Inc
Magneti Marelli SpA
Marelli

CONTACTS:

Note: Officers with more than one job title may be intentionally listed here more than once.

Beda Bolzenius, CEO
Shigeo Shingyoji, Exec. VP
Kosaku Hosokawa, Exec. VP
Koji Furukawa, Sr. VP
Akira Fujisaki, Exec. VP

GROWTH PLANS/SPECIAL FEATURES:

Calsonic Kansei Corporation manufactures automotive parts and accessories, with a focus on integrated modular assemblies such as cockpits, front-ends and exhaust systems. The company comprises 81 production plants and 14 research and development centers across North America, Europe, China and Asia, and operates through 34 consolidated subsidiaries and 14 affiliates (as of March 2019). Modules offer automakers reduced costs and lighter composite weights and provide drivers with engineered efficiencies that increase ease of use and comfort. Calsonic Kansei's cockpit modules integrate instrument panels, air conditioning systems, airbags, electric controls, power components, audio systems, steering columns and other related components in one consolidated unit. Other modules include front-end modules that combine in one unit a radiator, condenser, internal air cooler and oil cooler. Other Calsonic Kansei automotive components and products include air conditioners, exhaust systems, compressors and keyless entry devices. KKR & Co., Inc. holds 95.21% of Calsonic Kansei's shares. In early-2019, Fiat Chrysler Automobiles NV sold Magneti Marelli SpA, a manufacturer of high-tech systems and components for the automotive sector, to Calsonic Kansei for â‚¬6.2 billion ($7.2 billion). The combined business consists of nearly 200 facilities and research centers worldwide, with plans to possibly transition under one banner, Marelli.

FINANCIAL DATA:

Note: Data for latest year may not have been available at press time.

In U.S. $	2018	2017	2016	2015	2014	2013
Revenue	10,700,000,000	10,000,000,000	9,704,868,864	8,896,336,896	8,464,439,296	7,010,364,928
R&D Expense						
Operating Income						
Operating Margin %						
SGA Expense						
Net Income			207,453,808	192,739,648	233,417,776	58,036,572
Operating Cash Flow						
Capital Expenditure						
EBITDA						
Return on Assets %						
Return on Equity %						
Debt to Equity						

CONTACT INFORMATION:

Phone: 81 486602111 Fax:
Toll-Free:
Address: 2-1917 Nisshin, Kita-ku, Saitama, 331-8501 Japan

STOCK TICKER/OTHER:

Stock Ticker: CLKNF
Exchange: GREY
Employees: 22,424
Fiscal Year Ends: 03/31
Parent Company: KKR & Co Inc

SALARIES/BONUSES:

Top Exec. Salary: $ Bonus: $
Second Exec. Salary: $ Bonus: $

OTHER THOUGHTS:

Estimated Female Officers or Directors:
Hot Spot for Advancement for Women/Minorities:

Camping World Holdings Inc

www.campingworld.com/

NAIC Code: 441210

TYPES OF BUSINESS:

Recreational Vehicle Dealers

BRANDS/DIVISIONS/AFFILIATES:

Good Sam
Camping World
Gander Mountain Company
Overton's Inc
Active Sports Inc
TheHouse.com
EIGHTEENOTHREE LLC
Erehwon Mountain Outfitter

CONTACTS: *Note: Officers with more than one job title may be intentionally listed here more than once.*

Melvin Flanigan,
Marcus Lemonis, CEO
Brent Moody, Director
Thomas Wolfe, President, Subsidiary

GROWTH PLANS/SPECIAL FEATURES:

Camping World Holdings, Inc. is a provider of services, protection plans, products and resources for recreational vehicle enthusiast. The company is the largest national network of RV-centric retail locations, with more than 130 nationwide in 36 U.S. states. Whether customers are ready to buy or trade an RV, in need of service, repair or professional installation for an RV, or in need of specialized accessories designed for an RV, Camping World aims to meet those needs. The firm provides its offerings and services through two iconic brands: Good Sam and Camping World. Good Sam consumer services and plans include extended vehicle service contracts, emergency roadside assistance, property and casualty insurance, membership clubs, vehicle financing/refinancing, travel protection, credit cards, magazines and hosted online forums. Camping World consumer offerings are grouped into three categories: new and used vehicles, including travel trailers, fifth wheel trailers and motorhomes; parts and services, including repair and maintenance, installation, parts, accessories and supplies; and dealership finance and insurance, including vehicle financing and various protection plans. In 2017, the firm acquired certain assets of Gander Mountain Company and its Overton's, Inc. marine and watersports business through a bankruptcy auction; acquired Active Sports, Inc., including its TheHouse.com online retail component specializing in bikes, sailboards, skateboards, wakeboards, etc.; and acquired EIGHTEENOTHREE, LLC, (dba W82), which specializes in snowboarding, longboarding, swimwear and more; and acquired Uncle Dan's LTD, a specialty retailer of outdoor gear, apparel and camping supplies. During 2018, Camping World acquired Erehwon Mountain Outfitter, a specialty retailer of outdoor gear and apparel; and announced that 14 of its retail locations would operate with a co-branded offering, including Gander Outdoors' products and services for the outdoor enthusiast, and Camping World parts, accessories and services for the RV enthusiast.

FINANCIAL DATA: *Note: Data for latest year may not have been available at press time.*

In U.S. $	2018	2017	2016	2015	2014	2013
Revenue	4,792,017,000	4,285,255,000	3,526,706,000	3,333,261,000	2,634,998,000	2,356,595,000
R&D Expense						
Operating Income	244,251,000	361,634,000	282,022,000	245,452,000	185,109,000	158,825,000
Operating Margin %		.08%	.08%	.07%	.07%	.07%
SGA Expense	1,069,359,000	853,160,000	691,884,000	644,409,000	536,485,000	482,655,000
Net Income	10,398,000	28,362,000	191,661,000	178,530,000	123,626,000	20,817,000
Operating Cash Flow	136,292,000	-9,094,000	223,710,000	112,143,000	44,064,000	14,623,000
Capital Expenditure	254,359,000	89,515,000	56,859,000	71,709,000	41,413,000	47,442,000
EBITDA	247,337,000	492,150,000	301,011,000	269,791,000	207,811,000	128,696,000
Return on Assets %		.01%	.00%	.02%	.11%	
Return on Equity %		.43%				
Debt to Equity		16.059	8.273			

CONTACT INFORMATION:

Phone: 847-808-3000 Fax:
Toll-Free:
Address: 250 Parkway Dr., Ste. 270, Lincolnshire, IL 60069 United States

STOCK TICKER/OTHER:

Stock Ticker: CWH
Employees: 7,511
Parent Company:
Exchange: NYS
Fiscal Year Ends:

SALARIES/BONUSES:

Top Exec. Salary: $250,000 Bonus: $
Second Exec. Salary: $250,000 Bonus: $

OTHER THOUGHTS:

Estimated Female Officers or Directors:
Hot Spot for Advancement for Women/Minorities:

Canadian Tire Corporation Limited

corp.canadiantire.ca

NAIC Code: 441320

TYPES OF BUSINESS:

Retail-Auto Parts & Tires
Retail-Auto Accessories
Banking Services
Financial Services-Insurance & Loans
Roadside Assistance
Gas Stations
Convenience Stores
Retail-Sports & Work Apparel

BRANDS/DIVISIONS/AFFILIATES:

Canadian Tire
Sport Chek
Mark's
Helly Hanson
Sports Experts
Pro Hockey Life
PartSource
CT Real Estate Investment Trust

CONTACTS: *Note: Officers with more than one job title may be intentionally listed here more than once.*

Dean McCann, CFO
Jane Nakamachi, Senior VP, Divisional
Maureen Sabia, Chairman of the Board
Stephen Wetmore, Director
Allan MacDonald, Executive VP, Divisional
Iain Kennedy, Executive VP, Divisional
Mahes Wickramasinghe, Executive VP, Divisional
James Christie, Executive VP
Gregory Craig, President, Subsidiary
Douglas Nathanson, Secretary

GROWTH PLANS/SPECIAL FEATURES:

Canadian Tire Corporation, Limited (CTC) is a group of interrelated businesses. The company comprises 13 brands. Canadian Tire has been in business for over 95 years, with more than 500 tire retail locations throughout Canada. Sport Chek is a sports retailer offering an assortment of apparel and equipment for athletes and enthusiasts of all levels. Mark's is Canadian industrial apparel retailer known for casual clothing and footwear, with over 380 stores. Canadian Tire Financial Services offers credit card and related payment solutions to meet the everyday financial needs of its customers. Helly Hanson offers professional-grade outdoor gear, with core categories including sailing, skiing, mountain, urban, rainwear and workwear. Gas+ is a leading independent gasoline retailer in Canada, pumping more than 1 billion liters of gas each year across nearly 300 locations. Atmosphere is an outdoor retailer with 80 locations, offering related apparel and equipment, whether for camping, hiking, snowshoeing, skiing and other outdoor activity. Sports Experts offers a range of clothing, shoes and sports equipment for active families and sports enthusiasts. Pro Hockey Life is one of the world's largest hockey-centric retailer, with 16 megastores across five Canadian provinces, offering related equipment and apparel. National Sports offers equipment and apparel curated for team sports and their organizations. Trio Hockey offers players, whether beginner, novice or adult, a wide selection of products and services, including skate sharpening and equipment cleaning. PartSource is a chain of 90 automotive parts specialty stores that offer brand name auto parts to the medium and heavy do-it-yourselfers as well as to commercial installers. Last, CT Real Estate Investment Trust is a closed-end real estate investment trust formed to own income-producing commercial properties. Its portfolio is comprised of over 325 properties (primarily retail) totaling 26 million square feet of gross leasable area (GLA) throughout the country.

FINANCIAL DATA: *Note: Data for latest year may not have been available at press time.*

In U.S. $	2018	2017	2016	2015	2014	2013
Revenue	10,656,180,000	10,183,350,000	9,611,914,000	9,307,662,000	9,446,600,000	8,933,221,000
R&D Expense						
Operating Income	962,404,200	928,598,500	837,489,500	829,303,400	761,085,400	674,903,300
Operating Margin %		.09%	.09%	.08%	.08%	.12%
SGA Expense	2,308,648,000	2,236,944,000	2,154,930,000	2,031,608,000	2,037,141,000	1,882,513,000
Net Income	524,596,300	557,113,600	507,162,900	499,810,500	457,818,500	425,377,100
Operating Cash Flow	611,991,200	737,360,600	747,669,200	741,984,300	435,685,600	603,956,600
Capital Expenditure	414,083,200	479,496,700	591,829,000	462,821,200	522,019,200	386,720,200
EBITDA	1,256,424,000	1,291,442,000	1,190,935,000	1,161,904,000	1,044,721,000	951,868,400
Return on Assets %		.05%	.04%	.04%	.04%	.04%
Return on Equity %		.15%	.13%	.13%	.12%	.11%
Debt to Equity		0.657	0.54	0.595	0.439	0.453

CONTACT INFORMATION:

Phone: 416 480-3000 Fax: 416 544-7715
Toll-Free: 800-387-8803
Address: 2180 Yonge St., Toronto, ON M4P 2V8 Canada

STOCK TICKER/OTHER:

Stock Ticker: CTC
Employees: 31,686
Parent Company:
Exchange: TSE
Fiscal Year Ends: 12/31

SALARIES/BONUSES:

Top Exec. Salary: $ Bonus: $
Second Exec. Salary: $ Bonus: $

OTHER THOUGHTS:

Estimated Female Officers or Directors: 3
Hot Spot for Advancement for Women/Minorities: Y

Car Monkeys Group

www.carmonkeys.com

NAIC Code: 441310

TYPES OF BUSINESS:

Used Automotive Parts Stores

BRANDS/DIVISIONS/AFFILIATES:

Car Monkeys
www.carmonkeys.com

GROWTH PLANS/SPECIAL FEATURES:

Car Monkeys Group is an online used automobile parts distributor under the brand name Car Monkeys. The firm's website, www.carmonkeys.com, uses a proprietary search and consolidation algorithm that allows the site to show customers all parts that meet their specific needs. Far more sophisticated than normal search engines, this technology understands and accounts for the fact that many identical parts and assemblies are shared across multiple models, model years, and even across brands, a fact most car owners are unaware of. Another aspect of this technology is the ability to identify competitively-priced parts of verifiable quality, allowing Car Monkeys to offer a 5-year unlimited-mileage warranty on used parts purchased from them.

CONTACTS: *Note: Officers with more than one job title may be intentionally listed here more than once.*

Mariusz Girt, Pres.
Marek Kudlinski, CTO
Pawel Girt, Chmn.

FINANCIAL DATA: *Note: Data for latest year may not have been available at press time.*

In U.S. $	2018	2017	2016	2015	2014	2013
Revenue	902,226	859,263	818,346	779,377	672,858	3,210
R&D Expense						
Operating Income						
Operating Margin %						
SGA Expense						
Net Income				-59,156	94,583	-331,020
Operating Cash Flow						
Capital Expenditure						
EBITDA						
Return on Assets %						
Return on Equity %						
Debt to Equity						

CONTACT INFORMATION:

Phone: 765-744-8383 Fax:
Toll-Free:
Address: 361 N. Dalton Ave., Albany, IN 47320 United States

STOCK TICKER/OTHER:

Stock Ticker: Private Exchange:
Employees: 3 Fiscal Year Ends: 06/30
Parent Company:

SALARIES/BONUSES:

Top Exec. Salary: $ Bonus: $
Second Exec. Salary: $ Bonus: $

OTHER THOUGHTS:

Estimated Female Officers or Directors:
Hot Spot for Advancement for Women/Minorities:

Carlisle Companies Incorporated

www.carlisle.com

NAIC Code: 336300

TYPES OF BUSINESS:

Automotive Products, Motors & Parts Manufacturing
Construction Materials
Industrial Components
Transportation Products
Tires & Braking Systems
Rubber & Plastic Components
Foodservice Equipment
Wire & Cables

BRANDS/DIVISIONS/AFFILIATES:

Binks
DeVilbiss
Ransburg
BGK
MS Powder
Petersen Aluminum Corporation

CONTACTS: *Note: Officers with more than one job title may be intentionally listed here more than once.*

D. Koch, CEO
Robert Roche, CFO
David Roberts, Chairman of the Board
Titus Ball, Chief Accounting Officer
John Berlin, President, Divisional
Shelley Bausch, President, Divisional
Karl Messmer, President, Divisional
Amelia Murillo, President, Divisional
Douglas Taylor, Vice President, Divisional
Kevin Zdimal, Vice President, Divisional
Scott Selbach, Vice President

GROWTH PLANS/SPECIAL FEATURES:

Carlisle Companies Incorporated manufactures and distributes a range of products for the roofing, construction, trucking, automotive, industrial equipment and aerospace industries. The firm operates through four segments. The construction materials segment manufactures and sells ethylene propylene diene monomer (EPDM) rubber and thermoplastic polyolefin (TPO) roofing systems. In addition, the segment markets and sells polyvinyl chloride (PVC) membrane and accessories purchased from third-party suppliers. The interconnect technologies segment designs and manufactures high performance wire, cable, fiber-optic and RF/microwave connectors; specialty cable assemblies; integrated wired racks; and fully integrated airframe subsystem applications for the aerospace, defense, electronics and test and measurement industries. The fluid technologies segment designs, manufactures and sells engineered liquid finishing equipment and system components primarily to the automotive, automotive refinishing, aerospace, agriculture, construction, marine and rail industries. This division sells products under the Binks, DeVilbiss, Ransburg, BGK and MS Powder brand names. Last, the brake & friction segment includes braking systems and friction products for off-highway, on-highway, aircraft and other industrial applications. In January 2019, Carlisle Companies acquired Petersen Aluminum Corporation; and agreed to acquire MicroConnex as well as Hosco Fittings and Integrated Dispense Solutions later that year.

FINANCIAL DATA: *Note: Data for latest year may not have been available at press time.*

In U.S. $	2018	2017	2016	2015	2014	2013
Revenue	4,479,500,000	4,089,900,000	3,675,400,000	3,543,200,000	3,204,000,000	2,943,000,000
R&D Expense	55,100,000	54,900,000	48,100,000	42,800,000	33,800,000	29,300,000
Operating Income	509,000,000	505,700,000	582,600,000	501,900,000	408,300,000	366,800,000
Operating Margin %		.12%	.16%	.14%	.13%	.12%
SGA Expense	625,400,000	589,400,000	532,000,000	461,900,000	379,000,000	353,700,000
Net Income	611,100,000	365,500,000	250,100,000	319,700,000	251,300,000	209,700,000
Operating Cash Flow	339,200,000	458,700,000	531,200,000	529,200,000	295,900,000	414,700,000
Capital Expenditure	120,700,000	159,900,000	108,800,000	72,100,000	118,800,000	110,800,000
EBITDA	701,200,000	671,300,000	580,200,000	631,900,000	513,800,000	481,200,000
Return on Assets %		.08%	.06%	.08%	.07%	.06%
Return on Equity %		.15%	.10%	.14%	.12%	.11%
Debt to Equity		0.627	0.242	0.255	0.34	0.378

CONTACT INFORMATION:

Phone: 480-781-5000 Fax:
Toll-Free:
Address: 16430 N. Scotssdale Rd., Ste. 400, Scottsdale, AZ 85254 United States

STOCK TICKER/OTHER:

Stock Ticker: CSL
Exchange: NYS
Employees: 13,600
Fiscal Year Ends: 12/31
Parent Company:

SALARIES/BONUSES:

Top Exec. Salary: $1,140,000 Bonus: $
Second Exec. Salary: $663,000 Bonus: $

OTHER THOUGHTS:

Estimated Female Officers or Directors: 1
Hot Spot for Advancement for Women/Minorities: Y

CarMax Inc

www.carmax.com

NAIC Code: 441120

TYPES OF BUSINESS:

Used Auto Dealers
New Auto Dealers
Online Sales
Vehicle Repair Services
Financial Services

BRANDS/DIVISIONS/AFFILIATES:

CarMax Auto Finance

CONTACTS: *Note: Officers with more than one job title may be intentionally listed here more than once.*

William Nash, CEO
Thomas Reedy, CFO
Thomas Folliard, Chairman of the Board
Jill Livesay, Chief Accounting Officer
Shamim Mohammad, Chief Information Officer
James Lyski, Chief Marketing Officer
Edwin Hill, COO
Eric Margolin, Executive VP
Diane Cafritz, Other Executive Officer
Jon Daniels, Senior VP, Divisional
Darren Newberry, Senior VP, Divisional
Joe Wilson, Senior VP, Divisional

GROWTH PLANS/SPECIAL FEATURES:

CarMax, Inc. is a leading retailer of used cars in the U.S. The firm purchases, reconditions and sells used vehicles through more than 200 used car superstores across the U.S. CarMax vehicles are typically 0 to 10 years old and range in price from $11,000 to $35,000. The firm also sells new vehicles at two of its locations under franchise agreements with car manufacturers. The company offers a wide selection of makes and models of both domestic and imported vehicles to appeal to diverse consumer preferences and budgets, including popular brands from manufacturers such as Chrysler, Ford, General Motors, Honda, Hyundai, Kia, Mazda, Nissan, Toyota and Volkswagen, and luxury brands such as Acura, BMW, Infiniti, Lexus and Mercedes-Benz. The company will also transfer any used vehicle in its nationwide inventory to a local superstore. Vehicles purchased through the company's in-store appraisal process that fall short of retail standards are sold at onsite wholesale auctions restricted to licensed automobile dealers. All store locations provide vehicle repair service and used-car warranty service. In addition, through the company's web site, customers can search new and used cars as well as find information on Kelley Blue Book figures, car buying tips, rebates and incentives. CarMax offers financing options through CarMax Auto Finance, including revolving credit and automobile installment loans. The firm retailed approximately 748,961 used vehicles in fiscal 2019. Vehicles purchased through CarMax's appraisal process that do not meet its retail standards (average age, mileage or vehicle condition) are sold to licensed dealers through onsite wholesale auctions. In mid-2019, CarMax launched a new car-buying experience to customers in Florida, where they can choose to complete the entire purchase process from home and have the car delivered, including the ability to test drive prior to purchase.

CarMax offers comprehensive benefits.

FINANCIAL DATA: *Note: Data for latest year may not have been available at press time.*

In U.S. $	2018	2017	2016	2015	2014	2013
Revenue	17,120,210,000	15,875,120,000	15,149,670,000	14,268,720,000	12,574,300,000	
R&D Expense						
Operating Income	711,808,000	694,790,000	666,825,000	629,802,000	493,486,000	
Operating Margin %	.04%	.04%	.04%	.04%	.04%	
SGA Expense	1,617,051,000	1,488,504,000	1,351,935,000	1,257,725,000	1,155,215,000	
Net Income	664,112,000	626,970,000	623,428,000	597,358,000	492,586,000	
Operating Cash Flow	-80,550,000	-468,138,000	-148,893,000	-968,130,000	-613,163,000	
Capital Expenditure	296,816,000	418,144,000	315,584,000	309,817,000	310,317,000	
EBITDA	1,314,295,000	1,231,696,000	1,183,662,000	1,108,977,000	930,067,000	
Return on Assets %	.04%	.04%	.05%	.05%	.05%	
Return on Equity %	.21%	.21%	.21%	.18%	.16%	
Debt to Equity	3.845	3.804	3.56	2.794	2.213	

CONTACT INFORMATION:

Phone: 804 747-0422 Fax: 804 747-5848
Toll-Free: 800-519-1511
Address: 12800 Tuckahoe Creek Pkwy., Richmond, VA 23238 United States

STOCK TICKER/OTHER:

Stock Ticker: KMX
Exchange: NYS
Employees: 24,344
Fiscal Year Ends: 02/28
Parent Company:

SALARIES/BONUSES:

Top Exec. Salary: $1,063,157 Bonus: $
Second Exec. Salary: $744,210 Bonus: $

OTHER THOUGHTS:

Estimated Female Officers or Directors: 9
Hot Spot for Advancement for Women/Minorities: Y

CARQUEST Auto Parts

www.carquest.com

NAIC Code: 423120

TYPES OF BUSINESS:

Auto Parts Distribution

BRANDS/DIVISIONS/AFFILIATES:

Advance Auto Parts Inc
TECH-NET Professional Auto Service
CARQUEST eServices
CARQUEST Technical Institute
Direct-Hit

CONTACTS: *Note: Officers with more than one job title may be intentionally listed here more than once.*

David McCartney, Pres.
Randal Long, VP-Product Mgmt.
Mike DeSorbo, Dir.-Professional Markets

GROWTH PLANS/SPECIAL FEATURES:

CARQUEST Auto Parts, a subsidiary of Advance Auto Parts, Inc., operates a chain of over 1,210 automotive parts stores, independently and distributor-owned, located throughout the U.S. Items available in stores include temperature control and cooling products, steering and suspension products, engine and mechanical systems, brake systems, drivetrain systems, engine performance and emissions control systems, temperature control and cooling systems and electrical and vision systems. In addition, it provides parts, accessories, supplies and equipment for most models of light and heavy-weight trucks, recreational vehicles, agricultural equipment, buses and off-roading equipment. The firm also sells and distributes tools, equipment, chemicals, paint and accessories. CARQUEST's own branded line of products is sold to the distributor stores as well as to wholesalers for eventual resale to professional repair shops, service stations, dealerships and do-it-yourself (DIY) customers. CARQUEST owns TECH-NET Professional Auto Service, a network of independent automotive service facilities, and CARQUEST eServices, which provides professional customers with access to CARQUEST's inventory and catalog over the internet at any time. Through the CARQUEST Technical Institute, the firm offers online and instructor-led training programs for professional technicians and automotive repair facility owners. CARQUEST also offers Direct-Hit, an online vehicle diagnostic service.

The company offers its employees medical, dental and vision insurance; a 401(k); paid vacation; life, AD&D and long-term disability insurance; an employee stock ownership plan; flexible spending accounts; an employee assistance program; and education reimbursement.

FINANCIAL DATA: *Note: Data for latest year may not have been available at press time.*

In U.S. $	2018	2017	2016	2015	2014	2013
Revenue	3,060,225,000	3,045,000,000	2,900,000,000	3,400,000,000	3,000,000,000	2,300,000,000
R&D Expense						
Operating Income						
Operating Margin %						
SGA Expense						
Net Income						
Operating Cash Flow						
Capital Expenditure						
EBITDA						
Return on Assets %						
Return on Equity %						
Debt to Equity						

CONTACT INFORMATION:

Phone: 919-573-3000 Fax: 919-573-2501
Toll-Free: 877-735-2233
Address: 2635 E. Millbrook Rd., Raleigh, NC 27604 United States

STOCK TICKER/OTHER:

Stock Ticker: Subsidiary
Employees: 20,000
Parent Company: Advance Auto Parts Inc
Exchange:
Fiscal Year Ends: 12/31

SALARIES/BONUSES:

Top Exec. Salary: $ Bonus: $
Second Exec. Salary: $ Bonus: $

OTHER THOUGHTS:

Estimated Female Officers or Directors:
Hot Spot for Advancement for Women/Minorities:

Carvana Co

www.carvana.com

NAIC Code: 441120

TYPES OF BUSINESS:

Used Car Dealers
eCommerce Used Cars

BRANDS/DIVISIONS/AFFILIATES:

CONTACTS:

Note: Officers with more than one job title may be intentionally listed here more than once.

Ernie Garcia, CEO
Mark Jenkins, CFO
Benjamin Huston, Co-Founder
Ryan Keeton, Co-Founder
John Mckeon, Controller
Daniel Gill, Other Executive Officer
Paul Breaux, Vice President

GROWTH PLANS/SPECIAL FEATURES:

Carvana Co. operates an eCommerce platform for purchasing used cars. Consumers can research and identify a vehicle, inspect it using Carvana's proprietary 360-degree vehicle imaging technology, obtain financing and warranty coverage, purchase the vehicle and schedule delivery or pickup all from a computer or mobile device. The firm's transaction technologies and online platform enable customers to secure financing, complete the purchase and schedule delivery in as little as 10 minutes. Carvana's proprietary algorithms optimize its pool of over 15,000 vehicles, inspect and recondition the vehicles through a 150-point inspection process and manage a logistics network for delivering purchased cars directly to customers as soon as the following day. Customers in certain markets have the option to pick up their purchased vehicle at one of Carvana's proprietary vending machines. The firm's in-house distribution network serves more than 40 metropolitan markets. Car-owners can get an appraisal online, and either trade-in their vehicles in the form of a down payment or receive a check for selling the car to Carvana. Depending on the location, Carvana will either go to the car-owner's residence for a final trade-in/purchase inspection, or the vehicle can be dropped off at a vending machine. Every car sold comes with a seven-day money back guarantee. Vehicles offered include sport utility vehicles (SUVs), sedans, trucks, hatchbacks, six-cylinders, four-cylinders, all-wheel drives, four-wheel drives and more. Makes include Acura, Alfa Romeo, Audi, BMW, Buick, Cadillac, Chevrolet, Chrysler, Dodge, FIAT, Ford, Genesis, GMC, Honda, Hummer, Hyundai, Infiniti, Jaguar, Jeep, Kia, Land Rover, Lexus, Lincoln, Maserati, Mazda, Mercedes-Benz, MINI, Mitsubishi, Nissan, Porsche, Ram, Scion, Smart, Subaru, Tesla, Toyota, Volkswagen and Volvo. Most cars are no more than 10 years old.

Carvana offers health premiums and Carvana auto discounts to its employees.

FINANCIAL DATA:

Note: Data for latest year may not have been available at press time.

In U.S. $	2018	2017	2016	2015	2014	2013
Revenue	1,955,467,000	858,870,000	365,148,000	130,392,000	41,679,000	
R&D Expense						
Operating Income	-228,549,000	-155,309,000	-89,479,000	-35,332,000	-15,108,000	
Operating Margin %		-.18%	-.25%	-.27%	-.36%	
SGA Expense	425,258,000	223,400,000	108,676,000	36,678,000	14,684,000	
Net Income	-61,754,000	-18,313,000	-93,112,000	-4,009,000	-15,238,000	
Operating Cash Flow	-414,340,000	-199,924,000	-240,225,000	-53,508,000	-30,161,000	
Capital Expenditure	143,668,000	78,490,000	39,539,000	13,950,000	3,768,000	
EBITDA	-206,188,000	-145,089,000	-84,867,000	-32,568,000	-13,425,000	
Return on Assets %		-.04%	.05%	-.03%		
Return on Equity %						
Debt to Equity		1.694				

CONTACT INFORMATION:

Phone: 480-719-8809 Fax:
Toll-Free:
Address: 1930 W. Rio Salado Pkwy, Tempe, AZ 85821 United States

STOCK TICKER/OTHER:

Stock Ticker: CVNA
Exchange: NYS
Employees: 1,067
Fiscal Year Ends: 12/31
Parent Company:

SALARIES/BONUSES:

Top Exec. Salary: $400,000 Bonus: $
Second Exec. Salary: $375,000 Bonus: $

OTHER THOUGHTS:

Estimated Female Officers or Directors:
Hot Spot for Advancement for Women/Minorities:

CDK Global Inc

www.cdkglobal.com

NAIC Code: 0

TYPES OF BUSINESS:

Advertising-Automotive Dealerships & Manufacturers
Web-Based Software & CRM Tools
Training & Consulting Services
Media Services
Automotive Data Collection & Reporting
e-Commerce Services

BRANDS/DIVISIONS/AFFILIATES:

Progressus Media
ELEAD1ONE

CONTACTS: *Note: Officers with more than one job title may be intentionally listed here more than once.*

Brian Krzanich, CEO
Joseph Tautges, CFO
Leslie Brun, Chairman of the Board
Jennifer Williams, Chief Accounting Officer
Dean Crutchfield, Chief Information Officer
Rajiv Amar, Chief Technology Officer
Scott Mathews, Executive VP, Divisional
Lee Brunz, Executive VP
Ronald Frey, Executive VP
Amy Byrne, Executive VP
Neil Packham, President, Divisional
Daniel Flynn, President, Geographical

GROWTH PLANS/SPECIAL FEATURES:

CDK Global, Inc. provides integrated information technology and digital marketing solutions to the automotive retail and related industries. The firm operates through two business segments: CDK North America and CDK International. CDK North America comprises two divisions: retail solutions and advertising. The retail solutions division provides technology-based solutions such as automotive website platforms that help automotive retailers, original equipment manufacturers (OEMs) and other industry participants manage the acquisition, sale, financing, insuring, parts supply, repair and maintenance of vehicles in North America. These solutions help customers streamline operations, better target and serve customers and enhance the financial performance of their retail operations. This division also provides solutions to retailers and manufacturers of heavy trucks, construction equipment, agricultural equipment, motorcycles, boats and other marine and recreational vehicles. The advertising division provides advertising solutions such as management of digital advertising spend, for OEMs and automotive retailers. These solutions provide a coordinated offering across multiple marketing channels to help achieve customer marketing and sales objectives and coordinate execution between OEMs and their retailer networks. The CDK International segment provides technology-based solutions similar to the retail solutions division, but to approximately 100 countries outside the U.S. and Canada. Customers of this segment include automotive retail dealers and OEMs across Europe, the Middle East, Asia, Africa and Latin America. During 2018, CDK acquired: Progressus Media, a provider of mobile advertising solutions; and ELEAD1ONE, a customer relationship management software solutions provider.

The firm offers employees medical, dental and vision insurance; tuition reimbursement; relocation assistance; and a 401(k) plan.

FINANCIAL DATA: *Note: Data for latest year may not have been available at press time.*

In U.S. $	2018	2017	2016	2015	2014	2013
Revenue	2,273,200,000	2,220,200,000	2,114,600,000	2,063,500,000	1,973,600,000	1,839,200,000
R&D Expense						
Operating Income	615,400,000	507,600,000	422,700,000	359,200,000	352,700,000	313,700,000
Operating Margin %		.23%	.20%	.17%	.18%	.17%
SGA Expense	475,800,000	477,700,000	448,500,000	431,100,000	419,400,000	422,900,000
Net Income	380,800,000	295,600,000	239,300,000	178,400,000	226,900,000	199,400,000
Operating Cash Flow	461,600,000	431,000,000	320,100,000	267,900,000	258,300,000	263,300,000
Capital Expenditure	87,100,000	94,200,000	64,300,000	63,900,000	64,500,000	47,700,000
EBITDA	687,000,000	562,800,000	473,300,000	405,200,000	412,500,000	378,900,000
Return on Assets %		.11%	.10%	.07%	.09%	.08%
Return on Equity %		2.07%	.42%	.14%	.14%	.13%
Debt to Equity			3.308	1.261		

CONTACT INFORMATION:

Phone: 847-397-1700 Fax: 206-269-6350
Toll-Free: 800-909-8244
Address: 1950 Hassell Rd., Hoffman Estates, IL 60169 United States

STOCK TICKER/OTHER:

Stock Ticker: CDK
Employees: 8,900
Parent Company:
Exchange: NAS
Fiscal Year Ends: 06/30

SALARIES/BONUSES:

Top Exec. Salary: $595,833 Bonus: $400,000
Second Exec. Salary: $925,000 Bonus: $

OTHER THOUGHTS:

Estimated Female Officers or Directors: 1
Hot Spot for Advancement for Women/Minorities:

CFAO SA

www.cfaogroup.com

NAIC Code: 441110

TYPES OF BUSINESS:

New Car Dealers

BRANDS/DIVISIONS/AFFILIATES:

Toyota Motor Corporation
Toyota Tsusho Corporation
CFAO Automotive
CFAO Equipment
Eurapharma
Missionpharma
CFAO FMCG & AGRI
CFAO Retail

CONTACTS: *Note: Officers with more than one job title may be intentionally listed here more than once.*

Richard Bielle, CEO
Alain Pecheur, CFO
Cecile Desrez, VP-Human Resources
Richard Bielle, Chmn.

GROWTH PLANS/SPECIAL FEATURES:

CFAO SA is a specialized distributor of private and utility vehicles, pharmaceuticals, consumer goods, technology solutions and more. The company has operations in 36 countries in Africa, and access to 49 of the 54 markets of the continent, seven French overseas territories, in Denmark, in Portugal, in Italy and in Vietnam. CFAO is organized into four segments: mobility, healthcare, consumer goods and technology & energy. The mobility segment includes: CFAO Automotive sells passenger and commercial vehicles, tires, handling equipment and after-sales parts; CFAO Equipment serves mining and farming industries; LOXEA AVIS Fleet is a full-service rental company offering a range of vehicles and equipment to cover most construction, civil engineering, local authority, agricultural and industrial projects and needs; Africa Mobility Solutions provides import/export services in regards to passenger cars, commercial vehicles, trucks, buses, material handling machineries, motorcycles and spare parts; and production support offers specialized and tailored supply chain solutions in South Africa, with Toyota South Africa Manufacturing. The healthcare segment includes: Eurapharma, a pharmaceutical distributor in Africa and French overseas territories; and Missionpharma, offering intelligent solutions to the healthcare industry. The consumer goods segment includes: CFAO FMCG & AGRI produces and distributes consumer goods such as beverages, writing instruments, shaving products and cosmetics; and CFAO Retail, which is engaged in the shopping center development in Africa for grocery retailing and non-food retailing. Last, the technology & energy segment supplies integrated IT products and solutions as well as telecommunications systems, ATM management and radio communications operator services. This division's energy business provides development assistance for projects related to renewable energies such as geothermal power plants in Kenya. CFAO operates as a subsidiary of Toyota Tsusho Corporation, itself a subsidiary of Toyota Motor Corporation.

FINANCIAL DATA: *Note: Data for latest year may not have been available at press time.*

In U.S. $	2018	2017	2016	2015	2014	2013
Revenue	4,803,930,000	4,988,720,000	4,751,170,000	3,649,758,208	3,782,227,456	3,854,145,792
R&D Expense						
Operating Income						
Operating Margin %						
SGA Expense						
Net Income				113,241,624	106,761,568	106,655,336
Operating Cash Flow						
Capital Expenditure						
EBITDA						
Return on Assets %						
Return on Equity %						
Debt to Equity						

CONTACT INFORMATION:

Phone: 33 146235656 Fax: 33 146235710
Toll-Free:
Address: 18 rue Troyon, Sevres, 92310 France

STOCK TICKER/OTHER:

Stock Ticker: CFAO
Exchange: Paris
Employees: 15,200
Fiscal Year Ends:
Parent Company: Toyota Motor Corporation

SALARIES/BONUSES:

Top Exec. Salary: $ Bonus: $
Second Exec. Salary: $ Bonus: $

OTHER THOUGHTS:

Estimated Female Officers or Directors:
Hot Spot for Advancement for Women/Minorities:

Changan Automobile (Group) Co Ltd

www.globalchangan.com

NAIC Code: 336111

TYPES OF BUSINESS:

Automobile Manufacturing

BRANDS/DIVISIONS/AFFILIATES:

Chang An
Raeton
Eado
CS95
A800
CS15 EV400
Q20
Jiangling Motor Holdings

CONTACTS: *Note: Officers with more than one job title may be intentionally listed here more than once.*

Cui Yunjiang, Corp. Sec.
Cui Yunjiang, Chief Accountant
Wu Xueson, VP-China Automobile Group
Weidong Liu, Chmn.

GROWTH PLANS/SPECIAL FEATURES:

Changan Automobile (Group) Co., Ltd. is a government-owned Chinese automotive manufacturer that produces both consumer passenger cars and commercial vans and trucks under the Chang An brand name. Chang stands for lasting and An stands for safety. The company's current passenger car models include the Raeton, Eado and Alsvin; SUV models include the CS95, CS85, CS75, CS55, CS35, CS15 and CX70; MPV models include the A800, Ossan, Honor and S50; economy models include the CS15 EV400, Eado PHEV, Easo EV460, Benni EV360 and Benni EC260; and commercial models include the Star 5/9, G10, Star Truck and Q20. The firm's night vision technology, Thermal Imaging Technology, enlarges the visible range under difficult visibility conditions such as night and heavy fog via near-infrared, far-infrared and low-light intensifier lighting. Its full-automatic, one-key parking technology provides drivers automatic parking instructions outside the vehicle via a mobile phone app. Its self-adaptive cruise control and automatic emergency braking technologies detect vehicle distance and speed via radar, and controls the time-distance and braking systems for safety purposes. Changan's overseas research & development centers are located in China, Italy, Japan, England and the U.S. Changan sells its vehicles through independent retailer dealerships worldwide. During 2019, Changan rolled out its first vehicle in Pakistan through its production facility in Karachi; and Changan split its Jiangling Motor Holding joint venture (with Jiangling Motor Corporation Group and Aiways) into two separate companies, with one keeping the Jiangling Motor Holding name and one taking another name (to be announced) to secure production permits for new energy vehicles.

FINANCIAL DATA: *Note: Data for latest year may not have been available at press time.*

In U.S. $	2018	2017	2016	2015	2014	2013
Revenue	9,638,930,000	12,285,600,000	11,302,300,000	10,287,200,000	8,598,890,000	6,267,500,000
R&D Expense						
Operating Income						
Operating Margin %						
SGA Expense						
Net Income	105,167,000	1,106,830,000	1,478,800,000	1,528,720,000	1,221,740,000	544,891,000
Operating Cash Flow						
Capital Expenditure						
EBITDA						
Return on Assets %						
Return on Equity %						
Debt to Equity						

CONTACT INFORMATION:

Phone: 86-23-67594008 Fax: 86-23-67866055
Toll-Free:
Address: Yard 10, Chedaogou, Haidian Dist., Beijing 100089 China

STOCK TICKER/OTHER:

Stock Ticker: 625
Employees: 36,029
Parent Company:
Exchange: Shenzhen
Fiscal Year Ends: 12/31

SALARIES/BONUSES:

Top Exec. Salary: $ Bonus: $
Second Exec. Salary: $ Bonus: $

OTHER THOUGHTS:

Estimated Female Officers or Directors:
Hot Spot for Advancement for Women/Minorities:

Chapman Automotive Group LLC

www.chapmanchoice.com

NAIC Code: 441110

TYPES OF BUSINESS:

Auto Dealers, Retail
Parts & Service

BRANDS/DIVISIONS/AFFILIATES:

GROWTH PLANS/SPECIAL FEATURES:

Chapman Automotive Group, LLC sells new and pre-owned vehicles throughout the states of Nevada and Arizona. The firm has more than 25 dealership locations as well as five collision centers. The company sells Acura, Audi, BMW, Chevrolet, Chrysler, Dodge, Ford, Genesis, Honda, Hyundai, Jeep, Mazda, Mercedes-Benz, Porsche, RAM, Volkswagen, Isuzu and Sprinter automobiles. Chapman Automotive also provides part ordering, maintenance and repair services. The firm's website offers tools to search and locate centers; schedule appointments and courtesy vehicles and get quick estimates. Jerry Chapman founded the business in 1966.

Chapman offers employees health and dental plans, 401(k) retirement plans, paid vacations and an employee/family vehicle purchase plan.

CONTACTS: *Note: Officers with more than one job title may be intentionally listed here more than once.*

Edward Davault, CEO
Ted Chapman, Pres.

FINANCIAL DATA: *Note: Data for latest year may not have been available at press time.*

In U.S. $	2018	2017	2016	2015	2014	2013
Revenue	1,515,006,157	1,442,863,007	1,374,155,245	1,363,885,736		
R&D Expense						
Operating Income						
Operating Margin %						
SGA Expense						
Net Income						
Operating Cash Flow						
Capital Expenditure						
EBITDA						
Return on Assets %						
Return on Equity %						
Debt to Equity						

CONTACT INFORMATION:

Phone: 480-753-1234 Fax:
Toll-Free:
Address: 1150 N. 54th St. #5, Tempe, AZ 85284 United States

STOCK TICKER/OTHER:

Stock Ticker: Private
Employees: 1,700
Parent Company:
Exchange:
Fiscal Year Ends: 12/31

SALARIES/BONUSES:

Top Exec. Salary: $ Bonus: $
Second Exec. Salary: $ Bonus: $

OTHER THOUGHTS:

Estimated Female Officers or Directors:
Hot Spot for Advancement for Women/Minorities:

China Yuchai International Limited

www.cyilimited.com

NAIC Code: 336300

TYPES OF BUSINESS:

Diesel Engine Manufacturing
Hospitality and Property Management Services
Consumer Electronics, Distribution
Consumer Electronics, Contract Manufacturing

BRANDS/DIVISIONS/AFFILIATES:

Guangxi Yuchai Machinery Company Limited
HL Global Enterprises Limited
Guangxi Yuchau Exhaust Technology Co Ltd
Venture Delta Limited
Thakral Corporation Ltd

CONTACTS: *Note: Officers with more than one job title may be intentionally listed here more than once.*

Weng Ming Hoh, Pres.
Tak Chuen Kelvin Lai, VP-Operations
Thomas Khong Fock Phung, CFO
Shing Mei Foo (Deborah), General Counsel
Ira Stuart Outerbridge, III, Sec.

GROWTH PLANS/SPECIAL FEATURES:

China Yuchai International Limited (CYI) is a holding company with major interests in diesel engines and the hospitality industry. CYI's principal subsidiary is 76.4%-owned Guangxi Yuchai Machinery Company Limited (GYMC), which manufactures and sells diesel engines primarily for the Chinese market. GYMC also manufactures diesel generators and diesel engine parts at its facilities in the city of Yulin, in the Guangxi region of southern China. The subsidiary produces light-, medium- and heavy-duty diesel engines, and has benefitted in recent years from the continued expansion of the Chinese system of highways and toll roads, helping to fuel the general market demand for new trucks and buses to carry goods and passengers. Though the diesel engine business has historically represented CYI's primary investment and source of revenues, the firm has diversified into several additional business areas. The company holds a 48.9% share in HL Global Enterprises Limited (HLGE), a firm engaged in hospitality and property development activities primarily in Malaysia. Wholly-owned Guangxi Yuchai Exhaust Technology Co., Ltd. designs, produces and sells exhaust emission control systems for Chinese commercial vehicles. Wholly-owned Venture Delta Limited has a minority interest in Thakral Corporation Ltd. (TCL), which invests directly or with co-investors in real estate and other investment opportunities that include property-backed financial instruments. In mid-2019, CYI announced that its wholly-owned subsidiary Venture Lewis Limited had been dissolved.

FINANCIAL DATA: *Note: Data for latest year may not have been available at press time.*

In U.S. $	2018	2017	2016	2015	2014	2013
Revenue	2,362,676,000	2,356,748,000	1,985,187,000	1,995,153,000	2,387,794,000	2,310,247,000
R&D Expense	65,035,880	88,354,740	85,423,910	73,648,920	71,853,150	68,078,560
Operating Income	163,042,000	161,655,000	134,931,400	119,977,500	178,717,300	190,523,400
Operating Margin %		.07%	.07%	.06%	.07%	.08%
SGA Expense	225,834,900	263,801,800	218,549,000	217,592,200	232,250,000	225,212,500
Net Income	101,006,200	138,583,000	74,924,740	49,555,160	106,092,900	101,755,400
Operating Cash Flow	97,422,930	199,053,800	330,663,200	245,041,400	77,822,880	85,661,440
Capital Expenditure	85,477,090	42,053,640	51,060,810	57,793,680	100,349,400	73,367,090
EBITDA	250,354,600	314,596,000	208,787,700	184,052,800	253,983,600	248,133,600
Return on Assets %		.05%	.03%	.02%	.04%	.04%
Return on Equity %		.12%	.07%	.05%	.11%	.11%
Debt to Equity		0.003	0.002	0.008	0.154	0.161

CONTACT INFORMATION:

Phone: 65 6220-8411 Fax: 65 6221-1172
Toll-Free:
Address: 16 Raffles Quay, #39-01A, Hong Leong Bldg., Singapore, 048581 Singapore

STOCK TICKER/OTHER:

Stock Ticker: CYD
Employees: 9,887
Parent Company:
Exchange: NYS
Fiscal Year Ends: 12/31

SALARIES/BONUSES:

Top Exec. Salary: $ Bonus: $
Second Exec. Salary: $ Bonus: $

OTHER THOUGHTS:

Estimated Female Officers or Directors: 1
Hot Spot for Advancement for Women/Minorities:

Clarion Co Ltd

NAIC Code: 334310

www.clarion.com

TYPES OF BUSINESS:

Audio & Video Equipment, Manufacturing
Navigation Systems
Security Systems

BRANDS/DIVISIONS/AFFILIATES:

Hitachi Ltd

CONTACTS: *Note: Officers with more than one job title may be intentionally listed here more than once.*

Atsushi Kawabata, CEO
Toru Kaneko, Exec. Dir.
Hidetoshi Kawamoto, Exec. Dir.

GROWTH PLANS/SPECIAL FEATURES:

Clarion Co., Ltd., headquartered in Japan, develops safety, information and audio technology for automobiles and recreational vehicles. The safety and information systems division includes applications in automatic parking, safe driving support systems and autonomous driving technologies. Information systems comprise cloud information services that enhance connectivity for user information, vehicle operation and safety purposes. These cloud-based information networks include information management/control, cloud management, application management and policy management via onboard information devices that provide comfort and convenience in vehicles. The company's smart cockpit solutions integrate advanced connectivity technologies, safety, information, human machine interface and sound to create seamless connectivity within the vehicle. Clarion's proprietary map formats are used as a core source of information in its navigation systems. These formats comprise map readiness and map updates that cover the entire world, and provide data concerning road conditions in various regions, as well as a 3D locator that combines various sensor data with map data. Drive management systems encompass artificial intelligent (AI) technology for predicting driver behavior, route destinations and for controlling onboard devices. The audio technology segment features Clarion's sound processing technology, fully-digital speakers, emphasized bass sound and intelligent automatic tuning of audio settings based on the car model and speaker quality. Clarion continues to develop sound technologies that enable customers to enjoy better sound and sound options within their vehicles. The firm operates as a subsidiary of Hitachi Ltd.

FINANCIAL DATA: *Note: Data for latest year may not have been available at press time.*

In U.S. $	2018	2017	2016	2015	2014	2013
Revenue		2,050,000,000	1,981,080,000	1,832,380,000	1,859,092,000	1,621,700,000
R&D Expense						
Operating Income						
Operating Margin %						
SGA Expense						
Net Income			70,539,300	70,500,000	32,476,000	12,432,000
Operating Cash Flow						
Capital Expenditure						
EBITDA						
Return on Assets %						
Return on Equity %						
Debt to Equity						

CONTACT INFORMATION:

Phone: 81 486013700 Fax: 81 486013701
Toll-Free:
Address: 7-2 Shintoshin, Chuo-ku, Saitama-Shi, Saitama, 330-0081 Japan

STOCK TICKER/OTHER:

Stock Ticker: 6796
Employees: 10,000
Parent Company: Hitachi Ltd
Exchange: Tokyo
Fiscal Year Ends: 03/31

SALARIES/BONUSES:

Top Exec. Salary: $ Bonus: $
Second Exec. Salary: $ Bonus: $

OTHER THOUGHTS:

Estimated Female Officers or Directors:
Hot Spot for Advancement for Women/Minorities:

CODA Energy

www.codaenergy.com

NAIC Code: 335911

TYPES OF BUSINESS:

Energy Storage Systems

GROWTH PLANS/SPECIAL FEATURES:

CODA Energy designs, develops and manufactures scalable energy storage solutions. The company's energy storage systems support a smarter, cleaner and more reliable grid. UL Listed CODA Core, its safe and reliable storage and battery management system, helps commercial and industrial facilities reduce costs, control consumption and manage risk associated with energy use. CODA Energy develops, tests and implements battery and management systems for small- and large-scale applications ranging from electric vehicles to energy storage. The company's modular CODA Core Tower combines advanced lithium-ion cells with battery and temperature management systems and an integrated operating system designed to meet energy needs such as peak shaving, EV charging, renewable energy integration, backup power, frequency regulation and more. CODA Energy operates as a subsidiary of energy storage company, Exergonix, Inc.

BRANDS/DIVISIONS/AFFILIATES:

Exergonix Inc
UL Listed CODA Core
CODA Core Tower

CONTACTS: *Note: Officers with more than one job title may be intentionally listed here more than once.*

James Frasher, Dir.-Eng.
Clark Korbisch, Dir.-Field Oper.
Matt Sloustcher, Dir.-Gov't Rel. & Comm.
Michelle Mapel, Sr. Mgr.-Mktg.
Don Nissanka, Chmn.

FINANCIAL DATA: *Note: Data for latest year may not have been available at press time.*

In U.S. $	2018	2017	2016	2015	2014	2013
Revenue						
R&D Expense						
Operating Income						
Operating Margin %						
SGA Expense						
Net Income						
Operating Cash Flow						
Capital Expenditure						
EBITDA						
Return on Assets %						
Return on Equity %						
Debt to Equity						

CONTACT INFORMATION:

Phone: 626-775-3900 Fax:
Toll-Free: 855-377-2692
Address: 135 E. Maple Ave., Unit C, Monrovia, CA 91016 United States

STOCK TICKER/OTHER:

Stock Ticker: Private
Exchange:
Employees: 60
Fiscal Year Ends:
Parent Company: Exergonix Inc

SALARIES/BONUSES:

Top Exec. Salary: $ Bonus: $
Second Exec. Salary: $ Bonus: $

OTHER THOUGHTS:

Estimated Female Officers or Directors: 1
Hot Spot for Advancement for Women/Minorities:

Commercial Vehicle Group Inc (CVG)

www.cvgrp.com

NAIC Code: 336300

TYPES OF BUSINESS:

Commercial Cab Structures & Components
Suspension Seat Systems
Interior Trim Systems
Mirrors & Wiper Systems
Electronic Wire Harness Assemblies & Controls
Switches

BRANDS/DIVISIONS/AFFILIATES:

CVG
KAB Seating
Bostrom Seating
Sprague Devices
RoadWatch
Stratos
Moto Mirror
FinishTEK

CONTACTS: *Note: Officers with more than one job title may be intentionally listed here more than once.*

Patrick Miller, CEO
C. Trenary, CFO
Scott Arves, Chairman of the Board
Stacie Fleming, Chief Accounting Officer
Dale McKillop, Managing Director, Divisional

GROWTH PLANS/SPECIAL FEATURES:

Commercial Vehicle Group, Inc. (CVG) is a supplier of cab-related products and systems for the global commercial vehicle market. The commercial market includes the medium- and heavy-duty truck market, the medium- and heavy-construction vehicle market, as well as the military, bus, agriculture, specialty transportation, mining, industrial equipment and off-road recreational markets. Products include seats and seating systems, trim systems and components, cab structures, sleeper boxes, body panels and structural components, mirrors, wipers, control systems, as well as electronic wire harness and panel assemblies. CVG brands include CVG, KAB Seating, National Seating, Bostrom Seating, Sprague Devices, RoadWatch, Stratos, Moto Mirror and FinishTEK. In 2018, the medium- and heavy-duty truck original equipment manufacturer (OEM) market accounted for 43% of the company's revenues; construction OEMs, 24%; aftermarket and OE service derived 21%; bus OEMs, 8%; and other, 4%. CVG has manufacturing operations in the U.S., Mexico, China, the U.K., Czech Republic, Ukraine, Thailand, India and Australia. Products of the firm are primarily sold in North America, Europe and the Asia-Pacific region.

Employee benefits include medical, dental and vision coverage; a 401(k); and life insurance.

FINANCIAL DATA: *Note: Data for latest year may not have been available at press time.*

In U.S. $	2018	2017	2016	2015	2014	2013
Revenue	897,737,000	755,231,000	662,112,000	825,341,000	839,743,000	747,718,000
R&D Expense						
Operating Income	66,873,000	31,445,000	25,383,000	38,026,000	33,693,000	6,438,000
Operating Margin %		.04%	.04%	.05%	.04%	.01%
SGA Expense	60,679,000	59,800,000	60,542,000	71,469,000	72,480,000	71,711,000
Net Income	44,512,000	-1,705,000	6,785,000	7,060,000	7,630,000	-12,445,000
Operating Cash Flow	40,992,000	2,257,000	49,365,000	55,299,000	9,519,000	19,154,000
Capital Expenditure	14,150,000	13,458,000	11,429,000	14,685,000	13,704,000	12,626,000
EBITDA	83,602,000	48,138,000	42,603,000	55,888,000	51,725,000	26,882,000
Return on Assets %		.00%	.02%	.02%	.02%	-.03%
Return on Equity %		-.02%	.10%	.11%	.13%	-.20%
Debt to Equity		2.191	3.444	3.564	4.273	4.194

CONTACT INFORMATION:

Phone: 614 289-5360 Fax: 614 289-5367
Toll-Free:
Address: 7800 Walton Pkwy., New Albany, OH 43054 United States

STOCK TICKER/OTHER:

Stock Ticker: CVGI Exchange: NAS
Employees: 7,000 Fiscal Year Ends: 12/31
Parent Company:

SALARIES/BONUSES:

Top Exec. Salary: $608,769 Bonus: $
Second Exec. Salary: $430,000 Bonus: $

OTHER THOUGHTS:

Estimated Female Officers or Directors:
Hot Spot for Advancement for Women/Minorities:

Compagnie Plastic Omnium SA

www.plasticomnium.com

NAIC Code: 336300

TYPES OF BUSINESS:

Plastics & Rubber, Manufacturing
Automotive Fuel Systems
Exterior Panels & Trim
Waste Container Manufacturing & Related Services
Playgrounds

BRANDS/DIVISIONS/AFFILIATES:

Burelle SA
Hell Behr Plastic Omnium (HBPO)

GROWTH PLANS/SPECIAL FEATURES:

Compagnie Plastic Omnium SA (Omnium) develops and manufactures intelligent exterior systems, clean energy systems and automotive modules worldwide. Intelligent exterior systems include automotive bumper systems, fascias, body panels, spoilers, rear closure systems and semi-structural and structural parts. Clean energy systems include plastic fuel systems and diesel emissions reduction systems. Automotive modules primarily include front-end modules, which are assembled at the front of vehicles. The front-end module integrates the shock absorption beam, lighting and engine cooling systems, front grill flaps, radars and driving assistance sensors. Majority-owned (66.67%) Hell Behr Plastic Omnium (HBPO) operates Omnium's front-end module division. More than 6 million front-end modules are assembled by HBPO every year. Omnium operates as a subsidiary of Burelle SA.

CONTACTS: *Note: Officers with more than one job title may be intentionally listed here more than once.*

Laurent Burelle, CEO
Paul Henry Lemarie, COO
Rodolphe Lapillonne, CFO
Jean-Sebastien Blanc, Exec. VP-Human Resources
Jean-Michel Szczerba, Co-CEO
Jean-Luc Petit, Corp. Sec.
Adeline Mickeler, Exec. VP-Corp. Planning
Marc Szulewicz, Pres., Plastic Omnium Auto Exterior
Pierre Lecocq, Pres., Plastic Omnium Auto Inergy
Michel Kempinski, Chmn.-Plastic Omnium Environment
Jean-Michel Szczerba, Co-COO
Laurent Burelle, Chmn.

FINANCIAL DATA: *Note: Data for latest year may not have been available at press time.*

In U.S. $	2018	2017	2016	2015	2014	2013
Revenue	8,021,076,000	7,493,885,000	6,484,999,000	5,546,828,000	4,912,760,000	5,673,768,000
R&D Expense	226,216,800	188,231,900	161,359,600	119,662,300	115,184,900	133,617,100
Operating Income	598,693,500	619,726,600	558,497,600	473,156,600	388,502,000	411,377,300
Operating Margin %		.08%	.09%	.09%	.08%	.07%
SGA Expense	106,734,900	134,554,900	126,268,800	117,743,600	110,303,400	109,756,400
Net Income	590,451,700	470,745,100	345,562,500	286,065,100	248,619,300	213,918,300
Operating Cash Flow	863,182,000	711,863,400	711,676,300	580,869,100	453,118,900	498,719,000
Capital Expenditure	711,668,500	547,253,100	450,780,500	418,735,600	383,561,800	387,706,000
EBITDA	1,200,851,000	960,152,800	814,815,100	674,539,500	593,237,400	580,256,900
Return on Assets %		.08%	.07%	.07%	.06%	.06%
Return on Equity %		.27%	.23%	.22%	.23%	.23%
Debt to Equity		0.766	0.756	0.727	0.855	1.011

CONTACT INFORMATION:

Phone: 33-1-40-87-64-00 Fax: 33-1-47-39-78-98
Toll-Free:
Address: 1, allee Pierre Burelle, Levallois Cedex, 92593 France

STOCK TICKER/OTHER:

Stock Ticker: PASTF
Exchange: GREY
Employees: 22,812
Fiscal Year Ends: 12/31
Parent Company: Burelle SA

SALARIES/BONUSES:

Top Exec. Salary: $ Bonus: $
Second Exec. Salary: $ Bonus: $

OTHER THOUGHTS:

Estimated Female Officers or Directors: 4
Hot Spot for Advancement for Women/Minorities: Y

Continental AG

NAIC Code: 326200

www.conti-online.com

TYPES OF BUSINESS:

Automotive Components
Tires, Plastics & Rubber
Brake Products
Transmissions & Suspensions
Vehicle Interiors
Sealing Systems
Aviation Products
Protective Clothing

BRANDS/DIVISIONS/AFFILIATES:

ContiTech
Benecke-Kaliko Group
Kmart Tyre and Auto

CONTACTS:

Note: Officers with more than one job title may be intentionally listed here more than once.

Wolfgang Schafer, CFO
Ariane Reinhart, Head-Human Resources
Wolfgang Schafer, Dir.-Law
Nikolai Setzer, Dir.-Tire Div.
Jose A. Avila, Dir.-Powertrain Div.
Helmut Matschi, Dir.-Interior Div.
Ralf Cramer, Dir.-Chassis & Safety Div.
Elmar Degenhart, Chmn.

GROWTH PLANS/SPECIAL FEATURES:

Continental AG is one of Europe's largest manufacturers of tires and other automotive systems for cars and trucks. With a global presence in more than 55 countries, the company's operations consist of two business groups, automotive and rubber. The automotive group operates in three divisions: chassis and safety, powertrain and interior. The chassis and safety division offers electronic brake systems, hydraulic brake systems, dynamic driving control systems, advanced driver assistance systems (ADAS), airbag electronics, windshield washer systems, electronic air suspension systems and sensors. The powertrain segment provides products including engine system components, transmission control units, hybrid and electric vehicle components, sensors and actuators and fuel systems parts. The interior division combines all activities relating to the management and visualization of information in the vehicle, including body and security, connectivity, instrumentation and displays, interior modules and multimedia. The operations of the rubber group also include two divisions: tires and ContiTech. Tires offers tires for every application, including passenger cars, trucks, buses, construction site vehicles, special vehicles, bicycles and motorcycles. The ContiTech subsidiary, which has production locations in 30 countries, manufactures a variety of non-tire rubber products, such as transportation hoses for use in automotive fluid delivery as well as conveyor belts and accessories. ContiTech operates in nine units: air spring systems, Benecke-Kaliko Group, conveyor belt group, elastomer coatings, mobile fluid systems, power transmission group, compounding technology, industrial fluid systems and vibration control. In November 2018, Continental acquired Kmart Tyre and Auto, based in Australia, from Wesfarmers Limited.

FINANCIAL DATA:

Note: Data for latest year may not have been available at press time.

In U.S. $	2018	2017	2016	2015	2014	2013
Revenue	49,163,420,000	48,726,200,000	44,895,370,000	43,436,670,000	38,203,830,000	36,903,230,000
R&D Expense	4,738,928,000	3,436,337,000	3,112,821,000	2,712,135,000	2,366,807,000	2,079,717,000
Operating Income	4,316,541,000	5,016,608,000	4,785,540,000	4,867,582,000	4,101,417,000	3,752,547,000
Operating Margin %		.10%	.11%	.11%	.11%	.10%
SGA Expense	4,033,769,000	3,957,595,000	3,613,375,000	3,437,223,000	2,882,418,000	2,608,171,000
Net Income	3,207,817,000	3,304,473,000	3,102,857,000	3,019,708,000	2,629,872,000	2,129,207,000
Operating Cash Flow	5,510,629,000	5,780,004,000	5,467,339,000	5,442,427,000	4,615,035,000	4,120,682,000
Capital Expenditure	3,637,511,000	3,267,383,000	2,998,450,000	2,507,308,000	2,336,471,000	2,240,478,000
EBITDA	7,012,954,000	7,390,057,000	6,918,955,000	6,741,696,000	5,811,337,000	5,439,438,000
Return on Assets %		.08%	.08%	.09%	.08%	.07%
Return on Equity %		.20%	.21%	.23%	.24%	.22%
Debt to Equity		0.127	0.196	0.248	0.476	0.559

CONTACT INFORMATION:

Phone: 49 51193801 Fax: 49 51193881
Toll-Free:
Address: Vahrenwalder Strasse 9, Hanover, GM 30165 Germany

STOCK TICKER/OTHER:

Stock Ticker: CTTAF
Exchange: PINX
Employees: 243,226
Fiscal Year Ends: 12/31
Parent Company:

SALARIES/BONUSES:

Top Exec. Salary: $ Bonus: $
Second Exec. Salary: $ Bonus: $

OTHER THOUGHTS:

Estimated Female Officers or Directors: 1
Hot Spot for Advancement for Women/Minorities:

Continental Motors Group

www.continentalmotors.com

NAIC Code: 441110

TYPES OF BUSINESS:

Auto Dealers, Retail
New & Used Vehicles
Maintenance Services
Parts Sales

BRANDS/DIVISIONS/AFFILIATES:

Continental Acura
Continental Audi
Continental Autosports
Continental Ferrari
Continental Honda
Continental Mitsubishi
Continental Nissan
Continental Toyota

CONTACTS: *Note: Officers with more than one job title may be intentionally listed here more than once.*

Joel Weinberger, Dealer Principal
John F. Weinberger, Sr., Pres.
John Stanley, CFO

GROWTH PLANS/SPECIAL FEATURES:

Continental Motors Group is one of the largest car dealership groups in the state of Illinois, with nine locations. Founded in 1961, the company began as an import repair shop. Today, Continental Motors specializes in the sale of vehicles, with its dealerships including Continental Acura, Continental Audi, Continental Autosports, Continental Ferrari, Continental Honda, Continental Mazda, Continental Mitsubishi, Continental Nissan and Continental Toyota. The Continental Toyota dealership includes a Collision Center for paintless dent removal, and offers rental car services. Continental AutoSports specializes in vehicle repairs; classic and vintage service and restoration; and apparel, posters and accessories. The company's website offers options for both potential buyers and existing owners of vehicles to compare prices, review vehicle makes and models and determine the value of a trade-in vehicle. Customers are also able to search and view the new and used inventory available for purchase, buy a vehicle, inquire about financing and/or obtain a quick quote online. Existing car owners have the option of scheduling maintenance service, viewing and ordering parts and accessories and obtaining information about extending their warranties through online services.

FINANCIAL DATA: *Note: Data for latest year may not have been available at press time.*

In U.S. $	2018	2017	2016	2015	2014	2013
Revenue	523,687,500	498,750,000	475,000,000	468,000,000	455,000,000	413,714,321
R&D Expense						
Operating Income						
Operating Margin %						
SGA Expense						
Net Income						
Operating Cash Flow						
Capital Expenditure						
EBITDA						
Return on Assets %						
Return on Equity %						
Debt to Equity						

CONTACT INFORMATION:

Phone: 708-352-8080 Fax: 708-352-0678
Toll-Free:
Address: 5901 S. La Grange Rd., Countryside, IL 60525 United States

STOCK TICKER/OTHER:

Stock Ticker: Private
Employees: 550
Parent Company:
Exchange:
Fiscal Year Ends: 12/31

SALARIES/BONUSES:

Top Exec. Salary: $ Bonus: $
Second Exec. Salary: $ Bonus: $

OTHER THOUGHTS:

Estimated Female Officers or Directors:
Hot Spot for Advancement for Women/Minorities:

Cool Technologies Inc

NAIC Code: 332410

cooltechnologiesinc.com

TYPES OF BUSINESS:

Heat Transfer and Dispersion Technologies
Mobile Electric Power Generation Equipment

BRANDS/DIVISIONS/AFFILIATES:

Totally Enclosed Heat Pipe Cooled

CONTACTS:

Note: Officers with more than one job title may be intentionally listed here more than once.

Judson Bibb, CEO

GROWTH PLANS/SPECIAL FEATURES:

Cool Technologies, Inc. is an intellectual property and product development company with expertise in thermal dispersion technologies and their application to various product platforms. The firm has also developed and is commercializing a mobile power generation system designed to be retrofitted onto new and existing work trucks. Cool Technologies currently has one trademark: Totally Enclosed Heat Pipe Cooled (TEHPC). TEHPC and radial vent heat pipes deliver liquid-cooled results for rotating equipment, multi-plate clutches, brakes and rotors without the use of liquid. Markets for products utilizing this thermal dispersion technology include consumer, industrial and military markets, both in the U.S. and worldwide. The initial target markets include those involved in moving materials and moving people, such as: motors/generators; mobile auxiliary power; compressors; turbines (wind, micro); bearings; electric vehicles: rail, off-highway, mining, delivery, refuse; brakes/rotors/calipers; pumps/fans; passenger vehicles: autos, RVs, buses, trains, aircraft; commercial vehicles: SUVs, light trucks, trams, bucket trucks; military boats, Humvees, trucks, aircraft; and marine boats, ranging in size from 30 feet to 120 feet and beyond. In mid-2019, Cool Technologies announced that it entered into a joint venture agreement with KeyOptions Pty Ltd. based in Victoria, Australia, to obtain a license for the JV to market and sell CoolTech's entire product platform in Australia and neighboring countries in southeast Asia.

FINANCIAL DATA:

Note: Data for latest year may not have been available at press time.

In U.S. $	2018	2017	2016	2015	2014	2013
Revenue						
R&D Expense	501,342	348,424	251,724	824,711	1,518,807	486,160
Operating Income	-2,259,621	-2,378,961	-3,958,220	-5,049,658	-23,560,280	-2,979,152
Operating Margin %						
SGA Expense	1,758,279	2,030,537	3,706,496	4,224,947	22,041,480	2,492,992
Net Income	-4,618,388	-5,059,326	-844,169	-6,923,100	-23,562,980	-3,141,538
Operating Cash Flow	-2,402,282	-1,605,734	-1,324,076	-2,240,049	-4,334,071	-1,728,057
Capital Expenditure	22,486	17,086	12,968	18,634	68,603	25,115
EBITDA	-2,232,245	-2,353,025	-3,932,284	-5,023,805	-23,554,050	-2,959,506
Return on Assets %		-14.19%	-2.57%	-16.40%	-44.32%	-5.16%
Return on Equity %						-15.03%
Debt to Equity						

CONTACT INFORMATION:

Phone: 813 975-7467 Fax:
Toll-Free:
Address: 8875 Hidden River Pkwy, Ste 300, Tampa, FL 33637 United States

STOCK TICKER/OTHER:

Stock Ticker: WARM Exchange: PINX
Employees: 3 Fiscal Year Ends: 12/31
Parent Company:

SALARIES/BONUSES:

Top Exec. Salary: $ Bonus: $
Second Exec. Salary: $ Bonus: $

OTHER THOUGHTS:

Estimated Female Officers or Directors:
Hot Spot for Advancement for Women/Minorities:

Cooper Tire & Rubber Company

www.coopertire.com

NAIC Code: 326211

TYPES OF BUSINESS:

Tire Manufacturing
Tire design and sales

BRANDS/DIVISIONS/AFFILIATES:

Corporacion de Occidente SA de CV

CONTACTS:
Note: Officers with more than one job title may be intentionally listed here more than once.

Bradley Hughes, CEO
Christopher Eperjesy, CFO
Thomas Capo, Chairman of the Board
Mark Young, Chief Accounting Officer
Stephen Zamansky, General Counsel
John Bollman, Other Executive Officer

GROWTH PLANS/SPECIAL FEATURES:

Cooper Tire & Rubber Company is a manufacturer and marketer of replacement tires. The firm specializes in the design, manufacture, marketing and sales of passenger car, light truck, truck and bus radial (TBR), motorcycle and racing tires. Cooper operates through four geographical segments: North America (the U.S. and Canada), Latin America (Mexico, Central America and South America), Europe and Asia. The Americas (North & Latin) manufacture and market passenger car and light truck tires, primarily for sale in the U.S. replacement market. This segment also markets and distributes racing, TBR and motorcycle tires. Subsidiary Corporacion de Occidente SA de CV supplies passenger car tires to the U.S., Mexican, Central American and South American markets. These divisions also distribute tires for race cars, medium trucks and motorcycles. The Europe and Asia segments comprise Cooper's international tire operations. In the U.K., Cooper manufactures and markets passenger car, light truck, motorcycle and racing tires; and also manufactures tire retread material for the domestic and global markets. In Serbia, the company manufactures light vehicle tires primarily for the European markets and for export to the U.S. In Asia, Cooper's operations are located in China, in which light vehicle tires are made and sold domestically. Based in Findlay, Ohio, Cooper and its family of companies operate nine manufacturing facilities and 22 distribution centers in 14 countries. In early-2019, Cooper Tire announced plans to phase out its light truck tire business in the U.K. by year's end, therefore ceasing light vehicle tire production at its Melksham, England facility. Light vehicle tires will be obtained from other production sites within the company's network.

The firm offers employee comprehensive benefits and retirement plans.

FINANCIAL DATA:
Note: Data for latest year may not have been available at press time.

In U.S. $	2018	2017	2016	2015	2014	2013
Revenue	2,808,062,000	2,854,656,000	2,924,869,000	2,972,901,000	3,424,809,000	3,439,233,000
R&D Expense						
Operating Income	199,072,000	271,724,000	384,387,000	354,480,000	300,458,000	240,714,000
Operating Margin %		.10%	.13%	.12%	.09%	.07%
SGA Expense	244,221,000	244,779,000	267,963,000	262,970,000	272,300,000	275,477,000
Net Income	76,586,000	95,400,000	248,381,000	212,766,000	213,578,000	111,013,000
Operating Cash Flow	254,303,000	176,828,000	309,795,000	300,314,000	319,084,000	272,375,000
Capital Expenditure	193,299,000	197,186,000	175,437,000	182,544,000	145,041,000	180,448,000
EBITDA	293,400,000	416,201,000	523,954,000	479,256,000	515,823,000	375,628,000
Return on Assets %		.04%	.10%	.09%	.08%	.04%
Return on Equity %		.09%	.24%	.23%	.23%	.13%
Debt to Equity		0.263	0.276	0.303	0.354	0.324

CONTACT INFORMATION:

Phone: 419 423-1321 Fax:
Toll-Free: 800-854-6288
Address: 701 Lima Ave., Findlay, OH 45840 United States

STOCK TICKER/OTHER:

Stock Ticker: CTB
Exchange: NYS
Employees: 10,540
Fiscal Year Ends: 12/31
Parent Company:

SALARIES/BONUSES:

Top Exec. Salary: $958,479 Bonus: $
Second Exec. Salary: $525,000 Bonus: $

OTHER THOUGHTS:

Estimated Female Officers or Directors: 2
Hot Spot for Advancement for Women/Minorities:

Cooper-Standard Holdings Inc

www.cooperstandard.com

NAIC Code: 336300

TYPES OF BUSINESS:

Automotive Component Manufacturing
Automotive Body & Chassis Products
Automotive Fluid Handling Systems
Automotive Thermal Management Components

BRANDS/DIVISIONS/AFFILIATES:

CONTACTS:

Note: Officers with more than one job title may be intentionally listed here more than once.

Jonathan Banas, CFO
Jeffrey Edwards, Chairman of the Board
Peter Brusate, Chief Accounting Officer
Aleksandra Miziolek, Chief Compliance Officer
Susan Kampe, Chief Information Officer
Keith Stephenson, COO

GROWTH PLANS/SPECIAL FEATURES:

Cooper-Standard Holdings, Inc. manufactures sealing, fuel and brake delivery and fluid transfer systems. Substantially all of the firm's activities are conducted through its subsidiaries. Cooper-Standard manufactures its products primarily for use in passenger vehicles and light trucks made by global original equipment manufacturers (OEMs) such as Ford Motor Company, General Motors Company, Fiat Chrysler Automobiles, PSA Peugeot Citroen and Volkswagen Group, among others. Cooper-Standard designs and produces its products through 104 manufacturing locations as well as 55 design, engineering and administrative locations worldwide. The company's products are categorized into three lines: sealing systems, fuel & brank delivery systems and fluid transfer systems. Sealing systems protect vehicle interiors from weather, dust and noise intrusion for improved driving experience, and the provide aesthetic and functional exterior surface treatment. Fuel & brake delivery systems sense, deliver and control fluids to fuel and brake systems. Fluid transfer systems sense, deliver and control fluid and vapors for optimal powertrain and HVAC operation. During 2019, Cooper-Standard sold its anti-vibration systems business to Continental AG for $165.5 million; and announced that it was building a new world headquarters to be located in Northville, Michigan, with the project expected to be completed in early-2020.

FINANCIAL DATA:

Note: Data for latest year may not have been available at press time.

In U.S. $	2018	2017	2016	2015	2014	2013
Revenue		3,618,126,000	3,472,890,880	3,342,803,968	3,243,986,944	3,090,542,080
R&D Expense						
Operating Income						
Operating Margin %						
SGA Expense						
Net Income		135,503,000	138,988,000	111,880,000	42,779,000	47,941,000
Operating Cash Flow						
Capital Expenditure						
EBITDA						
Return on Assets %						
Return on Equity %						
Debt to Equity						

CONTACT INFORMATION:

Phone: 248 596-5900 Fax:
Toll-Free:
Address: 39550 Orchard Hill Place Dr., Novi, MI 48375 United States

STOCK TICKER/OTHER:

Stock Ticker: CPS
Exchange: NYS
Employees: 32,000
Fiscal Year Ends: 12/31
Parent Company:

SALARIES/BONUSES:

Top Exec. Salary: $ Bonus: $
Second Exec. Salary: $ Bonus: $

OTHER THOUGHTS:

Estimated Female Officers or Directors: 2
Hot Spot for Advancement for Women/Minorities:

Copart Inc

NAIC Code: 441120

www.copart.com

TYPES OF BUSINESS:

Salvage Vehicle Processing
Towing & Storage Services
Online Used Parts Database

BRANDS/DIVISIONS/AFFILIATES:

Virtual Bidding Third Generation

CONTACTS: *Note: Officers with more than one job title may be intentionally listed here more than once.*

A. Adair, CEO
Jeffrey Liaw, CFO
Willis Johnson, Chairman of the Board
William Franklin, Executive VP, Divisional

GROWTH PLANS/SPECIAL FEATURES:

Copart, Inc. provides online auctions and vehicle remarketing services, with operations in the U.S., Canada, the U.K., Brazil, Ireland, Germany, Finland, the United Arab Emirates, Oman, Bahrain and Spain. Some of the firm's goals is to promote vehicle and related parts restoration, repair and recycling, and to facilitate the recovery and resilience of communities affected by severe climate events. Copart provides vehicle sellers with a full range of services to process and sell vehicles primarily over the internet through its Virtual Bidding Third Generation (VB3) auction-style sales technology. Vehicle sellers primarily consist of insurance companies, but may also include banks, finance companies, charities, fleet operators, dealers and vehicles sourced directly from individual owners. Vehicles are principally sold to licensed vehicle dismantlers, rebuilders, repair licensees, used vehicle dealers and exporters, and at certain locations, to the general public. Value-added services include mobile applications, predictive analytics, Buy It Now purchase options, online payment capabilities, email notifications, vehicle processing (pictures, title, shop invoices), interactive online counter-bidding, second chance bidding and more.

Copart sponsors a 401(k) for eligible U.S. employees, and a contribution plan for eligible U.K. employees.

FINANCIAL DATA: *Note: Data for latest year may not have been available at press time.*

In U.S. $	2018	2017	2016	2015	2014	2013
Revenue	1,805,695,000	1,447,981,000	1,268,449,000	1,146,079,000	1,163,489,000	1,046,386,000
R&D Expense						
Operating Income	585,476,000	480,664,000	406,470,000	344,401,000	304,038,000	282,992,000
Operating Margin %		.33%	.32%	.30%	.26%	.27%
SGA Expense	176,890,000	151,364,000	138,116,000	138,975,000	164,535,000	137,930,000
Net Income	417,867,000	394,227,000	270,360,000	219,783,000	178,687,000	180,025,000
Operating Cash Flow	535,069,000	492,058,000	332,498,000	265,076,000	262,594,000	199,326,000
Capital Expenditure	287,910,000	172,178,000	173,917,000	79,153,000	81,510,000	130,265,000
EBITDA	661,919,000	521,320,000	469,114,000	399,083,000	332,529,000	343,867,000
Return on Assets %		.22%	.16%	.13%	.13%	.14%
Return on Equity %		.42%	.31%	.22%	.20%	.27%
Debt to Equity		0.502	0.729	0.614	0.222	0.389

CONTACT INFORMATION:

Phone: 707 639-5000 Fax: 707 644-7355
Toll-Free: 888-735-5481
Address: 14185 Dallas Parkway, Ste. 300, Dallas, TX 94534 United States

STOCK TICKER/OTHER:

Stock Ticker: CPRT
Employees: 5,323
Parent Company:
Exchange: NAS
Fiscal Year Ends: 07/31

SALARIES/BONUSES:

Top Exec. Salary: $494,230 Bonus: $600,000
Second Exec. Salary: $323,076 Bonus: $325,000

OTHER THOUGHTS:

Estimated Female Officers or Directors:
Hot Spot for Advancement for Women/Minorities:

Cox Automotive Inc

www.coxautoinc.com

NAIC Code: 519130

TYPES OF BUSINESS:

Internet Search Portals

BRANDS/DIVISIONS/AFFILIATES:

Cox Enterprises Inc
VinSolutions
Dealertrack
Manheim
vAuto
Autotrader
Kelly Blue Book
Clutch Technologies

CONTACTS: *Note: Officers with more than one job title may be intentionally listed here more than once.*

Sandy Schwartz, Pres.
Janet Barnard, Chief People Officer
David Brooks, CTO

GROWTH PLANS/SPECIAL FEATURES:

Cox Automotive, Inc. provides automotive resources and tools for consumers, dealers and manufacturers to maximize value at every step of the car buying and selling processes. These sources and tools consist of several brands, some of which provide multiple solutions. For example, VinSolutions provides a cloud-based internal management, sales, service and consumer engagement management platform that can be used from any PC, laptop or mobile device. Dealertrack is a dealer operations solution and brand. Inventory management brands include Manheim, NextGear Capital and vAuto. Inventory solutions address the acquisition and disposal of cars, vehicle floor plans, reconditioning of cars and transport of cars. Marketing brands include Autotrader, Dealer.com, HomeNet, Kelly Blue Book, vAuto and VinSolutions. Marketing solutions include advertising vehicles, attracting trade-in customers, creating a vehicle website, managing customer price expectations, managing the social community, measuring marketing performance and obtaining search results. Sales brands include Dealertrack, F&I Express, Kelley Blue Book, Manheim, vAuto and VinSolutions. Sales solutions include access to credit application information, connecting sales with the finance and insurance (F&I) processes, making deals online, managing rebates and incentives, and speeding up the registration and titling processes. Service solutions include the Dealertrack, VinSolutions and Xtime brands. Service solutions are for attracting and retaining business. And mobility solutions include the Clutch Technologies, Pivet and RideKleen brands. Mobility solutions provide end-to-end services for fleets, including in-fleeting, de-fleeting, reconditioning, maintenance and cleaning. Cox Automotive operates as a subsidiary of Cox Enterprises, Inc.

FINANCIAL DATA: *Note: Data for latest year may not have been available at press time.*

In U.S. $	2018	2017	2016	2015	2014	2013
Revenue	7,780,500,000	7,410,000,000	7,300,000,000	7,100,000,000	6,600,000,000	6,200,000,000
R&D Expense						
Operating Income						
Operating Margin %						
SGA Expense						
Net Income						
Operating Cash Flow						
Capital Expenditure						
EBITDA						
Return on Assets %						
Return on Equity %						
Debt to Equity						

CONTACT INFORMATION:

Phone: Fax:
Toll-Free: 855-449-0010
Address: 3003 Summit Blvd., Ste. 200, Atlanta, GA 30319 United States

STOCK TICKER/OTHER:

Stock Ticker: Subsidiary
Exchange:
Employees: 33,000
Fiscal Year Ends: 12/31
Parent Company: Cox Enterprises Inc

SALARIES/BONUSES:

Top Exec. Salary: $ Bonus: $
Second Exec. Salary: $ Bonus: $

OTHER THOUGHTS:

Estimated Female Officers or Directors:
Hot Spot for Advancement for Women/Minorities:

Cummins Filtration

www.cumminsfiltration.com

NAIC Code: 336300

TYPES OF BUSINESS:

Automobile Part Manufacturing
Filtration Products
Industrial Silencers & Mufflers
Exhaust Systems
Antifreeze & Coolant Additives

BRANDS/DIVISIONS/AFFILIATES:

Cummins Inc
Fleetguard

CONTACTS: *Note: Officers with more than one job title may be intentionally listed here more than once.*

Joseph Saoud, Pres.
K.C. Hall, Dir.-Bus. Dev.

GROWTH PLANS/SPECIAL FEATURES:

Cummins Filtration, a wholly-owned subsidiary of Cummins, Inc., designs, manufactures and sells heavy-duty air, fuel, hydraulic and lube filtration, as well as chemical technology products for diesel and gas-powered equipment worldwide. These products are marketed under the Fleetguard brand name. Cummins is a world leader in original equipment management and aftermarket filtration solutions for diesel engines, transmissions and industrial applications, including engines ranging from 1 to above 26 gallons (3 to 100 liters) in displacement. The company serves customers through a network of 600 company-owned and independent distributor facilities, as well as more than 7,200 dealer locations in over 190 countries and territories.

Cummins Filtration's employees receive access to child care centers, employee assistance, health and wellness programs, housing assistance and tuition reimbursement. Some employees have the option to telecommute.

FINANCIAL DATA: *Note: Data for latest year may not have been available at press time.*

In U.S. $	2018	2017	2016	2015	2014	2013
Revenue	1,265,000,000	1,153,000,000	1,010,000,000	1,423,000,000	1,924,000,000	1,465,000,000
R&D Expense						
Operating Income						
Operating Margin %						
SGA Expense						
Net Income						
Operating Cash Flow						
Capital Expenditure						
EBITDA						
Return on Assets %						
Return on Equity %						
Debt to Equity						

CONTACT INFORMATION:

Phone: 615-367-0040 Fax: 800-999-8664
Toll-Free: 800-223-4583
Address: 26 Century Blvd., Nashville, TN 37214 United States

STOCK TICKER/OTHER:

Stock Ticker: Subsidiary Exchange:
Employees: 4,250 Fiscal Year Ends: 12/31
Parent Company: Cummins Inc

SALARIES/BONUSES:

Top Exec. Salary: $ Bonus: $
Second Exec. Salary: $ Bonus: $

OTHER THOUGHTS:

Estimated Female Officers or Directors: 4
Hot Spot for Advancement for Women/Minorities: Y

Cummins Inc

www.cummins.com

NAIC Code: 336300

TYPES OF BUSINESS:

Automotive Products, Motors & Parts Manufacturing
Engines
Filtration Systems
Power Generation Systems
Alternators
Air Handling Systems
Filtration & Emissions Solutions
Fuel Systems

BRANDS/DIVISIONS/AFFILIATES:

CONTACTS: *Note: Officers with more than one job title may be intentionally listed here more than once.*

N. Linebarger, CEO
Peter Anderson, VP, Divisional
Mark Smith, CFO
Christopher Clulow, Chief Accounting Officer
Marya Rose, Chief Administrative Officer
Sherry Aaholm, Chief Information Officer
Jennifer Rumsey, Chief Technology Officer
Richard Freeland, Director
Sharon Barner, General Counsel
Jill Cook, Other Executive Officer
Livingston Satterthwaite, President, Divisional
Tracy Embree, President, Divisional
Norbert Nusterer, President, Divisional
Donald Jackson, Treasurer
Thaddeaus Ewald, Vice President, Divisional
Mark Osowick, Vice President, Divisional
Steven Chapman, Vice President, Geographical

GROWTH PLANS/SPECIAL FEATURES:

Cummins, Inc. designs, manufactures, distributes and services diesel and natural gas engines and powertrain-related component products. Cummins' products are sold to original equipment manufacturers (OEMs), distributors, dealers and other customers worldwide. These customers are served through a network of approximately 600 wholly-owned and independent distributor locations and over 7,600 dealer locations in more than 190 countries and territories. Cummins operates its business through five segments: engine, distribution, components, power systems and electrified power. The engine segment manufactures and markets a broad range of diesel and natural gas-powered engines under the Cummins brand name, as well as certain customer brand names, for the heavy- and medium-duty truck, bus recreational vehicle (RV), light-duty automotive, construction, mining, marine, rail, oil/gas, defense and agricultural markets. The distribution segment service and distribute the full range of Cummins' products to end-users at approximately 450 locations in more than 90 distribution territories. The components segment supplies products which complement Cummins' engine and power systems segments, including aftertreatment systems, turbochargers, transmissions, filtration products, electronics and fuel systems for commercial diesel and natural gas applications. The power systems segment offers three product lines: power generation, consisting of backup and prime power generators ranging from 2 kilowatts to 3.5 megawatts, as well as controls, paralleling systems and transfer switches for an array of applications; industrial, consisting of diesel and natural gas high-horsepower engines up to 5,500hp for a variety of equipment in the mining, rail, defense, oil/gas and commercial marine applications worldwide; and generator technologies, consisting of A/C generator/alternator products for internal consumption and for external generator set assemblers. Last, the electrified power segment offers electrified power systems, ranging from fully-electric to hybrid.

Cummins offers employees life, medical and dental insurance; and various employee assistance programs.

FINANCIAL DATA: *Note: Data for latest year may not have been available at press time.*

In U.S. $	2018	2017	2016	2015	2014	2013
Revenue	23,771,000,000	20,428,000,000	17,509,000,000	19,110,000,000	19,221,000,000	17,301,000,000
R&D Expense	902,000,000	752,000,000	636,000,000	735,000,000	754,000,000	713,000,000
Operating Income	2,467,000,000	2,046,000,000	1,822,000,000	2,100,000,000	2,061,000,000	1,791,000,000
Operating Margin %		.10%	.10%	.11%	.10%	.10%
SGA Expense	2,437,000,000	2,390,000,000	2,046,000,000	2,092,000,000	2,095,000,000	1,920,000,000
Net Income	2,141,000,000	999,000,000	1,394,000,000	1,399,000,000	1,651,000,000	1,483,000,000
Operating Cash Flow	2,378,000,000	2,277,000,000	1,935,000,000	2,059,000,000	2,266,000,000	2,089,000,000
Capital Expenditure	784,000,000	587,000,000	594,000,000	799,000,000	798,000,000	740,000,000
EBITDA	3,478,000,000	3,029,000,000	2,529,000,000	2,604,000,000	2,953,000,000	2,567,000,000
Return on Assets %		.06%	.09%	.09%	.11%	.11%
Return on Equity %		.14%	.20%	.18%	.22%	.21%
Debt to Equity		0.219	0.228	0.213	0.205	0.223

CONTACT INFORMATION:

Phone: 812 377-5000 Fax:
Toll-Free:
Address: 500 Jackson St., Columbus, IN 47202 United States

STOCK TICKER/OTHER:

Stock Ticker: CMI
Employees: 55,400
Parent Company:
Exchange: NYS
Fiscal Year Ends: 12/31

SALARIES/BONUSES:

Top Exec. Salary: $1,442,500 Bonus: $
Second Exec. Salary: $874,000 Bonus: $

OTHER THOUGHTS:

Estimated Female Officers or Directors: 2
Hot Spot for Advancement for Women/Minorities: Y

Daihatsu Motor Co Ltd

www.daihatsu.com

NAIC Code: 336111

TYPES OF BUSINESS:

Automobile Manufacturing
Industrial Engines

BRANDS/DIVISIONS/AFFILIATES:

Toyota Motor Corporation
Daihatsu Motor Kyushu Co Ltd
Daihatsu Business Support & Engineering Center
Daihatsu Credit Co Ltd
Daihatsu Transportation Co Ltd
Aoi Machine Industry Co Ltd
Daihatsu Metal Co Ltd
Akashi-Kikai Industry Co Ltd

CONTACTS: *Note: Officers with more than one job title may be intentionally listed here more than once.*

Soichiro Okudaira, Pres.
Tatsuya Kaneko, Exec. VP
Takashi Nomoto, Sr. Managing Exec. Officer
Yasunori Nakawaki, Sr. Managing Exec. Officer
Naoto Kitagawa, Sr. Managing Exec. Officer

GROWTH PLANS/SPECIAL FEATURES:

Daihatsu Motor Co., Ltd., headquartered in Osaka, Japan, develops, manufactures and sells mini vehicles that offer fuel efficiency, affordability and added value. Mini vehicles are super-small-sized cars unique to Japan. Their overall length is approximately 11 feet or less, with an overall width of less than 5 feet and a height of less than 6.5 feet. Daihatsu's mini cars are among the world's smallest class of vehicles, but can accommodate four adults, steadily drive at 62 miles per hour (100 km/h) and offer a level of safety equal to compact cars. The firm has been manufacturing mini vehicles since it was established in 1949, with plants located in Osaka, Shiga and Kyoto, and a parts center located in Nishinomiya. Wholly-owned subsidiaries include: Daihatsu Motor Kyushu Co. Ltd., which develops, designs, produces, sells and repairs automobiles, industrial vehicles and other types of vehicles and their parts; Daihatsu Business Support & Engineering Center Corp., which sells automotive accessories and materials, is engaged in research and development for automobiles and machines, and provides facility maintenance; Daihatsu Credit Co. Ltd., offering sales and lease financing; and Daihatsu Transportation Co. Ltd., providing cargo and vehicle transportation services. Majority-owned subsidiaries include: Aoi Machine Industry Co. Ltd., which manufactures stamped vehicle and agricultural equipment body parts; Daihatsu Metal Co. Ltd., a manufacturer of vehicle parts, diesel engine parts for marine and land vehicles, as well as hydraulic components and machinery; Akashi-Kikai Industry Co. Ltd., which manufactures vehicle control devices, engine parts, transmissions and hydraulic components; and Kanbishi Co. Ltd., which manufactures die cast parts, automobile door locks, switches and other functional parts. Daihatsu is a wholly-owned subsidiary of Toyota Motor Corporation.

FINANCIAL DATA: *Note: Data for latest year may not have been available at press time.*

In U.S. $	2018	2017	2016	2015	2014	2013
Revenue	17,587,500,000	16,750,000,000	16,570,347,520	17,813,338,112	18,755,971,072	17,302,329,344
R&D Expense						
Operating Income						
Operating Margin %						
SGA Expense						
Net Income			410,830,496	901,978,240	1,068,504,448	994,245,504
Operating Cash Flow						
Capital Expenditure						
EBITDA						
Return on Assets %						
Return on Equity %						
Debt to Equity						

CONTACT INFORMATION:

Phone: 81-72-751-8811 Fax:
Toll-Free:
Address: 1-1 Daihatsu-cho Ikeda-shi, Osaka, 563-8651 Japan

STOCK TICKER/OTHER:

Stock Ticker: Subsidiary
Exchange:
Employees: 12,796
Fiscal Year Ends: 03/31
Parent Company: Toyota Motor Corporation

SALARIES/BONUSES:

Top Exec. Salary: $ Bonus: $
Second Exec. Salary: $ Bonus: $

OTHER THOUGHTS:

Estimated Female Officers or Directors:
Hot Spot for Advancement for Women/Minorities:

Daimler AG

www.daimler.com

NAIC Code: 336111

TYPES OF BUSINESS:

Automobile Manufacturing
Financial Services & Insurance
Commercial Vehicles, Trucks & Buses
Aerospace & Defense Technology

BRANDS/DIVISIONS/AFFILIATES:

Mercedes-Benz
Daimler
Maybach
Freightliner
BharatBenz
car2go
Citan
BusStore

CONTACTS: *Note: Officers with more than one job title may be intentionally listed here more than once.*

Bodo Uebber, Dir.-Finance
Thomas Weber, Dir.-Group Research
Andreas Renschler, Dir.-Mfg.
Cristine Hohmann-Dennhardt, Dir.-Legal Affairs & Integrity
Bodo Uebber, Dir.-Controlling
Thomas Weber, Dir.-Mercedes-Benz Cars Dev.
Wolfgang Bernhard, Dir.-Trucks
Ola Kallenius, Chmn.
Andreas Renschler, Dir.-Procurement

GROWTH PLANS/SPECIAL FEATURES:

Daimler AG develops, manufactures, distributes and sells a wide range of automotive products, mainly passenger cars, trucks, vans and buses. The firm also provides financial and other services relating to its automotive businesses in more than 40 countries. The company reports in five segments: Mercedes-Benz cars, Daimler trucks, Daimler financial services, Mercedes-Benz vans and Daimler buses. The Mercedes-Benz cars segment designs, produces and sells Mercedes-Benz and Mercedes-AMG passenger cars, Maybach luxury sedans and smart micro compact cars. The Daimler trucks segment manufactures trucks and specialty vehicles under the Mercedes-Benz, Freightliner, Western Star, Fuso, Thomas and BharatBenz; it also maintains the components brand, Detroit. Daimler financial services primarily provides financing, leasing, insurance and fleet management services, with mobility services including the car2go, moovel and mytaxi brands. Mercedes-Benz vans comprises the Citan urban delivery vehicle, the Sprinter and Vito medium- and heavy-duty vans, as well as the V-Class MPV van and the Marco Polo line of camper vans. Daimler buses includes the Mercedes-Benz and Setra brands, as well as the Indian truck and bus brand BharatBenz. BusStore is a leading European brand for pre-owned buses from Mercedes-Benz and Setra. Daimler offers products and services primarily in Western Europe and in the NAFTA region, including the U.S., Canada and Mexico. In addition, Daimler's Mercedes me package of innovative services includes access to vehicles via smartphone and personalized home pages with relevant topics concerning entertainment, travel and lifestyle.

FINANCIAL DATA: *Note: Data for latest year may not have been available at press time.*

In U.S. $	2018	2017	2016	2015	2014	2013
Revenue	185,298,900,000	181,942,000,000	169,686,700,000	165,486,100,000	143,791,000,000	130,626,700,000
R&D Expense	7,286,316,000	6,574,402,000	5,820,417,000	5,270,151,000	5,017,715,000	4,540,522,000
Operating Income	11,135,960,000	14,375,550,000	13,368,030,000	13,887,290,000	10,494,910,000	8,648,140,000
Operating Margin %		.08%	.08%	.08%	.07%	.07%
SGA Expense	18,936,000,000	18,571,750,000	17,321,740,000	17,556,470,000	16,455,930,000	16,319,750,000
Net Income	8,025,908,000	11,653,010,000	9,439,770,000	9,326,838,000	7,708,149,000	7,575,288,000
Operating Cash Flow	379,760,900	-1,829,052,000	4,108,725,000	245,792,700	-1,410,540,000	3,637,068,000
Capital Expenditure	11,847,870,000	11,246,680,000	9,779,673,000	8,122,232,000	6,982,949,000	7,647,254,000
EBITDA	19,589,240,000	22,762,400,000	20,591,230,000	20,737,380,000	17,589,680,000	17,040,520,000
Return on Assets %		.04%	.04%	.04%	.04%	.04%
Return on Equity %		.17%	.15%	.17%	.16%	.16%
Debt to Equity		1.224	1.215	1.117	1.154	1.048

CONTACT INFORMATION:

Phone: 49 7111792543 Fax: 49 7111794116
Toll-Free:
Address: Mercedesstrasse 137, Stuttgart, 70546 Germany

STOCK TICKER/OTHER:

Stock Ticker: DAI N
Employees: 298,683
Parent Company:
Exchange: MEX
Fiscal Year Ends: 12/31

SALARIES/BONUSES:

Top Exec. Salary: $ Bonus: $
Second Exec. Salary: $ Bonus: $

OTHER THOUGHTS:

Estimated Female Officers or Directors: 6
Hot Spot for Advancement for Women/Minorities: Y

Daimler Mobility AG www.daimler.com/company/business-units/daimler-mobility/

NAIC Code: 522220

TYPES OF BUSINESS:

Vehicle Leasing & Financing
Fleet Management Services
Insurance Services
Consulting Services
Toll Collecting Systems
Traffic Routing Systems

BRANDS/DIVISIONS/AFFILIATES:

Daimler AG
FREE NOW
SHARE NOW
Blacklane
REACH NOW
PARK NOW
CHARGE NOW
Daimler Financial Services AG

CONTACTS: *Note: Officers with more than one job title may be intentionally listed here more than once.*

Franz Reiner, Pres.
Tilo Schmid-Sehl, CEO-Daimler Financial Svcs. Japan Co. Ltd.
Franz Reiner, Chmn.

GROWTH PLANS/SPECIAL FEATURES:

Daimler Mobility AG (formerly Daimler Financial Services AG) is a global financial and mobility services provider and the operating subsidiary of Daimler AG. The company offers a comprehensive range of solutions, from financing, leasing and rental services to fleet services and insurance options, through to app-based mobility solutions such as car-sharing and ride-hailing. These products and solutions are offered for Daimler vehicle brands, as well as other brands such as AMG, Maybach, smart, EQ, Freightliner, FUSO, Western Star, Thomas Built Buses, Bharat Benz, Setra and more. Daimler Mobility is also an investor in mobility services such as FREE NOW (ride hailing), SHARE NOW (car sharing) and Blacklane (chauffeur service). As of June 30, 2019, more than 75 million people had used the mobility services, as well as REACH NOW (on-demand mobility and multi-mobility rides), PARK NOW (parking) and CHARGE NOW (charging stations). In mid-2019, Daimler Financial Services changed its name to Daimler Mobility in order to place its financial services within the expanding mobility solutions field.

FINANCIAL DATA: *Note: Data for latest year may not have been available at press time.*

In U.S. $	2018	2017	2016	2015	2014	2013
Revenue	30,045,100,000	28,479,200,000	23,564,886,487	21,160,511,578	17,914,717,300	18,810,149,864
R&D Expense						
Operating Income						
Operating Margin %						
SGA Expense						
Net Income	1,583,010,000	2,359,790,000	2,042,227,529	1,191,809,634	989,379,425	1,390,250,264
Operating Cash Flow						
Capital Expenditure						
EBITDA						
Return on Assets %						
Return on Equity %						
Debt to Equity						

CONTACT INFORMATION:

Phone: 49-71125740 Fax: 41-71125748005
Toll-Free:
Address: Siemensstr. 7, Stuttgart, 70469 Germany

STOCK TICKER/OTHER:

Stock Ticker: Subsidiary
Employees: 14,070
Parent Company: Daimler AG
Exchange:
Fiscal Year Ends: 12/31

SALARIES/BONUSES:

Top Exec. Salary: $ Bonus: $
Second Exec. Salary: $ Bonus: $

OTHER THOUGHTS:

Estimated Female Officers or Directors:
Hot Spot for Advancement for Women/Minorities:

Daimler Trucks North America LLC

www.daimlertrucksnorthamerica.com

NAIC Code: 336120

TYPES OF BUSINESS:

Truck Manufacturing
Custom-Built Chassis
Van & Bus Manufacturing
Automobile Parts Manufacturing
Specialty Vehicle Manufacturing
Military Vehicle Manufacturing
Used Truck Dealerships
Truck Stops

BRANDS/DIVISIONS/AFFILIATES:

Daimler AG
Freightliner Trucks
Western Star Truck Sales Inc
Detroit Diesel Corporation
Thomas Built Buses
SelecTrucks
Alliance Truck Parts
Daimler Truck Financial

CONTACTS: *Note: Officers with more than one job title may be intentionally listed here more than once.*

Roger M. Nielsen, CEO
John O'Leary, CFO
Friedrich Baumann, Sr. VP-Aftermarket
Albert Kirchmann, Head-Daimler Truck Asia, Finance & Control

GROWTH PLANS/SPECIAL FEATURES:

Daimler Trucks North America, LLC (Daimler NA), a wholly-owned subsidiary of Daimler AG, is one of the largest manufacturers of medium- and heavy-duty trucks and specialized commercial vehicles in North America. The company is comprised of nine businesses. Freightliner Trucks manufactures Class 5-8 models of Freightliner-branded trucks with pickup and delivery, towing, municipal, construction and long-haul on-highway applications. Western Star Truck Sales, Inc. manufactures the Western Star brand of trucks, which are targeted at small and medium fleets, as well as owner-operators, with a focus on vocational and extreme-duty segments. Detroit Diesel Corporation manufactures a full portfolio of heavy-duty and mid-range diesel engines, as well as transmissions, axles, safety systems and telematics products for the on-highway and vocational commercial truck markets. Thomas Built Buses designs and builds school buses, including light- and medium-duty lines. Freightliner Custom Chassis Corporation manufactures premium chassis for recreational vehicles, walk-in vans, delivery vehicles, commercial vehicles, shuttle buses and school buses. SelecTrucks is Daimler Trucks' remarketing retail distributor, engaged in selling Freightliner-branded used trucks through retail locations in the U.S. and Canada. Alliance Truck Parts offers new and remanufactured parts to the commercial transportation industry. It has more than 30 product lines for all makes and all models of trucks and buses. Daimler Truck Financial offers financing for commercial vehicles such as Freightliner, Western Star, SelecTrucks, Thomas Built Buses, Mitsubishi Fuso and Sprinter. The firm customizes its financing solutions with a broad range of loan, lease and payment options. Daimler Truck Financial is a business unit of Mercedes-Benz Financial Services USA, LLC. Last, Elite Support are certified delivers that sell, maintain and repair Freightliner and Western Star trucks.

FINANCIAL DATA: *Note: Data for latest year may not have been available at press time.*

In U.S. $	2018	2017	2016	2015	2014	2013
Revenue	19,012,100,000	17,688,900,000	14,165,100,000	18,645,300,000	14,779,000,000	13,909,200,000
R&D Expense						
Operating Income						
Operating Margin %						
SGA Expense						
Net Income	1,345,100,000	1,068,490,000	1,943,440,000	2,930,071,200	2,136,131,100	3,013,038,603
Operating Cash Flow						
Capital Expenditure						
EBITDA						
Return on Assets %						
Return on Equity %						
Debt to Equity						

CONTACT INFORMATION:

Phone: 503-745-8000 Fax: 503-745-8921
Toll-Free:
Address: 4747 N. Channel Ave., Portland, OR 97217 United States

STOCK TICKER/OTHER:

Stock Ticker: Subsidiary
Employees: 23,588
Parent Company: Daimler AG
Exchange:
Fiscal Year Ends: 12/31

SALARIES/BONUSES:

Top Exec. Salary: $ Bonus: $
Second Exec. Salary: $ Bonus: $

OTHER THOUGHTS:

Estimated Female Officers or Directors:
Hot Spot for Advancement for Women/Minorities:

Dana Incorporated

www.dana.com

NAIC Code: 336300

TYPES OF BUSINESS:

Automotive Products, Motors & Parts Manufacturing
Engine Systems
Fluid Systems
Heavy Vehicle Technologies
Brake Components
Chassis & Drive Train Components
Filtration Products
Financial Services

BRANDS/DIVISIONS/AFFILIATES:

TM4 Inc

CONTACTS: *Note: Officers with more than one job title may be intentionally listed here more than once.*

Jonathan Collins, CFO
Keith Wandell, Chairman of the Board
James Kellett, Chief Accounting Officer
James Kamsickas, Director
Mark Wallace, Executive VP
Aziz Aghili, Executive VP
Douglas Liedberg, General Counsel
Robert Pyle, President, Divisional
Dwayne Matthews, President, Divisional

GROWTH PLANS/SPECIAL FEATURES:

Dana Incorporated supplies high technology driveline, sealing, thermal management and fluid-power products for global vehicle manufacturers. The company operates 135 facilities in 33 countries. Dana divides its operations into four segments: light vehicle, commercial vehicle, off-highway and power technologies. The light vehicle segment manufactures axles, driveshafts differentials, torque couplings, modular assemblies, drive units, power transfer units and electric vehicle (EV) gearboxes for the light vehicle market. The commercial vehicle segment manufactures parts for the medium/heavy duty vehicle market, including medium duty trucks, heavy duty trucks, buses and specialty vehicles. Products include axles, driveshafts and tire inflation systems. The off-highway segment manufactures axels, driveshafts, transmissions, torque converters, industrial gear boxes, tire inflation systems, hydraulic valves/pumps/motors and electronic controls for off-highway use such as construction, earth moving, agriculture, mining, forestry, rail and material handling. Last, the power technologies segment manufactures parts for the light vehicle, medium/heavy vehicle and off-highway markets. Products include gaskets, cover modules, heat shields, engine sealing systems, cooling and heat transfer products. Major customers of the company include: Ford Motor Company; Toyota Motor Company; General Motors Company; PACCAR, Inc.; Daimler AG; Deere & Company, Manitou Group; Cummins, Inc.; and Volkswagen AG, among others. During 2018, Dana acquired a 55% ownership interest TM4, Inc., which designs and manufactures motors, power inverters and control systems for electric vehicles. In March 2019, it acquired Oerlikon Group's drive systems segment.

FINANCIAL DATA: *Note: Data for latest year may not have been available at press time.*

In U.S. $	2018	2017	2016	2015	2014	2013
Revenue	8,143,000,000	7,209,000,000	5,826,000,000	6,060,000,000	6,617,000,000	6,769,000,000
R&D Expense						
Operating Income	662,000,000	547,000,000	448,000,000	451,000,000	456,000,000	452,000,000
Operating Margin %		.08%	.08%	.07%	.07%	.07%
SGA Expense	499,000,000	511,000,000	396,000,000	387,000,000	451,000,000	397,000,000
Net Income	427,000,000	111,000,000	640,000,000	159,000,000	319,000,000	244,000,000
Operating Cash Flow	568,000,000	554,000,000	384,000,000	406,000,000	510,000,000	577,000,000
Capital Expenditure	325,000,000	393,000,000	322,000,000	260,000,000	234,000,000	209,000,000
EBITDA	860,000,000	715,000,000	510,000,000	579,000,000	591,000,000	729,000,000
Return on Assets %		.02%	.14%	.03%	.06%	.00%
Return on Equity %		.10%	.68%	.18%	.31%	-.01%
Debt to Equity		1.736	1.379	2.133	1.494	1.672

CONTACT INFORMATION:

Phone: 419 887-3000 Fax: 419 535-4643
Toll-Free: 800-537-8823
Address: 3939 Technology Dr., Maumee, OH 43537 United States

STOCK TICKER/OTHER:

Stock Ticker: DAN
Exchange: NYS
Employees: 24,900
Fiscal Year Ends: 12/31
Parent Company:

SALARIES/BONUSES:

Top Exec. Salary: $1,146,950 Bonus: $
Second Exec. Salary: $605,000 Bonus: $

OTHER THOUGHTS:

Estimated Female Officers or Directors:
Hot Spot for Advancement for Women/Minorities: Y

Danfoss Power Solutions

powersolutions.danfoss.com

NAIC Code: 333996

TYPES OF BUSINESS:

Mobile Hydraulics Manufacturing

BRANDS/DIVISIONS/AFFILIATES:

Danfoss Group

CONTACTS:

Note: Officers with more than one job title may be intentionally listed here more than once.

Marc Weston, CMO
Charles Kells Hall, CTO
Kathy Laczniak, Mgr.-Investor Rel.
Kenneth D. McCuskey, VP
Helge Jorgensen, Exec. VP
Thomas Kaiser, Exec. VP

GROWTH PLANS/SPECIAL FEATURES:

Danfoss Power Solutions designs, manufactures and markets mobile hydraulic and electrification products and solutions for the construction, agriculture and other off-highway vehicle markets. Products include hydrostatic transmissions, control systems, sensors, displays and accessories, orbital motors, steering components, telematics solutions, piston pumps/motors and proportional valves. Danfoss's mobile hydraulic solutions include pressure and temperature monitoring, thermal management, hydrostatic drive solutions, steering components, systems integration solutions, thermal management and more. Other products include genuine parts, remanufacturing solutions, autonomous vehicle integration systems, and system kits. Danfoss Power Solutions operates as a U.S. subsidiary of the Danfoss Group, which is comprised of 55 companies worldwide. During 2018, Danfoss Power acquired the remote-control business of IKUSI, including its equipment and technologies for wireless operation and control of truck-mounted cranes, off-road machines and other applications; and acquired a majority share of Artemis Intelligent Power Ltd., which specializes in hydraulic system development (Mitsubishi Heavy Industries holds the remaining minority share of Artemis).

FINANCIAL DATA:

Note: Data for latest year may not have been available at press time.

In U.S. $	2018	2017	2016	2015	2014	2013
Revenue	2,412,260,000	2,242,400,000	1,693,210,000	1,693,260,000	1,862,130,000	2,027,980,000
R&D Expense						
Operating Income						
Operating Margin %						
SGA Expense						
Net Income						
Operating Cash Flow						
Capital Expenditure						
EBITDA						
Return on Assets %						
Return on Equity %						
Debt to Equity						

CONTACT INFORMATION:

Phone: 515 239-6000 Fax: 515 239-6318
Toll-Free:
Address: 2800 E. 13th St., Ames, IA 50010 United States

STOCK TICKER/OTHER:

Stock Ticker: Subsidiary
Exchange:
Employees: 7,625
Fiscal Year Ends: 12/31
Parent Company: Danfoss Group

SALARIES/BONUSES:

Top Exec. Salary: $ Bonus: $
Second Exec. Salary: $ Bonus: $

OTHER THOUGHTS:

Estimated Female Officers or Directors: 2
Hot Spot for Advancement for Women/Minorities:

Darcars Automotive Group

www.darcars.com

NAIC Code: 441110

TYPES OF BUSINESS:

Auto Dealers, Retail
Automotive Service & Parts

BRANDS/DIVISIONS/AFFILIATES:

GROWTH PLANS/SPECIAL FEATURES:

Darcars Automotive Group, founded in 1977, is a dealership holding company with more than 20 automobile dealerships in Maryland, Virginia, Washington DC and Florida. Each dealership is dedicated to one primary manufacturer selling new Ford, Chrysler, Jeep, Toyota, Kia, Dodge, Honda, Lexus, Volvo, Nissan, RAM and Volkswagen vehicles. However, the dealership's used cars may include Mitsubishi, Infiniti, Acura, BMW, Jaguar, Hummer, Cadillac, GMC, Mercedes-Benz and Audi makes, among other brands. The firm offers a range of additional automotive services through its 10 collision centers (including body repair) and more than 20 parts and service centers. Customers can use the company's website to locate each individual dealership's website, search for used and new cars, access finance options and order parts. Darcars is privately-owned and -operated by the founding Darvish family.

CONTACTS: *Note: Officers with more than one job title may be intentionally listed here more than once.*

John Darvish, CEO
Haman Baniamam, Dir.- Technology & eCommerce
Gary Higgins, Dir.-Fixed Oper.
Mike Quinn, Dir.-Finance
Tammy Darvish, VP

FINANCIAL DATA: *Note: Data for latest year may not have been available at press time.*

In U.S. $	2018	2017	2016	2015	2014	2013
Revenue	1,586,266,889	1,510,730,370	1,438,790,829	1,255,954,263	1,156,000,000	1,085,000,000
R&D Expense						
Operating Income						
Operating Margin %						
SGA Expense						
Net Income						
Operating Cash Flow						
Capital Expenditure						
EBITDA						
Return on Assets %						
Return on Equity %						
Debt to Equity						

CONTACT INFORMATION:

Phone: 301-622-0300 Fax: 301-622-4915
Toll-Free: 800-327-2277
Address: 12511 Prosperity Dr., Silver Spring, MD 20904 United States

STOCK TICKER/OTHER:

Stock Ticker: Private
Employees: 2,200
Parent Company:
Exchange:
Fiscal Year Ends: 12/31

SALARIES/BONUSES:

Top Exec. Salary: $ Bonus: $
Second Exec. Salary: $ Bonus: $

OTHER THOUGHTS:

Estimated Female Officers or Directors: 1
Hot Spot for Advancement for Women/Minorities: Y

David McDavid Auto Group

www.mcdavid.com

NAIC Code: 441110

TYPES OF BUSINESS:

Auto Dealers, Retail
Body Parts & Accessories
Wheels & Tires

BRANDS/DIVISIONS/AFFILIATES:

Asbury Automotive Group Inc
David McDavid Acura
David McDavid Acura of Austin
David McDavid Honda of Frisco
David McDavid Honda of Irving
David McDavid's Plano Lincoln
McDavid Performance Center

CONTACTS: *Note: Officers with more than one job title may be intentionally listed here more than once.*

David McDavid, Pres.
Charles Oglesby, CEO
Craig Monaghan, CFO
Michael Kearney, COO-Asbury Automotive Group

GROWTH PLANS/SPECIAL FEATURES:

David McDavid Auto Group is one of the largest car dealerships in Texas, as well as an operating subsidiary of Asbury Automotive Group, Inc. The company sells new and used cars, trucks, SUVs and minivans through its five dealerships in the Irving, Frisco, Plano and Austin areas. Dealerships owned and operated by firm include David McDavid Acura (in Plano), David McDavid Acura of Austin, David McDavid Honda of Frisco, David McDavid Honda of Irving, and David McDavid Plano Lincoln. The company sells pre-owned brands such as BMW, Audi, Nissan, Lexus, Acura, Land Rover, Infiniti, Cadillac, Lincoln, Porsche, FIAT, Hyundai, Jaguar, Jeep, Kia, Volkswagen and Mercedes-Benz. McDavid Performance Center offers body parts and other products such as performance apparel; engine, exhaust, suspension and electrical products; wheels and tires; and interior accessories and graphics. The company's website offers customers online financial help through its Second Chance Finance application. The company's founder, David McDavid, started his first car dealership in 1962 at the age of 19. McDavid sold 70% of the company to the Asbury Group in 1998.

.

FINANCIAL DATA: *Note: Data for latest year may not have been available at press time.*

In U.S. $	2018	2017	2016	2015	2014	2013
Revenue						
R&D Expense						
Operating Income						
Operating Margin %						
SGA Expense						
Net Income						
Operating Cash Flow						
Capital Expenditure						
EBITDA						
Return on Assets %						
Return on Equity %						
Debt to Equity						

CONTACT INFORMATION:

Phone: 972-790-6100 Fax: 972-986-5689
Toll-Free:
Address: 3700 W. Airport Freeway, Irving, TX 75062 United States

STOCK TICKER/OTHER:

Stock Ticker: Subsidiary Exchange:
Employees: Fiscal Year Ends: 12/31
Parent Company: Asbury Automotive Group Inc

SALARIES/BONUSES:

Top Exec. Salary: $ Bonus: $
Second Exec. Salary: $ Bonus: $

OTHER THOUGHTS:

Estimated Female Officers or Directors:
Hot Spot for Advancement for Women/Minorities:

David Wilson Automotive Group

www.wilsonautomotive.com/

NAIC Code: 441110

TYPES OF BUSINESS:

Auto Dealers, Retail
Auto Service
Auto Finance

BRANDS/DIVISIONS/AFFILIATES:

Weir Canyon Honda
Weir Canyon Acura
Tustin Lexus
Right Honda
Toyota of Orange
Villa Ford
Newport Lexus
South Coast Toyota

CONTACTS: *Note: Officers with more than one job title may be intentionally listed here more than once.*

David Wilson, CEO
Craig T. Whetter, Pres.
Shelly Jackley, CFO
Glenn Quintos, COO
Frank Romano, Head-Corp. Dev. & Training
Glenn Quintos, Corp. Controller
Craig Whetter, Exec. VP
Vikki Murphy, VP
Bob Wyrick, Dir.-Parts & Service
David Wilson, Chmn.

GROWTH PLANS/SPECIAL FEATURES:

David Wilson Automotive Group is a new and used automobile dealer. The firm has eight Toyota dealerships, two Lexus dealerships, three Honda dealerships, two Ford dealerships, one Acura and one Mazda dealership. California branches include Toyota of Orange, Mazda of Orange, Ford of Orange, Toyota of Riverside, Villa Ford (Orange County), Toyota of Huntington Beach, South Bay Toyota, South Coast Toyota, Freeway Honda, Tustin Lexus, Newport Lexus, Weir Canyon Honda and Weir Canyon Acura. The two branches in Arizona are Right Toyota and Right Honda. One branch in Nevada is Toyota of Las Vegas. The Mexican branch is Toyota Puerto Vallarta. Brands of new vehicles handled by the group include Toyota, Scion, Honda, Mazda, Acura, Ford and Lexus. In addition to new and used vehicles sales, David Wilson Automotive Group also comprise parts and services departments. Each branch operates its own website, with many listing the location's inventory online or offering a search engine to assist customers in finding the vehicle they are looking for. Customers can also apply for financing through the branch websites as well as check for dealership specials.

FINANCIAL DATA: *Note: Data for latest year may not have been available at press time.*

In U.S. $	2018	2017	2016	2015	2014	2013
Revenue	2,629,558,770	2,504,341,686	2,385,087,320	1,980,839,385	1,600,000,000	1,550,000,000
R&D Expense						
Operating Income						
Operating Margin %						
SGA Expense						
Net Income						
Operating Cash Flow						
Capital Expenditure						
EBITDA						
Return on Assets %						
Return on Equity %						
Debt to Equity						

CONTACT INFORMATION:

Phone: 714-516-3111 Fax: 714-997-9200
Toll-Free:
Address: 1400 N. Tustin Ave., Orange, CA 92867 United States

STOCK TICKER/OTHER:

Stock Ticker: Private
Employees: 2,600
Parent Company:
Exchange:
Fiscal Year Ends: 12/31

SALARIES/BONUSES:

Top Exec. Salary: $ Bonus: $
Second Exec. Salary: $ Bonus: $

OTHER THOUGHTS:

Estimated Female Officers or Directors: 1
Hot Spot for Advancement for Women/Minorities:

Delphi Technologies PLC

www.delphi.com

NAIC Code: 336300

TYPES OF BUSINESS:

Motor Vehicle Transmission and Power Train Parts Manufacturing

BRANDS/DIVISIONS/AFFILIATES:

Delphi Automotive PLC

CONTACTS:

Note: Officers with more than one job title may be intentionally listed here more than once.

Richard F. Dauch, CEO
Rodney ONeal, Pres.
Lucia V. Moretti, Sr. VP
David M. Sherbin, Sr. VP
James A. Spencer, Exec. VP-Oper.
Eleanor E. Mascheroni, Sr. VP-Corp. Comm.
Keith D. Stipp, VP
Majdi B. Abulaban, Sr. VP
James A. Bertrand, Sr. VP
Steven A. Kiefer, Sr. VP
Jugal K. Vijayvargiya, Sr. VP
Sidney Johnson, Sr. VP-Global Supply Mgmt.

GROWTH PLANS/SPECIAL FEATURES:

Delphi Technologies PLC develops, designs and manufactures vehicle propulsion systems. The company's propulsion products optimize engine performance, increase vehicle efficiency, reduce emissions, improve driving performance and support the electrification of vehicles. Delphi Technologies operates in two business segments: powertrain systems and aftermarket. The powertrain systems segment provides fuel injection systems as well as related powertrain products such as valvetrains, fuel delivery modules, ignition coils, canisters, sensors, valves and actuators. This division offers electronic control modules with the corresponding software, algorithms and calibration that provide centralized and reliable management of various powertrain components. It also provides power electronics solutions, including supervisory controllers and software and DC/DC converters and inverters. The aftermarket segment sells aftermarket products to independent aftermarket and original equipment service customers. It also supplies a wide range of aftermarket products and services covering the fuel injection, electronics and engine management, maintenance and test equipment and vehicle diagnostics categories. Delphi Technologies' operations include 24 manufacturing facilities and 12 technical centers, the majority of which are located in countries outside the U.S., including Mexico, China and other Asia-Pacific, European and South American countries.

FINANCIAL DATA:

Note: Data for latest year may not have been available at press time.

In U.S. $	2018	2017	2016	2015	2014	2013
Revenue	4,858,000,000	4,849,000,000	4,486,000,000	4,407,000,000	4,540,000,000	
R&D Expense						
Operating Income	469,000,000	544,000,000	481,000,000	515,000,000	494,000,000	
Operating Margin %		.11%	.11%	.12%	.11%	
SGA Expense	414,000,000	408,000,000	299,000,000	312,000,000	343,000,000	
Net Income	358,000,000	285,000,000	236,000,000	272,000,000	306,000,000	
Operating Cash Flow	419,000,000	389,000,000	372,000,000	429,000,000	533,000,000	
Capital Expenditure	265,000,000	197,000,000	171,000,000	201,000,000	322,000,000	
EBITDA	640,000,000	636,000,000	529,000,000	590,000,000	638,000,000	
Return on Assets %		.09%	.05%	.09%		
Return on Equity %		.52%	.14%	.23%		
Debt to Equity		22.279	0.006	0.008		

CONTACT INFORMATION:

Phone: 44-020305-74300 Fax:
Toll-Free:
Address: 1 Angel Court, 10/Fl, London, EC2R 7HJ United Kingdom

STOCK TICKER/OTHER:

Stock Ticker: DLPH
Exchange: NYS
Employees: 145,000
Fiscal Year Ends: 12/31
Parent Company:

SALARIES/BONUSES:

Top Exec. Salary: $582,500 Bonus: $307,406
Second Exec. Salary: $752,610 Bonus: $

OTHER THOUGHTS:

Estimated Female Officers or Directors: 2
Hot Spot for Advancement for Women/Minorities:

Denso Corporation

www.denso.com/global/en.html

NAIC Code: 336300

TYPES OF BUSINESS:

Automobile Parts Manufacturer
Engine Components
Automotive Electrical Systems
Automotive Electronic Systems
Thermal Systems
Small Motors
Semiconductors
Industrial Robots

BRANDS/DIVISIONS/AFFILIATES:

DENSO
Airbiquity Inc

CONTACTS:
Note: Officers with more than one job title may be intentionally listed here more than once.

Koji Arima, CEO
Nobuaki Katoh, Pres.
Hikaru Sugi, Exec. VP
Hiromi Tokuda, Exec. VP
Koji Kobayashi, Exec. VP
Masahiko Miyaki, Exec. VP

GROWTH PLANS/SPECIAL FEATURES:

Denso Corporation is a global automotive supplier of advanced technology, systems and components. As of mid-2018, the company has more than 220 subsidiaries in 35 countries worldwide, including Japan (73), North America (31). Europe (35), Asia (76) and South America/others (6). Denso's products and services are divided into the mobility and industry/home categories. Mobility products and services include electronics, powertrains, thermal control, information systems, safety systems, service parts, accessories and customer services. These products and services include electronic control units (ECUs), semiconductors, heat/cool generation and control, sensing systems, prediction systems, connectivity systems, protection systems and more. Industry/home's products and services include air conditioning equipment, industrial robots, barcode systems, QR code systems home energy management systems and carbon dioxide refrigerant heat pumps for water supply systems. All of the company's products are marketed under the DENSO brand name. In March 2019, Denso purchased a $5 million stake in Seattle-based Airbiquity, Inc., engaged in connected vehicle services and the development of automotive telematics technology. The investment will accelerate the development of over-the-air (OTA) systems for wirelessly updating automotive software from a remote location.

FINANCIAL DATA:
Note: Data for latest year may not have been available at press time.

In U.S. $	2018	2017	2016	2015	2014	2013
Revenue	46,942,580,000	41,602,170,000	41,578,040,000	39,604,740,000	37,639,450,000	
R&D Expense						
Operating Income	3,792,281,000	3,037,594,000	2,901,379,000	3,045,176,000	3,470,833,000	
Operating Margin %	.08%	.07%	.08%	.08%	.13%	
SGA Expense	4,114,427,000	3,962,434,000	3,786,207,000	3,670,870,000	390,544,000	
Net Income	2,945,791,000	2,367,387,000	2,244,541,000	2,374,398,000	2,640,948,000	
Operating Cash Flow	5,127,743,000	4,298,649,000	5,080,519,000	3,521,007,000	4,252,886,000	
Capital Expenditure	3,381,640,000	3,164,997,000	3,164,676,000	3,350,634,000	2,893,678,000	
EBITDA	6,690,168,000	5,622,717,000	5,448,769,000	5,526,586,000	5,742,915,000	
Return on Assets %	.06%	.05%	.05%	.05%	.07%	
Return on Equity %	.09%	.08%	.08%	.09%	.12%	
Debt to Equity	0.084	0.08	0.069	0.105	0.115	

CONTACT INFORMATION:

Phone: 81 566255511 Fax:
Toll-Free:
Address: 1-1 Showa-cho, Kariya, 448-8661 Japan

STOCK TICKER/OTHER:

Stock Ticker: DNZOF
Employees: 206,521
Parent Company:
Exchange: PINX
Fiscal Year Ends: 03/31

SALARIES/BONUSES:

Top Exec. Salary: $ Bonus: $
Second Exec. Salary: $ Bonus: $

OTHER THOUGHTS:

Estimated Female Officers or Directors:
Hot Spot for Advancement for Women/Minorities:

DEUTZ AG

NAIC Code: 333618

www.deutz.com

TYPES OF BUSINESS:

Diesel Engines
Maintenance Services

BRANDS/DIVISIONS/AFFILIATES:

Torqeedo GmbH

CONTACTS:

Note: Officers with more than one job title may be intentionally listed here more than once.

Frank Hiller, CEO
Andreas Strecker, CFO
Margarete Haase, Dir.-Investor Rel.
Margarete Haase, Dir.-Finance
Werner Scherer, Chmn. Cologne Works Council
Frank Hiller, Chmn.

GROWTH PLANS/SPECIAL FEATURES:

DEUTZ AG is a leading manufacturer of innovative drive systems, and has been in business for 155 years (as of 2019). The company's core competencies are the development, production, distribution and servicing of diesel, gas and electric drivetrains for professional applications. DEUTZ's engines range in power from 25 to more than 830 horsepower (19 to 620 kW), and include liquid-cooled engines with displacements under 4 liters and 4-to-8 liter engines. Customized solutions primarily include air-cooled engines, but also large liquid-cooled engines with displacements of more than 8 liters. DEUTZ comprises 13 distribution companies, seven sales offices and over 800 sales and service partners in more than 130 countries worldwide. The firm engages in research and development, and its technologies optimize temperature management, injection and charge air cooling strategies to achieve consistent engine performance and low fuel consumption capabilities. DEUTZ's engines are used in agricultural equipment, construction equipment, material handling equipment and ground support equipment, as well as marine, railway and automotive drive systems. Engine accessories are also produced by the company and include a broad portfolio of add-on components ranging from fuel pre-heaters to power packs. Customer-specific engineering support and application services are also offered by DEUTZ, as well as hand tools for customer workshops. During 2019, DEUTZ (51%) entered into a joint venture agreement with SANY Heavy Industry Co., Ltd. (49%), in which DEUTZ will take over production of SANY's current engine range with the aim of supplying SANY with approximately 75,000 new engines in 2022. These engines will comply with the China IV emissions standard for on- and off-road applications. The joint venture was expected to be fully established by the end of 2019.

FINANCIAL DATA:

Note: Data for latest year may not have been available at press time.

In U.S. $	2018	2017	2016	2015	2014	2013
Revenue	1,969,442,000	1,637,622,000	1,395,261,000	1,381,089,000	1,694,199,000	1,608,946,000
R&D Expense	101,860,100	9,964,571	85,806,020	84,477,420	82,263,060	64,991,140
Operating Income	75,841,460	39,747,560	37,422,500	11,514,620	29,561,560	43,179,810
Operating Margin %		.04%	.02%	.01%	.02%	.03%
SGA Expense	53,255,100	136,182,500	118,689,100	117,692,600	112,488,900	108,835,300
Net Income	77,391,500	134,189,600	18,379,100	5,978,743	23,472,100	40,301,150
Operating Cash Flow	107,949,500	124,778,600	70,637,740	114,371,100	126,328,600	116,253,300
Capital Expenditure	87,356,070	75,620,020	63,994,690	75,509,300	67,648,360	94,331,270
EBITDA	179,140,800	266,054,000	134,078,800	129,207,300	140,279,000	165,411,900
Return on Assets %		.11%	.02%	.00%	.02%	.03%
Return on Equity %		.22%	.03%	.01%	.04%	.08%
Debt to Equity		0.047	0.09	0.119	0.151	0.173

CONTACT INFORMATION:

Phone: 49 221822-0 Fax: 49 221822-3525
Toll-Free:
Address: Ottostrasse 1, Cologne, 51149 Germany

STOCK TICKER/OTHER:

Stock Ticker: DEUZF
Employees: 4,645
Parent Company:
Exchange: GREY
Fiscal Year Ends: 12/31

SALARIES/BONUSES:

Top Exec. Salary: $ Bonus: $
Second Exec. Salary: $ Bonus: $

OTHER THOUGHTS:

Estimated Female Officers or Directors: 2
Hot Spot for Advancement for Women/Minorities: Y

D'Ieteren SA/NV

www.dieteren.com

NAIC Code: 441110

TYPES OF BUSINESS:

New Car Dealers
Vehicle Financing
Long-Term Car Rental
Glass Repair & Replacement

BRANDS/DIVISIONS/AFFILIATES:

D'Ieteren Auto
Belron
Carglass
Safelite
Autoglass
Moleskin

CONTACTS: *Note: Officers with more than one job title may be intentionally listed here more than once.*

Francis Deprez, CEO
Arnaud Lviolette, CFO
Nicolas D'Ieteren, Chmn.

GROWTH PLANS/SPECIAL FEATURES:

D'Ieteren SA/NV imports and distributes automobiles and provides vehicle glass repair and replacement services. Its automotive business is divided into two segments: D'Ieteren Auto and Belron. Wholly-owned D'Ieteren Auto imports and distributes new and used Volkswagen, Audi, SEAT, Skoda, Bentley, Lamborghini, Bugatti and Porsche vehicles and parts across Belgium. Spare parts and accessories are also imported and distributed by this business segment, and after sales services are offered through its corporate-owned dealerships. Belron (54.10%-owned) is a leader in vehicle glass repair and replacement in 34 countries and six continents, serving approximately 16.5 million consumers annually. Operating through a network of subsidiaries and franchisees, its more than 10,000 branches and units enable Belron to offer services around the clock. The division uses more than ten major brands, including Carglass, Safelite and Autoglass. In addition, D'Ieteren comprises a non-automotive brand, Moleskine (100%-owned), which produces reading and writing accessories and hybrid products made from paper, including notebooks, diaries, journals and bags. D'Ieteren sells Moleskine products through a multi-channel distribution strategy in more than 115 countries. In August 2019, D'Ieteren agreed to acquire U.S.-based TruRoad Holdings, Inc., a vehicle glass repair and replacement, advanced driver assistance systems recalibration and claims management player.

FINANCIAL DATA: *Note: Data for latest year may not have been available at press time.*

In U.S. $	2018	2017	2016	2015	2014	2013
Revenue	3,961,581,000	3,825,399,000	7,165,301,000	6,682,242,000	6,135,519,000	6,056,798,000
R&D Expense						
Operating Income	126,992,900	106,620,900	148,029,200	259,964,600	27,015,060	221,324,200
Operating Margin %		.03%	.02%	.04%	.00%	.04%
SGA Expense	417,294,100	414,415,400	1,939,216,000	1,796,834,000	1,699,402,000	1,619,686,000
Net Income	1,160,319,000	124,667,800	55,248,010	144,707,700	-12,289,640	126,217,900
Operating Cash Flow	-30,336,580	94,552,700	429,030,100	366,696,200	288,308,300	313,551,800
Capital Expenditure	49,822,850	39,747,560	169,619,100	134,964,600	148,582,800	122,674,900
EBITDA	106,620,900	140,500,400	306,687,300	415,522,600	189,659,000	357,395,900
Return on Assets %		.03%	.01%	.04%	.00%	.03%
Return on Equity %		.06%	.03%	.08%	-.01%	.07%
Debt to Equity		0.075	0.452	0.409	0.45	0.402

CONTACT INFORMATION:

Phone: 32 25365111 Fax:
Toll-Free:
Address: rue du Mail, 50, Brussels, 1050 Belgium

STOCK TICKER/OTHER:

Stock Ticker: SIETY
Employees: 32,951
Parent Company:
Exchange: PINX
Fiscal Year Ends: 12/31

SALARIES/BONUSES:

Top Exec. Salary: $ Bonus: $
Second Exec. Salary: $ Bonus: $

OTHER THOUGHTS:

Estimated Female Officers or Directors:
Hot Spot for Advancement for Women/Minorities:

Discount Tire Company

www.discounttire.com

NAIC Code: 441320

TYPES OF BUSINESS:

Tire Stores
Mail-Order & Online Tire Sales
Roadside Assistance

BRANDS/DIVISIONS/AFFILIATES:

Discount Tire
America's Tire Co
Discount Tire Credit Card

CONTACTS: *Note: Officers with more than one job title may be intentionally listed here more than once.*

Michael Zuieback, CEO
Ed Kaminski, COO
Christian Roe, CFO

GROWTH PLANS/SPECIAL FEATURES:

Discount Tire Company, based in Arizona, is one of the largest independent tire dealers in the U.S. The firm operates over 1,035 stores in 35 states (as of July 2019). These stores primarily operate under the Discount Tire name, but also as America's Tire Co. in certain parts of California. Discount Tire carries leading tire brands such as BF Goodrich, Michelin, Goodyear, Pirelli and GT Radial as well as in-house exclusive brands Road Hugger, Arizonian, MB Wheels and Maxxim tires and wheels. Types of tires offered by the company are lawn/garden, ATV/UTV, trailer, temporary spares, winter, performance truck, ribbed, highway all-season, mud-terrain, all-terrain, all-purpose, track and competition, summer performance, all-season performance, grand touring and the standard all-season touring. The company also repairs tires, offers tire rotations and balancing and provides free air pressure checking to its customers. In addition, the firm sells and delivers tires through its mail-order/online division (Discount Tire direct), which provides fast free shipping to a customer's door as well as through its website. This website also provides extensive information for its customers on all aspects of wheel and tire care. The company offers a Discount Tire Credit Card, which can be applied for online and is underwritten by Synchrony Bank.

Discount Tires offers its employees benefits including flexible spending accounts; an employee assistance program; medical, vision, life and dental insurance; paid vacation; a 401(k) plan; and profit sharing plans. Part-time employees are eligible for medical insurance and a 401(k).

FINANCIAL DATA: *Note: Data for latest year may not have been available at press time.*

In U.S. $	2018	2017	2016	2015	2014	2013
Revenue	4,784,850,000	4,557,000,000	4,340,000,000	4,200,000,000	3,900,000,000	3,500,000,000
R&D Expense						
Operating Income						
Operating Margin %						
SGA Expense						
Net Income						
Operating Cash Flow						
Capital Expenditure						
EBITDA						
Return on Assets %						
Return on Equity %						
Debt to Equity						

CONTACT INFORMATION:

Phone: 480-606-6000 Fax: 480-951-8619
Toll-Free:
Address: 20225 N. Scottsdale Rd., Scottsdale, AZ 85254 United States

STOCK TICKER/OTHER:

Stock Ticker: Private
Employees: 18,635
Parent Company:
Exchange:
Fiscal Year Ends: 12/31

SALARIES/BONUSES:

Top Exec. Salary: $ Bonus: $
Second Exec. Salary: $ Bonus: $

OTHER THOUGHTS:

Estimated Female Officers or Directors:
Hot Spot for Advancement for Women/Minorities:

Dollar Thrifty Automotive Group Inc

www.thrifty.com/AboutUs/content.aspx

NAIC Code: 532111

TYPES OF BUSINESS:

Automobile Rental
Used Car Sales
Financial Services

BRANDS/DIVISIONS/AFFILIATES:

Hertz Global Holdings Inc
Dollar
Thrifty

CONTACTS: *Note: Officers with more than one job title may be intentionally listed here more than once.*

H. Clofford Buster, CFO

GROWTH PLANS/SPECIAL FEATURES:

Dollar Thrifty Automotive Group, Inc. (DTG) operates vehicle rental agencies under the brand names Dollar and Thrifty. These agencies comprise one of the largest car rental networks in the world. DTG itself is a wholly-owned subsidiary of Hertz Global Holdings, Inc. There are more than 4,000 corporately-owned and franchised Dollar and Thrifty stores, in conjunction with Hertz, strategically located in 77 countries throughout North, Central and South America, Africa, the Middle East, the Caribbean, Asia and the Pacific. DTG also sells vehicle rental franchises worldwide, and provides sales and marketing, reservations, data processing systems, insurance and other services to franchisees. DTG offers customers supplemental equipment and optional products, including global positioning system equipment, ski racks, infant/child seats, as well as rent-a-toll products for electronic toll payments.

The company offers employees medical, dental and vision coverage; domestic partner benefits; flexible spending accounts; a wellness program; short- and long-term disability; life and AD&D insurance; an employee assistance program; a 401(k); tuition reimbursement; and employee discounts.

FINANCIAL DATA: *Note: Data for latest year may not have been available at press time.*

In U.S. $	2018	2017	2016	2015	2014	2013
Revenue	1,620,000,000	1,600,000,000	1,528,500,000	1,800,000,000	1,910,000,000	1,875,000,000
R&D Expense						
Operating Income						
Operating Margin %						
SGA Expense						
Net Income						
Operating Cash Flow						
Capital Expenditure						
EBITDA						
Return on Assets %						
Return on Equity %						
Debt to Equity						

CONTACT INFORMATION:

Phone: 918-660-7700 Fax: 918-669-2934
Toll-Free: 888-700-9803
Address: 5330 E. 31st St., Tulsa, OK 74135 United States

STOCK TICKER/OTHER:

Stock Ticker: Subsidiary
Employees: 6,000
Parent Company: Hertz Global Holdings Inc
Exchange:
Fiscal Year Ends: 12/31

SALARIES/BONUSES:

Top Exec. Salary: $ Bonus: $
Second Exec. Salary: $ Bonus: $

OTHER THOUGHTS:

Estimated Female Officers or Directors: 2
Hot Spot for Advancement for Women/Minorities:

Dongfeng Motor Corporation

www.dongfeng-global.com/

NAIC Code: 336111

TYPES OF BUSINESS:

Automobile Manufacturing
Truck & Bus Manufacturing
Auto Parts & Components Manufacturing

BRANDS/DIVISIONS/AFFILIATES:

CONTACTS:

Note: Officers with more than one job title may be intentionally listed here more than once.

Zhu Yanfeng, CEO
Jun Seki, Pres.
Cai Wei, VP
Fan Zhong, Exec. Dir.
Li Shaozhu, Exec. Dir.
Hu Xindong, Joint Sec.
Susan Lo Yee Har, Joint Sec.

GROWTH PLANS/SPECIAL FEATURES:

Dongfeng Motor Corporation (DFM) is one of China's leading automakers. Established as a state-owned company in 1969, DFM was restructured in the 1990s and has since sought out numerous joint ventures as well as integrating its development with international automotive companies. Subsequently, the firm has become one of the Chinese automotive companies most heavily vested in foreign partnerships. DFM's products are categorized into two groups: commercial vehicles and passenger vehicles. Commercial vehicles include various types of heavy-duty trucks, semis, buses, motor coaches, sanitation vehicles, hybrids and tankers. Passenger vehicles include sedans, compact cars, sport utility vehicles (SUVs), vans and mini vans. During 2018, DFM introduced its Glory ix5 crossover vehicle to the Chinese market. It was made in conjunction with Baidu Apollo, a software platform for auto manufacturing partners to develop their own autonomous driving systems via on-vehicle and hardware platforms.

FINANCIAL DATA:

Note: Data for latest year may not have been available at press time.

In U.S. $	2018	2017	2016	2015	2014	2013
Revenue	15,199,200,000	18,444,100,000	17,621,700,000	19,576,351,777	13,028,413,251	6,069,000,000
R&D Expense						
Operating Income						
Operating Margin %						
SGA Expense						
Net Income	1,828,680,000	2,074,800,000	2,000,100,000	1,786,529,167	2,143,345,698	1,714,700,000
Operating Cash Flow						
Capital Expenditure						
EBITDA						
Return on Assets %						
Return on Equity %						
Debt to Equity						

CONTACT INFORMATION:

Phone: 86-719-8226-962 Fax: 86-719-8226-845
Toll-Free:
Address: 29 Baiye Rd., Wuhan, Hubei 430015 China

STOCK TICKER/OTHER:

Stock Ticker: 489
Employees: 176,000
Parent Company:
Exchange: Hong Kong
Fiscal Year Ends: 12/31

SALARIES/BONUSES:

Top Exec. Salary: $ Bonus: $
Second Exec. Salary: $ Bonus: $

OTHER THOUGHTS:

Estimated Female Officers or Directors: 1
Hot Spot for Advancement for Women/Minorities:

Dongfeng Motor Group Co Ltd

www.dfmg.com.cn

NAIC Code: 336111

TYPES OF BUSINESS:

Automobile Manufacturing

BRANDS/DIVISIONS/AFFILIATES:

Dongfeng Commercial Vehicles Co Ltd
Dongfeng Passenger Vehicle Company
Dongfeng Electric Vehicle Co
Dongfeng Motor Co Ltd

CONTACTS:

Note: Officers with more than one job title may be intentionally listed here more than once.

Fu Shou Zhu, Pres.
Li Kang, Head-Audit Dept.
Zhong Fan, Exec. Dir.
Shao Zhu Li, Exec. Dir.
Yanfeng Zhu, Chmn.

GROWTH PLANS/SPECIAL FEATURES:

Dongfeng Motor Group Co., Ltd. manufactures and sells commercial and passenger vehicles, both new and used, operating through a series of subsidiaries and joint ventures. Commercial vehicles include heavy duty trucks, medium trucks, light trucks, mini trucks and buses. The firm has multiple series of these commercial vehicle groups, most of which are trucks. Subsidiary Dongfeng Commercial Vehicles Co. Ltd. manages all operations in relation to commercial vehicles. Through this subsidiary, the company has a joint venture agreement with Volvo. Passenger vehicles include sedans, multipurpose vehicles and sport utility vehicles. The firm has multiple series of these vehicles, most of which are sedans, with SUVs coming in second and multi-purpose vehicles the remainder. Operations for these vehicles are managed by the Dongfeng Passenger Vehicle Company as well as a handful of joint ventures with of PSA Peugeot Citreon and Honda. Subsidiary Dongfeng Electric Vehicle Co. manages the operations of new energy vehicles. Additionally, the firm manufactures and sells parts and engines for both passenger and commercial vehicles and import and export vehicles and equipment; and offers financing options, vehicle insurance, and trades used cars. Dongfeng Motor Co. Ltd., a 50%-owned subsidiary, is in charge of the manufacture of vehicle equipment.

FINANCIAL DATA:

Note: Data for latest year may not have been available at press time.

In U.S. $	2018	2017	2016	2015	2014	2013
Revenue	15,187,700,000	18,161,950,000	17,785,110,000	18,387,130,000	11,760,760,000	5,413,458,000
R&D Expense						
Operating Income	687,596,200	849,870,700	1,069,965,000	1,014,905,000	592,294,500	123,340,200
Operating Margin %		.05%	.06%	.06%	.05%	.03%
SGA Expense	1,575,965,000	1,725,601,000	1,653,689,000	1,574,077,000	1,077,229,000	646,047,000
Net Income	1,885,551,000	2,043,031,000	1,940,175,000	1,677,950,000	1,866,083,000	1,529,477,000
Operating Cash Flow	-3,232,269,000	602,899,700	522,706,800	81,064,580	-143,097,900	-1,408,316,000
Capital Expenditure	704,012,500	650,114,700	568,904,900	551,326,400	508,614,900	193,509,000
EBITDA	2,470,581,000	2,642,444,000	2,621,088,000	2,327,919,000	2,396,345,000	1,691,751,000
Return on Assets %		.07%	.08%	.08%	.10%	.09%
Return on Equity %		.14%	.15%	.15%	.19%	.18%
Debt to Equity		0.022	0.073	0.089	0.005	

CONTACT INFORMATION:

Phone: 86-27-84285000 Fax:
Toll-Free:
Address: Special No 1 Dongfeng Rd., Wuhan Economic & Tech. Dev. Zone, Wuhan, Hubei 430056 China

STOCK TICKER/OTHER:

Stock Ticker: DNFGF
Employees: 139,602
Parent Company:
Exchange: PINX
Fiscal Year Ends: 12/31

SALARIES/BONUSES:

Top Exec. Salary: $ Bonus: $
Second Exec. Salary: $ Bonus: $

OTHER THOUGHTS:

Estimated Female Officers or Directors:
Hot Spot for Advancement for Women/Minorities:

Donlen Corporation

www.donlen.com

NAIC Code: 532112

TYPES OF BUSINESS:

Automobile Leasing
Business Vehicles
Fleet Management Services
License & Title Services
Maintenance Services
Asset Management Services

BRANDS/DIVISIONS/AFFILIATES:

Hertz Global Holdings Inc
Hertz Corporation (The)
FleetWeb
DriverPoint Telematics
Recall inSIGHT

CONTACTS: *Note: Officers with more than one job title may be intentionally listed here more than once.*

Tom Callahan, Pres.
Eric Hiller, CFO
Greg Hawes, Sr. VP-Sales & Client Relations
Sharon Peete, Sr. Dr.-HR
Dennis Straight, CTO
Brian Wright, Sr. VP-Prod. & Svcs.
Carla Garfinkle, General Counsel
Mike Lewis, Exec. VP
Jim Kachidurian, Sr. VP-Client Services

GROWTH PLANS/SPECIAL FEATURES:

Donlen Corporation provides a range of vehicle leasing, fleet administrative services and fleet management services. The company provides clients with flexible management programs to reduce operating costs and any administration needed to run an entire fleet. Programs include preventive maintenance, maintenance consultation, fuel management, accident management, acquisition, remarketing, transportation services and truck/equipment services, which are all accessed through the company's web-based tracking system, FleetWeb. FleetWeb covers all facets of fleet operations management and supplies a system for order entry and information maintenance. Donlen's DriverPoint Telematics platform is a multi-faceted program of telematics, online driver training and driver behavior scorecards that help reduce company cost, establish driver safety and increase productivity. Other solutions include fleet administrative services, vehicle maintenance, toll management, vehicle acquisition, fleet funding, remarketing, transportation services, global fleet solutions, violation management and vehicle optimization. Donlen's Recall inSIGHT is a recall management solution that gives fleet professionals full visibility to their vehicle fleet's open recalls, so they can take immediate action by working with their drivers to efficiently manage and address original equipment manufacturer (OEM) and National Highway Traffic Safety Administration (NHTSA) recalls. The firm is a wholly-owned subsidiary of The Hertz Corporation, which itself is a subsidiary of Hertz Global Holdings, Inc.

The company offers medical and dental insurance, life insurance, flexible spending accounts, a 401(k) plan, profit sharing and access to an onsite fitness center.

FINANCIAL DATA: *Note: Data for latest year may not have been available at press time.*

In U.S. $	2018	2017	2016	2015	2014	2013
Revenue	748,000,000	640,000,000	592,000,000	583,000,000	568,000,000	527,000,000
R&D Expense						
Operating Income						
Operating Margin %						
SGA Expense						
Net Income						
Operating Cash Flow						
Capital Expenditure						
EBITDA						
Return on Assets %						
Return on Equity %						
Debt to Equity						

CONTACT INFORMATION:

Phone: 847-714-1400 Fax:
Toll-Free: 800-323-1483
Address: 3000 Lakeside Dr., 2/Fl, Bannockburn, IL 60015 United States

STOCK TICKER/OTHER:

Stock Ticker: Subsidiary Exchange:
Employees: 300 Fiscal Year Ends: 08/31
Parent Company: Hertz Global Holdings Inc

SALARIES/BONUSES:

Top Exec. Salary: $ Bonus: $
Second Exec. Salary: $ Bonus: $

OTHER THOUGHTS:

Estimated Female Officers or Directors: 2
Hot Spot for Advancement for Women/Minorities:

Dorman Products Inc

www.dormanproducts.com

NAIC Code: 336300

TYPES OF BUSINESS:

Automobile Parts Manufacturer
Replacement & Aftermarket Parts

BRANDS/DIVISIONS/AFFILIATES:

Dorman OE Solutions
Dorman HELP!
Dorman HD Solutions
Dorman Premium
MAS
Dorman FirstStop
Dorman ConductTite
Dorman AutoGrade

CONTACTS: *Note: Officers with more than one job title may be intentionally listed here more than once.*

Kevin Olsen, CEO
David Hession, CFO
Steven Berman, Chairman of the Board
Michael Ginnetti, Controller
Michael Kealey, Executive VP, Divisional
Jeffery Darby, Senior VP, Divisional

GROWTH PLANS/SPECIAL FEATURES:

Dorman Products, Inc. is a leading supplier of original equipment automotive replacement parts, fasteners and service line products for the automotive aftermarket. The company markets over 75,000 different automotive replacement parts. Dorman's products are sold primarily in the U.S. through automotive aftermarket retailers (such as AutoZone, Advance Auto Parts and O'Reilly Auto Parts); national, regional and local warehouse distributors (such as Genuine Parts Co./NAPA); and specialty markets and salvage yards. The automotive replacements parts market is divided into two components: parts for passenger cars and light trucks and parts for medium and heavy-duty trucks, with most of the firm's parts designed for passenger cars and light trucks. Dorman categorizes its products into four classes: power-train, which accounted for 40% of 2018 sales; chassis, 29%; automotive body, 26%; and hardware, 5%. Most of the company's sales consist of original equipment dealer parts that include intake manifolds, exhaust manifolds, oil cooler lines, window regulators, radiator fan assemblies, power steering pulleys and harmonic balancers. Dorman currently sells its products under a number of proprietary brand names, including Dorman OE Solutions, Dorman HELP!, Dorman HD Solutions, Dorman Premium, MAS, Dorman FirstStop, Dorman ConductTite and Dorman AutoGrade.

Dorman offers its employees medical, dental and vision coverage; flexible spending accounts; a 401(k) plan; a 529 college savings plan; life, AD&D and disability insurance; tuition reimbursement; credit union membership; a company-sponsored health club membership; personal protection programs; and auto insurance.

FINANCIAL DATA: *Note: Data for latest year may not have been available at press time.*

In U.S. $	2018	2017	2016	2015	2014	2013
Revenue	973,705,000	903,221,000	859,604,000	802,957,000	751,476,000	664,466,000
R&D Expense						
Operating Income	171,143,000	176,240,000	168,601,000	146,157,000	140,734,000	127,939,000
Operating Margin %		.20%	.20%	.18%	.19%	.19%
SGA Expense	202,138,000	182,409,000	169,473,000	161,893,000	146,467,000	133,029,000
Net Income	133,602,000	106,599,000	106,049,000	92,329,000	89,987,000	81,920,000
Operating Cash Flow	78,112,000	94,241,000	121,539,000	92,060,000	59,640,000	61,559,000
Capital Expenditure	26,106,000	24,450,000	20,059,000	21,688,000	29,862,000	24,666,000
EBITDA	199,534,000	198,464,000	187,508,000	162,343,000	153,392,000	138,098,000
Return on Assets %		.14%	.16%	.15%	.16%	.18%
Return on Equity %		.17%	.19%	.19%	.21%	.22%
Debt to Equity						

CONTACT INFORMATION:

Phone: 215 997-1800 Fax:
Toll-Free:
Address: 3400 E. Walnut St., Colmar, PA 18915 United States

STOCK TICKER/OTHER:

Stock Ticker: DORM
Employees: 1,860
Parent Company:
Exchange: NAS
Fiscal Year Ends: 12/31

SALARIES/BONUSES:

Top Exec. Salary: $700,000 Bonus: $
Second Exec. Salary: $437,404 Bonus: $

OTHER THOUGHTS:

Estimated Female Officers or Directors:
Hot Spot for Advancement for Women/Minorities:

Double Coin Holdings Ltd

www.doublecoinholdings.com/en/about.aspx

NAIC Code: 326211

TYPES OF BUSINESS:

Tire Manufacturing (except Retreading)

BRANDS/DIVISIONS/AFFILIATES:

Shanghai Huayi Group Corp Ltd
Double Coin Heavy-Duty Radial Truck Tyre Co
Double Coin (Rugao) Tyre Co Ltd
Double Coin (Chongquin) Tyre Co Ltd
Huay Group (Thailand) Co Ltd
Double Coin Heavy-Duty Radial
Shanghai Tyre & Rubber Research Institute

CONTACTS: *Note: Officers with more than one job title may be intentionally listed here more than once.*

Xia Wang, Pres.
Zhang Wanyou, Exec. VP
Wang Wenhao, VP
Xie Huashun, VP

GROWTH PLANS/SPECIAL FEATURES:

Double Coin Holdings Ltd. is engaged in the development, manufacture and distribution of tires under the Double Coin and Warrior brands. The company's main products include truck and bus radial (TBR) tires; off-the-road (OTR) tires; industrial tires; and agricultural tires. Double Coin operates four plants: Double Coin Heavy-Duty Radial Truck Tyre Co., Double Coin (Rugao) Tyre Co. Ltd., Double Coin (Chongquin) Tyre Co. Ltd. and Huay Group (Thailand) Co. Ltd. Double Coin Heavy-Duty Radial is exclusively dedicated to the production of all-steel radial truck tires for trucks, light trucks, industrial, OTR, huge OTR and snow tires. The facility has more than 60 specifications and 500 varieties. Double Coin (Rugao) produces all-steel tires and approximately 100,000 all-steel radial OTR types, while Double Coin (Chongquin) produces all-steel radial truck tires. Both Double Coin (Rugao) and Double Coin (Chongquin) are co-investment companies. Huay Group (Thailand) manufactures TBR and OTR tires for the North American market. North American warehouses are located in Tennessee, California, Costa Rica and Mexico. Double Coin also manages an R&D center called the Shanghai Tyre & Rubber Research Institute. The firm sells its products in over 100 countries and supplies auxiliary products to approximately 30 major automobile manufacturers. Double Coin is majority-owned by Shanghai Huayi Group Corp. Ltd.

FINANCIAL DATA: *Note: Data for latest year may not have been available at press time.*

In U.S. $	2018	2017	2016	2015	2014	2013
Revenue		6,830,388,736	6,416,684,544	6,369,787,392	2,310,169,344	2,247,691,776
R&D Expense						
Operating Income						
Operating Margin %						
SGA Expense						
Net Income		97,096,848	65,600,716	110,418,616	53,685,112	47,939,536
Operating Cash Flow						
Capital Expenditure						
EBITDA						
Return on Assets %						
Return on Equity %						
Debt to Equity						

CONTACT INFORMATION:

Phone: 86 21-33024666 Fax: 86 21-63390367
Toll-Free:
Address: 63 Sichuan Middle Rd., Huangpu District, Shanghai 200002 China

STOCK TICKER/OTHER:

Stock Ticker: DCHLF Exchange: GREY
Employees: 2,481 Fiscal Year Ends: 12/31
Parent Company: Shanghai Huayi Group Corp Ltd

SALARIES/BONUSES:

Top Exec. Salary: $ Bonus: $
Second Exec. Salary: $ Bonus: $

OTHER THOUGHTS:

Estimated Female Officers or Directors:
Hot Spot for Advancement for Women/Minorities:

DRB-HICOM Berhad

www.drb-hicom.com/

NAIC Code: 336111

TYPES OF BUSINESS:

Automobile Manufacturing
Automobile Distribution

BRANDS/DIVISIONS/AFFILIATES:

Alam Flora Sdn Bhd
PUSPAKOM Sdn Bhd
Bank Muamalat Malaysia Berhad
DRB-HICOM University of Automotive Malaysia
Akademi Saga

CONTACTS: *Note: Officers with more than one job title may be intentionally listed here more than once.*

Syed Faisal Albar bin Syed A.R. Albar, Group Managing Dir.
Amalanathan Thomas, Dir.-Finance
Izham Ab Wahab, Group Head-Human Capital
Mohammad Zainal Shaari, Chmn.

GROWTH PLANS/SPECIAL FEATURES:

DRB-HICOM Berhad is an investment holding company that through its subsidiaries develops, assembles and sells motor and military vehicles, and is engaged in other businesses. The firm divides its activities into three core segments: automotive, services and properties. The automotive segment manufactures, assembles, inspects, distributes and sells a wide range of vehicles, including motorcycles, commercial vehicles, defense vehicles and customized vehicles (buses, ambulances, police vehicles, fire trucks and garbage compactor trucks). This division also provides contract manufacturing for national as well as global carmakers and original equipment manufacturers (OEMs). The services segment encompasses two units: the service unit offers waste management, vehicles inspection, banking, logistics and component manufacturing through Alam Flora Sdn Bhd, PUSPAKOM Sdn Bhd and Bank Muamalat Malaysia Berhad; and the education unit consists of two institutes that provide related education, including: DRB-HICOM University of Automotive Malaysia, a tertiary institution that focuses on building skills in all automotive-related disciplines; and Akademi Saga, a vocational training institution created specifically for building after-sales skills for the automotive industry. Last, the properties segment engages in the development of industrial properties throughout Malaysia, as well as high-tech and modern industrial parks in Singapore.

FINANCIAL DATA: *Note: Data for latest year may not have been available at press time.*

In U.S. $	2018	2017	2016	2015	2014	2013
Revenue	3,308,720,000	2,726,590,000	3,085,900,000	2,836,056,167	3,190,271,892	3,309,120,590
R&D Expense						
Operating Income						
Operating Margin %						
SGA Expense						
Net Income	76,396,300	-58,881,200	-220,960,000	-213,454,901	73,263,110	107,834,461
Operating Cash Flow						
Capital Expenditure						
EBITDA						
Return on Assets %						
Return on Equity %						
Debt to Equity						

CONTACT INFORMATION:

Phone: 60-3-2052-8000 Fax: 60-3-2052-8099
Toll-Free:
Address: Level 1 Wisma DRB-HICOM No. 2 Jalan Usahawan U1/8, Sec. U1, Shah Alam, Selangor 40150 Malaysia

STOCK TICKER/OTHER:

Stock Ticker: 1619
Employees: 56,000
Parent Company:
Exchange: Malaysia
Fiscal Year Ends: 03/31

SALARIES/BONUSES:

Top Exec. Salary: $ Bonus: $
Second Exec. Salary: $ Bonus: $

OTHER THOUGHTS:

Estimated Female Officers or Directors:
Hot Spot for Advancement for Women/Minorities:

DriveTime Automotive Group Inc

www.drivetime.com

NAIC Code: 441120

TYPES OF BUSINESS:

Used Auto Dealers
Auto Financing
Auto Leasing

BRANDS/DIVISIONS/AFFILIATES:

DriveCare Powertrain Protection Plan
Bridgecrest Acceptance Company

CONTACTS: *Note: Officers with more than one job title may be intentionally listed here more than once.*

Don Reese, CEO
Mary L. N. Phillips, CFO
Jon Ehlinger, General Counsel
Jon Ehlinger, VP-Public Rel.
Al Appelman, VP-Risk & Customer Analytics

GROWTH PLANS/SPECIAL FEATURES:

DriveTime Automotive Group, Inc. is a leading chain of buy-here-pay-here used car dealerships. The company targets its products and services to the sub-prime segment of the automobile financing industry. This segment serves customers with limited credit histories, low income or past credit problems who cannot access traditional financing. Advantages of buy-here-pay-here dealerships include the ability to offer customers expanded credit opportunities and flexible payment terms as well as the ability to make payments at the dealership. For each used vehicle sold, DriveTime offers a 30-day limited warranty, 5-day return guarantee, autocheck history report and a certified multi-point inspection. The firm finances all the used cars through retail installment contracts. DriveTime currently operates 145 dealerships nationwide. The dealerships are located in high-visibility, high-traffic commercial areas and comprise more than 11,300 available vehicles (all DriveTime dealerships combined), featuring a wide selection of makes and models. The ages of the cars typically range from three to seven years. DriveTime acquires its inventory primarily from used vehicle auctions. After purchase, the cars are delivered to one of the company's centers, where they are inspected thoroughly and reconditioned for sale. The company offers its DriveCare Powertrain Protection Plan to customers interested in extended protection coverage. Besides flexible auto loan financing, no-commitment lease options are also offered. Subsidiary Bridgecrest Acceptance Company is a licensed third-party servicer that services loans for DriveTime and other affiliated finance companies. All credit scoring, risk decision analytics and verifications remain the responsibility of DriveTime. In May 2018, DriveTime opened a new 110,000-square-foot inspection center in Morrisville, Pennsylvania.

DriveTime offers employees a choice of medical plans, tuition reimbursement plans, vacation pay, paid time off and fitness room.

FINANCIAL DATA: *Note: Data for latest year may not have been available at press time.*

In U.S. $	2018	2017	2016	2015	2014	2013
Revenue	1,764,000,000	1,680,000,000	1,600,000,000	1,525,000,000	1,475,000,000	1,400,896,000
R&D Expense						
Operating Income						
Operating Margin %						
SGA Expense						
Net Income						
Operating Cash Flow						
Capital Expenditure						
EBITDA						
Return on Assets %						
Return on Equity %						
Debt to Equity						

CONTACT INFORMATION:

Phone: 314-824-1170 Fax: 866-271-6010
Toll-Free: 888-418-1212
Address: 1720 W. Rio Salado Pkwy, Tempe, AZ 85281 United States

STOCK TICKER/OTHER:

Stock Ticker: Private
Employees: 5,000
Parent Company:
Exchange:
Fiscal Year Ends: 12/31

SALARIES/BONUSES:

Top Exec. Salary: $ Bonus: $
Second Exec. Salary: $ Bonus: $

OTHER THOUGHTS:

Estimated Female Officers or Directors:
Hot Spot for Advancement for Women/Minorities:

Ducati Motor Holding SpA

www.ducati.com

NAIC Code: 336991

TYPES OF BUSINESS:

Motorcycle Manufacturing & Retail
Apparel & Accessories
Online Retail
Racing Operations

BRANDS/DIVISIONS/AFFILIATES:

Volkswagen AG
Diavel
Hypermotard
Monster
Multistrada
Panigale
SuperSport
Scrambler

CONTACTS: *Note: Officers with more than one job title may be intentionally listed here more than once.*

Claudio Domencali, CEO

GROWTH PLANS/SPECIAL FEATURES:

Ducati Motor Holding SpA, founded in Italy in 1926, designs and manufactures road and sport motorcycles. The company manufactures eight lines of bikes: Diavel, a family of cruiser bikes; XDiavel, a combination of a cruiser and a sporty ride; Hypermotard, a family of dirt and road bikes; Monster, a family of racing bikes; Multistrada, family of tour and sport bikes; Panigale, a family of sport bikes; SuperSport, a relaxed sport bike with a much less radical riding position; and Scrambler, a youthful, spirited motorcycle line that enables the personalization of Ducati models, even via mobile devices. The Scrambler will configure several Ducati base models. Financial services are provided by the company, offering a wide range of options and flexible terms. Ducati Motor also offers apparel for men, women and kids, as well as safety gear, accessories, toys, books, art and DVDs. Ducati is engaged in the MotoGP World Championship, with its Ducati Marlboro Team; the Superbike World Championship, having won more than a dozen championships and over 300 race wins. Ducati is a subsidiary of Volkswagen AG.

FINANCIAL DATA: *Note: Data for latest year may not have been available at press time.*

In U.S. $	2018	2017	2016	2015	2014	2013
Revenue	680,556,000	718,718,000	821,555,812	781,401,447	651,762,500	617,745,455
R&D Expense						
Operating Income						
Operating Margin %						
SGA Expense						
Net Income			55,865,210	60,279,851	40,517,554	21,000,000
Operating Cash Flow						
Capital Expenditure						
EBITDA						
Return on Assets %						
Return on Equity %						
Debt to Equity						

CONTACT INFORMATION:

Phone: 39-051-641-3343 Fax:
Toll-Free:
Address: Via Cavalieri Ducati 3, Bologna, 40132 Italy

STOCK TICKER/OTHER:

Stock Ticker: Subsidiary
Employees: 1,278
Parent Company: Volkswagen AG
Exchange:
Fiscal Year Ends: 12/31

SALARIES/BONUSES:

Top Exec. Salary: $ Bonus: $
Second Exec. Salary: $ Bonus: $

OTHER THOUGHTS:

Estimated Female Officers or Directors:
Hot Spot for Advancement for Women/Minorities:

Eagle Ottawa LLC

NAIC Code: 336300

www.eagleottawa.com

TYPES OF BUSINESS:

Automobile Upholstery Manufacturing
Leather Treatment & Crafting
Engineering & Development Services
Durability Testing Services

BRANDS/DIVISIONS/AFFILIATES:

Lear Corporation
Eagle Ottawa Premium Leather

CONTACTS:

Note: Officers with more than one job title may be intentionally listed here more than once.

Jerry Sumpter, CEO
Tim Brennan, VP-Innovation
Pat Catlin, VP-Global Sales & Design
Cary Bean, Exec. VP
Craig Tonti, Pres., Americas & Europe
Eric Brooks, VP-Global Supply Chain Mgmt.

GROWTH PLANS/SPECIAL FEATURES:

Eagle Ottawa, LLC is a world leader in the manufacturing and marketing of performance and luxury upholstery leather for the automotive industry. The firm operates Eagle Ottawa Premium Leather sales and design centers in Germany, the U.K., the U.S., South Korea, Japan, Italy, Sweden, Thailand and China; and manufacturing facilities in Brazil, China, Thailand, Mexico, the U.S. and Hungary. The company offers finished hides, cut leather parts, complete seat cover engineering and development services as well as comprehensive material and seat durability testing services. Eagle Ottawa's product lines include natural shrunken grain leather, chrome-tanned and non-chrome tanned leather, high-durability leather and automotive-grade semi-aniline leather, varieties that are all used in luxury automotive interiors. Eagle Ottawa procures fresh and cured hides and has the tanning assembly line necessary to produce a colored, embossed and textured finished product for its clients. More than 100 vehicle models produced by major automakers worldwide use its leather, with customers such as BMW, Subaru, Honda, Kia, Nissan, Volkswagen, Mercedes-Benz, Lexus, Lincoln, Infiniti, Renault, Land Rover, Jaguar, Cadillac, Ford, Chevrolet and Toyota. Eagle Ottawa is a wholly-owned subsidiary of Lear Corporation.

FINANCIAL DATA:

Note: Data for latest year may not have been available at press time.

In U.S. $	2018	2017	2016	2015	2014	2013
Revenue	1,215,506,250	1,157,625,000	1,102,500,000	1,050,000,000	1,000,000,000	757,812,500
R&D Expense						
Operating Income						
Operating Margin %						
SGA Expense						
Net Income						
Operating Cash Flow						
Capital Expenditure						
EBITDA						
Return on Assets %						
Return on Equity %						
Debt to Equity						

CONTACT INFORMATION:

Phone: 248-364-7400 Fax: 248-364-7529
Toll-Free:
Address: 21557 Telegraph Rd., Southfield, MI 48033 United States

STOCK TICKER/OTHER:

Stock Ticker: Subsidiary
Exchange:
Employees: 6,500
Fiscal Year Ends: 11/30
Parent Company: Lear Corporation

SALARIES/BONUSES:

Top Exec. Salary: $ Bonus: $
Second Exec. Salary: $ Bonus: $

OTHER THOUGHTS:

Estimated Female Officers or Directors:
Hot Spot for Advancement for Women/Minorities:

Earnhardt Auto Centers

www.earnhardt.com

NAIC Code: 441110

TYPES OF BUSINESS:

Auto Dealers, Retail New & Used
Auto Service & Parts
Auto Loans & Insurance
Fleet Sales
RV Sales & Service

BRANDS/DIVISIONS/AFFILIATES:

Earnhardt Auto Body Shop

CONTACTS:

Note: Officers with more than one job title may be intentionally listed here more than once.

Tex Earnhardt, CEO
Hal J. Earnhardt, III, Pres.
Chris Kerr, VP-Mktg.
Hal J. Earnhardt, Jr., Chmn.

GROWTH PLANS/SPECIAL FEATURES:

Earnhardt Auto Centers operates new and used automobile dealerships, with 21 locations in Arizona and Nevada. The company sells and services 17 different automotive brands, including Ford, Honda, Chevrolet, Buick, GMC, Genesis, Toyota, Hyundai, Chrysler, Jeep, Dodge, RAM, Lexus, Kia, Cadillac, Mazda and Volkswagen. Each of the car dealerships has its own parts and service departments, and the company also has an Earnhardt Auto Body Shop in Gilbert, Arizona. The body shop provides full collision repair services and can service all makes and models, including those sold by other dealerships. It offers free repair estimates and rental service to customers. The company's website offers customers an advance look at each dealer's individual inventory and the opportunity to receive a quote on any particular vehicle. Commercial customers can use the website to locate Earnhardt's closest commercial fleet department and receive a quote. In addition, Earnhardt's provides related financing and auto insurance.

FINANCIAL DATA:

Note: Data for latest year may not have been available at press time.

In U.S. $	2018	2017	2016	2015	2014	2013
Revenue	1,707,644,777	1,626,328,359	1,548,884,151	1,287,390,026		
R&D Expense						
Operating Income						
Operating Margin %						
SGA Expense						
Net Income						
Operating Cash Flow						
Capital Expenditure						
EBITDA						
Return on Assets %						
Return on Equity %						
Debt to Equity						

CONTACT INFORMATION:

Phone: 480-926-4000 Fax: 480-632-7712
Toll-Free: 800-357-6070
Address: 7300 W. Orchid Ln., Chandler, AZ 85226 United States

STOCK TICKER/OTHER:

Stock Ticker: Private
Employees: 1,720
Parent Company:
Exchange:
Fiscal Year Ends: 12/31

SALARIES/BONUSES:

Top Exec. Salary: $ Bonus: $
Second Exec. Salary: $ Bonus: $

OTHER THOUGHTS:

Estimated Female Officers or Directors:
Hot Spot for Advancement for Women/Minorities:

East Penn Manufacturing Company Inc

www.eastpennmanufacturing.com

NAIC Code: 336300

TYPES OF BUSINESS:

Battery Manufacturing
Battery Recycling
Fuel Cell Technology
Electric Vehicle Battery Manufacturing

BRANDS/DIVISIONS/AFFILIATES:

Deka Battery
Navitas Systems

CONTACTS: *Note: Officers with more than one job title may be intentionally listed here more than once.*

Chris Pruitt, CEO
Bob Flicker, COO
Christopher E. Pruitt, Exec. VP-Admin.
Christopher E. Pruitt, Exec. VP-Finance
Dan Breidegam, Chmn.

GROWTH PLANS/SPECIAL FEATURES:

East Penn Manufacturing Company, Inc. manufactures lead-acid batteries, battery accessories, wire and cable products for the industrial, automotive, commercial, marine, stationary and specialty markets. The firm markets its products in four segments: transportation, motive power, reserve power, and wire cable and battery accessories. The transportation segment makes batteries for the automotive; marine; power sports; lawn and garden; golf care/electric vehicle (EV); agricultural; floor care equipment; and trucks and buses markets. The motive power segment offers products for industrial lift trucks; airline ground support; automatic guided vehicle (AGV); and rail and locomotive industries. The reserve power segment produces battery lines for telecommunications; uninterruptible power supply; grid optimization services; renewable energy; and community access television (CATV). The wire cable and battery accessories segment offers products that are used in the marine and fleet industries. Products are manufactured under the brand name Deka Battery. East Penn and operates a 520-acre single-site manufacturing complex in Berks County, Pennsylvania. The company safely reuses all parts of used batteries, reclaiming lead, plastic and sulfuric acid and turning sulfur fumes into liquid fertilizer. East Penn also traps its wastewater and separates it into liquid and solids for separate treatment, resulting in an overall reduction of pollution. The firm exports its products worldwide. During 2019, East Penn acquired a majority interest in Navitas Systems, a global leader in larger-format lithium battery technology and systems for heavy-duty commercial/industrial and government/defense market segments.

FINANCIAL DATA: *Note: Data for latest year may not have been available at press time.*

In U.S. $	2018	2017	2016	2015	2014	2013
Revenue	1,714,387,500	1,632,750,000	1,555,000,000	1,500,000,000	1,475,000,000	1,455,000,000
R&D Expense						
Operating Income						
Operating Margin %						
SGA Expense						
Net Income						
Operating Cash Flow						
Capital Expenditure						
EBITDA						
Return on Assets %						
Return on Equity %						
Debt to Equity						

CONTACT INFORMATION:

Phone: 610-682-6361 Fax: 610-682-4781
Toll-Free:
Address: Deka Rd., Lyon Station, PA 19536 United States

STOCK TICKER/OTHER:

Stock Ticker: Private
Exchange:
Employees: 8,000
Fiscal Year Ends: 12/31
Parent Company:

SALARIES/BONUSES:

Top Exec. Salary: $ Bonus: $
Second Exec. Salary: $ Bonus: $

OTHER THOUGHTS:

Estimated Female Officers or Directors: 1
Hot Spot for Advancement for Women/Minorities:

Eaton Corporation plc

www.eaton.com

NAIC Code: 336300

TYPES OF BUSINESS:

Hydraulic Products
Electrical Power Distribution & Control Equipment
Truck Transmissions & Axles
Engine Components
Aerospace & Military Components

BRANDS/DIVISIONS/AFFILIATES:

CONTACTS:
Note: Officers with more than one job title may be intentionally listed here more than once.

Craig Arnold, CEO
Uday Yadav, COO
Richard H. Fearon, CFO
Mark M. McGuire, General Counsel
Richard H. Fearon, Chief Planning Officer
Donald J. McGrath, Sr. VP-Comm.
Donald H. Bullock, Jr., Sr. VP-Investor Rel.
Ken D. Semelsberger, Controller
Uday Yadav, Pres., Aerospace Group
Curtis J. Hutchins, Pres., Asia Pacific Region
Craig Arnold, COO-Industrial Sector
Thomas S. Gross, COO-Electrical Sector
Frank C. Campbell, Pres., EMEA
Pavan Pattada, Sr. VP-Supply Chain Mgmt.

GROWTH PLANS/SPECIAL FEATURES:

Eaton Corporation plc is a global power management company, selling its products to customers in more than 175 countries. Customers are engaged in the aerospace, buildings, data center, food/beverage, government, military, healthcare, machine building, mining, metals, minerals, oil/gas, rail, utilities and vehicle industries. Eaton provides energy solutions that help these customers effectively manage electrical, hydraulic and mechanical power more efficiently, safely and sustainably. The firm's wide array of products include aerospace actuators, motion controls, backup power, IT power distribution, clutches, brakes, conduits, cable/wire management, cylinders, differentials, traction control, ducting solutions, electrical circuit protection, electronic components, engine solutions, filtration solutions, fuel systems, emissions, furniture, golf grips, hoses, tubing, fittings/connectors, hydraulic power units, heat exchangers, industrial controls, automation solutions, sensors, lighting, low- and medium-voltage power distribution, motors, generators, plastics, pumps, emergency communication systems, airflow management, steering systems, transmissions, grid solutions and much more. Based in Ireland, the firm has worldwide offices in the U.S., Canada and more.

FINANCIAL DATA:
Note: Data for latest year may not have been available at press time.

In U.S. $	2018	2017	2016	2015	2014	2013
Revenue	21,609,000,000	20,404,000,000	19,747,000,000	20,855,000,000	22,552,000,000	22,046,000,000
R&D Expense	584,000,000	584,000,000	589,000,000	625,000,000	647,000,000	644,000,000
Operating Income	2,966,000,000	2,499,000,000	2,253,000,000	2,342,000,000	2,449,000,000	2,147,000,000
Operating Margin %		.12%	.11%	.11%	.11%	.10%
SGA Expense	3,548,000,000	3,565,000,000	3,505,000,000	3,596,000,000	3,810,000,000	3,886,000,000
Net Income	2,145,000,000	2,985,000,000	1,922,000,000	1,979,000,000	1,793,000,000	1,861,000,000
Operating Cash Flow	2,658,000,000	2,666,000,000	2,552,000,000	2,371,000,000	1,878,000,000	2,285,000,000
Capital Expenditure	565,000,000	520,000,000	497,000,000	506,000,000	632,000,000	614,000,000
EBITDA	3,869,000,000	3,413,000,000	3,182,000,000	3,267,000,000	3,432,000,000	3,144,000,000
Return on Assets %		.09%	.06%	.06%	.05%	.05%
Return on Equity %		.19%	.13%	.13%	.11%	.12%
Debt to Equity		0.415	0.45	0.512	0.508	0.534

CONTACT INFORMATION:

Phone: 440-523-5000 Fax:
Toll-Free:
Address: Eaton House, 30 Pembroke Rd., Dublin, 4 Ireland

STOCK TICKER/OTHER:

Stock Ticker: ETN
Exchange: NYS
Employees: 95,000
Fiscal Year Ends: 12/31
Parent Company:

SALARIES/BONUSES:

Top Exec. Salary: $1,200,004 Bonus: $
Second Exec. Salary: $946,764 Bonus: $

OTHER THOUGHTS:

Estimated Female Officers or Directors: 4
Hot Spot for Advancement for Women/Minorities: Y

Edelbrock LLC

www.edelbrock.com

NAIC Code: 336300

TYPES OF BUSINESS:

Automobile Parts Manufacturer
Air Filters
Carburetors
Cylinder Heads
Camshafts
Intake Manifolds
Power Packages
Water Pumps

BRANDS/DIVISIONS/AFFILIATES:

Edelbrock Holdings Inc

GROWTH PLANS/SPECIAL FEATURES:

Edelbrock, LLC, founded in 1938, designs, manufactures, distributes and markets a wide range of performance replacement products designed for cars, light trucks, recreational vehicles, race cars and motorcycles. These products include air filters, camshafts, carburetors, chemicals, crate engines, cylinder heads, engine dress-ups, fittings, fuel injection systems, fuel systems, gaskets, ignitions, installation items, intake manifolds, nitrous oxide, power packages, sensors, superchargers, thermostats, tools, valvetrains and water pumps. Edelbrock offerings are sold in retail automotive chain stores, through mail-order catalog houses, warehouse distributors and performance specialty dealers. The company's products are planned and designed by its R&D staff, including computational fluid dynamic software and 3D rapid prototyping, all of which enable engineers to take a product from idea to reality. All products undergo a rigorous testing program. Edelbrock utilizes over 70 computer numerical control (CNC) machines and hundreds of staff members for machining and quality control purposes. The firm is based in Torrance, California with additional manufacturing locations in California and North Carolina, totaling more than 500,000 square feet in production space. Edelbrock is privately-held by Edelbrock Holdings, Inc.

CONTACTS: *Note: Officers with more than one job title may be intentionally listed here more than once.*

Don Barry, CEO
Mario Iannantuono, COO
Jay Wilson, CFO
Marissa Colwell, VP-Mktg.
Rob Simons, VP-R&D
Rick Roberts, Dir.-Eng.
Eric Blakely, Dir.-Advertising
Chrisite Edelbrock, VP-Purchasing

FINANCIAL DATA: *Note: Data for latest year may not have been available at press time.*

In U.S. $	2018	2017	2016	2015	2014	2013
Revenue	51,266,250	48,825,000	46,500,000	45,000,000	44,500,000	41,800,000
R&D Expense						
Operating Income						
Operating Margin %						
SGA Expense						
Net Income						
Operating Cash Flow						
Capital Expenditure						
EBITDA						
Return on Assets %						
Return on Equity %						
Debt to Equity						

CONTACT INFORMATION:

Phone: 310-781-2222 Fax: 310-320-1187
Toll-Free: 800-416-8628
Address: 2700 California St., Torrance, CA 90503 United States

STOCK TICKER/OTHER:

Stock Ticker: Private
Employees: 425
Parent Company: Edelbrock Holdings Inc
Exchange:
Fiscal Year Ends: 06/30

SALARIES/BONUSES:

Top Exec. Salary: $ Bonus: $
Second Exec. Salary: $ Bonus: $

OTHER THOUGHTS:

Estimated Female Officers or Directors:
Hot Spot for Advancement for Women/Minorities:

Elder Automotive Group

www.elderautogroup.com

NAIC Code: 441110

TYPES OF BUSINESS:

Auto Dealers, Retail
Parts & Service
Financing

GROWTH PLANS/SPECIAL FEATURES:

Elder Automotive Group (EAG), founded in 1967, is a new and pre-owned automobile dealer with dealerships located in Michigan and Florida. The firm retails vehicle brands such as Fisker, Ford, Genesis, Hyundai, Jaguar, Land Rover and Spyder. The dealerships sell parts as well as provide maintenance and repair services. Almost all EAG dealerships offer financing options to customers. The website provides details on new and used inventories, and allows shoppers to schedule test drives, make offers on vehicles and receive appraisals for trade-in vehicles. The website also displays vehicles priced below $10,000.

BRANDS/DIVISIONS/AFFILIATES:

CONTACTS: *Note: Officers with more than one job title may be intentionally listed here more than once.*

Robert Elder, Pres.

FINANCIAL DATA: *Note: Data for latest year may not have been available at press time.*

In U.S. $	2018	2017	2016	2015	2014	2013
Revenue	231,525,000	220,500,000	210,000,000	208,000,000	198,000,000	185,000,000
R&D Expense						
Operating Income						
Operating Margin %						
SGA Expense						
Net Income						
Operating Cash Flow						
Capital Expenditure						
EBITDA						
Return on Assets %						
Return on Equity %						
Debt to Equity						

CONTACT INFORMATION:

Phone: 248-585-4000 Fax: 248-585-4039
Toll-Free: 888-773-6290
Address: 777 John R. Rd., Troy, MI 48083 United States

STOCK TICKER/OTHER:

Stock Ticker: Private
Employees: 210
Parent Company:
Exchange:
Fiscal Year Ends: 12/31

SALARIES/BONUSES:

Top Exec. Salary: $ Bonus: $
Second Exec. Salary: $ Bonus: $

OTHER THOUGHTS:

Estimated Female Officers or Directors: 1
Hot Spot for Advancement for Women/Minorities:

ElringKlinger AG

NAIC Code: 336310

www.elringklinger.de

TYPES OF BUSINESS:

Gasoline Engine and Engine Parts Manufacturing

BRANDS/DIVISIONS/AFFILIATES:

ElringKlinger Logistic Services GmbH
Elring Klinger (Great Britain) Ltd
ElringKlinger Italia Srl
ElringKlinger Abschirmtechnik (Schweiz) AG
Elring Klinger do Brasil Ltda
Elring Klinger Mexico SA de CV
ElringKlinger USA Inc
Elring-Das Original

CONTACTS: *Note: Officers with more than one job title may be intentionally listed here more than once.*

Stefan Wolf, CEO
Reiner Drews, COO
Thomas Jessulat, CFO
Stefan Wolf, Chmn.

GROWTH PLANS/SPECIAL FEATURES:

ElringKlinger AG manufactures and distributes original equipment and replacement parts for automobiles. The company divides its operations into five segments: original equipment, aftermarket, engineered plastics, services and industrial parks. The original equipment segment develops, produces and sells parts and assemblies for vehicle engines and transmission units, as well as components for lithium-ion batteries and fuel cells. The aftermarket segment supplies a range of spare parts that primarily consist of cylinder-head gaskets and complete gasket sets. These gaskets are marketed under the Elring-Das Original brand. The engineered plastics segment develops, manufactures and sells products made of the high-performance plastic (PTFE), a synthetic fluoropolymer of tetrafluoroethylene that has numerous applications. The services segment provides development services for engines and transmissions using cutting-edge testing and measurement facilities. Last, the industrial parks segment leases and manages industrial park buildings located near Frankfurt, Germany and in Kecskemet, Hungary. Original equipment derives 82.9% of annual revenue (as of fiscal 2018), aftermarket derives 9.4%, engineered plastics derives 6.9%, services derives 0.6% and industrial parks derives 0.2%. Some of the company's many subsidiaries include ElringKlinger Logistic Services GmbH, Elring Klinger (Great Britain) Ltd., ElringKlinger Italia Srl, ElringKlinger Abschirmtechnik (Schweiz) AG, Elring Klinger do Brasil Ltda., Elring Klinger Mexico SA de CV and ElringKlinger USA, Inc.

FINANCIAL DATA: *Note: Data for latest year may not have been available at press time.*

In U.S. $	2018	2017	2016	2015	2014	2013
Revenue	1,881,090,000	1,842,384,000	1,724,361,000	1,668,792,000	1,467,930,000	1,301,186,000
R&D Expense	84,273,700	79,037,860	74,604,740	68,022,580	63,389,060	63,259,520
Operating Income	106,490,300	142,553,200	148,968,100	146,485,800	171,835,700	183,984,700
Operating Margin %		.08%	.09%	.09%	.12%	.14%
SGA Expense	256,867,800	243,141,100	216,736,000	206,677,400	172,425,800	144,186,200
Net Income	48,533,000	77,424,710	86,968,560	101,390,600	117,081,500	116,716,100
Operating Cash Flow	101,364,000	105,707,500	194,577,100	136,547,800	166,005,300	132,835,500
Capital Expenditure	197,704,800	184,021,300	202,709,300	210,070,900	180,615,600	140,921,200
EBITDA	218,645,900	248,825,300	259,349,000	253,141,100	270,302,200	262,459,000
Return on Assets %		.04%	.04%	.06%	.07%	.08%
Return on Equity %		.08%	.09%	.12%	.15%	.16%
Debt to Equity		0.00	0.377	0.397	0.361	0.351

CONTACT INFORMATION:

Phone: 49 071237240 Fax: 49 071237249006
Toll-Free:
Address: Max-Eyth Strasse 2, Dettingen/Erms, 72581 Germany

STOCK TICKER/OTHER:

Stock Ticker: EGKLF Exchange: GREY
Employees: 10,033 Fiscal Year Ends: 12/31
Parent Company:

SALARIES/BONUSES:

Top Exec. Salary: $ Bonus: $
Second Exec. Salary: $ Bonus: $

OTHER THOUGHTS:

Estimated Female Officers or Directors:
Hot Spot for Advancement for Women/Minorities:

EnerDel Inc

www.enerdel.com

NAIC Code: 335911

TYPES OF BUSINESS:

Battery Development & Manufacturing
Energy Storage Systems

BRANDS/DIVISIONS/AFFILIATES:

EnerZ
EnerTech
Moxie+
Secure+
Vigor+
Vigor+ Diagnostic & Service Software Tool
T100 Secure+

CONTACTS: *Note: Officers with more than one job title may be intentionally listed here more than once.*

Michael Canada, CEO
James Bowman, VP-Operations
Alexey Pikalov, CFO
John T. Warner, CMO
Tiara Hicks, Human Resources Director
Dr. Jin Sik Lee, CTO-ENER1
Sean Hendrix, VP-Eng.
Michael Alma, Sr. VP-Asia Business
Ben Wrightsman, Dir.-Procurement

GROWTH PLANS/SPECIAL FEATURES:

EnerDel, Inc. is an alternative energy company focused on designing, developing and manufacturing high-performance, rechargeable lithium-ion batteries and other systems for energy storage. The firm designs its batteries and energy systems to be of use for energy storage, transportation and other task-oriented services. EnerDel's energy storage solutions have been utilized in commercial, industrial and residential applications. The firm's products include lithium-Ion cells, such as Moxie+ prismatic cell; modules including a range of Moxie+ battery modules; battery and storage systems sold under the brand name Secure+, which are used in sub-station equipment back-up, micro-grids, frequency regulation and bulk energy storage and mobile hybrid power system (MHPS); a series of Vigor+ battery pack used in transportation including trains, commercial trucks, buses, trams, subways, marine vessels and other heavy-duty vehicles; Vigor+ Diagnostic & Service Software Tool, designed to be used with EnerDel's energy storage system in buses that have the Allison H40/50 hybrid power train; and T100 Secure+ battery management systems. The firm's task-oriented battery systems are designed to power items ranging from a lawn mower to a motorcycle or all-terrain vehicle. Enerdel also runs a technical training center to provide its customers, distributors, representatives and the public with hands-on training and experience with the firm's lithium-ion battery systems. The company also operates with two affiliated companies: EnerZ and EnerTech. EnerZ provides project management and technical and engineering support services for energy storage, transportation, mass transit and task-oriented applications in Russia. EnerTech, based in South Korea, manufactures both large and small format battery cells and packs for use in cell phones, GPS systems and other commercial utilities.

FINANCIAL DATA: *Note: Data for latest year may not have been available at press time.*

In U.S. $	2018	2017	2016	2015	2014	2013
Revenue	51,000,000	50,000,000	50,000,000	50,000,000	45,000,000	25,200,000
R&D Expense						
Operating Income						
Operating Margin %						
SGA Expense						
Net Income						
Operating Cash Flow						
Capital Expenditure						
EBITDA						
Return on Assets %						
Return on Equity %						
Debt to Equity						

CONTACT INFORMATION:

Phone: 317-703-1800 Fax:
Toll-Free:
Address: 8740 Hauge Rd., Bldg. 7, Indianapolis, IN 46256 United States

STOCK TICKER/OTHER:

Stock Ticker: Private
Employees: 164
Parent Company:
Exchange:
Fiscal Year Ends: 12/31

SALARIES/BONUSES:

Top Exec. Salary: $ Bonus: $
Second Exec. Salary: $ Bonus: $

OTHER THOUGHTS:

Estimated Female Officers or Directors: 1
Hot Spot for Advancement for Women/Minorities:

Enterprise Holdings Inc

www.enterpriseholdings.com

NAIC Code: 532111

TYPES OF BUSINESS:

Car & Truck Rental
Vanpool Services

BRANDS/DIVISIONS/AFFILIATES:

Alamo Rent A Car
National Car Rental
Enterprise Rent-A-Car
Enterprise Car Sales
Enterprise Truck Rental
Exotic Car Collection by Enterprise
Enterprise CarShare
Zimride

CONTACTS: *Note: Officers with more than one job title may be intentionally listed here more than once.*

Pamela Nicholson, CEO
Christine Taylor, Exec. VP
Rick Short, CFO
Frank Thurman, VP-Mktg.
Shelley Roither, VP-Human Resources
Michael Nolfo, CIO
Lee Kaplan, Chief Admin. Officer
Matthew G. Darrah, Exec. VP-North American Oper.
Greg Stubblefield, Chief Strategy Officer
Patrick T. Farrell, Chief Comm. Officer
Rose Langhorst, Treas.
Steve Bloom, Pres., Enterprise Fleet Mgmt.
Jo Ann Taylor Kindle, Pres., Enterprise Holdings Foundation
Andrew C. Taylor, Chmn.
Greg Stubblefield, Exec. VP-Global Sales & Mktg.

GROWTH PLANS/SPECIAL FEATURES:

Enterprise Holdings, Inc. is the parent company of Alamo Rent A Car, National Car Rental and Enterprise Rent-A-Car car rental agencies. The company also owns Enterprise Car Sales, Enterprise Truck Rental and Exotic Car Collection by Enterprise, as well as car/ride sharing programs Enterprise CarShare, Enterprise Rideshare and Zimride by Enterprise. The firm's combined rental fleet is the largest in the world, at nearly 2 million vehicles. It serves 10,000 fully-staffed neighborhood and airport locations in more than 90 countries worldwide. Alamo Rent A Car is a budget rental car company catering to leisure and vacation customers, particularly international travelers visiting North America. Enterprise Holdings operates self-service kiosks throughout the U.S. National Car Rental is a premium rental brand that serves frequent business travelers and offers the Emerald Club frequent-renter benefits program. Enterprise Rent-A-Car boasts over 7,600 retail and airport offices in the U.S. Enterprise Car Sales is a used-car reseller that provides non-negotiable pricing and after-market warranties on used cars acquired through trade-in or extracted from the rental fleet. Enterprise Truck Rental provides commercial-grade trucks such as Â¾- to 1-ton pickups, cargo vans, straight trucks, as well as stakebed trucks (from 16 to 26 feet long), all equipped for commercial use. Exotic Car Collection enables customers to rent vehicles such as exotic sports cars and luxury sedans, including Ferrari, Maserati, Porsche, Bentley, Range Rover and more. Enterprise CarShare is a car sharing program that allows customers to rent a car for flexible periods of time through an online membership portal. Enterprise Rideshare specializes in customized vanpool programs and commuter services for individuals and/or companies. Zimride is a ride-sharing platform for companies and universities.

Enterprise Holdings offers its employees medical, dental and vision insurance; prescription drug coverage; flexible spending accounts; life insurance; and long-term disability plans.

FINANCIAL DATA: *Note: Data for latest year may not have been available at press time.*

In U.S. $	2018	2017	2016	2015	2014	2013
Revenue	24,100,000,000	22,300,000,000	20,900,000,000	19,400,000,000	17,800,000,000	16,400,000,000
R&D Expense						
Operating Income						
Operating Margin %						
SGA Expense						
Net Income						
Operating Cash Flow						
Capital Expenditure						
EBITDA						
Return on Assets %						
Return on Equity %						
Debt to Equity						

CONTACT INFORMATION:

Phone: 314-512-2880 Fax: 314-512-4706
Toll-Free:
Address: 600 Corporate Park Dr., St. Louis, MO 63105 United States

STOCK TICKER/OTHER:

Stock Ticker: Private
Exchange:
Employees: 100,000
Fiscal Year Ends: 03/31
Parent Company:

SALARIES/BONUSES:

Top Exec. Salary: $ Bonus: $
Second Exec. Salary: $ Bonus: $

OTHER THOUGHTS:

Estimated Female Officers or Directors: 5
Hot Spot for Advancement for Women/Minorities: Y

Exco Technologies Limited

www.excocorp.com

NAIC Code: 336300

TYPES OF BUSINESS:

Automobile Parts Manufacturing
Industrial products
Automotive parts manufacture
Plastics
Design technology

BRANDS/DIVISIONS/AFFILIATES:

GROWTH PLANS/SPECIAL FEATURES:

Exco Technologies Limited is a global designer, developer and manufacturer of dies, molds, equipment, components and assemblies for the die-cast, extrusion and automotive industries. Exco operates through three business groups: automotive solutions, die cast and extrusion tooling solutions. The automotive solutions group designs, develops and manufactures automotive interior trim components and assemblies primarily for passenger and light truck vehicles. This division's facilities are located in Canada, the U.S., Mexico, Morocco and Bulgaria, and supply the North American, European and Asian markets. The die casting and extrusion technology groups design, develop and manufacture die-casting and extrusion tooling and equipment. Their operations are based in Canada, the U.S., Mexico, Colombia, Brazil and Thailand, and primarily serve automotive and industrial markets worldwide.

CONTACTS: *Note: Officers with more than one job title may be intentionally listed here more than once.*

William Schroers, CEO, Divisional
Brian Robbins, CEO
Drew Knight, CFO
Darren Kirk, COO
Paul Riganelli, Director
Paul Robbins, General Manager, Divisional
Jeff Blackburn, General Manager, Subsidiary
Nick Gnatyuk, General Manager, Subsidiary

FINANCIAL DATA: *Note: Data for latest year may not have been available at press time.*

In U.S. $	2018	2017	2016	2015	2014	2013
Revenue	436,257,100	442,814,300	446,440,500	377,696,500	279,131,300	185,408,900
R&D Expense						
Operating Income	41,390,890	47,441,820	49,320,850	47,004,470	31,439,400	26,153,260
Operating Margin %		.11%	.11%	.12%	.11%	.14%
SGA Expense	34,943,530	35,502,160	34,763,890	31,560,670	26,873,340	21,202,150
Net Income	32,039,720	32,228,450	36,047,140	30,894,410	23,236,560	17,912,530
Operating Cash Flow	37,014,320	50,334,260	49,624,800	31,255,210	30,602,590	17,345,560
Capital Expenditure	17,821,570	12,344,420	18,150,530	15,609,790	19,486,090	16,674,750
EBITDA	58,042,140	62,135,980	65,896,300	58,402,180	40,957,320	32,671,870
Return on Assets %		.10%	.12%	.13%	.13%	.13%
Return on Equity %		.15%	.18%	.18%	.17%	.15%
Debt to Equity		0.09	0.195	0.002	0.007	

CONTACT INFORMATION:

Phone: 905 477-3065 Fax:
Toll-Free:
Address: 130 Spy Ct.., Markham, ON L3R 5H6 Canada

STOCK TICKER/OTHER:

Stock Ticker: XTC Exchange: TSE
Employees: 6,757 Fiscal Year Ends: 09/30
Parent Company:

SALARIES/BONUSES:

Top Exec. Salary: $ Bonus: $
Second Exec. Salary: $ Bonus: $

OTHER THOUGHTS:

Estimated Female Officers or Directors: 3
Hot Spot for Advancement for Women/Minorities: Y

Fair Financial Corp

www.fair.com

NAIC Code: 532111

TYPES OF BUSINESS:

Car Subscription Service

BRANDS/DIVISIONS/AFFILIATES:

Fair
Fair Price Guarantee

CONTACTS:

Note: Officers with more than one job title may be intentionally listed here more than once.

Scott Painter, CEO
Craig Nehamen, Pres., Dealer Svcs & Servicing
Tyler Painter, CFO
Derek Callow, CMO
Lisa Russell, Exec. VP-People
George Bauer, Chmn.

GROWTH PLANS/SPECIAL FEATURES:

Fair Financial Corp. is the developer of a mobile application that enables the user to shop, get approved and pay for a pre-owned vehicle. Fair Financial streamlines the entire process of getting a car with a totally paperless, end-to-end solution. The potential car buyer launches the Fair app to get pre-qualified and shop for cars in their area, picks the one they want and signs for it on the phone. There are no long-term contracts, so the car buyer can drive the car for as long as they want and then walk away from it at any time. Fair Financial also offers the Fair Price Guarantee, guaranteeing that a user will not find a lower monthly payment on a comparable loan or lease. Every Fair car comes with a limited warranty, routine maintenance and roadside assistance included. In addition, optional Fair insurance, extra miles or excess wear-and-tear protection can all be bundled into one transparent monthly payment. The firm currently has over 3800 active dealer partners that users can buy vehicles from. In January 2018, Fair Financial acquired the active leasing portfolio of Xchange Leasing, a service Uber first established to lease new and nearly-new vehicles to drivers who did not come to the service with their own cars.

FINANCIAL DATA:

Note: Data for latest year may not have been available at press time.

In U.S. $	2018	2017	2016	2015	2014	2013
Revenue						
R&D Expense						
Operating Income						
Operating Margin %						
SGA Expense						
Net Income						
Operating Cash Flow						
Capital Expenditure						
EBITDA						
Return on Assets %						
Return on Equity %						
Debt to Equity						

CONTACT INFORMATION:

Phone: Fax:
Toll-Free: 833-387-6677
Address: 1540 2nd St., Fl. 2, Santa Monica, CA 90401 United States

STOCK TICKER/OTHER:

Stock Ticker: Private
Exchange:
Employees:
Fiscal Year Ends:
Parent Company:

SALARIES/BONUSES:

Top Exec. Salary: $ Bonus: $
Second Exec. Salary: $ Bonus: $

OTHER THOUGHTS:

Estimated Female Officers or Directors:
Hot Spot for Advancement for Women/Minorities:

Faulkner Organization (The)

www.tobesure.com

NAIC Code: 441110

TYPES OF BUSINESS:

Auto Dealers, Retail
Parts & Service
Financing
Fleet Services
Insurance

BRANDS/DIVISIONS/AFFILIATES:

Faulkner Collision Centers

CONTACTS:

Note: Officers with more than one job title may be intentionally listed here more than once.

Tom Joyce, Dir.-Oper.

GROWTH PLANS/SPECIAL FEATURES:

The Faulkner Organization, founded in 1932 by Henry Faulkner, Sr., is a family-owned and -operated car dealer in the Delaware Valley. The company operates a chain of 28 new and used vehicle dealerships located throughout Pennsylvania. The firm carries a wide range of domestic and international vehicle brands including Alfa Romeo, BMW, Buick, Cadillac, Chevrolet, Chrysler, Dodge, Fiat, GMC, Honda, Hyundai, Infiniti, Jeep, Mazda, Maserati, Nissan, RAM, Subaru, Toyota, Volkswagen and Volvo. The dealerships feature maintenance and service departments, financing, fleet services and insurance. Through the company's website, customers can search for new and used vehicle inventories, obtain quotes, find specials on service and repair work and apply for pre-qualified auto loans. In addition, internet specials are announced for auto parts and new and pre-owned vehicles. More than a dozen Faulkner Collision Centers are located in the state, including Trevose, Lancaster, West Chester, Bethlehem, Camp Hill, Carlisle, Fairless, Mechanicsburg, Plymouth Meeting, Philadelphia and Harrisburg.

FINANCIAL DATA:

Note: Data for latest year may not have been available at press time.

In U.S. $	2018	2017	2016	2015	2014	2013
Revenue						
R&D Expense						
Operating Income						
Operating Margin %						
SGA Expense						
Net Income						
Operating Cash Flow						
Capital Expenditure						
EBITDA						
Return on Assets %						
Return on Equity %						
Debt to Equity						

CONTACT INFORMATION:

Phone: 215-364-3980 Fax: 215-364-0706
Toll-Free:
Address: 4437 Street Rd., Trevose, PA 19053 United States

STOCK TICKER/OTHER:

Stock Ticker: Private
Employees: 1,440
Parent Company:
Exchange:
Fiscal Year Ends: 12/31

SALARIES/BONUSES:

Top Exec. Salary: $ Bonus: $
Second Exec. Salary: $ Bonus: $

OTHER THOUGHTS:

Estimated Female Officers or Directors:
Hot Spot for Advancement for Women/Minorities:

Faurecia SA

NAIC Code: 336300

www.faurecia.com

TYPES OF BUSINESS:

Automobile Part Manufacturing
Vehicle Component Modules
Vehicle Seats
Vehicle Doors
Exhaust Systems
Front End Modules
Acoustic Engineering & Equipment
Vehicle Electronics

BRANDS/DIVISIONS/AFFILIATES:

CONTACTS: *Note: Officers with more than one job title may be intentionally listed here more than once.*

Patrick Koller, CEO
Hagen Wiesner, Exec. VP-Oper.
Michel Favre, CFO
Thorsten Muschal, Exec. VP-Sales & Program Mgmt..
Jean-Pierre Sounillac, Exec. VP-Human Resources
Frank Imbert, Exec. VP
Herve Guyot, Exec. VP-Group Strategy
Kate Phillips, Exec. VP-Group Comm.
Herve Guyot, Exec. VP-Automotive Exteriors
Christophe Schmitt, Exec. VP-Emission Control Tech.
Patrick Koller, Exec. VP-Automotive Seating
Jean-Michel Renaude, Exec. VP-Interior Systems
MIchel De Rosen, Chmn.

GROWTH PLANS/SPECIAL FEATURES:

Faurecia SA, headquartered in France, is a global supplier of vehicle equipment. The firm has approximately 110 production facilities and 13 research and development centers in 37 countries spanning Europe, North America, South America and Asia. Faurecia divides its design and assembly operations into four business groups: seating, interiors, electronics and clean mobility. The seating group produces the full line of components that go into automotive seating: frames, mechanisms, mechatronics, foam pads, trim covers, accessories and electronic/pneumatic systems. Faurecia develops state-of-the-art technologies for enhanced seat performance, including mechanisms, cover technology, comfort systems and integrated safety. It also assembles complete seats, both front and rear, for just-in-time delivery to its customers' plants. The interiors group develops, produces and supplies: instrument panels and center consoles, cockpits, door panels and modules, acoustic products and modules, and decorative components. Faurecia is currently developing and integrating renewable, bio-based materials as part of a long-term campaign to produce lighter components. One of its technologies combines natural hemp fibers with a polypropylene resin to yield a 25% weight reduction over glass-reinforced polypropylene. The electronics group develops and produces in-vehicle infotainment and human machine interface (HMI) systems, full digital sound design, advanced driver assistance, connectivity and cloud services. Last, the clean mobility group contributes to the reduction of pollutant emissions by supplying carmakers with solutions in emissions control, as well as acoustic treatment, weight reduction and energy heat recovery. Its selective catalytic reduction systems curb nitrogen oxide emissions from diesel engines, eliminating up to 95% of engine NOx emissions; and its exhaust heat recovery system can capture up to 75% of the energy typically lost as heat when warming the cabin and engine. In December 2018, the firm changed its status to a European (Societas Europaea) company.

FINANCIAL DATA: *Note: Data for latest year may not have been available at press time.*

In U.S. $	2018	2017	2016	2015	2014	2013
Revenue	19,402,900,000	22,344,670,000	20,715,790,000	20,782,110,000	20,846,880,000	19,960,810,000
R&D Expense	330,823,700	293,401,200	320,527,000	308,237,400	260,739,600	281,222,300
Operating Income	1,398,361,000	1,294,398,000	1,074,181,000	924,380,000	749,225,000	595,992,100
Operating Margin %		.06%	.05%	.04%	.04%	.03%
SGA Expense	778,565,100	753,321,500	737,599,700	705,491,600	717,781,200	664,526,100
Net Income	775,907,900	675,597,900	706,155,900	411,647,500	183,458,800	96,988,490
Operating Cash Flow	1,818,645,000	1,785,430,000	1,435,673,000	1,383,082,000	1,148,583,000	1,026,794,000
Capital Expenditure	1,401,683,000	1,336,913,000	1,156,887,000	1,031,444,000	932,905,200	872,010,600
EBITDA	2,143,822,000	1,972,542,000	1,684,677,000	1,487,378,000	1,206,710,000	1,025,354,000
Return on Assets %		.06%	.06%	.04%	.02%	.01%
Return on Equity %		.20%	.24%	.18%	.10%	.06%
Debt to Equity		0.494	0.541	0.402	0.599	0.869

CONTACT INFORMATION:

Phone: 33 172367000 Fax: 33 172367007
Toll-Free:
Address: 2 rue Hennape, Nanterre, 92000 France

STOCK TICKER/OTHER:

Stock Ticker: FURCF Exchange: PINX
Employees: 114,693 Fiscal Year Ends: 12/31
Parent Company:

SALARIES/BONUSES:

Top Exec. Salary: $ Bonus: $
Second Exec. Salary: $ Bonus: $

OTHER THOUGHTS:

Estimated Female Officers or Directors: 1
Hot Spot for Advancement for Women/Minorities:

FAW Group Corporation (First Automotive Works) www.faw.com

NAIC Code: 336111

TYPES OF BUSINESS:

Automobile Manufacturing
Parts Manufacturing
Truck Manufacturing

BRANDS/DIVISIONS/AFFILIATES:

First Automotive Works
China FAW Group Import & Export Co Ltd
Hongqi
Besturn
Junpai
Senia
Advanced Technical Innovation Center
New Energy Vehicle R&D Center

CONTACTS: *Note: Officers with more than one job title may be intentionally listed here more than once.*

Guohua Xi, Pres.
Tieqi Teng, Chief Acct.
Xianping Xu, Chmn.

GROWTH PLANS/SPECIAL FEATURES:

FAW Group Corporation is a state-owned Chinese vehicle manufacturer. Founded in 1953 as First Automotive Works, the firm became one of the first vehicle producers in China, starting with the 1956 rollout of Jiefang trucks and the 1958 launch of Hongqi cars. Since then, FAW grew to produce more than 3 million vehicles annually (as of late-2018), with products including light-, medium- and heavy-duty trucks; automobiles; municipal buses; luxury tourist coaches; custom bus chassis; and mini-vehicles. As of early-2019, passenger vehicle models include the Hongqi, Besturn, Junpai and Senia lines; commercial trucks such as long-distance trucks, construction trucks and distribution trucks; and buses and coaches such as municipal transit buses, urban buses, luxury tourist coaches and school buses. Headquartered in Changchun, Jilin Province, the firm's domestic production facilities, subsidiaries and engineering development/test centers are located throughout China. FAW's Advanced Technical Innovation Center is located in Beijing, China; its New Energy Vehicle Research and Development (R&D) Center and Exterior/Interior Design Center are located in Shanghai; its forward-looking technology R&D center is located in Munich, Germany; and its artificial-intelligence (AI) R&D center is located in California, USA. Subsidiary China FAW Group Import & Export Co., Ltd. provides global marketing services and solutions for the group's passenger and commercial vehicles.

FINANCIAL DATA: *Note: Data for latest year may not have been available at press time.*

In U.S. $	2018	2017	2016	2015	2014	2013
Revenue	69,524,000,000	68,174,700,000	62,852,000,000	80,194,000,000	80,194,500,000	68,500,000,000
R&D Expense						
Operating Income						
Operating Margin %						
SGA Expense						
Net Income	2,855,800,000	2,330,332,800	3,253,000,000	4,248,000,000	3,000,000,000	2,285,816,000
Operating Cash Flow						
Capital Expenditure						
EBITDA						
Return on Assets %						
Return on Equity %						
Debt to Equity						

CONTACT INFORMATION:

Phone: 86-431-8590-0715 Fax: 86-431-8761-4780
Toll-Free:
Address: Dongfeng St., No. 3025, Changchun, 130011 China

STOCK TICKER/OTHER:

Stock Ticker: Government-Owned
Exchange:
Employees: 123,658
Fiscal Year Ends: 03/31
Parent Company:

SALARIES/BONUSES:

Top Exec. Salary: $ Bonus: $
Second Exec. Salary: $ Bonus: $

OTHER THOUGHTS:

Estimated Female Officers or Directors:
Hot Spot for Advancement for Women/Minorities:

FCA Canada Inc

www.chrysler.ca/en/dealers

NAIC Code: 336111

TYPES OF BUSINESS:

Automobile Manufacturing
Automobile Distribution
Parts Manufacturing

BRANDS/DIVISIONS/AFFILIATES:

Fiat Chrysler Automobiles NV
FCA US LLC
Chrysler
Dodge
Fiat
Jeep
Ram
Mopar

GROWTH PLANS/SPECIAL FEATURES:

FCA Canada, Inc. manufactures and wholesales passenger cars, trucks and automotive components in Canada. The firm markets Chrysler, Dodge, Fiat, Jeep and Ram brands. Chrysler Canada's vehicle production facilities include the Windsor and Brampton assembly plants, which build Chrysler and Dodge vehicles; and the Etobicoke Casting Plant in Toronto, which produces aluminum cast parts. Mopar (short for motor parts) is the parts, service and customer care organization within parent Fiat Chrysler Automobiles, operating in Canada and North America. To a lesser degree, Mopar also designs and builds customized vehicles. FCA Canada operates a research and development center in Windsor, and has sales offices and parts distribution centers throughout the country. FCA Canada operates as a wholly-owned subsidiary of FCA US, LLC, which covers the North American division of Fiat Chrysler Automobiles NV.

CONTACTS: *Note: Officers with more than one job title may be intentionally listed here more than once.*

Reid Bigland, CEO

FINANCIAL DATA: *Note: Data for latest year may not have been available at press time.*

In U.S. $	2018	2017	2016	2015	2014	2013
Revenue	9,726,535,174	9,263,366,832	8,822,254,126	9,433,558,455	7,900,000,000	7,731,000,000
R&D Expense						
Operating Income						
Operating Margin %						
SGA Expense						
Net Income						
Operating Cash Flow						
Capital Expenditure						
EBITDA						
Return on Assets %						
Return on Equity %						
Debt to Equity						

CONTACT INFORMATION:

Phone: 519-973-2000 Fax: 519-973-2226
Toll-Free:
Address: 1 Riverside Dr. W., Windsor, ON N9A 5K3 Canada

STOCK TICKER/OTHER:

Stock Ticker: Subsidiary Exchange:
Employees: 12,503 Fiscal Year Ends: 12/31
Parent Company: Fiat Chrysler Automobiles NV

SALARIES/BONUSES:

Top Exec. Salary: $ Bonus: $
Second Exec. Salary: $ Bonus: $

OTHER THOUGHTS:

Estimated Female Officers or Directors:
Hot Spot for Advancement for Women/Minorities:

FCA US LLC www.fcanorthamerica.com/company/AboutUs/Pages/AboutUs.aspx

NAIC Code: 336111

TYPES OF BUSINESS:

Automobile Manufacturing
Research & Development
Nanotechnology-Coatings
Light Truck Manufacturing
Financial Services

BRANDS/DIVISIONS/AFFILIATES:

Fiat Chrysler Automobiles NV
Chrysler
Jeep
Dodge
Ram
Fiat
Alfa Romeo
Uconnect

CONTACTS: *Note: Officers with more than one job title may be intentionally listed here more than once.*

Sergio Marchionne, CEO
Ralph V. Gilles, Sr. VP-Prod. Design
Mark M. Chernoby, Sr. VP-Eng.
Mauro Pino, Sr. VP-Mfg. & World Class Mfg.
Peter Grady, VP-Network Dev. & Fleet
Marjorie Loeb, General Counsel
Barbara J. Pilarski, VP-Bus. Dev.
Gualberto Ranieri, Sr. VP-Comm.
Laurie A. Macaddino, VP-Audit
Doug D. Betts, Sr. VP-Quality
Alistair Gardner, Pres.
Reid Bigland, Head-U.S. Sales
Sergio Marchionne, Chmn.
Steven G. Beahm, Sr. VP-Supply Chain Mgmt.

GROWTH PLANS/SPECIAL FEATURES:

FCA US, LLC is the U.S. division of Fiat Chrysler Automobiles NV. Based in Michigan, FCA US designs, engineers, manufactures and sells vehicles under the Chrysler, Jeep, Dodge, Ram, Fiat and Alfa Romeo brands, as well as the street and racing technology (SRT) performance vehicle designation. The company also distributes the Alfa Romeo model and Mopar parts and accessories. FCA US operates more than 30 manufacturing plants throughout the U.S. Engineering breakthroughs made by the company include: Uconnect, which allows drivers to easily adjust seat or cabin temperature, select a new music station or make a call without taking their eyes from the road; various fuel efficiency features in relation to power, transmissions, engines and electrified propulsion systems; and design, development and vehicle integration of technologies in relation to customer safety and security.

The firm offers employees medical, prescription, vision and dental coverage; life insurance; discounted auto and home insurance; discount new vehicle purchase programs; and educational and personal development programs.

FINANCIAL DATA: *Note: Data for latest year may not have been available at press time.*

In U.S. $	2018	2017	2016	2015	2014	2013
Revenue	11,777,000,000	11,750,000,000	11,700,000,000	11,676,910,000	10,913,000,000	72,140,000,000
R&D Expense						
Operating Income						
Operating Margin %						
SGA Expense						
Net Income			1,985,015,213	1,747,498,195	1,587,005,793	2,760,000,000
Operating Cash Flow						
Capital Expenditure						
EBITDA						
Return on Assets %						
Return on Equity %						
Debt to Equity						

CONTACT INFORMATION:

Phone: 248-576-5741 Fax:
Toll-Free: 800-992-1997
Address: 1000 Chrysler Dr., Auburn Hills, MI 48326-2766 United States

STOCK TICKER/OTHER:

Stock Ticker: Private Exchange:
Employees: 83,800 Fiscal Year Ends: 12/31
Parent Company: Fiat Chrysler Automobiles NV

SALARIES/BONUSES:

Top Exec. Salary: $ Bonus: $
Second Exec. Salary: $ Bonus: $

OTHER THOUGHTS:

Estimated Female Officers or Directors: 3
Hot Spot for Advancement for Women/Minorities: Y

Federal Signal Corporation

www.federalsignal.com

NAIC Code: 336300

TYPES OF BUSINESS:

Automobile Parts Manufacturing
Customer & Dealer Financing
Commercial Cleaning Equipment
Access Control Systems

BRANDS/DIVISIONS/AFFILIATES:

Federal Signal
Federal Signal VAMA
Victor
Elgin
Vactor
Guzzler
Mark Rite Lines Equipment Company Inc
HighMark Traffic Services Inc

CONTACTS: *Note: Officers with more than one job title may be intentionally listed here more than once.*

Jennifer Sherman, CEO
Ian Hudson, CFO
Dennis Martin, Chairman of the Board
Lauren Elting, Chief Accounting Officer
Mark Weber, COO
Daniel DuPre, General Counsel
Robert Fines, General Manager, Subsidiary
Svetlana Vinokur, Treasurer

GROWTH PLANS/SPECIAL FEATURES:

Federal Signal Corporation designs and manufactures signal, cleaning and safety equipment for municipal, governmental, commercial and industrial customers. The products manufactured by the firm are divided into two major operating groups: safety and security systems, and environmental solutions. The safety and security systems group designs and manufactures emergency vehicle warning lights and sirens; industrial and outdoor signaling, warning, lighting and communications devices and integrated systems; and parking revenue and access control systems. Products are sold under the Federal Signal, Federal Signal VAMA and Victor brand names, and the group operates manufacturing facilities in the U.S., Europe and South Africa. The environmental solutions group manufactures and supplies a full range of street sweeper vehicles, sewer cleaner and vacuum loader trucks, hydro-excavation trucks, high-performance waterblasting equipment, dump truck bodies and trailers. This division manufactures vehicles and equipment in the U.S. and Canada, which are sold under the Elgin, Vactor, Guzzler, Westech, Jetstream, OxBodies, Crysteel, J-Craft, Duraclass, Rugby and Travis brand names. In mid-2019, Federal Signal acquired Mark Rite Lines Equipment Company, Inc., a U.S. manufacturer of truck-mounted and ride-on road-marking equipment. The acquisition includes the operations of HighMark Traffic Services, Inc., a provider of road-marking services primarily in the state of Montana.

FINANCIAL DATA: *Note: Data for latest year may not have been available at press time.*

In U.S. $	2018	2017	2016	2015	2014	2013
Revenue	1,089,500,000	898,500,000	707,900,000	768,000,000	918,500,000	851,300,000
R&D Expense						
Operating Income	123,000,000	70,400,000	60,800,000	103,600,000	92,600,000	71,300,000
Operating Margin %		.08%	.09%	.13%	.10%	.08%
SGA Expense	159,100,000	150,800,000	122,300,000	122,000,000	140,700,000	133,800,000
Net Income	94,000,000	61,600,000	43,800,000	63,500,000	63,700,000	160,000,000
Operating Cash Flow	92,800,000	72,800,000	24,700,000	97,200,000	72,300,000	74,800,000
Capital Expenditure	14,100,000	8,000,000	6,100,000	9,600,000	19,500,000	17,000,000
EBITDA	157,300,000	98,300,000	77,800,000	114,500,000	106,100,000	76,000,000
Return on Assets %		.08%	.07%	.10%	.10%	.25%
Return on Equity %		.14%	.11%	.16%	.18%	.64%
Debt to Equity		0.606	0.161	0.108	0.118	0.241

CONTACT INFORMATION:

Phone: 630 954-2000 Fax: 630 954-2030
Toll-Free:
Address: 1415 W. 22nd St., Oak Brook, IL 60523 United States

STOCK TICKER/OTHER:

Stock Ticker: FSS
Exchange: NYS
Employees: 2,200
Fiscal Year Ends: 12/31
Parent Company:

SALARIES/BONUSES:

Top Exec. Salary: $702,975 Bonus: $
Second Exec. Salary: $432,981 Bonus: $

OTHER THOUGHTS:

Estimated Female Officers or Directors: 2
Hot Spot for Advancement for Women/Minorities: Y

Federal-Mogul LLC

www.federalmogul.com

NAIC Code: 336300

TYPES OF BUSINESS:

Aftermarket Products & Services
Powertrain Products
Sealing Systems
Vehicle Safety & Performance Products

BRANDS/DIVISIONS/AFFILIATES:

Tenneco Inc

CONTACTS:

Note: Officers with more than one job title may be intentionally listed here more than once.

Brian Kesseler, Co-CEO
Roger Wood, Co-CEO
Jason Hollar, CFO
Mark Bradbury, VP-IT
Kaled Awada, Sr. VP-Human Resources
Rusty Patel, CIO
Martin Hendricks, President, Divisional
Scott Pepin, Senior VP, Divisional
Jerome Rouquet, Senior VP
John Patouhas, Vice President

GROWTH PLANS/SPECIAL FEATURES:

Federal-Mogul, LLC is a global supplier of vehicle and industrial products for fuel economy, alternative energies and safety systems. The company operates two divisions: powertrain and motor parts. Powertrain focuses on original equipment (OE) products for automotive, heavy duty and industrial applications. This segment offers its customers a diverse array of market-leading products for OE applications, including pistons, piston rings, piston pins, cylinder liners, valve seats and guides, ignition products, dynamic seals, bonded piston seals, combustion & exhaust gaskets, static gaskets/seals, rigid heat shields, engine bearings, industrial bearings, brushings, washers, plus element resistant systems protection sleeving products, acoustic shielding and flexible heat shields. The motor parts segment sells and distributes a broad portfolio of products manufactured by Powertrain. Motor parts' products include brake disc pads, brake linings, brake linings, brake blocks, brake system components, chassis products, wipers and other product lines to OE and aftermarket customers. Federal-Mogul maintains manufacturing facilities and distribution centers in 24 countries. In late-2018, parent company Icahn Enterprises LP sold the firm to Tenneco, Inc. for $2.5 billion. Tenneco announced plans to separate its business to form two new independent companies by the end of 2019: an aftermarket and ride performance company as well as a powertrain technology company.

FINANCIAL DATA:

Note: Data for latest year may not have been available at press time.

In U.S. $	2018	2017	2016	2015	2014	2013
Revenue	8,190,000,000	7,800,000,000	7,434,000,000	7,418,999,808	7,317,000,192	6,785,999,872
R&D Expense						
Operating Income						
Operating Margin %						
SGA Expense						
Net Income			90,000,000	-110,000,000	-168,000,000	41,000,000
Operating Cash Flow						
Capital Expenditure						
EBITDA						
Return on Assets %						
Return on Equity %						
Debt to Equity						

CONTACT INFORMATION:

Phone: 248 354-7700   Fax: 248 354-8950
Toll-Free:
Address: 27300 West 11 Mile Rd., Southfield, MI 48034 United States

STOCK TICKER/OTHER:

Stock Ticker: Subsidiary   Exchange:
Employees: 53,000   Fiscal Year Ends: 12/31
Parent Company: Tenneco Inc

SALARIES/BONUSES:

Top Exec. Salary: $ Bonus: $
Second Exec. Salary: $ Bonus: $

OTHER THOUGHTS:

Estimated Female Officers or Directors: 1
Hot Spot for Advancement for Women/Minorities:

Ferrari SpA

www.ferrari.com

NAIC Code: 336111

TYPES OF BUSINESS:

Automobile Manufacturing
Magazine Publication
TV Content Production
Amusement Parks
Vehicle Financing

BRANDS/DIVISIONS/AFFILIATES:

812 superfast
SF90 Stradale
F8 Tributo
488 Pista Spider
GTC4Lusso
Ferrari Portofino
Ferrari Financial Services

CONTACTS: *Note: Officers with more than one job title may be intentionally listed here more than once.*

Louis C. Camilleri, CEO
Ervino Riccobon, VP-Prod. Processes
Italo Valenti, Dir.-Admin.
Mario Mairano, General Sec.
Stefano Lai, Dir.-Comm.
Italo Valenti, Dir.-Finance & Control
Piero Ferrari, Vice Chmn.
Vincenzo Regazzoni, Head-Tech & Infrastructure
Stefano Domenicali, Dir.-Gestione Sportiva
Andrea Perrone, Sr. VP-Brand
John Elkann, Chmn.
Sergio Carpentiere, Head-Purchasing & Supplier Dev.

GROWTH PLANS/SPECIAL FEATURES:

Ferrari SpA, founded in 1947, manufactures high-performance sports cars. Current Ferrari vehicles include the 812 superfast, the SF90 Stradale, the F8 Tributo, the 488 Pista Spider, the 488 Pista, the 488 Spider, the GTC4Lusso, the GTC4Lusso T and the Ferrari Portofino. Special limited series vehicles include the Ferrari Monza SP1 and SP2. 812 superfast has a maximum power output of 588 kW at 8,500 rpm; Stradale has a maximum power output of 574 kW @ 7,500 rpm; Tributo, 720 CV @7,000 rpm; Pista Sider has a maximum power of 530 kW; Pista, 720 CV @ 8,000 rpm; Spider has a retractable hard top, and a maximum torque 760 Nm @ 3,000 rpm; Lusso has a maximum power of 507 kW @ 8,000 rpm; Lusso T has a maximum torque of 760 Nm available between 3,000 and 5,250 rpm; and Portofino has a maximum power of 441 kW. Ferrari's service department offers original spare parts, restoration services, driving courses, vehicle insurance, road assistance and more. Tailor-made options are available for a personalized, one-of-a-kind Ferrari. Ferrari Financial Services is the company's own financial services provider, offering a flexible range of Ferrari-branded, basic and premium financial solutions. Ferrari also offers apparel, footwear, eyewear and accessories marketed under the Ferrari and other related brand names. Ferrari dealerships are located worldwide, including the Americas, Europe, the Middle East, Africa, Asia and Australasia.

FINANCIAL DATA: *Note: Data for latest year may not have been available at press time.*

In U.S. $	2018	2017	2016	2015	2014	2013
Revenue	3,786,892,000	3,783,094,000	3,437,870,000	3,160,285,000	3,058,415,000	2,585,551,000
R&D Expense	711,955,300	727,545,400	679,401,000	621,769,300	598,796,500	530,662,100
Operating Income	915,674,300	863,425,700	682,591,900	504,157,500	460,084,200	400,191,600
Operating Margin %		.23%	.20%	.16%	.15%	.15%
SGA Expense	362,423,600	364,332,400	326,884,400	374,918,000	332,252,000	287,732,500
Net Income	868,775,500	592,773,500	441,499,100	318,662,500	289,383,300	266,578,800
Operating Cash Flow	1,034,146,000	733,834,100	1,113,041,000	783,069,100	471,730,500	502,672,700
Capital Expenditure	706,749,400	433,359,200	378,639,300	394,091,000	365,365,400	299,936,900
EBITDA	1,235,369,000	1,151,962,000	956,857,900	808,361,400	780,037,600	699,405,400
Return on Assets %		.13%	.10%	.07%	.06%	.06%
Return on Equity %		.97%	2.66%	.24%	.11%	.11%
Debt to Equity		2.32	4.456		0.207	0.139

CONTACT INFORMATION:

Phone: 39-0-536-949-111 Fax: 39-0-536-949-714
Toll-Free:
Address: Via Abetone Inferiore 4, Maranello, 41053 Italy

STOCK TICKER/OTHER:

Stock Ticker: RACE
Employees: 3,248
Parent Company: Ferrari NV
Exchange: NYS
Fiscal Year Ends: 12/31

SALARIES/BONUSES:

Top Exec. Salary: $ Bonus: $
Second Exec. Salary: $ Bonus: $

OTHER THOUGHTS:

Estimated Female Officers or Directors:
Hot Spot for Advancement for Women/Minorities:

Fiat Chrysler Automobiles NV

www.fcagroup.com

NAIC Code: 336111

TYPES OF BUSINESS:

Automobile Manufacturing

BRANDS/DIVISIONS/AFFILIATES:

Abarth
Alfa Romeo
Chrysler
Fiat
Jeep
Mopar
Comau
Teksid

CONTACTS:

Note: Officers with more than one job title may be intentionally listed here more than once.

Michael Manley, CEO
Olivier Francois, CMO
Harald Wester, CTO

GROWTH PLANS/SPECIAL FEATURES:

Fiat Chrysler Automobiles NV is an international automotive group engaged in designing, engineering, manufacturing and selling vehicles, components and production systems. The firm is among the largest automakers in the world based on total vehicle sales. Fiat Chrysler operates 102 manufacturing facilities and 46 R&D centers, and sells vehicles through dealers and distributors in more than 135 countries. The company designs, engineers, manufactures, distributes and sells vehicles for the mass market under the Abarth, Alfa Romeo, Chrysler, Dodge, Fiat, Fiat Professional, Jeep, Lancia, Ram and Maserati brands. Fiat Chrysler supports its vehicle sales via after-sales services and products worldwide under the Mopar brand. Other brands of the firm include Comau, which produces systems; and Teksid, which produces iron and castings. From 2018 through 2022, the company plans to invest about $9 billion to enhance its line of electric vehicles. This will be part of a total $45 billion plan to expand and enhance the line of Jeep SUVs and Ram pickup trucks, as well as the sports-luxury cars of Maserati and Alfa Romeo. In 2019, Fiat Chrysler announced plans to invest $4.5 billion in a manufacturing plant in Detroit for building Jeeps, creating nearly 6,500 jobs. That same year, Fiat Chrysler sold auto parts maker Magneti Marelli SpA to Calsonic Kansei, a Japanese subsidiary of KKR & Co., Inc.

FINANCIAL DATA:

Note: Data for latest year may not have been available at press time.

In U.S. $	2018	2017	2016	2015	2014	2013
Revenue	122,245,300,000	122,823,300,000	122,916,300,000	122,448,000,000	106,388,400,000	
R&D Expense	3,377,990,000	3,576,174,000	3,624,889,000	3,170,948,000	2,808,902,000	
Operating Income	5,571,302,000	8,014,836,000	5,404,119,000	2,806,687,000	3,897,254,000	
Operating Margin %		.07%	.04%	.02%	.04%	
SGA Expense	8,102,303,000	8,176,484,000	8,379,097,000	8,556,244,000	7,843,225,000	
Net Income	3,994,686,000	3,865,146,000	1,996,236,000	369,796,300	628,875,100	
Operating Cash Flow	11,014,170,000	11,498,010,000	11,729,410,000	10,796,060,000	9,044,509,000	
Capital Expenditure	5,969,885,000	9,594,775,000	9,759,743,000	9,764,173,000	8,991,364,000	
EBITDA	11,705,050,000	14,726,530,000	11,770,370,000	9,304,695,000	9,243,801,000	
Return on Assets %		.03%	.02%	.00%	.01%	
Return on Equity %		.17%	.10%	.02%	.05%	
Debt to Equity		0.515	0.841	1.269	1.938	

CONTACT INFORMATION:

Phone: 44-207766-0311 Fax:
Toll-Free:
Address: 25 St. James's St., London, SW1A 1HA United Kingdom

STOCK TICKER/OTHER:

Stock Ticker: FCAU
Employees: 231,019
Parent Company:
Exchange: NYS
Fiscal Year Ends:

SALARIES/BONUSES:

Top Exec. Salary: $664,794 Bonus: $2,211,959
Second Exec. Salary: $2,187,559 Bonus: $315,181

OTHER THOUGHTS:

Estimated Female Officers or Directors:
Hot Spot for Advancement for Women/Minorities:

FinishMaster Inc

www.finishmaster.com

NAIC Code: 424600

TYPES OF BUSINESS:

Automotive Paints & Coatings-Distribution
Industrial & Automotive Paints

BRANDS/DIVISIONS/AFFILIATES:

Uni-Select Inc
SMART
WaterMasters

CONTACTS: *Note: Officers with more than one job title may be intentionally listed here more than once.*

Chris Adams, Pres.
Steve Yockey, VP-National Oper.
Travis Trott, CFO
Michael Good, VP-Mktg.
Zach Wickler, VP-Human Resources
Bart Chambers, VP-IT
Peter L. Lacy, VP-National Oper.
Travis N. Trott, VP-Supply Chain & Logistics

GROWTH PLANS/SPECIAL FEATURES:

FinishMaster, Inc., founded in Indianapolis, Indiana in 1968, distributes automotive paints, coatings and related accessories to the automotive industry. The firm has more than 200 locations throughout the U.S., and has more than 30,000 products available to its customers. FinishMaster's products are primarily marketed to collision repair shops, automotive dealerships and fleet operators. Many of the products distributed by FinishMaster are produced by manufacturers such as BASF, DuPont, PPG and 3M. Additionally, the firm markets its own private label, SMART, for refinishing accessory products such as body filler and putty, masking and plastic sheeting, undercoat products, detail products, wax and grease remover, glass cleaner, buffing pads, backing plates and adapters, sanders and buffers, paint suits, spray guns and work stands. Through its WaterMasters brand, the company markets waterborne basecoats for environmentally friendly finisher processes. FinishMaster operates as a wholly-owned subsidiary of Uni-Select, Inc., which specializes in the distribution of automotive refinish and industrial paint products in North America, as well as automotive aftermarket parts in Canada.

FINANCIAL DATA: *Note: Data for latest year may not have been available at press time.*

In U.S. $	2018	2017	2016	2015	2014	2013
Revenue	855,370,950	814,639,000	752,846,000	618,800,000	573,400,000	569,000,000
R&D Expense						
Operating Income						
Operating Margin %						
SGA Expense						
Net Income						
Operating Cash Flow						
Capital Expenditure						
EBITDA						
Return on Assets %						
Return on Equity %						
Debt to Equity						

CONTACT INFORMATION:

Phone: 317-237-3678 Fax: 317-237-2150
Toll-Free: 888-311-3678
Address: 115 W. Washington St., Ste. 700 S., Indianapolis, IN 46204 United States

STOCK TICKER/OTHER:

Stock Ticker: Subsidiary
Exchange:
Employees: 1,900
Fiscal Year Ends: 12/31
Parent Company: Uni-Select Inc

SALARIES/BONUSES:

Top Exec. Salary: $ Bonus: $
Second Exec. Salary: $ Bonus: $

OTHER THOUGHTS:

Estimated Female Officers or Directors:
Hot Spot for Advancement for Women/Minorities:

Fisher & Company Inc

www.fisherco.com

NAIC Code: 336300

TYPES OF BUSINESS:

Auto Parts Manufacturer
Seat Components
Seatbelts

BRANDS/DIVISIONS/AFFILIATES:

Fisher Dynamics
Fisher Dynamics Metal Forming

GROWTH PLANS/SPECIAL FEATURES:

Fisher & Company, Inc. is the parent company for Fisher Dynamics and Fisher Dynamics Metal Forming. Fisher Dynamics supplies the automotive industry with seat mechanisms. The firm designs and manufactures recliners, latches and specialty mechanisms for passenger vehicles, with offices in North America, Mexico, Germany, India and China. Fisher Dynamics Metal Forming manufactures high-strength, tight-tolerance stampings, complex fine blankings and precision broachings. This company forms many types of safety-critical precision metal parts for a variety of applications, serving customers in North America, Europe and Asia.

CONTACTS: *Note: Officers with more than one job title may be intentionally listed here more than once.*

Michael Fisher, Pres.
John Whalen, Dir.-Eng.
Alfred J. Fisher, IV, VP
Michael R. Fisher, Pres., Fisher Dynamics

FINANCIAL DATA: *Note: Data for latest year may not have been available at press time.*

In U.S. $	2018	2017	2016	2015	2014	2013
Revenue						
R&D Expense						
Operating Income						
Operating Margin %						
SGA Expense						
Net Income						
Operating Cash Flow						
Capital Expenditure						
EBITDA						
Return on Assets %						
Return on Equity %						
Debt to Equity						

CONTACT INFORMATION:

Phone: 586-746-2000 Fax: 586-296-1607
Toll-Free:
Address: 33300 Fisher Dr., St. Clair Shores, MI 48082 United States

STOCK TICKER/OTHER:

Stock Ticker: Private
Employees:
Parent Company:
Exchange:
Fiscal Year Ends:

SALARIES/BONUSES:

Top Exec. Salary: $ Bonus: $
Second Exec. Salary: $ Bonus: $

OTHER THOUGHTS:

Estimated Female Officers or Directors:
Hot Spot for Advancement for Women/Minorities:

Fletcher Jones Management Group Inc

www.fjautogroup.com/

NAIC Code: 441110

TYPES OF BUSINESS:

Auto Dealers, Retail
Vehicle Service
Vehicle Financing

BRANDS/DIVISIONS/AFFILIATES:

Fletcher Jones Motorcars
Fletcher Jones Imports
Fletcher Jones Imports-Sprinter Service

CONTACTS: *Note: Officers with more than one job title may be intentionally listed here more than once.*

Fletcher (Ted) Jones, Jr., CEO
Fletcher Jones, Jr., Pres.
Rhonda Brees, Corp. Controller

GROWTH PLANS/SPECIAL FEATURES:

Fletcher Jones Management Group, Inc. operates automobile dealerships located in the U.S. states of California, Hawaii, Nevada and Illinois. California dealerships are grouped into northern and southern regions: northern California locations include Fletcher Jones Motorcars of Fremont, Porsche Fremont and Audi Fremont; and southern California locations include Fletcher Jones Motorcars (Newport Beach), Audi Beverly Hills, Mercedes-Benz of Ontario and Audi Fletcher Jones (Costa Mesa). Hawaii dealerships include Mercedes-Benz of Honolulu and Mercedes-Benz of Maui. Nevada dealerships include Fletcher Jones Imports (Las Vegas), Fletcher Jones Imports-Sprinter Service (Las Vegas) and Mercedes-Benz of Henderson. Illinois dealerships include Fletcher Jones Audi (Chicago), Sprinter of Chicago and Mercedes-Benz of Chicago. Besides new and used vehicles, Fletcher Jones offers financing services such as leasing and car loans at its locations. The company's website offers different tools through which customers can look up new and used car inventory, promotional deals, schedule a service, and apply for credit. Customers can also order genuine original equipment manufacturer parts at some of the dealership locations.

FINANCIAL DATA: *Note: Data for latest year may not have been available at press time.*

In U.S. $	2018	2017	2016	2015	2014	2013
Revenue	2,577,201,064	2,454,477,204	2,337,597,337	2,273,420,217	2,000,000,000	1,850,000,000
R&D Expense						
Operating Income						
Operating Margin %						
SGA Expense						
Net Income						
Operating Cash Flow						
Capital Expenditure						
EBITDA						
Return on Assets %						
Return on Equity %						
Debt to Equity						

CONTACT INFORMATION:

Phone: 702-739-9800 Fax: 702-739-0486
Toll-Free:
Address: 7300 W. Sahara Ave., Las Vegas, NV 89117 United States

STOCK TICKER/OTHER:

Stock Ticker: Private
Employees:
Parent Company:
Exchange:
Fiscal Year Ends: 12/31

SALARIES/BONUSES:

Top Exec. Salary: $ Bonus: $
Second Exec. Salary: $ Bonus: $

OTHER THOUGHTS:

Estimated Female Officers or Directors: 1
Hot Spot for Advancement for Women/Minorities:

Ford Motor Company

www.ford.com

NAIC Code: 336111

TYPES OF BUSINESS:

Automobile Manufacturing
Automobile Financing
Fuel-Cell & Hybrid Research

BRANDS/DIVISIONS/AFFILIATES:

Ford
Lincoln
Ford Motor Credit Co
Ford Mustang
Ford F150
Ford Focus
Lincoln Navigator SUV
Ford Escape Hybrid SUV

CONTACTS: *Note: Officers with more than one job title may be intentionally listed here more than once.*

David McClelland, CEO, Subsidiary
James Hackett, CEO
Cathy O'Callaghan, CFO, Divisional
Tim Stone, CFO
William Ford, Chairman of the Board
Bradley Gayton, Chief Administrative Officer
Hau Thai-Tang, Other Corporate Officer
Kiersten Robinson, Other Executive Officer
Marcy Klevorn, President, Divisional
James Farley, President, Divisional
Joseph Hinrichs, President, Divisional

GROWTH PLANS/SPECIAL FEATURES:

Ford Motor Company is a designer and manufacturer of automobiles and automotive systems. The firm operates in two primary segments: automotive and financial services. The automotive segment designs, manufactures, sells and services cars, trucks, sport utility vehicles (SUVs), electrified vehicles and luxury vehicles under the Ford and Lincoln brand names. Ford is engaged in researching and developing human machine interaction (HMI) digital technology for the Ford brand, currently its F-150 truck (as of early-2019), and has developed My View, an innovative feature that lets owners customize the content and order of the truck's driver cockpit screens, and access them via touch. The company sells its vehicles to the public via independently owned dealerships, including more than 10,345 Ford; more than 260 Lincoln; and approximately 820 Ford/Lincoln dealerships. These dealerships are in North America, South America, Europe, Asia Pacific and Africa. In addition to new car sales, the firm also sells vehicles to its dealerships for sale to fleet customers, including commercial fleet customers, daily rental car companies and governments, and sells parts and accessories to authorized parts distributors. The firm's financial services segment, operating through Ford Motor Credit Company, LLC, offers vehicle-related financing, leasing and insurance. Some of Ford's most popular vehicles include the Ford Mustang sports car, the Ford F150 truck, the compact Ford Focus, the Lincoln Navigator SUV and the Ford Escape Hybrid SUV. In February 2019, Ford announced that it will exit the commercial heavy truck business in South America, ceasing production at the Sao Bernardo do Campo plant in Brazil that year, which will end sales of the F-4000, F-350 and Fiesta small car.

FINANCIAL DATA: *Note: Data for latest year may not have been available at press time.*

In U.S. $	2018	2017	2016	2015	2014	2013
Revenue	160,338,000,000	156,776,000,000	151,800,000,000	149,558,000,000	144,077,000,000	146,917,000,000
R&D Expense						
Operating Income	3,203,000,000	4,813,000,000	4,272,000,000	7,780,000,000	3,565,000,000	5,558,000,000
Operating Margin %		.05%	.03%	.06%	.03%	.04%
SGA Expense	11,403,000,000	11,527,000,000	12,196,000,000	14,999,000,000	14,117,000,000	13,176,000,000
Net Income	3,677,000,000	7,602,000,000	4,596,000,000	7,373,000,000	3,187,000,000	7,155,000,000
Operating Cash Flow	15,022,000,000	18,096,000,000	19,792,000,000	16,170,000,000	14,507,000,000	10,444,000,000
Capital Expenditure	7,785,000,000	7,049,000,000	6,992,000,000	7,196,000,000	7,463,000,000	6,597,000,000
EBITDA	13,881,000,000	17,734,000,000	16,407,000,000	18,991,000,000	12,562,000,000	14,286,000,000
Return on Assets %		.03%	.02%	.03%	.02%	.04%
Return on Equity %		.24%	.16%	.28%	.12%	.34%
Debt to Equity		2.943	3.199	3.137	3.225	2.904

CONTACT INFORMATION:

Phone: 313 322-3000 Fax: 313 222-4177
Toll-Free: 800-392-3673
Address: 1 American Rd., Dearborn, MI 48126 United States

STOCK TICKER/OTHER:

Stock Ticker: F
Employees: 201,000
Parent Company:
Exchange: NYS
Fiscal Year Ends: 12/31

SALARIES/BONUSES:

Top Exec. Salary: $1,800,000 Bonus: $
Second Exec. Salary: $1,700,000 Bonus: $

OTHER THOUGHTS:

Estimated Female Officers or Directors: 4
Hot Spot for Advancement for Women/Minorities: Y

Ford Motor Company of Canada Limited

www.ford.ca

NAIC Code: 336111

TYPES OF BUSINESS:

Automobile Manufacturing
Parts Manufacturing
Auto Financing & Leasing
Hybrid & Electric Vehicles

BRANDS/DIVISIONS/AFFILIATES:

Ford Motor Company
Mustang
F-150
Escape
Edge

CONTACTS:

Note: Officers with more than one job title may be intentionally listed here more than once.

Dean Stoneley, CEO
Dianne Craig, Pres.
Lauren More, VP-Public Affairs

GROWTH PLANS/SPECIAL FEATURES:

Ford Motor Company of Canada Limited, a subsidiary of Ford Motor Company, manufactures automobiles. The firm's manufacturing operations include the Windsor Operations, Windsor Engine and Essex Engine plants in Ontario. Assembly operations are located in Oakville, and include the Ford Edge, Lincoln MKX, Lincoln MKT and Ford Flex assembly lines. Ford Canada produces 320,000 vehicles each year for sale at Canadian dealerships. These vehicles include the categories of crossover utility vehicles, sport utility vehicles, trucks, cars, electric, commercial, fleet and mobility. Ford Motor Canada's innovative technology offers vehicle features such as blind spot information systems, connected information systems, connected sensors, smart suspensions and more. Popular Ford vehicle models include Mustang, F-150, Escape and Edge.

The firm offers employees healthcare coverage, a tuition refund plan, an employee assistance program, a stock investment program, vacation and paid holidays. Employees and their families can purchase Ford and Lincoln vehicles at dealer invoice cost.

FINANCIAL DATA:

Note: Data for latest year may not have been available at press time.

In U.S. $	2018	2017	2016	2015	2014	2013
Revenue	10,541,000,000	10,580,000,000	10,028,000,000	8,978,000,000	9,409,000,000	9,729,000,000
R&D Expense						
Operating Income						
Operating Margin %						
SGA Expense						
Net Income						
Operating Cash Flow						
Capital Expenditure						
EBITDA						
Return on Assets %						
Return on Equity %						
Debt to Equity						

CONTACT INFORMATION:

Phone: 905-845-2511 Fax: 905-844-8085
Toll-Free: 800-387-9333
Address: The Canadian Rd., PO Box 2000, Oakville, ON K6K 0C8 Canada

STOCK TICKER/OTHER:

Stock Ticker: Subsidiary
Employees:
Parent Company: Ford Motor Company
Exchange:
Fiscal Year Ends: 12/31

SALARIES/BONUSES:

Top Exec. Salary: $ Bonus: $
Second Exec. Salary: $ Bonus: $

OTHER THOUGHTS:

Estimated Female Officers or Directors: 3
Hot Spot for Advancement for Women/Minorities: Y

Ford Motor Credit Company LLC

www.fordcredit.com

NAIC Code: 522220

TYPES OF BUSINESS:

Automobile Financing
Insurance
Leasing
Loans & Mortgages
Fleet Financing
Dealer Financing

BRANDS/DIVISIONS/AFFILIATES:

Ford Motor Company
FCE Bank Plc

CONTACTS:

Note: Officers with more than one job title may be intentionally listed here more than once.

David McClelland, CEO
Brian Schaaf, CFO
Todd S. Murphy, Exec. VP-Oper. & Int'l Dir.

GROWTH PLANS/SPECIAL FEATURES:

Ford Motor Credit Company, LLC is an indirect, wholly-owned subsidiary of Ford Motor Company, offering financial services to vehicle buyers. The firm has a wide selection of automotive financing products offered to and through automotive dealers throughout the world. Its primary financing products fall into three categories: retail financing, wholesale financing and other financing. Retail financing includes purchasing retail-installment sale contracts and retail lease contracts from dealers, and offering financing to commercial customers, primarily vehicle leasing companies and fleet purchasers, to lease or purchase vehicle fleets. Wholesale financing provides loans to dealers to purchase vehicle inventory, also known as floor plan financing. Other financing includes loans to dealers to purchase/finance working capital and make improvements to dealership facilities. The company earns revenue primarily from payments made under retail-installment sale contracts and leases that it purchases; interest supplements; other support payments from Ford and affiliated companies; and payments made under wholesale and other dealer loan financing programs. Ford Motor Credit's online credit application and payment calculator can help the decision-making process, and can also be given to the dealer. The firm conducts business in the U.S. and Canada through business centers. In Europe, it conducts business through U.K. subsidiary, FCE Bank Plc, which has branches in several European countries.

FINANCIAL DATA:

Note: Data for latest year may not have been available at press time.

In U.S. $	2018	2017	2016	2015	2014	2013
Revenue	11,977,000,000	10,976,000,000	10,423,000,000	9,280,000,000	8,606,000,000	7,805,000,000
R&D Expense						
Operating Income						
Operating Margin %						
SGA Expense						
Net Income	2,224,000,000	3,007,000,000	1,373,000,000	1,363,000,000	1,705,000,000	1,479,000,000
Operating Cash Flow						
Capital Expenditure						
EBITDA						
Return on Assets %						
Return on Equity %						
Debt to Equity						

CONTACT INFORMATION:

Phone: 313-322-3000 Fax: 313-323-2959
Toll-Free: 800-727-7000
Address: 1 American Rd., Dearborn, MI 48126 United States

STOCK TICKER/OTHER:

Stock Ticker: Subsidiary
Employees: 7,600
Parent Company: Ford Motor Company
Exchange:
Fiscal Year Ends: 12/31

SALARIES/BONUSES:

Top Exec. Salary: $ Bonus: $
Second Exec. Salary: $ Bonus: $

OTHER THOUGHTS:

Estimated Female Officers or Directors:
Hot Spot for Advancement for Women/Minorities:

Galpin Motors Inc

NAIC Code: 441110

www.galpin.com

TYPES OF BUSINESS:

Auto Dealers, Retail
Car Rental Services
Vehicle Customization

BRANDS/DIVISIONS/AFFILIATES:

Fiesta
Focus
Edge
Escape
F-150
F-450
MKC
Navigator

CONTACTS:

Note: Officers with more than one job title may be intentionally listed here more than once.

Bert Boeckmann, CEO
Beau Boeckmann, Pres.
Phil Marshall, CFO
Laurie Knight, Dir.-Human Resources
Phil Marshall, Sec.
Bert Boeckmann, Chmn.

GROWTH PLANS/SPECIAL FEATURES:

Galpin Motors, Inc. operates a group of car dealerships and an integrated series of websites, selling new and used vehicles in southern California. Although founded by Frank Galpin in 1946, the company has been owned and operated by the Boeckmann family since the 1960s. The group sells Ford, Lincoln, Honda, Volkswagen, Mazda, Volvo, Lotus, Aston Martin and Jaguar, as well as additional makes as they are acquired. Galpin car dealers have more than 4,000 new and used cars, sport utility vehicles (SUVs) and trucks for sale. New Ford cars include: Ford Fiesta, Focus, Fusion, Flex, Roush, Shelby, EcoSport and Mustang; SUVs include Edge, Escape, Explorer and Expedition; and trucks include F-150, Super Duty F-250, F-350 and F-450. New and used Lincoln models include the MKC, MKT, MKX, MKZ, Nautilus and Navigator. Galpin Motors offers a wide range of flexible financing options, even for those with poor credit. Parts and related services are offered by the firm, including tire services, custom auto sports services, digital license plate services and more. Galpin Motors serves all of Southern California, including Los Angeles, Studio City, Burbank, North Hollywood, Van Nuys, North Hills, Glendale, Sherman Oaks, Culver City, Brentwood, Pasadena, Reseda, West Hollywood, Beverly Hills, Northridge, Woodland Hills, Sun Valley and Calabasas.

FINANCIAL DATA:

Note: Data for latest year may not have been available at press time.

In U.S. $	2018	2017	2016	2015	2014	2013
Revenue	1,349,574,632	1,285,309,173	1,128,865,879	1,053,268,389	1,660,000,000	1,477,000,000
R&D Expense						
Operating Income						
Operating Margin %						
SGA Expense						
Net Income						
Operating Cash Flow						
Capital Expenditure						
EBITDA						
Return on Assets %						
Return on Equity %						
Debt to Equity						

CONTACT INFORMATION:

Phone: 818-787-3800 Fax: 818-778-2210
Toll-Free: 800-256-7137
Address: 15505 Roscoe Blvd., North Hills, CA 91343 United States

STOCK TICKER/OTHER:

Stock Ticker: Private
Exchange:
Employees: 782
Fiscal Year Ends: 12/31
Parent Company:

SALARIES/BONUSES:

Top Exec. Salary: $ Bonus: $
Second Exec. Salary: $ Bonus: $

OTHER THOUGHTS:

Estimated Female Officers or Directors: 2
Hot Spot for Advancement for Women/Minorities:

GAZ Group

gazglobal.com/

NAIC Code: 336111

TYPES OF BUSINESS:

Automobile Manufacturing
Auto Parts & Components Manufacturing
Construction Equipment

BRANDS/DIVISIONS/AFFILIATES:

Basic Element Group of Companies
Russian Machines Corporation
Gazelle NEXT
Ural NEXT
Vector
PAZ
KAVZ
YMZ

CONTACTS: *Note: Officers with more than one job title may be intentionally listed here more than once.*

Vadim Sorokin, Pres.
Gunther Heiden, COO
Mikhail Kryukov, Dir.-Finance

GROWTH PLANS/SPECIAL FEATURES:

GAZ Group is one of Russia's largest commercial automobile manufacturers. The firm manufactures light- and medium-duty commercial vehicles, buses, heavy-duty trucks and powertrains. GAZ's commercial vehicles include the Gazelle NEXT line of drop-side trucks, vans, mini buses and framed buses. The company's trucks include the Ural NEXT line of dump and semi trucks. Buses are categorized by size or purpose, including: small and medium buses, and marketed under the Vector, PAZ and KAVZ models. GAZ Group's powertrains are multi-purpose in-line and V-shaped diesel engines offering high technical and economic performance and ranging from 130 to 800 in horsepower. Engine models include the YMZ-530, YMZ-650, YMZ V6, YMZ V8 and YMZ V12. Other related products by GAZ include gearboxes, clutches and diesel generating sets. The firm's products are offered through dealers in the Russian Federation and internationally, and include GAZ Grup Otomotive Sanayi ve Ticaret Anonim Sirketi (in Turkey), GAZKAR Automotive (in Madagascar) and ConEquip Philippines, Inc., among many others. GAZ is privately-owned by the Russian Machines Corporation, itself a subsidiary of Basic Element Group of Companies.

FINANCIAL DATA: *Note: Data for latest year may not have been available at press time.*

In U.S. $	2018	2017	2016	2015	2014	2013
Revenue	2,997,246,000	2,854,520,000	2,452,177,491	1,879,849,452	2,999,626,214	3,873,279,602
R&D Expense						
Operating Income						
Operating Margin %						
SGA Expense						
Net Income		60,697,600	18,072,000			
Operating Cash Flow						
Capital Expenditure						
EBITDA						
Return on Assets %						
Return on Equity %						
Debt to Equity						

CONTACT INFORMATION:

Phone: 7-831-299-0990 Fax:
Toll-Free:
Address: 88 Lenin Prospect, Nizhny Novgorod, 603950 Russia

STOCK TICKER/OTHER:

Stock Ticker: Private Exchange:
Employees: 40,000 Fiscal Year Ends: 12/31
Parent Company: Basic Element Group of Companies

SALARIES/BONUSES:

Top Exec. Salary: $ Bonus: $
Second Exec. Salary: $ Bonus: $

OTHER THOUGHTS:

Estimated Female Officers or Directors: 1
Hot Spot for Advancement for Women/Minorities:

Geely Automobile Holdings Limited

www.geelyauto.com.hk

NAIC Code: 336211

TYPES OF BUSINESS:

Motor Vehicle Body Manufacturing

BRANDS/DIVISIONS/AFFILIATES:

Zhejian Geely Holding Group Co Ltd
Lynk&Co JV
Geely
Emgrand
Vision

CONTACTS:

Note: Officers with more than one job title may be intentionally listed here more than once.

Sheng Yue Gui, CEO
Yang Jian, Pres.
Shu Fu Li, Chmn.

GROWTH PLANS/SPECIAL FEATURES:

Geely Automobile Holdings Limited is an automobile manufacturer focused on the development, manufacturing and sales of passenger vehicles. The company has nine manufacturing plants in Linhai, Ningbo/Cixi, Luqiao, Xiangtan, Jinan, Chunxiao, Baoji, Jinzhong and Chengdu. The company sells most of its products in China, but also has a sales and marketing division that exports to other countries. Geely's products consists of 17 major vehicle models, including the Lynk&Co models sold by the group's 50/50 joint venture, Lynk&Co JV. Other model series include Geely, Lotus, Emgrand and Vision, among others. At the end of 2018, nearly 980 dealers in China were marketing Geely branded vehicles. Lynk&Co serves customer through its more than 220 distribution centers, as well as 17 Lynk&Co spaces. Automobiles and related products are exported through Geely's network of sales agents and outlets to 24 countries, of which are primarily developing countries within in Eastern Europe, the Middle East and Africa. Geely Automobile operates as a subsidiary of Zhejian Geely Holding Group Co., Ltd.

FINANCIAL DATA:

Note: Data for latest year may not have been available at press time.

In U.S. $	2018	2017	2016	2015	2014	2013
Revenue	15,485,830,000	13,476,000,000	7,804,511,000	4,378,397,000	3,158,084,000	4,170,551,000
R&D Expense						
Operating Income	2,087,989,000	1,747,196,000	812,461,600	375,415,900	267,455,300	461,469,200
Operating Margin %		.13%	.10%	.09%	.08%	.11%
SGA Expense	1,205,862,000	1,013,820,000	735,483,600	543,849,700	439,156,500	492,104,900
Net Income	1,823,693,000	1,544,835,000	742,714,000	328,402,900	207,831,600	386,892,500
Operating Cash Flow	2,023,000,000	1,742,380,000	1,211,285,000	1,076,332,000	295,342,600	517,414,200
Capital Expenditure	1,092,973,000	1,110,156,000	471,282,400	538,785,600	351,658,300	293,743,200
EBITDA	2,540,324,000	2,153,332,000	1,158,401,000	598,662,300	421,039,000	651,046,600
Return on Assets %		.14%	.09%	.06%	.04%	.08%
Return on Equity %		.36%	.23%	.12%	.09%	.18%
Debt to Equity			0.085	0.099	0.105	

CONTACT INFORMATION:

Phone: 852-2598-3333 Fax: 852-2598-3399
Toll-Free:
Address: 23 Harbour Rd., 23/Fl, Great Eagle Centre Room, Wanchai, 2301 Hong Kong

STOCK TICKER/OTHER:

Stock Ticker: GELYY Exchange: PINX
Employees: 52,400 Fiscal Year Ends: 12/31
Parent Company: Zhejian Geely Holding Group Co Ltd

SALARIES/BONUSES:

Top Exec. Salary: $ Bonus: $
Second Exec. Salary: $ Bonus: $

OTHER THOUGHTS:

Estimated Female Officers or Directors:
Hot Spot for Advancement for Women/Minorities:

General Motors Company (GM)

www.gm.com

NAIC Code: 336111

TYPES OF BUSINESS:

Automobile Manufacturing
Security & Information Services
Automotive Electronics
Financing & Insurance
Parts & Service
Transmissions
Engines
Locomotives

BRANDS/DIVISIONS/AFFILIATES:

General Motors Financial Company Inc
OnStar LLC
Maven
GM Cruise
Buick
Cadillac
Chevrolet
GMC

CONTACTS: *Note: Officers with more than one job title may be intentionally listed here more than once.*

Daniel Ammann, CEO, Subsidiary
Mary Barra, CEO
Dhivya Suryadevara, CFO
Christopher Hatto, Chief Accounting Officer
Alicia Boler-Davis, Executive VP, Divisional
Craig Glidden, Executive VP
Barry Engle, Executive VP
Alan Batey, Executive VP
Matthew Tsien, Executive VP
Mark Reuss, President

GROWTH PLANS/SPECIAL FEATURES:

General Motors Company (GM) is engaged in the worldwide design, production and marketing of cars, crossovers, trucks and automotive parts. GM's automotive operations are grouped into two segments: GM North America, which derived 75.5% of vehicle sales in 2018; and GM International, 24.5%. GM North America serves customers in the U.S., Mexico and Canada, and develops, manufactures and/or markets vehicles under the Buick, Cadillac, Chevrolet and GMC brands. GM International develops, manufactures and/or markets vehicles under the Buick, Cadillac, Chevrolet, GMC and Holden brands. This division also has equity ownership stakes in entities located in China, which develop, manufacture and/or market vehicles under the Baojun, Buick, Cadillac, Chevrolet, Jiefang and Wuling brands. Subsidiary General Motors Financial Company, Inc. provides automotive financing services. OnStar, LLC provides subscription-based and complementary services to more than 20 million connected vehicles globally. OnStar products include connected safety, security and mobility solutions for retail and fleet customers, including automatic crash response, stolen vehicle assistance, roadside assistance, dealer maintenance notifications, remote door unlock, turn-by-turn navigation, vehicle location services, hands-free calling, smart driver and more. Maven is GM's shared vehicle marketplace that provides members with on-demand access to ride- and car-sharing vehicles through: Maven Gig and Maven Car Sharing. Last, GM Cruise is responsible for the development and commercialization of autonomous vehicle technology, as well as an autonomous vehicle (in partnership with Honda Motor Co., Ltd.).

FINANCIAL DATA: *Note: Data for latest year may not have been available at press time.*

In U.S. $	2018	2017	2016	2015	2014	2013
Revenue	147,049,000,000	145,588,000,000	166,380,000,000	152,356,000,000	155,929,000,000	155,427,000,000
R&D Expense						
Operating Income	4,445,000,000	10,016,000,000	9,545,000,000	4,897,000,000	1,650,000,000	5,672,000,000
Operating Margin %		.07%	.06%	.03%	.01%	.04%
SGA Expense	9,650,000,000	9,575,000,000	11,710,000,000	13,405,000,000	12,158,000,000	12,382,000,000
Net Income	8,014,000,000	-3,864,000,000	9,427,000,000	9,687,000,000	3,949,000,000	5,346,000,000
Operating Cash Flow	15,256,000,000	17,328,000,000	16,545,000,000	11,978,000,000	10,058,000,000	12,630,000,000
Capital Expenditure	25,497,000,000	27,633,000,000	29,166,000,000	23,032,000,000	11,867,000,000	9,819,000,000
EBITDA	22,873,000,000	24,699,000,000	22,664,000,000	16,178,000,000	11,887,000,000	15,833,000,000
Return on Assets %		-.02%	.05%	.05%	.02%	.02%
Return on Equity %		-.10%	.23%	.26%	.07%	.12%
Debt to Equity		1.921	1.268	1.092	0.898	0.558

CONTACT INFORMATION:

Phone: 313 556-5000 Fax:
Toll-Free:
Address: 300 Renaissance Ctr., Detroit, MI 48265-3000 United States

STOCK TICKER/OTHER:

Stock Ticker: GM
Employees: 135,000
Parent Company:
Exchange: NYS
Fiscal Year Ends: 12/31

SALARIES/BONUSES:

Top Exec. Salary: $2,100,000 Bonus: $
Second Exec. Salary: $1,450,000 Bonus: $

OTHER THOUGHTS:

Estimated Female Officers or Directors: 8
Hot Spot for Advancement for Women/Minorities: Y

General Motors of Canada Limited

www.gm.ca

NAIC Code: 336111

TYPES OF BUSINESS:

Automobile Manufacturing
Car & Truck Assembly
Parts Manufacturing & Assembly

BRANDS/DIVISIONS/AFFILIATES:

General Motors Company
Chevrolet
Buick
GMC
Cadillac

GROWTH PLANS/SPECIAL FEATURES:

General Motors of Canada Limited (GM Canada), a subsidiary of General Motors Company (GM) assembles and manufactures cars, trucks, engines and components. Brands produced by the firm include Chevrolet, Buick, GMC and Cadillac, as well as fleet vehicles. As of mid-2019, the firm's Oshawa assembly plant is being transformed toward mobility. In May 2019, GM Canada and Unifor announced a transformation agreement that will transform the Oshawa assembly operations to parts and manufacturing and advanced vehicle testing. Part of the plant will be converted into a test track for autonomous and advanced technology vehicles.

Employee benefits include tuition assistance, group insurance coverage, pension plan, comprehensive health care, a savings program, employee discounts and an employee and family assistance program.

CONTACTS: *Note: Officers with more than one job title may be intentionally listed here more than once.*

Travis Hester, Managing Dir.
Amy Martin, VP-Finance
Scott Bell, VP-Mktg. & Sales
Neil J. Macdonald, General Counsel
Neil J. Macdonald, VP-Corp. Affairs
Rick Westenberg, VP-Finance

FINANCIAL DATA: *Note: Data for latest year may not have been available at press time.*

In U.S. $	2018	2017	2016	2015	2014	2013
Revenue						
R&D Expense						
Operating Income						
Operating Margin %						
SGA Expense						
Net Income						
Operating Cash Flow						
Capital Expenditure						
EBITDA						
Return on Assets %						
Return on Equity %						
Debt to Equity						

CONTACT INFORMATION:

Phone: 905-644-5000 Fax: 905-644-4762
Toll-Free: 800-463-7483
Address: 1908 Colonel Sam Dr., Oshawa, ON L1H 8P7 Canada

STOCK TICKER/OTHER:

Stock Ticker: Subsidiary
Exchange:
Employees: 9,750
Fiscal Year Ends: 12/31
Parent Company: General Motors Company (GM)

SALARIES/BONUSES:

Top Exec. Salary: $ Bonus: $
Second Exec. Salary: $ Bonus: $

OTHER THOUGHTS:

Estimated Female Officers or Directors: 1
Hot Spot for Advancement for Women/Minorities:

Gentex Corporation

www.gentex.com

NAIC Code: 336300

TYPES OF BUSINESS:

Specialty Automobile Parts Manufacturer
Electro-Optic Technology
Rearview Mirrors & Mirror Sub-Assemblies
Headlight Systems
Smoke Alarms & Smoke Detectors
Electrochromic Window Shades

BRANDS/DIVISIONS/AFFILIATES:

HomeLink
HomeLink Connect
ActiveIRIS

CONTACTS: *Note: Officers with more than one job title may be intentionally listed here more than once.*

Steve Downing, CEO
Kevin Nash, CFO
Neil Boehm, Chief Technology Officer
James Wallace, Director
Scott Ryan, General Counsel
James Hollars, Independent Director
Matthew Chiodo, Vice President, Divisional

GROWTH PLANS/SPECIAL FEATURES:

Gentex Corporation is a global high-tech electronics company, specializing in a broad spectrum of technologies and processes that deliver products to the automotive, aerospace and fire protection industries. For the automotive industry, Gentex designs and manufactures automatic-dimming rearview and non-dimming mirrors and electronics. The electrochromic automatic-dimming rearview mirrors darken to reduce glare and improve visibility for the driver. These interior mirrors can also include additional electronic features such as compass, microphones, HomeLink applications (see below), lighting assist and driver assist forward safety camera systems, various lighting systems, telematic systems and a variety of displays. This division also ships interior non-automatic-dimming rearview mirrors with and without features. HomeLink is a wireless vehicle/home communications product that enables users to remotely activate doors, lighting, security systems and other connected things. HomeLink Connect is a home automation app that pairs with the vehicle and allows drivers to operate home automation devices from the vehicle's center console display. Gentex has a license agreement with Fingerprint Cards AB to deploy its ActiveIRIS iris-scanning biometric technology in automotive applications. For the aerospace industry, Gentex manufactures and sells variable dimmable windows for the passenger compartment on the Boeing 787 Dreamliner and 777X aircraft. For the fire protection industry, the firm manufactures photoelectric smoke detectors and alarms, visual signaling alarms, photoelectric smoke detectors and electrochemical carbon monoxide alarms, electrochemical carbon monoxide detectors and alarms, audible and visual signaling alarms, and bells and speakers for use in fire detection systems in office buildings, hotels and other commercial and residential establishments. Gentex owns 38 U.S. registered trademarks and 635 U.S. patents, and 309 foreign registered trademarks and 787 foreign patents. Genetex's manufacturing facilities are located in Zeeland and Holland, Michigan.

Gentex offers comprehensive health benefits, 401(k) and retirement plans, and a variety of employee assistance programs.

FINANCIAL DATA: *Note: Data for latest year may not have been available at press time.*

In U.S. $	2018	2017	2016	2015	2014	2013
Revenue	1,834,064,000	1,794,873,000	1,678,925,000	1,543,618,000	1,375,501,000	1,171,864,000
R&D Expense	107,134,900	99,726,440	94,238,030	88,392,920	84,175,740	76,495,050
Operating Income	508,125,500	523,358,300	511,742,900	458,766,400	398,834,200	304,741,800
Operating Margin %		.29%	.30%	.30%	.29%	.26%
SGA Expense	75,206,280	71,443,470	62,471,280	56,616,700	55,879,780	49,496,040
Net Income	437,883,100	406,791,900	347,591,300	318,469,900	288,604,600	222,930,000
Operating Cash Flow	552,418,600	501,002,800	471,464,800	351,578,400	327,223,100	317,338,800
Capital Expenditure	85,990,570	104,040,900	120,955,600	97,941,760	72,518,980	55,380,460
EBITDA	610,312,400	622,929,300	600,330,400	539,365,600	476,210,500	367,596,000
Return on Assets %		.17%	.16%	.15%	.15%	.15%
Return on Equity %		.21%	.19%	.19%	.20%	.18%
Debt to Equity			0.093	0.131	0.164	0.20

CONTACT INFORMATION:

Phone: 616 772-1800 Fax: 616 772-7348
Toll-Free:
Address: 600 N. Centennial St., Zeeland, MI 49464 United States

STOCK TICKER/OTHER:

Stock Ticker: GNTX
Employees: 5,315
Parent Company:
Exchange: NAS
Fiscal Year Ends: 12/31

SALARIES/BONUSES:

Top Exec. Salary: $618,173 Bonus: $180,000
Second Exec. Salary: $327,075 Bonus: $90,000

OTHER THOUGHTS:

Estimated Female Officers or Directors: 1
Hot Spot for Advancement for Women/Minorities:

Gentherm Incorporated

NAIC Code: 336300

www.gentherm.com

TYPES OF BUSINESS:

Automobile Parts Manufacturing
Thermoelectric Devices
Climate Control Seats
Temperature Controlled Mattresses

BRANDS/DIVISIONS/AFFILIATES:

GROWTH PLANS/SPECIAL FEATURES:

Gentherm Incorporated is a global technology and industry leader in the design, development and manufacturing of innovative thermal management technologies. For the automotive industry, Gentherm produces automotive climate control seat products, seat heaters, steering wheel heaters, automotive cables, battery thermal management products, electronics and other related products. For the industrial industry, Gentherm performs advanced research and development on thermal management systems, including those that utilize new proprietary comfort software algorithems, to enhance the efficiency and functionality of the company's automotive heating and cooling products. This division includes government-sponsored research projects. As of December 31, 2018, Gentherm held more than 635 issued patents, of which 273 were U.S. patents and 363 were foreign, and 17 were held jointly with other companies. In early-2019, Gentherm sold its Cincinnati Sub-Zero industrial test chamber business to Weiss Technik North America, Inc. for $47.5 million.

CONTACTS: *Note: Officers with more than one job title may be intentionally listed here more than once.*

Phillip Eyler, CEO
Matteo Anversa, CFO
Francois Castaing, Chairman of the Board
Mark Potesta, Chief Technology Officer
Kenneth Phillips, General Counsel
Barbara Runyon, Other Executive Officer
Frithjof Oldorff, President, Divisional
Ryan Gaul, Senior VP, Divisional
Paul Giberson, Senior VP, Divisional
Yijing Brentano, Senior VP, Divisional

FINANCIAL DATA: *Note: Data for latest year may not have been available at press time.*

In U.S. $	2018	2017	2016	2015	2014	2013
Revenue	1,038,259,000	985,683,000	917,600,000	856,445,000	811,300,000	662,082,000
R&D Expense	79,900,000	82,478,000	72,923,000	59,604,000	57,526,000	49,873,000
Operating Income	87,560,000	98,113,000	106,862,000	121,319,000	99,509,000	51,994,000
Operating Margin %		.10%	.12%	.14%	.12%	.08%
SGA Expense	127,152,000	130,522,000	115,252,000	95,456,000	84,647,000	72,895,000
Net Income	41,899,000	35,227,000	76,598,000	95,393,000	70,119,000	33,820,000
Operating Cash Flow	118,434,000	49,880,000	108,400,000	104,712,000	80,335,000	59,794,000
Capital Expenditure	41,541,000	50,785,000	66,316,000	55,490,000	38,887,000	35,861,000
EBITDA	113,699,000	119,112,000	151,584,000	162,577,000	132,512,000	81,022,000
Return on Assets %		.04%	.10%	.16%	.13%	.07%
Return on Equity %		.07%	.18%	.28%	.27%	.16%
Debt to Equity		0.255	0.368	0.242	0.29	0.262

CONTACT INFORMATION:

Phone: 248-504-0500 Fax: 248-348-9735
Toll-Free:
Address: 21680 Haggerty Rd., Ste. 101, Northville, MI 48167 United States

STOCK TICKER/OTHER:

Stock Ticker: THRM
Employees: 11,685
Parent Company:
Exchange: NAS
Fiscal Year Ends: 12/31

SALARIES/BONUSES:

Top Exec. Salary: $750,000 Bonus: $1,000,000
Second Exec. Salary: $404,330 Bonus: $100,000

OTHER THOUGHTS:

Estimated Female Officers or Directors: 1
Hot Spot for Advancement for Women/Minorities:

Genuine Parts Company

www.genpt.com

NAIC Code: 423120

TYPES OF BUSINESS:

Auto Parts, Distribution
Industrial Replacement Parts
Office Products Distribution
Electrical & Electronic Materials

BRANDS/DIVISIONS/AFFILIATES:

Motion Industries Inc
SP Richards Company
NAPA
Traction
Repco
Hennig Fahrzeugteile Group
Axis New England
PartsPoint Group

CONTACTS: *Note: Officers with more than one job title may be intentionally listed here more than once.*

Paul Donahue, CEO
Carol Yancey, CFO
Jerry Nix, Director
Kevin Herron, President, Divisional
Scott Sonnemaker, President, Geographical
Randall Breaux, President, Subsidiary
James Neill, Senior VP, Divisional

GROWTH PLANS/SPECIAL FEATURES:

Genuine Parts Company (GPC) distributes automotive and industrial replacement parts, office products and electrical/electronic materials. The company operates through three segments: automotive parts, industrial parts, and business products. The automotive parts segment distributes related parts and accessory items in the U.S., Canada, Mexico, Europe and Australasia via automotive parts distribution centers under the NAPA, Traction and Repco brand names, as well as others. Automotive parts are provided for substantially all motor vehicle makes and models in service in the U.S., including imported vehicles, trucks, SUVs, buses, motorcycles, recreational vehicles and farm vehicles. This division also distributes replacement parts for small engines, farm equipment and heavy-duty equipment. The industrial parts segment is operated through wholly-owned Motion Industries, Inc., which distributes replacement parts and supplies such as bearings, mechanical and electrical power transmission products, industrial automation, hose, hydraulic and pneumatic components, industrial and safety supplies and material handling products to maintenance, repair and operation (MRO) and original equipment manufacturers (OEM) customers throughout the U.S., Canada and Mexico. The business products segment operates through wholly-owned S. P. Richards Company, which is engaged in the wholesale distribution of a broad line of office and other business-related products through a diverse customer base of resellers. These products are used in businesses, schools, offices and other institutions, and fall into general categories such as office furniture, technology products, general office, school supplies, cleaning/janitorial, breakroom supplies, safety/security items, healthcare products and disposable food service products. In the first half of 2019, GPC acquired Hennig Fahrzeugteile Group, Axis New England, Axis New York, PartsPoint Group, and Inenco Group. In addition, GPC agreed to sell its EIS, Inc. subsidiary to Audax Private Equity.

GPC offers comprehensive health benefits; 401(k) and stock purchase plans; and various employee assistance programs.

FINANCIAL DATA: *Note: Data for latest year may not have been available at press time.*

In U.S. $	2018	2017	2016	2015	2014	2013
Revenue	18,735,070,000	16,308,800,000	15,339,710,000	15,280,040,000	15,341,650,000	14,077,840,000
R&D Expense						
Operating Income	1,109,715,000	1,019,639,000	1,069,772,000	1,124,414,000	1,124,226,000	1,058,236,000
Operating Margin %		.06%	.07%	.07%	.07%	.08%
SGA Expense	4,615,290,000	3,705,136,000	3,370,833,000	3,277,390,000	3,314,030,000	3,019,036,000
Net Income	810,474,000	616,757,000	687,240,000	705,672,000	711,286,000	684,959,000
Operating Cash Flow	1,145,164,000	815,043,000	946,078,000	1,159,373,000	790,145,000	1,056,731,000
Capital Expenditure	232,422,000	156,760,000	160,643,000	109,544,000	107,681,000	124,063,000
EBITDA	1,419,172,000	1,218,445,000	1,242,911,000	1,287,018,000	1,291,140,000	1,205,232,000
Return on Assets %		.06%	.08%	.09%	.09%	.09%
Return on Equity %		.19%	.22%	.22%	.21%	.22%
Debt to Equity		0.747	0.172	0.079	0.151	0.149

CONTACT INFORMATION:

Phone: 770 953-1700 Fax: 770 956-2211
Toll-Free:
Address: 2999 Wildwood Pkwy., Atlanta, GA 30339 United States

STOCK TICKER/OTHER:

Stock Ticker: GPC
Employees: 40,000
Parent Company:
Exchange: NYS
Fiscal Year Ends: 12/31

SALARIES/BONUSES:

Top Exec. Salary: $1,083,750 Bonus: $
Second Exec. Salary: $562,500 Bonus: $

OTHER THOUGHTS:

Estimated Female Officers or Directors: 2
Hot Spot for Advancement for Women/Minorities: Y

Georg Fischer Ltd

NAIC Code: 336300

www.georgfischer.com

TYPES OF BUSINESS:

Automotive Components
Iron Casting
Manufacturing Technology
Machine Tools
Piping Systems
Design
Control systems

BRANDS/DIVISIONS/AFFILIATES:

CONTACTS:

Note: Officers with more than one job title may be intentionally listed here more than once.

Andreas Muller, CEO
Mads Joergensen, CFO
Beat Romer, Head-Corp. Comm.
Daniel Bosiger, Head-Investor Rel.
Josef Edbauer, Head-Automotive
Pietro Lori, Head-Piping Systems
Pascal Boillat, Head-GF AgieCharmilles
Andreas Koopmann, Chmn.

GROWTH PLANS/SPECIAL FEATURES:

Georg Fischer Ltd. is a design and manufacturing firm with 140 subsidiaries operating through three divisions: casting solutions, piping systems and machining solutions. The casting solutions division designs and manufactures cast components and systems for the global automotive industry, aerospace and energy markets, off-highway vehicles as well as for industrial applications. The lightweight components are produced using various manufacturing technologies, from development to the ready-to-mount processes. This division manufactures at 14 production sites in Germany, Austria, Romania, Switzerland, China and the U.S., and its R&D centers are located in Switzerland and China. The piping systems division supplies piping systems made of plastics and metal. It focuses on system solutions and components for the safe transport of water, chemicals and gases, as well as corresponding services. Products include fittings, valves, pipes, automation and jointing technologies, covering all applications of the water cycle. Last, the machining solutions division provides complete solutions to the tool and mold-making industry, specializing in the manufacture of precision components. Its product portfolio includes milling, wire-cutting and die-sinking electrical discharge machining (EDM) machines. This division also offers spindles, laser texturing, additive manufacturing, tooling and automation as well as digitalization solutions and customer services. Primary machining customers include the aerospace, information and communication technology (ICT), medical and automotive industries. This division is present in more than 50 countries, and operates production facilities and R&D centers in Switzerland, the U.S., Sweden and China.

FINANCIAL DATA:

Note: Data for latest year may not have been available at press time.

In U.S. $	2018	2017	2016	2015	2014	2013
Revenue	4,643,400,000	4,250,570,000	3,673,690,000	3,764,608,920	4,069,203,960	4,262,801,797
R&D Expense						
Operating Income						
Operating Margin %						
SGA Expense						
Net Income	283,357,000	258,107,000	220,774,000	2,047,675,825	197,294,737	164,126,945
Operating Cash Flow						
Capital Expenditure						
EBITDA						
Return on Assets %						
Return on Equity %						
Debt to Equity						

CONTACT INFORMATION:

Phone: 41 526311111 Fax: 41 526312847
Toll-Free:
Address: Amsler-Laffon-Strasse 9, Schaffhausen, CH-8201 Switzerland

STOCK TICKER/OTHER:

Stock Ticker: GFIN
Exchange: Frankfurt
Employees: 15,027
Fiscal Year Ends: 12/31
Parent Company:

SALARIES/BONUSES:

Top Exec. Salary: $ Bonus: $
Second Exec. Salary: $ Bonus: $

OTHER THOUGHTS:

Estimated Female Officers or Directors: 2
Hot Spot for Advancement for Women/Minorities: Y

GKN plc

NAIC Code: 336300

www.gknplc.com

TYPES OF BUSINESS:

Automobile Parts-Manufacturing & Engineering
Aerospace Engineering
Driveshaft System Products
Powder Metallurgy
Off Highway Components
Engineering Support Services
Helicopters & Military Vehicles
Propulsion System Components

BRANDS/DIVISIONS/AFFILIATES:

Melrose Industries plc

GROWTH PLANS/SPECIAL FEATURES:

GKN plc is a global engineering company. The firm operates four primary segments: aerospace, automotive, powder metallurgy and wheels & structures. The aerospace segment is a multi-technology Tier 1 aerospace supplier, with 50 manufacturing locations in 14 countries, serving more than 90% of the world's aircraft and engine manufacturers. The automotive segment provides conventional, all-wheel and electrified drive systems and solutions. The powder metallurgy segment provides high-precision metal solutions for automotive and industrial applications. The wheels & structures segment manufactures off-highway wheels, and is a major supplier of structural assemblies. During 2018, GKN was acquired by Melrose Industries plc.

CONTACTS: *Note: Officers with more than one job title may be intentionally listed here more than once.*

Nigel Stein, CEO
Adam Walker, Finance
Judith Felton, Corp. Sec.
William Seeger, Jr., Dir.-Finance
Andrew Reynolds Smith, CEO-Automotive & Power Metallurgy
Marcus Bryson, CEO-Aerospace & Land Systems
Michael Turner, Chmn.

FINANCIAL DATA: *Note: Data for latest year may not have been available at press time.*

In U.S. $	2018	2017	2016	2015	2014	2013
Revenue		12,299,376,640	11,219,635,200	9,196,235,776	8,879,562,752	9,075,416,064
R&D Expense						
Operating Income						
Operating Margin %						
SGA Expense						
Net Income		639,704,896	307,770,560	250,540,496	214,930,688	502,352,768
Operating Cash Flow						
Capital Expenditure						
EBITDA						
Return on Assets %						
Return on Equity %						
Debt to Equity						

CONTACT INFORMATION:

Phone: 44 1527517715 Fax: 44 1527517700
Toll-Free:
Address: Ipsley House, Ipsley Church Ln., P.O. Box 55, Worcestershire, B98 OTL United Kingdom

STOCK TICKER/OTHER:

Stock Ticker: GKN
Employees: 74,200
Parent Company:
Exchange: DE
Fiscal Year Ends: 12/31

SALARIES/BONUSES:

Top Exec. Salary: $ Bonus: $
Second Exec. Salary: $ Bonus: $

OTHER THOUGHTS:

Estimated Female Officers or Directors: 2
Hot Spot for Advancement for Women/Minorities:

GM Cruise LLC (Cruise)

getcruise.com

NAIC Code: 511210

TYPES OF BUSINESS:

Technology for Self-Driving Vehicles
Self-Driving Hardware
Self-Driving Software

BRANDS/DIVISIONS/AFFILIATES:

GM Cruise LLC
Cruise
Chevy Bolt
Cruise Anywhere

GROWTH PLANS/SPECIAL FEATURES:

GM Cruise LLC, doing business as Cruise, is a self-driving car company based in San Francisco, CA. The firm is a subsidiary of the General Motors Company (GM) and forms the core of GM's self-driving interests. Cruise's hardware and software for the self-driving car are designed to be fully integrated into vehicles. Cruise's Chevy Bolt; designed, engineered and manufactured by GM in Orion; Michigan, is made with AV software and hardware that are unique to the vehicle itself. In fact, 40% of the Bolt is composed of parts unique to self-driving. With a fleet of approximately 30 vehicles and a permit from the California Department of Motor Vehicles, Cruise has been testing its self-driving technology throughout the streets of San Francisco. Recently, through its Cruise Anywhere program, the firm lets its San Francisco employees use its self-driving cars as a rideshare service.

CONTACTS: *Note: Officers with more than one job title may be intentionally listed here more than once.*

Dan Ammann, CEO
Kyle Vogt, Pres.
Geoff Richardson, CFO
Lucas Watson, CMO
Arden Hoffman, Chief People Officer
Dan Kan, Chief Product Officer

FINANCIAL DATA: *Note: Data for latest year may not have been available at press time.*

In U.S. $	2018	2017	2016	2015	2014	2013
Revenue						
R&D Expense						
Operating Income						
Operating Margin %						
SGA Expense						
Net Income						
Operating Cash Flow						
Capital Expenditure						
EBITDA						
Return on Assets %						
Return on Equity %						
Debt to Equity						

CONTACT INFORMATION:

Phone: 415-335-4097 Fax:
Toll-Free:
Address: 201 11th St., San Francisco, CA 94103 United States

STOCK TICKER/OTHER:

Stock Ticker: Subsidiary
Exchange:
Employees:
Fiscal Year Ends:
Parent Company: General Motors Company

SALARIES/BONUSES:

Top Exec. Salary: $ Bonus: $
Second Exec. Salary: $ Bonus: $

OTHER THOUGHTS:

Estimated Female Officers or Directors:
Hot Spot for Advancement for Women/Minorities:

GM Korea

www.gm-korea.co.kr

NAIC Code: 336111

TYPES OF BUSINESS:

Automobile Manufacturing
Auto Marketing

BRANDS/DIVISIONS/AFFILIATES:

General Motors Company (GM)
Chevrolet

GROWTH PLANS/SPECIAL FEATURES:

GM Korea designs, develops, produces and sells vehicles in South Korea. The company has been 96%-owned by General Motors Company since 2002. GM Korea manufactures passenger vehicles, sports cars and light commercial vehicles primarily under the Chevrolet brand. The firm's luxury division also offers Cadillac vehicles. GM Korea offers vehicle kits for assembly at GM facilities in China, Uzbekistan, Mexico, India, Columbia, Russia and other countries. GM Korea exports to automakers internationally. Its production facilities are located in Bupyeong, Changwon and Boryeong. During 2018, GM Korea closed its Gunsan factory, and a South Korean supplier of Tesla agreed to buy the plant's land and buildings in March 2019. Tesla wants to use it to manufacture electric vehicles for the U.S. and European markets.

CONTACTS: *Note: Officers with more than one job title may be intentionally listed here more than once.*

Kaher Kazem, CEO
Sergio Rocha, Pres.

FINANCIAL DATA: *Note: Data for latest year may not have been available at press time.*

In U.S. $	2018	2017	2016	2015	2014	2013
Revenue	9,518,620,000	10,019,600,000	10,608,526,500	11,166,870,000	11,754,600,000	
R&D Expense						
Operating Income						
Operating Margin %						
SGA Expense						
Net Income		-842,768,000	-547,000,000	-855,000,000	-303,000,000	
Operating Cash Flow						
Capital Expenditure						
EBITDA						
Return on Assets %						
Return on Equity %						
Debt to Equity						

CONTACT INFORMATION:

Phone: 8280-3000-5000 Fax: 833-2520-4613
Toll-Free:
Address: 233 Chongcheon-dong, Bupyeong-gu, Incheon, 403-714 South Korea

STOCK TICKER/OTHER:

Stock Ticker: Subsidiary
Exchange:
Employees: 13,000
Fiscal Year Ends: 12/31
Parent Company: General Motors Company (GM)

SALARIES/BONUSES:

Top Exec. Salary: $ Bonus: $
Second Exec. Salary: $ Bonus: $

OTHER THOUGHTS:

Estimated Female Officers or Directors:
Hot Spot for Advancement for Women/Minorities:

Goodyear Tire & Rubber Company (The)

www.goodyear.com

NAIC Code: 326211

TYPES OF BUSINESS:

Tire Manufacturing
Automotive Service Shops
Resins & Latex
Synthetic Polymers
Industrial Chemicals
Belts & Hoses
Blimps
Retail Sales

BRANDS/DIVISIONS/AFFILIATES:

Goodyear
Dunlop
Kelly
Fulda
Debica
Sava

CONTACTS: *Note: Officers with more than one job title may be intentionally listed here more than once.*

Richard Kramer, CEO
Evan Scocos, Chief Accounting Officer
Christopher Helsel, Chief Technology Officer
Laura Thompson, Executive VP
Darren Wells, Executive VP
David Bialosky, General Counsel
Stephen McClellan, President, Geographical
Ryan Patterson, President, Geographical
Christopher Delaney, President, Geographical
Laura Duda, Senior VP, Divisional
Jonathan Bellissimo, Senior VP, Divisional
Gary VanderLind, Senior VP, Divisional

GROWTH PLANS/SPECIAL FEATURES:

The Goodyear Tire & Rubber Company (Goodyear) is a leading manufacturer of tires and rubber-related chemicals. Goodyear is also one of the world's largest operators of commercial truck service and tire retreading centers. It operates approximately 1,000 tire and auto service center outlets and manufactures products at 47 manufacturing facilities in 21 countries. Goodyear is comprised of three geographic business segments: Americas; Europe, Middle East and Africa (EMEA); and Asia Pacific. Goodyear manufactures rubber tires for automobiles, trucks, buses, aviation, motorcycles, farm implements, earthmoving and mining equipment, industrial equipment and numerous other applications. The company sells tires under the Goodyear, Dunlop, Kelly, Fulda, Debica and Sava brands and various other Goodyear-owned brands and the private-label brands of certain customers. It also retreads truck, aviation and off-road tires; manufactures and sells tread rubber and other tire retreading materials; provides automotive repair services; and manufactures and sells flaps for truck tires and other types of tires. Approximately 85% of net sales are from the sale of new tires.

FINANCIAL DATA: *Note: Data for latest year may not have been available at press time.*

In U.S. $	2018	2017	2016	2015	2014	2013
Revenue	15,475,000,000	15,377,000,000	15,158,000,000	16,443,000,000	18,138,000,000	19,540,000,000
R&D Expense						
Operating Income	1,149,000,000	1,221,000,000	1,596,000,000	1,576,000,000	1,392,000,000	1,287,000,000
Operating Margin %		.08%	.10%	.09%	.08%	.07%
SGA Expense	2,312,000,000	2,302,000,000	2,407,000,000	2,614,000,000	2,720,000,000	2,758,000,000
Net Income	693,000,000	346,000,000	1,264,000,000	307,000,000	2,452,000,000	629,000,000
Operating Cash Flow	916,000,000	1,158,000,000	1,504,000,000	1,687,000,000	340,000,000	938,000,000
Capital Expenditure	811,000,000	881,000,000	996,000,000	983,000,000	923,000,000	1,168,000,000
EBITDA	2,110,000,000	1,994,000,000	2,306,000,000	1,718,000,000	1,847,000,000	1,927,000,000
Return on Assets %		.02%	.08%	.02%	.14%	.03%
Return on Equity %		.08%	.30%	.08%	1.04%	1.23%
Debt to Equity		1.103	1.065	1.306	1.722	5.571

CONTACT INFORMATION:

Phone: 330 796-2121 Fax: 330 796-2222
Toll-Free:
Address: 200 Innovation Way, Akron, OH 44316 United States

STOCK TICKER/OTHER:

Stock Ticker: GT
Exchange: NAS
Employees: 66,000
Fiscal Year Ends: 12/31
Parent Company:

SALARIES/BONUSES:

Top Exec. Salary: $1,300,000 Bonus: $
Second Exec. Salary: $195,417 Bonus: $500,000

OTHER THOUGHTS:

Estimated Female Officers or Directors: 4
Hot Spot for Advancement for Women/Minorities: Y

Grammer AG

www.grammer.com

NAIC Code: 336360

TYPES OF BUSINESS:

Motor Vehicle Seating and Interior Trim Manufacturing
Automotive Interiors

BRANDS/DIVISIONS/AFFILIATES:

CONTACTS:
Note: Officers with more than one job title may be intentionally listed here more than once.

Thorsten Seehars, CEO
Jens Ohlenschlager, COO
Jurate Keblyte, CFO
Manfred Pretscher, Head-R&D
Manfred Pretscher, Head-Oper.
Volker Walprecht, Head-Finance
Klaus Probst, Chmn.

GROWTH PLANS/SPECIAL FEATURES:

Grammer AG is a Germany-based developer and manufacturer of components and systems for car interiors as well as driver and passenger seats for off-road vehicles, trucks, buses and trains. The company operates in two business segments: automotive and commercial. The automotive segment produces headrests, armrests, center consoles, interior components and functional plastics to auto manufacturers and system suppliers worldwide. The commercial segment develops and produces driver and passenger seats for agricultural and construction machinery, forklifts, trucks, buses and trains worldwide. Grammer is present on four continents, with more than 50 production, distribution and logistics sites in 20 countries across the Americas, Europe, the Middle East, Africa and Asia-Pacific. In early-2019, Grammer and Allygrow Technologies formed a joint venture in India to develop products and solutions for the automotive and commercial vehicle industry through a new tech center in Pune.

FINANCIAL DATA:
Note: Data for latest year may not have been available at press time.

In U.S. $	2018	2017	2016	2015	2014	2013
Revenue	2,060,775,000	1,977,930,000	1,877,196,000	1,578,483,000	1,512,287,000	1,401,306,000
R&D Expense						
Operating Income	53,962,580	73,595,000	80,876,890	47,226,530	63,159,880	64,227,190
Operating Margin %						
SGA Expense	204,047,800	182,238,700	152,921,800	140,487,200	131,003,100	123,831,900
Net Income	25,801,590	35,969,880	49,801,820	26,133,750	38,396,810	33,210,810
Operating Cash Flow	158,953,700	76,667,410	94,959,040	31,928,700	71,988,490	65,858,060
Capital Expenditure	81,863,380	65,415,190	61,912,090	51,544,510	52,196,640	47,380,430
EBITDA	110,172,700	127,927,400	135,196,000	95,490,480	106,023,000	98,458,820
Return on Assets %						
Return on Equity %						
Debt to Equity						

CONTACT INFORMATION:

Phone: 49 9621660 Fax: 49 9621661000
Toll-Free:
Address: Postfach 1454, Amberg, D-92204 Germany

STOCK TICKER/OTHER:

Stock Ticker: GMEGF
Exchange: GREY
Employees: 14,657
Fiscal Year Ends: 12/31
Parent Company:

SALARIES/BONUSES:

Top Exec. Salary: $ Bonus: $
Second Exec. Salary: $ Bonus: $

OTHER THOUGHTS:

Estimated Female Officers or Directors: 1
Hot Spot for Advancement for Women/Minorities:

Great Dane Limited Partnership

www.greatdanetrailers.com

NAIC Code: 336212

TYPES OF BUSINESS:

Manufacturing-Truck Trailers
Used Trailer Sales
Accessories & Apparel
Replacement Parts

BRANDS/DIVISIONS/AFFILIATES:

GROWTH PLANS/SPECIAL FEATURES:

Great Dane Limited Partnership is a leading truck trailer manufacturer in North America, with nine manufacturing plants and 20 sales branches throughout the U.S. The company manufactures high-performance commercial transportation equipment, including dry and refrigerated trailers and truck bodies, as well as steel, aluminum and combo platform trailers. Great Dane's network of corporate-owned branches, full-line independent dealers and parts-only independent distributors offers a broad range of distribution points for new and used trailers, as well as aftermarket services across North and South America. Headquartered in Chicago, Illinois, Great Dane has additional corporate offices in Savannah, Georgia.

CONTACTS: *Note: Officers with more than one job title may be intentionally listed here more than once.*

Dean Engelage, Pres.
John J. Sobota, VP-Finance
Phillip Pines, Pres., Pines Trailers Div.

FINANCIAL DATA: *Note: Data for latest year may not have been available at press time.*

In U.S. $	2018	2017	2016	2015	2014	2013
Revenue						
R&D Expense						
Operating Income						
Operating Margin %						
SGA Expense						
Net Income						
Operating Cash Flow						
Capital Expenditure						
EBITDA						
Return on Assets %						
Return on Equity %						
Debt to Equity						

CONTACT INFORMATION:

Phone: 773-254-5533 Fax:
Toll-Free:
Address: 222 N. LaSalle St., Suite 920, Chicago, IL 60601 United States

STOCK TICKER/OTHER:

Stock Ticker: Private
Employees:
Parent Company:
Exchange:
Fiscal Year Ends: 12/31

SALARIES/BONUSES:

Top Exec. Salary: $ Bonus: $
Second Exec. Salary: $ Bonus: $

OTHER THOUGHTS:

Estimated Female Officers or Directors: 1
Hot Spot for Advancement for Women/Minorities:

Great Wall Motor Company Limited

www.gwm-global.com

NAIC Code: 336112

TYPES OF BUSINESS:

Light Truck and Utility Vehicle Manufacturing
Parts and Accessories

BRANDS/DIVISIONS/AFFILIATES:

Great Wall
Haval
Wingle
C30
P Series

CONTACTS:

Note: Officers with more than one job title may be intentionally listed here more than once.

Xu Hui, Sec.
Jian Hun Wei, Chmn.

GROWTH PLANS/SPECIAL FEATURES:

Great Wall Motor Company Limited is a Chinese firm engaged in the manufacture of automobiles. It is one of China's largest manufacturers of sport utility vehicles (SUVs) and pickups, but also produces sedans and multi-purpose vehicles (MPVs). The company's vehicles are sold under the Great Wall, Haval and WEY brands. Its current sedan models include the Great Wall C30 and C30EV (electric vehicle); SUV models include the Great Wall H6 and M4; and the pickup truck models include the Wingle 5, 6 and 7, as well as the P Series. Great Wall has sales locations across Asia, and offers after-sales services to its customers. The firm has more than 30 holding subsidiaries and four vehicle production bases. Great Wall's annual production capacity is about 1 million vehicles. Additionally, Great Wall Motor has the ability to independently produce core vehicle parts and accessories such as engines and transmissions. The company's technology center comprises a team that designs and develops passenger vehicles and powertrains, and also tests its engines, transmissions and other vehicle parts/components.

FINANCIAL DATA:

Note: Data for latest year may not have been available at press time.

In U.S. $	2018	2017	2016	2015	2014	2013
Revenue	14,208,070,000	14,599,120,000	14,301,600,000	11,034,460,000	9,093,002,000	8,249,457,000
R&D Expense	253,272,900					
Operating Income	961,129,500	786,798,100	1,816,038,000	1,355,757,000	1,329,330,000	1,386,903,000
Operating Margin %		.05%	.13%	.12%	.15%	.17%
SGA Expense	908,199,700	1,361,164,000	1,125,915,000	998,368,400	858,165,600	674,474,800
Net Income	756,503,200	730,350,900	1,532,841,000	1,170,836,000	1,168,250,000	1,194,624,000
Operating Cash Flow	2,861,642,000	-156,415,400	1,283,582,000	1,457,665,000	885,577,500	1,313,165,000
Capital Expenditure	967,906,800	845,863,200	971,052,100	850,863,500	1,050,200,000	1,036,303,000
EBITDA	1,614,689,000	1,414,858,000	2,194,117,000	1,702,013,000	1,645,227,000	1,609,497,000
Return on Assets %		.05%	.13%	.12%	.14%	.17%
Return on Equity %		.10%	.25%	.22%	.26%	.33%
Debt to Equity		0.009	0.001	0.001		

CONTACT INFORMATION:

Phone: 86 3122196670 Fax: 86 3122197680
Toll-Free:
Address: 226 Chaoyang South St., Baoding, Hebei Province 071000 China

STOCK TICKER/OTHER:

Stock Ticker: GWLLF
Employees: 71,617
Parent Company:
Exchange: PINX
Fiscal Year Ends: 12/31

SALARIES/BONUSES:

Top Exec. Salary: $ Bonus: $
Second Exec. Salary: $ Bonus: $

OTHER THOUGHTS:

Estimated Female Officers or Directors:
Hot Spot for Advancement for Women/Minorities:

Group 1 Automotive Inc

www.group1auto.com

NAIC Code: 441110

TYPES OF BUSINESS:

Auto Dealers
Auto Repair Services
Insurance Services
Automotive Replacement Parts
Financing Services
Collision Service Centers

BRANDS/DIVISIONS/AFFILIATES:

CONTACTS:
Note: Officers with more than one job title may be intentionally listed here more than once.

Earl Hesterberg, CEO
John Rickel, CFO
Stephen Quinn, Chairman of the Board
Lincoln Pereira, Director
Daryl Kenningham, President, Divisional
Peter DeLongchamps, Senior VP, Divisional
Frank Grese, Senior VP, Divisional

GROWTH PLANS/SPECIAL FEATURES:

Group 1 Automotive, Inc. is a leading operator in the automotive retail industries, with locations throughout the U.S., the U.K. and Brazil. The company, through its subsidiaries, sells new and used cars and light trucks, provides maintenance and repair services, sells replacement parts and arranges vehicle financing and insurance through its dealerships and franchises. In total, Group 1 owns and operates 184 dealerships, 238 franchises and 48 collision centers (as of July 2019). The dealerships offer approximately 30 brands of automobiles, which may include Toyota, BMW, Ford, Audi, Mercedes-Benz, Honda, Nissan, Lexus, Chevrolet, MINI, Volkswagen, GMC, Hyundai, Jeep, Acura, RAM, Land Rover, Kia, Cadillac, Dodge, Subaru, Jaguar, Buick, Sprinter, Chrysler, SEAT, Lincoln, Mazda, Skoda, Vauxhall, Volvo and Smart. Group 1's dealerships have taken several steps toward building customer confidence in their used vehicle inventory, including participation in manufacturer certification processes. These processes make used vehicles eligible for new vehicle benefits such as new vehicle finance rates and extended manufacturer warranties. In July 2019, Group 1 acquired five Volkswagen franchises in the U.K., which includes one commercial vehicle franchise.

FINANCIAL DATA:
Note: Data for latest year may not have been available at press time.

In U.S. $	2018	2017	2016	2015	2014	2013
Revenue	11,601,360,000	11,123,720,000	10,887,610,000	10,632,510,000	9,937,889,000	8,918,581,000
R&D Expense						
Operating Income	384,966,000	361,378,000	373,072,000	365,900,000	343,630,000	279,864,000
Operating Margin %		.03%	.03%	.03%	.03%	.03%
SGA Expense	1,273,057,000	1,226,195,000	1,170,763,000	1,120,833,000	1,061,964,000	976,856,000
Net Income	157,772,000	213,442,000	147,065,000	93,999,000	93,004,000	113,992,000
Operating Cash Flow	269,978,000	198,925,000	384,857,000	141,047,000	198,288,000	52,372,000
Capital Expenditure	141,033,000	215,832,000	156,521,000	120,252,000	150,392,000	102,858,000
EBITDA	408,153,000	399,808,000	391,468,000	325,577,000	298,051,000	308,359,000
Return on Assets %		.04%	.03%	.02%	.02%	.03%
Return on Equity %		.20%	.15%	.10%	.09%	.11%
Debt to Equity		1.172	1.304	1.311	1.032	0.624

CONTACT INFORMATION:

Phone: 713 647-5700 Fax: 713 647-5858
Toll-Free:
Address: 800 Gessner, Ste. 500, Houston, TX 77024 United States

STOCK TICKER/OTHER:

Stock Ticker: GPI
Exchange: NYS
Employees: 13,500
Fiscal Year Ends: 12/31
Parent Company:

SALARIES/BONUSES:

Top Exec. Salary: $1,150,000 Bonus: $
Second Exec. Salary: $624,000 Bonus: $

OTHER THOUGHTS:

Estimated Female Officers or Directors:
Hot Spot for Advancement for Women/Minorities: Y

Group Lotus plc

www.lotuscars.com

NAIC Code: 336111

TYPES OF BUSINESS:

Automobile Manufacturing
Sports Car Design & Manufacturing
Design & Engineering Services
Consulting Services
Driving Instruction Facilities
New & Pre-owned Sports Car Sales
Automotive Accessories
Lightweight Aluminum Manufacturing

BRANDS/DIVISIONS/AFFILIATES:

Zhejiang Geely Holding Group
Etika Automotive Sdn Bhd
Evija
Evora GT
Evora 400

CONTACTS: *Note: Officers with more than one job title may be intentionally listed here more than once.*

Qingfeng Feng, CEO
Caudio Berro, Dir.-Motorsport
Donato Coco, Dir.-Design
Russell Carr, Head-Lotus Design

GROWTH PLANS/SPECIAL FEATURES:

Group Lotus plc designs, manufactures and sells luxury sports cars. The company's vehicles range from sports cars to racing machines, each of which are hand-built at its factory in Hethel, Norfolk, U.K. The plant builds approximately 2,000 cars each year. Lotus' sports cars include the Evija, the Evora GT and the Evora 400. The vehicles' light weight, advanced suspension and weight distribution capabilities allow for sharp handling, high-speed cornering balance, body and roll control and comfort. The Evija model is an all-electric hypercar, with a maximum speed of more than 200 mph. The Evora GT features functional aerodynamics, bonded aluminum chassis, Bilstein dampers and more, for an immersive driving experience on the road. The Evora 400 produces 400 horsepower from its 3.5-liter supercharged V6 engine, while its weight ratio is combined with an aerodynamic package that maintains zero lift, but increases downforce at high speeds. Interested drivers can experience the agility and precision of Lotus vehicles at the firm's test track in Hethel. Factory tours are also available. Group Lotus provides comprehensive and versatile engineering consultancy services to many of the world's original equipment manufacturers (OEMs) and Tire-1 suppliers. Its high-tech research expertise reaches the areas of advanced powertrain design and validation, lightweight materials, ride and handling. Group Lotus sells its products through a dealer network, with global locations in the U.K., mainland Europe, North America, Japan and China. Zhejiang Geely Holding Group holds a majority stake (51%) in Group Lotus, with the remaining 49% held by Etika Automotive Sdn Bhd.

FINANCIAL DATA: *Note: Data for latest year may not have been available at press time.*

In U.S. $	2018	2017	2016	2015	2014	2013
Revenue	130,710,000	131,250,000	125,000,000	110,521,870	234,486,633	151,281,699
R&D Expense						
Operating Income						
Operating Margin %						
SGA Expense						
Net Income	1,122,500	1,362,400	-26,351,600	-1,338,020	-3,527,000	-436,091,000
Operating Cash Flow						
Capital Expenditure						
EBITDA						
Return on Assets %						
Return on Equity %						
Debt to Equity						

CONTACT INFORMATION:

Phone: 44-1953-608-000 Fax: 44-1953-608-300
Toll-Free:
Address: Potash Ln., Norwich, Norfolk NR14 8EZ United Kingdom

STOCK TICKER/OTHER:

Stock Ticker: Subsidiary
Exchange:
Employees: 1,100
Fiscal Year Ends: 03/31
Parent Company: Zhejiang Geely Holding Group

SALARIES/BONUSES:

Top Exec. Salary: $ Bonus: $
Second Exec. Salary: $ Bonus: $

OTHER THOUGHTS:

Estimated Female Officers or Directors:
Hot Spot for Advancement for Women/Minorities:

Grupo Kuo SAB de CV

NAIC Code: 336350

www.kuo.com.mx

TYPES OF BUSINESS:

Motor Vehicle Transmission and Power Train Parts Manufacturing
Industrial Chemicals & Plastics
Processed Foods
Pork
Aerospace Components
Aftermarket Automotive Components
Synthetic Rubber

BRANDS/DIVISIONS/AFFILIATES:

Herdez Del Fuerte
MegaMex
Keken
Tremec

CONTACTS: *Note: Officers with more than one job title may be intentionally listed here more than once.*

Alejandro de la Barreda Gomez, CEO
Marisol Vazquez-Mellado Mollon, Chief Admin. Officer
Ramon F. Estrada Rivero, Dir.-Legal Affairs
Felipe Varela Hernandez, Dir.-Elastomers Bus. Unit
Cesar Ramos Valdes, Dir.-Plastics Bus. Unit
Benjamin Centurion Diaz, Dir.-Aftermarket Bus. Unit
Ignacio Marco Arboli, Dir.-Dynasol Bus. Unit
Fernando Senderos Mestre, Chmn.

GROWTH PLANS/SPECIAL FEATURES:

Grupo Kuo, SAB de CV is a diversified holding company with interests in consumer products, foods, chemicals, automotive parts and other businesses. Kuo markets its products in 70 countries and comprises 26 manufacturing plants across the globe. The firm's business is divided into three primary units: consumer, chemical and automotive. The consumer business unit is made up of three divisions: pork, Herdez Del Fuerte and MegaMex. The pork division comprises the Keken brand, and produces, markets and distributes pork in the following forms: live, cuts, seasoned meats and frozen. Herdez Del Fuerte is a joint venture between Grupo Kuo and Herdez that produces packaged food products such as canned tuna, tomato puree, canned vegetables and fruits, salsas, fruit juices and other products. MegaMex is a 50-50 joint venture between Herdez Del Fuerte and Hormel Foods, and produces and distributes a variety of Mexican food products (frozen, sauces and guacamole) throughout the U.S. The chemical business unit manufactures: synthetic hule, a synthetic rubber used in a variety of applications (primarily tire and asphalt, but also in adhesives and sealants); and polystyrene, producing more than 160,000 tons per year for customers in the disposable packaging, bags, utensils, personal hygiene and office markets, among others. The polystyrene division also distributes acetone, phenol and styrene. Last, the automotive business unit manufactures: transmissions marketed under the Tremec brand, including manual transmissions for light, medium and heavy use, as well as various related automotive parts and components; and spare parts, including pistons, bearings, seals, brakes, powertrains and other products.

FINANCIAL DATA: *Note: Data for latest year may not have been available at press time.*

In U.S. $	2018	2017	2016	2015	2014	2013
Revenue	1,425,664,000	1,278,879,000	1,129,682,000	1,025,326,000	979,945,900	868,822,300
R&D Expense						
Operating Income	123,063,600	139,726,800	94,462,460	64,597,700	55,029,920	41,000,660
Operating Margin %		.11%	.08%	.10%	.06%	.05%
SGA Expense	76,790,740	71,928,570	67,051,810	66,204,060	50,621,640	40,460,540
Net Income	115,839,700	89,777,910	56,403,360	29,818,360	-36,592,480	64,985,180
Operating Cash Flow	81,378,680	128,975,200	103,742,600	21,967,390	3,431,192	59,876,520
Capital Expenditure	287,589,500	205,596,200	65,533,140	48,863,950	50,092,390	53,953,490
EBITDA	214,398,600	192,388,300	98,298,380	104,612,400	63,404,230	77,260,420
Return on Assets %		.06%	.04%	.02%	-.03%	.05%
Return on Equity %		.17%	.12%	.08%	-.09%	.18%
Debt to Equity		0.89	0.923	1.019	0.829	0.838

CONTACT INFORMATION:

Phone: 52 5552618000 Fax:
Toll-Free:
Address: Paseo de los Tamarindos No. 400-B, Piso 31, Mexico DF, 05120 Mexico

STOCK TICKER/OTHER:

Stock Ticker: GKSDF
Employees: 12,417
Parent Company:
Exchange: GREY
Fiscal Year Ends: 12/31

SALARIES/BONUSES:

Top Exec. Salary: $ Bonus: $
Second Exec. Salary: $ Bonus: $

OTHER THOUGHTS:

Estimated Female Officers or Directors:
Hot Spot for Advancement for Women/Minorities:

GT Technologies Inc

www.gttechnologies.com

NAIC Code: 336300

TYPES OF BUSINESS:

Automotive Systems & Components Manufacturing

BRANDS/DIVISIONS/AFFILIATES:

Industrial Opportunity Partners LLC

CONTACTS:

Note: Officers with more than one job title may be intentionally listed here more than once.

Paul Schwarzbaum, CEO
Daniel Brinker, Sr. VP-Eng.

GROWTH PLANS/SPECIAL FEATURES:

GT Technologies, Inc. designs, develops and manufactures performance-critical valve actuation components and systems for diesel, gasoline and flex fuel engines. The company's primary markets include the power generation, transportation, motorsports and recreational vehicle industries. Its applications range from less than one liter to more than 14 liters in size. GT's products include hydraulic lash adjusting capsules, rocker shaft assemblies, stamped rocker arms and roller finger followers, roller bearings and axles, hydraulic and mechanical roller tappets and valvetrain actuation assemblies with hydraulic lash compensation. For heavy-duty diesel clients, the firm also offers mechanical roller tappets and roller bearings for high pressure fuel injector pumps. GT's products are all custom-designed to address the specific applications and functional requirements of each client. The company is headquartered in Westland, Michigan, with manufacturing and assembly operations in Ohio, Florida and Tennessee (USA), as well as in Brazil and Czech Republic. It has a prototype center in Millbury, Ohio. GT is privately-owned by Industrial Opportunity Partners, LLC.

FINANCIAL DATA:

Note: Data for latest year may not have been available at press time.

In U.S. $	2018	2017	2016	2015	2014	2013
Revenue						
R&D Expense						
Operating Income						
Operating Margin %						
SGA Expense						
Net Income						
Operating Cash Flow						
Capital Expenditure						
EBITDA						
Return on Assets %						
Return on Equity %						
Debt to Equity						

CONTACT INFORMATION:

Phone: 734-467-8371 Fax:
Toll-Free:
Address: 5859 Executive Dr., Westland, MI 48185 United States

STOCK TICKER/OTHER:

Stock Ticker: Private Exchange:
Employees: 541 Fiscal Year Ends:
Parent Company: Industrial Opportunity Partners LLC

SALARIES/BONUSES:

Top Exec. Salary: $ Bonus: $
Second Exec. Salary: $ Bonus: $

OTHER THOUGHTS:

Estimated Female Officers or Directors:
Hot Spot for Advancement for Women/Minorities:

Guardian Industries

NAIC Code: 327215

www.guardian.com

TYPES OF BUSINESS:

Glass Manufacturing
Automotive Products
Building Materials

BRANDS/DIVISIONS/AFFILIATES:

Koch Industries Inc
Guardian Glass
SRG Global Inc

CONTACTS: *Note: Officers with more than one job title may be intentionally listed here more than once.*

Ron Vaupel, CEO
David Jaffe, Sec.
Scott Thomsen, Pres., Guardian Glass

GROWTH PLANS/SPECIAL FEATURES:

Guardian Industries is a leading global manufacturer of float glass (a flat, clear glass) and fabricated glass products. The company's product lines include automotive replacement glass, automotive products, building products, glass products and architect resources. Guardian has locations across five continents, with operations in over 25 countries, serving customers in more than 100 countries. The company operates through two business divisions and companies: Guardian Glass and SRG Global, Inc. Guardian Glass manufactures float, value-added and fabricated glass products and solutions. It comprises float plants around the globe, producing high performance glass for architectural, residential, interior, transportation and technical glass applications. The Guardian Glass Science & Technology Center continuously works to create new glass products and solutions using the most advanced technology to offer customers innovative products. SRG Global is a leading manufacturer of high-value coatings on plastic for automotive, commercial truck and consumer goods industries. This company has a manufacturing presence in North America, Europe and Asia. Its advanced development centers enhance manufacturing processes and accelerate development and delivery of the next generation of materials, coating technologies and subsystems. Guardian Industries is privately-owned by Koch Industries, Inc. In May 2019, Guardian Industries inaugurated a new laminating line at its float glass plant in Oroshaza, Hungary, to support the increasing demand for laminated glass in Europe. The line produces both standard and coated laminated glass, as well as specialty products such as acoustic, thick, coated and colored laminated glass.

FINANCIAL DATA: *Note: Data for latest year may not have been available at press time.*

In U.S. $	2018	2017	2016	2015	2014	2013
Revenue	6,129,900,000	5,838,000,000	5,560,000,000	5,670,000,000	5,660,000,000	5,650,000,000
R&D Expense						
Operating Income						
Operating Margin %						
SGA Expense						
Net Income						
Operating Cash Flow						
Capital Expenditure						
EBITDA						
Return on Assets %						
Return on Equity %						
Debt to Equity						

CONTACT INFORMATION:

Phone: 248-340-1800 Fax: 248-340-9988
Toll-Free:
Address: 2300 Harmon Rd., Auburn Hills, MI 48326 United States

STOCK TICKER/OTHER:

Stock Ticker: Private
Employees: 18,000
Parent Company: Koch Industries Inc
Exchange:
Fiscal Year Ends: 12/31

SALARIES/BONUSES:

Top Exec. Salary: $ Bonus: $
Second Exec. Salary: $ Bonus: $

OTHER THOUGHTS:

Estimated Female Officers or Directors:
Hot Spot for Advancement for Women/Minorities:

Gulf States Toyota Inc

www.gstcareers.com

NAIC Code: 423110

TYPES OF BUSINESS:

Vehicle Distribution-Wholesale
Parts & Accessories Distribution-Wholesale

BRANDS/DIVISIONS/AFFILIATES:

Friedkin Group (The)
Toyota

CONTACTS:

Note: Officers with more than one job title may be intentionally listed here more than once.

Thomas N. Hynes, CEO
Frank Gruen, CFO
Dan Friedkin, Chmn.

GROWTH PLANS/SPECIAL FEATURES:

Gulf States Toyota, Inc. distributes Toyota, Scion and Lexus branded vehicles to all the Toyota dealerships in Texas, Arkansas, Louisiana, Oklahoma and Mississippi. These vehicles include passenger cars, trucks, vans, minivans and sports utility vehicles. The firm is responsible for receiving cars from Toyota when shipped to Houston, as well as performing services in preparation for distribution to dealers. Gulf States provides dealership support to more than 155 dealers in its five-state region. The firm distributes over 260,000 vehicles per year. Thomas Friedkin founded Gulf States in 1969, and it is now owned by The Friedkin Group. The company is one of two privately-owned entities with exclusive rights to distribute vehicles within the North American Toyota distribution network. Gulf States' corporate office is based in Houston, Texas. Its vehicle processing center is also in Houston; its parts distribution center is based in Sealy, Texas; its technical training centers are located in Houston and Dallas; and its field operations are located in Texas, Oklahoma, Arkansas, Mississippi and Louisiana.

Employee benefits include medical, dental, vision and prescription plans; life and disability insurance; a 401(k) plan; an employee assistance program; tuition and adoption assistance; discounted pricing on Toyota vehicles and parts; and fitness programs and facilities.

FINANCIAL DATA:

Note: Data for latest year may not have been available at press time.

In U.S. $	2018	2017	2016	2015	2014	2013
Revenue	9,240,000,000	8,800,000,000	8,450,000,000	8,400,000,000	8,000,000,000	7,500,000,000
R&D Expense						
Operating Income						
Operating Margin %						
SGA Expense						
Net Income						
Operating Cash Flow						
Capital Expenditure						
EBITDA						
Return on Assets %						
Return on Equity %						
Debt to Equity						

CONTACT INFORMATION:

Phone: 713-580-3300 Fax: 713-580-3332
Toll-Free:
Address: 1375 Enclave Pkwy., Houston, TX 77077 United States

STOCK TICKER/OTHER:

Stock Ticker: Private
Employees: 2,200
Parent Company: Friedkin Group (The)
Exchange:
Fiscal Year Ends: 12/31

SALARIES/BONUSES:

Top Exec. Salary: $ Bonus: $
Second Exec. Salary: $ Bonus: $

OTHER THOUGHTS:

Estimated Female Officers or Directors:
Hot Spot for Advancement for Women/Minorities:

Gulf Stream Coach Inc

www.gulfstreamcoach.com/

NAIC Code: 336214

TYPES OF BUSINESS:

Travel Trailer and Camper Manufacturing

BRANDS/DIVISIONS/AFFILIATES:

BT Cruiser
Conquest
Innsbruck
Ameri-Lite
Track & Trail
GSX
Sedona
Conquest Lodge Series

GROWTH PLANS/SPECIAL FEATURES:

Gulf Stream Coach, Inc. is a leading manufacturer of recreational vehicles such as motor homes, several lines of trailers and fifth wheels. Gulf Stream's motor home model brands include the BT Cruiser and the Conquest Class C. Travel trailer models include the Conquest, Innsbruck, Kingsport and TrailMaster. Light-weight trailers include the Ameri-Lite, Vintage Cruiser, Envision, Capri, Geo, Vista Cruiser, Cabin Cruiser, Gulf Breeze, Streamlite, Matrix, Northern Express, Innsbruck Lite and Conquest Lite. Toy haulers include the Track & Trail and GSX models. Fifth wheels include the Sedona model. Destination trailers include the Conquest Lodge Series, the Innsbruck Lodge Series and the Kingsport Lodge Series. The company has more than 700 dealers and over 250 service centers throughout the U.S. and Canada.

CONTACTS: *Note: Officers with more than one job title may be intentionally listed here more than once.*

Paul Campbell, Dir.-Mktg.

FINANCIAL DATA: *Note: Data for latest year may not have been available at press time.*

In U.S. $	2018	2017	2016	2015	2014	2013
Revenue	180,258,750	171,675,000	163,500,000	162,000,000	139,000,000	131,000,000
R&D Expense						
Operating Income						
Operating Margin %						
SGA Expense						
Net Income						
Operating Cash Flow						
Capital Expenditure						
EBITDA						
Return on Assets %						
Return on Equity %						
Debt to Equity						

CONTACT INFORMATION:

Phone: 574-773-7761 Fax: 574-773-5761
Toll-Free: 800-289-8787
Address: 503 S. Oakland Ave., Nappanee, IN 46550 United States

STOCK TICKER/OTHER:

Stock Ticker: Subsidiary
Employees: 1,350
Parent Company:
Exchange:
Fiscal Year Ends: 12/31

SALARIES/BONUSES:

Top Exec. Salary: $ Bonus: $
Second Exec. Salary: $ Bonus: $

OTHER THOUGHTS:

Estimated Female Officers or Directors:
Hot Spot for Advancement for Women/Minorities:

Hahn Automotive Warehouse Inc

www.hahnauto.com

NAIC Code: 423120

TYPES OF BUSINESS:

Auto Parts, Retail Stores
Auto Parts, Wholesale Distribution
Auto Repair Instruction & Publications

BRANDS/DIVISIONS/AFFILIATES:

Advantage Auto Stores
Genuine Auto Parts
Nu-Way Auto Parts
Norwood Auto Parts
Prime Automotive Parts
Speedway Auto Parts
United Consolidated Warehouses
RAAC Warehouse

CONTACTS: *Note: Officers with more than one job title may be intentionally listed here more than once.*

Eli Futerman, CEO
Daniel Chessin, Pres.

GROWTH PLANS/SPECIAL FEATURES:

Hahn Automotive Warehouse, Inc. sells automotive aftermarket products to commercial service establishments. The company's products primarily consist of nationally branded automotive hard parts as well as many maintenance items, accessories and private label products for domestic and foreign cars, vans and light trucks. On the retail side, Hahn Automotive owns 90 Advantage Auto Stores and Genuine Auto Parts stores that sell parts to the professional service dealer and the do-it-yourselfer. The firm's Nu-Way Auto Parts stores deal directly with the professional service dealer and the do-it-yourselfer, and operates nine locations in western New York and northwest Pennsylvania. Nu-Way features ACDelco and Motorcraft brands, among others. Subsidiary Norwood Auto Parts is a distribution center that allows stores to provide rapid service to local areas in New Jersey. Its parts warehouse is marketed as Prime Automotive Parts. More than 200 brands of parts are stocked in the distribution center and warehouse, which are supplied by leading manufacturers in the industry. Subsidiary Speedway Auto Parts is a full-line supplier of domestic and imported auto parts located throughout Indiana. Speedway has access to millions of parts and accessories through its 40-warehouse network. United Consolidated Industries Warehouses has locations throughout New York, Ohio, North Carolina, Virginia and Maryland that service more than 500 parts stores. RAAC Warehouse is based in Batavia, New York, and provides accessories and unique products required by part store customers. The warehouse stocks over 70 product lines, including snow brushes and hand tools. RAAC has export capabilities for import/export needs.

FINANCIAL DATA: *Note: Data for latest year may not have been available at press time.*

In U.S. $	2018	2017	2016	2015	2014	2013
Revenue	259,087,500	246,750,000	235,000,000	230,000,000	220,000,000	215,000,000
R&D Expense						
Operating Income						
Operating Margin %						
SGA Expense						
Net Income						
Operating Cash Flow						
Capital Expenditure						
EBITDA						
Return on Assets %						
Return on Equity %						
Debt to Equity						

CONTACT INFORMATION:

Phone: 585-235-1595 Fax: 585-235-8615
Toll-Free:
Address: 415 W. Main St., Rochester, NY 14608 United States

STOCK TICKER/OTHER:

Stock Ticker: Private
Employees: 685
Parent Company:
Exchange:
Fiscal Year Ends: 09/30

SALARIES/BONUSES:

Top Exec. Salary: $ Bonus: $
Second Exec. Salary: $ Bonus: $

OTHER THOUGHTS:

Estimated Female Officers or Directors:
Hot Spot for Advancement for Women/Minorities:

Halfords Group plc

NAIC Code: 441310

www.halfordscompany.com

TYPES OF BUSINESS:

Automotive Parts and Accessories Stores
Cycling Products
Repair services

BRANDS/DIVISIONS/AFFILIATES:

Halfords
Cycle Republic
Tredz
Halfords Autocentres
Apollo
Carrera
Boardman
HalfordsAutocentres.com

CONTACTS: *Note: Officers with more than one job title may be intentionally listed here more than once.*

Graham Stapleton, CEO
Loraine Woodhouse, CFO
Alex Henderson, Head-Legal
Andrew Findlay, Group Dir.-Finance
Rob Swyer, Dir.-Retail
Clive West, Dir.-Digital
Andrew Mason, Dir.-Property
Bill Duffy, CEO-Autocenters
Robin Caley, Dir.-Supply Chain & Store Dev.

GROWTH PLANS/SPECIAL FEATURES:

Halfords Group plc, together with its subsidiaries, is engaged in the retailing of automotive, leisure and cycling parts and products across the U.K. and Ireland. Its two operating segments are retail and auto centers. The retail segment comprises more than 450 Halfords retail stores, which sell both motoring and cycling products; and 22 Cycle Republic stores and three Tredz stores, which both operate in the performance cycling market. The retail division generates 86% of annual revenue. Halford stores is a destination for consumers who want assistance with their cars, and delivers a wide range of products. Bikes sold by Halfords include its own brands such as Apollo, Carrera and Boardman, as well as third-party brands such as Specialized, Giant, Cannondale, Cube, Scott, Haibike, Brompton and G-tech. Cycle Republic and Tredz bike stores service the needs of all cyclists, from mainstream to commuter to enthusiast. The auto center segment comprises more than 315 Halfords Autocentres, a car service network serving the car aftercare market offering both a do-it-yourself or a do-it-for-me business approach. Autocenters offer retail parts sales, in-store fitting service and vehicle maintenance packages and services, including hybrid and electric vehicles. Services provided include diagnostics, tires, brakes, fluids, repairs and more. Halfords auto centers is the largest service network in U.K. with do-it-yourself and do-it-for-me concept stores. Customers can access booking and location tools online at HalfordsAutocentres.com, and can order parts and accessories from the website as well.

FINANCIAL DATA: *Note: Data for latest year may not have been available at press time.*

In U.S. $	2018	2017	2016	2015	2014	2013
Revenue	1,379,574,000	1,330,838,000	1,241,507,000	1,246,247,000	1,142,090,000	
R&D Expense						
Operating Income	91,031,730	93,340,940	102,699,300	106,467,000	94,556,320	
Operating Margin %	.07%	.07%	.08%	.09%	.08%	
SGA Expense	602,340,800	585,204,000	557,371,800	557,493,400	518,236,700	
Net Income	66,481,110	68,547,260	77,176,430	79,971,800	67,453,420	
Operating Cash Flow	96,136,310	87,628,670	101,970,100	146,088,300	82,037,940	
Capital Expenditure	44,968,940	41,808,960	46,792,010	48,128,920	32,450,560	
EBITDA	126,520,700	127,493,000	135,636,100	135,514,500	119,957,700	
Return on Assets %	.07%	.08%	.09%	.10%	.09%	
Return on Equity %	.13%	.14%	.16%	.19%	.18%	
Debt to Equity	0.223	0.203	0.09	0.167	0.29	

CONTACT INFORMATION:

Phone: 44 1527517601 Fax: 44 1527513201
Toll-Free:
Address: Icknield St., Worcestershire, B98 0DE United Kingdom

STOCK TICKER/OTHER:

Stock Ticker: HLFDY
Exchange: PINX
Employees: 10,200
Fiscal Year Ends: 03/31
Parent Company:

SALARIES/BONUSES:

Top Exec. Salary: $656,703 Bonus: $
Second Exec. Salary: $177,242 Bonus: $

OTHER THOUGHTS:

Estimated Female Officers or Directors: 1
Hot Spot for Advancement for Women/Minorities:

Hankook Tire Co Ltd

www.hankooktire.com

NAIC Code: 326200

TYPES OF BUSINESS:

Manufacturing-Tires
Batteries
Alloy Rims & Wheels
Brake Pads & Linings
System Integration Services

BRANDS/DIVISIONS/AFFILIATES:

Hankook
Laufenn
Aurora
Route Master
Kingstar
Road Fit

CONTACTS:
Note: Officers with more than one job title may be intentionally listed here more than once.

Hyun Bum Cho, CEO
Soo Il Lee, COO
Ki Yeul Huh, Co-Pres.

GROWTH PLANS/SPECIAL FEATURES:

Hankook Tire Co., Ltd., based in Korea, is a leading global tire manufacturer. The firm produced more than 100 million units in 2018. Hankook manufactures radial tires for passenger cars, sport utility vehicles (SUVs), crossovers, light trucks, heavy-duty trucks and buses. The company's four tire brands cater to the diverse needs of its global customers. These brands include: Hankook (flagship), which has several sub-brands that cover diverse segments in terms of trims and compatible vehicle types; Laufenn, a global brand that serves markets in North and Latin America, Europe, the Middle East and Asia-Pacific; Aurora, a brand for customers outside Korea, and has a product brand name of Route Master in relation to tires that master the road; and Kingstar, another brand sold outside Korea, with tires that deliver optimal on-road performance under the product brand name of Road Fit. Hankook Tire's global network consists of: offices throughout 30 countries; five R&D centers in Korea, Germany, China, Japan and the U.S.; and eight production facilities in Korea (2), China (3), the U.S., Hungary and Indonesia. Distribution is available in more than 180 countries.

FINANCIAL DATA:
Note: Data for latest year may not have been available at press time.

In U.S. $	2018	2017	2016	2015	2014	2013
Revenue		6,091,066,368	5,920,216,576	5,759,495,168	5,929,308,160	6,274,007,552
R&D Expense						
Operating Income						
Operating Margin %						
SGA Expense						
Net Income		535,595,808	780,376,640	587,248,128	621,575,680	654,915,968
Operating Cash Flow						
Capital Expenditure						
EBITDA						
Return on Assets %						
Return on Equity %						
Debt to Equity						

CONTACT INFORMATION:

Phone: 82 222221000 Fax: 82 222221100
Toll-Free:
Address: 133 Teheran-ro, Gangnam-gu, Seoul, South Korea

STOCK TICKER/OTHER:

Stock Ticker: HAOOF
Exchange: GREY
Employees: 14,000
Fiscal Year Ends:
Parent Company:

SALARIES/BONUSES:

Top Exec. Salary: $ Bonus: $
Second Exec. Salary: $ Bonus: $

OTHER THOUGHTS:

Estimated Female Officers or Directors:
Hot Spot for Advancement for Women/Minorities:

Harley-Davidson Inc

www.harley-davidson.com

NAIC Code: 336991

TYPES OF BUSINESS:

Motorcycle Manufacturing
Parts & Accessories
Financial Services

BRANDS/DIVISIONS/AFFILIATES:

Harley-Davidson Financial Services

CONTACTS: *Note: Officers with more than one job title may be intentionally listed here more than once.*

John Olin, CFO
Michael Cave, Chairman of the Board
Mark Kornetzke, Chief Accounting Officer
Luke Mansfield, Chief Strategy Officer
Michelle Kumbier, COO, Divisional
Lawrence Hund, COO, Subsidiary
Julie Anding, Other Executive Officer
Paul Jones, Other Executive Officer
Matthew Levatich, President
David Cox, Senior Executive VP, Divisional
Heather Malenshek, Senior VP, Divisional

GROWTH PLANS/SPECIAL FEATURES:

Harley-Davidson, Inc. specializes in the manufacturing and marketing of motorcycles and related products and accessories. The company operates in two segments: motorcycles & related products and financial services. The motorcycles & related products segment designs, manufactures and sells at wholesale on-road Harley-Davidson motorcycles as well as related parts, accessories, general merchandise and services. It conducts business on a global basis, with sales in North America, Latin America, Asia Pacific and Europe/Middle East/Africa (EMEA). Harley-Davidson currently manufactures five families of motorcycles: cruiser, emphasizing styling and owner customizations; touring, emphasizing rider comfort and load capacity, incorporating features such as fairings (shields for reducing air drag) and luggage compartments; standard, featuring a basic motorcycle which usually features upright seating for one or two passengers; sport bike, which incorporates racing technology, aerodynamic styling, low handlebars and high-performance tires; and dual, offering the capability for use on public roads as well as for some off-highway recreational use. This division distributes its motorcycles and products via independent dealers located in approximately 100 countries. The financial services segment does business as Harley-Davidson Financial Services, and finances and services wholesale inventory receivables and retail consumer loans, primarily for the purchase of Harley-Davison motorcycles. This division also works with unaffiliated insurance companies to provide motorcycle insurance and protection products to motorcycle owners. Financial business is primarily conducted in the U.S. and Canada, with other countries having access to finance through other third-party financial institutions, some of which have licensing or branding agreements with Harley-Davidson Financial Services. In March 2019, Harley-Davidson acquired StaCyc, Inc., the producer of the 12 and 16 EDRIVE electric-powered two-wheelers specifically designed for kids.

Harley-Davidson offers comprehensive health benefits; 401(k) and retirement plans; and a variety of employee assistance programs.

FINANCIAL DATA: *Note: Data for latest year may not have been available at press time.*

In U.S. $	2018	2017	2016	2015	2014	2013
Revenue	5,716,875,000	5,647,224,000	5,996,458,000	5,995,402,000	6,228,508,000	5,899,872,000
R&D Expense						
Operating Income	806,924,000	891,263,000	1,048,936,000	1,155,695,000	1,280,983,000	1,151,571,000
Operating Margin %		.16%	.17%	.19%	.21%	.20%
SGA Expense	1,258,098,000	1,181,641,000	1,217,439,000	1,220,095,000	1,159,502,000	1,126,884,000
Net Income	531,451,000	521,759,000	692,164,000	752,207,000	844,611,000	733,993,000
Operating Cash Flow	1,205,921,000	1,005,061,000	1,174,339,000	1,100,118,000	1,146,677,000	977,093,000
Capital Expenditure	213,516,000	206,294,000	256,263,000	259,974,000	232,319,000	208,321,000
EBITDA	982,376,000	1,117,031,000	1,263,136,000	1,360,354,000	1,466,782,000	1,326,633,000
Return on Assets %		.05%	.07%	.08%	.09%	.08%
Return on Equity %		.28%	.37%	.32%	.29%	.26%
Debt to Equity		2.487	2.431	2.634	1.293	1.135

CONTACT INFORMATION:

Phone: 414 342-4680 Fax: 414 343-4621
Toll-Free:
Address: 3700 W. Juneau Ave., Milwaukee, WI 53208 United States

STOCK TICKER/OTHER:

Stock Ticker: HOG
Exchange: NYS
Employees: 5,400
Fiscal Year Ends: 12/31
Parent Company:

SALARIES/BONUSES:

Top Exec. Salary: $1,076,250 Bonus: $
Second Exec. Salary: $671,375 Bonus: $

OTHER THOUGHTS:

Estimated Female Officers or Directors: 2
Hot Spot for Advancement for Women/Minorities: Y

Hella GmbH & Co KGaA

www.hella.com

NAIC Code: 336300

TYPES OF BUSINESS:

Manufacturing, Automotive Parts
Lighting
Electronics
Complete Vehicle Modules
Air Conditioning Systems
Vehicle Wiring Systems
Signal Processing

BRANDS/DIVISIONS/AFFILIATES:

CONTACTS: *Note: Officers with more than one job title may be intentionally listed here more than once.*

Rolf Breidenbach, CEO
Bernard Schaferbarthold, Dir.-Finance & IT
Nicole Schneider, Dir.-Human Resources
Markus Richter, Company Spokesperson
Wolfgang Ollig, VP-Finance & Controlling
Carsten Albrecht, VP-Aftermarket & Original Equipment Sales
Jurgen Behrend, Chmn.-Exec. Committee
Rolf Breidenbach, VP-Original Equipment
Michael Hoffman-Becking, Chmn.
Stefan Osterhage, VP-Logistics

GROWTH PLANS/SPECIAL FEATURES:

HELLA GmbH & Co. KGaA develops and manufactures lighting and electronics for the automobile industry, with a focus on products that improve environmental impact, driver safety and comfort. The firm operates in three segments: automotive, aftermarket and special applications. The automotive segment manages the development, production and marketing of lighting and electronic components and systems for vehicle manufacturers and suppliers. Lighting products range from headlamps and combination rear lamps to signal lamps, interior lamps and lighting electronics. Electronic components consist of complex body electronics such as central control units and access systems to various electronics components, including sensors and vacuum pumps, battery sensors and radar-based driver assistance systems. The aftermarket segment produces over 38,000 items for wholesalers of automotive parts and independent garages ranging from diagnostic, calibration, lighting, electrical equipment, electronics, thermal management and garage equipment. This division is also engaged in producing digital and mobility products for the aftermarket sector. The special applications segment develops and manufactures lighting and electronics products for special vehicles such as construction and agricultural vehicles, buses, trailers and motorhomes, as well as for the marine sector. This division transfers its technological expertise to these groups in order to develop unique products for them. Fiscal 2018-19 sales by business segment includes 82% automotive, 10% aftermarket and 6% special applications.

FINANCIAL DATA: *Note: Data for latest year may not have been available at press time.*

In U.S. $	2018	2017	2016	2015	2014	2013
Revenue	7,817,031,000	7,290,465,000	7,032,650,000	6,460,021,000	5,915,996,000	5,534,852,000
R&D Expense	766,201,300	704,432,100	690,278,000	602,226,600	568,583,900	518,353,600
Operating Income	568,492,000	495,933,400	405,785,000	400,906,800	373,590,600	326,781,400
Operating Margin %		.07%	.06%	.07%	.06%	.06%
SGA Expense	237,105,900	279,408,800	275,792,700	229,821,800	461,828,000	683,035,900
Net Income	430,335,500	378,358,000	297,276,400	317,753,600	246,775,900	223,054,700
Operating Cash Flow	914,354,600	788,885,100	666,688,500	619,931,300	592,304,100	512,826,600
Capital Expenditure	692,916,300	737,072,700	620,686,500	551,304,300	571,037,400	598,884,000
EBITDA	1,127,699,000	1,004,918,000	897,259,800	853,378,000	731,876,700	647,202,200
Return on Assets %		.06%	.05%	.06%	.05%	.06%
Return on Equity %		.16%	.14%	.18%	.18%	.18%
Debt to Equity		0.467	0.54	0.553	0.854	0.897

CONTACT INFORMATION:

Phone: 49-29-41-38-0 Fax: 49-29-41-38-71-33
Toll-Free:
Address: Rixbecker Str. 75, Lippstadt, 59552 Germany

STOCK TICKER/OTHER:

Stock Ticker: HLLGY
Exchange: PINX
Employees: 40,263
Fiscal Year Ends: 05/31
Parent Company:

SALARIES/BONUSES:

Top Exec. Salary: $ Bonus: $
Second Exec. Salary: $ Bonus: $

OTHER THOUGHTS:

Estimated Female Officers or Directors:
Hot Spot for Advancement for Women/Minorities:

Hendrick Automotive Group

www.hendrickauto.com

NAIC Code: 441110

TYPES OF BUSINESS:

Auto Dealers
Parts & Service
Accessories
Racing & Motorsports

BRANDS/DIVISIONS/AFFILIATES:

Hendrick Motorsports

CONTACTS:

Note: Officers with more than one job title may be intentionally listed here more than once.

Edward J. Brown, III, CEO
Edward J. Brown, III, Pres.
Brian Williams, VP-Mktg. & Advertising
Veronica Zayatz, VP-Acct., Audits & Taxes
Rick Hendrick, Chmn.

GROWTH PLANS/SPECIAL FEATURES:

Hendrick Automotive Group sells new and used automobiles from 27 automakers. These automakers include Acura, Audi, BMW, Buick, Cadillac, Chevrolet, Chrysler, Dodge, Fiat, GMA, Harley-Davidson, Honda, Jaguar, Jeep, Kia, Land Rover, Lexus, MINI, Mazda, Mercedes-Benz, Nissan, Porsche, RAM, Subaru, Toyota, Volkswagen and Volvo. The firm boasts a network of 96 dealerships in 14 U.S. states as well as 130 franchise locations. Hendrick's automobile offerings include cars as well as light trucks. The company offers other services, including financing, maintenance, body repair and parts and accessories. The group has 29 collision centers and four accessories distributor installers located across the U.S. Customers can access a database of pre-owned and new cars on the company website. Hendrick offers financing, warranties, automobile parts, accessories and autobody repair services. In addition, Hendrick Automotive operates Hendrick Motorsports, which sponsors a number of NASCAR teams.

FINANCIAL DATA:

Note: Data for latest year may not have been available at press time.

In U.S. $	2018	2017	2016	2015	2014	2013
Revenue	9,427,756,576	8,978,815,787	8,551,253,132	8,400,000,000	7,500,000,000	7,000,000,000
R&D Expense						
Operating Income						
Operating Margin %						
SGA Expense						
Net Income						
Operating Cash Flow						
Capital Expenditure						
EBITDA						
Return on Assets %						
Return on Equity %						
Debt to Equity						

CONTACT INFORMATION:

Phone: 704-568-5550 Fax: 704-566-3295
Toll-Free:
Address: 6000 Monroe Rd., Ste. 100, Charlotte, NC 28212 United States

STOCK TICKER/OTHER:

Stock Ticker: Private
Employees: 10,000
Parent Company:
Exchange:
Fiscal Year Ends: 12/31

SALARIES/BONUSES:

Top Exec. Salary: $ Bonus: $
Second Exec. Salary: $ Bonus: $

OTHER THOUGHTS:

Estimated Female Officers or Directors: 1
Hot Spot for Advancement for Women/Minorities:

Herb Chambers Companies (The)

www.herbchambers.com

NAIC Code: 441110

TYPES OF BUSINESS:

Auto Dealers, Retail
Parts & Service

BRANDS/DIVISIONS/AFFILIATES:

CONTACTS:

Note: Officers with more than one job title may be intentionally listed here more than once.

Alan McLaren, CEO
Herbert G. Chambers, Pres.

GROWTH PLANS/SPECIAL FEATURES:

The Herb Chambers Companies operates approximately 60 dealerships and three collision centers throughout Massachusetts and Rhode Island. It specializes in selling more than 10,000 new and pre-owned upscale automobiles, including models from Maserati, Lamborghini, Audi, Mercedes-Benz, BMW, MINI, Porsche, Infiniti, Lexus, Saab, Cadillac, Land Rover, Lincoln, Alfa Romeo, Jaguar, Volvo, Bentley and Hummer. The company also has dealerships offering Dodge, Chevrolet, Ford, Kia, Hyundai, Kia and Honda makes, as well as A2B electric bikes and Vespa motor scooters. In addition to Herb Chambers' three distinct collision centers, the dealerships offer repair and maintenance service, OEM (original equipment manufacturer) parts and lubricants and other accessories. The company's website offers online credit applications, vehicle inventory, vehicle reviews, a payment calculator and search tools. During 2018, more than 55,000 customers either purchased or leased a new or pre-owned vehicle, and another 420,000 chose to have their car serviced or repaired at a Herb Chambers dealership.

FINANCIAL DATA:

Note: Data for latest year may not have been available at press time.

In U.S. $	2018	2017	2016	2015	2014	2013
Revenue	2,898,436,267	2,760,415,492	2,628,967,135	2,522,762,046	2,106,000,000	1,990,000,000
R&D Expense						
Operating Income						
Operating Margin %						
SGA Expense						
Net Income						
Operating Cash Flow						
Capital Expenditure						
EBITDA						
Return on Assets %						
Return on Equity %						
Debt to Equity						

CONTACT INFORMATION:

Phone: 617-666-8333 Fax: 617-666-8448
Toll-Free:
Address: 259 McGrath Hwy., Somerville, MA 02145 United States

STOCK TICKER/OTHER:

Stock Ticker: Private
Employees: 2,400
Parent Company:
Exchange:
Fiscal Year Ends: 12/31

SALARIES/BONUSES:

Top Exec. Salary: $ Bonus: $
Second Exec. Salary: $ Bonus: $

OTHER THOUGHTS:

Estimated Female Officers or Directors:
Hot Spot for Advancement for Women/Minorities:

Hero MotoCorp Ltd

NAIC Code: 336991

www.heromotocorp.com

TYPES OF BUSINESS:

Motorcycle Manufacturing & Sales

BRANDS/DIVISIONS/AFFILIATES:

Xpulse
Xtreme
Karizma
Achiever
Splendor
Destini
Hero Tech Center Germany GmbH
Hero MotoSports Team Rally

CONTACTS: *Note: Officers with more than one job title may be intentionally listed here more than once.*

Pawan Munjal, Managing Dir.
Vikram Kasbekar, Dir.-Operations
Niranjan Gupta, CFO
Vikram Kasbekar, CTO
Sanjay Bhan, Dir.-Sales & Parts
Harjeet Singh, VP-R&D
Vijay Sethi, CIO
Ilam C. Kamboj, Corp. Sec.
Vikram Kasbekar, Head-Oper. & Supply Chain
Anadi Pande, VP-Corp. Planning & Strategy
Neeraj Mathur, VP-Supply Chain & Strategic Sourcing

GROWTH PLANS/SPECIAL FEATURES:

Hero MotoCorp Ltd., based in India, is a leading manufacturer and marketer of scooters and motorcycles, as well as related parts. The firm is owned by Hero Group, which is controlled by India's Munjal family. Hero MotorCorp's models include the Xpulse, Xtreme, Karizma, Achiever, Glamour, Passion, Splendor, Destini, Duet and Maestro lines. The company's products are sold and supported through a network of more than 6,000 dealers, authorized representatives and service centers located in both rural and urban India. The firm has five domestic manufacturing plants in India, and one each in Colombia and Bangladesh, with a combined capacity of approximately 9 million units of two-wheelers per year. The capacity will increase to 11 million units when the Andhra Pradesh manufacturing facility becomes operational. In addition, Hero MotoCorp operates offices in New Delhi, Bangalore, Kolkata and Pune as well as 24 regional offices throughout the country. Though India remains the company's primary market, the firm has rapidly expanded to 37 countries across Asia, Africa and South and Central America. In 2019, Hero MotoCorp set up the Hero Tech Center Germany GmbH, which will supplement the ongoing work at the Centre of Innovation and Technology (CIT), and will be the home of Hero MotoSports Team Rally, the firm's professional racing team.

FINANCIAL DATA: *Note: Data for latest year may not have been available at press time.*

In U.S. $	2018	2017	2016	2015	2014	2013
Revenue	4,689,151,488	4,129,706,496	4,135,585,024	3,980,639,232	3,657,366,016	3,465,056,768
R&D Expense						
Operating Income						
Operating Margin %						
SGA Expense						
Net Income	536,565,440	516,932,416	446,192,736	341,042,976	303,250,912	305,486,336
Operating Cash Flow						
Capital Expenditure						
EBITDA						
Return on Assets %						
Return on Equity %						
Debt to Equity						

CONTACT INFORMATION:

Phone: 91-11-2614-2451 Fax: 91-11-2614-3321
Toll-Free:
Address: 34 Community Centre, Basant Lok, Vasant Vihar, New Delhi, 110057 India

STOCK TICKER/OTHER:

Stock Ticker: HRTQY
Employees: 8,266
Parent Company:
Exchange: GREY
Fiscal Year Ends: 03/31

SALARIES/BONUSES:

Top Exec. Salary: $ Bonus: $
Second Exec. Salary: $ Bonus: $

OTHER THOUGHTS:

Estimated Female Officers or Directors: 1
Hot Spot for Advancement for Women/Minorities:

Hertz Global Holdings Inc

www.hertz.com

NAIC Code: 532111

TYPES OF BUSINESS:

Automobile Rental
Truck Rental
Claims Management
Heavy Equipment Rental
Used Automobile Sales
Leasing
Actuarial Services
Franchising

BRANDS/DIVISIONS/AFFILIATES:

Hertz
Dollar
Thrifty
Firefly
Donlen Corporation

GROWTH PLANS/SPECIAL FEATURES:

Hertz Global Holdings, Inc. owns one of the largest worldwide airport general-use car rental brands and one of the largest equipment rental businesses in the U.S. and Canada. Hertz has approximately 1,600 airport rental locations in the U.S. and approximately 1,500 airport rental locations internationally. The company operates in three segments: U.S. car rental, international car rental and other operations. U.S. car rental rents cars, crossovers and light trucks, and provides ancillary products and services. This segment has franchises and associates that operate rental locations under the Hertz, Dollar, Thrifty, and Firefly brands throughout the USA. International car rental rents the same vehicles and provides the same products and services as the U.S. division, only internationally. This segment maintains a network of company-operated car rental locations, most which are in Europe. Its franchisees and associates also operate rental locations in approximately 150 countries and jurisdictions. Other operations comprise the firm's Donlen Corporation, which provides fleet leasing and management services. U.S. car rental derives 68% of company revenues, international car rental derives 25% and other operations derives 7%. The firm has an agreement with Lyft to supply rental car rates for drivers who can either use the cars for Lyft business or for personal driving. Lyft provides ridesharing in more than 200 U.S. cities.

CONTACTS: *Note: Officers with more than one job title may be intentionally listed here more than once.*

Kathryn Marinello, CEO
Jamere Jackson, CFO
Eric Esper, Chief Accounting Officer
Opal Perry, Chief Information Officer
Henry Keizer, Director
Jodi Allen, Executive VP
David Galainena, Executive VP
Paul Stone, Executive VP
Murali Kuppuswamy, Executive VP

FINANCIAL DATA: *Note: Data for latest year may not have been available at press time.*

In U.S. $	2018	2017	2016	2015	2014	2013
Revenue	9,504,000,000	8,803,000,000	8,803,000,000	10,535,000,000	11,046,000,000	10,771,900,000
R&D Expense						
Operating Income	442,000,000	167,000,000	371,000,000	832,000,000	610,000,000	1,472,200,000
Operating Margin %		.02%	.04%	.08%	.06%	.14%
SGA Expense	1,017,000,000	880,000,000	899,000,000	1,045,000,000	1,088,000,000	1,022,200,000
Net Income	-225,000,000	327,000,000	-491,000,000	273,000,000	-82,000,000	346,200,000
Operating Cash Flow	2,556,000,000	2,394,000,000	2,529,000,000	3,332,000,000	3,452,000,000	3,589,600,000
Capital Expenditure	12,670,000,000	10,769,000,000	11,091,000,000	12,985,000,000	11,663,000,000	10,612,200,000
EBITDA	3,246,000,000	3,024,000,000	2,950,000,000	4,005,000,000	3,945,000,000	4,150,900,000
Return on Assets %		.02%	-.02%	.01%	.00%	.01%
Return on Equity %		.25%	-.32%	.12%	-.03%	.13%
Debt to Equity		9.78	12.596	7.879	6.491	5.885

CONTACT INFORMATION:

Phone: 239-301-7000 Fax:
Toll-Free: 800-654-3131
Address: 8501 Williams Road, Estero, FL 33928 United States

STOCK TICKER/OTHER:

Stock Ticker: HTZ
Employees: 30,400
Parent Company:
Exchange: NYS
Fiscal Year Ends: 12/31

SALARIES/BONUSES:

Top Exec. Salary: $1,450,000 Bonus: $
Second Exec. Salary: $223,558 Bonus: $1,029,000

OTHER THOUGHTS:

Estimated Female Officers or Directors: 6
Hot Spot for Advancement for Women/Minorities: Y

Hilite International Inc

www.hilite.com

NAIC Code: 336300

TYPES OF BUSINESS:

Automobile Parts Manufacturer
Transmission Components
Engine Components
Emission Control Systems
Automotive Valves
Clutches
Cam-phasing Systems

BRANDS/DIVISIONS/AFFILIATES:

Aviation Industry Corporation of China
Vanecam
StepCom

CONTACTS: *Note: Officers with more than one job title may be intentionally listed here more than once.*

Karl Hammer, CEO

GROWTH PLANS/SPECIAL FEATURES:

Hilite International, Inc., owned by Aviation Industry Corporation of China, develops and produces systems and components to improve fuel consumption and reduce emissions. Hilite partners with original equipment manufacturers (OEMs) and other customers in the automotive industry to develop engine and transmission applications for their specific requirements and needs. The company's products are divided into two groups: engine and transmission. Engine products include: the Vanecam line of camphaser systems, which control intake and exhaust valve timing for improved fuel economy, emissions and performance; camphaser modules; oil control valves; fast phaser systems; and diesel and other engine valves. In addition, Hilite's StepCom variable compression ratio (VCR) system is a connecting element between the piston and crankshaft within the engine. StepCom enables engine operation at different compression ratios, and is ideal for optimum efficiency (high compression) and high performance (low compression). Transmission products include: double clutch transmissions, which combines automatic transmissions with the efficiency and dynamics of a manual one; control valves; and torque transfer products, which are used in four-wheel-drive, all-wheel-drive and torque vectoring systems. Hilite has offices and production plants located in the U.S., Germany and China.

FINANCIAL DATA: *Note: Data for latest year may not have been available at press time.*

In U.S. $	2018	2017	2016	2015	2014	2013
Revenue	631,373,000	584,156,000	577,000,391	537,728,037	545,000,000	504,259,201
R&D Expense						
Operating Income						
Operating Margin %						
SGA Expense						
Net Income						
Operating Cash Flow						
Capital Expenditure						
EBITDA						
Return on Assets %						
Return on Equity %						
Debt to Equity						

CONTACT INFORMATION:

Phone: 49-9391 911-0 Fax: 49-9391 911-222
Toll-Free:
Address: Am Schlossfeld 5, Marktheidenfeld, 97828 Germany

STOCK TICKER/OTHER:

Stock Ticker: Subsidiary Exchange:
Employees: 1,700 Fiscal Year Ends: 06/30
Parent Company: Aviation Industry Corporation of China

SALARIES/BONUSES:

Top Exec. Salary: $ Bonus: $
Second Exec. Salary: $ Bonus: $

OTHER THOUGHTS:

Estimated Female Officers or Directors:
Hot Spot for Advancement for Women/Minorities:

Hino Motors Ltd

www.hino-global.com

NAIC Code: 336120

TYPES OF BUSINESS:

Truck & Misc. Automotive Manufacturing
Truck & Bus Sales
Commissioned Auto Manufacturing
Diesel Engine & Parts Manufacturing
Low Emissions Technology

BRANDS/DIVISIONS/AFFILIATES:

Toyota Motor Corporation
Hino 300 Series
Hino 300 Hybrid
Hino 500 Series
Hino 600 Series
Hino 700 Series
Hino 195h
Toyoace

CONTACTS: *Note: Officers with more than one job title may be intentionally listed here more than once.*

Yoshio Shimo, CEO
Seiei Okazaki, Exec. VP
Kenji Wagy, Sr. Managing Dir.
Hiroshi Kokaji, Sr. Managing Dir.
Yoshihide Maeda, Sr. Managing Dir.
Yasuhiko Ichihashi, Chmn.

GROWTH PLANS/SPECIAL FEATURES:

Hino Motors Ltd., founded in 1910, manufactures and markets trucks, buses, light commercial vehicles, passenger vehicles and various engines and spare parts. A consolidated subsidiary of Toyota Motor Corporation (50.1%-owned), Hino brings together a global network of production and distribution facilities, regional subsidiaries and specialized operations. In Japan, the company produces vehicles, components and engines at domestic plants. Its manufacturing operations in other nations include plants for producing trucks, buses and components in Thailand, Vietnam, Indonesia, China, Pakistan, Malaysia, Philippines, Mexico, Canada and the U.S. Hino's product lines include the Hino 300 Series light-duty trucks, the Hino 300 Hybrid, the Hino 500 Series medium-duty trucks, the Hino 600 Series medium-duty truck, the Hino 700 Series heavy-duty trucks, the Hino 195h heavy hybrid truck, bus chassis and both automotive and industrial diesel engines. In addition to trucks and buses, the company is engaged in the commissioned manufacture of vehicles and parts for Toyota Motor Corporation, including sport-utility vehicles and passenger cars such as the Land Cruiser Prado, FJ Cruiser, Dyna trucks and ToyoAce commercial vehicles. Hino Motors has domestic offices and dealers throughout Japan, as well as offices internationally in Asia, North America, Central America, the Caribbean, Europe, the Middle East and Oceania. In April 2019, Hino Motors began construction on a new factory in Russia, which will produce up to 3,000 light- and medium-duty trucks per year. The plant is slated to begin production in mid-2020. That July, Hino Motors announced the construction of a new development and production base in Thailand, to be called the Suvarnabhumi Monozukuri Center.

FINANCIAL DATA: *Note: Data for latest year may not have been available at press time.*

In U.S. $	2018	2017	2016	2015	2014	2013
Revenue	16,890,110,000	15,472,520,000	16,040,620,000	15,487,020,000	15,618,200,000	
R&D Expense						
Operating Income	738,246,700	654,144,400	903,243,900	969,711,500	1,030,969,000	
Operating Margin %	.04%	.08%	.09%	.10%	.10%	
SGA Expense	413,701,500	382,337,800	391,426,200	345,690,100	327,816,600	
Net Income	471,981,300	454,034,200	598,511,300	684,616,800	819,031,500	
Operating Cash Flow	794,642,600	696,177,200	1,023,396,000	714,537,800	1,313,554,000	
Capital Expenditure	617,873,500	870,244,500	803,436,900	699,246,500	604,208,800	
EBITDA	1,332,852,000	1,175,501,000	1,404,255,000	1,411,358,000	1,490,241,000	
Return on Assets %	.04%	.04%	.06%	.07%	.09%	
Return on Equity %	.11%	.11%	.15%	.20%	.29%	
Debt to Equity	0.062	0.082	0.105	0.098	0.096	

CONTACT INFORMATION:

Phone: 81 425865494 Fax:
Toll-Free:
Address: 1-1 Hinodai 3-chome, Hino-shi, Tokyo, 191-8660 Japan

STOCK TICKER/OTHER:

Stock Ticker: HINOY
Exchange: PINX
Employees: 45,442
Fiscal Year Ends: 03/31
Parent Company: Toyota Motor Corporation

SALARIES/BONUSES:

Top Exec. Salary: $ Bonus: $
Second Exec. Salary: $ Bonus: $

OTHER THOUGHTS:

Estimated Female Officers or Directors:
Hot Spot for Advancement for Women/Minorities:

Hino Motors Manufacturing (Thailand) Ltd

www.hinomanufacturing.co.th/EN/Index.aspx

NAIC Code: 336120

TYPES OF BUSINESS:

Truck & Bus Distribution
Spare Parts Distribution

BRANDS/DIVISIONS/AFFILIATES:

Hino Motors Ltd
Hino
Series 3
Series 5
RM1E

CONTACTS:

Note: Officers with more than one job title may be intentionally listed here more than once.

Somchai Pleankaew, Pres.
Kimiyoshi Kawano, Exec. VP
Amnuay Pongwicharn, Sr. Managing Dir.
Vinai Daopalangphrom, VP
Supapong Permsuwan, VP

GROWTH PLANS/SPECIAL FEATURES:

Hino Motor Manufacturing (Thailand) Ltd., a 98.3%-owned subsidiary of Japanese firm Hino Motors Ltd., manufactures and distributes Hino-brand trucks, buses and related parts in Thailand. It offers 11 different basic truck configurations and one bus model. In addition, the firm manufactures auto components for trucks, pickup trucks, multi-purpose vehicles and passenger cars. Its smallest trucks, collectively called Series 3, are comprised of four models of small freight trucks, available in 4- or 6-wheeled configurations. The largest trucks comprise the seven models in the Series 5, and generally consist of 6-, 10- or 12-wheeled freight trucks and semi-truck tractor heads. Hino Motor's bus model is the RM1E. Moreover, Hino Motor Manufacturing produces auto parts such as frame, hub, knuckle, rear bumper, side panel, lower control arm and back panel. These component parts are supplied to manufacturers in Thailand, as well as neighboring regions such as Indonesia, Singapore, Malaysia, Taiwan and Japan. The vehicles are marketed locally, as well as in the Southeast Asian region and Australia.

FINANCIAL DATA:

Note: Data for latest year may not have been available at press time.

In U.S. $	2018	2017	2016	2015	2014	2013
Revenue						
R&D Expense						
Operating Income						
Operating Margin %						
SGA Expense						
Net Income						
Operating Cash Flow						
Capital Expenditure						
EBITDA						
Return on Assets %						
Return on Equity %						
Debt to Equity						

CONTACT INFORMATION:

Phone: 660-2384-2900 Fax: 660-2384-0329
Toll-Free:
Address: 99 Moo 3, Teparak Rd., Teparak, Muang Samutprakarn, 10270 Thailand

STOCK TICKER/OTHER:

Stock Ticker: Subsidiary
Employees: 3,400
Parent Company: Hino Motors Ltd
Exchange:
Fiscal Year Ends:

SALARIES/BONUSES:

Top Exec. Salary: $ Bonus: $
Second Exec. Salary: $ Bonus: $

OTHER THOUGHTS:

Estimated Female Officers or Directors: 1
Hot Spot for Advancement for Women/Minorities: Y

Holden

www.holden.com.au

NAIC Code: 336111

TYPES OF BUSINESS:

Automobile Manufacturing
Light Commercial Vehicle Manufacturing
Engine and Parts Manufacturing
Retail Dealerships
Fleet Leasing and Management

BRANDS/DIVISIONS/AFFILIATES:

General Motors Company
Holden Eye
OnStar

GROWTH PLANS/SPECIAL FEATURES:

Holden, a subsidiary of General Motors Company, imports and sells GM cars as a national sales company. These vehicles include small cars, hatchbacks, sedans, sport utility vehicles (SUVs), trucks and four-wheel drives. Models include Acadia, Astra, Colorado, Commodore, Equinox, Trailblazer and Trax. Technology-wise, Holden vehicles are equipped with the intelligently-integrated Holden Eye safety drive system, which features forward collision alerts, parking assistance, lane departure warning and keeping within the lane assistance. Vehicles are also connected for Apple and Android devices. Its OnStar technology is currently being developed in collaboration with GM, which will help thwart car theft, coordinate emergency responders, provide enhanced navigation services and more.

CONTACTS: *Note: Officers with more than one job title may be intentionally listed here more than once.*

Dave Buttner, Managing Dir.
Jason Thorley, CFO
Greg Tyus, Exec. Dir.-Eng.
Peter Keley, Exec. Dir.-Planning & Program Mgmt.
Sean Liang, Exec. Dir.-Global Purchasing & Supply Chain

FINANCIAL DATA: *Note: Data for latest year may not have been available at press time.*

In U.S. $	2018	2017	2016	2015	2014	2013
Revenue	1,379,124,500	1,451,710,000	1,683,680,000	2,616,210,000	2,952,540,000	3,593,440,000
R&D Expense						
Operating Income						
Operating Margin %						
SGA Expense						
Net Income		122,381,000	90,687,600	93,425,800	-294,439,000	-491,370,000
Operating Cash Flow						
Capital Expenditure						
EBITDA						
Return on Assets %						
Return on Equity %						
Debt to Equity						

CONTACT INFORMATION:

Phone: 61-3-9647-1111 Fax: 61-3-9647-1237
Toll-Free: 800-033-349
Address: 191 Salmon St., Port Melbourne, VIC 3207 Australia

STOCK TICKER/OTHER:

Stock Ticker: Subsidiary
Exchange:
Employees: 14,000
Fiscal Year Ends: 12/31
Parent Company: General Motors Company (GM)

SALARIES/BONUSES:

Top Exec. Salary: $ Bonus: $
Second Exec. Salary: $ Bonus: $

OTHER THOUGHTS:

Estimated Female Officers or Directors: 1
Hot Spot for Advancement for Women/Minorities:

Holman Automotive Group Inc

www.holmanauto.com

NAIC Code: 441110

TYPES OF BUSINESS:

Auto Dealers, Retail
Fleet Management Services
Parts & Service
Auto Leasing

BRANDS/DIVISIONS/AFFILIATES:

Holman Enterprises
Automotive Rentals Inc
Auto Truck Group Inc
Holman Parts Distribution Inc
Steward Financial Services
Holman Insurance Services
Kuni Automotive
CarFinder

CONTACTS: *Note: Officers with more than one job title may be intentionally listed here more than once.*

Gene Welsh, Pres.
Laura Carlisle, CFO
Rick Deeck, Sr. VP-Mktg.
Katherine Andreola Mullin, General Counsel
William Cariss, VP-Dealership Oper.
Robert Campbell, VP-Finance
Angelo J. Nori, VP
Glenn A. Gardner, VP
Frank H. Beideman, VP-Resource Dev.

GROWTH PLANS/SPECIAL FEATURES:

Holman Automotive Group, Inc., part of Holman Enterprises, is a family-owned automobile retailer founded in 1924 by Steward Holman. The group consists of more than 35 car and truck dealership franchises, most of which include service and parts departments. The firm has collision centers in New Jersey and Florida, as well as other operating companies (listed below). Holman sells and leases new and used vehicles through its dealerships located in New Jersey, Florida and Pennsylvania. Brands sold include Aston Martin, Audi, Bentley, BMW, Cadillac, Chevrolet, Ford, Honda, Infiniti, Land Rover, Lexus, Lincoln, MINI, Porsche, Rolls-Royce, Toyota and Volkswagen. The company's website offers tools to search new and used vehicle inventory, promotional offers, CarFinder alert and a payment calculator. Other operating companies include: Automotive Rentals, Inc., a New Jersey-based fleet management corporation; Auto Truck Group, Inc., an Illinois-based truck equipment company; Holman Parts Distribution, Inc., a New Jersey-based original equipment and aftermarket powertrain products supplier; Steward Financial Services, a New Jersey-based automobile finance company; and Holman Insurance Services, which provides consumer insurance to retail customers, as well as customized insurance and risk management solutions to commercial clients. Subsidiary Kuni Automotive, a Holman Enterprise, comprises luxury dealerships in four western states (California, Oregon, Washington and Colorado).

Holman offers its employees medical, dental and vision insurance, a 401(k) plan, flexible spending account, short and long-term disability and life insurance, an employee purchase plan, paid vacation and holidays, and educational assistance.

FINANCIAL DATA: *Note: Data for latest year may not have been available at press time.*

In U.S. $	2018	2017	2016	2015	2014	2013
Revenue	3,267,879,776	3,112,266,453	2,964,063,289	1,449,599,272	1,222,000,000	1,150,000,000
R&D Expense						
Operating Income						
Operating Margin %						
SGA Expense						
Net Income						
Operating Cash Flow						
Capital Expenditure						
EBITDA						
Return on Assets %						
Return on Equity %						
Debt to Equity						

CONTACT INFORMATION:

Phone: 856-663-5200 Fax: 856-665-3444
Toll-Free:
Address: 244 E Kings Highway, Maple Shade, NJ 08052 United States

STOCK TICKER/OTHER:

Stock Ticker: Private
Exchange:
Employees: 3,400
Fiscal Year Ends: 12/31
Parent Company: Holman Enterprises

SALARIES/BONUSES:

Top Exec. Salary: $ Bonus: $
Second Exec. Salary: $ Bonus: $

OTHER THOUGHTS:

Estimated Female Officers or Directors: 2
Hot Spot for Advancement for Women/Minorities:

Honda Motor Co Ltd

world.honda.com

NAIC Code: 336111

TYPES OF BUSINESS:

Automobile Manufacturing
Motorcycles
ATVs & Personal Watercraft
Generators
Marine Engines
Lawn & Garden Equipment
Fuel Cell & Hybrid Vehicles
Airplanes

BRANDS/DIVISIONS/AFFILIATES:

Acura
Honda
Civic
Accord
Fit
CR-V
HondaJet
Odyssey

CONTACTS: *Note: Officers with more than one job title may be intentionally listed here more than once.*

Takahiro Hachigo, CEO

GROWTH PLANS/SPECIAL FEATURES:

Honda Motor Co. Ltd. develops, produces and manufactures a variety of motor products, ranging from small general-purpose engines and scooters to specialty sports cars. Comprised of 440 company subsidiaries and affiliates in Japan and internationally, Honda operates through four segments: motorcycles, automobiles, power products and aircrafts and jet engines. The motorcycle unit produces sport, business and commuter model bikes, which utilize air- or water-cooled gasoline engines with 1-6 cylinders, manufactured by the company. This segment also includes the production of all-terrain vehicles (ATVs), personal watercraft and multi-utility vehicles (MUVs). The automobiles segment manufactures vehicles under the Acura and Honda trademarks. Honda models include the Civic, a sub-compact car; the Accord, an intermediate passenger car; the Fit, a compact passenger car; the Odyssey, a minivan; the Accord, Fit/Jazz, Freed, Jade, Legend and Shuttle hybrid cars; and the CR-V, an SUV. Through its power products unit, Honda produces tillers, portable generators, general purpose engines, grass cutters, outboard marine engines, water pumps, snow throwers, power carriers, power sprayers, lawn mowers and lawn tractors. Products include internal combustion engines, electric-powered products, Butane gas powered systems and hybrid systems. The aircrafts and het engines segment, also known as HondaJet, manufactures business jets and jet engines; and manufactures advanced humanoid robots, as well as walking assisted devices and stride management systems for people with weakened leg muscles. Innovations include over-the-wing mounted engines, the HF120 turbofan engine, natural laminar flow wing and nose and more. In March 2018, the firm expanded HondaJet sales to India. In 2018, Honda opened plants in China and Bangladesh.

U.S. employee benefits include paid time off, credit union access, health care plans, domestic partner benefits, onsite fitness facilities, education reimbursement and retirement plans.

FINANCIAL DATA: *Note: Data for latest year may not have been available at press time.*

In U.S. $	2018	2017	2016	2015	2014	2013
Revenue	141,161,100,000	128,645,500,000	134,177,100,000	122,478,400,000	108,826,100,000	
R&D Expense	6,909,171,000	6,353,878,000	6,032,917,000	5,570,318,000	5,827,330,000	
Operating Income	7,659,971,000	7,725,703,000	4,625,767,000	6,162,498,000	6,894,698,000	
Operating Margin %	.05%	.06%	.03%	.05%	.06%	
SGA Expense	16,312,730,000	14,714,320,000	19,379,470,000	15,810,970,000	15,594,160,000	
Net Income	9,734,765,000	5,665,953,000	3,166,063,000	4,681,446,000	5,275,749,000	
Operating Cash Flow	9,076,190,000	8,133,367,000	12,782,530,000	9,376,989,000	11,295,640,000	
Capital Expenditure	5,260,890,000	5,857,858,000	8,012,856,000	8,115,420,000	17,476,990,000	
EBITDA	16,918,180,000	15,565,030,000	12,077,840,000	13,321,630,000	14,118,390,000	
Return on Assets %	.06%	.03%	.02%	.03%	.04%	
Return on Equity %	.14%	.09%	.05%	.08%	.10%	
Debt to Equity	0.489	0.551	0.553	0.552	0.546	

CONTACT INFORMATION:

Phone: 81 3 3423 1111 Fax:
Toll-Free:
Address: 2-1-1, Minami-Aoyama, Minato-ku, Tokyo, 107-8556 Japan

STOCK TICKER/OTHER:

Stock Ticker: HMC
Employees: 211,915
Parent Company:
Exchange: NYS
Fiscal Year Ends: 03/31

SALARIES/BONUSES:

Top Exec. Salary: $937,328 Bonus: $487,043
Second Exec. Salary: $ Bonus: $

OTHER THOUGHTS:

Estimated Female Officers or Directors:
Hot Spot for Advancement for Women/Minorities:

Hyster-Yale Materials Handling Inc

www.Hyster-Yale.com

NAIC Code: 333924

TYPES OF BUSINESS:

Industrial Truck, Tractor, Trailer, and Stacker Machinery Manufacturing
Hydrogen Production

BRANDS/DIVISIONS/AFFILIATES:

Hyster-Yale Group Inc
Nuvera Fuel Cells LLC
Bolzoni SpA
Zhejiang Maximal Forklift Co Ltd
Hyster
Yale
Hyster-Yale
Bolzoni Auramo

CONTACTS: *Note: Officers with more than one job title may be intentionally listed here more than once.*

Colin Wilson, CEO, Subsidiary
Gopichand Somayajula, Vice President, Subsidiary
Alfred Rankin, CEO
Kenneth Schilling, CFO
Lauren Miller, Chief Marketing Officer
Jennifer Langer, Controller
Suzanne Taylor, General Counsel
Rajiv Prasad, Other Corporate Officer
Charles Pascarelli, President, Subsidiary
Harry Sands, Senior VP, Subsidiary
Anthony Salgado, Senior VP, Subsidiary
Brian Frentzko, Treasurer
David LeBlanc, Vice President, Divisional
Gregory Breier, Vice President, Divisional
Raymond Ulmer, Vice President, Subsidiary
Mark Trivett, Vice President, Subsidiary

GROWTH PLANS/SPECIAL FEATURES:

Hyster-Yale Materials Handling, Inc. is a designer, engineer, manufacturer, seller and servicer of a comprehensive line of lift trucks and aftermarket parts marketed globally primarily under the Hyster and Yale brand names. The company operates through its subsidiaries, but primarily via Hyster-Yale Group, Inc. Lift trucks and component parts are manufactured in the U.S., Northern Ireland, Mexico, the Netherlands, Italy, the Philippines, Vietnam, Japan, Brazil and China. The firm operates through three geographical and three subsidiary segments: the Americas; EMEA (Europe, Middle East, Africa); JAPIC (Japan, Asia Pacific, India, China); Nuvera Fuel Cells, LLC; Bolzoni SpA; and Zhejiang Maximal Forklift Co., Ltd. In each region, certain marketing support functions for the Hyster and Yale brands are carried out by shared services teams, including sales and service training, information systems support, product launch coordination, specialized sales material development, help desks, order entry, marketing strategy and field service support. Hyster-Yale dealers are located in 129 countries, and generally independently owned and operated. The Americas segment has 13 Hyster, 28 Yale and 30 dual-branded (Hyster-Yale) dealers; EMEA has 69 Hyster, 90 Yale and five dual-branded dealers; and JAPIC has 51 Hyster, eight Yale and five dual-branded dealers. Nuvera is based in Massachusetts and is an alternative-power technology company focused on fuel-cell stacks and related systems. It also supports on-site hydrogen production and dispensing systems designed to deliver clean energy solutions to customers. Bolzoni is a worldwide producer of attachments, forks and lift tables under the Bolzoni Auramo and Meyer brand names. Maximal is a Chinese manufacturer of utility and standard lift trucks, as well as specialized material handling equipment, marketed under the Maximal brand name. The sales of lift trucks represent approximately 77% of the company's annual revenue (2018), including internal combustion engine units (49%) and electric units (28%).

FINANCIAL DATA: *Note: Data for latest year may not have been available at press time.*

In U.S. $	2018	2017	2016	2015	2014	2013
Revenue	3,174,400,000	2,885,200,000	2,569,700,000	2,578,100,000	2,767,200,000	2,666,300,000
R&D Expense						
Operating Income	38,800,000	76,000,000	34,600,000	103,500,000	131,000,000	134,300,000
Operating Margin %		.03%	.01%	.04%	.05%	.05%
SGA Expense	458,300,000	426,600,000	392,900,000	327,300,000	316,700,000	326,700,000
Net Income	34,700,000	48,600,000	42,800,000	74,700,000	109,800,000	110,000,000
Operating Cash Flow	67,600,000	164,700,000	-48,900,000	89,400,000	100,000,000	152,900,000
Capital Expenditure	38,800,000	41,000,000	42,700,000	46,600,000	48,500,000	36,500,000
EBITDA	96,600,000	151,200,000	84,100,000	138,100,000	183,700,000	166,600,000
Return on Assets %		.03%	.04%	.07%	.10%	.10%
Return on Equity %		.09%	.09%	.16%	.24%	.28%
Debt to Equity		0.382	0.177	0.043	0.026	0.015

CONTACT INFORMATION:

Phone: 440 449-9600 Fax:
Toll-Free:
Address: 5875 Landerbrook Dr., Ste. 300, Cleveland, OH 44124-4069 United States

STOCK TICKER/OTHER:

Stock Ticker: HY
Employees: 6,500
Parent Company:
Exchange: NYS
Fiscal Year Ends: 12/31

SALARIES/BONUSES:

Top Exec. Salary: $954,965 Bonus: $
Second Exec. Salary: $737,883 Bonus: $

OTHER THOUGHTS:

Estimated Female Officers or Directors:
Hot Spot for Advancement for Women/Minorities:

Hyundai Mobis Co Ltd

www.mobis.co.kr

NAIC Code: 336300

TYPES OF BUSINESS:

Automotive Parts Manufacturing
Automotive Parts Development
Automotive Parts Testing

BRANDS/DIVISIONS/AFFILIATES:

Hyundai Motor Group

CONTACTS: *Note: Officers with more than one job title may be intentionally listed here more than once.*

Kook Park Chung, CEO
Jun Ho-Suck, Pres.
Chae Gui-Hwan, Managing Dir.
Bae Ki-Eop, Head-Multi Parts Design Dept.

GROWTH PLANS/SPECIAL FEATURES:

Hyundai Mobis Co., Ltd. is a leading Korean automotive parts manufacturer. The company operates through three business divisions: automobile modules manufacturing, auto parts manufacturing and after-sales parts. The automobile modules manufacturing division utilizes cutting-edge modularization technology to manufacture and supply chassis modules, cockpit modules and front-end modules, the three core modules for carmakers. The auto parts manufacturing division develops and manufactures safety systems such as airbags, braking systems steering systems, lamp/lighting systems and air suspension systems. Air suspension systems minimize air resistance and secures handling by lowering the height of the vehicle during high-speed driving as well as driving on rough roads. It also facilitates loading and unloading passengers or cargo by adjusting the height of the vehicles accordingly. Last, the after-sales parts division supplies aftermarket service parts to approximately 57 million Hyundai and Kia Motors vehicles worldwide. This division also engages in the innovation of the parts supply system, including streamlining logistics hubs and establishing hi-tech distribution systems. In addition, Hyundai Mobis offers customized products and services, as well as related vehicle accessories. Hyundai Mobis operates as a subsidiary of Hyundai Motor Group. The firm announced plans to develop all autonomous driving sensors by 2020, including cameras and lidars, actively using artificial intelligence (AI) and deep learning to induce quantum leap concerning sensor technologies.

FINANCIAL DATA: *Note: Data for latest year may not have been available at press time.*

In U.S. $	2018	2017	2016	2015	2014	2013
Revenue	29,629,030,000	29,625,120,000	32,252,740,000	30,362,850,000	29,609,980,000	28,827,700,000
R&D Expense	637,663,800	580,675,400	527,659,700	484,539,500	410,670,000	332,843,800
Operating Income	1,706,937,000	1,706,914,000	2,448,510,000	2,473,697,000	1,696,211,000	2,465,126,000
Operating Margin %		.06%	.08%	.08%	.06%	.09%
SGA Expense	619,958,500	603,674,400	614,897,400	567,570,000	612,609,700	581,428,900
Net Income	1,592,167,000	1,321,874,000	2,560,701,000	2,575,561,000	2,884,920,000	2,884,168,000
Operating Cash Flow	1,357,257,000	1,642,692,000	1,700,893,000	3,668,404,000	713,630,500	1,584,405,000
Capital Expenditure	472,309,900	610,317,700	1,119,973,000	3,485,956,000	936,308,400	591,398,500
EBITDA	2,741,930,000	2,945,518,000	4,045,533,000	4,036,160,000	4,310,580,000	4,327,546,000
Return on Assets %		.04%	.08%	.08%	.09%	.11%
Return on Equity %		.05%	.11%	.13%	.16%	.18%
Debt to Equity		0.045	0.058	0.051	0.049	0.06

CONTACT INFORMATION:

Phone: 82 220185114 Fax: 82 220186000
Toll-Free:
Address: 203, Teheran-ro Gangnam-gu, Seoul, 06141 South Korea

STOCK TICKER/OTHER:

Stock Ticker: HYPLF
Exchange: PINX
Employees: 7,222
Fiscal Year Ends: 12/31
Parent Company: Hyundai Motor Group

SALARIES/BONUSES:

Top Exec. Salary: $ Bonus: $
Second Exec. Salary: $ Bonus: $

OTHER THOUGHTS:

Estimated Female Officers or Directors:
Hot Spot for Advancement for Women/Minorities:

Hyundai Motor America

www.hyundaiusa.com

NAIC Code: 336111

TYPES OF BUSINESS:

Automobile Manufacturing
Automobile Manufacturing

BRANDS/DIVISIONS/AFFILIATES:

Hyundai Motor Company
Elantra
Sonata
Tucson
Kona
Veloster
Genesis
Ioniq

CONTACTS: *Note: Officers with more than one job title may be intentionally listed here more than once.*

Kenny Lee, CEO
Dean Evans, CMO
Michael J. O'Brien, VP-Prod. Planning
Michael J. O'Brien, VP-Corp. Planning
Christopher Hosford, Exec. Dir.-Comm.
Frank Ferrara, Exec. VP-Customer Satisfaction
Christopher Chapman, Chief Designer

GROWTH PLANS/SPECIAL FEATURES:

Hyundai Motor America is the U.S. subsidiary of Hyundai Motor Company, which is based in Korea. It is responsible for the distribution of Hyundai vehicles nationwide and for manufacturing Hyundai vehicles. The company sells Hyundai models such as the Elantra and Sonata sedans; Tucson, Kona and Santa Fe SUVs and crossovers; Accent, Veloster and Elantra compact hatchbacks; Genesis luxury vehicles; and Ioniq and Sonata hybrid/fuel cell vehicles. Hyundai Motor America supports over 800 U.S. Hyundai dealers through its manufacturing facilities in Michigan, Alabama and California. The firm operates one of the most technologically advanced manufacturing facilities in the world in Alabama, comprised of over 2 million square-feet, with nearly 300 welding robots and the capability to produce approximately 300,000 vehicles annually. The company's website possesses shopping tools that allow customers to build their own cars, receive quotes, schedule test drives, locate dealers and obtain trade-in appraisals.

Hyundai Motor America offers its employees medical, dental and vision coverage; life, disability, business travel and AD&D insurance; flexible spending accounts; a 401(k); dependent and long-term care programs; an employee assistance program; employee discounts; corporate onsite fitness centers and convenience stores with laundry and tailoring services; education reimbursement; training and mentoring; and relocation assistance.

FINANCIAL DATA: *Note: Data for latest year may not have been available at press time.*

In U.S. $	2018	2017	2016	2015	2014	2013
Revenue	13,689,800,000	15,060,100,000	16,144,000,000	15,397,949,697	15,052,444,331	16,359,450,809
R&D Expense						
Operating Income						
Operating Margin %						
SGA Expense						
Net Income	-295,529,000	-812,911,000	-55,295,882	-146,794,703	338,785,997	483,362,165
Operating Cash Flow						
Capital Expenditure						
EBITDA						
Return on Assets %						
Return on Equity %						
Debt to Equity						

CONTACT INFORMATION:

Phone: 714-965-3000 Fax: 714-965-3149
Toll-Free: 800-633-5151
Address: 10550 Talbert Ave., Fountain Valley, CA 92708 United States

STOCK TICKER/OTHER:

Stock Ticker: Subsidiary
Exchange:
Employees: 31,100
Fiscal Year Ends: 12/31
Parent Company: Hyundai Motor Company

SALARIES/BONUSES:

Top Exec. Salary: $ Bonus: $
Second Exec. Salary: $ Bonus: $

OTHER THOUGHTS:

Estimated Female Officers or Directors:
Hot Spot for Advancement for Women/Minorities:

Hyundai Motor Company Limited

worldwide.hyundai.com

NAIC Code: 336111

TYPES OF BUSINESS:

Automobile Manufacturing
Trucks
Buses
Light Commercial Vehicles
Machine Tools
Factory Automation Equipment
Material Handling Equipment
Specialty Vehicle Manufacturing

BRANDS/DIVISIONS/AFFILIATES:

Accent
Sonata
Elantra
Xcient
Genesis
Kia Motors Corporation
Hyundai Motor America
Hyundai Capital Germany GmbH

CONTACTS:

Note: Officers with more than one job title may be intentionally listed here more than once.

Mong-Koo Chung, CEO
Choong Ho Kim, Co-CEO
Mong-Koo Chung, Chmn.

GROWTH PLANS/SPECIAL FEATURES:

Hyundai Motor Company, headquartered in South Korea, is one of the world's leading automobile manufacturers. The firm designs and manufactures passenger cars; recreational vehicles; commercial vehicles, including trucks, buses and tractors; and specialty vehicles, including crane trucks, refrigerated vans and tank trucks for fuel and water transport. Popular export models include the Accent, a sub-compact; the Sonata, a mid-size sedan; the Elantra, a compact sedan; the Santa Fe SUV; and the Tucson SUV. Light commercial vehicles include the H-1 cargo van, the Xcient truck and a variety of mini buses. Heavy commercial vehicles include small/medium size HD36L, HD35-78 and HD120 trucks and busses as well as cargo, dump, mixer and tractor trucks. Hyundai's i30 N vehicle offers the feeling of driving a racecar with up to 275 horsepower and high-performance cornering capabilities; KONA is a compact SUV; and the IONIQ model offers a line of electric and hybrid sedans. Genesis is the firm's luxury car unit. Hyundai also makes machine tools for factory automation and material handling and owns approximately 34% of Kia Motors Corporation. Subsidiary Hyundai Motor America oversees U.S. operations, including primary facilities in Alabama, Michigan and California. The subsidiary also distributes Hyundai vehicles in the U.S. In addition to its U.S. operations, the firm has other overseas plants in Brazil, Turkey, the Czech Republic, Russia, India and China, as well as research and development centers in North America, Japan and Europe. The company offers automotive financing services to European customers through joint venture Hyundai Capital Germany GmbH.

FINANCIAL DATA:

Note: Data for latest year may not have been available at press time.

In U.S. $	2018	2017	2016	2015	2014	2013
Revenue	81,608,180,000	81,240,210,000	78,941,450,000	77,516,610,000	75,238,600,000	73,595,970,000
R&D Expense	948,826,900	876,044,200	859,124,500	783,336,600	668,219,100	609,226,900
Operating Income	2,041,764,000	3,856,215,000	4,377,861,000	5,359,396,000	6,364,260,000	7,009,548,000
Operating Margin %			.06%	.07%	.08%	.10%
SGA Expense	7,068,858,000	7,452,180,000	7,020,550,000	6,586,103,000	6,590,123,000	6,375,935,000
Net Income	1,271,239,000	3,399,469,000	4,557,354,000	5,409,465,000	6,192,991,000	7,200,338,000
Operating Cash Flow	3,173,087,000	3,306,405,000	840,390,700	1,052,351,000	1,787,766,000	1,018,676,000
Capital Expenditure	4,096,060,000	3,808,554,000	3,690,024,000	7,889,898,000	3,983,693,000	3,508,490,000
EBITDA	5,561,886,000	6,997,309,000	9,220,213,000	9,704,560,000	10,790,960,000	12,298,000,000
Return on Assets %			.03%	.04%	.05%	.07%
Return on Equity %			.08%	.11%	.13%	.18%
Debt to Equity			0.742	0.722	0.654	0.654

CONTACT INFORMATION:

Phone: 82 234641114 Fax: 82 234643477
Toll-Free:
Address: 12 Heolleung-ro Seocho-gu, Seoul, 06797 South Korea

STOCK TICKER/OTHER:

Stock Ticker: HYMLF
Exchange: PINX
Employees: 61,410
Fiscal Year Ends: 12/31
Parent Company:

SALARIES/BONUSES:

Top Exec. Salary: $ Bonus: $
Second Exec. Salary: $ Bonus: $

OTHER THOUGHTS:

Estimated Female Officers or Directors:
Hot Spot for Advancement for Women/Minorities:

Inchcape plc

NAIC Code: 441110

www.inchcape.com

TYPES OF BUSINESS:

Auto Dealers, Retail
Import & Distribution Services
Financial Services
Logistics
Refurbishment
e-Commerce

BRANDS/DIVISIONS/AFFILIATES:

GROWTH PLANS/SPECIAL FEATURES:

Inchcape plc is an international automotive services company, present in 32 national markets. The firm operates across the full spectrum of the post-factory automotive value chain for original equipment manufacturers (OEMs). This value chain includes product planning and logistics, product specification, land/sea distribution, brand management, appoint and manage the dealer network (of which Inchcape typically owns and operates 15-20% of the network themselves), national marketing, price positioning, new and used car retailing, vehicle sales, customer engagement/retention, vehicle finance, insurance, aftersales care, vehicle servicing and parts. Inchcape has seven core OEM partnerships, which are primarily built around exclusive distribution contracts in multiple markets. These partners include Toyota Motor Corporation, Jaguar Land Rover Limited, Suzuki, Mercedes-Benz Retail Group, Volkswagen Group, BMW Group and Subaru. In total, the company has relationships with approximately 40 brands, including Aston Martin, Bentley, Daihatsu, Kia, Mack, Peugeot, smart and Volvo. Inchcape operates in the U.K., Europe, Russia, Asia, Africa, Australasia and South America.

CONTACTS: *Note: Officers with more than one job title may be intentionally listed here more than once.*

Stefan Bomhard, CEO
Richard Howes, CFO
Katherine Milliken, Group General Counsel
Ken Lee, Group Dir.-Comm.
John McConnell, Group Dir.-Finance
Nigel Stein, Chmn.

FINANCIAL DATA: *Note: Data for latest year may not have been available at press time.*

In U.S. $	2018	2017	2016	2015	2014	2013
Revenue	11,275,050,000	10,876,650,000	9,526,610,000	8,308,681,000	8,146,307,000	7,930,212,000
R&D Expense						
Operating Income	468,041,600	495,266,100	436,441,800	394,632,900	361,696,200	336,173,200
Operating Margin %		.05%	.05%	.04%	.04%	.04%
SGA Expense	1,122,157,000	1,043,401,000	907,035,800	810,777,900	806,038,000	801,419,500
Net Income	58,581,160	326,814,800	224,115,500	213,663,200	218,281,700	236,026,200
Operating Cash Flow	456,617,100	473,389,300	330,096,400	293,392,000	407,758,900	195,068,000
Capital Expenditure	152,165,200	154,595,900	114,002,400	84,104,080	84,833,300	141,591,400
EBITDA	284,033,600	566,122,600	421,735,800	406,665,100	392,931,300	399,737,400
Return on Assets %		.06%	.05%	.05%	.05%	.06%
Return on Equity %		.19%	.14%	.14%	.13%	.13%
Debt to Equity		0.252	0.217	0.256	0.237	0.203

CONTACT INFORMATION:

Phone: 44 2075460022 Fax: 44 2075460010
Toll-Free:
Address: 22A St. James's Sq., London, SW1Y 5LP United Kingdom

STOCK TICKER/OTHER:

Stock Ticker: INCPY
Exchange: PINX
Employees: 18,827
Fiscal Year Ends: 12/31
Parent Company:

SALARIES/BONUSES:

Top Exec. Salary: $898,164 Bonus: $522,612
Second Exec. Salary: $514,104 Bonus: $345,167

OTHER THOUGHTS:

Estimated Female Officers or Directors: 2
Hot Spot for Advancement for Women/Minorities: Y

Inoue Rubber (Thailand) Public Company Limited

www.ircthailand.com

NAIC Code: 326200

TYPES OF BUSINESS:

Industrial Rubber Parts Manufacturing
Motorcycle Tire & Tube Manufacturing
Motorcycle Wheel Set Assembly

BRANDS/DIVISIONS/AFFILIATES:

Inoue Rubber Company Limited
Kinno Hoshi Engineering Company Limited
IRC (Asia) Research Company Limited

CONTACTS:

Note: Officers with more than one job title may be intentionally listed here more than once.

Pimjai Laochinda, Pres.
Sopa Lumlerdvoravith, Sr. Mgr.-Acct.
Koji Matsuda, Vice Chmn.
Pornthip Sethiwan, Dir.-IRC (Asia) Research Co.
Koji Yamauchi, Exec. Dir.
Nareothai Boothong, Exec. Dir.
Pimjai Leeissaranukul, Chmn.

GROWTH PLANS/SPECIAL FEATURES:

Inoue Rubber (Thailand) Public Company Limited (IRC) manufactures industrial elastomer parts as well as motorcycle tires and tubes. The company started in 1969 as a collaboration between Japanese firm Inoue Rubber Company Limited (Inoue Japan) and shareholders from the Leeissaranukul family, who have a long history in Thailand's automotive industry. Today, Inoue Japan owns 34.3% of the firm. IRC's industrial elastomer parts mainly consist of rubber components for automobiles and motorcycles, including gaskets, bumpers, weather stripping, door sponges and engine mountings. The firm also supplies rubber parts used in other industries (including agriculture), such as insulators, gaskets and hoses. Its customers include automotive manufacturers such as Chevrolet, Ford, Toyota, Suzuki, Honda, Isuzu, Mazda, Nissan, Hino and Mitsubishi. IRC's motorcycle tires, comprised of off-road tires, on-road tires, heavy tires and scooter tires, as well as its motorcycle tubes, are supplied to both domestic and overseas motorcycle manufacturers. As a value-added service, the company also assembles its tires and tubes into complete wheels. IRC has two primary facilities, both located in Thailand, which manufacture products under the IRC brand name. At its headquarters in Prachathipat, the company manufactures motorcycle tires and tubes and assembles wheel sets; it manufactures industrial rubber parts at its plant in Lam Sai. Subsidiary Kinno Hoshi Engineering Company Limited produces metal molds for IRC's industrial elastomer products; and IRC (Asia) Research Company Limited engages in the research and development of industrial elastomer products and motorcycle tires and tubes in order to respond to and supply the specific needs of IRC customers.

FINANCIAL DATA:

Note: Data for latest year may not have been available at press time.

In U.S. $	2018	2017	2016	2015	2014	2013
Revenue	172,828,000	159,677,000	148,876,494	195,947,997	150,800,000	213,500,000
R&D Expense						
Operating Income						
Operating Margin %						
SGA Expense						
Net Income	11,039,800	12,692,400	13,279,181	11,727,665	8,700,000	12,800,000
Operating Cash Flow						
Capital Expenditure						
EBITDA						
Return on Assets %						
Return on Equity %						
Debt to Equity						

CONTACT INFORMATION:

Phone: 66-2-996-0890 Fax: 66-2-996-1439
Toll-Free:
Address: 258 Soi Rangsit-Nakornnayok 49, Prachatipat, 12130 Thailand

STOCK TICKER/OTHER:

Stock Ticker: IRC Exchange: Bangkok
Employees: 1,679 Fiscal Year Ends: 09/30
Parent Company: Inoue Rubber Company Limited

SALARIES/BONUSES:

Top Exec. Salary: $ Bonus: $
Second Exec. Salary: $ Bonus: $

OTHER THOUGHTS:

Estimated Female Officers or Directors: 4
Hot Spot for Advancement for Women/Minorities: Y

International Automotive Components Group SA

www.iacgroup.com

NAIC Code: 336300

TYPES OF BUSINESS:

Automotive Components Manufacturing
Automotive Components

BRANDS/DIVISIONS/AFFILIATES:

Coreback
FastKast
FiberFrame
HybridFleece Molding
Safe-TEC
SmartFoil
ThinFoam
TwinSurface

CONTACTS: *Note: Officers with more than one job title may be intentionally listed here more than once.*

Manfred Gingl, CEO
David Prystash, CFO
David Pascoe, CTO
Bruce Banks, VP-Mfg. Eng.
Janis N. Acosta, General Counsel
Tim Moore, VP-Continuous Improvement
Dan Griffin, VP-Sales & Program Mgmt., Asia
Kelli Carney, Sr. VP-Global Purchasing

GROWTH PLANS/SPECIAL FEATURES:

International Automotive Components Group SA (IAC Group) is a leading supplier of automotive components and systems to original equipment manufacturers (OEMs) across the globe. IAC Group's operations comprise more than 50 manufacturing facilities and 17 design, technical and commercial centers located in 17 countries. The company specializes in the production of: door and trim systems; instrument panels, consoles and cockpits; flooring and acoustic systems; headliner and overhead systems; and other interior and exterior components. Globally, IAC Group's products are incorporated into more than 300 different models, with major OEM customers including Opel, Ford, Volkswagen, BMW, Jaguar Land Rover, Hyundai/Kia, Daimler, Volvo, Fiat Chrysler, General Motors, Honda, Mercedes, Nissan and Toyota. The company's branded and trademarked innovations include: Coreback, a proprietary process that adds a chemical foaming agent to the resin when molding a vehicle interior component; FastKast, a process with polyvinyl chloride (PVC) and thermoplastic polyurethane (TPU) materials that improves quality, reduces cycle times and is environmentally friendly; FiberFrame, a lightweight natural fiber sunroof frame made of 70% renewable, raw-material content; HybridFleece Molding, a process for combining the pressing of a thermoplastic-mixed fiber fleece of natural fiber, glass or recycled carbon fiber with the molding of stiffening ribs and clips into a one-step process in the same molding tool with no need for additional welding or gluing; and Safe-TEC, a 100% recyclable injection-molded safety countermeasure and integrated module that provides solutions for side-impact protection and performance in Federal Motor Vehicle Safety Standards testing. Other trademark brands include SmartFoil, SprayPUR, ThinFoam, TwinFoil, TwinSurface and TAC2. Based in Luxembourg, the firm's international headquarters are located in: the U.S., serving North America; Germany, serving Europe; and China, serving Asia and Africa.

FINANCIAL DATA: *Note: Data for latest year may not have been available at press time.*

In U.S. $	2018	2017	2016	2015	2014	2013
Revenue	4,620,000,000	4,400,000,000	6,000,000,000	5,900,000,000	5,900,000,000	5,200,000,000
R&D Expense						
Operating Income						
Operating Margin %						
SGA Expense						
Net Income						
Operating Cash Flow						
Capital Expenditure						
EBITDA						
Return on Assets %						
Return on Equity %						
Debt to Equity						

CONTACT INFORMATION:

Phone: 352-267-50422 Fax: 352-276-50499
Toll-Free:
Address: 4, rue Lou Hemmer, Findel, Luxembourg L-1748 Luxembourg

STOCK TICKER/OTHER:

Stock Ticker: Private
Employees: 22,000
Parent Company:
Exchange:
Fiscal Year Ends: 11/10

SALARIES/BONUSES:

Top Exec. Salary: $ Bonus: $
Second Exec. Salary: $ Bonus: $

OTHER THOUGHTS:

Estimated Female Officers or Directors: 2
Hot Spot for Advancement for Women/Minorities:

Interstate Battery System of America Inc

www.interstatebatteries.com

NAIC Code: 335911

TYPES OF BUSINESS:

Battery Manufacturing
Retail Battery Sales
Battery Distribution

BRANDS/DIVISIONS/AFFILIATES:

Interstate All Battery Centers
PowerCare and Service Solutions Inc
Interstate Batteries Recycling Inc

CONTACTS: *Note: Officers with more than one job title may be intentionally listed here more than once.*

Scott Miller, CEO
Dale Herold, COO
Will McDade, CFO
Onyeka Nchege, CIO
Walt Holmes, Chief Legal Officer
Jane Koenecke, VP-Creative Comm. & Events
Wendell Samuel, VP-PowerCare
Scott Miller, VP-Independent Distributor Group
Billy Norris, VP-National Accounts
Norm Miller, Chmn.
Jon Savage, VP-Intl. Dev. & Interstate Batteries Recycling
Chris Antoniou, Chief Supply Chain Officer

GROWTH PLANS/SPECIAL FEATURES:

Interstate Battery System of America, Inc. (IBSA) produces and distributes batteries through its distributors, dealers, Interstate All Battery Center stores and the internet. The company's batteries are used in the automotive and marine industries as well as in motorcycles, snowmobiles, 4-wheelers, watercrafts, recreational vehicles, lawn mowers, watches, households, laptops, hearing-aids, wheelchairs/mobility scooters, forklifts, cordless/cellular phones and backup power supplies. More than 200,000 retail dealers and 200 All Battery Center franchise stores sell IBSA batteries throughout the U.S. and Canada. The firm also has roughly 300 wholesale warehouses. At its retail locations, an IBSA regional manager comes at regular intervals to rotate stock and pick up old batteries for recycling in order to keep the stock fresh. Through Interstate Batteries Recycling, Inc., IBSA recycles lead-acid batteries, industrial batteries and household batteries, recycling approximately 25 million vehicle batteries each year. The firm's PowerCare and Service Solutions, Inc. subsidiary provides batteries and battery services to the power industry. Interstate All Battery Centers offer more than 12,000 different types of household and business batteries. These batteries utilize NiCad, NiMH, SLA, lithium, alkaline, zinc air and silver oxide cell technology. Household batteries are used for products such as flashlights and camcorders, and business batteries are used for products such as pagers and computer backup power. In addition, consumers are able to purchase many of the company's batteries online. IBSA does business with automotive manufacturers.

The company offers its employees health and life insurance, paid holidays, tuition reimbursement and wellness programs.

FINANCIAL DATA: *Note: Data for latest year may not have been available at press time.*

In U.S. $	2018	2017	2016	2015	2014	2013
Revenue	1,890,000,000	1,800,000,000	1,600,000,000	1,575,000,000	1,555,000,000	1,550,000,000
R&D Expense						
Operating Income						
Operating Margin %						
SGA Expense						
Net Income						
Operating Cash Flow						
Capital Expenditure						
EBITDA						
Return on Assets %						
Return on Equity %						
Debt to Equity						

CONTACT INFORMATION:

Phone: 972-991-1444 Fax: 972-458-8288
Toll-Free: 866-842-5368
Address: 12770 Merit Dr., Ste. 300, Dallas, TX 75251 United States

STOCK TICKER/OTHER:

Stock Ticker: Private
Employees: 1,500
Parent Company:
Exchange:
Fiscal Year Ends: 12/31

SALARIES/BONUSES:

Top Exec. Salary: $ Bonus: $
Second Exec. Salary: $ Bonus: $

OTHER THOUGHTS:

Estimated Female Officers or Directors: 2
Hot Spot for Advancement for Women/Minorities:

Isuzu Motors Limited

www.isuzu.co.jp

NAIC Code: 336111

TYPES OF BUSINESS:

Automobile Manufacturing
Trucks & Buses
Diesel Engines
Logistics Services

BRANDS/DIVISIONS/AFFILIATES:

mu-X
Panther
Isuzu D-MAX
Erga Mio
Isuzu (China) Holding Co Ltd
Isuzu Malaysia Sendirian Berhad
Isuzu Philippines Corporation
Isuzu Motors India Private Limited

CONTACTS: *Note: Officers with more than one job title may be intentionally listed here more than once.*

Masanori Katayama, Pres.
Susumu Hosoi, Chmn.

GROWTH PLANS/SPECIAL FEATURES:

Isuzu Motors Limited, headquartered in Tokyo, manufactures and sells sport-utility vehicles (SUVs), pickups, freight trucks, buses, automobile parts and diesel engines. Its SUV line includes the mu-X in Thailand and the Panther in Indonesia, while its pick-up truck offering is the Isuzu D-MAX, popular throughout Thailand. Commercial truck models come in heavy, medium and light-duty varieties, with models that include tractor-trailers, dump trucks and concrete trucks. Isuzu sells its buses under the Erga brand name, offering a standard-size version and a smaller version known as the Erga Mio, both of which offer natural gas and diesel-run options. The company has focused on the development of fuel-efficient and low-emissions diesel engines for years, and currently produces a wide variety of diesel engine models sold to the automotive, industrial and maritime markets. Additionally, the firm produces snowmobile engines as well as industrial engines, such as cooler power sources for use in construction machinery, boats, agricultural tractors and refrigerated trucks. Isuzu Motors has more than 40 subsidiaries worldwide, and its products are currently sold in more than 100 countries. Its Fujisawa plant performs the company's research and development activities, and handles the assembly of heavy/medium/light-duty trucks. The Tochigi plant manufactures engines. Overseas subsidiaries include Isuzu (China) Holding Co. Ltd.; Isuzu Motors Asia Ltd. (Singapore); Isuzu Malaysia Sendirian Berhad; Isuzu Vietnam Co. Ltd.; PT Isuzu Astra Motor Indonesia: Isuzu Motors Co. (Thailand) Ltd.; Isuzu Philippines Corporation; Isuzu Motors India Private Limited; and Isuzu Motors Saudi Arabia Company Limited, among others.

FINANCIAL DATA: *Note: Data for latest year may not have been available at press time.*

In U.S. $	2018	2017	2016	2015	2014	2013
Revenue	19,025,540,000	17,948,780,000	17,707,840,000	17,271,110,000	16,181,380,000	
R&D Expense						
Operating Income	1,532,522,000	1,345,791,000	1,576,576,000	1,572,478,000	1,601,305,000	
Operating Margin %	.08%	.09%	.11%	.11%	.12%	
SGA Expense	500,900,600	446,544,700	478,570,100	429,084,700	364,510,200	
Net Income	970,988,800	862,506,900	1,053,814,000	1,075,721,000	1,096,453,000	
Operating Cash Flow	1,624,738,000	1,390,847,000	1,221,945,000	1,392,740,000	1,463,049,000	
Capital Expenditure						
EBITDA	2,268,618,000	1,978,965,000	2,278,037,000	2,175,758,000	2,143,145,000	
Return on Assets %	.05%	.05%	.06%	.07%	.08%	
Return on Equity %	.12%	.12%	.15%	.17%	.21%	
Debt to Equity	0.22	0.249	0.249	0.189	0.131	

CONTACT INFORMATION:

Phone: 81 354711141 Fax: 81 354711043
Toll-Free:
Address: 6-26-1 Minami-Oi, Shinagawa-Ku, Tokyo, 140-8722 Japan

STOCK TICKER/OTHER:

Stock Ticker: ISUZF
Employees: 47,255
Parent Company:
Exchange: PINX
Fiscal Year Ends: 03/31

SALARIES/BONUSES:

Top Exec. Salary: $ Bonus: $
Second Exec. Salary: $ Bonus: $

OTHER THOUGHTS:

Estimated Female Officers or Directors:
Hot Spot for Advancement for Women/Minorities:

Jaguar Land Rover Limited

www.jaguarlandrover.com

NAIC Code: 336111

TYPES OF BUSINESS:

Automobile Manufacturing
Racing
Financial Services

BRANDS/DIVISIONS/AFFILIATES:

Tata Motors Limited
XE
XF
XJ
F-Type
I-Pace
E-Pace
F-Pace

CONTACTS: *Note: Officers with more than one job title may be intentionally listed here more than once.*

Ralf D. Speth, CEO
Kenneth Gregor, CFO
Ian Harnett, Exec. Dir.-Human Resources
Ian Callum, Dir.-Jaguar Design

GROWTH PLANS/SPECIAL FEATURES:

Jaguar Land Rover Limited, founded in 1922 and based in the U.K., manufactures a distinctive line of luxury sedans, sports cars and electric/hybrid vehicles. The company is part of India-based Tata Motors Limited. Jaguar's current line includes six models: the XE, XF, XJ, F-Type, I-Pace, E-Pace and F-Pace. The Jaguar XE is a line of sports saloon cars comprising lightweight aluminum intensive architecture and packed with systems that deliver premium handling and performance. The XF is a sports sedan with a 5.0-liter V8 supercharged engine as well as features such as Bluetooth phone connectivity, a portable audio interface and voice-controlled navigation options. The company's flagship model, the XJ sedan, features a monocoque alloy body shell, a 470 hp supercharged engine and 510 hp engine, Bluetooth wireless technology and automatic climate control. The F-Type is a convertible sports car with 3.0 Litre V6 engines, quick shift transmission and a stiffer body for more precise and intuitive control. The I-Pace is an all-electric performance sport utility vehicle (SUV). The E-Pace is a compact SUV. The F-Pace is a sports car based on the C-X17 crossover concept vehicle, and also includes the lightweight aluminum intensive architecture. In total, Jaguar operates five engineering and production facilities in the Midlands and North West of England, three of which it shares with sister company Land Rover. Jaguar Land Rover recently announced that all new Jaguar and Land Rover models launched from the 2020 model year will have an all-electric or hybrid powertrain option.

FINANCIAL DATA: *Note: Data for latest year may not have been available at press time.*

In U.S. $	2018	2017	2016	2015	2014	2013
Revenue	36,181,100,000	32,783,700,000	25,605,600,000	31,098,153,190	29,784,165,750	26,669,822,970
R&D Expense						
Operating Income						
Operating Margin %						
SGA Expense						
Net Income	1,589,750,000	2,158,600,000	1,613,970,000	2,898,474,170	2,886,848,625	2,835,626,104
Operating Cash Flow						
Capital Expenditure						
EBITDA						
Return on Assets %						
Return on Equity %						
Debt to Equity						

CONTACT INFORMATION:

Phone: 44-24-7640-2121 Fax:
Toll-Free:
Address: Abbey Rd., Whitley, Coventry, CV3 4LF United Kingdom

STOCK TICKER/OTHER:

Stock Ticker: Subsidiary
Employees: 43,224
Parent Company: TATA Motors Limited
Exchange:
Fiscal Year Ends: 03/31

SALARIES/BONUSES:

Top Exec. Salary: $ Bonus: $
Second Exec. Salary: $ Bonus: $

OTHER THOUGHTS:

Estimated Female Officers or Directors:
Hot Spot for Advancement for Women/Minorities:

Jardine Cycle & Carriage Limited

www.jcclgroup.com

NAIC Code: 336111

TYPES OF BUSINESS:

Automobiles, Retailing
Auto Distribution
Auto Dealers
Auto Service
Auto Insurance

BRANDS/DIVISIONS/AFFILIATES:

Jardine Matheson Group
Cycle & Carriage
Tunas Ridean Tbk
Truong Hai Auto Corporation
PT Astra International Tbk
Siam City Cement pcl
Refrigeration Electrical Engineering Corporation

CONTACTS: *Note: Officers with more than one job title may be intentionally listed here more than once.*

Alex Newbigging, Managing Dir.
Stephen Gore, Dir-Finance
Ho Yeng Tat, Sec.
Cheah Kim Teck, CEO-Group Motor Oper.
Ho Yeng Tat, Dir.-Corp. Affairs
Chiew Sin Cheok, Dir.-Group Finance
Wong Kin Foo, CEO-Cycle & Carriage Bintang Berhad
Rico Setiawan, Pres.
Tran Ba Duong, Chmn.
Prijono Sugiarto, Pres.
Benjamin Keswick, Chmn.

GROWTH PLANS/SPECIAL FEATURES:

Jardine Cycle & Carriage Limited manages a variety of Singapore and Southeast Asian business interests in regards to motor vehicle distribution and retailing. The company operates its motor vehicle distribution, sales and after-sales businesses in Singapore, Malaysia and Myanmar under the Cycle & Carriage banner; through Tunas Ridean Tbk in Indonesia; and through Truong Hai Auto Corporation in Vietnam. Jardine has a strategic interest in PT Astra International Tbk, an independent automotive group in Southeast Asia. Astra itself has further interests in financial services, heavy equipment and mining, agribusiness, infrastructure and logistics, information technology and property. Other Jardine business interests include: 25.5%-owned Siam City Cement pcl, as well as 22%-owned Refrigeration Electrical Engineering Corporation (known as REE), which both serve key Southeast Asian markets. Jardine Cycle & Carriage itself is 75%-owned by the Jardine Matheson Group, which operates in the fields of engineering, insurance broking, property investment, retailing, hotels, motor vehicles, financial services, mining and agribusiness.

FINANCIAL DATA: *Note: Data for latest year may not have been available at press time.*

In U.S. $	2018	2017	2016	2015	2014	2013
Revenue	18,991,800,000	17,701,200,000	15,764,000,000	15,718,300,000	18,675,400,000	19,787,800,000
R&D Expense						
Operating Income	1,719,900,000	1,762,900,000	1,499,700,000	1,165,500,000	1,778,000,000	2,063,000,000
Operating Margin %		.10%	.10%	.07%	.11%	.10%
SGA Expense	1,945,600,000	1,877,600,000	1,623,800,000	1,634,500,000	1,738,200,000	1,729,900,000
Net Income	419,600,000	811,200,000	701,700,000	688,100,000	820,200,000	915,000,000
Operating Cash Flow	1,994,600,000	1,654,900,000	1,399,700,000	1,876,900,000	1,239,900,000	1,930,800,000
Capital Expenditure	1,017,200,000	847,200,000	573,100,000	594,700,000	876,600,000	941,600,000
EBITDA	3,069,700,000	3,013,500,000	2,514,500,000	2,293,600,000	3,080,400,000	3,446,700,000
Return on Assets %		.03%	.03%	.03%	.04%	.05%
Return on Equity %		.13%	.13%	.14%	.18%	.21%
Debt to Equity		0.363	0.325	0.474	0.568	0.522

CONTACT INFORMATION:

Phone: 65 6473-3122 Fax: 65 6475-7088
Toll-Free:
Address: 239 Alexandra Rd., Singapore, 159930 Singapore

STOCK TICKER/OTHER:

Stock Ticker: JCYGY Exchange: PINX
Employees: 250,000 Fiscal Year Ends: 12/31
Parent Company: Jardine Matheson Group

SALARIES/BONUSES:

Top Exec. Salary: $ Bonus: $
Second Exec. Salary: $ Bonus: $

OTHER THOUGHTS:

Estimated Female Officers or Directors:
Hot Spot for Advancement for Women/Minorities:

Jason Industries Inc

www.jasoninc.com

NAIC Code: 336300

TYPES OF BUSINESS:

Automobile Parts Manufacturing
Seats
Non-Woven Acoustical Fiber Insulation
Finishing Products
Precision Components

BRANDS/DIVISIONS/AFFILIATES:

Osborn
Sealeze
JacksonLea
Lippert Unipol
Load Runners
Metalex
Morton
Schaffner Manufacturing Company Inc

CONTACTS: *Note: Officers with more than one job title may be intentionally listed here more than once.*

Chad Paris, CFO
Brian Kobylinski, Chairman of the Board
Kevin Kuznicki, General Counsel
Srivas Prasad, General Manager, Divisional
Keith Walz, Senior VP
John Hengel, Vice President, Divisional

GROWTH PLANS/SPECIAL FEATURES:

Jason Industries, Inc. is a diversified manufacturing corporation. The firm operates in four segments: seating, which derived 26.2% of 2018 sales revenue; finishing, 33.9%; acoustics, 26.4%; and components, 13.5%. Through its four businesses, Jason Industries delivers an array of industrial consumables and critical manufactured components to industries such as industrial equipment, motorcycle, outdoor lawn, power equipment, rail, automotive and smart meters. The seating segment manufactures motorcycle seats; operator seats for the construction, agriculture and lawn/garden markets; and seating for the power sports market. The finishing segment manufactures abrasives products, industrial brushes, buffing wheels and buffing compounds. Brands within this segment include Osborn, Sealeze, JacksonLea, Lippert Unipol, Load Runners and DRONCO. The acoustics segment manufactures engineered non-woven, fiber-based acoustical products for the automotive industry. The components segment manufactures a broad range of stamped, formed, expanded and perforated metal components and subassemblies. These products include small gas engines, smart meters, outdoor equipment, hardware, railcars and off-road equipment, which are all branded under the Metalex and Morton labels. Jason Industries' global network comprises 28 manufacturing facilities, 15 sales offices, warehouses and joint venture facilities throughout the U.S. and 13 foreign countries. In April 2019, Jason Industries acquired Schaffner Manufacturing Company, Inc., a North American manufacturer of polishing and finishing products. That August, Jason Industries agreed to sell its fiber solutions business (Janesville) to Motus Integrated Technologies, reducing Jason's automotive market exposure and increasing its focus on the industrial and engineered components segments.

FINANCIAL DATA: *Note: Data for latest year may not have been available at press time.*

In U.S. $	2018	2017	2016	2015	2014	2013
Revenue	612,948,000	648,616,000	705,519,000	708,366,000		680,845,000
R&D Expense						
Operating Income	19,810,000	26,997,000	17,805,000	17,919,000		44,585,000
Operating Margin %		.04%	.03%	.03%		.07%
SGA Expense	106,470,000	103,855,000	113,797,000	129,371,000		108,889,000
Net Income	-19,317,000	-4,478,000	-66,879,000	-74,458,000		24,088,000
Operating Cash Flow	29,757,000	30,091,000	35,117,000	37,886,000		58,078,000
Capital Expenditure	13,905,000	15,977,000	19,866,000	33,033,000		25,770,000
EBITDA	60,776,000	57,166,000	-8,465,000	-34,773,000		90,056,000
Return on Assets %		-.01%	-.11%	-.10%		.05%
Return on Equity %				-1.18%		.71%
Debt to Equity				16.687		7.739

CONTACT INFORMATION:

Phone: 414-277-9300 Fax: 414-277-9445
Toll-Free:
Address: 833 East Michigan St., Ste. 900, Milwauke, WI 53202 United States

STOCK TICKER/OTHER:

Stock Ticker: JASN
Employees: 4,400
Parent Company:
Exchange: NAS
Fiscal Year Ends: 12/31

SALARIES/BONUSES:

Top Exec. Salary: $718,773 Bonus: $
Second Exec. Salary: $310,961 Bonus: $150,000

OTHER THOUGHTS:

Estimated Female Officers or Directors:
Hot Spot for Advancement for Women/Minorities:

Jayco Inc

NAIC Code: 336214

www.jayco.com

TYPES OF BUSINESS:

Travel Trailer and Camper Manufacturing
Motor Homes
Camping Trailers

BRANDS/DIVISIONS/AFFILIATES:

Thor Industries Inc

CONTACTS:

Note: Officers with more than one job title may be intentionally listed here more than once.

Derald L. Bontrager, CEO

GROWTH PLANS/SPECIAL FEATURES:

Jayco, Inc. is a leading manufacturer of recreational vehicles (RVs). The company began in a farmhouse in 1968, and now consists of a large-scale production operation with dealerships throughout the U.S. Jayco's recreational vehicles include camping trailers, travel trailers, fifth wheels, toy haulers and motorhomes. Jayco's camping trailers sleep six to eight people and includes wall-to-wall vinyl flooring, acrylic sinks and faucets, stainless steel indoor/outdoor stoves and residential cabinetry. Travel trailers offer modern kitchen designs, spacious living areas and relaxing bedroom features, with weights ranging from 1,545 to 9,500 or more pounds. Fifth wheels can include lightweight and luxurious features, with some models sleeping up to 11 people. Toy haulers are built to be durable and can haul small recreational vehicles such as motorcycles, quads, ATVS and more, with some models sleeping up to 8 people. Class C motorhomes include a 7,500-lb hitch and sleeps up to 10 people; and some models come with a Mercedes 3500 chasses and V6 turbo diesel engine. Class A motorhomes feature wide windshields, premium handling and ride features, recessed lighting and more, and range in price from approximately $120,000 to more than $300,000. Jayco's craftmanship includes its Magnum roof systems, Climate Shield heating and air system, custom-manufactured frames, and JRide precision handling. The firm operates as a subsidiary of Thor Industries, Inc., a manufacturer of recreational vehicles.

FINANCIAL DATA:

Note: Data for latest year may not have been available at press time.

In U.S. $	2018	2017	2016	2015	2014	2013
Revenue	1,934,887,500	1,842,750,000	1,755,000,000	1,500,000,000	1,125,000,000	800,000,000
R&D Expense						
Operating Income						
Operating Margin %						
SGA Expense						
Net Income			81,900,000	70,000,000		
Operating Cash Flow						
Capital Expenditure						
EBITDA						
Return on Assets %						
Return on Equity %						
Debt to Equity						

CONTACT INFORMATION:

Phone: 574-825-5861 Fax: 574-825-7354
Toll-Free:
Address: 903 S. Main St., Middlebury, IN 46540 United States

STOCK TICKER/OTHER:

Stock Ticker: Subsidiary
Exchange:
Employees: 4,000
Fiscal Year Ends: 08/31
Parent Company: Thor Industries Inc

SALARIES/BONUSES:

Top Exec. Salary: $ Bonus: $
Second Exec. Salary: $ Bonus: $

OTHER THOUGHTS:

Estimated Female Officers or Directors:
Hot Spot for Advancement for Women/Minorities:

JB Poindexter & Co Inc

www.jbpoindexter.com

NAIC Code: 336211

TYPES OF BUSINESS:

Truck Body Manufacturing
Step Van Manufacturing
Truck Accessories
Specialty Industrial Products
Contract Machining
Expandable Foam Products
Cargo Handling Equipment
Specialty Vehicles

BRANDS/DIVISIONS/AFFILIATES:

Morgan Corporation
Morgan Olson LLC
Reading Truck Body LLC
Specialty Vehicle Group
Truck Accessories Group LLC
EFP Corporation
MIC Group
Masterack LLC

CONTACTS: *Note: Officers with more than one job title may be intentionally listed here more than once.*

John B. Poindexter, CEO
John B. Poindexter, Pres.
Larry Wolfe, VP-Admin.
Larry Wolfe, Sec.
Michael Ownbey, Pres., Morgan Olson, LLC
Norbert Markert, Pres., Morgan Truck Body, LLC
James E. Donohue, Pres., Truck Accessories Group, LLC
Tim Lautermilch, Pres., Federal Coach, LLC & Eagle Coach, LLC

GROWTH PLANS/SPECIAL FEATURES:

J.B. Poindexter & Co., Inc. is a diversified manufacturing company serving the transportation industry and the industrial products market. The firm comprises over 30 facilities located in the U.S., Canada and Mexico, operating through eight primary subsidiaries. Business focus areas of these companies include truck bodies, step vans, truck accessories, specialty manufacturing and commercial vehicle interiors. Morgan Corporation manufactures truck bodies, and the largest manufacturer of Class 3 to 7 dry freight and refrigerated truck bodies in the U.S. Morgan Olson, LLC produces walk-in vans and dry freight delivery vehicle bodies. Reading Truck Body, LLC is a leading vocational work truck equipment manufacturer in the U.S., serving the equipment needs of municipalities, construction, utility, telecom, oil and gas, and landscape and nursery industries. Specialty Vehicle Group is a vehicle manufacturer of funeral coaches, limousines and other specialty vehicles. Truck Accessories Group, LLC manufactures fiberglass and aluminum truck caps and tonneaus (the part of an automobile that is occupied by the back seats). EFP Corporation, a manufacturer and converter of expanded foam products serving the consumer protective packaging, thermal temperature assurance, recreational vehicles, building and construction products markets. MIC Group supplies comprehensive machining and electro-mechanical assembly solutions to help meet complex manufacturing challenges. MIC's services range from new product development to final production via concurrent engineering services, quick turnaround prototypes, production runs and continuing cost improvements. Last, Masterack, LLC serves the commercial vehicle market with interiors and accessories designed to meet the unique needs of fleet customers.

FINANCIAL DATA: *Note: Data for latest year may not have been available at press time.*

In U.S. $	2018	2017	2016	2015	2014	2013
Revenue	1,470,000,000	1,400,000,000	1,270,000,000	1,250,000,000	1,100,000,000	950,000,000
R&D Expense						
Operating Income						
Operating Margin %						
SGA Expense						
Net Income						
Operating Cash Flow						
Capital Expenditure						
EBITDA						
Return on Assets %						
Return on Equity %						
Debt to Equity						

CONTACT INFORMATION:

Phone: 713-655-9800 Fax: 713-951-9038
Toll-Free:
Address: 600 Travis St., Ste. 200, Houston, TX 77002 United States

STOCK TICKER/OTHER:

Stock Ticker: Private
Employees: 3,300
Parent Company:
Exchange:
Fiscal Year Ends: 12/31

SALARIES/BONUSES:

Top Exec. Salary: $ Bonus: $
Second Exec. Salary: $ Bonus: $

OTHER THOUGHTS:

Estimated Female Officers or Directors:
Hot Spot for Advancement for Women/Minorities:

JD Power & Associates

www.jdpower.com

NAIC Code: 541910

TYPES OF BUSINESS:

Global Marketing Information Services
Automotive Industry Research
Consumer Satisfaction Surveys

BRANDS/DIVISIONS/AFFILIATES:

XIO Group

CONTACTS: *Note: Officers with more than one job title may be intentionally listed here more than once.*

Dave Habiger, CEO
Kevin Keegan, Sr. VP-Global Research Oper.
John Humphrey, Sr. VP-Global Automotive Oper.
Frances Caille, VP-Strategy & Planning
Peter Marlow, Gen. Mgr.-Corp. Comm.
Nilo Ramos, VP-Corp. Finance
John Tews, Dir.-Media Rel.
Syvetril Perryman, Media Rel. Supervisor
Andrew Teachout, Media Rel. Specialist
Gary B. Tucker, Sr. VP-Global Svcs. & Emerging Markets

GROWTH PLANS/SPECIAL FEATURES:

J.D. Power & Associates is a market research company specializing in consumer satisfaction. Although it covers a wide variety of industries, the company is best known for its research work in the automotive industry. Since its founding in 1968 by James D. Power, III, the firm has specialized in analyzing market information such as product quality and buyer behavior. In addition, the company conducts private tracking studies, media studies, forecasting and training services, often using independent, unbiased surveys to cull information. The company surveys recent new car buyers each year in order to create its well-known automobile quality ratings. With this consumer data, the firm can establish the qualifications of customer satisfaction, identify the strengths and weaknesses of individual companies and provide recommendations on how companies can improve themselves. J.D. Power has an intelligence network that links forecasting experts in the Americas, Europe and Asia Pacific regions. Automotive forecasting services include production and sales forecasting, global product advance and engine and transmission reports. Other industries served by J.D. Power include telecommunications, travel, real estate, finance, marine, health care, utilities, commercial vehicles, sports/entertainment, retail, electronics and professional services. In addition to its market research business, the company also provides consultation services in the areas of design, manufacturing and development, and sales and marketing services on a product by product basis. Moreover, the firm offers market consultant training services. J.D. Power is owned by XIO Group. In mid-2019, parent XIO Group agreed to sell J.D. Power to Thoma Bravo, LLC.

FINANCIAL DATA: *Note: Data for latest year may not have been available at press time.*

In U.S. $	2018	2017	2016	2015	2014	2013
Revenue	385,875,000	367,500,000	350,000,000			
R&D Expense						
Operating Income						
Operating Margin %						
SGA Expense						
Net Income						
Operating Cash Flow						
Capital Expenditure						
EBITDA						
Return on Assets %						
Return on Equity %						
Debt to Equity						

CONTACT INFORMATION:

Phone: 805-418-8000 Fax: 805-418-8900
Toll-Free: 888-537-6937
Address: 2625 Townsgate Rd., Westlake Village, CA 91361 United States

STOCK TICKER/OTHER:

Stock Ticker: Subsidiary
Employees: 800
Parent Company: XIO Group
Exchange:
Fiscal Year Ends: 12/31

SALARIES/BONUSES:

Top Exec. Salary: $ Bonus: $
Second Exec. Salary: $ Bonus: $

OTHER THOUGHTS:

Estimated Female Officers or Directors: 3
Hot Spot for Advancement for Women/Minorities: Y

Jiangling Motors Corporation Ltd

www.jmc.com.cn

NAIC Code: 336111

TYPES OF BUSINESS:

Automobile Manufacturing

BRANDS/DIVISIONS/AFFILIATES:

Ford Motor Company
Ford
JMC
Yu Sheng

GROWTH PLANS/SPECIAL FEATURES:

Jiangling Motors Corporation, Ltd., together with its subsidiaries, develops, manufactures and sells automobiles, engines and related parts, dies and tools in China and abroad. JMC operates more than 400 first-tier dealers and 1,000 dealers in total. The company's products are marketed under the brand names Ford, JMC and Yu Sheng. Jiangling's vehicle types include light trucks, pickups, sport utility vehicles (SUVs), commercial vehicles and heavy-duty trucks. The company's plants in Qingyunpu, Xiaolan, Taiyuan and Fushan cover stamping, welding, painting and assembly, as well as gas and diesel engine production. The firm is 32%-owned by Ford Motor Company, which is based in the U.S.

CONTACTS: *Note: Officers with more than one job title may be intentionally listed here more than once.*

Thomas Fann, Pres.
Yuan-Ching Chen, Pres.
Tiangao Qiu, Chmn.

FINANCIAL DATA: *Note: Data for latest year may not have been available at press time.*

In U.S. $	2018	2017	2016	2015	2014	2013
Revenue	4,103,981,000	4,553,817,000	3,869,301,000	3,563,340,000	3,709,982,000	3,034,795,000
R&D Expense	241,676,300					
Operating Income	189,757,200	-7,861,957	112,496,300	228,502,200	248,581,700	233,793,900
Operating Margin %		.00%	.03%	.06%	.07%	.08%
SGA Expense	290,421,400	784,412,200	642,614,800	586,287,200	562,958,900	456,598,600
Net Income	13,341,280	100,377,500	191,477,500	322,814,500	306,222,500	246,714,200
Operating Cash Flow	-14,758,780	98,035,000	667,314,500	279,711,000	608,720,400	457,130,900
Capital Expenditure	201,254,500	148,157,900	166,246,300	224,147,900	187,065,900	154,916,700
EBITDA	150,660,300	241,638,600	326,525,700	454,166,800	435,550,400	350,656,400
Return on Assets %		.03%	.06%	.11%	.12%	.11%
Return on Equity %		.06%	.11%	.20%	.21%	.20%
Debt to Equity		0.00	0.00	0.00	0.00	0.001

CONTACT INFORMATION:

Phone: 86 79185266000 Fax: 86 79185266677
Toll-Free:
Address: 509, Yingbin North Rd., Nanchang, Jiangxi 330001 China

STOCK TICKER/OTHER:

Stock Ticker: JGLMY
Employees: 16,865
Parent Company:
Exchange: GREY
Fiscal Year Ends: 12/31

SALARIES/BONUSES:

Top Exec. Salary: $ Bonus: $
Second Exec. Salary: $ Bonus: $

OTHER THOUGHTS:

Estimated Female Officers or Directors:
Hot Spot for Advancement for Women/Minorities:

Jiffy Lube International Inc

www.jiffylube.com

NAIC Code: 811191

TYPES OF BUSINESS:

Automotive Oil Change & Lubrication Shops

BRANDS/DIVISIONS/AFFILIATES:

Shell Oil Company
Jiffy Lube
Jiffy Lub Signature Service

CONTACTS:
Note: Officers with more than one job title may be intentionally listed here more than once.

Patrick Southwick, Pres.
Douglas W. Roan, VP-Dev.
Kendall A. Carr, VP-Finance
Douglas W. Roan, VP-Purchasing

GROWTH PLANS/SPECIAL FEATURES:

Jiffy Lube International, Inc., a subsidiary of Shell Oil Company, operates more than 2,000 franchised service centers in North America, serving 20+ million customers annually. Jiffy Lube is one of the largest systems of franchised vehicle service centers in the fast lube industry. The firm's service centers offer basic maintenance services that address a vehicle's oil, filters, air conditioning, air filtration, alignment, battery maintenance/replacement, brake, cooling system, drivetrain, engine, fuel system cleaning, transmission, suspension and more. The company also provides vehicle inspections and emissions, as well as windshield services. Jiffy Lube accesses manufacturer recommendations for maintenance, service and inspections, and is a resource center for common diagnostics as well as fuel efficiency. The firm also provides service for fleet drivers, and accepts most fleet credit cards. Fleets the company currently services include ARI, Donlen, EMKAY, Enterprise Fleet Management, Fuelman, GE, LeasePlan, Element, Mike Albert Fleet Solutions, Shell Fleet Navigator, Union Leasing, Voyager, Wright Express and Wheels. Jiffy Lube and Jiffy Lube Signature Service are registered trademarks of Jiffy Lube International.

FINANCIAL DATA:
Note: Data for latest year may not have been available at press time.

In U.S. $	2018	2017	2016	2015	2014	2013
Revenue	275,000,000	262,500,000	250,000,000	243,000,000	233,000,000	230,000,000
R&D Expense						
Operating Income						
Operating Margin %						
SGA Expense						
Net Income						
Operating Cash Flow						
Capital Expenditure						
EBITDA						
Return on Assets %						
Return on Equity %						
Debt to Equity						

CONTACT INFORMATION:

Phone: 713-546-4100 Fax: 713-546-8762
Toll-Free: 800-344-6933
Address: P.O. Box 4427, Houston, TX 77210-4458 United States

STOCK TICKER/OTHER:

Stock Ticker: Subsidiary Exchange:
Employees: 2,035 Fiscal Year Ends: 12/31
Parent Company: Shell Oil Company

SALARIES/BONUSES:

Top Exec. Salary: $ Bonus: $
Second Exec. Salary: $ Bonus: $

OTHER THOUGHTS:

Estimated Female Officers or Directors:
Hot Spot for Advancement for Women/Minorities:

Jim Koons Automotive Companies Inc

www.koons.com

NAIC Code: 441110

TYPES OF BUSINESS:

Auto Dealers, Retail
Collision Repair Centers
Commercial Sales
Online Sales
Parts

BRANDS/DIVISIONS/AFFILIATES:

Koons Tysons Toyota
Lexus of Wilmington
Koons Sterling Ford
Koons Tysons Chevy Buick GMC
Mercedes-Benz of Catonsville
Koons Kia of Owing Mills

CONTACTS: *Note: Officers with more than one job title may be intentionally listed here more than once.*

Jim O'Connell, Pres.

GROWTH PLANS/SPECIAL FEATURES:

Jim Koons Automotive Companies, Inc. sells new and used vehicles, with 19 dealerships throughout the Arlington, Washington DC and Baltimore, Maryland area. Founded in 1964 by John Koons, Sr., it was the first auto dealer to enter the Automotive Hall of Fame. The firm is now run by son Jim Koons. Brands include Toyota, Ford, Jeep, Chevrolet, Kia, Mercedes-Benz, Lexus, Chrysler, Dodge, RAM, Volvo, Buick, GMC and AMG. Koons' commercial sales department offers manufactured and customized vehicles to meet the needs of any business. The company also operates several collision repair centers. Koons' website features a virtual showroom of its new and used vehicles with information regarding special purchase deals, rebates and repair service specials. In addition, customers are able to value a trade-in vehicle, schedule a maintenance appointment, order customized vehicles, purchase accessories and parts and apply for credit online. The company's locations include, but are not limited to, Koons Tysons Toyota, which provides an expansive location for car tune-ups as well as new car sales; Lexus of Wilmington; Koons Sterling Ford; Koons Tysons Chevy Buick GMC; Mercedes-Benz of Catonsville; and Koons Kia of Owing Mills.

Koons offers its employees a benefits package including health, dental, life and disability insurance as well as a 401(k) plan.

FINANCIAL DATA: *Note: Data for latest year may not have been available at press time.*

In U.S. $	2018	2017	2016	2015	2014	2013
Revenue	2,464,900,769	2,347,524,542	2,235,737,659	1,980,361,662	102,532,500	97,650,000
R&D Expense						
Operating Income						
Operating Margin %						
SGA Expense						
Net Income						
Operating Cash Flow						
Capital Expenditure						
EBITDA						
Return on Assets %						
Return on Equity %						
Debt to Equity						

CONTACT INFORMATION:

Phone: 703-356-0400 Fax: 703-442-5765
Toll-Free: 800-782-0191
Address: 2000 Chain Bridge Rd., Vienna, VA 22182 United States

STOCK TICKER/OTHER:

Stock Ticker: Private
Employees: 4,850
Parent Company:
Exchange:
Fiscal Year Ends: 12/31

SALARIES/BONUSES:

Top Exec. Salary: $ Bonus: $
Second Exec. Salary: $ Bonus: $

OTHER THOUGHTS:

Estimated Female Officers or Directors:
Hot Spot for Advancement for Women/Minorities:

JM Family Enterprises Inc

www.jmfamily.com

NAIC Code: 423110

TYPES OF BUSINESS:

Automobile Distribution-Wholesale
Automobile Dealer
Parts Distribution
Financing & Insurance
Dealership Financing
Consulting Services

BRANDS/DIVISIONS/AFFILIATES:

Southeast Toyota Distributors LLC
Southeast Toyota Finance
JM Lexus
JM&A Group
Home Franchise Concepts
Budget Blinds
Concrete Craft
AdvantaClean

CONTACTS: *Note: Officers with more than one job title may be intentionally listed here more than once.*

Brent Burns, Pres.
Ron Coombs, VP
Carmen Johnson, VP-Human Resources
Carmen Johnson, General Counsel
Frank Armstrong, Exec. VP
Ron Coombs, Sr. VP
Forrest Heathcott, Exec. VP
Ed Sheehy, Exec. VP
Colin Brown, Chmn.

GROWTH PLANS/SPECIAL FEATURES:

JM Family Enterprises, Inc. is a leading family-owned diversified automotive company. Through its subsidiaries, JM is a distributor of Toyotas, operates a Lexus dealership, provides finance and insurance products, and operates a franchise network in the home improvement goods and services space. Subsidiary Southeast Toyota Distributors, LLC is an independent distributor of Toyotas, distributing vehicles, parts and accessories to more than 175 independent Toyota dealers in Alabama, Florida, Georgia, North Carolina and South Carolina. JM Lexus is located in Margate, Florida, and is a Lexus Plus dealership which also maintains state-of-the-art service and parts departments as well as a Lexus Certified Collision Center. Southeast Toyota Finance is a finance company for JM's Toyota dealers, servicing more than 730,000 finance and lease accounts. The finance firm is part of World Omni Financial Corporation, a global leader in wholesale floorplan accounting and risk management systems. JM&A Group is an independent provider of finance and insurance products to more than 3,800 automobile dealerships, including protection programs for new and used vehicles. Last, Home Franchise Concepts is among the world's largest franchise businesses, encompassing four brands: Budget Blinds, a provider of custom window coverings; Tailored Living, providing whole-home organization solutions; Concrete Craft, offering decorative concrete products; and AdvantaClean, offering professional home cleaning services. Through these brands, Home Franchise Concepts has a total 1,700 franchises located in the U.S., Canada and Mexico.

JM offers its employees educational assistance and development programs; flextime; adoption assistance; an onsite fitness center and access to a cafeteria and credit union; massage therapy; health and dependent care spending accounts; and medical, dental, vision, prescription, life and disability insurance.

FINANCIAL DATA: *Note: Data for latest year may not have been available at press time.*

In U.S. $	2018	2017	2016	2015	2014	2013
Revenue	16,300,000,000	15,100,000,000	14,900,000,000	14,500,000,000	13,750,000,000	12,500,000,000
R&D Expense						
Operating Income						
Operating Margin %						
SGA Expense						
Net Income						
Operating Cash Flow						
Capital Expenditure						
EBITDA						
Return on Assets %						
Return on Equity %						
Debt to Equity						

CONTACT INFORMATION:

Phone: 954-429-2000 Fax: 954-429-2300
Toll-Free:
Address: 100 Jim Moran Blvd., Deerfield Beach, FL 33442 United States

STOCK TICKER/OTHER:

Stock Ticker: Private Exchange:
Employees: 4,300 Fiscal Year Ends: 12/31
Parent Company:

SALARIES/BONUSES:

Top Exec. Salary: $ Bonus: $
Second Exec. Salary: $ Bonus: $

OTHER THOUGHTS:

Estimated Female Officers or Directors: 1
Hot Spot for Advancement for Women/Minorities:

Joe Rizza Auto Group

www.rizzacars.com

NAIC Code: 441110

TYPES OF BUSINESS:

Auto Dealers, Retail
Parts & Service
Financing

BRANDS/DIVISIONS/AFFILIATES:

Rizzacars.com

GROWTH PLANS/SPECIAL FEATURES:

Joe Rizza Auto Group operates a chain of new and used car dealerships in the Chicago, Illinois area under the Joe Rizza Cars brand. The group has nine locations that serve surrounding customers from the Orland Park and Tinley Park regions. Rizza carries makes including Acura, Buick, Cadillac, GMC and Lincoln, as well as the high-end Alfa Romeo, Maserati and Porsche brands. The company also sells pre-owned vehicles and Ford fleets sales, and each dealership has a parts and services department. At the Rizzacars.com website, customers can search new and used inventory, schedule a test drive and access the company's finance department. In addition, the firm provides separate websites to search vehicle inventory, including used cars and the bargain lot (which contains all of the company's bargain-priced vehicles).

CONTACTS: *Note: Officers with more than one job title may be intentionally listed here more than once.*

Jim Allegretti, Gen. Mgr.
Jim Mac, Gen. Sales Mgr.-Joe Rizza Acura

FINANCIAL DATA: *Note: Data for latest year may not have been available at press time.*

In U.S. $	2018	2017	2016	2015	2014	2013
Revenue						
R&D Expense						
Operating Income						
Operating Margin %						
SGA Expense						
Net Income						
Operating Cash Flow						
Capital Expenditure						
EBITDA						
Return on Assets %						
Return on Equity %						
Debt to Equity						

CONTACT INFORMATION:

Phone: 708-403-7770 Fax:
Toll-Free:
Address: 8150 W. 159th St., Orland Park, IL 60462 United States

STOCK TICKER/OTHER:

Stock Ticker: Private
Employees: 480
Parent Company:
Exchange:
Fiscal Year Ends: 12/31

SALARIES/BONUSES:

Top Exec. Salary: $ Bonus: $
Second Exec. Salary: $ Bonus: $

OTHER THOUGHTS:

Estimated Female Officers or Directors:
Hot Spot for Advancement for Women/Minorities:

Jordan Automotive Group

www.jordanauto.com

NAIC Code: 441110

TYPES OF BUSINESS:

Auto Dealers, Retail
Fleet Sales
Repair Services

BRANDS/DIVISIONS/AFFILIATES:

RFJ Auto Partners Inc

GROWTH PLANS/SPECIAL FEATURES:

Jordan Automotive Group sells new and used vehicles through its Indiana franchises. The group sells Ford and Toyota vehicles. Jordan also provides repair services for these brands and operates a body shop. In addition, the firm has a national and commercial fleet sales division through both its Ford and Toyota dealerships. Potential customers and pre-existing owners can obtain a quick quote, schedule a maintenance appointment and view images and information on new and used vehicles through the company's website. Online customers can apply for financing through the Jordan's finance department. Jordan Automotive operates as a wholly-owned subsidiary of RFJ Auto Partners, Inc.

CONTACTS: *Note: Officers with more than one job title may be intentionally listed here more than once.*

Rick Ford, CEO
Robert Hayden, VP-Oper.

FINANCIAL DATA: *Note: Data for latest year may not have been available at press time.*

In U.S. $	2018	2017	2016	2015	2014	2013
Revenue						
R&D Expense						
Operating Income						
Operating Margin %						
SGA Expense						
Net Income						
Operating Cash Flow						
Capital Expenditure						
EBITDA						
Return on Assets %						
Return on Equity %						
Debt to Equity						

CONTACT INFORMATION:

Phone: 574-259-1981 Fax: 574-254-7552
Toll-Free: 800-837-1981
Address: 609 E. Jefferson Blvd., Mishawaka, IN 46545 United States

STOCK TICKER/OTHER:

Stock Ticker: Subsidiary Exchange:
Employees: Fiscal Year Ends: 12/31
Parent Company: RFJ Auto Partners Inc

SALARIES/BONUSES:

Top Exec. Salary: $ Bonus: $
Second Exec. Salary: $ Bonus: $

OTHER THOUGHTS:

Estimated Female Officers or Directors:
Hot Spot for Advancement for Women/Minorities:

Joyson Safety Systems

joysonsafety.com/

NAIC Code: 336300

TYPES OF BUSINESS:

Automotive Safety Components Manufacturing
Seat Belts
Steering Wheels
Airbags
Electronic Sensors
Testing & Engineering Services

BRANDS/DIVISIONS/AFFILIATES:

Ningbo Joyson Electronic Corporation
KSS Abhishek Safety Systems Pvt Ltd
Takata India Pvt Ltd
Joyson ANAND Abhishek Safety Systems Pvt Ltd

CONTACTS: *Note: Officers with more than one job title may be intentionally listed here more than once.*

Guido Durrer, CEO/Pres.
Jean-Luc Hemmert, COO
Karen Hong, CFO
Mark Decker, Chief Human Resources Officer
Noha White, CIO
Jim Scarpa, Sr. VP-Mfg. & Quality
Tom Dono, General Counsel
David Gunther, VP-Bus. Dev.
Laura Miller, Corp. Controller
Mark Wehner, Pres., Global Safety Products
Greg Heald, CEO/Pres., Hamlin, Inc.
Fritz Nelson, VP-Strategic Planning
Greg Heald, Pres., Asia
Greg Heald, Sr. VP-Procurement

GROWTH PLANS/SPECIAL FEATURES:

Joyson Safety Systems designs and manufactures safety-critical components, systems and technology to automotive and non-automotive markets on a global scale. The firm's safety systems include seat belts, airbags, steering wheels and child seats, as well as other automotive products, technologies and related solutions. Joyson Safety Systems operates as a subsidiary of Ningbo Joyson Electronic Corporation and is present in 25 countries, including facilities in the Americas, Europe/Middle East/Africa and Asia. In mid-2019, Joyson announced the formation of a tri-party joint venture, merging its two JVs in India: KSS Abhishek Safety Systems Pvt. Ltd. and Takata India Pvt. Ltd. KSS is a joint venture with Abhishek Industries, and Takata is a joint venture with ANAND Group. Merging these two subsidiaries among the three parent companies will create a new, tri-party JV called Joyson ANAND Abhishek Safety Systems Private Limited. The merger is subject to approval of the National Company Law Tribunal. When the merger is complete, Joyson will own 65% of the JV, ANAND 30% and Abhishek 5%.

FINANCIAL DATA: *Note: Data for latest year may not have been available at press time.*

In U.S. $	2018	2017	2016	2015	2014	2013
Revenue	7,350,000,000	7,000,000,000	1,800,000,000	1,450,000,000	1,400,000,000	1,200,000,000
R&D Expense						
Operating Income						
Operating Margin %						
SGA Expense						
Net Income						
Operating Cash Flow						
Capital Expenditure						
EBITDA						
Return on Assets %						
Return on Equity %						
Debt to Equity						

CONTACT INFORMATION:

Phone: 248-373-8040 Fax:
Toll-Free:
Address: 2500 Innovation Dr., Auburn Hills, MI 48326 United States

STOCK TICKER/OTHER:

Stock Ticker: Private Exchange:
Employees: 50,000 Fiscal Year Ends: 12/31
Parent Company: Ningbo Joyson Electronic Corporation

SALARIES/BONUSES:

Top Exec. Salary: $ Bonus: $
Second Exec. Salary: $ Bonus: $

OTHER THOUGHTS:

Estimated Female Officers or Directors: 1
Hot Spot for Advancement for Women/Minorities:

KAR Auction Services Inc

www.karauctionservices.com

NAIC Code: 425120

TYPES OF BUSINESS:

Automobile Auctions, Wholesale
Financial Services
Inventory Services
Logistics
Vehicle Inspection
Titling

BRANDS/DIVISIONS/AFFILIATES:

ADESA Inc
Insurance Auto Auctions Inc (IAA)
Automotive Finance Corporation (AFC)
ADESA.com
LiveBlock
DealerBlock
Impact Auto Auctions
HBC Vehicle Services Limited

CONTACTS: *Note: Officers with more than one job title may be intentionally listed here more than once.*

John Kett, CEO, Subsidiary
James Hallett, CEO
Eric Loughmiller, CFO
Thomas Fisher, Chief Information Officer
Rebecca Polak, Chief Legal Officer
Donald Gottwald, Chief Strategy Officer
Lisa Price, Executive VP, Divisional
Benjamin Skuy, Executive VP, Divisional
Peter Kelly, President
James Money, President, Subsidiary
John Hammer, President, Subsidiary

GROWTH PLANS/SPECIAL FEATURES:

KAR Auction Services, Inc. provides auction services for both whole car and salvage vehicles via more than 255 locations. In 2018, the company facilitated the sale of approximately 6 million used and salvage vehicles. The firm operates through three primary subsidiaries: ADESA, Inc.; Insurance Auto Auctions, Inc. (IAA); and Automotive Finance Corporation (AFC). ADESA is the second largest auction services provider in North America, in which vehicles are typically sold by used vehicle dealers, vehicle manufacturers, as well as finance companies, commercial fleet operators and rental car companies. This business serves customers through online auctions and auction facilities via ADESA.com, LiveBlock and DealerBlock. ADESA provides the marketing and advertising for auctioned vehicles, dealer registration, storage of inventory, clearing of funds, auction vehicle registration, condition report processing, post-sale inspections, title processing, sales results reports and auctioning of vehicles by licensed auctioneers. IAA provides salvage vehicle auctions and related services in the U.S. under the IAA name, in Canada under the Impact Auto Auctions name, and in the U.K. under the HBC Vehicle Services Limited name. This business facilitates the remarketing of sellers such as insurance companies, dealerships, rental car companies, fleet lease companies and charitable organizations. Auction buyers bid and buy the salvage vehicles needed to fulfill scrap demand, replacement part or vehicle rebuild requirement. AFC provides short-term inventory-secured financing (known as floorplan financing) to independent used vehicle dealers. The company services more than 1.8 million loan transactions annually (in fiscal 2018-19), which includes both loans paid off and loans extended. AFC has approximately 12,300 active dealers with an average line of credit of $270,000. In August 2019, KAR expanded its U.S. footprint in the U.S. with the launch of two new markets, Kansas City and Minneapolis.

KAR offers comprehensive benefits, 401(k) and a variety of employee assistance programs.

FINANCIAL DATA: *Note: Data for latest year may not have been available at press time.*

In U.S. $	2018	2017	2016	2015	2014	2013
Revenue	3,769,600,000	3,458,000,000	3,150,100,000	2,639,600,000	2,364,500,000	2,173,300,000
R&D Expense						
Operating Income	624,200,000	566,000,000	499,000,000	427,300,000	377,700,000	256,700,000
Operating Margin %		.16%	.16%	.16%	.16%	.12%
SGA Expense	732,800,000	640,200,000	583,100,000	502,000,000	471,400,000	490,000,000
Net Income	328,000,000	362,000,000	222,400,000	214,600,000	169,300,000	67,700,000
Operating Cash Flow	749,800,000	588,800,000	360,800,000	475,000,000	431,300,000	434,000,000
Capital Expenditure	198,000,000	152,200,000	155,100,000	134,700,000	101,000,000	96,600,000
EBITDA	897,600,000	826,600,000	734,700,000	644,700,000	547,800,000	448,300,000
Return on Assets %		.05%	.04%	.04%	.03%	.01%
Return on Equity %		.25%	.16%	.15%	.11%	.05%
Debt to Equity		1.797	1.693	1.24	1.122	1.171

CONTACT INFORMATION:

Phone: Fax:
Toll-Free: 800-923-3725
Address: 13085 Hamilton Crossing Blvd., Carmel, IN 46032 United States

STOCK TICKER/OTHER:

Stock Ticker: KAR
Employees: 17,400
Parent Company:
Exchange: NYS
Fiscal Year Ends: 12/31

SALARIES/BONUSES:

Top Exec. Salary: $975,000 Bonus: $
Second Exec. Salary: $432,692 Bonus: $400,000

OTHER THOUGHTS:

Estimated Female Officers or Directors: 1
Hot Spot for Advancement for Women/Minorities:

Karma Automotive LLC

www.karmaautomotive.com

NAIC Code: 336111

TYPES OF BUSINESS:

Automobile Manufacturing--Electric
Plug-in Hybrids (PHEVs)

BRANDS/DIVISIONS/AFFILIATES:

Wanxiang Group Corporation
Revero
Revero GT
Karma GT

CONTACTS: *Note: Officers with more than one job title may be intentionally listed here more than once.*

Tom Corcoran, CEO
Cameron Adamson, CFO
James Taylor, CMO
Gary L. Horvat, VP-Prod. Dev.
Alberto Gonzalez, VP-Mfg.
Matthew K. Paroly, General Counsel
Bernhard Koehler, Chief Bus. Dev. Officer
Mark P. Decker, VP-External Affairs
Samuel S. Koroglu, Treas.
Alexander C. Klatt, VP-Global Design
Joseph Chao, CEO-China & Asia

GROWTH PLANS/SPECIAL FEATURES:

Karma Automotive, LLC is a California-based designer, marketer and manufacturer of premium plug-in hybrid automobiles. The company's Revero model is a luxury electric hybrid based on the Fisker Karma. It offers an A123 battery, charger and electrical controls, an endless torque via dual electric motors, six piston calipers and regenerative braking. Those driving less than 50 miles a day will not need to purchase gas. By driving the Revero, the battery recharges itself to provide up to 300 miles of range. The overall length of the car is nearly 200 inches (16.4 feet), 84 inches wide (7 feet, mirrors included) and 52.4 inches high (4.3 feet). The Revero GT comprises a BMW TwinPower Turbo three-cylinder in-line engine to power the on-board electric generator. It delivers 536 horsepower, 550-pound force foot of torque and 0-60 mph in 4.5 seconds. Karma GT is a bespoke, Italian-designed two-door coupe with next-generation styling and technology. Karma Automotive is a wholly-owned subsidiary of Wanxiang Group Corporation.

FINANCIAL DATA: *Note: Data for latest year may not have been available at press time.*

In U.S. $	2018	2017	2016	2015	2014	2013
Revenue						
R&D Expense						
Operating Income						
Operating Margin %						
SGA Expense						
Net Income						
Operating Cash Flow						
Capital Expenditure						
EBITDA						
Return on Assets %						
Return on Equity %						
Debt to Equity						

CONTACT INFORMATION:

Phone: 949-629-7502 Fax:
Toll-Free: 855-565-2762
Address: 9950 Jeronimo Rd., Irvine, CA 92618 United States

STOCK TICKER/OTHER:

Stock Ticker: Private Exchange:
Employees: 625 Fiscal Year Ends:
Parent Company: Wanxiang Group Corporation

SALARIES/BONUSES:

Top Exec. Salary: $ Bonus: $
Second Exec. Salary: $ Bonus: $

OTHER THOUGHTS:

Estimated Female Officers or Directors: 1
Hot Spot for Advancement for Women/Minorities:

Kawasaki Heavy Industries Ltd

www.khi.co.jp

NAIC Code: 336999

TYPES OF BUSINESS:

Recreational Vehicle & Machinery Manufacturing
Motorcycles, ATVs & Personal Watercraft
Helicopter & Aerospace Manufacturing
Industrial Machinery and Robotics
Gas Turbines, Engines & Generators
Locomotives, Ships & Submarines
Plant & Infrastructure Manufacturing
Power Plant Construction

BRANDS/DIVISIONS/AFFILIATES:

Wipro Kawasaki Precision Machinery Pvt Ltd

CONTACTS: *Note: Officers with more than one job title may be intentionally listed here more than once.*

Yoshinori Kanehana, CEO
Masahiko Hirohata, Gen. Mgr.-Corp. Planning
Hiroshi Takata, Sr. VP
Joji Iki, Sr. VP
Shigeru Murayama, Sr. VP
Kyohei Matsuoka, Sr. VP
Shigeru Murayama, Chmn.

GROWTH PLANS/SPECIAL FEATURES:

Kawasaki Heavy Industries, Ltd. manufactures a range of transportation equipment and industrial goods. The firm operates through four main business segments: mobility, energy, industrial equipment and leisure. The mobility segment consists of air unit, which includes airplanes, helicopters and space-related products; rail unit, which manufactures a wide range of rail cars; and marine, which makes marine machinery and ships. The energy segment consists of solutions unit, which includes distributed power generation, energy generation plants, power management systems for electric and thermal energy, nickel-metal hydride batteries production and technologies for renewable energy; and the equipment unit includes advanced products, such as gas turbines, efficient green gas engines, boiler facilities, oil/gas supply systems, industrial steam turbines, absorption chillers and high-end gasoline engines. The industrial equipment segment includes hydraulics components and systems such as motors, valves and pumps for agricultural and industrial use; robotics solutions for variety of industrial applications; industrial facilities and solutions, including cement and fertilizer plants, recycling and waste treatment facilities, construction machinery, technical products for defense and security, airport and material logistics systems, noise reduction hangers and rocket launch complexes. The leisure segment includes motorcycles, ATVs, recreation utility vehicles, utility vehicles, Jet Ski watercraft and general-purpose gasoline engines. In February 2019, Kawasaki Heavy Industries completed a new plant in India to produce hydraulic equipment for India's construction industry. The new plant is operated by subsidiary Wipro Kawasaki Precision Machinery Pvt. Ltd.

FINANCIAL DATA: *Note: Data for latest year may not have been available at press time.*

In U.S. $	2018	2017	2016	2015	2014	2013
Revenue	14,466,480,000	13,957,270,000	14,161,880,000	13,656,710,000	12,731,870,000	
R&D Expense	417,515,200	400,909,800	400,762,800	382,337,800	371,236,900	
Operating Income	513,931,300	422,367,200	882,181,600	801,893,100	664,896,100	
Operating Margin %	.04%	.09%	.12%	.11%	.11%	
SGA Expense	109,841,900	103,299,000	110,889,500	96,315,020	97,711,820	
Net Income	265,714,000	240,801,300	423,111,600	474,535,900	354,723,400	
Operating Cash Flow	515,070,800	859,345,700	790,838,100	1,173,047,000	1,394,238,000	
Capital Expenditure	755,725,100	637,208,300	730,224,200	710,898,700	736,758,000	
EBITDA	844,789,600	857,342,400	1,171,412,000	1,218,719,000	947,794,600	
Return on Assets %	.02%	.02%	.03%	.03%	.03%	
Return on Equity %	.06%	.06%	.11%	.13%	.11%	
Debt to Equity	0.681	0.638	0.655	0.629	0.698	

CONTACT INFORMATION:

Phone: 81 783719530 Fax: 81 783719568
Toll-Free:
Address: Kobe Crystal Tower,1-3 Higashikawasaki-cho 1-chome, Kobe, 650-8680 Japan

STOCK TICKER/OTHER:

Stock Ticker: KWHIF Exchange: PINX
Employees: 35,691 Fiscal Year Ends: 03/31
Parent Company:

SALARIES/BONUSES:

Top Exec. Salary: $ Bonus: $
Second Exec. Salary: $ Bonus: $

OTHER THOUGHTS:

Estimated Female Officers or Directors: 1
Hot Spot for Advancement for Women/Minorities:

Kelley Automotive Group LLC

www.drivekelley.com

NAIC Code: 441110

TYPES OF BUSINESS:

Auto Dealers, Retail
New & Used Cars
Automotive Parts & Service

BRANDS/DIVISIONS/AFFILIATES:

Tom Kelley Buick GMC
Kelley Chevrolet
Tom Kelley Cadillac
Tom Kelley Ford
Tom Kelley Chevrolet Buick
Tom Kelley Volvo
Kelley Body Shop

GROWTH PLANS/SPECIAL FEATURES:

Kelley Automotive Group, LLC is a family-owned and -operated business that sells new and pre-owned automobiles in the Fort Wayne, Indiana area. The group's six dealerships include Tom Kelley Buick GMC, Kelley Chevrolet, Tom Kelley Cadillac, Tom Kelley Ford, Tom Kelley Chevrolet Buick and Tom Kelley Volvo. The firm's finance team helps customers obtain vehicle loans or leases. Online applications are available as well, which can speed up the car-buying process but also come with no obligation to purchase. Kelley Automotive's service departments are equipped to handle advanced diagnostics, maintenance and repairs for every make and model using only factory-designed and engineered parts. There are two Kelley Body Shop locations that specialize in repairing/restoring vehicles involved in collisions. These shops work on all makes and models, and work with all insurance providers.

CONTACTS: *Note: Officers with more than one job title may be intentionally listed here more than once.*

Thomas W. Kelley, Pres.
Matt Bennett, CFO
Jim Kelly, VP-Oper.
Matthew Bennett, Controller

FINANCIAL DATA: *Note: Data for latest year may not have been available at press time.*

In U.S. $	2018	2017	2016	2015	2014	2013
Revenue						
R&D Expense						
Operating Income						
Operating Margin %						
SGA Expense						
Net Income						
Operating Cash Flow						
Capital Expenditure						
EBITDA						
Return on Assets %						
Return on Equity %						
Debt to Equity						

CONTACT INFORMATION:

Phone: 260-434-4750 Fax: 260-434-4707
Toll-Free: 877-853-5539
Address: 633 Ave. of Autos, Fort Wayne, IN 46804 United States

STOCK TICKER/OTHER:

Stock Ticker: Private
Employees:
Parent Company:
Exchange:
Fiscal Year Ends:

SALARIES/BONUSES:

Top Exec. Salary: $ Bonus: $
Second Exec. Salary: $ Bonus: $

OTHER THOUGHTS:

Estimated Female Officers or Directors:
Hot Spot for Advancement for Women/Minorities:

Kia Motors Corporation

www.kia.com

NAIC Code: 336111

TYPES OF BUSINESS:

Automobile Manufacturing
Buses
Military Vehicles
Passenger Vehicles

BRANDS/DIVISIONS/AFFILIATES:

Hyundai Motor Company
Rio
Forte
Optima
K900
Soul EV
READ System
V-Touch

CONTACTS: *Note: Officers with more than one job title may be intentionally listed here more than once.*

Han-Woo Park, Pres.
Mong-Koo Chung, Chmn.

GROWTH PLANS/SPECIAL FEATURES:

Kia Motors Corporation is one of the largest automobile manufacturers in Korea. It is an affiliate of Hyundai Motor Company, which controls 33.88% of the firm. The majority of Kia's car production is conducted in South Korea, China, Europe, the U.S. and Mexico. In 2019, the firm plans to enter the Indian market with their SUV-SP2 concept via Kia Motors India, with a production facility based in the Anantapur district of Andhra Pradesh. As a whole, Kia's passenger sedans (2019 and 2020) include the Rio, Forte, Optima, Stinger, Cadenza and K900 models. Crossovers, sports utility vehicles and minivans include the Soul, Niro, Sportage, Sorento, Telluride and Sedona models. Hybrids and Electric vehicles include the Niro, Optima Hybrid, Niro Plug-In Hybrid, Soul EV and Optima Plug-In Hybrid models. Hatchbacks include the Rio 5-door and Forte5 models. The company is engaged in innovative technology, including its R.E.A.D. System (real-time emotion adaptive driving system), a future mobility technology that deciphers drivers' emotions and simultaneously optimizes the in-vehicle environment for seamless comfort and pleasure. The R.E.A.D. System includes artificial intelligent (AI) machine learning technology. Kia's V-Touch (virtual touch) technology reads eyes and fingertips. It is a long-range virtual gesture recognition technology that enables control of numerous vehicle features with a swipe of a finger.

FINANCIAL DATA: *Note: Data for latest year may not have been available at press time.*

In U.S. $	2018	2017	2016	2015	2014	2013
Revenue	45,662,440,000	45,127,900,000	44,434,340,000	41,744,100,000	39,700,460,000	40,122,650,000
R&D Expense	728,318,900	651,267,400	667,983,100	645,784,800	525,666,100	474,808,400
Operating Income	975,693,400	558,223,400	2,074,904,000	1,984,534,000	2,168,530,000	2,678,136,000
Operating Margin %		.01%	.05%	.05%	.05%	.07%
SGA Expense	3,723,662,000	4,947,610,000	4,745,484,000	4,398,294,000	3,950,510,000	4,138,831,000
Net Income	974,402,100	815,990,700	2,322,024,000	2,217,464,000	2,523,449,000	3,217,590,000
Operating Cash Flow	3,768,631,000	2,186,772,000	2,761,405,000	2,845,165,000	1,992,586,000	4,026,429,000
Capital Expenditure	2,597,727,000	2,016,081,000	2,000,410,000	3,857,364,000	1,702,296,000	1,470,039,000
EBITDA	3,040,746,000	2,710,951,000	4,440,509,000	3,887,536,000	4,392,461,000	5,158,494,000
Return on Assets %		.02%	.06%	.06%	.08%	.11%
Return on Equity %		.04%	.11%	.11%	.14%	.21%
Debt to Equity		0.182	0.148	0.146	0.128	0.084

CONTACT INFORMATION:

Phone: 82 234641114 Fax: 82 234646816
Toll-Free:
Address: 12 Heolleung-ro Seocho-gu, Seoul, 06797 South Korea

STOCK TICKER/OTHER:

Stock Ticker: KIMTF
Exchange: PINX
Employees: 49,500
Fiscal Year Ends: 12/31
Parent Company: Hyundai Motor Company

SALARIES/BONUSES:

Top Exec. Salary: $ Bonus: $
Second Exec. Salary: $ Bonus: $

OTHER THOUGHTS:

Estimated Female Officers or Directors:
Hot Spot for Advancement for Women/Minorities:

KION Group AG

www.kiongroup.com

NAIC Code: 333924

TYPES OF BUSINESS:

Industrial Truck, Tractor, Trailer, and Stacker Machinery Manufacturing
Industrial Trucks
Forklifts
Supply Chain Solutions

BRANDS/DIVISIONS/AFFILIATES:

Linde
STILL
Baoli
Fenwick
KION North America
KION Warehouse Systems
KION IoT Systems GmbH
KION Financial Services

CONTACTS:

Note: Officers with more than one job title may be intentionally listed here more than once.

Gordon Riske, CEO
Anke Groth, CFO
Eike Bohm, Chief Technology Officer

GROWTH PLANS/SPECIAL FEATURES:

KION Group AG is a world-leading manufacturer of industrial trucks, and a provider of related supply chain solutions. The company's automated trucks and forklifts are marketed under the Linde, STILL and Baoli international brands, and the Fenwick, OM STILL and OME Voltas regional brands. These include counterbalance trucks with electric drives, counterbalance trucks with IC engines, autonomous trucks and automated trucks. KION'S supply chain solutions encompasses integrated technology and software solutions that are used to optimize supply chains, from in-house goods and multi-shuttle warehouse systems to picking and value-added packing. Products within this segment include conveyors, sorters, storage systems, retrieval systems, picking equipment and palletizers. This division's products and solutions are marketed under the Dematic brand. More than 1.4 million industrial trucks and over 6,000 installed supply chain systems from the KION Group are currently deployed by customers in all industries and of varied sizes across six continents (as of December 2018). KION's production sites and sales and service network are present in more than 100 countries worldwide, including Europe, North America, South America, Asia and Australia. Subsidiaries include KION North America, KION Warehouse Systems, KION IoT Systems GmbH, KION Financial Services and KION Group IT. In July 2019, KION Group and BMZ Holding GmbH announced plans to launch a 50/50 joint venture for lithium-ion batteries, named KION Battery Systems GmbH. Plans include a new production facility at BMZ's Karlstein headquarters.

FINANCIAL DATA:

Note: Data for latest year may not have been available at press time.

In U.S. $	2018	2017	2016	2015	2014	2013
Revenue	8,852,636,000	8,473,871,000	6,186,006,000	5,644,265,000	5,179,251,000	4,976,307,000
R&D Expense	152,457,900	151,682,900	106,842,300	158,326,000	139,171,800	125,775,000
Operating Income	709,034,600	614,592,600	466,563,300	459,256,000	401,572,200	385,075,300
Operating Margin %		.07%	.08%	.08%	.08%	.08%
SGA Expense	1,497,564,000	1,424,269,000	1,188,663,000	1,078,277,000	989,924,700	916,961,900
Net Income	442,759,100	470,327,700	271,811,300	240,367,600	195,637,700	153,675,800
Operating Cash Flow	847,542,100	681,798,100	458,702,400	750,553,700	668,512,000	372,121,300
Capital Expenditure	286,204,600	241,696,200	184,566,000	404,672,300	350,420,700	139,282,600
EBITDA	1,755,093,000	1,385,518,000	1,032,883,000	961,581,100	880,535,900	827,945,100
Return on Assets %		.04%	.03%	.03%	.03%	.02%
Return on Equity %		.15%	.11%	.12%	.11%	.12%
Debt to Equity		1.019	1.563	0.807	0.815	0.991

CONTACT INFORMATION:

Phone: 49 69 201 100   Fax: 49 69 201 107 690
Toll-Free:
Address: Thea-Rasche-Strasse 8, Frankfurt am Main, 60549 Germany

STOCK TICKER/OTHER:

Stock Ticker: KGXN   Exchange: MEX
Employees: 33,128   Fiscal Year Ends:
Parent Company:

SALARIES/BONUSES:

Top Exec. Salary: $ Bonus: $
Second Exec. Salary: $ Bonus: $

OTHER THOUGHTS:

Estimated Female Officers or Directors:
Hot Spot for Advancement for Women/Minorities:

Koenigsegg Automotive AB

www.koenigsegg.com

NAIC Code: 336111

TYPES OF BUSINESS:

Automobile Manufacturing

BRANDS/DIVISIONS/AFFILIATES:

Regera
Jesko
One:1
Agera RS

CONTACTS:

Note: Officers with more than one job title may be intentionally listed here more than once.

Christian V. Koenigsegg, CEO
Halldora Von Koenigsegg, Exec. Mgr.
Jonathan Palm, Dir.-Art
Magnus Arntell, Mgr.-Purchasing

GROWTH PLANS/SPECIAL FEATURES:

Koenigsegg Automotive AB is a Swedish sports car manufacturer that focuses on individually-crafted automobiles designed for speed and handling. The company produces its cars at the former site of a Swedish Air Force squadron. Every car Koenigsegg makes is crafted by a team made up of engineers, researchers, designers, composite technicians, pre-assemblers, engine assembly technicians, final assemblers and storagers, as well as public relations, sales, administration and leadership staff. Koenigsegg has a production capacity of seven cars simultaneously. Koenigsegg's current (2019) cars includes the Regera and the Jesko. The Regera was created as a luxury megacar alternative to Koenigsegg's traditional extreme, light weight, race-like cars of the One:1 and the Agera RS. Regera has a nearly 1,500-horsepower engine, eight-way electrically-adjustable memory foam seats, a 9-inch infotainment system, 4G and Wi-Fi connectivity, a front/inner/rear camera system with recording capability, Apple CarPlay, a supreme sound system, ambient lighting and remote diagnostic update capability. The company robotized the entire Regera with active front and rear wings, as well as chassis control and lifting systems, allowing it to be the first car in the world that operates all body closures completely automatically. The Jesko is a megacar with a 5.0-liter twin-turbo V8 engine producing 1280 horsepower on standard gasoline and 1600hp on E85 biofuel. The way Jesko's carbon fiber chassis is designed offers enhanced legroom, headroom and visibility. Jesko is the name of Christian's father. Historical car model lines include Agera, One:1 and CC. International sales offices are located in North America, Europe, Asia and the Middle East.

FINANCIAL DATA:

Note: Data for latest year may not have been available at press time.

In U.S. $	2018	2017	2016	2015	2014	2013
Revenue						
R&D Expense						
Operating Income						
Operating Margin %						
SGA Expense						
Net Income						
Operating Cash Flow						
Capital Expenditure						
EBITDA						
Return on Assets %						
Return on Equity %						
Debt to Equity						

CONTACT INFORMATION:

Phone: 46-421-45-44-60 Fax: 46-431-45-44-61
Toll-Free:
Address: Valhall Park, Angelholm, Skane, 262 74 Sweden

STOCK TICKER/OTHER:

Stock Ticker: Private
Employees: 89
Parent Company:
Exchange:
Fiscal Year Ends:

SALARIES/BONUSES:

Top Exec. Salary: $ Bonus: $
Second Exec. Salary: $ Bonus: $

OTHER THOUGHTS:

Estimated Female Officers or Directors: 1
Hot Spot for Advancement for Women/Minorities:

Koito Manufacturing Co Ltd

www.koito.co.jp/english

NAIC Code: 336300

TYPES OF BUSINESS:

Automotive Lighting Systems
LED Products
Airplane, Train & Railway Components
Electrical Devices
Measuring Equipment
Adaptive Front Lighting Systems
Near Infrared Lamps

BRANDS/DIVISIONS/AFFILIATES:

North American Lighting Inc
Koito Europe NV
Koito Europe Limited
Koito Czech sro
Shanghai Koito Automotive Lamp Co Ltd
Fuzhou Koito Tayih Automotive Lamp Co
Thai Koito Company Limited
India Japan Lighting Pvt Ltd

CONTACTS:

Note: Officers with more than one job title may be intentionally listed here more than once.

Masahiro Otake, CEO
Hiroshi Mihara, Pres.
Yuji Yokoya, Exec. VP
Mitsuo Kikuchi, Exec. VP
Hiroshi Mihara, Sr. Managing Dir.
Koichi Sakakibara, Sr. Managing Dir.

GROWTH PLANS/SPECIAL FEATURES:

Koito Manufacturing Co., Ltd., established in 1915, is a global manufacturer of automotive lighting equipment; components for airplanes, trains and railways; electrical devices; and measuring equipment. The firm is also involved in related financial and distribution operations. Koito's research and development activities include developing adaptive front lighting systems (AFS), which are capable of automatically controlling headlights to respond to changing road conditions such as turns, weather conditions, road types and other driving factors. Koito was the first company to receive approval from the Japanese Ministry of Land, Infrastructure and Transport (MLIT) for testing its Intelligent AFS prototype on public roads. The company is also researching a near infrared lamp to assist with night driving by helping drivers detect pedestrians and other obstacles outside the reach of headlamp illumination. It operates four domestic plants (Shizuoka, Haibara, Sagara and Fujikawa), and an overseas network of subsidiaries located in the U.S., the U.K., Czech Republic, China, Thailand, Taiwan and India. Koito's primary U.S. subsidiary, North American Lighting, Inc., is a leading independent auto lamp manufacturer in North America, serving both U.S. and Japanese transplant automakers. Koito Europe NV, the firm's primary European subsidiary, oversees its European operations, which have two manufacturing bases: Koito Europe Limited in England and Koito Czech sro in Zatec, Czech Republic. Some of its other subsidiaries include Shanghai Koito Automotive Lamp Co. Ltd.; Fuzhou Koito Tayih Automotive Lamp Co. Ltd.; Thai Koito Company Limited; and India Japan Lighting Pvt. Ltd.

FINANCIAL DATA:

Note: Data for latest year may not have been available at press time.

In U.S. $	2018	2017	2016	2015	2014	2013
Revenue	7,800,662,000	7,732,550,000	7,475,437,000	6,492,098,000	5,490,737,000	
R&D Expense						
Operating Income	953,740,100	850,239,000	755,550,500	589,560,800	454,944,000	
Operating Margin %	.12%	.11%	.10%	.09%	.08%	
SGA Expense	485,370,400	503,979,000	502,710,900	421,374,800	401,332,500	
Net Income	766,375,700	520,970,400	425,500,800	331,372,900	196,452,900	
Operating Cash Flow	871,099,100	904,135,300	678,441,500	673,488,300	326,888,400	
Capital Expenditure	377,835,000	361,836,100	388,016,900	393,594,900	302,389,300	
EBITDA	1,441,095,000	1,141,380,000	994,109,500	833,725,400	633,578,400	
Return on Assets %	.13%	.09%	.08%	.07%	.05%	
Return on Equity %	.22%	.18%	.17%	.15%	.10%	
Debt to Equity	0.032	0.039	0.046	0.014	0.024	

CONTACT INFORMATION:

Phone: 81-3-3443-7111 Fax: 81-3-3447-1520
Toll-Free:
Address: 4-8-3 Takanawa, Minato-ku, Tokyo, 108-8711 Japan

STOCK TICKER/OTHER:

Stock Ticker: KOTMY
Exchange: PINX
Employees: 27,588
Fiscal Year Ends: 03/31
Parent Company:

SALARIES/BONUSES:

Top Exec. Salary: $ Bonus: $
Second Exec. Salary: $ Bonus: $

OTHER THOUGHTS:

Estimated Female Officers or Directors:
Hot Spot for Advancement for Women/Minorities:

KR Motors Co Ltd

www.krmotors.com/

NAIC Code: 336991

TYPES OF BUSINESS:

Manufacturing-Motorcycles
Manufacturing-Scooters
Manufacturing-ATVs

BRANDS/DIVISIONS/AFFILIATES:

Kolao Holdings Pty Ltd
Miragu
Aquila
Grantus
Beaver
WOW 100 2
Ai Tango
Npro

CONTACTS:

Note: Officers with more than one job title may be intentionally listed here more than once.

Jung Min Seo, CEO
Taekwon Kim, Pres.

GROWTH PLANS/SPECIAL FEATURES:

KR Motors Co., Ltd. is a Korean company which manufactures motorcycles, scooters and recreational vehicles. The company's products span motorcycles, scooters, ATVs and electric vehicles. KR Motors' bike models include the Miragu650Pro, Mirage 250DR and Aquila 125. Scooter models include the Grantus 125, Beaver 125V DLX, Beaver 125V STD, Raon 100F, Delhi Road A and Delhi Road W, as well as the business scooter models DD110 STD, DD110 DLX and DD100. ATV models include the WOW 100 2 and the Agle 125. Electric vehicles encompass the Alley, Ai Tango and Npro scooter models. KR Motors' service network spans Seoul, Busan, Daegu, Incheon, Guangju, Daejeon, Ulsan, Sejong, Gyeonggi-do, Gangwon-do, Chung-cheong bukdo, Chungcheongnam-do, Jeollabuk do, Jeollanam do, Gyeongsangbuk-do, Gyeongsangnam-do and Jeju Island. KR Motors operates as a subsidiary of Kolao Holdings Pty Ltd. During 2019, KR Motors completed construction on a new plant it built in China, which began production mid-year. KR Motors also signed a memorandum of understanding with Hyundai KEFICO Corporation to build a technology collaboration system for electric motorcycles to be sold domestically and internationally.

FINANCIAL DATA:

Note: Data for latest year may not have been available at press time.

In U.S. $	2018	2017	2016	2015	2014	2013
Revenue	32,730,400	39,012,700	73,000,272	76,857,213	68,366,593	97,255,963
R&D Expense						
Operating Income						
Operating Margin %						
SGA Expense						
Net Income	-20,924,800	-28,765,600	-875,454	-14,129,937	-10,600,000	-6,100,000
Operating Cash Flow						
Capital Expenditure						
EBITDA						
Return on Assets %						
Return on Equity %						
Debt to Equity						

CONTACT INFORMATION:

Phone: 82-55-269-7011 Fax:
Toll-Free:
Address: 28 Wanam-ro, Seongsan-gu, Changwon-si, Gyeongnam, 641-314 South Korea

STOCK TICKER/OTHER:

Stock Ticker: 40
Employees: 123
Parent Company: Kolao Holdings Pty Ltd
Exchange: Seoul
Fiscal Year Ends: 12/31

SALARIES/BONUSES:

Top Exec. Salary: $ Bonus: $
Second Exec. Salary: $ Bonus: $

OTHER THOUGHTS:

Estimated Female Officers or Directors:
Hot Spot for Advancement for Women/Minorities:

Kumho Tire Co Ltd

www.kumhotire.com

NAIC Code: 326200

TYPES OF BUSINESS:

Tire Manufacturing
Ultra-High-Performance Tires

BRANDS/DIVISIONS/AFFILIATES:

CONTACTS:

Note: Officers with more than one job title may be intentionally listed here more than once.

Dae-Jin Jeon, CEO
Young-Nam Byun, Sr. Managing Dir.
Hyeon-Cheol Baek, Managing Dir.

GROWTH PLANS/SPECIAL FEATURES:

Kumho Tire Co., Ltd., headquartered in Seoul, South Korea, is a leading global manufacturer of tires. The company operates eight overseas sales corporations and 14 branch offices. Additionally, Kumho maintains three primary research and development centers, located in the U.S., Germany and China. The firm sells its tires, which include passenger car, sport utility vehicle (SUV), light truck, commercial truck, competition and specialty tires, in roughly 180 countries. Some of the company's specialty tires include aviation tires, racing tires, ultra-high-performance (UHP) tires, run-flat tires, aroma tires and colored-smoke tires. Kumho was among the first Korean companies to develop military aviation tires and is one of the only Korean companies to produce aviation tires. Its run-flat tires can be safely driven at speeds of up to 50-miles-an-hour after sustaining significant puncture damage. Aroma tires contain scented oils that release slowly over the tire's lifespan. Colored-smoke tires use a dye mixture built into the tread of the tire to produce a colored smoke effect for racing applications. The company supplies original equipment tires to international automobile manufacturers.

FINANCIAL DATA:

Note: Data for latest year may not have been available at press time.

In U.S. $	2018	2017	2016	2015	2014	2013
Revenue	2,156,840,000	2,424,678,000	2,484,366,000	2,562,911,000	2,897,951,000	3,117,686,000
R&D Expense						
Operating Income	-66,467,870	-132,478,000	101,196,600	114,609,700	302,112,400	291,606,600
Operating Margin %		-.05%	.04%	.04%	.10%	.09%
SGA Expense	237,920,900	356,833,900	360,439,700	378,348,200	400,719,000	389,177,100
Net Income	-146,863,400	-105,226,200	-30,387,800	-58,472,620	109,204,600	80,451,700
Operating Cash Flow	47,880,980	60,104,980	158,767,700	189,697,300	421,340,000	399,161,900
Capital Expenditure	134,027,900	245,757,400	308,899,200	569,901,200	239,253,500	207,020,900
EBITDA	130,722,300	182,945,700	252,440,500	210,389,900	425,254,200	419,818,200
Return on Assets %		-.03%	-.01%	-.01%	.03%	.02%
Return on Equity %		-.12%	-.03%	-.06%	.12%	.10%
Debt to Equity		0.893	1.04	0.948	1.261	0.027

CONTACT INFORMATION:

Phone: 82 263038114 Fax: 82 263038297
Toll-Free:
Address: 555, Sochon-dong, Gwangsan-gu, Seoul, 506-711 South Korea

STOCK TICKER/OTHER:

Stock Ticker: KMHTY
Employees: 4,979
Parent Company:
Exchange: GREY
Fiscal Year Ends: 12/31

SALARIES/BONUSES:

Top Exec. Salary: $ Bonus: $
Second Exec. Salary: $ Bonus: $

OTHER THOUGHTS:

Estimated Female Officers or Directors:
Hot Spot for Advancement for Women/Minorities:

Lacks Enterprises Inc

www.lacksenterprises.com

NAIC Code: 336300

TYPES OF BUSINESS:

Plastic Parts & Accessories
Injection Molding
Wheel Components & Systems
Automotive Trim
Turn-Key Solutions
Logistics & Supply Chain Management

BRANDS/DIVISIONS/AFFILIATES:

Lacks Wheel Trim Systems LLC
Lacks Trim Systems LLC
Plastic-Plate LLC
High Impact Plated Plastic (HIPP-140)
Spinelle Metal Finish
Flexlamp
Lacks Europe LLC
Lacks Japan Godo-Kaisha

CONTACTS: *Note: Officers with more than one job title may be intentionally listed here more than once.*

Richard Lacks, Jr., CEO
Nick Hrnyak, Pres.
Colin Snyder, Dir.-Technology
Kurt Lacks, Chmn.

GROWTH PLANS/SPECIAL FEATURES:

Lacks Enterprises, Inc. is a manufacturer and supplier of plastic parts and accessories for the automotive and consumer electronics industries. The company comprises three business operations: Lacks Wheel Trim Systems, LLC, a supplier of automotive wheel components and systems; Lacks Trim Systems, LLC, a global provider of complex components and systems for the exterior and interior automotive trim market; and Plastic-Plate, LLC, a provider of plastic molding and plating services. The company introduced High Impact Plated Plastic (HIPP-140), a chrome-plated plastic alternative to expensive metal trim for grilles and bumper molding, with enhanced impact, fatigue and temperature performance. Lacks' electroplating process provides a smooth matte finish. The firm's Spinelle Metal Finish is a multi-coat metal finishing technique. Lacks' patented Flexlamp uses advanced composite polymers to create external automotive lighting that can be located in the vehicle's impact zone. In addition, Lacks' technology division is engaged in finish technologies, industrial design, product development, testing, analytics, electrochemistry research and development, as well as organic coatings research and development. Germany-based Lacks Europe LLC serves the European market and Lacks Japan Godo-Kaisha serves the Asian market.

Employees receive medical and dental coverage, flexible spending accounts, life insurance, educational assistance, wellness programs and additional product discounts.

FINANCIAL DATA: *Note: Data for latest year may not have been available at press time.*

In U.S. $	2018	2017	2016	2015	2014	2013
Revenue	574,623,000	547,260,000	521,200,000	520,000,000	500,000,000	461,000,000
R&D Expense						
Operating Income						
Operating Margin %						
SGA Expense						
Net Income						
Operating Cash Flow						
Capital Expenditure						
EBITDA						
Return on Assets %						
Return on Equity %						
Debt to Equity						

CONTACT INFORMATION:

Phone: 616-949-6570 Fax: 616-285-2367
Toll-Free:
Address: 5460 Cascade Rd. SE, Grand Rapids, MI 49546 United States

STOCK TICKER/OTHER:

Stock Ticker: Private
Employees: 2,800
Parent Company:
Exchange:
Fiscal Year Ends: 12/31

SALARIES/BONUSES:

Top Exec. Salary: $ Bonus: $
Second Exec. Salary: $ Bonus: $

OTHER THOUGHTS:

Estimated Female Officers or Directors:
Hot Spot for Advancement for Women/Minorities:

Land Rover

www.landrover.co.uk

NAIC Code: 336111

TYPES OF BUSINESS:

Automobile Manufacturing
Luxury Vehicles
Off-Road Vehicles

BRANDS/DIVISIONS/AFFILIATES:

Tata Motors Limited
Jaguar Land Rover Limited
Range Rover
Range Rover Sport
Range Rover Velar
Range Rover Evoque
Discovery

CONTACTS: *Note: Officers with more than one job title may be intentionally listed here more than once.*

Ralf D. Speth, CEO
John Edwards, Dir.-Global Brands

GROWTH PLANS/SPECIAL FEATURES:

Land Rover is a world leader in the design and production of 4x4 vehicles. The company is a brand of the Jaguar Land Rover Limited division of India-based Tata Motors Limited. Currently (mid-2019), Land Rover markets seven models in the U.S. and internationally: Range Rover, Range Rover Sport, Range Rover Velar, Range Rover Evoque, Discovery, Discovery Sport and a plug-in hybrid. The U.S. is Land Rover's largest export market. The firm's 2020 Range Rover starts at about $102,500 (â‚¬83,655) and comes with either a 3.0-liter V6 supercharged engine or as a 2.0-liter plug-in electric hybrid. If customers choose to design their own vehicle, they can do so through the company's website. Land Rover models are designed for durability and off-road capability, and the company duly hosts a number of expeditions for adventurers and environmental researchers around the globe. The company has dealerships available in nearly every state in the U.S. and most areas of the U.K. On its website, Land Rover offers a range of technical information, special tools, diagnostic equipment and training materials.

FINANCIAL DATA: *Note: Data for latest year may not have been available at press time.*

In U.S. $	2018	2017	2016	2015	2014	2013
Revenue	7,966,332,277	7,586,983,121	7,225,698,210	7,190,525,000	4,500,000,000	4,231,028,531
R&D Expense						
Operating Income						
Operating Margin %						
SGA Expense						
Net Income			365,985,236	520,641,972	244,711,151	325,685,468
Operating Cash Flow						
Capital Expenditure						
EBITDA						
Return on Assets %						
Return on Equity %						
Debt to Equity						

CONTACT INFORMATION:

Phone: 44-2476-564-600 Fax:
Toll-Free:
Address: Abbey Rd., Whitely, Coventry, CV3 4LF United Kingdom

STOCK TICKER/OTHER:

Stock Ticker: Subsidiary
Employees: 7,500
Parent Company: Tata Motors Limited
Exchange:
Fiscal Year Ends: 03/31

SALARIES/BONUSES:

Top Exec. Salary: $ Bonus: $
Second Exec. Salary: $ Bonus: $

OTHER THOUGHTS:

Estimated Female Officers or Directors:
Hot Spot for Advancement for Women/Minorities:

Larry H Miller Group of Companies

www.lhm.com

NAIC Code: 441110

TYPES OF BUSINESS:

Auto Dealers, Retail
Auto Financing & Service
Sports Arenas
Movie Theaters
Professional Sports Teams
TV Station
Sports Apparel Stores

BRANDS/DIVISIONS/AFFILIATES:

Larry H Miller Dealerships
Prestige Financial
Total Care Auto Powered by Lancar
Larry H Miller Megaplex Theaters
Vivint Smart Home Arena
Larry H Miller's Tour of Utah
Larry H Miller's Jordan Commons
Larry H Miller Real Estate

CONTACTS: *Note: Officers with more than one job title may be intentionally listed here more than once.*

Steve Starks, CEO
Robert Tingey, General Counsel
Jay Francis, Exec. VP-Oper.
Clark Whitworth, CFO-Automotive
Robert Hyde, CFO-Sports & Entertainment
Steve Starks, Exec. VP-Oper.
Gail Miller, Owner

GROWTH PLANS/SPECIAL FEATURES:

Larry H Miller Group of Companies (LMG) is a holding firm that operates a large number of subsidiaries engaged in automotive dealerships, finance, insurance, sports, entertainment and retail. LMG has more than 80 businesses and properties located in 46 U.S. states. Larry H. Miller Dealerships sells a wide variety of automotive brands including Ford, Cadillac, Lexus, Toyota, Honda, Chevrolet and Jeep via 60 dealership locations under 20 different automotive brands in seven western states. Prestige Financial is a provider of consumer financial solutions for both franchised and independent automobile dealerships across America. Total Care Auto Powered by Landcar provides vehicle insurance coverage. The sports and entertainment and retail divisions include: Larry H. Miller Megaplex Theaters, which comprise more than 180 screens at 16 locations within Nevada and Utah; the Vivint Smart Home Arena, which seats more than 20,000 people for concerts, events and the Utah Jazz basketball games; the Larry H. Miller's Tour of Utah showcases professional cyclists for a week of racing during the month of August; the Salt Lake Bees are a triple-A affiliate of the Los Angeles Angels; the Salt Lake City Stars, NBA D-League team; Jazz Gaming, an NBA eSport team; the Saxton Horne advertising and communications agency, specializing in marketing and media buying services; and the Zone (1280 AM) and FOX Sports Radio (97.5 FM) are 50,000-watt sports radio stations in Utah. In addition, Larry H. Miller's Jordan Commons comprises restaurants, offices, a theatre and an event complex in Sandy, Utah; Larry H. Miller Management Corporation, which directs corporate governance, mergers/acquisitions, finance, human resource and related services; and Larry H. Miller Real Estate purchases, develops and manages properties for the firm's group of companies.

The company offers comprehensive benefits, 401(k) and retirement options, as well as a variety of employee assistance programs.

FINANCIAL DATA: *Note: Data for latest year may not have been available at press time.*

In U.S. $	2018	2017	2016	2015	2014	2013
Revenue	5,159,425,257	4,913,738,335	4,679,750,795	3,933,621,552	4,565,000,000	4,300,000,000
R&D Expense						
Operating Income						
Operating Margin %						
SGA Expense						
Net Income						
Operating Cash Flow						
Capital Expenditure						
EBITDA						
Return on Assets %						
Return on Equity %						
Debt to Equity						

CONTACT INFORMATION:

Phone: 801-563-4100 Fax: 801-563-4198
Toll-Free:
Address: 9350 S.150 E., Ste. 1000, Sandy, UT 84070 United States

STOCK TICKER/OTHER:

Stock Ticker: Private
Exchange:
Employees: 10,000
Fiscal Year Ends: 12/31
Parent Company:

SALARIES/BONUSES:

Top Exec. Salary: $ Bonus: $
Second Exec. Salary: $ Bonus: $

OTHER THOUGHTS:

Estimated Female Officers or Directors:
Hot Spot for Advancement for Women/Minorities:

LDI Ltd

www.ldiltd.com

NAIC Code: 336991

TYPES OF BUSINESS:

Auto Parts Distribution
Aftermarket Parts & Accessories-Motorcycles & Specialty
Automotive Paints & Coatings Distribution
Harley-Davidson Accessories
Specialty Services

BRANDS/DIVISIONS/AFFILIATES:

UltiMed Incorporated
Motorsport Aftermarket Group (MAG)
OIA Global Logistics Solutions
FinishMaster Automotive & Industrial Paint
Answer Products
Major Video Concepts (MVC)
US Corrugated Fiber Box Company
Polygon Company

CONTACTS: *Note: Officers with more than one job title may be intentionally listed here more than once.*

J.A. Lacy, CEO
Marty Brown, VP-Operations & Strategy
Bill Himebrook, CFO
Marc D. Johnson, VP-Corp. Dev.
Michael P. Hutson, Sr. VP-Finance
Marc D. Johnson, VP-Investments
Ryan L. Polk, VP-Business Unit Strategy & Performance
Gary M. Bilsland, Treas.

GROWTH PLANS/SPECIAL FEATURES:

LDI, Ltd. is an Indiana-based holding company that pursues acquisition opportunities with long-term growth potential and prefers majority-position investments. LDI stands for Lacy Diversified Industries. LDI aims to help build the companies it purchases via customer focus and continuous improvement strategies, and provides the resources and tools they need for success. LDI's expertise is in the manufacturing, distribution and logistics industries. The firm's eight current business units are UltiMed Incorporated, Motorsport Aftermarket Group (MAG), OIA Global Logistics Solutions, FinishMaster Automotive & Industrial Paint, Answer Products, Major Video Concepts (MVC), U.S. Corrugated Fiber Box Company and Polygon Company. UltiMed manufactures injection devices for human diabetes, veterinary diabetes and medical/surgical supply markets. MAG manufactures and distributes online retailer and aftermarket powersports parts, accessories and apparel brands. OIA Global is a worldwide transportation, supply chain management and packaging solutions provider. FinishMaster distributes automotive paint and refinish products nationwide. Answer is an international manufacturer of bicycle suspensions. MVC distributes movies for major film studios. U.S. Corrugated Fiber Box Company manufactures corrugated boxes, and has been in business since 1912. Polygon manufactures performance-improving composite components for end markets such as construction, agriculture, medical devices and municipal utilities. Its components include self-lubricating bearings, pneumatic and hydraulic cylinders, surgical tubing and double insulation tubing. In addition, LDI's Andre B. Lacy School of Business provides accredited undergraduate degrees in the fields of liberal arts and professional education, and is located in Indiana.

FINANCIAL DATA: *Note: Data for latest year may not have been available at press time.*

In U.S. $	2018	2017	2016	2015	2014	2013
Revenue	1,260,000,000	1,200,000,000				
R&D Expense						
Operating Income						
Operating Margin %						
SGA Expense						
Net Income						
Operating Cash Flow						
Capital Expenditure						
EBITDA						
Return on Assets %						
Return on Equity %						
Debt to Equity						

CONTACT INFORMATION:

Phone: 317-237-5400 Fax: 317-655-4721
Toll-Free:
Address: 54 Monument Cir., Ste. 800, Indianapolis, IN 46204 United States

STOCK TICKER/OTHER:

Stock Ticker: Private
Employees: 3,000
Parent Company:
Exchange:
Fiscal Year Ends: 12/31

SALARIES/BONUSES:

Top Exec. Salary: $ Bonus: $
Second Exec. Salary: $ Bonus: $

OTHER THOUGHTS:

Estimated Female Officers or Directors: 1
Hot Spot for Advancement for Women/Minorities:

Lear Corporation

www.lear.com

NAIC Code: 336300

TYPES OF BUSINESS:

Automobile Components
Automotive Interiors
Electrical Systems
Instrument Panels
Seat Systems
Flooring Systems
Entertainment & Wireless Systems
Keyless Entry Systems

BRANDS/DIVISIONS/AFFILIATES:

CONTACTS:

Note: Officers with more than one job title may be intentionally listed here more than once.

Raymond Scott, CEO
Jeffrey Vanneste, CFO
Henry Wallace, Chairman of the Board
Amy Doyle, Chief Accounting Officer
Thomas DiDonato, Chief Administrative Officer
Terrence Larkin, Executive VP, Divisional
Frank Orsini, President, Divisional
Shari Burgess, Treasurer

GROWTH PLANS/SPECIAL FEATURES:

Lear Corporation is one of the world's largest automotive interior systems suppliers. The firm serves every major automotive manufacturer, including General Motors, Ford, BMW, Fiat Chrysler and Daimler. The company currently operates 145 facilities in 22 countries. Its business is conducted through two segments: seating and e-systems. The seating segment consists of the design, engineering, just-in-time assembly and delivery of complete seat systems as well as the manufacture of all major seat components, including seat structures and mechanisms, seat covers, seat forms and headrests. The segment produces seat systems that are fully assembled and ready for installation in automobiles and light trucks. These include luxury and performance automotive seating required by premium automakers, including Alfa Romeo, Audi, Lamborghini, BMW, Cadillac, Ferrari, Jaguar Land Rover, Lincoln, Maserati, Mercedes-Benz and Porsche. The e-systems segment consists of the design, manufacture, assembly and supply of electrical distribution systems, electronic modules and related components and software for light vehicles globally. Its electrical distribution systems route electrical signals and manage electrical power within the vehicle for traditional vehicle architectures, as well as high power and hybrid electric systems. Electronics control various functions within the vehicle, and include body control modules, smart junction boxes, gateway modules, wireless control modules, lighting control modules and audio amplifiers. Connectivity capabilities facilitate secure, wireless communication between the vehicle's systems and external networks, as well as other vehicles. As of December 31, 2018, the company had 16 operating joint ventures located in five countries, of which 12 operated in Asia and four in North America. In April 2019, Lear agreed to acquire Seattle-based Xevo, Inc., an automotive software supplier that develops solutions for cloud, car and mobile devices.

FINANCIAL DATA:

Note: Data for latest year may not have been available at press time.

In U.S. $	2018	2017	2016	2015	2014	2013
Revenue	21,148,500,000	20,467,000,000	18,557,600,000	18,211,400,000	17,727,300,000	16,234,000,000
R&D Expense						
Operating Income	1,654,100,000	1,608,300,000	1,427,200,000	1,186,800,000	929,200,000	736,600,000
Operating Margin %		.08%	.08%	.07%	.05%	.05%
SGA Expense	612,800,000	635,200,000	621,900,000	580,500,000	529,900,000	528,700,000
Net Income	1,149,800,000	1,313,400,000	975,100,000	745,500,000	672,400,000	431,400,000
Operating Cash Flow	1,779,800,000	1,783,100,000	1,619,300,000	1,271,100,000	927,800,000	820,100,000
Capital Expenditure	677,000,000	594,500,000	528,300,000	485,800,000	424,700,000	460,600,000
EBITDA	2,106,900,000	2,040,100,000	1,799,000,000	1,466,000,000	1,165,800,000	964,000,000
Return on Assets %		.12%	.10%	.08%	.08%	.05%
Return on Equity %		.36%	.33%	.25%	.22%	.13%
Debt to Equity		0.47	0.621	0.66	0.499	0.347

CONTACT INFORMATION:

Phone: 248 447-1500 Fax:
Toll-Free: 800-413-5327
Address: 21557 Telegraph Rd., Southfield, MI 48033 United States

STOCK TICKER/OTHER:

Stock Ticker: LEA
Exchange: NYS
Employees: 161,000
Fiscal Year Ends: 12/31
Parent Company:

SALARIES/BONUSES:

Top Exec. Salary: $1,109,183 Bonus: $
Second Exec. Salary: $855,098 Bonus: $

OTHER THOUGHTS:

Estimated Female Officers or Directors: 1
Hot Spot for Advancement for Women/Minorities:

Les Schwab Tire Centers

www.lesschwab.com

NAIC Code: 441320

TYPES OF BUSINESS:

Tires, Retail
Alignments, Shock & Brake Service
Battery & Shock Retail

BRANDS/DIVISIONS/AFFILIATES:

Fleet Tire System

CONTACTS:

Note: Officers with more than one job title may be intentionally listed here more than once.

John Cuniff, CEO
Scott Robins, Mgr.-Fleet Tire Systems
Brian Capp, VP-Mktg.
Ken Edwards, VP-Supply Chain Mgmt.

GROWTH PLANS/SPECIAL FEATURES:

Les Schwab Tire Centers independently operates a chain of stores that sell tires, wheels and batteries in addition to performing alignment, shock and brake services. Founder Les Schwab started the company in 1952 with the purchase of one tire store, and has expanded the group since to include over 400 company-owned stores and member dealer locations in the western U.S. Stores are located throughout Alaska, California, Colorado, Idaho, Montana, Nevada, Oregon, Utah, Washington and Wyoming. The company's corporate operations are in central Oregon, where it runs one of the largest retreading facilities in the U.S. and maintains a distribution center. The firm provides tires for passenger cars, light trucks, SUVs and farm vehicles as well as specialty tires such as ATV, motor home, boat and trailer, golf cart and lawn and garden tires. The firm's Fleet Tire System offers services to commercial accounts. Additionally, the company markets custom wheels and snow tires. Les Schwab Tire Centers also retails a variety of batteries for cars, buses, farm equipment, lawn and garden, aircraft and military, light trucks, motor homes, industrial equipment, RVs and boat trailers, golf carts, heavy trucks and equipment, motorcycles, ATVs and floor sweepers. Moreover, the firm retails a variety of shocks for light trucks, SUVs, lifted light trucks and passenger cars. Services include complete front-disc brake service, complete rear-drum brake services, performance suspension lifting and lowering solutions as well as standard, thrust and four-wheel alignment services.

Les Schwab Tire Centers offer its employees a benefits package that includes a retiree health plan; medical, dental, life and vision coverage; a retirement program; and vacation pay.

FINANCIAL DATA:

Note: Data for latest year may not have been available at press time.

In U.S. $	2018	2017	2016	2015	2014	2013
Revenue	1,786,050,000	1,701,000,000	1,620,000,000	1,670,000,000	1,660,000,000	1,650,000,000
R&D Expense						
Operating Income						
Operating Margin %						
SGA Expense						
Net Income						
Operating Cash Flow						
Capital Expenditure						
EBITDA						
Return on Assets %						
Return on Equity %						
Debt to Equity						

CONTACT INFORMATION:

Phone: 541-447-4136 Fax: 541-416-5488
Toll-Free:
Address: 20900 Cooley Rd., Bend, OR 97701 United States

STOCK TICKER/OTHER:

Stock Ticker: Private
Employees: 8,200
Parent Company:
Exchange:
Fiscal Year Ends: 12/31

SALARIES/BONUSES:

Top Exec. Salary: $ Bonus: $
Second Exec. Salary: $ Bonus: $

OTHER THOUGHTS:

Estimated Female Officers or Directors: 1
Hot Spot for Advancement for Women/Minorities:

Sales, profits and employees may be estimates. Financial information, benefits and other data can change quickly and may vary from those stated here.

Linamar Corporation

www.linamar.com

NAIC Code: 336300

TYPES OF BUSINESS:

Automobile Parts Manufacturing
Machined Components, Assemblies & Castings
Industrial Products

BRANDS/DIVISIONS/AFFILIATES:

Skyjack
MacDon
OROS

CONTACTS:
Note: Officers with more than one job title may be intentionally listed here more than once.

Linda Hasenfratz, CEO
Dale Schneider, CFO
Frank Hasenfratz, Chairman of the Board
Jim Jarrell, COO
Mark Stoddart, Director
Roger Fulton, Executive VP, Divisional
Brian Ahlborn, President, Divisional
Kenneth McDougall, President, Geographical
Wenzhang Huang, President, Geographical
Brad Boehler, President, Subsidiary

GROWTH PLANS/SPECIAL FEATURES:

Linamar Corporation designs, develops and manufactures precision machined components and other engineered products, the bulk of which are sold to original equipment manufacturers (OEMs) and Tier 1 customers in the automotive industry. The company operates through two segments, transportation and industrial, which are further divided into groups such as machining and assembly, forging, Skyjack, light metals and agriculture. Linamar's products include the Skyjack line of material handling equipment, the MacDon line of harvesting equipment, the OROS line of headers/rake equipment/track equipment and other agriculture-related systems, engine components for automotive markets, automotive/freight logistics solutions, and components/modules/systems for renewable energy markets. Precision metallic components and systems for light vehicle powertrains include cylinder blocks, rods, camshafts, differentials, clutch modules, power transfer units, engineered gears and many other products. Aerial work platforms by Linamar's Skyjack division includes vertical mast lifts, DC electric scissor lifts, rough terrain scissor lifts, booms and telehandlers. Large precision machined castings for the renewable energy markets include gearbox housings, planetary carrier housings, bearing housings, hollow shafts, torque arms and downhole drill heads. Linamar has more than 60 manufacturing locations, 10 R&D centers and 25 sales offices in 17 countries across North and South America, Europe and Asia.

FINANCIAL DATA:
Note: Data for latest year may not have been available at press time.

In U.S. $	2018	2017	2016	2015	2014	2013
Revenue	5,776,231,000	4,962,069,000	4,552,098,000	3,913,022,000	3,161,950,000	2,725,300,000
R&D Expense						
Operating Income	604,209,800	552,493,700	513,534,400	444,501,600	337,868,500	243,946,000
Operating Margin %		.11%	.11%	.11%	.11%	.09%
SGA Expense	334,608,500	266,931,700	246,618,600	201,603,100	165,600,700	138,896,400
Net Income	448,329,400	416,410,200	395,760,600	330,986,900	242,977,300	174,174,900
Operating Cash Flow	523,944,500	595,713,600	680,714,800	524,412,200	414,269,700	442,458,100
Capital Expenditure	422,975,800	323,957,400	268,256,600	261,343,100	204,533,400	197,127,200
EBITDA	899,581,600	789,609,500	790,044,700	667,540,400	525,126,900	409,038,800
Return on Assets %		.10%	.12%	.13%	.11%	.09%
Return on Equity %		.19%	.22%	.22%	.21%	.19%
Debt to Equity		0.414	0.474	0.238	0.26	0.36

CONTACT INFORMATION:

Phone: 519 836-7550 Fax: 519 836-9175
Toll-Free:
Address: 287 Speedvale Ave. W., Guelph, ON N1H 1C5 Canada

STOCK TICKER/OTHER:

Stock Ticker: LIMAF
Exchange: PINX
Employees: 25,979
Fiscal Year Ends: 12/31
Parent Company:

SALARIES/BONUSES:

Top Exec. Salary: $ Bonus: $
Second Exec. Salary: $ Bonus: $

OTHER THOUGHTS:

Estimated Female Officers or Directors: 1
Hot Spot for Advancement for Women/Minorities:

Lithia Motors Inc

www.lithia.com

NAIC Code: 441110

TYPES OF BUSINESS:

Auto Dealers
Automotive Repair & Maintenance
Insurance & Financing

BRANDS/DIVISIONS/AFFILIATES:

CONTACTS:

Note: Officers with more than one job title may be intentionally listed here more than once.

Bryan Deboer, CEO
Tina Miller, CFO
Sidney Deboer, Chairman of the Board
Thomas Dobry, Chief Marketing Officer
Christopher Holzshu, Executive VP
Erik Lewis, Other Executive Officer
Bryan Osterhout, Senior VP
Scott Hillier, Senior VP, Divisional
Chun-Wai Liang, Senior VP, Divisional

GROWTH PLANS/SPECIAL FEATURES:

Lithia Motors, Inc. is a leading operator of automotive dealerships, retailing both new and used vehicles through 182 U.S. locations and over the internet. California and Oregon represent the firm's two largest markets. Lithia sells new and used cars and light trucks; sells replacement parts; provides vehicle maintenance, warranty, paint and repair services; and arranges related financing, service contracts, protection products and credit insurance for its automotive customers. Lithia's dealerships offer new vehicles marketed under nearly 30 brands, and all brands of used vehicles. The locations and other facilities consist primarily of automobile showrooms, display lots, service facilities, collision repair and paint shops, supply facilities, vehicle storage lots, parking lots and offices. Lithia notifies owners of vehicles purchased at its franchises when their vehicles are due for periodic service. Other marketing services include direct-mail ads to previous customers as well as newspaper, television and radio ads. Lithia's various websites offers users several services, such as viewing new and used vehicle inventories and scheduling service appointments. Lithia lists its inventory on listing services such as cars.com, autotrader.com, cargurus.com, kbb.com, edmunds.com, craigslist and local webpages, as well as its own websites. The company also offers financing and insurance to customers that purchase new or used vehicles. In 2018, Lithia Motors sold approximately 184,600 new and 151,230 vehicles, with the average price of new vehicles selling for about $35,750 and the average selling price of used vehicles being $20,350.

Lithia offers employees medical, dental, vision, life and disability insurance; and employee stock and 401(k) plans.

FINANCIAL DATA:

Note: Data for latest year may not have been available at press time.

In U.S. $	2018	2017	2016	2015	2014	2013
Revenue	11,821,400,000	10,086,510,000	8,678,157,000	7,864,252,000	5,390,326,000	4,005,749,000
R&D Expense						
Operating Income	433,500,000	408,986,000	352,356,000	322,859,000	233,752,000	183,518,000
Operating Margin %		.04%	.04%	.04%	.04%	.05%
SGA Expense	1,196,100,000	993,565,000	855,707,000	771,437,000	529,445,000	402,957,000
Net Income	265,700,000	245,217,000	197,058,000	182,999,000	138,720,000	106,000,000
Operating Cash Flow	519,700,000	148,856,000	86,516,000	74,209,000	30,319,000	32,059,000
Capital Expenditure	158,000,000	105,378,000	100,761,000	83,244,000	85,983,000	50,025,000
EBITDA	531,200,000	478,903,000	381,630,000	343,329,000	261,461,000	206,546,000
Return on Assets %		.06%	.06%	.06%	.06%	.07%
Return on Equity %		.25%	.23%	.24%	.23%	.22%
Debt to Equity		0.949	0.845	0.732	0.905	0.459

CONTACT INFORMATION:

Phone: 541 776-6401 Fax: 541 776-6362
Toll-Free: 877-331-3084
Address: 150 N. Bartlett St., Medford, OR 97501 United States

STOCK TICKER/OTHER:

Stock Ticker: LAD
Employees: 11,170
Parent Company:
Exchange: NYS
Fiscal Year Ends: 12/31

SALARIES/BONUSES:

Top Exec. Salary: $1,020,000 Bonus: $
Second Exec. Salary: $600,000 Bonus: $

OTHER THOUGHTS:

Estimated Female Officers or Directors:
Hot Spot for Advancement for Women/Minorities:

LKQ Corporation

www.lkqcorp.com

NAIC Code: 336300

TYPES OF BUSINESS:

Remanufactured OEM Parts
Aftermarket Replacement Parts
Vehicle Salvage
Scrap/Bulk Automotive Parts
Refurbished Aluminum Wheels

BRANDS/DIVISIONS/AFFILIATES:

CONTACTS:
Note: Officers with more than one job title may be intentionally listed here more than once.

John Quinn, CEO, Geographical
Dominick Zarcone, CEO
Varun Laroyia, CFO
Ashley Brooks, Chief Information Officer
Michael Clark, Controller
Joseph Holsten, Director
Victor Casini, General Counsel
Walter Hanley, Senior VP, Divisional
Justin Jude, Senior VP, Divisional
Matthew McKay, Senior VP, Divisional

GROWTH PLANS/SPECIAL FEATURES:

LKQ Corporation is a global distributor of vehicle products, including replacement parts, components and systems used in the repair and maintenance of vehicles. The company also distributes specialty products and accessories that improve the performance, functionality and appearance of vehicles. LKQ operates through three segments: North America, Europe and specialty. The North America segment comprises the company's wholesale operations, which include aftermarket, recycled, remanufactured, refurbished and original equipment manufacturer (OEM) parts supplied to professional collision and mechanical automobile repair businesses throughout the U.S. and Canada. The Europe segment provides mechanical aftermarket parts for the repair of vehicles 3 to 15 years old. Top-selling products within this division include brake pads, discs, sensors, clutches, spark plugs, batteries, steering systems and components, suspension systems and components, filters, and oil/automotive fluids. Last, the specialty segment sells and distributes recreational vehicle appliances, vehicle air conditioners, tow hitches, truck bed covers, vehicle protection products, cargo management products, wheels, tires and suspension products. This division primarily supplies small- to medium-sized businesses that focus on a narrow product or market niche. In August 2019, LKQ divested AeroVision International, its recycled aviation parts business.

FINANCIAL DATA:
Note: Data for latest year may not have been available at press time.

In U.S. $	2018	2017	2016	2015	2014	2013
Revenue	11,876,670,000	9,736,909,000	8,584,031,000	7,192,633,000	6,740,064,000	5,062,528,000
R&D Expense						
Operating Income	947,913,000	866,990,000	801,160,000	724,138,000	664,674,000	540,353,000
Operating Margin %		.09%	.09%	.10%	.10%	.11%
SGA Expense	3,352,731,000	1,915,699,000	1,670,192,000	1,431,230,000	1,340,229,000	1,028,999,000
Net Income	480,118,000	533,744,000	463,975,000	423,223,000	381,519,000	311,623,000
Operating Cash Flow	710,739,000	518,900,000	635,014,000	529,837,000	370,897,000	428,056,000
Capital Expenditure	250,027,000	179,090,000	207,074,000	170,490,000	140,950,000	90,186,000
EBITDA	1,183,885,000	1,098,470,000	971,630,000	835,082,000	777,867,000	613,474,000
Return on Assets %		.06%	.07%	.08%	.08%	.08%
Return on Equity %		.14%	.14%	.15%	.15%	.14%
Debt to Equity		0.781	0.951	0.491	0.662	0.538

CONTACT INFORMATION:

Phone: 312 621-1950 Fax: 312 621-1969
Toll-Free: 877-557-2677
Address: 500 W. Madison St., Ste. 2800, Chicago, IL 60661 United States

STOCK TICKER/OTHER:

Stock Ticker: LKQ
Employees: 42,500
Parent Company:
Exchange: NAS
Fiscal Year Ends: 12/31

SALARIES/BONUSES:

Top Exec. Salary: $955,069 Bonus: $
Second Exec. Salary: $592,343 Bonus: $

OTHER THOUGHTS:

Estimated Female Officers or Directors:
Hot Spot for Advancement for Women/Minorities:

LoJack Corporation

www.lojack.com

NAIC Code: 334290

TYPES OF BUSINESS:

Lost Automobile Location Services and Products
Asset Monitoring & Recovery

BRANDS/DIVISIONS/AFFILIATES:

CalAmp Corporation
LoJack Stolen Vehicle Recovery System
LoJack SureDrive
LoJack Asset Recovery for Equipment
LoJack LotSmart

CONTACTS: *Note: Officers with more than one job title may be intentionally listed here more than once.*

Kenneth Dumas, CFO
Kenneth L. Dumas, CFO
Jose Oxholm, General Counsel
Harold Dewsnap, General Manager, Divisional

GROWTH PLANS/SPECIAL FEATURES:

LoJack Corporation creates and markets technology products and services for the tracking and recovery of valuable mobile assets. LoJack Corporation is wholly-owned by CalAmp Corporation. With operations in the U.S. and abroad, the company's proprietary wireless technology network recovers stolen vehicles globally, comprising a more than 90% recovery rate on cars, trucks and sport utility vehicles (SUVs). The LoJack Stolen Vehicle Recovery System integrates with state and local law enforcement and encompasses radio frequency that tracks the vehicle, oftentimes enabling the recovery of vehicles within hours. The LoJack system combined with an early warning feature will alert the vehicle owner of potential auto theft via a keychain fob. The fob communicates directly with the LoJack system inside the vehicle. The LoJack system is also available for classic, custom and collective vehicles, as well as motorcycles. LoJack SureDrive connects the owner with their vehicle no matter who is driving it. SureDrive informs if the car is in an accident, if it is moved in such a way as being towed/stolen) and where it is parked. It will also notify when the driver of the vehicle arrives at the expected destination. LoJack Asset Recovery for Equipment is for business operations that want to further protect their equipment assets from theft. This equipment recovery system is currently for light-duty and car fleets (as of mid-2019). Last, LoJack LotSmart is an inventory lot management solution for dealerships.

FINANCIAL DATA: *Note: Data for latest year may not have been available at press time.*

In U.S. $	2018	2017	2016	2015	2014	2013
Revenue	126,000,000	120,000,000	117,500,000	129,552,000	133,568,000	140,207,008
R&D Expense						
Operating Income						
Operating Margin %						
SGA Expense						
Net Income				3,197,000	-17,924,000	3,167,000
Operating Cash Flow						
Capital Expenditure						
EBITDA						
Return on Assets %						
Return on Equity %						
Debt to Equity						

CONTACT INFORMATION:

Phone: 781 302-4200 Fax: 781 326-7255
Toll-Free: 800-445-6522
Address: 40 Pequot Way, Canton, MA 02021 United States

STOCK TICKER/OTHER:

Stock Ticker: Subsidiary
Employees: 670
Parent Company: CalAmp Corporation
Exchange:
Fiscal Year Ends: 12/31

SALARIES/BONUSES:

Top Exec. Salary: $ Bonus: $
Second Exec. Salary: $ Bonus: $

OTHER THOUGHTS:

Estimated Female Officers or Directors: 1
Hot Spot for Advancement for Women/Minorities: Y

Lucid Motors Inc

lucidmotors.com

NAIC Code: 336111

TYPES OF BUSINESS:

Automobile Manufacturing
Electric Automobile Manufacturing

BRANDS/DIVISIONS/AFFILIATES:

Lucid Air

CONTACTS:

Note: Officers with more than one job title may be intentionally listed here more than once.

Peter Rawlinson, CEO
Doug Coates, Sr. Dir.-Finance
Doreen Allen, Dir.-Sales
Andrew Liveris, Chmn.

GROWTH PLANS/SPECIAL FEATURES:

Lucid Motors, Inc. is an American automotive company that specializes in the design, manufacture and marketing of electric cars. The Lucid Air 4-door, 5-seat luxury sedan is designed to maximize interior space without being too large of a vehicle. Its proprietary technology and electric drivetrain deliver an ultimate driver and passenger experience. At top speeds or tight corners, the EV's calibrated air springs, advanced damper technology and low center of gravity offers precision handling and a smooth ride. Lucid's battery technology and power electronics enable over 400 miles of range, over 200 mph and going from 0-60 mph in 2.5 seconds' time. Its seamless intelligent technology presents a connected lifestyle inside and outside the vehicle. Lucid Air's on-board assistance tracks usage patterns and preferences, integrating with the connected user's digital life, including favorite music, preferred temperature and more. Controls can react via voice technology, and software upgrades will allow the Lucid Air to transition through progressive levels of autonomy. Lucid has designed, developed, manufactured and supplied battery packs for all race teams in Formula E's 2018-19 season, and will do so for the 2019-20 season as well. This is made capable through its collaboration with McLaren Applied Technologies and Sony.

FINANCIAL DATA:

Note: Data for latest year may not have been available at press time.

In U.S. $	2018	2017	2016	2015	2014	2013
Revenue						
R&D Expense						
Operating Income						
Operating Margin %						
SGA Expense						
Net Income						
Operating Cash Flow						
Capital Expenditure						
EBITDA						
Return on Assets %						
Return on Equity %						
Debt to Equity						

CONTACT INFORMATION:

Phone: 510-648-3553 Fax:
Toll-Free:
Address: 7373 Gateway Blvd., Newark, CA 94560 United States

STOCK TICKER/OTHER:

Stock Ticker: Private
Employees:
Parent Company:
Exchange:
Fiscal Year Ends:

SALARIES/BONUSES:

Top Exec. Salary: $ Bonus: $
Second Exec. Salary: $ Bonus: $

OTHER THOUGHTS:

Estimated Female Officers or Directors:
Hot Spot for Advancement for Women/Minorities:

Lund International Inc

www.lundinternational.com

NAIC Code: 336300

TYPES OF BUSINESS:

Automobile Parts Manufacturer
Appearance Products, Automotive
Exterior Visors
Running Boards
Hood Shields
Bumpers
Truck Liners
Spoilers

BRANDS/DIVISIONS/AFFILIATES:

Highlander Partners LP
Auto Ventshade (AVS)
Ventvisor
Powerstep
Lund
Belmor
Roadworks Manufacturing Inc
Roll-N-Lock

CONTACTS: *Note: Officers with more than one job title may be intentionally listed here more than once.*

Mitch Fogle, Pres.
Billy Bibb, Chief Designer
Luis Serentill, Mgr.-Eng.
Jarrod Holland, Media Contact
Jeff L. Hull, Chmn.

GROWTH PLANS/SPECIAL FEATURES:

Lund International, Inc. is a group of specialty companies that design, manufacture and market accessories for the automotive market. The company operates out of a 541,000-square-foot facility at its global headquarters and distribution warehouse, with strategic access for shipping via air and land. Lund's aftermarket accessories are primarily applied to light and heavy trucks, sport utility vehicles (SUVs), crossover utility vehicles (CUVs), vans and passenger cars. The firm also serves a diversified distribution network including warehouse distributors, automotive parts retailers, online retailers and original equipment manufacturers (OEMs). Products include hood protections, running boards, tonneau covers, floor coverings, exterior accessories, storage boxes, cargo management, bed accessories, scoops, vent decals, bed and grille coverings. Branded products include accessories such as the Auto Ventshade (AVS), a vent shade that is mounted above car windows in order to keep rain out and allow fresh air to come in; the Ventvisor family of side window deflectors; and the Powerstep line of electric running boards. Other brand names include Lund, AVS, Belmor, AMP Research, Rampage Products, RoadWorks Manufacturing, Roll-N-Lock, Stampede Automotive and Tonno Pro, which offer a range of functional body and appearance products that provide customers with ways to customize and personalize their vehicles. Lund International is a subsidiary of Highlander Partners LP, and holds more than 100 patents.

FINANCIAL DATA: *Note: Data for latest year may not have been available at press time.*

In U.S. $	2018	2017	2016	2015	2014	2013
Revenue	155,452,500	148,050,000	141,000,000	139,000,000	131,000,000	120,000,000
R&D Expense						
Operating Income						
Operating Margin %						
SGA Expense						
Net Income						
Operating Cash Flow						
Capital Expenditure						
EBITDA						
Return on Assets %						
Return on Equity %						
Debt to Equity						

CONTACT INFORMATION:

Phone: 678-804-3767 Fax:
Toll-Free: 888-588-6049
Address: 4325 Hamilton Mill Rd., Buford, GA 30518 United States

STOCK TICKER/OTHER:

Stock Ticker: Subsidiary
Exchange:
Employees: 1,200
Fiscal Year Ends: 12/31
Parent Company: Highlander Partners LP

SALARIES/BONUSES:

Top Exec. Salary: $ Bonus: $
Second Exec. Salary: $ Bonus: $

OTHER THOUGHTS:

Estimated Female Officers or Directors: 1
Hot Spot for Advancement for Women/Minorities:

Lupient Automotive Group Inc

www.lupient.com

NAIC Code: 441110

TYPES OF BUSINESS:

Auto Dealers, Retail
Auto Finance
Auto Service
Fleet Sales
Water Park

BRANDS/DIVISIONS/AFFILIATES:

Jim Lupient INFINITI
INFINITI Milwaukee
Lupient Buick GMC
Lupient Chevrolet
Lupient Kia
Lupient Nissan of Rochester
Lupient Collision Center
Jim Lupient Water Park

CONTACTS:

Note: Officers with more than one job title may be intentionally listed here more than once.

Jeff Lupient, CEO

GROWTH PLANS/SPECIAL FEATURES:

Lupient Automotive Group, Inc. is one of the largest new and pre-owned automotive dealers in Minnesota. The company features eight dealership locations in the Great Lakes area, including Jim Lupient INFINITI, INFINITI Milwaukee, Lupient Buick GMC, Lupient Chevrolet, Lupient Kia, Lupient Kia Milwaukee, Lupient Nissan of Rochester, and Lupient Buick GMC of Rochester. Lupient's inventory includes cars, trucks, SUVs and vans. In addition to individual automobiles, the firm generates revenue from large fleet sale operations. It also offers title and license administration, nationwide delivery, as well as warranty, maintenance and service services. Through the company's website, customers can link to each dealership and view inventory, get an instant quote on any vehicle or schedule service appointments. Additionally, Lupient operates three Lupient Collision Center body shops, based in Brooklyn Park, Bloomington and Rochester, Minnesota. The firm also funds and operates the Jim Lupient Water Park, featuring three large water slides, various related activities and covered shelters (available by reservation).

FINANCIAL DATA:

Note: Data for latest year may not have been available at press time.

In U.S. $	2018	2017	2016	2015	2014	2013
Revenue	716,625,000	682,500,000	650,000,000	634,000,000	615,000,000	585,000,000
R&D Expense						
Operating Income						
Operating Margin %						
SGA Expense						
Net Income						
Operating Cash Flow						
Capital Expenditure						
EBITDA						
Return on Assets %						
Return on Equity %						
Debt to Equity						

CONTACT INFORMATION:

Phone: 763-544-6666 Fax: 763-513-5517
Toll-Free:
Address: 7100 Wayzata Blvd., Ste. 200, Minneapolis, MN 55426 United States

STOCK TICKER/OTHER:

Stock Ticker: Private
Employees: 1,320
Parent Company:
Exchange:
Fiscal Year Ends: 12/31

SALARIES/BONUSES:

Top Exec. Salary: $ Bonus: $
Second Exec. Salary: $ Bonus: $

OTHER THOUGHTS:

Estimated Female Officers or Directors:
Hot Spot for Advancement for Women/Minorities:

Lydall Inc

www.lydall.com

NAIC Code: 336360

TYPES OF BUSINESS:

Motor Vehicle Seating and Interior Trim Manufacturing

BRANDS/DIVISIONS/AFFILIATES:

LydAir

CONTACTS:

Note: Officers with more than one job title may be intentionally listed here more than once.

Dale Barnhart, CEO
Randall Gonzales, CFO
Marc Giles, Chairman of the Board
James Laughlan, Chief Accounting Officer
Chad McDaniel, Chief Administrative Officer
Scott Deakin, President, Divisional
Paul Marold, President, Divisional
Joseph Abbruzzi, President, Divisional

GROWTH PLANS/SPECIAL FEATURES:

Lydall, Inc. designs and manufactures specialty engineered nonwoven filtration media, industrial thermal insulating solutions, thermal/acoustical barriers and thermal/acoustical applications. Lydall operates through two business segments: performance materials and thermal acoustical solutions. The firm's performance materials segment includes filtration media solutions for air, fluid power, industrial and life science applications. This division also produces sealing and gasket solutions, thermal insulation, energy storage and other engineered products. Filtration products include LydAir MG (micro-glass) air filtration media, LydAir MB (melt blown) air filtration media, LydAir SC (synthetic composite) air filtration media and Arioso membrane composite media. Interface fiber-reinforced gasket materials serve the heavy-duty diesel, automobile, small engine, transmission and compressor markets. These products handle demanding sealing challenges with a diverse range of metallic, non-metallic, rubber-coated and laminate materials. Interface engineered components are ready-to-use soft and hard gasket parts sold directly to original equipment manufacturers (OEMs) and aftermarket applications. The thermal acoustical solutions segment comprises technical nonwovens and thermal acoustical solutions. Technical nonwovens consist of needle punch nonwovens for an array of industries and applications. These products include nonwoven rolled felt media and filter bags used primarily in industrial air and liquid filtration applications, and for industries such as power, cement, steel, asphalt, incineration, mining, food and pharmaceutical. Thermal acoustical solutions are tailored for the transportation and industrial sectors to thermally shield sensitive components from high heat, to improve exhaust gas treatment and to lower emissions and reduce vibration and noise. Lydall's thermal products are found in the interior, underbody and under hood of vehicles, such as dashes, wheel wells, fuel tanks, engine compartments, powertrains, turbo chargers and more. Lydall has global manufacturing facilities, including the U.S., Germany, France, China, Canada and the U.K. In May 2019, Lydall sold Texel Geosol, Inc., its geosynthetic installation business, to FC Geosynthetiques, Inc.

FINANCIAL DATA:

Note: Data for latest year may not have been available at press time.

In U.S. $	2018	2017	2016	2015	2014	2013
Revenue	785,897,000	698,437,000	566,852,000	524,505,000	535,829,000	397,969,000
R&D Expense						
Operating Income	49,188,000	65,427,000	54,792,000	52,477,000	34,048,000	28,713,000
Operating Margin %		.09%	.10%	.10%	.06%	.07%
SGA Expense	103,457,000	97,635,000	83,750,000	70,020,000	80,930,000	56,512,000
Net Income	34,944,000	49,317,000	37,187,000	46,259,000	21,847,000	19,155,000
Operating Cash Flow	44,739,000	62,936,000	69,727,000	36,110,000	41,628,000	30,280,000
Capital Expenditure	31,291,000	27,006,000	25,466,000	20,645,000	13,971,000	13,826,000
EBITDA	82,639,000	90,169,000	75,566,000	89,053,000	52,395,000	41,239,000
Return on Assets %		.09%	.08%	.13%	.07%	.07%
Return on Equity %		.16%	.14%	.20%	.11%	.10%
Debt to Equity		0.218	0.469	0.082	0.19	0.005

CONTACT INFORMATION:

Phone: 860 646-1233 Fax: 860 646-8847
Toll-Free:
Address: One Colonial Rd., Manchester, CT 06042 United States

STOCK TICKER/OTHER:

Stock Ticker: LDL
Employees: 2,700
Parent Company:
Exchange: NYS
Fiscal Year Ends: 12/31

SALARIES/BONUSES:

Top Exec. Salary: $631,720 Bonus: $
Second Exec. Salary: $430,246 Bonus: $

OTHER THOUGHTS:

Estimated Female Officers or Directors: 1
Hot Spot for Advancement for Women/Minorities:

MAACO Franchising Inc

www.maaco.com

NAIC Code: 811100

TYPES OF BUSINESS:

Automotive Repair & Maintenance
Auto Painting
Collision Repair

BRANDS/DIVISIONS/AFFILIATES:

Driven Brands Inc
MAACO Collision Repair & Auto Painting Centers

CONTACTS:

Note: Officers with more than one job title may be intentionally listed here more than once.

Jonathan Fitzpatrick, CEO
Jonathan Fitzpatrick, Pres.
Dave Schaefers, Sr. VP-Franchise Dev.
David M. Lapps, Pres., MAACO Collision Repair & Auto Painting
Jason T. Ryan, VP-New Ctr. Dev.

GROWTH PLANS/SPECIAL FEATURES:

MAACO Franchising, Inc. provides auto body repair and painting through its franchise network of more than 500 MAACO Collision Repair & Auto Painting Centers. Since 1972, these franchised centers across the U.S., Canada and Puerto Rico have repaired more than 20 million vehicles. MAACO offers free estimates, vehicle body repair, vehicle surface preparation, vehicle surface sealer, vehicle paint services, vehicle protection and finishing, as well as advice and products for proper car care. For work that involves filing insurance claims, MAACO helps handle those details and works with every major insurance company so as to coordinate a complete repair for customers. MAACO also recommends options that help save money when paying for repairs are solely out-of-pocket. These services come with a coast-to-coast warranty, quality assurance, central billing, original factory color matching and quality name-brand paints and parts. The firm has color match systems in its auto body shops designed to match paint using Sherwin-Williams and DuPont paint systems. In addition to personal vehicle repair, the company offers fleet maintenance services. These services include accident management, remarketing and re-identification. Moreover, the company's eStore offers car care kits, food and beverage cooler bags for vehicles, hats, t-shirts and other items. MAACO is owned by Driven Brands, Inc.

FINANCIAL DATA:

Note: Data for latest year may not have been available at press time.

In U.S. $	2018	2017	2016	2015	2014	2013
Revenue	540,225,000	514,500,000	490,000,000	475,000,000	460,000,000	465,000,000
R&D Expense						
Operating Income						
Operating Margin %						
SGA Expense						
Net Income						
Operating Cash Flow						
Capital Expenditure						
EBITDA						
Return on Assets %						
Return on Equity %						
Debt to Equity						

CONTACT INFORMATION:

Phone: 800-521-6282 Fax:
Toll-Free: 800-521-6282
Address: 440 S. Church St., Ste. 700, Charlotte, NC 28202 United States

STOCK TICKER/OTHER:

Stock Ticker: Subsidiary Exchange:
Employees: Fiscal Year Ends: 10/31
Parent Company: Driven Brands Inc

SALARIES/BONUSES:

Top Exec. Salary: $ Bonus: $
Second Exec. Salary: $ Bonus: $

OTHER THOUGHTS:

Estimated Female Officers or Directors:
Hot Spot for Advancement for Women/Minorities:

Mack Trucks Inc

www.macktrucks.com

NAIC Code: 336120

TYPES OF BUSINESS:

Truck Manufacturer
Heavy-Duty Trucks
Replacement Parts
Customer Support Services
Construction Services

BRANDS/DIVISIONS/AFFILIATES:

AB Volvo
Mack Canada Inc
Mack Trucks Australia Pty Ltd
Mack de Mexico
Mack de Peru
Mack de Venezuela CA
Mack Anthem
TerraPro

CONTACTS: *Note: Officers with more than one job title may be intentionally listed here more than once.*

Martin Weissburg, Pres.
Dennis McDaniel, VP-Southeast Region
John Thomas, VP-Western Region
David Barletta, VP-Central Region
Patrick Meehan, VP-Northeast Region
Kevin Flaherty, Pres., North American Sales & Mktg.

GROWTH PLANS/SPECIAL FEATURES:

Mack Trucks, Inc., a subsidiary of AB Volvo, produces heavy-duty and medium-duty trucks and product components in the U.S. The firm's trucks are grouped into five series: Mack Anthem, Pinnacle, Granite, LR and TerraPro. Mack Anthem is a sleeper truck built for businesses and designed for drivers, comprising smart tracking and serviceability as well as modern aerodynamic components. The Pinnacle series comprises the day cab, a versatile truck for regional trips; and the sleeper, designed for comfort, heavy loads, steep grades and long hauls. The Granite series comprises the Granite lightweight chassis truck, which can carry loads while staying nimble; and the Mack Granite MHD (medium heavy duty), which is configured for shorter runs and lighter-duty cycles. The LR series comprises the light rigid (LR) models, which come with multiple driving and door options. The TerraPro series is a cabover truck comprised of a rugged exterior, provides visibility on all sides, and is primarily used for the construction and refuse industries. The company also offers Mack Parts, with round-the-clock parts purchasing, 24/7 online access. Remanufactured parts are branded under the REMACK name. Road Choice Truck Parts is a private label brand for more than 40 all-makes heavy-duty parts categories available at over 500 authorized dealer locations. Mack's powertrain and suspensions are designed to work together for optimum performance, increased fuel efficiency and lower maintenance costs. Mack MP engines are designed to be fuel-efficient and clean running, with a range of 325 to 605 horsepower, and torque ratings of 2,060 lb-feet. Mack also manufactures transmissions, axles, suspensions and more. Components are sold in over 45 countries. International subsidiaries include Mack Canada, Inc.; Mack Trucks Australia Pty. Ltd.; Mack de Mexico; Mack de Peru; and Mack de Venezuela CA.

FINANCIAL DATA: *Note: Data for latest year may not have been available at press time.*

In U.S. $	2018	2017	2016	2015	2014	2013
Revenue	2,870,000,000	2,677,500,000	2,550,000,000	2,448,000,000	1,800,000,000	1,750,000,000
R&D Expense						
Operating Income						
Operating Margin %						
SGA Expense						
Net Income			26,520,592	24,093,303	20,160,841	
Operating Cash Flow						
Capital Expenditure						
EBITDA						
Return on Assets %						
Return on Equity %						
Debt to Equity						

CONTACT INFORMATION:

Phone: 336-291-9001 Fax: 336-291-9202
Toll-Free: 800-866-1177
Address: 7900 National Service Rd., Greensboro, NC 27409 United States

STOCK TICKER/OTHER:

Stock Ticker: Subsidiary
Employees: 1,750
Parent Company: AB Volvo
Exchange:
Fiscal Year Ends: 12/31

SALARIES/BONUSES:

Top Exec. Salary: $ Bonus: $
Second Exec. Salary: $ Bonus: $

OTHER THOUGHTS:

Estimated Female Officers or Directors:
Hot Spot for Advancement for Women/Minorities:

MacNeil Automotive Products Limited (WeatherTech)

www.weathertech.com

NAIC Code: 336360

TYPES OF BUSINESS:

Floor Mats for Cars & Trucks

BRANDS/DIVISIONS/AFFILIATES:

WeatherTech
DigitalFit
TechFloor
WeatherTech AVM
WeatherTech Pet Barrier
WeatherTech PetSTEP
BumpStep
TechShade

CONTACTS: *Note: Officers with more than one job title may be intentionally listed here more than once.*

David MacNeil, CEO

GROWTH PLANS/SPECIAL FEATURES:

MacNeil Automotive Products Limited, operating under the WeatherTech brand name, is a manufacturer and distributor of custom rubber floor liners and other plastic products. Floor liners created by the firm are primarily designed to be used within various automobiles. Products include floor mats, cargo liners, mud flaps, bed liners, side window deflectors, car covers and bug deflectors, to name a few. The most popular of these automotive products is the DigitalFit floorliner. This floorliner is a laser-measured, heavy-duty floorliner that incudes channels and reservoirs to carry away and store liquids and other debris in order to help keep shoes and clothing clean. The DigitalFIt is available for both front and back seat floor wells. WeatherTech AVM (all-vehicle mat) is a universal all-weather floor mat and is the company's trim-to-fit product. The WeatherTech Pet Barrier product is an adjustable, expandable tubing barrier/gate that helps protect vehicle upholstery when transporting pets; and its WeatherTech PetSTEP product is a folding ramp for pet exit and entry into vehicles. The BumpStep is a hitch-mounted step that can be used as a step to reach the top roof of vehicles or can be used as a bumper protector from rear-end accidents, dents and scratches. The TechShade is a custom-fit windshield and window sun shade that protects vehicle interiors from UV rays. The shade helps keep interior temperatures cool in hot weather and when flipped around, prevents frost build-up in the winter. TechFloor, a non-automotive product, is a plastic flooring used to cover garage floors and other high foot traffic areas. Other products include license plate frame protective coverings, boot trays, drink coasters, cleaning products and more.

FINANCIAL DATA: *Note: Data for latest year may not have been available at press time.*

In U.S. $	2018	2017	2016	2015	2014	2013
Revenue	551,250,000	525,000,000	500,000,000	450,000,000	425,000,000	400,000,000
R&D Expense						
Operating Income						
Operating Margin %						
SGA Expense						
Net Income						
Operating Cash Flow						
Capital Expenditure						
EBITDA						
Return on Assets %						
Return on Equity %						
Debt to Equity						

CONTACT INFORMATION:

Phone: 630-769-1500 Fax: 630-769-0300
Toll-Free: 800-441-6287
Address: 841 Remington Blvd., Bolingbrook, IL 60440 United States

STOCK TICKER/OTHER:

Stock Ticker: Private Exchange:
Employees: 1,250 Fiscal Year Ends: 12/31
Parent Company:

SALARIES/BONUSES:

Top Exec. Salary: $ Bonus: $
Second Exec. Salary: $ Bonus: $

OTHER THOUGHTS:

Estimated Female Officers or Directors:
Hot Spot for Advancement for Women/Minorities:

Magna International Inc

www.magna.com

NAIC Code: 336300

TYPES OF BUSINESS:

Automobile Parts Manufacturer
Vehicle Assembly Services
Seating & Interior Products
Closure Systems
Body & Chassis Systems
Mirror, Lighting & Glass Systems
Exterior Decorative Systems
Solar Photovoltaic Components

BRANDS/DIVISIONS/AFFILIATES:

VIZA Geca SL

CONTACTS:

Note: Officers with more than one job title may be intentionally listed here more than once.

Donald Walker, CEO
William Young, Chairman of the Board
Riccardo Trecroce, Chief Legal Officer
James Tobin, Chief Marketing Officer
Seetarama Kotagiri, Chief Technology Officer
Tommy Skudutis, COO
Francis Seguin, Executive VP
Vincent Galifi, Executive VP
Aaron McCarthy, Executive VP
Indira Samarasekera, Independent Director
Cynthia Niekamp, Independent Director
Guenther Apfalter, President, Geographical

GROWTH PLANS/SPECIAL FEATURES:

Magna International, Inc. is a global supplier of high-tech automotive components, systems and complete modules. Its services span the design, engineering and manufacture of a full range of interior and exterior systems as well as providing complete vehicle assembly services to major automotive manufacturers. The company's operations include 348 manufacturing facilities and 91 product development, engineering and sales centers located in 28 countries across three geographic segments: North America, Europe and the rest of the world. Through its divisions and subsidiaries, the company provides services in four main product areas. These include: body exteriors & structures, consisting of the body, chassis, exteriors and roof systems; power & vision, consisting of powertrain, electronics, vision systems and closures; seating systems, including complete seats, structural seating products, foam and trim; and complete vehicles, consisting of vehicle engineering and contract manufacturing. In December 2018, Magna acquired VIZA Geca SL, based in Spain, an operator of four seating production facilities. In March 2019, Magna sold its fluid pressure and controls business to Hanon Systems.

FINANCIAL DATA:

Note: Data for latest year may not have been available at press time.

In U.S. $	2018	2017	2016	2015	2014	2013
Revenue	40,827,000,000	38,946,000,000	36,445,000,000	32,134,000,000	36,641,000,000	34,835,000,000
R&D Expense						
Operating Income	2,830,000,000	2,847,000,000	2,665,000,000	2,325,000,000	2,421,000,000	1,869,000,000
Operating Margin %		.07%	.07%	.07%	.06%	.05%
SGA Expense	1,664,000,000	1,668,000,000	1,601,000,000	1,448,000,000	1,707,000,000	1,616,000,000
Net Income	2,296,000,000	2,206,000,000	2,031,000,000	2,013,000,000	1,882,000,000	1,561,000,000
Operating Cash Flow	3,718,000,000	3,329,000,000	3,386,000,000	2,332,000,000	2,792,000,000	2,567,000,000
Capital Expenditure	1,650,000,000	1,858,000,000	1,807,000,000	1,591,000,000	1,586,000,000	1,169,000,000
EBITDA	4,342,000,000	4,262,000,000	3,936,000,000	3,511,000,000	3,476,000,000	3,002,000,000
Return on Assets %		.09%	.10%	.11%	.10%	.09%
Return on Equity %		.21%	.22%	.23%	.21%	.16%
Debt to Equity		0.285	0.245	0.262	0.094	0.011

CONTACT INFORMATION:

Phone: 905 726-2462 Fax:
Toll-Free:
Address: 337 Magna Dr., Aurora, ON L4G 7K1 Canada

STOCK TICKER/OTHER:

Stock Ticker: MGA
Employees: 131,225
Parent Company:
Exchange: NYS
Fiscal Year Ends: 12/31

SALARIES/BONUSES:

Top Exec. Salary: $325,000 Bonus: $
Second Exec. Salary: $325,000 Bonus: $

OTHER THOUGHTS:

Estimated Female Officers or Directors: 2
Hot Spot for Advancement for Women/Minorities:

Magna Mirrors

www.magna.com/capabilities/vision-systems

NAIC Code: 336300

TYPES OF BUSINESS:

Automobile Parts Manufacturer
Window & Door Systems
Vision Systems
Glass & Coating Products
Automotive Mirrors

BRANDS/DIVISIONS/AFFILIATES:

Magna International Inc
VideoMirror
Frameless
Total BlindZoneManagement System
ClearView

CONTACTS:

Note: Officers with more than one job title may be intentionally listed here more than once.

John O'Hara, Pres.
Vincent J. Galifi, CFO
Jeffrey O. Palmer, Chief Legal Officer
Herbert Demel, Chief Strategy Officer
Tom J. Skudutis, COO-Exteriors, Interiors, Seating & Mirrors
Jim Tobin, Pres., Magna Asia
Guenther Apfalter, Pres., Magna Europe

GROWTH PLANS/SPECIAL FEATURES:

Magna Mirrors is a wholly-owned operating unit of auto parts firm Magna International, Inc. Magna Mirrors provides a variety of exterior and interior mirror systems, as well as actuators. The company's manufacturing divisions and engineering facilities are located in the U.S., Mexico, Austria, Germany, France, Spain, Sweden, Slovakia, China, Japan and India. Among the firm's strengths is its ability to invent new products and technological solutions to enhance driving experience. Innovations and technologies include Magna Mirrors' VideoMirror, a rearview mirror that conceals a 2.5- or 3.5-inch LCD video screen which provides information displayed in heads-up situations (such as a child riding a tricycle nearby the vehicle); Frameless exterior electronic mirrors that provide maximum view; the Total BlindZoneManagement System, which combines camera technology, enhanced mirrors and lighting, and information/telematics to help eliminate blind zones around the vehicle; and ClearView, which helps improve visibility while changing lanes, backing out of parking spaces or driving with a vehicle full of cargo. Actuators enable features like automatic power folding mirrors and mirror memory functions, as well as controlling the movement of the flaps used in HVAC systems. They are designed to operate in all conditions with low noise. Customers of the firm include original equipment manufacturers, Tier-1 automobile manufacturers, medium- and heavy-truck manufacturers and non-automotive manufacturers such as Caterpillar, E-Z-Go, John Deere, Kubota and BRP. Nearly 30 million interior mirrors and 30 million exterior mirrors are produced by the company annually.

Employee benefits include an employee assistance program as a part of a larger benefits package.

FINANCIAL DATA:

Note: Data for latest year may not have been available at press time.

In U.S. $	2018	2017	2016	2015	2014	2013
Revenue						
R&D Expense						
Operating Income						
Operating Margin %						
SGA Expense						
Net Income						
Operating Cash Flow						
Capital Expenditure						
EBITDA						
Return on Assets %						
Return on Equity %						
Debt to Equity						

CONTACT INFORMATION:

Phone: 905-898-6744 Fax:
Toll-Free:
Address: 521 Newpark Blvd., Newmarket, ON L3Y 4X7 Canada

STOCK TICKER/OTHER:

Stock Ticker: Subsidiary
Exchange:
Employees: 124,000
Fiscal Year Ends: 12/31
Parent Company: Magna International Inc

SALARIES/BONUSES:

Top Exec. Salary: $ Bonus: $
Second Exec. Salary: $ Bonus: $

OTHER THOUGHTS:

Estimated Female Officers or Directors:
Hot Spot for Advancement for Women/Minorities:

Magneti Marelli SpA

www.magnetimarelli.com

NAIC Code: 336300

TYPES OF BUSINESS:

Automotive Components
Power Train Systems
Motor Sport Components
Lighting
Automotive Performance Research Equipment

BRANDS/DIVISIONS/AFFILIATES:

Fiat Chrysler Automobiles NV
FCA Italy SpA
Freechoice
Magneti Marelli Checkstar Service Network

CONTACTS:

Note: Officers with more than one job title may be intentionally listed here more than once.

Ermanno Ferrari, CEO
Eugenio Razelli, Pres.
A.C. Ferrara, Head-Mfg.
G. Acossato, General Counsel
A. Tanganelli, Head-Bus. Dev.
M. Bellone, Head-Comm.
M. Mamavello, Coordinator-Purchasing

GROWTH PLANS/SPECIAL FEATURES:

Magneti Marelli SpA designs and manufactures high-tech systems and components for the automotive sector. The firm has 85 production units and 15 research and development centers across 20 countries. Magneti Marelli has supplied major car manufacturers such as Renault, Citroen, Peugeot, the Fiat Group, Ford, Volkswagen, Audi, Seat, BMW, DaimlerChrysler, GM-Opel, Volvo, Saab, Nissan, Toyota and Daewoo. Magneti Marelli operates through seven business segments. Automotive lighting comprises front and rear lighting systems and body electronics. Powertrain comprises engine control systems for gasoline, diesel and multi-fuel engines; and automated manual transmission Freechoice gearboxes. Electronic systems include instrument clusters, as well as infotainment and telematics. Suspension systems include suspension systems, shock absorbers and dynamic systems. Exhaust systems include exhaust systems, catalytic converters and silencing systems. Aftermarket parts and services is a commercial division dedicated to spare parts and services, relying on an organized network of over 5,000 authorized workshops spread throughout the world under the Magneti Marelli Checkstar Service Network brand. Finally, the motorsport segment designs and produces electronic and electro-mechanical systems for 2- and 4-wheels racing vehicles. Specific products in this division include data acquisition, display, lap trigger, electronic control systems, engine components, power supply systems, software and technological excellences. The motorsport department is engaged in the research and production of kinetic energy recovery systems (KERS) for Formula 1 and other motorsports series. Magneti Marelli is a subsidiary of FCA Italy SpA, the Italian branch of Fiat Chrysler Automobiles NV. In October 2018, Fiat Chrysler announced that it was selling Magneti to Calsonic Kansei Corporation, a manufacturer of automotive parts and accessories, for â,¬6.2 billion ($7.2 billion). The combined business would have nearly 200 facilities and research centers around the world, and would be renamed as Magneti Marelli CK Holdings.

FINANCIAL DATA:

Note: Data for latest year may not have been available at press time.

In U.S. $	2018	2017	2016	2015	2014	2013
Revenue	10,313,604,000	9,822,480,000	8,323,120,000	8,263,066,700	7,349,550,000	8,323,457,820
R&D Expense						
Operating Income						
Operating Margin %						
SGA Expense						
Net Income			321,236,521	359,020,750	230,665,860	191,088,300
Operating Cash Flow						
Capital Expenditure						
EBITDA						
Return on Assets %						
Return on Equity %						
Debt to Equity						

CONTACT INFORMATION:

Phone: 39-02-9722-7454 Fax: 39-02-9722-7510
Toll-Free:
Address: Viale Aldo Borletti 61/63, Milano, 20011 Italy

STOCK TICKER/OTHER:

Stock Ticker: Subsidiary
Exchange:
Employees: 44,000
Fiscal Year Ends: 12/31
Parent Company: Fiat Chrysler Automobiles NV

SALARIES/BONUSES:

Top Exec. Salary: $ Bonus: $
Second Exec. Salary: $ Bonus: $

OTHER THOUGHTS:

Estimated Female Officers or Directors: 1
Hot Spot for Advancement for Women/Minorities:

Mahindra & Mahindra Limited

www.mahindra.com

NAIC Code: 336111

TYPES OF BUSINESS:

Automotive & Farm Equipment Manufacturing & Distribution
Software Engineering
Real Estate Development
Hotels
Financial Services
Automobile Finance
Housing Finance
Information Technology

BRANDS/DIVISIONS/AFFILIATES:

Mahindra Group

CONTACTS: *Note: Officers with more than one job title may be intentionally listed here more than once.*

Pawan Kumar Goenka, Managing Dir.
V.S. Parthasarathy, Group CFO
Rajan Wadhera, Chief Exec.-Prod. Dev.
S.P. Shukla, Pres., Group Strategy
Anita Arjundas, CEO-Real Estate Sector
Anoop Mathur, Pres., Two Wheeler Sector
S. Durgassankar, Exec. VP-Mergers & Acquisitions
Pravin Shah, CEO-Automotive Div.
Anand Gopal Mahindra, Chmn.
Ruzbeh Irani, Chief Exec.-Intl Oper.

GROWTH PLANS/SPECIAL FEATURES:

Mahindra & Mahindra Limited is one of the largest industrial companies in India and a leading producer of multi-utility vehicles. Mahindra & Mahindra is the flagship business of the Mahindra Group. The firm operates in eight sectors: mobility, farm equipment, IT, financial services, clean energy, urban lifestyle, business-to-business (B2B) and defense. Mobility comprises the firm's utility vehicle company, which includes sports utility vehicles, electric vehicles, pickups and commercial vehicles, as well as small aircraft and boats. Farm equipment includes agricultural and post-harvest advisory services, machines, tractors, tilling equipment and components and accessories for farmers. IT provides solutions that optimize productivity and connect enterprises globally, including networking, mobility, analytics, cloud, security, social channels and sensors. Financial services provides life and non-life insurance products, as well as various loans, including home, auto and equipment. Clean energy produces solar panels, as well as related energy engineering solutions. This division currently comprises more than 256 megawatts (MW) of commissioned solar power, with over 288MW under construction. Urban lifestyle focuses on creating sustainable urbanization, including smart housing and retail spaces, innovative rental living, green urban commuting and electric vehicle manufacturing. B2B comprises the firm's steel trading company, including steel consulting, logistics, industrial equipment, engineering and diesel services. Last, for the defense industry, Mahindra & Mahindra manufactures all-terrain transportation vehicles utilized by defense and police forces, as well as land systems, naval systems and defense electronics. This division also provides security consulting services.

FINANCIAL DATA: *Note: Data for latest year may not have been available at press time.*

In U.S. $	2018	2017	2016	2015	2014	2013
Revenue	11,938,220,000	10,817,780,000	10,054,890,000	9,201,434,000	9,643,537,000	
R&D Expense						
Operating Income	229,477,700	86,689,720	106,081,700	119,353,100	409,170,800	
Operating Margin %	.11%	.01%	.01%	.01%	.04%	
SGA Expense	912,718,100	740,184,400	869,703,900	807,263,200	735,500,400	
Net Income	1,082,111,000	532,820,400	462,684,300	452,052,500	672,419,800	
Operating Cash Flow	98,243,640	9,486,348	139,858,800	151,986,200	-35,118,510	
Capital Expenditure	850,915,600	724,177,000	624,489,600	685,675,400	528,100,300	
EBITDA	2,519,193,000	1,851,024,000	1,451,263,000	1,362,683,000	1,557,028,000	
Return on Assets %	.06%	.03%	.03%	.03%	.06%	
Return on Equity %	.23%	.13%	.12%	.13%	.22%	
Debt to Equity	0.919	1.014	0.877	0.864	1.094	

CONTACT INFORMATION:

Phone: 91 2224901441 Fax:
Toll-Free:
Address: Mahindra Towers, B Wing Dr., GM Bhosale Marg, Mumbai, Maharashtra 400001 India

STOCK TICKER/OTHER:

Stock Ticker: MAHDY
Exchange: PINX
Employees: 42,875
Fiscal Year Ends: 03/31
Parent Company:

SALARIES/BONUSES:

Top Exec. Salary: $ Bonus: $
Second Exec. Salary: $ Bonus: $

OTHER THOUGHTS:

Estimated Female Officers or Directors: 1
Hot Spot for Advancement for Women/Minorities:

Major Automotive Companies Inc

www.majorworld.com

NAIC Code: 441110

TYPES OF BUSINESS:

Auto Dealers-Retail
Auto Financing
Parts & Repair Service
Used Car Sales

BRANDS/DIVISIONS/AFFILIATES:

Major World Dealer Group
Major World
MajorWorld.com

CONTACTS: *Note: Officers with more than one job title may be intentionally listed here more than once.*

Alan A. Pearson, CEO
Bruce Bendell, Pres.

GROWTH PLANS/SPECIAL FEATURES:

Major Automotive Companies, Inc. is a holding company for Major World Dealer Group, an automobile retailer in the New York metropolitan area. From its dealerships in Long Island City and Queens, Major World sells used cars of virtually all makes, such as Acura, BMW, Toyota, Honda, Nissan, Land Rover, Audi, Lexus, Porsche and Mercedes-Benz. Major Automotive focuses on the sale of used vehicles, which affords it the opportunity to generate customer traffic from a wide variety of prospective buyers, increase vehicle sales by aggressively pursuing customer trade-ins and generate incremental revenues from customers financially unable or indisposed to purchase a new vehicle. Major Automotive has established the Major World brand and MajorWorld.com internet brand for its operations and those of the group's participating regional dealerships. Customers can search for available cars, obtain a valuation of a used vehicle trade-in and apply for financing through the company's website. In order to serve diverse populations, the company employs a multilingual sales force. Additionally, its customized telephone interactive voice response provides price quotes, places orders, answers frequently asked questions and approves credit in multiple languages. The firm also offers related replacement parts and vehicle repair services through its dealership locations.

FINANCIAL DATA: *Note: Data for latest year may not have been available at press time.*

In U.S. $	2018	2017	2016	2015	2014	2013
Revenue						
R&D Expense						
Operating Income						
Operating Margin %						
SGA Expense						
Net Income						
Operating Cash Flow						
Capital Expenditure						
EBITDA						
Return on Assets %						
Return on Equity %						
Debt to Equity						

CONTACT INFORMATION:

Phone: 718-937-3700 Fax: 718-520-6879
Toll-Free:
Address: 43-40 Northern Blvd, Long Island City, NY 11101 United States

STOCK TICKER/OTHER:

Stock Ticker: Private
Employees: 495
Parent Company:
Exchange:
Fiscal Year Ends: 12/31

SALARIES/BONUSES:

Top Exec. Salary: $ Bonus: $
Second Exec. Salary: $ Bonus: $

OTHER THOUGHTS:

Estimated Female Officers or Directors:
Hot Spot for Advancement for Women/Minorities:

MAN SE

NAIC Code: 336120

www.corporate.man.eu/en/

TYPES OF BUSINESS:

Heavy Duty Truck Manufacturing

BRANDS/DIVISIONS/AFFILIATES:

MAN Truck & Bus AG
MAN Latin America
Renk AG

CONTACTS:

Note: Officers with more than one job title may be intentionally listed here more than once.

Joachim Drees, CEO
Jan-Henrik Lafrentz, Finance
Carsten Intra, Chief Human Resources Officer
Anders Nielsen, CEO-MAN Truck & Bus AG
Rene Umlauft, CEO-MAN Diesel & Turbo SE
Andreas Renschler, Chmn.
Antonio Roberto Cortes, Pres., MAN Latin America
Ulf Vberkenhagen, Chief Procurement Officer

GROWTH PLANS/SPECIAL FEATURES:

MAN SE is a manufacturer of commercial vehicles, engines and mechanical engineering equipment. The company supplies buses, trucks, diesel engines, turbo machinery and special gear, with a focus on transportation and energy market segments. MAN's operations are divided into two segments: commercial vehicles, which comprises MAN Truck & Bus and MAN Latin America; and power engineering, comprising MAN Energy Solutions and Renk AG. Within the commercial vehicles segment, MAN Truck & Business is based in Munich, Germany, and is one of Europe's leading manufacturers of commercial vehicles. The firm has production facilities in Russia, South Africa, India and Turkey. MAN Latin America produces trucks and buses in Resende, Brazil and Queretaro, Mexico. The firm has a nationwide sales and service network in Brazil, as well as in neighboring Latin American countries. Its sales are primarily made through Volkswagen Camnhoes e Onibus. Within the power engineering segment, MAN Energy Solutions is based in Augsburg, Germany, and is a leading developer and manufacturer of large-bore diesel engines, turbocompressors, industrial turbines and chemical reactor systems. The firm has a strong market position in: the development of two-stroke diesel engines for propulsion systems in large ships; the development and manufacture of four-stroke diesel engines for smaller vessels and used as auxiliary engines; and in four-stroke engines for electricity generation at power plants. Renk is also based in Augsburg, and provides gear and drive technology for various applications.

FINANCIAL DATA:

Note: Data for latest year may not have been available at press time.

In U.S. $	2018	2017	2016	2015	2014	2013
Revenue	13,402,350,000	15,879,100,000	15,017,720,000	15,170,500,000	15,817,100,000	17,342,780,000
R&D Expense						597,874,200
Operating Income	379,760,900	575,730,800	171,612,000	146,147,000	450,620,000	486,049,600
Operating Margin %		.04%	.01%	.01%	.03%	.03%
SGA Expense	2,047,166,000	2,652,790,000	2,570,859,000	2,573,074,000	2,569,752,000	2,240,921,000
Net Income	747,342,800	344,331,300	-19,929,140	155,004,400	281,222,300	-580,159,400
Operating Cash Flow	602,302,900	296,722,800	922,276,400	1,286,537,000	-769,486,300	150,575,700
Capital Expenditure	756,200,200	906,775,900	946,634,200	761,736,100	669,840,600	617,803,400
EBITDA	1,896,590,000	1,963,020,000	1,355,182,000	1,436,005,000	1,448,184,000	1,061,780,000
Return on Assets %		.02%	.00%	.01%	.01%	-.02%
Return on Equity %		.05%	.00%	.03%	.05%	-.10%
Debt to Equity		0.248	0.073	0.226	0.278	0.44

CONTACT INFORMATION:

Phone: 49 89360980 Fax: 49 8936098250
Toll-Free:
Address: Dachauer Strasse 641, Munich, 80995 Germany

STOCK TICKER/OTHER:

Stock Ticker: MAGOF
Exchange: PINX
Employees: 38,430
Fiscal Year Ends: 12/31
Parent Company:

SALARIES/BONUSES:

Top Exec. Salary: $ Bonus: $
Second Exec. Salary: $ Bonus: $

OTHER THOUGHTS:

Estimated Female Officers or Directors:
Hot Spot for Advancement for Women/Minorities:

Marangoni SpA

www.marangoni.com

NAIC Code: 326200

TYPES OF BUSINESS:

Plastics & Rubber, Manufacturing
Tire Sales & Distribution
Retreading Systems
Tire Technology & Equipment
Car Accessories

BRANDS/DIVISIONS/AFFILIATES:

RINGTREAD
Borrachas Vipal SA
Marangoni Tread North America Inc
Leader Rubber Company SA (Pty) Ltd

CONTACTS:

Note: Officers with more than one job title may be intentionally listed here more than once.

Vittorio Marangoni, Pres.

GROWTH PLANS/SPECIAL FEATURES:

Marangoni SpA operates integrated businesses that design, develop, manufacture, retread and distribute tires. It engages in every aspect of tire production and retreading, from the processing of raw materials through development, manufacture, sales and distribution to scrap tire disposal. Marangoni's four business solution segments include: retreading systems, which supplies the systems and technology for retreading; new tire machinery, which provides innovation technology for new and future tires; tires, which provides tires to the industrial, earthmover, truck and bus sectors; and technical compounding, which manufactures and sells rubber compounds through its wide range of elastomers. Marangoni owns and operates 12 manufacturing production sites as well as commercial offices through various global brands worldwide, including Italy, France, the U.K., Germany, Turkey, Brazil, Argentina, the U.S., Russia and China. Its RINGTREAD tire retreading process has been utilized in production for more than 40 years. The RINGTREAD concept arose from an idea destined to revolutionize the cold retreading system: the construction of a pre-cured tread ring applied on truck tires. Retreaded tires using the ring are spliceless, and therefore eliminate the limitation of flat strip retreading. Maragoni holds 11 active patents, and invests $10 million in research and development every year. The firm's advanced R&D center is based in Rovereto, Italy, and operates across all of the group's business areas. In late-2018, Marangoni SpA and Borrachas Vipal SA announced a partnership agreement to increase the synergies and productivity of both groups; subsequently, in March 2019, Borrachas acquired a 51% stake in Marangoni Tread North America, Inc., completing the first phase of the agreement involving activities in the Americas. In early-2019, Marangoni increased its share from 25% to 51%, taking a majority stake in South African tread maker, Leader Rubber Company SA (Pty) Ltd.

FINANCIAL DATA:

Note: Data for latest year may not have been available at press time.

In U.S. $	2018	2017	2016	2015	2014	2013
Revenue	387,450,000	369,000,000	371,000,000	373,649,000	374,790,698	470,790,698
R&D Expense						
Operating Income						
Operating Margin %						
SGA Expense						
Net Income						
Operating Cash Flow						
Capital Expenditure						
EBITDA						
Return on Assets %						
Return on Equity %						
Debt to Equity						

CONTACT INFORMATION:

Phone: 39-0464-301111 Fax: 39-0464-436169
Toll-Free:
Address: Via del Garda, 6, Rovereto, 38068 Italy

STOCK TICKER/OTHER:

Stock Ticker: Private
Employees: 1,300
Parent Company:
Exchange:
Fiscal Year Ends: 12/31

SALARIES/BONUSES:

Top Exec. Salary: $ Bonus: $
Second Exec. Salary: $ Bonus: $

OTHER THOUGHTS:

Estimated Female Officers or Directors:
Hot Spot for Advancement for Women/Minorities:

Martinrea International Inc

www.martinrea.com

NAIC Code: 336300

TYPES OF BUSINESS:

Industrial Products - Autos & Parts
Metal forming
Fluid management

BRANDS/DIVISIONS/AFFILIATES:

NanoXplore Inc

CONTACTS: *Note: Officers with more than one job title may be intentionally listed here more than once.*

Fred Di Tosto, CFO
Robert Wildeboer, Chairman of the Board
Ganesh Iyer, Chief Information Officer
Robert Fairchild, Executive VP, Divisional
Alfredo Alonso, Executive VP, Divisional
Bruce Johnson, Executive VP, Divisional
Armando Pagliari, Executive VP, Divisional
Hany Morsy, Other Executive Officer
Pat DEramo, President
Kerri Pope, Secretary
Peter Cirulis, Vice President, Divisional
Megan Hunter, Vice President, Divisional
Mike Leal, Vice President, Divisional
Larry Paine, Vice President, Divisional

GROWTH PLANS/SPECIAL FEATURES:

Martinrea International, Inc. is a Canadian-based global automotive supplier, engaged in the design, development and manufacture of metal parts, assemblies, modules, complex fluid management systems and aluminum products. The firm's manufacturing, engineering and technical centers are located in Canada, the U.S., Mexico, Brazil, Germany, Slovakia, Spain and China, with more than 45 facilities worldwide. Martinrea focuses on innovation and uses its lightweighting expertise in metal forming, aluminum casting, fluid systems and related assembly to help automakers curb vehicle weight while also improving the vehicle's overall strength, safety and efficiency. Aluminum products include engine blocks, oil pans, cam carriers, camshaft housings, transmission housings, subframes, knuckles, control arms, shock towers, plate and coils, among others. Flexible manufacturing products include front and rear suspension modules, front vertical corner modules, bus frame assemblies, structural parts and fabrications, metallic tanks and reservoirs, and metallic racks and containers. Fluid systems include fuel and brake lines, fuel tanks, fuel fillers, EOC/TOC lines, powertrain lines, steering lines, heater core inlet/outlet assemblies, DPS lines, EGR tubes and AC lines. Metal parts and services include frame rail assemblies, engine cradle/sub-frames, suspension arms, cross members, suspension twist axles, door beams, bumpers, structural assemblies, dash assemblies, mufflers, exhaust manifold tubes, roof ditch moldings, window belts, decorative sounds, and more. In early-2019, Martinrea invested an additional share in NanoXplore, Inc., for a total 16% stake. NanoXplore manufactures and supplies high-volume graphene powder for use in industrial markets.

FINANCIAL DATA: *Note: Data for latest year may not have been available at press time.*

In U.S. $	2018	2017	2016	2015	2014	2013
Revenue	2,776,396,000	2,797,316,000	3,007,964,000	2,930,926,000	2,727,693,000	2,442,114,000
R&D Expense	20,134,920	20,159,930	18,838,020	16,497,380	13,915,710	12,742,360
Operating Income	215,601,400	177,864,800	150,120,500	134,342,400	102,905,300	102,092,800
Operating Margin %		.06%	.05%	.05%	.04%	.04%
SGA Expense	176,088,100	160,337,300	150,162,200	146,752,000	139,846,100	124,296,200
Net Income	140,895,200	120,930,000	70,021,980	81,126,350	54,046,840	12,847,720
Operating Cash Flow	224,893,500	229,561,900	196,859,700	146,007,000	200,374,400	102,932,600
Capital Expenditure	244,993,500	207,542,600	181,561,400	147,632,100	169,878,700	147,781,400
EBITDA	341,820,600	315,949,300	234,850,300	231,786,500	194,298,500	163,936,900
Return on Assets %		.06%	.04%	.05%	.04%	.01%
Return on Equity %		.18%	.12%	.16%	.14%	.04%
Debt to Equity		0.656	0.835	0.868	1.137	0.936

CONTACT INFORMATION:

Phone: 416 749-0314 Fax: 289 982-3004
Toll-Free:
Address: 3210 Langstaff Rd., Vaughan, ON L4K 5B2 Canada

STOCK TICKER/OTHER:

Stock Ticker: MRE
Employees: 15,000
Parent Company:
Exchange: TSE
Fiscal Year Ends: 12/31

SALARIES/BONUSES:

Top Exec. Salary: $ Bonus: $
Second Exec. Salary: $ Bonus: $

OTHER THOUGHTS:

Estimated Female Officers or Directors: 2
Hot Spot for Advancement for Women/Minorities:

Maruti Suzuki India Limited

www.marutisuzuki.com

NAIC Code: 336111

TYPES OF BUSINESS:

Automobile Manufacturing
Financial Services
Auto Accessories
Driving Training School

BRANDS/DIVISIONS/AFFILIATES:

Suzuki Motor Corporation
True Value
Maruti Driving School
Maruti Finance
Maruti Leasing
Maruti AutoCard
Alto
DZire

CONTACTS: *Note: Officers with more than one job title may be intentionally listed here more than once.*

Kenichi Ayukawa, CEO
Tsuneo Ohashi, Managing Exec. Officer-Prod.
Keiichi Asai, Managing Exec. Officer-Eng.
S. Ravi Aiyar, Chief Legal Officer
R. C. Bhargava, Chmn.
Kazuhiko Ayabe, Managing Exec.-Supply Chain

GROWTH PLANS/SPECIAL FEATURES:

Maruti Suzuki India Limited is a majority-owned subsidiary of Suzuki Motor Corporation and one of India's foremost automobile manufacturing companies, accounting for more than half of the domestic car market. The company began in 1982 as a joint venture between the government of India and Suzuki. The firm operates in five segments: marketing and sales, research and development, manufacturing, administration and supply chain. Maruti Suzuki has two integrated production facilities in India (Gurugram and Manesar), which together have a goal of reaching 2 million units sold in 2020. Current vehicles include hatchbacks, sedans, multi-utility and sports utility vehicles (MUVs and SUVs), and vans, which include the Alto, DZire, Ertiga and EECO models, among many others. Maruti Suzuki exports its vehicles to over 100 countries, primarily in Africa, Latin America and Southeast Asia. Maruti Suzuki's pre-owned sales channel, True Value, comprises more than 250 digitally-integrated independent showrooms in 151 cities. Every car sold goes through a 376-check quality evaluation, refurbishment and certification process, and come with an up to 1-year warranty and three free services. True Value buyers are typically aged between 25 and 45 years old. The firm also offers automobile accessories, such as wheel and body covers, graphics kits, seat and steering wheel covers, mud flaps, door visors, sun visors, fog lamps, floor mats, media systems, car frames, security systems and car care products. The Maruti Driving School (MDS) offers on-the-road, classroom and simulator training. Maruti Finance offers a variety of vehicle finance options. Maruti Insurance provides auto insurance products. Maruti Leasing offers vehicle leasing options as well as comprehensive maintenance packages. The Maruti AutoCard is the firm's loyalty program offering 3% back on every Maruti Suzuki transaction, additional discounts for trade-ins, reward points and emergency services.

FINANCIAL DATA: *Note: Data for latest year may not have been available at press time.*

In U.S. $	2018	2017	2016	2015	2014	2013
Revenue	11,510,311,936	9,819,389,952	8,453,169,152	7,326,705,152	6,410,777,088	6,389,691,904
R&D Expense						
Operating Income						
Operating Margin %						
SGA Expense						
Net Income	1,136,473,472	1,083,096,576	667,735,808	546,516,800	408,149,696	352,955,744
Operating Cash Flow						
Capital Expenditure						
EBITDA						
Return on Assets %						
Return on Equity %						
Debt to Equity						

CONTACT INFORMATION:

Phone: 91-11-4678-1000 Fax: 91-11-4615-0275
Toll-Free:
Address: 1, Nelson Mandela Rd., Vasant Kunj, New Delhi, 110 070 India

STOCK TICKER/OTHER:

Stock Ticker: MRZUY
Employees: 34,515
Parent Company: Suzuki Motor Corporation
Exchange: PINX
Fiscal Year Ends: 03/31

SALARIES/BONUSES:

Top Exec. Salary: $ Bonus: $
Second Exec. Salary: $ Bonus: $

OTHER THOUGHTS:

Estimated Female Officers or Directors: 1
Hot Spot for Advancement for Women/Minorities:

Maxion Wheels USA LLC

www.maxionwheelsandrims.com/

NAIC Code: 336300

TYPES OF BUSINESS:

Automobile Part Manufacturing
Automotive & Light Truck Wheels
Commercial Highway Vehicle Wheels

BRANDS/DIVISIONS/AFFILIATES:

Iochpe-Maxion SA
GemTech
Novachrome
VersaStyle

CONTACTS:

Note: Officers with more than one job title may be intentionally listed here more than once.

Pieter Klinkers, CEO
Roger Poussen, CFO
Mark Gerardts, VP-Global Mktg. & Sales
Mark Sinar, VP-Human Resources
Esteban Remecz, CIO
Steve Esau, General Counsel
Donald Hampton, VP-Oper.
John A. Salvette, VP-Bus. Dev.
Don Polk, Pres., Americas
Pieter Klinkers, Pres., Europe, Africa & Asia-Pacific

GROWTH PLANS/SPECIAL FEATURES:

Maxion Wheels USA, LLC is a world-leader in the manufacture of wheels and wheel-end attachments for major automobile original equipment manufacturers (OEMs). The company's primary operation is the designing and manufacturing of fabricated steel and cast aluminum wheels for OEMs. Maxion Wheels manufactures aluminum wheels with bright finishes such as GemTech machining, Novachrome plating, chrome cladding and premium paints. Its aluminum wheels are produced in sizes from 13-22 inches. Steel wheels manufactured by the company include drop well, bead seat, full face, VersaStyle and cladded steel. They range in sizes from 13-20 inches for passenger cars and up to 24.5 inches for commercial vehicles, with diameters to 14 inches. Maxion Wheels offers multiple agriculture and off-road construction applications including tractors, combines, sprayers, planters, compactors and graders, all with a variety of diameters and widths. It also offers a variety of tubeless wheels and rims for commercial and military vehicles. Apart from its U.S. locations in Missouri, Michigan and Ohio, the company maintains sales, production and distribution facilities in 12 countries on five continents. Maxion Wheels serves OEM customers from 22 locations via state-of-the-art technical centers across the Americas, Europe and Asia. The firm operates as a subsidiary of Iochpe-Maxion SA.

Employee benefits include medical coverage, wellness programs, education assistance and retirement plans.

FINANCIAL DATA:

Note: Data for latest year may not have been available at press time.

In U.S. $	2018	2017	2016	2015	2014	2013
Revenue	1,984,500,000	1,890,000,000	1,800,000,000	1,716,528,973	1,406,939,934	
R&D Expense						
Operating Income						
Operating Margin %						
SGA Expense						
Net Income						
Operating Cash Flow						
Capital Expenditure						
EBITDA						
Return on Assets %						
Return on Equity %						
Debt to Equity						

CONTACT INFORMATION:

Phone: 734-737-5000 Fax: 734-737-2198
Toll-Free: 800-521-0515
Address: 39500 Orchard Hill Place, Ste 500, Novi, MI 48375 United States

STOCK TICKER/OTHER:

Stock Ticker: Subsidiary
Exchange:
Employees: 6,400
Fiscal Year Ends: 01/31
Parent Company: Iochpe-Maxion SA

SALARIES/BONUSES:

Top Exec. Salary: $ Bonus: $
Second Exec. Salary: $ Bonus: $

OTHER THOUGHTS:

Estimated Female Officers or Directors:
Hot Spot for Advancement for Women/Minorities: Y

Mazda Motor Corporation

www.mazda.com

NAIC Code: 336111

TYPES OF BUSINESS:

Automobile Manufacturing
Commercial Vans & Trucks
Hydrogen Engine Technology

BRANDS/DIVISIONS/AFFILIATES:

Demio
Axela
Atenza
CX-5
Mazda3
MX-5 Miata RF
Scrum
Bongo

CONTACTS: *Note: Officers with more than one job title may be intentionally listed here more than once.*

Akira Marumoto, CEO
Masamichi Kogai, Pres.
Kiyoshi Fujiwara, Gen. Mgr.-R&D
Masafumi Nakano, Managing Exec. Officer-Prod. & Brand Quality
Kiyotaka Shobuda, Gen. Mgr.-Eng.
Koji Kurosawa, Sec.
Akira Marumoto, Exec. VP-Corp. Planning & American Oper.
Yuji Nakamine, Sr. Managing Exec. Officer-Corp. Comm.
Seita Kanai, Vice Chmn.
Nobuhide Inamoto, Sr. Managing Exec. Officer-China & Domestic Sales
Koji Kurosawa, Pres.
Keishi Egawa, Managing Exec. Officer-Latin America
Yuji Nakamine, Sr. Managing Exec. Officer-EMEA, Asia & Oceania
Kazuki Imai, Managing Exec. Officer-Purchasing

GROWTH PLANS/SPECIAL FEATURES:

Mazda Motor Corporation, established in 1920, is one of Japan's largest automakers. Mazda manufactures passenger and commercial vehicles through its production facilities located in Japan, China, Thailand, Mexico, Vietnam, Malaysia and Russia. Mazda's research and development sites are located in Japan, the U.S., Germany and China. The company has been exporting cars to the U.S. and Europe for nearly 40 years, while Mazda cars and trucks are currently sold in approximately 140 countries. Overseas sales account for more than two-thirds of the firm's annual revenues. Current passenger vehicle models (2018-2019) include Demio, Axela, Atenza, CX-3, CX-5, CX-8, Roadster, Premacy and Biante. Additional passenger vehicle models which are sold outside Japan include the Mazda3 and Mazda6 sedans, the CX-4 compact crossover, the CX-9 seven-passenger SUV, the MX-5 Miata RF roadster and the BT-50 mid-sized pickup truck. Micro-mini vehicle models include Flair, Flair Wagon, Scrum Wagon, Carol and Flair Crossover. Commercial vehicle models include the Bongo van, Bongo truck, Familia van, Titan flatbed, Scrum van and Scrum truck. Special needs features can be configured through the Demio, Premacy, Biante, Flair Wagon and CX-5 models. Mazda produced approximately 1.6 million units in 2018.

FINANCIAL DATA: *Note: Data for latest year may not have been available at press time.*

In U.S. $	2018	2017	2016	2015	2014	2013
Revenue	31,924,500,000	29,538,350,000	31,304,940,000	27,879,980,000	24,740,290,000	
R&D Expense						
Operating Income	1,345,534,000	1,154,999,000	2,083,946,000	1,864,437,000	1,673,599,000	
Operating Margin %	.04%	.04%	.07%	.07%	.07%	
SGA Expense						
Net Income	1,029,746,000	861,790,100	1,235,242,000	1,459,364,000	1,247,004,000	
Operating Cash Flow	1,909,529,000	1,480,399,000	2,414,722,000	1,878,873,000	1,253,253,000	
Capital Expenditure	911,441,000	824,361,400	809,400,800	1,250,947,000	1,094,404,000	
EBITDA	2,314,648,000	2,023,635,000	2,378,396,000	2,682,531,000	1,544,201,000	
Return on Assets %	.04%	.04%	.05%	.07%	.06%	
Return on Equity %	.10%	.09%	.15%	.21%	.23%	
Debt to Equity	0.268	0.264	0.374	0.561	0.799	

CONTACT INFORMATION:

Phone: 81 822821111 Fax:
Toll-Free:
Address: 3-1 Shinchi, Fuchu-cho, Aki-gun, Hiroshima, 100-0011 Japan

STOCK TICKER/OTHER:

Stock Ticker: MZDAF
Exchange: PINX
Employees: 49,998
Fiscal Year Ends: 03/31
Parent Company:

SALARIES/BONUSES:

Top Exec. Salary: $ Bonus: $
Second Exec. Salary: $ Bonus: $

OTHER THOUGHTS:

Estimated Female Officers or Directors:
Hot Spot for Advancement for Women/Minorities:

Mazda North American Operations

www.mazdausa.com

NAIC Code: 336111

TYPES OF BUSINESS:

Automobile Distribution
Customer Parts & Services Operations
Vehicle Research & Development

BRANDS/DIVISIONS/AFFILIATES:

Mazda Motor Corporation
Mazda Motor of America Inc
Mazda Motor de Mexico S de RL de SV
Mazda3
Mazda6
Mazda CX-3
MX-5 Miata
Mazda CX-30

CONTACTS:

Note: Officers with more than one job title may be intentionally listed here more than once.

Masahiro Moro, CEO
Norio Minato, VP-R&D
Phil Johnson, VP-Eng.
Shawn Murphy, General Counsel
Robert T. Davis, Sr. VP-U.S. Oper.
Akira Kofa, Exec. VP-Corp. & Prod. Planning
Barbara Nocera, Dir.-Gov't Affairs
Leopoldo Orellana, Pres., Mazda Motor De Mexico
Derek Jenkins, Dir.-Design
Rob Mllne, Dir.-Retail Oper.
Shusuke Koreeda, Pres., Mazda Canada
Keving Fuschetto, Mgr.-Dist.

GROWTH PLANS/SPECIAL FEATURES:

Mazda North American Operations (Mazda NA), a subsidiary of Mazda Motor Corporation, provides sales, marketing, parts and customer service support of Mazda vehicles in the U.S. and Mexico. The company is comprised of Mazda Motor of America, Inc., which handles the firm's U.S. sales and distribution operations as well as providing product planning, product development, research, evaluation testing and vehicle certification services; and Mazda Motor de Mexico S de RL de SV, based in Mexico City, controlling operations in Mexico. Mazda NA sells and leases its line of new and used cars, trucks, minivans and SUVs through nearly 700 dealerships across North America. The firm's models include the Mazda3 4-door and Mazda6 4-door sedans; the Mazda3 5-door hatchback; the Mazda CX-3, CX-5 and CX-9 crossovers and SUVs; the MX-5 Miata sports car; and the Mazda MX-5 Miata RF 2-door, open-top roadster. The Mazda CX-30 compact SUV is planned for a 2020 release in the U.S., and is the first Mazda model to offer a form of driver monitoring features. The CX-30's powertrain offers a 2.0-liter four-cylinder engine, 6-speed automatic and 6-speed manual transmissions, and a front- or all-wheel drive. Over half of Mazda vehicles sold in North America are done so via dealerships that exclusively offer the Mazda brand. All recent model Mazda cars are equipped with Bluetooth hands-free voice-command or steering mounted controls for making and receiving phone calls. Mazda NA's online shopping tools allow customers to build their own vehicles, search existing inventory, appraise trade-ins, request quotes, estimate payments, compare vehicles, locate a dealer and apply for credit.

Mazda offers comprehensive benefits, 401(k) and retirement plans, and a varity of employee assistance programs.

FINANCIAL DATA:

Note: Data for latest year may not have been available at press time.

In U.S. $	2018	2017	2016	2015	2014	2013
Revenue	12,784,900,000	9,659,850,000	10,251,575,000	10,143,143,037	8,078,689,000	6,258,794,694
R&D Expense						
Operating Income						
Operating Margin %						
SGA Expense						
Net Income	254,116,000	239,939,000	165,225,690	157,563,408	1,346,389,489	329,719,338
Operating Cash Flow						
Capital Expenditure						
EBITDA						
Return on Assets %						
Return on Equity %						
Debt to Equity						

CONTACT INFORMATION:

Phone: 949-727-6220 Fax: 949-727-6813
Toll-Free: 800-222-5500
Address: 7755 Irvine Center Dr., Irvine, CA 92623 United States

STOCK TICKER/OTHER:

Stock Ticker: Subsidiary
Exchange:
Employees: 25,000
Fiscal Year Ends: 03/31
Parent Company: Mazda Motor Corporation

SALARIES/BONUSES:

Top Exec. Salary: $ Bonus: $
Second Exec. Salary: $ Bonus: $

OTHER THOUGHTS:

Estimated Female Officers or Directors: 2
Hot Spot for Advancement for Women/Minorities:

Mercedes-Benz USA LLC

www.mbusa.com

NAIC Code: 336111

TYPES OF BUSINESS:

Automobile Manufacturing
Marketing & Sales Services
Dealership

BRANDS/DIVISIONS/AFFILIATES:

Daimler AG
Mercedex-Benz US International Inc
AMG Driving Academy

CONTACTS:
Note: Officers with more than one job title may be intentionally listed here more than once.

Dietmar Exler, CEO
Matthew E. Roy, VP-Admin.
Michelle D. Spreitzer, General Counsel
Donna Boland, Mgr.-Corp. Comm.

GROWTH PLANS/SPECIAL FEATURES:

Mercedes-Benz USA LLC (MBUSA), a wholly-owned subsidiary of Daimler AG, sells, services, distributes and markets Mercedes-Benz cars and light trucks and Maybach super-luxury sedans throughout the U.S. MBUSA's vehicles include the A-, C-, E- and S-Class and Maybach sedans; C-, E- and S-Class, CLA, CLS and AMG GT S coupes; G- and E-Class, GLA, GLC, GLE, GLE Coupe and GLS sport utility vehicles (SUVs) and wagons; SLC- and SL-Class roadsters; the C-, E- and S-Class Cabriolet convertibles; and the GLC hybrid and electric SUV. The firm sells these vehicles through a network of more than 300 independently owned dealerships in the U.S. MBUSA also provides sales, marketing and other services to Mercedes-Benz dealerships. Company certified collision centers are located in Alabama, Alaska, Arizona, California, Colorado, Connecticut, Delaware, District of Columbia, Florida, Georgia, Hawaii and Idaho. Mercedes-Benz U.S. International, Inc. (MBUSI), a division of Mercedes-Benz and a subsidiary of Daimler AG, operates a Mercedes-Benz automobile manufacturing plant near Vance, Alabama, which is approximately 5 million square feet in size and sits on a 966-acre plot. The factory produces more than 300,000 vehicles annually. In addition, the company operates the AMG Driving Academy, a teen driving school in Los Angeles; and a 71,000-square-foot research and development facility in Sunnyvale, California.

Employee benefits include medical, dental, vision, short- and long-term disability, life, AD&D, automobile, home and pet insurance; domestic partner benefits; flexible spending accounts; paid holidays; and a 401(k).

FINANCIAL DATA:
Note: Data for latest year may not have been available at press time.

In U.S. $	2018	2017	2016	2015	2014	2013
Revenue	48,171,422,250	45,877,545,000	43,692,900,000	43,260,000,000	41,197,513,000	38,394,700,000
R&D Expense						
Operating Income						
Operating Margin %						
SGA Expense						
Net Income			155,231,879	152,378,099	219,621,273	94,128,328
Operating Cash Flow						
Capital Expenditure						
EBITDA						
Return on Assets %						
Return on Equity %						
Debt to Equity						

CONTACT INFORMATION:

Phone: Fax:
Toll-Free: 800-367-6372
Address: 1 Mercedes-Benz Dr., Sandy Springs, GA 30328 United States

STOCK TICKER/OTHER:

Stock Ticker: Subsidiary
Employees: 23,750
Parent Company: Daimler AG
Exchange:
Fiscal Year Ends: 12/31

SALARIES/BONUSES:

Top Exec. Salary: $ Bonus: $
Second Exec. Salary: $ Bonus: $

OTHER THOUGHTS:

Estimated Female Officers or Directors: 2
Hot Spot for Advancement for Women/Minorities:

Meritor Inc

www.meritor.com

NAIC Code: 336300

TYPES OF BUSINESS:

Auto Parts Manufacturer
Drivetrain Systems & Components
Exhaust Systems
Braking Systems
Driveline Systems & Axles
Undercarriage Systems
Third-Party Logistics (3PL) Services

BRANDS/DIVISIONS/AFFILIATES:

Transportation Power Inc (TransPower)

CONTACTS: *Note: Officers with more than one job title may be intentionally listed here more than once.*

Carl Anderson, CFO
Timothy Heffron, Chief Information Officer
Paul Bialy, Controller
William Newlin, Director
April Miller, Other Executive Officer
Chris Villavarayan, President, Divisional
Joseph Plomin, President, Divisional
Jeffrey Craig, President

GROWTH PLANS/SPECIAL FEATURES:

Meritor, Inc., headquartered in Troy, Michigan, is a global supplier of a broad range of integrated systems, modules and components serving commercial truck, trailer and specialty original equipment manufacturers (OEMs) and certain aftermarkets. The company has 26 manufacturing facilities and 25 engineering facilities, sales offices, warehouses and services centers in the U.S., Europe, South America, Canada, Mexico and the Asia Pacific regions. The firm's primary operating segments are commercial truck and industrial, and aftermarket and trailer. The commercial truck and industrial segment supplies drivetrain systems and components, including axles, drivelines and braking and suspension systems, primarily for medium- and heavy-duty trucks in North America, South America, Europe and Asia Pacific. Its industrial components include drivetrain systems for off-highway, military, construction, bus and coach, fire and emergency and other industrial applications. This segment also includes all of the firm's aftermarket businesses in Asia-Pacific and South America, including all on- and off-highway activities. The aftermarket and trailer segment supplies axles, brakes, drivelines, suspension parts and other replacement and remanufactured parts to commercial vehicle aftermarket customers. This segment also supplies a wide variety of undercarriage products and systems for trailer applications in North America. In April 2019, Meritor announced an additional investment in Transportation Power, Inc. (TransPower), a developer and provider of clean vehicle and stationary energy storage technologies and products. Through TransPower, Meritor wants to support future growth in the area of electric commercial vehicle technologies.

The company offers employees medical, dental and vision insurance; life and AD&D insurance; flexible spending accounts; disability coverage; a retirement plan; a 401(k); and business travel accident insurance.

FINANCIAL DATA: *Note: Data for latest year may not have been available at press time.*

In U.S. $	2018	2017	2016	2015	2014	2013
Revenue	4,178,000,000	3,347,000,000	3,199,000,000	3,505,000,000	3,766,000,000	3,701,000,000
R&D Expense						
Operating Income	328,000,000	228,000,000	219,000,000	164,000,000	230,000,000	37,000,000
Operating Margin %		.07%	.07%	.05%	.06%	.01%
SGA Expense	285,000,000	235,000,000	240,000,000	299,000,000	235,000,000	346,000,000
Net Income	117,000,000	324,000,000	573,000,000	64,000,000	249,000,000	-22,000,000
Operating Cash Flow	251,000,000	176,000,000	204,000,000	97,000,000	215,000,000	-96,000,000
Capital Expenditure	104,000,000	95,000,000	93,000,000	79,000,000	77,000,000	54,000,000
EBITDA	412,000,000	303,000,000	286,000,000	229,000,000	297,000,000	104,000,000
Return on Assets %		.12%	.24%	.03%	.10%	-.01%
Return on Equity %		11.37%				
Debt to Equity		2.799				

CONTACT INFORMATION:

Phone: 248 435-1000 Fax:
Toll-Free:
Address: 2135 W. Maple Rd., Troy, MI 48084 United States

STOCK TICKER/OTHER:

Stock Ticker: MTOR Exchange: NYS
Employees: 8,000 Fiscal Year Ends: 09/30
Parent Company:

SALARIES/BONUSES:

Top Exec. Salary: $900,000 Bonus: $
Second Exec. Salary: $566,666 Bonus: $

OTHER THOUGHTS:

Estimated Female Officers or Directors: 3
Hot Spot for Advancement for Women/Minorities: Y

Michelin (Compagnie Generale des Etablissements Michelin SCA)

www.michelin.com

NAIC Code: 326200

TYPES OF BUSINESS:

Plastics & Rubber, Manufacturing
Tire Production
Tourism Services
Maps, Guidebooks & Atlases

BRANDS/DIVISIONS/AFFILIATES:

Michelin
BFGoodrich
Riken
Taurus
Tiger
Camso

CONTACTS: *Note: Officers with more than one job title may be intentionally listed here more than once.*

Florent Menegaux, CEO
Terry Gettys, Dir.-R&D
Laurent Noual, Dir.-Corp. Dev.
Francois Corbin, Dir.-Geographic Zones
Eric de Cromieres, Dir.-Commercial Performance
Jean-Cristophe Guerin, Dir.-Materials Prod. Line
Serge Lafon, Dir.-Truck Prod. Line

GROWTH PLANS/SPECIAL FEATURES:

Compagnie Generale des Etablissements Michelin (CGEM), based in France, is a worldwide corporation best known for its production of Michelin tires for cars, trucks, aircraft, earthmovers and motorcycles. The company is one of the world's largest tire producers, with 67 Michelin tire and semi-finished production facilities in 25 countries and marketing operations in 170 countries. CGEM produces roughly 190 million tires annually. The company produces three main lines of products: passenger car and light truck tires, truck tires and specialty business products and services. Passenger car and light truck tires account for most of CGEM's annual sales. Tires range from premium, mid-range and entry level qualities. The Michelin brand sells only premium tires, and BFGoodrich markets mid-range. The company currently has approximately 5,000 dealerships and service centers across the globe where it sells its tires. The truck tires division sells specialty tires for aviation, agriculture, earth mover and industrial vehicles. Specialty business products and services are comprised of travel services and lifestyle products. Products are marketed under the brands Michelin, Riken, Taurus and Tiger, among others. The majority (approximately 85%) of sales come from the Michelin brand. In December 2018, CGEM acquired Camso, a manufacturer of off-the-road tires, tracks and accessories for power sports, agriculture, material handling and construction markets.

FINANCIAL DATA: *Note: Data for latest year may not have been available at press time.*

In U.S. $	2018	2017	2016	2015	2014	2013
Revenue	24,388,840,000	24,313,550,000	23,147,700,000	23,470,990,000	21,648,580,000	22,416,960,000
R&D Expense	717,449,100	709,698,900	794,951,300	762,843,300	726,306,500	711,913,200
Operating Income	3,025,908,000	3,044,730,000	3,321,523,000	2,873,118,000	2,223,206,000	2,459,035,000
Operating Margin %		.12%	.13%	.12%	.11%	.11%
SGA Expense	4,083,260,000	4,126,439,000	4,058,902,000	4,025,687,000	3,806,466,000	3,858,503,000
Net Income	1,856,732,000	1,882,197,000	1,855,624,000	1,293,180,000	1,141,497,000	1,247,786,000
Operating Cash Flow	3,134,411,000	3,034,765,000	3,061,337,000	2,983,835,000	2,792,294,000	3,420,062,000
Capital Expenditure	1,922,055,000	1,874,446,000	2,032,772,000	1,976,306,000	2,048,273,000	2,192,206,000
EBITDA	4,277,015,000	4,417,627,000	4,649,026,000	3,950,399,000	3,383,525,000	3,353,631,000
Return on Assets %		.07%	.07%	.05%	.05%	.05%
Return on Equity %		.15%	.17%	.12%	.11%	.13%
Debt to Equity		0.197	0.158	0.247	0.163	0.156

CONTACT INFORMATION:

Phone: 33 473985900 Fax: 33 473985904
Toll-Free:
Address: 23, place des Carmes-Dechaux, Clermont-Ferrand, 63040 France

STOCK TICKER/OTHER:

Stock Ticker: MLN
Employees: 117,400
Parent Company:
Exchange: MEX
Fiscal Year Ends: 12/31

SALARIES/BONUSES:

Top Exec. Salary: $ Bonus: $
Second Exec. Salary: $ Bonus: $

OTHER THOUGHTS:

Estimated Female Officers or Directors: 4
Hot Spot for Advancement for Women/Minorities: Y

Midas Inc

NAIC Code: 811100

www.midas.com

TYPES OF BUSINESS:

Automotive Repair & Maintenance
Real Estate Operations

BRANDS/DIVISIONS/AFFILIATES:

TBC Corporation
Midas
Midas SpeeDee
Midas Touch Maintenance Package
Midas Touch Courtesy Check

CONTACTS: *Note: Officers with more than one job title may be intentionally listed here more than once.*

Alan Feldman, CEO
Alvin K. Marr, General Counsel
John A. Warzecha, Sr. VP-Franchise Bus. Dev.
John E. Brisson, Jr., VP-Finance & Franchise Sales
Audrey L. Gualandri, VP

GROWTH PLANS/SPECIAL FEATURES:

Midas, Inc., a subsidiary of TBC Corporation, provides auto repair and maintenance services primarily in the U.S. and Canada. Its more than 1,200 Midas stores are company-owned or franchised, and in other countries it operates in service centers that are either licensed or franchised. Midas' services include brakes and brake repair, oil changes, tires and tire repair, mufflers, exhaust systems, engine light check, belts, hoses, lights, wipers, car heating and air conditioning, steering, suspension, batteries, charging, starting, radiator, engine cooling and fleet services. The Midas Touch Maintenance Package is a discounted package program that includes routine maintenance such as oil and filter changes. Midas Touch Courtesy Check is a multi-point visual inspection that helps identify areas that could need attention. This courtesy check includes major systems and components such as engine, transmission, brakes, steering, starting/charging, heating/cooling and lighting; under-the-hood items such as battery, radiator, water pump, air filter, belts and hoses; fluids such as engine, oil, transmission, power steering, brake and windshield washer; under-the-vehicle such as shocks/struts, brake and fuel lines, exhaust system and driveline; and tires such as tread depth, wear patterns and inflation pattern. The company sells Midas and Midas SpeeDee co-branded franchises.

FINANCIAL DATA: *Note: Data for latest year may not have been available at press time.*

In U.S. $	2018	2017	2016	2015	2014	2013
Revenue	234,045,750	222,915,000	212,300,000	200,000,000	195,000,000	190,000,000
R&D Expense						
Operating Income						
Operating Margin %						
SGA Expense						
Net Income			6,800,000	5,500,000	5,200,000	4,800,000
Operating Cash Flow						
Capital Expenditure						
EBITDA						
Return on Assets %						
Return on Equity %						
Debt to Equity						

CONTACT INFORMATION:

Phone: 630-438-3000 Fax: 630-438-3880
Toll-Free: 800-621-8545
Address: 1300 Arlington Heights Rd., Itasca, IL 60143 United States

STOCK TICKER/OTHER:

Stock Ticker: Subsidiary
Exchange:
Employees: 1,130
Fiscal Year Ends: 12/31
Parent Company: TBC Corporation

SALARIES/BONUSES:

Top Exec. Salary: $ Bonus: $
Second Exec. Salary: $ Bonus: $

OTHER THOUGHTS:

Estimated Female Officers or Directors: 1
Hot Spot for Advancement for Women/Minorities:

Miller Industries Inc

www.millerind.com

NAIC Code: 336300

TYPES OF BUSINESS:

Wrecker Equipment
Trailer Body & Car Carrier Manufacturing

BRANDS/DIVISIONS/AFFILIATES:

Century
Vulcan
Challenger
Holmes
Champion
Eagle
Titan
Boniface

CONTACTS: *Note: Officers with more than one job title may be intentionally listed here more than once.*

Debbie Whitmire, CFO
William Miller, Chairman of the Board
Josias Reyneke, Chief Information Officer
Jeffrey Badgley, Co-CEO
William Miller, Co-CEO
Frank Madonia, Executive VP

GROWTH PLANS/SPECIAL FEATURES:

Miller Industries, Inc. is one of the world's leading integrated providers of vehicle towing and recovery equipment and services. It offers a broad range of towing and recovery equipment products that meet most customer design, capacity and cost requirements. Miller manufactures the bodies of wreckers, trailer bodies and car carriers for installation on truck chassis manufactured by third parties. The wreckers range in capacity from 4-75 tons and are used to remove abandoned, illegally parked or disabled vehicles as well as for commercial towing. Other uses of wreckers include removing vehicles from accident scenes or recovering overturned tractor trailers, buses, motor homes and other large vehicles. The firm's trailer bodies are used primarily by auto dealers, leasing companies and similar businesses and can generally haul 6-7 vehicles. The firm's specialized trailers are designed, engineered and manufactured for military applications. The car carriers are primarily used for long-distance hauling of autos and industrial equipment. Miller markets towing and recovery equipment under several brand names: Century, Vulcan, Challenger, Holmes, Champion, Chevron, Eagle, Titan, Jige and Boniface. The company's products are sold primarily through independent distributors that serve all 50 U.S. states, Canada and Mexico as well as other foreign markets in Australia, Chile, Costa Rica, England, France, Japan, New Zealand, Norway, Puerto Rico, South Africa, Taiwan and Trinidad. The firm's domestic manufacturing operations are located in Tennessee and Pennsylvania, while its foreign manufacturing operations are located in France and the U.K.

FINANCIAL DATA: *Note: Data for latest year may not have been available at press time.*

In U.S. $	2018	2017	2016	2015	2014	2013
Revenue	711,706,000	615,101,000	601,119,000	540,966,000	492,776,000	404,170,000
R&D Expense						
Operating Income	43,794,000	31,927,000	32,238,000	25,782,000	24,052,000	14,232,000
Operating Margin %		.05%	.05%	.05%	.05%	.03%
SGA Expense	39,542,000	35,561,000	32,318,000	31,491,000	28,496,000	28,323,000
Net Income	33,746,000	23,016,000	19,922,000	15,976,000	14,904,000	9,230,000
Operating Cash Flow	21,897,000	13,953,000	20,926,000	20,059,000	9,913,000	1,192,000
Capital Expenditure	13,342,000	24,693,000	25,026,000	11,900,000	5,345,000	2,430,000
EBITDA	51,539,000	38,074,000	37,066,000	30,099,000	28,067,000	17,995,000
Return on Assets %		.07%	.07%	.06%	.06%	.04%
Return on Equity %		.12%	.11%	.09%	.09%	.06%
Debt to Equity		0.05	0.027			

CONTACT INFORMATION:

Phone: 423 238-4171 Fax: 423 238-5371
Toll-Free: 800-292-0330
Address: 8503 Hilltop Dr., Ooltewah, TN 37363 United States

STOCK TICKER/OTHER:

Stock Ticker: MLR
Employees: 1,103
Parent Company:
Exchange: NYS
Fiscal Year Ends: 12/31

SALARIES/BONUSES:

Top Exec. Salary: $475,565 Bonus: $153,690
Second Exec. Salary: $475,565 Bonus: $ 925

OTHER THOUGHTS:

Estimated Female Officers or Directors:
Hot Spot for Advancement for Women/Minorities:

Mitsubishi Fuso Truck of America Inc

www.mitfuso.com

NAIC Code: 336120

TYPES OF BUSINESS:

Commercial Truck Manufacturing

BRANDS/DIVISIONS/AFFILIATES:

Daimler AG
Mitsubishi Fuso Truck and Bus Corporation
Canter FE-130
Canter FE-160
Canter FE-160 Crew Cab
Canter FE-180
e-CANTER

CONTACTS: *Note: Officers with more than one job title may be intentionally listed here more than once.*

Justin Palmer, CEO/Pres.
Gina Harlan, CFO
Leighton Good, Mgr.-Prod. & Applications
Len Doherty, Dir.-Parts Oper.
Joshua Treager, Mgr.-Corp. Comm.
Albert Kirchmann, CEO/Pres., Mitsubishi Fuso Truck & Bus Corp.
Gene Hedbany, Mgr.-Prod. Support
Jim Metz, Mgr.-National Service

GROWTH PLANS/SPECIAL FEATURES:

Mitsubishi Fuso Truck of America, Inc. (MFTA) is the U.S. operating arm of Mitsubishi Fuso Truck and Bus Corporation (MFTBC), a part of Daimler AG's trucks division. The company manufactures and markets Class 3 through Class 7 diesel- and gas-powered, medium-duty cabover trucks through more than 200 dealers across the U.S., Puerto Rico and Canada. The firm's trucks are used for dry freight, landscaping, refrigerated delivery, vehicle recovery, public works and beverage vending applications, and are also used as contractor vehicles for carpenters, plumbers, electricians and energy, utility and telecommunications companies. The company's FUSO FE series of cabover trucks come with enhanced engine durability and fuel economy features. FE models include: FE-130 (13,200 pounds), FE-160 (15,995 pounds) and FE-180 (17,995 pounds). The FE-160 Crew Cab can hold up to seven people. MFTA's e-CANTER model (15,995 pounds) is an electric-powered light truck, featuring a state-of-the-art modular high-voltage battery pack, permanent synchronous e-motor and an output of 185 Kw of power. e-CANTER is quiet and emission-free, and available in a flatbed and van body option.

FINANCIAL DATA: *Note: Data for latest year may not have been available at press time.*

In U.S. $	2018	2017	2016	2015	2014	2013
Revenue						
R&D Expense						
Operating Income						
Operating Margin %						
SGA Expense						
Net Income						
Operating Cash Flow						
Capital Expenditure						
EBITDA						
Return on Assets %						
Return on Equity %						
Debt to Equity						

CONTACT INFORMATION:

Phone: 856-467-4500 Fax: 856-467-2781
Toll-Free:
Address: 2015 Center Square Rd., Swedesboro, NJ 08085 United States

STOCK TICKER/OTHER:

Stock Ticker: Subsidiary
Employees:
Parent Company: Daimler AG
Exchange:
Fiscal Year Ends: 12/31

SALARIES/BONUSES:

Top Exec. Salary: $ Bonus: $
Second Exec. Salary: $ Bonus: $

OTHER THOUGHTS:

Estimated Female Officers or Directors:
Hot Spot for Advancement for Women/Minorities:

Mitsubishi Motors (Thailand) Co Ltd www.mitsubishi-motors.co.th/th/home

NAIC Code: 336111

TYPES OF BUSINESS:

Automobile Manufacturing

BRANDS/DIVISIONS/AFFILIATES:

Mitsubishi Motors Corporation
MMTh Engine Co Ltd
Pajero Sport
Triton
Xpander
Attrage
Mirage

GROWTH PLANS/SPECIAL FEATURES:

Mitsubishi Motors (Thailand) Co. Ltd. is the Thai subsidiary of international car manufacturer Mitsubishi Motors Corporation. The firm manufactures, distributes and exports Mitsubishi pickup trucks and passenger cars. While the vast majority of manufactured vehicles are exported worldwide, approximately 10% of them are produced specifically for Thailand's domestic market. The company's three manufacturing facilities have an annual production capacity of 510,000 units. Its vehicles include the SUV Pajero Sport line of two and four-wheel-drive SUVs, as well as the Xpander SUV, comprising a 12-volt power outlet in each row (3) for connected devices; the Triton 4-door truck series; and the Attrage and Mirage sedan models. The firm offers its products in over 120 countries. Mitsubishi Thailand also runs a subsidiary that manufactures engines, MMTh Engine Co. Ltd., producing more than 500,000 engines a year for its Thai manufacturing plants.

CONTACTS: *Note: Officers with more than one job title may be intentionally listed here more than once.*

Morikazu Chokki, CEO
Koji Nakahara, Exec. VP

FINANCIAL DATA: *Note: Data for latest year may not have been available at press time.*

In U.S. $	2018	2017	2016	2015	2014	2013
Revenue	1,583,352,200	1,507,954,476	1,436,147,120	1,058,605,000	1,571,064,000	2,857,255,000
R&D Expense						
Operating Income						
Operating Margin %						
SGA Expense						
Net Income						
Operating Cash Flow						
Capital Expenditure						
EBITDA						
Return on Assets %						
Return on Equity %						
Debt to Equity						

CONTACT INFORMATION:

Phone: 66-2-908-8000 Fax:
Toll-Free:
Address: 88 MU 11 Phaholyothin Rd., Pathum Thani, Klongluang 12120 Thailand

STOCK TICKER/OTHER:

Stock Ticker: Subsidiary Exchange:
Employees: 4,000 Fiscal Year Ends: 03/31
Parent Company: Mitsubishi Motors Corporation

SALARIES/BONUSES:

Top Exec. Salary: $ Bonus: $
Second Exec. Salary: $ Bonus: $

OTHER THOUGHTS:

Estimated Female Officers or Directors:
Hot Spot for Advancement for Women/Minorities:

Mitsubishi Motors Corporation

www.mitsubishi-motors.com

NAIC Code: 336111

TYPES OF BUSINESS:

Automobile Manufacturing
Automobile Parts
Agricultural Machinery & Industrial Engines
Automotive Sales
Financial Services

BRANDS/DIVISIONS/AFFILIATES:

Nissan Motor Co Ltd
Mitsubishi Corporation
Renault-Nissan
Eclipse Cross
Xpander
Outlander
i-MiEV
eK

CONTACTS: *Note: Officers with more than one job title may be intentionally listed here more than once.*

Osamu Masuko, CEO
Ryugo Nakao, Managing Dir.-Prod. Projects & Strategy
Hiizu Ichikawa, Exec. VP-Corp. Planning
Shuichi Aoto, Managing Dir.-Corp. Affairs
Hiizu Ichikawa, Exec. VP-Finance
Shuichi Aoto, Chief Bus. Ethics Officer
Seiji Izumisawa, Head-Quality Affairs Group
Hiroshi Harunari, Exec. VP-Overseas Oper.
Shuichi Aoto, Head-Procurement Group

GROWTH PLANS/SPECIAL FEATURES:

Mitsubishi Motors Corporation (MMC) designs, manufactures, sells and distributes automobiles, trucks, buses and parts. The firm also designs, manufactures, sells and imports agricultural machinery and industrial engines. The Mitsubishi brand includes the Eclipse Cross, Xpander, Outlander, Triton, Pajero/Montero, Lancer, Attrage, Delica, i-MiEV and eK models, as well as the MiEV minicab model. MMC has six car manufacturing facilities; 11 car manufacturing facilities of affiliated companies and business partners worldwide; seven engine, transmission and parts manufacturing facilities; and nine research & development centers. In addition, the company has 34 consolidated subsidiaries. MMC itself is majority-owned by Nissan Motor Co. Ltd. (34%), and is part of the Renault-Nissan alliance. Mitsubishi Corporation maintains a 20% stake in MMC, and Renault-Nissan owns a major share of the firm's stock. In mid-2018, the Renault-Nissan-Mitsubishi alliance opened a state-of-the-art national distribution center in Melbourne, Australia, the first shared parts and accessories warehouse for the member companies.

FINANCIAL DATA: *Note: Data for latest year may not have been available at press time.*

In U.S. $	2018	2017	2016	2015	2014	2013
Revenue	20,146,930,000	17,520,970,000	20,840,370,000	20,039,770,000	19,237,360,000	
R&D Expense	515,217,800	530,040,400	413,637,200	414,050,700	337,382,800	
Operating Income	902,453,600	47,059,360	1,271,650,000	1,248,998,000	1,134,332,000	
Operating Margin %	.04%	.03%	.09%	.09%	.08%	
SGA Expense	1,400,138,000	1,183,891,000	1,352,417,000	1,476,962,000	1,495,479,000	
Net Income	988,963,500	-1,824,334,000	666,927,000	1,085,922,000	961,808,500	
Operating Cash Flow	1,099,283,000	-421,145,000	1,816,679,000	1,626,613,000	1,933,863,000	
Capital Expenditure	769,601,200	624,921,900	634,074,700	786,601,800	833,440,600	
EBITDA	1,462,038,000	-1,017,414,000	1,554,227,000	1,803,483,000	1,706,956,000	
Return on Assets %	.07%	-.14%	.05%	.08%	.07%	
Return on Equity %	.15%	-.29%	.11%	.20%	.24%	
Debt to Equity	0.001	0.002	0.003	0.043	0.136	

CONTACT INFORMATION:

Phone: 81 334561111 Fax:
Toll-Free:
Address: 33-8, Shiba 5-chome, Minato-ku, Tokyo, 108-8410 Japan

STOCK TICKER/OTHER:

Stock Ticker: MMTOF
Exchange: PINX
Employees: 39,996
Fiscal Year Ends: 03/31
Parent Company: Nissan Motor Co Ltd

SALARIES/BONUSES:

Top Exec. Salary: $ Bonus: $
Second Exec. Salary: $ Bonus: $

OTHER THOUGHTS:

Estimated Female Officers or Directors:
Hot Spot for Advancement for Women/Minorities:

Mobileye NV

www.mobileye.com

NAIC Code: 334220

TYPES OF BUSINESS:

Camera-Based Driver Assistance Technology

BRANDS/DIVISIONS/AFFILIATES:

Intel Corporation

CONTACTS:

Note: Officers with more than one job title may be intentionally listed here more than once.

Amnon Shashua, CEO
Ziv Aviram, Pres.
Ofer Maharshak, CFO
Gaby Hayon, Sr. VP-R&D
Itay Gat, VP-Production Programs
Elchanan Rushinek, Sr. VP-Eng.
Norio Ichihashi, Sr. VP-Pacific Region
Isaac Litman, CEO-Mobileye Products
Shotaro Kawahara, CEO-Mobileye Japan
Gideon Stein, Chief Research Scientist

GROWTH PLANS/SPECIAL FEATURES:

Mobileye NV is a technology company that offers advanced image sensing and processing technology for automotive applications. The company designs, develops, manufactures and supplies camera-based advanced driver assistance systems for the automotive industry worldwide. It delivers advanced driver assistance systems with forward collision warning, pedestrian collision warning, headway monitoring warning, lane departure warning, intelligent high-beam control and speed limit indicator features; and a smartphone application which allows users to receive critical real-time warnings to their personal smartphones via Bluetooth connectivity. Mobileye provides vision applications for onboard driving assistant systems. Its products are used in various applications such as lane detection, vehicle detection, radar vision fusion, general object detection, pedestrian detection, traffic sign detection, head lamp control, rear camera and surround view systems. Mobileye offers its products to automakers as well as to aftermarket solutions companies. The firm's range of diverse markets include OEM (original equipment manufacturing), Tier 1, insurance, lease companies, consumer, fleet management systems provider (telematics) and off-highway industrial vehicles. Mobileye offers its products through distributors, with more than 40 million vehicle models currently comprising Mobileye products (as of mid-2019). The firm's technology has been made available to more than 25 OEMs. Mobileye is currently developing the next evolution of driver assistance systems (DAS) technology in order to provide OEM partners with hands-free capable driving at highway speeds and in congested traffic situations. The technology is enabled by a number of forward-facing cameras, as well as low-cost radars for redundancy. Mobileye anticipates the inclusion of country roads and city traffic capabilities in the near future. The firm has a partnership with Intel, BMW and other automakers to develop production-ready fully autonomous vehicles, with a production launch planned for 2021. Mobileye operates as a wholly-owned subsidiary of Intel Corporation.

FINANCIAL DATA:

Note: Data for latest year may not have been available at press time.

In U.S. $	2018	2017	2016	2015	2014	2013
Revenue		460,000,000	358,161,984	240,872,000	143,636,992	81,245,000
R&D Expense						
Operating Income						
Operating Margin %						
SGA Expense						
Net Income			108,370,000	68,450,000	-30,084,000	19,920,000
Operating Cash Flow						
Capital Expenditure						
EBITDA						
Return on Assets %						
Return on Equity %						
Debt to Equity						

CONTACT INFORMATION:

Phone: 972-2-541-7333 Fax: 972-2-541-7300
Toll-Free:
Address: Har Hotzvin, 13 Hartom St., Jerusalem, 9777513 Israel

STOCK TICKER/OTHER:

Stock Ticker: MBBYF
Exchange: PINX
Employees: 663
Fiscal Year Ends:
Parent Company: Intel Corporation

SALARIES/BONUSES:

Top Exec. Salary: $ Bonus: $
Second Exec. Salary: $ Bonus: $

OTHER THOUGHTS:

Estimated Female Officers or Directors:
Hot Spot for Advancement for Women/Minorities:

Modine Manufacturing Company

www.modine.com

NAIC Code: 336300

TYPES OF BUSINESS:

Automobile Parts Manufacturer
Heat Exchangers & Systems
Oil Cores
Electronics Cooling
Heating & Air Conditioning Products
Radiator Cores
Fuel Cells

BRANDS/DIVISIONS/AFFILIATES:

CONTACTS:

Note: Officers with more than one job title may be intentionally listed here more than once.

Thomas Burke, CEO
Michael Lucareli, CFO
Scott Wollenberg, Chief Technology Officer
Scott Bowser, COO
Sylvia Stein, General Counsel
Matthew McBurney, Vice President, Divisional
Scott Miller, Vice President, Divisional
Dennis Appel, Vice President, Divisional
Brian Agen, Vice President, Divisional
Joel Casterton, Vice President, Divisional

GROWTH PLANS/SPECIAL FEATURES:

Modine Manufacturing Company is a worldwide leader in thermal management technology. The firm provides engineered heat transfer systems and heat transfer components for us in on- and off-highway original equipment manufacturer (OEM) vehicular applications. Modine also develops and markets thermal management technology and solutions for commercial, industrial and building, heating, ventilating, air conditioning and refrigeration markets. The company's primary product groups include: powertrain cooling and engine cooling; coils, coolers and coatings; and heating, ventilation and air conditioning. These products and systems help to solve heat transfer challenges requiring effective thermal management. Modine's top five customers are engaged in the automotive, commercial vehicle and off-highway markets, and its 10-largest customers accounted for 50% of fiscal 2019 sales. Nearly 60% of total sales are generated outside the U.S. During fiscal 2019, Modine sold its AIAC Air Conditioning South Africa Pty Ltd. business. In July 2019, the firm agreed to sell its 50% stake in its Nikkei Heat Exchanger Company, Ltd. joint venture to its JV partner, Nippon Light Metal Company, Ltd.

Modine offers employees medical benefits, educational assistance, retirement plans, life insurance and flexible spending accounts.

FINANCIAL DATA:

Note: Data for latest year may not have been available at press time.

In U.S. $	2018	2017	2016	2015	2014	2013
Revenue	2,103,100,000	1,503,000,000	1,352,500,000	1,496,400,000	1,477,600,000	
R&D Expense						
Operating Income	107,400,000	48,300,000	19,000,000	62,000,000	56,500,000	
Operating Margin %	.05%	.03%	.01%	.04%	.04%	
SGA Expense	249,100,000	205,000,000	204,500,000	184,500,000	181,700,000	
Net Income	22,200,000	14,200,000	-1,600,000	21,800,000	130,400,000	
Operating Cash Flow	123,800,000	41,600,000	72,400,000	63,500,000	104,500,000	
Capital Expenditure	71,000,000	65,400,000	104,500,000	75,000,000	57,300,000	
EBITDA	165,600,000	96,300,000	51,400,000	104,500,000	94,500,000	
Return on Assets %	.01%	.01%	.00%	.02%	.14%	
Return on Equity %	.05%	.04%	.00%	.06%	.38%	
Debt to Equity	0.788	0.98	0.334	0.364	0.309	

CONTACT INFORMATION:

Phone: 262 636-1200 Fax: 262 636-1424
Toll-Free:
Address: 1500 DeKoven Ave., Racine, WI 53403 United States

STOCK TICKER/OTHER:

Stock Ticker: MOD
Exchange: NYS
Employees: 11,200
Fiscal Year Ends: 02/28
Parent Company:

SALARIES/BONUSES:

Top Exec. Salary: $965,000 Bonus: $
Second Exec. Salary: $448,500 Bonus: $

OTHER THOUGHTS:

Estimated Female Officers or Directors: 4
Hot Spot for Advancement for Women/Minorities: Y

Monro Muffler Brake Inc

www.monro.com

NAIC Code: 811100

TYPES OF BUSINESS:

Automotive Repair & Maintenance
Under-Car Repair Services
Inspection Services
Tires

BRANDS/DIVISIONS/AFFILIATES:

Monro Service Corporation
Car-X LLC
Monro Muffler Brake & Service
Tread Quarters Discount tire
Mr Tire
Autotire Car Care Center
Ken Towery's Tire & Auto Care
Free Service Tire Company

CONTACTS: *Note: Officers with more than one job title may be intentionally listed here more than once.*

Brett Ponton, CEO
Brian DAmbrosia, CFO
Robert Mellor, Chairman of the Board
Maureen Mulholland, General Counsel
Deborah Brundage, Senior VP, Divisional
Samuel Senuk, Vice President, Divisional
Raymond Pickens, Vice President, Divisional

GROWTH PLANS/SPECIAL FEATURES:

Monro Muffler Brake, Inc. operates through a chain of 1,248 company-operated stores, 98 franchised locations, eight wholesale locations, three retread facilities and two dealer-operated stores, providing automotive under-car repair and tire services in 30 U.S. states. These stores are typically located in high-visibility locations in suburban areas and small towns, and operate under the names Monro Muffler Brake & Service, Tread Quarters Discount Tire, Mr. Tire, Autotire Car Care Center, Tire Warehouse, Tire Barn Warehouse, Ken Towery's Tire & Auto Care, The Tire Choice, Car-X, McGee Tire, and Certified Tire. The firm's stores service more than 6.2 million vehicles annually (as of mid-2019). Monro provides a range of services on passenger cars, light trucks and vans for brakes; mufflers and exhaust systems; and steering, drive train, suspension and wheel alignment. Other products and services offered by the company include tires and routine maintenance services, such as state inspections. It specializes in the repair and replacement of parts that must be periodically replaced due to normal wear and tear. Typically, the firm does not perform under-the-hood repair, except for oil change services, heating and cooling system flush and fill services and some minor tune-ups. Monro operates through two wholly-owned subsidiaries: Monro Service Corporation, which provides purchasing, distribution, merchandising, advertising, accounting and other store support functions; and Car-X, LLC, which operates as a franchisor, with 101 Car-X franchised locations. In May 2019, Monro acquired 40 Certified Tire stores in California, entering its 30th state.

Monro offers its employees Automotive Service Excellence (ASE) certification reimbursement; recreational discounts; an employee assistance program; tool insurance; and medical, dental, life and disability insurance.

FINANCIAL DATA: *Note: Data for latest year may not have been available at press time.*

In U.S. $	2018	2017	2016	2015	2014	2013
Revenue	1,127,815,000	1,021,511,000	943,651,000	894,492,000	831,432,000	
R&D Expense						
Operating Income	127,296,000	116,384,000	120,589,000	109,789,000	95,347,000	
Operating Margin %	.11%	.11%	.13%	.12%	.11%	
SGA Expense	308,278,000	280,505,000	265,114,000	243,561,000	224,627,000	
Net Income	63,935,000	61,526,000	66,805,000	61,799,000	54,459,000	
Operating Cash Flow	121,235,000	129,935,000	126,504,000	126,349,000	93,943,000	
Capital Expenditure	39,122,000	34,640,000	36,834,000	34,750,000	32,150,000	
EBITDA	176,631,000	161,013,000	160,358,000	145,510,000	127,035,000	
Return on Assets %	.05%	.06%	.07%	.07%	.07%	
Return on Equity %	.11%	.11%	.13%	.14%	.14%	
Debt to Equity	0.597	0.68	0.502	0.54	0.45	

CONTACT INFORMATION:

Phone: 585-647-6400 Fax: 585-647-0945
Toll-Free:
Address: 200 Holleder Pkwy., Rochester, NY 14615 United States

STOCK TICKER/OTHER:

Stock Ticker: MNRO
Employees: 7,878
Parent Company:
Exchange: NAS
Fiscal Year Ends: 03/31

SALARIES/BONUSES:

Top Exec. Salary: $550,000 Bonus: $
Second Exec. Salary: $350,000 Bonus: $

OTHER THOUGHTS:

Estimated Female Officers or Directors: 1
Hot Spot for Advancement for Women/Minorities:

Montupet SA

NAIC Code: 336300

www.montupet.fr

TYPES OF BUSINESS:

Automobile Parts Manufacturing
Cast Aluminum Parts
Parts-Retail & Distribution

BRANDS/DIVISIONS/AFFILIATES:

Linamar Corporation

CONTACTS:

Note: Officers with more than one job title may be intentionally listed here more than once.

Stephane Magnan, CEO

GROWTH PLANS/SPECIAL FEATURES:

Montupet SA, established in 1894, is a major manufacturer of molded car parts in aluminum alloys. The company makes three product ranges in cast aluminum: finished motor parts, including cylinder heads, cylinder blocks and intake manifolds; machined and painted wheels and rims; and finished structure parts, suspension and braking parts. The firm also manufactures some of the tooling necessary for its production activities. Montupet's products are made either through gravity casting, which relies on the weight of the liquid metal to fill a die; or through low pressure casting, which forces liquid metal into a die via a tube to more accurately control how the die fills. Montupet designs and manufactures parts mainly for Audi, BMW, Daimler, Ford, General Motors, Peugeot-Citroen, Renault-Nissan and Volvo. It also manufactures parts for Volkswagen, Bosch, Iveco, Jaguar, Bentley, Daewoo, Fiat, MINI, Seat and John Deere. The firm owns and operates nine facilities in France, the U.K., Spain, Mexico, Bulgaria and India. It also maintains a Technical Centre near Paris, France. Montupet operates as a subsidiary of Canada-based Linamar Corporation.

FINANCIAL DATA:

Note: Data for latest year may not have been available at press time.

In U.S. $	2018	2017	2016	2015	2014	2013
Revenue	700,087,500	666,750,000	635,000,000	627,172,960	524,096,800	467,982,528
R&D Expense						
Operating Income						
Operating Margin %						
SGA Expense						
Net Income						
Operating Cash Flow						
Capital Expenditure						
EBITDA						
Return on Assets %						
Return on Equity %						
Debt to Equity						

CONTACT INFORMATION:

Phone: 33-1-47-56-47-56 Fax: 33-1-47-39-77-93
Toll-Free:
Address: 202, Quai de Clichy, Clichy, 92112 France

STOCK TICKER/OTHER:

Stock Ticker: Private
Employees: 1,585
Parent Company: Linamar Corporation
Exchange:
Fiscal Year Ends: 12/31

SALARIES/BONUSES:

Top Exec. Salary: $ Bonus: $
Second Exec. Salary: $ Bonus: $

OTHER THOUGHTS:

Estimated Female Officers or Directors:
Hot Spot for Advancement for Women/Minorities:

Morgan Motor Company (The)

www.morgan-motor.co.uk

NAIC Code: 336111

TYPES OF BUSINESS:

Automobile Manufacturing
Insurance

BRANDS/DIVISIONS/AFFILIATES:

Aero 8
Aero SuperSport
Aero GT
Classic
4-Apr
Roadster
Plus 6
3 Wheeler

CONTACTS:
Note: Officers with more than one job title may be intentionally listed here more than once.

Steve Morris, CEO
Colin Boden, Dir.-Finance
Tim Whitworth, Company Sec.
Steve Morris, Dir.-Oper.
Tim Whitworth, Dir.-Finance
Dominic Riley, Chmn.

GROWTH PLANS/SPECIAL FEATURES:

The Morgan Motor Company specializes in designing and building high-quality retro-stylized vehicles. The Morgan factory in Malvern, England builds approximately 700 cars per year. The company's Aero 8 was launched in 2000, with a continual evolution of eight dramatic Aero SuperSport cars, as well as the Aero GT. The Classic range continues to be the company's flagship line, with models including the 4/4, Plus 4, Roadster and Plus 6. The Plus 4 has a top speed of 118 mph, and the Roadster has a top speed of 140 mph. Morgan's current 3 Wheeler offerings come as a gasoline-powered vehicle or an all-electric, zero-emissions EV3 vehicle. The 3 Wheeler vehicles are 2-seaters that accelerate from 0 to 62 mph in six seconds, with a top speed of 116 mph. Cars are sold in the U.S., the U.K., Australia, New Zealand, South Africa, Austria, Belgium, Denmark, France, Germany, Italy, Japan and many other countries. In addition, Morgan rents its cars for hire, with prices ranging per day, overnight, for a weekend or an entire week. Vehicles for rent include the Plus 4 and the 3 Wheeler. The company is also willing to meet specific requests about renting Morgan vehicles. While the Morgan family still act as the stewards of the brand and own a minority stake in the business, the firm is majority owned by Investindustrial.

FINANCIAL DATA:
Note: Data for latest year may not have been available at press time.

In U.S. $	2018	2017	2016	2015	2014	2013
Revenue	42,893,000	48,568,500	36,314,300	39,229,400	41,702,700	55,151,560
R&D Expense						
Operating Income						
Operating Margin %						
SGA Expense						
Net Income	4,060,880	2,528,080	546,356	125,090	-32,237	1,156,700
Operating Cash Flow						
Capital Expenditure						
EBITDA						
Return on Assets %						
Return on Equity %						
Debt to Equity						

CONTACT INFORMATION:

Phone: 44-1684-573104 Fax: 44-1684-892295
Toll-Free:
Address: Pickersleigh Rd., Malvern, Worcestershire WR14 2LL United Kingdom

STOCK TICKER/OTHER:

Stock Ticker: Private
Employees: 180
Parent Company: Investindustrial
Exchange:
Fiscal Year Ends: 12/31

SALARIES/BONUSES:

Top Exec. Salary: $ Bonus: $
Second Exec. Salary: $ Bonus: $

OTHER THOUGHTS:

Estimated Female Officers or Directors:
Hot Spot for Advancement for Women/Minorities:

Morse Operations Inc

NAIC Code: 441110

www.edmorse.com

TYPES OF BUSINESS:

Auto Dealers, Retail
Fleet Sales
Maintenance Services

BRANDS/DIVISIONS/AFFILIATES:

Ed Morse Automotive Group
Ed Morse Collision Center

CONTACTS:

Note: Officers with more than one job title may be intentionally listed here more than once.

Teddy Morse, CEO
Carmine Colella, Pres.
Dennis MacInnes, VP

GROWTH PLANS/SPECIAL FEATURES:

Morse Operations, Inc., headquartered in Fort Lauderdale, Florida, sells new and pre-owned vehicles through 16 dealerships throughout Florida and Texas. The 16 dealership locations house 22 automotive franchises and 13 different brands of cars, both domestic and import. New vehicle makes include Alfa Romeo, Buick, Cadillac, Chevrolet, Chrysler, Dodge, Fiat, GMC, Honda, Jeep, Mazda, RAM and Toyota. Pre-owned vehicles can include virtually all makes. Morse Operations also sells buses, commercial sales vans and trucks. Dealerships are branded under the Ed Morse Automotive Group name. The company maintains auto body shops under the Ed Morse Collision Center brand line, which are equipped to serve both automotive paint and body needs. Morse Operations offers financing for its vehicles as well as service and parts, which are available at all dealerships. The firm's website allows customers to search inventory, research new and used vehicles, schedule maintenance and service and order parts.

Morse Operations offers employees benefits which include health, dental, vision, paid vacation and 401(k) savings plans.

FINANCIAL DATA:

Note: Data for latest year may not have been available at press time.

In U.S. $	2018	2017	2016	2015	2014	2013
Revenue	1,456,635,327	1,387,271,740	1,321,211,181	1,050,988,732	834,001,513	682,808,217
R&D Expense						
Operating Income						
Operating Margin %						
SGA Expense						
Net Income						
Operating Cash Flow						
Capital Expenditure						
EBITDA						
Return on Assets %						
Return on Equity %						
Debt to Equity						

CONTACT INFORMATION:

Phone: 561-276-5000 Fax:
Toll-Free:
Address: 2850 South Federal Highway, Delray Beach, FL 33483 United States

STOCK TICKER/OTHER:

Stock Ticker: Private
Employees: 1,120
Parent Company:
Exchange:
Fiscal Year Ends: 12/31

SALARIES/BONUSES:

Top Exec. Salary: $ Bonus: $
Second Exec. Salary: $ Bonus: $

OTHER THOUGHTS:

Estimated Female Officers or Directors:
Hot Spot for Advancement for Women/Minorities:

Motor Coach Industries International Inc

www.mcicoach.com

NAIC Code: 336120

TYPES OF BUSINESS:

Motor Coach Manufacturing
Luxury Buses
Customization
Parts & Service
Refurbishing
Apparel & Accessories
Financing

BRANDS/DIVISIONS/AFFILIATES:

New Flyer Industries Inc
MCI J4500
MCI University Coach
MCI D4005
MCI Commuter Coach
MCI Hybrid Commuter Coach
MCI ISTV
Diesel Particulate Filters

CONTACTS: *Note: Officers with more than one job title may be intentionally listed here more than once.*

Ian Smart, Pres.
Sandra Morison, VP-Finance
Patrick Scully, Exec. VP-Mktg. & Sales
Denis Sutton, VP-Human Resources

GROWTH PLANS/SPECIAL FEATURES:

Motor Coach Industries International, Inc. (MCI) designs, builds, sells, services and finances motor coaches. The firm is headquartered in Schaumburg, Illinois, with sales and service centers located across the U.S., as well as in Canada and Mexico. MCI creates vehicles as intercity coaches and for long-distance travel. It also offers motor coach conversion and coach-related parts and services for the North American market. Customers include local transit authorities, prison authorities and other organizations. The company's certified pre-owned program assures customers of better access to select late-model MCI coaches. The firm also assists in the customization of vehicles, such as that of NFL broadcaster John Madden's fully equipped luxury coach. MCI constructs luxury buses under the following model names: MCI J4500, MCI University Coach, MCI D 4505, MCI D4005, MCI Commuter Coach, MCI CNG (compressed natural gas) Commuter Coach, MCI Hybrid Commuter Coach and MCI ISTV (inmate security transportation vehicle). MCI's luxury buses can feature hot showers, and commuter coaches often feature vacuum flush toilets and six-monitor video systems. MCI also manufactures coaches for public transit, government agencies, universities and correctional facilities. The firm offers motor coach service, financing and refurbishing. Its Diesel Particulate Filters reduce muffler components and therefore helps to reduce particulate matter or black smoke by up to 90%. MCI is owned by transit bus and motor coach manufacturer, New Flyer Industries, Inc.

FINANCIAL DATA: *Note: Data for latest year may not have been available at press time.*

In U.S. $	2018	2017	2016	2015	2014	2013
Revenue	550,000,000	546,525,000	520,500,000	443,000,000	605,000,000	600,000,000
R&D Expense						
Operating Income						
Operating Margin %						
SGA Expense						
Net Income						
Operating Cash Flow						
Capital Expenditure						
EBITDA						
Return on Assets %						
Return on Equity %						
Debt to Equity						

CONTACT INFORMATION:

Phone: 847-285-2000 Fax: 847-285-2013
Toll-Free: 866-624-2622
Address: 200 E. Oakton St., Des Plaines, IL 60018 United States

STOCK TICKER/OTHER:

Stock Ticker: Subsidiary
Exchange:
Employees: 2,359
Fiscal Year Ends: 12/31
Parent Company: New Flyer Industries Inc

SALARIES/BONUSES:

Top Exec. Salary: $ Bonus: $
Second Exec. Salary: $ Bonus: $

OTHER THOUGHTS:

Estimated Female Officers or Directors: 2
Hot Spot for Advancement for Women/Minorities: Y

Motorcar Parts of America Inc

www.motorcarparts.com

NAIC Code: 336300

TYPES OF BUSINESS:

Replacement Alternators & Starters

BRANDS/DIVISIONS/AFFILIATES:

CONTACTS:

Note: Officers with more than one job title may be intentionally listed here more than once.

Selwyn Joffe, CEO
David Lee, CFO
Kevin Daly, Chief Accounting Officer
Michael Umansky, General Counsel
Douglas Schooner, Other Executive Officer

GROWTH PLANS/SPECIAL FEATURES:

Motorcar Parts of America, Inc. (MPA) remanufactures, remanufactures and distributes aftermarket automotive parts for import and domestic cars, light trucks, heavy duty, agricultural and industrial applications. The company primarily sells its products in North America to large auto parts retail and traditional warehouse chains, as well as to major automobile manufacturers for both aftermarket programs and warranty replacement programs. Customers include Advance, AutoZone, Genuine Parts (NAPA) and O'Reilly, which comprise an aggregate of approximately 25,000 retail outlets. MPA's aftermarket for automobile parts is divided into two markets: the do-it-yourself (DIY) market, which is generally served by large retail chain outlets; and the professional installer market, which is serviced by the traditional warehouse distributors, the dealer networks and the commercial divisions of retail chains. Products of the firm include rotating electrical products such as alternators, starters, wheel hub assemblies, bearings and new brake master cylinders. MPA recycles nearly all materials; nearly all parts, including metal from the Used Cores (raw material) and corrugated packaging are recycled. The firm carries more than 35,500 stock keeping units for automotive parts that are sold under customer labels such as Quality-Built, Pure Energy, Xtreme, Talon, Reliance, D&V Electronics, E&M Power, Dixie Electric, DelStar, Select Power Source, among others. The company has remanufacturing, warehousing, shipping and/or office operations in California, Mexico, Canada, India, Singapore, Malaysia and China.

FINANCIAL DATA:

Note: Data for latest year may not have been available at press time.

In U.S. $	2018	2017	2016	2015	2014	2013
Revenue	428,072,000	421,253,000	368,970,000	301,711,000	258,669,000	
R&D Expense	5,692,000	3,824,000	3,008,000	2,273,000	1,940,000	
Operating Income	49,624,000	67,972,000	38,286,000	33,586,000	32,104,000	
Operating Margin %	.12%	.16%	.10%	.11%	.12%	
SGA Expense	50,557,000	43,250,000	59,630,000	45,714,000	47,522,000	
Net Income	16,316,000	37,573,000	10,563,000	11,453,000	107,359,000	
Operating Cash Flow	-13,944,000	-5,269,000	15,334,000	-9,457,000	13,517,000	
Capital Expenditure	9,933,000	4,929,000	3,747,000	3,734,000	2,978,000	
EBITDA	54,132,000	71,686,000	41,222,000	36,107,000	34,846,000	
Return on Assets %	.04%	.09%	.03%	.03%	.31%	
Return on Equity %	.06%	.16%	.05%	.08%	2.02%	
Debt to Equity	0.051	0.068	0.095	0.38	0.725	

CONTACT INFORMATION:

Phone: 310 212-7910 Fax: 310 212-6315
Toll-Free: 800-890-9988
Address: 2929 California St., Torrance, CA 90503 United States

STOCK TICKER/OTHER:

Stock Ticker: MPAA
Exchange: NAS
Employees: 2,817
Fiscal Year Ends: 03/31
Parent Company:

SALARIES/BONUSES:

Top Exec. Salary: $728,960 Bonus: $ 100
Second Exec. Salary: $506,000 Bonus: $ 100

OTHER THOUGHTS:

Estimated Female Officers or Directors:
Hot Spot for Advancement for Women/Minorities:

Navistar International Corp (Holding Co.)

www.navistar.com

NAIC Code: 336120

TYPES OF BUSINESS:

Truck Manufacturing
Diesel Engines
Financial Services
Bus Manufacturing
Low-Emission Vehicles
Diesel-Electric Hybrid Vehicles

BRANDS/DIVISIONS/AFFILIATES:

Navistar Inc
International Industria Automotiva da America
Navistar Financial Corporation
International
Navistar Defense
IC

CONTACTS: *Note: Officers with more than one job title may be intentionally listed here more than once.*

Richard Bond, Assistant General Counsel
Troy Clarke, CEO
Walter Borst, CFO
Samara Strycker, Chief Accounting Officer
Persio Lisboa, Executive VP
Curt Kramer, General Counsel
William McMenamin, President, Divisional

GROWTH PLANS/SPECIAL FEATURES:

Navistar International Corporation is a manufacturer of commercial trucks, buses, diesel engines, chassis, recreational vehicles and military vehicles. Additionally, the firm provides service parts for trucks and trailers and is a private-label designer and manufacturer of diesel engines for the pickup truck, van and SUV markets. The company operates in four industry segments: truck, parts, global operations and financial services. In its truck segment, which includes subsidiary Navistar, Inc., the firm manufactures and distributes Class 4 through 8 trucks and buses in the common carrier, private carrier, government, leasing, construction, energy, military, student and commercial transportation markets under the International, Navistar Defense and IC brands. Its parts segment supports its brands of International commercial trucks, IC buses, proprietary engines, as well as other product lines by providing proprietary products and standard truck, trailer and engine service parts. Goods are delivered to our customers through eleven regional parts distribution centers. The global operations segment includes businesses that derive revenue from outside core North America markets and consists of the operations of wholly-owned subsidiary, International Industria Automotiva da America do Sul Ltda. (IIAA). IIAA caters to the South American mid-range diesel engine market, manufacturing and distributing mid-range diesel engines with additional engine offerings in the agriculture, marine and light truck markets. Through Navistar Financial Corporation, the financial services segment provides retail, wholesale and lease financing for products sold by its truck and parts segments and its dealers within the U.S. and Mexico. The segment also provides wholesale financing for 100% of the company's new truck inventory sold in the U.S. each year. In November 2018, Navistar agreed to sell a 70% interest in its Navistar Defense business to Cerberus Capital Management LP.

Navistar offers its employees medical, dental, vision and short/long-term disability insurance; tuition reimbursement; and flexible spending accounts.

FINANCIAL DATA: *Note: Data for latest year may not have been available at press time.*

In U.S. $	2018	2017	2016	2015	2014	2013
Revenue	10,250,000,000	8,570,000,000	8,111,000,000	10,140,000,000	10,806,000,000	10,775,000,000
R&D Expense	297,000,000	251,000,000	247,000,000	288,000,000	331,000,000	406,000,000
Operating Income	714,000,000	404,000,000	250,000,000	274,000,000	-38,000,000	-607,000,000
Operating Margin %		.05%	.03%	.03%	.00%	-.06%
SGA Expense	922,000,000	878,000,000	802,000,000	908,000,000	979,000,000	1,215,000,000
Net Income	340,000,000	30,000,000	-97,000,000	-184,000,000	-619,000,000	-898,000,000
Operating Cash Flow	269,000,000	109,000,000	267,000,000	46,000,000	-336,000,000	100,000,000
Capital Expenditure	345,000,000	239,000,000	248,000,000	202,000,000	277,000,000	599,000,000
EBITDA	958,000,000	638,000,000	520,000,000	485,000,000	90,000,000	-236,000,000
Return on Assets %		.01%	-.02%	-.03%	-.08%	-.10%
Return on Equity %						
Debt to Equity						

CONTACT INFORMATION:

Phone: 630 753-5000 Fax: 630 753-3982
Toll-Free: 800-448-7825
Address: 2701 Navistar Dr., Lisle, IL 60532 United States

STOCK TICKER/OTHER:

Stock Ticker: NAV
Employees: 15,400
Parent Company:
Exchange: NYS
Fiscal Year Ends: 10/31

SALARIES/BONUSES:

Top Exec. Salary: $1,027,183 Bonus: $
Second Exec. Salary: $766,711 Bonus: $

OTHER THOUGHTS:

Estimated Female Officers or Directors: 1
Hot Spot for Advancement for Women/Minorities:

Sales, profits and employees may be estimates. Financial information, benefits and other data can change quickly and may vary from those stated here.

Newmar Corporation

www.newmarcorp.com

NAIC Code: 336213

TYPES OF BUSINESS:

Motor Home Manufacturing

BRANDS/DIVISIONS/AFFILIATES:

Bay Star
Canyon Star
Kountry Star
Ventana
Mountain Aire
London Aire
Kountry Klub
Newmar Express Limited Warranty

CONTACTS: *Note: Officers with more than one job title may be intentionally listed here more than once.*

Matt Miller, CEO
Kevin Bogan, VP-Mfg.
Mahlon Miller, Chmn.

GROWTH PLANS/SPECIAL FEATURES:

Newmar Corporation is a recreational vehicle manufacturer specializing in motorhomes and luxury motorhomes. The company's motor coaches are divided into three groups: gas motor coaches, diesel motor coaches and luxury motor coaches. Gas motor coaches include the Bay Star, Bay Star Sport and Canyon Star models. Diesel motor coaches include the Kountry Star, Ventana and Dutch Star models. Luxury motor coaches include the Mountain Aire, London Aire, Essex, King Aire and New Aire models. All motorhomes come equipped with wood cabinetry, furniture, a television, an oven, a bathroom with plumbing, a sound system, air conditioning and many other features. Newmar also offers full-paint exterior graphics on its vehicles. These graphics are applied in its 18,900-square-foot paint facility. Chassis manufacturers include Ford, Freightliner and Spartan, as well as Star Foundation's steel superstructure. The company's Canyon Star features a rear garage that can store most sizes of off-road vehicles. Some Dutch Star, Ventana and Canyon Star models offer a wheelchair-accessible floor plan. The firm owns a company country club, which goes by the name Kountry Klub, for RV owners. All purchases come with a Newmar Express Limited Warranty, which insures the vehicle for the first year after purchase.

FINANCIAL DATA: *Note: Data for latest year may not have been available at press time.*

In U.S. $	2018	2017	2016	2015	2014	2013
Revenue	507,150,000	483,000,000	460,000,000	450,000,000	440,000,000	425,000,000
R&D Expense						
Operating Income						
Operating Margin %						
SGA Expense						
Net Income						
Operating Cash Flow						
Capital Expenditure						
EBITDA						
Return on Assets %						
Return on Equity %						
Debt to Equity						

CONTACT INFORMATION:

Phone: 574-773-7791 Fax: 574-773-2895
Toll-Free: 800-731-8300
Address: 355 N. Delaware St., Nappanee, IN 46550 United States

STOCK TICKER/OTHER:

Stock Ticker: Private
Employees: 1,015
Parent Company:
Exchange:
Fiscal Year Ends: 12/31

SALARIES/BONUSES:

Top Exec. Salary: $ Bonus: $
Second Exec. Salary: $ Bonus: $

OTHER THOUGHTS:

Estimated Female Officers or Directors:
Hot Spot for Advancement for Women/Minorities:

NFI Group Inc

www.newflyer.com

NAIC Code: 336111

TYPES OF BUSINESS:

Bus Manufacturer
Buses
Alternative Fuel Drive Systems
Diesel-Electric Hybrids
Electric Trolleys
Parts, Publications, Training & Svcs.

BRANDS/DIVISIONS/AFFILIATES:

New Flyer
Alexander Dennis Limited
Plaxton
MCI
ARBOC
NFI Parts

CONTACTS: *Note: Officers with more than one job title may be intentionally listed here more than once.*

Paul Soubry, CEO
Glenn Asham, CFO
Brian Tobin, Chairman of the Board
David White, Executive VP, Divisional
Janice Harper, Executive VP, Divisional
Colin Pewarchuk, Executive VP
Chris Stoddart, President, Divisional
Ian Smart, President, Divisional
Brian Dewsnup, President, Divisional

GROWTH PLANS/SPECIAL FEATURES:

NFI Group, Inc. is a leading bus and motor coach manufacturer and parts distributor, with more than 50 facilities across 10 countries. The firm also provides a comprehensive suite of mass transportation solutions under the following brands: New Flyer, representing heavy-duty transit buses; Alexander Dennis Limited, single- and double-deck buses; Plaxton, motor coaches; MCI, motor coaches; ARBOC, low-floor cutaway and medium-duty buses; and NFI Parts (also a trademark of the group). NFI buses and motor coaches incorporate the widest range of drive systems available, including clean diesel, natural gas, diesel-electric hybrid and zero-emission electric (trolley, battery and fuel-cell). The company also supports infrastructure development through its New Flyer Infrastructure Solutions service, which is dedicated to providing safe and reliable charging and mobility solutions. NFI currently (as of mid-2019) supports more than 105,000 buses and coaches in service throughout the world. In May 2019, NFI Group acquired Alexander Dennis Limited (ADL), with more than 31,000 vehicles in service in the U.K., Europe, Hong Kong, Singapore, New Zealand, Mexico, Canada and the U.S., sold under the Alexander Dennis and Plaxton brands.

FINANCIAL DATA: *Note: Data for latest year may not have been available at press time.*

In U.S. $	2018	2017	2016	2015	2014	2013
Revenue	2,519,021,000	2,381,858,000	2,274,176,000	1,538,900,000	1,451,100,000	1,199,424,000
R&D Expense						
Operating Income	245,786,000	255,436,000	212,909,000	93,550,000	56,998,000	51,227,000
Operating Margin %		.11%	.09%	.06%	.04%	.04%
SGA Expense	210,560,000	195,957,000	186,420,000	103,898,000	81,285,000	69,540,000
Net Income	159,942,000	191,368,000	124,894,000	53,894,000	26,719,000	26,761,000
Operating Cash Flow	175,144,000	172,059,000	149,704,000	42,581,000	45,823,000	29,979,000
Capital Expenditure	71,041,000	53,006,000	24,916,000	8,764,000	10,889,000	20,951,000
EBITDA	302,283,000	314,697,000	274,123,000	125,576,000	84,531,000	73,575,000
Return on Assets %		.10%	.07%	.04%	.02%	.03%
Return on Equity %		.27%	.22%	.12%	.06%	.07%
Debt to Equity		0.769	0.77	1.123	0.45	0.44

CONTACT INFORMATION:

Phone: 204-224-1251 Fax: 204-224-4214
Toll-Free:
Address: 711 Kernaghan Ave., Winnipeg, MB R2C 3T4 Canada

STOCK TICKER/OTHER:

Stock Ticker: NFI
Employees: 6,200
Parent Company:
Exchange: TSE
Fiscal Year Ends: 12/31

SALARIES/BONUSES:

Top Exec. Salary: $ Bonus: $
Second Exec. Salary: $ Bonus: $

OTHER THOUGHTS:

Estimated Female Officers or Directors: 3
Hot Spot for Advancement for Women/Minorities: Y

Nihon Plast Co Ltd

www.n-plast.co.jp

NAIC Code: 336300

TYPES OF BUSINESS:

Manufacturing-Automobile Components
Airbags
Steering Wheels
Instrument Panel Parts
Interior & Exterior Trim Parts
Air Spoilers

BRANDS/DIVISIONS/AFFILIATES:

NP Service Co Ltd
Neaton Auto Products Manufacturing Inc
P.T. Nihon Plast Indonesia
Nihon Plast Mexicana SA de CV
Nihon Magnesio SA de CV
Nihon Plast (Zhongshan) Co Ltd
Nihon Plast (Wuhan) Co Ltd
Nihon Plast Thailand Co Ltd

CONTACTS: *Note: Officers with more than one job title may be intentionally listed here more than once.*

Hirohisa Nagano, Pres.
Takahiro Mori, Managing Dir.
Wataru Sudo, Managing Dir.
Makoto Hirose, Chmn.

GROWTH PLANS/SPECIAL FEATURES:

Nihon Plast Co., Ltd. makes airbag, plastic molding and occupant protection components primarily for passenger cars. The company manufactures, processes and sells synthetic resins, die cast metal mold, automotive parts and electrical components. Nihon Plast's products are divided into five categories: safety parts, instrument panel parts, interior trim parts, exterior trim parts and aero parts. The safety parts division includes steering wheels and supplemental restraint system (SRS) airbag modules. Instrumental panel parts consist of glove boxes, ventilators, air conditioning ducts, console boxes, cup holders, column covers and shift knobs. Its interior trim parts include interior components with decorative covering. Its exterior trim parts include cover cowl tops and fender protectors. Its aero parts include air spoilers and front under covers, which both improve aerodynamics and fuel economy. The firm has manufacturing facilities in Fuji, Isesaki, Suzuka and Kyushu, which utilize various molding and manufacturing techniques, including injection molding, blow molding, decorative processing, reaction injection molding (RIM), combination molding, high reflective coating applicators and vibration welding. Nihon Plast technical centers test company equipment via crash simulation, airbag deployment and burst and durability tests. The facility also has vibration test equipment to simulate high-speed driving and rough road testing conditions. Subsidiaries of the firm include NP Service Co. Ltd.; Neaton Auto Products Manufacturing Inc.; Neaton Rome Inc.; P.T. Nihon Plast Indonesia; Nihon Plast Mexicana SA de CV; Nihon Magnesio SA de CV; Nihon Plast (Zhongshan) Co. Ltd.; Nihon Plast (Wuhan) Co. Ltd.; Nihon Plast Thailand Co. Ltd.; and Neaton Auto Mexicana SA de CV.

FINANCIAL DATA: *Note: Data for latest year may not have been available at press time.*

In U.S. $	2018	2017	2016	2015	2014	2013
Revenue	1,079,420,000	1,156,130,000	1,177,204,987	1,378,478,633	1,026,100,000	896,084,122
R&D Expense						
Operating Income						
Operating Margin %						
SGA Expense						
Net Income	18,964,600	35,820,100	36,510,282	34,846,503	19,900,000	-34,381,691
Operating Cash Flow						
Capital Expenditure						
EBITDA						
Return on Assets %						
Return on Equity %						
Debt to Equity						

CONTACT INFORMATION:

Phone: 81-544-58-6830 Fax: 81-544-48-6850
Toll-Free:
Address: 3507-15 Yamamiya, Fujinomiya City, Shizuoka 418-0111 Japan

STOCK TICKER/OTHER:

Stock Ticker: 7291
Exchange: Tokyo
Employees: 6,290
Fiscal Year Ends: 03/31
Parent Company:

SALARIES/BONUSES:

Top Exec. Salary: $ Bonus: $
Second Exec. Salary: $ Bonus: $

OTHER THOUGHTS:

Estimated Female Officers or Directors:
Hot Spot for Advancement for Women/Minorities:

Nikola Corporation

nikolamotor.com

NAIC Code: 336120

TYPES OF BUSINESS:

Electric Semi-Truck Manufacturing
Electric Off-Road Vehicle Manufacturing
Design and Installation of Solar Panels

BRANDS/DIVISIONS/AFFILIATES:

Nikola Motor Company
Nikola Powersports
Nikola Hydrogen
Nikola One
Nikola Two
Nikola Tre

CONTACTS:

Note: Officers with more than one job title may be intentionally listed here more than once.

Trevor Milton, CEO
Kim Brady, CFO
Joseph Pike, Chief Human Resources Officer

GROWTH PLANS/SPECIAL FEATURES:

Nikola Corporation operates subsidiaries involved in the transportation and energy segments. Nikola Motor Company is a pioneer in electric heavy-duty applications, offering both pure electric and hydrogen electric powertrains to cover class 6-8 in transportation. Nikola Motor's current products include: Nikola One, a fully-electric hydrogen-powered sleeper semi-truck, which is available in North and South America; Nikola Two, a fully-electric hydrogen-powered day cab semi-truck, also available in North and South America; and Nikola Tre, a fully-electric hydrogen-powered day cab semi-truck available in Europe, Asia and Australia. The firm plans to create the largest hydrogen station network in the world, and has partnered with Ryder System, Inc. as well as Thompson Machinery to provide sales and service for its vehicles. Nikola Powersports produces electric off-road and powersport applications. The subsidiary currently designs electric off-highway vehicles (OHVs) and personal watercrafts for commercial and military markets. Its products include: the Nikola NZT, a fully-electric four-seater OHV; and the military grade, fully-electric tactical all-terrain vehicle. Last, Nikola Hydrogen works in partnership with Nel ASA, who supplies equipment so that Nikola Hydrogen can create hydrogen stations. This subsidiary has created two of the planned 16 stations, which will cover more than 2,000 miles and will initially produce up to eight tons daily, but can be expanded up to 32 tons per day. Each Nikola truck is anticipated to consume about 50-75 kilograms per day, and each truck will store between 2-3MWh of energy. Each station is anticipated to produce hydrogen at 700 bar (10,000 psi) and 350 (5,000 psi). Nikola will allow all hydrogen vehicles to fill at their stations.

FINANCIAL DATA:

Note: Data for latest year may not have been available at press time.

In U.S. $	2018	2017	2016	2015	2014	2013
Revenue						
R&D Expense						
Operating Income						
Operating Margin %						
SGA Expense						
Net Income						
Operating Cash Flow						
Capital Expenditure						
EBITDA						
Return on Assets %						
Return on Equity %						
Debt to Equity						

CONTACT INFORMATION:

Phone: 435-862-9544 Fax:
Toll-Free:
Address: 1130 S. 3800 W., Ste. 200, Salt Lake, UT 84104 United States

STOCK TICKER/OTHER:

Stock Ticker: Private
Employees:
Parent Company:
Exchange:
Fiscal Year Ends:

SALARIES/BONUSES:

Top Exec. Salary: $ Bonus: $
Second Exec. Salary: $ Bonus: $

OTHER THOUGHTS:

Estimated Female Officers or Directors:
Hot Spot for Advancement for Women/Minorities:

NIO Inc

NAIC Code: 336111

www.nio.io

TYPES OF BUSINESS:

Automobile Manufacturing, All-Electric
Self-Driving Cars

BRANDS/DIVISIONS/AFFILIATES:

EP9
ES8
ES6
EVE
NIO Pilot
NOMI

CONTACTS:
Note: Officers with more than one job title may be intentionally listed here more than once.

Bin Li, CEO
Qin Lihong, Pres.
Louis T. Hsieh, CFO
Bin Li, Chmn.

GROWTH PLANS/SPECIAL FEATURES:

NIO, Inc. is a Chinese startup that designs, jointly manufactures and markets premium smart electric vehicles. The company offers its cars under the EP9, ES8, ES6 and EVE brand names. The EP9 offers a 777-volt full electric powertrain, has a maximum speed of 194 miles per hour (313 kph), a peak power of 1 megawatts (MW) and the downforce of a current Formula One car. ES8 is a 7-seat, high-performance electric sport utility vehicle (SUV) built exclusively for the China market. The car's onboard NIO Pilot system offers advanced autonomous driving assistance, and its artificial intelligence (AI) learns the preferences and driving styles of its authorized drivers. ES8 offers a dual motor and is an all-wheel drive vehicle that reaches 62 miles per hour (100km/h) in 4.4 seconds' time. ES6 is a long-range smart electric SUV with maximum 544 horsepower, taking 4.7 seconds to accelerate from 0 to 62 mph. EVE is the company's concept car that features NOMI, a digital companion powered by AI, which continually learns about its passenger's interests, tailoring information to meet individual needs. It can seat six passengers and is primarily intended for enhanced autonomous driving, but the steering and pedals can be activated when required so that manual driving can occur. Active glass across the entire upper canopy becomes a canvas of NOMI to provide personalized information or entertainment. Power is provided in several ways: a battery swap within a modular NIO power station; power mobile, a power supply delivery service in which NIO vans serve as mobile power banks that go to the NIO vehicle; and a public NIO power charger, which is powered by the mobile internet to provide charging services for all electric vehicles.

FINANCIAL DATA:
Note: Data for latest year may not have been available at press time.

In U.S. $	2018	2017	2016	2015	2014	2013
Revenue	719,291,500					
R&D Expense	580,809,200	378,140,000	212,882,100			
Operating Income	-1,394,022,000	-719,643,700	-378,089,300			
Operating Margin %						
SGA Expense	739,754,300	322,774,900	159,647,700			
Net Income	-1,394,264,000	-724,167,400	-368,468,400			
Operating Cash Flow	-1,149,398,000	-664,601,600	-319,836,700			
Capital Expenditure	384,107,200	161,823,100	95,077,280			
EBITDA	-1,310,264,000	-701,299,600	-366,504,600			
Return on Assets %						
Return on Equity %						
Debt to Equity						

CONTACT INFORMATION:

Phone: 86-21-6908-3306 Fax:
Toll-Free:
Address: No. 56 AnTuo Rd., Bldg 20, AnTing Town, JiaDing Dist., Shanghai, Shanghai 201804 China

STOCK TICKER/OTHER:

Stock Ticker: NIO
Employees: 6,231
Parent Company:
Exchange: NYS
Fiscal Year Ends:

SALARIES/BONUSES:

Top Exec. Salary: $ Bonus: $
Second Exec. Salary: $ Bonus: $

OTHER THOUGHTS:

Estimated Female Officers or Directors:
Hot Spot for Advancement for Women/Minorities:

Nippon Piston Ring Co Ltd

www.npr.co.jp

NAIC Code: 336300

TYPES OF BUSINESS:

Automobile Parts Manufacturing
Internal Combustion Engine Components
Piston Rings, Cylinder Liners & Valve Train Parts
Appliance Components
Industrial Machinery Components

BRANDS/DIVISIONS/AFFILIATES:

Toyota Motor Corporation
Japan Trustee Services Bank Ltd
NPR ASIMCO Powdered Metals Manufacturing (Yizheng)
NPR of America Inc
SIAM NPR Co Ltd
NPR Auto Parts Manufacturing India Pvt Ltd

CONTACTS: *Note: Officers with more than one job title may be intentionally listed here more than once.*

Yuji Sakamoto, Managing Dir.
Akira Yamamoto, Pres.
Masaaki Fujita, Dir-Finance

GROWTH PLANS/SPECIAL FEATURES:

Nippon Piston Ring Co., Ltd. (NPR) is a leading Japanese manufacturer and marketer of production and replacement parts for domestic and overseas automobile, marine and land engines. These components include piston rings, cylinder liners and seal rings; valve train parts for internal combustion engines, such as valve seat inserts, cast iron and composite camshafts, valve rocker arms, valve guides and rocker bridges; engine parts; synchronizer rings; compressor parts for household electronic appliances; components for industrial machinery; and casting, sintering and plastic working parts. Most of the company's business relates to domestic operations, supplying both original equipment components to Japanese auto makers and aftermarket parts to distributors, with overseas operations serving markets in the U.S., Germany, India, China and other parts of Southeast Asia. NPR utilizes a technique called metal injection molding (MIM). MIM products are manufactured using a multi-stage compacting press technique and are used as functional parts for various engines and automobiles. Some of the firm's major shareholders include Toyota Motor Corporation; Japan Trustee Services Bank Ltd.; The Master Trust Bank of Japan Ltd.; and Asahi Mutual Life Insurance Company. NPR's overseas subsidiaries include, but are not limited to, NPR ASIMCO Powdered Metals Manufacturing (Yizheng) Co. Ltd.; NPR of America, Inc.; SIAM NPR Co. Ltd; and NPR Auto Parts Manufacturing India Pvt. Ltd.

FINANCIAL DATA: *Note: Data for latest year may not have been available at press time.*

In U.S. $	2018	2017	2016	2015	2014	2013
Revenue	537,089,000	453,188,000	477,741,291	517,096,727	429,800,000	443,800,000
R&D Expense						
Operating Income						
Operating Margin %						
SGA Expense						
Net Income	17,769,300	12,149,700	22,143,917	25,251,049	18,100,000	19,000,000
Operating Cash Flow						
Capital Expenditure						
EBITDA						
Return on Assets %						
Return on Equity %						
Debt to Equity						

CONTACT INFORMATION:

Phone: 81-48-856-5022 Fax: 81-48-856-5038
Toll-Free:
Address: 12-10, 5-Chome, Honmachi-Higashi, Chuo-ku, Saitama City, 338-8503 Japan

STOCK TICKER/OTHER:

Stock Ticker: 6461
Employees: 3,021
Parent Company:
Exchange: Tokyo
Fiscal Year Ends: 03/31

SALARIES/BONUSES:

Top Exec. Salary: $ Bonus: $
Second Exec. Salary: $ Bonus: $

OTHER THOUGHTS:

Estimated Female Officers or Directors:
Hot Spot for Advancement for Women/Minorities:

Nissan Diesel (Thailand) Co Ltd

www.tanchong.com/en/nissan_diesel_thailand.aspx

NAIC Code: 336120

TYPES OF BUSINESS:

Commercial Truck Manufacturing
Automotive Parts Manufacturing

BRANDS/DIVISIONS/AFFILIATES:

Tan Chong International Ltd
Foton Truck (Thailand) Co Ltd
MAN Commercial Vehicles (Thailand) Co Ltd
Motor Image Subaru (Thailand) Co Ltd

CONTACTS: *Note: Officers with more than one job title may be intentionally listed here more than once.*

Ramesh Narasimhan, Pres.
Chua Tong Guan, Dir.-Finance & Acct.
Kiyoshi Chigira, VP

GROWTH PLANS/SPECIAL FEATURES:

Nissan Diesel (Thailand) Co., Ltd. (NDT) primarily manufactures heavy-duty trucks for the Thai market. It was established in 1987 as a joint venture between two Thai firms (Siam Motor Co., Ltd. and Marubeni Thailand Co., Ltd.) and two Japanese firms (Marubeni Corporation and Nissan Diesel Motor Co., Ltd.). Subsequently, the company became a wholly-owned subsidiary of Tan Chong International Ltd. in 2002. NDT's vehicles are comprised of 6- and 10-wheeled freight trucks, bus chassis and semi-truck tractors. The company also sells replacement parts, as well as other automotive materials such as engine coolant. The firm's products are distributed by dozens of dealers all across Thailand, divided into six areas: Central Thailand, Northern Thailand, Eastern Thailand, Northeastern Thailand, Southern Thailand and the Bangkok area. Besides its domestic sales network, NDT exports its vehicles worldwide. The company maintains one factory, located in Bang Sao Thong, in Thailand's Samut Prakarn province. Sister companies of NDT include: Foton Truck (Thailand) Co., Ltd.; MAN Commercial Vehicles (Thailand) Co., Ltd.; and Motor Image Subaru (Thailand) Co., Ltd.

FINANCIAL DATA: *Note: Data for latest year may not have been available at press time.*

In U.S. $	2018	2017	2016	2015	2014	2013
Revenue						
R&D Expense						
Operating Income						
Operating Margin %						
SGA Expense						
Net Income						
Operating Cash Flow						
Capital Expenditure						
EBITDA						
Return on Assets %						
Return on Equity %						
Debt to Equity						

CONTACT INFORMATION:

Phone: 66-2567-2882-88 Fax: 66-2567-2886-7
Toll-Free:
Address: 59 Moo 1, Rangsit-Pathumthani Rd., Ban Klang, 12000 Thailand

STOCK TICKER/OTHER:

Stock Ticker: Subsidiary Exchange:
Employees: Fiscal Year Ends:
Parent Company: Tan Chong International Ltd

SALARIES/BONUSES:

Top Exec. Salary: $ Bonus: $
Second Exec. Salary: $ Bonus: $

OTHER THOUGHTS:

Estimated Female Officers or Directors:
Hot Spot for Advancement for Women/Minorities:

Nissan Motor Co Ltd

www.nissan-global.com

NAIC Code: 336111

TYPES OF BUSINESS:

Automobile Manufacturing
Research & Development
Industrial Machinery
Marine Equipment
Logistics Services
Alternative Fuels Research
Financial Services

BRANDS/DIVISIONS/AFFILIATES:

Versa
Sentra
Altima
370Z
NV
QX80
GO
Datsun CROSS

CONTACTS:
Note: Officers with more than one job title may be intentionally listed here more than once.

Hiroto Saikawa, CEO
Hiroshi Karube, CFO

GROWTH PLANS/SPECIAL FEATURES:

Nissan Motor Co., Ltd. develops, manufactures, sells and services automotive products in over 160 countries. The company's products, which are sold both in Japan and overseas (principally in North America and Europe), include passenger cars, zero emission vehicles, busses and trucks, along with related components. Brands include Nissan, Infiniti and Datsun. Nissan's model offerings include Versa, Sentra, Altima, Maxima, 370Z, GT-R, Juke, Rogue, Murano, Pathfinder, Armada, Frontier, Kicks Titan, NV and Leaf. Nissan's commercial vehicle models include NV200 Compact Cargo, NV Cargo and NV Passenger. Infiniti models include Q50, Q70, Q60, QX30, QX50, QX60 and QX80. The Datsun brand offers hatchback vehicles GO, redi-GO and GO+, as well as the on-DO 4-door sedan, the mi-DO mini SUV and the Datsun CROSS (crossover). Through Nissan Marine, the firm also produces/sells pleasure boats, operates a marina business and exports outboard engines. The company operates offices and production plants in Japan, Africa, North America, Australia, Europe, Asia and the Middle East. Nissan and Renault SA, a French company, manage an alliance that allows each company to maintain its distinct corporate culture and brand identity while enduring the challenges of market globalization and the accelerating change of technology. Renault-Nissan ranks as one of the world's leading automotive groups, and the two companies operate a joint venture factory in the eastern Indian city of Chennai. Renault SA owns approximately 43% of Nissan. Nissan, an allied firm, promotes intensive research and development in alternative fuel technologies. In 2018, Nissan announced that Infiniti will introduce new vehicles with electrified powertrains beginning in 2021, and that electrified vehicles will comprise more than half of Infiniti's global sales by 2025.

FINANCIAL DATA:
Note: Data for latest year may not have been available at press time.

In U.S. $	2018	2017	2016	2015	2014	2013
Revenue	109,825,100,000	107,701,200,000	112,015,400,000	104,532,300,000	96,328,980,000	
R&D Expense						
Operating Income	5,281,750,000	6,820,695,000	7,289,819,000	5,417,763,000	4,579,719,000	
Operating Margin %	.05%	.08%	.08%	.07%	.07%	
SGA Expense	5,834,433,000	5,954,714,000	6,534,645,000	6,337,659,000	5,494,790,000	
Net Income	6,863,555,000	6,097,215,000	4,813,830,000	4,204,870,000	3,575,023,000	
Operating Cash Flow	9,844,238,000	12,272,310,000	8,518,774,000	6,365,990,000	6,691,077,000	
Capital Expenditure	13,146,120,000	11,889,730,000	12,736,540,000	9,838,762,000	9,227,542,000	
EBITDA	14,532,070,000	16,728,010,000	14,617,040,000	13,773,800,000	11,352,170,000	
Return on Assets %	.04%	.04%	.03%	.03%	.03%	
Return on Equity %	.15%	.14%	.11%	.10%	.10%	
Debt to Equity	0.921	0.95	0.792	0.792	0.835	

CONTACT INFORMATION:

Phone: 81 455235523 Fax:
Toll-Free:
Address: 1-1, Takashima 1-chome, Nishi-ku, Kanagawa, 220-8686 Japan

STOCK TICKER/OTHER:

Stock Ticker: NSANF
Employees: 158,133
Parent Company:
Exchange: PINX
Fiscal Year Ends: 03/31

SALARIES/BONUSES:

Top Exec. Salary: $ Bonus: $
Second Exec. Salary: $ Bonus: $

OTHER THOUGHTS:

Estimated Female Officers or Directors:
Hot Spot for Advancement for Women/Minorities:

Nissan North America Inc

www.nissanusa.com

NAIC Code: 336111

TYPES OF BUSINESS:

Automobile Manufacturing
Car & Truck Manufacturing
Engine & Part Manufacturing
Car & Parts Distribution
Car Design & Engineering
Financing & Leasing

BRANDS/DIVISIONS/AFFILIATES:

Nissan Motor Co Ltd
Versa
Sentra
Altima
LEAF
Pathfinder
ProPILOT Assist
Safety Shield 360

CONTACTS: *Note: Officers with more than one job title may be intentionally listed here more than once.*

Nobao Araki, CEO
Bill Krueger, Sr. VP-Mfg.
Scott E. Becker, Sr. VP-Admin.
Alan J. Buddendeck, VP-Corp. Comm.
Scott E. Becker, Sr. VP-Finance
Victor Nacif, VP-Design Bus. Aspects, Nissan Design America
Bill Krueger, Sr. VP-Supply Chain & Purchasing

GROWTH PLANS/SPECIAL FEATURES:

Nissan North America, Inc. (Nissan NA), a subsidiary of Nissan Motor Co., Ltd., coordinates Nissan's operations in the U.S., Canada and Mexico, including automotive styling, consumer and corporate financing and engineering. Current (2019) passenger and commercial vehicle models by Nissan include Versa, Sentra, Altima, Maxima, LEAF, 370Z, GT-R, Kicks, Rogue, Murano, Pathfinder, Armada, Frontier, Titan and NV. These automobiles comprise sedans, coupes, electric cars, sports cars, crossovers, sport utility vehicles, minivans, vans, trucks and commercial vehicles. Nissan NA sells its vehicles and related accessories through a network of dealers and centers. During 2018, the company sold 10.76 million vehicles combined. Nissan NA's production plants are located in Tennessee and Mississippi. The firm's intelligent mobility division is engaged in three core areas of innovation: Nissan intelligent driving, Nissan intelligent power and Nissan intelligent integration. The 2019 Altima is available with hands-on driving assistant, ProPILOT Assist. In September 2018, the intelligent mobility division introduced Safety Shield 360, a suite of six advanced active safety and driver-assist technologies that will be regarded as standard equipment on all of Nissan's top-selling models by 2021. In February 2019, Nissan NA broke ground on an advanced technology training center in Decherd, Tennessee, which will have the capacity to train 180 employees simultaneously in the areas of production, maintenance, engineering and management.

FINANCIAL DATA: *Note: Data for latest year may not have been available at press time.*

In U.S. $	2018	2017	2016	2015	2014	2013
Revenue	56,743,807,500	56,461,500,000	58,250,613,400	55,902,700,000	45,252,000,000	38,924,000,000
R&D Expense						
Operating Income						
Operating Margin %						
SGA Expense						
Net Income		2,557,810,000	2,110,236,609	1,832,057,000	2,383,203,000	1,546,714,000
Operating Cash Flow						
Capital Expenditure						
EBITDA						
Return on Assets %						
Return on Equity %						
Debt to Equity						

CONTACT INFORMATION:

Phone: 615-725-1000 Fax: 615-725-8535
Toll-Free:
Address: 932 Nissan Dr., Smyrna, TN 37167 United States

STOCK TICKER/OTHER:

Stock Ticker: Subsidiary
Exchange:
Employees: 24,000
Fiscal Year Ends: 03/31
Parent Company: Nissan Motor Co Ltd

SALARIES/BONUSES:

Top Exec. Salary: $ Bonus: $
Second Exec. Salary: $ Bonus: $

OTHER THOUGHTS:

Estimated Female Officers or Directors: 1
Hot Spot for Advancement for Women/Minorities:

Nissan Shatai Co Ltd

www.nissan-shatai.co.jp

NAIC Code: 336211

TYPES OF BUSINESS:

Automobile Manufacturer
Vehicle Bodies

BRANDS/DIVISIONS/AFFILIATES:

Nissan Motor Co Ltd
Nissan Shatai Kyushu Co Ltd
Shonan Plant
Auto Works Kyoto Co Ltd
Nissan Shatai Manufacturing Co Ltd
Nissan Shatai Engineering Co Ltd
Pro Staff Co Ltd
Nissan Shatai Computer Service Co Ltd

CONTACTS: *Note: Officers with more than one job title may be intentionally listed here more than once.*

Shohei Kimura, Pres.

GROWTH PLANS/SPECIAL FEATURES:

Nissan Shatai Co., Ltd., based in Japan, manufactures car bodies and parts exclusively for Nissan Motor Co., Ltd. The firm has manufacturing divisions for commercial vehicle bodies, passenger vehicle bodies and small bus bodies. It manufactures three categories of products: light commercial vehicles (LCVs), multipurpose vehicles (MPVs) and specially-equipped vehicles. Specially-equipped vehicles include taxis, ambulances, children's school buses and refrigerator vans, all custom-designed for customer/client needs. The firm uses 3D-CAD and intelligent body assembly system (IBS) technologies to design and assemble vehicle bodies. Nissan Shatai Kyushu Co., Ltd. is a vehicle manufacturing plant with a capacity to produce 120,000 vehicles per year and focuses on manufacturing MPVs. Vehicle models from this plant include Infiniti QX80, Patrol, Armada, Elgrand and NV350. The Shonan Plant primarily manufactures LCVs, with models including NV200, NV150, Armada, NV200, Patrol and Patrol pickup. Auto Works Kyoto Co., Ltd. manufactures microbuses and trucks, with models including Atlas and Civilian. Other affiliates of the firm include Nissan Shatai Manufacturing Co., Ltd., a producer of pressed parts for Nissan Shatai; Nissan Shatai Engineering Co., Ltd., which provides maintenance of equipment and distribution at Nissan Shatai and Nissan Shatai Kyushu; Pro Staff Co., Ltd., providing temporary staff placement and outsourcing services; and Nissan Shatai Computer Service Co., Ltd, which provides IT-related services for Nissan Shatai companies.

FINANCIAL DATA: *Note: Data for latest year may not have been available at press time.*

In U.S. $	2018	2017	2016	2015	2014	2013
Revenue	4,825,000,000	4,750,000,000	4,668,960,000	4,356,750,000	3,945,700,000	4,252,980,000
R&D Expense						
Operating Income						
Operating Margin %						
SGA Expense						
Net Income			72,762,800	143,292,000	55,800,000	51,386,000
Operating Cash Flow						
Capital Expenditure						
EBITDA						
Return on Assets %						
Return on Equity %						
Debt to Equity						

CONTACT INFORMATION:

Phone: 81-463-21-8001 Fax: 81-463-8155
Toll-Free:
Address: 2-1, Tsutsumicho, Hiratsuka, Kanagawa, 254-8610 Japan

STOCK TICKER/OTHER:

Stock Ticker: 7222
Employees: 4,035
Parent Company:
Exchange: Tokyo
Fiscal Year Ends: 12/31

SALARIES/BONUSES:

Top Exec. Salary: $ Bonus: $
Second Exec. Salary: $ Bonus: $

OTHER THOUGHTS:

Estimated Female Officers or Directors:
Hot Spot for Advancement for Women/Minorities:

Niu Technologies

www.niu.com

NAIC Code: 336991

TYPES OF BUSINESS:

Electric Mopeds
eScooter

BRANDS/DIVISIONS/AFFILIATES:

N
M
U
NIU

CONTACTS:

Note: Officers with more than one job title may be intentionally listed here more than once.

Hardy Peng Zhang, CFO

GROWTH PLANS/SPECIAL FEATURES:

Niu Technologies designs, manufactures and sells high-performance smart electric two-wheeled vehicles, which the China-based company refers to as eScooters. The company's product portfolio consists of three series, N, M and U, with multiple models or specifications for each series. The eScooters are powered by lithium-ion batteries. The N series consists of the N model and the NGT model, equipped with halo light-emitting diode (LED) daytime running lights, a cloud-based central controller that collects and analyzes vehicle information, has on-board computer and cloud technology and enables NIU app users to receive real-time data such as vehicle diagnostics, anti-theft alerts, daily riding habits and battery status. The M series consist of the M and M+ models, which are based on Niu's 48V powertrain platform and is NIU app compatible. The U series is smaller and lighter than the N and M series. Niu Technologies has an omnichannel retail model, integrating office and online channels, to sell its products and provide services. The firm sells and services its products through more than 230 partners that have more than 750 franchised stores in 175+ cities throughout China, as well as through 22 distributors in 27 countries overseas, and through online stores and third-party eCommerce platforms.

FINANCIAL DATA:

Note: Data for latest year may not have been available at press time.

In U.S. $	2018	2017	2016	2015	2014	2013
Revenue	214,687,700	111,771,500	51,545,750			
R&D Expense	13,338,160	5,737,389	4,807,154			
Operating Income	-45,915,210	-20,838,280	-32,709,370			
Operating Margin %						
SGA Expense	61,635,460	23,168,310	26,236,050			
Net Income	-50,705,680	-26,827,270	-33,809,010			
Operating Cash Flow	1,130,163	11,631,360	-17,876,880			
Capital Expenditure	7,741,731	3,376,890	1,499,267			
EBITDA	-46,840,860	-24,953,190	-32,718,270			
Return on Assets %						
Return on Equity %						
Debt to Equity						

CONTACT INFORMATION:

Phone: 86 1064321899 Fax:
Toll-Free:
Address: No. 10 Wangjing St., Bldg. A, 11/Fl, Beijing, 100102 China

STOCK TICKER/OTHER:

Stock Ticker: NIU
Employees:
Parent Company:
Exchange: NAS
Fiscal Year Ends: 12/31

SALARIES/BONUSES:

Top Exec. Salary: $ Bonus: $
Second Exec. Salary: $ Bonus: $

OTHER THOUGHTS:

Estimated Female Officers or Directors:
Hot Spot for Advancement for Women/Minorities:

Nokian Tyres plc

www.nokiantyres.com

NAIC Code: 326211

TYPES OF BUSINESS:

Tire Manufacturing (except Retreading)

BRANDS/DIVISIONS/AFFILIATES:

Nokian Tyres Ltd
Nokia Tyres
Vianor

CONTACTS: *Note: Officers with more than one job title may be intentionally listed here more than once.*

Hille Korhonen, CEO
Teemu Kangas-Karki, CFO
Petteri Wallden, Chmn.

GROWTH PLANS/SPECIAL FEATURES:

Nokian Tyres plc develops and manufactures tires for passenger cars, vans and trucks. The firm is knowns for its innovative winter tires, while also developing summer and all-season tire ranges. Nokian Tyres owns factories in Nokia, Finland; Vsevolozhsk, Russia; and Tennessee, USA; and also engages in contract manufacturing in other countries worldwide. The firm markets globally, although it primarily serves the Nordic market and areas with harsh driving conditions. Nokian Tyres often cooperates with machinery and equipment manufacturers for the innovation and development of their tire products. The car tires business unit offers products including studded and non-studded winter tires as well as high-speed and ultra-high-performance summer tires. It develops and manufactures tires for passenger cars, vans and sport utility vehicles (SUVs). Subsidiary Nokian Heavy Tyres Ltd. develops and manufactures tires for trucks and heavy equipment. It develops solutions for the most extreme conditions found in forests, modern-day farming, municipal contracting, transportation terminals and underground applications. All heavy tires are manufactured in Nokia, and new truck and bus tires are manufactured via contract partners. Primary markets for the heavy tire division include the Nordic countries, central Europe, the Americas and Russia. Nokian Tyres' authorized dealer network comprises branded stores throughout Europe, China and other countries. In addition, the firm's owned or franchised Vianor tire chain comprises approximately 1,500 service centers in more than 25 countries. Vianor sells car and van tires as well as truck tires, including the Nokian and other brands. The product range also features other automotive products and services, such as rims, batteries and shock absorbers. In August 2019, Nokian Tyres agreed to acquire Finnish heavy equipment wheel company, Levpyora Oy, which has two business lines: wheels and steel structures.

FINANCIAL DATA: *Note: Data for latest year may not have been available at press time.*

In U.S. $	2018	2017	2016	2015	2014	2013
Revenue	1,766,608,000	1,740,921,000	1,540,190,000	1,505,979,000	1,537,976,000	1,684,012,000
R&D Expense	23,029,230	24,136,400	22,475,640	20,704,160	18,379,100	17,825,510
Operating Income	412,090,400	403,122,200	343,002,700	326,173,600	340,788,300	424,269,300
Operating Margin %		.23%	.22%	.22%	.22%	.25%
SGA Expense	370,128,400	384,189,600	350,974,300	322,741,400	311,116,000	316,319,700
Net Income	326,837,900	245,128,400	278,786,500	266,496,900	230,735,200	203,388,000
Operating Cash Flow	594,442,000	259,189,600	403,454,400	313,773,200		
Capital Expenditure	250,775,000	149,357,800	112,378,200	110,717,400	90,456,160	168,069,100
EBITDA	508,082,400	483,946,000	449,955,700	424,380,000	309,012,400	366,806,900
Return on Assets %		.11%	.13%	.14%	.11%	.09%
Return on Equity %		.15%	.19%	.20%	.16%	.13%
Debt to Equity		0.092	0.094	0.161	0.227	0.133

CONTACT INFORMATION:

Phone: 358 104017000 Fax: 358 104017799
Toll-Free:
Address: Pirkkalaistie 7, Nokia, 37101 Finland

STOCK TICKER/OTHER:

Stock Ticker: NKRKF
Employees: 4,719
Parent Company:
Exchange: PINX
Fiscal Year Ends: 12/31

SALARIES/BONUSES:

Top Exec. Salary: $ Bonus: $
Second Exec. Salary: $ Bonus: $

OTHER THOUGHTS:

Estimated Female Officers or Directors:
Hot Spot for Advancement for Women/Minorities:

Novares Group SA

www.novaresteam.com

NAIC Code: 336300

TYPES OF BUSINESS:

Automotive Part Manufacturing
Injection Molding

BRANDS/DIVISIONS/AFFILIATES:

Mecaplast-Key Plastics LLC
Mecaplast Group

CONTACTS:

Note: Officers with more than one job title may be intentionally listed here more than once.

Pierre Boulet, CEO

GROWTH PLANS/SPECIAL FEATURES:

Novares Group SA, formerly Mecaplast-Key Plastics L.L.C., offers a full range of engineering, program management and production services to the automotive industry. Novares is part of the Mecaplast Group. The company operates 47 manufacturing sites, 17 customer service centers, eight skill centers, eight technical centers in 2s countries throughout Asia, Europe and North America. Novares provides exterior, interior and under hood products. Exterior products include handles and LED (light-emitting diode) lighting for ambient and proximity technology. The company's interior products include air vents and ducts; bezels and fascias for radio, climate, navigation and steering wheel controls; cup holders; ashtrays; glove boxes; control panel covers; instrument clusters; speaker grilles; decorative trims; assist handles; floor console assemblies; seat belt adjusters; and head rest assemblies. Novares' under hood products include battery trays, electric and electronic component supports, cable channels and fan and shrouds. Additionally, the firm offers program management and technical services, which include in-house rapid prototyping, painting, thermoforming, in-house performance testing and layouts and local program management for all services. Customers include most domestic and transplant original equipment manufacturers (OEMs) and Tier 1 suppliers in the industry.

FINANCIAL DATA:

Note: Data for latest year may not have been available at press time.

In U.S. $	2018	2017	2016	2015	2014	2013
Revenue	1,715,690,000	1,437,440,000	1,158,920,000	801,924,000	850,000,000	909,933,000
R&D Expense						
Operating Income						
Operating Margin %						
SGA Expense						
Net Income						
Operating Cash Flow						
Capital Expenditure						
EBITDA						
Return on Assets %						
Return on Equity %						
Debt to Equity						

CONTACT INFORMATION:

Phone: Fax: 45-29-0661
Toll-Free:
Address: 361 Ave. du General de Gaull, Clamart, Paris, 92140 France

STOCK TICKER/OTHER:

Stock Ticker: Private
Employees: 10,000
Parent Company: Mecaplast Group
Exchange:
Fiscal Year Ends: 12/31

SALARIES/BONUSES:

Top Exec. Salary: $ Bonus: $
Second Exec. Salary: $ Bonus: $

OTHER THOUGHTS:

Estimated Female Officers or Directors:
Hot Spot for Advancement for Women/Minorities:

Nuro Inc

nuro.ai

NAIC Code: 336111

TYPES OF BUSINESS:

Automobile Manufacturing
Self-Driving, Electric Delivery Vehicles

BRANDS/DIVISIONS/AFFILIATES:

R1

GROWTH PLANS/SPECIAL FEATURES:

Nuro, Inc. is a robotics company that develops autonomous delivery vehicles. To date, the firm's sole product is the R1. The R1 is an electric, self-driving vehicle designed for the delivery of local commerce. The vehicle carries only cargo, with the first model capable of carrying 12 grocery bags. Currently, Nuro has teamed up with The Kroger Co., the supermarket chain, to launch a pilot program to test the fully autonomous delivery of groceries in Scottsdale, Arizona. In December 2018, the R1 joined the pilot. In February 2019, Nuro raised $940 million from SoftBank Group, the Japanese multinational holding conglomerate.

CONTACTS: *Note: Officers with more than one job title may be intentionally listed here more than once.*

Jiajun Zhu, Co-Founder
Dave Ferguson, Co-Founder

FINANCIAL DATA: *Note: Data for latest year may not have been available at press time.*

In U.S. $	2018	2017	2016	2015	2014	2013
Revenue						
R&D Expense						
Operating Income						
Operating Margin %						
SGA Expense						
Net Income						
Operating Cash Flow						
Capital Expenditure						
EBITDA						
Return on Assets %						
Return on Equity %						
Debt to Equity						

CONTACT INFORMATION:

Phone: 650-476-2687 Fax:
Toll-Free:
Address: 1300 Terra Bella Ave., Ste. 100, Mountain View, CA 94043 United States

STOCK TICKER/OTHER:

Stock Ticker: Private
Employees: 200
Parent Company:
Exchange:
Fiscal Year Ends:

SALARIES/BONUSES:

Top Exec. Salary: $ Bonus: $
Second Exec. Salary: $ Bonus: $

OTHER THOUGHTS:

Estimated Female Officers or Directors:
Hot Spot for Advancement for Women/Minorities:

NYX Incorporated

www.nyxinc.com

NAIC Code: 336300

TYPES OF BUSINESS:

Automobile Parts Manufacturer
Interior & Exterior Components
Under-Hood Assemblies
Plastics Processing
Steel Stamping
Design Services

BRANDS/DIVISIONS/AFFILIATES:

GROWTH PLANS/SPECIAL FEATURES:

NYX Incorporated provides custom-engineered automotive interior, under-hood and related technology systems and parts. The firm specializes in plastics processing, engineered plastics, rubber extrusion, steel stamping and assembly. NYX's solutions include door panels, center consoles, overhead consoles, glove box systems, knee bolster assemblies, interior garnish, seating components, rear shelf packaging trays and design and engineering. Based in Michigan, the company's production facilities are located throughout Michigan, Tennessee and Mexico. NYX also maintains a design and engineering center in India. Customers of NYX include General Motors, Ford, Honda, TRW, Chrysler, Volkswagen, Faurecia, LEAR, Autoliv, Nissan and Magna.

CONTACTS: *Note: Officers with more than one job title may be intentionally listed here more than once.*

Jatinder-Bir Sandhu, CEO
Jatinder-bir Sandhu, Pres.
Chain S. Sandhu, Chmn.

FINANCIAL DATA: *Note: Data for latest year may not have been available at press time.*

In U.S. $	2018	2017	2016	2015	2014	2013
Revenue	471,870,000	449,400,000	428,000,000	424,000,000	411,000,000	380,000,000
R&D Expense						
Operating Income						
Operating Margin %						
SGA Expense						
Net Income						
Operating Cash Flow						
Capital Expenditure						
EBITDA						
Return on Assets %						
Return on Equity %						
Debt to Equity						

CONTACT INFORMATION:

Phone: 734-462-2385 Fax: 734-464-4830
Toll-Free:
Address: 36111 Schoolcraft Rd., Livonia, MI 48150 United States

STOCK TICKER/OTHER:

Stock Ticker: Private
Employees: 2,136
Parent Company:
Exchange:
Fiscal Year Ends: 12/31

SALARIES/BONUSES:

Top Exec. Salary: $ Bonus: $
Second Exec. Salary: $ Bonus: $

OTHER THOUGHTS:

Estimated Female Officers or Directors:
Hot Spot for Advancement for Women/Minorities:

O Reilly Automotive Inc

www.oreillyauto.com

NAIC Code: 441310

TYPES OF BUSINESS:

Auto Parts Stores
Tools
Auto Accessories

BRANDS/DIVISIONS/AFFILIATES:

O'Reilly Auto Parts
Power Torque
BrakeBest
Prestone
Master Pro
Omnispark
Super Start
Ultima

CONTACTS: *Note: Officers with more than one job title may be intentionally listed here more than once.*

Thomas McFall, CFO
Jonathan Andrews, Senior VP, Divisional
David OReilly, Chairman of the Board
Jeremy Fletcher, Controller
Gregory Johnson, Co-President
Jeff Shaw, Co-President
Lawrence OReilly, Co-Vice Chairman of the Board
Gregory Henslee, Co-Vice Chairman of the Board
Brad Beckham, Executive VP, Divisional
Jeffrey Lauro, Senior VP, Divisional
Scott Kraus, Senior VP, Divisional
Carl Wilbanks, Senior VP, Divisional
Robert Dumas, Senior VP, Divisional
Doug Bragg, Senior VP, Divisional
Richard Venosdel, Senior VP, Divisional
Jason Tarrant, Senior VP, Divisional
Larry Ellis, Senior VP, Divisional
Brent Kirby, Senior VP, Divisional
Jeffrey Groves, Senior VP, Divisional

GROWTH PLANS/SPECIAL FEATURES:

O'Reilly Automotive, Inc. is one of the largest specialty retailers of automotive aftermarket parts, tools, supplies, equipment and accessories in the U.S., selling products to both do-it-yourself (DIY) customers and professional installers. The company operates 5,344 stores under the O'Reilly Auto Parts name in 47 states across the U.S. Stores carry an average of 48,000 stock keeping units (SKUs) with an extensive product line consisting of new and remanufactured automotive hard parts, such as alternators, starters, brake system components, batteries, chassis parts and engine parts; maintenance items, such as oil, antifreeze, fluids, wiper blades, lighting, engine additives and appearance products; accessories, such as floor mats, truck accessories and seat covers; and a complete line of auto body paint and related materials, automotive tools and professional service equipment. Store merchandise generally consists of nationally recognized, well-advertised, name brand products such as AC Delco, Armor All, Bosch, BWD, Cardone, Castrol, Gates Rubber, Monroe, Moog, Pennzoil, Prestone, Quaker State, STP, Turtle Wax, Valvoline, Wagner and Wix. In addition to name-brand products, stores carry a wide variety of high-quality private-label products under the BestTest, BrakeBest, Import Direct, Master Pro, Micro-Gard, Murray, Omnispark, Precision, Power Torque, Super Start and Ultima brands. O'Reilly operates 27 distribution centers and 342 hub stores, each equipped with highly automated material handling equipment that expedites the movement of products to loading areas for shipment to individual stores on a nightly basis. In August 2019, O'Reilly agreed to acquire an auto parts company in Guadalajara, Mexico, called Mayoreo de Autopartes Y Aceites SA de CV.

O'Reilly offers its employees medical, dental, vision, pharmacy and life insurance; a credit union membership; a 401(k) plan with company match; a profit sharing plan; paid time off; a discount stock purchase plan; and an employee assistance program.

FINANCIAL DATA: *Note: Data for latest year may not have been available at press time.*

In U.S. $	2018	2017	2016	2015	2014	2013
Revenue	9,536,428,000	8,977,726,000	8,593,096,000	7,966,674,000	7,216,081,000	6,649,237,000
R&D Expense						
Operating Income	1,815,184,000	1,725,400,000	1,699,206,000	1,514,021,000	1,270,374,000	1,103,485,000
Operating Margin %		.19%	.20%	.19%	.18%	.17%
SGA Expense	3,224,782,000	2,995,283,000	2,809,805,000	2,648,622,000	2,438,527,000	2,265,516,000
Net Income	1,324,487,000	1,133,804,000	1,037,691,000	931,216,000	778,182,000	670,292,000
Operating Cash Flow	1,727,555,000	1,403,687,000	1,454,167,000	1,281,476,000	1,190,430,000	908,026,000
Capital Expenditure	504,268,000	465,940,000	476,344,000	414,020,000	429,987,000	395,881,000
EBITDA	2,075,153,000	1,962,998,000	1,925,988,000	1,727,751,000	1,469,677,000	1,291,196,000
Return on Assets %		.15%	.15%	.14%	.12%	.11%
Return on Equity %		.99%	.58%	.47%	.39%	.33%
Debt to Equity		4.561	1.16	0.709	0.692	0.71

CONTACT INFORMATION:

Phone: 417 862-6708 Fax: 417 863-2242
Toll-Free: 800-755-6759
Address: 233 S. Patterson Ave., Springfield, MO 65802 United States

STOCK TICKER/OTHER:

Stock Ticker: ORLY
Exchange: NAS
Employees: 74,580
Fiscal Year Ends: 12/31
Parent Company:

SALARIES/BONUSES:

Top Exec. Salary: $803,846 Bonus: $
Second Exec. Salary: $771,154 Bonus: $

OTHER THOUGHTS:

Estimated Female Officers or Directors: 1
Hot Spot for Advancement for Women/Minorities: Y

OnStar LLC

NAIC Code: 517210

www.onstar.com

TYPES OF BUSINESS:

Vehicle Telematics
Safety Services
Roadside Assistance
Accident Assistance
Communications Services
Stolen Vehicle Recovery
GPS Systems

BRANDS/DIVISIONS/AFFILIATES:

General Motors Company (GM)

GROWTH PLANS/SPECIAL FEATURES:

OnStar, LLC, a subsidiary of General Motors Company, provides in-vehicle safety and security services. These services include 24-hour-a-day access to trained service advisors. The company's safety and security services include automatic crash response, emergency services, roadside assistance, crisis assist, stolen vehicle assistance and turn-by-turn navigation. OnStar currently offers three service plans: the connected access plan, the remote access plan and the unlimited access plan. Each plan offers a range of diagnostic and vehicle location services, with the services becoming more in depth as the monthly fee increases. The connected access plan comes free with the purchase of a Chevrolet, Buick, GMC or Cadillac. The remote access plan costs $14.99 a month and the unlimited costs $39.99 a month.

CONTACTS:

Note: Officers with more than one job title may be intentionally listed here more than once.

Santiago Chamorro, VP
Greg Ross, Dir.-Prod. Strategy
Phil Abram, Exec. Dir.

FINANCIAL DATA:

Note: Data for latest year may not have been available at press time.

In U.S. $	2018	2017	2016	2015	2014	2013
Revenue	2,100,000,000	2,021,250,000	1,925,000,000	1,880,000,000	1,680,000,000	1,657,000,000
R&D Expense						
Operating Income						
Operating Margin %						
SGA Expense						
Net Income						
Operating Cash Flow						
Capital Expenditure						
EBITDA						
Return on Assets %						
Return on Equity %						
Debt to Equity						

CONTACT INFORMATION:

Phone: 248-588-6050   Fax: 313-667-0822
Toll-Free: 888-466-7827
Address: 400 Renaissance Ctr., Detroit, MI 48265 United States

STOCK TICKER/OTHER:

Stock Ticker: Subsidiary   Exchange:
Employees: Fiscal Year Ends: 12/31
Parent Company: General Motors Company (GM)

SALARIES/BONUSES:

Top Exec. Salary: $ Bonus: $
Second Exec. Salary: $ Bonus: $

OTHER THOUGHTS:

Estimated Female Officers or Directors: 1
Hot Spot for Advancement for Women/Minorities:

Opel Automobile GmbH

www.opel.com

NAIC Code: 336111

TYPES OF BUSINESS:

Automobile Manufacturing

BRANDS/DIVISIONS/AFFILIATES:

Opel Group GmbH
Vauxhall
ADAM
Ampera-e
Corsa
Grandland X Hybrid
KARL
Zafira

CONTACTS:

Note: Officers with more than one job title may be intentionally listed here more than once.

Michael Lohscheller, CEO
Stephen J. Girsky, Pres., GM Europe
Frederic Brunet, Dir.-Finance & IT
Xavier Duchemin, Dir.-Sales & Mktg.
Ralph Wangemann, Dir.-Human Resources
Michael F. Ableson, VP-Eng.
Peter Thom, VP-Mfg.
Johan Willems, Communications
Susanna Webber, VP-Supply Chain & Purchasing

GROWTH PLANS/SPECIAL FEATURES:

Opel Automobile GmbH, along with its Vauxhall sister brand in the U.K., is a European manufacturer of passenger cars, trucks, commercial vehicles, automobile parts and accessories. Beginning with the manufacture of sewing machines and bikes, the firm's founder, Adam Opel, began making automobiles in 1899. Opel operates 12 plants and four development & test centers in eight European countries, and its cars are sold in more than 50 countries, including locations in the Middle East, Asia Pacific and South America. Opel sells more than 1 million passenger cars and light commercial vehicles every year. In the interest of cutting down on carbon dioxide emissions, the company offers compressed natural gas (CNG) and liquefied petroleum gas (LPG) powered models for several of its vehicles. Subsidiary Opel Group GmbH is responsible for Opel/Vauxhall. Passenger car models offered by Opel include the ADAM, Ampera-e, Astra, Cascada, Corsa, Crossland Insignia, KARL, Mokka X, Vivaro and Zafira. Commercial vehicle models include the Combo, Corsavan, Movano, and Vivaro. After having brought seven new automobile models to market in 2017, the firm followed in 2018 with three new models: the Insignia GSi, Corsa GSi and a new edition of the Combo. For 2019 Opel is planning a new generation of the Corsa, to be followed by nine new models in 2020.

FINANCIAL DATA:

Note: Data for latest year may not have been available at press time.

In U.S. $	2018	2017	2016	2015	2014	2013
Revenue	9,103,647,000	8,670,140,000	18,900,000,000	20,000,000,000	20,400,000,000	20,100,000,000
R&D Expense						
Operating Income						
Operating Margin %						
SGA Expense						
Net Income			-10,200,000	-15,000,000	-260,000,000	-837,000,000
Operating Cash Flow						
Capital Expenditure						
EBITDA						
Return on Assets %						
Return on Equity %						
Debt to Equity						

CONTACT INFORMATION:

Phone: 49-061-42-7-70 Fax: 49-061-42-7-88-00
Toll-Free:
Address: Bahnhofspl 1, Russelsheim, D-65423 Germany

STOCK TICKER/OTHER:

Stock Ticker: Subsidiary
Exchange:
Employees: 37,000
Fiscal Year Ends: 12/31
Parent Company: Peugeot SA (Groupe PSA)

SALARIES/BONUSES:

Top Exec. Salary: $ Bonus: $
Second Exec. Salary: $ Bonus: $

OTHER THOUGHTS:

Estimated Female Officers or Directors: 1
Hot Spot for Advancement for Women/Minorities: Y

Orbital Corporation Limited

orbitalcorp.com.au/

NAIC Code: 336300

TYPES OF BUSINESS:

Automobile Parts Manufacturer
Fuel Injection Engines
Combustion Engines
Control System Technologies
Engineering Services

BRANDS/DIVISIONS/AFFILIATES:

ORBITAL UAV
FlexDI

CONTACTS:

Note: Officers with more than one job title may be intentionally listed here more than once.

Todd Alder, CEO
Geoff Paul Cathcart, Dir.-Eng.
Ian Veitch, Sec.
Luke Colzato, Gen. Mgr.-Orbital Autogas Systems
Steven Ahern, Dir.-Intellectual Property Mgmt. & Planning
John Welborn, Chmn.

GROWTH PLANS/SPECIAL FEATURES:

Orbital Corporation Limited invents and builds smart technology for the aerospace and military industries. The company operates on a global scale, and is headquartered in Perth, Australia. Within the aerospace industry, the company's ORBITAL UAV offering comprises engine development technology used to design, develop and construct engines and propulsion systems for unmanned aerial vehicles (UAVs). Orbital's proprietary FlexDI technology provides heavy fuel solutions for military applications, and is used to secure a commercial production contract for the development of large-scale commercial UAV production facilities in the U.S. Its patented fuel injection system enables advanced spark ignition using heavy fuel-a requirement for military applications due to fuel, logistics, defense policy and site safety. FlexDI's combustion systems allows vehicles to use almost any type of common fuel (including gasoline, ethanol, compressed natural gas and hydrogen, or mixtures of these) without redesigning the base engine. Orbital UAV provides testing, validation and refurbishment services in its facilities.

FINANCIAL DATA:

Note: Data for latest year may not have been available at press time.

In U.S. $	2018	2017	2016	2015	2014	2013
Revenue	15,508,900	11,214,800	8,491,390	7,039,720	5,651,430	23,689,200
R&D Expense						
Operating Income						
Operating Margin %						
SGA Expense						
Net Income	1,638,030	-9,582,050	1,950,320	-3,446,260	1,366,980	322,966
Operating Cash Flow						
Capital Expenditure						
EBITDA						
Return on Assets %						
Return on Equity %						
Debt to Equity						

CONTACT INFORMATION:

Phone: 61 894412311 Fax: 61 894412111
Toll-Free:
Address: 4 Whipple St., Balcatta, WA 6021 Australia

STOCK TICKER/OTHER:

Stock Ticker: OEC
Exchange: ASX
Employees: 62
Fiscal Year Ends: 06/30
Parent Company:

SALARIES/BONUSES:

Top Exec. Salary: $ Bonus: $
Second Exec. Salary: $ Bonus: $

OTHER THOUGHTS:

Estimated Female Officers or Directors: 1
Hot Spot for Advancement for Women/Minorities:

Oshkosh Corporation

www.oshkoshcorporation.com

NAIC Code: 336120

TYPES OF BUSINESS:

Fire & Emergency Vehicles
Military Trucks
Truck Bodies
Specialty Trucks
Cement Mixers
Refuse Trucks

BRANDS/DIVISIONS/AFFILIATES:

JLG Industries Inc
Pierce Manufacturing Inc
Jerr-Dan

CONTACTS: *Note: Officers with more than one job title may be intentionally listed here more than once.*

William Jones, CEO
Tina Schoner, Other Executive Officer
David Sagehorn, CFO
Craig Omtvedt, Chairman of the Board
James Freeders, Chief Accounting Officer
Anupam Khare, Chief Information Officer
Bryan Brandt, Chief Marketing Officer
John Pfeifer, COO
Ignacio Cortina, Executive VP
Robert Sims, Executive VP
John Bryant, Executive VP
James Johnson, Executive VP
Frank Nerenhausen, Executive VP
Bradley Nelson, President, Divisional
Robert Messina, Senior VP, Divisional
Marek May, Senior VP, Divisional

GROWTH PLANS/SPECIAL FEATURES:

Oshkosh Corporation is a leading designer, manufacturer and marketer of specialty vehicles and vehicle bodies. The company operates in four segments: access equipment, defense, fire and emergency and commercial. The access equipment segment, accounting for 49% of the firm's sales, is formed through JLG Industries, Inc. a global manufacturer of aerial work platforms and telehandlers used in a wide variety of construction, agricultural, industrial, institutional and general maintenance applications to position workers and materials at elevated heights. This segment also manufactures towing and recovery equipment in the U.S. under the Jerr-Dan brand name. The defense segment, accounting for roughly 24% of the company's sales, supplies severe-duty, heavy-payload tactical trucks to the U.S. Department of Defense (DoD). The fire and emergency segment (14%), through subsidiary Pierce Manufacturing, Inc., is a leading domestic manufacturer of fire apparatus assembled on custom chassis. It also manufactures fire apparatus assembled on commercially-available chassis, snow removal vehicles and emergency vehicles, including pumpers; aerial and ladder trucks; tankers; light-, medium- and heavy-duty rescue vehicles; rough terrain response vehicles; mobile command and control centers; bomb squad vehicles; and hazardous materials control vehicles. The segment sells aircraft rescue and fire fighting (ARFF) vehicles to domestic and international airports. The commercial segment (13%), manufactures rear- and front-discharge concrete mixers, refuse collection vehicles, mobile and stationary compactors and waste transfer units, portable and stationary concrete batch plants and vehicle components. Oshkosh Corporation purchased part of the Lake Shore Municipal Golf Course in Oshkosh, Wisconsin to build its new headquarters on the property, with construction occurring through 2019. The city plans to redevelop the rest of the golf course into a new public space.

The firm offers employees medical, prescription, dental, vision, AD&D, disability and life insurance; 401(k), pension and stock purchase programs; and tuition reimbursement.

FINANCIAL DATA: *Note: Data for latest year may not have been available at press time.*

In U.S. $	2018	2017	2016	2015	2014	2013
Revenue	7,705,500,000	6,829,600,000	6,279,200,000	6,098,100,000	6,808,200,000	7,665,100,000
R&D Expense						
Operating Income	653,500,000	463,000,000	390,900,000	398,600,000	503,300,000	514,700,000
Operating Margin %		.07%	.06%	.07%	.07%	.07%
SGA Expense	663,900,000	665,600,000	612,400,000	587,400,000	624,100,000	620,500,000
Net Income	471,900,000	285,600,000	216,400,000	229,500,000	309,300,000	318,000,000
Operating Cash Flow	436,300,000	246,500,000	577,700,000	82,500,000	170,400,000	438,000,000
Capital Expenditure	100,100,000	113,200,000	127,300,000	158,000,000	124,900,000	59,900,000
EBITDA	786,000,000	601,400,000	496,200,000	520,700,000	630,100,000	637,800,000
Return on Assets %		.06%	.05%	.05%	.07%	.07%
Return on Equity %		.13%	.11%	.12%	.15%	.16%
Debt to Equity		0.35	0.418	0.447	0.441	0.422

CONTACT INFORMATION:

Phone: 920 235-9151 Fax:
Toll-Free:
Address: 2307 Oregon St., Oshkosh, WI 54902 United States

STOCK TICKER/OTHER:

Stock Ticker: OSK
Employees: 13,800
Parent Company:
Exchange: NYS
Fiscal Year Ends: 09/30

SALARIES/BONUSES:

Top Exec. Salary: $1,161,923 Bonus: $
Second Exec. Salary: $700,818 Bonus: $

OTHER THOUGHTS:

Estimated Female Officers or Directors: 5
Hot Spot for Advancement for Women/Minorities: Y

Otokar Otomotiv ve Savunma Sanayi AS

www.otokar.com.tr

NAIC Code: 336111

TYPES OF BUSINESS:

Automobile Manufacturing

BRANDS/DIVISIONS/AFFILIATES:

Koc Holding AS
Navigo
Vectio
Ulyso
Territo
Otokar Atlas
AKREP
TULPAR

CONTACTS: *Note: Officers with more than one job title may be intentionally listed here more than once.*

Rildirim Ali Koc, Chmn.

GROWTH PLANS/SPECIAL FEATURES:

Otokar Otomotiv ve Savunma Sanayi AS is a Turkey-based automotive design firm. Otokar designs, manufactures and sells vehicles including minibuses, medium-sized buses, trailers and military vehicles, among other related products. The firm operates in four segments: bus, truck, trailer and military. The bus segment comprises city buses such as the Navigo C, Vectio C and Kent C; tourism buses such as the Navigo T and the Ulyso T; and intercity buses such as the Navigo U, Vectio U, Vectio U LE and Territo U. The truck segment includes the Otokar Atlas, a medium-class truck with a maximum loaded weight of 8.5 tons and comes as either a short or long wheelbase. The trailer segment offers tanker semi-trailers and refrigerated trailers. Tanker semi-trailers include cylindrical, elliptical and maxi sectioned semi-trailer and truck body applications for transporting dangerous goods with aluminum sheet construction. Refrigerated trailers are used for the transport of perishable goods. The military segment designs, develops and manufactures state-of-the-art tactical vehicles in various configurations, covering the full range of armored vehicles, from 4.4 tons (4 tonnes) to battle tanks. Oktar's military vehicles are grouped into three categories: wheeled armored, tracked armored and turret systems. They operate under different geographical and extreme climate conditions worldwide. Wheeled armored vehicle models include AKREP, ARMA, COBRA, KALE, KAYA, URAL and ISV; and tracked vehicle models include TULPAR and ALTAY. This segment also produces turret systems, primarily for tank guns, which contain a bearing system that enables the rotation around a fixed part. The firm's single manufacturing plant is a nearly 6-million-square-foot facility located in Sakarya. Koc Holding AS is the company's major shareholder.

FINANCIAL DATA: *Note: Data for latest year may not have been available at press time.*

In U.S. $	2018	2017	2016	2015	2014	2013
Revenue		435,963,904	399,148,896	350,175,328	300,765,280	342,259,584
R&D Expense						
Operating Income						
Operating Margin %						
SGA Expense						
Net Income		24,279,122	17,027,074	19,415,422	17,770,746	23,580,402
Operating Cash Flow						
Capital Expenditure						
EBITDA						
Return on Assets %						
Return on Equity %						
Debt to Equity						

CONTACT INFORMATION:

Phone: 90-216-489-2950 Fax: 90-216-489-2967
Toll-Free:
Address: Aydinevler Mah. Dumlupinar Cad., No.58, A Blok, Istanbul, 34854 Turkey

STOCK TICKER/OTHER:

Stock Ticker: OTKAR Exchange: IST
Employees: 2,147 Fiscal Year Ends:
Parent Company:

SALARIES/BONUSES:

Top Exec. Salary: $ Bonus: $
Second Exec. Salary: $ Bonus: $

OTHER THOUGHTS:

Estimated Female Officers or Directors:
Hot Spot for Advancement for Women/Minorities:

Ourisman Automotive Enterprises

www.ourisman.com

NAIC Code: 441110

TYPES OF BUSINESS:

Auto Dealers, Retail
Auto Service
Auto Financing
Fleet Sales

BRANDS/DIVISIONS/AFFILIATES:

CONTACTS:

Note: Officers with more than one job title may be intentionally listed here more than once.

Chris Ourisman, Pres.

GROWTH PLANS/SPECIAL FEATURES:

Ourisman Automotive Enterprises is a family-owned automobile dealership company headquartered in the Washington, D.C. area. The company operates approximately 30 new and pre-owned automobile franchise dealerships primarily located in Maryland and Virginia, as well as one in Chicago, Illinois. Ourisman sells vehicles from automakers such as Audi, Buick, Chevrolet, Chrysler, Dodge, Ford, GMC, Honda, Hyundai, Jeep, Kia, Lincoln, Mazda, Mitsubishi, Ram, Toyota, Volkswagen and Volvo. Vehicle models include cargo vans, convertibles, coups, crossovers, hatchbacks, sedans, sport utility vehicles (SUVs), trucks, minivans, vans and wagons. Ourisman's Ford dealership sells and services a full line of commercial trucks. Via the company's website, customers can link to individual dealership sites for searching all of Ourisman's new and pre-owned inventory, schedule service appointments and apply for financing. The site also provides credit checks, payment calculations and detailed information regarding each used vehicle, including lemon checks and history reports.

FINANCIAL DATA:

Note: Data for latest year may not have been available at press time.

In U.S. $	2018	2017	2016	2015	2014	2013
Revenue	1,400,000,000	1,362,454,497	1,297,575,711	1,249,628,119	1,087,818,338	904,133,882
R&D Expense						
Operating Income						
Operating Margin %						
SGA Expense						
Net Income						
Operating Cash Flow						
Capital Expenditure						
EBITDA						
Return on Assets %						
Return on Equity %						
Debt to Equity						

CONTACT INFORMATION:

Phone: 301-423-4028 Fax: 301-423-5725
Toll-Free:
Address: 4400 Branch Ave., Marlow Heights, MD 20748 United States

STOCK TICKER/OTHER:

Stock Ticker: Private
Employees: 1,660
Parent Company:
Exchange:
Fiscal Year Ends: 12/31

SALARIES/BONUSES:

Top Exec. Salary: $ Bonus: $
Second Exec. Salary: $ Bonus: $

OTHER THOUGHTS:

Estimated Female Officers or Directors:
Hot Spot for Advancement for Women/Minorities:

PACCAR Inc

NAIC Code: 336120

www.paccar.com

TYPES OF BUSINESS:

Truck Manufacturing
Premium Truck Manufacturer
Parts Distribution
Finance, Lease and Insurance Services

BRANDS/DIVISIONS/AFFILIATES:

Kenworth Truck Company
Peterbilt Motors
DAF Trucks
PACCAR Financial Services
Carco
Braden
Gearmatic

CONTACTS: *Note: Officers with more than one job title may be intentionally listed here more than once.*

Ronald Armstrong, CEO
Jack LeVier, VP, Divisional
Harrie Schippers, CFO
Mark Pigott, Chairman of the Board
Michael Barkley, Chief Accounting Officer
A Ley, Chief Information Officer
T. Quinn, Chief Technology Officer
Gary Moore, Executive VP
Preston Feight, Executive VP, Subsidiary
David Danforth, General Manager, Divisional
Jason Skoog, General Manager, Subsidiary
Michael Dozier, General Manager, Subsidiary
Harry Wolters, President, Subsidiary
Darrin Siver, Senior VP
Marco Davila, Vice President
Todd Hubbard, Vice President, Divisional
Douglas Grandstaff, Vice President

GROWTH PLANS/SPECIAL FEATURES:

PACCAR, Inc. is a leading manufacturer of premium light-, medium- and heavy-duty trucks. The firm operates in three major divisions: trucks, parts and financial services. Truck division subsidiaries include Kenworth Truck Company, Peterbilt Motors and DAF Trucks. The vehicles are used worldwide for over-the-road and off-highway hauling of freight, petroleum, wood products, construction and other materials. The Kenworth and Peterbilt nameplates are manufactured and distributed by separate divisions in the U.S. and foreign plants in Canada, Mexico and Australia. Headquartered in the Netherlands, DAF Trucks comprises the European component of PACCAR, with distribution throughout Europe, Asia and Africa. Products and services are available worldwide, with customer call centers operating continuously. Substantially all trucks and related parts are sold to independent dealers, and this division accounts for 76% of net sales. The parts division includes the distribution of aftermarket parts for trucks and related commercial vehicles in the U.S., Canada, Europe, Australia, Mexico and South America. Aftermarket truck parts are sold and delivered to the company's independent dealers through the firm's 18 strategically-located distribution centers. The parts segment accounts for 17% of net sales. The company's financial services segment (7% of net sales), which operates through wholly-owned subsidiary PACCAR Financial Services, maintains a presence in over 24 countries. This division provides financing and leasing arrangements, mainly for its manufactured trucks. The company's share of the U.S. and Canadian Class 8 truck market is roughly 30.7%. In addition, other businesses (less than 1% of net sales) consists of a manufacturing division, which makes industrial winches in two U.S. plants and markets them under the Braden, Carco and Gearmatic nameplates. PACCAR also designs and manufactures advanced diesel engines, provides financial services, IT and distributes truck parts.

FINANCIAL DATA: *Note: Data for latest year may not have been available at press time.*

In U.S. $	2018	2017	2016	2015	2014	2013
Revenue	23,495,700,000	19,456,400,000	17,033,300,000	19,115,100,000	18,997,000,000	17,123,800,000
R&D Expense	306,100,000	264,700,000	247,200,000	239,800,000	215,600,000	251,400,000
Operating Income	2,688,500,000	2,143,600,000	1,947,400,000	2,327,600,000	2,000,800,000	1,671,700,000
Operating Margin %		.12%	.12%	.11%	.09%	.08%
SGA Expense	644,700,000	555,000,000	540,200,000	541,500,000	561,400,000	559,500,000
Net Income	2,195,100,000	1,675,200,000	521,700,000	1,604,000,000	1,358,800,000	1,171,300,000
Operating Cash Flow	2,992,300,000	2,715,800,000	2,300,800,000	2,556,000,000	2,123,600,000	2,375,700,000
Capital Expenditure	1,952,300,000	1,846,600,000	1,964,900,000	1,725,200,000	1,537,300,000	1,872,800,000
EBITDA	3,742,600,000	3,251,100,000	2,940,500,000	3,234,700,000	2,918,500,000	2,482,400,000
Return on Assets %		.08%	.02%	.08%	.07%	.06%
Return on Equity %		.23%	.08%	.23%	.20%	.19%
Debt to Equity		0.739	0.889	0.835	0.828	0.906

CONTACT INFORMATION:

Phone: 425 468-7400 Fax: 425 468-8216
Toll-Free:
Address: 777 106th Ave. NE, Bellevue, WA 98004 United States

STOCK TICKER/OTHER:

Stock Ticker: PCAR
Exchange: NAS
Employees: 23,000
Fiscal Year Ends: 12/31
Parent Company:

SALARIES/BONUSES:

Top Exec. Salary: $1,373,077 Bonus: $
Second Exec. Salary: $798,077 Bonus: $

OTHER THOUGHTS:

Estimated Female Officers or Directors:
Hot Spot for Advancement for Women/Minorities:

Pendragon PLC

NAIC Code: 441110

www.pendragonplc.com

TYPES OF BUSINESS:

New Car Dealers

BRANDS/DIVISIONS/AFFILIATES:

Evans Halshaw
Stratstone
Hornburg
Pinewood Technologies

CONTACTS:

Note: Officers with more than one job title may be intentionally listed here more than once.

Martin Casha, COO
Mark Willis, CFO
Chris Chambers, Chmn.

GROWTH PLANS/SPECIAL FEATURES:

Pendragon PLC sells vehicles through retail and online channels, primarily serving the U.K. and the U.S. markets. The company's businesses encompass the sale of new and used vehicles, aftersales and repair services. Within the U.K., the Evans Halshaw and Stratstone brands focus on the retail and repair of used and new cars, vans, trucks and motorcycles. In California, USA, the Hornburg brand focuses on the retail and repair of new and used cars. Pendragon provides the following services and solutions: dealer management systems globally through its Pinewood Technologies brand; vehicle leasing management through its tailored fleet solutions; and new, used and aftersales vehicle solutions for the group. Pendragon's new car division sells vehicle units to individual customers, and also sells multiple vehicles to businesses (fleet market). Aftersales services encompass maintenance and repair of motor vehicles, including body shop repair, and the retailing of parts and other motor-related accessories. The aftersales division derives the majority of annual revenues, with new car sales coming in second and used car sales third. Support and services derive the remainder of revenues. In July 2019, Pendragon sold certain dealerships from its U.S. division, including its Jaguar Land Rover dealership in Mission Viejo, California.

FINANCIAL DATA:

Note: Data for latest year may not have been available at press time.

In U.S. $	2018	2017	2016	2015	2014	2013
Revenue	5,042,113,000	5,759,793,000	5,514,165,000	5,413,167,000	4,861,993,000	4,677,864,000
R&D Expense						
Operating Income	-47,035,080	105,008,600	115,217,700	111,814,700	104,522,400	90,180,960
Operating Margin %		.02%	.02%	.02%	.02%	.02%
SGA Expense		566,973,300	564,907,100	555,305,700	530,633,500	517,385,900
Net Income	-61,376,530	64,779,590	67,453,420	88,600,980	60,525,770	47,642,770
Operating Cash Flow	63,685,750	112,787,000	73,044,150	90,545,580	83,982,540	127,250,000
Capital Expenditure	161,888,200	234,567,700	178,660,400	166,385,100	117,526,900	82,767,160
EBITDA	2,066,141	142,563,700	156,419,000	177,931,200	149,612,900	111,207,000
Return on Assets %		.03%	.03%	.04%	.03%	.03%
Return on Equity %		.13%	.14%	.20%	.15%	.14%
Debt to Equity		0.417	0.471	0.553	0.589	0.649

CONTACT INFORMATION:

Phone: 44 1623725000 Fax: 44 1623725015
Toll-Free:
Address: Loxley House, 2 Oakwood Court, Little Oak Drive, Annesley, Nottingham NG15 0DR United Kingdom

STOCK TICKER/OTHER:

Stock Ticker: PDGNF
Employees: 9,199
Parent Company:
Exchange: GREY
Fiscal Year Ends: 12/31

SALARIES/BONUSES:

Top Exec. Salary: $563,935 Bonus: $
Second Exec. Salary: $354,890 Bonus: $

OTHER THOUGHTS:

Estimated Female Officers or Directors:
Hot Spot for Advancement for Women/Minorities:

Penske Automotive Group Inc

NAIC Code: 441110

www.penskeautomotive.com

TYPES OF BUSINESS:

Auto Dealers
Automotive Leasing
Parts & Service

BRANDS/DIVISIONS/AFFILIATES:

CarSense
CarShop
Penske Commercial Vehicles Australia
Penske Power Systems
Penske Truck Leasing Co LP

CONTACTS: *Note: Officers with more than one job title may be intentionally listed here more than once.*

Roger Penske, CEO
J. Carlson, Chief Accounting Officer
Robert Kurnick, Director
Bud Denker, Executive VP, Divisional
Shane Spradlin, Executive VP

GROWTH PLANS/SPECIAL FEATURES:

Penske Automotive Group, Inc. (PAG) is an international transportation services company operating automotive and commercial truck dealerships primarily in the U.S., Canada and western Europe. PAG also distributes commercial vehicles, diesel engines, gas engines, power systems and related parts and services principally in Australia and New Zealand. As of December 31, 2018, PAG operated 345 automotive retail franchises, of which 154 are located in the U.S. and 191 outside of the U.S. The franchises outside the U.S. are located primarily in the U.K. This division also operates 14 stand-alone used vehicle supercenters in the U.S. and U.K., which retail and wholesale pre-owned vehicles under a one price, no haggle methodology. Through subsidiary CarSense operates five U.S. retail locations and five U.K. retail locations, as well as a vehicle preparation center under the CarShop name. In 2018, PAG company retailed and wholesaled more than 644,000 vehicles. The commercial vehicle is the exclusive importer and distributor of Western Star heavy-duty trucks (a Daimler brand), MAN heavy- and medium-duty trucks and buses (a Volkswagen brand), and Dennis Eagle refuse collection vehicles across Australia and New Zealand, as well as portions of the Pacific. This business is known as Penske Commercial Vehicles Australia, which distributes commercial vehicles and parts to more than 70 dealership locations, including nine company-owned retail commercial vehicle dealerships. The commercial vehicle segment also distributes engines and power systems for MTU, Detroit Diesel, Allison Transmission and Rolls Royce Power Systems. Penske Power Systems offers products across the on- and off-highway markets, construction, mining, marine and defense. Penske Truck Leasing Co., LP provides transportation and supply chain services.

Employee benefits include medical, dental, prescription, vision and life insurance; a 401(k) with company match; flexible spending accounts; an employee assistance program; and paid time off.

FINANCIAL DATA: *Note: Data for latest year may not have been available at press time.*

In U.S. $	2018	2017	2016	2015	2014	2013
Revenue	22,785,100,000	21,386,900,000	20,118,500,000	19,284,900,000	17,177,200,000	14,705,400,000
R&D Expense						
Operating Income	664,900,000	611,400,000	574,900,000	566,500,000	504,100,000	436,200,000
Operating Margin %		.03%	.03%	.03%	.03%	.03%
SGA Expense	2,646,300,000	2,516,000,000	2,302,000,000	2,223,000,000	1,999,600,000	1,761,900,000
Net Income	471,000,000	613,300,000	342,900,000	326,100,000	286,700,000	244,200,000
Operating Cash Flow	614,700,000	623,500,000	367,100,000	386,000,000	366,600,000	320,100,000
Capital Expenditure	305,600,000	247,000,000	203,100,000	199,500,000	174,800,000	169,900,000
EBITDA	903,400,000	814,100,000	734,100,000	683,800,000	630,900,000	528,600,000
Return on Assets %		.06%	.04%	.04%	.04%	.04%
Return on Equity %		.30%	.19%	.19%	.18%	.17%
Debt to Equity		0.873	1.044	0.701	0.796	0.687

CONTACT INFORMATION:

Phone: 248 648-2500 Fax: 248 648-2525
Toll-Free:
Address: 2555 Telegraph Rd., Bloomfield Hills, MI 48302 United States

STOCK TICKER/OTHER:

Stock Ticker: PAG
Employees: 24,000
Parent Company:
Exchange: NYS
Fiscal Year Ends: 12/31

SALARIES/BONUSES:

Top Exec. Salary: $1,400,000 Bonus: $
Second Exec. Salary: $547,917 Bonus: $350,000

OTHER THOUGHTS:

Estimated Female Officers or Directors: 2
Hot Spot for Advancement for Women/Minorities:

Penske Corporation

www.penske.com

NAIC Code: 532120

TYPES OF BUSINESS:

Truck Rental
Auto Racing
Auto Sales & Service
Supply Chain Solutions
Auto Accessories Manufacturing & Retail
Fuel Management Systems
Fleet Management Services
Vehicle Components & Systems

BRANDS/DIVISIONS/AFFILIATES:

Penske Automotive Group
Penske Motor Group
Penske Truck Leasing
Penske Logistics
Truck-Lite
Davco Technology LLC
Penske Racing
Ilmor Engineering Inc

CONTACTS: *Note: Officers with more than one job title may be intentionally listed here more than once.*

Roger S. Penske, CEO
Robert H. Kurnick Jr., Pres.
Gregory J. Houfley, CFO
Robert H. Kurnick, Jr., Pres., Penske Automotive Group
Calvin C. Sharp, Exec. VP-Human Resources, Penske Automotive Group
David K. Jones, CFO
Shane M. Spradlin, General Counsel
Roger S. Penske, Chmn.
Marc Althen, Pres., Penske Logistics

GROWTH PLANS/SPECIAL FEATURES:

Penske Corporation is a diversified transportation company that participates in a variety of automotive markets through its network of subsidiaries. Its markets include auto sales and service, truck rental, supply chain solutions, vehicle headlight design and development, vehicle lighting and harness safety systems, fluid management and automobile racing. Penske Automotive Group is an international transportation services company that operates retail automotive dealerships, Hertz car rental franchises and commercial vehicle distribution. It operates primarily in the U.S., Western Europe, Australia and New Zealand. Penske Motor Group owns and operates automobile dealerships in California. Penske Truck Leasing operates over 240,000 vehicles, serving customers from more than 3,000 locations in North America, South America, Europe, Australia and Asia. This division comprises Penske Truck Rental, which offers fleet management services including service leasing, truck rentals, logistics, used trucks for sale and felt services for utility and transit companies with municipalities at more than 1,000 Penske facilities nationwide. Penske Logistics focuses on supply chain solutions, providing services designed to cut costs, reduce cycle time, improve service and integrate technology into the operations of its customers. Truck-Lite is responsible for creating vehicle lighting and harness safety systems for fleet vehicles through its affiliated subsidiaries: Truck-Lite Co., LLC and Truck-Lite Europe Limited. Davco Technology, LLC provides diesel fuel management with its line of filters, fuel/water separators and fuel warmers. Davco products include the Sea Pro for marine applications, Diesel Pro for medium trucks and the Industrial Pro for fuel filtration and water separation for industrial applications such as power generation, mining, oil and gas exploration. Penske Racing's operations include teams competing in NASCAR Sprint Cup Series, IndyCar Series, NASCAR Nationwide Series and American Le Mans Series. Other subsidiaries include Premier Truck Group, Penske Vehicle Service, Penske Logistics, and Ilmor Engineering, Inc.

FINANCIAL DATA: *Note: Data for latest year may not have been available at press time.*

In U.S. $	2018	2017	2016	2015	2014	2013
Revenue	27,000,000,000	26,500,000,000	26,000,000,000	23,000,000,000	20,500,000,000	20,000,000,000
R&D Expense						
Operating Income						
Operating Margin %						
SGA Expense						
Net Income						
Operating Cash Flow						
Capital Expenditure						
EBITDA						
Return on Assets %						
Return on Equity %						
Debt to Equity						

CONTACT INFORMATION:

Phone: 248-648-2000 Fax: 248-648-2525
Toll-Free:
Address: 2555 Telegraph Rd., Bloomfield Hills, MI 48302 United States

STOCK TICKER/OTHER:

Stock Ticker: Private
Employees: 52,000
Parent Company:
Exchange:
Fiscal Year Ends: 12/31

SALARIES/BONUSES:

Top Exec. Salary: $ Bonus: $
Second Exec. Salary: $ Bonus: $

OTHER THOUGHTS:

Estimated Female Officers or Directors:
Hot Spot for Advancement for Women/Minorities:

Pep Boys-Manny Moe & Jack (The)

www.pepboys.com

NAIC Code: 441310

TYPES OF BUSINESS:

Auto Parts, Retail
Automotive Services
Installation Services
Used Vehicle Inspections

BRANDS/DIVISIONS/AFFILIATES:

Icahn Automotive Group LLC
Pep Boys Supercenter
Pep Boys Service & Tire Center
Pep Express

CONTACTS: *Note: Officers with more than one job title may be intentionally listed here more than once.*

Anthony Brent Windom, CEO
David Stern, CFO
Brian Zuckerman, General Counsel
Thomas Carey, Other Executive Officer
James Flanagan, Other Executive Officer
Christopher Adams, Senior VP, Divisional
John Kelly, Senior VP, Divisional
Joseph Cirelli, Senior VP, Divisional

GROWTH PLANS/SPECIAL FEATURES:

The Pep Boys-Manny, Moe & Jack, a subsidiary of Icahn Automotive Group, LLC, operates a leading automotive retail and service chain specializing in the sale, installation and servicing of automotive parts, tires and accessories. Pep Boys has approximately 975 locations in 36 U.S. states and Puerto Rico, consisting of Pep Boy Supercenters, Pep Boys Service & Tire Centers and Pep Express stores. Supercenters average approximately 20,000 square feet; and carry more than 25,000 items; and Service & Tire Centers average 6,000 square feet, carrying more than 2,000 items. These items include: parts, such as tires, batteries, shocks, struts, brakes and new and used auto parts; car care, such as motor oil, car soap, wax, additives, chemicals and antifreeze; performance, such as air and fuel delivery, brake kits, ignition and suspension; tools, such as hand tools, jacks, ramps, jump starters, diagnostic tools and canopies/shelters; electronics, such as radar detectors, stereos, GPS/navigation, and backup and dash cameras; and accessories, such as floor mats, seat covers, trunk accessories and travel accessories. The company sells products under national brand names and private labels, including Cornell, Futura, Definity, Pro and Value. Professional automotive services are available at Supercenters or Service & Tire locations, with the average Service & Tire location housing six service bays. Services cover oil changes, transmission flushes, brake services, tire alignments, suspension work, tune-ups and diagnostics, state inspections and emissions testing and air conditioning services.

Employee benefits include medical, dental, vision, life and disability insurance; flexible spending accounts; 401(k)-company match; paid time off; tuition reimbursement; and merchandise discounts.

FINANCIAL DATA: *Note: Data for latest year may not have been available at press time.*

In U.S. $	2018	2017	2016	2015	2014	2013
Revenue	2,315,250,000	2,205,000,000	2,100,000,000	2,084,603,008	2,066,567,936	2,090,729,984
R&D Expense						
Operating Income						
Operating Margin %						
SGA Expense						
Net Income				-27,293,000	6,865,000	12,810,000
Operating Cash Flow						
Capital Expenditure						
EBITDA						
Return on Assets %						
Return on Equity %						
Debt to Equity						

CONTACT INFORMATION:

Phone: 215 430-9000 Fax: 215 227-4067
Toll-Free: 800-737-2697
Address: 3111 W. Allegheny Ave., Philadelphia, PA 19132 United States

STOCK TICKER/OTHER:

Stock Ticker: Subsidiary Exchange:
Employees: 18,914 Fiscal Year Ends: 01/31
Parent Company: Icahn Automotive Group LLC

SALARIES/BONUSES:

Top Exec. Salary: $ Bonus: $
Second Exec. Salary: $ Bonus: $

OTHER THOUGHTS:

Estimated Female Officers or Directors: 1
Hot Spot for Advancement for Women/Minorities:

Peterson Manufacturing Company

www.pmlights.com

NAIC Code: 336300

TYPES OF BUSINESS:

Automotive Lighting Products
Mirrors & Reflectors
Antennas

BRANDS/DIVISIONS/AFFILIATES:

Peterson Corporation LLC
Piranha
PM
Auto Select
Nightwatcher
BladeLights
Maxi-Seal
Great White

CONTACTS:

Note: Officers with more than one job title may be intentionally listed here more than once.

Don R. Armacost, Jr., CEO
Steven Ham, VP-Corp. Mfg.
Steve Hickerson, VP-Finance
Allyn Leake, Mgr.-Heavy Duty Sales
Ryan Eichhorn, Mgr.-OEM Sales
Kristen Goodson, Dir.-Prod. Mgmt.

GROWTH PLANS/SPECIAL FEATURES:

Peterson Manufacturing Company develops and manufactures a complete line of vehicle safety lights, mirrors, reflectors, antennas and other related products. The company sells products both to automotive manufacturers and to major retailers. Some of its major customers have included Harley-Davidson, John Deere, Caterpillar, Wal-Mart, Fleetwood and EZ Loader. Peterson offers over 2,200 products, which include LED (light-emitting diode) lights, incandescent lights, specialty lights (such as dome and interior lights, as well as tow and snow plow lights), halogen lights, mounting and electrical accessories. The firm also offers a line of reflectors, emergency lights, mirrors and antennas. Peterson's Piranha LED light brand lights up faster than ordinary lights and has six times the life expectancy. The company's standard lighting products are sold under the PM brand. The Auto Select brand covers its imported automotive products. Nightwatcher is Peterson's trademark for fog driving and off-road lights. Other brands include BladeLights, for snowplow and emergency lights; Maxi-Seal, for custom wire harness systems for the heavy-duty trucking industry and for its aftermarket electrical accessory program; Great White, for back-up and utility lights; and Spitfire, for micro-prismatic, wide angle reflectors. Although the group is primarily focused on automotive lighting products, Peterson oversees more than 10 business units in different industries, including the agriculture, waste handling, marine, emergency, aviation and military. Peterson Manufacturing operates as a wholly-owned subsidiary of Peterson Corporation, LLC.

FINANCIAL DATA:

Note: Data for latest year may not have been available at press time.

In U.S. $	2018	2017	2016	2015	2014	2013
Revenue	358,312,500	341,250,000	325,000,000	300,000,000	285,000,000	275,000,000
R&D Expense						
Operating Income						
Operating Margin %						
SGA Expense						
Net Income						
Operating Cash Flow						
Capital Expenditure						
EBITDA						
Return on Assets %						
Return on Equity %						
Debt to Equity						

CONTACT INFORMATION:

Phone: 816-765-2000 Fax: 816-761-6693
Toll-Free:
Address: 4200 E. 135th St., Grandview, MO 64030 United States

STOCK TICKER/OTHER:

Stock Ticker: Subsidiary Exchange:
Employees: 725 Fiscal Year Ends: 09/30
Parent Company: Peterson Corporation LLC

SALARIES/BONUSES:

Top Exec. Salary: $ Bonus: $
Second Exec. Salary: $ Bonus: $

OTHER THOUGHTS:

Estimated Female Officers or Directors: 2
Hot Spot for Advancement for Women/Minorities:

Peugeot SA

NAIC Code: 336111

www.groupe-psa.com

TYPES OF BUSINESS:

Automobile Manufacturing
Automotive Equipment & Components
Transportation & Logistics Services
Motorcycles
Financial Services
Industrial Equipment
Engines
Clean Diesel & Hybrid Engine Technology

BRANDS/DIVISIONS/AFFILIATES:

Peugeot
Citroen
DS Automobiles
Free2 Move
PSA Powertrain
Banque PSA Finance
Mister Auto
AutoButler

CONTACTS: *Note: Officers with more than one job title may be intentionally listed here more than once.*

Philippe de Rovira, Dir.-Finance
Xavier Chereau, Exec. VP-Human Resources
Guillaume Faury, Exec. VP-R&D
Pierre Todorov, Corp. Sec.
Denis Martin, Exec. VP-Industrial Oper.
Yves Bonnefont, Exec. VP-Strategy
Jonathan Goodman, Exec. VP-Corp. Comm.
Olivier Sartoris, Investors Rel. Mgr.
Frederic Saint-Geours, VP-Finance
Frederic Saint Geours, Exec. VP-Brands
Christian Peugeot, Exec. VP- Public Affairs & External Rel.
Carlos Gomes, Sr. VP-Latin America
Bernd Schantz, Sr. VP- Russia, Ukraine & CIS
Carlos Tavares, Chmn.
Gregoire Olivier, Exec. VP-Asia
Yannick Bezard, VP-Purchasing

GROWTH PLANS/SPECIAL FEATURES:

Peugeot SA (Groupe PSA) is a leading automobile manufacturer in Europe, producing cars and light commercial vehicles under the Peugeot, Citroen, DS Automobiles, Opel and Vauxhall brand names. Groupe PSA firm sold more than 3.6 million vehicles in fiscal 2017-18, which includes vehicles sold in Europe, Latin America, China, Southeast Asia, Middle East, Africa, Eurasia and India/Pacific. Style ranges include small, super-mini, city, sport utility and hatchback passenger vehicles. Peugot's 3008 model is an SUV; Citrogen's C5 Aircross is the brand's flagship SUV; the DS 7 is a crossback model; and the Opel/Vauxhall Ampera-e is a 100% electric vehicle. During 2018, Opel announced plans to replace Amerpa-e for an all-electric version of the new generation of Opel Corsa, a subcompact hatchback, in 2020. In addition to vehicles, Groupe PSA owns Free2Move, a worldwide mobility service provider offering shared vehicle, scooter or bike services; PSA Powertrain, which adapts the engines and components made by the Group for sale to other vehicle brands and manufacturers; Banque PSA Finance, which provides financing for vehicles sold by the three brands in 18 network countries; Mister Auto, an automotive spare parts eCommerce site, managing approximately 12,000 daily orders; Europar, offering a range of multi-brand spare parts and accessories for the maintenance and repair of vehicles over three years old; and AutoButler, an online platform that allows motorists to find a garage offering the service best suited to their needs by taking into consideration their location, budget and availability. In late-2018, Groupe PSA announced that Toyota Motor Corporation would be acquiring its stake in their joint production of small cars by 2021, but would be expanding their partnership in the production of light commercial vehicles in France and Spain.

FINANCIAL DATA: *Note: Data for latest year may not have been available at press time.*

In U.S. $	2018	2017	2016	2015	2014	2013
Revenue	81,960,800,000	72,198,850,000	59,820,640,000	60,535,870,000	59,352,300,000	59,887,070,000
R&D Expense	2,009,522,000	1,545,616,000	2,120,239,000	2,057,130,000	2,242,028,000	2,087,024,000
Operating Income	6,298,716,000	4,418,734,000	3,581,710,000	3,025,908,000	1,001,993,000	-195,969,900
Operating Margin %		.06%	.06%	.05%	.02%	.00%
SGA Expense	7,332,817,000	6,520,151,000	5,725,199,000	6,173,605,000	6,547,830,000	7,105,846,000
Net Income	3,129,982,000	2,135,740,000	1,915,412,000	995,349,900	-781,665,200	-2,565,323,000
Operating Cash Flow	9,294,730,000	5,842,560,000	7,163,419,000	13,322,630,000	4,499,557,000	1,804,694,000
Capital Expenditure	5,280,115,000	4,826,174,000	3,957,042,000	3,286,094,000	2,764,615,000	2,855,403,000
EBITDA	8,012,622,000	6,240,035,000	5,469,443,000	4,827,281,000	2,926,262,000	2,341,674,000
Return on Assets %		.04%	.04%	.02%	-.01%	-.04%
Return on Equity %		.14%	.15%	.09%	-.09%	-.28%
Debt to Equity		0.328	0.357	0.404	0.697	1.173

CONTACT INFORMATION:

Phone: 33-1-40-66-55-11 Fax:
Toll-Free:
Address: 75, Ave. de la Grande-Armee, Paris, 75116 France

STOCK TICKER/OTHER:

Stock Ticker: PUGOY Exchange: PINX
Employees: 211,013 Fiscal Year Ends: 12/31
Parent Company:

SALARIES/BONUSES:

Top Exec. Salary: $ Bonus: $
Second Exec. Salary: $ Bonus: $

OTHER THOUGHTS:

Estimated Female Officers or Directors: 3
Hot Spot for Advancement for Women/Minorities: Y

Phil Long Dealerships Inc

www.phillong.com

NAIC Code: 441110

TYPES OF BUSINESS:

Auto Dealers
Auto Service
Auto Finance
Collision Repair

BRANDS/DIVISIONS/AFFILIATES:

Phil Long Collision Center
Phil Long Expo Center

CONTACTS: *Note: Officers with more than one job title may be intentionally listed here more than once.*

Jay Cimino, CEO
Dan Jonuska, Operations Mngr.
Shawn Flynn, Dir.-IT
Michelle Narron, Mgr.-Corp. Comm.

GROWTH PLANS/SPECIAL FEATURES:

Phil Long Dealerships, Inc. is a new and used automobile dealer that operates 16 dealerships in Colorado and one in New Mexico. The dealer showrooms offer new and used cars, trucks, vans and SUVs. The dealerships sell and service eight different makes, including Ford, Hyundai, Chevrolet, Mercedes-Benz, Audi, Lincoln and Kia. Phil Long's website offers a link to each individual dealership's website, where customers can apply for credit, obtain and insurance quote, search both new and pre-owned inventory, configure the approximately value of a trade-in, and make appointments with the service or collision departments. Each Phil Long dealership has its own parts and service department as well as a signature Phil Long Collision Center. Phil Long Collision Centers are exclusive to the company's dealerships and stock parts with equivalent fit and finish of the original equipment manufacturer. The firm also operates the Phil Long Expo Center, an indoor, multi-purpose event venue.

FINANCIAL DATA: *Note: Data for latest year may not have been available at press time.*

In U.S. $	2018	2017	2016	2015	2014	2013
Revenue	788,280,347	750,743,188	714,993,512	664,000,000	559,000,000	438,000,000
R&D Expense						
Operating Income						
Operating Margin %						
SGA Expense						
Net Income						
Operating Cash Flow						
Capital Expenditure						
EBITDA						
Return on Assets %						
Return on Equity %						
Debt to Equity						

CONTACT INFORMATION:

Phone: 719-575-7000 Fax: 719-575-7837
Toll-Free:
Address: 1212 A Motor City Dr., Colorado Springs, CO 80906 United States

STOCK TICKER/OTHER:

Stock Ticker: Private
Employees: 1,425
Parent Company:
Exchange:
Fiscal Year Ends: 12/31

SALARIES/BONUSES:

Top Exec. Salary: $ Bonus: $
Second Exec. Salary: $ Bonus: $

OTHER THOUGHTS:

Estimated Female Officers or Directors: 1
Hot Spot for Advancement for Women/Minorities:

Piaggio & C SpA

www.piaggio.com

NAIC Code: 336991

TYPES OF BUSINESS:

Motorcycle Manufacturing
Scooters
Mopeds
Accessories
Engines
Two-Wheel Recreational Vehicles

BRANDS/DIVISIONS/AFFILIATES:

Immsa SpA
Piaggio
Vespa
Scarabeo
Liberty
Beverly
Gita
Piaggio Fast Forward

CONTACTS: *Note: Officers with more than one job title may be intentionally listed here more than once.*

Roberto Colaninno, CEO
Simone Montanari, CFO
Davide Scotti, Dir.-Prod. Dev. & Strategies
Carlo Coppola, Dir.-Mfg. Tech.
Alessandra Simonotto, Dir.-Admin.
Ulisse Spada, Head-Legal
Davide Scotti, Dir.-Strategies
Roberto Maria Zerbi, Mgr.-External Rel. & Institutional Affairs
Gabrielle Galli, Dir.-Finance Mgmt.
Alessandra Simonotto, Dir.-Credit Management
Luciana Franciosi, Dir.-Customer & Dealer Satisfaction System
Ravinder Chopra, Managing Dir.-Piaggio Vehicles Private Ltd.
Stefano Sterpone, Dir- Americas Sales & Mktg.
Roberto Colaninno, Chmn.
Stefano Sterpone, Dir.-EMEA

GROWTH PLANS/SPECIAL FEATURES:

Piaggio & C. SpA is a leading manufacturer of motorized two-wheel vehicles, including racing scooters, mopeds, motorcycles and personal two-wheel recreational vehicles. The company has a commercial presence in over 50 countries in Europe, Asia and the Americas. Piaggio also produces light commercial vehicles, as well as robotics. The firm's two-wheel operations comprise six production facilities located in Italy, Spain, China, India and Vietnam. The company's scooters and motorcycles range from 50cc to 1,400cc and are marketed under the Piaggio, Vespa, Aprilia, Moto Guzzi, Gilera, Derbi and Scarabeo brands. Scooter models include the Liberty, Beverly, Medley and MP3. Piaggio's engine division manufactures a variety of engines, which cover the range of company vehicles and work-related robotics. Through VespaVintage.com, customers can purchase an exclusive line of replacement parts for classic Vespas. Together, Piaggio and Vespa engage in the development of hybrid electric scooters. Piaggio is 55%-owned by Immsi SpA. Piaggio formed a partnership agreement with Foton Motor to co-develop new light-duty commercial vehicles in Italy, with the marketing of its vehicles scheduled to begin mid-2020. Robotics-wise, Piaggio Fast Forward (PFF) is the group's research center based in Boston, Massachusetts, USA, and engaged in mobility activities. PFF produced Gita, an autonomous vehicle designed to assist people.

The firm offers employees benefits such as a company car and medical coverage.

FINANCIAL DATA: *Note: Data for latest year may not have been available at press time.*

In U.S. $	2018	2017	2016	2015	2014	2013
Revenue	1,538,470,000	1,486,327,000	1,453,841,000	1,434,108,000	1,343,304,000	1,342,488,000
R&D Expense						
Operating Income	86,460,370	77,633,970	63,590,570	61,141,500	73,315,990	73,246,240
Operating Margin %		.05%	.04%	.04%	.05%	.05%
SGA Expense						
Net Income	39,941,320	22,125,780	15,544,730	13,145,480	17,786,760	-7,248,672
Operating Cash Flow	163,916,100	166,206,800	140,589,000	142,649,500	73,474,310	39,991,140
Capital Expenditure	127,632,900	95,998,670	107,033,900	112,810,000	105,063,100	96,991,810
EBITDA	229,144,200	212,495,600	186,079,500	176,219,000	171,584,400	162,590,800
Return on Assets %		.01%	.01%	.01%	.01%	.00%
Return on Equity %		.05%	.04%	.03%	.04%	-.02%
Debt to Equity		1.159	1.31	1.228	1.185	1.089

CONTACT INFORMATION:

Phone: 39 0587272111 Fax: 39 0587272344
Toll-Free:
Address: Via Rinaldo Piaggio, n. 25, Pisa, 56025 Italy

STOCK TICKER/OTHER:

Stock Ticker: PIAN Exchange: MEX
Employees: 6,515 Fiscal Year Ends: 12/31
Parent Company: IMMSI SpA

SALARIES/BONUSES:

Top Exec. Salary: $ Bonus: $
Second Exec. Salary: $ Bonus: $

OTHER THOUGHTS:

Estimated Female Officers or Directors: 3
Hot Spot for Advancement for Women/Minorities: Y

Pilkington Group Limited www.pilkington.com/en-gb/uk/about/uk-and-ireland-operations

NAIC Code: 327215

TYPES OF BUSINESS:

Glass Production
Auto Glass
Building Glass
Glass Fiber

BRANDS/DIVISIONS/AFFILIATES:

Nippon Sheet Glass Company Limited
Pilkington Automotive Limited
Pilkington Activ
Pilkington energiKare
Pilkington Pyrodur
Pilkington Suncool
Pilkington K Glass
Pilkington Insulight

CONTACTS: *Note: Officers with more than one job title may be intentionally listed here more than once.*

Shigeki Mori, CEO-NSG
David Roycroft, Head-Corp. Affairs
David Roycroft, Head-Investor Rel.
Mark Lyons, Pres., Building Prod. Worldwide
Mike Fallon, Pres., Automotive Prod. Worldwide

GROWTH PLANS/SPECIAL FEATURES:

Pilkington Group Limited, a subsidiary of Nippon Sheet Glass Company Limited (NSG), is a leading glass manufacturer and supplier in the U.K. The company develops glass technology, with some of the NSG Group's major manufacturing facilities across the nation. Its glass solutions include float, rolled and coated glass, as well as glass processing. The firm distributes its products to various merchants, building/construction industries and automotive original equipment/automotive glass replacement manufacturers. Pilkington is based in St. Helens, U.K., as well as at the NSG European technical center in Lathom, Lancashire. The firm operates two float glass lines in St. Helens (Greengate and Cowley Hill), a rolled glass operation at Watson Street and an advanced offline coating line at Cowley Hill. Pilkington also supplies laminated glass and fire-resistant glass from its St. Helens facility. Pilkington's architectural division manufactures the patented Pilkington Planar structural glazing system for distribution worldwide. The company's insulating glazing units incorporate toughened, laminated and fire-resistant glass products, as well as a range of coated glass for solar control and thermal insulation for distribution worldwide. Brands of the firm include Pilkington Activ, Pilkington energiKare, Pilkington Pyrostop, Pilkington Pyrodur, Pilkington Suncool, Pilkington K Glass, Pilkington Optitherm and Pilkington Insulight. Subsidiary Pilkington Automotive Limited offers specific glass technology for the automotive industry. This division operates three facilities in the U.K., supplying glass solutions for original equipment and replacement glass manufacturers. These facilities are located in Kings Norton, Redditch and Worcestershire.

FINANCIAL DATA: *Note: Data for latest year may not have been available at press time.*

In U.S. $	2018	2017	2016	2015	2014	2013
Revenue	102,716,000	3,035,929,256	2,891,361,196	3,589,851,565	4,215,762,538	4,760,000,000
R&D Expense						
Operating Income						
Operating Margin %						
SGA Expense						
Net Income	317,004,000	501,679,000	246,686,584	229,366,888		
Operating Cash Flow						
Capital Expenditure						
EBITDA						
Return on Assets %						
Return on Equity %						
Debt to Equity						

CONTACT INFORMATION:

Phone: 44-1744-692837 Fax: 44-1744-692550
Toll-Free:
Address: European Technical Centre, Hall Lane Lathom Nr, Lancashire, L40 5UF United Kingdom

STOCK TICKER/OTHER:

Stock Ticker: Subsidiary Exchange:
Employees: 27,371 Fiscal Year Ends: 03/31
Parent Company: Nippon Sheet Glass Company Limited

SALARIES/BONUSES:

Top Exec. Salary: $ Bonus: $
Second Exec. Salary: $ Bonus: $

OTHER THOUGHTS:

Estimated Female Officers or Directors:
Hot Spot for Advancement for Women/Minorities:

Pininfarina SpA

www.pininfarina.it

NAIC Code: 541330

TYPES OF BUSINESS:

Automotive Design & Engineering Services
Aeronautics Design
Mass Transit Design
Consumer Products Design
Retractable Roof Systems
Engineering Services
Prototype Testing
Automobile Design

BRANDS/DIVISIONS/AFFILIATES:

Mahindra Group
Pininfarina Engineering SRL
Pininfarina Deutschland GmbH
Pininfarina Shanghai Co Ltd
Pininfarina of America Corp
Signature SRL (Pininfarina Segno)
GOODMIND SRL

CONTACTS: *Note: Officers with more than one job title may be intentionally listed here more than once.*

Silvio Pietro Angori, CEO
Andrea Maria Benedetto, VP-Prod. Dev.
Gabriella Isoardi, Dir.-Legal
Silvio Pietro Angori, Interim Dir.-Comm. & Image
Gianfranco Albertini, Gen. Mgr.-Investor Rel.
Fabio Filippini, Dir.-Design
Paolo Pininfarina, Chmn.

GROWTH PLANS/SPECIAL FEATURES:

Pininfarina SpA specializes in providing automotive and general manufacturers with services through all stages of product development, from planning, designing and development to engineering, manufacturing and end-product consultation. Wholly-owned subsidiaries engaged in these business activities include Pininfarina Engineering SRL, Pininfarina Deutschland GmbH, Pininfarina Shanghai Co. Ltd., and Pininfarina of America Corp. In the aerodynamics and aeroacoustics industry, the company designs the interior and exterior forms of its vehicles using its own automotive wind tunnels. It does design work for trains, planes and boats, as well as non-transportation products such as shoes, cellular phones, coffee machines, ski boots and watches. The firm's customers include car makers such as Ferrari, GM, Lancia, Maserati, Fiat, Alfa Romeo, Hyundai, Peugeot, Citroen, Jaguar, Daewoo, Honda, Brillance, Chery, JAC, Ford Europe, Volvo, Mitsubishi Europe and Rolls-Royce; industrial vehicle makers, including BMC; bus and truck makers, including BredaMenarinibus, IVECO and Hispano; railway makers, including AnsaldoBreda, Bombardier and Eurostar; nautical and aeronautical clients, including Beneteau, Derecktor Shipyards, Ferretti Yachts and BAE Systems; and other clients, including Leitner Ropeways, Poma and Solex. Additional subsidiaries include: Signature SRL (also referred to as Pininfarina Segno) creates writing instruments such as pens and related accessories; and minority-owned GOODMIND SRL, is an advertising agency offering brand strategy and communication services and solutions. The Mahindra Group owns a majority stake in Pininfarina SpA (76.06%).

FINANCIAL DATA: *Note: Data for latest year may not have been available at press time.*

In U.S. $	2018	2017	2016	2015	2014	2013
Revenue	120,472,000	104,335,000	72,556,600	90,468,900	105,224,000	109,795,000
R&D Expense						
Operating Income						
Operating Margin %						
SGA Expense						
Net Income	2,485,460	1,570,400	21,630,600	-19,849,300	-1,533,940	-14,297,400
Operating Cash Flow						
Capital Expenditure						
EBITDA						
Return on Assets %						
Return on Equity %						
Debt to Equity						

CONTACT INFORMATION:

Phone: 39-011-9438111 Fax:
Toll-Free:
Address: Via Nazionale, 30, Cambiano, TO 10020 Italy

STOCK TICKER/OTHER:

Stock Ticker: PINF
Exchange: Milan
Employees: 656
Fiscal Year Ends: 12/31
Parent Company: Mahindra Group

SALARIES/BONUSES:

Top Exec. Salary: $ Bonus: $
Second Exec. Salary: $ Bonus: $

OTHER THOUGHTS:

Estimated Female Officers or Directors: 2
Hot Spot for Advancement for Women/Minorities:

Pirelli & C SpA

www.pirelli.com

NAIC Code: 326200

TYPES OF BUSINESS:

Tire Manufacturing
Solar Energy Investments
Fashion Collections
Eco-Fuels

BRANDS/DIVISIONS/AFFILIATES:

Pirelli Connesso
Run Flat
Pirelli Noise Cancelling System

CONTACTS: *Note: Officers with more than one job title may be intentionally listed here more than once.*

Marco Tronchetti Provera, CEO
Francesco Tanzi, Exec. Dir.-Admin.
Francesco Chiappetta, General Counsel
G. Pomati, Dir.-Oper.
M. Abet, Dir.-Comm. & Media
V. Leone, Dir.-Investor Rel.
A. Imperiali, Dir.-Image & Brand Equity Mgmt.
M. Borchert, Head-Central Europe
A. Pirelli, Head-Africa, the Middle East & India
Ning Gaoning, Chmn.
G. Borgo, Head-Asia Pacific
L. Staccoli, Exec. Dir.-Purchasing

GROWTH PLANS/SPECIAL FEATURES:

Pirelli & C. SpA is an Italian company known for its sale of high-performance consumer tires, such as tires for cars, motorcycles and bicycles. The firm continuously engages in the development of its products and applications. Recent innovations include the Pirelli Connesso system, which enables tires to communicate digitally with the customer about tire temperature, pressure and wear. Pirelli offers a range of colors for the tire's compound name, including white, yellow, red, green and blue (for the 2019 season). Other product offerings include the Run Flat and Seal Inside lines of tires that enable cars to continue driving after a puncture; and the Pirelli Noise Cancelling System, which are tires that reduce road noise during driving. Pirelli manufactures more than 70 million vehicle tires per year, with 55% being derived from high-value tires. The company participates in over 460 car and motorcycle sport events and has been an exclusive tire supplier to the Formula One World Championship, supplying an average of 40,000 racing tires each year. The firm has 19 production plants in 12 countries, and a commercial presence in over 160. Pirelli holds 6,500 patents. Automotive tires are categorized into summer tires, all-season tires and winter tires. Motorcycle tires are categorized into racing tires, on-road tires, on/off road tires, off-road tires and scooter tires. Bicycle tires are grouped into road racing, mountain biking and city trekking.

FINANCIAL DATA: *Note: Data for latest year may not have been available at press time.*

In U.S. $	2018	2017	2016	2015	2014	2013
Revenue	6,900,000,000	6,800,000,000	6,790,440,448	7,071,993,856	6,745,195,008	6,888,769,536
R&D Expense						
Operating Income						
Operating Margin %						
SGA Expense						
Net Income			151,381,984	-438,652,800	357,869,312	340,253,312
Operating Cash Flow						
Capital Expenditure						
EBITDA						
Return on Assets %						
Return on Equity %						
Debt to Equity						

CONTACT INFORMATION:

Phone: 39 264421 Fax: 39 264424444
Toll-Free:
Address: 25 Viale Piero e Alberto Pirelli N., Milano, 20126 Italy

STOCK TICKER/OTHER:

Stock Ticker: PPAMF Exchange: PINX
Employees: 37,050 Fiscal Year Ends: 12/31
Parent Company:

SALARIES/BONUSES:

Top Exec. Salary: $ Bonus: $
Second Exec. Salary: $ Bonus: $

OTHER THOUGHTS:

Estimated Female Officers or Directors: 1
Hot Spot for Advancement for Women/Minorities: Y

Polaris Industries Inc

www.polarisindustries.com

NAIC Code: 336999

TYPES OF BUSINESS:

All-Terrain Vehicle Manufacturing
Snowmobile Manufacturing
Parts & Accessories
Motorcycles
Clothing
Low-Emission Vehicles (LEV)

BRANDS/DIVISIONS/AFFILIATES:

RZR
FTR
GEM
Goupil
DAGOR
Pro Comp
Rubicon Express
Bennington

CONTACTS: *Note: Officers with more than one job title may be intentionally listed here more than once.*

Scott Wine, CEO
Michael Speetzen, CFO
Lucy Clark Dougherty, Chief Compliance Officer
Kenneth Pucel, Executive VP, Divisional
James Williams, Other Executive Officer
Michael Dougherty, President, Divisional
Stephen Eastman, President, Divisional
Christopher Musso, President, Divisional
Robert Mack, President, Divisional

GROWTH PLANS/SPECIAL FEATURES:

Polaris Industries, Inc. designs, engineers and manufactures powersports vehicles. These range of vehicles include: off-road vehicles (ORV) such as all-terrain vehicles (ATVs) and side-by-side vehicles for recreational and utility use; snowmobiles; motorcycles; global adjacent vehicles such as commercial, government and defense; and boats. Polaris also produces and markets parts, apparel and accessories. The company's products are sold through dealers, distributors and retail stores principally located in the U.S., Canada, western Europe, Australia and Mexico. ORVs are four-wheel vehicles designed for off-road use and traversing through rough terrain, dunes, swamps and marshland. The vehicles can be single- or multi-passenger, and used for fishing, hunting, trail/dune riding and for utility purposes on farms, ranches and construction sites. Motorcycles are utilized as a mode of transportation as well as for recreational purposes, and include cruiser, touring, sport and standard bike models. Global adjacent vehicles are designed to support people-mobility and for commercial work applications, and include products in the light-duty hauling, people mover, industrial and urban/suburban commuting subsectors, as well as tactical defense vehicles. Polaris entered the boat sector in 2018, with models primarily used for recreational purposes and therefore including pontoon, deck, bowrider, cruiser and fishing boats. The company serves more than 100 countries worldwide. Its brands include RZR, FTR, GEM, Goupil, DAGOR, Pro Comp, Rubicon Express, Kolpin, Klim, Trail Tech, Bennington, Rinker, Striper and many more.

Polaris offers its employees tuition and health club reimbursement, a flexible spending plan and an employee assistance program.

FINANCIAL DATA: *Note: Data for latest year may not have been available at press time.*

In U.S. $	2018	2017	2016	2015	2014	2013
Revenue	6,078,540,000	5,428,477,000	4,516,629,000	4,719,290,000	4,479,648,000	3,777,068,000
R&D Expense	259,682,000	238,299,000	185,126,000	166,460,000	148,458,000	139,193,000
Operating Income	487,412,000	359,657,000	350,278,000	716,139,000	714,690,000	577,914,000
Operating Margin %		.07%	.08%	.15%	.16%	.15%
SGA Expense	841,536,000	803,001,000	648,677,000	525,746,000	517,697,000	449,673,000
Net Income	335,257,000	172,492,000	212,948,000	455,361,000	454,029,000	377,292,000
Operating Cash Flow	477,112,000	579,980,000	571,783,000	440,231,000	529,270,000	492,240,000
Capital Expenditure	225,414,000	184,388,000	209,137,000	249,485,000	205,079,000	251,401,000
EBITDA	697,252,000	542,054,000	497,082,000	849,331,000	838,063,000	672,739,000
Return on Assets %		.06%	.08%	.20%	.24%	.24%
Return on Equity %		.19%	.23%	.49%	.65%	.62%
Debt to Equity		0.929	1.313	0.467	0.26	0.531

CONTACT INFORMATION:

Phone: 763 542-0500 Fax: 763 542-0599
Toll-Free: 800-765-2747
Address: 2100 Hwy. 55, Medina, MN 55340 United States

STOCK TICKER/OTHER:

Stock Ticker: PII
Employees: 10,000
Parent Company:
Exchange: NYS
Fiscal Year Ends: 12/31

SALARIES/BONUSES:

Top Exec. Salary: $540,000 Bonus: $1,035,825
Second Exec. Salary: $1,006,923 Bonus: $

OTHER THOUGHTS:

Estimated Female Officers or Directors: 2
Hot Spot for Advancement for Women/Minorities:

Porsche Automobil Holding SE

www.porsche-se.com

NAIC Code: 336111

TYPES OF BUSINESS:

Automobile Manufacturing
Sports Cars
Apparel & Accessories

GROWTH PLANS/SPECIAL FEATURES:

Porsche Automobil Holding SE is a German-based holding company comprised of 12 brands from seven European countries. Primarily, Porsche holds the majority (50.7%) of the ordinary shares in the Volkswagen Group, which is one of the world's leading automobile manufacturers. The firm's 12 brands include: Volkswagen passenger cars, Audi, SEAT, SKODA, Bentley, Bugatti, Lamborghini, Porsche, Ducati, Volkswagen commercial vehicles, Scania and MAN. The company also retains interest in after-sales of automobiles, parts distribution and the investment in the automotive value chain, which encompasses vehicle related services, supporting the developments and production process and offering its technological resources. In addition to its 12 brands, Porsche Automobil owns interests in other auto-related businesses, including: a nearly 100% stake in Planung Transport Verkehr AG, a German provider of software for traffic planning and traffic management, as well as transport logistics; a minority stake in the U.S.-technology company, INRIX, Inc.; and in two 3D printing specialists, Markforged, Inc. and Suerat Technologies, Inc., each based in the U.S.

BRANDS/DIVISIONS/AFFILIATES:

Volkswagen Group
Audi
SEAT
SKODA
Bentley
Bugatti
Lamborghini
Porsche

CONTACTS: *Note: Officers with more than one job title may be intentionally listed here more than once.*

Hans Dieter Potsch, CFO
Matthias Muller, Dir.-Strategy & Corp. Dev.
Philipp von Hagen, Dir.-Investment Management
Wolfgang Porsche, Chmn.

FINANCIAL DATA: *Note: Data for latest year may not have been available at press time.*

In U.S. $	2018	2017	2016	2015	2014	2013
Revenue	114,039,000	37,643,930	1,107,175			
R&D Expense						
Operating Income	-139,504,000	-56,465,900	-52,037,200	-43,179,810	-79,716,570	-55,358,720
Operating Margin %			-47.00%			
SGA Expense	29,893,710	24,357,840	24,357,840	13,286,090	25,465,010	26,572,190
Net Income	3,845,217,000	3,689,105,000	1,521,258,000	-302,258,700	3,352,525,000	2,666,076,000
Operating Cash Flow	617,803,400	276,793,600	-107,395,900	663,197,500	344,331,300	736,271,000
Capital Expenditure	4,428,698	2,214,349				
EBITDA	3,967,006,000	3,731,178,000	1,556,687,000	-457,263,100	3,735,607,000	2,972,763,000
Return on Assets %			.05%	-.01%	.10%	.08%
Return on Equity %			.05%	-.01%	.10%	.08%
Debt to Equity				0.011	0.01	0.01

CONTACT INFORMATION:

Phone: 49-711-911-0 Fax: 49-711-911-25777
Toll-Free:
Address: Porscheplatz 1, Stuttgart, 70435 Germany

STOCK TICKER/OTHER:

Stock Ticker: POAHY
Employees: 935
Parent Company:
Exchange: PINX
Fiscal Year Ends: 07/31

SALARIES/BONUSES:

Top Exec. Salary: $ Bonus: $
Second Exec. Salary: $ Bonus: $

OTHER THOUGHTS:

Estimated Female Officers or Directors:
Hot Spot for Advancement for Women/Minorities:

Potamkin Automotive Group

www.potamkin.com

NAIC Code: 441110

TYPES OF BUSINESS:

Auto Dealers, Retail
Auto Service & Repair

BRANDS/DIVISIONS/AFFILIATES:

GROWTH PLANS/SPECIAL FEATURES:

Potamkin Automotive Group is a privately-owned car dealership network based in Florida. Vehicle brands sold by Potamkin dealerships include Alfa Romero, Buick, Cadillac, Chevrolet, Chrysler, Dodge, Fiat, GMC, Genesis, Hyundai, Jeep, Ram and Toyota. Model types include new and used cars, trucks and SUVs. The firm supports its dealerships financial backing, financial contracts, appealing advertising rates on a local and regional basis, manufacturer relationships and discounts from suppliers and vendors. After having given its dealer partners the tools needed to succeed, Potamkin allows them to remain individually operated and managed in order to best serve the local markets. This style of partnership is known as corporate decentralizing. All Potamkin dealerships offer clients several exclusive deals: a no-haggle, no-hassle pricing program; a 3-Day/100-Mile money back guarantee; a 10% discount on service, parts and accessories; free car washes for the life of the vehicle ownership; and numerous financing plans.

Potamkin provides its employees with a 401(k) plan; flexible spending accounts; disability, basic life, dependent life and accident insurance; business travel insurance; and a medical, dental and vision plan.

CONTACTS: *Note: Officers with more than one job title may be intentionally listed here more than once.*

Robert Potamkin, Co-Chmn.
Barry Frieder, COO
Mike Cunningham, CFO
David Frieder, VP-Purchasing
William Rignack, CIO
John Hickey, Exec- Legal Council
Andrew Pfeifer, Sr. VP-Corp. Oper.
David Winton, Treas.
Robert Potamkin, Co-Chmn.
Bill Mercado, VP-Fixed Oper.
Alan Potamkin, Co-Chmn.
David Frieder, VP-Purchasing & Vendor Rel.

FINANCIAL DATA: *Note: Data for latest year may not have been available at press time.*

In U.S. $	2018	2017	2016	2015	2014	2013
Revenue	1,703,972,815	1,622,831,250	1,545,553,571	1,492,413,801	1,315,000,000	1,216,589,457
R&D Expense						
Operating Income						
Operating Margin %						
SGA Expense						
Net Income						
Operating Cash Flow						
Capital Expenditure						
EBITDA						
Return on Assets %						
Return on Equity %						
Debt to Equity						

CONTACT INFORMATION:

Phone: 305-779-4060 Fax:
Toll-Free:
Address: 5800 NW 171st, Miami, FL 33015 United States

STOCK TICKER/OTHER:

Stock Ticker: Private
Employees: 1,620
Parent Company:
Exchange:
Fiscal Year Ends: 12/31

SALARIES/BONUSES:

Top Exec. Salary: $ Bonus: $
Second Exec. Salary: $ Bonus: $

OTHER THOUGHTS:

Estimated Female Officers or Directors:
Hot Spot for Advancement for Women/Minorities:

Precision Auto Care Inc

www.precisiontune.com/

NAIC Code: 811111

TYPES OF BUSINESS:

General Automotive Repair

BRANDS/DIVISIONS/AFFILIATES:

Icahn Enterprises LP
Icahn Automotive Group LLC
Precision Franchising LLC
Precision Tune Auto Care
Precision Auto Wash
Precision Lube

CONTACTS:

Note: Officers with more than one job title may be intentionally listed here more than once.

Robert A. Falconi, CEO
Mark P. Francis, CFO

GROWTH PLANS/SPECIAL FEATURES:

Precision Auto Care, Inc. is a franchisor of automotive maintenance service centers which provide specialized automotive care services as well as fast oil change and lube services. Subsidiary Precision Franchising, LLC is a franchisor of automotive service centers located in the U.S., and in certain foreign countries. Auto care centers, both company-owned and franchised, operate under the Precision Tune Auto Care brand name. Precision Tune operations offer air conditioning/heating service and repair, aftermarket accessories, airbag diagnostics, alarm system service and repair, alignments, alternator service and replacement, automotive computer reprogramming services, battery service/testing, belts, hoses, filters, brake service, catalytic converter replacement, check engine light diagnostics, clutch repair, axle repair, electrical systems services, emission services and inspections, exhaust system inspection and repair, and much more. In addition, Precision Auto Care offers fleet services, along with complementary shuttle service at some locations. Precision Tune Auto Care operates more than 300 centers worldwide. Other franchises include Precision Auto Wash, providing automobile cleaning services; and Precision Lube, offering express vehicle oil and lubricant under-the-hood services. Precision Auto is owned by Icahn Automotive Group, LLC, itself a subsidiary of Icahn Enterprises LP.

FINANCIAL DATA:

Note: Data for latest year may not have been available at press time.

In U.S. $	2018	2017	2016	2015	2014	2013
Revenue	30,425,631	28,976,791	27,596,944	25,390,146	25,436,112	25,992,335
R&D Expense						
Operating Income						
Operating Margin %						
SGA Expense						
Net Income			1,121,782	646,816	971,341	592,531
Operating Cash Flow						
Capital Expenditure						
EBITDA						
Return on Assets %						
Return on Equity %						
Debt to Equity						

CONTACT INFORMATION:

Phone: 703-777-9095 Fax: 703-771-7108
Toll-Free:
Address: 748 Miller Drive, S.E., Leesburg, VA 20175 United States

STOCK TICKER/OTHER:

Stock Ticker: Subsidiary
Employees: 28
Parent Company: Icahn Enterprises LP
Exchange:
Fiscal Year Ends: 06/30

SALARIES/BONUSES:

Top Exec. Salary: $ Bonus: $
Second Exec. Salary: $ Bonus: $

OTHER THOUGHTS:

Estimated Female Officers or Directors:
Hot Spot for Advancement for Women/Minorities:

Primearth EV Energy Co Ltd

www.peve.jp

NAIC Code: 335911

TYPES OF BUSINESS:

Battery Manufacturing-Hybrid Cars
Battery Management Systems

BRANDS/DIVISIONS/AFFILIATES:

Panasonic Corporation
Toyota Motor Corporation
Battery ECU
Panasonic Automotive Systems of America
Automotive Systems Company
Sinogy Toyota Automotive Energy System Co Ltd
Corun Peve Automotive Battery Co Ltd

CONTACTS: *Note: Officers with more than one job title may be intentionally listed here more than once.*

Shigeki Suzuki, Pres.

GROWTH PLANS/SPECIAL FEATURES:

Primearth EV Energy Co., Ltd. develops, manufactures and sells nickel metal-hydride batteries, primarily for hybrid electric vehicles (HEVs). Founded in 1996, it is a joint venture between Panasonic Corporation and Toyota Motor Corporation (TMC), with Toyota holding a majority stake. Primearth manufactures two HEV rechargeable batteries, the metal case prismatic and the resin case prismatic modules, which both take up 14% less volume than conventional HEV batteries. Additionally, the metal case battery has a 40% higher cooling performance, and the plastic case battery is approximately 25% lighter than conventional HEV battery modules. Besides batteries, Primearth offers a battery management system known as Battery ECU, which monitors and controls the battery's functions, such as temperature and voltage. Battery pack systems can be configured to customer requirements. The firm's products are used in several current production model hybrid vehicles. Although not its primary line of business, the company has historically supplied batteries for pure electric vehicles as well. The firm's U.S. sales group consists of Panasonic Automotive Systems of America, a division of Panasonic Corporation of North America, while its Japanese sales group consists of the Automotive Systems Company of Panasonic Corporation. Primearth maintains three production facilities, two in Kosai (shizuoka), and one in Kurokawa-gun (Miyagi), Japan. Affiliate Sinogy Toyota Automotive Energy System Co. Ltd. is a hybrid-vehicle-battery production joint venture with TMC, and is based in the Jiangsu province of China; and TMC affiliate Corun Peve Automotive Battery Co. Ltd. manufactures nickel-metal-hydride (NiMH) batteries for HEVs in China.

FINANCIAL DATA: *Note: Data for latest year may not have been available at press time.*

In U.S. $	2018	2017	2016	2015	2014	2013
Revenue	1,562,001,000	1,487,620,000	1,401,600,000	1,154,900,000	1,390,770,000	1,483,170,000
R&D Expense						
Operating Income						
Operating Margin %						
SGA Expense						
Net Income						
Operating Cash Flow						
Capital Expenditure						
EBITDA						
Return on Assets %						
Return on Equity %						
Debt to Equity						

CONTACT INFORMATION:

Phone: 81-53-577-3111 Fax:
Toll-Free: 800-211-7262
Address: 20 Okasaki, Kosai-shi, Shizuoka-ken, 431-0422 Japan

STOCK TICKER/OTHER:

Stock Ticker: Joint Venture Exchange:
Employees: 3,743 Fiscal Year Ends: 03/31
Parent Company: Toyota Motor Corporation

SALARIES/BONUSES:

Top Exec. Salary: $ Bonus: $
Second Exec. Salary: $ Bonus: $

OTHER THOUGHTS:

Estimated Female Officers or Directors:
Hot Spot for Advancement for Women/Minorities:

Proton Holdings Berhad

www.proton.com

NAIC Code: 336111

TYPES OF BUSINESS:

Automobile Manufacturing
Motorcycles
Bicycles
Distribution
Manufacturing Consulting
Financial Services
Property Investments

BRANDS/DIVISIONS/AFFILIATES:

DRB-HICOM Berhad
Zhejiang Geely Holding Group
Proton Ertiga
Saga
Persona
Perdana
Iriz
X70

CONTACTS:

Note: Officers with more than one job title may be intentionally listed here more than once.

Li Chungrong, CEO
Tajul Zahari Bin Abu Bakar, Dir.-Eng.
Azmi Bin Idris, Dir.-Group Mfg.
Michelle Kythe Lim Beng Sze, Chief Legal Counsel
Terence Soo Thean Hin, Head-Group Finance
Mohammad Aris Bin Anuar, Dir.-Group Quality
Syed Faisal Albar, Chmn.
Brian Collier, Managing Dir.-Proton Cars U.K. Ltd.

GROWTH PLANS/SPECIAL FEATURES:

Proton Holdings Berhad designs, manufactures, distributes and sells automobiles in Malaysia, one of the very few in the country. The firm's manufacturing plant rolled out its first national car, the Proton Saga, in 1985, and now produces several vehicle models. The company's current portfolio includes the Proton Ertiga, Saga, Persona, Perdana, Iriz, Preve, X70 and Exora passenger vehicle models of sedans, hatchbacks and sport utility vehicles (SUVs). Proton's line of four-cylinder gasoline direct injection/turbocharged and three-cylinder variable valve timing engines are developed in collaboration with Ricardo and Lotus Engineering. Proton's Shah Alam manufacturing complex is a multi-vehicle factory which features engine machining, vehicle manufacturing and assembly. Proton currently exports its vehicles to several countries, including Singapore, Thailand, Egypt, Chile and Indonesia; but, is predominantly reliant on its domestic market. In addition, Proton builds competition cars for the racing sector. Its current race cars include the Iriz R3 MTC and the Suprima S R3 MTC, each comprising a 5-speed with an R3 CAMPRO 1597c 16-valve transmission. Proton is 50.1%-owned by DRB-HICOM Berhad and 49.9%-owned by Zhejiang Geely Holding Group.

FINANCIAL DATA:

Note: Data for latest year may not have been available at press time.

In U.S. $	2018	2017	2016	2015	2014	2013
Revenue	4,961,250,000	4,725,000,000	4,500,000,000	4,556,665,230	4,748,023,748	3,100,000,000
R&D Expense						
Operating Income						
Operating Margin %						
SGA Expense						
Net Income						
Operating Cash Flow						
Capital Expenditure						
EBITDA						
Return on Assets %						
Return on Equity %						
Debt to Equity						

CONTACT INFORMATION:

Phone: 8026-9999 Fax:
Toll-Free:
Address: KM33.8 Westbound, Shah Alam Expressway, Subang Jaya, Selangor Darul Ehsan, 47600 Malaysia

STOCK TICKER/OTHER:

Stock Ticker: Subsidiary
Employees: 15
Parent Company: DRB-HICOM Berhad
Exchange:
Fiscal Year Ends: 03/31

SALARIES/BONUSES:

Top Exec. Salary: $ Bonus: $
Second Exec. Salary: $ Bonus: $

OTHER THOUGHTS:

Estimated Female Officers or Directors: 2
Hot Spot for Advancement for Women/Minorities: Y

PT Astra International TbK

www.astra.co.id

NAIC Code: 336111

TYPES OF BUSINESS:

Automobile Manufacturing
Heavy Equipment
Financial Services
Agribusiness
Information Technology
Infrastructure
Motorcycles & Four-Wheelers
Customer Relationship Management

BRANDS/DIVISIONS/AFFILIATES:

CONTACTS: *Note: Officers with more than one job title may be intentionally listed here more than once.*

Prijono Sugiarto, CEO
Prijono Sugiarto, Pres.
Gita Tiffany Boer, Company Sec.
Simon Collier Dixon, Dir.-Corp. Finance
Gunawan Geniusahardja, Dir.-Financial Svcs. Group
Johannes Loman, Dir.-PT Astra Honda Motor
Johnney Darmawan, Dir.-Toyota Bus.
Angky Tisnadisasrea, Dir.-PT Asrtratel Nusantara

GROWTH PLANS/SPECIAL FEATURES:

PT Astra International TbK, based in Indonesia, is diversified company operating through seven segments via subsidiaries and joint ventures. These business segments include: automotive; financial services; heavy equipment, mining, construction and energy; agribusiness; infrastructure and logistics; information technology (IT); and property. Nearly 230 subsidiaries, joint ventures and associates operate within these segments. The automotive segment manufactures cars, motorcycles and automotive components, and offers related solutions and services. The financial services segment provides vehicle financing, motorcycle financing, heavy equipment financing, insurance and banking services and solutions. The heavy equipment, mining, construction and energy segment: manufactures and distributes construction machinery; engages in mining and construction contracting; coal mining; and energy production via coal. The agribusiness operates a palm oil plantation that is integrated from upstream to downstream activities. Crude palm oil (CPO) produced is marketed to domestic and international customers, while palm oil derivative products are exported. Derivative products include refined bleached deodorized palm oil (RBDPO), olein, stearin and palm fatty acid distillate (PFAD). The infrastructure and logistics segment: invests in and operates infrastructure assets, both land and sea, primarily consisting of toll roads and ports; and provides integrated transportation solutions, used vehicles sales solutions and logistics service solutions. The operational fleet available to transport solutions and logistics solutions are supplied by Astra automotive companies (among others). Used car sales units collaborate with Astra's automotive and financial services segments to provide support in serving customers regarding trade-in schemes, car sales financing and settlement of non-performing loans. The IT segment provides document management solutions and information, communication technology (ICT) solutions. Last, the property segment is engaged in property investment, management and development, primarily constructing office building and tower projects, public facilities and open areas, as well as residential/apartment projects.

FINANCIAL DATA: *Note: Data for latest year may not have been available at press time.*

In U.S. $	2018	2017	2016	2015	2014	2013
Revenue	16,887,050,000	14,546,910,000	12,783,900,000	13,003,600,000	14,239,390,000	13,687,260,000
R&D Expense						
Operating Income	1,903,283,000	1,439,110,000	1,242,358,000	1,221,885,000	1,430,568,000	1,317,826,000
Operating Margin %		.11%	.11%	.11%	.11%	.11%
SGA Expense	1,687,328,000	1,556,089,000	1,334,134,000	1,376,491,000	1,316,343,000	1,179,527,000
Net Income	1,530,039,000	1,332,933,000	1,069,961,000	1,021,108,000	1,354,112,000	1,370,773,000
Operating Cash Flow						
Capital Expenditure	1,023,720,000	750,441,300	545,005,300	578,750,500	745,428,900	700,176,500
EBITDA	2,689,728,000	2,205,295,000	1,694,176,000	1,482,527,000	2,028,027,000	2,021,320,000
Return on Assets %		.07%	.06%	.06%	.09%	.10%
Return on Equity %		.16%	.14%	.15%	.21%	.25%
Debt to Equity		0.254	0.224	0.338	0.341	0.323

CONTACT INFORMATION:

Phone: 62 2165084-3888 Fax: 021-6530-4957
Toll-Free:
Address: Menara Astra 59/Fl, Jl. Jenderal Sudirman Kav 5-6, Jakarta, 10220 Indonesia

STOCK TICKER/OTHER:

Stock Ticker: PTAIF Exchange: PINX
Employees: 226,140 Fiscal Year Ends: 12/31
Parent Company: Jardine Cycle & Carriage Limited

SALARIES/BONUSES:

Top Exec. Salary: $ Bonus: $
Second Exec. Salary: $ Bonus: $

OTHER THOUGHTS:

Estimated Female Officers or Directors: 1
Hot Spot for Advancement for Women/Minorities:

Qingling Motors (Group) Co Ltd

www.qingling.com.cn

NAIC Code: 336112

TYPES OF BUSINESS:

Light Truck and Utility Vehicle Manufacturing

BRANDS/DIVISIONS/AFFILIATES:

Isuzu Motors Limited

CONTACTS: *Note: Officers with more than one job title may be intentionally listed here more than once.*

Yuguang Luo, Chmn.

GROWTH PLANS/SPECIAL FEATURES:

Qingling Motors (Group) Co., Ltd. is a Chinese automobile manufacturer and a subsidiary of Isuzu Motors Limited. The firm maintains factories, several subsidiaries and one research & development center. Qingling's vehicles are categorized into five groups: heavy, light heavy, medium, light and SUV. Heavy vehicles include pickup trucks comprised with Isuzu electric 6UZ1 diesel engines, strong chassis, durable transmissions and modified adaptability. Light heavy vehicles include various models that can come with more than 10 options of chassis parameters, can include just the chassis, whole vehicles, van trucks or refrigerator trucks, and can comprise the Isuzu rail engines. Medium-sized vehicles come with Isuzu engines, a variety of chassis parameters, and can include just the chassis, whole vehicles, van trucks or refrigerator trucks. Light vehicles come with the Isuzu engines (including electric), a variety of chassis parameters, and can include just the chassis, whole vehicles, van trucks or refrigerator trucks. The SUV group includes the Isuzu-branded sport utility vehicle comprised of either a 3.2-liter V6/2.6-liter petrol engine or a 2.8-liter diesel turbo engine, and comes in an SUV model or a van-truck model. Qingling Motors Group operates through 14 joint ventures, three state-owned companies and a factory.

FINANCIAL DATA: *Note: Data for latest year may not have been available at press time.*

In U.S. $	2018	2017	2016	2015	2014	2013
Revenue	763,176,900	737,039,200	673,182,500	799,647,800	842,618,100	840,120,700
R&D Expense	27,300,900	18,034,260	8,327,861	5,290,118	3,470,087	4,417,294
Operating Income	33,780,400	81,603,860	80,028,180	81,224,400	71,104,680	61,751,600
Operating Margin %		.11%	.12%	.10%	.08%	.07%
SGA Expense	72,561,960	66,716,740	61,123,860	85,724,930	70,419,410	79,814,040
Net Income	65,922,650	72,191,940	69,919,950	69,716,560	64,582,760	53,996,710
Operating Cash Flow	79,197,630	56,634,510	125,117,500	215,375,800	55,367,980	74,549,490
Capital Expenditure	21,125,750	9,714,094	12,124,100	14,214,200	7,065,258	8,812,941
EBITDA	40,757,040	92,743,850	93,151,640	112,780,700	109,736,200	105,896,500
Return on Assets %		.05%	.05%	.05%	.04%	.04%
Return on Equity %		.06%	.06%	.06%	.06%	.05%
Debt to Equity						

CONTACT INFORMATION:

Phone: 8623-65262277 Fax: 8623-65262920

Toll-Free:

Address: 1 Xiexing Village, Zhongliangshan, Chongqing, 400052 China

STOCK TICKER/OTHER:

Stock Ticker: QGLHF

Employees: 3,008

Parent Company: Isuzu Motors Limited

Exchange: GREY

Fiscal Year Ends: 12/31

SALARIES/BONUSES:

Top Exec. Salary: $ Bonus: $

Second Exec. Salary: $ Bonus: $

OTHER THOUGHTS:

Estimated Female Officers or Directors:

Hot Spot for Advancement for Women/Minorities:

Rassini SAB de CV

NAIC Code: 336300

www.rassini.com

TYPES OF BUSINESS:

Parts-Suspension System Components
Parts-Brake Components
Parts-Elastomer Manufacturing

BRANDS/DIVISIONS/AFFILIATES:

Rassini

CONTACTS:

Note: Officers with more than one job title may be intentionally listed here more than once.

Eugenio Madero Pinson, Managing Dir.
Juan Pablo Sanchez Kanter, VP-Finance
Enrique Villasenor, CEO-SANLUIS Rassini South America
Robert Anderson, CEO
Sergio Davila, COO-Rassini Suspensions North America
Hector Galvan, CEO-Rassini Brakes
Antonio Madero Bracho, Chmn.
Eugenio Madero, CEO-SANLUIS Rassini North America

GROWTH PLANS/SPECIAL FEATURES:

Rassini SAB de CV designs and manufactures components for suspension, brakes and anti-vibration systems used by the automotive industry. These products are marketed under the Rassini brand and are included in a range of vehicles across urban, family, all-terrain, sport, luxury and commercial, and are included in both electric and internal combustion engines. Rassini has operations in Mexico, the U.S., Brazil, Germany, Japan and Israel, and divides its products into two groups: suspensions and brakes. The suspension group manufactures multi-leaf springs and parabolic leaf springs, coil springs, torsion bars and stabilizing bars. The brakes group sells rotors, disks, drums and hubs for brake systems. Rassini also produces high-density rubber components for anti-vibration purposes, and is engaged in the parts aftermarket. The firm has an R&D center in Plymouth, Michigan, which uses RASCAL, a type of software developed in-house specifically for coil spring design, as well as computer aided design (CAD) software and other off-the-shelf software.

FINANCIAL DATA:

Note: Data for latest year may not have been available at press time.

In U.S. $	2018	2017	2016	2015	2014	2013
Revenue		1,080,000,000	919,293,952	725,599,168	669,509,824	582,957,248
R&D Expense						
Operating Income						
Operating Margin %						
SGA Expense						
Net Income			80,518,384	49,728,908	48,610,520	-8,033,987
Operating Cash Flow						
Capital Expenditure						
EBITDA						
Return on Assets %						
Return on Equity %						
Debt to Equity						

CONTACT INFORMATION:

Phone: 52 5552295821 Fax: 52 5552025895
Toll-Free:
Address: 220 Monte Pelvoux, Mexico, 11000 Mexico

STOCK TICKER/OTHER:

Stock Ticker: RASSICPO
Employees: 4,400
Parent Company:
Exchange: MEX
Fiscal Year Ends: 12/31

SALARIES/BONUSES:

Top Exec. Salary: $ Bonus: $
Second Exec. Salary: $ Bonus: $

OTHER THOUGHTS:

Estimated Female Officers or Directors:
Hot Spot for Advancement for Women/Minorities:

Renault SA

www.renault.com

NAIC Code: 336111

TYPES OF BUSINESS:

Automobile Manufacturing
Financial Services
Commercial Vehicles
Scooters
Farm Machinery
Automotive Maintenance Service

BRANDS/DIVISIONS/AFFILIATES:

Renault
Renault Samsung Motors
Dacia
Renault-Nissan BV
AvtoVAZ OAO
Daimler AG
Nissan Motor Co Ltd
Renault Minute

CONTACTS: *Note: Officers with more than one job title may be intentionally listed here more than once.*

Thierry Bollore, COO
Philippe Klein, Exec. VP-Prod. Planning, Plan & Programs
Jean-Michel Billig, Exec. VP-Eng. & Quality
Jose Vicente de los Mosoz Obispo, Exec. VP-Mfg.
Philippe Klein, Exec. VP-Corp. Planning
Mouna Sepehri, Exec. VP-Office of CEO
Stefan Mueller, Exec. VP
Gerard Leclercq, Exec. VP-Supply Chain

GROWTH PLANS/SPECIAL FEATURES:

Renault SA is a leading automobile manufacturer in France. The company's automobile division consists of the Renault, Renault Samsung Motors (RSM) and Dacia brands. It designs, develops and markets a line of small- to mid-size cars, including hatchbacks and minivans, as well as light commercial vehicles and two-wheelers, such as scooters. Some of Renault's models include Kwid, Kadjar, Captur, Sandero, Clio, Duster, Megane, Kangoo and Trafic. RSM models include SM5, SM3, QM3, SM3 ZE, QM5, SM7 and SM6. Dacia's models include the Duster, an SUV; Logan, available in a 4-door sedan; and Sandero, a 4-door hatchback. Renault's sales and finance division is comprised of RCI Banque and its subsidiaries, which provide sales, services and cash management for the group. Renault SA operates a host of automotive maintenance locations under the names Renault Minute and Motrio. There are more than 750 Renault Minute centers throughout France. Motrio offers a range of multi-branded parts for the maintenance and light engineering of vehicles, as well as at-your-service auto repair shops throughout the country. Through its joint venture Renault-Nissan BV, Renault owns approximately 43.4% of Japan-based Nissan Motor Co. Ltd. Nissan, in turn, owns approximately 15% of Renault. In addition, the French government has a 19.73% stake in the company. The firm has a partnership and 25% stake in Russian automaker AvtoVAZ OAO, as well as a 1.55% stake in automaker Daimler AG of Germany.

FINANCIAL DATA: *Note: Data for latest year may not have been available at press time.*

In U.S. $	2018	2017	2016	2015	2014	2013
Revenue	63,572,860,000	65,068,650,000	56,734,950,000	50,184,900,000	45,455,050,000	45,318,870,000
R&D Expense	2,876,440,000	2,867,582,000	2,624,004,000	2,297,387,000	1,905,447,000	2,006,200,000
Operating Income	3,999,114,000	4,267,051,000	3,633,747,000	2,568,645,000	1,781,444,000	1,375,111,000
Operating Margin %		.07%	.06%	.05%	.04%	.03%
SGA Expense	6,412,755,000	6,475,864,000	5,906,776,000	5,335,474,000	4,888,176,000	4,724,314,000
Net Income	3,655,890,000	5,662,090,000	3,785,430,000	3,125,554,000	2,092,560,000	648,804,300
Operating Cash Flow	6,958,592,000	6,313,109,000	4,859,389,000	6,661,869,000	4,397,697,000	3,954,827,000
Capital Expenditure	4,879,318,000	3,986,935,000	3,428,919,000	3,101,196,000	2,780,115,000	3,043,623,000
EBITDA	8,654,783,000	10,643,270,000	8,696,856,000	7,109,168,000	5,965,456,000	5,302,259,000
Return on Assets %		.05%	.04%	.03%	.02%	.01%
Return on Equity %		.16%	.12%	.11%	.08%	.02%
Debt to Equity		0.144	0.134	0.186	0.282	0.295

CONTACT INFORMATION:

Phone: 33 176840404 Fax:
Toll-Free:
Address: 13-15 Quai Alponse le Gallo, Billancourt Cedex, 92513 France

STOCK TICKER/OTHER:

Stock Ticker: RNSDF
Exchange: PINX
Employees: 183,002
Fiscal Year Ends: 12/31
Parent Company:

SALARIES/BONUSES:

Top Exec. Salary: $ Bonus: $
Second Exec. Salary: $ Bonus: $

OTHER THOUGHTS:

Estimated Female Officers or Directors: 7
Hot Spot for Advancement for Women/Minorities: Y

REV Group Inc

www.revgroup.com/

NAIC Code: 336120

TYPES OF BUSINESS:

Trucks, RVs & Misc. Automotive, Manufacturing
Buses
Ambulances
Terminal Trucks
Road Construction Equipment
Sweeper Equipment

BRANDS/DIVISIONS/AFFILIATES:

Emergency One
Marque
Frontline
Collins Bus
Federal Coach
American Coach
Fleetwood RV
Lance Camper

CONTACTS: *Note: Officers with more than one job title may be intentionally listed here more than once.*

Timothy Sullivan, CEO
Dean Nolden, CFO
Ian Walsh, COO
Paul Bamatter, Director
Stephen Boettinger, General Counsel

GROWTH PLANS/SPECIAL FEATURES:

REV Group, Inc. designs, manufactures and distributes specialty vehicles and related aftermarket parts and services. The company provides customized vehicle solutions for applications such as ambulances, fire apparatus, school buses, mobility vans, municipal transit buses, street sweepers, recreational vehicles (RVs), luxury buses and more. REV's fire and emergency segment markets its vehicles under the Emergency One, Kovatch Mobile Equipment, Ferrara, American Emergency Vehicles, Horton Emergency Vehicles, Leader Emergency Vehicles, Marque, McCoy Miller, Road Rescue, Wheeled Coach and Frontline brands. The commercial segment produces small- and medium-sized buses, school buses, transit buses, terminal trucks and street sweepers in the U.S., with brands including Collins Bus, ENC, ElDorado National, Federal Coach, Champion and World Trans, among others. The recreation segment serves the RV market through seven principal brands: American Coach, Fleetwood RV, Monaco Coach, Holiday Rambler, Renegade RV, Midwest Automotive Designs and Lance Camper. REV's manufacturing and service network consists of 21 manufacturing facilities and 12 aftermarket service locations.

FINANCIAL DATA: *Note: Data for latest year may not have been available at press time.*

In U.S. $	2018	2017	2016	2015	2014	2013
Revenue	2,381,300,000	2,267,783,000	1,925,999,000	1,735,081,000	1,721,116,000	1,173,051,000
R&D Expense	6,500,000	4,219,000	4,815,000	5,106,000	8,275,000	1,863,000
Operating Income	70,600,000	87,204,000	75,922,000	65,953,000	34,354,000	20,668,000
Operating Margin %		.04%	.04%	.04%	.02%	.02%
SGA Expense	182,800,000	188,257,000	139,771,000	102,309,000	111,820,000	88,618,000
Net Income	13,000,000	31,371,000	30,193,000	22,877,000	1,488,000	25,026,000
Operating Cash Flow	-19,200,000	33,175,000	75,570,000	25,639,000	5,929,000	69,079,000
Capital Expenditure	60,700,000	79,345,000	48,542,000	15,430,000	12,067,000	9,110,000
EBITDA	116,600,000	125,016,000	100,515,000	85,037,000	53,255,000	35,045,000
Return on Assets %		.03%	.04%	.03%	.00%	
Return on Equity %		.08%	.13%	.11%	.01%	
Debt to Equity		0.40	1.076	0.946	1.105	

CONTACT INFORMATION:

Phone: 414-290-0190 Fax:
Toll-Free:
Address: 111 East Kilbourn Ave., Ste. 2600, Milwaukee, WI 53202 United States

STOCK TICKER/OTHER:

Stock Ticker: REVG
Exchange: NYS
Employees: 6,000
Fiscal Year Ends: 10/31
Parent Company:

SALARIES/BONUSES:

Top Exec. Salary: $880,000 Bonus: $
Second Exec. Salary: $400,000 Bonus: $

OTHER THOUGHTS:

Estimated Female Officers or Directors:
Hot Spot for Advancement for Women/Minorities:

Rheinmetall AG

www.rheinmetall.de

NAIC Code: 336300

TYPES OF BUSINESS:

Automotive Components Manufacturing
Military Vehicles
Weapons & Ammunition
Defense Electronics
Air Defense Systems
Command & Control Systems
Reconnaissance Systems
Training & Simulator Operations

BRANDS/DIVISIONS/AFFILIATES:

Rheinmetall Defence AG
Rheinmetall Automotive AG

CONTACTS: *Note: Officers with more than one job title may be intentionally listed here more than once.*

Armin Papperger, CEO
Helmut P. Merch, CFO
Horst Binnig, Chmn.-Automotive

GROWTH PLANS/SPECIAL FEATURES:

Rheinmetall AG, established in 1889, provides environmentally-friendly mobility and threat security technology. The company operates through two business segments: Rheinmetall Defence AG and Rheinmetall Automotive AG. Rheinmetall Defence provides innovative products for German and international armed forces, and offers systems and partial system solutions as well as a wide range of services in the areas of mobility, reconnaissance, management, effectiveness and protection. This division's products and services include armored vehicles, vehicle systems, weapons/ammunition, turret systems, weapon stations, protection systems, air defense systems, C4I systems, electro-optics, simulation/training, unmanned vehicles, infantry, naval applications, airborne applications aviation systems, tracked vehicles, military trucks, services vehicle systems, propulsion systems, ammunition disposal, manufacturing and testing. Rheinmetall Automotive provides air supply, emission control and pump products and component systems. It also develops, manufactures and supplies aftermarket pistons, engine blocks and plain bearings. Based in Dusseldorf, Germany, the firm has additional locations throughout Europe, the U.K., Asia, America, Africa and Australia. In January 2019, Rheinmetall agreed to acquire a 55% share of BAE Systems' land business, creating a joint venture to be called Rheinmetall BAE Systems Land. The transaction is subject to regulatory approval.

FINANCIAL DATA: *Note: Data for latest year may not have been available at press time.*

In U.S. $	2018	2017	2016	2015	2014	2013
Revenue	6,806,908,000	6,527,901,000	6,202,392,000	5,738,486,000	5,190,434,000	5,107,396,000
R&D Expense						
Operating Income	496,014,200	373,117,800	368,689,100	287,865,400	77,502,220	176,040,800
Operating Margin %						
SGA Expense	201,505,800	194,862,700	245,792,700	239,149,700	221,434,900	208,148,800
Net Income	337,688,200	248,007,100	221,434,900	167,183,300	19,929,140	32,108,060
Operating Cash Flow	267,936,200	604,517,300	491,585,500	375,332,200	112,931,800	215,899,000
Capital Expenditure	306,687,300	298,937,100	313,330,400	343,224,100	314,437,600	211,470,300
EBITDA	932,241,000	722,985,000	648,804,300	545,837,100	345,438,500	360,938,900
Return on Assets %		.04%	.03%	.03%	.00%	.01%
Return on Equity %		.13%	.13%	.12%	.02%	.02%
Debt to Equity		0.312	0.13	0.509	0.678	0.424

CONTACT INFORMATION:

Phone: 49-211-473-01 Fax: 49-21-473-4727
Toll-Free:
Address: Rheinmetall Platz 1, DÃ¼sseldorf, 40476 Germany

STOCK TICKER/OTHER:

Stock Ticker: RNMBF
Employees: 22,899
Parent Company:
Exchange: PINX
Fiscal Year Ends: 12/31

SALARIES/BONUSES:

Top Exec. Salary: $ Bonus: $
Second Exec. Salary: $ Bonus: $

OTHER THOUGHTS:

Estimated Female Officers or Directors:
Hot Spot for Advancement for Women/Minorities:

Rheinmetall Automotive AG

www.rheinmetall-automotive.com/en/company/kspg-ag/

NAIC Code: 336300

TYPES OF BUSINESS:

Automobile Parts Manufacturing
Pistons & Piston Compressors
Air Supply Products & Pumps
Emission Control Products
Bearings
Aluminum Engine Blocks
Hybrid & Fuel Cell Technologies

BRANDS/DIVISIONS/AFFILIATES:

KSPG AG
KS Kolbenschmidt GmbH
Pierburg GmbH
MS Motor Service International GmbH
Kolbenschmidt
Pierburg
Motorservice

CONTACTS: *Note: Officers with more than one job title may be intentionally listed here more than once.*

Olaf Hedden, CFO
Peter Sebastian Krause, Human Resources
Peter-Sebastian Krause, Dir.-Legal Affairs
Gerd Kleinert, Dir.-Oper.
Gerd Kleinert, Dir.-Strategy
Peter P. Merten, Dir.-Finance & Controlling

GROWTH PLANS/SPECIAL FEATURES:

Rheinmetall Automotive AG (formerly KSPG AG) is a German holding company which, through its subsidiaries, provides products for the automotive industry. The firm specializes in products for air supply, emission control and pumps, as well as in the development, manufacture and aftermarket supply of pistons, engine blocks and plain bearings. Rheinmetall is made up of three brands: Kolbenschmidt, Pierburg and Motorservice. The Kolbenschmidt brand includes KS Kolbenschmidt GmbH, which develops, produces and markets gasoline and diesel engine pistons for cars and commercial vehicles. Its products include bearings, castings, large bore pistons and small bore pistons. The Pierburg brand includes Pierburg GmbH, which specializes in emission control, air supply and valves. Its products include actuators, automotive emission systems, commercial diesel systems, pump technology such as on-demand controlled electric coolant pumps, solenoid valves and variable valve trains. The Motorservice brand includes MS Motor Service International GmbH, which is the sales organization for the worldwide aftermarket activities of Rheinmetall Automotive. This division serves wholesalers, engine repairers and independent workshops in 130 countries, and its product range is comprised of high-grade parts for engines that ensure optimal function even in extreme conditions.

FINANCIAL DATA: *Note: Data for latest year may not have been available at press time.*

In U.S. $	2018	2017	2016	2015	2014	2013
Revenue	3,351,310,000	3,427,090,000	3,176,919,521	2,901,502,325	5,306,112,800	3,234,002,040
R&D Expense						
Operating Income						
Operating Margin %						
SGA Expense						
Net Income	299,673,000	298,268,000	262,336,881	5,003,744	18,100,000	65,106,835
Operating Cash Flow						
Capital Expenditure						
EBITDA						
Return on Assets %						
Return on Equity %						
Debt to Equity						

CONTACT INFORMATION:

Phone: 49-7132-33-0 Fax: 49-7132-33-2796
Toll-Free:
Address: Karl-Schmidt-Strasse, Neckarsulm, 74172 Germany

STOCK TICKER/OTHER:

Stock Ticker: Subsidiary
Exchange:
Employees: 11,500
Fiscal Year Ends: 12/31
Parent Company: Rheinmetall AG

SALARIES/BONUSES:

Top Exec. Salary: $ Bonus: $
Second Exec. Salary: $ Bonus: $

OTHER THOUGHTS:

Estimated Female Officers or Directors:
Hot Spot for Advancement for Women/Minorities:

Ricart Automotive Inc

www.ricart.com

NAIC Code: 441110

TYPES OF BUSINESS:

Auto Dealers, Retail
Reconditioned Airplane Sales
Mortgage Services
Van & RV Sales

BRANDS/DIVISIONS/AFFILIATES:

Ricart Mega Mall
Ricart Super Duty Center

GROWTH PLANS/SPECIAL FEATURES:

Ricart Automotive, Inc. is a new and used car dealership serving the Columbus, Ohio region. The company offers new vehicle brands, including Ford, Genesis, Nissan, Hyundai, Kia, Mazda and Mitsubishi, as well as virtually any model of pre-owned vehicles. The Ricart dealership is situated on a 67-acre property known as the Ricart Mega Mall. The mega-dealership has thousands of vehicles in stock on any given day. Ricart also provides a range of services, as well as parts and financing. Moreover, the Ricart Super Duty Center provides heavy duty and diesel repair. From the firm's website, customers can search inventory by make, model, year and price; apply for financing; get a quote; or apply for their rewards program. The company has been family owned since its inception in 1953.

CONTACTS: *Note: Officers with more than one job title may be intentionally listed here more than once.*

Rhett Ricart, CEO
Fred Ricart, Partner
Rob Caruthers, CFO
Jeremy Tudor, Dir.-Digital Srvcs.
Julie Dyer, Dir.-Human Resources
Rick Ricart, Co-Pres.
Lynne Meadows Ricart, Spokeswoman
Lynne DeWitt, Dir.-Consumer Affairs
Rhett C. Ricart, Co-CEO
Jared Ricart, Co-Pres.

FINANCIAL DATA: *Note: Data for latest year may not have been available at press time.*

In U.S. $	2018	2017	2016	2015	2014	2013
Revenue	574,402,500	547,050,000	521,000,000			
R&D Expense						
Operating Income						
Operating Margin %						
SGA Expense						
Net Income						
Operating Cash Flow						
Capital Expenditure						
EBITDA						
Return on Assets %						
Return on Equity %						
Debt to Equity						

CONTACT INFORMATION:

Phone: 614-836-6265 Fax: 614-836-6563
Toll-Free:
Address: 4255 S. Hamilton Rd., Columbus, OH 43125 United States

STOCK TICKER/OTHER:

Stock Ticker: Private
Employees: 560
Parent Company:
Exchange:
Fiscal Year Ends: 12/31

SALARIES/BONUSES:

Top Exec. Salary: $ Bonus: $
Second Exec. Salary: $ Bonus: $

OTHER THOUGHTS:

Estimated Female Officers or Directors: 3
Hot Spot for Advancement for Women/Minorities: Y

Rieter Holding AG

www.rieter.com

NAIC Code: 336300

TYPES OF BUSINESS:

Auto Parts Manufacturing
Interior Trim
Noise Control Systems
Thermal Insulation Products
Dash Assemblies
Plastic Extrusion Systems
Textile Spinning Systems
Automotive Carpets

BRANDS/DIVISIONS/AFFILIATES:

Bracker
Graf
Novibra
Suessen

CONTACTS: *Note: Officers with more than one job title may be intentionally listed here more than once.*

Norbert Klapper, CEO
Kurt Ledermann, CFO
Thomas Anwander, General Counsel
Peter Gnagi, CEO-Textile Systems
Bernhard Jucker, Chmn.

GROWTH PLANS/SPECIAL FEATURES:

Rieter Holding AG is a Swiss industrial group that provides systems and services for the textile and plastics industries. The company comprises three business groups: machines & systems, after sales and components. The machines & systems group produces and supplies short staple yarns from natural and man-made fibers for all applications. This division's offerings range from complete installations from raw material to end-products, subsystems, machines, components, wear and tear parts, as well as spare parts. Operation plants are located in Europe, India and China, along with sales and service centers to support customers in those regions. The after sales group provides spare parts, as well as value-adding after sales services and solutions over the entire product life cycle. After sales services include technology support, maintenance audits, repair services and customer training. After sales solutions aim to make customer spinning mills productive, efficient and flexible, and to enable swift response to market changes. The components group is comprised of four companies: Bracker, Graf, Novibra and Suessen, which supply world-leading brands of technology components to the textile industry, from fiber to yarn and more. This division is therefore, a global provider of components for all spinning technologies. These products include technology parts for sliver preparation, spinning components, high-end and basic technologies, as well as global sales, service, engineering and manufacturing components. Rieter has 14 manufacturing locations worldwide, including Belgium, China, France, Germany, India, Italy, Netherlands, Switzerland and Uzbekistan.

FINANCIAL DATA: *Note: Data for latest year may not have been available at press time.*

In U.S. $	2018	2017	2016	2015	2014	2013
Revenue	1,081,908,000	971,624,100	950,895,600	1,043,268,000	1,160,596,000	1,041,759,000
R&D Expense	7,949,286					
Operating Income	42,966,390	55,141,880	50,613,810	63,393,040	81,706,580	60,575,570
Operating Margin %		.06%	.05%	.04%	.07%	.06%
SGA Expense	66,311,130	50,513,180	47,595,090	51,217,550	56,349,370	47,997,580
Net Income	32,099,010	13,282,350	42,664,520	50,010,060	53,129,400	39,645,800
Operating Cash Flow	78,889,110	20,728,520	102,837,600	89,555,250	90,158,980	108,371,900
Capital Expenditure	29,382,170	29,583,420	31,092,780	31,797,140	42,463,270	55,343,130
EBITDA	88,549,010	68,625,480	98,913,260	116,119,900	125,578,600	103,944,500
Return on Assets %		.01%	.04%	.04%	.05%	.04%
Return on Equity %		.03%	.09%	.11%	.13%	.10%
Debt to Equity		0.233	0.218	0.243	0.24	0.472

CONTACT INFORMATION:

Phone: 41 522087171 Fax: 41 522087060
Toll-Free:
Address: Klosterstrasse 32, Winterthur, CH-8406 Switzerland

STOCK TICKER/OTHER:

Stock Ticker: RTRZY
Employees: 5,134
Parent Company:
Exchange: GREY
Fiscal Year Ends: 12/31

SALARIES/BONUSES:

Top Exec. Salary: $ Bonus: $
Second Exec. Salary: $ Bonus: $

OTHER THOUGHTS:

Estimated Female Officers or Directors:
Hot Spot for Advancement for Women/Minorities:

Rivian Automotive LLC

www.rivian.com

NAIC Code: 336111

TYPES OF BUSINESS:

Electric Automobile Manufacturing
Electric Drive Technologies

BRANDS/DIVISIONS/AFFILIATES:

R1S
R1T

CONTACTS:
Note: Officers with more than one job title may be intentionally listed here more than once.

RJ Scaringe, CEO
JitenBehl, Chief Strategy Officer
Ryan Green, CFO
Mark Vinnels, Exec. Dir.-Eng. & Programs

GROWTH PLANS/SPECIAL FEATURES:

Rivian Automotive LLC is an American automaker that develops vehicles, products and services related to electric-powered transportation. Headquartered in Plymouth, Michigan, the firm also has facilities in San Jose and Irvine, California; Normal, Illinois; and in the U.K. Rivian is in the process of developing two vehicles, an electric sports utility vehicle (SUV), the R1S, and an electric pickup truck, the R1T. Both the R1S and R1T share the same electric chassis and battery, as well as sharing many of the same specifications. Both vehicles are designed to be capable of off-road travel, have the ability to cross three feet of water depth, a range of over 400 miles on a 180 kWh battery and be able to sprint from 0 to 60 in under three seconds, with a top speed of approximately 125 miles per hour. The firm plans to introduce both models to the American market in 2020. In February 2019, Amazon announced that it would lead an investment round of $700 million into Rivian. The company plans to sell vehicles directly to consumers, bypassing the traditional franchised dealer model used by most car makers. Initial production of 20,000 units in 2021 is hoped for. Retail prices for the vehicles will start in the $70,000 range. The firm may eventually license some of its unique technology platform to other firms.

FINANCIAL DATA:
Note: Data for latest year may not have been available at press time.

In U.S. $	2018	2017	2016	2015	2014	2013
Revenue						
R&D Expense						
Operating Income						
Operating Margin %						
SGA Expense						
Net Income						
Operating Cash Flow						
Capital Expenditure						
EBITDA						
Return on Assets %						
Return on Equity %						
Debt to Equity						

CONTACT INFORMATION:

Phone: 734-855-4350 Fax:
Toll-Free:
Address: 13250 Haggerty Rd., Plymouth, MI 48170 United States

STOCK TICKER/OTHER:

Stock Ticker: Private
Employees: 750
Parent Company:
Exchange:
Fiscal Year Ends:

SALARIES/BONUSES:

Top Exec. Salary: $ Bonus: $
Second Exec. Salary: $ Bonus: $

OTHER THOUGHTS:

Estimated Female Officers or Directors:
Hot Spot for Advancement for Women/Minorities:

Roark Capital Management LLC (Roark Caoital Group)

www.roarkcapital.com

NAIC Code: 551112

TYPES OF BUSINESS:

Private Equity Firm
Limited-Service Restaurants
Automotive Repair/Maintenance
Gyms
Massage Therapy

BRANDS/DIVISIONS/AFFILIATES:

Inspire Brands
CKE Restaurants
FOCUS Brands
Self Esteem Brands
Massage Envy
Great Expressions Dental Centers
Driven Brands
Batteries Plus Bulbs

CONTACTS: *Note: Officers with more than one job title may be intentionally listed here more than once.*

Neal K. Aronson, Managing Partner
Tracy A. Haas, CFO

GROWTH PLANS/SPECIAL FEATURES:

Roark Capital Management LLC, d/b/a Roark Caoital Group, is a private equity firm with investments in middle-market companies, primarily in the franchise/multi-unit, restaurant and food, retail healthcare and business services sectors. Since its inception, the firm has 68 franchise/multi-unit brands which generate approximately $37 billion in system revenues from 36,000 locations located in 50 states and 81 countries. Roark's portfolio companies span multiple industries including food and restaurants, specialty retail, health and wellness, retail healthcare, business services, and education. The food and restaurant sector encompasses 25 investments in brands such as: Inspire Brands, the owner of Arby's, Buffalo Wild Wings, Rusty Taco and Sonic; CKE Restaurants, the owner of Carl's Jr and Hardee's; Corner Bakery; Culver's; FOCUS Brands, the owner of Auntie Anne's Pretzels, Carvel Ice Cream, Cinnabon, Jamba Juice, McAlister's Deli, Moe's Southwest Grill and Schlotzsky's; Il Fornaio; Jim 'N Nick's BBQ; Jimmy John's; Miller's Ale House; Naf Naf Middle Eastern Grill; and Wingstop. The companies within the health and wellness sector include Self Esteem Brands, the parent company of Anytime Fitness, Basecamp Fitness and Waxing the City; Drybar; Fitness Connection; Massage Envy; and Orangetheory Fitness. Great Expressions Dental Centers comprises Roark's retail healthcare sector. The business services sector is comprised of Installation Made Easy and Solterra Recycling Solutions. The specialty retail sector encompasses investments in Driven Brands, the owner of a family of automotive brands including 1-800 Radiator, CARSTAR, MAACO, Meineke Car Care Centers, Merlin 200,000 Mile Shops, Pro Oil Change and Econo Lube & Tune; Take 5 Oil Change; International Car Wash Group; the pet store chains of Bosley's, Pet Supermarket and Pet Value; and Batteries Plus Bulbs. Investment in Primrose Schools is the extent of the firm's current educational holdings.

FINANCIAL DATA: *Note: Data for latest year may not have been available at press time.*

In U.S. $	2018	2017	2016	2015	2014	2013
Revenue						
R&D Expense						
Operating Income						
Operating Margin %						
SGA Expense						
Net Income						
Operating Cash Flow						
Capital Expenditure						
EBITDA						
Return on Assets %						
Return on Equity %						
Debt to Equity						

CONTACT INFORMATION:

Phone: 404-591-5200 Fax:
Toll-Free:
Address: 1180 Peachtree St. NE, Ste. 2500, Atlanta, GA 30309 United States

STOCK TICKER/OTHER:

Stock Ticker: Private
Employees:
Parent Company:
Exchange:
Fiscal Year Ends:

SALARIES/BONUSES:

Top Exec. Salary: $ Bonus: $
Second Exec. Salary: $ Bonus: $

OTHER THOUGHTS:

Estimated Female Officers or Directors:
Hot Spot for Advancement for Women/Minorities:

Robert Bosch GmbH

www.bosch.com

NAIC Code: 336300

TYPES OF BUSINESS:

Automobile Components Manufacturing
Software and Machine to Machine Data
Motor, Control & Motion Products
Chassis Systems
Electronics & Multimedia
Energy, Fuel & Body Systems
Security Systems
Power Tools

BRANDS/DIVISIONS/AFFILIATES:

Bosch Mahle TurboSystems
Bosch Engineering
Bosch Boxberg Proving Ground
Bosch Battery Systems
Bosch Rexroth
Bosch Packaging Technology

CONTACTS: *Note: Officers with more than one job title may be intentionally listed here more than once.*

Volkmar Denner, Dir.-Research
Volkmar Denner, Dir.-Prod. Planning
Volkmar Denner, Dir.-Eng.
Stefan Asenkerschbaumer, Dir.-Bus. Admin.
Christoph Kubel, Dir.-Legal Svcs., Taxes & Internal Auditing
Stefan Asenkerschbaumer, Dir.-Corp. Planning
Volkmar Denner, Dir.-Corp. Comm.
Stefan Asenkerschbaumer, Dir.-Finance & Controlling
Wolf-Henning Scheider, Dir.-Coordination Automotive Tech.
Uwe Raschke, Dir.-Consumer Goods & User Experience
Werner Struth, Dir.-North & South America
Volkmar Denner, Chmn.
Peter Tyroller, Dir.-Asia Pacific
Stefan Asenkerschbaumer, Dir.-Purchasing & Logistics

GROWTH PLANS/SPECIAL FEATURES:

Robert Bosch GmbH is one of the world's leading manufacturers of automotive components. It has operations in roughly 60 countries through over 440 subsidiaries. The company operates in four business sectors: mobility solutions, industrial technology, consumer goods and energy and building technology. Mobility solutions supplies independent parts to the automotive industry, including gasoline systems, diesel systems, chassis systems control, electrical drives, starter motors, generators, multimedia, automotive electronics, automotive aftermarket parts and steering systems. Subsidiaries and joint ventures (JVs) in this segment include Bosch Mahle TurboSystems, Bosch Engineering, Bosch Boxberg Proving Ground and Bosch Battery Systems. Industrial technology incorporates the drive, control technology and packaging technology divisions. Subsidiary Bosch Rexroth provides drive and control technologies for mobile applications, machinery applications/engineering and factory automation. Bosch Packaging Technology is a leading supplier in the field of processing and packaging technology, developing and producing solutions for the pharmaceutical, food and confectionary industries. Consumer goods provides a wide spectrum of products and solutions in the areas of power tools and household appliances. Energy and building technology offers products and solutions such as HVAC (heating, ventilating and air conditioning), solar energy and security systems. In addition, Robert Bosch's Internet of Things (IoT) solutions combines the fields of software, sensors and services to provide connectivity solutions in regards to industry, mobility, smart home, smart city and more. The company is very technology-driven and invests about 9% of revenues in research and development. During 2018, the firm opened a new global Internet of Things (IoT) campus in Berlin, Germany; and invested in ABAX Sensing, which is developing a full solid-state chip Lidar for consumer and automotive applications, in particular for advanced driver assistance systems and autonomous vehicles.

Bosch USA offers employees medical, dental, vision, disability and travel insurance; paid vacations; and an educational assistance program.

FINANCIAL DATA: *Note: Data for latest year may not have been available at press time.*

In U.S. $	2018	2017	2016	2015	2014	2013
Revenue	88,321,400,000	93,512,400,000	77,058,200,000	77,152,300,000	54,586,000,000	51,372,000,000
R&D Expense						
Operating Income						
Operating Margin %						
SGA Expense						
Net Income	6,008,870,000	3,921,810,000	2,805,000,000	4,178,000,000	2,941,000,000	1,395,000,000
Operating Cash Flow						
Capital Expenditure						
EBITDA						
Return on Assets %						
Return on Equity %						
Debt to Equity						

CONTACT INFORMATION:

Phone: 49-711-400-40990 Fax: 49-711-400-40999
Toll-Free:
Address: Robert-Bosch-Platz 1, Gerlingen-Schillerhohe, 70839 Germany

STOCK TICKER/OTHER:

Stock Ticker: Private
Employees: 410,000
Parent Company:
Exchange:
Fiscal Year Ends: 12/31

SALARIES/BONUSES:

Top Exec. Salary: $ Bonus: $
Second Exec. Salary: $ Bonus: $

OTHER THOUGHTS:

Estimated Female Officers or Directors: 3
Hot Spot for Advancement for Women/Minorities: Y

Sales, profits and employees may be estimates. Financial information, benefits and other data can change quickly and may vary from those stated here.

Rolls-Royce Motor Car Limited

www.rolls-roycemotorcars.com

NAIC Code: 336111

TYPES OF BUSINESS:

Automobile Manufacturing
Luxury Automobile Sales
Automobile Customizing
Pre-owned Luxury Automobile Sales

BRANDS/DIVISIONS/AFFILIATES:

Bayerische Motoren Werke AG (BMW)
Ghost
Phantom
Wraith
Dawn
Bespoke
Black Badge
Cullinan

CONTACTS: *Note: Officers with more than one job title may be intentionally listed here more than once.*

Torsten Muller-Otvos, CEO
Nigel Wonnacott, Mgr.-Prod. Comm.
Helmut Riedl, Dir.-Eng.
Xaver Franz, Dir.-Mfg.
Richard Carter, Dir.-Global Comm.
Paul Harris, Dir.-Asia Pacific
Brenda Pek, Gen. Mgr.-South & East Asia Pacific
Geoffrey Briscoe, Dir.-Middle East, Africa & Latin America
Peter Schwarzenbauer, Chmn.
James Crichton, Dir.-Europe & South Africa

GROWTH PLANS/SPECIAL FEATURES:

Rolls-Royce Motor Car Limited, a subsidiary of Bayerische Motoren Werke AG (BMW), is a predominant designer and manufacturer of fully customizable luxury automobiles. Bespoke, the company's automobile modification program, allows customers to intricately customize any aspect of the automobile. The firm currently offers six primary vehicle lines: the Ghost, the Phantom, the Wraith, the Black Badge, the Dawn and the Cullinan. The Ghost is a 4-door sedan with a V12 twin turbo engine and 8-speed automatic transmission. The Phantom 4-seater is larger than the Ghost and comprises a V12 engine and 8-speed automatic transmission. The Phantom also comes with an extended wheel base, known as the Phantom EWB model. The Wraith and the edgier Black Badge are 4-seat grand tourer vehicles, with a V12 twin turbo engine and 8-speed automatic transmission. The Dawn is a 4-seat, 2-door luxury convertible with a V12 twin turbo engine and 8-speed automatic transmission. The Cullinan is the firm's first sports utility vehicle (SUV) and first all-wheel drive vehicle. The SUV comes equipped with a twin-turbocharged V12 engine and 8-speed automatic transmission. Rolls-Royce distributes its bespoke vehicles worldwide and operates from production facilities located in Goodwood and West Sussex, England.

FINANCIAL DATA: *Note: Data for latest year may not have been available at press time.*

In U.S. $	2018	2017	2016	2015	2014	2013
Revenue	749,981,000	569,990,000	551,808,000	523,995,000	693,185,000	621,372,000
R&D Expense						
Operating Income						
Operating Margin %						
SGA Expense						
Net Income	80,604,600	28,374,800	17,011,900	19,272,200	21,277,300	21,436,000
Operating Cash Flow						
Capital Expenditure						
EBITDA						
Return on Assets %						
Return on Equity %						
Debt to Equity						

CONTACT INFORMATION:

Phone: 44-1243-384000 Fax: 44-1243-384100
Toll-Free:
Address: The Drive, Westhampnett, Chichester, PO18 0SH United Kingdom

STOCK TICKER/OTHER:

Stock Ticker: Subsidiary
Exchange:
Employees: 1,277
Fiscal Year Ends: 12/31
Parent Company: Bayerische Motoren Werke AG (BMW)

SALARIES/BONUSES:

Top Exec. Salary: $ Bonus: $
Second Exec. Salary: $ Bonus: $

OTHER THOUGHTS:

Estimated Female Officers or Directors: 2
Hot Spot for Advancement for Women/Minorities:

Rosenthal Automotive Organization

www.rosenthalauto.com

NAIC Code: 441110

TYPES OF BUSINESS:

Auto Dealer
Fleet Sales
Repair Service
Online Service Appointment Scheduling

BRANDS/DIVISIONS/AFFILIATES:

GROWTH PLANS/SPECIAL FEATURES:

Rosenthal Automotive Organization is an automotive dealership operating through 15 locations, of which 13 are in Virginia and two in Maryland. The firm sells cars, trucks and SUVs (sport utility vehicles). Brands sold include Audi, BMW, Porsche, Honda, Acura, Hyundai, Mazda, Jaguar, Land Rover, Volvo, Genesis and Volkswagen. Rosenthal Automotive additionally sells used cars and offers online service appointment scheduling and an online parts order form. The company also operates body shops, and sells parts and related accessories at select locations. Vehicle inventory can be searched online, as well as parts and accessories.

CONTACTS: *Note: Officers with more than one job title may be intentionally listed here more than once.*

George Liu, CEO

FINANCIAL DATA: *Note: Data for latest year may not have been available at press time.*

In U.S. $	2018	2017	2016	2015	2014	2013
Revenue	1,113,525,000	1,060,500,000	1,010,000,000	983,000,000	955,500,000	926,041,239
R&D Expense						
Operating Income						
Operating Margin %						
SGA Expense						
Net Income						
Operating Cash Flow						
Capital Expenditure						
EBITDA						
Return on Assets %						
Return on Equity %						
Debt to Equity						

CONTACT INFORMATION:

Phone: 703-553-4300 Fax: 703-553-8435
Toll-Free:
Address: 1902 Association Dr., Reston, VA 20191 United States

STOCK TICKER/OTHER:

Stock Ticker: Private
Employees:
Parent Company:
Exchange:
Fiscal Year Ends: 12/31

SALARIES/BONUSES:

Top Exec. Salary: $ Bonus: $
Second Exec. Salary: $ Bonus: $

OTHER THOUGHTS:

Estimated Female Officers or Directors:
Hot Spot for Advancement for Women/Minorities:

Rush Enterprises Inc

www.rushenterprises.com

NAIC Code: 441110

TYPES OF BUSINESS:

Truck Dealerships
New & Used Construction Equipment
Truck Parts
Repair Services
Financing & Insurance
Leasing
Construction Equipment Rental

BRANDS/DIVISIONS/AFFILIATES:

Rush Truck Centers
House of Trucks
Perfection Equipment
Rush Truck Leasing Centers
World Wide Tires

CONTACTS: *Note: Officers with more than one job title may be intentionally listed here more than once.*

Steven Keller, CFO
W. Rush, Chairman of the Board
Michael McRoberts, COO
Derrek Weaver, Executive VP
James Thor, Senior VP, Divisional
Scott Anderson, Senior VP, Divisional

GROWTH PLANS/SPECIAL FEATURES:

Rush Enterprises, Inc. is a full-service, integrated retailer and servicer of commercial vehicles and related services. Rush's truck segment operates a network of more than 100 Rush Truck Centers located in 22 U.S. states. The company provides retail sales of new and used medium-duty and heavy-duty trucks; aftermarket parts, service and body shop facilities; and financial services, including the financing of new and used truck purchases, insurance products and truck leasing and rentals. Each center is a franchised dealership for vehicles manufactured by Peterbilt, International, Hino, Ford, Isuzu, Mitsubishi Fuso, IC Bus or Blue Bird. The House of Trucks, a Rush subsidiary, sells used commercial vehicles, new and used trailers. Subsidiary Perfection Equipment offers installation of equipment, equipment repair, parts installation and paint and body repair. Rush Truck Leasing Centers offer leasing and rental opportunities for Class 4 through Class 8 trucks, heavy-duty cranes and refuse haulers. Custom Vehicle Solutions operates and Texas and Pennsylvania, and provides new vehicle pre-delivery inspections, truck modifications, natural gas fuel system installation, body and chassis upfitting and component installation. Additionally, Rush operates two World Wide Tires stores in Texas, which sell tires for use on commercial vehicles. All of Rush's centers offer third-party financing and a complete line of property and casualty insurance, including collision and liability insurance on commercial vehicles, cargo insurance and credit life insurance. In 2019, Rush Enterprises agreed to form a 50/50 joint venture with Tallman Group to operate Tallman Group's network of commercial vehicle dealerships in Canada.

FINANCIAL DATA: *Note: Data for latest year may not have been available at press time.*

In U.S. $	2018	2017	2016	2015	2014	2013
Revenue	5,506,190,000	4,713,882,000	4,214,614,000	4,979,733,000	4,727,356,000	3,384,705,000
R&D Expense						
Operating Income	202,554,000	148,814,000	78,973,000	121,820,000	141,590,000	91,749,000
Operating Margin %		.03%	.02%	.02%	.03%	.03%
SGA Expense	705,226,000	631,053,000	587,778,000	619,268,000	573,670,000	450,340,000
Net Income	139,062,000	172,129,000	40,582,000	66,053,000	79,957,000	49,217,000
Operating Cash Flow	215,364,000	152,737,000	521,170,000	227,250,000	88,937,000	173,488,000
Capital Expenditure	238,260,000	209,917,000	196,965,000	367,790,000	260,820,000	191,584,000
EBITDA	389,349,000	307,551,000	238,976,000	266,701,000	268,432,000	185,281,000
Return on Assets %		.06%	.01%	.02%	.03%	.02%
Return on Equity %		.18%	.05%	.08%	.11%	.08%
Debt to Equity		0.512	0.629	0.67	0.622	0.632

CONTACT INFORMATION:

Phone: 830 626-5200 Fax:
Toll-Free: 800-973-7874
Address: 555 IH-35 S., Ste. 500, New Braunfels, TX 78130 United States

STOCK TICKER/OTHER:

Stock Ticker: RUSHA
Employees: 6,180
Parent Company:
Exchange: NAS
Fiscal Year Ends: 12/31

SALARIES/BONUSES:

Top Exec. Salary: $1,549,948 Bonus: $2,500,000
Second Exec. Salary: $553,516 Bonus: $565,000

OTHER THOUGHTS:

Estimated Female Officers or Directors:
Hot Spot for Advancement for Women/Minorities:

Russ Darrow Group Inc

www.russdarrow.com

NAIC Code: 441110

TYPES OF BUSINESS:

Auto Dealers, Retail
Fleet Sales
Leasing
Repair Services
Financing

BRANDS/DIVISIONS/AFFILIATES:

Russ Darrow Leasing

CONTACTS:

Note: Officers with more than one job title may be intentionally listed here more than once.

Russell Darrow, Jr., CEO
Mike Darrow, Pres.

GROWTH PLANS/SPECIAL FEATURES:

Russ Darrow Group, Inc. is a leading automobile dealer in Wisconsin, with 15 locations throughout the state. The group sells both new and used vehicles, with a focus on Chrysler, Dodge, Honda, Jeep, Kia, Mazda, Mitsubishi, Nissan, RAM and Toyota brands. The firm also has parts, service and collision centers that are located within its dealerships. Russ Darrow's website features a search engine for new and pre-owned vehicles as well as vehicles priced below $10,000. Customers can also check internet specials; contact and make appointments with the service, parts and collision departments; and fill out a finance application. In addition to selling new and used vehicles, the company's Russ Darrow Leasing business leases and finances trucks and commercial fleets. Russ Darrow Leasing offers a fleet maintenance management program and a fleet fuel card program in conjunction with its commercial fleet services offering.

Russ Darrow offers its employees technician apprenticeship training; an employee assistance program; vehicle purchase discounts; a bi-annual family zoo party; tenure benefits; flexible spending accounts; and medical, dental, disability and life insurance.

FINANCIAL DATA:

Note: Data for latest year may not have been available at press time.

In U.S. $	2018	2017	2016	2015	2014	2013
Revenue	633,037,497	602,892,854	574,183,670	520,764,466	451,000,000	333,137,641
R&D Expense						
Operating Income						
Operating Margin %						
SGA Expense						
Net Income						
Operating Cash Flow						
Capital Expenditure						
EBITDA						
Return on Assets %						
Return on Equity %						
Debt to Equity						

CONTACT INFORMATION:

Phone: 262-250-9600 Fax: 262-253-7530
Toll-Free:
Address: W133 N8569 Executive Pkwy., Menomonee Falls, WI 53051 United States

STOCK TICKER/OTHER:

Stock Ticker: Private
Employees: 1,001
Parent Company:
Exchange:
Fiscal Year Ends: 12/31

SALARIES/BONUSES:

Top Exec. Salary: $ Bonus: $
Second Exec. Salary: $ Bonus: $

OTHER THOUGHTS:

Estimated Female Officers or Directors:
Hot Spot for Advancement for Women/Minorities:

Sales, profits and employees may be estimates. Financial information, benefits and other data can change quickly and may vary from those stated here.

Rybrook Holdings Limited

www.rybrook.co.uk

NAIC Code: 441110

TYPES OF BUSINESS:

Auto Dealers, Retail
Auto Leasing
Fleet Sales

BRANDS/DIVISIONS/AFFILIATES:

Ryland
Rybrook

GROWTH PLANS/SPECIAL FEATURES:

Rybrook Holdings Limited is a leading private car dealership in the U.K. The company operates its dealerships under the Ryland and Rybrook names. The firm carries 10 different makes of vehicles, including Bentley, BMW, Jaguar, Lamborghini, Land Rover, McLaren, MINI, Rolls-Royce, Porsche and Volvo, as well as specialist cars. The group also sells used cars. Ryland's web site assists customers in valuing their current automobiles and in selecting new models. For corporate customers, the firm offers car and fuel benefit calculators and a sales group committed to company fleet sales. Fleet services include up to 250 vehicles in most of the models of the dealerships' new cars. In addition, Ryland's dealerships feature parts and service departments and personal financing.

CONTACTS: *Note: Officers with more than one job title may be intentionally listed here more than once.*

Henry Whale, CEO
Keith Hampson, Dir.-Finance

FINANCIAL DATA: *Note: Data for latest year may not have been available at press time.*

In U.S. $	2018	2017	2016	2015	2014	2013
Revenue	780,404,625	743,242,500	707,850,000	640,977,000	680,319,000	621,744,000
R&D Expense						
Operating Income						
Operating Margin %						
SGA Expense						
Net Income			3,704,010	21,351,900	4,990,430	1,953,830
Operating Cash Flow						
Capital Expenditure						
EBITDA						
Return on Assets %						
Return on Equity %						
Debt to Equity						

CONTACT INFORMATION:

Phone: 44-1845-366-8243 Fax:
Toll-Free:
Address: 6 Athena Court, Tachbrook Park, Warwick, Birmingham CV34 6RT United Kingdom

STOCK TICKER/OTHER:

Stock Ticker: Private
Employees: 805
Parent Company:
Exchange:
Fiscal Year Ends: 12/31

SALARIES/BONUSES:

Top Exec. Salary: $ Bonus: $
Second Exec. Salary: $ Bonus: $

OTHER THOUGHTS:

Estimated Female Officers or Directors:
Hot Spot for Advancement for Women/Minorities:

Rygor Group Limited

www.rygor.co.uk

NAIC Code: 441110

TYPES OF BUSINESS:

Auto Dealers, Retail
Commercial Sales
Parts & Service
Distribution Services
Rental Services
Warehousing Services

BRANDS/DIVISIONS/AFFILIATES:

GROWTH PLANS/SPECIAL FEATURES:

Rygor Group Limited, based in southern England, is a dealer group for Mercedes-Benz commercial vehicles. Company branches are located at 11 sales and aftersales branches throughout the country. Its commercial vehicle offerings are divided into two groups: trucks and vans. Truck models currently being offered as new include rigid trucks, tractors/arctics, FUSO Canter and unimog trucks. Vans currently being offered as new are branded under the Citan, Vito and Sprinter labels, and include panel vans, crew vans, tourer/wagon vehicles and sport vehicles. The X-Class pickup concept contains a V-6 diesel engine in conjunction with 4MATIC permanent all-wheel drive, for enhanced driving dynamics both on and off regular roads. All used trucks, vans or unimogs can be searched on the firm's website. Rygor also provides financing, leasing and insurance services, as well as after sales parts and services.

CONTACTS: *Note: Officers with more than one job title may be intentionally listed here more than once.*

Tim Stacey, Managing Dir.
Jim Pascoe, Mgr.-Group Oper.
Graham Drake, Dir.-Finance

FINANCIAL DATA: *Note: Data for latest year may not have been available at press time.*

In U.S. $	2018	2017	2016	2015	2014	2013
Revenue	329,053,000	287,941,000	281,254,000	291,271,000	259,994,000	192,955,000
R&D Expense						
Operating Income						
Operating Margin %						
SGA Expense						
Net Income	-586,908	723,497	1,207,730	2,833,070	943,518	1,865,670
Operating Cash Flow						
Capital Expenditure						
EBITDA						
Return on Assets %						
Return on Equity %						
Debt to Equity						

CONTACT INFORMATION:

Phone: 44-1373-855-555 Fax:
Toll-Free:
Address: The Broadway, W. Wilts Trading Estate, Westbury, BA13 4JX United Kingdom

STOCK TICKER/OTHER:

Stock Ticker: Private
Employees: 450
Parent Company:
Exchange:
Fiscal Year Ends: 04/30

SALARIES/BONUSES:

Top Exec. Salary: $ Bonus: $
Second Exec. Salary: $ Bonus: $

OTHER THOUGHTS:

Estimated Female Officers or Directors:
Hot Spot for Advancement for Women/Minorities:

SAF-Holland SA

NAIC Code: 336214

www.safholland.com

TYPES OF BUSINESS:

Travel Trailer and Camper Manufacturing

BRANDS/DIVISIONS/AFFILIATES:

SAF
Holland
Neway

CONTACTS:
Note: Officers with more than one job title may be intentionally listed here more than once.

Alexander Geis, CEO
Andre Philipp, COO
Matthias Heiden, CFO
Jack Ginsinger, Pres., Powered Vehicles Systems & Group Tech.
Stefffen Schewerda, Pres., Trailer Systems Bus. & Group Oper.
Alexander Geis, Pres., Aftermarket Bus. Unit

GROWTH PLANS/SPECIAL FEATURES:

SAF-Holland SA manufactures and sells components and systems for trailers, semi-trailers, trucks, tractor units, buses and recreational vehicles. Products are distributed mainly to original equipment manufacturers (OEMs) and original equipment suppliers (OESs) under the brand names SAF, Holland and Neway. It operates in three segments: trailer systems, powered vehicle systems and aftermarket. The trailer systems division manufactures landing gear, kingpins, axle systems and suspension systems for trailer manufacturers. The powered vehicle systems segment consists of axle suspension systems and fifth wheels for the production of trucks and buses. The aftermarket segment supplies spare parts to the transport and automotive industry in North America and Europe through a global network of approximately 10,000 spare parts and service locations. Major clients include Mercedes-Benz, Peterbilt, Scania, Freightliner, Hyundai, Volvo, Iveco and Sisu. SAF-Holland has locations in more than 25 countries and is active on six continents.

FINANCIAL DATA:
Note: Data for latest year may not have been available at press time.

In U.S. $	2018	2017	2016	2015	2014	2013
Revenue	1,439,941,000	1,260,998,000	1,153,670,000	1,174,384,000	1,062,537,000	948,868,500
R&D Expense	21,669,620	22,598,540	21,799,160	23,186,450	21,716,120	19,843,890
Operating Income	90,642,160	80,515,940	90,469,450	88,294,950	64,013,510	57,163,420
Operating Margin %		.06%	.08%	.08%	.06%	.06%
SGA Expense	46,304,250	46,482,510	42,941,760	45,969,880	46,474,760	42,659,440
Net Income	53,311,560	47,483,390	48,974,760	57,160,100	36,141,500	26,976,310
Operating Cash Flow	45,150,580	62,828,830	102,599,600	69,848,320	39,911,430	59,745,350
Capital Expenditure	45,157,220	30,028,790	27,686,010	31,071,750	27,394,820	25,704,160
EBITDA	114,737,600	104,691,100	110,676,500	119,959,000	86,564,440	65,347,660
Return on Assets %		.04%	.05%	.07%	.06%	.05%
Return on Equity %		.14%	.15%	.19%	.14%	.12%
Debt to Equity		1.209	1.45	1.332	0.728	0.603

CONTACT INFORMATION:

Phone: 49 6095301400 Fax: 49 6095301200
Toll-Free:
Address: Hauptstrasse 26, Bessenbach, 63856 Luxembourg

STOCK TICKER/OTHER:

Stock Ticker: SFHLF
Employees: 4,293
Parent Company:
Exchange: GREY
Fiscal Year Ends: 12/31

SALARIES/BONUSES:

Top Exec. Salary: $ Bonus: $
Second Exec. Salary: $ Bonus: $

OTHER THOUGHTS:

Estimated Female Officers or Directors: 1
Hot Spot for Advancement for Women/Minorities:

SAIC Motor Corporation Limited

www.saicmotor.com

NAIC Code: 336111

TYPES OF BUSINESS:

Automobile Manufacturing
Motorcycle Manufacturing
Bus Manufacturing
Car Rental Services
Tractor & Heavy Equipment Manufacturing
Parts Manufacturing, Distribution & Retailing
Consumer Finance & Leasing
Insurance

BRANDS/DIVISIONS/AFFILIATES:

General Motors India Private Limited
SAIC USA Inc
SAIC Europe GmbH
SAIC Motor-CP Co ltd
SAIC Hong Kong Co Ltd
MG Motor UK Ltd
SAIC MAXUS
SAIC Volkswagen

CONTACTS: *Note: Officers with more than one job title may be intentionally listed here more than once.*

Chen Zhixin, Pres.
Wei Yong, CFO
Wang Jianzhang, Sec.
Chen Demei, VP
Chen Zhixin, Exec. VP
Xiao Guopu, Exec. VP
Yu Jianwei, VP-Nanjing Automotive Group
Zhu Genlin, VP
Chen Hong, Chmn.

GROWTH PLANS/SPECIAL FEATURES:

SAIC Motor Corporation Limited is a state-owned entity and one of China's largest automotive companies. The group operates manufacturing facilities, mainly near Shanghai, that make passenger cars, trucks, buses and automotive parts. SAIC has branches in Korea, Japan, Hong Kong, the U.S. and Europe. The firm sold nearly 7 million vehicles in 2018. SAIC Motor's business covers the research, production and vehicle sales of both passenger cars and commercial vehicles. The company actively promotes new energy vehicles, the commercialization of internet-connected cars and is exploring intelligent driving technology. SAIC is engaged in the research and development, production and sales of parts for motor drive systems, chassis systems, interior/exterior decoration, battery, electric drive and power electronics, as well as auto-related services such as logistics, eCommerce, travel, energy saving/charging services, finance, insurance and investments. Subsidiaries under SAIC include: General Motors India Private Limited; SAIC USA, Inc.; SAIC Europe GmbH; SAIC Motor-CP Co., Ltd.; SAIC Hong Kong Co., Ltd.; and MG Motor U.K. Ltd. Affiliated vehicle companies include Morris Garages, SAIC MAXUS, SAIC Volkswagen, SAIC-GM, Shanghai General Motors Wuling, NAVECO, SAIC-IVECO Hongyan and Shanghai Sunwin Bus Corporation.

FINANCIAL DATA: *Note: Data for latest year may not have been available at press time.*

In U.S. $	2018	2017	2016	2015	2014	2013
Revenue	198,711,000,000	132,474,000,000	108,846,000,000	100,370,000,000	101,389,843,328	91,756,700,000
R&D Expense						
Operating Income						
Operating Margin %						
SGA Expense						
Net Income	5,233,940,000	5,283,550,000	46,048,000	4,545,109,272	4,501,862,834	4,039,300,000
Operating Cash Flow						
Capital Expenditure						
EBITDA						
Return on Assets %						
Return on Equity %						
Debt to Equity						

CONTACT INFORMATION:

Phone: 86-21-2201-1888 Fax: 86-21-2201-1777
Toll-Free:
Address: 489 WeiHai Rd., Shanghai, Shanghai 200041 China

STOCK TICKER/OTHER:

Stock Ticker: 600104.SS
Employees: 180,749
Parent Company:
Exchange: Shanghai
Fiscal Year Ends: 12/31

SALARIES/BONUSES:

Top Exec. Salary: $ Bonus: $
Second Exec. Salary: $ Bonus: $

OTHER THOUGHTS:

Estimated Female Officers or Directors: 1
Hot Spot for Advancement for Women/Minorities:

SAIC-GM-Wuling Automobile Company

www.sgmw.com.cn

NAIC Code: 336111

TYPES OF BUSINESS:

Automobile Manufacturing
Gasoline Engine Manufacturing

BRANDS/DIVISIONS/AFFILIATES:

Shanghai Automotive Industry Corporation
General Motors China
Liuzhou Wuling Motors Co Ltd
Wuling
Po Chun
Baojun

CONTACTS: *Note: Officers with more than one job title may be intentionally listed here more than once.*

Shen Yang, Pres.
Ray Bierzynski, Exec. VP
Matthew Tsien, Exec. VP

GROWTH PLANS/SPECIAL FEATURES:

SAIC-GM-Wuling Automobile Company (SGMW) is a Chinese automaker that specializes in sedans, mini-vans, vans and light trucks. It is a three-way joint venture between Shanghai Automobile Industry Corporation (SAIC), General Motors China and Liuzhou Wuling Motors Co., Ltd. The firm manufactures several models sold under the Wuling moniker, as well as the Baojun name. Wuling models include minivans, long and extended-length vans, sport utility vehicles (SUVs) and small- and large-sized trucks. Po Chun models include SUVs, crossovers and sedans. Baojun models includes the small, four-passenger-door sedans with a hatchback, as well as SUV (which was renamed under the Wuling moniker). SGMW also produces Wuling gas engines. The company has vehicle manufacturing facilities in Liuzhou, Chongqing and Qingdao, China, as well as an engine factory. These plants benefit from the General Motors (GM) Global Manufacturing System. SGMW, which is highly-focused on exporting its products, currently sells its vehicles in 40 countries, including the Middle East, Africa, Southeast Asia and Center and South America. The firm sells more than 2 million cars annually. During 2019, SGMW Indonesia launched its first SUV, the Wuling Almaz.

FINANCIAL DATA: *Note: Data for latest year may not have been available at press time.*

In U.S. $	2018	2017	2016	2015	2014	2013
Revenue	2,154,951,960	2,052,335,200	1,192,700,190	1,132,455,326		
R&D Expense						
Operating Income						
Operating Margin %						
SGA Expense						
Net Income						
Operating Cash Flow						
Capital Expenditure						
EBITDA						
Return on Assets %						
Return on Equity %						
Debt to Equity						

CONTACT INFORMATION:

Phone: 86772-3751-337 Fax:
Toll-Free:
Address: Hexi Rd., No. 18, Liuzhou, 545007 China

STOCK TICKER/OTHER:

Stock Ticker: Joint Venture Exchange:
Employees: 20,000 Fiscal Year Ends: 03/31
Parent Company: SAIC Motor Corporation Limited

SALARIES/BONUSES:

Top Exec. Salary: $ Bonus: $
Second Exec. Salary: $ Bonus: $

OTHER THOUGHTS:

Estimated Female Officers or Directors:
Hot Spot for Advancement for Women/Minorities:

Sansone Auto Network

www.sansoneauto.com

NAIC Code: 441110

TYPES OF BUSINESS:

Auto Dealers, Retail
Parts
Service
Financing

BRANDS/DIVISIONS/AFFILIATES:

GROWTH PLANS/SPECIAL FEATURES:

Sansone Auto Network has a network of eight dealership locations in the state of New Jersey, all of which operate under the Sansone brand name. The dealerships offer new vehicle brands such as Genesis, Chrysler, Jeep, Dodge, Hyundai, Kia, Mazda, Nissan and Toyota, as well as an array of pre-owned vehicle makes and models. Sansone's automobile services include auto repair and financing. Customers can schedule service appointments and apply for financing online, as well as search for vehicles and obtain Internet specials on new and used vehicles. The online finance department has the ability to pre-qualify loan applicants.

CONTACTS: *Note: Officers with more than one job title may be intentionally listed here more than once.*

Dave Salsido, Pres.

FINANCIAL DATA: *Note: Data for latest year may not have been available at press time.*

In U.S. $	2018	2017	2016	2015	2014	2013
Revenue	358,098,938	368,724,910	351,166,581	336,100,528	315,651,300	255,562,320
R&D Expense						
Operating Income						
Operating Margin %						
SGA Expense						
Net Income						
Operating Cash Flow						
Capital Expenditure						
EBITDA						
Return on Assets %						
Return on Equity %						
Debt to Equity						

CONTACT INFORMATION:

Phone: 732-815-0500 Fax: 732-815-2395
Toll-Free: 866-328-3333
Address: 90-100 US Highway 1 N., Avenel, NJ 07001 United States

STOCK TICKER/OTHER:

Stock Ticker: Private
Employees: 500
Parent Company:
Exchange:
Fiscal Year Ends: 12/31

SALARIES/BONUSES:

Top Exec. Salary: $ Bonus: $
Second Exec. Salary: $ Bonus: $

OTHER THOUGHTS:

Estimated Female Officers or Directors: 1
Hot Spot for Advancement for Women/Minorities:

Sales, profits and employees may be estimates. Financial information, benefits and other data can change quickly and may vary from those stated here.

Santa Monica Ford Lincoln Mercury

www.smford.com

NAIC Code: 441110

TYPES OF BUSINESS:

Auto Dealers, Retail
Fleet Sales
Parts & Service

BRANDS/DIVISIONS/AFFILIATES:

GROWTH PLANS/SPECIAL FEATURES:

Santa Monica Ford Lincoln Mercury is a major dealership that services the greater Los Angeles area, selling over 40,000 vehicles a year. The company's high sales volume comes largely from fleet sales to corporate customers. Santa Monica Ford offers both new and pre-owned Ford, Lincoln, Dodge and Jeep vehicles at its dealership and to customers throughout the country through its online showrooms. Vehicle body styles include 2- and 4-door sedans, convertibles, passenger minivans, pickups, sport utility vehicles (SUVs) and station wagons. Santa Monica Ford's website provides detailed statistics and pictures for all of the vehicles in its inventory in addition to offering online quotes and finance application forms. The firm also operates an I-CAR certified collision center that offers free estimates and lifetime warranties as well as painting, refinishing and frame alignment and measuring services. Santa Monica Ford's other operational divisions include its auto financing and leasing services, a parts department and a service department.

CONTACTS: *Note: Officers with more than one job title may be intentionally listed here more than once.*

Ron Davis, Managing Dir.
Ronald Davis, Pres.
Billy Lourie, Bus. Dev.
Larry Rosen, Controller

FINANCIAL DATA: *Note: Data for latest year may not have been available at press time.*

In U.S. $	2018	2017	2016	2015	2014	2013
Revenue						
R&D Expense						
Operating Income						
Operating Margin %						
SGA Expense						
Net Income						
Operating Cash Flow						
Capital Expenditure						
EBITDA						
Return on Assets %						
Return on Equity %						
Debt to Equity						

CONTACT INFORMATION:

Phone: 310-451-1588 Fax: 310-394-0643
Toll-Free: 888-875-3867
Address: 1230 Santa Monica Blvd., Santa Monica, CA 90404 United States

STOCK TICKER/OTHER:

Stock Ticker: Private
Employees: 140
Parent Company:
Exchange:
Fiscal Year Ends:

SALARIES/BONUSES:

Top Exec. Salary: $ Bonus: $
Second Exec. Salary: $ Bonus: $

OTHER THOUGHTS:

Estimated Female Officers or Directors:
Hot Spot for Advancement for Women/Minorities:

Scania AB

www.scania.com

NAIC Code: 336120

TYPES OF BUSINESS:

Trucks & Buses, Manufacturing
Buses & Coaches
Industrial & Marine Engines
Auto Sales
Parts & Accessories
Construction & Specialty Vehicles
Fire & Rescue Vehicles
Repair & Assistance

BRANDS/DIVISIONS/AFFILIATES:

Volkswagen AG
Scania Power Magazine
Scania Assistance
Scania Fleet Management

CONTACTS: *Note: Officers with more than one job title may be intentionally listed here more than once.*

Henrik Henriksson, CEO
Mathias Carlbaum, Exec. VP-Oper.
Johan Haeggman, CFO
Karin Radstrom, Exec. VP-Sales & Mktg.
Kent Conradson, Sr. VP-Human Resources
Harald Ludanek, Exec. VP-R&D
Per Hallberg, Exec. VP-Prod. & Logistics
Henrik Henriksson, Exec. VP-Franchise & Factory Sales
Andreas Renschler, Chmn.
Andrea Funder, Exec. VP-Purchasing

GROWTH PLANS/SPECIAL FEATURES:

Scania AB, a unit of Volkswagen AG, manufactures heavy trucks and buses, selling them in approximately 100 countries worldwide. Scania manufactures a range of vehicles for construction and specialty purposes including tractors, trailers, concrete mixers, garbage trucks and fire and rescue vehicles. In addition, Scania manufactures industrial and marine engines for applications in boats, generators and other machinery; and manufactures intercity and city buses. One of the only bus manufacturers in the BioEthanol for Sustainable Transport (BEST) project, Scania began large-scale development of ethanol-powered vehicles in collaboration with Storstockholms Lokaltrafik (SL), the Swedish capital's regional transport company. Scania delivers its ethanol buses worldwide. The company also offers vehicles that run on ethanol, biogas or natural gas. The Scania Power Magazine offers information about Scania's products and services as well as news in the trucking industry. The firm offers its customers financial services, driver training, roadside assistance, computer-based fleet management rentals, parts and workshop services. It also maintains services such as Scania Assistance, which consists of professionals who send out service vehicles and arrange for replacement vehicles, as well as running credit checks and providing workshop estimates; and Scania Fleet Management, a program in which customers can monitor their fleet from an office computer. Scania is active in several partnerships that drive the shift toward sustainable transport systems.

FINANCIAL DATA: *Note: Data for latest year may not have been available at press time.*

In U.S. $	2018	2017	2016	2015	2014	2013
Revenue	15,258,400,000	14,566,900,000	12,738,893,237	10,514,600,000	11,043,009,536	10,400,968,704
R&D Expense						
Operating Income						
Operating Margin %						
SGA Expense						
Net Income	1,083,130,000	1,512,990,000	401,088,789	652,615,000	706,736,576	728,106,624
Operating Cash Flow						
Capital Expenditure						
EBITDA						
Return on Assets %						
Return on Equity %						
Debt to Equity						

CONTACT INFORMATION:

Phone: 46 855381000 Fax: 46 855381037
Toll-Free:
Address: Verkstadsvagen 1, Sodertalje, 151 87 Sweden

STOCK TICKER/OTHER:

Stock Ticker: Subsidiary
Employees: 52,103
Parent Company: Volkswagen AG
Exchange:
Fiscal Year Ends: 12/31

SALARIES/BONUSES:

Top Exec. Salary: $ Bonus: $
Second Exec. Salary: $ Bonus: $

OTHER THOUGHTS:

Estimated Female Officers or Directors: 3
Hot Spot for Advancement for Women/Minorities: Y

Schaeffler AG

NAIC Code: 332991

www.schaeffler.com

TYPES OF BUSINESS:

Rolling Bearing Manufacturing
Vehicle Components
Bearings

BRANDS/DIVISIONS/AFFILIATES:

CONTACTS:

Note: Officers with more than one job title may be intentionally listed here more than once.

Klaus Rosenfeld, CEO
Andreas Schick, COO
Dietmar Heinrich, CFO
Corinna Schittenhelm, Chief Human Resources Officer
Peter Gutzmer, Chief Technology Officer

GROWTH PLANS/SPECIAL FEATURES:

Schaeffler AG is a global integrated automotive and industrial supplier. The company's high-precision components and systems are integrated into engine, transmission and chassis applications, and its rolling and plain bearing solutions are utilized for a wide variety of industrial applications. Schaeffler's automotive original equipment manufacturer (OEM) division develops and manufactures products for engine, transmission and chassis applications based on internal combustion engines as well as for hybrid and electric vehicles. Its automotive aftermarket division delivers components and repair solutions to the automotive spare parts market. The company's industrial division supplies products such as rolling and plain bearings, linear and direct-drive technology as well as services such as maintenance products and monitoring systems to various industrial sectors via direct-sales and/or distribution partners. Innovation- and technology-wise, Schaeffler is engaged in the research and development of: Internet of Things that link with vehicles, machines and people (smartphones, digital websites); and motorsports such as vehicle, on-track competitions and races. Schaeffler is one of the world's largest family-owned companies, with approximately 170 locations in more than 50 countries. The firm's network includes manufacturing sites, research and development facilities and sales centers. Recently, Schaeffler announced that it had begun construction on a new assembly and packaging center in Halle, Germany, expanding its automotive aftermarket division and capabilities. Production was expected to begin in early 2020. In May 2019, the firm opened a new plant in Bien Hoa, Vietnam, creating about 300 new jobs.

FINANCIAL DATA:

Note: Data for latest year may not have been available at press time.

In U.S. $	2018	2017	2016	2015	2014	2013
Revenue	15,767,270,000	15,523,690,000	14,767,490,000	14,643,490,000	13,423,380,000	12,405,890,000
R&D Expense	937,776,800	936,669,600	831,488,100	797,165,600	693,091,300	676,483,600
Operating Income	1,530,115,000	1,773,694,000	1,731,621,000	1,571,081,000	1,678,477,000	1,079,495,000
Operating Margin %		.11%	.12%	.11%	.13%	.09%
SGA Expense	1,651,904,000	1,564,438,000	1,486,935,000	1,469,221,000	1,418,290,000	1,321,966,000
Net Income	975,420,700	1,085,031,000	951,062,900	654,340,200	724,092,200	140,611,200
Operating Cash Flow	1,778,122,000	1,968,556,000	2,077,059,000	1,519,043,000	996,457,100	1,137,068,000
Capital Expenditure	1,364,039,000	1,409,433,000	1,268,822,000	1,134,854,000	948,848,600	633,303,800
EBITDA	2,630,647,000	2,838,796,000	3,148,804,000	3,297,166,000	3,284,987,000	2,631,754,000
Return on Assets %		.08%	.07%	.05%	.07%	.02%
Return on Equity %		.45%	.51%	.71%		
Debt to Equity		1.256	1.953	3.841	34.294	

CONTACT INFORMATION:

Phone: 49-9132-82-0 Fax: 49-9132-82-4950
Toll-Free:
Address: IndustriestraÃŸe 1-3, Herzogenaurach, 91074 Germany

STOCK TICKER/OTHER:

Stock Ticker: SFFLY Exchange: GREY
Employees: 92,478 Fiscal Year Ends:
Parent Company:

SALARIES/BONUSES:

Top Exec. Salary: $ Bonus: $
Second Exec. Salary: $ Bonus: $

OTHER THOUGHTS:

Estimated Female Officers or Directors:
Hot Spot for Advancement for Women/Minorities:

SEAT SA

www.seat.com

NAIC Code: 336111

TYPES OF BUSINESS:

Automobile Manufacturing
Engine Manufacturing

BRANDS/DIVISIONS/AFFILIATES:

Volkswagon AG
Mii-e
Ibiza
Leon
Arona
Ateca
Alhambra
Tarraco

CONTACTS: *Note: Officers with more than one job title may be intentionally listed here more than once.*

Luca de Meo, Pres.
Xavier Ros, Dir.-Human Resources
Matthias Rabe, Exec. VP-R&D
Anfreas Tostmann, Exec. VP-Prod.
Luis Comas Martinez de Tejada, General Counsel
Serafi del Arco Majon, Head-Corp. Comm.
Holger Kintscher, Exec. VP-Finance
Ramon Paredes Sanchez-Collado, Exec. VP-Gov't & Institutional Rel.
Herbert Diess, Chmn.
Deiter Seemann, Exec. VP-Purchasing

GROWTH PLANS/SPECIAL FEATURES:

SEAT SA, a subsidiary of Volkswagen AG and a member of the Audi brand group, is a Spanish designer and manufacturer of automobiles with operations in more than 75 countries worldwide. SEAT has produced recent models such as the Mii-e, Ibiza, Leon, Leon ST, Arona, Ateca, Alhambra and Tarraco. The Mii-e is a 100% electric model that comes as a 5-door hatchback, heated seats, LED mirror lights and a 5-inch color display within the dashboard. Ibiza models come as a sports coupe hatchback, a 5-door hatchback or a sports wagon, and equipped with full link technology, rear view camera and an integrated navigation system. Leon models come as a sports coup hatchback, a 5-door hatchback and a sports wagon, with full LED headlamps, parking assist features, traffic sign recognition and adaptive cruise control features. Arona is a five-door hatchback crossover that comprises full link connectivity, wireless phone charging, keyless entry, blind spot detection, rear traffic alert and a navigation system. Ateca comes as a four-wheel-drive SUV for power and traction purposes, a wireless charger, top-view camera and park assist features and hands-free key system. Alhambra is a compact multi-purpose vehicle (MPV) designed as a small minivan with sliding side doors, Bi-Xenon LED headlights, a massage seat and blind spot detection. Tarraco is an SUV that seats up to seven passengers and comes with the latest in technology. The company sold more than 517,000 new cars in 2018.

FINANCIAL DATA: *Note: Data for latest year may not have been available at press time.*

In U.S. $	2018	2017	2016	2015	2014	2013
Revenue	11,427,600,000	11,441,800,000	9,057,770,000	9,103,150,000	9,111,970,000	8,395,378,194
R&D Expense						
Operating Income						
Operating Margin %						
SGA Expense						
Net Income	336,504,000	336,839,000	951,575,000	6,555,240	-79,857,000	-192,878,895
Operating Cash Flow						
Capital Expenditure						
EBITDA						
Return on Assets %						
Return on Equity %						
Debt to Equity						

CONTACT INFORMATION:

Phone: 34-93-708-5000 Fax: 34-93-708-5502
Toll-Free:
Address: Autovia A2, Km. 585, Martorell, 08760 Spain

STOCK TICKER/OTHER:

Stock Ticker: Subsidiary
Employees: 14,627
Parent Company: Volkswagen AG
Exchange:
Fiscal Year Ends: 12/31

SALARIES/BONUSES:

Top Exec. Salary: $ Bonus: $
Second Exec. Salary: $ Bonus: $

OTHER THOUGHTS:

Estimated Female Officers or Directors:
Hot Spot for Advancement for Women/Minorities:

Segway Inc

www.segway.com

NAIC Code: 336991

TYPES OF BUSINESS:

Personal Transportation Devices
Robotic Cargo Transportation Devices

BRANDS/DIVISIONS/AFFILIATES:

Segway i2 SE
Segway x2 SE
Ninebot
Segway S-Plus
i2 SE Patroller
SE-3 Patroller
Loomo
T60

CONTACTS: *Note: Officers with more than one job title may be intentionally listed here more than once.*

Matt Polimeno, VP-Operations
Judy Cai, Interim Pres.
Eric Fleming, Mgr.-Comm.
Claude Le Blond, VP-Int'l Bus.

GROWTH PLANS/SPECIAL FEATURES:

Segway, Inc. manufactures and distributes a range of battery-powered personal transportation (PT) devices. These products are grouped into four categories: professional, consumer, public safety and robotics. Professional PTs are primarily for employees who spend more than an hour a day walking or want to be more efficient cross-territorial-wise when working at construction sites, farms, vineyards or any outdoor area. Professional PTs feature two parallel wheels and are marketed under the Segway i2 SE and Segway x2 SE models. Consumer PTs include: the Ninebot line of go carts; the self-balancing TP, Segway S-Plus; the Ninebot One S1, a single-wheeled PT; and the Ninebot line of kick scooters. Public safety PTs are primarily used by law enforcement and private security agencies worldwide, for patrolling all sorts of indoor and outdoor environments. Two-wheel public safety models include the i2 SE Patroller, and the x2 SE Patroller equipped with ATV-style tires. This division's SE-3 Patroller model is a three-wheel Segway for situations that require a large yet versatile vehicles, or requires a rider to frequently mount and dismount the vehicle during a patrol. Last, the robotics category comprises a mobility platform. Its products include: the Loomo smart personal/companion robot; the T60 ride-share scooter, capable of automatic control; and artificial intelligence (AI)-based delivery robots. Segway's global dealer locations include the Americas, Europe, the Middle East, Africa, Asia and Asia-Pacific.

FINANCIAL DATA: *Note: Data for latest year may not have been available at press time.*

In U.S. $	2018	2017	2016	2015	2014	2013
Revenue						
R&D Expense						
Operating Income						
Operating Margin %						
SGA Expense						
Net Income						
Operating Cash Flow						
Capital Expenditure						
EBITDA						
Return on Assets %						
Return on Equity %						
Debt to Equity						

CONTACT INFORMATION:

Phone: 603-222-6000 Fax: 603-222-6001
Toll-Free: 866-473-4929
Address: 14 Technology Dr., Bedford, NH 03110 United States

STOCK TICKER/OTHER:

Stock Ticker: Private
Employees: 130
Parent Company:
Exchange:
Fiscal Year Ends:

SALARIES/BONUSES:

Top Exec. Salary: $ Bonus: $
Second Exec. Salary: $ Bonus: $

OTHER THOUGHTS:

Estimated Female Officers or Directors:
Hot Spot for Advancement for Women/Minorities:

Sequa Corporation

www.sequa.com

NAIC Code: 488190

TYPES OF BUSINESS:

Aircraft Maintenance and Repair Services (Except Factory Conversion, Factory Overhaul, Factory Rebuilding)
Automotive Accessories
Metal Coatings
Specialty Chemicals
Industrial Machinery

BRANDS/DIVISIONS/AFFILIATES:

Carlyle Group (The)
Chromalloy
Precoat Metals

GROWTH PLANS/SPECIAL FEATURES:

Sequa Corporation is a highly diversified industrial company servicing the aerospace and metal coating industries. The firm maintains its business operations through two business units: Chromalloy and Precoat Metals. Chromalloy, the company's largest business segment, provides a broad range of aftermarket services to the airline industry, and is a leading independent supplier of advanced repairs for jet engine parts. Chromalloy also serves the industrial and marine gas turbine market, as well as the military market. Precoat Metals provides decorative and protective coatings to continuous coiled steel for use in residential and commercial construction projects. Precoat also serves other industrial end users. Sequa is owned by The Carlyle Group.

CONTACTS: *Note: Officers with more than one job title may be intentionally listed here more than once.*

Thomas Mepham, CEO
Keith Howe, CFO
Marc Werbach, VP-Human Resources
Steven R. Lowson, General Counsel
Andrew Farrant, VP-Corp. Comm.
David G. Albert, VP-External Affairs
Carlo Luzzatto, Pres., Chromalloy
Gerard M. Dombek, Pres., Precoat Metals
David L. Squier, Chmn.

FINANCIAL DATA: *Note: Data for latest year may not have been available at press time.*

In U.S. $	2018	2017	2016	2015	2014	2013
Revenue	2,625,000,000	2,500,000,000	2,425,000,000	2,350,000,000	2,400,000,000	
R&D Expense						
Operating Income						
Operating Margin %						
SGA Expense						
Net Income						
Operating Cash Flow						
Capital Expenditure						
EBITDA						
Return on Assets %						
Return on Equity %						
Debt to Equity						

CONTACT INFORMATION:

Phone: 561-935-3571 Fax:
Toll-Free:
Address: 4100 RCA Blvd., Palm Beach Gardens, FL 33410 United States

STOCK TICKER/OTHER:

Stock Ticker: Private
Employees: 10,500
Parent Company: Carlyle Group (The)
Exchange:
Fiscal Year Ends: 12/31

SALARIES/BONUSES:

Top Exec. Salary: $ Bonus: $
Second Exec. Salary: $ Bonus: $

OTHER THOUGHTS:

Estimated Female Officers or Directors: 1
Hot Spot for Advancement for Women/Minorities:

Sheehy Auto Stores

NAIC Code: 441110

www.sheehy.com

TYPES OF BUSINESS:

Auto Dealers, Retail
Auto Service
Auto Finance
Collision Repair

BRANDS/DIVISIONS/AFFILIATES:

Sheehy Markdown

CONTACTS:

Note: Officers with more than one job title may be intentionally listed here more than once.

Vincent A. Sheehy, Pres.
Brand Fowler, COO
Joe Shine, CFO
Lisa Ziropoulos, Dir.-Sales
Shawn Lumpkin, Dir.-Human Resources
Neil Desmond, Dir.-Sales Oper.
Brand Fowler, VP-Service
Kevin Scrimgeour, Dir.-Mktg.
Gary Letkemann, Dir.-Fixed Oper.

GROWTH PLANS/SPECIAL FEATURES:

Sheehy Auto Stores is a new and pre-owned automobile and motorcycle dealer with 22 U.S. locations from Maryland to Virginia, including Annapolis, Gaithersburg, Springfield and Fredericksburg. The company was founded in 1965 as Sheehy Ford, a small, family-owned car dealership just off the Washington, D.C. beltway. Today, the company sells 11 brands of vehicles from manufacturers, including new cars and motorcycles from Ford, Nissan, Toyota, Hyundai, Subaru, Volkswagen, Honda, Infiniti, Lincoln, Lexus and Harley-Davidson. Sheehy is one of the largest retailers of Fords in the mid-Atlantic region, selling approximately 45,000 vehicles annually. All cars sold by Sheehy carry a three-day money back guarantee and the Sheehy Markdown, which ensures that all new vehicles are priced below list price and all used vehicles are priced below Blue Book value. It even features a bargain lot, on which customers can find automobiles for less than $15,000. The company has an in-house collision center as well. Sheehy's website provides links to each of the dealerships, where customers can browse inventory, schedule service appointments or apply for financing.

Sheehy offers its employees medical and dental insurance, flexible spending accounts, a 401(k) plan, paid vacation, short- and long-term disability insurance and life insurance.

FINANCIAL DATA:

Note: Data for latest year may not have been available at press time.

In U.S. $	2018	2017	2016	2015	2014	2013
Revenue	1,600,000,000	1,500,000,000	1,395,667,852	1,064,230,000	885,000,000	845,431,000
R&D Expense						
Operating Income						
Operating Margin %						
SGA Expense						
Net Income						
Operating Cash Flow						
Capital Expenditure						
EBITDA						
Return on Assets %						
Return on Equity %						
Debt to Equity						

CONTACT INFORMATION:

Phone: 703-802-3480 Fax: 703-802-3481
Toll-Free:
Address: 12701 Fair Lakes Cir., Ste. 250, Fairfax, VA 22033 United States

STOCK TICKER/OTHER:

Stock Ticker: Private
Employees: 4,200
Parent Company:
Exchange:
Fiscal Year Ends: 12/31

SALARIES/BONUSES:

Top Exec. Salary: $ Bonus: $
Second Exec. Salary: $ Bonus: $

OTHER THOUGHTS:

Estimated Female Officers or Directors:
Hot Spot for Advancement for Women/Minorities:

Shiloh Industries Inc

www.shiloh.com

NAIC Code: 336370

TYPES OF BUSINESS:

Motor Vehicle Metal Stamping

BRANDS/DIVISIONS/AFFILIATES:

ShilohCore
BlankLight
CastLight
StampLight

CONTACTS: *Note: Officers with more than one job title may be intentionally listed here more than once.*

Ramzi Hermiz, CEO
Lillian Etzkorn, CFO
Curtis Moll, Chairman of the Board
Gary DeThomas, Chief Accounting Officer

GROWTH PLANS/SPECIAL FEATURES:

Shiloh Industries, Inc. is a global solutions provider focused on light-weighting technologies that provide environmental and safety benefits to the mobility market. Based in Ohio, USA, the firm has manufacturing operations and technical centers in Asia, Europe and North America. Shiloh's multi-component, multi-material solutions are comprised of a variety of alloys in aluminum, magnesium and steel grades, along with its proprietary line of noise- and vibration-reducing ShilohCore acoustic laminate products. The firm's BlankLight, CastLight and StampLight brands combine to maximize light-weighting solutions without compromising safety or performance. These solutions are applied to body structure, chassis and propulsion systems to original equipment manufacturers (OEMs) and Tier 1 suppliers in the automotive and commercial vehicle markets. Body structure components include shock towers, instrument panel/crossbar beams, torque boxes, tunnel supports, seat supports, seat back frames, hinge pillars, liftgates, door inners, roof supports/roof panels, dash panels and body sides. Chassis systems components include cross members, frame rails, axle carriers, bearing caps, axle covers, PTU covers, axle tubes, rack and pinion housings, steering column housings, knuckles, links, wheel hubs, steering pumps, brake components, wheel blanks and flanges. Propulsion systems components include battery boxes and closures, beam axle housings, planetary carriers, clutch housings, transmission gear housings, engine valve covers, valve bodies, rocker arm spacers, heat shields, exhaust manifolds, cones, baffles, muffler shells, engine oil pans, transmission fluid pans, front covers and transmission covers. Shiloh serves more than 200 global customers, which include BMW, Faurecia, Fiat Chrysler Automobile, Ford Motor Company, General Motors Company, Hendrickson International, Linamar Corporation, Tesla Inc., Volvo AB/Volvo Car Corporation and ZF Friedrichshafen AG.

FINANCIAL DATA: *Note: Data for latest year may not have been available at press time.*

In U.S. $	2018	2017	2016	2015	2014	2013
Revenue	1,139,944,000	1,041,986,000	1,065,834,000	1,109,195,000	878,744,000	700,186,000
R&D Expense						
Operating Income	25,119,000	28,732,000	20,501,000	21,763,000	27,139,000	34,622,000
Operating Margin %		.03%	.02%	.02%	.03%	.05%
SGA Expense	88,604,000	83,142,000	73,417,000	63,028,000	50,207,000	37,073,000
Net Income	11,479,000	-697,000	3,669,000	8,264,000	22,444,000	21,570,000
Operating Cash Flow	53,226,000	76,315,000	69,361,000	3,501,000	29,583,000	38,813,000
Capital Expenditure	50,135,000	48,395,000	28,324,000	39,504,000	40,158,000	27,441,000
EBITDA	63,331,000	63,159,000	54,248,000	55,625,000	59,587,000	55,653,000
Return on Assets %		.00%	.01%	.01%	.04%	.07%
Return on Equity %		.00%	.03%	.06%	.16%	.18%
Debt to Equity		0.961	1.935	2.121	1.855	0.91

CONTACT INFORMATION:

Phone: 330 558-2600 Fax: 302 522-2275
Toll-Free:
Address: 880 Steel Dr., Valley City, OH 44280 United States

STOCK TICKER/OTHER:

Stock Ticker: SHLO
Exchange: NAS
Employees: 3,100
Fiscal Year Ends: 10/31
Parent Company:

SALARIES/BONUSES:

Top Exec. Salary: $875,000 Bonus: $
Second Exec. Salary: $263,642 Bonus: $

OTHER THOUGHTS:

Estimated Female Officers or Directors: 1
Hot Spot for Advancement for Women/Minorities:

Silvercar Inc

www.silvercar.com

NAIC Code: 532111

TYPES OF BUSINESS:

Passenger Car Rental

BRANDS/DIVISIONS/AFFILIATES:

Audi AG
Audi of America LLC

CONTACTS:

Note: Officers with more than one job title may be intentionally listed here more than once.

Christopher Donus, VP-Finance
Kay Stroman, VP-Human Resources
William Diffenderffer, Chmn.

GROWTH PLANS/SPECIAL FEATURES:

Silvercar, Inc. is an online/mobile car rental program operating through 25 locations throughout the U.S., offering only Audi vehicles. These operations are primarily located at airports in Austin, Charlotte, Chicago, Dallas, Denver, Ft. Lauderdale, Las Vegas, Los Angeles, Miami, Newark, New York City, Orange County, Orlando, Phoenix, Salt Lake City, San Diego, San Francisco, Seattle, Tampa and Washington Dulles. In-town car rental locations include Miami-South Beach, NYC-Brooklyn Downtown, NYC-Brooklyn Williamsburg, NYC-Columbus and NYC-Manhattan. Silvercar uses online and mobile technologies to connect clients to its rental services. Apps are available for download on iPhone and Android smartphones, and walk the user through each step of the rental process: making a reservation, accessing the car, receiving the receipt, etc. With the app, users unlock the rented car, assess it and pair their phones for hands-free calling and music capabilities. No lines and no paperwork are involved, and therefore eliminates the need for concierge services and gate checkpoints, as customers can simply walk off their plane and head to their vehicle. The Audi vehicles come with complementary services such as a navigation system, SiriusXM satellite radio, 4G LTE Wi-fi hot spot, Bluetooth pairing, toll tracking, quattro all-wheel drive, leather seats and road-side assistance. Car seats and ski racks are available upon request at no extra charge. There is no need to fuel the car before returning it to its location, as the company utilizes fuel sensors that track how much gas the client used and charges that exact amount, plus an additional $5 flat fee. Silvercar operates as a subsidiary of Audi of America, LLC, itself a subsidiary of Audi AG.

FINANCIAL DATA:

Note: Data for latest year may not have been available at press time.

In U.S. $	2018	2017	2016	2015	2014	2013
Revenue	80,000,000	70,000,000	50,000,000	30,000,000	10,000,000	
R&D Expense						
Operating Income						
Operating Margin %						
SGA Expense						
Net Income						
Operating Cash Flow						
Capital Expenditure						
EBITDA						
Return on Assets %						
Return on Equity %						
Debt to Equity						

CONTACT INFORMATION:

Phone: 855-359-2227 Fax:
Toll-Free:
Address: 2415 Highway 71 East, Del Valle, TX 78617 United States

STOCK TICKER/OTHER:

Stock Ticker: Subsidiary
Employees: 150
Parent Company: Audi AG
Exchange:
Fiscal Year Ends: 12/31

SALARIES/BONUSES:

Top Exec. Salary: $ Bonus: $
Second Exec. Salary: $ Bonus: $

OTHER THOUGHTS:

Estimated Female Officers or Directors:
Hot Spot for Advancement for Women/Minorities:

Sinotruk (Hong Kong) Limited

www.sinotruk.com

NAIC Code: 336120

TYPES OF BUSINESS:

Heavy Duty Truck Manufacturing

BRANDS/DIVISIONS/AFFILIATES:

Jinan Truck Co Ltd
Jinan Commercial Vehicle Co Ltd
Jinan Power Co Ltd
Jinan Axle Co Ltd
Datong Gear Co Ltd
China National Heavy Duty Truck Co Ltd
SITRAK
JK

CONTACTS: *Note: Officers with more than one job title may be intentionally listed here more than once.*

Cai Dong, Pres.
Kong Xiangquan, Group Financial Controller
Wang Bozhi, Chmn.

GROWTH PLANS/SPECIAL FEATURES:

Sinotruk (Hong Kong) Limited is an investment holding company headquartered in China. The company, along with its subsidiaries, is engaged in the research, development and manufacturing of heavy-duty trucks and related key components and parts. Sinotruk has generated a variety of models of heavy-duty, middle, light and mining dump trucks, as well as special purpose vehicles and buses. The firm also manufactures a variety of heavy engines including D10 and D12 diesel engines; T10 and T12 gas engines; and MC11, MC13, MC05 and MC07 engines. Its truck brands include SITRAK, HOWO, STEYR and Hohan; and bus models include the JK and ZZ lines. Bus models come in traditional energy, hybrid or electric power formats. In addition, Sinotruk recently (in 2018) launched an unmanned electric truck in Tianjin Port for commercial use. The L4 electric truck's laser radar, HD cameras and intelligent calculation unit enabled it to drive on the road, park and load/unload containers without human intervention. Subsidiaries of Sinotruk include: Jinan Truck Co., Ltd; Jinan Commercial Vehicle Co., Ltd.; Jinan Power Co., Ltd.; Jinan Axle Co., Ltd; and Datong Gear Co., Ltd. The firm sells its products in more than 90 countries worldwide. Sinotruk operates as a subsidiary of China National Heavy Duty Truck Group Co., Ltd.

FINANCIAL DATA: *Note: Data for latest year may not have been available at press time.*

In U.S. $	2018	2017	2016	2015	2014	2013
Revenue	8,975,894,000	8,056,763,000	4,788,171,000	4,112,051,000	4,766,453,000	4,417,844,000
R&D Expense						
Operating Income	797,393,500	574,944,500	140,916,100	72,005,980	158,952,100	154,490,100
Operating Margin %		.07%	.03%	.02%	.03%	.03%
SGA Expense	860,376,000	897,865,400	723,571,500	688,972,000	680,809,700	626,609,500
Net Income	631,162,600	439,175,800	77,302,640	29,919,220	59,277,680	39,426,300
Operating Cash Flow	614,680,500	748,955,500	760,970,400	151,026,100	825,265,300	93,874,690
Capital Expenditure	203,894,700	132,402,700	54,889,150	101,333,900	54,856,750	65,256,410
EBITDA	1,023,003,000	806,420,800	385,252,900	331,891,800	385,089,500	330,225,800
Return on Assets %		.05%	.01%	.00%	.01%	.01%
Return on Equity %		.14%	.03%	.01%	.02%	.01%
Debt to Equity				0.118	0.126	0.04

CONTACT INFORMATION:

Phone: 852-31023810 Fax: 852-31023812
Toll-Free:
Address: 168-200 Connaught Rd. Central, Units 2102-03, Hong Kong, 250002 Hong Kong

STOCK TICKER/OTHER:

Stock Ticker: SHKLY Exchange: PINX
Employees: 25,148 Fiscal Year Ends: 12/31
Parent Company: China National Heavy Duty Truck Group Co Ltd

SALARIES/BONUSES:

Top Exec. Salary: $ Bonus: $
Second Exec. Salary: $ Bonus: $

OTHER THOUGHTS:

Estimated Female Officers or Directors:
Hot Spot for Advancement for Women/Minorities:

Sixt SE

about.sixt.com/websites/sixt_cc/English/0/about-us.html

NAIC Code: 532111

TYPES OF BUSINESS:

Automobile Rental
e-Commerce
Automobile Leasing
Used Car Sales
Fleet Management
Insurance Services

BRANDS/DIVISIONS/AFFILIATES:

SIXT GmbH & Co. Autovermietung KG
Sixt Leasing SE
Sixt Rent-a-Truck
Sixt Ferienmietwagen
Sixt Sports and Luxury Cars
sixt-neuwagen.de
autohaus24.de
DriveNow

CONTACTS: *Note: Officers with more than one job title may be intentionally listed here more than once.*

Erich Sixt, CEO
Detlev Patsch, COO
Jorg Bremer, CFO
Frank Elsner, Head-Press Rel.
Julian zu Pulitz, Controller
Erich Sixt, Chmn.

GROWTH PLANS/SPECIAL FEATURES:

Sixt SE, along with its subsidiaries, provides automobile rentals, full-service leasing, used car sales and eCommerce services in over 105 countries worldwide with 2,200 locations. The company operates through two business units: rental and leasing. The vehicle rental unit is operated through wholly-owned subsidiary Sixt GmbH & Co. Autovermietung KG, which rents automobiles, including cars, trucks and holiday cars, to corporate and private customers. It possesses one of the largest fleets of BMW and Mercedes Benz vehicles in the world. Other related subsidiaries include: Sixt Rent-a-Truck, renting trucks up to 12 tons; Sixt Ferienmietwagen, an international holiday car rental service; Six Limousine Service, a limousine rental service available in 60 countries; Sixt Sports and Luxury Cars, offering luxury saloons, sports cars and SUVs; myDriver, providing transfer services at fixed prices and operates in 150 cities in 60 countries; FLIZZR, the value rental division of Sixt; and integrated mobility concepts, personalized concepts for customers, including fixed monthly rates. The leasing unit is operated through 41.9%-owned Sixt Leasing SE, Pullach and other German subsidiaries in 35 countries. The segment operates in two business fields: fleet leasing and online retail. The fleet leasing business, Sixt Leasing SE, offers lease financing and associated services to corporate customers. Along with leasing the segment also offers vendor-neutral online car configuration, vehicle selection, online approval procedures following specific corporate guidelines and more. The online retail business offers private and commercial customers from more than 35 different car manufacturers through online platforms sixt-neuwagen.de and autohaus24.de. The company has partnership collaborations with various airlines and hotel groups worldwide. Sixt's portfolio consists of 238,800 vehicles and more than 2,210 rental, leasing and related locations. During 2018, Sixt sold its DriveNow stake to BMW Group, which held the other half of the joint venture's shares, and became BMW's wholly-owned subsidiary.

FINANCIAL DATA: *Note: Data for latest year may not have been available at press time.*

In U.S. $	2018	2017	2016	2015	2014	2013
Revenue	3,351,310,000	3,118,040,000	2,050,000,000	2,004,479,680	2,016,900,000	2,414,730,000
R&D Expense						
Operating Income						
Operating Margin %						
SGA Expense						
Net Income	502,125,000	244,364,000	184,938,989	122,768,800	123,500,000	122,300,000
Operating Cash Flow						
Capital Expenditure						
EBITDA						
Return on Assets %						
Return on Equity %						
Debt to Equity						

CONTACT INFORMATION:

Phone: 49-89-74444-0 Fax: 49-89-74444-86666
Toll-Free:
Address: Zugspitzstrasse 1, Pullach im Isartal, 82049 Germany

STOCK TICKER/OTHER:

Stock Ticker: SIX2
Employees: 7,000
Parent Company:
Exchange: Frankfurt
Fiscal Year Ends: 12/31

SALARIES/BONUSES:

Top Exec. Salary: $ Bonus: $
Second Exec. Salary: $ Bonus: $

OTHER THOUGHTS:

Estimated Female Officers or Directors:
Hot Spot for Advancement for Women/Minorities:

Skoda Auto AS

www.skoda-auto.com

NAIC Code: 336111

TYPES OF BUSINESS:

Automobile Manufacturing
Automobile Parts Manufacturer

BRANDS/DIVISIONS/AFFILIATES:

Volkswagen AG
Citigo
Fabia
Rapid
Octavia
Karoq
Yeti
Superb

CONTACTS: *Note: Officers with more than one job title may be intentionally listed here more than once.*

Klaus-Dieter Schurmann, Dir.-Finance & IT
Alain Favey, Dir.-Sales & Mktg.
Bohdan Wojnar, Dir.-Human Resources
Michael Oeljeklaus, Dir.-Prod. & Logistics
Jan Miller, Sec.
Winfried Krause, Dir.-Comm. Affairs
Bernhard Maier, Chmn.
Karlheinz Hell, Dir.-Purchasing

GROWTH PLANS/SPECIAL FEATURES:

Skoda Auto AS, a subsidiary of Volkswagen AG, designs and manufactures automobiles in the Czech Republic, operating in more than 100 global markets. The company develops, produces and sells passenger and utility cars, engines, components, original parts and car accessories, as well as providing related repair and maintenance services. Skoda offers nine different models: Citigo, Fabia, Rapid, Octavia, Karoq, Kodiaq, Yeti, Kamiq and Superb. Models come with gasoline or diesel engine options and many feature a Combi variant model, extending the car's interior space and capacity. Citigo comes as a 3- and 5-door small car, as well as the environmentally friendly G-TEC model, the Monte Carlo sports model, and the Fun city car model. The Fabia is a small hatchback based on the Volkswagen Polo platform. The line also includes the Fabia Monte Carlo, which contains a sunroof and alloy wheels, sports seats and 3-spoke leather steering wheel. The Rapid vehicle is a compact hatchback with modern technology. Octavia is a 4-door sedan that comes in basic, racy sports, fuel efficient and high-tech models. Karoq is a compact sport utility vehicle (SUV) with four passenger doors and a hatchback. Kodiaq is an off-road SUV with an optional third row of seating for a total seven passengers. Yeti is a compact 4-door SUV. Kamiq is a subcompact crossover built exclusively for the Chinese market. The Superb is a comfortable sedan with the practicality of a liftback and comes equipped with bi-xenon headlights, LED daylights, as well as the GreenLine, Superb Combi, Superb Combi GreenLine and Superb Sportline models and styles. Skoda's Vision concept for an electric car with level 3 autonomy capability and a 310-mile range is planned to be for sale in 2020.

Employee benefits include company auto insurance, pension plans and a variety of employee assistance programs.

FINANCIAL DATA: *Note: Data for latest year may not have been available at press time.*

In U.S. $	2018	2017	2016	2015	2014	2013
Revenue	18,486,200,000	19,078,400,000	13,562,215,832	13,048,722,957	12,382,248,686	12,719,061,122
R&D Expense						
Operating Income						
Operating Margin %						
SGA Expense						
Net Income	1,281,760,000	1,491,100,000	1,135,738,784	1,276,955,470	883,598,562	560,491,363
Operating Cash Flow						
Capital Expenditure						
EBITDA						
Return on Assets %						
Return on Equity %						
Debt to Equity						

CONTACT INFORMATION:

Phone: 42-326-811-111 Fax: 42-326-721-328
Toll-Free:
Address: Tr. Vaclava Klementa 869, Mlada Boleslav, 293 01 Czech Republic

STOCK TICKER/OTHER:

Stock Ticker: Subsidiary
Employees: 33,696
Parent Company: Volkswagen AG
Exchange:
Fiscal Year Ends: 12/31

SALARIES/BONUSES:

Top Exec. Salary: $ Bonus: $
Second Exec. Salary: $ Bonus: $

OTHER THOUGHTS:

Estimated Female Officers or Directors:
Hot Spot for Advancement for Women/Minorities:

Smart GmbH

NAIC Code: 336111

www.smart.com

TYPES OF BUSINESS:

Automobile Manufacturing
Ultra-Compact Cars
Electric Bikes
Electric Vehicles
Car Sharing

BRANDS/DIVISIONS/AFFILIATES:

Daimler AG
Geely
Smart Fortwo
Smart Fortwo Cabrio
Smart Forfour

CONTACTS:

Note: Officers with more than one job title may be intentionally listed here more than once.

Katrin Adt, CEO
Dieter Zetsche, Chmn.-Daimler AG
Wilried Porth, VP-Human Resources-Daimler AG
Wolfgang Bernhard, VP-Prod. & Procurement-Daimler AG

GROWTH PLANS/SPECIAL FEATURES:

Smart GmbH, a 50/50 joint venture between Daimler AG and Geely, manufactures ultra-compact cars primarily sold in the European market. Its Smart Fortwo model, a two-seater, is eight feet long and five feet wide, with 7.8 cubic feet (3.9 square feet) of trunk space and 12 cubic feet (5.2 square feet) total storage space, including the roof. It is commonly referred to and branded as a smart car. Smart Fortwo ranges from 61 to 90 in horsepower, depending on a gas or turbo gas engine, and has a max speed of nearly 93 miles per hour. The Smart Fortwo Cabrio model, a two-seater sporty convertible, ranges from 71 to 90 in horsepower (gas or turbo gas). The Fortwo Cabrio models include: standard, smart EQ, BRABUS, tailor made and special. The Smart Forfour model, a four-door four-seater, is 11 feet long, five and one-half feet wide and five feet high. It ranges from 61 to 90 in horsepower (gas and turbo gas), with a max speed of 93 miles per hour. All the Smart vehicles have a 3-cylinder engine. The vehicles' fuel efficiencies range from approximately 87 to 105 miles per gallon equivalent. The electric drive models require no gas and no oil changes. In March 2019, Geely acquired a 50% share of Smart GmbH. That same year, Daimler announced plans to construct a new production plant in China, with support from Geely, to build next-generation smart cars in 2022.

FINANCIAL DATA:

Note: Data for latest year may not have been available at press time.

In U.S. $	2018	2017	2016	2015	2014	2013
Revenue						
R&D Expense						
Operating Income						
Operating Margin %						
SGA Expense						
Net Income						
Operating Cash Flow						
Capital Expenditure						
EBITDA						
Return on Assets %						
Return on Equity %						
Debt to Equity						

CONTACT INFORMATION:

Phone: 49-7031-9071-163 Fax: 49-7031-9071-241
Toll-Free:
Address: 2 Leibnizstrasse, Boeblingen, D-71032 Germany

STOCK TICKER/OTHER:

Stock Ticker: Joint Venture
Exchange:
Employees:
Fiscal Year Ends: 12/31
Parent Company: Daimler AG

SALARIES/BONUSES:

Top Exec. Salary: $ Bonus: $
Second Exec. Salary: $ Bonus: $

OTHER THOUGHTS:

Estimated Female Officers or Directors:
Hot Spot for Advancement for Women/Minorities:

Sogefi SpA

www.sogefi.it

NAIC Code: 336300

TYPES OF BUSINESS:

Automotive Parts Manufacturing
Fluid Filters
Suspension Parts

BRANDS/DIVISIONS/AFFILIATES:

SogefiPro
Allevard Rejna
Coopers FIAAM
FRAM
LP-DN
Purflux
United Springs

CONTACTS: *Note: Officers with more than one job title may be intentionally listed here more than once.*

Laurent Hebenstreit, CEO
Francesca Muratori, Group Comm. Mgr.
Giancarlo Coppa, Mgr.-Investor Rel.
Pierre L'Alloret, Gen. Mgr.-Fluid Filtration Subdivision
Pierangelo Rota, Gen. Mgr. Suspension Components Div. Sales & Dev.
Keith Drew, Gen. Mgr.-Filters Div.
Giorgio F. Imposimato, Mgr.-Internal Audit & Risk
Monica Mondardini, Chmn.
Roberto Fabris, Mgr.-Purchasing

GROWTH PLANS/SPECIAL FEATURES:

Sogefi SpA is a global supplier of original parts for the automotive industry. The firm designs and manufactures filtration systems, flexible suspension components and air management and engine cooling systems. The filtration division produces a range of filter products, including oil, petrol, diesel fuel, and air and cabin air filters that are used in motorcycles, three-wheelers, cars and heavy-duty vehicles. The suspension division produces its products in close collaboration with automotive manufacturers. These products include helical springs, stabilizer bars, torsion bars, stabilinks, leaf springs and track tensioners. They are designed for use on cars, light and heavy commercial vehicles, earth-moving equipment, armored vehicles and rolling wagons. This division's customers range from automotive and industrial vehicle manufacturers to major railway vehicle manufacturers. The air and cooling division engineers and manufactures high-tech plastic automotive components, including intake manifold systems, charged air ducting, air induction systems, thermostat housing, ducts, coolant pumps and modules. Brands of the company include SogefiPro, Allevard Rejna, Coopers FIAAM, FRAM, LP-DN (Luhn & Pulvermacher/Dittmann & Neuhaus), Purflux, United Springs and more. Sogefi has more than 40 manufacturing sites worldwide, and is present in 23 countries on four continents.

FINANCIAL DATA: *Note: Data for latest year may not have been available at press time.*

In U.S. $	2018	2017	2016	2015	2014	2013
Revenue	1,857,260,000	2,003,310,000	1,842,638,337	1,760,482,487	1,527,100,000	1,721,700,000
R&D Expense						
Operating Income						
Operating Margin %						
SGA Expense						
Net Income	16,018,800	31,863,200	10,961,937	1,314,493	4,100,000	27,200,000
Operating Cash Flow						
Capital Expenditure						
EBITDA						
Return on Assets %						
Return on Equity %						
Debt to Equity						

CONTACT INFORMATION:

Phone: 39-02-467501 Fax: 39-02-43511201
Toll-Free:
Address: Via Ciovassino 1/A, Milan, 20121 Italy

STOCK TICKER/OTHER:

Stock Ticker: SO
Employees: 6,967
Parent Company:
Exchange: Milan
Fiscal Year Ends: 12/31

SALARIES/BONUSES:

Top Exec. Salary: $ Bonus: $
Second Exec. Salary: $ Bonus: $

OTHER THOUGHTS:

Estimated Female Officers or Directors: 2
Hot Spot for Advancement for Women/Minorities:

Sonic Automotive Inc

www.sonicautomotive.com

NAIC Code: 441110

TYPES OF BUSINESS:

Auto Dealers, Retail
Collision Repair Centers
Auto Parts
Insurance
Financing

BRANDS/DIVISIONS/AFFILIATES:

EchoPark

CONTACTS:

Note: Officers with more than one job title may be intentionally listed here more than once.

David Smith, CEO
Heath Byrd, CFO
O. Smith, Chairman of the Board
Jeff Dyke, President

GROWTH PLANS/SPECIAL FEATURES:

Sonic Automotive, Inc. is a leading U.S. automotive retailer, operating more than 100 vehicle franchises in 13 states nationwide, as well as 15 collision repair centers. The franchises are primarily Sonic dealerships, with a handful being EchoPark stores. Sonic dealerships offer new and used cars and light trucks; replacement parts; and services such as repair, finance and insurance, including collision repair. Dealerships also arrange extended warranties, service contracts, financing, insurance and other aftermarket products for its customers. The dealerships feature 24 brands, including Acura, BMW, Mercedes, Lexus, Audi, Cadillac, Land Rover, Porsche, Mini, Honda, Toyota, Volkswagen, Hyundai and Ford. The EchoPark business operates independently from the dealership franchised business. EchoPark stores sell used cars and light trucks and arranges finance and insurance products. Some EchoPark vehicles originate as trade-ins and would normally be wholesaled; but, are instead sold at value prices. Sonic's dealership and EchoPark locations include California, Texas, Tennessee, Alabama, Florida, Colorado, North Carolina, Ohio, Maryland, Georgia, Virginia, Nevada and South Carolina. In early-2019, Sonic sold two dealerships to Graham Holdings, the Lexus of Rockville in Maryland and the Honda location in Vienna, Virginia.

FINANCIAL DATA:

Note: Data for latest year may not have been available at press time.

In U.S. $	2018	2017	2016	2015	2014	2013
Revenue	9,951,630,000	9,867,208,000	9,731,779,000	9,624,298,000	9,197,099,000	8,843,168,000
R&D Expense						
Operating Income	207,177,000	220,959,000	240,972,000	235,248,000	240,207,000	244,475,000
Operating Margin %		.02%	.02%	.02%	.03%	.03%
SGA Expense	1,145,325,000	1,147,773,000	1,110,856,000	1,110,565,000	1,067,433,000	1,003,125,000
Net Income	51,650,000	92,983,000	93,193,000	86,311,000	97,217,000	81,618,000
Operating Cash Flow	143,675,000	162,883,000	216,368,000	69,491,000	160,650,000	126,448,000
Capital Expenditure	163,619,000	234,245,000	206,232,000	173,249,000	146,432,000	157,617,000
EBITDA	270,047,000	286,630,000	310,566,000	286,191,000	293,129,000	259,229,000
Return on Assets %		.02%	.03%	.03%	.03%	.03%
Return on Equity %		.12%	.13%	.12%	.15%	.14%
Debt to Equity		1.225	1.158	1.071	1.114	1.19

CONTACT INFORMATION:

Phone: 704 566-2400 Fax:
Toll-Free:
Address: 4401 Colwick Rd., Charlotte, NC 28211 United States

STOCK TICKER/OTHER:

Stock Ticker: SAH
Employees: 9,800
Parent Company:
Exchange: NYS
Fiscal Year Ends: 12/31

SALARIES/BONUSES:

Top Exec. Salary: $1,284,921 Bonus: $
Second Exec. Salary: $1,109,821 Bonus: $

OTHER THOUGHTS:

Estimated Female Officers or Directors:
Hot Spot for Advancement for Women/Minorities:

Spartan Motors Inc

www.spartanmotors.com

NAIC Code: 336300

TYPES OF BUSINESS:

Heavy-Duty Chassis Manufacturing
Custom Chassis
Aerial Ladder Components

BRANDS/DIVISIONS/AFFILIATES:

Spartan Motors USA Inc
Spartan-Gimaex Innovations LLC
Utilimaster
Smeal Fire Apparatus Company

CONTACTS: *Note: Officers with more than one job title may be intentionally listed here more than once.*

Daryl Adams, CEO
Frederick Sohm, CFO
James Sharman, Chairman of the Board
Thomas Schultz, Chief Administrative Officer
Ryan Roney, Chief Legal Officer
Todd Heavin, COO
Chad Heminover, President, Divisional
Steve Guillaume, President, Divisional

GROWTH PLANS/SPECIAL FEATURES:

Spartan Motors, Inc. is a world leader in the engineering, design and manufacturing of heavy-duty custom platforms and emergency vehicles. Its operating activities are conducted through wholly-owned subsidiary, Spartan Motors USA, Inc. The firm has three operating segments: emergency response vehicles (ERV), specialty chassis and vehicles (SCV) and fleet vehicles and services. The ERV segment engineers and manufactures emergency chassis, emergency response bodies and aerial equipment at its Michigan, South Dakota, Nebraska, Wisconsin and Pennsylvania manufacturing locations. This division's aerial ladders and ERV bodies are products that are mounted on custom chassis. Joint venture Spartan-Gimaex Innovations, LLC and wholly-owned Smeal Fire Apparatus Company, among others, operate within the ERV segment. ERV represents 30% of Spartan's consolidated annual sales. The SCV segment engineers and manufactures motor home chassis, defense vehicles and other specialty chassis manufactured at Spartan's Michigan operations. SCV represents 23% of consolidated annual sales. Last, the fleet vehicles and services segment manufactures fleet vehicles used in the parcel delivery, mobile retail, trades and construction industries at Spartan's Indiana operations. Spartan's fleet vehicles are marketed under the Utilimaster brand name. This division also sells aftermarket parts and accessories, as well as customer-specific upfit equipment for walk-in vans and other delivery vehicles. This division represents 47% of consolidated annual sales.

FINANCIAL DATA: *Note: Data for latest year may not have been available at press time.*

In U.S. $	2018	2017	2016	2015	2014	2013
Revenue	816,164,000	707,098,000	590,777,000	550,414,000	506,764,000	469,538,000
R&D Expense	7,332,000	6,523,000	6,772,000	4,560,000	11,676,000	10,911,000
Operating Income	17,844,000	17,423,000	9,720,000	-9,624,000	1,006,000	-3,344,000
Operating Margin %		.02%	.02%	-.02%	.00%	-.01%
SGA Expense	73,381,000	65,497,000	56,172,000	52,695,000	51,205,000	45,496,000
Net Income	15,012,000	15,935,000	8,610,000	-16,972,000	1,173,000	-5,971,000
Operating Cash Flow	8,026,000	22,016,000	23,451,000	12,900,000	6,506,000	13,046,000
Capital Expenditure	8,985,000	5,340,000	13,410,000	4,895,000	3,463,000	3,526,000
EBITDA	28,723,000	26,825,000	17,016,000	-4,798,000	7,645,000	1,699,000
Return on Assets %		.06%	.04%	-.07%	.00%	-.02%
Return on Equity %		.10%	.06%	-.11%	.01%	-.03%
Debt to Equity		0.106	0.00	0.034	0.031	0.031

CONTACT INFORMATION:

Phone: 517 543-6400 Fax: 517 543-7728
Toll-Free:
Address: 1541 Reynolds Rd., Charlotte, MI 48813 United States

STOCK TICKER/OTHER:

Stock Ticker: SPAR
Employees: 2,340
Parent Company:
Exchange: NAS
Fiscal Year Ends: 12/31

SALARIES/BONUSES:

Top Exec. Salary: $674,719 Bonus: $
Second Exec. Salary: $166,154 Bonus: $150,000

OTHER THOUGHTS:

Estimated Female Officers or Directors:
Hot Spot for Advancement for Women/Minorities:

Special Devices Inc

NAIC Code: 336300

www.specialdevices.com

TYPES OF BUSINESS:

Airbags Initiator Systems
Propellants
Electronic Detonator Products
Micro Gas Generators
Composite Molded Assemblies

BRANDS/DIVISIONS/AFFILIATES:

Daicel Corporation

GROWTH PLANS/SPECIAL FEATURES:

Special Devices, Inc. (SDI), a subsidiary of Daicel Corporation, provides precision engineered devices for the automotive, industrial and medical devices industries. The automotive segment manufactures automotive airbag initiators, micro gas generators (for safety device applications), power disconnect devices and composite molded products. These products are key elements in driver, passenger and impact automotive safety systems. The industrial segment produces pyrotechnic products for a wide array of industrial applications where high speed, precision and extreme/critical reliability are crucial factors. Some of this division's applications include gas generators, power disconnect devices, cable cutters, fire suppression systems, pin pullers/pushers, propelling cartridges and explosive bolts/nuts. The company is headquartered in California, with manufacturing facilities in Arizona, Japan and Thailand.

CONTACTS: *Note: Officers with more than one job title may be intentionally listed here more than once.*

Christopher Hunter, CEO
Christopher Hunter, Pres.

FINANCIAL DATA: *Note: Data for latest year may not have been available at press time.*

In U.S. $	2018	2017	2016	2015	2014	2013
Revenue						
R&D Expense						
Operating Income						
Operating Margin %						
SGA Expense						
Net Income						
Operating Cash Flow						
Capital Expenditure						
EBITDA						
Return on Assets %						
Return on Equity %						
Debt to Equity						

CONTACT INFORMATION:

Phone: 805-387-1000 Fax: 805-387-1001
Toll-Free:
Address: 2655 First St., Ste. 300, Simi Valley, CA 93065 United States

STOCK TICKER/OTHER:

Stock Ticker: Subsidiary
Employees: 570
Parent Company: Daicel Corporation
Exchange:
Fiscal Year Ends:

SALARIES/BONUSES:

Top Exec. Salary: $ Bonus: $
Second Exec. Salary: $ Bonus: $

OTHER THOUGHTS:

Estimated Female Officers or Directors:
Hot Spot for Advancement for Women/Minorities:

Spectra Premium Industries Inc

www.spectrapremium.com

NAIC Code: 336300

TYPES OF BUSINESS:

Aftermarket Remanufactured Parts
Heat-Transfer Products
Underbody Components

BRANDS/DIVISIONS/AFFILIATES:

CONTACTS:

Note: Officers with more than one job title may be intentionally listed here more than once.

Mark Church, VP-Sales & Mktg.

GROWTH PLANS/SPECIAL FEATURES:

Spectra Premium Industries, Inc. designs, manufactures and distributes cooling systems, fuel delivery, ignition and engine management, climate control and under car components for automotive vehicles as well as light and heavy trucks. Spectra develops and provides its products for original equipment manufacturers, automotive technicians and consumers. Heating and cooling systems and services include radiators, charge air coolers, active grille shutters, cooling fan assembly, heaters, intercoolers, coolant reservoirs, exhaust gas recirculation coolers and heavy-duty radiators. Fuel delivery products include fuel modules, fuel pumps (electric, mechanical, direct injection), emission control components, fuel tanks, fuel filler necks, fuel pump driver modules and fuel tank straps. Ignition and engine management products include mass air flow sensors, electronic throttle body, camshaft sensors, crankshaft position sensors, variable valve timing solenoids, ignition distributors, camshaft synchronizers, oxygen sensors, ignition coils and manifold absolute pressure sensors. Climate control products include condensers, A/C compressors, A/C evaporators and A/C accumulator-driver. Under car components primarily consist of oil pans. Spectra develops and builds its own tooling for its automotive and power sport parts. The company's tool shop has the capacity of processing tools up to five meters in length and 65,000 pounds in weight. Spectra also specializes in medium and large progressive dies, and has created internal templates, casting construction or plate dies using lifter racks assemblies or rails. The firm owns and operates five manufacturing plants, 16 warehouses and a distribution network throughout North America, including the U.S., Canada and Mexico.

FINANCIAL DATA:

Note: Data for latest year may not have been available at press time.

In U.S. $	2018	2017	2016	2015	2014	2013
Revenue	482,343,750	459,375,000	437,500,000	388,000,000	375,000,000	330,000,000
R&D Expense						
Operating Income						
Operating Margin %						
SGA Expense						
Net Income						
Operating Cash Flow						
Capital Expenditure						
EBITDA						
Return on Assets %						
Return on Equity %						
Debt to Equity						

CONTACT INFORMATION:

Phone: 450-641-3090 Fax: 450-641-3866
Toll-Free: 888-910-8888
Address: 1421 Ampere St., Boucherville, QC J4B 5Z5 Canada

STOCK TICKER/OTHER:

Stock Ticker: Private
Employees: 1,300
Parent Company:
Exchange:
Fiscal Year Ends: 01/31

SALARIES/BONUSES:

Top Exec. Salary: $ Bonus: $
Second Exec. Salary: $ Bonus: $

OTHER THOUGHTS:

Estimated Female Officers or Directors: 1
Hot Spot for Advancement for Women/Minorities:

Spitzer Management Inc

NAIC Code: 441110

www.spitzer.com

TYPES OF BUSINESS:

Auto Dealers, Retail
Property Management
Parts & Service
Marina Management
Golf Course Management
Financing

BRANDS/DIVISIONS/AFFILIATES:

Spitzer Collision Center

GROWTH PLANS/SPECIAL FEATURES:

Spitzer Management, Inc. is a new and pre-owned automobile dealer with 14 automobile dealerships in Ohio, Pennsylvania and Florida. Spitzer offers vehicle financing and insurance services, and sells both new and used makes such as Acura, Chevrolet, Chrysler, Dodge, Jeep, Ford, Kia, RAM, Toyota and Volkswagen. Through the company's website, customers are able to search inventory, build a vehicle, compare vehicles, apply for credit and obtain product information. The Spitzer Collision Center offers complete auto body repair with frame and unibody repair, state-of-the-art color matching, lifetime guarantees, replacement car rentals and 24-hour-a-day towing. Vehicle owners can schedule service and maintenance, request parts and set up an appointment with the collision center via the company's website.

CONTACTS: *Note: Officers with more than one job title may be intentionally listed here more than once.*

Alan Spitzer, CEO

FINANCIAL DATA: *Note: Data for latest year may not have been available at press time.*

In U.S. $	2018	2017	2016	2015	2014	2013
Revenue						
R&D Expense						
Operating Income						
Operating Margin %						
SGA Expense						
Net Income						
Operating Cash Flow						
Capital Expenditure						
EBITDA						
Return on Assets %						
Return on Equity %						
Debt to Equity						

CONTACT INFORMATION:

Phone: 440-323-4671 Fax: 440-323-3623
Toll-Free:
Address: 150 E. Bridge St., Elyria, OH 44035 United States

STOCK TICKER/OTHER:

Stock Ticker: Private
Employees:
Parent Company:
Exchange:
Fiscal Year Ends: 12/31

SALARIES/BONUSES:

Top Exec. Salary: $ Bonus: $
Second Exec. Salary: $ Bonus: $

OTHER THOUGHTS:

Estimated Female Officers or Directors:
Hot Spot for Advancement for Women/Minorities:

SRG Global Inc

www.srgglobal.com

NAIC Code: 326100

TYPES OF BUSINESS:

Automotive Components
Trim Products & Systems
Front End Systems
Bodyside Systems
Rear End Systems
Greenhouse Systems
Interior systems
Non-Automotive Products

BRANDS/DIVISIONS/AFFILIATES:

Koch Industries Inc
Guardian Industries Corporation
Integrille

CONTACTS: *Note: Officers with more than one job title may be intentionally listed here more than once.*

Dave Prater, CEO
Dave Prater, VP-Prod. Dev.
Dave Prater, VP-Prod. Eng.

GROWTH PLANS/SPECIAL FEATURES:

SRG Global, Inc. is a world-leading industrial manufacturer of high value coatings on plastic for the automotive and commercial truck industries. SRG is a wholly-owned subsidiary of Guardian Industries Corporation, which itself is a subsidiary of Koch Industries, Inc. The company's products are divided into four groups: exteriors, interiors, subsystems and non-automotive products. Exteriors include front and rear end: grilles, emblems/nameplates, fascia appliques, lift gate moldings, spoilers and rear appliques; green house: ditch moldings, window surround moldings, cowls and A/B/C/D pillars; body side: moldings, fuel filler systems, claddings, rocker panels, wheel flares/arches, wheel covers, door handles; and other parts such as roof appliques. Interiors include accents: center consoles, instrument panels, overhead panels, seat trim, door panel accents, steering wheel trim components and interior assemblies. Subsystems include integrated systems such as active grille shutters, including SRG's Integrille brand of grill shutters. Non-automotive products include trim, grilles and fairings for motorcycles and commercial vehicles. SRG is headquartered near Detroit, Michigan, with 13 manufacturing and assembly facilities worldwide, including North America, Western and Central Europe and Asia Pacific. The company's advanced development centers enhance manufacturing processes and accelerates development and delivery of the next generation of materials, coating technologies and sub-systems. They are located in Michigan, USA; Liria, Spain; and Suzhou, China.

FINANCIAL DATA: *Note: Data for latest year may not have been available at press time.*

In U.S. $	2018	2017	2016	2015	2014	2013
Revenue	546,000,000	520,000,000	511,000,000	500,000,000	485,000,000	480,000,000
R&D Expense						
Operating Income						
Operating Margin %						
SGA Expense						
Net Income						
Operating Cash Flow						
Capital Expenditure						
EBITDA						
Return on Assets %						
Return on Equity %						
Debt to Equity						

CONTACT INFORMATION:

Phone: 248-509-1100 Fax: 248-509-1300
Toll-Free:
Address: 800 Stephenson Hwy., Troy, MI 48083 United States

STOCK TICKER/OTHER:

Stock Ticker: Subsidiary
Employees: 6,500
Parent Company: Koch Industries Inc
Exchange:
Fiscal Year Ends: 12/31

SALARIES/BONUSES:

Top Exec. Salary: $ Bonus: $
Second Exec. Salary: $ Bonus: $

OTHER THOUGHTS:

Estimated Female Officers or Directors:
Hot Spot for Advancement for Women/Minorities:

SsangYong Motor Company

www.smotor.com

NAIC Code: 336111

TYPES OF BUSINESS:

Automobile Manufacturing
SUVs
Passenger Cars
Multi-Purpose Vehicles

BRANDS/DIVISIONS/AFFILIATES:

Mahindra & Mahindra Limited
Musso
Tivoli
Rexton
XLV
Korando
Rodius

CONTACTS: *Note: Officers with more than one job title may be intentionally listed here more than once.*

Yea Byung-tae, CEO

GROWTH PLANS/SPECIAL FEATURES:

SsangYong Motor Company is a leading Korean automobile manufacturer specializing in luxury SUVs, passenger cars, sports utility trucks and multi-purpose vehicles (MPVs). The company has historically manufactured commercial trucks, jeeps, special purpose vehicles and construction equipment, but now focuses mainly on light commercial vehicles. SsangYong was the first company to introduce a sports utility truck (SUT)to the Korean market, with its Musso model. Currently, the company produces four SUVs, the Tivoli, Rexton, XLV and Korando; the Rodius MPV van; and the Musso SUT. The Rodius features seating for up to 11 passengers, and has swing doors similar to passenger car doors, a rear obstacle warning system and an immobilizer for panic alarm, vehicle-finding and automatic door lock functions. The company's global network spans Europe, including the Commonwealth of Independent States; the Middle East; Asia, with particular focus on China; the Pacific region and Oceania, including Australia; Central and South America; Africa; and Russia. SsangYong's primary manufacturing plant is located just south of Seoul in Pyeongtaek, which has an annual manufacturing capacity of 220,000 vehicles. This facility also contains the company's head office and R&D center. A second plant in Changwon, South Korea manufactures gasoline and diesel engines, transmissions, transaxles and rear ends for SsangYong's SUVs and passenger cars. Indian conglomerate Mahindra & Mahindra Limited owns a majority stake in SsangYong (approximately 75%).

FINANCIAL DATA: *Note: Data for latest year may not have been available at press time.*

In U.S. $	2018	2017	2016	2015	2014	2013
Revenue	3,316,450,000	3,272,410,000	3,090,924,056	2,915,471,091	2,812,265,400	2,400,529,490
R&D Expense						
Operating Income						
Operating Margin %						
SGA Expense						
Net Income	-55,320,300	-61,635,400	20,192,066	-71,110,946	-43,000,000	-2,316,579
Operating Cash Flow						
Capital Expenditure						
EBITDA						
Return on Assets %						
Return on Equity %						
Debt to Equity						

CONTACT INFORMATION:

Phone: 82-31-610-1114 Fax: 82-31-610-3700
Toll-Free:
Address: 455-12 dongsakro, Pyeongtaek City, Gyeonggi Province, South Korea

STOCK TICKER/OTHER:

Stock Ticker: Subsidiary Exchange:
Employees: 4,698 Fiscal Year Ends: 12/31
Parent Company: Mahindra & Mahindra Limited

SALARIES/BONUSES:

Top Exec. Salary: $ Bonus: $
Second Exec. Salary: $ Bonus: $

OTHER THOUGHTS:

Estimated Female Officers or Directors:
Hot Spot for Advancement for Women/Minorities:

Stackpole International Inc

www.stackpole.com

NAIC Code: 336350

TYPES OF BUSINESS:

Automobile Parts Manufacturing
Engine & Transmission Components
Gears

BRANDS/DIVISIONS/AFFILIATES:

Johnson Electric Holdings Limited

CONTACTS:

Note: Officers with more than one job title may be intentionally listed here more than once.

Nick Albu, Global Dir.-IT
Ronald J. Duke, VP-New Bus. Dev.

GROWTH PLANS/SPECIAL FEATURES:

Stackpole International designs and manufactures highly-engineered systems for customers in the automotive sector. The firm's products and solutions are grouped into three categories: fluid power solutions, powder metal technology and custom solutions. Stackpole's fluid power solutions include electric pumps, engine oil pumps, tandem pumps, transmission oil pumps, vacuum pumps and coolant pumps, all of which are utilized within hydraulic powertrain systems. This division is a single-source provider for every step of the electrically-driven power transfer system development process. The powder metal technology category produces sophisticated automotive components and assemblies that have complex geometries and superior strength. Products within this division includes chassis components, clutch components, gears, high-strength synchronizer hubs, planetary carriers, pump components, WT components and alternative energy components. The custom solutions division provides a wide range of applications for global automotive brands, from conceptualization, modeling, prototyping and process development to manufacture. Stackpole's corporate services are based in Ontario, Canada, with manufacturing facilities and technical centers located throughout North America, Europe and Asia. The firm continually engages in research and development, power system solutions, advanced engineering and product/process engineering innovation activities in order to have a leading edge in the industry. Stackpole International is a subsidiary of Johnson Electric Holdings Limited, a global leader in electric motors and motion subsystems.

FINANCIAL DATA:

Note: Data for latest year may not have been available at press time.

In U.S. $	2018	2017	2016	2015	2014	2013
Revenue	647,400,000	475,200,000	427,600,000			
R&D Expense						
Operating Income						
Operating Margin %						
SGA Expense						
Net Income						
Operating Cash Flow						
Capital Expenditure						
EBITDA						
Return on Assets %						
Return on Equity %						
Debt to Equity						

CONTACT INFORMATION:

Phone: 905-304-9455 Fax:
Toll-Free:
Address: 1325 Cormorant Rd., Ancaster, ON L9G 4V5 Canada

STOCK TICKER/OTHER:

Stock Ticker: Private
Exchange:
Employees: 2,500
Fiscal Year Ends: 12/31
Parent Company: Johnson Electric Holdings Limited

SALARIES/BONUSES:

Top Exec. Salary: $ Bonus: $
Second Exec. Salary: $ Bonus: $

OTHER THOUGHTS:

Estimated Female Officers or Directors:
Hot Spot for Advancement for Women/Minorities:

Stanadyne LLC

www.stanadyne.com

NAIC Code: 336300

TYPES OF BUSINESS:

Engine Components Manufacturing
Parts Distribution & Sale

BRANDS/DIVISIONS/AFFILIATES:

Stanadyne Holdings Inc
Pure Power Technologies Inc

CONTACTS: *Note: Officers with more than one job title may be intentionally listed here more than once.*

David P. Galuska, CEO
John A. Pinson, Pres.
Stephen Langin, CFO
Greg Butler, Dir..-Global Operations
Brad Stroia, CTO
Stephen S. Langin, Corp. Sec.
Robert Isaman, Chmn.
Joseph M. Vorih, VP-Int'l
Edward May, VP-Global Supply Chain

GROWTH PLANS/SPECIAL FEATURES:

Stanadyne, LLC designs and manufactures engine components, including fuel injection equipment for diesel engines and hydraulic valve lifters primarily for gasoline engines. The firm manufactures its own proprietary products, including pumps for gasoline engines and diesel engines, fuel injectors and fuel filtration systems for diesel engines, and various non-proprietary products manufactured under contract for other companies. These products are used in a variety of applications, including agricultural and construction vehicles and equipment, industrial products, power generation equipment, utility equipment, passenger automobiles, light- and heavy-duty trucks and racing vehicles. Stanadyne also sells replacement parts through service organizations and its own network of dealers and distributors. The company possesses a broad range of manufacturing technologies and is capable of high-volume production runs, machining high-quality components within tolerances of smaller than one micron. The firm's primary focus is the agricultural and industrial off-highway segments of the automotive market. Stanadyne's primary customers are original equipment manufacturers (OEMs) of diesel engines. International locations in Italy, China, India and the United Arab Emirates. Stanadyne operates as a wholly-owned subsidiary of Stanadyne Holdings, Inc. In April 2019, Stanadyne acquired Pure Power Technologies, Inc., which engineers and manufactures diesel fuel injectors and turbochargers, and is based in South Carolina, USA.

FINANCIAL DATA: *Note: Data for latest year may not have been available at press time.*

In U.S. $	2018	2017	2016	2015	2014	2013
Revenue	281,137,500	267,750,000	255,000,000	238,000,000	220,000,000	200,000,000
R&D Expense						
Operating Income						
Operating Margin %						
SGA Expense						
Net Income						
Operating Cash Flow						
Capital Expenditure						
EBITDA						
Return on Assets %						
Return on Equity %						
Debt to Equity						

CONTACT INFORMATION:

Phone: 860-525-0821 Fax: 860-683-4500
Toll-Free:
Address: 92 Deerfield Rd., Windsor, CT 06095 United States

STOCK TICKER/OTHER:

Stock Ticker: Private
Employees: 1,755
Parent Company: Stanadyne Holdings Inc
Exchange:
Fiscal Year Ends: 12/31

SALARIES/BONUSES:

Top Exec. Salary: $ Bonus: $
Second Exec. Salary: $ Bonus: $

OTHER THOUGHTS:

Estimated Female Officers or Directors: 1
Hot Spot for Advancement for Women/Minorities:

Standard Motor Products Inc

www.smpcorp.com

NAIC Code: 336300

TYPES OF BUSINESS:

Automobile Parts Manufacturer
Engine Management Products
Ignition Parts
Emission Control Parts
Fuel System Parts
Battery Cables

BRANDS/DIVISIONS/AFFILIATES:

Standard
Blue Streak
Four Seasons
LockSmart
EVERCO
Intermotor
Hayden
GP Sorensen

CONTACTS: *Note: Officers with more than one job title may be intentionally listed here more than once.*

Eric Sills, CEO
James Burke, CFO
Lawrence Sills, Chairman of the Board
William Fazio, Chief Accounting Officer
Ray Nicholas, Chief Information Officer
Peter Sills, Director Emeritus
Arthur Sills, Director Emeritus
Dale Burks, Executive VP
Carmine Broccole, General Counsel
Erin Pawlish, Treasurer
Thomas Tesoro, Vice President, Divisional

GROWTH PLANS/SPECIAL FEATURES:

Standard Motor Products, Inc. (SMP) is a leading independent manufacturer and distributor of replacement parts for motor vehicles, primarily in the automotive aftermarket industry. It is organized into two major operating segments, each of which focuses on a specific line of replacement parts. The engine management segment manufactures ignition and emission parts, ignition wires, battery cables and fuel system parts. The temperature control segment manufactures and remanufactures air conditioning compressors, clutch assemblies, small motors, fan clutches, filter dryers, evaporators, transmission coolers, accumulators and hoses, heater cores and valves, engine cooling system parts, power window accessories, windshield washer system parts and other air conditioning and heating parts. SMP sells its products primarily to warehouse distributors and large auto parts retail chains, original equipment manufacturers (OEMs) and original equipment service part operations in the U.S., Canada, Latin America and Europe. The company distributes parts under its own brand names, such as Standard, Blue Streak, BWD, Select, Intermotor, GP Sorensen, TechSmart, Tech Expert, OEM, LockSmart, Four Seasons, EVERCO, ACi and Hayden, and through co-labels and private labels such as NAPA Echlin and NAPA Belden. In April 2019, SMP acquired the Pollak business of Stoneridge, Inc., which manufactures and distributes a range of engine management products such as sensors, switches and connectors.

SMP offers its employee medical, dental, life and disability insurance; flexible spending accounts; and tuition assistance.

FINANCIAL DATA: *Note: Data for latest year may not have been available at press time.*

In U.S. $	2018	2017	2016	2015	2014	2013
Revenue	1,092,051,000	1,116,143,000	1,058,482,000	971,975,000	980,392,000	983,704,000
R&D Expense						
Operating Income	85,778,000	104,347,000	102,024,000	75,726,000	97,185,000	90,220,000
Operating Margin %		.09%	.10%	.08%	.09%	.09%
SGA Expense	231,336,000	223,584,000	221,658,000	206,287,000	193,525,000	201,256,000
Net Income	43,003,000	37,976,000	60,430,000	46,018,000	43,029,000	51,450,000
Operating Cash Flow	70,258,000	64,617,000	97,805,000	65,171,000	46,987,000	57,616,000
Capital Expenditure	20,141,000	24,442,000	20,921,000	18,047,000	13,904,000	11,410,000
EBITDA	104,961,000	122,687,000	120,583,000	93,277,000	100,664,000	104,459,000
Return on Assets %		.05%	.08%	.07%	.07%	.09%
Return on Equity %		.08%	.15%	.12%	.12%	.16%
Debt to Equity		0.00	0.00	0.00	0.00	0.00

CONTACT INFORMATION:

Phone: 718 392-0200 Fax: 718 472-0122
Toll-Free:
Address: 37-18 Northern Blvd., Long Island City, NY 11101 United States

STOCK TICKER/OTHER:

Stock Ticker: SMP Exchange: NYS
Employees: 4,100 Fiscal Year Ends: 12/31
Parent Company:

SALARIES/BONUSES:

Top Exec. Salary: $590,000 Bonus: $963,000
Second Exec. Salary: $600,000 Bonus: $

OTHER THOUGHTS:

Estimated Female Officers or Directors: 1
Hot Spot for Advancement for Women/Minorities:

Stoneridge Inc

NAIC Code: 336300

www.stoneridge.com

TYPES OF BUSINESS:

Automotive Electronic Components
Vehicle Power Distribution Systems
Actuator & Sensor Products
Instrumentation & Display Products
Wiring Systems
Switch Products

BRANDS/DIVISIONS/AFFILIATES:

PST Eletronica Ltda

CONTACTS: *Note: Officers with more than one job title may be intentionally listed here more than once.*

Jonathan DeGaynor, CEO
Robert Krakowiak, CFO
Robert Hartman, Chief Accounting Officer
Thomas Dono, Chief Legal Officer
Laurent Borne, Chief Technology Officer
William Lasky, Director
Daniel Kusiak, Other Executive Officer
Caetano Ferraiolo, President, Divisional
Robert Willig, President, Divisional
Thomas Beaver, President, Divisional
Anthony Moore, Vice President, Divisional

GROWTH PLANS/SPECIAL FEATURES:

Stoneridge, Inc. is an independent designer and manufacturer of highly-engineered electrical and electronic components, modules and systems primarily for the automotive, commercial, off-highway, motorcycle and agricultural vehicle markets. Stoneridge encompasses 26 locations in 13 countries that enable it to supply global and regional automotive, commercial, motorcycle, off-highway and agricultural vehicle manufacturers around the world. Custom-engineered products and systems are used to activate equipment and accessories, monitor and display vehicle performance and control, distribute electrical power and signals and provide vehicle security and convenience. Product offerings consist of sensors; application-specific actuators, switches and valves; vehicle and driver information systems; vehicle management electronics; power and switch distribution modules and telematics; camera-based vision systems and monitors; security alarms and vehicle tracking devices and monitoring services; and convenience accessories. Stoneridge operates under three reportable segments: electronics, control devices and PST Eletronica Ltda. The electronics segment includes design and manufacturing of electronic instrument clusters, electronic control units, driver information systems and electrical distribution systems; control devices includes design and manufacturing of sensors, switches, valves and actuators; and PST, which specializes in the design, manufacture and sale of electronic vehicle security alarms, convenience accessories, vehicle tracking devices and monitoring services and in-vehicle audio and video devices in South America. In April 2019, Stoneridge sold product lines and assets related to certain non-core switches and connectors to Standard Motor Products, Inc. for approximately $40 million. The company also announced plans to close its Canton, Massachusetts manufacturing facility by year's end, consolidating operations.

Stoneridge offers employees health and life insurance, a 401(k), flexible spending accounts and long-term disability coverage.

FINANCIAL DATA: *Note: Data for latest year may not have been available at press time.*

In U.S. $	2018	2017	2016	2015	2014	2013
Revenue	866,199,000	824,444,000	695,977,000	644,812,000	660,579,000	947,830,000
R&D Expense	51,074,000	48,877,000	40,212,000	38,792,000	41,609,000	
Operating Income	67,004,000	57,370,000	44,082,000	27,815,000	25,635,000	39,704,000
Operating Margin %		.07%	.06%	.04%	.04%	.04%
SGA Expense	138,553,000	141,893,000	111,145,000	110,371,000	123,630,000	186,317,000
Net Income	53,848,000	45,179,000	77,461,000	22,774,000	-47,108,000	15,131,000
Operating Cash Flow	80,772,000	78,908,000	65,277,000	54,805,000	19,815,000	43,684,000
Capital Expenditure	29,027,000	32,170,000	24,476,000	28,735,000	24,754,000	25,344,000
EBITDA	96,521,000	85,624,000	67,695,000	50,612,000	55,716,000	74,929,000
Return on Assets %		.09%	.20%	.06%	-.10%	.03%
Return on Equity %		.21%	.57%	.25%	-.39%	.10%
Debt to Equity		0.512	0.421	1.122	1.213	1.242

CONTACT INFORMATION:

Phone: 248-489-9300 Fax: 248-489-3970
Toll-Free:
Address: 39675 MacKenzie Dr., Ste. 400, Novi, MI 48377 United States

STOCK TICKER/OTHER:

Stock Ticker: SRI
Employees: 4,200
Parent Company:
Exchange: NYS
Fiscal Year Ends: 12/31

SALARIES/BONUSES:

Top Exec. Salary: $750,000 Bonus: $
Second Exec. Salary: $433,800 Bonus: $

OTHER THOUGHTS:

Estimated Female Officers or Directors: 1
Hot Spot for Advancement for Women/Minorities:

Strattec Security Corporation

www.strattec.com

NAIC Code: 336300

TYPES OF BUSINESS:

Vehicle Security Systems
Automotive Locks & Keys
Electronic Security Systems
Ancillary Automotive Power Systems

BRANDS/DIVISIONS/AFFILIATES:

CONTACTS: *Note: Officers with more than one job title may be intentionally listed here more than once.*

Frank Krejci, CEO
Patrick Hansen, CFO
Harold Stratton, Chairman of the Board
Rolando Guillot, Senior VP, Divisional
Al-Waleed Hamdan, Vice President, Divisional
Brian Reetz, Vice President, Divisional
Richard Messina, Vice President, Divisional

GROWTH PLANS/SPECIAL FEATURES:

Strattec Security Corporation designs, produces and distributes automotive vehicle access systems, which are both theft deterrent and consumer friendly. The firm's engineering and manufacturing expertise is in electro-mechanical products, which include vehicle access latches, keys with remote entry electronic systems, and ignition interface systems with passive start capabilities. Strattec Security's primary raw materials are high-grade zinc, brass, nickel, steel, aluminum and plastic resins, which are generally purchased from a number of suppliers. Approximately 60% of Strattec Security's annual sales are to General Motors Company, Fort Motor Company and Fiat Chrysler Automobiles. The products sold to these customers, among others, are model specific, fitting only certain defined applications. Products include locksets, fobs, push-button ignition systems, steering column lock housings, seatback and secondary latches, power-sliding door systems, power liftgate systems, power decklids, door handle components and trim and other access products unique to vehicles. Strattec Security has four manufacturing plants, one warehouse and one sales office, all of which are located in the U.S. and Mexico.

Employees of Strattec receive medical, dental, vision and life insurance as well as disability plans.

FINANCIAL DATA: *Note: Data for latest year may not have been available at press time.*

In U.S. $	2018	2017	2016	2015	2014	2013
Revenue	439,195,000	417,325,000	401,419,000	411,475,000	348,419,000	298,179,000
R&D Expense						
Operating Income	13,275,000	13,702,000	20,908,000	31,126,000	26,524,000	18,932,000
Operating Margin %		.03%	.05%	.08%	.08%	.06%
SGA Expense	41,168,000	46,460,000	43,917,000	41,534,000	39,274,000	34,934,000
Net Income	12,283,000	7,197,000	9,149,000	20,654,000	16,424,000	9,375,000
Operating Cash Flow	6,940,000	23,142,000	8,218,000	31,459,000	11,519,000	15,665,000
Capital Expenditure	24,134,000	37,010,000	23,496,000	26,097,000	12,812,000	12,515,000
EBITDA	33,420,000	28,229,000	29,487,000	42,819,000	36,126,000	24,403,000
Return on Assets %		.03%	.04%	.09%	.09%	.06%
Return on Equity %		.05%	.07%	.16%	.14%	.10%
Debt to Equity		0.199	0.144	0.071	0.02	

CONTACT INFORMATION:

Phone: 414 247-3333 Fax: 414 247-3329
Toll-Free:
Address: 3333 W. Good Hope Rd., Milwaukee, WI 53209 United States

STOCK TICKER/OTHER:

Stock Ticker: STRT
Employees: 3,892
Parent Company:
Exchange: NAS
Fiscal Year Ends: 07/03

SALARIES/BONUSES:

Top Exec. Salary: $428,833 Bonus: $1,000
Second Exec. Salary: $287,200 Bonus: $1,000

OTHER THOUGHTS:

Estimated Female Officers or Directors: 1
Hot Spot for Advancement for Women/Minorities:

Subaru Corporation

www.subaru.co.jp/en/

NAIC Code: 336111

TYPES OF BUSINESS:

Automobile Manufacturing
Aircraft Manufacturing & Components
Heavy-Duty Engines & Equipment
Sanitation Vehicles
Specialty Vehicles
Waste Treatment, Recycling & Alternative Energy Technologies
Industrial Robotics

BRANDS/DIVISIONS/AFFILIATES:

AH-64D
Subaru
Outback
Forester
Impreza
Baja
Legacy
Levor

CONTACTS: *Note: Officers with more than one job title may be intentionally listed here more than once.*

Tomomi Nakamura, CEO
Yasuyuki Yoshinaga, Chmn.

GROWTH PLANS/SPECIAL FEATURES:

Subaru Corporation, best known for its Subaru cars, is a transportation conglomerate that also manufactures engines, aircraft components and specialty vehicles. It operates in two main divisions: automotive and aerospace products. The automotive division does business as Subaru, producing symmetrical all-wheel-drive vehicles (AWD), such as the Legacy and Forester models, which are built on small-car platforms but maintain the look and feel of an SUV. Other models include the Tribeca, Legacy Outback, Levorg, Exiga, Stella, WRX/STI, Impreza, Pleo and Justy. The Subaru engine incorporates an unusual design, called the horizontally-opposed "Boxer" Engine, which the firm claims reduces vibration and is generally more compact than other designs and has a low center of gravity. The aerospace division manufactures, sells and repairs fixed wing aircraft and parts. It also conducts research specifically for the Japan Aerospace Exploration Agency. The company developed the Flying Forward Observation System (FFOS), an unmanned aircraft technology, for its primary contractor, the Japan Military of Defense (MOD). Its branded offerings consist of the T-1, T-7 and T-5 defense trainer jets. The firm is also the sole manufacturer of attack helicopters, AH-64D and UH-1J, in Japan. Additionally, Subaru Corporation's aerospace division is responsible for the design and building of the center wing section of the Boeing 777 and 787. The Subaru Corporation has four plants dedicated to automotive manufacturing and three plants dedicated to aerospace manufacturing, with corporate and distribution offices in Japan, China, Singapore, the U.S., Canada, Belgium, Italy and the Netherlands. In July 2018, Subaru Corporation and SBI Investment Co. Ltd. established a joint private fund, the Subaru-SBI Innovation Fund, to invest in promising start-up companies in Japan.

FINANCIAL DATA: *Note: Data for latest year may not have been available at press time.*

In U.S. $	2018	2017	2016	2015	2014	2013
Revenue	31,292,240,000	30,564,160,000	29,702,800,000	26,446,540,000	22,129,470,000	
R&D Expense						
Operating Income	3,486,923,000	3,775,133,000	5,197,473,000	3,887,567,000	3,000,267,000	
Operating Margin %	.11%	.12%	.17%	.15%	.14%	
SGA Expense						
Net Income	2,024,940,000	2,594,689,000	4,012,627,000	2,406,479,000	1,898,695,000	
Operating Cash Flow	3,366,091,000	3,174,435,000	5,644,698,000	2,862,920,000	2,876,530,000	
Capital Expenditure					669,500,200	
EBITDA	3,683,340,000	4,431,116,000	6,381,548,000	4,290,847,000	3,612,893,000	
Return on Assets %	.08%	.11%	.18%	.13%	.12%	
Return on Equity %	.15%	.20%	.37%	.29%	.30%	
Debt to Equity	0.014	0.042	0.069	0.123	0.214	

CONTACT INFORMATION:

Phone: 81-3 6447-8000 Fax: 81-3 6447-8184
Toll-Free:
Address: 1-20-8, Ebisu, Shibuya-ku, Tokyo, 150-8554 Japan

STOCK TICKER/OTHER:

Stock Ticker: FUJHF Exchange: PINX
Employees: 43,057 Fiscal Year Ends: 03/31
Parent Company:

SALARIES/BONUSES:

Top Exec. Salary: $ Bonus: $
Second Exec. Salary: $ Bonus: $

OTHER THOUGHTS:

Estimated Female Officers or Directors:
Hot Spot for Advancement for Women/Minorities:

Sumitomo Electric Industries Ltd

www.sei.co.jp/

NAIC Code: 336320

TYPES OF BUSINESS:

Motor Vehicle Electrical and Electronic Equipment Manufacturing
Cable Manufacturing
Insulated Electrical Wiring
Electrical Apparatus and Related Equipment Wholesalers
Internet of Things

BRANDS/DIVISIONS/AFFILIATES:

Sumiden Wire Products Corporation
Sumitomo Electric Device Innovations USA Inc
Sumidenso do Brasil Industrias Eletricas Ltda
SEWS Canada Ltd
Sumitomo Electric Hardmetal de Mexico SA de CV

CONTACTS: *Note: Officers with more than one job title may be intentionally listed here more than once.*

Masayoshi Matsumoto, CEO
Osamu Inoue, Pres.
Masayoshi Matsumoto, Chmn.

GROWTH PLANS/SPECIAL FEATURES:

Sumitomo Electric Industries Ltd. manufactures electric wires, cables and related equipment to automotive, electronics, communications, industrial material, energy and environmental industries. Wiring harnesses are used to transmit information and electrical power within vehicles; steel cords and bead wires are used for tire reinforcement; steel wires are used to make springs and spring materials; thermoplastic engineering materials are used to create infrared devices and optical lenses, as well as abrasion-resistant parts; heat shrink tubing and tapes are used in a variety of fields such as automobiles, IT, electronics and more; and electric vehicle quick-chargers and connector assemblies keep environmental-friendly vehicles running. Sumitomo Electric's research and development division develops new technologies and products that contribute to improving the environment, safety and security performance of end-products. The firm's domestic manufacturing plants, labs and offices are located throughout Japan, including Osaka, Tokyo, Hyogo, Yokohama and Okinawa. Through the collective efforts of these plants, Sumitomo's Internet of Things (IoT) research and development center is engaged in the development of IoT technologies such as sensing systems, wireless communications, artificial intelligence (AI) and big data analysis to support its manufacturing processes. The Sumitomo group comprises approximately 400 subsidiaries located in countries across Asia, the Americas and Europe. Just a few of these subsidiaries include: Sumiden Wire Products Corporation; Sumitomo Electric Device Innovations USA, Inc.; Sumidenso do Brasil Industrias Eletricas Ltda.; SEWS Canada Ltd.; and Sumitomo Electric Hardmetal de Mexico SA de CV.

FINANCIAL DATA: *Note: Data for latest year may not have been available at press time.*

In U.S. $	2018	2017	2016	2015	2014	2013
Revenue	28,324,270,000	25,863,660,000	26,953,580,000	25,940,190,000	23,605,760,000	
R&D Expense						
Operating Income	1,591,059,000	1,383,045,000	1,318,471,000	1,235,591,000	1,103,272,000	
Operating Margin %	.06%	.05%	.05%	.05%	.05%	
SGA Expense						
Net Income	1,105,753,000	988,439,700	836,252,600	1,100,634,000	613,379,900	
Operating Cash Flow	2,201,553,000	1,922,744,000	2,212,636,000	1,410,669,000	1,357,333,000	
Capital Expenditure	1,580,142,000	1,609,722,000	1,473,158,000	1,343,117,000	1,310,991,000	
EBITDA	3,147,354,000	2,803,979,000	2,711,735,000	2,774,793,000	2,237,677,000	
Return on Assets %	.04%	.04%	.03%	.04%	.03%	
Return on Equity %	.08%	.08%	.07%	.09%	.06%	
Debt to Equity	0.196	0.222	0.207	0.226	0.257	

CONTACT INFORMATION:

Phone: 81 662204141 Fax: 81 662223380
Toll-Free:
Address: 5-33, Kitahama 4-chome, Chuo-ku, Osaka, 541-0041 Japan

STOCK TICKER/OTHER:

Stock Ticker: SMTOY
Exchange: PINX
Employees: 312,930
Fiscal Year Ends: 03/31
Parent Company:

SALARIES/BONUSES:

Top Exec. Salary: $ Bonus: $
Second Exec. Salary: $ Bonus: $

OTHER THOUGHTS:

Estimated Female Officers or Directors:
Hot Spot for Advancement for Women/Minorities:

Superior Industries International Inc

www.supind.com

NAIC Code: 336300

TYPES OF BUSINESS:

Automobile Parts Manufacturer
Aluminum Road Wheels

BRANDS/DIVISIONS/AFFILIATES:

ATS
RIAL
ALUTEC
ANZIO

CONTACTS:

Note: Officers with more than one job title may be intentionally listed here more than once.

Timothy Mcquay, CEO
Majdi Abulaban, CEO
Karsten Obenaus, CFO, Geographical
Matti Masanovich, CFO
Michael Hatzfeld, Chief Accounting Officer
Joanne Finnorn, General Counsel
Shawn Pallagi, Other Executive Officer
Parveen Kakar, Senior VP, Divisional
Robert Tykal, Senior VP, Geographical
Wolfgang Hiller, Senior VP, Geographical

GROWTH PLANS/SPECIAL FEATURES:

Superior Industries International, Inc. designs and manufactures aluminum wheels to original equipment manufacturers (OEMs) in North America and Europe, and aftermarket distributors in Europe. The firm operates nine manufacturing plants in North America and Europe, with a combined annual manufacturing capacity of about 21 million wheels. The raw materials used in manufacturing its products are obtained through numerous suppliers, with aluminum accounting for the majority of Superior Industries' total raw material requirements. The company's OEM wheels accounted for more than 90% of 2018 sales. These wheels are primarily sold for factory installation on many vehicle models manufactured by BMW-Mini, Daimler AG, FCA, Ford, GM, Honda, Jaguar-Land Rover, Mazda, Nissan, Renault, Peugeot, PSA, Subaru, Suzuki, Toyota, VW Group and Volvo. Superior Industries also sells aluminum wheels to the European aftermarket under the brands ATS, RIAL, ALUTEC and ANZIO.

FINANCIAL DATA:

Note: Data for latest year may not have been available at press time.

In U.S. $	2018	2017	2016	2015	2014	2013
Revenue	1,501,827,000	1,108,055,000	732,677,000	727,946,000	745,447,000	789,564,000
R&D Expense						
Operating Income	85,805,000	21,518,000	54,602,000	36,294,000	17,913,000	34,593,000
Operating Margin %		.02%	.07%	.05%	.02%	.04%
SGA Expense	77,722,000	81,379,000	31,602,000	34,923,000	32,309,000	29,468,000
Net Income	25,961,000	-6,203,000	41,381,000	23,944,000	8,803,000	22,824,000
Operating Cash Flow	156,116,000	63,710,000	78,491,000	59,349,000	11,627,000	69,252,000
Capital Expenditure	77,697,000	70,937,000	39,575,000	39,543,000	112,556,000	67,980,000
EBITDA	180,861,000	90,853,000	88,863,000	70,824,000	53,495,000	63,059,000
Return on Assets %		-.02%	.08%	.04%	.01%	.04%
Return on Equity %		-.08%	.10%	.06%	.02%	.05%
Debt to Equity		2.728				

CONTACT INFORMATION:

Phone: 248-352-7300 Fax: 248-352-6989
Toll-Free:
Address: 26600 Telegraph Rd., Ste. 400, Southfield, MI 48033 United States

STOCK TICKER/OTHER:

Stock Ticker: SUP
Exchange: NYS
Employees: 4,871
Fiscal Year Ends: 12/31
Parent Company:

SALARIES/BONUSES:

Top Exec. Salary: $900,024 Bonus: $
Second Exec. Salary: $416,412 Bonus: $

OTHER THOUGHTS:

Estimated Female Officers or Directors: 2
Hot Spot for Advancement for Women/Minorities:

Supreme Industries Inc

www.supremeindustries.com/

NAIC Code: 336211

TYPES OF BUSINESS:

Specialized Vehicles

BRANDS/DIVISIONS/AFFILIATES:

Wabash National Corporation
Supreme Forest Products
ER Hinman & Sons
Quantum BioPower

CONTACTS: *Note: Officers with more than one job title may be intentionally listed here more than once.*

Kevin J. Boucher, Pres.
William Barrett, Assistant Treasurer
Michael Oium, Vice President, Divisional

GROWTH PLANS/SPECIAL FEATURES:

Supreme Industries, Inc. is a comprehensive specialty contractor that provides industry expertise to complex right-of-way clearing, access road and site preparation projects. Founded in 1974, the company has been helping power, pipeline, the Department of Transportation, municipalities and site construction professionals complete their projects for decades. Supreme Industries' core services include road building, land clearing, erosion control and site development. Subsidiaries of Supreme include: Supreme Forest Products, a source for mulch, topsoil, compost and playground safety fiber; E. R. Hinman & Sons, which operates a mill in the New England area that provides forestry services and lumber mill products; and Quantum BioPower, which specialize in organics management and renewable energy, and developed Connecticut's first anaerobic digestion facility. Supreme Industries itself operates as a wholly-owned subsidiary of Wabash National Corporation.

FINANCIAL DATA: *Note: Data for latest year may not have been available at press time.*

In U.S. $	2018	2017	2016	2015	2014	2013
Revenue	327,600,000	312,000,000	298,971,680	278,424,800	236,308,928	282,273,312
R&D Expense						
Operating Income						
Operating Margin %						
SGA Expense						
Net Income			19,037,338	12,875,269	6,902,531	6,425,876
Operating Cash Flow						
Capital Expenditure						
EBITDA						
Return on Assets %						
Return on Equity %						
Debt to Equity						

CONTACT INFORMATION:

Phone: 860-485-0343 Fax: 860-485-0349
Toll-Free:
Address: 216 Bogue Rd., Harwinton, CT 06791 United States

STOCK TICKER/OTHER:

Stock Ticker: Subsidiary Exchange:
Employees: 1,450 Fiscal Year Ends: 12/31
Parent Company: Wabash National Corporation

SALARIES/BONUSES:

Top Exec. Salary: $ Bonus: $
Second Exec. Salary: $ Bonus: $

OTHER THOUGHTS:

Estimated Female Officers or Directors:
Hot Spot for Advancement for Women/Minorities:

Suzuki Motor (Thailand) Co Ltd

www.suzuki.co.th

NAIC Code: 423110

TYPES OF BUSINESS:

Automobile Imports & Exports
Automobile Production

BRANDS/DIVISIONS/AFFILIATES:

Suzuki Motor Corporation
Thai Suzuki Motor Co Ltd
Carry
Celerio
Swift
Ertiga
Ciaz
Jimny

GROWTH PLANS/SPECIAL FEATURES:

Suzuki Motor (Thailand) Co., Ltd., established in 2003, produces, imports and distributes Suzuki branded cars and parts in Thailand. The firm's product line includes the Carry commercial vehicle as well as passenger vehicle models such as the Celerio and Swift five-door hatchbacks, the Ertiga SUV, the Ciaz sedan and the Jimny four-wheel drive mini SUV. Suzuki Thailand affiliates include auto manufacturer Thai Suzuki Motor Co. Ltd., a fellow Suzuki subsidiary that produces and markets Suzuki motorcycles and outboard motors. Suzuki Thailand operates as a subsidiary of Suzuki Motor Corporation.

CONTACTS: *Note: Officers with more than one job title may be intentionally listed here more than once.*

Takayuki Sugiyama, Pres.
Osamu Suzuki, Chmn.-Suzuki Motor Corporation

FINANCIAL DATA: *Note: Data for latest year may not have been available at press time.*

In U.S. $	2018	2017	2016	2015	2014	2013
Revenue						
R&D Expense						
Operating Income						
Operating Margin %						
SGA Expense						
Net Income						
Operating Cash Flow						
Capital Expenditure						
EBITDA						
Return on Assets %						
Return on Equity %						
Debt to Equity						

CONTACT INFORMATION:

Phone: 66-2245-5734 Fax: 66-2727-5925
Toll-Free: 800-600-900
Address: Nut Road, 855 Rd., Prawet Dist., Bangkok, 10250 Thailand

STOCK TICKER/OTHER:

Stock Ticker: Subsidiary
Exchange:
Employees: 600
Fiscal Year Ends: 03/31
Parent Company: Suzuki Motor Corporation

SALARIES/BONUSES:

Top Exec. Salary: $ Bonus: $
Second Exec. Salary: $ Bonus: $

OTHER THOUGHTS:

Estimated Female Officers or Directors:
Hot Spot for Advancement for Women/Minorities:

Suzuki Motor Corporation

www.globalsuzuki.com

NAIC Code: 336111

TYPES OF BUSINESS:

Automobile Manufacturing
Motorcycles
ATVs
Marine Products
Wheelchairs
Industrial Equipment

BRANDS/DIVISIONS/AFFILIATES:

Suzuki Auto Parts Mfg Co Ltd
Snic Co Ltd
Suzuki Akita Auto Parts Mfg Co Ltd
Celerio
Suzuki Toyama Auto Parts Mgf Co Ltd
Suzuki Transportation & Packing Co Ltd
Suzuki Engineering Co Ltd
Suzuki Finance Co Ltd

CONTACTS: *Note: Officers with more than one job title may be intentionally listed here more than once.*

Toshihiro Suzuki, CEO
Minoru Tamura, Exec. VP
Osamu Honda, Exec. VP
Toshihiro Suzuki, Exec. VP
Yasuhito Harayama, Exec. VP
Osamu Suzuki, Chmn.

GROWTH PLANS/SPECIAL FEATURES:

Suzuki Motor Corporation designs and manufactures all-terrain vehicles (ATVs), motorcycles, outboard motors, passenger cars, compact and subcompact cars, commercial vehicles and other products. The firm also manufactures boats, electric scooters, motorized wheelchairs and industrial equipment. Suzuki is one of the largest manufacturers of minicars and motorcycles in Japan. Its production facilities are spread throughout 20 countries. Overall, the company's network serves approximately 200 countries and territory areas. The firm's products include the Celerio, Ignis, Swift, Swift Sport, Dzire, Baleno, Jimny, Vitara, SX4 S-Cross, Grand Vitara, Ciaz, Ertiga and APV automobiles; the GSX, Hayabusa, Katana, SV650, V-Strom, Suzuki Boulevard, Burgman, Address, Inazuma, DR-Z, TU, VanVan, RMX and RM-Z motorcycles and scooters; the KingQuad, OZARK and QuadSport ATVs; and the 2- and 4-stroke outboard marine engine models. Suzuki has developed an ultra-low-emission, direct-injection turbo engine for the minicar category in Japan as well as a line of motorcycles incorporating an electronically controlled, continuously variable transmission. Manufacturing companies of the firm include Suzuki Auto Parts Mfg. Co. Ltd.; Snic Co. Ltd.; Suzuki Akita Auto Parts Mfg. Co. Ltd.; and Suzuki Toyama Auto Parts Mfg. Co. Ltd.; non-manufacturing companies include Suzuki Transportation & Packing Co. Ltd.; Suzuki Business Co. Ltd.; Suzuki Engineering Co. Ltd.; Suzuki Support Co. Ltd.; Suzuki Finance Co. Ltd.; and Suzuki Consultant Co. Ltd.; as well as sales company Suzuki Marine Co. Ltd and 54 domestic and 44 overseas managed distribution companies.

FINANCIAL DATA: *Note: Data for latest year may not have been available at press time.*

In U.S. $	2018	2017	2016	2015	2014	2013
Revenue	34,526,920,000	29,126,470,000	29,228,630,000	27,710,540,000	27,001,600,000	
R&D Expense						
Operating Income	3,438,541,000	2,450,698,000	1,794,780,000	1,648,824,000	1,725,299,000	
Operating Margin %	.10%	.08%	.06%	.06%	.06%	
SGA Expense						
Net Income	1,982,448,000	1,469,914,000	1,072,046,000	890,112,200	987,722,800	
Operating Cash Flow	4,090,893,000	3,366,247,000	2,702,582,000	2,343,659,000	2,967,423,000	
Capital Expenditure	1,891,693,000	1,764,878,000	1,493,972,000	1,770,759,000	1,881,447,000	
EBITDA	4,990,461,000	4,258,114,000	3,862,590,000	3,097,372,000	2,944,643,000	
Return on Assets %	.07%	.05%	.04%	.03%	.04%	
Return on Equity %	.18%	.15%	.10%	.07%	.09%	
Debt to Equity	0.298	0.378	0.274	0.184	0.158	

CONTACT INFORMATION:

Phone: 81-53-440-2061 Fax:
Toll-Free:
Address: 300 Takatsuka-cho, Minami-ku, Hamamatsu, 432-8611 Japan

STOCK TICKER/OTHER:

Stock Ticker: SZKMF
Exchange: PINX
Employees: 101,523
Fiscal Year Ends: 03/31
Parent Company:

SALARIES/BONUSES:

Top Exec. Salary: $ Bonus: $
Second Exec. Salary: $ Bonus: $

OTHER THOUGHTS:

Estimated Female Officers or Directors:
Hot Spot for Advancement for Women/Minorities:

Sytner Group Limited

www.sytner.co.uk

NAIC Code: 441110

TYPES OF BUSINESS:

Auto Dealers, Retail
Auto Parts & Service
Auto Finance
Auto Rental

BRANDS/DIVISIONS/AFFILIATES:

Penske Automotive Group Inc
Graypaul Classic Cars

CONTACTS: *Note: Officers with more than one job title may be intentionally listed here more than once.*

Darren Edwards, Managing Dir.

GROWTH PLANS/SPECIAL FEATURES:

Sytner Group Limited is a retailer of new and pre-owned vehicles, specializing in high-end, luxury vehicles, with dealership locations throughout the U.K. The firm is a wholly-owned subsidiary of the Penske Automotive Group, Inc., a Detroit-based automotive company. Sytner's brands of new vehicles include MINI, Audi, Ferrari, Jaguar, Bentley, BMW, Lamborghini and Mercedes-Benz. The firm also offers used cars from many of the same brands. Sytner allows customers to order customized new cars that meet their specifications, and works with specialist builder ALPINA to offer individually-tailored BMWs. In addition, the company offers after-sale body shop, parts and repair services, including tailored solutions for most of its brands, and its Sytner Drive vehicle replacement plan, which provides customers with a replacement vehicle of the same standard as their own vehicle, if it is damaged in an accident. Sytner's website provides links to each individual dealership where customers can browse new and used inventory, as well as obtaining finance or lease information. The company's Graypaul Classic Cars dealership works to source and sell only the finest, hand-picked classic and sports cars.

FINANCIAL DATA: *Note: Data for latest year may not have been available at press time.*

In U.S. $	2018	2017	2016	2015	2014	2013
Revenue	6,621,151,950	6,305,859,000	6,005,580,000	6,276,930,000	5,677,710,000	5,135,970,000
R&D Expense						
Operating Income						
Operating Margin %						
SGA Expense						
Net Income			106,329,000	108,073,000	94,759,200	79,653,500
Operating Cash Flow						
Capital Expenditure						
EBITDA						
Return on Assets %						
Return on Equity %						
Debt to Equity						

CONTACT INFORMATION:

Phone: 44-845-481-0148 Fax: 44-116-282-1010
Toll-Free:
Address: 2 Penman Way, Grove Park, Leicester, LE19 1ST United Kingdom

STOCK TICKER/OTHER:

Stock Ticker: Subsidiary Exchange:
Employees: 7,100 Fiscal Year Ends: 12/31
Parent Company: Penske Automotive Group Inc

SALARIES/BONUSES:

Top Exec. Salary: $ Bonus: $
Second Exec. Salary: $ Bonus: $

OTHER THOUGHTS:

Estimated Female Officers or Directors:
Hot Spot for Advancement for Women/Minorities:

Tata Group

www.tata.com

NAIC Code: 331110

TYPES OF BUSINESS:

Steel Production
Communication & Information Systems
Engineered Products
Energy Utilities
Solar Power
Automobiles
Hotels & Resorts
Pharmaceuticals & Chemicals

BRANDS/DIVISIONS/AFFILIATES:

Tata Sons Private Limited
Tata Motors
Tata Steel
Tata Chemicals
Tata Global Beverages
Titan
Tata Capital
Tata Power

CONTACTS: *Note: Officers with more than one job title may be intentionally listed here more than once.*

Madhu Kannan, Head-Bus. Dev.
Mukund G. Rajan, Chief Ethics Officer
Nirmalya Kumar, Head-Strategy
Natarajan Chandrasekaran, Chmn.

GROWTH PLANS/SPECIAL FEATURES:

Tata Group, owned by Tata Sons Private Limited, is an Indian conglomerate that comprises 10 companies across 10 verticals, operating in more than 100 countries across six continents. These companies include: Tata Consultancy Services, offering information technology (IT) services, consulting and business solutions; Tata Motors, which designs, manufactures and markets automobiles, such as luxury sedans, sports cars, performance SUVs and all-terrain vehicles; Tata Steel, a diversified steel producer operating in 26 countries, with a commercial presence in over 50 countries; Tata Chemicals, which has interests in basic chemistry products, consumer products and specialty products, and is a world-leading producer of soda ash, with manufacturing facilities in North America, Europe, Asia and Africa; Tata Global Beverages, a natural beverages company with a focus on tea, coffee and water, and a presence in more than 40 countries; Titan, which produces jewelry, watches, eyewear, perfume and silk sarees under the Titan, Fastrack, Sonata, Raaga, Skinn and Taneira brands; Tata Capital, offering one-stop financial solutions to retail, corporate and institutional customers; Tata Power, a leading integrated power company in India, offering conventional and renewable energy, power services and next-generation customer solutions such as solar rooftop and electric vehicle charging stations; Tata Advanced Systems, which develops and manufactures critical aerospace and defense solutions for the country of India, including unmanned vehicles, missiles, radars, command and control systems and homeland security solutions; Indian Hotels, which includes India's famous Taj Mahal Palace within its portfolio of 170 hotels (including 25 under development) in over 80 locations in 12 countries on four continents; and Tata Communications, a global digital infrastructure provider that serves over 7,000 customers, with services including managed services such as network, cloud, mobility, Internet of Things (IoT), collaboration and security.

FINANCIAL DATA: *Note: Data for latest year may not have been available at press time.*

In U.S. $	2018	2017	2016	2015	2014	2013
Revenue	109,670,000,000	94,620,050,000	90,672,600,000			
R&D Expense						
Operating Income						
Operating Margin %						
SGA Expense						
Net Income	1,381,820,000	3,702,500,000	6,947,020,000			
Operating Cash Flow						
Capital Expenditure						
EBITDA						
Return on Assets %						
Return on Equity %						
Debt to Equity						

CONTACT INFORMATION:

Phone: 91 22-6665-8282 Fax: 91-22-6665-8160
Toll-Free:
Address: 24 Homi Mody St., Mumbai, 400 001 India

STOCK TICKER/OTHER:

Stock Ticker: Private
Employees: 706,511
Parent Company: Tata Sons Private Limited
Exchange:
Fiscal Year Ends: 03/31

SALARIES/BONUSES:

Top Exec. Salary: $ Bonus: $
Second Exec. Salary: $ Bonus: $

OTHER THOUGHTS:

Estimated Female Officers or Directors:
Hot Spot for Advancement for Women/Minorities:

Tata Motors Limited

www.tatamotors.com

NAIC Code: 336111

TYPES OF BUSINESS:

Automobile Manufacturing
Light & Medium Commercial Vehicles Manufacturing
Heavy Commercial Vehicles Manufacturing
Passenger Vehicles Manufacturing

BRANDS/DIVISIONS/AFFILIATES:

Tata Group
Jaguar
Land Rover
Nex-Gen ULTRA
NEXON AMT
Tata Hispano Motors Carrocera SA
Tata Marcopolo Motors Limited
Marcopolo SA Brazil

CONTACTS: *Note: Officers with more than one job title may be intentionally listed here more than once.*

Guenter Butschek, CEO
Satish Borwankar, COO
P.B. Balaji, CFO
Ravindra Kumar, Chief Human Resources Officer
Rajendra Parker, CTO
Rajesh Bagga, VP-Legal
Ravindra Pisharody, Pres., Commercial Vehicles
S.B. Borwankar, Exec. Dir.
Ravi Kant, Vice Chmn.
N. Chandrasekaran, Chmn.
Venkatram Mamillapalle, Sr. VP

GROWTH PLANS/SPECIAL FEATURES:

Tata Motors Limited, part of Tata Group, is one of India's largest automobile manufacturers with vehicles sold in over 170 countriescountries. The company manufactures commercial and passenger vehicles and also provides automobile financing services. Tata Motors' products include passenger vehicles; utility vehicles; light commercial vehicles, including pick-up trucks; and medium and heavy commercial vehicles. Through its subsidiaries, the firm is also engaged in areas such as engineering, construction equipment manufacturing, vehicle components manufacturing, supply chain management, factory automation and automotive retailing and servicing. The company also produces defense vehicles. The company employs a significant number of engineers and scientists and maintains R&D centers in India, South Korea, Spain and the U.K. Tata Motors is among the world's leading bus manufacturers, and the company has expanded these activities through strategic partnerships with: Tata Hispano Motors Carrocera SA, a Spanish bus and coach manufacturer; and Tata Marcopolo Motors Limited, a strategic partnership between Tata and Brazilian bus manufacturer, Macropolo S.A. Brazil. The firm has also expanded its international presence through such activities as the manufacture and marketing of pick-up trucks in Thailand, and the marketing of Fiat-branded cars in India as well as through vehicle sales in several countries in Europe, Africa, the Middle East, Australia and Asia. Tata Motors also owns the Jaguar and Land Rover brands through Jaguar Land Rover Automotive plc, with an additional 97 direct and indirect subsidiaries in its portfolio. In early-2018, the firm announced the nation-wide launch of Nex-Gen ULTRA range of trucks; opened bookings for the new NEXON AMT with HyprDrive Self-Shift Gears; and celebrated the first anniversary of the Tata Hexa, a crossover lifestyle vehicle.

FINANCIAL DATA: *Note: Data for latest year may not have been available at press time.*

In U.S. $	2018	2017	2016	2015	2014	2013
Revenue	41,538,090,000	38,275,270,000	38,864,950,000	37,825,310,000	33,740,520,000	
R&D Expense	508,878,300	491,833,400	499,786,800	410,853,700	369,587,200	
Operating Income	-1,667,567,000	-921,491,300	401,780,900	1,345,766,000	1,061,463,000	
Operating Margin %		.04%	.07%	.09%	.09%	
SGA Expense	4,408,626,000	4,145,367,000	4,205,186,000	3,649,505,000	3,122,628,000	
Net Income	960,461,100	881,932,200	1,381,506,000	1,848,443,000	1,883,396,000	
Operating Cash Flow	3,437,421,000	4,367,226,000	5,398,934,000	5,264,770,000	5,351,656,000	
Capital Expenditure	5,054,236,000	4,417,514,000	4,489,628,000	4,345,553,000	3,729,037,000	
EBITDA	5,214,664,000	4,649,168,000	4,904,148,000	5,546,568,000	4,941,466,000	
Return on Assets %		.02%	.04%	.06%	.07%	
Return on Equity %		.09%	.15%	.22%	.26%	
Debt to Equity		1.135	0.662	1.02	0.726	

CONTACT INFORMATION:

Phone: 91-22-66658282 Fax:
Toll-Free:
Address: Homi Mody St., Bombay House, 24, Mumbai, 400 001 India

STOCK TICKER/OTHER:

Stock Ticker: TTM
Exchange: NYS
Employees: 79,558
Fiscal Year Ends: 03/31
Parent Company: Tata Group

SALARIES/BONUSES:

Top Exec. Salary: $3,794,943 Bonus: $
Second Exec. Salary: $1,194,194 Bonus: $

OTHER THOUGHTS:

Estimated Female Officers or Directors:
Hot Spot for Advancement for Women/Minorities:

TBC Corporation

www.tbccorp.com

NAIC Code: 441320

TYPES OF BUSINESS:

Tire Stores
Wholesale Tire Distribution

BRANDS/DIVISIONS/AFFILIATES:

TCB Brands
NTW
TBC International
Tire America
NTB
Tire Kingdom
Big O Tires
Midas

CONTACTS: *Note: Officers with more than one job title may be intentionally listed here more than once.*

Erik R. Olsen, CEO
Timothy J. Miller, CFO
Scott Stoughton, CMO
Terri Hoskins, Sr. VP - Chief Human Resources Officer
William Gearhart, CIO
Brian Maciak, General Counsel
Timothy J. Miller, Treas.
J. Glen Gravatt, Pres., Purchasing & Dist. Div.

GROWTH PLANS/SPECIAL FEATURES:

TBC Corporation markets and distributes replacement automobile tires through wholesale, retail and franchise operations. The firm serves wholesale customers in the U.S., Canada and Mexico through TCB Brands, NTW, TBC International and TBC de Mexico. TBC Brands is a leading marketer of private brand tires in North America, with a core program designed to service independent wholesale and retail dealers. NTW (National Tire Wholesale) is one of the largest U.S. tire distributors in the wholesale distribution market, with 144 distribution centers serving 92 metropolitan areas. TBC International is a global distributor of tires, primarily passenger and commercial tires. The firm has established dealer networks in Latin America, Mexico and the Middle East. TBC de Mexico is a leading tire dealer in Mexico, distributing car, van, truck, agricultural, industrial and specialty tires as well as oil, wheels and other automotive equipment. This brand has 44 branch locations throughout the country, each with a dedicated warehouse to provide quick and efficient supply for its customers. The retail division operates more than 730 locations throughout North America under the Tire America, NTB and Tire Kingdom brands. Tire America provides seamless online purchasing (tireamerica.com) and local installation options, with millions of tires in stock and thousands of installers nationwide. NTB, Tire Kingdom and Merchant's tire and service centers are automotive maintenance facilities that specialize in fast car care and complete tire services, including oil change, brakes, batteries, wheel alignment, tire rotation, flat tire repair, steering, suspension, fluid services and more. Its Premier Fleet Program offers business owners and company drivers with discounts on all auto services. Last, the franchise division comprises more than 2,500 locations throughout North America under the Big O Tires and Midas brand names. These businesses offer tire and auto repair services for vehicles as well as for fleets.

FINANCIAL DATA: *Note: Data for latest year may not have been available at press time.*

In U.S. $	2018	2017	2016	2015	2014	2013
Revenue	3,570,000,000	3,400,000,000	3,230,000,000	3,400,000,000	3,500,000,000	3,000,000,000
R&D Expense						
Operating Income						
Operating Margin %						
SGA Expense						
Net Income						
Operating Cash Flow						
Capital Expenditure						
EBITDA						
Return on Assets %						
Return on Equity %						
Debt to Equity						

CONTACT INFORMATION:

Phone: 561-383-3100 Fax: 531-383-3149
Toll-Free:
Address: 4300 TBC Way, Palm Beach Gardens, FL 33410 United States

STOCK TICKER/OTHER:

Stock Ticker: Joint Venture
Employees: 11,322
Parent Company: Sumitomo Corporation
Exchange:
Fiscal Year Ends: 12/31

SALARIES/BONUSES:

Top Exec. Salary: $ Bonus: $
Second Exec. Salary: $ Bonus: $

OTHER THOUGHTS:

Estimated Female Officers or Directors:
Hot Spot for Advancement for Women/Minorities:

Tenneco Inc

NAIC Code: 336300

www.tenneco.com

TYPES OF BUSINESS:

Automotive Parts Manufacturer
Advanced Suspension Technologies
Ride Control Products
Emissions Systems
Performance Mufflers
Noise Control Systems

BRANDS/DIVISIONS/AFFILIATES:

Federal-Mogul LLC
Ohlinus Racing AB

CONTACTS: *Note: Officers with more than one job title may be intentionally listed here more than once.*

Jason Hollar, CFO
John Patouhas, Chief Accounting Officer
Benny Patel, Chief Technology Officer
Brian Kesseler, Co-CEO
Roger Wood, Co-CEO
Gregg Sherrill, Director
Rainer Jueckstock, Executive VP
Peng Guo, Executive VP
Bradley Norton, Executive VP
Brandon Smith, General Counsel
Kaled Awada, Other Executive Officer
Gregg Bolt, Senior VP, Divisional

GROWTH PLANS/SPECIAL FEATURES:

Tenneco, Inc. designs, manufactures and sells innovative products and services for light vehicle, commercial truck, off-highway, industrial and aftermarket customers. The firm serves both original equipment manufacturers (OEMs) and replacement markets worldwide. Tenneco is among the world's leading manufacturers of clean air, powertrain and ride performance systems and products. The clean air division invests in core sciences, including combustion and thermal management, materials science and thermoelectrical energy, all of which enables the development of creative solutions that help Tenneco better meet its customer's current and future emissions control needs. The powertrain division utilizes technology and expertise to help customers adopt hybrid and fully-electric powertrains, which offer enhanced vehicle ride performance via noise, vibration and harshness reduction capabilities for smoother rides. The ride performance division offers advanced suspension technologies that deliver performance, comfort and power to differentiate vehicles. Tenneco's 64 manufacturing plants are located throughout Asia Pacific (27), Europe (20) and North America (15), as well as in South America (2). In October 2018, Tenneco acquired Federal-Mogul LLC, a global supplier of technology and innovation in vehicle and industrial products for fuel economy, emissions reduction and safety systems. Subsequently, in mid-2019, Tenneco expects to separate its businesses to form two new independent, publicly-traded companies: an aftermarket and ride performance company and a powertrain technology company. In January 2019, Tenneco acquired Ohlinus Racing AB, which offers suspension systems and components to automotive and motorsport industries.

FINANCIAL DATA: *Note: Data for latest year may not have been available at press time.*

In U.S. $	2018	2017	2016	2015	2014	2013
Revenue	11,763,000,000	9,274,000,000	8,599,000,000	8,209,000,000	8,420,000,000	7,964,000,000
R&D Expense	204,000,000	158,000,000	154,000,000	146,000,000	169,000,000	144,000,000
Operating Income	349,000,000	432,000,000	533,000,000	524,000,000	499,000,000	428,000,000
Operating Margin %		.05%	.06%	.06%	.06%	.05%
SGA Expense	794,000,000	648,000,000	589,000,000	491,000,000	519,000,000	453,000,000
Net Income	55,000,000	207,000,000	363,000,000	247,000,000	226,000,000	183,000,000
Operating Cash Flow	439,000,000	629,000,000	489,000,000	517,000,000	341,000,000	503,000,000
Capital Expenditure	507,000,000	419,000,000	345,000,000	309,000,000	344,000,000	269,000,000
EBITDA	651,000,000	641,000,000	740,000,000	722,000,000	700,000,000	629,000,000
Return on Assets %		.05%	.09%	.06%	.06%	.05%
Return on Equity %		.32%	.71%	.53%	.49%	.54%
Debt to Equity		1.951	2.201	2.596	2.151	2.353

CONTACT INFORMATION:

Phone: 847 482-5000 Fax: 847 482-5940
Toll-Free:
Address: 500 N. Field Dr., Lake Forest, IL 60045 United States

STOCK TICKER/OTHER:

Stock Ticker: TEN Exchange: NYS
Employees: 31,000 Fiscal Year Ends: 12/31
Parent Company:

SALARIES/BONUSES:

Top Exec. Salary: $1,050,000 Bonus: $
Second Exec. Salary: $670,000 Bonus: $

OTHER THOUGHTS:

Estimated Female Officers or Directors: 4
Hot Spot for Advancement for Women/Minorities: Y

Tesla Inc

www.teslamotors.com

NAIC Code: 336111

TYPES OF BUSINESS:

Automobile Manufacturing, All-Electric
Battery Manufacturing
Lithium Ion Battery Storage Technologies
Energy Storage Systems

BRANDS/DIVISIONS/AFFILIATES:

Model S
Model X
Model 3
Model Y
Roadster
Tesla Semi

CONTACTS: *Note: Officers with more than one job title may be intentionally listed here more than once.*

Elon Musk, CEO
Zachary Kirkhorn, CFO
Vaibhav Taneja, Chief Accounting Officer
Jeffrey Straubel, Chief Technology Officer
Jerome Guillen, President, Divisional

GROWTH PLANS/SPECIAL FEATURES:

Tesla, Inc. manufactures high-performance, all-electric automobiles and energy storage products. Its sales have been impressive, and the company is widely admired for its innovation, design, engineering and marketing. The Model S features a lightweight aluminum body and has a 335-mile range, as well as 360-degree cameras for maximum visibility. The Model X sport utility vehicle has a 295-mile range and room to seat up to seven adult passengers. The Model 3 is an all-wheel drive vehicle with a 310-mile range. Unveiled in 2019, the Model Y will have up to three rows of seats (up to seven people) and a range of up to 300 miles. The Roadster, slated for 2020, will also comprise a lightweight, removable glass roof that stores in the trunk for a convertible driving experience. The Tesla Semi, expected in 2020, is a commercial truck that goes from 0-60 mph in 20 seconds. Battery-wise, each Tesla car has thousands of small, lithium-ion batteries linked together, similar to the batteries found in consumer electronics. The firm's network of car charging stations can fully-charge a Tesla in 75 minutes and are located in North America, Europe and Asia; but Tesla vehicles can be charged anywhere with standard equipment and convenient options. In addition to vehicles, Tesla manufactures solar panels and solar roofs for converting sunlight into energy; manufactures an easy-to-install home-sized energy storage system intended to store local, solar-generated power for later use; and manufactures a giant battery designed for commercial and utility purposes. In March 2019, Tesla made a few announcements: that a cost-saving measure would allow them to decrease the price of the Model 3; that it would be closing most of its stores and galleries (it had about 130 at the time of the announcement); and that future sales would occur over the internet.

FINANCIAL DATA: *Note: Data for latest year may not have been available at press time.*

In U.S. $	2018	2017	2016	2015	2014	2013
Revenue	21,461,270,000	11,758,750,000	7,000,132,000	4,046,025,000	3,198,356,000	2,013,496,000
R&D Expense	1,460,370,000	1,378,073,000	834,408,000	717,900,000	464,700,000	231,976,000
Operating Income	-252,840,000	-1,632,086,000	-667,340,000	-716,629,000	-186,689,000	-61,283,000
Operating Margin %		-.14%	-.10%	-.18%	-.06%	-.03%
SGA Expense	2,834,491,000	2,476,500,000	1,432,189,000	922,232,000	603,660,000	285,569,000
Net Income	-976,091,000	-1,961,400,000	-674,914,000	-888,663,000	-294,040,000	-74,014,000
Operating Cash Flow	2,097,802,000	-60,654,000	-123,829,000	-524,499,000	-57,337,000	257,994,000
Capital Expenditure	2,319,516,000	4,081,354,000	1,440,471,000	1,634,850,000	969,885,000	264,224,000
EBITDA	1,559,376,000	-101,770,000	399,561,000	-334,183,000	48,181,000	67,591,000
Return on Assets %		-.08%	-.04%	-.13%	-.07%	-.04%
Return on Equity %		-.44%	-.23%	-.89%	-.37%	-.19%
Debt to Equity		2.223	1.258	1.912	2.059	0.898

CONTACT INFORMATION:

Phone: 650 681-5000 Fax:
Toll-Free:
Address: 3500 Deer Creek Rd., Palo Alto, CA 94304 United States

STOCK TICKER/OTHER:

Stock Ticker: TSLA
Employees: 17,782
Parent Company:
Exchange: NAS
Fiscal Year Ends: 12/31

SALARIES/BONUSES:

Top Exec. Salary: $501,923 Bonus: $
Second Exec. Salary: $301,154 Bonus: $

OTHER THOUGHTS:

Estimated Female Officers or Directors: 1
Hot Spot for Advancement for Women/Minorities:

Thor Industries Inc

www.thorindustries.com

NAIC Code: 336214

TYPES OF BUSINESS:

Recreational Vehicle Manufacturing
Motor Homes
Automotive Parts & Accessories
Buses

BRANDS/DIVISIONS/AFFILIATES:

Airstream Inc
Thor Motor Coach Inc
KZ Inc
Postle Operating LLC
Jayco Inc
Dutchman
Bison Coach
Erwin Hymer Group SE

CONTACTS: *Note: Officers with more than one job title may be intentionally listed here more than once.*

Robert Martin, CEO
Colleen Zuhl, CFO
Peter Orthwein, Chairman of the Board
W. Woelfer, General Counsel
Kenneth Julian, Senior VP, Divisional

GROWTH PLANS/SPECIAL FEATURES:

Thor Industries, Inc. is a leading manufacturer of a wide range of recreational vehicles (RVs). The company's primary RV subsidiaries are Airstream, Inc.; Thor Motor Coach, Inc.; Keystone RV Company, which includes Crossroads and Dutchman; Heartland Recreational Vehicles LLC, which includes Bison Horse Trailers, LLC (dba Bison Coach), Cruiser RV, LLC and DRV, LLC; K.Z., Inc., which includes Venture RV; Postle Operating, LLC; and Jayco, Inc. (which includes Jayco, StarCraft, Highland Ridge and Entegra Coach). Together these businesses produce towable RVs, which account for 72.1% of annual net sales, as well as motorized RVs, which account for 25.8% of sales (3.7% goes toward other/related sales). Towable RVs include conventional travel trailers, fifth wheels and park models; truck and folding campers; and equestrian and other specialty towable vehicles. Park models are recreational dwellings towed to a permanent site such as a lake, woods or park, with the maximum size of park models in the U.S. being 400 square feet. Motorized RVs include Class A, B and C motorhomes, which are self-powered vehicles built on a chassis and self-contained with their own lighting, heating, cooking, refrigeration, sewage holding and water storage facilities. Thor also manufactures and sells related parts and accessories. During 2019, Thor acquired Germany RV manufacturer, Erwin Hymer Group SE, its first acquisition outside the U.S.

FINANCIAL DATA: *Note: Data for latest year may not have been available at press time.*

In U.S. $	2018	2017	2016	2015	2014	2013
Revenue	8,328,909,000	7,246,952,000	4,582,112,000	4,006,819,000	3,525,456,000	3,241,795,000
R&D Expense						
Operating Income	632,104,000	559,811,000	392,094,000	290,639,000	248,764,000	219,429,000
Operating Margin %		.08%	.09%	.07%	.07%	.07%
SGA Expense	477,444,000	419,847,000	306,269,000	250,891,000	208,712,000	194,650,000
Net Income	430,151,000	374,254,000	256,519,000	199,385,000	179,002,000	152,862,000
Operating Cash Flow	466,508,000	419,333,000	341,209,000	247,860,000	149,261,000	145,066,000
Capital Expenditure	138,197,000	115,027,000	51,976,000	42,283,000	30,406,000	24,305,000
EBITDA	731,439,000	664,374,000	437,480,000	324,456,000	278,663,000	246,965,000
Return on Assets %		.15%	.13%	.14%	.13%	.12%
Return on Equity %		.26%	.22%	.20%	.19%	.18%
Debt to Equity		0.092	0.285			

CONTACT INFORMATION:

Phone: 574-970-7460 Fax:
Toll-Free:
Address: 601 E. Beardsley Ave., Elkhart, IN 46514-3305 United States

STOCK TICKER/OTHER:

Stock Ticker: THO
Exchange: NYS
Employees: 17,800
Fiscal Year Ends: 07/31
Parent Company:

SALARIES/BONUSES:

Top Exec. Salary: $750,000 Bonus: $
Second Exec. Salary: $600,000 Bonus: $

OTHER THOUGHTS:

Estimated Female Officers or Directors:
Hot Spot for Advancement for Women/Minorities:

TI Fluid Systems plc

www.tiautomotive.com

NAIC Code: 336350

TYPES OF BUSINESS:

Automobile Parts Manufacturing
Fuel Storage & Fluid Transfer Systems
Fluid Systems Analysis

BRANDS/DIVISIONS/AFFILIATES:

TI Automotive

CONTACTS:

Note: Officers with more than one job title may be intentionally listed here more than once.

William L. Kozyra, CEO
Tim Knutson, CFO
Domenico Milicia, Chief Human Resources Officer
Al Deane, CTO
Tim Guerriero, General Counsel
Domenico Milicia, Chief Comm. Officer
Jay Phillion, Chief Purchasing & Quality Officer
David Murrell, Exec. VP-Global Pump & Module Systems
Hans Dieltjens, Exec. VP-Global Tank Systems
Jan Svec, VP-Global Pump & Module Systems

GROWTH PLANS/SPECIAL FEATURES:

TI Fluid Systems plc is a global supplier of integrated fuel storage and delivery systems, as well as fluid carrying systems for braking and powertrain applications for both cars and trucks. TI has manufacturing facilities in 118 locations across 29 countries, serving every major automobile maker in the world. The firm's components are used in roughly half of the cars built worldwide. TI operates through two products groups: fluid carrying systems and fuel tank and delivery systems. The fluid carrying systems division designs and manufactures a wide range of products designed to move fluid throughout the vehicle. These systems are also designed and manufactured to meet assembly, design and performance requirements of vehicles, and does this by using a range of materials and manufacturing processes. This division's brake and fuel lines and bundles consist of multi-layer low-permeation plastic tubes, high-pressure steel double-wall and single-wall tubes, quick connectors and flexible lines. TI has developed specialty internal and external coatings designed to withstand corrosion, abrasion and other hazards on all of its fluid-carrying systems products. This division's thermal products are light-weight yet durable through the use of innovative materials and a variety of sizes. These thermal products reduce noise, boost efficiency and provide solutions to meet glycol formulations and refrigerant regulations. This division's powertrain products improve fuel economy and reduce emissions, and include fuel injection systems, cooling and lubrication systems and more. The fuel tank and delivery systems division develops and manufactures fuel tank systems for diesel, gasoline, flex-fuel and hybrid vehicle applications. Fuel delivery products consist of pumps and modules for gasoline, diesel and flex-fuel vehicles, and designed for quiet, efficient, low-voltage performance and durability. This division offers a comprehensive line of pumps and modules to effectively handle fuel systems. Aftermarket parts are manufactured by U.S. subsidiary TI Automotive.

FINANCIAL DATA:

Note: Data for latest year may not have been available at press time.

In U.S. $	2018	2017	2016	2015	2014	2013
Revenue	3,972,390,000	4,181,620,000	3,527,950,000	3,381,630,000	3,277,300,000	3,000,000,000
R&D Expense						
Operating Income						
Operating Margin %						
SGA Expense						
Net Income	160,245,000	137,994,000	46,251,300	-44,357,100	19,204,600	
Operating Cash Flow						
Capital Expenditure						
EBITDA						
Return on Assets %						
Return on Equity %						
Debt to Equity						

CONTACT INFORMATION:

Phone: 44 1865 871820 Fax:
Toll-Free:
Address: 4650 Kingsgate, Cascade Way, Oxford Business Park South, Oxford, OX4 2SU United Kingdom

STOCK TICKER/OTHER:

Stock Ticker: TIFS
Employees: 28,000
Parent Company:
Exchange: London
Fiscal Year Ends: 12/31

SALARIES/BONUSES:

Top Exec. Salary: $ Bonus: $
Second Exec. Salary: $ Bonus: $

OTHER THOUGHTS:

Estimated Female Officers or Directors:
Hot Spot for Advancement for Women/Minorities:

Titan International Inc

NAIC Code: 336300

www.titan-intl.com

TYPES OF BUSINESS:

Tire Manufacturing
Specialty Tires & Wheels

BRANDS/DIVISIONS/AFFILIATES:

Voltyre-Prom

CONTACTS:

Note: Officers with more than one job title may be intentionally listed here more than once.

Paul Reitz, CEO
David Martin, CFO
Maurice Taylor, Chairman of the Board
Amy Evans, Chief Accounting Officer
Michael Troyanovich, General Counsel

GROWTH PLANS/SPECIAL FEATURES:

Titan International, Inc. and its subsidiaries are a global wheel, tire and undercarriage industrial manufacturer and supplier, serving customers across the globe. As a leading manufacturer in the off-highway industry, Titan produces a broad range of specialty products to meet the specifications of original equipment manufacturers (OEMs) and aftermarket customers in the agricultural, earthmoving/construction and consumer markets. Titan's agricultural market includes rims, wheels, tires and undercarriage systems and components manufactured for use on various agricultural and forestry equipment. Titan's earthmoving/construction market includes wheels, tires and undercarriage systems and components supplied to the mining industry, while the consumer market includes bias truck tires in Latin America, products for all-terrain vehicles (ATVs) and recreational/utility trailers. Minority-owned Voltyre-Prom produces agricultural and industrial tires at its more than 2 million-square-foot manufacturing facility in Russia. Other businesses are located throughout North America, as well as in Australia and Latin America.

FINANCIAL DATA:

Note: Data for latest year may not have been available at press time.

In U.S. $	2018	2017	2016	2015	2014	2013
Revenue	1,602,408,000	1,468,922,000	1,265,497,000	1,394,771,000	1,895,527,000	2,163,595,000
R&D Expense	11,146,000	10,302,000	9,971,000	11,162,000	14,005,000	11,165,000
Operating Income	42,244,000	-3,267,000	-21,333,000	-24,279,000	-21,122,000	102,395,000
Operating Margin %		-.01%	-.01%	-.02%	-.03%	.05%
SGA Expense	134,789,000	150,676,000	144,988,000	140,393,000	173,614,000	167,371,000
Net Income	16,087,000	-60,042,000	-33,987,000	-75,633,000	-80,461,000	35,205,000
Operating Cash Flow	-36,176,000	-1,289,000	43,500,000	63,930,000	114,072,000	116,649,000
Capital Expenditure	39,000,000	32,626,000	41,948,000	48,429,000	58,439,000	80,131,000
EBITDA	107,881,000	35,797,000	59,451,000	51,644,000	-26,976,000	182,476,000
Return on Assets %		-.05%	-.03%	-.07%	-.05%	.02%
Return on Equity %		-.22%	-.14%	-.21%	-.13%	.05%
Debt to Equity		1.269	1.391	1.392	0.885	0.724

CONTACT INFORMATION:

Phone: 217 228-6011 Fax: 217 228-7499
Toll-Free:
Address: 2701 Spruce St., Quincy, IL 62301 United States

STOCK TICKER/OTHER:

Stock Ticker: TWI Exchange: NYS
Employees: 6,100 Fiscal Year Ends: 12/31
Parent Company:

SALARIES/BONUSES:

Top Exec. Salary: $900,000 Bonus: $975,000
Second Exec. Salary: $350,000 Bonus: $175,000

OTHER THOUGHTS:

Estimated Female Officers or Directors: 1
Hot Spot for Advancement for Women/Minorities:

Titan Machinery Inc

titanmachinery.com

NAIC Code: 811310

TYPES OF BUSINESS:

Commercial and Industrial Machinery and Equipment (except Automotive and Electronic) Repair and Maintenance
Equipment Sales & Rental

BRANDS/DIVISIONS/AFFILIATES:

CNH Industrial NV

CONTACTS:

Note: Officers with more than one job title may be intentionally listed here more than once.

Mark Kalvoda, CFO
David Meyer, Chairman of the Board
Bryan Knutson, COO

GROWTH PLANS/SPECIAL FEATURES:

Titan Machinery, Inc. owns and operates a network of full-service agricultural and construction equipment stores. The firm has built extensive, geographically contiguous network of 74 stores in the U.S. and 30 stores in Europe. Titan sells and rents agricultural and construction equipment, and also services the equipment in the areas surrounding its stores. Agricultural equipment the company sells and services includes machinery and attachments for uses ranging from large-scale farming to home and garden use. The construction equipment it sells and services includes heavy construction and light industrial machinery for commercial and residential construction, road and highway construction, as well as mining. The company engages in four core business activities: new and used equipment sales, parts sales, repair and maintenance services and equipment rental and other activities. New equipment parts are supplied primarily by CNH Industrial NV, or its U.S. subsidiaries. This division acquires used equipment for resale through trade-ins from its customers and selective purchases. Parts are sold via in-store departments and through its on-site repair and maintenance services. Last, the firm rents equipment and provides other ancillary services such as equipment transportation, GPS signal subscriptions and finance/insurance products. Therefore, Titan offers its customers a one-stop solution by providing equipment and parts sales, repair and maintenance services and rental functions in each of its stores.

FINANCIAL DATA:

Note: Data for latest year may not have been available at press time.

In U.S. $	2018	2017	2016	2015	2014	2013
Revenue	1,202,938,000	1,213,080,000	1,367,835,000	1,900,246,000	2,226,446,000	
R&D Expense						
Operating Income	12,097,000	2,357,000	-14,610,000	35,113,000	56,872,000	
Operating Margin %	.01%	.00%	-.01%	.02%	.16%	
SGA Expense						
Net Income	-7,049,000	-14,179,000	-37,892,000	-32,157,000	8,851,000	
Operating Cash Flow	95,812,000	140,997,000	231,884,000	41,058,000	-82,243,000	
Capital Expenditure	26,115,000	12,425,000	8,411,000	17,596,000	23,858,000	
EBITDA	27,665,000	26,020,000	4,950,000	28,219,000	79,778,000	
Return on Assets %	-.01%	-.02%	-.03%	-.02%	.01%	
Return on Equity %	-.02%	-.04%	-.10%	-.08%	.02%	
Debt to Equity	0.303	0.395	0.511	0.53	0.549	

CONTACT INFORMATION:

Phone: 701-356-0130 Fax: 701 356-0139
Toll-Free:
Address: 644 E. Beaton Dr., West Fargo, ND 58078-2648 United States

STOCK TICKER/OTHER:

Stock Ticker: TITN
Exchange: NAS
Employees: 2,431
Fiscal Year Ends: 01/31
Parent Company:

SALARIES/BONUSES:

Top Exec. Salary: $475,000 Bonus: $
Second Exec. Salary: $366,667 Bonus: $

OTHER THOUGHTS:

Estimated Female Officers or Directors:
Hot Spot for Advancement for Women/Minorities:

Tofas Turk Otomobil Fabrikasi AS

www.tofas.com.tr

NAIC Code: 336111

TYPES OF BUSINESS:

Automobile Manufacturing
After Sales Services
Spare Parts
Financing Services

BRANDS/DIVISIONS/AFFILIATES:

Fiat Chrysler Automobiles NV
FCA Italy SpA
Koc Fiat Kredi
Fer Mas Oto Ticaret AS
Fiat
Alfa Romeo
Jeep
Opar

CONTACTS: *Note: Officers with more than one job title may be intentionally listed here more than once.*

Cengiz Eroldu, CEO
Fabrizio Renzi, Dir.-Financial
Ozgur Suslu, Dir.-Mktg.
Burhan CakÄ±r, Dir.-Human Resources
Filippo Sesia, Dir.-R&D
Omer Ozgur Cetinoglu, Dir.-Info. & Comm. Technologies
M. Osman Soyogul, Dir.-Prod.
Cengiz Eroldu, Dir.-Finance
Altan Aytac, Dir.-Supply Chain
Akin Aydemir, Dir.-Industrial Oper.
Selcuk Oncer, Dir.-Acct.
Mahmut Karacan, Dir.-Sales
Yuksel Ozturk, Dir-Purchasing

GROWTH PLANS/SPECIAL FEATURES:

Tofas Turk Otomobil Fabrikasi AS, based in Turkey, is a leading production and research and development center for vehicle manufacturer FCA Italy SpA of Fiat Chrysler Automobiles NV. Tofas has an annual manufacturing capacity of 450,000 vehicles. The company's production lines include: Fiat, Alfa Romeo and Jeep vehicles, as well as the Opar and Magneti Marelli lines of spare parts, accessories and maintenance products. Subsidiaries of Tofas include: Koc Fiat Kredi, which provides finance and insurance products for all of the group's new and used vehicles manufactured in Turkey under a Fiat Chrysler Automobiles license and/or are imported into Turkey; and Fer Mas Oto Ticaret AS, a provider of Ferrari and Maserati automobiles and related aftersales services. Tofas continually invests in expansion and advanced technology in order to develop value-added systems and innovative products for its global customers. The Tofas R&D center submitted 48 new patent applications in 2018. Tofas' headquarters is in Istanbul, and its factory is in Bursa.

Tofas offers its employees access to onsite health, sports and shopping facilities. Company social activities range from tennis, basketball and volleyball tournaments to bowling, painting, diving, folk dancing and other activities. The firm also provides summer schools for employees' children.

FINANCIAL DATA: *Note: Data for latest year may not have been available at press time.*

In U.S. $	2018	2017	2016	2015	2014	2013
Revenue		3,009,405,440	2,459,795,456	1,595,090,560	1,167,078,656	1,131,929,472
R&D Expense						
Operating Income						
Operating Margin %						
SGA Expense						
Net Income		216,049,920	163,404,064	130,323,776	90,077,968	68,114,480
Operating Cash Flow						
Capital Expenditure						
EBITDA						
Return on Assets %						
Return on Equity %						
Debt to Equity						

CONTACT INFORMATION:

Phone: 90 2122753390 Fax: 90 2122753988
Toll-Free:
Address: Buyukdere Cad. No. 145, Tofas Han Zincirlikuyu, Istanbul, 34394 Turkey

STOCK TICKER/OTHER:

Stock Ticker: THYAO Exchange: Istanbul
Employees: 9,712 Fiscal Year Ends: 12/31
Parent Company:

SALARIES/BONUSES:

Top Exec. Salary: $ Bonus: $
Second Exec. Salary: $ Bonus: $

OTHER THOUGHTS:

Estimated Female Officers or Directors:
Hot Spot for Advancement for Women/Minorities:

Tokai Rika Co Ltd

www.tokai-rika.co.jp

NAIC Code: 336300

TYPES OF BUSINESS:

Automobile Parts Manufacturing
Human Interface Systems
Security Systems
Seat Belts
Controls
Aftermarket Parts
Housing Facilities & Equipment

BRANDS/DIVISIONS/AFFILIATES:

TRAM Inc
TAC Manufacturing Inc
TRMI Inc
Wuxi Risho Technology Co Ltd
TRP Inc
Thai Seat Belt Co Ltd
Tokai Rika Belgium NV
Tokai Rika Mexico SA de CV

CONTACTS: *Note: Officers with more than one job title may be intentionally listed here more than once.*

Kenji Miura, Pres.
Kiyoshi Tsunekawa, Exec. VP
Mineo Hattori, Senior Managing Dir.
Shoji Ishida, Senior Managing Dir.
Hitoshi Iwata, Senior Managing Dir.

GROWTH PLANS/SPECIAL FEATURES:

Tokai Rika Co. Ltd. is a manufacturer of automobile parts and components. The company divides it products into six categories: human interface systems & controls, security systems, safety systems, electronics, ornaments and non-vehicle. Human interface systems & controls include remote control touchpads for GPS, audio or air conditioner accessories; switches such as multi-function, power window, steering, heater control, rear seat and push start; and transmission shift levers. Security systems include Smart keys, emergency key systems, electronic key systems, mechanical steering lock systems and immobilizers. Safety systems include seatbelts, steering wheel systems, door mirrors and interior mirrors. Electronics includes systems such as: the power supply engine control unit (ECU), used to control the power source of a vehicle; the immobilizer ECU, which prevents vehicle theft with a duplicated key; the motor rotation sensor, which makes it possible to control the motor; the speed sensor; the steering angle sensor; and the semiconductor. Ornaments include full wheel covers, center caps (hub caps) and vehicle emblems. Non-vehicle products include an entrance electric door lock for any kind of door, window lock monitoring systems, electrical connector systems and alarms. Just a few of Tokai Rika's many subsidiaries include: TRAM, Inc.; TAC Manufacturing, Inc.; TRMI, Inc.; Wuxi Risho Technology Co., Ltd.; TRP, Inc.; Thai Seat Belt Co., Ltd.; TRB Limited; Tokai Rika Belgium NV; and Tokai Rika Mexico SA de CV. During 2019, Tokai Rika established a joint venture agreement with Datatec Co., Ltd. to create a digital key distribution business. The JV combines Tokai's key authentication and digital key distribution technology with Datatec's vehicle operations management and safe driving diagnostics technologies.

FINANCIAL DATA: *Note: Data for latest year may not have been available at press time.*

In U.S. $	2018	2017	2016	2015	2014	2013
Revenue	4,535,930,000	4,125,420,000	4,363,710,000	4,122,143,232	3,990,984,192	3,390,477,568
R&D Expense						
Operating Income						
Operating Margin %						
SGA Expense						
Net Income	-40,809,200	-31,443,700	-39,730,800	190,849,504	157,321,408	52,097,100
Operating Cash Flow						
Capital Expenditure						
EBITDA						
Return on Assets %						
Return on Equity %						
Debt to Equity						

CONTACT INFORMATION:

Phone: 81-587-95-5211 Fax:
Toll-Free:
Address: 3-260 Toyota, Oguchi-Cho, Niwa-Gun, Aichi, 480-0195 Japan

STOCK TICKER/OTHER:

Stock Ticker: 6995
Employees: 19,390
Parent Company:
Exchange: Tokyo
Fiscal Year Ends: 03/31

SALARIES/BONUSES:

Top Exec. Salary: $ Bonus: $
Second Exec. Salary: $ Bonus: $

OTHER THOUGHTS:

Estimated Female Officers or Directors:
Hot Spot for Advancement for Women/Minorities:

Toresco Enterprises Inc

NAIC Code: 441110

www.1800autoland.com

TYPES OF BUSINESS:

Auto Dealers, Retail
Fleet Sales
Repair Services
Financing

BRANDS/DIVISIONS/AFFILIATES:

Autoland

GROWTH PLANS/SPECIAL FEATURES:

Toresco Enterprises, Inc., established in the mid-1940s by the Toresco family, operates Autoland, an automobile mall in New Jersey. The mega dealership sells both used and pre-owned automobiles and offers financing, maintenance services and parts. Autoland Toyota Chrysler Jeep Dodge Ram is located in Springfield. Through the firm's website, customers can search new and used inventories, schedule a test drive, schedule a service appointment, place an order for parts and fill out a finance application. Its website also provides a financing payment calculator and coupons for its cars, services and parts. Founder Donald Toresco opened the first Autoland location in 1985.

CONTACTS: *Note: Officers with more than one job title may be intentionally listed here more than once.*

Mark Montenero, Pres.
Joe Catena, VP
Mark Montenero, Dir.-Oper.
Kashif Qureshi, Dir.-Finance

FINANCIAL DATA: *Note: Data for latest year may not have been available at press time.*

In U.S. $	2018	2017	2016	2015	2014	2013
Revenue	722,137,500	687,750,000	655,000,000	642,000,000	635,000,000	600,000,000
R&D Expense						
Operating Income						
Operating Margin %						
SGA Expense						
Net Income						
Operating Cash Flow						
Capital Expenditure						
EBITDA						
Return on Assets %						
Return on Equity %						
Debt to Equity						

CONTACT INFORMATION:

Phone: 973-467-2900 Fax: 973-467-1824
Toll-Free:
Address: 170 Rte. 22 E., Springfield, NJ 07081 United States

STOCK TICKER/OTHER:

Stock Ticker: Private
Employees: 600
Parent Company:
Exchange:
Fiscal Year Ends: 12/31

SALARIES/BONUSES:

Top Exec. Salary: $ Bonus: $
Second Exec. Salary: $ Bonus: $

OTHER THOUGHTS:

Estimated Female Officers or Directors:
Hot Spot for Advancement for Women/Minorities:

Tower International Inc

www.towerinternational.com

NAIC Code: 336300

TYPES OF BUSINESS:

Automobile Parts Manufacturer
Body Components & Assemblies

BRANDS/DIVISIONS/AFFILIATES:

GROWTH PLANS/SPECIAL FEATURES:

Tower International, Inc. is a manufacturer of engineered automotive structural metal components and assemblies. The company primarily serves original equipment manufacturers (OEMs), supplying body-structure stampings, frame and other chassis structures, as well as complex welded assemblies for small and large cars, crossovers, pickups and sport utility vehicles (SUVs). Tower Chicago is the firm's 400,000-square-foot facility that supports the Ford Chicago Assembly Plant. Tower International's capabilities include both hot and cold forming and joining, and process and product technologies. In mid-2019, Tower International agreed to be acquired by Autokiniton Global Group (AGG), a North American supplier of metal-formed components and complex assemblies to the automotive industry. Earlier that year, Tower International sold its entire European operations to Financiere SNOP Dunois SA.

CONTACTS: *Note: Officers with more than one job title may be intentionally listed here more than once.*

Jeffrey Kersten, CFO
Gregory Guastella, Chief Accounting Officer
James Gouin, Director
Thomas Brown, Director
Reid Southby, Executive VP
Par Malmhagen, President
Nanette Dudek, Secretary
Mark Flynn, Senior VP, Divisional

FINANCIAL DATA: *Note: Data for latest year may not have been available at press time.*

In U.S. $	2018	2017	2016	2015	2014	2013
Revenue	1,571,853,000	1,988,046,000	1,913,641,000	1,955,709,000	2,067,771,000	2,102,019,000
R&D Expense						
Operating Income	101,533,000	126,031,000	106,408,000	87,578,000	95,014,000	107,085,000
Operating Margin %		.06%	.06%	.04%	.05%	.05%
SGA Expense	89,527,000	118,061,000	131,552,000	130,650,000	132,635,000	133,588,000
Net Income	48,900,000	47,625,000	38,579,000	194,052,000	21,516,000	-20,275,000
Operating Cash Flow	98,247,000	167,207,000	143,740,000	122,169,000	121,150,000	153,350,000
Capital Expenditure	83,141,000	104,153,000	116,283,000	124,641,000	98,440,000	84,754,000
EBITDA	153,049,000	192,335,000	167,621,000	159,360,000	168,454,000	133,476,000
Return on Assets %		.04%	.03%	.16%	.02%	-.02%
Return on Equity %		.20%	.19%	1.61%	.37%	-.29%
Debt to Equity		1.277	1.714	2.118	10.774	6.24

CONTACT INFORMATION:

Phone: 248 675-6000 Fax: 248-675-6800
Toll-Free:
Address: 17672 N. Laurel Park Dr., Ste. 400 E, Livonia, MI 48152 United States

STOCK TICKER/OTHER:

Stock Ticker: TOWR
Exchange: NYS
Employees: 7,900
Fiscal Year Ends: 12/31
Parent Company:

SALARIES/BONUSES:

Top Exec. Salary: $800,000 Bonus: $
Second Exec. Salary: $675,000 Bonus: $

OTHER THOUGHTS:

Estimated Female Officers or Directors:
Hot Spot for Advancement for Women/Minorities:

Toyo Tire Corporation

www.toyotires.co.jp

NAIC Code: 326200

TYPES OF BUSINESS:

Plastics & Rubber Manufacturing
Tire Production
Auto Racing
Chemical & Industrial Products
Thermal Insulation

BRANDS/DIVISIONS/AFFILIATES:

Toyo Tire Canada Inc
Toyo Tire USA Corp
NT Mexico de RL de CV
Toyo Tyre Rubber Australia Ltd
Toyo Tire (Shanghai) Co Ltd
Toyo Tyre Sales and Marketing Malaysia Sdn Bhd
Toyo Tire Europe GmbH
Toyo Tyre Europe GmbH

CONTACTS: *Note: Officers with more than one job title may be intentionally listed here more than once.*

Takashi Shimizu, Pres.
Tetsuo Tatara, Gen. Mgr.-Prod. Eng. Center
Kazuyuki Ito, Gen. Mgr.-Tire Prod. Mgmt. Div.
Koichi Ono, Gen. Mgr.-Corp. Planning Div.
Hidenori Fukutomi, Sr. Corp. Officer
Tetsuya Kuze, Sr. Corp. Officer
Takuji Yamamoto, Sr. Corp. Officer
Tamotsu Sakuramoto, Gen. Mgr.-Europe
James L. Hawk, Pres., Toyo Tire North America Mfg., Inc.
Sadao Ichihara, Gen. Mgr.-Corp. Purchasing Div.

GROWTH PLANS/SPECIAL FEATURES:

Toyo Tire Corporation (formerly Toyo Tire & Rubber Co., Ltd.) is a worldwide producer tires, automotive parts and related components. The company's tire division manufactures and sells tires for passenger vehicles, trucks and buses, as well as for construction vehicles. Brands within this division include Toyo and Nitto. Tire plants are located worldwide, and operate through subsidiaries such as Toyo Tire Canada, Inc.; Toyo Tire USA Corp.; NT Mexico de RL de CV; Toyo Tyre Rubber Australia Ltd.; Toyo Tire (Shanghai) Co., Ltd.; Toyo Tyre Sales and Marketing Malaysia Sdn Bhd.; Toyo Tyre Europe GmbH; Toyo Tire Benelux BV; Toyo Tire Italia SpA; and Toyo Tire Rus, LLC. Toyo's automotive parts division develops products such as anti-vibration rubber for cars, utilizing its rubber-related and vibration control technologies. These products help enhance stable maneuverability and reduce noise for vehicles. Anti-vibration rubber products include engine mounts, motor mounts, member mounts, differential mounts, strut mounts, brushes, couplings, exhaust mounts and dampers. Other parts include a constant verlocity universal joint boot and air suspension. In January 2019, Toyo Tire & Rubber Co., Ltd. changed its corporate name to Toyo Tire Corporation.

FINANCIAL DATA: *Note: Data for latest year may not have been available at press time.*

In U.S. $	2018	2017	2016	2015	2014	2013
Revenue	3,613,490,000	3,721,733,000	3,507,030,000	3,747,372,000	3,618,655,000	
R&D Expense						
Operating Income	389,542,400	416,357,300	453,179,600	582,438,900	436,592,500	
Operating Margin %		.11%	.13%	.16%	.12%	
SGA Expense						
Net Income	96,976,660	142,216,500	-112,663,100	15,383,200	287,079,600	
Operating Cash Flow	175,179,200	123,414,800	357,149,400	379,571,800	347,261,500	
Capital Expenditure	262,920,400	201,314,100	227,669,600	424,811,600	336,960,100	
EBITDA	417,772,500	456,717,500	113,444,200	305,238,000	693,117,100	
Return on Assets %		.03%	-.02%	.00%	.07%	
Return on Equity %		.10%	-.08%	.01%	.20%	
Debt to Equity		0.479	0.525	0.589	0.507	

CONTACT INFORMATION:

Phone: 81 72789-9100 Fax:
Toll-Free:
Address: 2-2-13 Fujinoki, Itami, Hyogo, 664 0847 Japan

STOCK TICKER/OTHER:

Stock Ticker: TOTTF
Exchange: GREY
Employees: 12,804
Fiscal Year Ends: 03/31
Parent Company:

SALARIES/BONUSES:

Top Exec. Salary: $ Bonus: $
Second Exec. Salary: $ Bonus: $

OTHER THOUGHTS:

Estimated Female Officers or Directors:
Hot Spot for Advancement for Women/Minorities:

Toyoda Gosei Co Ltd

www.toyoda-gosei.com

NAIC Code: 336300

TYPES OF BUSINESS:

Automotive Components
LEDs & Optoelectronics
Consumer Products
Airbags

BRANDS/DIVISIONS/AFFILIATES:

Toyota Motor Corporation
Toyoda Gosei Minda India Pvt Ltd

CONTACTS: *Note: Officers with more than one job title may be intentionally listed here more than once.*

Naoki Miyazaki, Pres.
Nobuo Fujiwara, Sr. Managing Dir.
Tetsumi Ichioka, Pres., Europe
Kyoji Ikki, Pres., Asia
Toru Koyama, Pres., North America

GROWTH PLANS/SPECIAL FEATURES:

Toyoda Gosei Co., Ltd., a member of Toyota Motor Corporation, produces and distributes automotive components. The company has approximately 65 consolidated subsidiaries operating in 17 nations and regions around the world. Toyoda's automotive business operates in four segments: interior and exterior parts, automotive sealing products, functional components and safety system products. The interior and exterior parts division produces instrument panel modules and components, such as integrated center clusters, registers, cup holders, audio covers and glove compartments; interior parts, such as assist grips, front pillar garnishes and lighting illumination scuff plates; exterior parts, such as radiator grilles, side protection molding, roof spoilers, hybrid wheels, mud guards and wheel caps; applied LED products; and automobile accessories, such as console boxes, blue light grilles and front bumper spoilers. The automotive sealing products division primarily makes weather stripping rubber products which are attached to door or window frames to keep out rain, wind and noise. The functional components division develops fuel tanks and components; power train parts (such as water and air hoses), cylinder head covers and insulation plates for hybrid cars; and chassis and drive-train parts, including brake hoses, piston cups, pinion boots and dust covers. The safety system products division makes steering wheels and airbags. Toyoda Gosei also produces optoelectronic products and general industry products. In the optoelectronic products division, the firm offers LED lighting and LED lamps/chips. The company also produces a variety of other consumer products, including communications equipment components, air-conditioning products, home-related components and construction and production machinery components. The firm also engages in partnership agreements with various worldwide companies for the development, manufacturing and distribution of LED products. In February 2019, Toyoda Gosei's Indian subsidiary Toyoda Gosei Minda India Pvt. Ltd. opened its new Gujarat plant, its sixth location in the country.

FINANCIAL DATA: *Note: Data for latest year may not have been available at press time.*

In U.S. $	2018	2017	2016	2015	2014	2013
Revenue	7,415,347,000	6,943,586,000	7,185,132,000	6,688,532,000	6,335,940,000	
R&D Expense						
Operating Income	378,055,500	373,828,400	393,567,400	382,347,000	402,518,000	
Operating Margin %	.05%	.09%	.09%	.09%	.10%	
SGA Expense	319,261,200	291,628,400	308,050,000	278,910,100	272,514,200	
Net Income	194,587,400	149,172,900	186,133,100	194,403,600	240,893,200	
Operating Cash Flow	559,161,900	555,054,200	714,620,500	471,264,500	509,538,700	
Capital Expenditure	564,308,000	505,458,600	517,423,300	551,185,500	410,981,400	
EBITDA	753,106,000	677,384,700	763,462,700	742,124,600	790,185,700	
Return on Assets %	.03%	.03%	.03%	.04%	.05%	
Return on Equity %	.07%	.05%	.07%	.07%	.10%	
Debt to Equity	0.196	0.182	0.147	0.137	0.111	

CONTACT INFORMATION:

Phone: 81 524005131 Fax:
Toll-Free:
Address: 1 Haruhinagahata Kiyosu, Kiyosu, 452-8564 Japan

STOCK TICKER/OTHER:

Stock Ticker: TGOSY
Exchange: PINX
Employees: 46,243
Fiscal Year Ends: 03/31
Parent Company: Toyota Motor Corporation

SALARIES/BONUSES:

Top Exec. Salary: $ Bonus: $
Second Exec. Salary: $ Bonus: $

OTHER THOUGHTS:

Estimated Female Officers or Directors:
Hot Spot for Advancement for Women/Minorities:

Toyota Auto Body Co Ltd

NAIC Code: 336211

www.toyota-body.co.jp

TYPES OF BUSINESS:

Motor Vehicle Body Manufacturing
Commercial Vans & Trucks
Auto Parts Manufacturing

BRANDS/DIVISIONS/AFFILIATES:

Toyota Motor Corporation
PT Sugity Creatives Co Ltd
Chun Shyang Shin Yeh Industry Co Ltd
Thai Auto Conversion Co Ltd
PT Toyota Auto Body-Tokai Extrusion
Toyota Auto Body (Malaysia) Sdn Bhd
Toyota Auto Works Co Ltd
Auto Parts Manufacturing Mississippi Inc

CONTACTS: *Note: Officers with more than one job title may be intentionally listed here more than once.*

Keiji Masui, Pres.

GROWTH PLANS/SPECIAL FEATURES:

Toyota Auto Body Co., Ltd., founded in 1945 in Japan, operates as a wholly-owned subsidiary of Toyota Motor Corporation. The firm's primary business is comprised of body assembly for minivans, SUVs and commercial vehicles and, through a series of subsidiaries, parts manufacturing. The firm also assembles special purpose vehicles, including container vans, refrigerator/freezer vehicles, load labor-saving vehicles and vans with power lifters. Vehicles and equipment for the physically impaired are assembled by the company as well, including passenger lift-up seat vehicles, side lift-up seat vehicles, wheelchari accessible vehicles and Friendmatic (Wel Carry) vehicles. Other Toyota models assembled by Toyota Auto Body include Alphard, Vellfire, Estima, Voxy, Noah, Esquire, Land Cruiser, Lexus, Hiace, Regiusace and Coaster. Toyota Auto Body also produces the super-compact electric vehicle known as COMS. The firm's domestic plants include Kariya, Inabe, Yoshiwara and Fujimatsu, along with the Kotobuki New Development Center in Aichi. Internationally, the company operates subsidiaries in Asian countries such as Indonesia, Thailand and Taiwan. Subsidiaries include: PT. Sugity Creatives Co. Ltd.; Chun Shyang Shin Yeh Industry Co., Ltd.; Thai Auto Conversion Co. Ltd.; PT. Toyota Auto Body-Tokai Extrusion; Toyota Auto Body (Malaysia) Sdn. Bhd.; Toyota Auto Works Co. Ltd.; Auto Parts Manufacturing Mississippi, Inc.; Tab Minth Mobility Equipment Co. Ltd.; and PT. Resin Plating Technology.

FINANCIAL DATA: *Note: Data for latest year may not have been available at press time.*

In U.S. $	2018	2017	2016	2015	2014	2013
Revenue	21,388,500,000	20,370,000,000	19,400,000,000	19,100,000,000	17,000,000,000	16,500,000,000
R&D Expense						
Operating Income						
Operating Margin %						
SGA Expense						
Net Income						
Operating Cash Flow						
Capital Expenditure						
EBITDA						
Return on Assets %						
Return on Equity %						
Debt to Equity						

CONTACT INFORMATION:

Phone: 81-566-36-2121 Fax:
Toll-Free:
Address: 100 Kanayama, Ichiriyama-cho Kariya, Aichi, 448-8666 Japan

STOCK TICKER/OTHER:

Stock Ticker: Subsidiary
Exchange:
Employees: 11,191
Fiscal Year Ends: 03/31
Parent Company: Toyota Motor Corporation

SALARIES/BONUSES:

Top Exec. Salary: $ Bonus: $
Second Exec. Salary: $ Bonus: $

OTHER THOUGHTS:

Estimated Female Officers or Directors:
Hot Spot for Advancement for Women/Minorities:

Toyota Motor Corporation

www.toyota.co.jp

NAIC Code: 336111

TYPES OF BUSINESS:

Automobile Manufacturing
Manufactured Housing
Advertising & e-Commerce Services
Financial Services
Telecommunications Services
Information Technology
Nanotechnology Research

BRANDS/DIVISIONS/AFFILIATES:

Daihatsu Motor Co Ltd
Hino Motors Ltd
Toyota Financial Services Corporation
Toyota Motor Credit Corporation
Toyota Research Institute Inc
Toyota
Lexus
Hino

CONTACTS: *Note: Officers with more than one job title may be intentionally listed here more than once.*

Akio Toyoda, Pres.
Satoshi Ozawa, Exec. VP-Gen. Admin.
Mitsuhisa Kato, Exec. VP-Customer Service Oper.
Mamoru Furuhashi, CEO-Govt & Public Affairs
Satoshi Ozawa, Exec. VP-Acct.
Takeshi Uchiyamada, Chmn.
Satoshi Ozawa, Exec VP-European Oper.

GROWTH PLANS/SPECIAL FEATURES:

Toyota Motor Corporation designs, manufactures, assembles and sells passenger cars, minivans, commercial vehicles and related parts and accessories in 190 countries under the Toyota, Lexus, Daihatsu and Hino brands. The firm operates in three segments: automotive, financial and other. Its primary automotive markets are Japan, which generates approximately 25.2% of fiscal 2018 sales; North America, 31.3%; Asia, 17.2%; Europe, 10.8%; and other countries generate the remainder. Toyota produces both conventional engine vehicles and hybrid vehicles, with automobile types including subcompact and compact cars; mini-vehicles; mid-size, luxury, sports and specialty cars; recreational and sport-utility vehicles; pickup trucks; minivans; and buses. Wholly-owned subsidiary Daihatsu Motor Co. Ltd. produces and sells mini-vehicles and compact cars. Hino Motors Ltd. produces and sells commercial vehicles such as trucks and buses. Toyota produces automobiles and related components through over 50 manufacturing companies in 26 countries. Approximately 71.1% of the firm's vehicles sold in North America are produced in North America, and 81.5% of its vehicles sold in Europe are produced in Europe. The company offers financial services in 35 countries through subsidiary Toyota Financial Services Corporation, and in the U.S. through subsidiary Toyota Motor Credit Corporation. The company's Toyota Research Institute, Inc. is a research and development enterprise with a focus on artificial intelligence technology and robotics. In August 2018, Toyota announced an investment of $500 million in Uber's autonomous cars.

FINANCIAL DATA: *Note: Data for latest year may not have been available at press time.*

In U.S. $	2018	2017	2016	2015	2014	2013
Revenue	269,982,600,000	253,604,100,000	261,010,100,000	250,271,300,000	236,095,500,000	
R&D Expense						
Operating Income	22,053,500,000	18,327,260,000	26,226,530,000	25,276,270,000	21,063,330,000	
Operating Margin %	.08%	.07%	.10%	.10%	.09%	
SGA Expense	28,400,060,000	26,359,910,000	27,050,930,000	24,281,210,000	23,880,350,000	
Net Income	22,918,420,000	16,826,950,000	21,252,470,000	19,971,860,000	16,753,530,000	
Operating Cash Flow	38,687,830,000	31,375,090,000	40,992,990,000	33,870,180,000	33,505,190,000	
Capital Expenditure	33,070,270,000	32,543,990,000	37,302,110,000	30,854,330,000	24,615,800,000	
EBITDA	40,268,780,000	35,233,670,000	42,681,690,000	39,742,460,000	34,107,360,000	
Return on Assets %	.05%	.04%	.05%	.05%	.05%	
Return on Equity %	.14%	.11%	.14%	.14%	.14%	
Debt to Equity	0.534	0.566	0.584	0.597	0.591	

CONTACT INFORMATION:

Phone: 81 565282121 Fax: 81 565235800
Toll-Free:
Address: 1 Toyota-Cho, Toyota City, Toyota, Aichi Prefecture 471-8571 Japan

STOCK TICKER/OTHER:

Stock Ticker: TM
Employees: 364,445
Parent Company:
Exchange: NYS
Fiscal Year Ends: 03/31

SALARIES/BONUSES:

Top Exec. Salary: $2,288,182 Bonus: $7,140,232
Second Exec. Salary: $909,759 Bonus: $2,573,057

OTHER THOUGHTS:

Estimated Female Officers or Directors:
Hot Spot for Advancement for Women/Minorities:

Toyota Motor Credit Corporation

www.toyotafinancial.com

NAIC Code: 522220

TYPES OF BUSINESS:

Automobile Financing
Leasing
Insurance

BRANDS/DIVISIONS/AFFILIATES:

Toyota Motor Corporation
Toyotal Financial Services
Toyota Motor Insurance Services Inc
Toyota Financial Services Corporation

GROWTH PLANS/SPECIAL FEATURES:

Toyota Motor Credit Corporation (TMCC) is a financial and insurance firm. Its Toyota Financial Services (TFS) name is a service mark that acts as an umbrella brand used to market the products of TMCC and Toyota Motor Insurance Services, Inc. TMCC provides retail and wholesale financing, retail leasing, vehicle protection plans and other financial services to authorized Toyota and Lexus dealers, affiliates and their customers in most of the United States. TFS is part of the worldwide financial services operations for Toyota Financial Services Corporation, which is a wholly-owned subsidiary of Toyota Motor Corporation in Japan. TFS has regional offices, customer service centers, dealer sales and service offices throughout the U.S., as well as an affiliate financial services company in Puerto Rico.

Toyota Motor Credit Corporation offers comprehensive health benefits, retirement plans and a variety of employee assistance programs.

CONTACTS:

Note: Officers with more than one job title may be intentionally listed here more than once.

Mark Templin, CEO

FINANCIAL DATA:

Note: Data for latest year may not have been available at press time.

In U.S. $	2018	2017	2016	2015	2014	2013
Revenue	10,717,000,000	10,046,000,000	9,403,000,000	8,310,000,000	7,397,000,000	7,244,000,000
R&D Expense						
Operating Income						
Operating Margin %						
SGA Expense						
Net Income	3,410,000,000	267,000,000	932,000,000	1,197,000,000	857,000,000	1,331,000,000
Operating Cash Flow						
Capital Expenditure						
EBITDA						
Return on Assets %						
Return on Equity %						
Debt to Equity						

CONTACT INFORMATION:

Phone: 469-486-9300 Fax:
Toll-Free:
Address: 6565 Headquarters Dr., Plano, TX 75024 United States

STOCK TICKER/OTHER:

Stock Ticker: Subsidiary
Employees: 3,300
Parent Company: Toyota Motor Corporation
Exchange:
Fiscal Year Ends: 03/31

SALARIES/BONUSES:

Top Exec. Salary: $ Bonus: $
Second Exec. Salary: $ Bonus: $

OTHER THOUGHTS:

Estimated Female Officers or Directors:
Hot Spot for Advancement for Women/Minorities:

Toyota Motor East Japan Inc

www.toyota-ej.co.jp

NAIC Code: 336211

TYPES OF BUSINESS:

Motor Vehicle Body Manufacturing
Automobile Assembly
Housing Manufacturing
Engineering Services
Food Services

BRANDS/DIVISIONS/AFFILIATES:

Toyota Motor Corporation
Sienta
Corolla
Prius
Porte
JPN Taxi
Patrafour

CONTACTS: *Note: Officers with more than one job title may be intentionally listed here more than once.*

Takeshi Shirane, Pres.

GROWTH PLANS/SPECIAL FEATURES:

Toyota Motor East Japan, Inc. (TMEJ) is involved in the planning, research and development (R&D) and production of cars for Toyota Motor Corporation. TMEJ currently manufactures passenger vehicles, welfare vehicles, automobile parts and all-wheel-drive wheelchairs. Passenger vehicles are manufactured at the following TMEJ plants: Miyagi Ohira plant, which produces the Sienta and Corolla models; Iwate plant, producing the C-HR, Prius and Yaris models; and Higashi Fuji plant, producing the Porte, Spade, Century and JPN Taxi models. Welfare vehicles are developed and produced with automatic vehicle maintenance lift options for the disabled, the elderly and caregivers. These options are described as Welcabs, which can be configured in the following vehicle models: Sienta, Porte, Spade, Prius and Corolla. The automobile parts division produces engines, brake actuators, vehicle dynamics management systems, electronic modulated suspension systems, height control suspension systems, axles and torque converters. Patrafour is an all-wheel-drive powered wheelchair built by the company, is capable of going down slopes and going up curbs, and comes in a variety of colors. TMEJ has overseas bases in Brazil and Thailand.

FINANCIAL DATA: *Note: Data for latest year may not have been available at press time.*

In U.S. $	2018	2017	2016	2015	2014	2013
Revenue	6,812,477,697	6,488,073,997	6,179,118,092	7,700,000,000	7,671,894,500	7,400,000,000
R&D Expense						
Operating Income						
Operating Margin %						
SGA Expense						
Net Income						
Operating Cash Flow						
Capital Expenditure						
EBITDA						
Return on Assets %						
Return on Equity %						
Debt to Equity						

CONTACT INFORMATION:

Phone: 81-22-765-6000 Fax:
Toll-Free:
Address: 1, Chuo-daira, Ohira-mura, Kurokawa-gun, Miyagi 9891-3609 Japan

STOCK TICKER/OTHER:

Stock Ticker: Subsidiary
Employees: 7,700
Parent Company: Toyota Motor Corporation
Exchange:
Fiscal Year Ends: 03/31

SALARIES/BONUSES:

Top Exec. Salary: $ Bonus: $
Second Exec. Salary: $ Bonus: $

OTHER THOUGHTS:

Estimated Female Officers or Directors:
Hot Spot for Advancement for Women/Minorities:

Toyota Motor Sales USA Inc (TMS)

www.toyota.com/usa/operations

NAIC Code: 336111

TYPES OF BUSINESS:

Automobile Manufacturing

BRANDS/DIVISIONS/AFFILIATES:

Toyota Motor Corporation
4Runner
Avalon
C-HR
Camry
Highlander
Safety Connect
Hui

CONTACTS:

Note: Officers with more than one job title may be intentionally listed here more than once.

James Lentz, CEO

GROWTH PLANS/SPECIAL FEATURES:

Toyota Motor Sales, USA, Inc. manufactures and sells vehicles. Through various subsidiaries, Toyota operates 10 plants in the U.S., manufacturing models such as sport utility vehicles (SUVs), trucks, cars, crossovers, minivans and hybrids. Model brands include 4Runner, 86, Avalon, C-HR, Camry, Corolla, Highlander, Land Cruiser, Mirai, Prius, RAV, Sequoia, Sienna, Tacoma, Tundra and Yaris. In total, Toyota produced about 2.1 million vehicles in North America in 2018. Toyota's vehicles are primarily leased or sold through dealers located throughout the U.S., from which used vehicles are also sold. The company exports eight of its U.S. models to more than 30 countries. Connected vehicles are smart device compatible. Toyota Motor Sales' Safety Connect offering is a subscription-based service that provides help after an emergency. Drivers can be connected to Toyota's 24/7 response center at the touch of a button, and obtain emergency assistance, roadside assistance, automatic collision notification and the connected vehicle can be located more easily through the GPS system if stolen. In addition, Toyota Motor Sales has a carshare service in Honolulu that is operated through Servco Pacific, Inc., the company's vehicle distributor in Hawaii. The service utilizes Toyota's proprietary global mobility service platform and a consumer-facing app called Hui, which was developed by Toyota USA's connected division, and enables users to reserve a vehicle either by the hour or day. Hui vehicles are parked in marked, reserved stalls for easy pickup and drop-off. Toyota Motor Sales operates as a subsidiary of Toyota Motor Corporation.

FINANCIAL DATA:

Note: Data for latest year may not have been available at press time.

In U.S. $	2018	2017	2016	2015	2014	2013
Revenue	95,578,770,000	91,027,400,000	98,245,124,503	93,053,000,000	78,110,000,000	61,283,000,000
R&D Expense						
Operating Income						
Operating Margin %						
SGA Expense						
Net Income						
Operating Cash Flow						
Capital Expenditure						
EBITDA						
Return on Assets %						
Return on Equity %						
Debt to Equity						

CONTACT INFORMATION:

Phone: Fax: 310-468-7814
Toll-Free: 800-331-4331
Address: P.O. Box 259001, Plano, TX 75025-9001 United States

STOCK TICKER/OTHER:

Stock Ticker: Subsidiary
Exchange:
Employees: 5,510
Fiscal Year Ends: 03/31
Parent Company: Toyota Motor Corporation

SALARIES/BONUSES:

Top Exec. Salary: $ Bonus: $
Second Exec. Salary: $ Bonus: $

OTHER THOUGHTS:

Estimated Female Officers or Directors:
Hot Spot for Advancement for Women/Minorities:

Toyota Motor Thailand Co Ltd

www.toyota.co.th

NAIC Code: 336111

TYPES OF BUSINESS:

Automobile Manufacturing
Automotive Repair Services
Rice Production
Ethanol-based Fuel Production

BRANDS/DIVISIONS/AFFILIATES:

Toyota Motor Corporation
HINO Motor Manufacturing (Thailand) Co Ltd
Toyota Auto Body (Thailand) Co Ltd
Siam Toyota Manufacturing Co Ltd
Toyota Auto Works Co Ltd
Toyota Daihatsu Engineering & Manufacturing Co Ltd
Avanza
Alphard

CONTACTS: *Note: Officers with more than one job title may be intentionally listed here more than once.*

Michinobu Sugata, Pres.
Toshiyuki Oya, Exec. VP-Mfg.
Chatchai Taveesakulvadchara, Sr. VP-Admin.
Kohei Nakao, Treas.
Ninnart Chaithirapinyo, Vice Chmn.
Sitachai Jeeratunyasakul, VP-Mktg.
Chusak Yiengsakul, VP-Mfg.
Ninnart Chaithirapinyo, Chmn.

GROWTH PLANS/SPECIAL FEATURES:

Toyota Motor Thailand Co., Ltd. (TMT), a subsidiary of Toyota Motor Corporation, is a Thai manufacturer of Toyota brand automobiles. TMT currently produces 15 models, with some having variations. These models consist of passenger, commercial and multipurpose vehicles. TMT's passenger vehicles include the Yaris ATIV, Yaris, Vios, Altis, C-HR and Camry models. Commercial vehicle models include: the Hilux Revo, with variations including a standard cab, a smart cab or a double cab; the Commuter 4-row passenger van; and the Hiace 3-row passenger van. TMT's multipurpose vehicles consist of the Avanza, Sietna, Innova Crysta, Fortuner, Coaster, Majesty and Alphard sport utility vehicles (SUVs), buses and vans. TMT has three manufacturing facilities: the Samrong Plant, with a production capacity of 240,000 units per year; the Gateway Plant, 300,000 units per year; and the Ban Pho Plant, 220,000 units per year. TMT's vehicles are sold through Toyota dealerships and are on display in hundreds of showrooms nationwide. Many of these dealerships also offer repair services. To facilitate repairs covered under warranty, the firm offers the Warranty Plus Card, which stores all the most pertinent information about the customer's car, including model, vehicle identification number (VIN), maintenance history and claim record. Permanent information, such as the model and VIN, is printed on the card, while changeable information, such as repair history, is stored in a memory chip implanted in the card. Other companies in Toyota's Thailand Group, which serve as affiliates of TMT, include: HINO Motor Manufacturing (Thailand) Co., Ltd.; Toyota Auto Body (Thailand) Co., Ltd.; Siam Toyota Manufacturing Co., Ltd.; Toyota Auto Works Co., Ltd.; and Toyota Daihatsu Engineering & Manufacturing Co., Ltd., among others.

FINANCIAL DATA: *Note: Data for latest year may not have been available at press time.*

In U.S. $	2018	2017	2016	2015	2014	2013
Revenue	6,174,000,000	5,880,000,000	5,600,000,000	5,480,000,000	5,478,330,000	6,385,000,000
R&D Expense						
Operating Income						
Operating Margin %						
SGA Expense						
Net Income						
Operating Cash Flow						
Capital Expenditure						
EBITDA						
Return on Assets %						
Return on Equity %						
Debt to Equity						

CONTACT INFORMATION:

Phone: 66-2-386-1000 Fax: 66-2-386-1000
Toll-Free: 800-238444
Address: 186/1 Moo Old Railway Rd., Samrong Tai, 10130 Thailand

STOCK TICKER/OTHER:

Stock Ticker: Subsidiary
Exchange:
Employees: 14,900
Fiscal Year Ends: 03/31
Parent Company: Toyota Motor Corporation

SALARIES/BONUSES:

Top Exec. Salary: $ Bonus: $
Second Exec. Salary: $ Bonus: $

OTHER THOUGHTS:

Estimated Female Officers or Directors:
Hot Spot for Advancement for Women/Minorities:

Traton SE

traton.com

NAIC Code: 336120

TYPES OF BUSINESS:

Heavy Duty Truck Manufacturing
Commercial Vehicle Manufacture

BRANDS/DIVISIONS/AFFILIATES:

Volkswagen AG
MAN
Scania
Volkswagen Caminhoes e Onibus
RIO

CONTACTS:

Note: Officers with more than one job title may be intentionally listed here more than once.

Andreas Renschler, CEO
Christian Levin, COO
Christian Schulz, Exec. Board-Finance & Bus. Dev.
Carsten Intra, Dir.-Human Resources & IT
Hans Dieter Potsch, Chmn.

GROWTH PLANS/SPECIAL FEATURES:

Traton SE, a subsidiary of Volkswagen AG, is a global commercial vehicle manufacturer, with brands including MAN, Scania and Volkswagen Caminhoes e Onibus (VWCO). The MAN brand offers a full range of products, including vans, long-distance vans, light- to heavy-duty trucks, construction vehicles, city buses and intercity and travel coaches. MAN has production sites in three European countries as well as Russia, South Africa and Turkey. The Scania brand offers city buses, intercity and travel coaches, heavy-duty vehicles and construction vehicles. Its production sites are located in Europe, South America and Asia, and the Scania company offers a variety of supplementary sales and services aligned with its product range. The VWCO brand provides light-to-heavy-duty trucks and bus chassis, all of which are customized for markets such as Latin America and Africa. VWCO's commercial vehicle brand has a sales and service network in Brazil, along with its neighboring countries. VWCO also offers aftersales services and custom digital solutions. RIO is Traton's global brand for digital services in the transport industry. Its goal is to increase efficiency and profitability in freight transport via data-driven intelligence. RIO offers an open, vendor-neutral and cloud-based platform for freight transport, and delivers recommendations for action in real-time.

FINANCIAL DATA:

Note: Data for latest year may not have been available at press time.

In U.S. $	2018	2017	2016	2015	2014	2013
Revenue	29,655,100,000	29,187,100,000				
R&D Expense						
Operating Income						
Operating Margin %						
SGA Expense						
Net Income						
Operating Cash Flow						
Capital Expenditure						
EBITDA						
Return on Assets %						
Return on Equity %						
Debt to Equity						

CONTACT INFORMATION:

Phone: 49 89 36098 70 Fax:
Toll-Free:
Address: Dachauer Str. 641, Munich, 80995 Germany

STOCK TICKER/OTHER:

Stock Ticker: 8TRA
Employees: 80,940
Parent Company: Volkswagen AG
Exchange: Frankfurt
Fiscal Year Ends: 12/31

SALARIES/BONUSES:

Top Exec. Salary: $ Bonus: $
Second Exec. Salary: $ Bonus: $

OTHER THOUGHTS:

Estimated Female Officers or Directors:
Hot Spot for Advancement for Women/Minorities:

Trelleborg AB

www.trelleborg.com

NAIC Code: 326100

TYPES OF BUSINESS:

Polymer Technology-Based Customized Solutions
Polymer-Based Automotive Components
Industrial Fluid Systems
Building Materials

BRANDS/DIVISIONS/AFFILIATES:

Trelleborg Coated Systems
Trellborg Industrial Solutions
Trelleborg Offshore & Construction
Trelleborg Sealing Solutions
Trelleborg Wheel Systems
Axcyl
Provana Solutions srl
Provana Quality Center srl

CONTACTS: *Note: Officers with more than one job title may be intentionally listed here more than once.*

Peter Nilsson, CEO
Ulf Berghult, CFO
Paolo Astarita, Sr. VP-Human Resources
Ulf Graden, General Counsel
Patrik Romberg, Sr. VP-Corp. Comm.
Christofer Sjogren, VP-Investor Rel.
Mikael Fryklund, Pres., Trelleborg Industrial Solutions
Maurizio Vischi, Pres., Trelleborg Wheel Systems
Fredrik Meuller, Pres., Trelleborg Offshore & Construction
Claus Barsoe, Pres., Trelleborg Sealing Solutions
Hans Biorck, Chmn.

GROWTH PLANS/SPECIAL FEATURES:

Trelleborg AB, provides customized products and services based on polymer technology and application. The firm has operations in 50 countries, and comprises five business units: Trelleborg Coated Systems, Trelleborg Industrial Solutions, Trelleborg Offshore & Construction, Trelleborg Sealing Solutions and Trelleborg Wheel Systems. Trelleborg Coated Systems develops and produces polymer-coated fabrics for a variety of industry applications, with brands such as Axcyl, Printec, Rollin and Vulcan. Trelleborg Industrial Solutions creates fluid handling solutions, such as hoses, expansion joints and elastomer materials; industrial antivibration solutions, such as dampers and precision components; and sealing solutions for waste and water systems. Brands include Epros, Cryoline and DIPRO. Trelleborg Offshore & Construction provides polymer-based solutions for offshore oil and gas exploration and infrastructure for civil engineering services. Trelleborg Sealing Solutions supplies advanced sealing products in specialty materials designed for a range of industrial applications. The largest product groups are O-rings, rotary seals and hydraulic seals. It also produces safety-critical aircraft seals for engines, flight control actuators, airframes and landing gear; vehicle seals for fuel systems, steering, climate control and exhaust systems; and seals for trains, construction and agricultural machinery. Trelleborg Wheel Systems produces tires and complete wheel systems for farm and forest machines, lift trucks and other materials-handling vehicles. In March 2019, Trelleborg acquired Provana Solutions srl and Provana Quality Center srl, with Provana Solutions specializing in the distribution and service of tires and wheels to tractor dealers and farmers in Italy, and Provana Quality providing testing and various tire solutions to original equipment manufacturers (OEMs) of agricultural machinery.

Trelleborg offers internships and summer work opportunities, as well as offering employee training and management programs.

FINANCIAL DATA: *Note: Data for latest year may not have been available at press time.*

In U.S. $	2018	2017	2016	2015	2014	2013
Revenue	3,519,268,000	3,268,402,000	2,809,309,000	2,566,929,000	2,330,137,000	2,222,298,000
R&D Expense	58,473,360	53,402,220	44,812,330	39,637,690	34,256,070	31,979,230
Operating Income	463,957,600	421,111,700	352,185,600	299,818,300	290,090,000	261,629,500
Operating Margin %		.13%	.11%	.11%	.11%	.10%
SGA Expense	624,060,800	586,286,000	544,060,900	494,177,500	498,213,700	462,301,700
Net Income	330,141,600	297,437,900	681,499,200	269,391,400	229,857,200	166,519,700
Operating Cash Flow	410,555,400	396,790,900	360,051,000	420,594,200	298,886,800	190,944,000
Capital Expenditure	201,086,300	148,719,000	118,809,600	135,989,400	106,080,000	95,420,240
EBITDA	611,331,200	541,473,700	437,567,000	448,847,700	395,445,500	336,765,200
Return on Assets %		.06%	.16%	.08%	.07%	.06%
Return on Equity %		.11%	.30%	.14%	.14%	.11%
Debt to Equity		0.294	0.387	0.283	0.234	0.328

CONTACT INFORMATION:

Phone: 46 41067000 Fax: 46 41042763
Toll-Free:
Address: Johan Kocksgatan 10, Trelleborg, SE- 23122 Sweden

STOCK TICKER/OTHER:

Stock Ticker: TBABF
Exchange: PINX
Employees: 24,045
Fiscal Year Ends: 12/31
Parent Company:

SALARIES/BONUSES:

Top Exec. Salary: $ Bonus: $
Second Exec. Salary: $ Bonus: $

OTHER THOUGHTS:

Estimated Female Officers or Directors: 4
Hot Spot for Advancement for Women/Minorities: Y

Tri Petch Isuzu Sales Co Ltd

NAIC Code: 336120

www.isuzu-tis.com

TYPES OF BUSINESS:

Passenger Truck Manufacturing
Diesel Engine Manufacturing

BRANDS/DIVISIONS/AFFILIATES:

Mitsubishi Corporation
Isuzu
D-Max
Miu-X

GROWTH PLANS/SPECIAL FEATURES:

Tri Petch Isuzu Sales Co., Ltd. produces, distributes and services Isuzu pickups trucks, medium-duty trucks and multipurpose vehicles in Thailand. All of the firm's products are sold under the Isuzu banner. Tri Petch's pickups include the D-Max X-Series, V-Cross 4x4, Spark and various 2-door/4 door models. Its commercial trucks include 6- and 10-wheel tractors, 10-wheel/2-axle cars, 10-axles cars, medium- and large-6-wheel vehicles, 4-wheel trucks and cement mixers. Multipurpose vehicles include the Miu-X Onyx and Miu-X Blue Power models. Tri Petch's distribution and service centers network includes approximately 300 locations throughout Thailand. The company operates as a subsidiary of Mitsubishi Corporation.

CONTACTS: *Note: Officers with more than one job title may be intentionally listed here more than once.*

Panatda Chennavasin, VP-Corp. Strategies
Panatda Chennavasin, VP-Corp. Rel.

FINANCIAL DATA: *Note: Data for latest year may not have been available at press time.*

In U.S. $	2018	2017	2016	2015	2014	2013
Revenue	19,459,125,000	18,532,500,000	17,650,000,000	17,500,000,000	17,109,003,000	16,000,000,000
R&D Expense						
Operating Income						
Operating Margin %						
SGA Expense						
Net Income						
Operating Cash Flow						
Capital Expenditure						
EBITDA						
Return on Assets %						
Return on Equity %						
Debt to Equity						

CONTACT INFORMATION:

Phone: 66-2966-2111 Fax: 66-2966-1291
Toll-Free:
Address: 1088 Vibhavadi Rangsit Rd., Chatuchak, Bangkok, 10900 Thailand

STOCK TICKER/OTHER:

Stock Ticker: Subsidiary
Employees: 500
Parent Company: Mitsubishi Corporation
Exchange:
Fiscal Year Ends: 03/31

SALARIES/BONUSES:

Top Exec. Salary: $ Bonus: $
Second Exec. Salary: $ Bonus: $

OTHER THOUGHTS:

Estimated Female Officers or Directors: 1
Hot Spot for Advancement for Women/Minorities:

TrueCar Inc

www.truecar.com

NAIC Code: 519130

TYPES OF BUSINESS:

Internet Publishing and Broadcasting and Web Search Portals

BRANDS/DIVISIONS/AFFILIATES:

TrueCar.com
TrueCar Certified Dealer

CONTACTS:

Note: Officers with more than one job title may be intentionally listed here more than once.

Michael Darrow, CEO
Charles Thomas, CFO
Christopher Claus, Chairman of the Board
Jeff Swart, Executive VP

GROWTH PLANS/SPECIAL FEATURES:

TrueCar, Inc. provides comparative sales information for car makes and models in specific areas through its TrueCar.com website. The online portal also provides information related to where vehicles are available, estimated prices for that make and model of car (referred to as upfront pricing information) all derived from the company's network of TrueCar Certified Dealers. The upfront pricing information generally includes guaranteed savings off MSRP which the consumer may then take to one of 16,000 TrueCar Certified Dealer in the form of a Guaranteed Savings Certificate that applies toward the purchase of the specified make and model of car. TrueCar benefits its network of TrueCar Certified Dealers by enabling them to attract these informed, in-market consumers in a cost-effective, accountable manner, which helps them to sell more cars. The network covers the entire U.S. and has accounted for millions of cars sold. Most of the firm's revenue is derived from the fee that TrueCar Certified Dealers pay when a TrueCar.com user purchases a car from them. The remaining revenue comes from the sale of data and consulting services to the automotive and financial services industries. In early-2019, TrueCar acquired a 20% stake in Accu-Trade, LLC, the developer of a vehicle appraisal technology for dealers and consumers.

FINANCIAL DATA:

Note: Data for latest year may not have been available at press time.

In U.S. $	2018	2017	2016	2015	2014	2013
Revenue	353,571,000	323,149,000	277,507,000	259,838,000	206,649,000	133,958,000
R&D Expense	61,348,000	59,070,000	53,580,000	48,021,000	36,563,000	23,685,000
Operating Income	-29,163,000	-33,663,000	-38,899,000	-63,982,000	-47,505,000	-22,628,000
Operating Margin %		-.10%	-.14%	-.25%	-.23%	-.17%
SGA Expense	267,555,000	247,043,000	214,314,000	234,496,000	186,865,000	106,037,000
Net Income	-28,321,000	-32,849,000	-41,708,000	-64,911,000	-48,429,000	-25,056,000
Operating Cash Flow	24,833,000	22,118,000	2,768,000	-11,369,000	3,104,000	-3,911,000
Capital Expenditure	17,099,000	19,809,000	16,639,000	29,836,000	15,896,000	8,404,000
EBITDA	-3,172,000	-9,931,000	-15,178,000	-46,216,000	-34,196,000	-10,920,000
Return on Assets %		-.10%	-.14%	-.22%	-.21%	-.16%
Return on Equity %		-.12%	-.18%	-.27%	-.27%	-.24%
Debt to Equity		0.093	0.128	0.116	0.024	

CONTACT INFORMATION:

Phone: Fax:
Toll-Free: 800-200-2000
Address: 120 Broadway, Ste. 200, Santa Monica, CA 90401 United States

STOCK TICKER/OTHER:

Stock Ticker: TRUE
Employees: 650
Parent Company:
Exchange: NAS
Fiscal Year Ends:

SALARIES/BONUSES:

Top Exec. Salary: $800,000 Bonus: $238,848
Second Exec. Salary: $400,000 Bonus: $106,302

OTHER THOUGHTS:

Estimated Female Officers or Directors:
Hot Spot for Advancement for Women/Minorities:

TuanChe Limited

NAIC Code: 423110

www.tuanche.com

TYPES OF BUSINESS:

All Other Information Services

BRANDS/DIVISIONS/AFFILIATES:

tuanche.com

CONTACTS:

Note: Officers with more than one job title may be intentionally listed here more than once.

Zhihai Mao, CFO

GROWTH PLANS/SPECIAL FEATURES:

TuanChe Limited operates an omni-channel automotive marketplace in China. The company organizes auto shows to create a consumption environment for prospective local auto-buying customers. TuanChe's two primary business offerings include: integrated marketing solutions and virtual dealership services. Integrated marketing solutions turn individual and isolated automobile purchase transactions into large-scale collective purchase activities at TuanChe's sales events, such as auto shows and group-purchase events. By attracting a large number of consumers, these events serve as integrated marketing solutions to the firm's industry customers, including automakers, franchised dealerships, secondary dealers and automotive service providers. Virtual dealership services connects automakers and franchised dealerships with secondary dealers by providing a suite of services traditionally undertaken by franchised dealerships, without setting up permanent physical presence. Mostly directed at lower-tier cities, these services include distribution channel expansion services for automakers and sourcing services for secondary dealers. TuanChe's online channels consist of the tuanche.com website, mobile apps, and its WeChat account and WeChat mini program. Approximately 11 million consumers have entered their information on the company's online platform. In 2018, TuanChe attracted 6.8 million consumers to sign up for its offline events via online channels. Offline, the firm works with various partners to attract participants to the events, such as print media, television, radio and billboards. In 2018, TuanChe's offline events facilitated the sale of more than 347,000 automobiles.

FINANCIAL DATA:

Note: Data for latest year may not have been available at press time.

In U.S. $	2018	2017	2016	2015	2014	2013
Revenue	94,577,240	40,774,320	17,048,700			
R&D Expense	2,798,326	2,313,537	2,843,943			
Operating Income	-9,884,214	-10,422,320	-11,781,240			
Operating Margin %						
SGA Expense	75,023,820	36,426,760	23,407,620			
Net Income	-11,433,300	-13,172,410	-12,576,340			
Operating Cash Flow	-7,748,787	-8,667,519	-7,858,326			
Capital Expenditure	3,008,397	39,515	9,443			
EBITDA	-9,730,220	-10,282,130	-11,605,750			
Return on Assets %						
Return on Equity %						
Debt to Equity						

CONTACT INFORMATION:

Phone: 86 1063982942 Fax:

Toll-Free:

Address: 9/Fl, Ruihai Bldg., No. 21 Yangfangdian Rd., Beijing, 100038 China

STOCK TICKER/OTHER:

Stock Ticker: TC

Exchange: NAS

Employees: 679

Fiscal Year Ends: 12/31

Parent Company:

SALARIES/BONUSES:

Top Exec. Salary: $ Bonus: $

Second Exec. Salary: $ Bonus: $

OTHER THOUGHTS:

Estimated Female Officers or Directors:

Hot Spot for Advancement for Women/Minorities:

Tuttle-Click Automotive Group

www.tuttleclick.com

NAIC Code: 441110

TYPES OF BUSINESS:

Auto Dealers, Retail
Maintenance & Repair

BRANDS/DIVISIONS/AFFILIATES:

Tuttle-Click
Tuttle-Click Commercial

CONTACTS: *Note: Officers with more than one job title may be intentionally listed here more than once.*

Jim Click, Jr., Co-CEO
Robert Holmes Tuttle, Co-CEO
Chris Cotter, Pres.

GROWTH PLANS/SPECIAL FEATURES:

Tuttle-Click Automotive Group sells new and used cars at 10 dealerships in California. The company's dealership network represents several franchises operating under the Tuttle-Click and Tuttle-Click Commercial names, including Chrysler, Dodge, Ford, Genesis, Hyundai, Jeep, Lincoln, Mazda and RAM. The group retails new and pre-owned vehicles from a variety of manufacturers and include body styles such as cargo vans, convertibles, coupes, hatchbacks, sedans, SUVs, trucks, vans/minivans and wagons. Dealerships comprise service centers which provide repair and maintenance services. The company also operates an online dealership that assists customers in choosing, purchasing and financing any of its new or used vehicles. The website displays detailed information about each car in its inventory, including specifications, prices, mileage and pictures. Customers purchasing new cars and trucks have the option to customize their vehicle online to satisfy personal preferences. Founded by Holmes Tuttle and James Click, the company has been in business since 1946.

FINANCIAL DATA: *Note: Data for latest year may not have been available at press time.*

In U.S. $	2018	2017	2016	2015	2014	2013
Revenue	1,046,302,869	996,478,923	949,027,546	838,041,661	775,651,322	645,605,200
R&D Expense						
Operating Income						
Operating Margin %						
SGA Expense						
Net Income						
Operating Cash Flow						
Capital Expenditure						
EBITDA						
Return on Assets %						
Return on Equity %						
Debt to Equity						

CONTACT INFORMATION:

Phone: 949-598-4800 Fax: 949-830-0980
Toll-Free: 888-251-0584
Address: 40 Auto Center Dr., Irvine, CA 92782 United States

STOCK TICKER/OTHER:

Stock Ticker: Private
Employees: 1,320
Parent Company:
Exchange:
Fiscal Year Ends: 12/31

SALARIES/BONUSES:

Top Exec. Salary: $ Bonus: $
Second Exec. Salary: $ Bonus: $

OTHER THOUGHTS:

Estimated Female Officers or Directors:
Hot Spot for Advancement for Women/Minorities:

UD Trucks Corporation

www.udtrucks.com

NAIC Code: 336120

TYPES OF BUSINESS:

Truck & Bus Manufacturing
Engines & Transmissions
Vehicle & Parts Distribution

BRANDS/DIVISIONS/AFFILIATES:

AB Volvo
Quester
Quon
Condor
Croner
Kuzer

CONTACTS: *Note: Officers with more than one job title may be intentionally listed here more than once.*

Satoru Takeuchi, Pres.
Toshimitsu Kurihara, Sr. VP-Eng.
Toshimitsu Kurihara, Sr. VP-Prod. Control
Toshimitsu Kurihara, Sec.
Keishi Abe, Sr. VP-Domestic Strategy Planning
Yusuke Sakaue, Exec. VP-Public Relations & Comm.
Yusuke Sakaue, Exec. VP-Acct. & Finance Dept.
Tadamichi Harada, Sr. VP-Volvo PT Japan
Claes Svedberg, Sr. VP-Overseas Sales

GROWTH PLANS/SPECIAL FEATURES:

UD Trucks Corporation, a wholly-owned subsidiary of AB Volvo, manufactures medium- and heavy-duty diesel trucks, specialty vehicles and engines. The firm's products include the Quester heavy-duty line of trucks that range from 220 to 420 horsepower and have axle configurations of 6x2, 8x4, 4x2 and 6x4; the Quon heavy-duty line of trucks that range from 16 to 33 feet in length, range in power from 257 to 360 kilowatts (kW) and have axle configurations of 6x2, 8x4, 4x2, 4x4, 6x6 and 6x4; the Condor maximum medium-duty line of trucks that range from 8 to 20 feet in length, range in power from 158 to 206 kW and have axle configurations of 4x2 and 6x4; the Croner medium-duty line of trucks that range from 10.4 to 17 feet in length, range in horsepower from 180 to 280 and have an axle configuration of 4x2; and the Kuzer medium-duty truck with 150 horsepower and an axle configuration of 4x2. UD also provides parts and services to automotive/transport industries, as well as telematics services for wireless communication systems between management and fleet. The company's trucks are marketed in over 60 countries, with distributors throughout Asia, the Americas, Oceania, the Middle East and Africa.

FINANCIAL DATA: *Note: Data for latest year may not have been available at press time.*

In U.S. $	2018	2017	2016	2015	2014	2013
Revenue						
R&D Expense						
Operating Income						
Operating Margin %						
SGA Expense						
Net Income						
Operating Cash Flow						
Capital Expenditure						
EBITDA						
Return on Assets %						
Return on Equity %						
Debt to Equity						

CONTACT INFORMATION:

Phone: 81-48-726-7601 Fax: 81-48-781-6349
Toll-Free:
Address: 1-1 Ageo-shi, Saitama, 362-8523 Japan

STOCK TICKER/OTHER:

Stock Ticker: Subsidiary
Exchange:
Employees: 3,267
Fiscal Year Ends: 03/31
Parent Company: AB Volvo

SALARIES/BONUSES:

Top Exec. Salary: $ Bonus: $
Second Exec. Salary: $ Bonus: $

OTHER THOUGHTS:

Estimated Female Officers or Directors:
Hot Spot for Advancement for Women/Minorities:

Unipart Group of Companies

www.unipart.co.uk

NAIC Code: 336300

TYPES OF BUSINESS:

Automobile Parts Manufacturer
Supply Chain Management
Consulting Services
Railroad Supplies
Automobile Parts Warehousing & Distribution
Marine Parts & Accessories
Recreational Vehicle & Camping Accessories

BRANDS/DIVISIONS/AFFILIATES:

Unipart Logistics
Unipart Rail
Unipart Manufacturing
Unipart Expert Practices
Unipart International
Unipart Autoparts
Unipart Security
MetLease

CONTACTS: *Note: Officers with more than one job title may be intentionally listed here more than once.*

John M. Neill, CEO
Carl Powell, Head-Mftg.
Debbie Daly, Group Mgr.-Comm.
Tony Morgue, Dir.-Finance
Frank Nigriello, Dir.-Corp. Affairs
Carl Powell, Head-Logistics

GROWTH PLANS/SPECIAL FEATURES:

Unipart Group of Companies is a leading provider of manufacturing, logistics and consultancy services. This business system enables Unipart to provide productivity improvement and innovation for its customers. The company operates its business through eight divisions and one joint venture. Unipart Logistics works with organizations in order to optimize inventory and end-to-end supply chain processes. Unipart Rail provides two primary solutions to the rail industry: supply chain and technology and product. Supply chain solutions cover stock planning and coordination, and the execution of product movement, including receipt, storage, tracking, maintenance, issuing and disposal of materials, plant and tools. Technology and product solutions span across infrastructure, signaling, rolling stock and train operations, offering optimized delivery of materials, engineering product support, warranty and reliability management, asset management, safety and incident management, product innovation and quality and risk management. The Unipart Manufacturing division consults and delivers tailored solutions to manufacturing, engineering and supply chain problems. Unipart Expert Practices manufactures car parts and provides logistics and consulting services. Unipart International provides services and products to the truck and bus aftermarket, the collision parts industry and the automotive heat exchange markets throughout Europe and North America. UTL provides logistics, field services and repair solutions to the mobile telecoms, consumer electronics and consumer retail sectors. Unipart Autoparts is a global distributor of car, van, truck and trailer components. Last, Unipart Security provides manned guarding, monitoring and cyber security products and solutions, installation and maintenance services, and investigation and consultancy services. In addition, joint venture MetLase (with Rolls-Royce) offers mechanical engineering consultancy services.

FINANCIAL DATA: *Note: Data for latest year may not have been available at press time.*

In U.S. $	2018	2017	2016	2015	2014	2013
Revenue	1,073,205,000	1,022,100,000	962,603,677	1,071,010,000	1,079,780,000	1,741,630,000
R&D Expense						
Operating Income						
Operating Margin %						
SGA Expense						
Net Income		18,752,800	10,087,300	129,114,000	3,727,680	-30,997,400
Operating Cash Flow						
Capital Expenditure						
EBITDA						
Return on Assets %						
Return on Equity %						
Debt to Equity						

CONTACT INFORMATION:

Phone: 44-1865-778-966 Fax: 44-1865-383-763
Toll-Free:
Address: Unipart House, Garsington Rd., Cowley, Oxford, OX4 2PG United Kingdom

STOCK TICKER/OTHER:

Stock Ticker: Private
Employees: 6,049
Parent Company:
Exchange:
Fiscal Year Ends: 12/31

SALARIES/BONUSES:

Top Exec. Salary: $ Bonus: $
Second Exec. Salary: $ Bonus: $

OTHER THOUGHTS:

Estimated Female Officers or Directors: 1
Hot Spot for Advancement for Women/Minorities:

Unipres Corporation

www.unipres.co.jp

NAIC Code: 336370

TYPES OF BUSINESS:

Motor Vehicle Metal Stamping

BRANDS/DIVISIONS/AFFILIATES:

Unipres R&D Co Ltd
Unipres Butsuryu Co Ltd
Unipres North America Inc
MA Automotive Brazil Ltd
Unipres (UK) Limited
Unipres (China) Corporation
PT Unipres Indonesia
Unipres India Private Limited

CONTACTS: *Note: Officers with more than one job title may be intentionally listed here more than once.*

Masanobu Yoshizawa, Pres.
Masahide Masuda, Exec. VP-Eng. Div.
Yoshio Ito, Exec. VP-Admin.
Shigeru Asahi, Exec. VP-Corp. Planning
Yukihiko Morita, Sr. VP-Finance & Acct.
Hiroyoshi Yamakawa, Sr. VP-Transmission Parts & Plastics Bus.
Hideki Ogoshi, Pres., Unipres North America, Inc.
Tetsuo Uotsu, Exec. VP-Purchasing

GROWTH PLANS/SPECIAL FEATURES:

Unipres Corporation is a Japanese company engaged in manufacturing press-formed automotive parts. The firm operates through five primary divisions: total press engineering, car body press technology, precision press technology, plastic press technology and production technologies. Total press engineering designs products that match automaker's needs through a lifecycle of parts development, prototyping and mass production. Car body press technology develops body structural parts that are light in weight yet strong for safety purposes. Precision press technology improves upon casting and forging methods in the production of transmission parts such as clutch packs, carrier packs and torque converters. Plastic press technology produces plastic parts for automobiles such as floor under-covers made with foam molding material, which is also aerodynamic, heat resistant and sound absorbent. Other plastic press parts include front fender protectors, trunk trim, rear diffusers, which are all up to 50% lighter in weight than conventional products. Production technologies merges the company's press and assembly technologies with digital technology in all processes from development to production. The pressing of high-tensile materials requires highly advanced technology; therefore, this division's forming simulations discover potential problems in the pressing processes in order to optimize production methods, the number of steps, equipment setup and die speculations before transferring the presses on a global scale. Unipres has manufacturing facilities throughout Asia, North America and Europe. Domestic subsidiaries include Unipres R&D Co. Ltd., Unipres Butsuryu Co. Ltd. and Unipres Service Corporation. Among Unipres' many overseas subsidiaries and affiliates include: Unipres North America, Inc.; MA Automotive Brazil Ltd.; Unipres Europe SAS; Unipres (UK) Limited; Unipres (China) Corporation; PT. Unipres Indonesia; and Unipres India Private Limited.

FINANCIAL DATA: *Note: Data for latest year may not have been available at press time.*

In U.S. $	2018	2017	2016	2015	2014	2013
Revenue	3,040,709,000	2,951,369,000	2,990,471,000	2,837,153,000	2,660,274,000	
R&D Expense						
Operating Income	239,358,600	211,597,100	202,481,200	163,545,300	141,839,700	
Operating Margin %	.08%	.07%	.07%	.06%	.05%	
SGA Expense						
Net Income	146,563,100	132,135,600	89,597,500	66,228,640	75,427,310	
Operating Cash Flow	304,852,100	307,204,600	267,478,400	236,179,000	351,543,900	
Capital Expenditure	214,813,500	169,977,900	170,207,700	219,031,400	261,707,400	
EBITDA	405,798,600	381,924,300	345,230,700	345,975,000	316,614,600	
Return on Assets %	.06%	.06%	.04%	.03%	.04%	
Return on Equity %	.12%	.12%	.08%	.07%	.08%	
Debt to Equity	0.022	0.035	0.074	0.116	0.10	

CONTACT INFORMATION:

Phone: 81-45-470-8250 Fax: 81-45-470-8797
Toll-Free:
Address: Sun Hamada Bldg., 5/Fl., 1-19-20 Shin-Yokohama, Kanagawa, 222-8581 Japan

STOCK TICKER/OTHER:

Stock Ticker: UPRZF Exchange: GREY
Employees: 11,557 Fiscal Year Ends: 03/31
Parent Company:

SALARIES/BONUSES:

Top Exec. Salary: $ Bonus: $
Second Exec. Salary: $ Bonus: $

OTHER THOUGHTS:

Estimated Female Officers or Directors:
Hot Spot for Advancement for Women/Minorities:

Uni-Select Inc

www.uniselect.com

NAIC Code: 423120

TYPES OF BUSINESS:

Automobile Parts Manufacturer
Auto Parts Dealer
Auto Parts Distribution
Product & Market Development Services
Marketing & Support Services

BRANDS/DIVISIONS/AFFILIATES:

FinishMaster Inc
Canadian Automotive Group
Parts Alliance (The)
Auto Parts Plus
Bumper to Bumper
Uni-Pro
SAX
Carrossier ProColor

CONTACTS: *Note: Officers with more than one job title may be intentionally listed here more than once.*

Peter Septhon, CEO, Divisional
Andre Courville, CEO
Eric Bussieres, CFO
Brent Windom, COO, Divisional
Marie-Noelle Gagnon, Other Executive Officer
Me Louis Juneau, Other Executive Officer

GROWTH PLANS/SPECIAL FEATURES:

Uni-Select, Inc. is a wholesale distributor and marketer of automotive and heavy-duty replacement parts and accessories. The firm operates through a network of 17 warehouse distribution centers and more than 440 corporate stores, and also serves 1,100+ independent customers across Canada, the U.K. and the U.S. Uni-Select's products include domestic and foreign nameplate replacement parts, paint and paint-related products, as well as tools and equipment. Brands include Auto Parts Plus, Auto-Plus, Bumper to Bumper, Auto Select, Uni-Pro, SAX and Carrossier ProColor. Subsidiary FinishMaster, Inc. is a leading national independent distributor of automotive paints, coatings and related accessories in the U.S. FinishMaster services a network of over 30,000 customers annually, of which more than 6,800 are collision repair center customers. Uni-Select's automotive products distributor businesses include Canadian Automotive Group and The Parts Alliance (serving the U.K. and Ireland). In mid-2019, Uni-Select announced the official opening of a new Bumper to Bumper distribution center in Calgary, Alberta, its largest yet with more than 296,000-square-feet of space.

FINANCIAL DATA: *Note: Data for latest year may not have been available at press time.*

In U.S. $	2018	2017	2016	2015	2014	2013
Revenue	1,751,965,000	1,448,272,000	1,197,319,000	1,355,434,000	1,784,359,000	1,788,085,000
R&D Expense						
Operating Income	79,827,000	87,885,000	90,140,000	83,800,000	71,840,000	63,082,000
Operating Margin %		.06%	.08%	.06%	.04%	.04%
SGA Expense	308,546,000	236,684,000	175,621,000	213,666,000	283,085,000	293,809,000
Net Income	36,497,000	44,616,000	58,265,000	-40,221,000	50,125,000	21,328,000
Operating Cash Flow	94,579,000	124,005,000	136,905,000	15,396,000	123,534,000	76,812,000
Capital Expenditure	22,660,000	18,272,000	15,005,000	21,794,000	19,466,000	22,819,000
EBITDA	104,189,000	107,799,000	106,616,000	-54,925,000	106,201,000	57,419,000
Return on Assets %		.04%	.06%	-.04%	.04%	.02%
Return on Equity %		.09%	.13%	-.08%	.10%	.04%
Debt to Equity		0.795	0.276	0.201	0.41	0.655

CONTACT INFORMATION:

Phone: 450 641-2440 Fax: 450 449-4908
Toll-Free:
Address: 170 Industriel Blvd., Boucherville, QC J4B 2X3 Canada

STOCK TICKER/OTHER:

Stock Ticker: UNS
Exchange: TSE
Employees: 1,385
Fiscal Year Ends: 12/31
Parent Company:

SALARIES/BONUSES:

Top Exec. Salary: $ Bonus: $
Second Exec. Salary: $ Bonus: $

OTHER THOUGHTS:

Estimated Female Officers or Directors: 1
Hot Spot for Advancement for Women/Minorities:

US Auto Parts Network Inc

www.usautoparts.net

NAIC Code: 454111

TYPES OF BUSINESS:

Auto Parts Online

BRANDS/DIVISIONS/AFFILIATES:

CONTACTS:
Note: Officers with more than one job title may be intentionally listed here more than once.

Lev Peker, CEO
David Meniane, CFO
Houman Akhavan, Chief Marketing Officer
Sanjiv Gomes, Chief Technology Officer
Warren Phelps, Director
Sol Khazani, Founder
Alfredo Gomez, General Counsel

GROWTH PLANS/SPECIAL FEATURES:

U.S. Auto Parts Network, Inc. is an online provider of automotive aftermarket parts. The company principally sells its products (stock keeping units/SKUs) to individual consumers through its network of websites and online marketplace. U.S. Auto's websites offer a comprehensive selection of more than 1.5 million SKUs with detailed product descriptions, attributes and photographs. The firm has developed a proprietary product database that maps its SKUs to product applications based on vehicle makes, models and years. U.S. Auto's products are grouped into three categories: collision parts, engine parts and performance parts and related accessories. Collision parts consists of parts for the exterior of an automobile, and are typically replacement parts for original body parts that have been damaged as a result of a collision or through general wear and tear. In addition, this category sells an extensive line of mirror products which are marketed and sold as aftermarket replacement parts and upgrades to existing parts. The engine parts category consists of engine and chassis components and other mechanical and electrical parts. These serve as replacement parts for existing engine parts and are generally used by professionals and do-it-yourselfers for engine and mechanical maintenance and repair. The performance parts and related accessories category offers performance versions of many parts sold in each of the other categories, and generally consist of parts that enhance the performance of the automobile, upgrade existing functionality of a specific part or improve the physical appearance or comfort of the automobile. U.S. Auto Parts fulfills customer orders through two methods: stock-and-ship, where it takes physical delivery of merchandise and stores it in one of its distribution centers until it is shipped to a customer; and drop-ship, where merchandise is shipped directly to customers from the company's suppliers.

FINANCIAL DATA:
Note: Data for latest year may not have been available at press time.

In U.S. $	2018	2017	2016	2015	2014	2013
Revenue	289,467,000	303,366,000	303,571,000	291,091,000	283,508,000	254,753,000
R&D Expense		4,711,000	5,843,000	5,000,000	4,863,000	5,128,000
Operating Income	-5,006,000	4,635,000	1,520,000	-2,055,000	-5,912,000	-8,690,000
Operating Margin %		.02%	.01%	-.01%	-.02%	-.03%
SGA Expense	58,044,000	79,995,000	84,437,000	80,025,000	79,077,000	77,314,000
Net Income	-4,889,000	24,015,000	731,000	-1,281,000	-6,879,000	-15,634,000
Operating Cash Flow	6,181,000	11,634,000	21,571,000	5,745,000	1,243,000	867,000
Capital Expenditure	5,689,000	4,896,000	6,478,000	7,805,000	5,756,000	8,325,000
EBITDA	2,368,000	11,405,000	8,428,000	5,955,000	3,498,000	-2,063,000
Return on Assets %		.26%	.01%	-.02%	-.09%	-.20%
Return on Equity %		.75%	.02%	-.08%	-.35%	-.64%
Debt to Equity		0.227	0.428	0.50	0.481	0.455

CONTACT INFORMATION:

Phone: 310 735-0085 Fax: 310 632-1681
Toll-Free:
Address: 16941 Keegan Ave, Carson, CA 90746 United States

STOCK TICKER/OTHER:

Stock Ticker: PRTS
Exchange: NAS
Employees: 1,080
Fiscal Year Ends: 12/31
Parent Company:

SALARIES/BONUSES:

Top Exec. Salary: $409,423 Bonus: $
Second Exec. Salary: $321,038 Bonus: $

OTHER THOUGHTS:

Estimated Female Officers or Directors:
Hot Spot for Advancement for Women/Minorities:

Utilimaster Corporation

www.spartanmotors.com/fleet-vehicles/

NAIC Code: 336120

TYPES OF BUSINESS:

Truck Manufacturer
Custom Vehicles

BRANDS/DIVISIONS/AFFILIATES:

Spartan Motors Inc
Utilimaster Holdings Inc

CONTACTS: *Note: Officers with more than one job title may be intentionally listed here more than once.*

Chad Heminover, Pres.
John Knudtson, VP-Prod. Dev.

GROWTH PLANS/SPECIAL FEATURES:

Utilimaster Corporation designs and builds custom commercial vehicles. The company operates as a subsidiary of Utilimaster Holdings, Inc., which itself is wholly-owned by Spartan Motors, Inc. Utilimaster works extensively with, and offers specialized solutions to, industries such as food/beverage, parcel delivery, textile, utility service, emergency response, mobile sales, mobile maintenance, trades & construction, specialty uplift, commercial truck and stock trucks. Its products include walk-in vans, truck bodies and refrigerated trucks. Walk-in vans are built on a strip chassis, and used for delivery and service vehicles. Sizes vary from 12 to 30 feet long, 81 to 85 inches high and 86.5 to 93.5 inches wide. Truck bodies are built on a cab chassis for heavy-duty commercial delivery and come in 10 to 28 feet long, 72 to 108 inches high and 96 inches wide configurations. Refrigerated trucks include standard modes and custom-engineered solutions. Trade & construction vehicles are built on a cutaway (cab chassis) for contractors and come in 10, 12 or 14 feet long, 60.5 or 75 to 78 inches high and 80 or 96 inches wide sizes. Utility vans are built on a cutaway chassis for medium-duty commercial delivery and range from 10 to 17 feet long, 72, 78, 84 or 90 inches high and 96 inches wide. Delivery and mobile retail vehicles are built on a cutaway chassis, are fuel efficient for inner city delivery and come in 10 or 12 feet long, 78 inches high and 81 inches wide configurations. Reach trucks are built on an Isuzu diesel chassis and are smaller, fuel-efficient delivery vehicles available in 12 or 14 feet in length, up to 27 inches in headroom and either 540 or 630 cubic feet of storage. Other vehicles include full stand-up height, varied cargo capacity options, and curbside sliding or walk-through doors.

FINANCIAL DATA: *Note: Data for latest year may not have been available at press time.*

In U.S. $	2018	2017	2016	2015	2014	2013
Revenue						
R&D Expense						
Operating Income						
Operating Margin %						
SGA Expense						
Net Income						
Operating Cash Flow						
Capital Expenditure						
EBITDA						
Return on Assets %						
Return on Equity %						
Debt to Equity						

CONTACT INFORMATION:

Phone: 574-848-2000 Fax: 574-862-4517
Toll-Free: 800-582-3454
Address: 603-605 Earthway Dr., Bristol, IN 46507 United States

STOCK TICKER/OTHER:

Stock Ticker: Subsidiary
Employees: 792
Parent Company: Spartan Motors Inc
Exchange:
Fiscal Year Ends: 12/31

SALARIES/BONUSES:

Top Exec. Salary: $ Bonus: $
Second Exec. Salary: $ Bonus: $

OTHER THOUGHTS:

Estimated Female Officers or Directors:
Hot Spot for Advancement for Women/Minorities:

Utility Trailer Manufacturing Company

www.utilitytrailer.com

NAIC Code: 336212

TYPES OF BUSINESS:

Truck Trailer Manufacturing
Parts & Service

BRANDS/DIVISIONS/AFFILIATES:

Barrier Door
Tautliner
3000R
4000D-X Composite
4000D
4000A
4000S
Utilitopics

CONTACTS: *Note: Officers with more than one job title may be intentionally listed here more than once.*

Paul Bennett, CEO
Craig Bennett, Sr. VP-Sales & Mktg.
Todd Bennett, Dir.-Finance
Stephen F. Bennett, VP-Purchasing

GROWTH PLANS/SPECIAL FEATURES:

Utility Trailer Manufacturing Company designs, engineers, builds and services a complete line of trailers, including flatbeds, refrigerated trailers (reefers), dry-freight vans and curtain-sided trailers. It has developed numerous technologies including the cold flow floor design, its patented Barrier Door, the use of polyurethane foam in refrigerated trailers, the shockless pintle hook and a completely waterproof electrical system. The firm was one of the first companies in the U.S. to introduce and manufacture curtain-sided trailers. Sold under the brand Tautliner, these trailers feature load-bearing curtains that slide back for immediate access to the load. The Tautliner is one of the company's most popular brands. The firm's 3000R reefer, one of the top selling reefers in the world, is used on five continents and is available in three different size models. Its 4000D-X Composite and 4000D models are dry vans, and its 4000A and 4000S models are drop deck flatbeds. The company operates five trailer manufacturing plants throughout the U.S., and its products are sold by more than 100 dealers in the U.S., Canada, Mexico and South America. Its North American facilities also offer parts and servicing for all of the company's trailers. The firm publishes Utilitopics, a newsletter sent to company employees, customers and dealers, covering market conditions and other topics. Utility Trailer has been owned and operated by the Bennett family since brothers H. C. and E. W. Bennett founded the company in 1914. During 2019, Utility Trailer announced the opening of a new, dual-use facility located in Eagle Pass, Texas, a state-of-the-art dealer facility on 40 acres of land, which services the new utility refrigerated trailer factory in Coahuila, Mexico, three miles away.

FINANCIAL DATA: *Note: Data for latest year may not have been available at press time.*

In U.S. $	2018	2017	2016	2015	2014	2013
Revenue	1,391,505,503	1,325,243,336	1,262,136,510	1,353,375,000	1,125,000,000	1,100,000,000
R&D Expense						
Operating Income						
Operating Margin %						
SGA Expense						
Net Income						
Operating Cash Flow						
Capital Expenditure						
EBITDA						
Return on Assets %						
Return on Equity %						
Debt to Equity						

CONTACT INFORMATION:

Phone: 626-965-1541 Fax: 626-965-2790
Toll-Free:
Address: 17295 E. Railroad St., City of Industry, CA 91748 United States

STOCK TICKER/OTHER:

Stock Ticker: Private
Employees: 3,758
Parent Company:
Exchange:
Fiscal Year Ends:

SALARIES/BONUSES:

Top Exec. Salary: $ Bonus: $
Second Exec. Salary: $ Bonus: $

OTHER THOUGHTS:

Estimated Female Officers or Directors:
Hot Spot for Advancement for Women/Minorities:

Valeo SA

www.valeo.com

NAIC Code: 336300

TYPES OF BUSINESS:

Automobile Parts Manufacturing
Security Systems
Electrical & Electronic Systems
Lighting Systems
Thermal Systems
Aftermarket Products
Transmission Components

BRANDS/DIVISIONS/AFFILIATES:

Valeo Service

CONTACTS: *Note: Officers with more than one job title may be intentionally listed here more than once.*

Jacques Aschenbroich, CEO
Jean-Francois Tarabbia, Sr. VP-R&D & Product Mktg.
Geric Lebedoff, General Counsel
Francois Marion, VP-Corp. Strategy & Planning
Axel Joachim Maschka, Sr. VP-Bus. Dev.
Fabienne de Brebisson, VP-Comm.
Antoine Doutriaux, Pres., Visibility Systems
Alain Marmugi, Pres., Thermal Systems
Marc Vrecko, Pres., Comfort & Driving Assistance Systems
Catherine Delhaye, Chief Ethics & Compliance Officer
Sergio-Pancini Sa, National Dir.-South America

GROWTH PLANS/SPECIAL FEATURES:

Valeo SA is a global automotive supplier operating approximately 186 production sites, 59 research and development centers and 15 distribution platforms, with a presence in 33 countries. The firm's business activities are divided into six segments: comfort & driving assistance systems, powertrain systems, thermal systems, visibility systems, Valeo Service and heavy commercial vehicles. The comfort & driving assistance systems segment offers a wide range of smart sensors and features that improve vehicle safety and comfort, including automated parking systems and automated driving systems. The powertrain systems segment develops and manufactures innovative powertrain solutions designed to reduce CO2 emissions and fuel consumption. These innovations revolved around three approaches: electrification, transmissions automation and clean engine solutions. The thermal systems segment designs and manufactures systems, modules and components to optimize thermal management of vehicles and passenger comfort in the cabin. Thermal systems reduce pollution emissions, optimizes battery range and lifespan in hybrid and electric vehicles, and protect the health and well-being of passengers. The visibility systems segment is made up of two product groups: wiper systems and lighting systems, each of which designs and produces innovative technologies to ensure the best possible visibility and safety for drivers in all weather conditions, in both day and night. The Valeo Service segment is an aftermarket specialist serving both auto manufacturers with original equipment spares and the independent aftermarket with replacement parts and accessories for passenger cars and commercial vehicles. Last, the heavy commercial vehicles segment offers technological innovations that fulfill the needs and expectations of transportation players in relation to electrical systems, driving assistance systems and digital solutions.

FINANCIAL DATA: *Note: Data for latest year may not have been available at press time.*

In U.S. $	2018	2017	2016	2015	2014	2013
Revenue	21,173,610,000	20,538,090,000	18,289,420,000	16,102,750,000	14,088,800,000	13,407,880,000
R&D Expense	1,502,436,000	1,459,256,000	1,283,215,000	1,044,066,000	921,169,200	863,596,100
Operating Income	1,331,931,000	1,610,939,000	1,409,433,000	1,173,605,000	954,384,400	880,203,700
Operating Margin %		.08%	.08%	.07%	.07%	.07%
SGA Expense	1,008,636,000	984,278,100	875,775,000	792,737,000	726,306,500	703,055,800
Net Income	604,517,300	980,956,600	1,024,136,000	807,130,200	622,232,100	486,049,600
Operating Cash Flow	2,402,568,000	2,257,529,000	2,092,560,000	1,914,305,000	1,447,077,000	1,481,400,000
Capital Expenditure	2,289,637,000	1,976,306,000	1,439,327,000	1,238,928,000	1,060,673,000	1,011,958,000
EBITDA	2,436,891,000	2,602,967,000	2,412,533,000	1,956,377,000	1,651,904,000	1,421,612,000
Return on Assets %		.06%	.07%	.07%	.06%	.05%
Return on Equity %		.21%	.24%	.23%	.22%	.20%
Debt to Equity		0.733	0.503	0.33	0.532	0.639

CONTACT INFORMATION:

Phone: 33 140552020 Fax: 33 140552171
Toll-Free:
Address: 43 rue Bayen Cedex 17, Paris, 75848 France

STOCK TICKER/OTHER:

Stock Ticker: VLEEF
Employees: 113,600
Parent Company:
Exchange: PINX
Fiscal Year Ends: 12/31

SALARIES/BONUSES:

Top Exec. Salary: $ Bonus: $
Second Exec. Salary: $ Bonus: $

OTHER THOUGHTS:

Estimated Female Officers or Directors: 4
Hot Spot for Advancement for Women/Minorities: Y

Vauxhall Motors Limited

www.vauxhall.co.uk

NAIC Code: 336111

TYPES OF BUSINESS:

Automobile Manufacturing
Vehicle Manufacture
Automotive Parts
Automotive Maintenance

BRANDS/DIVISIONS/AFFILIATES:

Peugeot SA (Groupe PSA)
Viva
Astra
Insignia
Crossland
Combo
Vivaro
Movano

CONTACTS: *Note: Officers with more than one job title may be intentionally listed here more than once.*

Stephen Norman, Managing Dir.

GROWTH PLANS/SPECIAL FEATURES:

Vauxhall Motors Limited is a U.K. manufacturer of passenger and light commercial vehicles. Current car models: Viva, Viva Rocks, Corsa 3- and 5-door, Adam, Astra, Astra Sports Tourer, Insignia Grand Sport, Insignia Sports Tourer, Insignia Country Tourer, Mokka X, Crossland X, Grandland X, Combo Life, Combo Life 7-seater and Vivaro Life. Van models: Combo Cargo, Vivaro, Movano and Movano Conversions. Vauxhall operates manufacturing plants in Ellesmere Port, and its warehouse and lead office is based in Luton. The Luton plant builds Vivaro and Astra vehicles. Vauxhall technology is utilized to design and manufacture economy and performance vehicles. Its ecoTEC technology helps to improve fuel consumption as well as keep CO2 emission, tax and whole life costs to a minimum. Vauxhall's proprietary BlueInjection diesel engine uses a selective catalytic reduction system to effectively reduce NOx emissions. An additive called AdBlue is injected into the exhaust. The ammonia from AdBlue mixes with NOx from the vehicle and turns it into nitrogen and water, which is emitted via the exhaust. AdBlue ages, so it is imperative not to use out-of-date AdBlue. Vauxhall Heritage Centre houses a variety of classic Vauxhall models as well as the PA Cresta, Viva and multiple generations of the Cavalier model. Vauxhall Heritage Services offers owners or prospective owners of classic Vauxhall vehicles parts and technical support services, as well as information on related clubs and events. Vauxhall Network Q provides performance certification and warranty services for used Vauxhall vehicles. Vauxhall announced it may re-enter commercialization of its HydroGen4 fuel cell vehicle by 2020. Vauxhall Motors is owned by Peugeot SA (referred to as Groupe PSA).

FINANCIAL DATA: *Note: Data for latest year may not have been available at press time.*

In U.S. $	2018	2017	2016	2015	2014	2013
Revenue	2,093,830,000					
R&D Expense						
Operating Income						
Operating Margin %						
SGA Expense						
Net Income						
Operating Cash Flow						
Capital Expenditure						
EBITDA						
Return on Assets %						
Return on Equity %						
Debt to Equity						

CONTACT INFORMATION:

Phone: 44-1582-721-122 Fax: 44-1582-427-400
Toll-Free:
Address: UK1-101-135 Osborne Rd., Griffin House, Luton, Beds LU1 3YT United Kingdom

STOCK TICKER/OTHER:

Stock Ticker: Subsidiary
Exchange:
Employees: 2,793
Fiscal Year Ends: 12/31
Parent Company: Peugeot SA (Groupe PSA)

SALARIES/BONUSES:

Top Exec. Salary: $ Bonus: $
Second Exec. Salary: $ Bonus: $

OTHER THOUGHTS:

Estimated Female Officers or Directors:
Hot Spot for Advancement for Women/Minorities:

Visteon Corporation

www.visteon.com

NAIC Code: 336300

TYPES OF BUSINESS:

Automobile Parts
Climate Control Products
Fuel Storage & Delivery Products
Chassis & Power Train Components
Multimedia Systems

BRANDS/DIVISIONS/AFFILIATES:

SmartCore
DriveCore

CONTACTS: *Note: Officers with more than one job title may be intentionally listed here more than once.*

Sachin Lawande, CEO
Christian Garcia, CFO
Markus Schupfner, Chief Technology Officer
Francis Scricco, Director
Brett Pynnonen, General Counsel
Kristin Trecker, Other Executive Officer
Matthew Cole, Senior VP, Divisional
Robert Vallance, Senior VP, Divisional
Sunil Bilolikar, Senior VP, Divisional

GROWTH PLANS/SPECIAL FEATURES:

Visteon Corporation is a global automotive supplier that designs, engineers and manufactures innovative electronics products for nearly every original equipment vehicle manufacturer (OEM). The company operates through a single segment, electronics. The electronics division provides vehicle cockpit electronics products to its customers, including instrument clusters, information displays, infotainment systems, audio systems, telematics solutions and head up displays. Instrument clusters include standard analog gauge clusters to high-resolutions, all-digital, fully reconfigurable, 2d and 3D display-based devices. Information displays are utilized alongside various applications within the cockpit and can integrate a range of user interface technologies and graphics management capabilities such as 3D, dual view, cameras, optics, haptic feedback, light effects and dual organic light-emitting diode (OLED) displays. Infotainment and audio systems include the company's Phoenix display audio and embedded infotainment platform, and the Android embedded infotainment open-source system. These systems are designed to allow vehicle occupants to easily connect their mobile devices and safely access phone functions, listen to music, stream media and more. Visteon's telematics solution uses a single hardware and flexible software architecture to support regional telematics service providers and mobile networks. It also offers a hands-free telephone unit that provides Bluetooth and Universal Serial Bus (USB) connectivity. Head up displays provide critical information to the driver in a convenient vehicle location and at a comfortable focal distance through a compact, transparent screen mounted on a panel. In addition, Visteon's SmartCore domain controller can independently operate the infotainment system, instrument cluster, head-up display and other features on a single, multi-core chip; and its DriveCore technology platform consists of the hardware, middleware and frameworks to develop machine learning algorithms for autonomous driving applications of Level 3 and above. The firm's customers include Ford, Mazda, Renault/Nissan, General Motors, Volkswagen, Jaguar/Land Rover, Daimler, Honda and BMW.

FINANCIAL DATA: *Note: Data for latest year may not have been available at press time.*

In U.S. $	2018	2017	2016	2015	2014	2013
Revenue	2,984,000,000	3,146,000,000	3,161,000,000	3,245,000,000	7,509,000,000	7,439,000,000
R&D Expense						
Operating Income	218,000,000	277,000,000	244,000,000	185,000,000	413,000,000	317,000,000
Operating Margin %		.09%	.08%	.06%	.06%	.04%
SGA Expense	193,000,000	222,000,000	220,000,000	245,000,000	377,000,000	367,000,000
Net Income	164,000,000	176,000,000	75,000,000	2,284,000,000	-295,000,000	690,000,000
Operating Cash Flow	204,000,000	217,000,000	120,000,000	338,000,000	284,000,000	312,000,000
Capital Expenditure	127,000,000	99,000,000	75,000,000	187,000,000	340,000,000	269,000,000
EBITDA	321,000,000	331,000,000	263,000,000	257,000,000	568,000,000	1,191,000,000
Return on Assets %		.08%	.02%	.46%	-.05%	.12%
Return on Equity %		.29%	.09%	2.38%	-.21%	.42%
Debt to Equity		0.545	0.59	0.328	0.97	0.325

CONTACT INFORMATION:

Phone: 734 710-5800 Fax:
Toll-Free: 800-847-8366
Address: 1 Village Center Dr., Van Buren Township, MI 48111 United States

STOCK TICKER/OTHER:

Stock Ticker: VC
Employees: 10,000
Parent Company:
Exchange: NAS
Fiscal Year Ends: 12/31

SALARIES/BONUSES:

Top Exec. Salary: $1,030,000 Bonus: $
Second Exec. Salary: $590,000 Bonus: $

OTHER THOUGHTS:

Estimated Female Officers or Directors:
Hot Spot for Advancement for Women/Minorities: Y

Volkswagen AG (VW)

www.volkswagenag.com

NAIC Code: 336111

TYPES OF BUSINESS:

Automobile Manufacturing
Truck Manufacturing
Car Rental Services
Consumer Financing
Digital Services
Electric Cars

BRANDS/DIVISIONS/AFFILIATES:

Volkswagen
Audi
Bentley
Bugatti
Lamborghini
SEAT
Skoda
Ducati

CONTACTS: *Note: Officers with more than one job title may be intentionally listed here more than once.*

Herbert Diess, CEO
Frank Witter, CFO
Gunnar Kilian, Dir.-Human Resources
Michael Macht, Dir.-Group Production
Hans Dieter Potsch, Dir.-Finance
Leif Ostling, Dir.-Group Commercial Vehicles
Herbert Diess, Chmn.
Jochem Heizmann, Dir.-China
Francisco Javier Garcia Sanz, Dir.-Procurement

GROWTH PLANS/SPECIAL FEATURES:

Volkswagen AG (VW) is a world-leading automobile manufacturer. The firm's production base consists of 120 plants in more than 30 countries worldwide. The company's automobiles are made up of twelve brands from seven European countries: passenger cars, including Volkswagen, Audi, Bentley, Bugatti, Lamborghini, SEAT, Skoda and Porsche; motorcycles under the Ducati brand; trucks, buses and diesel engines under the Scania and MAN brand names; and Volkswagen commercial vehicles. Each brand operates as an independent entity on the market, with products ranging from low-consumption small cars to luxury class vehicles to motorcycles. Models offered under the Volkswagen brand include the Up!, eco up!, e-up!, up! GTI, load up!, e-load up!, cross up!, Golf, Passat, Touran, Sharan, Tiguan, Atlas, Tourareg, Ameo (Russia/India), Polo, Voyage (South America), Gol (South America), Fox (South America), Jetta (North America/China), Sagitar (China), The Beetle (North America), and many more. The Arteon model is due in 2019, featuring driver assistance capabilities. In the commercial vehicle segment, products include pick-ups, busses and heavy trucks. VW is also active in other fields of business, manufacturing large-bore diesel engines for marine and stationary applications, turbochargers and machinery, special gear units, compressors and chemical reactors. In addition, the group offers a wide range of financial services, including dealer and customer financing, leasing, banking and insurance activities, as well as fleet management services. In 2018, the firm announced plans to produce battery-powered vehicles at nine more plants worldwide within the next two years (it currently produces them at three), and at 16 locations worldwide by the end of 2022. In June 2019, VW spun off its heavy-truck unit, renamed it Traton SE and began trading shares of it on both the Frankfurt and Stockholm stock exchanges.

FINANCIAL DATA: *Note: Data for latest year may not have been available at press time.*

In U.S. $	2018	2017	2016	2015	2014	2013
Revenue	261,126,000,000	255,405,200,000	240,553,600,000	236,151,500,000	224,156,300,000	218,122,200,000
R&D Expense						
Operating Income	15,980,960,000	14,883,750,000	9,220,550,000	-1,369,575,000	13,430,030,000	12,730,290,000
Operating Margin %		.06%	.04%	-.01%	.06%	.06%
SGA Expense	32,472,320,000	34,282,550,000	33,255,090,000	34,003,540,000	30,040,970,000	29,387,730,000
Net Income	13,436,670,000	12,874,230,000	5,944,420,000	-1,517,936,000	12,161,200,000	10,067,540,000
Operating Cash Flow	8,051,373,000	-1,312,002,000	10,440,650,000	15,145,040,000	11,939,770,000	13,944,860,000
Capital Expenditure	20,995,350,000	20,274,580,000	20,927,810,000	20,188,220,000	18,393,490,000	17,057,130,000
EBITDA	43,824,180,000	42,360,500,000	33,793,180,000	22,972,760,000	37,912,980,000	32,599,650,000
Return on Assets %		.03%	.01%	.00%	.03%	.03%
Return on Equity %		.11%	.06%	-.02%	.12%	.11%
Debt to Equity		0.73	0.686	0.819	0.749	0.69

CONTACT INFORMATION:

Phone: 49 536190 Fax:
Toll-Free:
Address: Brieffach 1848-2, Wolfsburg, 38436 Germany

STOCK TICKER/OTHER:

Stock Ticker: VLKPF
Exchange: PINX
Employees: 615,081
Fiscal Year Ends: 12/31
Parent Company:

SALARIES/BONUSES:

Top Exec. Salary: $ Bonus: $
Second Exec. Salary: $ Bonus: $

OTHER THOUGHTS:

Estimated Female Officers or Directors:
Hot Spot for Advancement for Women/Minorities:

Volkswagen Group of America Inc www.volkswagengroupamerica.com

NAIC Code: 336111

TYPES OF BUSINESS:

Automobile Manufacturing
Vehicle Importing
Vehicle Financing & Leasing

BRANDS/DIVISIONS/AFFILIATES:

Volkswagen AG
VW Credit Inc
Audi
Bentley
Bugatti
Lamborghini
Beetle
TT Coupe

CONTACTS: *Note: Officers with more than one job title may be intentionally listed here more than once.*

Scott Keogh, CEO/Pres.
Cian O'Brien, COO
David Geanacopoulos, General Counsel
Tony Cervone, Exec. VP-Corp. Comm.
Scott Keogh, Pres., Audi of America, Inc.
Christophe Georges, COO-Bentley Motors, Inc.
Andrew Stuart, CEO/Pres., Volkswagen Credit, Inc.
David Geanacopoulos, Exec. VP-Public Affairs

GROWTH PLANS/SPECIAL FEATURES:

Volkswagen Group of America, Inc. (VGA) is the U.S. importing and distribution branch of Volkswagen AG (VW). The firm handles all of Volkswagen's brands including Volkswagen, Audi, Bentley, Bugatti and Lamborghini. Wholly-owned subsidiary VW Credit, Inc. offers leasing and financial services through brands Volkswagen Credit, Audi Financial Services and Bentley Financial Services. It also manages and markets co-branded financial services through third-party providers. VGA operates parts distribution centers in California, Florida, New Jersey, Texas and Wisconsin; ports and post production facilities in California, Georgia, Rhode Island and Texas; corporate research, development and technical facilities in California, Arizona and New Jersey; financial service centers in Illinois and Oregon; and a production facility in Chattanooga, Tennessee. The company operates over 1,000 Volkswagen and Audi dealerships in the U.S. Volkswagen models include Arteon, Beetle, Golf, Jetta, Passat, Tiguan and Atlas. Audi models include the TT Coupe, TTS Coupe, A3-A8, S3-S8, Q3, Q5, Q7, Q8, SQ5, RS3, RS5, RS7, R8 and Spyder. VGA also retails car accessories, apparel and other logo merchandise through its eCommerce website.

FINANCIAL DATA: *Note: Data for latest year may not have been available at press time.*

In U.S. $	2018	2017	2016	2015	2014	2013
Revenue	43,070,600,000	45,142,700,000	41,614,324,599	39,269,949,924	33,853,809,882	30,332,711,223
R&D Expense						
Operating Income						
Operating Margin %						
SGA Expense						
Net Income						
Operating Cash Flow						
Capital Expenditure						
EBITDA						
Return on Assets %						
Return on Equity %						
Debt to Equity						

CONTACT INFORMATION:

Phone: 703-364-7000 Fax:
Toll-Free:
Address: 2200 Ferdinand Porsche Dr., Herndon, VA 20171 United States

STOCK TICKER/OTHER:

Stock Ticker: Subsidiary
Employees: 6,335
Parent Company: Volkswagen AG
Exchange:
Fiscal Year Ends: 12/31

SALARIES/BONUSES:

Top Exec. Salary: $ Bonus: $
Second Exec. Salary: $ Bonus: $

OTHER THOUGHTS:

Estimated Female Officers or Directors:
Hot Spot for Advancement for Women/Minorities:

Volvo Car Corporation

www.volvocars.com

NAIC Code: 336111

TYPES OF BUSINESS:

Automobile Manufacturing

BRANDS/DIVISIONS/AFFILIATES:

Zhejiang Geely Holding Group Co Ltd
Volvo Cars of North America
Volvo Cars Financial Services US LLC
260
S90
V60
XC60
XC90

CONTACTS: *Note: Officers with more than one job title may be intentionally listed here more than once.*

Hakan Samuelsson, Pres.
Peter Mertens, Sr. VP-R&D
Lars Wrebo, Sr. VP-Mfg. & Purchasing
Maria Hemberg, General Counsel
Anders Karrberg, Acting Sr. VP-Corp. Comm.
Nils Mosko, Head-Investor Rel.
Thomas Ingenlath, VP-Design
Paul Gustavsson, Sr. VP-Bus. Office Dev.
Lex Kerssemakers, Sr. VP-Prod. Strategy & Vehicle Line Mgmt.
Paul Welander, Sr. VP-Quality & Customer Satisfaction
Li Shufu, Chmn.
Lars Danielson, Sr. VP-China Oper.

GROWTH PLANS/SPECIAL FEATURES:

Volvo Car Corporation, founded in 1927, is a Swedish designer, developer and manufacturer of cars known for safety and reliability. Volvo is owned by Zhejiang Geely Holding Group Co. Ltd, based in Hangzhou, China. Its largest markets are the U.K., Sweden, China and Germany. Volvo cars are manufactured at seven facilities, with the largest facilities in Sweden and Belgium and smaller plants in China. Its current models include the S60 and S90 sedans; the V60 and V90 crossover/wagon models; and the XC40, XC60 and XC90 SUVs. The firm's cars have won numerous awards for safety, design, environmental issues and overall value. It offers environmentally savvy FlexiFuel cars (so named because they can run on either ethanol or gasoline), and hopes to expand its production of those models. Available in certain states in the U.S., Volvo's PZEV (partial zero emission vehicle) engines produce exhaust which, in heavy city traffic, may be cleaner than the ambient air. Volvo's U.S. companies include Volvo Cars of North America and Volvo Cars Financial Services U.S., LLC (VCFS). Polestar is the performance brand of Volvo cars, where customers can optimize their vehicles for increased engine performance. Volvo has a partnership with Uber to develop fully-autonomous driving cars, the XC90 SUVs. Volvo announced that beginning in 2019, all of its new models will include an electric motor in their powertrain, and that between 2019 and 2021, the company plans to launch three electric cars under the Volvo brand and two under the Polestar brand.

FINANCIAL DATA: *Note: Data for latest year may not have been available at press time.*

In U.S. $	2018	2017	2016	2015	2014	2013
Revenue	28,113,500,000	25,664,200,000	21,604,490,000	20,166,314,523	15,361,045,464	18,654,768,151
R&D Expense						
Operating Income						
Operating Margin %						
SGA Expense						
Net Income	1,098,380,000	1,244,200,000	106,675,000	74,648,800	62,453,113	146,497,535
Operating Cash Flow						
Capital Expenditure						
EBITDA						
Return on Assets %						
Return on Equity %						
Debt to Equity						

CONTACT INFORMATION:

Phone: 46-31-59-00-00 Fax:
Toll-Free:
Address: VAK Bldg., Assar Gabrielssons vag, Goteborg, 418 78 Sweden

STOCK TICKER/OTHER:

Stock Ticker: Subsidiary Exchange:
Employees: 39,000 Fiscal Year Ends: 12/31
Parent Company: Zhejiang Geely Holding Group Co Ltd

SALARIES/BONUSES:

Top Exec. Salary: $ Bonus: $
Second Exec. Salary: $ Bonus: $

OTHER THOUGHTS:

Estimated Female Officers or Directors: 3
Hot Spot for Advancement for Women/Minorities: Y

Volvo Cars of North America Inc

www.volvocars.com/us

NAIC Code: 441110

TYPES OF BUSINESS:

Automobiles-Distribution & Marketing
Fleet Sales
Auto Financing
Roadside Assistance
Replacement Parts

BRANDS/DIVISIONS/AFFILIATES:

Volvo Car Corporation
Zhejiang Geely Holding Group Co Ltd
Volvo Car Finance
XC90
XC60
V90
S60
S90

CONTACTS: *Note: Officers with more than one job title may be intentionally listed here more than once.*

Anders Gustafsson, CEO
Michael Thomas, General Counsel
Wendi McAden, VP-Corp. Comm.

GROWTH PLANS/SPECIAL FEATURES:

Volvo Cars of North America, Inc. distributes, sells and markets Volvo-branded sedans, crossover/wagons and sport utility vehicles (SUVs) in the U.S. and Canada. The firm is a subsidiary of Sweden-based Volvo Car Corporation, itself a subsidiary of Zhejiang Geely Holding Group Co., Ltd. Volvo Cars' website includes a customization tool through which a purchaser can create and order a personalized vehicle. Its current vehicle models include sport utility vehicles: XC90, XC60 and XC40; crossover-wagons: V90 and V60; and sedans: S60 and S90. Vehicle accessories include backseat entertainment systems, portable navigation systems, booster cushions, stereo systems, parking assist software, reversible luggage compartment mats, electric coolers, protective bumper covers, bicycle carriers, specialized trim, gearshift knobs, steering wheels and other merchandise. Volvo Cars is connected with Volvo Car Finance, which provides leasing and financing for new vehicles, including variable and customized payment plans, as well as advance payment programs. In addition, the firm provides overseas delivery, pre-owned vehicles, special internet offers, fleet sales for corporations, care and maintenance services, spare and replacement parts, roadside assistance, and high-definition and satellite radio services for its vehicles. This division's U.S. plant is located in South Carolina, which currently produces the S60 mid-size sedan, with plans to produce the next-generation XC90 SUV in 2022. The plant has the capacity to produce up to 150,000 cars annually.

The company offers employees a lease car and purchase plan, tuition reimbursement and 401(k).

FINANCIAL DATA: *Note: Data for latest year may not have been available at press time.*

In U.S. $	2018	2017	2016	2015	2014	2013
Revenue						
R&D Expense						
Operating Income						
Operating Margin %						
SGA Expense						
Net Income						
Operating Cash Flow						
Capital Expenditure						
EBITDA						
Return on Assets %						
Return on Equity %						
Debt to Equity						

CONTACT INFORMATION:

Phone: 201-768-7300 Fax: 201-767-4816
Toll-Free: 800-458-1552
Address: 1 Volvo Dr., Rockleigh, NJ 07647 United States

STOCK TICKER/OTHER:

Stock Ticker: Subsidiary
Exchange:
Employees:
Fiscal Year Ends: 12/31
Parent Company: Zhejiang Geely Holding Group Co Ltd

SALARIES/BONUSES:

Top Exec. Salary: $ Bonus: $
Second Exec. Salary: $ Bonus: $

OTHER THOUGHTS:

Estimated Female Officers or Directors: 1
Hot Spot for Advancement for Women/Minorities:

Vroom

NAIC Code: 441120

www.vroom.com

TYPES OF BUSINESS:

Used Car Dealers
Electronic Shopping

BRANDS/DIVISIONS/AFFILIATES:

GROWTH PLANS/SPECIAL FEATURES:

Vroom is an online direct car retailer that allows customers to buy, sell and finance used cars. Customers can use its online database and filters to find a desirable car. The firm offers over 400 makes and models of primarily newer, low-mileage vehicles. Vroom has made over 250,000 sales and offers free delivery. Customers can test out the vehicle for a seven-day test drive before making the full purchase, which they can pay full in cash, finance through Vroom or through over 30 partnering bank services. In addition to purchasing vehicles, users can sell or trade in their vehicles through an online appraisal center. Once the user's car information is submitted, a Vroom expert will email a guaranteed cash offer for the vehicle within 30 minutes (during business hours). Vroom's investors include Auto Nation, L. Catterton, T.RowePrice, General Catalyst, PICO/Partners and Allen & Company.

CONTACTS: *Note: Officers with more than one job title may be intentionally listed here more than once.*

Paul Hennessy, CEO
Dave Jones, CFO
Peter Scherr, CMO
Deni Stott, Sr. VP-People & Culture
Mitch Berg, CTO

FINANCIAL DATA: *Note: Data for latest year may not have been available at press time.*

In U.S. $	2018	2017	2016	2015	2014	2013
Revenue	1,155,000,000	1,100,000,000	1,000,000,000	900,000,000	10,000,000	
R&D Expense						
Operating Income						
Operating Margin %						
SGA Expense						
Net Income						
Operating Cash Flow						
Capital Expenditure						
EBITDA						
Return on Assets %						
Return on Equity %						
Debt to Equity						

CONTACT INFORMATION:

Phone: 855-524-1300 Fax:
Toll-Free:
Address: 2615 W Interstate 20 2615 W Interstate 20 2615 W Interstate 20, Grand Prairie, TX 10010 United States

STOCK TICKER/OTHER:

Stock Ticker: Private
Employees: 600
Parent Company:
Exchange:
Fiscal Year Ends: 12/31

SALARIES/BONUSES:

Top Exec. Salary: $ Bonus: $
Second Exec. Salary: $ Bonus: $

OTHER THOUGHTS:

Estimated Female Officers or Directors:
Hot Spot for Advancement for Women/Minorities:

Wabash National Corporation

www.wabashnational.com

NAIC Code: 336212

TYPES OF BUSINESS:

Trailer Manufacturer
Trailer Dealerships
Repair Parts
Leasing & Financing
Trailer Rental

BRANDS/DIVISIONS/AFFILIATES:

Supreme Industries Inc
Wabash
DuraPlate
ArcticLite
RoadRailer
Transcraft
Benson

CONTACTS: *Note: Officers with more than one job title may be intentionally listed here more than once.*

Brent Yeagy, CEO
Jeffery Taylor, CFO
Martin Jischke, Director
Melanie Margolin, General Counsel
Mary Glazner, Other Executive Officer
Michael Pettit, President, Divisional
Kevin Page, President, Divisional
Dustin Smith, President, Divisional

GROWTH PLANS/SPECIAL FEATURES:

Wabash National Corporation designs, manufactures and markets standard and customized truck trailers and related transportation equipment. The firm divides its operations into three segments: commercial trailer products, diversified products and final mile products. The commercial trailer products segment manufactures standard and customized dry van, refrigerated van, and platform trailers and other transportation related equipment to customers who purchase directly from Wabash, through independent dealers or company-owned branch locations. This segment's transportation equipment is marketed under the following trademarks: Wabash, DuraPlate, DuraPlateHD, DuraPlate XD-35, ArcticLite, RoadRailer, Transcraft and Benson. The diversified products segment is comprised of four business units: tank trailer, aviation and truck equipment, process systems and composites. The tank trailer unit sells products that represent leading positions in liquid transportation systems and include a full line of stainless steel and aluminum tank trailers for the North American chemical, dairy, food and beverage, petroleum and energy services markets. The aviation and truck equipment unit manufactures truck-mounted tanks used in the aviation, refined fuel, heating oil, propane and liquid waste industries. The process systems unit produces isolators, stationary silos and downflow booths for the chemical, dairy, food and beverage, pharmaceutical and nuclear markets. Last, the composites unit utilizes DuraPlate panel technology to develop numerous proprietary products. The final mile products segment consists of subsidiary Supreme Industries, Inc., a manufacturer of specialized commercial vehicles, including cutaway and dry-freight van bodies, refrigerated units and stake bodies.

FINANCIAL DATA: *Note: Data for latest year may not have been available at press time.*

In U.S. $	2018	2017	2016	2015	2014	2013
Revenue	2,267,278,000	1,767,161,000	1,845,444,000	2,027,489,000	1,863,315,000	1,635,686,000
R&D Expense						
Operating Income	136,023,000	140,421,000	202,532,000	180,369,000	122,386,000	104,074,000
Operating Margin %		.08%	.11%	.09%	.07%	.06%
SGA Expense	128,160,000	103,413,000	101,399,000	100,728,000	88,370,000	89,263,000
Net Income	69,421,000	111,422,000	119,433,000	104,289,000	60,930,000	46,529,000
Operating Cash Flow	112,471,000	144,379,000	178,750,000	131,795,000	92,635,000	128,669,000
Capital Expenditure	34,009,000	26,056,000	20,342,000	20,847,000	19,957,000	18,352,000
EBITDA	165,446,000	173,991,000	237,850,000	220,857,000	159,456,000	142,267,000
Return on Assets %		.10%	.13%	.11%	.07%	.05%
Return on Equity %		.23%	.26%	.25%	.17%	.16%
Debt to Equity		0.998	0.497	0.63	0.846	1.135

CONTACT INFORMATION:

Phone: 765 771-5300 Fax:
Toll-Free: 800-937-4784
Address: 1000 Sagamore Pkwy. S., Lafayette, IN 47905 United States

STOCK TICKER/OTHER:

Stock Ticker: WNC
Employees: 5,100
Parent Company:
Exchange: NYS
Fiscal Year Ends: 12/31

SALARIES/BONUSES:

Top Exec. Salary: $726,153 Bonus: $
Second Exec. Salary: $690,666 Bonus: $

OTHER THOUGHTS:

Estimated Female Officers or Directors: 1
Hot Spot for Advancement for Women/Minorities:

WABCO Holdings Inc

www.wabco-auto.com

NAIC Code: 336340

TYPES OF BUSINESS:

Brake Systems Manufacturing
Suspension Systems

BRANDS/DIVISIONS/AFFILIATES:

Asset Trackr

CONTACTS:
Note: Officers with more than one job title may be intentionally listed here more than once.

Jacques Esculier, CEO
Sean Deason, CFO
Lisa Brown, Chief Legal Officer
Christian Brenneke, Chief Technology Officer
Mazen Mazraani, Other Executive Officer
Nicolas Bardot, Other Executive Officer
Nick Rens, President, Geographical

GROWTH PLANS/SPECIAL FEATURES:

WABCO Holdings, Inc. is a provider of electronic, mechanical, electro-mechanical and aerodynamic products for commercial truck, trailer, bus and passenger car manufacturers. The firm engineers, develops, manufactures and sells integrated systems controlling advanced braking, stability, suspension, steering, transmission automation, as well as air compression and processing. These systems improve vehicle safety, efficiency and performance while reducing overall vehicle operating costs. WABCO's largest-selling products are pneumatic anti-lock braking systems (ABS), electronic braking systems (EBS), electronic stability control (ESC) systems, brake controls, automated manual transmission systems, air disc brakes and a variety of conventional mechanical products such as actuators, air compressors and air control valves for medium- and heavy-duty trucks, buses and trailers. WABCO is also a global leader in hydraulic components, controls and brake systems for heavy-duty, off-highway vehicles used in agriculture, construction and mining. Aerodynamic products reduce the air drag of commercial trucks traveling long distance at highway speeds, thereby lowering consumption and CO2 emissions. The company's advanced electronic suspension controls and vacuum pumps primarily serve the passenger car and SUV markets in Europe, North America and Asia. WABCO also supplies replacement parts, fleet management solutions, diagnostic tools, training and other services to commercial vehicle aftermarket distributors and service partners. The firm's global Asset Trackr fleet management solutions platform helps commercial fleets to track, analyze and optimize their transportation resources and assets in real-time via cloud-based solutions. In March 2019, WABCO agreed to be acquired by ZF Friedrichshafen AG for approximately $7 billion; the transaction is expected to close in 2020.

FINANCIAL DATA:
Note: Data for latest year may not have been available at press time.

In U.S. $	2018	2017	2016	2015	2014	2013
Revenue	3,831,000,000	3,304,200,000	2,810,000,000	2,627,500,000	2,851,000,000	2,720,500,000
R&D Expense	184,400,000	147,000,000	135,200,000	139,500,000	145,000,000	119,400,000
Operating Income	511,400,000	452,200,000	357,500,000	272,600,000	333,200,000	333,900,000
Operating Margin %		.13%	.13%	.10%	.12%	.12%
SGA Expense	476,000,000	411,200,000	377,700,000	368,400,000	386,800,000	352,800,000
Net Income	394,100,000	406,100,000	223,000,000	275,200,000	291,500,000	653,200,000
Operating Cash Flow	468,500,000	421,500,000	405,400,000	395,300,000	314,400,000	665,800,000
Capital Expenditure	132,100,000	110,500,000	114,000,000	100,600,000	135,900,000	121,500,000
EBITDA	636,100,000	559,300,000	455,500,000	369,300,000	434,800,000	419,100,000
Return on Assets %		.11%	.08%	.11%	.12%	.32%
Return on Equity %		.45%	.30%	.34%	.29%	.71%
Debt to Equity		0.913	1.367	0.634	0.365	0.041

CONTACT INFORMATION:

Phone: 248-260-9032 Fax:
Toll-Free:
Address: 1220 Pacific Dr., Auburn Hills, MI 48326-1589 United States

STOCK TICKER/OTHER:

Stock Ticker: WBC
Exchange: NYS
Employees: 12,860
Fiscal Year Ends: 12/31
Parent Company:

SALARIES/BONUSES:

Top Exec. Salary: $1,100,000 Bonus: $
Second Exec. Salary: $405,000 Bonus: $

OTHER THOUGHTS:

Estimated Female Officers or Directors: 2
Hot Spot for Advancement for Women/Minorities:

Wanxiang Automotive Components LLC

www.wanxiang.com

NAIC Code: 336300

TYPES OF BUSINESS:

Automobile Parts Manufacturer
LED Lighting Systems

BRANDS/DIVISIONS/AFFILIATES:

Wanxiang Group Corporation
Wanxiang America Corporation

CONTACTS:

Note: Officers with more than one job title may be intentionally listed here more than once.

Pin Ni, Pres.
Michael J. Schaal, Gen. Mgr.

GROWTH PLANS/SPECIAL FEATURES:

Wanxiang Automotive Components, LLC is a contract manufacturer and marketer of automotive systems and components. The firm's products include drivelines, brakes and bearings, as well as related components such as universal joints, constant-velocity joints, automotive bearings and hubs, windshield wipers, various 12-volt applications, industrial bearings and drive shafts, and electric motors for seating. Wanxiang Automotive operates as a wholly-owned subsidiary of Wanxiang America Corporation, which itself is a subsidiary of China-based Wanxiang Group Corporation.

FINANCIAL DATA:

Note: Data for latest year may not have been available at press time.

In U.S. $	2018	2017	2016	2015	2014	2013
Revenue						
R&D Expense						
Operating Income						
Operating Margin %						
SGA Expense						
Net Income						
Operating Cash Flow						
Capital Expenditure						
EBITDA						
Return on Assets %						
Return on Equity %						
Debt to Equity						

CONTACT INFORMATION:

Phone: 847-622-8838 Fax: 847-931-4838
Toll-Free:
Address: 88 Airport Rd., Elgin, IL 60123 United States

STOCK TICKER/OTHER:

Stock Ticker: Subsidiary
Exchange:
Employees:
Fiscal Year Ends:
Parent Company: Wanxiang Group Corporation

SALARIES/BONUSES:

Top Exec. Salary: $ Bonus: $
Second Exec. Salary: $ Bonus: $

OTHER THOUGHTS:

Estimated Female Officers or Directors:
Hot Spot for Advancement for Women/Minorities:

Wanxiang Group Corporation

www.wanxiang.com.cn

NAIC Code: 336300

TYPES OF BUSINESS:

Automotive Parts Manufacturer
Agricultural Engineering
Aquaculture
Restaurant & Hotel Management
Road & Bridge Construction
Power Plant Construction
Leasing & Financial Services
Trade Consulting

BRANDS/DIVISIONS/AFFILIATES:

Wanxiang Innovative Energy Fusion City
Xanxiang Sannong
Zhejiang Ocean Family Co Ltd
Chengde Lolo Co Ltd
Beijing Doneed Seeds Industry Co Ltd

CONTACTS: *Note: Officers with more than one job title may be intentionally listed here more than once.*

Weiding Lu, CEO
Gary E. Wetzel, COO
Pin Ni, Pres., Wanxiang America Corp.

GROWTH PLANS/SPECIAL FEATURES:

Wanxiang Group Corporation is one of China's largest auto parts manufacturers, with strategically-situated factories supplying automotive components throughout the world. Within China, the group's manufacturing facilities hold more than a 60% market share in the relevant industry. Internationally, the firm's overseas subsidiaries and more than 40 factories are located in the U.S., Great Britain, Germany and other countries. Wanxiang Group's automotive parts and accessories include the development, production and selling of drive shafts, brakes, shock absorbers, rolling elements and related components. The company has supporting partnerships with mainstream automotive manufacturers such as General Motors, Volkswagen, Ford and Chrysler. Wanxiang Group has recently invested billions in new energy, innovation and transformation technologies and solutions for the purpose of becoming a clean energy company. Subsidiary Wanxiang Innovative Energy Fusion City is a hub focused on manufacturing new energy automobile components and batteries, as well as battery/electric passenger buses and vehicles. Other subsidiaries include: Wanxiang Sannong, an agricultural industry group that provides services to agriculture, farmer and rural areas; Zhejiang Ocean Family Co. Ltd., which owns and operates ocean fisheries, and is engaged in seafood processing as well as the import/export of seafood products; Chengde Lolo Co Ltd., a provider of healthy, plant-based food and beverages; and Beijing Doneed Seeds Industry Co. Ltd., a high-tech comprehensive seed enterprise, focusing on the research, production, management and service of seeds for the agricultural industry.

FINANCIAL DATA: *Note: Data for latest year may not have been available at press time.*

In U.S. $	2018	2017	2016	2015	2014	2013
Revenue	2,050,000,000	20,000,000,000	19,000,000,000	18,000,000,000	17,500,000,000	16,000,000,000
R&D Expense						
Operating Income						
Operating Margin %						
SGA Expense						
Net Income						
Operating Cash Flow						
Capital Expenditure						
EBITDA						
Return on Assets %						
Return on Equity %						
Debt to Equity						

CONTACT INFORMATION:

Phone: 86-571-8283-2999 Fax: 86-571-8283-3999
Toll-Free:
Address: Wang Xiang Rd., Xiao Shan Dist., Hangzhou, Zhejiang 311215 China

STOCK TICKER/OTHER:

Stock Ticker: Private
Exchange:
Employees: 48,500
Fiscal Year Ends: 03/31
Parent Company:

SALARIES/BONUSES:

Top Exec. Salary: $ Bonus: $
Second Exec. Salary: $ Bonus: $

OTHER THOUGHTS:

Estimated Female Officers or Directors:
Hot Spot for Advancement for Women/Minorities:

Waymo LLC

www.waymo.com

NAIC Code: 511210

TYPES OF BUSINESS:

Technology for Self-Driving Vehicles
Self-Driving Hardware
Self-Driving Software

BRANDS/DIVISIONS/AFFILIATES:

Alphabet Inc
Google
Waymo One

CONTACTS:

Note: Officers with more than one job title may be intentionally listed here more than once.

John Krafcik, CEO

GROWTH PLANS/SPECIAL FEATURES:

Waymo, LLC is an autonomous car development company and subsidiary of Alphabet, Inc., the owner of Google. Waymo was enabled as a separate entity in order to commercialize and distribute the self-driving vehicle technology that Google developed. Waymo has an exceptional amount of experience in this regard, as its test vehicles have completed several million miles on the road, as well as 2.7 billion miles in simulation in 2017 alone. Waymo offers both software and hardware for self-driving vehicles, enabling auto makers and truck makers an opportunity to purchase complete technology platforms. In early-2018, the firm placed separate orders for thousands of hybrid-drive Pacifica minivans and Jaguar I-PACE electric sedans for the purpose of launching a driverless ride-hailing service. How the Waymo One driverless system works: vehicles have sensors and software designed to detect pedestrians, cyclists, vehicles, road work and more from up to three football fields away in all 360 degrees. The sensors and software detect and predict the behavior of all road users within the range. The sensors can even observe when a cyclist has extended his/her arm as a traffic signal. This signals the Waymo vehicle to slow down and make room for the cyclist to pass safely. The Waymo app enables users to locate and hire a self-driving car.

FINANCIAL DATA:

Note: Data for latest year may not have been available at press time.

In U.S. $	2018	2017	2016	2015	2014	2013
Revenue						
R&D Expense						
Operating Income						
Operating Margin %						
SGA Expense						
Net Income						
Operating Cash Flow						
Capital Expenditure						
EBITDA						
Return on Assets %						
Return on Equity %						
Debt to Equity						

CONTACT INFORMATION:

Phone: 650-253-0000 Fax:
Toll-Free:
Address: 1600 Amphitheatre Pkwy., Mountain View, CA 94043 United States

STOCK TICKER/OTHER:

Stock Ticker: Subsidiary
Employees:
Parent Company: Alphabet Inc
Exchange:
Fiscal Year Ends:

SALARIES/BONUSES:

Top Exec. Salary: $ Bonus: $
Second Exec. Salary: $ Bonus: $

OTHER THOUGHTS:

Estimated Female Officers or Directors:
Hot Spot for Advancement for Women/Minorities:

Weichai Power Co Ltd

en.weichai.com/wmdgs/ssgs/wcdlgfyxgs/

NAIC Code: 333618

TYPES OF BUSINESS:

Engines, Diesel and Semidiesel, Manufacturing
Diesel Engines
Vehicle Parts
Heavy Duty Vehicles
Light Duty Vehicles
Components

BRANDS/DIVISIONS/AFFILIATES:

Shandong Heavy Industry Group Co Ltd
Weichai Holding Group Co Ltd

GROWTH PLANS/SPECIAL FEATURES:

Weichai Power Co., Ltd. researches, develops, manufactures and sells diesel engines for light- and heavy-duty vehicles. Based in China, the company also sells related parts and components, and repairs diesel engines. Light- and heavy-duty vehicles include trucks, construction machinery, passenger vehicles, coaches, vessels, power generators, forklift trucks and more. Weichai also provides gear boxes, spark plugs, axles, chassis, air conditioner compressors and hydraulic controlling parts, as well as warehouses technology services, supply chain solutions. Weichai Power operates as a subsidiary of Weichai Holding Group Co., Ltd., which itself is owned by Shandong Heavy Industry Group Co., Ltd.

CONTACTS: *Note: Officers with more than one job title may be intentionally listed here more than once.*

Xuguang Tan, CEO
Kwan Tong Kwong, CFO

FINANCIAL DATA: *Note: Data for latest year may not have been available at press time.*

In U.S. $	2018	2017	2016	2015	2014	2013
Revenue	23,136,220,000	22,019,550,000	13,537,430,000	10,709,810,000	11,569,450,000	8,471,353,000
R&D Expense	627,626,200					
Operating Income	2,644,001,000	1,828,511,000	775,252,300	487,511,400	774,321,000	688,963,100
Operating Margin %		.08%	.06%	.05%	.07%	.08%
SGA Expense	2,452,084,000	2,896,731,000	2,222,202,000	1,949,617,000	1,669,718,000	1,018,259,000
Net Income	1,257,740,000	989,095,800	354,648,600	202,018,900	729,944,800	518,754,000
Operating Cash Flow	3,234,104,000	2,361,962,000	1,198,599,000	984,092,400	1,622,996,000	838,017,600
Capital Expenditure	535,143,000	369,246,200	647,892,000	631,277,700	480,822,800	213,321,900
EBITDA	3,246,358,000	2,787,872,000	1,723,121,000	1,388,842,000	1,681,621,000	1,028,695,000
Return on Assets %		.04%	.02%	.01%	.05%	.05%
Return on Equity %		.20%	.08%	.04%	.17%	.14%
Debt to Equity		0.742	1.039	0.418	0.404	0.456

CONTACT INFORMATION:

Phone: 86 5368197069 Fax: 86 5368197073
Toll-Free:
Address: 197, Fu Shou East St., Sect. A, Weifang, Shandong 261001 China

STOCK TICKER/OTHER:

Stock Ticker: WEICY
Exchange: PINX
Employees: 69,800
Fiscal Year Ends: 12/31
Parent Company: Shandong Heavy Industry Group Co Ltd

SALARIES/BONUSES:

Top Exec. Salary: $ Bonus: $
Second Exec. Salary: $ Bonus: $

OTHER THOUGHTS:

Estimated Female Officers or Directors:
Hot Spot for Advancement for Women/Minorities:

Wescast Industries Inc

www.wescast.com

NAIC Code: 336300

TYPES OF BUSINESS:

Engine Components
Powertrain Components
Exhaust Manifolds
Turbine Housing

BRANDS/DIVISIONS/AFFILIATES:

Sichuan Bohong Industry Co Ltd
United Machining Sterling
Wescast Industries (China) Co Ltd
Wescast Hungary Atoipari Zrt

CONTACTS: *Note: Officers with more than one job title may be intentionally listed here more than once.*

Ed Frackowiak, CEO
David Fowler, VP-Manufacturing, Innovation & Tech.

GROWTH PLANS/SPECIAL FEATURES:

Wescast Industries, Inc., based in Ontario, Canada, is one of the world's largest suppliers of cast exhaust manifolds for passenger cars and light trucks. The firm designs, casts, machines and assembles exhaust system components for automotive original equipment manufacturers (OEMs) worldwide. The production of cast iron exhaust manifolds consists of casting, which is the pouring of molten iron into sand molds, and then machining, which is the finishing of the raw exhaust manifold by milling, drilling, tapping, assembling and testing by highly-automated machines. In this way, the company prepares the exhaust manifold for final assembly on the engine. In addition to exhaust manifolds, the firm produces integrated turbo manifolds, turbine housings, catalytic converter containers, differential cases and wheel hubs. The company operates manufacturing facilities, sales offices and design centers in North America, Asia and Europe. Wescast also maintains several subsidiaries, including wholly-owned subsidiary United Machining Sterling, which operates a flexible machining facility in Michigan. In addition, the firm has a foundry and machining operation located in Wuhan, China. Its Asian operations, which are conducted through Wescast Industries (China) Co. Ltd., provide production and prototype parts for a number of customers within Asia (China, Japan and Malaysia) as well as exporting to other regions in support of global customers (North America, Europe, Africa and South America). The firm's European power-train operations are managed by subsidiary Wescast Hungary Autoipari Zrt. Wescast itself operates as a wholly-owned subsidiary of Sichuan Bohong Industry Co., Ltd.

FINANCIAL DATA: *Note: Data for latest year may not have been available at press time.*

In U.S. $	2018	2017	2016	2015	2014	2013
Revenue	358,312,500	341,250,000	325,000,000	310,000,000	300,000,000	295,000,000
R&D Expense						
Operating Income						
Operating Margin %						
SGA Expense						
Net Income						
Operating Cash Flow						
Capital Expenditure						
EBITDA						
Return on Assets %						
Return on Equity %						
Debt to Equity						

CONTACT INFORMATION:

Phone: 519 750-0000 Fax: 519 720-1629
Toll-Free:
Address: 150 Savannah Oaks Dr., Brantford, ON N3T 5L8 Canada

STOCK TICKER/OTHER:

Stock Ticker: Subsidiary Exchange:
Employees: 2,946 Fiscal Year Ends: 12/31
Parent Company: Sichuan Bohong Industry Co Ltd

SALARIES/BONUSES:

Top Exec. Salary: $ Bonus: $
Second Exec. Salary: $ Bonus: $

OTHER THOUGHTS:

Estimated Female Officers or Directors:
Hot Spot for Advancement for Women/Minorities: Y

Winnebago Industries Inc

www.winnebagoind.com

NAIC Code: 336213

TYPES OF BUSINESS:

Motor Home Manufacturing
Commercial Vehicles
Component Products
Extruded Aluminum

BRANDS/DIVISIONS/AFFILIATES:

Winnebago
Grand Design
Chris-Craft
Adventurer
Benchmark
Cambria
Dynomax
Glide & Dine

CONTACTS: *Note: Officers with more than one job title may be intentionally listed here more than once.*

Michael Happe, CEO
Bryan Hughes, CFO
Robert Chiusano, Chairman of the Board
Jeff Kubacki, Chief Information Officer
Stacy Bogart, General Counsel
Brian Hazelton, General Manager, Divisional
Donald Clark, President, Subsidiary
Christopher West, Vice President, Divisional
Ashis Bhattacharya, Vice President, Divisional
Bret Woodson, Vice President, Divisional
Steven Degnan, Vice President

GROWTH PLANS/SPECIAL FEATURES:

Winnebago Industries, Inc. is a leading U.S. manufacturer of recreational vehicles (RVs) and marine products used primarily in leisure travel and outdoor recreation activities. The firm produces Winnebago's motorhomes in manufacturing facilities in Iowa and Oregon; travel trailers and fifth wheel trailers in Indiana; and marine products in Florida. The company distributes these products through independent dealers throughout the U.S. and Canada, who then retail the products to end customers. Marine products are also distributed through independent dealers outside the U.S. and Canada. The firm operates through five segments: Winnebago motorhomes, Winnebago towables, Grand Design towables, Winnebago specialty vehicles and Chris-Craft marine. Motorhomes are comprised of products that include a motorized chassis as well as other related manufactured products and services, and grouped as either Class A, B or C. Towables are comprised of non-motorized products and generally towed by another vehicle. The towables consist of additional manufactured products and solutions. Winnebago specialty vehicles are custom designed for the buyer's specific needs and requirements, such as law enforcement command centers, mobile medical clinics and mobile office space. This division also provides commercial vehicles as bare shells to third-party up-fitters for conversion at their facilities. Chris-Craft manufactures premium quality boats for the recreational powerboat industry, which are then sold through a global network of independent authorized dealers. Winnebago's RV dealer network in the U.S. and Canada includes approximately 550 motorhome and towable physical dealer locations, many of which carry both products. Other domestic and foreign trademarks of the company include Adventurer, Benchmark, Cambria, Dynomax, Ellipse, Fuse, Glide & Dine, Grand Design and Winnebago.

Winnebago offers its employees medical, life and dental insurance; paid holidays and vacation; and a 401(k).

FINANCIAL DATA: *Note: Data for latest year may not have been available at press time.*

In U.S. $	2018	2017	2016	2015	2014	2013
Revenue	2,016,829,000	1,547,119,000	975,226,000	976,505,000	945,163,000	803,165,000
R&D Expense						
Operating Income	162,569,000	106,902,000	65,741,000	59,881,000	63,280,000	44,426,000
Operating Margin %		.08%	.07%	.06%	.07%	.06%
SGA Expense	127,939,000	91,015,000	46,908,000	44,999,000	40,717,000	40,205,000
Net Income	102,357,000	71,330,000	45,496,000	41,210,000	45,053,000	31,953,000
Operating Cash Flow	83,346,000	97,127,000	52,746,000	45,183,000	23,236,000	10,238,000
Capital Expenditure	28,668,000	13,993,000	24,551,000	16,573,000	10,476,000	4,422,000
EBITDA	180,063,000	157,411,000	71,486,000	64,394,000	70,287,000	51,498,000
Return on Assets %		.11%	.12%	.11%	.14%	.11%
Return on Equity %		.20%	.19%	.20%	.25%	.20%
Debt to Equity		0.615				

CONTACT INFORMATION:

Phone: 641 585-3535 Fax: 641 585-6966
Toll-Free:
Address: 605 W. Crystal Lake Rd., Forest City, IA 50436 United States

STOCK TICKER/OTHER:

Stock Ticker: WGO
Employees: 4,700
Parent Company:
Exchange: NYS
Fiscal Year Ends: 08/25

SALARIES/BONUSES:

Top Exec. Salary: $657,692 Bonus: $
Second Exec. Salary: $472,588 Bonus: $

OTHER THOUGHTS:

Estimated Female Officers or Directors: 1
Hot Spot for Advancement for Women/Minorities:

WM Motor Technology Co Ltd

www.wm-motor.com

NAIC Code: 336111

TYPES OF BUSINESS:

Automobile Manufacturing, All-Electric
Self-Driving Cars

BRANDS/DIVISIONS/AFFILIATES:

Weltmeister
EX5

GROWTH PLANS/SPECIAL FEATURES:

WM Motor Technology Co Ltd WM Motor Technology Co., Ltd. designs, develops and manufactures intelligent electric motor automobiles. Based in Shanghai, China, WM Motor revealed its first car in December 2017 under the Weltmeister brand, the EX5 model, and began taking orders domestically in April 2018. EX5 is a sport utility vehicle (SUV) with an electric range of approximately 323 miles (520 km) and a maximum power of 160kW, torque 315N-m. The SUV features WM's own next-generation lithium ceramic battery, a full car interaction system, hidden door handles, light-emitting diode (LED) headlights, integrated luggage rack and an intelligent interaction system that recognizes authorized users.

CONTACTS: *Note: Officers with more than one job title may be intentionally listed here more than once.*

Freeman Shen, CEO

FINANCIAL DATA: *Note: Data for latest year may not have been available at press time.*

In U.S. $	2018	2017	2016	2015	2014	2013
Revenue						
R&D Expense						
Operating Income						
Operating Margin %						
SGA Expense						
Net Income						
Operating Cash Flow						
Capital Expenditure						
EBITDA						
Return on Assets %						
Return on Equity %						
Debt to Equity						

CONTACT INFORMATION:

Phone: 4006 - 999 - 666 Fax:
Toll-Free:
Address: 333 SongZe Ave., 5/Fl, Twr. C, National Exhibition and Convention Ctr., Shanghai, Shanghai China

STOCK TICKER/OTHER:

Stock Ticker: Private
Employees:
Parent Company:
Exchange:
Fiscal Year Ends:

SALARIES/BONUSES:

Top Exec. Salary: $ Bonus: $
Second Exec. Salary: $ Bonus: $

OTHER THOUGHTS:

Estimated Female Officers or Directors:
Hot Spot for Advancement for Women/Minorities:

Xiaopeng Motors (Xpeng)

www.xiaopeng.com/en/

NAIC Code: 336111

TYPES OF BUSINESS:

Electric Automobile Manufacturing

BRANDS/DIVISIONS/AFFILIATES:

G3
Xpeng Auto Finance

CONTACTS: *Note: Officers with more than one job title may be intentionally listed here more than once.*

He Xiaopeng, CEO
Henry Xia, Co-Pres.
Brain Gu, Co-Pres.
He Tao, VP
He Xiaopeng, Chmn.

GROWTH PLANS/SPECIAL FEATURES:

Xiaopeng Motors (Xpeng), founded in 2014, is a Chinese electric vehicle and technology company that designs and manufactures automobiles that are seamlessly integrated with advanced internet, artificial intelligence (AI) and autonomous driving technologies. More than half of Xpeng's employees work in research and development (R&D)-related areas. In December 2018, Xpeng began delivering its G3 sport utility vehicle (SUV) model to customers, having received more than 1,570 new orders within 24 hours of its launch. G3 is equipped with a concealed smart driving system, light-emitting diode (LED) lighting systems, various intelligent radars, cameras and sensors for autonomous driving, parking and operation purposes. G3 offers both touch control as well as voice control, and can be synced to a smartphone for temperature settings, seat settings and more. Personal driving habits, customized services and individual preferences can be uploaded for cloud backup. A remote intelligent diagnostic system detects vehicle problems and provides free inquiry for vehicle rule violation. Road assistance is offered by Xpeng, as well as maintenance services and replacement services. It takes approximately 30 minutes to charge G3 to 80% capacity, with Xpeng-branded charging systems available throughout China, as well as through 100,000 third-party charging stations in major cities via Xpeng Motors' app. Tailored finance options are provided by Xpeng Auto Finance, including leasing, lending and auto insurance services. There are approximately 100 Xpeng retail sales and service centers in China, but vehicle sales are available online as well. Xpeng is headquartered in Guangzhou, with additional offices in Beijing, Shanghai and California, USA. Investors of the company include Alibaba Group, University Corporation for Atmospheric Research, GGV Capital, Morningside, IDG Capital, Foxconn and more.

FINANCIAL DATA: *Note: Data for latest year may not have been available at press time.*

In U.S. $	2018	2017	2016	2015	2014	2013
Revenue						
R&D Expense						
Operating Income						
Operating Margin %						
SGA Expense						
Net Income						
Operating Cash Flow						
Capital Expenditure						
EBITDA						
Return on Assets %						
Return on Equity %						
Debt to Equity						

CONTACT INFORMATION:

Phone: 86-20-6680-6680 Fax: 86-20-6680-6689
Toll-Free:
Address: No. 8 Songgang Rd., Changxing St., Cencun, Tianhe Distr., Guangdong 510640 China

STOCK TICKER/OTHER:

Stock Ticker: Private
Exchange:
Employees:
Fiscal Year Ends:
Parent Company:

SALARIES/BONUSES:

Top Exec. Salary: $ Bonus: $
Second Exec. Salary: $ Bonus: $

OTHER THOUGHTS:

Estimated Female Officers or Directors:
Hot Spot for Advancement for Women/Minorities:

Yamaha Motor Company Limited

www.yamaha-motor.co.jp

NAIC Code: 336991

TYPES OF BUSINESS:

Motorcycle Manufacturing
Personal Water Vehicles
Snowmobiles
Boats
Golf Carts
Motors
Generators
All-Terrain Vehicles

BRANDS/DIVISIONS/AFFILIATES:

CONTACTS: *Note: Officers with more than one job title may be intentionally listed here more than once.*

Tetsuya Tashiro, Gen. Mgr-Mfg.
Kozo Shinozaki, Sr. Dir.-Corp. Planning
Kozo Shinozaki, Sr. Dir.-Finance
Takaaki Kimura, Sr. Exec. Officer
Hiroyuki Yanagi, Chmn.
Tetsuya Tashiro, Gen. Mgr.-Procurement Center

GROWTH PLANS/SPECIAL FEATURES:

Yamaha Motor Company Limited is a Japanese manufacturer and seller of motorcycles, boats, outboard motors, personal watercraft, snowmobiles, all-terrain vehicles (ATVs), golf carts, water pumps, automotive engines, intelligent machinery, industrial-use unmanned helicopters and electrical power units for wheelchairs. The company operates in four segments: motorcycles, marine products, power products and other products. The motorcycles segment manufactures and sells motorcycles and parts for overseas production. The marine products segment manufactures and sells outboard motors, personal watercraft, recreational-use boats, fiberglass-reinforced plastic pools, fishing boats, utility boats and diesel engines as well as related products. The power products segment offers ATVs, side-by-side vehicles, snowmobiles, generators, golf carts, multipurpose engines and snow throwers. The other products segment provides automobile engines, surface mounters, industrial robots, electro-hybrid bicycles, industrial-use unmanned helicopters, electrically powered wheelchairs and intermediate parts for all business segments. Additionally, the company imports and sells various types of products used in the development of tourist businesses and the management of leisure and recreational facilities. As of June 2019, the firm comprised 131 consolidated subsidiaries, four non-consolidated subsidiaries and 31 affiliates, all of which operate worldwide. Asia represents 43.8% of 2018 annual sales revenue; North America, 21.9%; Europe, 13%; Japan, 10%; and others, 11.3%.

U.S. employee benefits include 401(k); medical, dental, vision, life and AD&D insurance; flexible spending accounts; paid vacation and holidays; and an employee assistance program.

FINANCIAL DATA: *Note: Data for latest year may not have been available at press time.*

In U.S. $	2018	2017	2016	2015	2014	2013
Revenue	15,375,270,000	15,347,270,000	13,810,270,000	14,844,240,000	13,979,110,000	12,961,510,000
R&D Expense						
Operating Income	1,293,760,000	1,376,420,000	997,932,400	1,106,745,000	801,773,600	506,680,800
Operating Margin %		.09%	.07%	.07%	.06%	.04%
SGA Expense						
Net Income	857,985,700	933,679,500	580,343,700	551,580,600	629,038,800	404,861,300
Operating Cash Flow	540,874,900	1,161,018,000	1,315,595,000	220,437,400	860,301,400	615,475,100
Capital Expenditure	496,094,500	591,361,900	463,563,700	620,327,200	568,415,700	491,150,500
EBITDA	1,715,236,000	1,852,784,000	1,349,090,000	1,598,493,000	1,318,765,000	926,300,400
Return on Assets %		.07%	.05%	.05%	.06%	.04%
Return on Equity %		.18%	.12%	.13%	.16%	.13%
Debt to Equity		0.261	0.341	0.306	0.392	0.363

CONTACT INFORMATION:

Phone: 81 538321103 Fax: 81 538374252
Toll-Free:
Address: 2500 Shingai, Iwata-shi, Iwata-shi, 438-8501 Japan

STOCK TICKER/OTHER:

Stock Ticker: YAMHF
Exchange: PINX
Employees: 67,071
Fiscal Year Ends: 12/31
Parent Company:

SALARIES/BONUSES:

Top Exec. Salary: $ Bonus: $
Second Exec. Salary: $ Bonus: $

OTHER THOUGHTS:

Estimated Female Officers or Directors:
Hot Spot for Advancement for Women/Minorities:

YAZAKI Corporation

NAIC Code: 336320

www.yazaki-group.com

TYPES OF BUSINESS:

Motor Vehicle Electrical and Electronic Equipment Manufacturing

BRANDS/DIVISIONS/AFFILIATES:

Yazaki Parts Co Ltd
Yazaki Meter Co Ltd
Yazaki Energy System Corporation
Yazaki (China) Investment Corporation
Yazaki Brasil Minas Gerais Sistemas Eletoricos Ltd
Yazaki North America Inc
Yazaki Uruguay SA
Yazaki Europe Ltd

CONTACTS: *Note: Officers with more than one job title may be intentionally listed here more than once.*

Shinji Yazaki, Pres.

GROWTH PLANS/SPECIAL FEATURES:

YAZAKI Corporation is an independent automotive component manufacturer headquartered in Tokyo, Japan. Founded in 1941, the firm's core product is automotive wire harnesses. An automotive wire harness is the computerized nervous system of an automobile, consisting of tightly bound information circuits. In addition to its core product, YAZAKI also manufactures automotive meters, such as speedometer and tachometer displays; electrical wires for building and residential use; in-vehicle safety & service systems, such as tachographs, taximeters and telematics services; charging connectors, a quick charging method for battery electric vehicles; air conditioning equipment; gas equipment, such as gas meters, residential fire alarms and gas alarms; and solar equipment, such as solar water heaters and commercial solar power systems. Japanese subsidiaries include Yazaki Parts Co. Ltd., Yazaki Meter Co. Ltd. and Yazaki Energy System Corporation. Among YAZAKI Corporation's numerous international subsidiaries include: Yazaki (China) Investment Corporation; Yazaki Brasil Minas Gerais Sistemas Eletoricos Ltda.; Yazaki North America, Inc.; Yazaki Uruguay SA; Yazaki Europe Ltd.; Yazaki Europe Ltd.; and Yazaki Automotive Products Tunisia Sarl. YAZAKI has operations in more than 45 countries, including Europe, Africa, the Americas, Asia and Oceania. Japan represented 34.5% of 2018 net sales, the Americas 30.5%, Asia and Oceania 17.8% and Europe 17.2%.

FINANCIAL DATA: *Note: Data for latest year may not have been available at press time.*

In U.S. $	2018	2017	2016	2015	2014	2013
Revenue	18,435,012,750	17,557,155,000	16,721,100,000	14,179,100,000	16,011,100,000	15,687,100,000
R&D Expense						
Operating Income						
Operating Margin %						
SGA Expense						
Net Income						
Operating Cash Flow						
Capital Expenditure						
EBITDA						
Return on Assets %						
Return on Equity %						
Debt to Equity						

CONTACT INFORMATION:

Phone: 81 33 455 8811 Fax: 81 33 455 8808
Toll-Free:
Address: 17/Fl, Mita-Kokusai Bldg., 4-28 Mita 1-chome, Minato-Ku, Tokyo, 108-8333 Japan

STOCK TICKER/OTHER:

Stock Ticker: Private
Employees: 27,900
Parent Company:
Exchange:
Fiscal Year Ends: 06/30

SALARIES/BONUSES:

Top Exec. Salary: $ Bonus: $
Second Exec. Salary: $ Bonus: $

OTHER THOUGHTS:

Estimated Female Officers or Directors:
Hot Spot for Advancement for Women/Minorities:

Yazaki North America Inc

www.yazaki-na.com

NAIC Code: 336300

TYPES OF BUSINESS:

Vehicle Power & Data Networks
Wire Products
Electric Motor Products

BRANDS/DIVISIONS/AFFILIATES:

Yazaki Corporation
Yazaki Energy Systems Inc
Y-Connect
YTC America Inc

CONTACTS: *Note: Officers with more than one job title may be intentionally listed here more than once.*

Bo Andersson, CEO
Jim Romine, Exec. VP-Eng.
Lois Bingham, General Counsel
Ernesto Gonzalez-Beltran, Exec. VP-Mfg. Oper.
Barbara Long, VP-New Bus. Dev.
Don Winn, VP-Finance
Colleen Haley, Exec. VP-U.S. OEM Bus. Unit
Toshihiro Inoue, Exec. VP-Advisor Mfg. Oper.
Rich Tajer, Exec. VP-Component Bus. Unit
Mariano Mar, VP-Quality
Takashige Miyashita, Exec. VP-Trans Pacific Oper.
Olga Alavanou, Exec. VP-Supply Chain Management

GROWTH PLANS/SPECIAL FEATURES:

Yazaki North America, Inc. is a manufacturer of vehicle power, data networks and electronic technologies for the automotive industry. The firm is a subsidiary of Yazaki Corporation and produces high-voltage hybrid and electric vehicle solutions such as connectors, sensors, power distribution components, power control systems, charge couplers, battery interconnectors and wire harnesses. Yazaki's innovative driver information products include instrument clusters, head-up displays and safety warning devices. These systems and components seamlessly integrate into the vehicle's networks to provide driver information flow while also reducing driver distraction. North American subsidiaries include: Yazaki Energy Systems, Inc., which manufactures and supplies non-chloroflurocarbon-based space cooling and heating systems; Y-Connect, which manufactures connectivity solutions; and YTC America, Inc., which manufactures and supplies next-generation vehicle information communication technology. Yazaki North America has operations throughout the U.S., as well as select locations in Canada and Mexico.

The company offers employees life, medical and dental insurance; flexible spending accounts; an employee assistance program; a 401(k) savings and retirement plan; and disability coverage.

FINANCIAL DATA: *Note: Data for latest year may not have been available at press time.*

In U.S. $	2018	2017	2016	2015	2014	2013
Revenue	5,300,000,000	5,127,368,720	4,883,208,305	4,249,711,116	3,737,558,982	3,300,000,000
R&D Expense						
Operating Income						
Operating Margin %						
SGA Expense						
Net Income						
Operating Cash Flow						
Capital Expenditure						
EBITDA						
Return on Assets %						
Return on Equity %						
Debt to Equity						

CONTACT INFORMATION:

Phone: 734-983-1000 Fax: 734-983-1105
Toll-Free:
Address: 6801 Haggerty Rd., Canton, MI 48187 United States

STOCK TICKER/OTHER:

Stock Ticker: Subsidiary
Employees: 1,751
Parent Company: YAZAKI Corporation
Exchange:
Fiscal Year Ends: 12/31

SALARIES/BONUSES:

Top Exec. Salary: $ Bonus: $
Second Exec. Salary: $ Bonus: $

OTHER THOUGHTS:

Estimated Female Officers or Directors: 5
Hot Spot for Advancement for Women/Minorities: Y

YHI International Limited

NAIC Code: 423120

www.yhigroup.com/

TYPES OF BUSINESS:

Automobile Products Distribution
Alloy Tire Manufacturing
Industrial Products Distribution

BRANDS/DIVISIONS/AFFILIATES:

YHI Singapre Pte Ltd
YHI Malaysia Sdn Bhd
PT YHI Indonesia
YHI Hong Kong Co Ltd
Advanti Wheels
YHI Australia Limited
YHI Canada Inc
YHI Power New Zealand Ltd

CONTACTS: *Note: Officers with more than one job title may be intentionally listed here more than once.*

Tay Tian Hoe, Managing Dir.
Alex Ong Chin Kiong, COO
Gary Su Thiam Huat, CFO
Amy Soo Wee Hsien, Gen. Mgr.-Human Resources
Amy Soo, Gen. Mgr.-Admin.
Tay Tiang Guan, Exec. Dir.
Alex Ong, General Mgr.-Industrial Prod. Div.
Steve Liew, General Mgr.-Tires Div.
Robert Tan, Gen. Mgr.-ASEAN Mgmt.
Tay Tian Hoe, Chmn.
Joseph Schaefer, Pres., Pan-Mar Corp.

GROWTH PLANS/SPECIAL FEATURES:

YHI International Ltd., based in Singapore, is a global distributor of automotive and industrial products and an original design manufacturer (ODM) of alloy wheels. The company's distribution division distributes a range of high-quality automotive and industrial products worldwide with the aim of building YHI into a global brand name. Currently, its presence primarily exists in the Asia Pacific region, North America and Europe, representing brands such as Yokohama, Nitto, Nankang, Nexen, Pirelli, Achilles and YHI's proprietary brand, Neuton Tyres. Overall, YHI is present in more than 100 countries, operating through more than 30 entities. The ODM division is comprised of four alloy wheels manufacturing plants located in China, Taiwan and Malaysia with a combined capacity of producing appoximately 2.6 million alloy wheels per year. As an ODM, YHI provides integrated services from the design and development to the manufacturing, marketing and distribution of alloy wheels. Alloy wheel brands include Enkei, OZ, Konig and Breyton, as well as its proprietary Advanti Racing brand. Company subsidiaries include YHI Singapore Pte. Ltd.; YHI Malaysia Sdn. Bhd.; YHI East Malaysia Sdn. Bhd.; PT. YHI Indonesia; YHI Hong Kong Co. Ltd.; YHI Taiwan Limited; Advanti Wheels; YHI Australia Limited; YHI Canada, Inc.; YHI Power Australia Pty. Ltd.; YHI New Zealand Ltd.; and YHI Power New Zealand Ltd.

FINANCIAL DATA: *Note: Data for latest year may not have been available at press time.*

In U.S. $	2018	2017	2016	2015	2014	2013
Revenue		345,000,000	353,030,080	378,512,000	387,652,992	385,904,416
R&D Expense						
Operating Income						
Operating Margin %						
SGA Expense						
Net Income			2,801,074	6,255,782	5,328,410	6,690,275
Operating Cash Flow						
Capital Expenditure						
EBITDA						
Return on Assets %						
Return on Equity %						
Debt to Equity						

CONTACT INFORMATION:

Phone: 65 6264-2155 Fax: 65 6265-9927
Toll-Free:
Address: 2 Pandan Rd., Singapore, 609254 Singapore

STOCK TICKER/OTHER:

Stock Ticker: YHIIF
Employees:
Parent Company:
Exchange: GREY
Fiscal Year Ends: 12/31

SALARIES/BONUSES:

Top Exec. Salary: $ Bonus: $
Second Exec. Salary: $ Bonus: $

OTHER THOUGHTS:

Estimated Female Officers or Directors: 1
Hot Spot for Advancement for Women/Minorities:

Yuasa Battery (Thailand) Public Company Limited

www.yuasathai.com

NAIC Code: 335910

TYPES OF BUSINESS:

Automotive Battery Manufacturing
Industrial Battery Manufacturing
Battery Sales & Distribution

BRANDS/DIVISIONS/AFFILIATES:

GS Yuasa International Ltd
Yuasa Sales and Distribution Co Ltd
Yuasa
Yucon
Thunderlite

CONTACTS: *Note: Officers with more than one job title may be intentionally listed here more than once.*

Ichiro Murata, CEO
Sukthae Ruangwattanachot, COO
Phatcharee Apirak, Dir-Finance
Sukthae Ruengwattanachot, Sec.
Pataraporn Tasanasewee, Mgr.-Finance & Acct.
Ichiro Murata, Acting Chmn.

GROWTH PLANS/SPECIAL FEATURES:

Yuasa Battery (Thailand) Public Company Limited manufactures and imports batteries, primarily for automobiles and industrial applications. The firm was initially owned by Japanese firm Yuasa Corporation, which subsequently merged with Japan Storage Battery Co., Ltd. to form GS Yuasa International Ltd. (GYIN). GYIN is currently the largest shareholder of Yuasa, owning a 40.69% interest. Yuasa's batteries are sold under the Yuasa, Yucon and Thunderlite brand names. The company pays GYIN a royalty fee for all its batteries regardless of the brand, based on either the number of batteries sold or the number manufactured, depending on the type of battery. In general, Yuasa produces car batteries, motorcycle batteries and industrial power supply batteries. Although all of the automobile batteries utilize a lead-acid design, the company does offer a range of nickel-cadmium industrial batteries often used in marine or rail vehicles or for emergency power supplies, as well as some solar powered industrial batteries. The firm has two factories located in the Samut Prakan and Cha Cheang Sao provinces. Subsidiary Yuasa Sales and Distribution Co., Ltd. markets Yuasa's batteries.

FINANCIAL DATA: *Note: Data for latest year may not have been available at press time.*

In U.S. $	2018	2017	2016	2015	2014	2013
Revenue	73,693,900	71,262,600	58,029,000	48,577,300	46,822,426	49,115,046
R&D Expense						
Operating Income						
Operating Margin %						
SGA Expense						
Net Income	3,922,120	3,412,920	3,169,200	1,216,900	-208,217	428,699
Operating Cash Flow						
Capital Expenditure						
EBITDA						
Return on Assets %						
Return on Equity %						
Debt to Equity						

CONTACT INFORMATION:

Phone: 66-2769-7300 Fax: 66-2769-7349
Toll-Free:
Address: 164 Moo 5, Soi 55 Sukhumvit Rd., Prakam, 10280 Thailand

STOCK TICKER/OTHER:

Stock Ticker: YUASA Exchange: Bangkok
Employees: 638 Fiscal Year Ends: 12/31
Parent Company: GS Yuasa International Ltd

SALARIES/BONUSES:

Top Exec. Salary: $ Bonus: $
Second Exec. Salary: $ Bonus: $

OTHER THOUGHTS:

Estimated Female Officers or Directors: 3
Hot Spot for Advancement for Women/Minorities: Y

Yulon Motor Co Ltd

NAIC Code: 336111

www.yulon-motor.com.tw

TYPES OF BUSINESS:

Automobile Manufacturing
Automotive Components & Accessories

BRANDS/DIVISIONS/AFFILIATES:

Yulon Group

GROWTH PLANS/SPECIAL FEATURES:

Yulon Motor Co., Ltd., established in 1953 and operated by Yulon Group, is one of Taiwan's largest automobile manufacturers, with an annual production capacity of 445,000 units. The company makes vehicles, automotive components, automobile accessories and peripherals for multiple market brands. Yulon Motor's smart manufacturing assembly lines encompass applications with cyber-physical systems and Internet of Things (IoT), and offer flexible customization for select production models, hybrid and sequential assembly, synchronized serial production and welding production lines. The firm's facilities also encompass molding equipment and fixture equipment, and provide aftermarket service parts, distribution and logistics services. Yulon Motor's current hybrid production line produces at least 10 models of automobiles. The company continually upgrades product and service differentiation via innovative business process to meet both brand and consumer demand.

CONTACTS: *Note: Officers with more than one job title may be intentionally listed here more than once.*

Chen-Hsiang Yao, Pres.
Chen Li-Lien, Chmn.

FINANCIAL DATA: *Note: Data for latest year may not have been available at press time.*

In U.S. $	2018	2017	2016	2015	2014	2013
Revenue	2,649,000,000	3,104,790,000	3,864,139,000	4,040,905,962	3,977,586,453	3,109,700,000
R&D Expense						
Operating Income						
Operating Margin %						
SGA Expense						
Net Income	125,633,000	101,559,000	43,861,951	110,479,351	72,883,393	79,100,000
Operating Cash Flow						
Capital Expenditure						
EBITDA						
Return on Assets %						
Return on Equity %						
Debt to Equity						

CONTACT INFORMATION:

Phone: 886-37-871801 Fax: 886-37-874790
Toll-Free:
Address: 39-1 Pau-Kon Keun, Xihu, Sanyi, Taiwan

STOCK TICKER/OTHER:

Stock Ticker: 2201
Employees: 12,402
Parent Company: Yulon Group
Exchange: Taipei
Fiscal Year Ends: 12/31

SALARIES/BONUSES:

Top Exec. Salary: $ Bonus: $
Second Exec. Salary: $ Bonus: $

OTHER THOUGHTS:

Estimated Female Officers or Directors: 1
Hot Spot for Advancement for Women/Minorities:

ZF Friedrichshafen AG (ZF)

www.zf.com

NAIC Code: 336350

TYPES OF BUSINESS:

Automotive Components
Transmissions & Power Trains
Axles
Steering Systems
Chassis Components
Repair Services
Agricultural & Construction Machinery
Boat & Helicopter Transmissions

BRANDS/DIVISIONS/AFFILIATES:

Zeppelin Foundation
Friction Material Group North America Inc
ASAP Holding GmbH

CONTACTS: *Note: Officers with more than one job title may be intentionally listed here more than once.*

Wolf-Henning Scheider, CEO
Stefan Sommer, Dir.-Corp. Dev
Stefan Sommer, Dir.-Corp. Comm.
Konstantin Sauer, Exec. VP-Finance & Controlling
Wilhelm Rehm, Exec. VP-Industrial Tech.
Gerhard Wagner, Exec. VP-Powertrain Tech. Div.
Reinhard Buhl, Exec. VP-Car Chassis Tech. Div.
Rolf Lutz, Exec. VP-Commercial Vehicles, South America
Peter Ottenbruch, Exec. VP-Tech., Asia Pacific

GROWTH PLANS/SPECIAL FEATURES:

ZF Friedrichshafen AG designs and manufactures transmissions, steering systems, chassis components and axle systems and modules. Zeppelin Foundation, which is administered by the city of Friedrichsafen, holds a majority interest in the firm. ZF's business units mostly operate as jointly- or wholly-owned subsidiaries. The company operates through eight divisions: car powertrain technology, car chassis technology, commercial vehicle technology, industrial technology, e-mobility, aftermarket, electronics and active & passive safety technology. Car powertrain technology includes automatic, manual and dual clutch transmissions, axle drives, powertrain modules, electric drive technology and die casting technology. Car chassis technology includes chassis systems and components and suspension technology. Commercial vehicle (CV) technology includes truck and van driveline technology, axle and transmission systems for buses and coaches, CV chassis modules, damper technology and powertrain modules. Industrial technology includes off-highway systems, test systems, special driveline technology, marine propulsion systems, aviation technology and wind power technology. The e-mobility segment includes electronic systems, system house and electric traction drive systems. The aftermarket segment includes original equipment services, specific original equipment, manufacturing services and Friction Material Group North America, Inc., which specializes in automotive brakes. The electronics division includes advanced driver assistance systems (ADAS) and related safety electronics. Last, the active & passive safety technology division includes systems for braking, steering, occupant safety and body control, as well as electronics and parts and services. ZF's global presence spans 230 locations in approximately 40 countries. In April 2018, ZF announced it was building a new production facility in Pancevo, Serbia to produce electric and hybrid drives. Production was scheduled for early-2019. That October, ZF acquired a 35% stake in ASAP Holding GmbH, which offers engineering services with a focus on e-mobility, autonomous driving and connected cars. In March 2019, the firm agreed to be acquired by Wabco Holdings, Inc. for approximately $7 billion.

FINANCIAL DATA: *Note: Data for latest year may not have been available at press time.*

In U.S. $	2018	2017	2016	2015	2014	2013
Revenue	42,236,100,000	43,654,900,000	37,230,900,000	32,785,130,700	20,538,000,000	22,108,636,677
R&D Expense						
Operating Income						
Operating Margin %						
SGA Expense						
Net Income	1,103,760,000	1,397,910,000	978,257,000	1,145,916,450	749,412,000	606,598,851
Operating Cash Flow						
Capital Expenditure						
EBITDA						
Return on Assets %						
Return on Equity %						
Debt to Equity						

CONTACT INFORMATION:

Phone: 49-7541-77-0 Fax: 49-7541-77-908000
Toll-Free:
Address: Lowentaler Strasse 20, Friedrichshafen, 88046 Germany

STOCK TICKER/OTHER:

Stock Ticker: Private
Employees: 148,969
Parent Company: Zeppelin Foundation
Exchange:
Fiscal Year Ends: 12/31

SALARIES/BONUSES:

Top Exec. Salary: $ Bonus: $
Second Exec. Salary: $ Bonus: $

OTHER THOUGHTS:

Estimated Female Officers or Directors:
Hot Spot for Advancement for Women/Minorities:

Zhengzhou Yutong Bus Co Ltd

en.yutong.com

NAIC Code: 336120

TYPES OF BUSINESS:

Heavy Duty Truck Manufacturing
Buses

BRANDS/DIVISIONS/AFFILIATES:

GROWTH PLANS/SPECIAL FEATURES:

Zhengzhou Yutong Bus Co., Ltd. is a China-based company engaged in the research, development, manufacture and sale of passenger bus products. Yutong Bus has four manufacturing bases. Its primary plant is located in the Zhengzhou Yutong Industrial Park, covering an area of 3.67 million square feet (1.12m sm). Yutong Bus recently built an energy vehicle plant located in the Eastern International Logistics Park of Zhengzhou, and covers more than 4.36 million square feet (1.33m sm), with an expected annual output of 30,000 units. During 2018, Yutong Bus delivered 63,526 units of buses and construction machinery. The company's model lineup consists of over 140 series, covering various segment markets, including intercity, long-haul coaches, school buses, airport airfield buses and specialty vehicles. Yutong Bus sells to more than 30 countries and regions, including France, the U.K., Australia, Cuba, Venezuela, Russia and Saudi Arabia, with a 30% market share in China and over 15% outside of China. In August 2019, Yutong Bus delivered more than 30 pure electric buses to Helsinki, Finland; this is the first time the company had entered the Finnish market.

CONTACTS: *Note: Officers with more than one job title may be intentionally listed here more than once.*

Xueqing Lu, CFO
Yuxiang Tang, Chmn.

FINANCIAL DATA: *Note: Data for latest year may not have been available at press time.*

In U.S. $	2018	2017	2016	2015	2014	2013
Revenue	4,615,440,000	5,100,980,000	5,158,820,000	4,808,370,000	4,181,030,000	3,613,530,000
R&D Expense						
Operating Income						
Operating Margin %						
SGA Expense						
Net Income	338,517,000	486,283,000	590,278,000	552,631,000	426,586,000	297,843,000
Operating Cash Flow						
Capital Expenditure						
EBITDA						
Return on Assets %						
Return on Equity %						
Debt to Equity						

CONTACT INFORMATION:

Phone: 86-371-66718999 Fax:
Toll-Free:
Address: Yutong Industrial Park, Yutong Rd., Zhengzhou, Henan 450061 China

STOCK TICKER/OTHER:

Stock Ticker: 600066
Employees: 19,527
Parent Company:
Exchange: Shanghai
Fiscal Year Ends:

SALARIES/BONUSES:

Top Exec. Salary: $ Bonus: $
Second Exec. Salary: $ Bonus: $

OTHER THOUGHTS:

Estimated Female Officers or Directors:
Hot Spot for Advancement for Women/Minorities:

Zhongsheng Group Holdings Limited

www.zs-group.com.cn

NAIC Code: 423110

TYPES OF BUSINESS:

Automobile and Other Motor Vehicle Merchant Wholesalers

BRANDS/DIVISIONS/AFFILIATES:

GROWTH PLANS/SPECIAL FEATURES:

Zhongsheng Group Holdings Limited is an automobile dealership group in China. The firm owns a comprehensive dealership network throughout China, covering affluent cities and regions. Zhongsheng Group focuses on luxury and mid- to high-end automobile brands, namely luxury brands such as Mercedes-Benz, Lexus, Porsche, Land Rover and Audi, and mid- to high-end brands such as Toyota, Nissan, Volkswagen and Chrysler. Its dealership network operates primarily on the Chinese coast, but also has operations in Sichuan, Yunnan and Shannxi provinces. In addition to new automobile sales at its dealerships, the group's aftersales businesses offer spare parts, automobile accessories, repair and maintenance services, detailing services and other automobile-related products and services.

CONTACTS: *Note: Officers with more than one job title may be intentionally listed here more than once.*

Li Guoqiang, CEO
Mak Sze Man, Joint Sec.
Zhang Zhicheng, VP-Luxury Brand Automobile
Kam Mei Ha, Joint Sec.
Du Qingshan, Deputy Exec. Mgr.
Yu Guangming, Deputy Exec. Mgr.
Huang Yi, Chmn.

FINANCIAL DATA: *Note: Data for latest year may not have been available at press time.*

In U.S. $	2018	2017	2016	2015	2014	2013
Revenue	15,651,520,000	12,536,000,000	10,401,720,000	8,592,062,000	7,959,243,000	7,631,022,000
R&D Expense						
Operating Income	927,459,600	860,210,200	568,252,600	286,939,600	334,858,400	347,254,100
Operating Margin %		.07%	.05%	.03%	.04%	.04%
SGA Expense	879,787,100	674,284,700	579,000,800	546,736,900	487,396,500	444,498,700
Net Income	528,319,700	486,738,100	270,248,400	66,967,480	109,089,300	146,739,500
Operating Cash Flow	336,746,800	760,452,800	655,583,100	675,780,400	134,603,200	262,457,800
Capital Expenditure	372,011,400	338,050,700	225,686,600	261,224,800	310,868,700	327,368,100
EBITDA	1,105,003,000	1,000,026,000	698,178,900	410,023,200	445,441,200	446,678,400
Return on Assets %		.08%	.05%	.01%	.02%	.03%
Return on Equity %		.24%	.16%	.04%	.08%	.13%
Debt to Equity		0.157	0.155	0.397	0.255	0.066

CONTACT INFORMATION:

Phone: 86 41139798800 Fax: 86 1057580111
Toll-Free:
Address: No.1 Dongzhimen South St., Raffles City Beijing Office Tower, 7/Fl, Beijing, 100007 China

STOCK TICKER/OTHER:

Stock Ticker: ZSHGY
Employees: 26,969
Parent Company:
Exchange: PINX
Fiscal Year Ends: 12/31

SALARIES/BONUSES:

Top Exec. Salary: $ Bonus: $
Second Exec. Salary: $ Bonus: $

OTHER THOUGHTS:

Estimated Female Officers or Directors: 2
Hot Spot for Advancement for Women/Minorities:

Ziebart International Corporation

www.ziebart.com

NAIC Code: 811100

TYPES OF BUSINESS:

Automotive Repair & Maintenance
Aftermarket Accessories Installation
Detailing
Paint & Fabric Protection
Window Tinting
Rust Protection

BRANDS/DIVISIONS/AFFILIATES:

Aquapel
Renu-A-Shine
Z-Shield
Diamond Gloss
Z-Liner
ZeeGuard
Shatter Bloc
Inner Guard

CONTACTS: *Note: Officers with more than one job title may be intentionally listed here more than once.*

Thomas E. Wolfe, CEO
Sue Spriet, VP-Admin.
William R. Patterson, Treas.
Bruce Weir, VP-Intl. Oper.

GROWTH PLANS/SPECIAL FEATURES:

Ziebart International Corporation is a leading global provider of automotive appearance and protection services, with a network of over 1,000 franchise locations in 34 countries. The company's services include interior and exterior detailing; paint and fabric protection; vehicle restoration, including paint restoration, polishing, scratch removal and windshield repair; interior protection; leather conditioning; window tinting; rust protection; and installation of electronic systems, sunroofs and alarm systems. Ziebart also specializes in truck accessories, such as bed liners, trailer hitches, toolboxes and bedrails as well as scratch and scuff paint repair for bed liners. The firm's detailing products include Aquapel, Renu-A-Shine and Inner-Clean. Other brand names include Z-Shield, Protect-A-Shine, Diamond Gloss, Z-Liner, Ziebart TidyCar, Ziebart Shield, ZeeGaurd, Formula Z, Express Shine, Preserv-A-Shine, Shatter Bloc, Artech, Gold Shield, Ziebart Anti-Bacterial Process and Inner Guard. In addition, the company provides spray-on truck bed liners, glass repair and replacement and remote starter installation. Ziebart maintains strategic business partnerships with groups such as Speedy Auto Glass and Rhino Linings. Moreover, Ziebart offers management, marketing, construction design, location scouting and layout of a new store; business development; grand opening support; monthly publications; ongoing support for franchise owners; marketing meetings; and technical, sales and marketing training for its franchisees.

FINANCIAL DATA: *Note: Data for latest year may not have been available at press time.*

In U.S. $	2018	2017	2016	2015	2014	2013
Revenue	167,580,000	159,600,000	152,000,000	150,000,000	155,400,000	140,000,000
R&D Expense						
Operating Income						
Operating Margin %						
SGA Expense						
Net Income						
Operating Cash Flow						
Capital Expenditure						
EBITDA						
Return on Assets %						
Return on Equity %						
Debt to Equity						

CONTACT INFORMATION:

Phone: 248-588-4100 Fax: 248-588-1444
Toll-Free: 800-877-1312
Address: 1290 E. Maple Rd., Troy, MI 48083 United States

STOCK TICKER/OTHER:

Stock Ticker: Private
Exchange:
Employees: 200
Fiscal Year Ends: 06/30
Parent Company:

SALARIES/BONUSES:

Top Exec. Salary: $ Bonus: $
Second Exec. Salary: $ Bonus: $

OTHER THOUGHTS:

Estimated Female Officers or Directors: 1
Hot Spot for Advancement for Women/Minorities:

Zipcar Inc

www.zipcar.com

NAIC Code: 532111

TYPES OF BUSINESS:

Car Sharing Service
Car Rental
Fleet Management Software

BRANDS/DIVISIONS/AFFILIATES:

Avis Budget Group Inc
Zipcards

CONTACTS: *Note: Officers with more than one job title may be intentionally listed here more than once.*

Tracey Zhen, Pres.
Nicole Mozeliak, VP-Operations & Revenue Mgmt.
Sherrill Kaplan, VP-Mktg.
Maura Haley, Human Resources
Scott Rudberg, VP-IT
Dean Breda, General Counsel
Gretchen Effgen, VP-Strategy & Corp. Dev.

GROWTH PLANS/SPECIAL FEATURES:

Zipcar, Inc., a subsidiary of Avis Budget Group, Inc., provides membership-based car-sharing services for users in a growing number of urban areas across the U.S., Canada and Europe. Originating in Boston in 1999, Zipcar has since established a presence in urban areas such as New York, Philadelphia, San Francisco, Chicago, Portland and Seattle. Internationally, the company has operations in Belgium, Canada, Costa Rica, France, Iceland, Spain, Taiwan, Turkey and the U.K. Zipcar members reserve vehicles ahead of time, then pay an hourly, monthly or annual fee for the use of the vehicle. The rental price includes all gas and insurance costs. Driving rates vary by city and car model. The program is marketed to drivers who normally use public transportation but occasionally want access to a car and to those who need a car as a primary mode of transportation but wish to avoid the costs associated with car ownership. To create an account, users need to create a Zipcar log-in, enter their driver's license number as well as credit or debit card information. Members use Zipcards, which operate on radio frequency identification (RFID) technology, to unlock cars, while global positioning system (GPS) technology combined with smartphone software allows members to locate cars nearby and make reservations from their mobile phones. Zipcar has a work week access program, giving unlimited and exclusive access to a car from 5 a.m. Monday to 7 p.m. Friday for a monthly fee, dependent upon the city, and a few cents per mile in the U.S. Also, in partnership with the Maryland Department of Transportation Transit Administration, Zipcar has car-sharing vehicles at select transit stations throughout the state, providing on-demand access to transit riders.

FINANCIAL DATA: *Note: Data for latest year may not have been available at press time.*

In U.S. $	2018	2017	2016	2015	2014	2013
Revenue	400,000,000	385,000,000	380,000,000	378,000,000	363,000,000	296,000,000
R&D Expense						
Operating Income						
Operating Margin %						
SGA Expense						
Net Income						
Operating Cash Flow						
Capital Expenditure						
EBITDA						
Return on Assets %						
Return on Equity %						
Debt to Equity						

CONTACT INFORMATION:

Phone: 617 995-4231 Fax: 617 995-4300
Toll-Free: 866-494-7227
Address: 35 Thomson Pl., Boston, MA 02210 United States

STOCK TICKER/OTHER:

Stock Ticker: Subsidiary
Exchange:
Employees: 855
Fiscal Year Ends: 12/31
Parent Company: Avis Budget Group Inc

SALARIES/BONUSES:

Top Exec. Salary: $ Bonus: $
Second Exec. Salary: $ Bonus: $

OTHER THOUGHTS:

Estimated Female Officers or Directors: 2
Hot Spot for Advancement for Women/Minorities: Y

Zoox Inc

zoox.com

NAIC Code: 336111

TYPES OF BUSINESS:

Autonomous Automobile Technologies
Self-Driving Taxis
Software for Autonomous Vehicles

BRANDS/DIVISIONS/AFFILIATES:

GROWTH PLANS/SPECIAL FEATURES:

Zoox, Inc. is engaged in developing autonomous mobility. The firm is applying its technology to the automotive, robotics and renewable energy segments by designing a symmetrical, bi-directional, zero-emissions vehicle from the ground up to solve the unique challenges of autonomous mobility. Zoox tests its software and sensors on conventional vehicles with safety drivers. The company's plans are to operate a series of fully autonomous battery electric vehicles optimized for ride-sharing cities, creating a next-generation mobility society of riders as opposed to drivers.

CONTACTS: *Note: Officers with more than one job title may be intentionally listed here more than once.*

Aicha Evans, CEO
Jesse Levinson, Pres.
Carl Bass, Chmn.

FINANCIAL DATA: *Note: Data for latest year may not have been available at press time.*

In U.S. $	2018	2017	2016	2015	2014	2013
Revenue						
R&D Expense						
Operating Income						
Operating Margin %						
SGA Expense						
Net Income						
Operating Cash Flow						
Capital Expenditure						
EBITDA						
Return on Assets %						
Return on Equity %						
Debt to Equity						

CONTACT INFORMATION:

Phone: 650-539-9669 Fax:
Toll-Free:
Address: 1149 Chess Dr., Foster City, CA 94404 United States

STOCK TICKER/OTHER:

Stock Ticker: Private
Employees: 700
Parent Company:
Exchange:
Fiscal Year Ends:

SALARIES/BONUSES:

Top Exec. Salary: $ Bonus: $
Second Exec. Salary: $ Bonus: $

OTHER THOUGHTS:

Estimated Female Officers or Directors:
Hot Spot for Advancement for Women/Minorities: Y

ADDITIONAL INDEXES

Contents:

INDEX OF FIRMS NOTED AS HOT SPOTS FOR ADVANCEMENT FOR WOMEN & MINORITIES

INDEX OF SUBSIDIARIES, BRAND NAMES AND AFFILIATIONS

Brand or subsidiary, followed by the name of the related corporation

INDEX OF SUBSIDIARIES, BRAND NAMES AND AFFILIATIONS, CONT.

INDEX OF SUBSIDIARIES, BRAND NAMES AND AFFILIATIONS, CONT.

INDEX OF SUBSIDIARIES, BRAND NAMES AND AFFILIATIONS, CONT.

INDEX OF SUBSIDIARIES, BRAND NAMES AND AFFILIATIONS, CONT.

INDEX OF SUBSIDIARIES, BRAND NAMES AND AFFILIATIONS, CONT.

INDEX OF SUBSIDIARIES, BRAND NAMES AND AFFILIATIONS, CONT.

INDEX OF SUBSIDIARIES, BRAND NAMES AND AFFILIATIONS, CONT.

INDEX OF SUBSIDIARIES, BRAND NAMES AND AFFILIATIONS, CONT.

INDEX OF SUBSIDIARIES, BRAND NAMES AND AFFILIATIONS, CONT.

INDEX OF SUBSIDIARIES, BRAND NAMES AND AFFILIATIONS, CONT.

INDEX OF SUBSIDIARIES, BRAND NAMES AND AFFILIATIONS, CONT.

INDEX OF SUBSIDIARIES, BRAND NAMES AND AFFILIATIONS, CONT.

INDEX OF SUBSIDIARIES, BRAND NAMES AND AFFILIATIONS, CONT.

INDEX OF SUBSIDIARIES, BRAND NAMES AND AFFILIATIONS, CONT.

INDEX OF SUBSIDIARIES, BRAND NAMES AND AFFILIATIONS, CONT.

INDEX OF SUBSIDIARIES, BRAND NAMES AND AFFILIATIONS, CONT.

INDEX OF SUBSIDIARIES, BRAND NAMES AND AFFILIATIONS, CONT.

INDEX OF SUBSIDIARIES, BRAND NAMES AND AFFILIATIONS, CONT.

INDEX OF SUBSIDIARIES, BRAND NAMES AND AFFILIATIONS, CONT.

A Short Automobile Industry Glossary

3-D Printing: See "Additive Manufacturing."

3PL: See "Third-Party Logistics (3PL)."

802.15.1: See "Bluetooth."

ACC: See "Adaptive Cruise Control (ACC)."

Active Anti-Theft Device: An active device that renders a vehicle inoperative by disabling the fuel, ignition or starting system. The word active refers to a separate manual step, which is needed to engage the device. Also see "Passive Anti-Theft Device."

Active Safety Features: Safety features that are controlled by or interact with the driver (e.g., traction control and anti-lock braking systems).

Actual Cash Value (ACV): An insurance-related term that refers to the amount an insurance company will pay when a vehicle is damaged or declared as a total loss. Actual cash value is recognized as the cost of replacement minus depreciation.

Adaptive Cruise Control (ACC): A technology, based on radar or lasers, that is able to gauge the distance between one vehicle and the vehicle directly in front of it. Adaptive Cruise Control (ACC) can maintain a steady and safe distance, automatically slowing or speeding up a vehicle as needed. The technology could potentially harmonize speeds among vehicles and increase traffic efficiency while reducing traffic jams and enabling more vehicles to travel at once on a highway. The technology is also known as "active cruise control" or "intelligent cruise control."

Additive: A resin or chemical from a compounded substance that is designed to improve or enhance certain characteristics such as fuel efficiency.

Additive Manufacturing: The use of 3-D "printers" that that build up layers of materials such as plastics, ceramic powders or metallic powders in order to create a finished product. Such printers follow instructions from computerized design files. Originally used mainly for creating prototypes of product concepts, this process is growing in popularity as a final manufacturing process.

Aftermarket (Replacement Market): All products and services used to maintain, enhance and repair vehicles after they leave the factory.

AI: See "Artificial Intelligence (AI)."

All-Wheel Drive (AWD): A vehicle drive train in which all wheels are powered by the vehicle's engine at all times. Also see "Four-Wheel Drive (4WD)."

American Automobile Labeling Act (AALA): A regulation requiring manufacturers of vehicles to include content information on vehicle labels for trucks and cars sold in the U.S. after October 1, 1994.

Analytics: Generally refers to the deep examination of massive amounts of data, often on a continual or real-time basis. The goal is to discover deeper insights, make recommendations or generate predictions. Advanced analytics includes such techniques as big data, predictive analytics, text analytics, data mining, forecasting, optimization and simulation.

ANPR: See "Automatic Number Plate Recognition (ANPR)."

ANSI: American National Standards Institute. Founded in 1918, ANSI is a private, non-profit organization that administers and coordinates the U.S. voluntary standardization and conformity assessment system. Its mission is to enhance both the global competitiveness of U.S. business and the quality of U.S. life by promoting and facilitating voluntary consensus standards and conformity assessment systems, and safeguarding their integrity. See www.ansi.org.

Antilock Brake System (ABS): A system that senses when wheels lock up or are about to and reduces the braking forces intermittently, lessening the chance of a skid.

APAC: Asia Pacific Advisory Committee. A multi-country committee representing the Asia and Pacific region.

Applied Research: The application of compounds, processes, materials or other items discovered during basic research to practical uses. The goal is to move discoveries along to the final development phase.

Artificial Intelligence (AI): The use of computer technology to perform functions somewhat like those normally associated with human intelligence, such as reasoning, learning and self-improvement.

ASEAN: Association of Southeast Asian Nations. A regional economic development association established in 1967 by five original member countries: Indonesia, Malaysia, Philippines, Singapore, and Thailand. Brunei joined on 8 January 1984, Vietnam on 28 July 1995, Laos and Myanmar on 23 July 1997, and Cambodia on 30 April 1999.

Asia Pacific Economic Cooperation (APEC): An organization established to promote investment and trade in the Pacific basin.

Automated Guided Vehicle System (AGVS): A vehicle equipped with AGVS follows a specific path, stopping at machining or assembly stations for manual loading and unloading of parts.

Automatic Number Plate Recognition (ANPR): A traffic safety and crime prevention technology that uses large numbers of traffic cameras in urban areas. Violators of traffic laws will be automatically photographed, and citations are mailed to them. Britain leads the world in use of this technology, but dozens of U.S. cities have implemented it as well.

Base Model: The least expensive model of a car or truck, often featuring few accessories, a manual transmission and a small engine.

Basic Research: Attempts to discover compounds, materials, processes or other items that may be largely or entirely new and/or unique. Basic research may start with a theoretical concept that has yet to be proven. The goal is to create discoveries that can be moved along to applied research. Basic research is sometimes referred to as "blue sky" research.

Big Three: Ford, Chrysler and General Motors, the three largest car makers in North America.

Biodiesel: A fuel derived when glycerin is separated from vegetable oils or animal fats. The resulting byproducts are methyl esters (the chemical name for biodiesel) and glycerin which can be used in soaps and cleaning products. It has lower emissions than petroleum diesel and is currently used as an additive to that fuel since it helps with lubricity.

Bioethanol: A fuel produced by the fermentation of plant matter such as corn. Fermentation is enhanced through the use of enzymes that are created through biotechnology. Also, see "Ethanol."

Bluetooth: An industry standard for a technology that enables wireless, short-distance infrared connections between devices such as cell phone headsets, Palm Pilots or PDAs, laptops, printers and Internet appliances.

Body Shop: A service outlet that specializes in vehicle body repair work.

BPO: See "Business Process Outsourcing (BPO)."

Brand: A marketing strategy that places a focus on the brand name of a product, service or firm in order to increase the brand's market share, increase sales, establish credibility, improve satisfaction, raise the profile of the firm and increase profits. Also, see "Brand."

Brand Development Index (BDI): A measure of how a brand's sales in a particular market compare to the number of people in that market, as a portion of the national totals.

Brand Name: See "Brand."

Branding: A marketing strategy that places a focus on the brand name of a product, service or firm in order to increase the brand's market share, increase sales, establish credibility, improve satisfaction, raise the profile of the firm and increase profits. Also, see "Brand."

B-to-B, or B2B: See "Business-to-Business."

B-to-C, or B2C: See "Business-to-Consumer."

Business Process Outsourcing (BPO): The process of hiring another company to handle business activities. BPO is one of the fastest-growing segments in the offshoring sector. Services include human resources management, billing and purchasing and call centers, as well as many types of customer service or marketing activities, depending on the industry involved. Also, see "Knowledge Process Outsourcing (KPO)" and Business Transformation Outsourcing (BTO)."

Business Transformation Outsourcing (BTO): A segment within outsourcing in which the client company revamps its business processes with the goal of transforming its business by following a collaborative approach with its outsourced services provider.

Business-to-Business: An organization focused on selling products, services or data to commercial customers rather than individual consumers. Also known as B2B.

Business-to-Consumer: An organization focused on selling products, services or data to individual consumers rather than commercial customers. Also known as B2C.

CAFÉ: See "Corporate Average Fuel Economy (CAFÉ)."

CAFTA-DR: See "Central American-Dominican Republic Free Trade Agreement (CAFTA-DR)."

Capex: Capital expenditures.

Captive Finance Company: A finance or leasing company that is affiliated with an automobile distributor or manufacturer.

Captive Import: An imported part or motor vehicle manufactured by another automaker and sold under the brand name of the importer.

Captive Offshoring: Used to describe a company-owned offshore operation. For example, Microsoft owns and operates significant captive offshore research and development centers in China and elsewhere that are offshore from Microsoft's U.S. home base. Also see "Offshoring."

Casting: The process of pouring molten liquid metal into a purpose-built mold.

CEM: Contract electronic manufacturing. See "Contract Manufacturing."

Central American-Dominican Republic Free Trade Agreement (CAFTA-DR): A trade agreement signed into law in 2005 that aimed to open up the Central American and Dominican Republic markets to American goods. Member nations include Guatemala, Nicaragua, Costa Rica, El Salvador, Honduras and the Dominican Republic. Before the law was signed, products from those countries could enter the U.S. almost tariff-free, while American goods heading into those countries faced stiff tariffs. The goal of this agreement was to create U.S. jobs while at the same time offering the non-U.S. member citizens a chance for a better quality of life through access to U.S.-made goods.

Changeover: The refitting of equipment to either neutralize the effects of the just completed model production or to prepare equipment for production of the next scheduled model, or both. This term is frequently used in connection with automotive manufacturing.

Chassis: The structural frame of a vehicle to which wheels, tires, brakes and suspension are attached.

Climate Change (Greenhouse Effect): A theory that assumes an increasing mean global surface temperature of the Earth caused by gases (sometimes referred to as greenhouse gases) in the atmosphere (including carbon dioxide, methane, nitrous oxide, ozone and chlorofluorocarbons). The greenhouse effect allows solar radiation to penetrate the Earth's atmosphere but absorbs the infrared radiation returning to space.

Coachwork: The non-mechanical body and shell work that sit on top of a vehicle's frame.

Coinjection Molding: A hybrid technology, also known as multimaterial injection molding, that creates composite pieces made of plastic and metal parts locked together via injection molding or extrusion. The process combines the strength of steel with the corrosion-resistant properties of plastic. Overall weight is reduced, the need for exterior paint is eliminated and assembly and labor costs are slashed due to more efficient use of machinery.

Collaborative Planning, Forecasting and Replenishment (CPFR): An inventory management practice that evaluates and fills inventory needs throughout the supply chain. It is a cooperative effort between suppliers and retailers.

Commerce Chain Management (CCM): Refers to Internet-based tools to facilitate sales, distribution, inventory management and content personalization in the e-commerce industry. Also see "Supply Chain."

Component: In the automobile manufacturing sector, considered to be several distinct parts that have been assembled by a supplier into a subproduct with recognizable features. A component is the next step up from a part such as a bolt. Also see "System" and "Module."

Computer-Aided Design (CAD): A tool used to provide three-dimensional, on-screen design for everything from buildings to automobiles to clothing. It generally runs on workstations.

Computer-Aided Manufacturing (CAM): The use of computers to assist with manufacturing processes, thereby increasing efficiency and productivity.

Concept Vehicle: A vehicle (not currently being produced) that has been modified for new concepts or designs and evaluated for functional feasibility.

Consumer Telematics: In-vehicle consumer devices including GPS and advanced entertainment and information systems. Ford's Sync is an example of consumer telematics. See "Telematics."

Contract Manufacturing: A business arrangement whereby a company manufactures products that will be sold under the brand names of its client companies. For example, a large number of consumer electronics, such as laptop computers, are manufactured by contract manufacturers for leading brand-name computer companies such as Dell and Apple. Many other types of products, such as shoes and apparel, are made under contract manufacturing. Also see "Original Equipment Manufacturer (OEM)" and "Original Design Manufacturer (ODM)."

Corporate Average Fuel Economy (CAFE): Standards that were first issued by federal regulators in the 1970s as a method of setting average fuel economy standards for carmakers. Each manufacturer must meet a minimum average mpg for passenger cars and a lesser minimum average for SUVs, pickups and minivans.

Coupe: A two-door car.

CPFR: See "Collaborative Planning, Forecasting and Replenishment (CPFR)."

CRM: See "Customer Relationship Management (CRM)."

Crossover Utility Vehicle (CUV): A vehicle that has the looks of a sport utility vehicle (SUV), but handling and chassis characteristics more like those of a passenger car than of true SUVs, which tend to handle like light trucks.

Customer Relationship Management (CRM): Refers to the automation, via sophisticated software, of business processes involving existing and prospective customers. CRM may cover aspects such as sales (contact management and contact history), marketing (campaign management and telemarketing) and customer service (call center history and field service history). Well known providers of CRM software include Salesforce, which delivers via a Software as a Service model (see "Software as a Service (Saas)"), Microsoft and Oracle.

CUV: See "Crossover Utility Vehicle (CUV)."

Days' Supply: An estimate of the number of days needed to sell all inventory vehicles, based on the sales rate of the previous month.

DBA: Doing business as.

Dealer Principal: A corporation or individual that owns and controls one or more automobile dealerships.

Demand Chain: A similar concept to a supply chain, but with an emphasis on the end user.

Demographics: The breakdown of the population into statistical categories such as age, income, education and sex.

Design Patent: A patent that may be granted by the U.S. Patent and Trademark Office to anyone who invents a new, original, and ornamental design for an article of manufacture.

Development: The phase of research and development (R&D) in which researchers attempt to create new products from the results of discoveries and applications created during basic and applied research.

Die: A solid or hollow form used to shape materials by pressing, stamping, drawing, threading or extruding.

Displacement Taxes: Taxes levied on vehicles with larger engines.

Distributor: An individual or business involved in marketing, warehousing and/or shipping of products manufactured by others to a specific group of end users. Distributors do not sell to the general public. In order to develop a competitive advantage, distributors often focus on serving one industry or one set of niche clients. For example, within the medical industry, there are major distributors that focus on providing pharmaceuticals, surgical supplies or dental supplies to clinics and hospitals.

Do-it-Yourself (DIY) Market: Market for parts purchased and installed by individual car owners.

Door Rates: Hourly rates charged by a dealer for standard units of service work, which may or may not correspond to an actual hour of work.

EDI: See "Electronic Data Interchange (EDI)."

Electronic Data Interchange (EDI): An accepted standard format for the exchange of data between various companies' networks. EDI allows for the transfer of e-mail as well as orders, invoices and other files from one company to another.

Electronic Stability Control (ESC): An advanced safety feature in cars that helps prevent roll over and other control problems.

EMEA: The region comprised of Europe, the Middle East and Africa.

Emission: The release or discharge of a substance into the environment. Generally refers to the release of gases or particulates into the air.

EMS: Electronics Manufacturing Services. See "Contract Manufacturing."

Enterprise Resource Planning (ERP): An integrated information system that helps manage all aspects of a business, including accounting, ordering and human resources, typically across all locations of a major corporation or organization. ERP is considered to be a critical tool for management of large organizations. Suppliers of ERP tools include SAP and Oracle.

ERP: See "Enterprise Resource Planning (ERP)."

ESC: See "Electronic Stability Control (ESC)."

Ethanol: A clear, colorless, flammable, oxygenated hydrocarbon, also called ethyl alcohol. In the U.S., it is used as a gasoline octane enhancer and oxygenate in a 10% blend called E10. Ethanol can be used in higher concentrations (such as an 85% blend called E85) in vehicles designed for its use. It is typically produced chemically from ethylene or biologically from fermentation of various sugars from carbohydrates found in agricultural crops and cellulose residues from crops or wood. Grain ethanol production is typically based on corn or sugarcane. Cellulosic ethanol production is based on agricultural waste, such as wheat stalks, that has been treated with enzymes to break the waste down into component sugars.

EU: See "European Union (EU)."

EU Competence: The jurisdiction in which the European Union (EU) can take legal action.

European Community (EC): See "European Union (EU)."

European Union (EU): A consolidation of European countries (member states) functioning as one body to facilitate trade. Previously known as the European Community (EC). The EU has a unified currency, the Euro. See europa.eu.int.

Fab Lab: See "3-D Printing."

FASB: See "Financial Accounting Standards Board (FASB)."

Federation International de Automobile (FIA): The sanctioning body of all international car racing.

Financial Accounting Standards Board (FASB): An independent organization that establishes the Generally Accepted Accounting Principles (GAAP).

Fleet Sales: The sale of large quantities of vehicles to business or government agencies.

Forging: A process that transforms solid metal into various thicknesses and shapes, often by heating.

Fourth Screen: Refers to the information/entertainment dashboard panel in vehicles as a viewing device that is beyond the three primary screens used by consumers--the TV, the computer monitor and the cellphone.

Fourth-Party Logistics (4PL): A service that integrates a company's third-party logistics providers into a single entity for ease of use. Often formed by a telecommunications company, a 4PL is also called a lead logistics provider. A 4PL service provider provides a top layer of business processes, generally technology-driven, to the client's supply chain. Also see "Third-Party Logistics (3PL)."

Four-Wheel Drive (4WD): A vehicle drive train in which all four wheels are driven by a transfer case sending power to both axles. Also see "All-Wheel Drive (AWD)."

Franchise: 1) A contractual agreement between a franchisor (for example, a company or organization owning all rights to a brand, type of business, retail operation, restaurant concept or sports league) and a franchisee (person or organization desiring to license the use of those rights for a specific purpose within a specific region) that allows the franchisee to operate a retail outlet or other type of business using a brand, trade secrets, formulas and format developed and supported by the franchisor. Typically, a franchisee pays an upfront fee and then continuing fees to the franchisor. 2) A generic term used to describe a very well established business or brand.

Franchisee: See "Franchise."

Free Trade Agreement of the Americas (FTAA): The effort to unite the economies of the Western Hemisphere into a single free trade agreement.

Front-Wheel Drive: A drive train in which a vehicle is steered by and power is put into the front wheels, pulling the vehicle forward.

Fuel Cell: An environmentally friendly electrochemical engine that generates electricity using hydrogen and oxygen as fuel, emitting only heat and water as byproducts.

GAAP: See "Generally Accepted Accounting Principles (GAAP)."

GDP: See "Gross Domestic Product (GDP)."

Generally Accepted Accounting Principles (GAAP): A set of accounting standards administered by the Financial Accounting Standards Board (FASB) and enforced by the U.S. Security and Exchange Commission (SEC). GAAP is primarily used in the U.S.

GHG: See "Greenhouse Gas (GHG)."

Global Positioning System (GPS): A satellite system, originally designed by the U.S. Department of Defense for navigation purposes. Today, GPS is in wide use for consumer and business purposes, such as navigation for drivers, boaters and hikers. It utilizes satellites orbiting the earth at 10,900 miles to enable users to pinpoint precise locations using small, electronic wireless receivers.

Globalization: The increased mobility of goods, services, labor, technology and capital throughout the world. Although globalization is not a new development, its pace has increased with the advent of new technologies.

GPS: See "Global Positioning System (GPS)."

Gray Market: The market for vehicles that have been imported through individual channels outside of authorized dealers.

Greenhouse Gas (GHG): See "Climate Change (Greenhouse Effect)."

Gross Domestic Product (GDP): The total value of a nation's output, income and expenditures produced with a nation's physical borders.

Gross National Product (GNP): A country's total output of goods and services from all forms of economic activity measured at market prices for one calendar year. It differs from Gross Domestic Product (GDP) in that GNP includes income from investments made in foreign nations.

Group of Eight (G8): The eight major industrial countries, including the United States, Japan, Germany, France, the United Kingdom, Italy, Russia and Canada, whose leaders meet at annual economic summits to coordinate economic policies. The group was formerly known as the G7, before Russia was admitted in June 2002.

Heavy-Duty Truck: A vehicle weighing from 26,001 to 33,001 pounds.

Hydraulic Hybrid System: A patented fuel-saving system developed by the Environmental Protection Agency. Used in heavy service vehicles such as garbage trucks and UPS delivery vans, the system utilizes a hydraulic pump and storage tanks that store and use energy that is typically lost when brakes are applied.

ICE (in vehicles): Internal Combustion Engine.

IFRS: See "International Financials Reporting Standards (IFRS)."

Ignition System: An electrical system that includes a battery, induction coil, capacitor, distributor, spark plugs and relevant switches and wiring that produce timed sparks from spark plugs.

Import Nameplate: Vehicles sold by manufacturers primarily located outside North America, whether assembled in North America or overseas.

IMVP: See "International Motor Vehicle Program (IMVP)."

Independent Repair Shop: A service outlet that offers specialized repair services but does not usually sell gasoline and is not associated with a new car dealer.

Industry Code: A descriptive code assigned to any company in order to group it with firms that operate in similar businesses. Common industry codes include the NAICS (North American Industrial Classification System) and the SIC (Standard Industrial Classification), both of which are standards widely used in America, as well as the International Standard Industrial Classification of all Economic Activities (ISIC), the Standard International Trade Classification established by the United Nations (SITC) and the General Industrial Classification of Economic Activities within the European Communities (NACE).

Initial Public Offering (IPO): A company's first effort to sell its stock to investors (the public). Investors in an up-trending market eagerly seek stocks offered in many IPOs because the stocks of newly public companies that seem to have great promise may appreciate very rapidly in price, reaping great profits for those who were able to get the stock at the first offering. In the United States, IPOs are regulated by the SEC (U.S. Securities Exchange Commission) and by the state-level regulatory agencies of the states in which the IPO shares are offered.

Intellectual Property (IP): The exclusive ownership of original concepts, ideas, designs, engineering plans or other assets that are protected by law. Examples include items covered by trademarks, copyrights and patents. Items such as software, engineering plans, fashion designs and architectural designs, as well as games, books, songs and other entertainment items are among the many things that may be considered to be intellectual property. (Also, see "Patent.")

Intelligent Transportation Systems (ITS): ITS includes a broad number of information technologies that can provide an electronic communications link to cars and trucks, enabling drivers to be alerted to road hazards, delays, construction and accidents. At the same time, ITS can transmit driving directions and a wealth of additional driving-related information. ITS enables automated drive-through toll collection and truck pre-clearance along highways and at bridge and tunnel crossings. ITS technologies are likewise in use at border stations, points of entry and customs checkpoints, especially in the NAFTA zone. ITS also includes vehicle-to-vehicle communications for improved safety and collision avoidance.

International Financials Reporting Standards (IFRS): A set of accounting standards established by the International Accounting Standards Board (IASB) for the preparation of public financial statements. IFRS has been adopted by much of the world, including the European Union, Russia and Singapore.

International Motor Vehicle Program (IMVP): A research project, launched in 1979, funded by leading global car makers as well as government agencies, focused on research that can enhance automotive design and manufacturing methods. More than 50 senior scientists, management experts, social scientists and engineers have conducted interdisciplinary automotive research at more than 25 universities on six continents. One of IMVP's researchers coined the phrase "lean production."

IP: See "Intellectual Property (IP)."

ISO 9000, 9001, 9002, 9003: Standards set by the International Organization for Standardization. ISO 9000, 9001, 9002 and 9003 are the highest quality certifications awarded to organizations that meet exacting standards in their operating practices and procedures.

IT-Enabled Services (ITES): The portion of the Information Technology industry focused on providing business services, such as call centers, insurance claims processing and medical records transcription, by utilizing the power of IT, especially the Internet. Most ITES functions are considered to be back-office procedures. Also, see "Business Process Outsourcing (BPO)."

Jigs: An accurate machining device that holds goods in place while guiding tools exactly into position.

Just-in-Time (JIT) Delivery: Refers to a supply chain practice whereby manufacturers receive components on or just before the time that they are needed on the assembly line, rather than bearing the cost of maintaining several days' or weeks' supply in a warehouse. This adds greatly to the cost-effectiveness of a manufacturing plant and puts the burden of warehousing and timely delivery on the supplier of the components.

Kaizen: A Japanese manufacturing process concept that is widely studied by the global automotive industry. It is a philosophy based on continuous improvement of the manufacturing and business process. Facets of Kaizen may include just-in-time delivery of components, zero defects, productivity enhancement and a customer-oriented mindset.

Kanban: From the Japanese word for "visual record," a just-in-time methodology, initially attributed to Toyota, whereby sub-assemblies are delivered to a product line at the time required in the appropriate number. Kanban has also come to refer to tag-like cards used to track flow along the product line.

Knowledge Process Outsourcing (KPO): The use of outsourced and/or offshore workers to perform business tasks that require judgment and analysis. Examples include such professional tasks as patent research, legal research, architecture, design, engineering, market research, scientific research, accounting and tax return preparation. Also, see "Business Process Outsourcing (BPO)."

LAC: An acronym for Latin America and the Caribbean.

LDCs: See "Least Developed Countries (LDCs)."

Lean Manufacturing: See "Lean Production."

Lean Production: An enhancement of the mass production concept. Lean production, also known as lean manufacturing, involves optimizing the factory floor, design team, supply chain and other areas in order to manufacture a higher-quality product in less time, with less labor at less cost.

Lease (Automotive): A form of contract transferring the use of a vehicle, typically in consideration of a monthly payment. Ownership is retained by the lease company.

Least Developed Countries (LDCs): Nations determined by the U.N. Economic and Social Council to be the poorest and weakest members of the international community. There are currently 50 LDCs, of which 34 are in Africa, 15 are in Asia Pacific and the remaining one (Haiti) is in Latin America. The top 10 on the LDC list, in descending order from top to 10th, are Afghanistan, Angola, Bangladesh, Benin, Bhutan, Burkina Faso, Burundi, Cambodia, Cape Verde and the Central African Republic. Sixteen of the LDCs are also Landlocked Least Developed Countries (LLDCs) which present them with additional difficulties often due to the high cost of transporting trade goods. Eleven of the LDCs are Small Island Developing States (SIDS), which are often at risk of extreme weather phenomenon (hurricanes, typhoons, Tsunami); have fragile ecosystems; are often dependent on foreign energy sources; can have high disease rates for HIV/AIDS and malaria; and can have poor market access and trade terms.

Light Truck: In the U.S., a light truck is a vehicle that weights no more than 13,000 pounds (about 6,300 kg). These are vehicles that are used both by individuals and commercial entities. Vehicles that fall within this classification may include pickups, full-size passenger vans and commercial vans, minivans and SUVs.

LOHAS: Lifestyles of Health and Sustainability. A marketing term that refers to consumers who choose to purchase and/or live with items that are natural, organic, less polluting, etc. Such consumers may also prefer products powered by alternative energy, such as hybrid cars.

Loss Leaders: The use of very low prices to attract customers where merchandise may be sold at or below cost.

Low Emission Vehicle (LEV) Standards: Standards set by federal and state governments for automakers developing vehicles that will output lower emission levels.

Machine Learning: The ability of a computer or computerized device to learn based on the results of previous actions or the analysis of a stream of related data. It is a vital branch of Artificial Intelligence that uses advanced software in order to identify patterns and make decisions or predictions.

Machining: An operation which shapes metal parts by carving away excess material in a sequential process of turning, milling and grinding.

Make-to-Order (MTO): A term applied to products that are manufactured only when an order is confirmed. MTO differs from ETO in that no additional engineering or design is required to make the product.

Manufacturer's Suggested Retail Price (MSRP): The suggested selling price of a vehicle as stated by its manufacturer.

Manufacturing Resource Planning (MRP II): A methodology that supports effective planning with regard to all resources of a manufacturing company, linking MRP with sales and operations planning, production planning and master production scheduling.

Maquila (Maquiladora): A production plant, located in Mexico near the U.S.-Mexican border, that manufactures components but does not perform final assembly of completed products. The U.S. allows duty-free import of these components, which then undergo final assembly at a U.S. plant. Also see "Original Equipment Manufacturer (OEM)."

Market Segmentation: The division of a consumer market into specific groups of buyers based on demographic factors.

Marketing: Includes all planning and management activities and expenses associated with the promotion of a product or service. Marketing can encompass advertising, customer surveys, public relations and many other disciplines. Marketing is distinct from selling, which is the process of sell-through to the end user.

Mass Production: The use of specialized labor, and in some cases moving assembly lines, to manufacture large quantities. This is much faster and much more cost-effective than low-quantity or custom production. Henry Ford is generally credited with making mass production the standard in the automobile industry. He installed the first moving assembly line in 1913 in his Highland Park, Michigan plant.

Material Requirements Planning (MRP): An integrated management technique that uses bill of material data, inventory data and master production schedules to calculate requirements for material. MRP generates recommendations to release or reschedule replenishment orders for materials.

Mechanic Installed Market (MIL): The sale of parts for installation by professional mechanics.

Media Oriented Systems Transport (MOST): A standard adopted in 2004 by the Consumer Electronics Association for the integration of or interface with consumer electronics (such as iPods) into entertainment systems in automobiles.

Medium-Duty Truck: In the U.S., a medium-duty truck is a commercial vehicle weighing between 13,000 pounds and 33,000 pounds.

Merchandising: Any marketing method utilized to foster sales growth.

Model Line: A group of vehicles having the same model name or platform.

Module: In the automobile manufacturing sector, a module is considered to be several distinct systems that have been assembled into a major functional unit of a vehicle, such as an engine. A module is the next step up from a system, which is the next step up from a component, the next step up from a part such as a bolt. Also see "Component" and "System."

Multimaterial Injection Molding: See "Coinjection Molding."

NAFTA: See "North American Free Trade Agreement (NAFTA)."

NAICS: North American Industrial Classification System. See "Industry Code."

Natural Gas Vehicle (NGV): A car, truck or bus that runs on compressed natural gas (CNG) or liquified natural gas (LNG).

NGV: See "Natural Gas Vehicle (NGV)."

No Fault Insurance: A system of insurance where both parties in an accident file claims and neither party is held primarily responsible.

North American Free Trade Agreement (NAFTA): A trade agreement signed in December 1992 by U.S. President George H. W. Bush, Canadian Prime Minister Brian Mulroney and Mexican President Carlos Salinas de Gortari. The agreement eliminates tariffs on most goods originating in and traveling between the three member countries. It was approved by the legislatures of the three countries and had entered into force by January 1994. When it was created, NAFTA formed one of the largest free-trade areas of its kind in the world.

ODM: See "Original Design Manufacturer (ODM)."

OECD: See "Organisation for Economic Co-operation and Development (OECD)."

OEM: See "Original Equipment Manufacturer (OEM)."

Off-Highway Vehicle: A vehicle intended to be operated on rough terrain or unpaved surfaces.

Offshoring: The rapidly growing tendency among U.S., Japanese and Western European firms to send knowledge-based and manufacturing work overseas. The intent is to take advantage of lower wages and operating costs in such nations as China, India, Hungary and Russia. The choice of a nation for offshore work may be influenced by such factors as language and education of the local workforce, transportation systems or natural resources. For example, China and India are graduating high numbers of skilled engineers and scientists from their universities. Also, some nations are noted for large numbers of workers skilled in the English language, such as the Philippines and India. Also see "Captive Offshoring" and "Outsourcing."

On Board Diagnostics (OBD): A system that monitors a vehicle for problems and unit failures during normal vehicle operations.

Onshoring: The opposite of "offshoring." Providing or maintaining manufacturing or services within or nearby a company's domestic location. Sometimes referred to as reshoring.

Optimum Lean Production: See "Lean Production."

Organisation for Economic Co-operation and Development (OECD): A group of more than 30 nations that are strongly committed to the market economy and democracy. Some of the OECD members include Japan, the U.S., Spain, Germany, Australia, Korea, the U.K., Canada and Mexico. Although not members, Estonia, Israel and Russia are invited to member talks; and Brazil, China, India, Indonesia and South Africa have enhanced engagement policies with the OECD. The Organisation provides statistics, as well as social and economic data; and researches social changes, including patterns in evolving fiscal policy, agriculture, technology, trade, the environment and other areas. It publishes over 250 titles annually; publishes a corporate magazine, the OECD Observer; has radio and TV studios; and has centers in Tokyo, Washington, D.C., Berlin and Mexico City that distributed the Organisation's work and organizes events.

Original Design Manufacturer (ODM): A contract manufacturer that offers complete, end-to-end design, engineering and manufacturing services. ODMs design and build products, such as consumer electronics, that client companies can then brand and sell as their own. For example, a large percentage of laptop computers, cell phones and PDAs are made by ODMs. Also see "Original Equipment Manufacturer (OEM)" and "Contract Manufacturing."

Original Equipment Manufacturer (OEM): 1) A company that manufactures a component (or a completed product) for sale to a customer that will integrate the component into a final product. The OEM's customer will put its own brand name on the end product and distribute or resell it to end users. 2) A firm that buys a component and then incorporates it into a final product, or buys a completed product and then resells it under the firm's own brand name. This usage is most often found in the computer industry, where OEM is sometimes used as a verb. Also see "Original Design Manufacturer (ODM)" and "Contract Manufacturing."

Outbound Logistics: The process related to the movement and storage of products from the end of the production line to the end user.

Outsourcing: The hiring of an outside company to perform a task otherwise performed internally by the company, generally with the goal of lowering costs and/or streamlining work flow. Outsourcing contracts are generally several years in length. Companies that hire outsourced services providers often prefer to focus on their core strengths while sending more routine tasks outside for others to perform. Typical outsourced services include the running of human resources departments, telephone call centers and computer departments. When outsourcing is performed overseas, it may be referred to as offshoring. Also see "Offshoring."

Partnership for a New Generation of Vehicles: A partnership between the U.S. Federal Government and the automotive industry created to establish global technical leadership in the development and production of affordable, fuel-efficient, low-emission vehicles to meet performance standards.

Passenger Vehicle: A four-wheeled motor vehicle, including sport utility vehicles and minivans. The primary purpose of these vehicles is to carry passengers, not cargo.

Passive Anti-Theft Device: A passive device that renders a vehicle inoperative by disabling the fuel, ignition or starting system. The device is passive because a separate manual step is not needed to engage the device. Also see "Active Anti-Theft Device."

Patent: An intellectual property right granted by a national government to an inventor to exclude others from making, using, offering for sale, or selling the invention throughout that nation or importing the invention into the nation for a limited time in exchange for public disclosure of the invention when the patent is granted. In addition to national patenting agencies, such as the United States Patent and Trademark Office, and regional organizations such as the European Patent Office, there is a cooperative international patent organization, the World Intellectual Property Organization, or WIPO, established by the United Nations.

Platform: The primary load-bearing structural assembly of a motor vehicle, which determines its basic size and supports its suspension components and driveline.

Plug-in Hybrid Electric Vehicles (PHEV): A PHEV is an automobile that features an extra high-capacity battery bank that gives the vehicle a longer electric-only range than standard hybrids. These cars are designed so that they can be plugged into a standard electric outlet for recharging. The intent is to minimize or eliminate the need to use the car's gasoline engine and rely on the electric engine instead.

Pneumatic Tire: A tire with an outer part made of flexible, hollow rubber which is inflated by air pressure.

Positioning: The design and implementation of a merchandising mix, price structure and style of selling to create an image of the retailer, relative to its competitors, in the customer's mind.

Predictive Analytics: See "Analytics."

Product Lifecycle (Product Life Cycle): The prediction of the life of a product or brand. Stages are described as Introduction, Growth, Maturity and finally Sales Decline. These stages track a product from its initial introduction to the market through to the end of its usefulness as a commercially viable product. The goal of Product Lifecycle Management is to maximize production efficiency, consumer acceptance and profits. Consequently, critical processes around the product need to be adjusted during its lifecycle, including pricing, advertising, promotion, distribution and packaging.

Production Car: A model of vehicle that is in production and for sale to the general public.

Program Cars: Vehicles sold for fleet use, usually in large fleets such as those used by car rental companies.

R&D: Research and development. Also see "Applied Research" and "Basic Research."

Rapid Prototyping: See "3-D Printing."

Rear-Wheel Drive: A drive train in which the front wheels of the vehicle steer while the rear wheels push the vehicle forward.

Reefer: A refrigerated trailer.

Refit: In manufacturing, the closure of a plant for the purpose of retooling or conversion.

Registration: Vehicle ownership details that are filed with the state/province and printed out on a certificate of ownership called a title.

SaaS: See "Software as a Service (SaaS)."

SCM: See "Supply Chain Management."

Securitization: The process of financing a pool of similar assets (such as mortgages, automobile loans, corporate debt instruments or credit card debts) by issuing to investors interests in the funds generated by that pool. Such pools are generally in the range of $100 million or higher, and may represent the debts of dozens of companies or thousands of consumers. Securitization enables banks and other lenders to have ready markets into which they may sell loans that they generate.

SIC: Standard Industrial Classification. See "Industry Code."

Six Sigma: A quality enhancement strategy designed to reduce the number of products coming from a manufacturing plant that do not conform to specifications. Six Sigma states that no more than 3.4 defects per million parts is the goal of high-quality output. Motorola invented the system in the 1980s in order to enhance its competitive position against Japanese electronics manufacturers.

Software as a Service (SaaS): Refers to the practice of providing users with software applications that are hosted on remote servers and accessed via the Internet. Excellent examples include the CRM (Customer Relationship Management) software provided in SaaS format by Salesforce. An earlier technology that operated in a similar, but less sophisticated, manner was called ASP or Application Service Provider.

Specialty Repair Shop: A retail outlet that focuses on specialized service and repair, such as brake or muffler repair.

Sport Utility Vehicle (SUV): A vehicle designed as a hybrid of a truck and a passenger car. SUVs frequently have four-wheel drive for rough or off-road driving, in addition to extra space for people or cargo and comforts such as additional suspension and luxury options.

Stamping: A process that creates shaped parts from rolled sheet metal by bending or stretching it in a sequence of purpose-built tools fitted to a general-purpose press.

Stop-Start: A technology that enables a gasoline-powered vehicle to turn off and then restart upon demand, automatically and with split-second timing. This gasoline savings over traditional idling of engines can run in the 4% to 10% range, depending on the vehicle and its usage. Advanced software along with a special battery that can deal with the strain are integral parts of the package.

Subsidiary, Wholly-Owned: A company that is wholly controlled by another company through stock ownership.

Supply Chain: The complete set of suppliers of goods and services required for a company to operate its business. For example, a manufacturer's supply chain may include providers of raw materials, components, custom-made parts and packaging materials.

Supply Chain Management: The coordination of all supply chain activities. Also referred to as "SCM."

SUV: See "Sport Utility Vehicle (SUV)."

System: In the automobile manufacturing sector, a system is considered to be several distinct components that have been assembled by a supplier into a subproduct that is a functional part of a vehicle, such as an instrument panel. A system is the next step up from a component, which is the next step up from a part such as a bolt. Also see "Component" and "Module."

Telematics: The use of cellular or radio transmission to exchange information between an automobile or truck and a base data center or customer service center. In the trucking industry, telematics is used to provide a headquarters with information about the location and routing of a truck. Telematics can also be used to alert a central service office about the temperature, oil pressure and other vital statistics of a gas or diesel engine. In passenger automobiles, telematics may be used to provide emergency response during accidents or breakdowns. Such emergency response may occur automatically, for example, when an air bag inflates. GM's OnStar service is a well-known example of telematics services for passenger car owners. Consumer telematics may provide advanced information, location-based services and entertainment to passenger vehicles.

Third-Party Logistics (3PL): A specialist firm in logistics, which may provide a variety of transportation, warehousing and logistics-related services to buyers or sellers. These tasks were previously performed in-house by the customer. When 3PL services are provided within the client's own facilities, it can also be referred to as insourcing. Also see "Fourth-Party Logistics (4PL)."

Tier 1 Supplier: A component manufacturer to final vehicle assemblers, responsible for delivery of the finished assembly, product development and continued technology renewal. Tier 1 suppliers work hand-in-hand with automobile manufacturers to design, manufacture and deliver complicated automobile systems and modules, such as significant interior, exterior or drivetrain units. Tier 1 suppliers in turn purchase from tier 2 and tier 3 suppliers, which rank below tier 1.

Tier 2 Supplier: A producer of value-adding parts in the minor sub-assembly phase. Tier 2 suppliers buy from tier 3 and sell to tier 1.

Tier 3 Supplier: A supplier of engineered materials and special services, such as rolls of sheet steel, heat treating and surface treatments. Tier 3 suppliers rank below tier 2 and tier 1 suppliers in terms of the complexity of the products that they provide.

Title: See "Registration."

Total Quality Management (TQM): The management of an operation with the goal of producing a product with zero defects.

V2I: Vehicle-to-infrastructure, as in wireless communications between cars or trucks and nearby bridges, intersections or traffic warnings. Possible uses include warnings sent to vehicles regarding pedestrians, slow curves in the road, rail crossings and bridge clearance. This is part of the intelligent transportation trend. See "Intelligent Transportation Systems (ITS)."

V2V: Vehicle-to-vehicle, as in wireless communications between cars and trucks for improved safety and collision avoidance. This is part of the intelligent transportation trend. See "Intelligent Transportation Systems (ITS)."

V2X: See "Vehicle-to-Everything (V2X)."

Value Added Tax (VAT): A tax that imposes a levy on businesses at every stage of manufacturing based on the value it adds to a product. Each business in the supply chain pays its own VAT and is subsequently repaid by the next link down the chain; hence, a VAT is ultimately paid by the consumer, being the last link in the supply chain, making it comparable to a sales tax. Generally, VAT only applies to goods bought for consumption within a given country; export goods are exempt from VAT, and purchasers from other countries taking goods back home may apply for a VAT refund.

Vehicle Identification Number (VIN): The unique number assigned to a vehicle by its manufacturer for identification and registration purposes.

Vehicle-to-Everything (V2X): The digital connection of data between vehicles and other entities such as infrastructure systems, other vehicles, networks, pedestrians, devices or grids. V2X are WLAN-based or cellular-based, and can be used to increase road safety and traffic and energy efficiency.

Vendor: Any firm, such as a manufacturer or distributor, from which a retailer obtains merchandise.

Vertical Integration: A business model in which one company owns many (or all) of the means of production of the many goods that comprise its product line. For example, founder Henry Ford designed Ford Motor Company's early River Rouge plant so that coal, iron ore and other needed raw materials arrived at one end of the plant and were processed into steel, which was then converted on-site into finished components. At the final stage of the plant, completed automobiles were assembled.

World Trade Organization (WTO): One of the only globally active international organizations dealing with the trade rules between nations. Its goal is to assist the free flow of trade goods, ensuring a smooth, predictable supply of goods to help raise the quality of life of member citizens. Members form consensus decisions that are then ratified by their respective parliaments. The WTO's conflict resolution process generally emphasizes interpreting existing commitments and agreements, and discovers how to ensure trade policies to conform to those agreements, with the ultimate aim of avoiding military or political conflict.

WTO: See "World Trade Organization (WTO)."

Zero-Emission Vehicle (ZEV): Describes a vehicle meeting either the EPA's CFV ZEV standards or CARB's California Low-Emission Vehicle Program ZEV standards. ZEV standards, usually met with electric vehicles, require zero vehicle emissions.

CPSIA information can be obtained
at www.ICGtesting.com
Printed in the USA
BVHW091755160919
558564BV00016B/1653/P